Life is Short. Enjoy the Best Music.

(These helpful guides will show you the way.)

MUSICHOUND™ ROCK
The Essential Album Guide

Everything you need to know about buying the best rock albums is right here. Look up any of 2,000 pivotal artists who perform classic, alternative and modern rock and you'll find not only reviews of all their albums, but also suggestions for what to buy, what to avoid and what's worth searching for. Includes a free rock CD sampler and a huge resources section with Web page information and more.

Gary Graff • 1996 • paperback with music CD • **ISBN 0-7876-1037-2**

MUSICHOUND™ JAZZ
The Essential Album Guide

Building your jazz collection doesn't have to be intimidating. This essential jazz buyer's guide makes the genre more accessible with foolproof selections from the work of 1,500 performers of Dixieland and big band, bebop, scat, fusion and jazzy pop. Includes a free CD sampler of cool jazz sounds.

Steve Holtje and Nancy Ann Lee • October 1997 • paperback with music CD **ISBN 1-57859-031-0**

MUSIC FESTIVALS
from Bach to Blues

Music loving travel hound Tom Clynes takes you on a cross-country tour of more than 1,000 great festivals celebrating all kinds of music, from bluegrass to Chicago blues and from alternative to opera. You'll read all about where to go and what to expect when you get there.

Tom Clynes • 1996 • paperback • **ISBN 0-7876-0823-8**

VISIBLE
I N K
P R E S S

Available at bookstores everywhere.

MusicHound™ Rock: The Essential Album Guide

"This is a thoughtful and opinionated guide for newcomers. For longtime fans, this tome will spark some fun arguments."
—**Minneapolis Star Tribune**

MusicHound Rock profiles and reviews the work of nearly 2,000 pivotal artists and groups who perform classic, alternative, and modern rock. Provides a complete list of albums, with suggestions for "What to Buy," "What to Buy Next," and "What to Avoid," as well as details on the performer's career, influences, and impact on other musicians. Plus, a Producer Index, Record Label Directory, Web Site Guide, and Resources Section. Also includes a free music CD sampler from RCA Records.

Gary Graff • ISBN 0-7876-1037-2 • 911 pages

MusicHound™ Country: The Essential Album Guide

"Finally, a country music reference book with some real musical meat on its bones! Definitive and doggone indispensable."
—**Neil Pond, Country America Magazine**

The second in a series of *MusicHound* buyers' guides that help consumers build their CD collections, *Country* profiles and reviews the work of more than 1,000 acts, from Patsy Cline and Bill Monroe to Garth Brooks, Shania Twain, and BR5-49. Includes a Resources Section, Web Site Guide, Fan Club Directory, Music Festival Directory, Awards Section, Band Member Index, and Producer Index. Features forewords by Jim Lauderdale and Suzy Bogguss and a free music CD sampler from Mercury Nashville.

Brian Mansfield and Gary Graff • ISBN 1-57859-006-X • 642 pages

MusicHound™ R&B: The Essential Album Guide

The only definitive guide to rhythm & blues, *R&B* covers more than 1,000 acts from all areas of R&B, including soul, funk, old school, rap, hip-hop, gospel, Motown, Stax, and the Philly Sound. Using the familiar *MusicHound* format, *R&B* steers you toward the essential album purchases for each performer. Includes a Resources Section, Web Site Guide, Radio Station Directory, Band Member Index, and Producer Index. Features forewords by Eddie Levert (of the O'Jays), Kurtis Blow, and Huey Lewis, and a free music CD sampler from Mercury Records.

Gary Graff, Josh Freedom du Lac, and Jim McFarlin • ISBN 1-57859-026-4 • 800 pages

MusicHound™ Jazz: The Essential Album Guide

A mammoth work of musical scholarship, *Jazz* reviews the work of 1,500 artists and groups from all facets of jazz, including Dixieland, big band, bebop, scat, fusion, and more. Essential album purchases are targeted by *MusicHound*'s familiar format, enabling both the novice and jazz buff to expand their collections wisely. Includes a Resources Section, Web Site Guide, Music Festival Directory, Band Member Index, and Producer Index. Also features a free music CD sampler from Verve Records.

Steve Holtje and Nancy Ann Lee • ISBN 1-57859-031-0 • 1,100 pages

Music Festivals from Bach to Blues: A Traveler's Guide

"A unique listener's guide to all genres of tuneful revelry across North America."
—**Time International**

Music lovers, vacationers, and students alike will welcome this comprehensive travel guide. Seasoned traveler Tom Clynes takes you to a wide variety of music festivals in the U.S. and Canada. More than 1,001 entries provide full descriptions of the artistic focus, who's performing, and what festival-goers can expect from headliners. Also includes a guide to music workshops.

Tom Clynes • ISBN 0-7876-0823-8 • 582 pages

600 Blues Artists, Including:

Luther Allison	Howlin' Wolf	Jimmy Rogers
Marcia Ball	Etta James	Roomful of Blues
Jeff Beck	Robert Johnson	Son Seals
Michael Bloomfield	Albert King	Kenny Wayne Shepherd
Ray Charles	B.B. King	Percy Sledge
Eric Clapton	Al Kooper	Bessie Smith
Albert Collins	Jonny Lang	Koko Taylor
James Cotton	Taj Mahal	Irma Thomas
Robert Cray	John Mayall	Jimmie Vaughan
Willie Dixon	Steve Miller	Stevie Ray Vaughan
Al Green	Maria Muldaur	Dinah Washington
Buddy Guy	Charlie Musselwhite	Muddy Waters
Ted Hawkins	Doc Pomus	Junior Wells
Jimi Hendrix	Professor Longhair	Josh White
Billie Holiday	Bonnie Raitt	Chris Whitley
John Lee Hooker	Duke Robillard	Johnny Winter

musicHound
blues

The Essential Album Guide

edited by Leland Rucker
foreword by Al Kooper

DETROIT • NEW YORK • TORONTO • LONDON

musicHound™ blues
The
Essential
Album
Guide

Published by Visible Ink Press®
a division of Gale Research
835 Penobscot Building
Detroit, MI 48226-4094

Visible Ink Press, MusicHound, and A Cunning Canine Production are trademarks of Gale Research.

Most Visible Ink Press books are available at special quantity discounts when purchased in bulk by corporations, organizations, or groups. Customized printings, special imprints, messages, and excerpts can be produced to meet your needs. For more information, contact Special Markets Manager, Gale Research, 835 Penobscot Bldg., Detroit, MI 48226. Or call 1-800-776-6265.

Cover photo of Buddy Guy © Jack Vartoogian

Library of Congress Cataloging-in-Publication Data

MusicHound blues : the essential album guide / edited by Leland
 Rucker.
      p.   cm.
    Includes bibliographical references (p.   ), list of World Wide
 Web pages (p.   ), and indexes.
     ISBN 1-57859-030-2 (alk. paper)
      1. Blues (Music)—Discography. 2. Sound recordings—Reviews.
 I. Rucker, Leland, 1947-
 ML156.4.B6M85 1998
 781.643'0266—dc21   97-37693
                                      CIP
                                          MN

ISBN 1-57859-030-2
Printed in the United States of America
All rights reserved

10 9 8 7 6 5 4 3 2

musicHound contents

musicHound m o n s t e r s o l o s

the yin and yang of the blues

If I have a yin and yang, one is a love for the blues and the other is a hatred of revisionism. Here, finally, is a book that satisfies my yin and yang.

I was first brought into the blues genre as a youngster, when my father played me his Bessie Smith 78s, and then by the crossover hits of Jimmy Reed in the 1950s. "Big Boss Man," "Baby, What You Want Me to Do," and "Caress Me Baby" took me down into a world of from-the-heart singing, out-of-tune guitars, and a harp sound that bragged of nothing less than the graveyard at midnight.

Later, in the mid-1960s, when I joined a band called the Blues Project, the other members of that band finished my education with many late-night outpourings of their record collections.

When I was growing up in New York City, it was rare to hear a Muddy Waters or B.B. King record. The hard-core stations either played slick R&B or gospel music, or both. But no amount of dial-twisting could produce an all-blues station such as WLAC out of Nashville. Today, blues shows abound on most radio stations, but in the 1950s in New York City, it was another story.

MusicHound, which in the past has published guides to country and rock music, now jumps headfirst into the blues with this edition. For the novice, it's a great way to start a collection. However, history is a great adjunct in the enjoyment of music. I would recommend that the neophyte listener purchase almost exclusively from the Chess and Vee-Jay catalogs.

This is where the blues were popularized in Chicago, beginning in the mid-1940s. With just these two labels, one can hear the best works of Muddy Waters, John Lee Hooker, Howling Wolf, Chuck Berry, Jimmy Reed, and Sonny Boy Williamson II, to name but a few. These artists remain the cornerstones of today's blues.

For modern blues, a plethora of indie labels maintain the spirit of Chess and Vee-Jay: Alligator, Black Top, Rounder, and HighTone are just a few of a great bunch. With just these four you can enjoy Luther Allison, Robert Cray, Robert Ward, Tracy Nelson, and Irma Thomas, to just cherry-pick off the top of my head.

We live in an age of bad information. You would not believe the amount of errors in today's books of musical history documentation. And when these books are employed in research, their errors are compounded geometrically, until they become erroneous fact. This is the bane of my existence.

It was once said, by a man greater than I, that writing about music is like dancing about architecture, so *MusicHound* keeps the verbiage to a minimum. You get a thumbnail sketch of the artist's career, a discography, and some recommended releases to get you on your way. No long-winded speeches or proselytizing paragraphs. They know that if you've bought this book, you're committed to the genre and don't need any further convincing.

Even a jaded collector like myself can enjoy a book like this. I'll be searching for names and titles I might have missed in my quest for, say, a CD version of Percy Mayfield's long-lost *My Jug and I* album. And I know I'm getting good information, based on *MusicHound*'s intensive research and their love for the music herein. So, come on aboard, and let's ride these blues all the way to the end of the line.

Al Kooper has been a vital part of the music business for the last 40 years. He was a member of the Blues Project and Blood, Sweat & Tears, has played keyboards for Bob Dylan, the Rolling Stones, and the Who, and produced and discovered Lynyrd Skynyrd and the Tubes. He has always been a gospel and blues lover, having played with B.B. King, Howlin' Wolf, Muddy Waters, John Lee Hooker, Jimi Hendrix, the Staple Singers, and many others. He currently teaches at the Berklee College of Music in Boston and writes a monthly column for EQ magazine. His autobiography, Backstage Passes and Backstabbing Bastards, *will be published by Billboard Books in August 1998.*

So how do you use *MusicHound Blues*? Here's what you'll find in the entries, and what we intend to accomplish with each point:

• An introductory paragraph, which will give you not only biographical information but also a sense of the artist's or group's sound and its stature in the blues—and overall music—pantheon.

• **What to Buy:** The album or albums that we feel are essential purchases for consuming this act. It may be a greatest hits set, or it may be a particular album that captures the essence of the artist in question. In any event, this is where you should start—and don't think it wasn't hard to make these choices when eyeballing the catalogs of Muddy Waters, B.B. King, John Lee Hooker, and some of the other blues titans.

• **What to Buy Next:** In other words, once you're hooked, these will be the most rewarding next purchases.

• **What to Avoid:** Seems clear enough. This is Hound poop.

• **The Rest:** Everything else that's available for this act, rated with the Hound's trusty bone scale (see below for more on this). Note that for some artists with sizeable catalogs, we've condensed this section down to **Best of the Rest.**

• **Worth Searching For:** An out-of-print gem. A bootleg. An import. A guest appearance on another artist's album or a film soundtrack. Something that may require some investigating but will reward you for the effort.

• ◀◀: The crucial influences on this act's music.

• ▶▶: The acts that have been influenced by this artist or group. Used only where applicable; it's a little early for Jonny Lang to have influenced anybody.

Now, you ask, what's with those bones? (Down, boy! Sheesh. . . .) It's not hard to figure out—𝄢𝄢𝄢𝄢𝄢 is nirvana (not Nirvana), a **woof!** is dog food. Keep in mind that the bone ratings don't pertain just to the act's own catalog, but to its worth in the whole music realm. Therefore a lesser act's **What to Buy** choice might rate no more than 𝄢𝄢𝄢; some even rate 𝄢𝄢, a not-so-subtle sign that you might want to think twice about that act.

As with any opinions, all of what you're about to read is subjective and personal. The MusicHound has a bit of junkyard dog in it, too; it likes to start fights. We hope it does, too. Ultimately, we think the Hound will point you in the right direction, and if you buy the 𝄢𝄢𝄢𝄢𝄢 and 𝄢𝄢𝄢𝄢 choices, you'll have an album collection to howl about. But if you've got a bone to pick, the Hound wants to hear about it—and promises not to bite (but maybe bark a little bit). If you think we're wagging our tails in the wrong direction or lifting our leg at something that doesn't deserve it, let us know. If you think an act has been capriciously excluded—or charitably included—tell us. Your comments and suggestions will serve the greater *MusicHound* audience and future projects, so don't be shy.

Editor

Leland Rucker has been a music and popular culture journalist for 23 years. He has been managing editor of *Blues Access,* an internationally distributed quarterly blues journal, since 1994. He grew up in Kansas City, Missouri, and studied for the Lutheran ministry before becoming popular music critic for *The Kansas City Times* (now *The Kansas City Star*). He moved to Boulder, Colorado, where he now lives, in 1983, and was entertainment editor and popular culture columnist for *The Colorado Daily* from 1986 to 1993. With Gil Asakawa, he wrote *The Toy Book* (Knopf, 1992), a study of the play things of the post–World War II generation. He loves fresh catfish, crawfish, and peaches, and spends his free time reading, traveling, listening to music, and playing guitar.

Supervising Editor

Gary Graff is an award-winning music journalist and supervising editor of the *MusicHound* album guide series. A native of Pittsburgh, Pennsylvania, his work is published regularly by Reuters, *Replay, Guitar World, ICE,* the *San Francisco Chronicle,* the *Cleveland Plain Dealer,* Michigan's *Oakland Press,* SW Radio Networks, *Country Song Roundup,* Mr. Showbiz/Wall of Sound, Jam TV, Electric Village, and other publications. His weekly "Rock 'n' Roll Insider" report airs on Detroit rock station WRIF-FM (101.1), and he also appears on public TV station WTVS' *Backstage Pass* program. He is a board member of the North American Music Critics Association and co-producer of the annual Detroit Music Awards. He lives in the Detroit suburbs with his wife, daughter, and two stepsons.

Managing Editor

Dean Dauphinais is an editor at Visible Ink Press and a contributor to *MusicHound Rock* and *MusicHound R&B.* The co-author of two books, *Astounding Averages!* and *Car Crazy,* he lives in suburban Detroit with his wife, Kathy, and two sons, Sam and Josh.

Copy Editor

Jan Klisz is a former reference book editor and currently provides freelance editorial services as the proprietor of Upper Woods Word Shop. She works out of her almost-rural-enough Michigan home, where her husband and two daughters are both the cause of and cure for her working-mom blues.

Publisher

Martin Connors

MusicHound Staff

Michelle Banks, Christa Brelin, Jim Craddock, Beth Fhaner, Judy Galens, Jeff Hermann, Brad Morgan, Leslie Norback, Terri Schell, Carol Schwartz, Devra Sladics, Christine Tomassini

Art Director

Tracey Rowens

Photographers Extraordinaire

Jack and Linda Vartoogian grew up in late 1950s Detroit and heard, but did not get to see, the best performers in blues and R&B. To compensate, they have devoted themselves to photographing musicians (and dancers) from across the country and around the world. While their New York City home virtually guarantees that, eventually, most acts come to them, they continue to seek opportunities to discover new talent and new venues—the farther from home the better. Their images appear regularly in *The New York Times, Time, Newsweek, Living Blues,* and *Jazz Times,* among many others, as well as in innumerable books, including their own *Afropop!* (Chartwell Books, 1995) and *The Living World of Dance* (Smithmark, 1997), and *MusicHound R&B* and *MusicHound Jazz.*

Ken Settle is a Detroit-area photographer who has specialized in music photography for over 16 years. His photos have been published worldwide in magazines such as *Rolling Stone, People, Guitar Player, Playboy, Audio,* Japan's *Player,* France's *Guitarist,* and Australia's *Who Weekly.* His work also appears in *MusicHound Country* and *MusicHound R&B.*

Graphic Services
Randy Bassett, Pam Reed, Barbara Yarrow

Permissions
Maria Franklin

Production
Mary Beth Trimper, Dorothy Maki, Evi Seoud, Shanna Heilveil

Data Entry
Kathy Dauphinais

Technology Wizard
Jeffrey Muhr

Typesetting Virtuoso
Marco Di Vita of The Graphix Group

Marketing & Promotion
Marilou Carlin, Kim Intindola, Betsy Rovegno, Susan Stefani

MusicHound Development
Julia Furtaw

Contributors
Gil Asakawa is the content editor for Digital City Denver, a site on America Online. He's written for *Rolling Stone, Pulse, Creem, No Depression,* and *New Country,* co-authored *The Toy Book* (Knopf, 1992), and has contributed entries to *MusicHound Rock* and *MusicHound Country.*

Steve Braun is a Chicago-based national correspondent for *The Los Angeles Times.* He covered the second Woodstock and the Rock and Roll Hall of Fame concert and has written about Jerry Lee Lewis's brushes with the law.

John C. Bruening is a freelance writer from Cleveland, Ohio. He has written CD reviews, concert reviews, and artist profiles for *Blues Access* magazine, the *Cleveland Plain Dealer,* and the *Pittsburgh City Paper.*

Ken Burke is a singer/songwriter whose column "The Continuing Saga of Dr. Iguana" has inspired a loyal (albeit deeply disturbed) following in small press publications since 1985.

Salvatore Caputo is a freelance writer living in Phoenix with his wife and three kids. The pop music columnist for the *Arizona Republic* from 1990 to 1997, he has been a judge in the Arizona Blues Showdown for three years.

Nadine Cohodas writes for *Blues Access* and *Living Blues* magazines. She is the author of *Strom Thurmond and the Politics of Southern Change* (Mercer University Press, 1994) and *The Band Played Dixie: Race and the Liberal Conscience at Ole Miss* (Free Press, 1997).

Cary Darling is an entertainment editor at the *Orange County Register* in California. He also writes a syndicated column on world and dance music.

Michael Dixon is a contributor to *Blues Access* magazine and writes for various Maine publications, including the *Southern Maine Blues Society Newsletter* and Lewiston's *Sun-Journal.* He also hosts a weekly blues show on the Bates College radio station, WRBC.

Daniel Durchholz is editor of *Replay* magazine and a contributor to *MusicHound Rock, MusicHound Country,* and *MusicHound R&B.*

Tom Ellis III has been writing about blues and playing harmonica since 1968. From 1995 to 1997 he authored a five-part series on the life of Paul Butterfield for *Blues Access* magazine and is currently at work on a book about Butterfield. He lives in Dallas, Texas, and owns Tom's Mics, selling vintage microphones to professional and amateur harmonica players worldwide.

David Feld is a contributing writer for *Blues Access* magazine and plays guitar and bass in the Diminished Capacity Revue. By day, he is a deputy public defender in Alameda County, California.

Lawrence Gabriel is the editor of Detroit's *Metro Times* and is a contributor to *MusicHound Rock, MusicHound R&B,* and *MusicHound Jazz.*

Gary Graff is supervising editor of Visible Ink Press' *MusicHound* series.

Jeff Hannusch is a New Orleans–based freelance writer who has written hundreds of articles on the subject of music. His book, *I Hear You Knockin': The Sound of Rhythm and Blues* (Swallow, 1985), won the American Book Award.

Steve Holtje has contributed to all the *MusicHound* volumes and is co-editor of *MusicHound Jazz*. He has written for *The Wire, Jazziz, Newsday, Rhythm Music*, Allstarmag.com, and many other magazines, newspapers, and online publications. He was a senior editor at the late, lamented *Creem*.

B.J. Huchtemann is a freelance music journalist who writes for *Blues Access* magazine and Chicago's *Screamin'* magazine. She is a staff music reviewer and interviewer for *The Reader* in Omaha, Nebraska. When not out supporting live music, she also writes advertising and promotional copy for radio and television.

Rob Hutten founded BluesNet (http://www.hub.org/blues net/), the World Wide Web's first blues site, in 1993, and his writings on Son House and Jack Owens have appeared in *Blues & Rhythm* magazine. A UNIX Systems administrator by trade, Rob also studies and performs traditional blues and old-time music and is a member of an Andean folk music group called Fiesta Andina.

Scott Jordan writes the "Bluesworthy" column and is a frequent contributor to New Orleans' *OffBeat* magazine. His work has appeared in *A B.B. King Companion, Bam, Blues Revue, Relix*, and other publications.

Steve Knopper is a Chicago-based freelancer who writes a regular blues column for the Knight-Ridder Newspapers wire service. His work has also appeared in *Rolling Stone, George*, the *Chicago Tribune, Newsday, Blues Access, Request, Billboard*, and *Yahoo! Internet Life*. He is the former music critic for Boulder, Colorado's *Daily Camera* and obituary writer for Richmond, Virginia's *News Leader*. A contributor to *MusicHound Rock* and *MusicHound Country*, he's editing *MusicHound Lounge*, to be published by Visible Ink Press in 1998.

John Koetzner is a freelance music critic who has written for *Down Beat, Bass Player, Mix, Relix, BAM*, the *Reno News & Review*, California's *Press Democrat* and *Healdsburg Tribune*, and numerous other publications. He attended his first blues concert, performed by John Lee Hooker and Johnny Shines, at age 16 and has followed the blues for the past 27 years.

Greg Kot is the rock critic for the *Chicago Tribune* and has contributed articles to numerous publications, including *Rolling Stone, Request, Replay*, and *Guitar World*. He's also a contribu-

tor to *MusicHound Rock, MusicHound Country*, and *Music-Hound R&B*.

Tali Madden is a contributing writer to *Blues Access* magazine and a freelance music journalist. A former NPR-affiliate jazz and blues broadcaster/programmer, he is currently based in Portland, Oregon.

David Menconi is the music critic at the *Raleigh* (North Carolina) *News and Observer* and has written for *Spin, Billboard*, and *Request* magazines. A contributor to *MusicHound Rock, MusicHound Country*, and *MusicHound R&B*, he is also a contributing editor for *No Depression* magazine.

D. Thomas Moon is a Chicago-based educator, guitarist, and music journalist. His writings have appeared in CD liner notes and in *Blues Access, Living Blues, Blues Revue*, and *Latin Beat* magazines. He is currently working on a children's picture book, *Wang Dang Doodle Day*.

Craig Morrison gives private music lessons and teaches courses on country, blues, and rock 'n' roll through McGill University's department of continuing education. He is the author of *Go Cat Go!: Rockabilly Music and Its Makers* (University of Illinois Press, 1996). He lives in Montreal.

Allan Orski has written extensively for the *MusicHound* series. He's also contributed to *Rolling Stone* Online, *Replay, Requestline*, SW Radio Networks, *Black Book*, and *New Review*. He lives and starves in Brooklyn, New York.

Mark Pasman is co-author of the "Monster Solo" sidebars in *MusicHound Blues*. He hosts the weekly "Motor City Blues Project" show on WCSX-FM in Detroit and plays guitar in the band Mudpuppy.

Alan Paul is a senior editor of *Guitar World* and the editor of *Guitar World* Online (www.guitarworld.com). His proudest professional moment was interviewing Albert King for *Guitar World* in 1991.

Matt Pensinger is a music writer and columnist for the *Colorado Springs Gazette* and Digital City Denver, a site on America Online. He has also written for national music publications such as *Blues Access* and *No Depression*.

Doug Pullen is the music and media writer for the *Flint* (Michigan) *Journal* and Booth Newspapers. He is a contributor to *MusicHound Rock* and *MusicHound Country*.

Bryan Powell is a musician and freelance writer/editor based in Lawrenceville, Georgia, near Atlanta. He is a regular contributor to *Blues Access* magazine and *Acoustic Guitar*, a monthly guitar publication.

Dave Ranney writes about blues and jazz for the *Wichita Eagle*. He is the former editor of the *Wichita Blues Society Newsletter*.

Rob Reuteman is business editor of Denver's *Rocky Mountain News*.

Steven Rosen has written about music for the *Denver Post* and other newspapers and magazines, as well as for his own fanzine, *One Shot: The Magazine of One-Hit Wonders*. He is also the founder of "National One-Hit Wonder Day," celebrated each year on September 25. The winner of a 1997 Music Journalism Award for commentary, he is currently the movie critic at the *Denver Post*.

Robert Sacré is a professor at the University of Liege in Belgium, where, since the early 1980s, he has taught ethnomusicology ("Story of African American Music & Literature"). He has conducted research in Africa and the United States and has published numerous articles on the blues, gospel, Cajun, and zydeco music. Among his books are *The Voice of the Delta: Charley Patton and the Mississippi Delta Blues Traditions* (Presses Universitaires de Liege, 1987) and *Saints and Sinners: Religion, Blues, and Evil in African-American Music and Literature* (Presses Universitaires de Liege, 1996).

Tim Schuller was a factory worker/Teamster/rock musician in Ohio and Chicago before moving to Texas in 1977. He presently writes for the *Dallas Observer* and *Blues Access* magazine. His sidebar passions include European horror videos, guns, and Mexican beer.

Joel Selvin is the longtime *San Francisco Chronicle* pop music critic and a contributor to *MusicHound Rock, MusicHound Country,* and *MusicHound R&B*. He'll publish his seventh book, *Sly and the Family Stone: On the Record,* in the spring of 1998.

Steven Sharp is a newspaper journalist whose freelance features and reviews appear regularly in *Living Blues* magazine. His profiles of blues artists have also been published in the British *Juke* magazine and the *Milwaukee Journal Sentinel*. He has provided liner notes for numerous CD releases on the Evidence and Wolf labels.

John Sinclair is a poet, performer (with his Blues Scholars), music journalist, radio host (WWOZ-FM), and record producer (Big Chief Productions) based in New Orleans. His recordings include *Full Moon Night; Full Circle* (with Wayne Kramer); *If I Could Be with You* (with Ed Moss & the Society Jazz Orchestra; and *thelonius: a book of monk—volume one.*

Todd Wicks is a Detroit freelance writer whose work has appeared in the fanzines *Jam Rag* and *Renegade, The Detroit Jewish News,* and the suburban Detroit *Observer & Eccentric* newspapers.

Cary Wolfson is the editor and publisher of *Blues Access* magazine and the producer of one of the longest-running nationally distributed blues radio programs, "Blues from the Red Rooster Lounge." He lives in Boulder, Colorado.

Jennifer Zogott currently writes about blues for *Blues Access, Blue Suede News,* and *Folk Roots*. She is also a contributor to the forthcoming *Rolling Stone Jazz & Blues Album Guide*. She lives in New York City.

A project as expansive as this involves too many folks to properly acknowledge them all; people from literally all over the globe have helped in one way or the other to make this book happen.

Billie Gutgsell and Gus watched and waited patiently, offering only positive support as I ranted and raved downstairs in my office through much of 1997—they are truly the greatest. Gary Graff had the temerity to hire me on the basis of a brief business card exchange at SXSW in March of 1996 in Austin, Texas, and some entries I wrote for *MusicHound Rock*. Everybody at Visible Ink Press was efficient and helpful, especially Dean Dauphinais, managing editor of the *MusicHound* series, who was a rock, ever helpful and sympathetic, keeping things on target as the original manuscript deadlines came and went and came and went. Copy editor Jan Klisz was thorough and persevering, trying to keep straight which Sonny Boy Williamson was which and coming up with the Rich Text Format transfer trick that speeded things up considerably.

My special appreciation goes to the contributors, all of whom managed to endure my pestering for producers' names, spellings, and other seemingly trivial queries with as much dignity as they could muster, even though they all had real lives and jobs and families to deal with. Their writing reflects the artists because of the many long hours each has spent with the music they know well. I'm proud to have worked with each and every one.

Special thanks to Steve Knopper, who went far beyond the call of duty time and again without complaint. *Living Blues* magazine's Brett Bonner discovered some choice oversights in the original list and pointed me in the direction of the pre–WWII

artists whose stories and music form the backbone of the book. Jeff Hannusch and Steve Braun came onboard late and helped significantly to fill in the cracks. Cary Wolfson, publisher of *Blues Access* magazine, cut me an awful lot of slack during the production of two issues of the magazine. Gil Asakawa and Noah Saunders offered generous counsel when I needed it most.

Among others who were ever helpful with advice, information, and much more were Mary Katherine Aldin; Mark Pucci of Mark Pucci Media; David Dorn at Rhino; Lisa Shively and the Press Network; Bill Bentley; Cary Baker; Mindy Giles, Kat Stratton, Glenn Dicker, and Steve Burton of Rounder; Tom Cording at Sony-Legacy; Jennifer Ballantyne of MCA/Chess; Sharon Liviten at House of Blues; Kris Drey at Blind Pig; Dave Bartlett at Tone-Cool; Alligator's Marc Lipkin; Jerry Gordon at Evidence; Delmark's Doug Engel; and Annie Johnston at Arhoolie.

I turned often to *Blues Access* and *Living Blues* magazines. (An invaluable tool to enjoying both is Mary Katherine Aldin's self-produced *Blues Magazine Selective Index*, which also includes indexes for *Juke Blues* and *Blues & Rhythm* magazines.) The Tower Records Internet and AOL sites, both of which list thousands of blues releases in print, answered a lot of questions.

Of all the features of the Internet revolution, none came in more handy than electronic mail. Despite its inconsistencies, translation, and attached-file woes, e-mail really made this project a reality. Most contributors sent me copy in that form, and I passed it along to the home office in Detroit via the same method. I've never met more than half the contributors in person, but we all got to know each other pretty well by tapping into our computer screens, reviving the somewhat lost art of letter writing.

Among others who helped our contributors along the way, in no particular order: Anson and Renee Funderburgh; Black Top Records; Ronnie Narmour of RNA Booking; Antone's Records; Cheryl Neeley at Icehouse; Jay Sheffield Management; Johnny Reno; Bob H. Bell, Roomful of Blues manager; Joel Dorn of 32 Records; Shane Tappendorf of Double Tee Promotions, Inc.; Shannon D. Love of *Jet City Blues Review*; John Brenes, owner of the Music Coop in Petaluma, California; Pete Frame (for his scholarly book *Rock Family Trees*); Joanna Connor; Kathleen Cherrier, Floyd Dixon's manager; Sujata Murthy of Capitol;

David Maxwell; Paul Oscher; Arnie Goodman of Viceroy Music; Drink Small and his manager, Charles Derrick; Sherry Broyles of Ichiban; Rick Hallock of Mapleshade Productions; Kim Simmonds; Greg Spencer of Blue Wave; Les Kippel of *Relix*; Arnie Goodman at Viceroy Music; Steve Karas of PGD; Randi Hill of GNP Crescendos; Studebaker John Grimaldi; Jim English at Intrepid Artists; Louis Sahagun; Janis Johnson; Josh Jackson of WWOZ-FM; and Jerry Brock and Barry Smith at the Louisiana Music Factory. Thanks to them and anybody else we missed along the way.

Leland Rucker

musicHound
blues

A

Johnny Ace

Born John Marshall Alexander Jr., June 9, 1929, in Memphis, TN. Died December 25, 1954, in Houston, TX.

The son of a Memphis preacher, John Alexander was playing piano for the Beale Streeters, a blues collective that included B.B. King, Bobby "Blue" Bland and Roscoe Gordon, when producer David Mattis asked him to take over for Bland at a Duke Records session in 1952. The resulting single, "My Song," released under the name Johnny Ace, was a major R&B hit and gave the fledgling vocalist a brief but spectacular career that ended abruptly on Christmas Day, 1954, when the singing star shot himself in the head while waiting to go on stage in Houston. "Pledging My Love," a plaintive avowal of undying adoration issued posthumously in 1955, touched the hearts of teenagers of every description and became one of the biggest records of that pivotal year, crossing over to the pop charts to help open the door for black artists like Little Willie John, Sam Cooke, Jackie Wilson and James Brown to reach a vast new audience. But it was too late for Johnny Ace, who left us only two short years' worth of intensely personal recordings to remember him by.

what to buy: *Johnny Ace Memorial Album* 🎵🎵🎵🎵 (MCA, 1988) was first issued by Duke Records in the early days of R&B LPs and happily has been kept in print ever since. It collects the striking series of singles cut in Memphis under the guidance of original label owner David Mattis, and in Houston by his successor, Don Robey (with the valuable assistance of Johnny Otis and Joe Scott). Johnny's soulful, heartfelt blues ballads—"My

Song," "The Clock," "Never Let Me Go," "Cross My Heart," "Pledging My Love"—were the key to his popularity, but he could deliver a jump blues like "How Can You Be So Mean" or "Don't You Know" with all the energy and drive of the great blues shouters of the post-war era. Most of his releases were blues ballads, however, and if an entire album of tear-jerkers seems excessive, you can sample Ace's output on a pair of MCA anthologies: *Duke Peacock's Greatest Hits* 🎵🎵🎵 (MCA, 1992) has "The Clock" and "Pledging My Love," while *The Best of Duke-Peacock Blues* 🎵🎵🎵🎵 (MCA, 1992) includes the hot jump blues "How Can You Be So Mean."

influences:

◄◄ Billy Eckstine, Cecil Gant, Lonnie Johnson, B.B. King

►► Bobby "Blue" Bland, Sam Cooke, Little Willie John, James Brown, O.V. Wright, Little Milton

John Sinclair

The Aces

Formed c. 1949, in Chicago, IL. Disbanded 1956.

Dave Myers (born October 30, 1926, in Byhalia, MS), bass; Louis Myers (born September 18, 1929, in Byhalia, MS; died September 4, 1994, in Chicago, IL), guitar; Fred Below (born September 6, 1926, in Chicago, IL; died August 13, 1988, in Chicago, IL), drums.

As the Little Boys, the Myers brothers added Junior Wells to become the Three Deuces and the Three Aces, and Fred Below for the Four Aces and finally just the Aces. From the beginning the group was a dream team for anyone eager to record or perform with the most energetic and, at the same time, the most subtle of Chicago backing groups. With Wells, their urban and sophisticated style, ahead of its time, became ever more popular as their tight cohesion and jazz-influenced playing and instrumental versatility and skills improved. Little Walter was happy to hire the famous trio, who stayed with Walter as the Jukes until 1956, when they went their separate ways. In the early 1970s Louis Myers reformed the original Aces with Below and brother Dave. Below, an innovative drummer with a be-bop approach, invented the blues backbeat. With him the drums became a lead instrument in blues bands, and he influenced all modern blues drummers. Dave Myers is duly praised as the master of electric bass, his heavy and subtle lines still a favorite of recording musicians. An innovative stylist, Louis Myers was a great band leader and a talented accompanist with a captivating voice and a special sensitivity for melody. His harp work and guitar playing—he was a master of the bottleneck style—were brilliant.

what to buy: *The Essential Little Walter* ♪♪♪♪♪ (MCA/Chess 1993, prod. Andy McKaie) captures the essential Little Walter and his best sides with the Aces. *Chicago Beat* ♪♪♪♪♪ (Black & Blue, 1970, prod. Jacques Morgantini) was recorded in Bordeaux, France, with guests Eddie Taylor, Jimmy Rogers, Willie Mabon and Mickey Baker.

what to buy next: Louis' first solo album with West Coast partners, *Louis Myers—I'm a Southern Man* ♪♪♪♪ (Advent, 1978/Testament, 1995, prod. Pete Welding), is an opportunity to show his abilities as singer, songwriter, guitarist and harmonica player. *Louis Myers—Tell My Story Movin'* ♪♪♪♪ (Earwig, 1991, prod. Michael Frank) is the last recording of a giant of the blues.

the rest:

The Aces ♪♪♪♪ (Vogue, 1971/Vivid)
The Aces & Their Guests ♪♪♪ (MGM, 1975)

influences:

◄◄ Ransom Knowling, Little Walter, Lonnie Johnson, Big Bill Broonzy

►► Willie Kent, Jimmy Dawkins

Robert Sacré

Johnny Adams

Born January 5, 1932, in New Orleans, LA.

Johnny Adams' warm vocals and extraordinary range have earned him the title of "the Tan Canary" in New Orleans. He is equally comfortable singing blues, jazz, R&B and country in a

rich, strong tenor that soars from round, low notes to a soulful falsetto, from a whisper to a scream. Among New Orleans singers, only Aaron Neville comes close to approaching the elegance and grace that Adams brings to each song. One can still hear in his voice his beginnings as a gospel singer with groups such as the Soul Revivers and Bessie Griffin and her Soul Consolators. In 1959, he started recording rhythm & blues for Ric Records and scored a big local hit with "I Won't Cry." Legend has it that Berry Gordy loved Adams' voice and wanted him for Motown, but a threatened lawsuit by Ric president Joe Ruffino ended that possibility. Adams continued recording for regional labels and charted with the country-flavored "Release Me" and "Reconsider Me" on SSS International Records in the late 1960s. For many years, Adams teamed up with guitarist Walter "Wolfman" Washington every weekend at Dorothy's Medallion Lounge, a club that featured 300-pound go-go dancers performing with snakes. In 1984, Adams began an association with Rounder Records and producer Scott Billington which resulted in a series of excellent recordings and well-deserved national renown.

what to buy: *Johnny Adams Sings Doc Pomus: The Real Me* ♪♪♪♪♪ (Rounder, 1991, prod. Scott Billington, Mac Rebennack) is a glorious tribute to the literate and complex songs of the great Doc Pomus. Rebennack gets high marks for co-producing, playing keyboards and co-writing seven of the 11 tunes, and Red Tyler adds exquisite arrangements to songs like the clever and poignant "Imitation of Love" and the jazzy ballad "Blinded by Love." Adams finds his way to the heart of lyrics like this from "My Baby's Quit Me": "The dust is three inches thick/Ain't a clock in the house sayin' tick." *I Won't Cry: From the Vaults of Ric & Ron Records* ♪♪♪♪ (Rounder, 1991, prod. Jeff Hannusch) is a collection of Adams' earliest recordings from 1959–62. The youthful singer displays almost overwhelming power and emotion on these dates, which also feature the young Mac Rebennack. The title tune, Adams' first recording, is a doo-wop number with huge vocals penned by "Tutti Frutti" composer Dorothy Labostrie, a neighbor of Adams who brought him to Ruffino after hearing him sing "Precious Lord" in the bathtub. *Good Morning Heartache* ♪♪♪♪ (Rounder, 1993, prod. Scott Billington) is a dream match-up: legendary arranger Wardell Quezergue meets the Tan Canary on a set of jazz standards. This is late-night, brandy-sniffing, romance-enhancing music, as Adams wraps his chords around gorgeous songs like "You Don't Know What Love Is" and "Come Rain or Come Shine." *One Foot in the Blues* ♪♪♪♪ (Rounder, 1996, prod. Scott Billington) is another inspired grouping, matching Adams with

Dr. Lonnie Smith's Hammond B-3 organ for a satisfying set of soulful blues.

what to buy next: Adams' other tribute album, *Walking on a Tightrope: The Songs of Percy Mayfield* ♫♫♫ (Rounder, 1989, prod. Scott Billington), features the songs of "the poet laureate of the blues." A contract writer for Ray Charles for many years as well as a distinctive vocalist in his own right, Mayfield composed hundreds of songs. Backed by various jazz and blues musicians (including Walter "Wolfman" Washington and Duke Robillard on guitars), Adams brings elegance and emotion to the slow blues of the title cut and swing tunes like "Look the Whole World Over." The highlight is a brilliant reading of "Danger Zone," one of the greatest songs ever written.

the rest:

From the Heart ♫♫♫ (Rounder, 1984)
After Dark ♫♫♫ (Rounder, 1986)
Room with a View of the Blues ♫♫♫ (Rounder, 1987)
The Verdict ♫♫♫ (Rounder, 1995)

worth searching for: Adams shows up as a guest vocalist on a diverse group of recordings. Look for him on Maria Muldaur's *Fanning the Flames* (Telarc, 1996, prod. Maria Muldaur, John Snyder, Elaine Martone) and *Lost in the Stars: The Music of Kurt Weill* (A&M, 1985, prod. Hal Willner, John Telfer).

influences:

◀◀ Percy Mayfield, Johnny Hartman, Bobby "Blue" Bland

David Feld

Garfield Akers

Born 1901, reportedly in Bates, MS. Died 1959, in Memphis, TN.

Little is known about Garfield Akers, a mysterious presence who lived most of his life in the southern Memphis suburb that produced bluesmen Robert Wilkins and Joe Callicott and was the long-time home of rock wildman Jerry Lee Lewis. But on his four known recordings made in Memphis' Peabody Hotel in 1929 and 1930, Akers moaned an unearthly croon, backing himself on guitar with some of the most throbbing crosscut-saw guitar work heard in the pre-war blues era. His "Dough Roller Blues" contains one of the earliest permutations of Hambone Willie Newbern's "Roll and Tumble." Akers' version is even more insistent than the original; he cries over his departed dough-roller, wringing his hands in despair. A year earlier, Akers recorded the equally-driving, two-part "Cottonfield Blues," weaving against Joe Callicott's polyrhythmic guitar fills. In interviews after his own rediscovery in the 1960s, Callicott

said that he and Akers played together at northern Mississippi house parties at night and sharecropped by day throughout the 1930s. But unlike Callicott, Akers never recorded again after 1930, dying in obscurity like so many early bluesmen who offered only tantalizing shreds of their talent.

what to buy: *Son House and the Great Delta Blues Singers* ♫♫♫♫ (Document, 1990, prod. Johnny Parth) is an indispensable collection of the Delta's greatest—and phantom-like—bluesmen. In addition to Akers, it offers Son House's classic Paramount performances and definitive standards by Willie Brown, Kid Bailey, Jim Thompkins, Blind Joe Reynolds, Rube Lacey and Callicott.

what to buy next: If the previous collection didn't exist, *Mississippi Masters* ♫♫♫ (Yazoo, 1994, prod. Richard Nevins, Don Kent) would be the pick. The mastering of the old 78s is even better than Parth's, but Akers' work fits more snugly among the Delta greats in the latter disc. Still, this may be more easily found than Parth's Austrian import, and its other blues masters—Callicott, King Solomon Hill, Otto Virgial and Geeshie Wiley—are hardly slouches.

influences:

▶▶ Muddy Waters, Elmore James, Canned Heat

Steve Braun

Alger Alexander

See: Texas Alexander

John Marshall Alexander Jr.

See: Johnny Ace

Texas Alexander

Born Alger Alexander, September 12, 1900, in Jewett, TX. Died c. 1955, in TX.

When Texas Alexander walked into a New York studio in August 1927, he was already a singing relic, even among the crowd of pre-war blues session men who played behind him. Alexander was a novelty among the first generation of blues masters, a vocalist who played no instruments. He wandered the expanse of Texas with future guitar legends such as T-Bone Walker (then known as Oak Cliff T-Bone). Alexander emerged from the arid Texas cotton fields that Leadbelly sang about, taking work as a field hand and singing for tips. Imprisoned for a period in Ft. Worth, reportedly for attempted murder, Alexander settled in Dallas, singing in the Central Tracks neighborhood of tough bars. Discovered by barrelhouse pianist Sammy Price, Alexander was brought to record in New York. His first accompanist was blues guitar king Lonnie Johnson, who later complained that Alexander could not sing on tempo. Johnson survived by keeping the pace slow, and what resulted were drawn-out classics like "Long Lonesome Day Blues" and the evocative "Levee Camp Moan." Between 1927 and 1929 Alexander cut 66 songs, backed by a parade of artists as varied as pianist Eddie Heywood, guitarist Eddie Lang, the Mississippi Sheiks, Texas bluesman Little Hat Jones and jazzmen King Oliver and Clarence Williams. Alexander continued his wanderings through the 1930s but in 1940 was sent back to jail for murdering his wife. Released in 1945, he played for several years with Lightnin' Hopkins before his death.

what to buy: The three separate volumes of *Texas Alexander: Complete Recorded Works 1927 to 1929* ♪♪♪♪ (Matchbox, 1993) collect all 66 of Alexander's recordings. Of the three, the most enduring is the first, which features Alexander moaning to the lonesome backing of Lonnie Johnson.

influences:
▶▶ Lightnin' Hopkins, Smokey Hogg

Steve Braun

Fulton Allen
See: Blind Boy Fuller

Luther Allison
Born August 17, 1939, in Widener, AR. Died August 12, 1997, in Madison, WI.

Frustrated by a stalled career, Chicago guitarist Luther Allison moved to Paris in 1983. After establishing himself as something of a superstar in Europe, Allison commenced a strong domestic comeback with 1994's *Soul Fixin' Man*, reclaiming the sterling domestic reputation he earned as a young man. All of his Alligator releases feature a wide range of material spotlighting his slashing guitar work and gravelly, soulful vocals. From uptempo rockers to contemplative acoustic blues, from bouncy, horn-driven soul tunes to organ-fueled, gospel-style ballads, Allison performed with the fiery energy of a teenager and the grizzled soul of a veteran. His only weakness was an occasional tendency to do a little too much, go over the top. Usually, however, his guitar playing was reckless in the best sense of the word, dancing on a razor's edge, remaining just this side of out-of-control. Allison came from the same school of West Side Chicago guitar as Buddy Guy, Otis Rush, Magic Sam, Freddie King and Jimmy

Dawkins, favoring hard-driving, piercing single-note leads with a soul base and a rock edge. He also played a mean slide.

what to buy: *Soul Fixin' Man* ♪♪♪♪ (Alligator, 1994, prod. Jim Gaines) launched Allison's American comeback, and it is a gem—soulful, intense, varied and never out of control. You also won't go wrong with *Reckless* ♪♪♪♪ (Alligator, 1997, prod. Jim Gaines). *Where Have You Been? Live in Montreaux 1976–94* ♪♪♪♪ (Ruf, 1996, prod. Thomas Ruf) is an excellent live collection, spotlighting Allison's transcendent performance powers.

what to buy next: More straightforward than most of what followed, Allison's debut, *Love Me Mama* ♪♪♪♪ (Delmark, 1969, prod. Robert Koester), makes clear why he was considered a rising star of the blues at the time of its release. Similarly, *Love Me Papa* ♪♪♪♪ (Disques Black & Blue, 1978/Evidence, 1992) is a straight-ahead Chicago-style session performed with flair and a sort of off-handed charm.

what to avoid: *Motown Sessions, 1972–76* ♪♪♪ (Motown, 1996) collects Allison's best work as Motown's only bluesman. Even as the creme de la creme, it is not what it could and should have been.

the rest:
Serious ♪♪♪♪ (Blind Pig, 1987)
Blue Streak ♪♪♪♪ (Alligator, 1995)

influences:
◀◀ Robert Nighthawk, Magic Sam, Freddie King
▶▶ Kenny Neal, Joe Louis Walker

Alan Paul

Mose Allison
Born Mose John Allison Jr., November 11, 1927, in Tippo, MS.

Though Allison's light, improvisational piano style has more in common with jazz than blues, he built his early reputation by personalizing Sonny Boy Williamson's "Eyesight to the Blind," Willie Dixon's "Seventh Son" and Muddy Waters' "Rollin' Stone." Interpreting blues standards in his lazy and smart-alecky—but always warm—voice, he also influenced rockers Pete Townshend, Van Morrison, the Clash and the Yardbirds. Townshend in particular, who liked the blues but didn't want the Who to become another blues-reviving Yardbirds or Rolling Stones, found inspiration in "Eyesight to the Blind" and Alli-

Luther Allison (© Linda Vartoogian)

son's most enduring anthem, "Young Man's Blues." But all the rock influence has distorted Allison's legend. He has been recording albums and touring nightclubs (where he refuses to let anybody smoke) for 40 years, and his devastating sense of humor led to such wonderful jazz songs as "Your Mind Is on Vacation" and "If You're Going to the City." His piano style, reminiscent of long-time Waters sideman Otis Spann, is fast and playful but never so busy it clutters up the lyrics. Not much has changed over the past several decades for Allison, though he collaborated on *Tell Me Something* with Van Morrison (who once covered his "If You Only Knew") and occasionally does joint interviews with his country-rocking daughter, the talented Parlor James singer Amy Allison.

what to buy: *Allison Wonderland: The Mose Allison Anthology* ♫♫♫♫♫ (Rhino, 1994, prod. Joel Dorn, James Austin) shows why Allison was such an important link between mid-century Chicago blues and early-1960s British rock 'n' roll. The compilation displaced *The Best of Mose Allison* ♫♫♫♫ (Atlantic, 1988, prod. Bob Porter) and *Greatest Hits* ♫♫♫♫ (Prestige, 1959/1988, prod. Bob Weinstock) as the essential places to find "The Seventh Son," "Eyesight to the Blind," "Young Man's Blues" and "Your Mind Is on Vacation."

what to buy next: His original studio albums are hard to find, but *Back Country Suite* ♫♫♫ (Prestige, 1957, engineer Rudy Van Gelder), *Local Color* ♫♫♫ (Prestige, 1958, prod. Bob Weinstock) and *Ramblin' with Mose Allison* ♫♫♫ (Prestige, 1961) are among the best of a prolific recording career. His 1980s Elektra period, which produced *Middle Class White Boy* ♫♫♫ (Elektra, 1982, prod. Esmond Edwards) and *Lesson in Living* ♫♫♫ (Elektra, 1983, prod. Philippe Rault), allowed him to revitalize his style with a more soulful touch. *Tell Me Something* ♫♫♫ (Verve, 1996, prod. Van Morrison, Ben Sidran, Georgie Fame), a collaboration with Morrison and Fame, is a nice tribute and return to form after years of nondescript studio albums.

what to avoid: Allison has been churning out records with incredible regularity for four decades, and sometimes he releases a rushed batch of stuff: *Mose Alive!* ♫♫♫ (Atlantic, 1966), *Western Man* ♫♫ (Atlantic, 1971) and *Mose in Your Ear* ♫♫ (Atlantic, 1972) are examples of this lack of inspiration.

the rest:
Parchman Farm ♫♫♫ (Original Jazz Classics)
Creek Bank ♫♫♫ (Prestige, 1958)
Ol' Devil Mose ♫♫♫ (Prestige, 1958)
Young Man Mose ♫♫♫ (Prestige, 1958)
Autumn Song ♫♫♫ (Prestige, 1959)

Mose Allison Plays for Lovers ♫♫♫ (Prestige, 1959)
Transfiguration of Hiram Brown ♫♫♫ (Columbia, 1960)
I Love the Life I Live ♫♫ (Columbia, 1961)
V-8 Ford Blues ♫♫♫ (Epic/Legacy, 1961)
I Don't Worry about a Thing ♫♫ (Atlantic/Rhino, 1962)
Mose Allison Takes to the Hills ♫♫♫ (Epic/Legacy, 1962)
Mose Allison Sings ♫♫♫ (Prestige, 1963)
Swingin' Machine ♫♫ (Atlantic, 1963)
The Word from Mose Allison ♫♫♫ (Atlantic, 1964)
Wild Man on the Lane ♫♫ (Atlantic, 1966)
I Been Doin' Some Thinkin' ♫♫ (Atlantic, 1968)
Mose Goes ♫♫ (Columbia, 1968)
Hello There Universe ♫♫ (Atlantic, 1970)
Retrospective ♫♫♫ (Columbia, 1971)
Mose Allison ♫♫♫ (Prestige, 1972)
The Seventh Son ♫♫♫ (Prestige, 1973)
Your Mind Is on Vacation ♫♫♫ (Atlantic, 1976)
Ever Since the World Ended ♫♫ (Blue Note, 1988)
My Backyard ♫♫ (Blue Note, 1990)
Mose Allison Sings and Plays ♫♫♫ (Prestige, 1991)
I Don't Worry about a Thing ♫♫♫ (Rhino, 1993)
The Earth Wants You ♫♫ (Blue Note, 1994)
High Jinks!: The Mose Allison Trilogy ♫♫♫ (Columbia, 1994)

influences:

◄◄ Muddy Waters, Willie Dixon, Art Tatum, Ray Charles, Charles Brown, Sonny Boy Williamson II, Otis Spann

►► Pete Townshend, Bonnie Raitt, Van Morrison, Elvis Costello, Ray Davies

Steve Knopper

The Allman Brothers Band

Formed 1969, in Jacksonville, FL.

Duane Allman (died October 29, 1971), guitar; Gregg Allman, keyboards, vocals; Dickey Betts, guitar, vocals; Berry Oakley (died November 11, 1972), bass; Butch Trucks, drums; Jaimoe Johanson, drums; Chuck Leavell, keyboards (1972–76); Lamar Williams (died January 25, 1983), bass (1972–76); Bonnie Bramlett, vocals (1979–80); Dan Toler, guitar (1979–82); David Goldflies, bass (1979–82); David "Frankie" Toler, drums (1981–82); Johnny Neel, keyboards (1989–90); Warren Haynes, guitar (1989–present); Allen Woody, bass (1989–present); Marc Quinones, percussion (1991–present); Jack Pearson, guitar (1997); Oteil Burbridge, bass (1997).

In the late 1960s there were countless rock artists trying to simultaneously embrace and expand the blues. Only Jimi Hendrix had success equal to that of the Allman Brothers Band, who sounded perfectly at home playing material by the likes of Muddy Waters, Elmore James and Sonny Boy Williamson. Formed in 1969 by Duane Allman, a young session guitarist who had recorded with Wilson Pickett, Aretha Franklin, King Curtis and other R&B greats, the group quickly created an utterly distinct, highly improvisational style. They rocked hard while reflecting a profound understanding of virtually every indigenous American musical form: not just blues, but also country, folk, R&B and jazz. Driven by the relentlessly propulsive, inventive drumming of Trucks and Johanson, Gregg Allman's bluesy organ riffing and Oakley's free-range bass lines, Betts and Duane Allman crafted a remarkable twin lead guitar approach. Taking cues from jazz horn players, particularly Miles Davis and John Coltrane, and the twin fiddles of western swing music, they rewrote the rule book on how rock guitarists can play together, paving the way for every two-guitar band that has followed. But Hall-of-Fame careers are not built on instrumental virtuosity alone, and the root of the Allman Brothers' success has been a strong, varied songbook. The band has overcome a variety of obstacles, most notably the deaths of Duane Allman and Oakley and two break-ups, to return to nearly peak form in the 1990s. It is a development few could have predicted.

what to buy: *At Fillmore East* 𝄞𝄞𝄞𝄞𝄞 (Capricorn, 1971, prod. Tom Dowd) captured the band's instrumental glory and improvisational magic remarkably well. The double album holds only seven (very long) songs—and nary a wasted note—and also features some of the Allmans' best straight blues, including "Statesboro Blues," "Stormy Monday" and "Done Somebody Wrong." *Eat a Peach* 𝄞𝄞𝄞𝄞 (Capricorn, 1972, prod. Tom Dowd) contains more tunes from the Fillmore shows, including the 33-minute "Mountain Jam" and Sonny Boy Williamson's "One Way Out," as well as great new tunes like "Melissa" and "Blue Sky." *Brothers and Sisters* 𝄞𝄞𝄞𝄞 (Capricorn, 1975, prod. Johnny Sandlin, Allman Brothers Band), the group's first post-Duane album, includes the band's biggest hits—"Ramblin' Man," "Jessica" and "Southbound." If you want to see what the band's up to now, *An Evening With: First Set* 𝄞𝄞𝄞𝄞 (Epic, 1992, prod. Tom Dowd) provides a pretty good overview.

what to buy next: *Beginnings* 𝄞𝄞𝄞𝄞 (Capricorn, 1973, prod. Joel Dorn, Tom Dowd) combines the band's first two albums in full. Once you're hooked, you won't want to be without *Dreams* 𝄞𝄞𝄞𝄞 (Polydor, 1989, prod. various), a four-disc collection that does everything a boxed set should. *Where It All Begins* 𝄞𝄞𝄞 (Epic, 1994, prod. Tom Dowd), while quite inconsistent, contains the best material the new Brothers have produced.

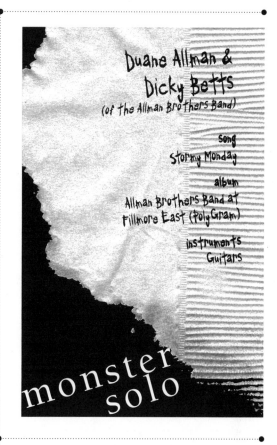

Duane Allman & Dicky Betts (of the Allman Brothers Band)

song
Stormy Monday

album
Allman Brothers Band at Fillmore East (PolyGram)

instruments
Guitars

monster solo

what to avoid: The Allmans' worst albums, *Brothers of the Road* 𝄞𝄞 (Arista, 1980) and *Reach for the Sky* 𝄞 (Arista, 1981), were both recently reissued by Razor & Tie after years of being out of print. One can only wonder why.

the rest:
The Allman Brothers Band 𝄞𝄞𝄞𝄞 (Capricorn, 1969)
Idlewild South 𝄞𝄞𝄞𝄞 (Capricorn, 1970)
Win, Lose or Draw 𝄞𝄞𝄞 (Capricorn, 1975)
The Road Goes on Forever 𝄞𝄞𝄞𝄞 (Capricorn, 1976)
Wipe the Windows, Check the Oil, Dollar Gas 𝄞𝄞𝄞 (Capricorn, 1976)
Enlightened Rogues 𝄞𝄞𝄞 (Capricorn, 1979)
Best of the Allman Brothers Band 𝄞𝄞𝄞 (Polydor, 1981)
Live at Ludlow Garage, 1970 𝄞𝄞𝄞𝄞 (Polydor, 1990)
Seven Turns 𝄞𝄞𝄞𝄞 (Epic, 1990)
Decade of Hits (1969–79) 𝄞𝄞𝄞𝄞 (Polydor, 1991)
Shades of Two Worlds 𝄞𝄞𝄞 (Epic, 1991)
The Fillmore Concerts 𝄞𝄞𝄞𝄞𝄞 (PolyGram, 1992)
Hell and High Water 𝄞𝄞 (Arista, 1994)

An Evening With: Second Set 🎵🎵🎵 (Epic, 1995)
February, 1970, Fillmore East 🎵🎵🎵🎵 (Grateful Dead Records, 1997)

worth searching for: *The Allman Brothers Band at the R&R Cafe* 🎵🎵🎵🎵 was a promotional-only acoustic performance which is well worth the effort to find. Excellent live bootlegs abound, but *New York City Blues* 🎵🎵🎵🎵, recorded in 1970, is exceptional.

solo outings:
Duane Allman:
An Anthology 🎵🎵🎵🎵 (Capricorn, 1972)
An Anthology Vol. 2 🎵🎵🎵 (Capricorn, 1974)

Gregg Allman:
Laid Back 🎵🎵🎵🎵 (PolyGram, 1973)
The Gregg Allman Tour 🎵🎵🎵🎵 (PolyGram, 1974)
Playin' up a Storm 🎵🎵🎵 (Razor & Tie, 1977)
I'm No Angel 🎵🎵🎵🎵 (Epic, 1987)
Just before the Bullets Fly 🎵🎵🎵 (Epic, 1988)
One More Try 🎵🎵🎵 (Polydor, 1997)

Dickey Betts:
Highway Call 🎵🎵🎵🎵 (PolyGram, 1974)
Pattern Disruptive 🎵🎵 (Epic, 1988)

Govt Mule:
Govt Mule 🎵🎵🎵 (Relativity, 1995)
Live at Roseland Ballroom 🎵🎵🎵🎵 (Foundation, 1996)

influences:
⏪ Albert King, Cream, Miles Davis, Bob Willis, Texas Playboys
⏩ Eagles, Lynyrd Skynyrd, Little Feat, Black Crowes

Alan Paul

Dave Alvin

Born November 11, 1955, in Los Angeles, CA.

If this excellent songwriter could sing, he might well be a superstar. But the Lord, alas, gave the vocal gifts to his brother, Phil Alvin, and decreed that the two would almost never get along. Fortunately, in the solo years since the brothers' band, the Blasters, broke up, Dave Alvin has developed his limited voice almost to the acquired-taste level of Lyle Lovett or John Hiatt. Either way, he always rocks, which is more than you can say for most performing musicologists. Though his songs are rooted in twangy country and rockabilly music, Alvin regularly pays tribute to his blues influences. There's a line in his Blasters classic, "American Music," about the Chicago blues, and there's that

point in every Alvin concert where he shifts to the 12-bar and plays like Buddy Guy with his teeth gritted. He has shown the most maturity, though, in his songwriting; where his solo debut, *Romeo's Escape*, held together solely because of Alvin's passion, his last few albums have been remarkably cohesive. His 1990s songs, including "Haley's Comet," "Wanda and Duane," "Thirty Dollar Room" and "Museum of Heart," stack up perfectly next to Blasters classics "So Long Baby Goodbye" and "Border Radio." To adapt to his lack of commercial potential, Alvin has become the big fish at the little label HighTone, where he produces and performs with Rosie Flores, Big Sandy & His Fly-Rite Boys and several other artists, coordinated the excellent 1994 Merle Haggard tribute album, *Tulare Dust,* and, of course, churns out his own solo records. Every few years he and Phil will get on a stage together and do old Blasters songs; they stand many feet apart, barely acknowledging each other and conclude by walking off separately.

what to buy: *Blue Blvd.* 🎵🎵🎵🎵 (HighTone, 1991, prod. Chris Silagyi, Dave Alvin, Bruce Bromberg) contains some of Alvin's best songwriting, from the lonely-driving title track to the depressing rock fairy tale and Bill Haley tribute, "Haley's Comet"; you can practically hear his voice maturing as the record goes on.

what to buy next: *King of California* 🎵🎵🎵🎵 (HighTone, 1994, prod. Greg Leisz) is Alvin's acoustic album, with revamped versions of the Blasters' "Border Radio" and X's "Fourth of July," and the tangible sense of desperation taps into both blues and country history.

what to avoid: Despite a few typically well-written songs, including the title track and "Thirty Dollar Room," the music and images on *Museum of Heart* 🎵🎵🎵 (HighTone, 1993, prod. Chris Silagyi, Bruce Bromberg, Dave Alvin) aren't as memorable as Alvin's other solo material.

the rest:
Romeo's Escape 🎵🎵🎵 (Epic, 1987)
Interstate City 🎵🎵🎵 (HighTone, 1996)

worth searching for: Alvin co-produced *Tulare Dust: A Songwriters' Tribute to Merle Haggard* 🎵🎵🎵🎵 (HighTone, 1994, prod. Tom Russell, Dave Alvin), and you can hear his fingerprints all over it; he performs the closing song, "Kern River," and puts his trademark blues-and-country loneliness sheen on tracks by Barrence Whitfield, Katy Moffatt and Marshall Crenshaw.

influences:
⏪ Willie Dixon, Howlin' Wolf, Lightnin' Hopkins, Elvis Presley, Carl Perkins, Johnny Cash, Patsy Cline, Charlie Rich, Merle Haggard

Gregg Allman of the Allman Brothers Band **(© Ken Settle)**

▶▶ Stray Cats, Los Lobos, Big Sandy & His Fly-Rite Boys, Lucinda Williams, X, Social Distortion, Jason & the Scorchers, Stevie Ray Vaughan

Steve Knopper

Phil Alvin

Born March 6, 1953, in Los Angeles, CA.

As the frontman for the Blasters, Alvin effortlessly sang blues, R&B and big-band classics—including some written by his brother and bandmate, Dave Alvin—like he was born to do so. But the Blasters broke up, the brothers' relationship splintered and Phil was left without his own songs to sing. On two great eclectic solo records, though, he adapted. Despite the absence of his often-estranged brother, Phil Alvin has been touring with the Blasters for several years.

what to buy: Alvin's fascination with American music history found perfect collaborators, on *Un "Sung Stories"* ♫♫♫ (Slash, 1986, prod. Phil Alvin, Pat Burnett), in Sun Ra's Arkestra and the Dirty Dozen Brass Band. It's a tribute to the legendary R&B singer Big Joe Turner, and though it shifts quickly from jumping swing jazz ("The Ballad of Smokey Joe") to stark acoustic blues ("Gangster's Blues"), Alvin's distinctive sound and unyielding enthusiasm hold it together. The lesser-known contributors to his follow-up, *County Fair 2000* ♫♫♫ (HighTone, 1994, prod. Phil Alvin), include Billy Boy Arnold and the Faultline Syncopators.

influences:

◀◀ Big Joe Turner, Sun Ra, Hank Williams, Cab Calloway

Steve Knopper

Little Willie Anderson

Born May 21, 1920, in West Memphis, AR. Died June 20, 1991, in Chicago, IL.

Little Willie Anderson was wholly enamored of the great harpist Little Walter. He imitated Walter so thoroughly—and also became his friend, chauffeur and valet—that he probably doomed his own recording career. The association, of course, made him an incredible harmonica expert, and when he finally got around to recording an album in the early 1980s, he proved to be a nice contemporary bridge between old-school blues harp and modern studio techniques.

what to buy: *Swinging the Blues* ♫♫♫ (Blues on Blues, 1981) is surprisingly Little Walter-free and experimental, tackling a

Lester Young jazz standard and featuring a genuinely raucous band for the singer's original material.

influences:

◀◀ Little Walter, Sonny Boy Williamson I, Robert Nighthawk, Muddy Waters

▶▶ Charlie Musselwhite, Sugar Blue, Sonny Boy Williamson II, Junior Wells

Steve Knopper

Pink Anderson

Born February 12, 1900, in Laurens, SC. Died October 12, 1974, in Spartanburg, SC.

Pink Anderson sang East Coast acoustic folk music, blues, minstrel tunes and ballads. He hit the road at age 14 as a performer in the Indian Remedy Company's traveling medicine show, staying with the group until 1945. As captured in his recordings, he performed diverse material in a plaintive style, drawing from both black and white country traditions. Like many of his peers from the Piedmont region of the Southeast (and unlike countless Mississippi Delta bluesmen), his legacy in modern blues or rock 'n' roll, or even folk music, is not substantial. That fact makes his recordings all the more unique and valuable as documents of a musical heritage that—though not embraced by contemporary culture—certainly is worth remembering.

what to buy: *The Blues of Pink Anderson: Ballad & Folksinger, Vol. 3* ♫♫♫♫ (Prestige/Bluesville, 1961/Original Blues Classics, 1995, supervised by Samuel Charters) captures some of Anderson's best work, including "The Titanic," "Boweevil" and "John Henry." One negative: at less than 35 minutes, it's over too soon!

what to buy next: *Pink Anderson: Carolina Blues Man, Vol. 1* ♫♫♫ (Original Blues Classics, 1992, supervised by Samuel Charters) packages Anderson's more overtly blues-based material. It's well-executed, but less unique and more familiar than *Ballad & Folksinger*, including tunes such as "Baby Please Don't Go" and Brownie McGhee's "Meet Me in the Bottom." *Rev. Gary Davis and Pink Anderson: Gospel, Blues and Street Songs, Vol. 3* ♫♫♫ (Original Blues Classics, 1987) includes seven tunes from Anderson recorded in 1950 in Charlottesville, Virginia, among them the irresistible "Greasy Greens." The sound quality does not measure up to Anderson's 1961 recordings, or even to the standard of the day, however.

worth searching for: Inexplicably, the second volume of the series mentioned above, which captured Anderson's medicine show recordings, is not available and not scheduled for reissue at press time. The Prestige/Bluesville LP version is worth finding, though.

influences:

▶▶ Paul Geremia, Roy Book Binder, Steve James

Bryan Powell

The Animals

Formed 1962, in Newcastle Upon Tyne, England. Disbanded 1969. Reformed 1976 and 1983.

Eric Burdon, vocals; Alan Price, keyboards (1962–65); Bryan "Chas" Chandler (died July 17, 1996), bass (1962–66); John Steel, drums (1962–66); Hilton Valentine, guitar (1962–66); Dave Rowberry, keyboards (1965–66); Barry Jenkins, drums (1966–present); John Weider, guitar (1966–present); Danny McCullough, bass (1966–68); Tom Parker, organ (1966–67); Vic Briggs, guitar (1967–68); Zoot Money, keyboards (1968–69); Andrew Somers, guitar (1968–69).

During the early 1960s British Invasion, the Animals prided itself on being one of the stalwarts of the blues, even after the Rolling Stones went pop. Yet the band will be remembered as one of the first to marry a folk song to a rock beat for its breakthrough hit, "House of the Rising Sun." Front man Burdon was one of the great vocalists of the era, with gritty, soulful delivery and his James Brown-style collapse routine on stage. The original Animals split up in 1966, but an altered band—billed with Burdon's name out front—was at the front line of West Coast psychedelia, having been to the Monterey Pop Festival (and writing a hit single about it) and later singing convincingly of such American concerns as Vietnam and San Francisco nights. As they left, the individual Animals made their marks elsewhere: Chandler was Jimi Hendrix's first manager; Price scored the soundtrack to *O Lucky Man!*; Somers became Andy Summers and joined the Police; and Burdon went on to a solo career, with War as his first backing band. The Animals' reunions have never stuck, but the group's performances showed it could still call up the ferocious attack of its 1960s blues peak at will.

what to buy: There's never been a fully satisfying Animals collection—at least not on these shores. But *The Best of the Animals* 𝄢𝄢𝄢𝄢 (MGM, 1966/Abkco, 1987, prod. Mickie Most) covers the extraordinary early singles, the Abkco set in digitally remastered sound.

what to buy next: *The Best of Eric Burdon and the Animals, Vol. 2* 𝄢𝄢𝄢 (MGM, 1967, prod. various) captures the later, psychedelicized version of the band. *Animalization* 𝄢𝄢𝄢 (MGM, 1966, prod. Mickie Most) is the most fully realized early album.

what to avoid: Of Burdon's many mediocre solo albums, *Black Man's Burdon* 𝄢𝄢 (MGM, 1971/Avenue, 1993, prod. Jerry Goldstein)—his second with War—was incredibly indulgent and self-consciously arty.

best of the rest:

The Animals 𝄢𝄢𝄢 (MGM, 1964)
The Animals on Tour 𝄢𝄢𝄢 (MGM, 1965)
Animal Tracks 𝄢𝄢𝄢 (MGM, 1965)
Animalism 𝄢𝄢𝄢 (MGM, 1966)
The Greatest Hits of Eric Burdon and the Animals 𝄢𝄢𝄢 (MGM, 1969)
Before We Were So Rudely Interrupted 𝄢𝄢𝄢 (United Artists, 1977)
Rip It to Shreds: Greatest Hits Live 𝄢𝄢𝄢 (I.R.S., 1984)

worth searching for: That illusive 1962–69 Animals collection exists in the form of the strong Australian import *The Most of the Animals* 𝄢𝄢𝄢𝄢 (Raven, 1989, prod. various), which tracks the hits from "House of the Rising Sun" through the group's resurrections of Johnny Cash's "Ring of Fire" and Traffic's "Coloured Rain."

influences:

◀◀ John Lee Hooker, Alex Korner

▶▶ Bruce Springsteen, John Mellencamp, Blue Oyster Cult

Roger Catlin

Rodney Armstrong

See: Guitar Slim Jr.

Billy Boy Arnold

Born William Arnold, September 16, 1935, in Chicago, IL.

Billy Boy Arnold has been a major figure on the Chicago blues scene since the early 1950s. As a teenager he was influenced by John Lee "Sonny Boy" Williamson, who he met in his neighborhood and tutored for a short time. Arnold assimilated Sonny Boy's choking style and wah-wah vibrato on a plastic harmonica, then on a Marine Band instrument, before going on to learn with local talents Little Walter, Earl Hooker and Junior Wells. An original stylist with a clear, sensitive voice and stop-time harmonica phrases, he combined urban modernity and country Mississippi roots and was a key actor in the emergence of modern Chicago blues (1955–57) and early rock 'n' roll (through his work with Bo Diddley in 1954). He then recorded under his own name for Vee-Jay and produced some hits between 1955 and 1957 ("I Wish You Would," "I Ain't Got You," "Kissing at Midnight," "Don't Stay out All Night") that influenced the British blues revival in the 1960s. In the early 1970s he toured Europe successfully, then stayed semi-retired from 1975 until 1993, playing occasional gigs in Chicago before coming back on Alligator Records.

what to buy: *Crying and Pleading* 🎵🎵🎵🎵 (Charly, 1980/1994, prod. Alan Balfour) includes the Vee-Jay classics "I Wish You Would" and "I Ain't Got You." *Checkin' It Out* 🎵🎵🎵 (Red Lightnin, 1979/Sequel, 1996, prod. Peter Shertser) is a 1977 London session with British partners ("Dirty Mother Fucker," "Eldorado Cadillac," "I Ain't Got You") and new personal compositions. *Back Where I Belong* 🎵🎵🎵🎵 (Alligator, 1992, prod. Randy Chortkoff) has tributes to his masters and new songs, or try *Eldorado Cadillac* 🎵🎵🎵 (Alligator, 1996, prod. Bruce Iglauer, Billy Boy Arnold, Scott Dirks), with nine Arnold originals ("Man of Considerable Taste" is especially nice) and more deep, dark vocals.

what to buy next: *More Blues on the Southside* 🎵🎵🎵 (Prestige, 1963, prod. Samuel Charters) includes Lafayette Leake and Mighty Joe Young in the band.

the rest:

Johnny Jones—B.B. Arnold Live 🎵🎵🎵 (Alligator, 1979)
Bo Diddley—Bo's Blues 🎵🎵🎵🎵 (Ace, 1993)

influences:

◀◀ Sonny Boy Williamson I, Little Walter

▶▶ Yardbirds, Animals

Robert Sacré

James "Kokomo" Arnold

Born February 15, 1901, in Lovejoy's Station, GA. Died November 8, 1968, in Chicago, IL.

A hell-bent slide guitar player and an occasional bootlegger when he needed spending money, Kokomo Arnold recorded prolifically in the 1930s. Among his more than 80 recordings, three stand out for their embryonic impact on the songwriting of mythic Delta blues wanderer Robert Johnson and the generations of blues singers who followed. Arnold's 1934 "Milkcow Blues" begat Johnson's "Milkcow's Calf Blues" and, nearly 20 years later, Elvis Presley's "Milkcow Blues Boogie." Cut at the same session, "Old Original Kokomo Blues" spawned Johnson's "Sweet Home Chicago" and dozens of copycat versions. The last song cut at the session, "Sagefield Woman Blues," is probably even more influential. Its immortal trebly guitar lick and the line "I believe I'll dust my broom" not only spurred Johnson's "Dust My Broom" but indirectly launched slide master Elmore James on his career. An itinerant who worked the steel mills of Buffalo,

Pittsburgh and Gary in the 1920s, Arnold played in Mississippi Delta clubs and sold illegal liquor on the side until he settled in Chicago in 1929. Playing solo or backing up piano legends like Peetie Wheatstraw and Roosevelt Sykes, Arnold recorded extensively for Decca, backing up his own lazy vocals with a plangent slide that he either plucked randomly or hammered like a mad carpenter. Like many blues musicians of his era, he tended to repeat himself, and by the late 1930s was deep in a musical rut. He returned to work in the steel mills, grumpily waving off blues rediscoverers in the late 1950s. He was finished with "that mad way of life," he told French interviewers in 1959.

what to buy: To get Arnold's trend-setting 1934 cuts, *Kokomo Arnold Vol. 1* 🎵🎵🎵🎵 (Document, 1991, prod. Johnny Parth) is the collection to find. It also includes his anarchic "Paddlin' Madeline Blues," recorded under a brief nom-de-blues, "Gitfiddle Jim."

worth searching for: A nice compilation, *Bottleneck Trendsetters* 🎵🎵🎵🎵 (Yazoo, prod. Nick Perls) balances Arnold's classic recordings with Hawaiian slide wizard Casey Bill Weldon.

influences:

◀◀ Sam Collins

▶▶ Robert Johnson, Elmore James, Elvis Presley

Steve Braun

Etta Baker

Born 1913, in Caldwell County, NC.

In her quietly unassuming way, Etta Baker has lived a remarkable life. She is among the greatest practitioners of acoustic Piedmont finger picking (an open-tuned guitar style that owes a great deal to bluegrass-style banjo) but toils in obscurity because she spent the better part of her musical career never playing outside of family gatherings. Born to a musical lineage, Baker began playing guitar at an early age and learned the traditional folk-blues dance tunes, rags and ballads from her father. She remains active on the folk and blues festival circuit.

what to buy: Baker first appeared on vinyl with her father and other relatives on the 1956 field recording *Instrumental Music of the Southern Appalachians* 🎵🎵🎵🎵 (Rykodisc, 1997, prod. Diane Hamilton, Liam Clancy, Paul Clayton), resulting in the closest thing to being at a Baker family house party. It would be 35 years before Baker recorded again, during which time she worked in the textile mills of western North Carolina and raised nine children before finally turning pro as a musician in her sixties. *One-Dime Blues* ♫♫♫♫ (Rounder, 1991, prod. Wayne Martin, Lesley Williams) arrived seemingly out of nowhere, a stunning 20-song collection of some of the finest folk-blues guitar you'll hear anywhere, especially the title track (popularized by Woody Guthrie as "New York Town").

worth searching for: The Rykodisc reissue of *Instrumental Music of the Southern Appalachians* (Tradition, 1956) has a different cover from the original. For that reason, the vinyl version is worth finding for the cover—a borderline offensive hillbilly caricature that is simply not to be believed (and which has absolutely nothing to do with the music). A landmark in political incorrectness.

influences:

◀◀ Elizabeth Cotten, Blind Boy Fuller

David Menconi

LaVern Baker

Born Delores LaVern Baker, November 11, 1929, in Chicago, IL. Died March 10, 1997, in New York, NY.

Everyone remembers "Tweedle Dee," that novelty song by Georgia Gibbs, right? The fact that you probably don't is a perfect example of art's eventual triumph over commerce. With the passage of time, it is LaVern Baker's original recording that strikes a chord with the public and not the insipid white cover version. In spite of this, LaVern Baker herself never wavered in her hatred for the song. She resented being labeled a rock 'n' roll singer, period. A brief survey of her illustrious career provides ample clues as to the reasons why. Niece of Merline Johnson, a prolifically recorded blues singer who attained stardom as "the Yas Yas Girl" in the 1930s and was a distant cousin of Memphis Minnie, Baker burst on the scene in the late 1940s as "Little Miss Sharecropper." Her comic, jump-blues routine was so well-received that she was whisked into both the Columbia and RCA studios within two years of her professional debut. In 1952 she joined "sock-instrumental" blues pianist Todd Rhodes' band, with whom she recorded for King, and in 1953 was signed by the jazz hounds at Atlantic, who were eager to dress up her jazz balladry with heavier R&B sensibilities. Her first Atlantic single, the tough, gospel-inflected blues ballad "Soul on Fire," is a fine illustration of the origins of her style. By the time of her third single, however, Baker was already a reluc-

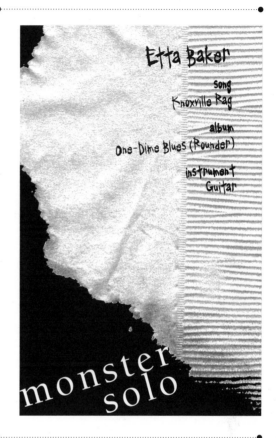

Etta Baker
song
Knoxville Rag
album
One-Dime Blues (Rounder)
instrument
Guitar

monster solo

tant pop commodity, regularly featured on Alan Freed's all-star stage shows belting out "Jim Dandy," "Jim Dandy Got Married" and other hits. In 1958, at the height of her popularity, she defiantly recorded a blues album, *LaVern Baker Sings Bessie Smith*, but most listeners paid considerably more attention to chart-toppers like "I Cried a Tear" (her biggest hit) and "I Waited Too Long." When the soul era eventually brought an end to her commercial appeal, Baker left Atlantic and soon disappeared from the scene. When she re-emerged in the late 1980s, her adaptable vocal style had lost none of its punch. Her final recordings find her in fine form, singing in the jazzy blues tradition that was always closest to her heart.

what to buy: *Soul on Fire* ♫♫♫♫ (Atlantic, 1991, prod. Ahmet Ertegun) gathers up all of her Atlantic hits recorded between 1953–62. Classics like "Tweedle Dee," "Play It Fair," "Jim Dandy," "Jim Dandy Got Married," "I Cried a Tear," "Saved" and "See See Rider" deserve a prominent place in any basic R&B

$\frac{1}{4}$ *lee baker jr.*

LaVern Baker (© Jack Vartoogian)

collection. The set is rounded out nicely by several uncharted obscurities, including the magnificent Ben E. King collaborations, "How Often" and "You Said." *LaVern Baker Sings Bessie Smith* ♫♫♫♫ (Atco, 1958/1988, prod. Nesuhi Ertegun) shows best Baker's overlooked talent for mature blues singing. Others have been intrepid enough to cover Bessie Smith, but Baker is the only one who doesn't come off sounding like some vaudeville pop artist without soul.

what to buy next: The best of her "comeback" recordings, *Live in Hollywood '91* ♫♫♫ (Rhino, 1996, prod. Mark Linett, Andy Paley) finds Baker in good form singing in front of a lively crowd at Hollywood's Cinegrill nightclub.

what to avoid: *Blues Side of Rock 'n' Roll* ♫♫♫ (Star Club, 1995, prod. Ahmet Ertegun) duplicates 14 tracks found on the Atlantic collection with vastly inferior sound quality. It does, however, contain 12 cuts otherwise unavailable on CD, including "Tra La La," "Oh Johnny Oh Johnny" and "Bumble Bee."

the rest:

Woke Up This Morning ♫♫ (DRG, 1992)

worth searching for: *Blues Ballads* ♫♫♫♫ (Atlantic, 1959, prod. Ahmet Ertegun) is another rare set of jazzy blues well worth hunting down. Muddy Waters once said that to sing the blues, you first have to go to church; the gospel LP *Precious Memories* ♫♫♫♫ (Atlantic, 1959, prod. Ahmet Ertegun) is proof that he was right.

influences:

◀◀ Bessie Smith, Dinah Washington

▶▶ Denise LaSalle

D. Thomas Moon

Lee Baker Jr.

See: Lonnie Brooks

Marcia Ball (© Jack Vartoogian)

Marcia Ball

Born March 20, 1949, in Orange, TX.

Say the phrase "The Girls" to anyone familiar with the blues scene in Austin, Texas, and they'll know you're talking about Angela Strehli, Lou Ann Barton and "Long, Tall Marcia Ball." Of the three, Ball is the only one notable as a player as well as a singer. She's a pianist, and a good one, drawing from the fertile influence of New Orleans legends like Professor Longhair and Allen Toussaint. Like most blues acts in Austin during that city's mid-1970s progressive country heyday, Ball put in some time playing country, leading the group Freda and the Firedogs. But her heart was always in Gulf Coast rhythm & blues, and Ball truly found her voice when she moved in that direction.

what to buy: *Soulful Dress* 𝄞𝄞𝄞 (Rounder, 1983, prod. Denny Bruce) was the first album on which Ball really clicked, exuding an earthy common sense and appealing sensuality that was largely absent from her country phase. Particularly notable is "Jailbird,"

because a song about whomping your man takes on all sorts of meanings when sung by a woman who towers over most anyone who doesn't play in the NBA. Better still is *Blue House* 𝄞𝄞𝄞 (Rounder, 1994, prod. Marcia Ball, Miles Wilkinson), with an ace version of the Joe Ely piano-playing classic "Fingernails."

what to buy next: Ball teamed up with Barton and Strehli for *Dreams Come True* 𝄞𝄞𝄞 (Antone's, 1990, prod. Mac Rebennack), a fine sampler of the three queens of Austin blues that should nevertheless be better than it is. But that's the likely by-product of the fact that it was pieced together patchwork-style over a period of several years. It's still recommended for anyone with an interest in contemporary Texas blues.

what to avoid: Ball's debut, *Circuit Queen* 𝄞𝄞 (Capitol, 1978, prod. Neil Wilburn), isn't terrible, but it doesn't really work, either. *Circuit Queen* miscasts Ball as an Emmylou Harris-type country-rock singer, a guise she sounds uncomfortable with. Dated, fussy Nashville arrangements don't help, either.

the rest:

Hot Tamale Baby 𝄢𝄢𝄢 (Rounder, 1985)
Gatorhythms 𝄢𝄢𝄢𝄢 (Rounder, 1989)
Let Me Play with Your Poodle 𝄢𝄢𝄢𝄢 (Rounder, 1997)

worth searching for: Rounder put out a promotional interview CD for *Blue House* that includes music from Ball's first three Rounder releases, plus interview snippets of Ball holding forth on everything from food to why she kicks her piano when she plays it.

influences:

⏪ Professor Longhair, Allen Toussaint, Bonnie Raitt, Etta James, Irma Thomas

David Menconi

L.V. Banks

Born October 28, 1932, in Stringtown, MS.

Like Vance Kelly and Johnny Laws, L.V. Banks is a Chicago guitarist who gained fame outside his South Side neighborhood only recently. Unlike the Chicago-born Kelly and Laws, however, Banks' musical history can be traced to the Mississippi Delta of his birth. Banks was friends with such notables as Little Milton, Willie Love and "Booba" Barnes, and was a part of the musical cross-pollination that created so many great Mississippi guitarists. Banks used to play the hometown birthday parties of B.B. King, and King showed his appreciation by teaching Banks his popular and influential string-bending technique. It is an art form that Banks, at the age of 65, has perfected for himself. Banks, a former picker of cotton, now prides himself on being one of Chicago's better guitar pickers. "I picks the blues, you know what I'm sayin'?" he told *Living Blues* magazine in 1993. "A lot of people don't pick. I pick." The result? A stinging guitar sound that keeps his ghetto club audiences on the South Side in fits of ecstasy all night. His son is Tre.

what to buy: It was a long wait, but Banks' first full-length album, *Teddy Bear* 𝄢𝄢𝄢𝄢 (Wolf, 1996, prod. L.V. Banks, John Primer, Hannes Folterbauer), reveals Banks' affinity for traditional post-war Chicago blues and the guitar style of his mentor, B.B. King. Banks' cover of his Clicke Records side, "Teddy Bear," is a high point.

worth searching for: A real find would be the "Teddy Bear" 45 single by L.V. Banks and the Soul Swingers', with its b-side, "That's the Way Our Love Goes," on the Clicke label.

influences:

⏪ B.B. King, Little Milton, Howlin' Wolf, Bobby "Blue" Bland, Z.Z. Hill

⏩ Tre

Steven Sharp

Barbecue Bob

Born Robert Hicks, September 11, 1902, in Walnut Grove, GA. Died October 21, 1931, in Atlanta, GA.

Barbecue Bob Hicks was one of two great country blues exports from Atlanta, along with Blind Willie McTell. His thrumming six-string guitar work echoed McTell's, as did his quavering delivery and broad choice of material, which ranged from sly, sexual ditties and chilling ballads to Christian hymns. His first record in 1927, "Barbecue Blues," was a bald advertisement for his then-employer, Tidwell's Barbecue Place. The record sold well enough regionally that Columbia Records rushed him to New York three months later. Hicks unleashed a string of stunning performances—his flood classic, "Mississippi Heavy Water Blues," and the standards "Poor Boy" and "Easy Rider Don't Deny My Name." In Atlanta the same year, he was back in the studio with his brother, "Laughing Charlie" Hicks, who had taught him guitar. Hicks stayed busy through 1930, cutting more than 60 titles until the Depression put an end to most blues sessions. Within the year, Hicks caught a fatal case of pneumonia, stilling one of the greatest Georgia blues singers at age 29.

what to buy: All three of the discs on *Complete Recorded Works, 1927–30* 𝄢𝄢𝄢𝄢 (Document, 1991, prod. Johnny Parth) are essential, crammed with ample evidence of his mastery of country blues, hymns, folk ballads and topical fare. Some tracks are marred by the scratchy distortion typical of 1920s-era 78s, but even bad sound can't obscure Hicks' power.

what to buy next: *Chocolate to the Bone* 𝄢𝄢𝄢𝄢 (Yazoo, 1990) is a well-chosen selection of 14 Hicks cuts, including the title cut, a paean to African-American loving that anticipates the Rolling Stones' "Brown Sugar" by some 40 years.

influences:

⏪ Charlie Hicks

⏩ Willie Baker

Steve Braun

John Henry Barbee

Born November 14, 1905, in Henning, TN. Died November 3, 1964, in Chicago, IL.

Save for a tragic end, this singer-guitarist's blues career followed the same pattern as many of his peers. As a young man, he worked briefly with John Lee "Sonny Boy" Williamson before forming a long, lucrative partnership with Sunnyland Slim. Then he moved to Chicago, recording occasional singles, but made his name at the Maxwell Street Market. He drifted away from blues, but returned during the 1960s revival, touring Europe with the American Folk and Blues Festival. His popularity may have grown further if it weren't for a tragic car wreck; he died of a heart attack in jail, with the resultant court case pending.

what to buy: *Memphis Blues 1927–38* ♪♪♪♪ (Document) offers five recordings by Barbee, including "Six Weeks Old Blues," as well as material from Ollie Rupert, Pearl Dickson, Charlie "Bozo" Nickerson and others. He's also included on *Blues Masters, Vol. 3: I Ain't Gonna Pick No More Cotton* ♪♪♪♪ (Storyville, 1992).

influences:

◀◀ Sunnyland Slim, Sonny Boy Williamson I, Robert Nighthawk, Robert Junior Lockwood, Muddy Waters

▶▶ Buddy Guy, Otis Rush, Son Seals, Eric Clapton

Steve Knopper

Joshua Barnes

See: Peg Leg Howell

Roosevelt "Booba" Barnes

Born Roosevelt Melvin Barnes, September 25, 1936, in Longwood, MS. Died April 2, 1996, in Chicago, IL.

Booba Barnes should have been one of Chicago's most popular blues personalities of the 1990s. He wasn't. Before Booba had time to conquer the city's scene, cancer took his life. Until his death, however, Barnes continued to present his heart-rending, hypnotic blues with fire, flair and guts. He had the ability to instantly transform even the most staid club into a rocking juke joint. Duck walking, playing behind his back, then licking his guitar strings in a lewd manner, Booba's performances were pure celebrations of life. Playing in his own demented guitar tunings, Barnes often seemed the musical equivalent of a stunt driver squealing down the pavement, careening wildly, but always in complete control. His unorthodox string-bending technique and haunting harp style were often overwhelming in their intensity. Before moving to Chicago permanently in the early

Marcia Ball

song
Crawfishin

album
Let Me Play with
Your Poodle (Rounder)

instrument
Piano

monster solo

1990s, Barnes worked his magic onstage at juke joints in and around Greenville, Mississippi. In the early 1980s he opened his infamous Playboy Club on Nelson Street in Greenville, and it was in this down-home environment that Barnes made some of the finest of his few recordings.

what to buy: After being entranced by Booba's Mississippi juke joint performances, journalist turned record-maker Jim O'Neal brought Barnes into studios in Holly Springs, Mississippi and Memphis to record the classic *The Heartbroken Man* ♪♪♪♪♪ (Rooster Blues, 1990, prod. Jim O'Neal, Booba Barnes). Barnes' manic, chicken-clucking guitar, twisted harp blowing and Howlin' Wolf impersonations are captured in all their glory. The movie soundtrack *Deep Blues* ♪♪♪♪ (Anxious/Atlantic, 1992, prod. Robert Palmer) is also essential to any collection of modern blues. Gathered here are three live tracks by Barnes recorded inside the Playboy Club in 1990: "Heartbroken Man," "Ain't Gonna Worry about Tomorrow" and "Love Like I Wanna,"

the last tracks Barnes released. Other featured performers include Junior Kimbrough, R.L. Burnside, Jessie Mae Hemphill and Big Jack Johnson.

influences:

◀◀ Howlin' Wolf, Little Milton, Sonny Boy Williamson II, Jimmy Reed

▶▶ Big Bad Smitty, L.V. Banks, David Thompson

Steven Sharp

Lou Ann Barton

Born February 17, 1954, in Austin, TX.

Lou Ann Barton is a blues belter with an uncanny knack for making everything she sings sound like an illicit roadhouse rendezvous. Barton has kept her sound mostly blues guitar-oriented, with only occasional sidesteps into brass-augmented soul. A 20-year veteran of the Austin blues scene, she helped Stevie Ray Vaughan assemble his first band, sang with Roomful of Blues for a short while and worked extensively with early line-ups of the Fabulous Thunderbirds. She has also guested with Ray Campi, Roky Erickson and Jimmie Vaughan (who has played lead guitar on at least one cut of every Barton record). In 1982, legendary producer Jerry Wexler and Glenn Frey of the Eagles got her a deal with Asylum. Backed by the Muscle Shoals Horns, Barton's debut, *Old Enough*, was hailed by critics but a commercial failure. For such a big talent, Barton's recorded output is frustratingly small. Yet her ability to rage like a rocker and purr like a soul chanteuse continues to earn her the respect of bigger name acts and an enthusiastic cult following.

what to buy: Thankfully, Antone's has reissued all of Barton's fine records onto disc, including the critically acclaimed *Old Enough* ♪♪♪ (Antone's, 1997, prod. Glenn Frey, Jerry Wexler, Lou Ann Barton) and the supreme *Read My Lips* ♪♪♪♪ (Antone's, 1989, prod. Paul Ray, Lou Ann Barton), which features wild covers of Wanda Jackson's "Mean Mean Man," Hank Ballard's "Sexy Ways," Koko Taylor's "You Can Have My Husband," Jimmy Longsdon's "Rocket in My Pocket" and Little Richard's "Can't Believe You Wanna Leave." The guitars snarl and sneer almost as much as Barton's vocals.

what to buy next: If you just gotta have more by this great Texas vocalist, *Forbidden Tones* ♪♪♪ (Antone's, 1997, prod. Lou

Ann Barton) is a reissue of her 1986 Spindletop LP. The song selection isn't as incendiary, but Barton enlivens everything with her heartfelt, powerhouse style.

worth searching for: Barton's collaboration with Marcia Ball and Angela Strehli on *Dreams Come True* ♪♪♪♪ (Antone's, 1990, prod. Mac Rebennack) is a high-water mark for all three artists. On cuts like "Good Rockin' Daddy" and "Bad Thing," Barton joyously rocks with seduction and sass.

influences:

◀◀ Irma Thomas, Fabulous Thunderbirds, Wanda Jackson

▶▶ Sarah Brown, Angela Strehli

Ken Burke

Will Batts

Born January 24, 1904, in Michigan, MS. Died April 16, 1954, in Memphis, TN.

Will Batts' tough fiddle was the lead instrument in Jack Kelly's South Memphis Jug Band, perhaps the most blues-oriented of all the string bands that clustered in Memphis street corners and parks in the first half of the century. Batts and Kelly both cut tributes to the fabled northern Mississippi route, Highway 61, some 20 years before Bob Dylan was born. Batts abandoned his life as a farm hand to play on Beale Street, joining Kelly (guitar), D.M. Higgs (jug) and Dane Sane (guitar), the occasional partner of minstrel singer Frank Stokes, in competition against such vaunted groups as the Memphis Jug Band. Batts recorded behind Stokes and other Memphis acts and continued playing through the 1950s, still heard as late as 1952 behind harmonica virtuoso Big Walter Horton.

what to buy: Ten of the South Memphis Jug Band's 14 recordings from 1933 can be found on *The Sounds of Memphis 1933–39* ♪♪♪♪ (Story of Blues, 1987, prod. Johnny Parth), which also features four tracks by Little Jimmy Doyle, a blues-singing dwarf, and Tennessee journeyman Charlie Pickett. All of the jug band's cuts are stellar and in surprisingly powerful sound.

Steve Braun

Beck

Born Beck Hansen, July 8, 1970, in Los Angeles, CA.

Blues is just one of the many musical styles Beck, a Bob Dylan-influenced singer-songwriter who became a major rock star in 1996, pastes into a complex collage. His first hit, 1994's "Loser," was hyped as a "slacker anthem," but few paid atten-

tion to its major musical inspiration. Underneath all the catchy but indecipherable rambling and George Bush vocal samples is the foundation of Dr. John's weird, spooky "I Walk on Gilded Splinters." Though Beck is a bluesman only to the extent that Dylan was a bluesman in the mid-1960s, you can hear traces of Mississippi John Hurt, Lightnin' Hopkins and other country-blues legends in his style. His breakthrough album, *Mellow Gold*, is much more folk-oriented than *Odelay*, which, like all great rock albums, basically creates its own genre.

what to buy: *Odelay* ✧✧✧✧ (Geffen, 1996, prod. Beck Hansen, Dust Brothers) captures a daunting number of styles, from thrashing heavy metal to bouncy elevator music to electronic techno to, yes, the blues, in catchy summer singles like "Where It's At" and the screechy "Devil's Haircut."

what to buy next: *Mellow Gold* ✧✧✧ (Geffen, 1994, prod. Beck Hansen, Tom Rothrock, Rob Schnapf, Karl Stephenson) is weaker all around than *Odelay*, but it shows more promise than many critics, who labeled the "Loser" singer a one-hit wonder, gave him credit for.

what to avoid: Beck has tried to maintain dual personalities, as a formidable rock superstar and a noisy underground punk—the latter side, documented on *Stereopathetic Soul Manure* ✧✧ (Flipside, 1994, prod. Beck Hansen) and *One Foot in the Grave* ✧✧ (K, 1994, prod. Beck Hansen), is by far the least interesting.

worth searching for: *Golden Feelings* ✧✧ (Sonic Enemy, 1993) and the EP *A Western Harvest Field by Moonlight* ✧✧ (Finger Paint, 1994), Beck's first two albums, while not cohesive or well-produced by any standard, reflect his participation in New York City's creatively lucrative "antifolk" scene.

influences:

◄◄ Bob Dylan, Dr. John, Mississippi John Hurt, Beastie Boys, Public Enemy, Esquivel, Woody Guthrie, Leadbelly, Sonic Youth, Jon Spencer

►► Mary Lou Lord, G. Love & Special Sauce, Preacher Boy

Steve Knopper

Jeff Beck

Born June 24, 1944, in Surrey, England.

These days it's hard to tell whether Beck is a guitar hero first

Beck (© Ken Settle)

and classic car mechanic second or vice-versa. Back in the mid-1960s he filled Eric Clapton's vacant Yardbirds position with feedback and daredevil solos and seemed unstoppable. Although steeped in blues tradition, Beck carried a love for Gene Vincent and distortion as well. What has troubled his career is a dictatorial egomania that has resulted in transient musical relationships with little adherence to a group dynamic. Which is too bad, since his first solo stab had him playing with Rod Stewart, Ronnie Wood and the mesmerizing Mick Waller on drums. Subsequent incarnations of rough-and-tumble rock withstood ups and downs without much fanfare until Beck decided to shuck singers all together in the mid-1970s, freeing himself to create instrumental music that flirted with jazz and fusion. An unpredictable pastiche of styles has been his calling card ever since, though the infrequency of his album releases makes you wonder if he isn't happier at home tinkering with vintage sports cars.

what to buy: The startling Beck/Stewart/Wood/Waller debut, *Truth* ✧✧✧✧ (Epic, 1968, prod. Mickie Most), strips the blues down to a thick distorted buzz. Although Stewart is not quite in full blossom, the configuration's hard blooze would've undoubtedly gone on to further glories had Beck allowed for some sense of democracy. Defying skeptics, Beck released *Blow by Blow* ✧✧✧✧ (Epic, 1975, prod. George Martin), an instrumental album of fluid guitar work extending into jazz fusion with dazzling prowess. And without meddlesome vocalists hogging the spotlight, Beck is free to let wail without restraint.

what to buy next: *There and Back* ✧✧✧ (Epic, 1980, prod. Jeff Beck, Ken Scott) is clearly the highlight of his collaboration with former Mahavishnu Orchestra keyboardist Jan Hammer. Punchy, tight and aggressive, it's the most precise of his rock-and-fusion period. Beck made waves in the 1980s with a heart-felt remake of Curtis Mayfield's "People Get Ready," marked by emotive performances by the briefly reunited Stewart and Beck. The album from which it sprang, *Flash* ✧✧✧ (Epic, 1985), is a pleasant if altogether lightweight pop affair, mixing instrumentals and over-the-top vocals (supplied by Jimmy Hall). *Crazy Legs* ✧✧✧ (Epic, 1993) is an all-out love letter to Gene Vincent and Vincent's own guitar wizard, Cliff Gallup. Beck pledges undying allegiance with note-for-note rave-ups of the fallen 1950s idol's suggestive rock 'n' roll.

what to avoid: *Jeff Beck and Jan Hammer Group Live* ✧ (Epic, 1977, prod. Jan Hammer), the nadir of the duo's union, is fraught with synthesizers which point a sterile finger to the *Miami Vice* theme song Hammer would later create.

the rest:

Beck-Ola ♫♫♫ (Epic, 1969)
Rough and Ready ♫♫♫ (Epic, 1971)
Jeff Beck Group ♫♫ (Epic, 1972)
Beck, Bogart and Appice ♫♫ (Epic, 1973)
Wired ♫♫♫ (Epic, 1976)
Jeff Beck's Guitar Shop ♫♫♫ (Epic, 1989)
Beckology ♫♫♫ (Epic, 1991)
Frankie's House ♫♫♫♫ (Epic, 1992)
Best of Beck ♫♫♫♥ (Epic, 1995)

worth searching for: Beck has recorded with numerous musicians over the years, and the import *Rock 'n' Roll Spirit Vol. 2: Jeff Beck Session Works* ♫♫♫ (Epic, 1994, prod. various) covers many of his cameos.

influences:

◀◀ Les Paul, Jimmy Page, Cliff Gallup

▶▶ Joe Satriani, Eric Johnson

Allan Orski

Carey Bell

Born Carey Bell Harrington, November 14, 1936, in Macon, MS.

A harmonicist of oft-boggling deftness and skill, Carey Bell started out playing behind his stepfather, pianist Lovey Lee, with whom he moved to Chicago in 1956. He immediately fell in with heavy company, taking lessons from Little Walter and Big Walter Horton and gigging with Johnny Young, Eddie Taylor and Earl Hooker. His first session work was with the latter on an Arhoolie LP in 1968. In the early 1970s he toured and recorded with Muddy Waters and Willie Dixon. As the post-war elders died out, Bell was kept from harmonica primacy by James Cotton and Junior Wells, who were easier for the emergent, rock-oriented blues audience to lock on to. Not that Bell's talent was ever in doubt! For a harp blower schooled by the Walters, he developed a style apart from theirs (though he can muster their sort of wall-rattling tones at will) hallmarked by a head-twisting deftness and seemingly inexhaustible improvisational inventiveness.

what to buy: Harpmeister though he is, bland material, production and/or accompaniment have frequently underserved Bell. His genius is best showcased through the precision production on *Deep Down* ♫♫♫♫ (Alligator, 1995, prod. Carey Bell, Bruce Iglauer, Scott Dirks). Backed by chronic badmen Lurrie Bell (his

Jeff Beck (© Ken Settle)

son), Lucky Peterson and Carl Weathersby, Bell blows explosively on this set, which includes a cut titled "When I Get Drunk" that's one of the best paeans to booze ever written. A tough, tough disc.

what to buy next: *Mellow Down Easy* ♫♫♫♫ (Blind Pig, 1991, prod. Steve Jacobs, Jerry Del Giudice, Mark Hurwitz) shows Bell can blow the breath of life into standards ("Fine Long Years," "St. Louis Blues," the title cut) even when backed by just a fair band. Tough luck. *Carey Bell's Blues Harp* ♫♫♫ (Delmark, 1995, prod. Robert Koester), a reissue of a 1969 LP, is a tad schizoid, with Bell backed by two bands, one led by Eddie Taylor (good), the other by Jimmy Dawkins (not good). The former's cuts are confident and strong, the latter's tense and herky jerky, but Bell's blowing saves all. *Goin' on Main Street* ♫♫♫ (Evidence, 1994, prod. Horst Lippmann) is an old German LP with two cuts from Bell's set at the landmark American Folk Blues Tour of 1981. He's in his usual, idiosyncratic form and joined by fellow harp-blower Billy Branch on "Tribute to Big Walter."

what to avoid: *Last Night* ♥ (One Way, 1995, prod. Al Smith) gets a bone fragment only for the doom-laden title cut, but otherwise this is dull, dull, dull, originally released c. 1972.

the rest:

Big Walter and Big Walter Horton ♫♫♫ (Alligator, 1973)
(With Billy Branch, James Cotton and Junior Wells) *Harp Attack* ♫♫♫♥ (Alligator, 1990)
Harpmaster ♫♫♫ (JSP, 1993)
Dynasty ♫♫ (JSP, 1996)

influences:

◀◀ Big Walter Horton, Little Walter, Sonny Boy Williamson II

▶▶ Charlie Musselwhite, Sugar Blue

Tim Schuller

Lurrie Bell

Born 1958, in Chicago, IL.

Lurrie Bell is a central figure among the ranks of a younger generation of black performers who are keeping the blues tradition alive and legitimizing its place in their cultural heritage. Son of harp ace Carey Bell, Lurrie was quite literally born into the blues. Before he was even out of diapers, he was receiving instruction from his father and other graduates of Muddy Waters' blues school. While still in his teens, Bell made the music world take notice with appearances on Eddie C. Campbell's critically acclaimed *King of the Jungle* and his father's only recently released Ralph Bass recordings. More sessions followed in the late 1970s, and Bell continued to generate a great deal of excitement while touring with the Sons of Blues, Koko Taylor and his father. Father and son recorded a few solid albums together in the 1980s, and Lurrie finally stepped out with his long overdue solo debut in 1989. Through his powerful vocal delivery and explosive guitar work, Bell has been able to bridge the gap separating down-and-dirty traditional blues and the funky, soul-tinged blues currently in vogue with many younger artists. Personal problems have plagued Bell's career over the past decade, but he is still active on the Chicago scene, and he remains one of the great hopes for the future.

what to buy: Technically not a solo endeavor, *Son of a Gun* ✧✧✧✧ (Rooster Blues, 1984, prod. Jim O'Neal) is his strongest album appearance to date. While his father's contributions are not to be discounted, Lurrie takes on most of the vocal chores here and tastefully complements the senior Bell's horn-like harp with his own inimitable high-energy guitar. *Mercurial Son* ✧✧✧✧ (Delmark, 1995, prod. Steve Cushing) represents the culmination of a decade's worth of stark disappointments and personal tragedy, pain never far from the surface in his gut-wrenched vocals and stinging guitar. Though padded with a few numbers that work better as basic tracks than as actual songs (the "Voo-Doo Whammy" numbers, "Longview Texas Trainwreck"), this haunting disc is steeped with blues essence.

the rest:
Everybody Wants to Win ✧✧✧ (JSP, 1989)
700 Blues ✧✧✧✧ (Delmark, 1997)

worth searching for: *The Blues Caravan Live at Pit Inn* ✧✧✧✧ (Yupiteru, 1982, prod. *Black Music Review* Editors) is a live set begging for release on disc and proof positive that on a good night, Lurrie can go blow-for-blow with the best of today's guitar heroes.

influences:
◀◀ Eddie Taylor, Robert Junior Lockwood, Magic Sam, Albert Collins

D. Thomas Moon

Fred Below

Born September 16, 1926, in Chicago, IL. Died August 13, 1988, in Chicago, IL.

Fred Below's straight-ahead, swinging percussion helped propel Little Walter's career as a solo act in the early 1950s and later transformed Muddy Waters' band from a voodoo choir into the stream-lined train that hissed out definitive smokers like "I'm Ready," "Hoochie Coochie Man" and "I Just Want to Make Love to You." A young jazz drummer who had played with the 427th Army band, Below returned to civilian life in 1951 to discover that he could earn more as a bluesman. Joining first with the teenaged Junior Wells, Below quickly became a crack rhythm man alongside guitarist Louis Myers and bassist Dave Myers. Then, in one of blues music's strangest trades, the Aces were hijacked by harpmaster Little Walter Jacobs, who decided to flee the Waters band; in return, Muddy hired Wells. After a few years on the road with the mercurial Jacobs, Below joined Muddy, too. The Chess producers increasingly relied on Below's impeccable time-keeping, using him on sessions with Willie Dixon, Otis Rush, Chuck Berry, Buddy Guy and Howlin' Wolf. Preferring to stay behind the scenes, Below never recorded as a leader. But to hear him in his glory, crank up "Hoochie Coochie Man." That addictive beat is Fred Below's legacy.

what to buy: Studded with rave-ups, *The Essential Little Walter* ✧✧✧✧✧ (Chess, 1993, prod. Andy McKaie), a Little Walter anthology, collects the cream of Below's work. On "Off the Wall" and "Mellow Down Easy," Below sounds like he was still in the Army. His arms were dangerous weapons.

what to buy next: Much of the drumming on *The Best of Muddy Waters* ✧✧✧✧ (Chess, 1959, prod. Leonard Chess, Phil Chess) was by Elgin Evans, but the classic, brash cuts are Below.

the rest:
Live and Cooking at Alice's Revisited ✧✧✧✧ (Chess, 1972)

influences:
◀◀ Elgin Evans

Steve Braun

Tab Benoit

Born 1965, in Baton Rouge, LA.

Guitarist Tab Benoit has carved a modest but noteworthy niche by pumping down-home blues and swampy Cajun riffs through an electric guitar and coming up with something beyond the Delta, but not quite embedded in the Chicago blues idiom. Although not a flashy or astounding guitar technician, Benoit takes a consistent, earnest approach to his music—both onstage and in the studio. With spontaneity as the primary rule, most of his gritty guitar and vocal tracks come together in one or two takes. Benoit developed his repertoire at weddings, local Cajun festivals and rock 'n' roll gigs, then moved to New Orleans and signed with Justice Records. A few of Benoit's tracks have

Buster Benton (© Jack Vartoogian)

made it to prime time TV, including episodes of *Northern Exposure*, *Melrose Place* and *Party of Five*. Additionally, he appeared in an early episode of *Baywatch Nights*, which has also had B.B. King and Robert Cray in other episodes.

what to buy: Benoit's debut, *Nice and Warm* 🎵🎵🎵🎵 (Justice, 1992, prod. Randall Hage Jamail), mixes his own competent songwriting with chestnuts from Buddy Guy, Howlin' Wolf and others. Fiery tracks like "Open Book" and "Voodoo on the Bayou" blend well with laid-back fare like Robert Johnson's "Ramblin' on My Mind" (with Dr. John on piano) and Benoit's own "Shining Moon."

what to buy next: Keyboardist Paul English, who spices up the debut album, reunites with Benoit on *Standing on the Bank* 🎵🎵🎵 (Justice, 1995, prod. Randall Hage Jamail) and makes a significant contribution to the record's swampy, bayou flavor. Willie Nelson joins in on guitar and vocals in a poignant reading of Nelson's "Rainy Day Blues."

the rest:
What I Live For 🎵🎵 (Justice, 1994)

influences:
◄◄ Buddy Guy, Duane Allman, Creedence Clearwater Revival

John C. Bruening

Arley Benton
See: Buster Benton

Buster Benton
Born Arley Benton, July 19, 1932, in Texarkana, AR. Died January 20, 1996, in Chicago, IL.

Buster Benton spent a substantial portion of his early career fending off accusations that he was just another B.B. King imitator. Although heavily influenced by King (as well as T-Bone Walker and Albert King), Benton never failed to inject his own soul and laid-back demeanor into the variety of funky grooves he conjured. It was Benton's frugal, understated guitar style that gained him entrance to stages in ghetto clubs on Chicago's South Side in 1959 and his versatility as an artist that later made him popular in Europe. Benton's recording career began in the early 1960s, when he waxed a stack of singles for obscure labels, including Melloway, Alteen and Sonic. His career gained momentum in the early 1970s when he was discovered by Willie Dixon, who promptly hired Benton as lead guitarist for his Chicago Blues All-Stars. Shortly thereafter, Dixon brought Benton into the studio to record what would be Buster's trademark song, "Spider in My Stew." In 1979, the song became the title track to an album Benton later called his "breakthrough." Benton told *Living Blues* 14 years after its release, "I never heard nobody say I sounded like B.B. King (again)."

what to buy: *Spider in My Stew* 🎵🎵🎵 (Ronn, 1994, prod. Ralph Bass) captures Benton in a session with the renowned Chess producer. Highlights include the title track and the Benton classics "Sweet 94," "Lonesome for a Dime" and the straight-forward "Do It in the Rain." *Blues at the Top* 🎵🎵🎵🎵 (Blue Phoenix, 1988/Evidence, 1993, prod. Disques Black and Blue) is Benton's finest work, recorded on visits to Paris in 1983 and 1985 and backed by stalwarts Billy Branch, Johnny Littlejohn, Bob Stroger and Carl Weathersby. *Money's the Name of the Game* 🎵🎵🎵 (Ichiban, 1989, prod. Gary B.B. Coleman) is the better of his two Ichiban releases, although it pales in comparison to *Spider in My Stew* and *Blues at the Top*. High points include remakes of the title track, "Sweet 94," and best of all, "As the Years Go Passing By."

the rest:
I Like to Hear My Guitar Sing 🎵🎵🎵 (Ichiban, 1991)

worth searching for: Benton's work with Willie Dixon in the early 1970s is displayed on *The All Star Blues World of Maestro Willie Dixon* 🎵🎵🎵 (Spivey, prod. Victoria Spivey, Len Kunstadt). Benton's obscure single, "Good to the Last Drop," along with versions of "Sweet 94" and "Money's the Name of the Game," are included on the British vinyl compilation *Good to the Last Drop* 🎵🎵🎵 (Charly, 1988, compiled by Neil Slaven). Benton churns out hypnotic boogie and blues with help from Carey Bell, Jimmy Johnson and Lafayette Leake on his tremendous *Buster Benton Is the Feeling* 🎵🎵🎵 (Ronn, 1981, prod. Buster Benton). This, along with *Why Me* 🎵🎵🎵 (Ichiban, 1988, prod. Gary B.B. Coleman), is available only on vinyl and cassette.

influences:
◀◀ B.B. King, Albert King, T-Bone Walker

▶▶ Tre, Michael Coleman

Steven Sharp

Chuck Berry

Born Charles Edward Anderson Berry, October 18, 1926, in St. Louis, MO.

Next to Elvis Presley, Chuck Berry is rock 'n' roll's most influential performer, yet in terms of innovation, he stands second to no one. Berry's ringing guitar gave the nascent genre its most identifiable sound, and his wide-ranging, poetic lyrics gave it a vision. A black man with a taste for country music as well as the blues, Berry's souped-up anthems to teendom were irresistible, and thanks to his well-enunciated, theoretically raceless vocals, acceptable for airplay on radio stations that refused to broadcast rhythm & blues. But how the mighty have fallen. Beyond these staggering accomplishments, Berry's contributions to rock 'n' roll include sexual deviancy—he was jailed for transporting a teenaged prostitute across state lines in the early 1960s and fined for videotaping the bathroom activities at his Wentzville, Missouri, restaurant in the early 1990s—and tax evasion, for which he was sent to prison in the late 1970s. Embittered, perhaps justifiably so, at the treatment he has received in exchange for his music, Berry for years has toured in a mercenary fashion, insisting on payment in cash, not rehearsing the pickup bands that back him and phoning in his performances. The father of rock 'n' roll somehow turned into its deadbeat dad.

what to buy: Featuring 71 cuts on three discs, *The Chess Box* 🎵🎵🎵🎵 (Chess/MCA, 1988, prod. Leonard Chess, Phil Chess) is an essential purchase for any serious fan of contemporary music. It covers all his essential hits—some of which topped the R&B charts while others went pop—and delves into other areas, such as his blues playing and some of the instrumental jams that the Chess brothers recorded surreptitiously in the studio and used to flesh out Berry's albums. Those on a tighter budget are directed to *The Great Twenty-Eight* 🎵🎵🎵🎵🎵 (Chess, 1982, prod. Leonard Chess, Phil Chess), which gets right down to the business of Berry's best, with no frills, though some essential material is missing. Still it's solid from start to finish.

what to buy next: Berry wasn't really an album-oriented artist, so which of his individual albums you might care to own largely depends on the hits contained therein. Of his many original classic albums, the two that remain in print are *Chuck Berry Is on Top* 🎵🎵🎵🎵🎵 (Chess, 1959, prod. Leonard Chess), which includes "Johnny B. Goode," "Maybelline," "Roll Over Beethoven," "Carol" and "Little Queenie," pretty much qualifying it as one of the best and most important albums ever, and *New Juke Box Hits* 🎵🎵🎵🎵 (Chess, 1961/1988) contains "Thirteen

Question Method," one of Berry's slyest pieces of writing ever. For those who own the basics, *Rock 'n' Roll Rarities* 𝄞𝄞𝄞𝄞 (Chess, 1986, prod. Leonard Chess, Phil Chess) offers a host of previously unreleased versions of Berry's hits as well as a number of stereo remixes.

what to avoid: Berry left Chess in the mid-1960s to record for Mercury, and most of the undistinguished work he turned in there is justifiably out of print. Still available, though, are *Golden Hits* **woof!** (Mercury, 1967, prod. Chuck Berry), which features rerecordings of the definitive Chess versions, and *Live at the Fillmore Auditorium* 𝄞𝄞 (Mercury, 1967, prod. Abe Kesh), a less than impressive concert recording. *The London Chuck Berry Sessions* 𝄞𝄞 (Chess, 1972, prod. Esmond Edwards) yielded one of Berry's biggest hits, the novelty song "My Ding-a-Ling," but the album is a marginal effort nonetheless. Finally, Berry's work has been repackaged many times on many labels. Unless you know enough to know what you're looking at, don't buy it.

the rest:

Hail! Hail! Rock 'n' Roll 𝄞𝄞𝄞𝄞 (MCA, 1987)
His Best, Volume 1 𝄞𝄞𝄞𝄞 (MCA/Chess, 1997)
His Best, Volume 2 𝄞𝄞𝄞𝄞 (MCA/Chess, 1997)

worth searching for: Nearly all of Berry's original Chess albums are worth a listen. In the wake of the boxed set, they were reissued a few years back on MCA, but are out of print once again. Still, there may be a few lingering in used-CD bins. The latter two volumes in the *Rarities* series, *More Rock 'n' Roll Rarities* 𝄞𝄞𝄞𝄞 (Chess, 1986, prod. Leonard Chess, Phil Chess) and *Missing Berries: Rarities, Vol. 3* 𝄞𝄞𝄞𝄞 (MCA/Chess, 1990, prod. Leonard Chess, Phil Chess) are also out of print, and die hard fans will dig 'em both.

influences:

◀◀ Muddy Waters, Louis Jordan, T-Bone Walker, Hank Williams

▶▶ Beatles, Rolling Stones, Beach Boys, Bob Dylan and the whole first and second generation of rock 'n' rollers

Daniel Durchholz

Richard Berry

Born April 11, 1935, in Extension, LA. Died January 23, 1997, in Los Angeles, CA.

Richard Berry died a happy man. For most of his life, he was a forgotten doo-wopper, practitioner of a musical genre that dated as fast as unrefrigerated milk. But a song he scribbled on a napkin between sets in an Los Angeles nightclub in 1957 be-

came the quintessential, mindless rock 'n' roll song, a Latin-tinged blues number by the name of "Louie Louie." Berry's own version sank without a trace, and even after the Seattle-based Kingsmen drove FBI agents goofy trying to decipher their gargled cover, he received little recognition and no residuals. It took radio, "Louie Louie" marathons and the support of lawyers, music critics and thousands of lovers of garage rock to win Berry the royalties and honor he deserved.

Stricken with polio not long after his family moved to Los Angeles during his childhood, Berry was on crutches until he was six. By high school, he was playing the ukulele and had met a pack of future doo-wop stars, among them crooner Jesse Belvin and future Coaster Cornell Gunter. The high school friends soon joined in a rotating roster of R&B groups—the Flairs, the Dreamers, the Pharoahs—and recorded for Dolphin, Modern and Flip. Berry was a natural songwriter, able to spin double entendres in "Jelly Roll" and satirize the mañana mentality in "Next Time." But it was his menacing, sex-dripping voice that became his stock-in-trade. Leiber and Stoller used him, uncredited, as the lead singer on the Robins' classic "Riot in Cellblock #9," and he was the nasty Henry voice in "The Wallflower," Etta James' answer to Hank Ballard's "Work with Me, Annie." Session work kept him in clover for awhile, but by the late 1950s, Berry's star was fading. He kept churning out records, among them "Louie Louie." The song took off on Chuck Berry's "Havana Moon" and the calypso craze but was so overlooked that Flip Records released it as the b-side to a fluffy version of "You are My Sunshine." Berry had already relinquished his rights when scuffling bands in Seattle found old copies of the song in the early 1960s. Soon, every Seattle band had "Louie Louie" in its repertoire; the Kingsmen and Paul Revere and the Raiders were the first to record it. It was the Kingsmen's noise-congested version, shouted up at a high-hung microphone, that sent dozens of FBI agents hunting around the country—and eventually interviewing a bewildered Berry—in a vain attempt to identify obscene lyrics. The song did nothing for Richard Berry until the 1980s, when new versions began to litter the landscape like forest toadstools—ranging from truly pornographic live Iggy Pop performances to kazoo band marches. Berry won some back some royalties, and when the song rights were sold again in 1992, he won a substantial settlement. In recent years, he had begun to perform again, mostly in the Los Angeles area—a promising development cut short by his death from a heart attack.

what to buy: *Get out of the Car* 𝄞𝄞𝄞𝄞 (Flair, 1994, prod. Joe Bihari) is funky, uptempo L.A. doo-wop and dreamy ballads, almost all written by Berry. It includes "Jelly Roll" and "The Big Break"—the sequel to "Riot in Cellblock #9"—but no "Louie Louie."

what to avoid: *Best of Louie Louie Vol. 1* 🐾🐾 (Rhino, 1988) is only for "Louie" fanatics. Berry's version is here, and so is the Kingsmen's, but can you really stand a second listen to the Sandpipers or the Rice University Marching Owl Band?

worth searching for: *The Best of Flip Records, Vols. 1–3* 🐾🐾🐾🐾 (Titanic, 1997, prod. Max Freitag) documents Berry's Pharoah recordings, mixed in among tough doo-wop by Arthur Lee Maye (who went on to a career as a Baltimore Orioles slugger) and some cloying girl group ditties. "Louie Louie" is on Vol. 3, and on Vol. 1 is "Have Love Will Travel," covered by the Sonics in the 1960s and 20 years later in a riotous version by Bruce Springsteen on his Tunnel of Love tour. The sound is spectacular, but these are Italian imports, so you'll have to dig.

influences:

◀◀ Jesse Belvin, Big Jay McNeely, Chuck Berry, Harry Belafonte

▶▶ Kingsmen, Kinks, Paul Revere & the Raiders, Sonics, Beach Boys, Iggy Pop, Toots & the Maytals, Bruce Springsteen, Dave Barry

Steve Braun

Big Brother & the Holding Company

See: Janis Joplin

Big Maceo

See: Big Maceo Merriweather

Big Maybelle

Born Maybelle Smith, May 1, 1924, in Jackson, TN. Died January 23, 1972, in Cleveland, OH.

Big Maybelle Smith had a perfect R&B body and voice; she was a bustling belter in the classic blues tradition with a singular capacity to go for the kill around a good slow one. She started early, but it wasn't until producer Fred Mendelsohn recorded her, dropped the last name and took the tapes to Columbia's OKeh subsidiary that things began happening. Besides many legendary dates at the famed Apollo Theater, she had a few modest hits and recorded a jumping blues version of the country-western tune "Whole Lotta Shakin' Goin' On" two years before Jerry Lee Lewis' world-wide hit version. She moved on to Savoy, where she scored again with "Candy" in 1956. Personal

and professional problems, including a debilitating heroin habit, kept her from ever reaching her potential. Her last appearance in 1967 on the R&B roster was her only time on the pop charts with her version of the Tex-Mex classic, "96 Tears."

what to buy: Recorded between 1952 and 1955, *The Complete OKeh Sessions* 🐾🐾🐾🐾 (Sony-Legacy, 1994, prod. Bob Irwin), captures Maybelle at her best on her biggest hits with sidemen Quincy Jones, Brownie McGhee and Mickey Baker, among others. Included are "Gabbin' Blues (Don't Run My Business)," "Maybelle's Blues," "One Monkey Don't Stop No Show" and "Whole Lot of Shakin' Goin' On." *Blues, Candy & Big Maybelle* 🐾🐾🐾🐾 (Savoy, 1994, prod. Ozzie Cadena, Fred Mendelsohn) rocks harder than the OKeh sessions, and includes "Candy," "Ring Dang Dilly," "Rockhouse" and "A Good Man Is Hard to Find."

what to buy next: The sometimes bizarre *The Last of Big Maybelle* 🐾🐾🐾 (Muse, 1996, prod. Jack Taylor, P. Taylor, Robert Steffany), with echo on the vocals and string orchestrations, shows how poorly producers were able to deal with Maybelle's talent. Still, there are a couple of ballads here that will stop your heart.

worth searching for: You can find three Big Maybelle tracks in the fine company of Smiley Lewis, Chuck Willis, Johnny Ray, Billy Stewart, Paul Gayten and others on the vinyl version of *OKeh Rhythm and Blues* 🐾🐾🐾🐾 (Epic/Legacy, 1982).

influences:

◀◀ Bessie Smith, Big Mama Thornton, Billie Holiday, Mamie Smith

Leland Rucker

Big Three Trio

Formed 1946, in Chicago, IL. Disbanded 1952.

Willie Dixon, bass; Leonard "Baby Doo" Caston, piano; Bernardo Dennis, guitar (1946–47); Ollie Crawford, guitar (1947–52).

Before Willie Dixon earned his legend as the house producer at Chicago's influential Chess Records, he hooked up with pianist Caston, who had just returned from service in World War II (Dixon had been a conscientious objector). Their R&B songs, recorded briefly for Bullet before the trio jumped more lucratively to Columbia, were slickly produced, like most of the chart hits at the time—they contained little of the grit and soul that became Dixon's specialty at Chess. When Caston left and the band

Big Time Sarah (© Jack Vartoogian)

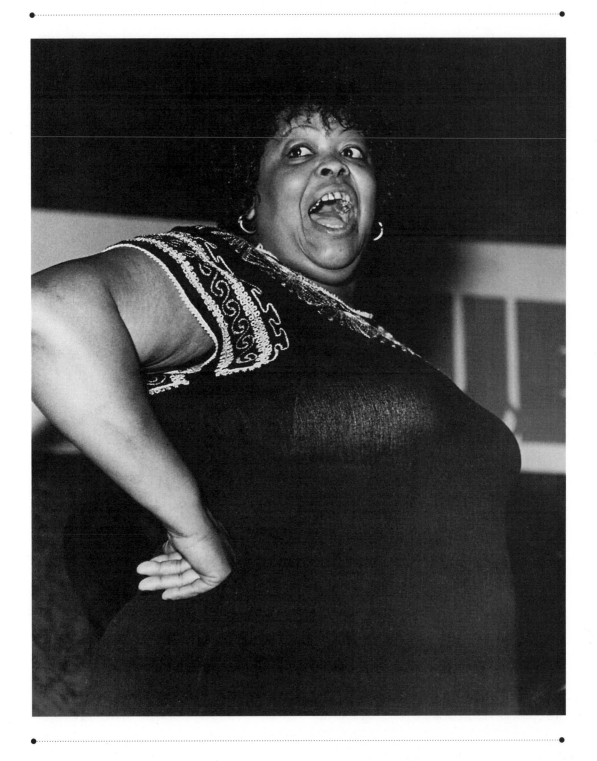

broke up in 1952, Dixon took several of his Big Three songs with him to his next stop, Cobra Records; Otis Rush recorded "My Love Will Never Die" and "Violent Love" in the late 1950s.

what to buy: *The Big Three Trio* 𝄢𝄢𝄢𝄢 (Columbia, 1990, prod. various) is most definitely a trio record, for Dixon hadn't developed his signature deep, rambling voice until a few years later. The harmonies are strong, especially "Signifying Monkey" and "Tell That Woman," although new Dixon fans will want to look elsewhere for his more individually definitive work.

what to buy next: *I Feel Like Steppin' Out* 𝄢𝄢𝄢 (Dr. Horse, 1986) complements the Columbia collection with weaker, but still interesting, material.

influences:

◀◀ Three Blazers, Nat "King" Cole Trio, Louis Jordan

▶▶ Otis Rush, Muddy Waters, Howlin' Wolf

Steve Knopper

Big Time Sarah

Born Sarah Streeter, January 31, 1953, in Coldwater, MS.

The influences on Big Time Sarah, one of several Chicago current blues belters, are easy to spot: Koko Taylor, perhaps the best known of these Windy City singers, and Etta James. Big Time Sarah can sing with the husky growl of Taylor, and on stage she enjoys shaking her amply endowed rear in good-natured fun a la James. The burly-voiced Sarah plays the tough and lusty woman singing about the travails of the heart, yet her version of George Gershwin's "Summertime"—more understated than much of her work—is surprisingly effective. Sarah moved to Chicago from Mississippi with her family in 1960, and like so many other singers got her start in a church choir. She made her debut as a singer at age 14 at a local club with a group called the Aces. From there she sang at a number of other local clubs when she got her biggest break from Sunnyland Slim, who let her sit in with him on a regular basis and go on his tours. His band members nicknamed her "Big Time" because of her big ambition. Sarah later played in Europe several times but really came into her own back home when she formed the BTS Express in 1989. Though her singing is heartfelt and the subject matter of her songs the same as Ma Rainey and Bessie Smith, the naturalness of their presentations is missing.

what to buy: One of the distinctive things about *Blues in the Year One-D-One* 𝄢𝄢𝄢 (Delmark, 1996, prod. Robert Koester) is the use of some fine saxophones where most blues bands use

guitars, which gives a new sound to old material. The title cut is a nice interplay between singer and band followed by a rollicking treatment of "Hound Dog." There's also a hefty version of the standard "Little Red Rooster," with Sarah's intermittent growls embellished by the sax players.

the rest:

Crying 𝄢𝄢 (MCA, 1993)
Lay It on 'Em Girls 𝄢𝄢𝄢 (Delmark, 1993)

influences:

◀◀ Ma Rainey, Big Mama Thornton, Koko Taylor, Etta James

Nadine Cohodas

Big Twist
& the Mellow Fellows

Formed 1978, in Chicago, IL.

Larry "Big Twist" Nolan (died March 1990), vocals; Pete Special, guitar; Terry Ogolini, tenor saxophone; Tango West, bass; Gene Barge, tenor saxophone; Steve Eisen, baritone saxophone; Don Tenuto, trumpet; Jim Exum, trombone; Willie Hayes, drums; Sid Wingfield, keyboards; Martin Allbritton, vocals (1990).

As the Blues Brothers were transforming traditional music into good-time party tunes for frat parties and campus bars, Big Twist & the Mellow Fellows were doing the same thing in real life for much of Illinois. With a 6'4", 300-pound frontman who wore impeccable ties and fedoras, they cranked up the horns and played soul music the way the Mar-Keys played it in the mid-1960s. Twist could croon like Bobby "Blue" Bland and lead the band into sloppy funk like Tony Joe White, and musical director Special learned precision from-the-heart soul from James Brown's bands. Their live shows are legendary, but the Mellow Fellows' albums tend to have a had-to-be-there feeling. When the band leader died of diabetes and kidney failure in 1990, it threw the Mellow Fellows into disarray. Substitute Martin Allbritton tried to carry on, but Special left the band, taking the Mellow Fellows name with him. The rest of them continue to tour as the Chicago Rhythm & Blues Kings.

what to buy: *Playing for Keeps* 𝄢𝄢𝄢 (Alligator, 1983, prod. Gene Barge, Pete Special) is a showcase for Nolan's voice, soft on his "I Want Your Love" and fun-loving on Tony Joe White's much-covered "Polk Salad Annie." The horns are impeccably arranged, but the missing sweaty bar feeling keeps the album restrained and occasionally lifeless.

what to buy next: Dominating live bands almost always get around to recording live albums, and *Live from Chicago! Bigger Than Life!!* ♪♪♪ (Alligator, 1984, prod. Gene Barge, Pete Special, Bruce Iglauer) is the best way to remember Big Twist, with horns popping in every direction and Twist using his considerable frame to hold everything into place.

what to avoid: Allbritton just wasn't on Twist's singing level, and despite shared vocals by Barge, *Street Party* ♪♪ (Alligator, 1990) is like those Doors albums recorded after Jim Morrison died. There's just no real point in buying it.

the rest:
Big Twist & the Mellow Fellows ♪♪♪ (Flying Fish, 1981)
One Track Mind ♪♪ (Flying Fish, 1982)

influences:

◀◀ Big Daddy Kinsey, Kinsey Report, T-Bone Walker, B.B. King, Fats Domino

▶▶ Squirrel Nut Zippers, Royal Crown Revue, Roomful of Blues, Blues Brothers

Steve Knopper

Elvin Bishop

Born October 21, 1942, in Tulsa, OK.

When singer-guitarist Elvin Bishop stomps clumsily onto the stage with electrified frizzy hair, clunky boots and a pair of overalls he looks like a psycho-hillbilly. But he quickly establishes his skill, first as a flashy, bombastic guitar player, then as a serious bluesman reverential and determined to honor his heroes, including Jimmy Reed and Jimi Hendrix. A voracious record collector and radio listener who grew up in the South, Bishop earned a University of Chicago scholarship in the late 1960s, hooked up with harpist Paul Butterfield and managed to score guest appearances with Buddy Guy and Muddy Waters. With Butterfield and guitarist Michael Bloomfield, Bishop co-founded the Paul Butterfield Blues Band, which helped introduce traditional blues to young white audiences and pioneered the spacey, stretched-out two-guitar jam that influenced both the Allman Brothers and the Grateful Dead. Jumping on the southern blues bandwagon, Bishop's post-Butterfield solo career yielded his first hit, "Fooled Around and Fell in Love," in 1976. After that, he slowly injected himself into the blues circuit and frequently plays package shows with such fellow guitarists as John Lee Hooker, Lonnie Brooks and Luther Allison.

what to buy: Though Bishop's first solo album came out in 1969, he didn't catch commercial fire until *Struttin' My Stuff* ♪♪♪ (Capricorn, 1976), an explosive collection containing "Fooled Around and Fell in Love." *Don't Let the Bossman Get You Down!* ♪♪♪ (Alligator, 1991, prod. Elvin Bishop) is the refreshing highlight of his pure-blues comeback phase after almost 10 years away from the studio.

what to buy next: A terrific document of Bishop's Marin County, California, phase—when he was represented by promoter Bill Graham and played frequently at San Francisco's Fillmore theaters—is *Best of Elvin Bishop: Tulsa Shuffle* ♪♪♪♪ (Epic/Legacy, 1994, prod. various), which samples his first four years, including the instrumental jam "Hogbottom" and other songs with Carlos Santana's Latin-dominated rock rhythm section.

what to avoid: In Bishop's long career, he has never been above coasting or releasing an album because it seemed like the right business move at the time. We recommend any best-of collection (even the mediocre *The Best of Elvin Bishop: Crabshaw Rising* ♪♪♪ (Epic, 1972)) above *Hometown Boy Makes Good!* ♪♪ (Capricorn, 1977), *Raisin' Hell* ♪♪ (Capricorn, 1977) and the over-soloed *Ace in the Hole* ♪♪ (Alligator, 1995).

the rest:
The Elvin Bishop Group ♪♪♪ (Fillmore, 1969)
Feel It! ♪♪♪ (Epic, 1970)
Applejack ♪♪♪ (Epic, 1971)
Rock My Soul ♪♪ (Epic, 1971)
Let It Flow ♪♪♪ (Capricorn, 1974)
Juke Joint Jump ♪♪♪ (Capricorn, 1975)
Hog Heaven ♪♪♪ (Capricorn, 1978)
Big Fun ♪♪♪ (Alligator, 1988)
Sure Feels Good: The Best of Elvin Bishop ♪♪♪ (PolyGram, 1992)

worth searching for: Bishop's work on all three classic Butterfield albums, *Paul Butterfield Blues Band* ♪♪♪♪ (Elektra, 1965), *East-West* ♪♪♪♪ (Elektra, 1966) and *The Resurrection of Pigboy Crabshaw* ♪♪♪♪ (Elektra, 1968), sound overly psychedelic and slightly dated today, but they're essential links between traditional Chicago blues and the late-1960s San Francisco rock scene and inspirations for contemporary bands like Blues Traveler and Phish.

influences:

◀◀ Muddy Waters, Buddy Guy, Jimi Hendrix, B.B. King, John Lee Hooker, Elmore James, Michael Bloomfield, Rev. Gary Davis

▶▶ Allman Brothers Band, Grateful Dead, Blues Traveler, Phish

Steve Knopper

Billy Bizor

Born 1917, in Centerville, TX. Died April 4, 1969, in Houston, TX.

Until the 1960s blues revival, even artists keeping track of their colleagues had never heard of Billy Bizor. He was a backup harpist, briefly, for his cousin, Lightnin' Hopkins, and didn't strike out as a solo artist until just before his death. The one major document of his existence, *Blowing My Blues Away*, has some surprisingly terrific harp grooves.

what to buy: *Blowing My Blues Away* ♫♫♫ (Collectables) won't make you think Bizor was the undiscovered Little Walter, but it's an excellent collection of slow, spooky Hopkins-like blues songs.

influences:

◀◀ Lightnin' Hopkins, Little Walter, Sonny Boy Williamson I, Billy Boy Arnold, Buster Brown

▶▶ Junior Wells, Sugar Blue, Charlie Musselwhite, Taj Mahal

Steve Knopper

Black Ace

Born Babe Karo Lemon Turner, 1905, in Hughes Springs, TX. Died November 7, 1972, in Ft. Worth, TX.

Black Ace (a.k.a. Buck Turner) was a great Texas blues singer and one of the few exponents of the flat Hawaiian blues style to have been recorded. During the 1930s he toured the Southwest and recorded for Decca—including his signature "Black Ace"—and Vocalion. After the war, Ace abandoned music and eventually became a photographer. Musicologist Paul Oliver found him in 1960 and convinced him to resume playing again. The sessions Ace recorded with Oliver were inspired.

what to buy: Sadly under-recorded, Ace's *I'm the Boss Card in Your Hand* ♫♫♫♫ (Arhoolie, 1992, prod. Chris Strachwitz, Paul Oliver) contains almost all of his recorded legacy.

influences:

◀◀ Kokomo Arnold, Oscar Woods, Robert Johnson

▶▶ L.C. Robinson, Sonny Rhodes, Freddy Roulette

Jeff Hannusch

Amos Blackmore

See: Junior Wells

Elvin Bishop (© Ken Settle)

Francis Hillman Blackwell

See: Scrapper Blackwell

Otis Blackwell

Born 1931, in Brooklyn, NY.

Most songwriters are fortunate if they can pen one song that neither time nor trends can diminish. Otis Blackwell can sleep at night wearing the pride that rightfully belongs to a man who's authored several undeniable classics that helped define rock's birth from R&B. The list reads like a roll call of rock's formative years: "Don't Be Cruel," "All Shook Up," "Great Balls of Fire," "Breathless," "Handy Man," "Return to Sender," "Paralyzed," "Rip It Up." Although the pungent forces of Elvis Presley and Jerry Lee Lewis are responsible for much of the raucous joy which springs from the tunes, they came from Blackwell's pen first. While he originally sought to make his name by performing his material himself, Blackwell has only recorded one album.

what to buy: Recorded in 1976, *All Shook Up* ♫♫♫♫ (Shanachie, 1995, prod. Herb Abramson, Otis Blackwell) runs through his hit list and then some. Blackwell's delivery bears more than a little resemblance to Presley's, whose shadow is felt in the album's bristling energy. Where Blackwell falters is in his lack of tonal colors, which renders the album a lively, but somewhat one-note affair that probably is best left for the history buffs.

the rest:

Otis Blackwell 1953–55 ♫♫♫ (Flyright)

influences:

◀◀ Chuck Willis, Larry Darnell

▶▶ Elvis Presley, Little Willie John, Jerry Lee Lewis, Jimmy Jones

Allan Orski

Scrapper Blackwell

Born Francis Hillman Blackwell, February 21, 1903, in Syracuse, SC. Died October 1962, in Indianapolis, IN.

Scrapper Blackwell was one of the most admired blues guitar instrumentalists of the late 1920s and the mid-1930s. In contrast to the rough-hewn sound of many other bluesmen, Blackwell played in a tight, cohesive style marked by hard, basic, chord progressions and precise single-string counterpoints. Blackwell is best known for his collaborations with pianist Leroy Carr; the duo's first 1928 recording session yielded "How Long Blues" and "My Own Lonesome Blues," both which were immediately successful. Carr and Blackwell quickly set the standard for guitar/piano duets of that era with tunes such as "(In the Evening) When the Sun Goes Down," "Blues before Sunrise" and "Sloppy Drunk," now familiar standards in the blues canon. Throughout their partnership Blackwell recorded on his own for several labels, including Vocalion and Bluebird. While at times lacking the verve of the duet recordings, his solo offerings are nonetheless outstanding examples of the kind of raw, finely crafted lead guitar work that was to become integral to post-war urban blues. Unfortunately, by the late 1930s Blackwell had disappeared from the blues scene entirely and remained inactive until his re-emergence in 1958. Subsequent to his rediscovery, he recorded a number of respectable records (particularly the Prestige/Bluesville sides) and appeared to be making a strong comeback when he was shot and killed in 1962.

what to buy: The best single collection of Blackwell's work as a solo artist is *The Virtuoso Guitar of Scrapper Blackwell 1925–34* 𝄞𝄞𝄞𝄞 (Yazoo, 1991, prod. Nick Perls), which also includes accompaniments to Leroy Carr and Black Bottom McPhail. While made up of only 14 tracks, it easily lives up to its title. There is plenty to inspire even the most accomplished guitar buffs. Particularly fine is the often-imitated "Kokomo Blues," a favorite of Robert Johnson, who fashioned his "Sweet Home Chicago" on the tune. Better yet is the whole enchilada, *Complete Recorded Works in Chronological Order, Vols. 1–2* 𝄞𝄞𝄞𝄞 (Document, 1993, prod. Johnny Parth). Each disc is crammed with more than an hour's worth of stellar solo performances (on guitar and piano), with occasional accompaniment from Leroy Carr, Josh White and Bumble Bee Slim.

what to buy next: Blackwell's rediscovery recordings are well worth seeking out. *Scrapper Blackwell with Brooks Berry* 𝄞𝄞𝄞𝄞 (Document, 1994, prod. Johnny Parth) features 10 tunes from a 1960 session along with 11 rare sides from a 1959 concert appearance, highlighted by some magnificent Brooks Berry collaborations. *Mr. Scrapper's Blues* 𝄞𝄞𝄞𝄞 (P-Vine, 1995, prod. Kenneth Goldstein, Arthur Rosenbaum) is a reissue of the Bluesville material, which includes outstanding covers, remakes and an unforgettable pair of guitar instrumentals, "A Blues" and "E Blues."

what to avoid: *Leroy Carr and Scrapper Blackwell 1930–58* 𝄞𝄞𝄞 (Story of Blues, 1993, prod. Johnny Parth) features four of Blackwell's superb 1958 recordings, but these are available in a better format elsewhere. The Carr/Blackwell duet performances, though interesting, do not present them at their best.

the rest:

Leroy Carr: 1930–35 𝄞𝄞𝄞𝄞 (Magpie, 1990)
Leroy Carr: 1929–35 𝄞𝄞𝄞𝄞 (Magpie, 1992)

influences:

◀◀ Payton Blackwell

▶▶ Robert Johnson, Johnny Shines, T-Bone Walker, B.B. King

D. Thomas Moon

Bobby "Blue" Bland

Born January 27, 1930, in Rosemark, TN.

Bobby "Blue" Bland's lack of impact on white audiences during his 1960s heyday speaks more of its fickle and often narrow view of bluesmen than it does his actual stake in the genre. The R&B charts and black clubs have known since the 1950s that although Bland is neither handsome, a guitar player or even distinctly urban, his meaty crooning and midtempo sexiness put him in company with Ray Charles and Sam Cooke. His cosmopolitan style of a spare, big-band brand of Texas blues allows him to inject even middling material with nearly unparalleled sweeps of emotion and delicate phrasing. Bland's subtle, lady-killer vocals incorporate his southern gospel beginnings, jazz, blues and soul. That confident versatility marked his watershed 20-year stint at Duke Records, his silky ballads influencing artists as far-reaching as Little Milton and the Band. Indeed, many a lesser singer has burnt out his throat attempting Bland's "squall," a climactic, strangled outburst punctuating his more dramatic moments. Ironically, Bland started to make more of a dent in white markets with the release of his mid-1970s albums (*California Album*, *Dreamer*), which were clear erosions of his Duke glories. Years of ceaseless touring, health problems and time itself have damaged and restricted his instrument as the hit-and-miss quality of his recent albums indicate.

what to buy: For a single album, the early classic *Two Steps from the Blues* 𝄞𝄞𝄞𝄞𝄞 (MCA, 1961/1989, prod. Joe Scott) is a model of Bland's sizzling ballads and strikingly mature delivery. *I Pity the Fool/The Duke Recordings, Vol. 1* 𝄞𝄞𝄞𝄞𝄞 (MCA, 1992, compilation prod. Andy McKaie) captures the singer struggling to find a hit while forming the Texas blues sound that would carry him for the next two decades. The title track and "Cry, Cry, Cry" are but two gems that indicate his ease with uncluttered, divergent styles. Certainly his unchecked zenith, *Turn on Your Love Light* 𝄞𝄞𝄞𝄞𝄞 (MCA, 1994, compilation prod. Andy McKaie) is a virtual tour-de-force of Bland's midperiod mastery; from the aching "Share Your Love with Me" to the supercharged title track and the pop-jumpiness of "Blue Moon" his command is undeniable, his approach intermittently gritty and smooth.

Bobby "Blue" Bland (© Jack Vartoogian)

what to buy next: There's a slight dip in quality inherent in *That Did It! The Duke Recordings, Vol. 3* &&&& (MCA, 1994, compilation prod. Andy McKaie), which documents his final years at Duke. Overall, his least-known period is more restrained and the songs lack the impact of his seminal work but there are plenty of rewarding moments to be unearthed.

what to avoid: The injustice of a singer of Bland's stature singing Rod Stewart's "Tonight's the Night" makes *Sad Street* & (Malaco, 1995, prod. Wolf Stephenson, Tommy Couch) that much more difficult to swallow. Never mind that his voice is a ravaged hulk by this point.

the rest:

Best of Bobby "Blue" Bland &&&& (MCA, 1972)
His California Album &&& (MCA, 1973/1991)
Dreamer &&& (MCA, 1974/1991)
(With B.B. King) *Together for the First Time . . . Live* &&&& (MCA, 1974)
(With B.B. King) *Together Again . . . Live* &&&& (MCA, 1976/1980)
Here We Go Again && (MCA, 1982)
Members Only && (Malaco, 1985)

After All && (Malaco, 1986)
Blues You Can Use && (Malaco, 1987)
First Class Blues & (Malaco, 1987)
Midnight Run &&& (Malaco, 1989)
Portrait of the Blues && (Malaco, 1991)
Years of Tears && (Malaco, 1993)
(With B.B. King) *I Like to Live the Love* &&& (MCA, 1994)
You've Got Me Loving You && (MCA, 1995)
How Blue Can You Get?: Classic Live Performances 1964–94 &&& (MCA, 1996)

worth searching for: Vinyl copies of anything from Bland's Duke heyday should be seized with a firm grip, whether it's *Call on Me* &&&&& (MCA, 1963), *Ain't Nothing You Can Do* &&&&& (Duke, 1964) or *Here's the Man* &&&&& (Duke, 1962). They're all stellar and should be treated as such.

influences:

◀◀ Ray Charles, Sam Cooke, Johnny Ace, B.B. King

▶▶ The Band, Little Milton, Mighty Sam McClain

Allan Orski

Blind Blake

Born Arthur Phelps, 1890s, in Jacksonville, FL. Died 1930s.

Though little is known of his life and death, Blind Blake was one of the leading exponents of the ragtime-influenced dance music that gained wide popularity along the southeastern seaboard states in the 1920s and 1930s. In stark contrast to the dense and driving rhythms that characterize Delta blues, Blake played in a relaxed, fingerpicking style. For most numbers, he employed a syncopated accompaniment with his thumb on the bass strings while fingering complex figures on the treble strings. Aspects of his inimitable technique influenced Blind Boy Fuller, the Rev. Gary Davis, Buddy Moss and others of the Piedmont blues school. He began his recording career in August 1926 and became one of Paramount's best-selling artists, turning out 80 titles over a mere six-year period. His adept picking is showcased in such tunes as "Blind Arthur's Breakdown," "Scoodle Loo Doo," "Southern Rag" and "Righteous Blues," the latter a particularly adroit example of his intuitive grasp of harmony. Always an adaptable player, Blake proved his competence in a number of stylistic contexts—he recorded as an accompanist with vaudeville artists such as Ma Rainey, Papa Charlie Jackson and Leola B. Wilson, and made some classic piano/guitar duet recordings, most notably the superb "Hastings Street." Blake even cut a handful of jazz-flavored sides with clarinetist Johnny Dodds, including "Southbound Rag," "Hot Potatoes" and "C.C. Pill Blues," each an awe-inspiring masterpiece. While much of his popularity can be credited to his instrumental prowess, Blake's penchant for outrageous and occasionally risqué lyrics ("Too Tight," "Notoriety Woman Blues," "Righteous Blues") also helps to account for his high sales figures. Indeed, few have been able to duplicate the multifarious scope of Blake's success.

what to buy: For an exceptional sampler of the breadth of Blake's musical legacy, one can do no better than *The Master of Ragtime Guitar* 🎵🎵🎵🎵 (Indigo Records, 1996). "He's in the Jailhouse Now" and "That Will Never Happen No More" hail from his repertoire of songs rooted in the vaudeville tradition, while "Early Morning Blues" and "Cold Hearted Mama" are proof of his authority in the blues arena. The fabulous recording made with pianist Charlie Spand, "Hastings Street," is included, along with three from the 1928 jazz session with Johnny Dodds and Jimmy Bertrand. There are plenty of incendiary finger-picking workouts on this disc, including "Diddie Wa Diddie," "Blind Arthur's Breakdown," "Come on Boys Let's Do That Messin' Around," "Skeedle Loo Doo" and "Police Dog Blues." *Ragtime Guitar's Foremost Fingerpicker* 🎵🎵🎵🎵🎵 (Yazoo, 1990, prod. Nick Perls) duplicates his best guitar rags, though on several numbers he is featured in a supporting role with various vaudeville singers. Missing is his glorious debut recording of "West Coast Blues," though the presence of the riotous and politically incorrect "Righteous Blues" more than makes up for the omission.

what to buy next: For a comprehensive look at Blake's recorded output, pick up *Complete Recorded Works in Chronological Order, Vols. 1–4* 🎵🎵🎵 (Document, 1991, prod. Johnny Parth). While not for the casual fan, Blake's music is engaging enough to sustain itself over four discs. Consider this *the* primer for any serious student of fingerstyle guitar.

what to avoid: Although there is much to enjoy on *Blind Blake: The Accompanist* 🎵🎵🎵 (Wolf, prod. Hannes Folterbauer), one must tolerate the rather awful singing of Daniel Brown as well as dubs from some well-worn 78s. The novelty dialogue between Blake and Charlie Jackson, "Papa Charlie and Blind Blake Talk about It, Parts 1 & 2," while interesting, becomes tiresome with repeated listenings.

the rest:

The Best of Blind Blake 🎵🎵🎵🎵 (Collectables, 1995)
The Best of Blind Blake 🎵🎵🎵🎵 (Wolf, 1995)

influences:

◀◀ Nineteenth century black dance music, minstrel/medicine shows, jazz ensembles

▶▶ Josh White, Big Bill Broonzy, Leon Redbone, Ry Cooder

D. Thomas Moon

Rory Block

Born Aurora Block, November 6, 1949, in Princeton, NJ.

Though she tried recording disco and R&B songs in the 1970s, Block found her muse in the Rev. Gary Davis, Son House and Robert Johnson in 1981 and has rarely strayed beyond acoustic blues ever since. She's an excellent guitarist and interpreter who loves to faithfully reproduce well-known classics like Skip James' "Devil Got My Woman" and unearth obscure gems like Mattie Delaney's "Tallahatchie Blues." Many compare Block to Bonnie Raitt, which is true in that they're both women who play the blues. But Block seems perfectly comfortable staying underneath the pop radar screen, and most of her influences recorded in the 1920s and 1930s. Block's father owned a sandal shop in Greenwich Village, so when she was growing up in the 1960s, she got to meet such folkies as Bob Dylan and Joan

Baez. She was more inspired, though, by the visits from Son House, "Mississippi" John Hurt and Fred McDowell, who were in town for blues festivals.

what to buy: *High Heeled Blues* 🐾🐾🐾 (Rounder, 1989, prod. Rory Block, John Sebastian) kick-started her blues career, and you can almost hear Block's sense of relief that she can play country blues covers instead of the pop slop in which she used to dabble. *Tornado* 🐾🐾 (Rounder, 1995) is slightly more pop-oriented, but Block's growing songwriting skills produced the country-blues gem "Gone Woman Blues," inspired by O.J. Simpson's murdered wife, Nicole Brown.

what to buy next: Blues history buffs will enjoy *Gone Woman Blues: The Country Blues Collection* 🐾🐾🐾 (Rounder, 1995), with its three Robert Johnson covers (including the stark "Hellhound on My Trail") and songs by Charley Patton, Skip James, Blind Willie McTell and many others.

what to avoid: *The Early Tapes 1975/1976* 🐾🐾 (Alacazam!, 1989, prod. Rory Block) are interesting, but Block still hadn't discovered her ultimate inner muse.

the rest:
Rhinestones and Steel Strings 🐾🐾🐾 (Rounder, 1983/1990)
Best Blues & Originals 🐾🐾🐾 (Rounder, 1987)
House of Hearts 🐾🐾 (Rounder, 1987)
Blue Horizon 🐾🐾🐾 (Rounder, 1989)
I've Got a Rock in My Sock! 🐾🐾🐾 (Rounder, 1989)
Mama's Blues 🐾🐾🐾 (Rounder, 1991)
Ain't I a Woman 🐾🐾🐾 (Rounder, 1992)
When a Woman Gets the Blues 🐾🐾 (Rounder, 1995)

worth searching for: Block's children's record, *Color Me Wild* 🐾🐾🐾 (Alacazam!, 1990), is fun and fresh, full of non-condescending blues humor.

influences:
◀◀ Son House, Robert Johnson, Tommy Johnson, Tommy Patton, Rev. Gary Davis, Mississippi John Hurt, Stefan Grossman

Steve Knopper

Michael Bloomfield

Born July 28, 1944, in Chicago, IL. Died February 15, 1981, in San Francisco, CA.

Born into an enormously wealthy Chicago family, Michael Bloomfield helped push the electric guitar into the forefront of the rock and blues revolution of the 1960s. Bloomfield immersed himself in Chicago's blues scene as a teenager and endeared himself to the older players as a sincere and passionate sup-

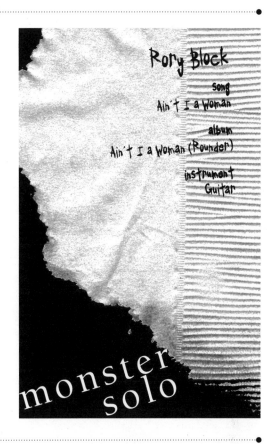

Rory Block

song
Ain't I a Woman

album
Ain't I a Woman (Rounder)

instrument
Guitar

monster solo

porter of the music and a quick study on electric guitar. His charisma, powerful attack and lyrical style, which he learned from Albert King, Muddy Waters and others, while not commercially successful, was influential nonetheless. He backed James Cotton and joined Paul Butterfield's hard-nosed blues unit in time for the group's seminal appearance at the Newport Folk Festival in 1965. That same year, his explosive guitar work kicked Bob Dylan's *Highway 61 Revisited* into the stratosphere. Bloomfield's contributions to the Butterfield Band were immense, especially the modal-scaled *East-West*, but he left in 1967 to form the horn-oriented Electric Flag. He lasted for one album before making *Super Session* with Stephen Stills and Al Kooper and *The Live Adventures of Michael Bloomfield and Al Kooper*, which raised his profile immensely. After the much-admired Flag, career-wise it was pretty much downhill for Bloomfield, with occasional solo records on small labels and low-budget soundtracks ("The Trip," "You Are What You Eat," "Steelyard Blues") before a debilitating heroin habit took its final toll in 1981.

what to buy: In general, Bloomfield was only as good as his surroundings dictated, so it's not a surprise his best work is in ensemble situations. Start with *The Lost Sessions* ♫♫♫ (Elektra, 1964/Rhino, 1995, prod. Paul Rothchild) and *East-West* ♫♫♫♫ (Elektra, 1966, prod. Paul Rothchild, Mark Abramson, Barry Friedman), his early recordings with the Paul Butterfield Band, and follow that with *Super Session* ♫♫♫♫ (Columbia, 1968, prod. Al Kooper) and *The Live Adventures of Michael Bloomfield and Al Kooper* ♫♫♫♫ (Columbia, 1969, prod. Al Kooper). The Electric Flag, with its hard-bitten horn section, provided a nice backdrop for Bloomfield's charms. Check out *Old Glory, the Best of Electric Flag* ♫♫♫♫ (Columbia/Legacy, 1995) and *A Long Time Coming* ♫♫♫ (Columbia, 1968/1988, prod. John Court).

what to buy next: Dylan's *Highway 61 Revisited* ♫♫♫♫ (Columbia, 1965, prod. Bob Johnston), is an excellent example of his sideman abilities, especially on the blues numbers. While none are great, *Don't Say That I Ain't Your Man! Essential Blues 1964–69* ♫♫♫ (Columbia/Legacy, 1994, prod. various), *It's Not Killing Me* ♫♫♫ (Columbia, 1969) and *Living in the Fast Lane* ♫♫♫ (Waterhouse, 1981, prod. Norman Dayron) offer sometime flashes of brilliance after his glory days.

what to avoid: *Triumvirate* ♫♫ (Columbia, 1973/1989) is a jam with Dr. John and John Hammond that just doesn't catch the fire it should have.

the rest:

Try It before You Buy It ♫♫♫ (CBS, 1975)
The Best of Michael Bloomfield ♫♫♫ (Takoma, 1987)
Blues, Gospel and Ragtime Guitar Instrumentals ♫♫♫ (Shanachie, 1993)
The Gospel of Blues ♫♫♫ (LaserLight, 1994)
Rx for the Blues ♫♫♫ (Eclipse, 1996)

worth searching for: Never miss a chance to see *Festival,* an obscure, long-out-of-print film on the Newport fest in the early 1960s. It includes part of the infamous 1965 Butterfield Band workshop, an interview with a bushy-tailed Bloomfield about his love for the blues and plenty of other worthwhile performances by famous bluesers of that era.

influences:

◀◀ B.B. King, Albert King, Muddy Waters, Elmore James, Son House, T-Bone Walker

Michael Bloomfield (© Peter Amft/Ken Settle)

▶▶ Peter Green, Bob Dylan, the Band, Blood, Sweat & Tears, Chicago, Black Crowes, Buddy Miles

Leland Rucker

Bluebirds

Formed 1987, in Shreveport, LA.

Buddy Flett, guitars, vocals; Bruce Flett, bass, vocals.

The bluesrockin' Bluebirds are as Louisiana as Justin Wilson, and cook just as well. Core members Bruce and Buddy Flett grew up in Shreveport grooving to R&B DJs Birdbrain and Gay Poppa on KOKA and rooting around in Stan's Record Shop (owned by Stan Lewis of Jewel/Paula fame). Buddy was inspired by local Albert King clone Raymond Blakes (with whom he played dates on Fannin Street), and later picked up on Johnny "Guitar" Watson and Elmore James. Both Fletts played in A-Train, a band that was popular throughout Louisiana and Texas from 1977–87. The Bluebirds started as a Tuesday night jam band, and has had on drums Kerry Hunter and Kevin Smith. The Fletts are not only exemplary musicians but skilled songwriters who inject a regional feel to their tunes without being stagy about it.

what to buy: *Swamp Stomp* ♫♫♫♫ (Icehouse, 1995, prod. Keith Sykes, John Hampton, Buddy Flett, Bruce Flett) is roiling, fervid blues rock rife with gut-pummeling slide. Buddy wrote the infectious title cut, and co-penned "First You Cry," a magnificent, southern-style soul ballad in the Dan Penn tradition (Percy Sledge selected it to sing on his Grammy-nominated *Blue Night*). Buddy's unplugged rendering of "No More Cane on the Brazos" (originally by another Fannin Street habitué, Leadbelly) is haunting and excellent. If you're among those who think blues rock is narrow and unimaginative, hear this and be enlightened.

what to buy next: From the opening rocker "Cleveland, MS," Buddy's slide bursts from the speakers and is in no short supply on the other selections on *South from Memphis* ♫♫♫♫ (Icehouse, 1996, prod. Buddy Flett). Highlights include the travelin' "Tehana Train" and another Leadbelly l'hommage, "Fannin Street." Unreservedly recommended, especially with a side of gumbo and a cold beer.

influences:

◀◀ Raymond Blakes, Johnny "Guitar" Watson, Elmore James, Rolling Stones

Tim Schuller

Blues Project

Formed 1965, in New York, NY. Disbanded 1972.

Danny Kalb, guitar; Roy Blumenfeld, drums; Andy Kulberg, bass, flute (1965–67); Steve Katz, guitar, harmonica (1965–67); Tommy Flanders, vocals (1965–66, 1972); Al Kooper, keyboards, vocals (1965–67); Don Kretmar, bass, saxophone, (1971–72); David Cohen, piano (1972); Bill Lussenden, guitar (1972).

"The Jewish Beatles," as this 1960s New York-based band was once dubbed, the Blues Project was more important and influential than its lack of success might first indicate. The Project was a transitional phase for many of its members: Kooper and Katz went on to found Blood, Sweat & Tears; Kooper became successful as a producer, sideman and performer; Kulberg and Blumenfield headed for Seatrain. The members, individualists all, came up with a potent, sophisticated, East Coast blast of blues, folk and rock with slightly jazzy overtones that found adherents from all genres. That sound lasted, in its original incarnation, only a couple years. Still, after Paul Butterfield and along with English bands like Cream, the group was instrumental in educating the 1960s rock audience to blues—as the members were learning it themselves.

what to buy: *The Best of the Blues Project* 𝄞𝄞𝄞𝄞 (Rhino, 1989) is a 16-track overview that includes all the essentials: strange covers of Blind Willie Johnson's "I Can't Keep from Crying" on acid and a live kidnapping of Muddy Waters' "Two Trains Running," with Kalb at his most-experimental. If you like it, you'll want *Anthology* 𝄞𝄞𝄞𝄞 (Polydor Chronicles, 1997), with all that and more outtakes and live tracks spread over two discs.

what to buy next: *Projections* 𝄞𝄞𝄞𝄞 (Verve-Forecast, 1966/ Polydor, 1989, prod. Tom Wilson), their only real studio album, is still the best indication of the breadth of their eclectic talent, from the lilting jazz melody of "Flute Thing" to the 11:20 live version of "Two Trains Running." *Live at the Cafe Au Go Go* 𝄞𝄞𝄞 (Verve-Forecast, 1966) is a gritty document of their early, blues/folk synthesis. Who else would have put "Catch the Wind" and "Violets of Dawn" alongside "Spoonful" and "Who Do You Love"?

what to avoid: *Lazarus* 𝄞 (Capitol, 1971, prod. Shel Talmy) was an uninspired, misguided attempt by Kalb, Blumenfeld and Flanders to bring back the magic.

the rest:

Live at Town Hall 𝄞𝄞 (Verve-Forecast, 1967/One Way, 1994)
Planned Obsolescence 𝄞𝄞 (Verve-Forecast, 1968/One Way, 1995)
Reunion in Central Park 𝄞𝄞𝄞 (MCA, 1973/One Way, 1995)

worth searching for: Not strictly a Blues Project reunion, *Soul of a Man: Al Kooper Live* 𝄞𝄞𝄞 (Musicmasters, 1995) does bring back the magic, with Kalb, Kulberg and Blumenthal together on four tracks and a great nod to BST.

influences:

◀◀ Muddy Waters, Willie Dixon, Bob Dylan, Rolling Stones

▶▶ Blood, Sweat & Tears, Seatrain

Leland Rucker

Bluestime

See: J. Geils Band

Deanna Bogart

Born 1960, in Detroit, MI.

The barrelhouse piano style fits comfortably into many different genres—New Orleans R&B, boogie-woogie blues, swing jazz, Jerry Lee Lewis-style rock 'n' roll—and this talented Maryland pianist has mastered them all. She's an energetic live performer, frequently talking to the audience and leaping from her bench, and her songwriting merges all the seemingly disparate styles more seamlessly with every album. Bogart always shows a keen eye for style, developing a black fedora into her trademark and whipping out a saxophone whenever she needs a break from the piano.

what to buy: Her playful style, which recalls Saffire—The Uppity Blueswomen on winking songs about aging like "Over Thirty"—is most refreshing on her debut, *Out to Get You* 𝄞𝄞𝄞 (Blind Pig, 1991).

what to buy next: Both follow-ups, *Crossing Borders* 𝄞𝄞𝄞 (Flying Fish, 1992) and *New Address* 𝄞𝄞𝄞 (Viceroots, 1996, prod. Jon Carrell) reflect a growing songwriting style that takes chances on funk and soul while staying close to the bottom-line piano boogie.

influences:

◀◀ Victoria Spivey, Sippie Wallace, Dorothy Donegan, Billie Holiday, Bessie Smith, Eddie Shaw

▶▶ Joanna Connor, Saffire—The Uppity Blueswomen

Steve Knopper

Zuzu Bollin

Born A.D. Bollin, 1922, in Frisco, TX. Died October 19, 1990, in Dallas, TX.

In a textbook rediscovery scenario, Bollin was tracked to a ramshackle rooming house near downtown Dallas by ex-cab driver Chuck Nevitt in 1987. The obscure singer/guitarist had been in the literature of the blues since the 1960s, when his 1951 cut "Why Don't You Eat Where You Slept Last Night?" was being cited as a masterpiece of the "jump" blues subgenre. Bollin had hung with Li'l Son Jackson, played with Ernie Fields and Jimmy Reed, pissed off Jack Ruby and even done a little time behind marijuana. With Nevitt's help he went blazing down the comeback trail, playing blues fests here and abroad and cutting *Texas Bluesman* for the Dallas Blues Society in 1989, the purest expression of the jump mode recorded in decades. He died the next year of cancer.

what to buy: *Texas Bluesman* ♫♫♫♫ (Antone's, 1992, prod. Chuck Nevitt) is the reissued DBS session, which evokes Eddie Vinson and T-Bone Walker in a swinging, jazz-style session.

influences:

◄◄ T-Bone Walker

►► Hash Brown

Tim Schuller

Juke Boy Bonner

Born Weldon Bonner, March 22, 1932, in Belleville, TX. Died June 28, 1978, in Houston, TX.

Juke Boy Bonner was a bluesman who considered himself an entertainer and commentator on social conditions. A limited guitarist who also sang and played the harp on a rack, Bonner recorded for the Irma label in 1956 and Goldband in 1960. The records sold poorly, but he survived by hustling gigs as a one-man trio in Houston's rough-and-tumble Third Ward beer joints. Bonner benefited from Europe's mid-1960s wave of blues interest, via new recordings, reissues of old recordings and concert tours. In the late 1960s, Bonner made some of his best recordings for Arhoolie and Sonet. However, by the mid-1970s, gigs were hard to find, and his career faded into an alcoholic cloud.

what to buy: Bonner's most introspective material is contained on *Life Gave Me a Dirty Deal* ♫♫♫♫ (Arhoolie, 1992, prod. Chris Strachwitz). *Juke Boy Bonner, 1960 to 1967* ♫♫♫♫ (Flyright, 1992, prod. Bruce Bastin) is a magnificent collection of early studio releases and live material recorded in Houston's Jungle Lounge.

what to avoid: While there are some fine songs collected on *The Adventures of Juke Boy Bonner* ♫♫ (Collectables, 1992), Bonner's accompaniment—vocal group and synthesizer—often overwhelms him.

worth searching for: A favorite Juke Bonner collectable is the LP *Blues Scene USA: The Louisiana Blues* ♫♫♫, which contains all of his energetic Goldband material.

influences:

◄◄ Lightnin' Hopkins, Blind Lemon Jefferson, John Lee Hooker, Jimmy Reed, Sonny Boy Williamson II, Frankie Lee Sims, Lightnin' Slim

►► Fabulous Thunderbirds

Jeff Hannusch

Roy Book Binder

Born Roy Bookbinder, October 5, 1943, in New York, NY.

A long-time acoustic guitar master, Roy Book Binder mixes Piedmont blues, folk, country and hillbilly with an affable performing style that has traveled many miles over three decades. Turned onto blues while in the service in the 1960s, he traded being chauffeur for the Rev. Gary Davis to learn the secrets of the master before beginning his own recording career. He has lived, literally, on the road since making a mobile home his primary residence in 1976.

what to buy: *Travelin' Man* ♫♫♫ (Adelphi, 1970/Genes, 1997, prod. Gene Rosenthal) is still the book on Book Binder, as he soaks up influences and turns them into his own folk/blues, including Pink Anderson's title track and Davis' "Delia," in Book Binder's ever-pleasant solo style. For a band experience, try the rockabilly-tinged *The Hillbilly Blues Cats* ♫♫♫♫ (Rounder, 1992).

what to buy next: *Bookeroo!* ♫♫♫♫ (Rounder, 1988, prod. Jerry Douglas) includes "Gonna Get Myself a Motorhome" with the tasty backing of Douglas' dobro, percussionist Kenny Malone and bassist Edgar Meyer.

the rest:

Goin' Back to Tampa ♫♫♫ (Rounder, 1979)
Live Book: Don't Start Me Talkin' ♫♫♫ (Rounder, 1994)

influences:

◄◄ Pink Anderson, Rev. Gary Davis, Mississippi John Hurt, Bo Carter, Blind Boy Fuller, Blind Willie McTell, Blind Blake

Leland Rucker

James Booker

Born December 17, 1939, in New Orleans, LA. Died November 8, 1983, in New Orleans, LA.

James Booker was the Piano Prince of New Orleans, the Bronze Liberace. A child prodigy, he studied both classical and barroom piano and could play virtually any style with ease. A medley might start with Chopin, segue into Jelly Roll Morton and end up on the "Sunny Side of the Street." Booker began performing in public in his early teens on black radio shows around New Orleans. At age 14 he formed a band called Booker Boy and the Rhythmaires, which played at local dances. His first recording session came in 1954 when Dave Bartholomew produced "Doing the Hambone" and "Thinkin' about My Baby" for Imperial. Booker's ability to duplicate other pianists' sound led to him ghosting on recordings for Fats Domino, among others. Booker struggled all his life against personal demons. Drug addiction and mental illness plagued him for many years and derailed a promising career. Even toward the end of his life, however, when Booker was *on*, there was no better piano player in the world.

what to buy: From 1977 to 1982, Booker played a weekly gig (when he showed up) at New Orleans' Maple Leaf, a bar-cum-laundromat frequented by Tulane University students and foreign blues freaks on a pilgrimage. Sixty hours of tapes have been edited down to two releases. The better half, *Spiders on the Keys* &&&&&, (Rounder, 1993, prod. Scott Billington, John Parsons), is all instrumental and reveals Booker playing at a stunning level of imagination and finesse. The highlights are a nearly eight-minute version of the autobiographical "Papa Was a Rascal," the dazzling pianistics of "Tico Tico" and a reworking of "Eleanor Rigby." All the lonely people, indeed. *Resurrection of the Bayou Maharajah* &&&& (Rounder, 1993, prod. Scott Billington, John Parsons) is almost as good and has the added pleasure of Booker's peculiar choked-off vocals. On these cuts, Booker combines the lightest classical technique with the darkest paranoid lyrics, culminating in his warning that "We all got to watch out for the CIA." Still, that doesn't stop him from including Chopin's "Minute Waltz." *Junco Partner* &&&& (Hannibal, 1993, prod. Joe Boyd) is the best of Booker's studio recordings and features more of a rolling stride style than the big block chords of the live performances. Booker adds soul to Chopin to come up with the "Black Minute Waltz." There's a definitive version of the title tune, one of Booker's theme songs, and a rollicking "Goodnight Irene," in which Booker makes note of the fact that both he and the song's composer, Leadbelly, spent time on "the Ponderosa," Louisiana's notorious Angola State Prison.

what to buy next: *Classified* &&&& (Rounder, 1983, prod. Scott Billington) is another studio date on which Booker is joined by the New Orleans all-star backup group of Red Tyler on sax, James Singleton on bass and Johnny Vidacovich on drums. Highlights include a Professor Longhair medley, a searing ver-

sion of the title song and a priceless "King of the Road." *New Orleans Piano Wizard: Live!* &&&& (Rounder, 1993), a live recording from Switzerland in 1977, finds Booker covering Percy Mayfield's "Please Send Me Someone to Love" and Joe Tex's "Come in My House." Novelty bonus: a ragtime version of "Something Stupid," one of the worst songs ever written. *Gonzo: More Than All the 45s* &&&& (Night Train, 1996, prod. Aaron Fuchs) gathers Booker's earliest recordings together in one release. Booker sounds even younger than his 15 years on his first date, "Doing the Hambone." The best parts are all the rocking organ instrumentals he made for Ace and Peacock, including his biggest hit, "Gonzo."

the rest:

The Lost Paramount Tapes &&& (DJM, 1995)

worth searching for: Booker has a strong following in Europe, where several additional recordings of his have been released over the years. Look for *King of the New Orleans Keyboard* &&&& (Junco Partner Records), *Piano Prince of New Orleans* &&&& (Aves) and *Blues and Ragtime from New Orleans* &&&& (Aves).

influences:

◀◀ Jelly Roll Morton, Edward Frank, Professor Longhair

▶▶ Dr. John, Harry Connick Jr.

David Feld

Pat Boyack

Born June 26, 1967, in Helper, UT.

Guitarist Pat Boyack is one of blues' young lions who traces his interest in the music to Stevie Ray Vaughan. Boyack grew up listening to his mother's Elvis Presley records before switching to KISS and Van Halen in his teenage years. Then came SRV's *Couldn't Stand the Weather* and *Soul to Soul*; from then on he was into Jimmie Vaughan, Anson Funderburgh and the Fabulous Thunderbirds—the whole Texas thing. Except for a short stint in Phoenix, when he joined the Rocket 88s, a big-league bar band that included singer and harmonica player Jimmy Morello, Boyack has lived in Dallas, where he formed the Prowlers, which continue to evolve.

what to buy: Hearing *Breaking In* &&&&& (Bullseye Blues, 1994, prod. Ron Levy), you realize it's true: these guys could have been the next the Fabulous Thunderbirds, as old buddy Morello bares the reincarnated soul of Howlin' Wolf while Boyack's guitar sizzles behind him. Where *Breaking In* rocks, *On the Prowl* &&&& (Bullseye Blues, 1996, prod. Ron Levy, Rusty McFarland) swings.

the rest:

Super Blue and Funky 🎵🎵🎵 (Bullseye Blues, 1997)

worth searching for: A few copies of the pre-Morello Prowlers' *Armed and Dangerous* 🎵🎵🎵 (1993, prod. Anson Funderburgh), can probably be found among the used CD stores in the Dallas/Ft. Worth area.

influences:

◀◀ Stevie Ray Vaughan, Jimmie Vaughan, Anson Funderburgh, Duke Robillard

Dave Ranney

Eddie Boyd

Born Edward Riley Boyd, November 25, 1914, in Stovall, MS. Died July 13, 1994.

Boyd lived a familiar bluesman's story: Born in Mississippi, moved to Chicago in the 1940s, tried desperately to make hit singles, had minor financial successes, drifted out of the American blues scene and relocated to Europe before his death. This pianist and organist's biggest hits were 1947's "Killroy Won't Be Back," 1952's "Five Long Years" and 1953's "24 Hours," and he backed Sonny Boy Williamson on 1945's "Elevator Woman." But he ended his American career in frustration with the music industry, staying in Helsinki, Finland, after touring there with the American Folk Blues Festival in 1965. He was a relatively minor character in the Chicago blues scene, but every now and then some nightclub performer gets around to performing "Five Long Years."

what to buy: With Buddy Guy on guitar and bass and Big Mama Thornton contributing some lead vocals, Boyd's 1965 London and Hamburg sessions became *Five Long Years* 🎵🎵🎵 (Evidence, 1994, prod. Mike Vernon); Boyd's high-pitched voice, which recalls Berry, stands out much more than his understated piano licks.

what to buy next: *Third Degree* 🎵🎵🎵 (Charly, 1993, prod. various) tours Boyd's 1951–59 singles for Chess Records, including "I Got the Blues" and "Nothing but Trouble."

worth searching for: With Peter Green, John McVie and Mick Fleetwood—better known as the early Fleetwood Mac—Boyd put out *7936 South Rhodes* 🎵🎵🎵 (Epic, 1968), a solid album despite the band's slight lack of confidence.

influences:

◀◀ Robert Junior Lockwood, Charles Brown, Muddy Waters, Otis Spann, Sonny Boy Williamson II, Tampa Red

▶▶ Ron Levy, Dr. John, Buddy Guy, Otis Rush

Steve Knopper

Ishmon Bracey

Born January 9, 1901, in Byram, MS. Died February 12, 1970, in Jackson, MS.

Often described as an acquired taste even among blues fanatics, Ishmon (sometimes Ishman) Bracey was nearly as talented as his frequent partner, Tommy Johnson, and a more serious and dedicated musician than his doomed, clowning friend. His trembling alto is not immediately warmed to, but over time Bracey becomes an easier listen than, say, the fevered falsetto of Skip James. In his most famous photograph, taken in 1925, Bracey seems so formal and reserved in suit and tie that he appears stuffed. He was anything but: a showman and bar fighter who eventually renounced the devil's music in the late 1930s, Bracey became an ordained preacher for the rest of his life. He could range between a gutty baritone and a raspy soprano, a tact he took on the powerful "Woman Woman Blues," with a harsh, almost-Eastern guitar style that Muddy Waters would revive on "Rolling Stone." Bracey also excelled in the sad, fatalistic laments that Tommy Johnson traded in—"Suitcase Full of Blues" and "Trouble Hearted Blues" are two stunning examples. Bracey and Johnson were frequent road partners throughout Jackson and the Mississippi Delta in the 1930s, but as Johnson became a hopeless alcoholic, Bracey began to replace his blues with gospel hymns. He stayed a churchman through the early 1960s, when he was rediscovered by blues researchers. He was proud of his 23 recordings made for Victor and Paramount in 1928 and 1929, but they were ancient history to him. The only music he made in his last years was in praise of his Lord.

what to buy: *Ishmon Bracey and Charley Taylor, 1928–29* 🎵🎵🎵🎵 (Document, 1991, prod. Johnny Parth) includes all of Bracey's work, from solemn blues backed by Charlie McCoy on guitar and mandolin to more halting efforts backed by the shambling support of the New Orleans Nehi Boys. And there are two strange comedy workouts featuring piano by Charley Taylor and bad jokes and jackdaw laughter by Bracey.

the rest:

Masters of the Delta Blues 🎵🎵🎵 (Yazoo, 1991)

influences:

◀◀ Tommy Johnson, Dick Bankston, Charley Patton, Willie Brown

▶▶ Muddy Waters, Alan Wilson

Steve Braun

Doyle Bramhall

Born 1949, in Dallas, TX.

Before he became a band leader, drummer and vocalist Doyle Bramhall kicked around Texas as a teenager, playing with Jimmie Vaughan in the Dallas outfit the Chessmen, and later, with Stevie Ray Vaughan on bass, Texas Storm. Soaking up the influences of acts such as Jimi Hendrix and the Animals (for which the Chessmen served as an opening act), Bramhall moved to Austin, where as a member of various acts, he helped spearhead that city's nascent blues/rock scene. Stardom beckoned several times, but Bramhall never quite answered the call. Toiling for years as a drummer, he gained notice as a songwriter when some of his songs (including "The House Is Rockin'") wound up on a couple Stevie Ray albums as well as the Vaughan Brothers *Family Style* collaboration. Bramhall finally got his shot as a band leader in 1989, and his debut album followed five years later. A master of roots-style drumming and with a voice as lived-in as a favorite pair of boots, Bramhall is the real deal. Too bad his talent still far outstrips his notoriety.

what to buy: An album that can only be described as a labor of love, *Bird Nest on the Ground* 𝅘𝅥𝅘𝅥𝅘𝅥𝅘𝅥 (Antone's, 1994, prod. Doyle Bramhall, Barbara Logan, David Watson, Clint Birdwell, Charley Wirz, Smokin' Joe Kubek, Chuck Nevitt) was recorded over a period of a dozen years, with Bramhall scraping together material and cash for sessions as he drummed for Marcia Ball, Mason Ruffner and Lou Ann Barton. The album is a virtual textbook of Texas rock 'n' blues styles, the very sort that took Stevie Ray Vaughan—whose vocal style was partially inspired by Bramhall's—to the top. What makes *Bird Nest* such a triumph is how much of a piece it sounds, given its extended gestation, numerous participants and wide range of material. Bramhall's extraordinarily soulful vocals hold everything together, from the Stax-style title track (a Muddy Waters tune) to the down 'n' dirty version of John Lee Hooker's "I'm in the Mood" and a chooglin' take on Johnny Nash's "I Can See Clearly Now." Look for cameos from Stevie Ray and Jimmie Vaughan, the Memphis Horns, and even Mike Judge (famous not as a bassist, but as the creator of *Beavis and Butt-head*).

influences:

◄◄ Bobby "Blue" Bland, Ray Charles, Muddy Waters, Albert King

►► Stevie Ray Vaughan, Doyle Bramhall II

Daniel Durchholz

Billy Branch

Born William Earl Branch, October 31, 1951, in Great Lakes, IL.

Raised in Los Angeles, Billy Branch returned to Chicago in 1969 and got slagged by a certain pundit. His dictum: since Branch counted Lee Oskar as a harmonica influence, you couldn't really regard him as a "pure" blues dude. Genre heavyweight Willie Dixon and the great, unsung piano patriarch Jimmy Walker had no idea he wasn't "pure" and welcomed him to their bandstands, accurately appraising his merit as a harp blower. Branch is of that breed of harmonica artist who can tuck into the tonal uproar of elder harpmen at will but will play with lightness, melody and jazz-like improvisational zest. Topping it all off, he also sings well. Branch's tremendously commendable "Blues in the Schools" program started in Chicago but has reached learning centers in other cities and states as well. Odds are it'll do kids more good than punditry ever will.

what to buy: *Blues Keep Following Me Around* 𝅘𝅥𝅘𝅥𝅘𝅥𝅘𝅥 (Verve, 1995, prod. John Snyder, Jay Newland) is very strong, very diverse; hard-line blues mixed with the unlikely success of "Polk Salad Annie" (one of three cuts spurred by horns) and Willie Dixon's almost vaudevillian "Flamin' Mamie."

what to buy next: Compared to the almost slick production of *Blues Keep Following Me Around*, *Where's My Money* 𝅘𝅥𝅘𝅥𝅘𝅥𝅘𝅥 (Red Beans, 1984/Evidence, 1995) seems back-alley, which is far from a pejorative term in these climes; it's Branch, the Sons of the Blues and guest pianist Jimmy Walker performing bumptious, feisty music in true Chicago tradition.

the rest:

Live '82 𝅘𝅥𝅘𝅥𝅘𝅥 (Evidence, 1994)

influences:

◄◄ Sonny Boy Williamson II, Howlin' Wolf, Big Walter Horton

►► Lee McBee

Tim Schuller

Jackie Brenston

Born August 15, 1930, in Clarksdale, MS. Died December 15, 1979, in Memphis, TN.

Jackie Brenston's fame rests on a whim of fate. One of a rotating crew of saxophonists who took turns fronting Ike Turner's slashing Kings of Rhythm, Brenston had the good fortune to be taking lead when Turner blasted off on "Rocket 88," a chart-topping R&B hit that some scholars insist is the first true rock 'n' roll record. Brenston happened to replace another Turner singer, Johnny O'Neal, just before the Oldsmobile tribute was waxed in March 1951 for producer Sam Phillips. Sold to Chicago's Chess brothers, the record was credited to Brenston "and his Delta Cats," a mistake Turner still laments. Starry-eyed, Brenston split from Turner's band, but despite gigs with pianist Phineas Newborn Jr. and guitar slinger Lowell Fulson, he was useless without Turner. Slinking back in the mid-1950s, Brenston began drinking heavily and left Ike for good in 1962 as Tina Turner's career was taking off.

what to buy: For true blues crazies who want "Rocket 88" and its flip side, "Independent Woman," the only way to go is *Sun Records: The Blues Years 1950–58* 𝄞𝄞𝄞𝄞 (Charly, 1996, prod. Sam Phillips), an eight-disc, 202-track set, an overwhelming survey of Sam Phillips' blues years.

what to buy next: Brenston rejoined Ike during sessions for Syd Nathan's Federal label in 1956 and 1957, blowing baritone sax and singing on four tracks on *Kings of Rhythm* 𝄞𝄞𝄞𝄞 (Charly, 1991, prod. Syd Nathan).

influences:
◄◄ Ike Turner

Steve Braun

John Brim

Born April 19, 1922, in Hopkinsville, TN.

It's easy to say that Brim gets overlooked on rosters of Chicago blues greats. Though he cut but a handful of sides in the 1950s, they are of a quality that assures his respect among genre buffs. But Brim always held the music biz at arm's length, preferring to rely on the dry-cleaning trade for his main buck. He wasn't in the least interested in recording covers. A talented writer, he cut with able sidemen like Roosevelt Sykes (with Random), Sunnyland Slim (JOB), Robert Lockwood and Fred Below (Chess/Checker) and Eddie Taylor (Parrot). Several of his songs, including "Ice Cream Man," "Tough Times" and "Rattlesnake" are absolute gems, clear-cut epitomizations of Chicago blues in its Golden Era. Jump cut to the 1970s, and there's Brim being overlooked again helming a band that on its best nights was a Windy City blues revue so stellar it's embarrassing there aren't recordings of it, with Brim's guitarist son John (a.k.a. "Boomie"), bassist Floyd Jones and sometimes Jimmy Reed (who Brim knew from days of yore) or Eddie Taylor. Whenever you hear musicians snivel about getting swindled by the Big, Bad Record Man, remember that they could have done what Brim did: He kept his publishing straight and today lives in comfortable retirement from royalties—several bands have

cut "Tough Times," J. Geils did "Be Careful" and Van Halen scored with "Ice Cream Man."

what to buy: Brim's discography is so scant he shares *Whose Muddy Shoes* 𝄞𝄞𝄞𝄞 (MCA/Chess 1991, prod. Leonard Chess, Phil Chess) with Elmore James. The James cuts are great, but the five Brim tunes alone make this essential (from 1950s Chess/Checker and Parrot sides).

what to avoid: *Ice Cream Man* **woof!** (Tone Cool, 1994) is a complete failure. The music was recorded and tapes sent to Brim, who dubbed in his vocals and sounds bored to tears. He was also irate that this tack left him no space for guitar solos.

influences:
◄◄ Big Bill Broonzy
►► Bob Margolin, Studebaker John

Tim Schuller

Hadda Brooks

Born Hadda Hopgood, October 29, 1916, in Los Angeles, CA.

This classically trained boogie-woogie pianist's time came and went quickly, but not before her mid-1940s singles were successful enough to establish jukebox operator Jules Bihari as a credible record company owner. (Later Bihari Records artists included B.B. King, Charles Brown, Elmore James and Etta James.) Brooks, known as "Queen of the Boogie," played with a pristine, jazzy style—like a torch singer—and became famous for "boogie-izing" pop standards like "I Hadn't Anyone Till You." She began singing when a Los Angeles bandleader told her to "fake it" on her first vocal hit, "You Won't Let Me Go." Brooks' sleek, friendly charisma led to several movie roles, including one where she sings to Humphrey Bogart in *In a Lonely Place*. But as with so many 1940s boogie experts, Brooks' career slowed down when first dirtier R&B, then explicitly sexy rock 'n' roll, made her music a pop anachronism. She retired in 1971, but a chapter in a "Whatever Became Of … ?" book gave her a second career performing in L.A. clubs (such as Johnny Depp's swanky Viper Room) and recording new albums (including a single on *The Crossing Guard* soundtrack).

what to buy: Her Modern tracks—"Out of the Blue" and "Anytime, Anyplace, Anywhere," among many others—return on *That's My Desire* 𝄞𝄞𝄞𝄞 (Virgin, 1994, prod. various), a collection of styles ranging from pure boogie to slick jazz.

what to buy next: Brooks' comeback album, *Time Was When* 𝄞𝄞𝄞 (Pointblank/Virgin, 1996, prod. John Wooler), travels in the Charles Brown zone between slick cocktail jazz and raunchy blues. In fact, Brooks' recent recordings make nice supplements to Brown's newer material in any piano/blues collection.

the rest:

Anytime, Anyplace, Anywhere 𝄞𝄞𝄞 (DRG, 1994)
Jump Back Honey: The Complete OKeh Sessions 𝄞𝄞𝄞 (Columbia, 1997)

worth searching for: The album *Femme Fatale* 𝄞𝄞𝄞 (Crown, prod. Jules Bihari) was a nice change of pace from Brooks' singles-dominated career, but it came out at the wrong time—just as Elvis Presley and Bill Haley were taking over the charts—and sunk commercially.

influences:

◀◀ Art Tatum, Victoria Spivey, Sippie Wallace, Bessie Smith, Billie Holiday, Nat "King" Cole

▶▶ Charles Brown, Dr. John, Rosemary Clooney, Etta James, Deanna Bogart

Steve Knopper

Lonnie Brooks

Born Lee Baker Jr., December 18, 1933, in Dubuisson, LA.

Once dubbed "the human juke box," Lonnie Brooks spent his early years learning every imaginable guitar style as a means of survival. These days, eclecticism has become his trademark. With his guitar-slinging sons, Ronnie and Wayne, adding a contemporary edge to his road show and studio efforts, Brooks has developed a reputation as a full-throttle yet tongue-in-cheek showman rooted in southern-fried blues, but fluent in Cajun, country and rock styles. As "Guitar Jr.," Brooks backed zydeco legend Clifton Chenier in the mid-1950s, and later cut a few R&B and rock-flavored singles of his own for Goldband. He toured briefly with Sam Cooke and worked as a sideman for Jimmy Reed, but struggled through the 1960s with a string of marginally successful singles on Mercury, Chess and several smaller labels. *Broke and Hungry*, his first full-length album, released in 1969, didn't fare much better. After some moderate successes on European labels, the breakthrough came when Brooks appeared on *Living Chicago Blues Vol. 3*, a 1978 compilation by the Chicago-based Alligator label. *Bayou Lightning*, released on Alligator a year later, marked the beginning of a two-decade relationship that has optimized Brooks' solid combination of musical versatility, vocal prowess and engaging showmanship.

what to buy: A full horn section on five of the 10 tracks on *Turn on the Night* 𝄞𝄞𝄞𝄞 (Alligator, 1981, prod. Bruce Iglauer, Lonnie

Brooks) add an extra kick to Brooks' already punchy arrangements. In addition to successfully capturing the rollicking flavor of Brooks' live show, *Live from Chicago: Bayou Lightning Strikes* 𝄞𝄞𝄞 (Alligator, 1988, prod. Bruce Iglauer) also marks guitarist Ronnie Baker Brooks' debut in his dad's band. Former SRV and Santana producer Jim Gaines replaces Brooks' road band for *Roadhouse Rules* 𝄞𝄞𝄞𝄞 (Alligator, 1996, prod. Jim Gaines) with a patchwork of solid studio musicians. These hired guns, along with guest appearances by the Memphis Horns, provide a more diverse platform for Brooks' songwriting and vocal performances.

what to buy next: Guest appearances by guitarist Johnny Winter (a life-long Brooks fan) and harpist Jim Liban on *Wound Up Tight* 𝄞𝄞𝄞 (Alligator, 1988, prod. Lonnie Brooks, Bruce Iglauer) heighten Brooks' southern rock and Cajun sensitivies. Tracks like "Jealous Man" and "Bewitched" have become mainstays of his live show. Although *Let's Talk It Over* 𝄞𝄞𝄞 (Delmark, 1993, prod. Ralph Bass) virtually ignores Brooks' southern roots, these 1977 sessions do a fine job of showcasing his Chicago blues sensibilities.

what to avoid: Brooks' lack of polish at age 35 isn't the real problem with *Live at Pepper's 1968* 𝄞 (Black Magic, 1985/Black Top, 1996, prod. George Adins); it's the abysmal production quality, inconsistent rhythm section and generally disinterested audience that make this record an uncomfortable—and sometimes painful—experience.

the rest:

Sweet Home Chicago 𝄞𝄞𝄞 (Capitol, 1975/Evidence, 1992)
Living Chicago Blues 𝄞𝄞𝄞 (Alligator, 1978)
Bayou Lightning 𝄞𝄞𝄞 (Alligator, 1979)
Hot Shot 𝄞𝄞𝄞 (Alligator, 1983)
The Crawl 𝄞𝄞𝄞 (Charly, 1984)
Satisfaction Guaranteed 𝄞𝄞𝄞 (Alligator, 1991)

worth searching for: The commercial failure of *Broke and Hungry* 𝄞𝄞𝄞 (Capitol, 1969) had more to do with poor marketing than poor quality. Long out of print, it features covers of tunes by Professor Longhair, Guitar Slim and Lightnin' Slim and offers a interesting glimpse of Brooks early in his solo career.

influences:

◀◀ Lightnin' Hopkins, Jimmy Reed

▶▶ Johnny Winter, Kenny Neal

John C. Bruening

Lonnie Brooks (© Jack Vartoogian)

Big Bill Broonzy

Born William Lee Conley Broonzy, June 26, 1893, in Scott, MS. Died August 15, 1958, in Chicago, IL.

Broonzy's body of work—including his enduring originals "Key to the Highway" and "Black, Brown and White"—ranks him among Muddy Waters, B.B. King and Robert Johnson in terms of influence. A storyteller as much as a lonesome singer, Broonzy was among the first performers to marry rough rural blues (like Johnson's brand of Mississippi Delta moaning) with upscale jazzy city blues (like Charles Brown's cocktail piano crooning). He began his career as a violinist (a skill he learned from an uncle) and learned from mentor Papa Charlie Jackson how to adapt those skills to the guitar. As his obvious talent gradually turned him into a star, he moved to Chicago and started hooking up with Memphis Slim, Brownie McGhee, John Lee "Sonny Boy" Williamson and Big Maceo; he also recorded for many different labels, including Columbia, OKeh and Blue-bird. Most refused to put out "Black, Brown and White"—a powerful attack on racism with the memorable tell-it-like-it-is chorus, "Get back"—after Broonzy wrote it in 1949; two years later, in France, writer-critic Hugues Panassie and record company officials helped him get it in circulation. Broonzy's pockets of regional popularity coagulated into an adoring national audience after he played John Hammond's From Spirituals to Swing concert (as a replacement for Robert Johnson, who had just died) at New York City's Carnegie Hall in 1938. Regular Chicago and southern gigs followed until the 1950s, when Broonzy—along with peers Leadbelly, Josh White and Sonny Terry and Brownie McGhee—became an avatar of the folk movement. While touring and recording in Europe throughout the 1950s, he wrote a fascinating biography, *Big Bill Blues*, with Danish writer Yannick Bruynoghe.

what to buy: Because Broonzy was such a prolific writer and because so many different big record companies put out his stuff, plenty of thorough CD collections document various stages of his career. Most impressive include *Good Time Tonight* 𝄢𝄢𝄢𝄢 (Columbia/Legacy, 1990, prod. various), which spans 1930 to 1940 (including, of course, his classic "I Can't Be Satisfied"); *Do That Guitar Rag (1928–35)* 𝄢𝄢𝄢𝄢 (Yazoo, 1973); and *Blues in the Mississippi Night* 𝄢𝄢𝄢𝄢 (Rykodisc, 1990), a sometimes chilling 1946 Alan Lomax-recorded no-holds-barred conversation between Broonzy, pianist Memphis Slim and harpist Sonny Boy Williamson about racism in the South.

what to buy next: As per usual with the archivist label, *Complete Recorded Works in Chronological Order, Vols. 1–11* 𝄢𝄢𝄢𝄢 (Document, 1991, prod. various) is far too complete unless you're a major fan or an obsessive collector; if you are, of course, you can't go wrong.

best of the rest:

Big Bill Broonzy Sings Folk Songs 𝄢𝄢𝄢𝄢 (Smithsonian/Folkways, 1962)
Big Bill Broonzy & Washboard Sam 𝄢𝄢𝄢 (MCA, 1962)
The Young Big Bill Broonzy (1928–35) 𝄢𝄢𝄢 (Yazoo, 1968)
Feelin' Low Down 𝄢𝄢𝄢 (GNP Crescendo, 1973)

worth searching for: *Big Bill's Blues* 𝄢𝄢𝄢𝄢 (Portrait) captures Broonzy's seriousness and humor as well as the spontaneity of his recording process.

influences:

◀◀ Papa Charlie Jackson, Son House, Robert Johnson, Jimmie Rodgers, Blind Lemon Jefferson

▶▶ Muddy Waters, Leadbelly, Bob Dylan, Woody Guthrie, Sonny Terry & Brownie McGhee, Eric Clapton, Taj Mahal, Cephas & Wiggins

Steve Knopper

Andrew Brown

Born February 25, 1937, in Jackson, MS. Died December 11, 1985.

Guitarist/vocalist Andrew Brown arrived in Chicago in the mid-1940s with strong songwriting capabilities, a fluent urban guitar style and a full, powerful vocal delivery. Like many Chicago musicians, while he played his blues at the night clubs, he also maintained a day job at a steel mill. He cut a few singles for the small U.S.A. and 4 Brothers labels in the early and mid-1960s, but there was little, if any notoriety for him beyond Chicago. His career got a needed boost in 1980 with his inclusion on an Alligator Records *Living Chicago Blues* series and subsequent signing to the Dutch Black Magic label before Brown succumbed to lung cancer.

what to buy: *On the Case* 𝄢𝄢𝄢𝄢 (Double Trouble, 1985, prod. Dick Shurman, Marcel Vos), Brown's last recording, reveals him for the polished guitarist/vocalist he was. His playing here is aggressive and his singing strong, despite the health problems that were soon to end his life. A tight band that includes noted blues keyboardist Professor Eddie Lusk provides a superb blues backdrop to this import. The instrumental title selection penned by Brown is a great example of his fluid yet pointed guitar style.

what to buy next: His most readily accessible recorded work is on *Living Chicago Blues Vol. 4* 𝄢𝄢𝄢 (Alligator, 1980, prod. Bruce

Iglauer), a compilation with three Brown selections: "I Got News for You," "Morning, Noon and Night" and "Two Years."

worth searching for: *Big Brown's Chicago Blues* ⅃⅃⅃ (Black Magic, 1982, prod. Marcel Vos) is pretty much unavailable except perhaps in used vinyl outlets and blues specialty shops.

influences:

◀◀ Earl Hooker, Fenton Robinson, T-Bone Walker

▶▶ Joe Louis Walker, Phillip Walker

Tali Madden

Buster Brown

Born either August 15, 1911 or August 11, 1914, in Crisp County, GA. Died January 31, 1976, in Brooklyn, NY.

Brown first recorded in 1943 for the Library of Congress during his performance at the Fort Valley State College (Georgia) Folk Festival. An energetic singer and harmonica player, he moved to Newark in the late 1950s and eventually sought out Bobby Robinson, who owned the Harlem-based Fire label. Robinson liked the down-home groove Brown had on a song called "Fannie Mae" and recorded it. Surprisingly, the song reached the #1 position on the R&B charts and even dented the Top 40 pop chart. Brown had a limited repertoire, but he followed up with minor hits like "Is You or Ain't You My Baby" and "Sugar Babe." After leaving Fire in 1962, he cut singles for several labels with little commercial success.

what to buy: *Raise a Ruckus Tonight* ⅃⅃⅃ (Relic, 1994, prod. Bobby Robinson) contains 21 lively tracks Brown recorded for Fire between 1959 and 1960.

the rest:

New King of the Blues Harmonica ⅃⅃⅃ (Collectables, 1990)

worth searching for: Brown's singles on Checker, Vest and Serock are all outstanding. Flyright also issued his Library of Congress material on LP back in the 1970s—but all is long out of print.

influences:

◀◀ Sonny Terry

Jeff Hannusch

Charles Brown

Born 1920, in Texas City, TX.

Ever wonder how pop piano music changed just after World War II from slick Gershwin tunes to hot, fast R&B? Blame Charles Brown. The blues pianist's first band, Johnny Moore's Three Blazers, modeled themselves after the slick hitmaker Nat "King" Cole and his trio. The band's primary talent, of course, was Brown; he penned the smooth 1945 hit "Driftin' Blues" and became a minor blues celebrity. Then Ray Charles, paying close attention to Brown's style and songwriting, copied the Three Blazers for his early bands. In "Driftin' Blues"—like Brown's later standards, "Merry Christmas, Baby" and "Trouble Blues"—you can hear both the cocktail-party-ready feeling of Cole's pop and the rocking-house-party feeling of Charles' R&B. Around 1956, not so coincidentally when Elvis Presley was pushing rock 'n' roll onto the radio, Brown's stardom started to dry up. He continued to record and tour throughout the 1960s and 1970s, making a decent living, but retired in the early 1980s. Then Bonnie Raitt, using her newfound star power to share fame with her blues influences, brought Brown on tour and recorded several duets. Since then, the revitalized singer-pianist has become prolific and multi-dimensional. His straightforward 1992 piano blues comeback, *Someone to Love*, is almost as excellent as his confident 1996 jazz release, *Honey Dripper*.

what to buy: *Driftin' Blues: The Best of Charles Brown* ⅃⅃⅃⅃ (EMI, 1992, prod. Adam Block) does a great job of collecting the early Three Blazers hits (including, of course, the title track) and Brown's later work, such as "Merry Christmas, Baby." His 1992 collaboration with Raitt, *Someone to Love* ⅃⅃⅃ (Bullseye Blues/Rounder, 1992, prod. Ron Levy) is the sound of an old musician tickled to have such high-profile fans. Much more confident is *Honey Dripper* ⅃⅃⅃ (Verve, 1996, prod. John Snyder), which stacks the goofy New Orleans novelty hit "Gee" against beautiful romantic ballads like "When Did You Leave Heaven" and "There Is No Greater Love."

what to buy next: Brown's pre-Raitt-tour comeback, *All My Life* ⅃⅃⅃ (Bullseye Blues/Rounder, 1990, prod. Ron Levy), is a solid piano blues album, but he hadn't yet hit his second recording career's stride. His post-Raitt material—*Just a Lucky So and So* ⅃⅃⅃ (Bullseye Blues/Rounder, 1994, prod. Ron Levy) and *These Blues* ⅃⅃⅃ (Verve, 1994, prod. John Snyder)—is much more versatile and finds Brown stretching out vocally.

what to avoid: Brown's best periods were the 1940s and 1990s, and his singles in between, documented on *Southern Blues 1957–63* ⅃⅃ (Paula, 1994, prod. Willie Dixon), are uneven at best.

Charles Brown (© Jack Vartoogian)

the rest:

Blues 'n' Brown 🎵🎵🎵 (Jewel, 1971)
One More for the Road 🎵🎵🎵 (Blueside, 1986/Alligator, 1989)
Driftin' Blues 🎵🎵🎵 (Mainstream, 1989)
Blues and Other Love Songs 🎵🎵🎵 (Muse, 1994)
Cool Christmas Blues 🎵🎵🎵 (Bullseye Blues/Rounder, 1994)

worth searching for: *The Complete Aladdin Recordings of Charles Brown* 🎵🎵🎵🎵 (Mosaic, 1994, prod. Michael Cuscuna), a limited-edition boxed set, gathers more than one hundred sides, every single that Brown and the Three Blazers recorded for Philo and Aladdin between 1945 and 1956, on five compact discs, with serious information about each one. For extreme fans and historians, it's the early Brown motherlode.

influences:

◄◄ Nat "King" Cole, T-Bone Walker, Art Tatum, Scott Joplin

►► Ray Charles, Bonnie Raitt, Otis Spann, Floyd Dixon

Steve Knopper

Clarence "Gatemouth" Brown

Born April 18, 1924, in Vinton, LA.

Clarence "Gatemouth" Brown is one of the foremost architects of modern blues guitar, second only to T-Bone Walker in terms of influential Texans. But with Gate, that's just the start of the story. A multi-instrumentalist (violin, harmonica, piano, mandolin, viola and drums as well as guitar), Brown embraces a host of musical categories, throwing Cajun, country, bluegrass and jazz into his blues-dominated arsenal. Gate's versatility sometimes works against him—even his best albums often include one misguided venture—but it also informs everything he does with a wide-ranging sense of possibility. And he remains a damn fined blues guitarist.

what to buy: *The Original Peacock Recordings* 🎵🎵🎵🎵 (Rounder, 1990, prod. Scott Billington, Clarence Brown) collects Brown's 1950s work and is the best indication of how and why his playing was so influential on several generations of Texan guitarists. He returned to a big band format more than 40 years later with *Gate Swings* ♪♪♪♪ (Verve, 1997, prod. John Snyder, Jim Bateman) with smashing, jazzy results. *Pressure Cooker* (Alligator, 1987, prod. Bruce Iglauer) reissues 1973 French sessions, in which Brown is backed by jazz greats including Jay McShann, Arnett Cobb and Milt Buckner. The result is a predictably swinging set.

what to buy next: Brown stuck to horn-driven blues on his comeback album, *Alright Again!* ♪♪♪♪ (Rounder, 1982, prod. Scott Billington, Jim Bateman), which won a Grammy and quickly reestablished him as an American original and a musical force to be reckoned with. Most of his many subsequent albums have been quite strong, but *Standing My Ground* ♪♪♪ (Alligator, 1989) stands out.

what to avoid: On *Long Way Home* ♪♪♥ (Verve, 1996), Brown is mostly just hindered by guest stars ranging from Eric Clapton, who lays down a few generic solos, to John Loudermilk, who sings a wretched version of his own "Tobacco Road." The album does, however, include several excellent and unexpected acoustic tracks. *Gate's on the Heat* ♪♪ (Verve, 1975) found him saddled with a lame, stiff band.

the rest:

One More Mile ♪♪♪ (Rounder, 1983)
Real Life ♪♪♪ (Rounder, 1987)
Texas Swing ♪♪♪♪ (Rounder, 1987)
Just Got Lucky ♪♪♪♪ (Evidence, 1993)
Man ♪♪♪ (Verve, 1995)
San Antonio Ballbuster ♪♪♪♪ (Drive Archives, 1995)

influences:

◀◀ T-Bone Walker, Louis Jordan

▶▶ Johnny Copeland, Johnny Winter, Albert Collins, Roy Clark

Alan Paul

J.T. Brown

Born John T. Brown, April 2, 1918, in MS. Died November 24, 1969, in Chicago, IL.

Possessing an instantly recognizable saxophone style, Brown was one of Chicago's most prolific sidemen and an occasional solo artist. Also known as "Sax Man," "Bep," "Nature Boy" and "Big Boy," Brown broke into show biz with the Rabbit Foot Minstrels, but by 1945 he was in Chicago backing Roosevelt Sykes and St. Louis Jimmy. Brown's first session as a leader was for the Harlem label in 1950, and he recorded again for JOB and United in 1952 before joining Elmore James' Broomdusters. Al-

though his last solo recordings took place in 1956, he stayed active as a sideman, recording with J.B. Lenoir, Johnny Jones and Muddy Waters.

what to buy: If you can procure a copy of *Rockin' with J.T.* ♪♪♪♥ (Flyright, 1975) or *Windy City Boogie* ♪♪♪♥ (Pearl, 1978), both still only on vinyl, you are indeed fortunate.

influences:

◀◀ King Kolax

▶▶ A.C. Reed, Eddie Shaw

Jeff Hannusch

James Brown

Born May 3, 1933, in Barnwell, SC.

In terms of soul music, nobody can top the contributions or pervasive influence of James Brown. He is a living link between

the R&B/swing/blues bands of Louis Jordan and today's rap minimalists. The great soul singers of the middle and late 1960s took lessons from his early records and that animalistic scream he called a voice. He literally invented funk in the 1960s, still the dominant influence on black music. Like no one save Ray Charles, Brown faced off the spiritual passion and cadences of black gospel preachers with the supercharged sexual beat and rhythms of R&B and blues. "Please, Please, Please," "Try Me" and "Think" introduced Brown's considerable skills to a generation of budding soul stars that would explode in the mid-1960s. His stage show, from the corny cape-and-crown routines to the rigorously rehearsed, ultra-professional, dapper Famous Flames Revue, set a sweaty standard for any other such wannabes. Nobody worked harder than "The Hardest Working Man in Show Business." In 1965 he began treating the recording studio with the same precision and exuberance of an Apollo midnight performance, and his incredibly high standards for band membership paid off with "Papa's Got a Brand New Bag" and "It's a Man's, Man's, Man's World," music as revolutionary and innovative as any from the better-known and higher-praised Beatles, Rolling Stones or Bob Dylan. As the 1960s wore on, Brown's lyrics became more strident and tied to the civil rights movement. The lyrics began stressing black individualism as much as sex and romance, and the music turned in on itself in ever more primal ways. Brown's band became an incubator of soul, home to innovative, talented musicians as stubborn, professional, moody and self-determined as their boss. Solos and verse-chorus patterns were dumped in favor of extended, repetitive grooves pushed to fever pitch by Brown's call-and-response vocal chants ("Take me to the bridge," "give the drummer some"). Soon every instrument was a percussion instrument, and this minimalist approach would evolve into the dance music that became known as funk and eventually disco and the even-more fragmented rap. He has achieved enormous wealth and success, but Brown never has gotten the recognition accorded many of his contemporaries. Drug and personal problems landed him in prison in the late 1980s, and his most recent work gets mighty repetitive. But there's no denying Brown's importance: the proof is in those grooves.

what to buy: Brown's recorded output is as fragmented as the funk he created. Brown was a singles artist, and whether you're at all interested in his importance or just want to shake it 'til it drops off, nothing could possibly top *Star Time* &&&&& (Polydor,

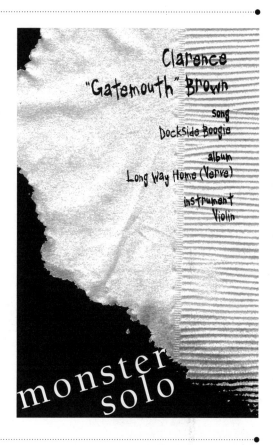

Clarence "Gatemouth" Brown (© **Jack Vartoogian**)

1991, prod. Harry Weinger), a comprehensive, chronological and funkifying solid four discs of his very best and most important work, with many of the singles expanded back to their original lengths and extensive liner notes. If you're not that interested, you shouldn't be without *Solid Gold 30 Golden Hits* &&&& (Polydor, 1986), about half of those incredibly visionary, exhausting, shake-your-booty singles. *Live at the Apollo, 1962* &&&&& (King, 1963/Polydor, 1990, prod. James Brown) is the midnight show of August 24, 1962, at the Harlem club that put Brown on the national map, a classroom lecture for every aspiring soul singer ever after and considered by many the greatest live album ever.

what to buy next: Brown was never known as a great organ player, but his intuitive style is much better than it's been credited. When King owner Sid Nathan objected to an instrumental called "(Do the) Mash Potatoes," Brown put it out on another label under a pseudonym, and, no surprise, it became a hit. His limitless proficiency on instrumental tracks matches (or at least augments) the creativity of the vocal hits, and many of the band's finest performances are included on *Soul Pride: The Instrumentals 1960–69* 🎜🎜🎜 (Polydor, 1993, prod. James Brown). *Roots of a Revolution* 🎜🎜🎜 (Polydor, 1983) is a producer's choice of recordings from 1956–64, showing how Brown and the Famous Flames went from imitative to innovative in the years leading up to "Papa's Got a Brand New Bag." *Messing with the Blues* 🎜🎜🎜 (Polydor, 1990, prod. James Brown) captures his individualistic approach to other's material and natural feel for the blues.

what to avoid: *Hooked on Brown* 🎜 (Scotti Brothers, 1996) is nothing more than remixes of his greatest hits. Settle for no less than the originals. *Black Caesar* 🎜 (Polydor, 1972/1992) and *Slaughter's Big Rip-Off* 🎜 (Polydor, 1972/1992) are blaxploitation soundtracks that prove Brown was mortal after all.

best of the rest:
Please Please Please 🎜🎜🎜 (King, 1959/PolyGram Chronicles, 1996)
Try Me 🎜🎜🎜 (King, 1959/PolyGram Chronicles, 1996)
Think 🎜🎜🎜 (King, 1960/PolyGram Chronicles, 1996)
Tell Me What You're Gonna Do 🎜🎜🎜 (King, 1961/Charly, 1995)
Live at the Apollo, 1962 Gold Disc 🎜🎜🎜🎜 (King, 1963/Ultradisc, 1993)
Papa's Got a Brand New Bag 🎜🎜🎜 (King, 1965/PolyGram Special Products, 1992)
James Brown Sings Raw Soul 🎜🎜🎜 (King, 1967/Polydor, 1996)
Out of Sight 🎜🎜🎜 (King, 1968/Polydor, 1996)
Say It Loud I'm Black and I'm Proud 🎜🎜🎜 (King, 1969/Polydor, 1996)
Sex Machine 🎜🎜🎜 (King, 1970/ITC Masters, 1997)
Hot Pants 🎜🎜🎜 (Polydor, 1971/1993)
20 All-Time Greatest Hits 🎜🎜🎜 (Polydor, 1991)
40th Anniversary Collection 🎜🎜🎜 (Polydor, 1996)
Foundations of Funk 1964–69 🎜🎜🎜 (PolyGram Chronicles, 1996)
Funk Power 1970: A Brand New Thang 🎜🎜🎜 (PolyGram Chronicles, 1996)
Make It Funky: The Big Payback 1971–75 🎜🎜🎜 (PolyGram Chronicles, 1996)

worth searching for: If you're interested in Brown's early recordings, *The Federal Years—Parts One and Two* 🎜🎜🎜 (Solid Smoke, 1984), still only available on vinyl, offer nascent versions of Brown's early vision and the growing pangs of the Famous Flames.

influences:
⏮ Hank Ballard & the Midnighters, Ray Charles, Louis Jordan, Bo Diddley, Wynonie Harris, Roy Brown, Dominos, Five Royales, Rev. J.M. Gates

⏭ Michael Jackson, Otis Redding, Sly & the Family Stone, Jimi Hendrix, Parliament, Funkadelic, George Clinton, Bootsy

Collins, Isaac Hayes, Chic, Afrika Bambaataa, Prince, Eric B. & Rakim, Mick Jagger, Rod Stewart, MC5

Leland Rucker

Nappy Brown
Born Napoleon Culp Brown, October 12, 1929, in Charlotte, NC.

"Don't Be Angry" was a big hit in 1955, its opening "so-li-li-li-li-li-li" nonsense syllables and driving beat earning enough attention for the decidedly non-bluesy Crewcuts to record it later. Brown, who co-wrote the song and sang it in his soul crooner's voice, didn't much like the Crewcuts' version—if only given the chance, he thought, he could cross over to the pop audience on his own. (Patti Page also blunted the popularity of his R&B hit "Piddly Patter Patter.") In a racist era with Pat Boone ruling the white pop charts, even such well-known black performers as Little Richard and Chuck Berry were often screwed out of much bigger success. Brown, who grew up testifying in the church choir, never had a chance. His fame, unjustly, lasted not much more than 15 minutes; by the early 1960s, the talented R&B singer was so forgotten he gave up recording entirely. He tried several comebacks, including a gospel project, but it wasn't until the late 1980s, after several supportive European tours, that he returned as a screaming, stage-stalking, innuendo-happy blues singer. Brown's songs—including the standard "Night Time Is the Right Time," quickly re-recorded by Ray Charles—will undoubtedly outlast the singer. It's just too bad he never got proper reimbursement for them, in terms of fame or money.

what to buy: The sides collected on *Don't Be Angry* 🎜🎜🎜🎜 (Savoy Jazz, 1990, prod. Fred Mendelsohn) are enough to make any rational R&B fan believe Brown was yet another victim of late-1950s music-industry racism. These songs are fun, especially the raucous "Don't Be Angry" and "I Wonder," and solemn, such as the ominous "Land I Love."

what to buy next: Brown's best post-comeback album, *Tore Up* 🎜🎜🎜 (Alligator, 1984, prod. Michael Rothschild, Ricky Keller, Eddy Offord), shows the singer posing like Groucho Marx on the cover, with a big smile, white cocktail jacket and cigarette dangling from his fingers. It's not quite as fun as that—or "Don't Be Angry"—but Atlanta guitarslinger Tinsley Ellis' backup band, the Heartfixers, supplements Brown's now-gritty voice with plenty of interesting solos. Also, there's a great version of Brown's early blues classic "Lemon Squeezin' Daddy."

what to avoid: *Aw! Shucks* 🎜🎜 (Ichiban, 1991, prod. Bryan Cole) proves that, unfortunately, Brown's most interesting days were in the late 1950s; though his voice carries some nice Jackie Wilson-style nuance, songs like "You Know It Ain't Right" and the "live jam" version of "Night Time" could be on any contemporary blues album.

the rest:

I Done Got Over 🎜🎜🎜 (Stockholm, 1985)
Just for Me 🎜🎜🎜 (JSP, 1988/1996)
Something Gonna Jump out the Bushes 🎜🎜🎜 (Black Top, 1988)
Deep Sea Diver 🎜🎜 (Meltone, 1989)
I'm a Wild Man 🎜🎜🎜 (New Moon, 1994)
Who's Been Fooling You? 🎜🎜🎜 (New Moon, 1997)

influences:

◄◄ Screamin' Jay Hawkins, Rufus Thomas, Bobby "Blue" Bland, Fats Domino, Charles Brown

►► Otis Redding, Jackie Wilson, Otis Rush, Otis Clay, Percy Sledge

Steve Knopper

Robert Brown

See: Washboard Sam

Roy Brown

Born September 10, 1925, in New Orleans, LA. Died May 25, 1981, in San Fernando, CA.

Like his contemporaries Champion Jack Dupree and Professor Longhair, Roy Brown entered show business as a professional boxer who sang on the side at talent shows and in little neighborhood joints. A great composer and a widely influential singer, Brown was signed to a recording contract by DeLuxe in 1947 as one of the first wave of Crescent City R&B artists to reach public consciousness, alongside Paul Gayten & Annie Laurie, Longhair, Smiley Lewis, Fats Domino and Larry Darnell. He peddled one of his first compositions, "Good Rocking Tonight," to Wynonie Harris one night at the Dew Drop Inn and watched it rise to the top of the R&B charts to become Harris' most successful recording, far surpassing Brown's own version on DeLuxe. A glorious succession of singles followed on DeLuxe: "Mighty Mighty Man," "Rockin' at Midnight," "Boogie at Midnight," "Cadillac Baby," "Bar Room Blues," "Beautician Blues" and "Blues for Big Town" are just a few. In the fall of 1953 Brown was switched to King, by now the parent company of DeLuxe, and continued to blast away with singles like "Laughing but Cry-

ing," "Black Diamond," "Queen of Diamonds" and "This Is My Last Goodbye." Unlike so many of his fellow R&B shouters from the Golden Age, Roy Brown had a second act under the aegis of Dave Bartholomew, who cut several hip sides of Roy for Imperial between 1956-58, including "The Tick of the Clock," "Let the Four Winds Blow," "Diddy-Y-Diddy-O" and a cover of Buddy Knox's "Party Doll," backed with Jimmy Bowen's "I'm Stickin' with You." He faded into relative obscurity until 1970, when Johnny Otis brought him out to be showcased with his Rhythm & Blues Revue, recorded live at Monterey that fall. While his personal fortunes may have waned, his influence on singers like Clyde McPhatter and fellow pugilist Jackie Wilson—and on the development of soul shouting in general—continued to flourish well past his moments in the sun.

what to buy: The best single collection of Roy Brown sides is *Good Rockin' Tonight* 🎜🎜🎜🎜 (Rhino, 1994, prod. James Austin), which contains 17 of his biggest DeLuxe and King singles and "Let the Four Winds Blow." *Blues DeLuxe* 🎜🎜🎜🎜 (Charly, 1994) gives us more of his DeLuxe output, including little-heard gems like "Double Crossin' Woman," "I've Got the Last Laugh Now," "Brown Angel" and the "Answer to Big Town." His King sides are explored in greater depth on *Mighty Mighty Man* 🎜🎜🎜🎜 (Ace, 1993), containing treasures from 1953-54 like "Bootleggin' Baby," "Everything's All Right" and "Up Jumped the Devil." If you have these three you won't need the British collection, *Good Rocking Tonight* 🎜🎜🎜🎜 (Charly), or the Swedish *Mr. Blues Is Coming to Town* 🎜🎜🎜🎜 (Route 66, 1991), which mine the same gold.

what to buy next: *Laughing but Crying* 🎜🎜🎜🎜 (Mr. R&B, 1994) combines DeLuxe and King masters and adds some early sides not available elsewhere. *Complete Imperial Recordings* 🎜🎜🎜 (Capitol, 1995, prod. Dave Bartholomew) gathers all of Roy's Imperial singles and unreleased masters from the Dave Bartholomew sessions. Most of these are not indispensable, but Roy Brown fans will find many things to enjoy. And you can hear the master in concert with the Johnny Otis Show on *Live at Monterey* 🎜🎜🎜🎜 (Sony, 1993).

worth searching for: King Records has coupled the Roy Brown hits with equally great singles by Wynonie Harris on *Battle of the Blues, Volume One* 🎜🎜🎜🎜🎜 (King, 1988) and *Battle of the Blues, Volume Two* 🎜🎜🎜🎜🎜 (King, 1988), and with Wynonie and Eddie "Cleanhead" Vinson on *Battle of the Blues, Volume Four* 🎜🎜🎜🎜🎜 (King, 1988), all which retain the original LP cover art and are sure to be CD collector's items ten years from now.

influences:

◀◀ Gene Autry, Billy Eckstine, Wynonie Harris, Eddie "Clean-head" Vinson

▶▶ Jackie Wilson, Clyde McPhatter

John Sinclair

Willie Brown

Born August 6, 1900, in Clarksdale, MS. Died December 30, 1952, in Tunica, MS.

Willie Brown was one of the most important of the early Delta blues guitarists. He is perhaps best known as the excellent second guitarist on many of Charley Patton's and Son House's recordings and as an associate of these and other Delta luminaries, including Robert Johnson. Brown was also a remarkable solo performer, as witnessed by his three extant solo recordings. Two of these, "M & O Blues" and "Future Blues," hail from the near-legendary 1930 Paramount session in Grafton, Wisconsin, that produced Son House's only pre-World War II recordings as well as excellent material by Patton and barrelhouse pianist Louise Johnson. Brown's only other solo title, "Make Me a Pallet on the Floor," was recorded by Alan Lomax during a 1941 Library of Congress field recording session at which Brown also accompanied House on some songs. Willie Brown was an emotive singer and a wonderful guitarist who shared many elements of style, technique and repertoire with fellow Mississippians Patton and House. A less powerful singer than the other two, Brown was arguably the superior guitarist and was regarded highly by his peers for his ability to "second" (accompany) another musician.

what to buy: This decision is simplified somewhat due to the unfortunate shortage of available material. Brown's two 1930 sides can be most easily found on *Son House and the Great Delta Blues Singers* ♪♪♪♪ (Document, 1990, prod. Johnny Parth), which also features important recordings by Son House (all of his pre-World War II material, including "Walking Blues" with Brown on second guitar), Kid Bailey (who some actually claim to be Brown recording under a pseudonym; others believe Brown played second guitar on Bailey's "Rowdy Blues" from 1929), Rube Lacy and others. "Make Me a Pallet on the Floor" from 1941 is available on *Mississippi Blues: Library of Congress Recordings 1940–42* ♪♪♪♪ (Travelin' Man, 1991).

what to buy next: All of Brown's other recordings feature him as an accompanist to Charley Patton and Son House. Search out the three-volume Patton set *Charley Patton: Vols. 1–3 (1929–34)* ♪♪♪♪ (Document, 1990, prod. Johnny Parth). Most of Patton's output has also been collected on *Founder of the Delta Blues* ♪♪♪♪ (Yazoo, 1995) and *King of the Delta Blues* ♪♪♪♪ (Yazoo, 1992). Son House's 1941 Library of Congress recordings, several of which feature Brown, are collected on *Son House: The Complete Library of Congress Sessions 1941–42* ♪♪♪♪ (Travelin' Man, 1990).

influences:

◀◀ Charley Patton, Son House

▶▶ Robert Johnson, Kid Bailey, Howlin' Wolf

Rob Hutten

Roy Buchanan

Born September 23, 1939, in Ozark, AR. Died August 14, 1988, in Reston, VA.

This soft-spoken, enigmatic guitarist poured his soul into a variety of styles that ranged from hillbilly to early rock 'n' roll to spirituals to blues to Jimi Hendrix. He first gained national attention when a 1971 article in *Rolling Stone* proclaimed him one of the three greatest living guitarists, based solely on the strength of his performances at bars in and around Washington, DC. His first album, *The Prophet*, was shelved by Poly-Gram, but he put out a home-made live LP, *Buch and the Snake Stretchers*. The recording quality was at about the standard of a mediocre bootleg, and it was packaged in a burlap bag, but it gave enough flashes of his incendiary guitar to prove that the *Rolling Stone* story was no hype. Problems with drugs and alcohol and a love/hate relationship with the limelight prevented Buchanan from ever becoming the mega-star he might have been, and his life came to an early end when he was found hanging by his belt in a Virginia drunk tank under what some maintain were suspicious circumstances.

what to buy: The two-disc set *Sweet Dreams: The Anthology* ♪♪♪♪ (Polydor Chronicles, 1992) collects many of his best tracks for PolyGram and Atlantic. It includes four songs from the unreleased *The Prophet* and five more that never came out in the U.S. *Roy Buchanan* ♪♪♪ (PolyGram, 1972, prod. Peter K. Siegel) mixes country tunes with some extended blues and the amazing spiritual "The Messiah Will Come Again." *Second Album* ♪♪♪ (PolyGram, 1973, prod. Peter K. Siegel) contains the most blues of any of his PolyGram releases. *When a Guitar Plays the Blues* ♪♪♪ (Alligator, 1985, prod. Roy Buchanan, Bruce Iglauer, Dick Shurman) was Roy's first recording for the Chicago label and spices up the vocals (always the weak suit on any Buchanan album) with contributions from Otis Clay and Gloria Hardiman.

what to buy next: *Live Stock* 𝄞𝄞𝄞 (PolyGram, 1975, prod. Jay Reich Jr.), recorded live in New York, is a favorite of many Roy aficionados for its bluesy flavor. *You're Not Alone* 𝄞𝄞𝄞 (Atlantic, 1978, prod. Ramon Silva), a spacey psychedelic "concept" album, works surprisingly well. Roy's workouts on "Turn to Stone" and "Down by the River" manage to cut the originals. *Buch and the Snake Stretchers: One of Three* 𝄞𝄞𝄞𝄞 (Genes, 1991) is the CD reissue of that original live album. The performances (including the definitive version of "The Messiah") are stellar, but the sound quality is lacking.

the rest:

That's What I Am Here For 𝄞𝄞𝄞 (Polydor, 1973)
In the Beginning 𝄞𝄞 (PolyGram, 1974)
Loading Zone 𝄞𝄞 (Atlantic, 1977)
My Babe 𝄞𝄞 (Waterhouse, 1980)
Hot Wires 𝄞𝄞𝄞 (Alligator, 1987)
Guitar on Fire: The Atlantic Session 𝄞𝄞𝄞 (Rhino, 1993)

influences:

◀◀ Blind Boy Fuller, Pete Lewis, Jimmy Nolen, James Burton

▶▶ Robbie Robertson, Gary Moore

Cary Wolfson

Norton Buffalo

Born September 28, 1951, in Oakland, CA.

Norton Buffalo has left a legacy of noted harp solos for soundtracks and albums (including "Runaway" on Bonnie Raitt's *Sweet Forgiveness*). After learning the fundamentals from his father, he developed into an in-demand musician proficient in many styles, including chromatic harmonica. His tone ranges from sweet, upper-register jazz stylings to fat-and-nasty, down-and-dirty blues. In addition to a busy session schedule, he's been a touring and recording member of the Steve Miller Band for more than 20 years, tours with his own band, the Knockouts, and is a capable vocalist, keyboard player and percussionist. In 1991 Buffalo teamed up with blues slide guitarist Roy Rogers.

what to buy: The acoustic, Delta-inspired *R&B* 𝄞𝄞𝄞𝄞 (Blind Pig, 1991, prod. Norton Buffalo, Roy Rogers) blends perfectly Norton's harp and Rogers' slide guitar. On their second outing, *Travellin' Tracks* 𝄞𝄞𝄞𝄞 (Blind Pig, 1992, prod. Norton Buffalo, Roy Rogers), they add a rhythm section and include some live selections, including K.C. Douglas' "Mercury Blues" and a studio cover of Elmore James' "Shake Your Moneymaker."

worth searching for: The rambunctious, high-energy *The Legendary Sy Klopps Blues Band: Walter Ego* 𝄞𝄞𝄞𝄞 (Guitar Recordings, 1993, prod. David Denny, Bobby Scott) features Norton on only one selection, and his solo on "Fannie Mae" is a Buffalo monster blow out, just one of many high points on this obscure but worthwhile recording. The elusive video, *Steve Miller: Blues in the Twentieth Century* (Capitol, 1986, prod. Steve Miller), offers a good opportunity to view Buffalo trading solos with James Cotton as the Miller band romps through a solid set.

influences:

◀◀ Sonny Terry, Charlie Musselwhite, Paul Butterfield

▶▶ Sugar Blue, John Popper, Pat O'Brien

Tali Madden

George "Mojo" Buford

Born November 10, 1929, in Hernando, MS.

A treasure from the old school, George Buford is one of the small nucleus of peerless harp players Muddy Waters employed. With his big leather belt of harps slung across his chest, Buford cuts an imposing figure. He has a classic, post-war amplified harp style reminiscent of the older Chicago harpmen. Raised on a cotton farm in Mississippi until his family moved to Memphis in 1943, he was taught harmonica from the age of five and by his teenage years was playing professionally. He arrived in Chicago in 1952 and formed a band called the Savage Boys. They soon hooked up with Muddy Waters, who provided them with bookings guidance and a new name, the Muddy Waters Jr. Band. Upon the departure of harpman George Smith from Muddy's band in 1959, Buford was invited to replace him. This first stint with Muddy lasted three years, at which time Buford struck out on his own, relocating to Minneapolis. He met with some success there as a local blues star, changing his nickname from "Little Jr. B." to "Mojo." Appropriately enough, his first single had "Got My Mojo Working" on it. "Mojo" gigged regularly at barbecue joints and clubs in Minneapolis through the early 1960s before returning to Chicago to rejoin Muddy's increasingly popular band, this time stepping in for the departed James Cotton. Buford would leave and rejoin Muddy's band two more times before finally making Minneapolis his home base. Buford's deep resonant singing is, not surprisingly, similar to that of Muddy Waters. Buford has remained active and is truly a link with the roots of blues harp.

what to buy: Buford is in top form on *Still Blowin' Strong* 𝄞𝄞𝄞𝄞 (Blue Moon, 1996, prod. Pat Dawson), with hard-hitting solos and impressive vocals.

5/8 *george "mojo" buford*

what to buy next: *Mojo Buford's Blues Summit* 🎵🎵🎵 (Red Rooster, 1981) is a high-energy set of Chicago blues with a number of notable guitarists, including Sammy Lawhorn and Little Smokey Smothers.

the rest:

Exciting Harmonica Sound of Mojo Buford 🎵🎵🎵 (Blues Recording Society, 1964)

Harpslinger 🎵🎵🎵 (Blue Moon, 1993)

worth searching for: *Luther Georgia Boy Snake Johnson: The Muddy Waters Blues Band* 🎵🎵🎵 (Douglas, 1994, prod. Alan Douglas) is a rare outing by the Waters group with Muddy letting his bandmates dominate. Great moments from Otis Spann, Mojo Buford and Sammy Lawhorn. Guitarist Georgia Boy Johnson leads on side one and Buford on side two of this vinyl treasure.

influences:

◀◀ Big Walter Horton, George "Harmonica" Smith, Junior Wells

▶▶ Curtis Salgado, Paul Butterfield, Jerry Portnoy

Tali Madden

Bumble Bee Slim

Born Amos Easton, May 7, 1905, in Brunswick, GA. Died April 1968, in Los Angeles, CA.

Though not much of an innovator, Bumble Bee Slim developed into an incredibly popular Chicago pianist in the 1930s. Inspired directly by the guitar-and-vocal duo Leroy Carr and Scrapper Blackwell, Slim churned out songs by the handful and recorded with Big Bill Broonzy and Clarence Lofton. In terms of influence, he wasn't exactly up there with Muddy Waters, but he sold a lot of records and a lot of people knew him, which have always been important factors in spreading blues to more listeners.

what to buy: All you really need is *Complete Recorded Works in Chronological Order 1931–37* 🎵🎵🎵 (Document), which collects his best work from the Bluebird, Decca and Vocalion labels, among others, and samples his output from 1935, a prolific year in which he put out 30 sides.

influences:

◀◀ Leroy Carr, Scrapper Blackwell, Big Bill Broonzy, Robert Johnson, Cripple Clarence Lofton

▶▶ Muddy Waters, B.B. King, Buddy Guy, Otis Rush

Steve Knopper

George "Mojo" Buford (© **Linda Vartoogian**)

William Bunch

See: Peetie Wheatstraw

Alden Bunn

See: Tarheel Slim

Solomon Burke

Born 1936, in Philadelphia, PA.

The Bishop, the King of Rock and Soul, Brother Solomon: it takes three titles to encompass the talent and girth of one of soul music's founders. A 250-plus-pound circuit preacher now, father of 21 kids and grandchildren by the bushel, Solomon Burke can lay claim—and often does—to having been present at soul's creation in the early 1960s. Like Al Green, he see-saws between the sacred and the corporeal, and, when the spirit is within him, Burke can get bluesy with the best of them. His glory days came in the early 1960s, when soul was being pioneered by artists like Sam Cooke, James Brown and Jerry Butler. Signed by Atlantic Records in 1960, Burke released several ballads, then hit with "Just Out of Reach (of My Two Open Arms)," a country-styled lament that pre-dated Ray Charles' own C&W move by two years. As Burke was challenged by stablemate Wilson Pickett and later by Otis Redding, he toughened up his a-sides, producing the blues-inflected stompers "Stupidity" and "You're Good for Me." But while his deep, mellifluous voice still packed them in at the Apollo (where Burke sold "magic popcorn" in the aisles at intermission), his act sounded more and more dated compared to Redding's love-crowd theatrics and Aretha Franklin's vocal thrills. In the years since soul shifted to funk and then disco, Burke returned to the church. He snagged a character role in the film *The Big Easy* and was the self-promoting hero of Peter Guralnick's R&B history, *Sweet Soul Music.* When the secular spirit moves him, Burke's booming, raspy tenor can still transport the ladies to ecstasy.

what to buy: *Home in Your Heart* 🎵🎵🎵🎵 (Rhino/Atlantic, 1992, prod. Yves Beauvais) is a two-disc survey of Burke's country, ballad and soul winners during a six-year span with Atlantic. Among them are the original versions of "Cry to Me" and "Everybody Needs Somebody to Love," which a young Mick Jagger tried to imitate in his best plastic-soul fashion for the Rolling Stones.

what to buy next: In a desperate period when Aretha and the Godfather flirted with disco, the Bishop struck back with poise, releasing *Soul Alive!* 🎵🎵🎵🎵 (Rounder, 1988, prod. Solomon Burke), a 1981 concert that showed he could still provoke swoons. For a seamless hour, singing as if it were 1963 at the Apollo (it was in a small club in the District of Columbia), Burke sang as if his life depended on it. It didn't—the Bishop is too much the hustler to sweat it. But the show ranks just a notch below James Brown's Apollo shows and Otis Redding's concert discs as a prime example of what soul is all about.

the rest:

A Change Is Gonna Come 𝄢𝄢𝄢 (Rounder, 1986)
Best of Solomon Burke 𝄢𝄢𝄢 (Curb, 1991)
Let Your Love Flow 𝄢𝄢𝄢 (Shanachie, 1993)
Soul of the Blues 𝄢𝄢𝄢𝄢 (Black Top, 1993)
Live at the House of Blues 𝄢𝄢𝄢 (Black Top, 1995)
The Definition of Soul 𝄢𝄢𝄢 (Point Blank, 1997)

influences:

◀◀ Sam Cooke, Ivory Joe Hunter

▶▶ Rolling Stones, Al Green

Steve Braun

Chester Arthur Burnett

See: Howlin' Wolf

Eddie Burns

Born February 8, 1928, near Belzoni, MS.

Eddie Burns (a.k.a. Big Daddy, Little Eddie, Big Ed) is a fine stylist on harmonica, with strong influences of both Sonny Boy Williamsons. He learned the rudiments of guitar and harmonica from his father, himself a musician, and from the records of Jazz Gillum and others. Then still a teenager, he sang on street corners for nickels and dimes. Burns moved to Detroit in 1947 and cut his first record for Sensation a year later. He met John Lee Hooker at house parties; they played together, and Hooker liked the way Burns was blowing harmonica enough to use him as a sideman on sessions recorded by Bernie Besman. He already had become a first-class harp player and a competent singer-guitarist with an eager intensity. Between 1952–57 he recorded for Joe Von Battle, with singles on JVB, DeLuxe, Modern, Checker, Harvey and Von, spent 1958–61 in Aaron Willis' Little Sonny Band and rejoined Hooker and recorded with him in the 1960s. Disillusioned by the hassles of show business and the hazards of an itinerant musician's life, he kept his day jobs in Detroit and played in festivals, touring Europe occasionally, where his old-fashioned style was popular. In the early 1990s he experienced something of a comeback, with new sides recorded for Blue Suit.

what to buy: *Treat Me Like I Treat You* 𝄢𝄢𝄢𝄢 (Moonshine, 1982, prod. Marcel Vos) has the sides recorded in the 1950s that underline Burns' mellow, bluesy voice and expressive harp playing. *Detroit* 𝄢𝄢𝄢 (Blue Suit, 1990/Evidence, 1995, prod. Robert Seeman, John Gibbs Rockwood, Gregory Oatis) is Eddie Burns in the 1990s, the same old-fashioned style with a modern band. *J.L. Hooker Detroit Blues* 𝄢𝄢𝄢 (Flyright 1987/1990, prod. Bruce Bastin) includes six additional 1951 tracks.

the rest:

Bottle Up and Go 𝄢𝄢𝄢𝄢 (Action, 1972)
Detroit Blackbottom 𝄢𝄢𝄢𝄢 (Big Bear, 1975)

influences:

◀◀ Sonny Boy Williamson I, Jazz Gillum, Sonny Boy Williamson II

Robert Sacré

Jimmy Burns

Born James Olin Burns, February 27, 1943, in Dublin, MS.

By day, Jimmy Burns runs his barbecue stand on Chicago's West Side. When the sun goes down, however, it's blues time, and he's off to his regular gig at the Smokedaddy. It is there that guitarist/singer Burns delivers his smooth, soul-inflected brand of down-home blues. As a young man, Burns, younger brother of Eddie Burns, sang in various vocal harmony groups on Chicago's West Side. He even waxed a few 45s with his colleagues and as a band leader over the years. Burns, however, married early and spent much of his adult life raising his family, performing only sporadically. Now, his children grown, Burns is making his music a priority. His reappearance on the Chicago blues scene in the early 1990s was nothing less than a blessing to fans of West Side blues.

what to buy: Burns introduced himself to the blues world with *Leaving Here Walking* 𝄢𝄢𝄢𝄢 (Delmark, 1996, prod. Scott Dirks), and after one listen it's easy to tell that Burns was way past ready to record. The disc captures him in a variety of musical styles and is laden with Burns' originals and his fresh and soulful—yet solidly blues-rooted—spin on old chestnuts like "Rollin' and Tumblin'" and "Catfish Blues."

influences:

◀◀ Muddy Waters, Howlin' Wolf, Lightnin' Hopkins, Nappy Brown, Eddie Taylor, Eddie Burns

▶▶ Johnny Burgin

Steven Sharp

R.L. Burnside

Born November 21, 1926, in Harmontown, MS.

Burnside is a welcome anomaly in the blues world: he's an old guitarist from Mississippi trained by the great Mississippi Fred McDowell, but was only recently "discovered" and stays far removed from tedious conventions. He draws inspiration from such luminaries as Muddy Waters and Elmore James, but he reaches for their spirits instead of trying to match their guitar solos. Burnside, who performed for years as a regional star in local juke joints, is a master of the sloppy blues groove; he plays it over and over, approximating John Lee Hooker's classic boogie style and mumbling vocal delivery, building tension until something explodes in the music. Burnside didn't come to national renown until 1992, when former *New York Times* critic Robert Palmer produced his recordings and stuck them in his excellent *Deep Blues* documentary film and soundtrack. After that, Burnside made one astounding solo record, *Too Bad Jim*, and pulled off a surprisingly successful and predictably raw collaboration with New York City punk Jon Spencer.

what to buy: *Too Bad Jim* 🎵🎵🎵🎵 (Fat Possum/Capricorn, 1994, prod. Robert Palmer) opens with Bukka White's 1930s hit, "Shake 'Em on Down," but it's like none of the many other versions available. The groove is tense but cathartic—like Howlin' Wolf, early Rolling Stones and punk rock—and it refuses to let up through the racy "Miss Glory B." and the violent ".44 Pistol."

what to buy next: Burnside and Jon Spencer, leader of the screaming New York City punk band Blues Explosion, adapt surprisingly well to each others' weaknesses on *A Ass Pocket of Whiskey* 🎵🎵🎵 (Matador, 1996, prod. Matthew Johnson), although the incomprehensible shouting sometimes makes the album difficult to listen to. The *Deep Blues* 🎵🎵🎵🎵 soundtrack (Atlantic, 1992, prod. Robert Palmer) is Burnside's first exposure to a national audience; the album also features his future Fat Possum labelmate Junior Kimbrough.

what to avoid: You can tell Burnside hasn't adapted comfortably to the studio on *Bad Luck City* 🎵🎵🎵 (Fat Possum, 1991, prod. Robert Palmer), his major recording debut.

the rest:
Sound Machine Groove 🎵🎵🎵 (High Water, 1980/HMG/HighTone, 1997)
Mr. Wizard 🎵🎵🎵 (Fat Possum/Epitaph, 1997)

worth searching for: Before Palmer found him, Burnside put out a few albums on small record labels: *R.L. Burnside Plays and Sings the Mississippi Delta Blues* 🎵🎵🎵 (Swingmaster, 1980) is almost impossible to find; a foreign-released single, "Bad

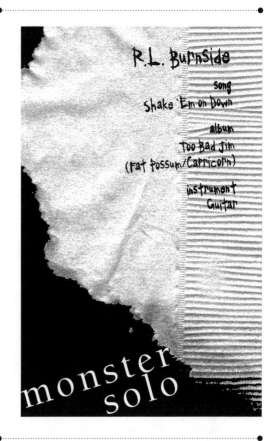

R.L. Burnside
song
Shake 'Em on Down
album
Too Bad Jim
(Fat Possum/Capricorn)
instrument
Guitar

monster solo

Luck City"/"Jumper on the Line" is available for listening through Memphis State University.

influences:
◀◀ Mississippi Fred McDowell, Muddy Waters, Bukka White, John Lee Hooker, Robert Johnson, Iggy Pop, Rolling Stones

▶▶ Jon Spencer Blues Explosion, Junior Kimbrough, Popa Chubby, Preacher Boy

Steve Knopper

Harold Burrage

Born March 30, 1931, in Chicago, IL. Died November 25, 1966, in Chicago, IL.

Harold Burrage was an obscure but important figure in the shaping of R&B music in Chicago. A gospel trained vocalist, Burrage first recorded in 1950, when Chicago was already a blues center. He then watched the city become a major player

in the development of soul. After some minor hits in the 1950s, Burrage signed with M-Pac in 1963, where he recorded some of the best Chicago soul of the era. His biggest record, "Got to Find a Way," charted in 1965, and he became a strong influence and mentor to other up-and-coming Chicago vocalists, including Otis Clay and Tyrone Davis. Sadly he died at the apex of his brief career after a heart attack in Davis' back yard.

what to buy: Burrage's most innovative material is contained on *The Pioneer of Chicago Soul* 𝄢𝄢𝄢𝄢 (P-Vine, 1979, prod. Otis Hayes), which collects his great M-Pac sides.

worth searching for: All of Burrage's singles are great but hard to find. A nice blues LP for your collection is *She Knocks Me Out* 𝄢𝄢𝄢𝄢 (Flyright, 1981), which contains his Cobra sides.

influences:

◀◀ Sam Cooke, Little Richard, Curtis Mayfield, Bobby "Blue" Bland

▶▶ Tyrone Davis, McKinley Mitchell, Otis Clay

Jeff Hannusch

Aron Burton

Born in MS.

Burton's career was influential on many more artists—including Big Jack Johnson, Honeyboy Edwards and Lonnie Brooks, to name just a few of the stars he has played with—before he became a solo performer than after. He had been bass player in Alligator Records' house band in the mid-1980s and one of Albert Collins' hot-shot Icebreakers. His voice is fine and he does an excellent job of preserving the Chicago blues, but his lot is clearly as a role player for other stars.

what's available: *Past, Present & Future* 𝄢𝄢𝄢 (Earwig, 1993, prod. Michael Robert Frank, Aron Burton) is stuff you've heard before—Percy Mayfield's "A Highway Is Like a Woman," Tony Joe White's "Rainy Night in Georgia" and electric guitar licks between every verse; the recordings are collected from sessions with pianist Champion Jack Dupree during the 1980s. His debut, *Usual Dangerous Guy* 𝄢𝄢𝄢 (Earwig, prod. Aron Burton), captures the notes and the sounds of his mentors, including Albert Collins, but it has none of the chaotic soul of the great ones.

influences:

◀◀ Albert Collins, Son Seals, B.B. King, Albert King, Freddie King, Big Jack Johnson, Honeyboy Edwards

R.L. Burnside (© Jack Vartoogian)

▶▶ Lonnie Brooks, Tinsley Ellis

Steve Knopper

George "Wild Child" Butler

Born October 1, 1936, in Autaugaville, AL.

George Butler, nicknamed by his mother to describe his behavior, once said his family "fed me greens juice in the morning, went out to the fields and didn't know if I would be alive or dead when they came back." He learned to play the harp and, despite his difficult early years, managed to find a long career in the blues. Butler's earlier material lived up to his nickname; his 1976 *Funky Butt Lover* (later retitled *Lickin' Gravy* for some reason), predicted rapper Sir Mix-A-Lot's posterior obsession by two decades. More recently, he has recorded for Bullseye Blues/Rounder and made a decent career as a conventional 12-bar bluesman.

what to buy: *Stranger* 𝄢𝄢𝄢 (Bullseye Blues/Rounder, 1994, prod. Mike Vernon) is full of very standard but well-played Butler originals, including "Weak in the Knees."

what to buy next: The import *Open Up Baby* 𝄢𝄢𝄢 (Charly, 1984) is an explosive collection of Butler's Jewel singles.

the rest:

These Mean Old Blues 𝄢𝄢𝄢 (Bullseye Blues/Rounder, 1991)

worth searching for: Butler's early albums, including his Mercury debut, *Keep on Doing What You're Doing* 𝄢𝄢𝄢 (Mercury, 1969) and *Lickin' Gravy* 𝄢𝄢𝄢 (Rooster Blues, 1977), are out of print and extremely difficult to find.

influences:

◀◀ Albert King, B.B. King, Muddy Waters, Albert Collins

Steve Knopper

Paul Butterfield Blues Band

Formed 1963, in Chicago, IL. Disbanded 1972.

Paul Butterfield (born December 17, 1941, in Chicago, IL; died May 4, 1987, in North Hollywood, CA), vocals, harmonica; Smokey Smothers, guitar (1963–64); Elvin Bishop (born October 21, 1942, in Tulsa, OK), guitar, vocals (1963–69); Jerome Arnold, bass (1963–67); Sam Lay (born March 20, 1935, in Birmingham, AL), drums, vocals (1963–65); Michael Bloomfield, (born July 28, 1944, in Chicago, IL; died February 15, 1981, in San Francisco, CA), guitar, vocals (1965–69); Mark Naftalin, piano/keyboards (1964–69); Billy Davenport, drums/percussion (1965–67); Gene Dinwiddie, tenor saxophone, mandolin, flute, vocals (1967–71); David Sanborn, tenor/alto/soprano saxophones (1967–71); Keith Johnson, trumpet, keyboards (1967–69); Philip Wilson, drums/percussion, vocals (1967–69); Bugsy Maugh, bass, vocals (1967–69); Buzzy Feiten, guitar (1968–69); Steve Madaio, trumpet (1968–71); Rod Hicks, bass, vocals (1969–71); Trevor Lawrence, baritone saxophone (1969–71); Ted Harris, keyboards (1968–69); Ralph Wash (died 1996), guitar, vocals (1970–71); George Davidson, drums (1970–71); Dennis Whitted (died 1990), drums (1971).

It's hard today to estimate the immeasurable impact the Butterfield Blues Band had on the course of blues, pop and rock 'n' roll music when it burst on the scene in the mid-1960s. Initially introduced on a 1965 sampler LP of Elektra artists by what became its signature tune—"Born in Chicago"—the Butterfield Band was no group of rank amateurs or folkies attempting to make the jump to amplification; these were already seasoned musicians, trained playing six sets a night in the South Side's legendary blues clubs. Butterfield, a child prodigy on flute, had left his middle-class home in Chicago's Hyde Park and moved into the South Side in his late teens. He immersed himself in the blues scene, studying with Little Walter and James Cotton, and became a respected member of the scene and an adopted son of Muddy Waters and Smokey Smothers. Bishop had taken a similar route from his home in Tulsa, as had Bloomfield, as much a blues musicologist as guitarist at first. The rhythm section of Arnold and Lay had served years with Howlin' Wolf. This fully integrated group floored the audience at the 1965 Newport Folk Festival, and the appearance there firmly established it as a leader in the new movement of amplified American bands on the East Coast. The band had a similar impact on the West Coast scene, especially in San Francisco and Los Angeles, where the level of its musicianship and professionalism placed it in a class separate from and high above any of the groups working there. The 1965 West Coast tour not only introduced the band's highly respectful, energetic take on the blues, but also a growing interest in jazz and Indian music, especially in the long, improvisational approach to Cannonball Adderly's "Work Song" and Bloomfield's raga/rock "East-West." The latter, based on Eastern scales and motifs, would set the tone for the entire San Francisco sound exemplified by the Grateful Dead, Jefferson Airplane, Quicksilver Messenger Service, et al. The band's impact on club owners like the Fillmore's Bill Graham was also immense and would lead to his reliance on its recommendations to book Muddy, B.B. King, Wolf and others, which would open a new white audience to these masters: Butterfield and Bloomfield are arguably the source point for the beginning of the popularity of the blues in the U.S.

By 1966 almost everyone in blues and rock—from coast to coast—was watching and aping the Butterfield Blues Band. Bloomfield left in 1967, claiming fatigue from the road, but his creative energies were clearly focused on other directions. Butterfield, always hearing a new and different type of blues in his head, elevated Bishop to the lead guitarist role, gave Naftalin more room as both pianist and arranger, and added bassist/vocalist Maugh, as well as a group of young jazz players—Dinwiddie, Johnson and Sanborn—heavily influenced by both the blues and avant jazz. This first big band reached its zenith with *In My Own Dream*, an assemblage of songs evocative of the blues but entirely unique to the genre, an album of democratic input and superb soloing by Sanborn and Bishop, whose squawking style would predate the similar efforts of New York's East Side jazz guitarists of the 1980s. Bishop would leave in 1969 to pursue solo fame but was followed by a stellar array of guitarists, including Buzz Feiten and Ralph Wash. By 1970 the band was as much a jazz outfit as a blues group, and Butterfield's harp playing was on another level from that of his Chicago predecessors—swinging, exploratory and highly emotional. The big band opened musical doors for its many progeny, including Blood, Sweat & Tears and Chicago. However, by 1971 musical trends were changing, and the band was suffering from a plague of drugs and recording inertia. Although still famous for its live shows and highly profitable on the road, the band disbanded after its final album, *Sometimes I Feel Like Smilin'*, stiffed.

what to buy: Invaluable for the long out-of-print tracks from the last four LPs, *The Box Set* ♪♪♪♪♪ (Elektra, 1997) finally collects the great examples of each evolution of the Butterfield Band, starting with its unreleased (until 1995) first studio effort through to the end. Taken as a tour-de-force of Butterfield's leadership abilities (proof of his harmonica genius and artistry) or of his bands' incredible blowing power, there's nary a wasted moment. The album that made Bloomfield and Butterfield legends, *The Paul Butterfield Blues Band* ♪♪♪♪♪ (Elektra, 1965, prod. Paul Rothchild) is the group's episodic debut, wherein a variety of blues styles are respectfully altered to the Butterfield sound—loud, aggressive and incredibly musical. *The Lost Sessions* ♪♪♪♪ (Elektra, 1964/Rhino, 1995, prod. Paul Rothchild) marks Bloomfield's initial days with the band but really showcases the tough unit of Lay, Arnold and Bishop that wowed Chicago audiences. *East-West* ♪♪♪♪ (Elektra, 1966, prod. Paul Rothchild, Mark Abramson, Barry Friedman) is Bloomfield's swan song, and although not representative of the band's live prowess, it sets the stage for all rock experimentation to follow and marked Bloomfield as a guitar deity.

what to buy next: The three versions of the title tune, at 12, 15 and 28 minutes, on *East-West Live* ♪♪♪♪ (Winner, 1997, prod. Mark Naftalin), a low-fi masterpiece mastered from live tapes, freeze-frame the brilliance of this band, whose playing seems modern and progressive even today—a timeless recording of ferocious artistry and proof this was possibly the greatest blues and rock band of its time. The final, 1967 version is pure musical genius, with all players firing off one another. Expect greatness from Bloomfield, but the real discovery is Davenport, and Butterfield's remarkable explorations on harp. Rushed out not long after the big band had been formed, there are a lot of covers on *The Resurrection of Pigboy Crabshaw* ♪♪♪ (Elektra, 1968, prod. John Court), but it's a harbinger of what would develop with the horn players.

what to avoid: Half of *An Offer You Can't Refuse* ♪♪ (Red Lightnin', 1997) features Butterfield with mentor Smokey Smothers, Lay and Arnold from a 1963 live date at Chicago's Big John's. Butterfield's harp style shows its uniqueness and rarely derivative punch in these blues standards.

worth searching for: Five cuts from the Butterfield Band's live set at the Monterey Pop Festival in 1967 can be found on *The Monterey International Pop Festival* ♪♪♪♪ (Rhino, 1992), alongside dozens of other influential musicians of the time. And watch for used copies of *In My Own Dream* ♪♪♪♪ (Elektra, 1968, prod. John Court), *Sometimes I Feel Like Smilin'* ♪♪ (Elektra, 1972, prod. Paul Rothchild) and *Keep on Movin'* ♪♪♪ (Elektra 1969, prod. Jerry Ragovoy). Tracks from each are included on *Box Set*, but all are now out of print, as are *The Butterfield Blues Band Live* ♪♪♪♪ (Elektra, 1974) and *Golden Butter: The Best of the Butterfield Blues Band* ♪♪♪ (Elektra, 1972).

influences:

◀◀ Little Walter, Sonny Boy Williamson II, James Cotton, Muddy Waters, Howlin' Wolf, Otis Rush, Bobby "Blue" Bland

▶▶ Eric Clapton, Cream, Electric Flag, Bob Dylan, the Band, Blood, Sweat & Tears, Chicago, Stephen Stills, Quicksilver Messenger Service, Grateful Dead, Robben Ford, Janis Joplin, Maria Muldaur, Bonnie Raitt, Charlie Musselwhite, Rod Piazza, J. Geils Band, Canned Heat, John Mayall

Tom Ellis III

Paul Butterfield's Better Days

Formed 1972, in Woodstock, NY. Disbanded 1973.

Paul Butterfield, vocals, harmonica, piano; Geoff Muldaur, vocals, guitar, keyboards; Amos Garrett, guitar, vocals; Ronnie Barron (born 1943; died March 21, 1997), vocals, piano/organ; Billy Rich, bass; Christopher Parker, drums.

After the big band folded, Paul Butterfield assembled another great group of players—Barron from New Orleans, Garrett from Canada, Muldaur a Cambridge folkie—and combined it with a very young rhythm section. The musical depth of Muldaur, Butterfield and Barron mixed with the stellar work of Garrett made for some great music reflecting blues traditions from around the U.S. Butterfield would carry on with three solo albums to follow; there were high points, but each showed his abilities were stronger in a band environment, not as a solo artist. He would also lend his harp to one of Muddy Waters' greatest albums, *Fathers and Sons*, wherein Butterfield shows himself the true successor to Little Walter, and the Grammy-winning *Muddy Waters—The Woodstock Album*. Many of his band members would springboard to great successes, including David Sanborn, Feiten, Garrett, Parker, Lawrence, Madaio, Bishop and Johnson, all of whom are still active today.

what to buy: The band's first album, *Better Days* ♪♪♪♪♪ (Bearsville, 1973, prod. Paul Butterfield, Geoff Muldaur) is a great collection of new and old blues compositions with Barron, Muldaur and Butterfield sharing the vocal chores. Barron's work is terrific throughout, and Muldaur's take on "Please Send Me Someone to Love" is a classic. Butterfield's singing is in top form, and his harp playing—acoustic to amplified— shows him to be the best of the best.

what to buy next: By the time *It All Comes Back* ♪♪♪♪ (Bearsville, 1973, prod. Paul Butterfield, Geoff Muldaur, Nick Jameson) arrived, the band was in the throes of break-up, and although it's strong, it doesn't capture the essence or completeness of the first release. Butterfield's playing, however, is stunning, and Muldaur's reading of "Small Town Talk" is beautiful.

solo outings:
Paul Butterfield:
Put It in Your Ear ♪♪♪♪ (Bearsville, 1974)
North-South ♪♪♪ (Bearsville, 1981)
Rides Again **woof!** (Amherst, 1986)

influences:

◀◀ Paul Butterfield Blues Band, Little Walter, Sonny Boy Williamson II, James Cotton, Muddy Waters, Howlin' Wolf, Otis Rush, Bobby "Blue" Bland

Tom Ellis III

Henry Roy Byrd

See: Professor Longhair

C

Chris Cain

Born November 19, 1955, in San Jose, CA.

Cain is a California native who came under the spell of the guitar styles of B.B. King and Albert King. He put together a tough band in the 1980s that included dazzling saxophonist Noel Catura, and they built a solid following in the blues clubs around the Bay Area. After recording a W.C. Handy Award-nominated album for Patrick Ford's tiny Blue Rock'It label in 1987, Chris hooked on with Blind Pig, where he still resides.

what to buy: *Late Night City Blues* ♫♫♫♫ (Blue Rock'It, 1987, prod. Victor Raposa, Chris Cain) was a stunning introduction for the small klatch of blues fans who were able to find the limited distribution LP. Since reissued on CD, Cain's throaty vocals were used as an effective counterpoint to his musical interplay with Catura. Nine originals, with a good mix of danceable numbers and slow, aching heartbreakers. *Somewhere Along the Way* ♫♫♫♫ (Blind Pig, 1995, prod. Pat Ford) features an all-new band and some of Cain's most consistent songwriting.

the rest:
Cuttin' Loose ♫♫♫♪ (Blind Pig, 1990)
Can't Buy a Break ♫♫♫♪ (Blind Pig, 1992)

influences:
◄◄ Albert King, B.B. King, Albert Collins

Cary Wolfson

Joe Callicott

Born October 11, 1901, in Nesbit, MS. Died 1970 or 1971, in Nesbit, MS.

Joe Callicott was not very prolific, his career a long silence bracketed on either end by several scant performances of undiluted magnificence. A stately performer who combined Mississippi John Hurt's dainty guitar work with the mournful moans that only true deep bluesmen like Muddy Waters and Son House could produce, Callicott always took his time, performing drawn-out songs that unreeled like anthems and never failed to hit their emotional mark. He came out of the fertile blues culture that pulsed in the early 1900s just south of Memphis, familiar with such early legends as Jim Jackson, Frank Stokes and Garfield Akers. Reportedly discovered by Jackson, Callicott recorded only two songs in 1930, "Traveling Mama Blues" and "Fare Thee Well Blues," both which would become highly prized by collectors decades later. But as those decades passed, Callicott played only to his Delta neighbors, sometimes accompanied by his good friend, Akers. After Akers died, Callicott put down his guitar, not picking it up again until 1968, when a blues researcher recorded him in his home. The performances were as vintage as the ones from 40 years earlier. Callicott performed a spare version of Akers' signature tune, "I Rolled and I Tumbled" and a lament, "Lonesome Katy Blues," as stirring as anything in Tommy Johnson's canon. Eight songs were recorded and no more. Callicott's death two years later muted a master's voice.

what to buy: Joe Callicott's collected works unfold over 10 tracks, two from 1930 and nine from 1967, on *Mississippi Delta Blues Vol. 2* ♫♫♫♫ (Arhoolie, 1994, prod. George Mitchell, Chris Strachwitz). His unhurried delivery masks a supremely confident voice that shines on anything he sings. In addition to Callicott's masterworks, *Vol. 2* contains the first unaccompanied recordings of R.L. Burnside, one of the last second-generation Delta masters still recording, and several cuts by Tommy Johnson acolyte Houston Stackhouse.

influences:
◄◄ Garfield Akers, Jim Jackson, Frank Stokes

Steve Braun

Eddie C. Campbell

Born May 6, 1939, in Duncan, MS.

One of the most innovative and hypnotic guitarists on today's Chicago blues scene, Eddie C. Campbell came to Chicago from his Mississippi birthplace in the mid-1940s and grew up listening to the guitarists who performed each Sunday at the Maxwell Street Market near his near West Side home. When Campbell was nine his mother helped him buy his first guitar, and by the age of 12 he was sitting in with Muddy Waters. Campbell spent the early part of his career backing Howlin' Wolf and Otis Rush; in the 1970s he joined Willie Dixon's Chicago Blues All-Stars. Under the tutelage of these masters, Campbell learned how to create a solid groove. He also perfected his distinctive and tasteful guitar style, dominated by lilting tremolo interspersed with blunted bursts of sound. After spending a decade living in London, Amsterdam and Germany, Campbell recently returned to the U.S. He now gigs frequently in Chicago. His live shows, like his recordings, are not to be missed.

what to buy: Campbell's most recent, *That's When I Know* ♫♫♫♫♫ (Blind Pig, 1994, prod. Eddie C. Campbell, Jerry Del Giudice) is one of the finest blues discs issued so far in the 1990s. Packed with original material, it captures Campbell at his best. His band swings insistently, with Campbell's guitar slicing over—and into—the layers of rhythm. Campbell displays a vocal style that has undergone considerable growth. With Robert "Huckleberry Hound" Wright shuffle-thumping the skins, an indelible, funky spell is cast. Originally issued on the Mr. Blues label, *King of the Jungle* 🎵🎵🎵 (Rooster Blues, 1996, prod. Steve Wisner, Dick Shurman) captures Campbell in the late 1970s backed by a star-studded line-up, including Carey and Lurrie Bell, Bob Stroger and Lafayette Leake. *Baddest Cat in the Block* 🎵🎵🎵🎵 (JSP, 1988, prod. John Stedman) contains several remakes of classic blues numbers, including "She's 19 Years Old" and "The Same Thing," and captures Campbell breathing new life and refreshing mellowness into some well-worn standards.

what to buy next: Campbell is heard in a rare solo acoustic session on *From West Helena to Chicago* 🎵🎵🎵 (Wolf, 1988, prod. Alex Munkas), a five-song session recorded in a Vienna studio in which Campbell delivers a rudimentary version of what would later appear as "My Sister Taught Me Guitar" on *That's When I Know*. Campbell also displays his talent for performing straight Delta blues on "Just Walking," and there are numbers by Honeyboy Edwards, Magic Slim, John Primer and Johnny B. Moore. On *Mind Trouble* 🎵🎵🎵 (Double Trouble, 1977/1986, prod. Marcel Vos, Steve Wisner), recorded in Amsterdam in 1986, Campbell all but abandons his strength—subtlety—when he enters the studio with an unnecessarily large band. Recorded in the Netherlands in 1984 and originally released on the Black Magic label, *Let's Pick It* 🎵🎵🎵 (Evidence, 1993) suffers from heavy-handed treatment from a monotonous backing band. Still, worthwhile moments can be found on the latter two releases, with Campbell's genius frequently managing to triumph.

influences:

◀◀ Magic Sam, Muddy Waters, Otis Rush, Howlin' Wolf

▶▶ Luther Allison, Jimmy Dawkins

Steven Sharp

John Campbell

Born January 20, 1952, in Shreveport, LA. Died June 13, 1993, in New York, NY.

Many people say that music saved their lives, but in John Campbell's case, it just might be true. Or was for a time, anyway. Campbell took up the guitar as a child and began playing professionally when he was barely a teen. But it was a near-

fatal drag-racing accident when he was 15 that taught him the meaning of the blues. Campbell lost his right eye in the crash, a lung collapsed and 5,000 stitches were required to reconstruct his face. While convalescing, he looked to the guitar for solace, and it was during that time that he discovered that music could provide an outlet for his emotions like nothing else. Seasoned by years of gigging in Louisiana and a residency at a club in New York's SoHo district, Campbell became a guitarist whose fierce licks matched the scarifying growl of his vocals. He achieved some degree of notoriety, though hardly commensurate with his talent, before he died an untimely death by heart attack while on a European tour.

what to buy: "I got the devil in my closet/and the wolf is at my door," Campbell growls over the opening bars of his major-label debut, *One Believer* 🎵🎵🎵🎵 (Elektra, 1991, prod. Dennis Walker, Peter Lubin), and after one jolt of his gruff baritone and a few stellar licks from his guitar, there's no way you'll accuse him of talking shit. The whole album is like that, combining metaphysics—check out the prescient, doom-laden "Angel of Sorrow"—and sad tales from this world, such as "Tiny Coffins," which describes the young, unintended victim of a drive-by shooting. Campbell's blues are utterly contemporary, but he plays and sings like he might have taken a long-ago trip to the crossroads, too.

the rest:

Howlin' Mercy 🎵🎵🎵🎵 (Elektra, 1993)

worth searching for: An early selection of tracks produced in 1985 by guitarist Ronnie Earl, *A Man and His Blues* 🎵🎵🎵🎵 (Crosscut, 1988) offers an indication of good things to come.

influences:

◀◀ Howlin' Wolf, Muddy Waters, John Lee Hooker

Daniel Durchholz

Milton Campbell

See: Little Milton

Canned Heat

Formed 1966, in Los Angeles, CA.

Bob "Bear" Hite (died April 5, 1981), vocals, harmonica (1966–81); Al "Blind Owl" Wilson (died September 3, 1970), guitar, vocals, harmonica (1966–70); Henry "The Sunflower" Vestine, guitar (1966–69, 1970); Frank Cook, drums (1966–68); Larry Taylor (born Samuel Taylor), bass (1966–70, 1994–present); Adolpho "Fito" de la Parra, drums (1968–present); Harvey Mandel, guitar (1969–70); Antonio de la

John Campbell (© Jack Vartoogian)

Barreda, bass (1970–72); Richard Hite, bass (1972–91); James Thornbury, guitar, harmonica, vocals (1984–present); Junior Watson, guitar, vocals (1994–present); Ron Shumake, bass, vocals (1994–present).

The boogie, ever since John Lee Hooker created it during the late 1940s in Detroit, has been a timeless thing. So it is that this bunch of players from southern California plugged in their jug band and started playing the rolling, loose-limbed blues they loved so much on their John Lee Hooker records. If Canned Heat was a new band today, it would be part of the H.O.R.D.E. festival. As it is, the group continues; though without original frontmen Bob Hite and Al Wilson, it returns as if coming back to the mothership for a bit of boogie nourishment.

what to buy: *Uncanned! The Best of Canned Heat* 𝄢𝄢𝄢𝄢 (Liberty/EMI, 1994, prod. various) is an expansive two-disc, 41-song set that has the hits ("On the Road Again," "Going up the Country," "Fannie Mae") and a disarming number of highly listenable jams. How quickly we forget.

what to avoid: *The King Biscuit Flower Hour Presents Canned Heat* 𝄢𝄢 (KBFH, 1996), a radio concert taken from a flat and forgettable 1979 show.

the rest:
The Best of Canned Heat 𝄢𝄢𝄢 (EMI America, 1987)
Internal Combustion 𝄢𝄢𝄢 (River Road, 1994)
Gamblin' Woman 𝄢𝄢 (Mausoleum, 1996)

worth searching for: One of the group's most consistent albums was *Future Blues* 𝄢𝄢𝄢𝄢 (Liberty, 1970/See for Miles, 1993, prod. Skip Taylor, Canned Heat), now only available as an import.

influences:
◀◀ John Lee Hooker, Howlin' Wolf, Sonny Boy Williamson II
▶▶ Grateful Dead, Fabulous Thunderbirds, Blues Traveler

Gary Graff

Hayward "Chuck" Carbo

Born January 11, 1926, in Houma, LA.

Chuck Carbo, "The Voice of New Orleans," sang lead for hit Crescent City vocal group the Spiders on their brilliant series of singles produced by Dave Bartholomew for Imperial during 1953–56. "Witchcraft" and the oft-banned "I Didn't Wanna Do It" made noise nationally, while "I'm Slippin' In" was a big local hit. After the Spiders faded, Carbo cut a few singles for local labels and then retired from the performing life. He was brought back on-stage by radio station WWOZ in the early 1980s, and Carbo continues to croon with consummate strength and artistry well into his early seventies.

what to buy: *The Spiders: Complete Imperial Recordings* ♫♫♫♫ (Bear Family, 1992) boasts everything recorded by Carbo and the Spiders for Imperial. Not everything is worth repeated listening, but "Witchcraft," "I Didn't Wanna Do It" and "I'm Slippin' In" are as good as any records ever made. The liner notes by reissue producer Rick Coleman and the typically thorough Bear Family research add a welcome bonus for fiendish R&B scholars. Chuck Carbo's first compact disc, *Drawers Trouble* ♫♫♫ (Rounder, 1993, prod. Ron Levy), recorded 40 years after he cut his first single with the Spiders, is a tour-de-force for the singer with what Jeff Hannusch calls "probably the richest baritone voice in the Crescent City," backed by an all-star rhythm section—Ed Frank, Walter Payton and Shannon Powell—and featuring special guest Dr. John on piano, organ and "low guitar."

the rest:

The Barber's Blues ♫♫♫ (Rounder, 1996)

worth searching for: The first Carbo album, *Life's Ups and Downs* (504, 1992) is still not available on CD, but it's worth nabbing on cassette or LP for infectious party anthems like "Second Line on Monday," "Meet Me with Your Black Drawers On" and "Bad Water."

influences:

◀◀ Zion Harmonizers

▶▶ Johnny Adams, Art Neville, Ernie K-Doe, Davell Crawford

John Sinclair

James Carr

Born June 13, 1942, in Memphis, TN.

There is not a sorrier story in the annals of soul music than the unfulfilled promise of James Carr. Beset by personal demons that left him mute in mid-performance on stage and froze him out of recording studios for two decades, Carr remains a major R&B figure for the furious power of his deep soul recordings of the 1960s. In more than 40 minor-mode gems made for Gold-wax in Memphis, Carr unleashed himself like a man at the end of his rope, keening in ragged shrieks at unfaithful women and betraying friends. He could top the urbane blues of Little Johnny Taylor in "You Don't Want Me" or topple into full-blown cheating misery in "The Dark End of the Street." But if one song was emblematic of his power and his instability, it was "You've Got My Mind Messed Up," a Redding-style raver in which Carr's squawks mounted over the shrill backing of Memphis horns. Carr's recordings, carried by the lowly Goldwax label, sold well, but never challenged the rival Stax label. When Goldwax shut down in 1969, Carr seemed to go under, too. Seemingly dropped from the face of the earth, Carr stunned soul fanatics by recording for the revived Goldwax label in 1991. Carr could not turn back the years; at times he sounded shell-shocked, but there were still traces of soul mastery in his voice. He tours on occasion, then drops out of sight. Only James Carr knows if he will ever record again.

what to buy: *Essential James Carr* ♫♫♫♫ (Razor & Tie, 1995, prod. Quinton Claunch) is the cream of Carr's Goldwax years. Backed by top Memphis musicians, he raves on over 20 cuts, including those mentioned above and the fatalistic "Pouring Water on a Drowning Man."

what to buy next: One of two Japanese imports that collect all of Carr's Goldwax cuts, *A Man Needs a Woman* ♫♫♫♫ (Vivid Sound, 1990, prod. Quinton Claunch) includes only a few clinkers among 21 majestic soul performances. For soul addicts who have to have them all, there is *You Got My Mind Messed Up* ♫♫♫♫ (Vivid Sound, 1990, prod. Quinton Claunch).

what to avoid: Painful as it is to say, Carr's comeback attempt, *Take Me to the Limit* ♫♫ (Goldwax, 1991, prod. Quinton Claunch), shows how hard it is to recapture the ephemeral essence of soul. Carr brings a muted intensity to "I Can't Leave Your Love" and "She's Already Gone," but the rest is sub-par, standard funk workouts that never quite gel.

the rest:

The Complete James Carr Vol. 1 ♫♫♫ (Goldwax, 1993)

influences:

◀◀ O.V. Wright, Otis Redding

Steve Braun

Leroy Carr

Born March 27, 1905, in Nashville, TN. Died April 29, 1935, in Indianapolis, IN.

In its earliest incubation, the blues was a country music suffused with rural themes and down-home lyrics. It took the mellow, rolling cadence of Leroy Carr's piano and vocals to give urban blues its own distinct presence—and its first master. Carr's relaxed style became so overwhelmingly popular—and so suddenly—that he created an instant genre: the big city blues piano crooner. Cecil Gant, Charles Brown, Amos Milburn, Charles Brown and Ray Charles all might have eventually taken flight without Carr. But Carr surely set the standard for them and dozens of other piano men. Recording nearly 200 songs over the course of his seven-year career, Carr could hardly help to avoid getting mired in old grooves and repetition. But much of his music remained fresh and influential—both because of Carr's simple tunes and piano noodling and the exquisite guitar backing of longtime partner Francis "Scrapper" Blackwell. Carr churned out blues standards that became part of the music's lexicon so easily it seemed as if they had always been there. His classics, "How Long, How Long Blues," "Blues before Sunrise," "When the Sun Goes Down," "I Believe I'll Make a Change" and "Sloppy Drunk Blues," have been reinterpreted over scores of recordings by everyone from Muddy Waters to Hot Tuna. Carr had only an inkling of his influence, a full-fledged alcoholic who died at the age of 30. What little is known of his early years is that he had become proficient on the piano as a teenager, joining the Army and a traveling circus before he set out as a musician. In Indianapolis, he met up with Blackwell and the two were soon inseparable. A group of Vocalion field recorders sent there to cut Blackwell ended up using Carr as well. One of his first two sides, "How Long," a variation of Ida Carr's melancholic "Crow Jane," became an overnight sensation. Five months later Carr returned with a second version of "How Long," a habit that he adopted too often. But recording as regularly as he and Blackwell did, as often as every three months, the pair rarely put out inferior efforts—at least not until Carr's alcoholism raged into its advanced stages. His recording activity tailed off when the Depression curtailed many blues sessions in 1932. By then, his liver was becoming ravaged. Bedridden in Indianapolis, he died of alcoholism and nephritis, leaving Blackwell to soldier on alone in increasing anonymity for another 30 years.

what to buy: *Leroy Carr 1930–35* ♪♪♪♪ (Magpie, 1990, prod. Francis Wilford Smith) came as part of the estimable series of early barrelhouse and boogie-woogie piano recordings compiled by British 78 collectors. Among the 20 tracks are some of Carr's most sublime efforts, including his second version of "How Long," "Sloppy Drunk Blues" and the eternal "How Long Has That Evening Train Been Gone?" The mastering remains the crispest among all Carr re-releases.

what to buy next: The cleanly-mastered Carr tracks on *Leroy Carr Vol. 2* ♪♪♪♪ (Magpie, 1990, prod. Francis Wilford Smith) are almost as uniformly fine as those on Magpie's first disc. They pale against the first only because there is slightly more of a sameness to some of the sides. It took five long-playing CDs to contain all of Carr and Blackwell's inimitable duets, and even with the pair's dross discarded, you would still need all five to encompass their best stuff. The biggest surprise is the first one, *Leroy Carr 1928–35* ♪♪♪♪ (Document, 1992, prod. Johnny Parth), with a bright sound and selection of such early classics as the first "How Long," "Mean Old Train Blues" and the doomy "Prison Bound Blues."

what to avoid: Once upon a time *Blues before Sunrise* ♪♪ (Columbia/Portrait, 1989), a re-release of a late-1950s Columbia LP, was the only way to find Leroy Carr on an album, let alone on record. But Columbia apparently did little work on the dismal sound the second time around, making the Magpie and Document collections essential and this one superfluous.

influences:

◀◀ Scrapper Blackwell, Ida Cox

▶▶ Jimmy Rushing, Cecil Gant, Charles Brown, Ray Charles, Sonny Boy Williamson I, Robert Johnson, Elmore James, Muddy Waters, Hot Tuna

Steve Braun

Sam Carr

See: Frank Frost & Sam Carr

Karen Carroll

Born January 30, 1958, in Chicago, IL.

It's not a stretch to say that blues is in Karen Carroll's blood. She is the daughter of Jeanne Carroll, a blues/gospel/jazz singer, and since childhood, Carroll wanted to follow in her mother's footsteps. She had ample encouragement: Her godmother is fellow Delmark recording artist Bonnie Lee; guitarist George Freeman is her godfather; and she learned one of her favorite blues tunes, "Vicksburg Blues," straight from Little Brother Montgomery, the man who made it famous. Carroll started singing at age nine and joined her mother on stage at

14 to play guitar in her band. By the time she was 18 she was ready to try singing on her own, honing her craft in small South Side Chicago clubs. Carroll has one of the deeper voices among the city's many blues belters, adding a husky growl now and then for effect when she sings. She credits her mother for learning the jazz phrasings that crop up now and then in her performance of standard blues. Carroll enjoys a call-and-response with the audience, especially when talking about rocky romance with "the mens" or joking about "the nasty girls."

what to buy: Carroll's debut album, *Had My Fun* &&& (Delmark, 1995, prod. Steve Wagner), offers basic blues, long and slow. Only three of the 10 tracks are less than five minutes; one runs nearly nine. This allows a good opportunity to feel Carroll's full, husky voice and to hear keyboardist Ken Saydak and guitarist Johnny B. Moore strut their stuff. The first four tracks were recorded live at Blue Chicago; the remainder were done in the studio—most, the notes say, in one take and with the same mike Carroll used at the club, providing the opportunity for that pleasantly raw feeling that comes from a live performance.

worth searching for: On her first recording, *Professor Strut* && (Delmark, 1989, prod. Robert Koester) Carroll sings solo on three tracks with Professor Eddie Lusk and his band. "Everything Is You," with its scat section, shows her jazz bent, and it has a lighter, less confident feel. Four tracks, including a swinging version of "All of Me," feature Carroll on *Stock Yards Stomp* && (Delmark, 1995, prod. Robert Koester). She's backed by the Dixie Stompers, and this, too, has a lighter feel. Carroll sounds like she's having fun.

influences:
◄◄ Jeanne Carroll

Nadine Cohodas

Bo Carter

Born Armenter Chatmon, March 21, 1893, in Bolton, MS. Died September 21, 1964, in Memphis, TN.

Though he frequently performed with his brothers' band, the Mississippi Sheiks, Carter was most famous as the salacious singer and complex guitarist behind "My Pencil Won't Write No More" and "Ram Rod Daddy." The blind street singer lived a much cleaner life than the dirty songs he wrote, which he admitted were just for the money, but they landed him many recording sessions throughout the 1930s and 1940s. Carter's thinly disguised innuendo predated such clever blues and rock 'n' roll classics as John Lee Hooker's "Crawling King Snake" and Jerry Lee Lewis' "Whole Lotta Shaking Goin' On."

what to buy: *Greatest Hits 1930–40* &&& (Yazoo, 1970) supplements Carter's sexy songs with a few Sheiks tracks. Much more complete, as usual, is *Complete Recorded Works in Chronological Order Vols. 1–5* &&& (Document, 1991), a collection of separate discs with just about everything Carter ever did.

influences:
◄◄ Mississippi Sheiks, Robert Johnson, Son House, Memphis Jug Band, Emmett Miller
►► John Lee Hooker, Blind Boy Fuller, Lightnin' Hopkins, Memphis Slim, Muddy Waters, Taj Mahal

Steve Knopper

Clarence Carter

Born January 14, 1936, in Montgomery, AL.

For a blind guy, Clarence Carter sure did a lot of cheatin' and homewreckin'. Bad for the monogamists but good for us, as his lecherous ways produced a bona-fide classic, "Slip Away." A back door proposition with Carter woefully copping to the tawdriness of it all as he slides his foot in the door, the song is a close second to "Dark End of the Street" as the greatest stolen-love R&B song ever. The rest of his body of work follows the tracks that "Slip Away" laid down, with no less lascivious results, as his trademark "heh-heh-heh" growl can still make the dudes pull their girlfriends a little closer.

what to buy: *Snatching It Back: The Best of Clarence Carter* &&&& (Rhino, 1992, prod. Rick Hall), a solid 21-track compilation, contains "Slip Away" and "Patches" as well as other important tracks, such as his absurdly profound reworking of "Dark End of the Street." Preaching over the song's subtle groove, Carter fuses the sexual and the spiritual into a dizzying stir of desire.

what to buy next: In a handshake deal with Ichiban, Carter still releases albums sporadically. *Dr. C.C.* && (Ichiban, 1987, prod. Clarence Carter) is highlighted by the gloriously lewd "Strokin'."

what to avoid: *The Dr.'s Greatest Prescriptions* && (Ichiban) isn't a bad compilation, but the Rhino package renders it obsolete.

the rest:
Hooked on Love && (Ichiban, 1988)
Messin' with My Mind && (Ichiban, 1988)
Touch of Blues &&& (Ichiban, 1988)
Between a Rock and a Hard Place && (Ichiban, 1990)
Have You Met Clarence Carter? && (Ichiban, 1992)
Legendary && (MCA Special Products, 1995)

worth searching for: Carter's out of print final session with the Muscle Shoals gang, *Sixty Minutes with Clarence Carter* ♪♪♪ (Fame, 1973, prod. Rick Hall), brought some new and more modern elements into his mix.

influences:

◀◀ Lightnin' Hopkins, Otis Redding, Solomon Burke

▶▶ Rick James, Aerosmith, Keith Sweat, R. Kelly

Allan Orski

Goree Carter

Born 1930, in Houston, TX. Died December 29, 1990, in Houston, TX.

A guitar-playing master of jump blues, Carter emulated T-Bone Walker and Charlie Christian and, like those more-famous contemporaries, predated rock 'n' roll's prototypical electric-guitar sound. His licks jump out of *Unsung Hero*, a reissue of sides he cut for Freedom before he was drafted into the Army. Though he later recorded for several different labels, including Peacock, Modern and Coral, he never had a long-term contract and eventually quit playing and sold his guitar. In liner notes, modern Texas blues guitarist Pete Mayes says Carter's death came because "he just didn't care anymore."

what to buy: *Unsung Hero* ♪♪♪ (Collectables, 1992, prod. Roy Ames) documents a hot, hungry guitarist who could have been as big as Chuck Berry if more opportunities had rolled his way; but that's the story of the blues. Most notable are the sweaty "Hoy Hoy" and the horn-piano-and-guitar interplay on "Back Home Blues."

influences:

◀◀ T-Bone Walker, Charlie Christian, Duke Ellington

▶▶ Elmore James, Ike Turner, Chuck Berry, Rolling Stones

Steve Knopper

Leonard "Baby Doo" Caston

See: Big Three Trio

Tommy Castro

Born 1955, in San Jose, CA.

A young Bay Area guitarist-vocalist, Tommy Castro plays blues-rock that falls right smack into the "party" category. This is the band you hope to luck into at some out-of-the-way roadhouse on a Saturday night. Long a favorite live band in the San Francisco area, Castro's high-energy sound doesn't lose much in the studio. He has a husky, punchy vocal style and a fiery, straight-ahead way with a guitar. His small band (Keith Crossan, sax; Randy McDonald, bass; Shad Harris, drums) plays hard, tight and usually fast. Castro writes or co-writes most of the material, and though it isn't blindingly original, it certainly suits his style.

what to buy: The producer's touch is evident on *Can't Keep a Good Man Down* ♪♪♪ (Blind Pig, 1997, prod. Jim Gaines). There are a couple of slow, deep ones, like "My Time After Awhile," but Castro mostly goes for the funk, like "High on the Hog," or a good fast boogie, like "Nobody Loves Me Like My Baby," with Commander Cody guesting on piano.

the rest:
Exception to the Rule ♪♪♪ (Blind Pig, 1995)

influences:

◀◀ Johnny Winter

Jennifer Zogott

Cate Brothers

Formed 1960, in Fayetteville, AR.

Earl Cate (born December 26, 1942, in Fayetteville, AR), keyboards, vocals; Ernie Cate (born December 26, 1942, in Fayetteville, AR), guitar, vocals.

Twin brothers who started their first band while in their teens, Earl and Ernie Cate have become a legendary blues outfit anywhere within overnight range of their Fayetteville home base. Briefly, way back when, they had Levon Helm, later of the Band, in their group (and he introduced them to his cousin, Terry Cagle, who became their drummer for a spell). It was the Cates that Helm called to fill in at the New Jersey club the Hawks were playing when they got the call from Bob Dylan to join him to be booed around the world for playing electric music. Singer Ernie Cate's smoky voice is reminiscent of Ray Charles or Bobby Bland, and guitarist Earl Cate can burn like Eric Clapton or smolder like Stevie Ray Vaughan. They recorded four prized-to-collectors soul albums in the 1970s, flirted with a hit with "Union Man" and backed the Band off-and-on in the 1980s. Depending on the place and the time of night, they can be the tightest cover group or the best damned original band you *never* heard of; if you're somewhere between Fayetteville and Memphis and see their name on the marquee, take the chance.

what to buy: Their only compact disc, *Radioland* ♪♪♪♪ (Blue Sun/Icehouse, 1996), is also their first recording since 1979, and it shows a fully mature blues band stretching out all over

Phil Wiggins (l) and John Cephas (© **Linda Vartoogian**)

the place. Ernie Cates burns like Ray Charles on "Damned Guilty Blues" and "Solid Ground," while guitar master Earl Cate, generally throttled in the studio, has never sounded better than on "Am I Losing You."

worth searching for: None of their 1970s albums have been issued on compact disc, which makes them particularly noteworthy finds. While all are recommended, in order of preference, they are *In One Eye and out the Other* ♪♪♪♪ (Elektra, 1976, prod. Steve Cropper) (the great lost Steve Cropper album with the great road song, "Travelin' Man"); *Cate Brothers* ♪♪♪♪ (Elektra, 1975, prod. Steve Cropper), with "Union Man"; *The Cate Brothers Band* ♪♪♪♪ (Asylum, 1977, prod. Jim Mason); and *Fire on the Tracks* ♪♪♪ (Atlantic, 1979, prod. Tom Dowd).

influences:

◀◀ Jerry Lee Lewis, Bo Diddley, Ray Charles, Bobby "Blue" Bland

Leland Rucker

Cephas & Wiggins

John Cephas born September 4, 1930, in Washington, DC. Phil Wiggins born May 8, 1954, in Washington, DC.

This acoustic duo lovingly preserves the "Piedmont Blues" tradition—which basically means the heavily rhythmic, almost playful, East Coast style of legends Sonny Terry, Blind Boy Fuller, the Rev. Gary Davis and Blind Blake. "Bowling Green" Cephas met the much younger Wiggins at the Smithsonian Folklife Festival in 1976. (Cephas had made his name in the 1960s, when he lured pianist Big Chief Ellis out of retirement and established him as a solid festival performer and recording artist.) Like John Hammond Jr. and Taj Mahal, these historians and blues fanatics put out an album of traditional standards every couple of years and go into great depth about the material's origins in accompanying liner notes. They mimic the style and instrumentation of the great Sonny Terry and Brownie McGhee, and they're distinctive in their own way. But despite the occasional fun, driving blues song—such as "Action Man"—they tend to put out the same album over and over.

what to buy: The duo won a W.C. Handy award for *Dog Days of August* 𝄞𝄞𝄞 (Flying Fish, 1986), which established their reverential, sometimes playful and sometimes soulful take on traditional country-blues standards.

what to buy next: One of their best songs, the snappy "Action Man," opens *Cool Down* 𝄞𝄞 (Alligator, 1995, prod. Joe Wilson), which then reverts to the usual solemnly-remake-the-classics style.

the rest:

Sweet Bitter Blues 𝄞𝄞 (L&R Music, 1984/Evidence, 1994)
Let It Roll: Bowling Green 𝄞𝄞 (Marimac, 1985)
Guitar Man 𝄞𝄞𝄞 (Flying Fish, 1987)
Walking Blues 𝄞𝄞𝄞 (Marimac, 1988)
Flip, Flop & Fly 𝄞𝄞𝄞 (Flying Fish, 1992)
Bluesmen 𝄞𝄞 (Chesky, 1993)

influences:

◄◄ Sonny Terry & Brownie McGhee, Blind Boy Fuller, Blind Blake, Taj Mahal, John Hammond Jr., Big Chief Ellis

►► Rory Block, Keb' Mo'

Steve Knopper

Ray Charles

Born Ray Charles Robinson, September 23, 1930, in Albany, GA.

Not for nothing is Ray Charles known as "the Genius." In a career almost unparalleled in American popular music, he has done more than anyone to obliterate the lines that once existed between R&B, gospel, country, pop, jazz and rock. Beginning as an imitator of the urbane vocal stylings of Nat "King" Cole and the uptown blues of Charles Brown, Charles eventually forged his own style, combining gospel music and the country and blues music of his youth with decidedly earthier lyrics reflecting love, lust, heartbreak and hard times. Though Charles' increase in popularity occurred simultaneously with the rise of rock 'n' roll, he correctly commented in his autobiography that his work has little to do with the nascent genre; it contained too much despair to compete on the charts with the uptempo ravings of Little Richard, Jerry Lee Lewis and Elvis Presley. Yet Charles remains a seminal influence on rock, and he was rightfully inducted into the Rock and Roll Hall of Fame in 1986. Charles is revered both for his voice, which reveals a capacity for heartache seemingly without depth, and for his deftly intuitive ideas, which find him mining influences as vari-

ous as Count Basie and Hank Williams, and turning the result into works of staggering originality. A man of Herculean determination, few opponents from the world of music—or from life in general, for that matter—have faced him down. Not all of his decisions have been right ones, but he stands behind them all. And why not? He is one of the most recognizable figures in all of music, thanks to such timeless hits as "I Got a Woman," "What'd I Say," "The Night Time Is the Right Time," "Hit the Road Jack," "Georgia on My Mind," "Unchain My Heart," "You Don't Know Me," "Busted" and countless others, to say nothing of his famous "Uh-huh" Diet Pepsi commercials. There is no one else like him.

what to buy: Charles' illustrious career has been documented with several excellent boxed sets, but *Genius & Soul: The 50th Anniversary Collection* 𝄞𝄞𝄞𝄞𝄞 (Rhino, 1997, prod. various) stands above them all, if only for pulling together for the first time material from all facets of Charles career and from all of the labels he's recorded for. At five discs, it's a hefty investment in time and money, but it's an absolute treasure. Starting with an early single from his Seattle days, the set moves through his "genius" phase at Atlantic, to the even more unbridled innovation of his ABC days—recording soulful country and western classics and covering the Beatles—to the quiet classics (such as his recent reading of Leon Russell's "A Song for You") that he records to this day. *Genius & Soul* is simply one of the best boxed sets ever assembled. For those unwilling or unable to treat themselves, start with both *Anthology* 𝄞𝄞𝄞𝄞𝄞 (Rhino, 1988, prod. Sid Feller, Joe Adams) and *The Best of Ray Charles: The Atlantic Years* 𝄞𝄞𝄞𝄞𝄞 (Rhino, 1994, prod. Jerry Wexler, Zenas Sears, Nesuhi Ertegun, Ahmet Ertegun). The 20-track *Anthology* contains the ABC material, including "Georgia on My Mind," "Let's Go Get Stoned," "Eleanor Rigby," "Hit the Road Jack" and "Unchain My Heart." *The Atlantic Years*, which also contains 20 tracks, features "I Got a Woman," "What'd I Say," "The Night Time Is the Right Time" and "Drown in My Own Tears." Both are the best single-disc representations of those periods of Charles' music currently available.

what to buy next: They're advertised as country and western, but there are few recordings as soulful as Charles' takes on Eddy Arnold's "You Don't Know Me," Hank Williams' "You Win Again" and Frankie Laine's "That Lucky Old Sun." On *Modern Sounds in Country and Western Music* 𝄞𝄞𝄞𝄞 (ABC, 1963, prod. Sid Feller, Joe Adams) those songs and others stand as monuments to Charles' innovation and sheer audacity. During the heightened racial tensions of the early 1960s, what other black

Ray Charles (© Jack Vartoogian)

man could have pulled this off? *Live* 𝄞𝄞𝄞𝄞𝄞 (Atlantic, 1987/Rhino 1990, prod. Nesuhi Ertegun, Zenas Sears) combines a pair of essential late-1950s live recordings, *Ray Charles at Newport* and *Ray Charles in Person*. The sets reveal Charles' intensity and charisma as a concert performer and includes explosive versions of "The Right Time," "What'd I Say" and "Drown in My Own Tears."

what to avoid: Some of Charles' albums are ill-conceived or carried out, but none are truly wretched. The thing to beware of, however, are the numerous cheap repackagings of his hits. If it's not on Atlantic, ABC, Rhino, or DCC, proceed with caution.

best of the rest:

The Great Ray Charles/The Genius After Hours 𝄞𝄞𝄞 (Atlantic, 1958/ 1961/Rhino, 1987)
(With Milt Hinton) *Soul Brothers/Soul Meeting* 𝄞𝄞𝄞 (Atlantic, 1958/ 1962/Rhino, 1989)
The Genius of Ray Charles 𝄞𝄞𝄞𝄞 (Atlantic, 1959/ Rhino, 1990)
The Genius Hits the Road 𝄞𝄞𝄞 (ABC, 1960/ Rhino, 1997)

The Best of Ray Charles 𝄞𝄞𝄞 (Atlantic, 1970/ Rhino, 1988)
Would You Believe? 𝄞𝄞 (Warner Bros., 1990)
The Birth of Soul: The Complete Atlantic Rhythm & Blues Recordings, 1952–59 𝄞𝄞𝄞𝄞 (Rhino, 1991)
My World 𝄞𝄞𝄞 (Warner Bros., 1993)
Ain't That Fine 𝄞𝄞 (Drive Archive, 1994)
Blues + Jazz 𝄞𝄞𝄞 (Rhino, 1994)
The Early Years 𝄞𝄞𝄞 (Tomato, 1994)
Berlin, 1962 𝄞𝄞𝄞𝄞 (Pablo, 1996)
Strong Love Affair 𝄞𝄞 (Qwest, 1996)

worth searching for: Rhino Records is in the midst of an extensive program of reissuing Charles' ABC sides. One worth waiting for is *A Message from the People* 𝄞𝄞𝄞 (ABC, 1972), which includes "Abraham, Martin, and John," "There'll Be No Peace without All Men As One," and Charles' brilliant readings of "Look What They Done to My Song, Ma" and "America the Beautiful." It's a protest album of sorts, from a man whose politics, before this album and since, have seldom been on display.

influences:

◀◀ Nat "King" Cole, Charles Brown, Count Basie, Grand Ole Opry, Louis Jordan, Claude Jeter

▶▶ Van Morrison, Joe Cocker, Billy Joel

Daniel Durchholz

Rockie Charles

Born Charles Merick, November 14, 1942, in Boothville, LA.

Nobody paid much attention to Rockie Charles until he reactivated his career in the mid-1990s. Influenced originally by Guitar Slim, Earl King and Chuck Berry, Charles played guitar and sang with several small New Orleans R&B combos. He auditioned for Minit and Imperial but was turned down. His first single, "Sinking Like a Ship," on the obscure Black Patch label, didn't do much. In the late 1960s, Charles relocated to Nashville and he played behind artists like O.V. Wright, Roscoe Shelton and Little Johnny Taylor when they toured the area. By 1970 he was back in New Orleans and started his own label, Soulgate, which provided a local hit, "The President of Soul," one of the first records done at the Malaco studio in Jackson, Mississippi. Once disco reared its head, work as a musician slowed and he hired on as a tug boat captain and oyster fisherman. His career got a jump start in 1994 when Orleans Records producer Carlo Ditta saw an ad Charles placed in a local entertainment magazine.

what to buy: Their meeting resulted in an introspective, original CD that received lots of attention upon its release. *Born for You* 𝄢𝄢𝄢𝄢 (Orleans, 1996, prod. Carlo Ditta) sounds like the great lost Al Green record.

worth searching for: In addition to the singles on Black Patch and Soulgate, search for the sides Charles played for the New Orleans Watch label in the mid-1960s.

influences:

◀◀ Earl King, Al Green

Jeff Hannusch

John Len "Peter" Chatman

See: Memphis Slim

Armenter Chatman

See: Bo Carter

Lonnie Chatman

See: Mississippi Sheiks

Sam Chatmon

Born January 10, 1897, in Bolton, MS. Died February 2, 1983, in Hollandale, MS.

The Chatmon family string band was the Jackson 5 of its time, featuring extraordinarily talented brothers who performed as successful solo artists (Bo Carter) or a popular and influential folk/blues band (the Mississippi Sheiks). Though Lonnie Chatmon was the family's most dominant personality, Sam was a versatile songwriter and multi-instrumentalist (guitar, bass, mandolin, banjo and harmonica). But the life of a street singer, working for low tips, was never particularly lucrative, so Sam moved to Hollandale to work on plantations. The 1960s blues revival offered a chance of a comeback, and he performed in festivals around the world before he died in 1984.

what to buy: Both *Sam Chatmon's Advice* 𝄢𝄢𝄢𝄢 (Rounder, 1979) and *Mississippi Sheiks and Chatmon Brothers (Lonnie & Sam), Vol. 4 (1934–36)* 𝄢𝄢𝄢𝄢 (Document) sample the essential subsections of Chatmon's career. The former is a playful, sexy singing session he did after he "unretired" from music; the latter, part of Document's thorough four-volume Mississippi Sheiks library, collects his early-career sides, with and without the family band.

the rest:

Sam Chatmon and His Barbecue Boys 𝄢𝄢𝄢 (Flying Fish, 1987)

influences:

◀◀ Charley Patton, Son House, Emmett Miller, Jimmie Rodgers, Robert Johnson, Lonnie Johnson

▶▶ Bob Dylan, Muddy Waters, Taj Mahal, John Hammond Jr., Frank Frost & Sam Carr, Sonny Terry & Brownie McGhee

Steve Knopper

Jeannie & Jimmy Cheatham

Birth information unavailable.

This husband-and-wife team, overseers of hot weekly San Diego jam sessions since the 1980s, recreate classic jazz and big-band music with affection and flawless skill. Their great strength isn't in breaking new ground or adding a different perspective to the old styles, but in lovingly rescuing old songs and finding wonderful old jazz and blues sidepeople to play in their venerable Sweet Baby Blues Band. They met in 1956, married three years later and have been together ever since. They've blended Percy Mayfield's "What a Fool I Was" and "Please Send Me Someone to Love," Billie Holiday's "Fine and Mellow" and Pete Johnson's "Piney Brown" into their horn-heavy cocktail swing style. Singer-pianist Jeannie Cheatham and bass trombonist Jimmy Cheatham also write terrific songs, including "Meet Me with Your Black Drawers On" (a hit for singer Chuck Carbo in 1989 and a Nawlins' club standard) and the dark "Line in the Sand."

what to buy: Their bluesiest album, *Blues and the Boogie Masters* 𝄢𝄢𝄢 (Concord Jazz, 1993, prod. Nick Phillips), features Ray Charles' former musical director Hank Crawford on alto sax and nine tear-jerking Cheatham-and-Cheatham originals.

what to buy next: *Gud Nuz Blues* 𝄢𝄢𝄢 (Concord Jazz, 1996, prod. Nick Phillips), like most of their albums, gets your attention with a master sideman, this time ex-Henry Mancini orchestra saxophonist Plas Johnson. Unfortunately, it suffers from too many requisite rounds of solos.

the rest:
Homeward Bound 𝄢𝄢𝄢 (Concord Jazz)
Midnight Mama 𝄢𝄢 (Concord Jazz, 1986)
Back to the Neighborhood 𝄢𝄢 (Concord Jazz, 1989)
Sweet Baby Blues 𝄢𝄢 (Concord Jazz, 1989)
Basket Full of Blues 𝄢𝄢𝄢 (Concord Jazz, 1992)

worth searching for: *Luv in the Afternoon* 𝄢𝄢𝄢 (Concord Jazz) features guest bluesman Clarence "Gatemouth" Brown.

influences:
◄◄ Percy Mayfield, Duke Ellington, Sidney Bechet, Billie Holiday
►► Squirrel Nut Zippers, Royal Crown Revue, Setters

Steve Knopper

C.J. Chenier

Born Clayton Joseph Chenier, September 28, 1957, in Port Arthur, TX.

Son of Clifton Chenier, the "King of Zydeco," C.J. Chenier learned to play alto saxophone (and flute, piano and keyboards) in school. He liked James Brown and Funkadelic as well as John Coltrane and Miles Davis. After gaining experience in Top 40 bands, he was expected to make it as a jazz or funk player. But in the early 1980s his father asked him to replace John Hart in his own group. By 1984 C.J. switched to accordion, became the leader of the band when Clifton died in December 1987 and led it to stardom under his own (first) name. Open-minded, he introduced modernity to traditional zydeco music, keeping the blues elements, Cajun waltzes and two-steps and mixing them with the jazz and funk rhythms he had practiced before. He also opened the band's repertoire to New Orleans R&B and rock 'n' roll. With Nathan Williams, Lynn August and a

small handful of others he is now the head of one of the best zydeco bands in the business, with dynamic live shows and meaty songs. "We play real songs that tell a story, not this new type of zydeco where they just play one riff over and over and shout out some words and don't even ever change chords," Chenier has said in interviews. C.J. Chenier is a soulful singer, a master of bluesy ballads and strong zydeco tunes and a brilliant accordion player whose infectious rhythm brings everyone on the dance floor wherever he plays.

what to buy: *Too Much Fun* 𝄢𝄢𝄢𝄢 (Alligator, 1995, prod. C.J. Chenier, Bruce Iglauer) offers 13 songs and a lot of variety, with nice arrangements of Clifton's "You Used to Call Me," "Louisiana Two-Step" and "Zydeco Cha Cha," sentimental songs ("Got You on My Mind"), catchy ballads ("Bad Luck," "Richest Man"), energetic material ("Too Much Fun"—indeed!—"Squeaky Wheel" or "Man Smart, Woman Smarter") and blues covers ("Louisiana Down Home Blues"). C.J.'s Red Hot Louisiana Band is partly made of Clifton's ex-partners and guests Vasti Jackson on guitar and the Memphis Horns. His latest album, *The Big Squeeze* 𝄢𝄢𝄢𝄢 (Alligator, 1996, prod. C.J. Chenier, Bruce Iglauer), is equally fine, with more covers of Clifton's blues and zydeco tunes ("No Shoes Zydeco," "Mon Cher 'Tite Bèbè," "The Moon Is Rising"), bluesy ballads ("I Have the Right" or the lovely, slow waltz "Everyday I Have to Cry Some") and fast numbers.

what to buy next: *My Baby Don't Wear No Shoes* 𝄢𝄢𝄢𝄢 (Arhoolie, 1992, prod. Chris Strachwitz, C.J. Chenier) offers a nice mixture of blues and zydeco, while *I Ain't No Playboy* 𝄢𝄢𝄢𝄢 (Slash, 1992, prod. Joe Hardy) is more soul-oriented.

the rest:
Hot Rod 𝄢𝄢𝄢 (Slash, 1989)

influences:
◄◄ Clifton Chenier, Lynn August
►► Lil' Brian, Geno Delafosse

Robert Sacré

Clifton Chenier

Born June 25, 1925, in Opelousas, LA. Died December 12, 1987, in Lafayette, LA.

Clifton Chenier was the undisputed King of Zydeco, the music of the "black Cajuns" of rural Louisiana which mixes traditional Cajun instruments with rhythm & blues. In the early part of the twentieth century, French "lala" musicians played a style of music not much different from their white neighbors, based on the accordion, fiddle, triangle and washboard. Amadee Ardoin and other accordionists added elements of blues to create a distinctive black French vocabulary. Chenier went further, incorporating modern sounds from electric blues and rock. In his words, "I was the first one to put the pep to it." Chenier recorded his first hit, "Ay Tete Fee" (a variation of "Eh, Petite Fille" or "Hey Little Girl") in 1955. By the mid-1960s, however, his career had stalled, until Chris Strachwitz of Arhoolie Records heard him play one night in Houston. That led to a long-term affiliation with Arhoolie Records that resulted in many classic recordings. Chenier was the most popular and most visible exponent of zydeco, playing at festivals and French dances across the U.S. and Europe. Performing for other French-speaking blacks from Louisiana and Texas, Chenier and his band would play for four hours or more without a break, one fast dance tune after another, with an occasional waltz to slow things down. In the mid-1970s, Clifton put together a classic band with blind John Hart on saxophone and Paul Senegal on guitar, who turned the music more in the direction of electric blues. Chenier continued to perform in the 1980s, although he was clearly suffering the effects of the diabetes which eventually led to his death.

what to buy: *Zydeco Dynamite* 🎵🎵🎵🎵 (Rhino, 1993, prod. James Austin) is a two-disc compilation of Chenier's best and most important recordings from 1954–84, when, although past his prime, he won a Grammy. The set draws from many different labels and includes rare singles and unreleased recordings. Here you'll find his first recording, "Louisiana Stomp," a truly stomping instrumental. Chenier's greatest hits are included—from "Eh Petite Fille" in 1955 to the rocking "I'm a Hog for You." There are many more fierce two-steps, as well as slow drags like "The Cat's Dreamin'" and "real" blues tunes like "If I Get Lucky" and "My Soul." This package absolutely establishes Chenier's claim to the crown. "We're goin' way out in the woods, where the crawfish got soul," Chenier tells the crowd at the start of *Live at St. Mark's* 🎵🎵🎵🎵 (Arhoolie, 1989, prod. Chris Strachwitz), recorded live at a "French dance" in Richmond, California, in 1971. This is as close as you'll get to experiencing Chenier in his element. The set list of two-steps and blues is guaranteed to get you on the floor. Chenier's earliest recordings for Arhoolie, *Louisiana Blues and Zydeco* 🎵🎵🎵🎵 (Arhoolie, 1991, prod. Chris Strachwitz), feature bare-bones zydeco, often with Chenier's accordion backed only by drums and rubboard (a metal vest played with bottle openers). This is the source: two-steps and waltzes that pull the body into the music. Extra tracks include a bluesier band with Chenier blowing harmonica. The best record-

ing of Chenier's great band of the mid-1970s, *Bogalusa Blues* 🎵🎵🎵🎵 (Arhoolie, 1990, prod. Chris Strachwitz), offers blues and zydeco in an almost perfect match. John Hart's soulful sax compliments Chenier's most emotional vocals and accordion work. From the opening rocking blues of "One Step at a Time" to the final chorus of "Bogalusa Boogie", this band serves notice that it has created a new form of roots-based music.

what to buy next: All the Arhoolie recordings are worthwhile and have great dance music. *Bon Ton Roulet* 🎵🎵🎵🎵 (Arhoolie, 1990, prod. Chris Strachwitz) includes 11 tunes recorded by Strachwitz in Houston in 1966. Chenier's band that day included his uncle Morris Chenier on fiddle, who adds a strong backwoods element to this terrific set of black French music. The band achieves a perfect balance of deep blues and Cajun exuberance on songs like "Baby, Please Don't Go" and "Blues de Ma Negresse." They even cover the classic Cajun waltz, "Jole Blonde." The remaining 10 tunes come from various sessions and include Chenier's hit "Black Snake Blues" and the blues standard, "Key to the Highway." The Bogalusa Blues band, featuring John Hart on sax and Paul Senegal on guitar, recorded *Out West* 🎵🎵🎵🎵 (Arhoolie, 1991, prod. Chris Strachwitz) in San Francisco, accompanied by Elvin Bishop on electric slide and pianist Steve Miller. Romping R&B tunes like "The Hucklebuck" and "Just Like a Woman" highlight this set, along with driving zydeco dance numbers and three songs from a live broadcast done with a smaller, more traditional group. *Live! At the Long Beach and San Francisco Blues Festivals* 🎵🎵🎵🎵 (Arhoolie, 1993, prod. Chris Strachwitz, Tom Mazzolini) are early-1980s festival dates that showcase Chenier's tight big band, led by his son, C.J., on alto sax. Chenier's instrument sounds more like an electric piano, although there are still flashes of brilliance on tunes like "Louisiana Two-Step."

what to avoid: *I'm Here* 🎵🎵 (Alligator, 1982, prod. Sam Charters) is a listless and dispirited affair on which Chenier sounds tired and sick—he probably was. The recording lacks the punch and verve of the Arhoolie recordings. Too much "Zydeco Disco."

the rest:
Frenchin' the Boogie 🎵🎵🎵 (Verve, 1993)
King of the Bayous 🎵🎵🎵 (Arhoolie, 1993)
Zodico Blues & Boogie 🎵🎵🎵 (Specialty, 1993)

worth searching for: On the only-on-vinyl *Boogie in Black and White* 🎵🎵🎵🎵 (Jin, 1976) Chenier and Rod Bernard combine for an enjoyable set of blues and swamp pop featuring Warren Storm on drums.

influences:

◀◀ Amadee Ardoin, Alphonse "Bois Sec" Ardoin

▶▶ Buckwheat Zydeco, C.J. Chenier and every other zydeco accordionist

David Feld

Chicken Shack

Formed 1965, in the Birmingham, England, area.

Stan Webb, guitar, vocals; Andy Sylvester, bass (1965–70); Dave Bidwell, drums (1965–70); Christine Perfect, keyboards (1967–69).

Chicken Shack was part of a British blues and R&B scene whose development, along with that of the more acoustically-oriented skiffle, had its roots in the English take on Dixieland and New Orleans music, the so-called trad jazz. Both Muddy Waters and Big Bill Broonzy had performed in England during the 1950s, and their influence showed up in the work of the scene's progenitors, Alexis Korner and Cyril Davies, who together formed the backbone of the loose aggregation known as Blues Incorporated. This group gave woodshedding opportunity to players who went on to form mainstays of the scene, most importantly the Rolling Stones and John Mayall's Bluesbreakers. These groups, along with the Animals and the Yardbirds, formed the movement's vanguard in the early 1960s, and in turn provided the impetus, and sometimes members for, the scene's second generation, which featured groups like Cream, Fleetwood Mac, Savoy Brown, Ten Years After, Climax Blues Band and Chicken Shack. Chicken Shack, which reportedly took its name from the poultry coop that was the group's early practice space, helped popularize, by imitation, the Chicago blues form for British and European audiences, taking a version of Etta James' "I'd Rather Go Blind" to the U.K. Top 20. Founder Stan Webb, heavily influenced by Freddy King, was a decent if derivative guitarist, but his thin wavering vocals were a taste some never acquired. In its heyday, the group was perhaps better served by the vocals of Christine Perfect, who as Christine McVie went on to megastardom in a later, poppier incarnation of Fleetwood Mac. After 1970, Webb continued Chicken Shack with a variety of side players, including Blodwyn Pig bassist Andy Pyle.

worth searching for: Not much of a recorded legacy is left at this late date. Worth seeking out, however, is the British import *The Collection* ♫♫♫♫ (Castle Communications, 1988, prod. Mike Vernon), which presents the best of Chicken Shack's four albums for Vernon's Blue Horizon label. It features several Perfect songs and includes the bizarre between-track patter from the group's second album *OK, Ken*. Unfortunately missing is Chicken Shack's over-the-top version of the Don Nix song, "Going Down."

influences:

◀◀ Freddie King, Blues Incorporated, Rolling Stones

▶▶ Savoy Brown, Fleetwood Mac

Michael Dixon

Eric Clapton

Born March 30, 1945, in Surrey, England.

Eric Clapton's reputation as a great guitarist and a towering figure has overtaken reality to such a large extent that it is nearly impossible to consider his music objectively. Which may help explain how Clapton has remained so revered over the last 20 years as he has released one middling album after another—with occasional forays into outright wretchedness. Whatever one thinks of his pop efforts, Clapton's prowess as a blues guitarist is particularly distorted. His work on *Bluesbreakers—John Mayall with Eric Clapton* was certainly groundbreaking, but more because it revealed that a young white man could indeed master the past (in his case, Freddie King, specifically) than because it trod much new ground. Clapton's subsequent work with Cream and Blind Faith is truly brilliant and groundbreaking, and his sole studio album with Derek & the Dominos, *Layla and Other Assorted Love Songs,* is a certifiable masterpiece. His first few solo albums range from very good to pretty good, as he seemed to be settling into a laid-back, singer-songwriter groove, something which he did pretty well, even if it displeased old fans waiting to hear fiery, innovative guitar soloing. In retrospect, these early and mid-1970s albums, most of which were largely dismissed at the time, sound like high points. Since then, he has made some truly despicable records. In 1989, Clapton seemed content with the comfortable plateau he had reached, actually titling one album *Journeyman.* His next release, *Unplugged,* however, catapulted him to international stardom greater than any he had previously known. Clapton *can* still play, and he continues to sparkle sporadically, largely on guest appearances, like Chuck Berry's *Hail, Hail Rock and Roll,* Gatemouth Brown's *Long Way Home* and Jimmie Vaughn's *Tribute to Stevie Ray Vaughan,* but he seems to have long since stalled creatively.

what to buy: Clapton's work on *Bluesbreakers—John Mayall with Eric Clapton* ♫♫♫♫ (Deram, 1966, prod. Mike Vernon)

proved that a white boy could indeed play the blues, giving confidence to countless palefaced prodigies. On Derek & the Dominos' *Layla and Other Assorted Love Songs* 𝄞𝄞𝄞𝄞 (Polydor, 1970, prod. Tom Dowd), Clapton was spurred to perhaps the greatest playing of his career by the presence of Duane Allman. The results speak for themselves: a blues-rock classic. *461 Ocean Boulevard* 𝄞𝄞𝄞 (Polydor, 1974, prod. Tom Dowd) and *Slowhand* 𝄞𝄞𝄞 (Polydor, 1977, prod. Glyn Johns) are the best of Clapton's mellow-period albums.

what to buy next: Though the fourth CD is filled with padding, illustrating Clapton's decline, *Crossroads* 𝄞𝄞𝄞 (Polydor, 1988, prod. Bill Levenson) is pretty much a model boxed set. Clapton's self-titled debut album *Eric Clapton* 𝄞𝄞𝄞 (Polydor, 1970, prod. Delaney Bramlett) is loose and filled with great playing, though in many ways it sounds more like a Delaney Bramlett album than a Clapton recording.

what to avoid: *Behind the Sun* 𝄞 (Duck/Warner Bros., 1985, prod. Phil Collins) and *August* 𝄞 (Duck/Warner Bros., 1986, prod. Phil Collins) are vile albums: soulless, pandering, overdone and inexcusable. *From the Cradle* 𝄞𝄞𝄞 (Warner Bros., 1994, prod. Russ Titelman, Eric Clapton) was hailed as Clapton's return to his blues roots and includes lots of great guitar playing. Unfortunately, his all-English backing band wouldn't know a groove if it fell into one, and Clapton's singing is overemotive, patronizing blues belting at its worst. For lessons on how to effectively cover blues classics, he should listen back to his own versions of Robert Johnson's "Steady Rollin' Man" (*461 Ocean Boulevard*) Elmore James' "The Sky Is Crying" (*There's One in Every Crowd*) or Arthur Crudup's "Mean Old Frisco" (*Slowhand*), where he took them at his own speed and made them his own, rather than slavishly—and pointlessly—mimicking the originals.

the rest:

The Rainbow Concert 𝄞𝄞𝄞 (Polydor, 1973/1995)
There's One in Every Crowd 𝄞𝄞𝄞 (Polydor, 1974)
E.C. Was Here 𝄞𝄞𝄞 (Polydor, 1975)
No Reason to Cry 𝄞𝄞𝄞 (Polydor, 1976)
Backless 𝄞𝄞𝄞 (Polydor, 1978)
Just One Night 𝄞𝄞𝄞 (Polydor, 1980)
Another Ticket 𝄞𝄞𝄞 (Polydor, 1981)
Timepieces (The Best of Eric Clapton) 𝄞𝄞𝄞𝄞 (Polydor, 1982)
Money and Cigarettes 𝄞𝄞 (Duck/Warner Bros., 1983)

Eric Clapton (© Ken Settle)

Timepieces Vol. II: Live in the Seventies 𝄞𝄞𝄞 (Polydor, 1983)
Journeyman 𝄞𝄞𝄞 (Reprise, 1989)
24 Nights 𝄞𝄞𝄞 (Reprise, 1991)
Rush 𝄞𝄞𝄞 (Reprise, 1992)
Unplugged 𝄞𝄞𝄞 (Reprise, 1992)
Crossroads 2 𝄞𝄞𝄞 (Polydor, 1996)

influences:

◀◀ Albert King, Freddie King, Jimi Hendrix, the Band, J.J. Cale
▶▶ Stevie Ray Vaughan, Allman Brothers Band

Alan Paul

W.C. Clark

Born Wesley Curley Clark, November 16, 1939, in Austin, TX.

A skilled mechanic as well as the bane of Texas crappies and sand bass, W.C. Clark is called the Godfather of Austin blues. Denny Freeman, the brothers Vaughan, Doyle Bramhall and Freddie Walden were all Dallasites who moved to Austin and helped establish the city as a blues mecca, but Clark had been there all along. He came up watching Big Pete Pierson, T.D. Bell, and Erbie Bowser at the Victory Grille and entered music full-time with Blues Boy Hubbard and the Jets at Charlie's Playhouse before taking the road with Joe Tex. He wed and settled down to the domestic life with a day gig as a mechanic. Not for long. Stevie Ray Vaughan had gotten acquainted with him and was determined to pester him back into the blues biz. With Vaughan on guitar and Clark on bass, Triple Threat formed, and with hard-boozing Lou Ann Barton on vocals, played all over Texas, Louisiana, Oklahoma and Arkansas. Post-SRV, Clark formed the W.C. Clark Blues Revue, though it's anybody's guess who'll be in it on a given gig. Clark is tremendously talented and is a true band leader (not just a frontman). A fluid guitarist with a high but lustrous, full-bodied voice, he can access a great variety of material, as able with Memphis-style soul as well as with get-down blues.

what to buy: *Heart of Gold* 🎵🎵🎵 (Black Top, 1994, prod. Hammond Scott, Mark Kazanoff) is classic Clark, kicking off with his own, irrepressible soul-romp "Heart of Gold," ranging through Benny Latimore's "Let's Straighten It Out" to the oily blues, "Come Back." Some cuts feature horns (arranged by Kazanoff), others thick 'n' rich B3 from talented Riley Osborne. Clark gets high marks for singing, guitar playing and songwriting, and his accompaniment is top-notch.

what to buy next: The Godfather scores again with *Texas Soul* 🎵🎵🎵🎵 (Black Top, 1996, prod. Hammond Scott, Mark Kazanoff), a blend of cool covers (Roy Hawkins' hard blues, "Why Do Things Happen to Me?" and "Funny How Time Slips Away" by fellow Texan Willie Nelson), and well-wrought originals ("Reminiscing"). Clark sings sublimely, again accompanied by fine musicians from the Austin talent pool.

influences:

◀◀ Albert Collins, T.D. Bell

▶▶ Jimmie Vaughan, Mike Campbell, Charlie Sexton

Tim Schuller

William Clarke

Born March 21, 1951, in Inglewood, CA. Died November 3, 1996, in Fresno, CA.

A student and close friend of George "Harmonica" Smith and a veteran of the West Coast blues scene, William Clarke developed a reputation for punchy, high-energy recordings that mixed elements of jazz with blues and swing. The full extent of his talent had yet to be realized when he died at age 45. The son of Ken-

tucky parents who relocated to Los Angeles, Clarke immersed himself in the club scene of the L.A. ghetto, where he played with Smokey Wilson and Shakey Jake Harris. In 1977 he began a longtime friendship and apprenticeship with Smith and developed a reputation throughout southern California for his solid, innovative harp playing. Clarke released five albums on small, regional independent labels throughout the late 1970s and 1980s before signing with Alligator. Clarke continued to fuse jazz and blues, but health problems combined with a rigorous touring schedule exacted their toll. Although he had trimmed down his massive frame and stopped drinking after a bout with congestive heart failure in Indianapolis in early 1996, he died as a result of complications from a bleeding ulcer later that year.

what to buy: His Alligator debut, *Blowin' Like Hell* 🎵🎵🎵🎵 (Alligator, 1990, prod. William Clarke), features "Must Be Jelly," the Handy winner for blues song of 1991.

what to buy next: Clarke's last album, *The Hard Way* 🎵🎵🎵 (Alligator, 1996, prod. William Clarke), is arguably his furthest leap into jazz, without sacrificing his trademark swing blues and jump blues rhythms.

the rest:

Serious Intentions 🎵🎵🎵 (Alligator, 1992)
Groove Time 🎵🎵🎵 (Alligator, 1994)

worth searching for: Clarke's indie label recordings prior to signing with Alligator are out of print and hard to come by, especially since his death at the end of 1996. Nevertheless, his early recordings between 1978 and 1989 garnered him no less than six Handy Awards. Be on the lookout for *Hitting Heavy* 🎵🎵🎵 (Good Time, 1978), *Blues from Los Angeles* 🎵🎵🎵 (Hitting Heavy, 1980), *Can't You Hear Me Calling* 🎵🎵🎵 (Watch Dog, 1980), *Tip of the Top* 🎵🎵🎵 (Satch, 1987), *Rockin' the Boat* 🎵🎵🎵 (Riviera, 1988) and *Smokey Wilson & the William Clarke Band* 🎵🎵🎵 (Black Magic, 1989). Clarke had been negotiating with Alligator to release a compilation CD of his early work, but there has been no word on the project since his death.

influences:

◀◀ George "Harmonica" Smith, Eddie "Cleanhead" Vinson, Big Joe Turner

John C. Bruening

Otis Clay

Born February 11, 1942, in Waxhaw, MS.

Few artists straddle the line separating the sacred and the secular like legendary vocalist Otis Clay. Clay began singing in church in his hometown at age four. After moving to Chicago in 1957, Clay sang in various gospel groups before going secular in 1963 to record his hits, "That's How It Is" and "I'm Satisfied," for the One-der-ful label. From there, he switched to Atlantic's Cotillion and, in 1971, made his pivotal move to the Memphis-based Hi. It was at Hi that Clay created some of his greatest and most commercially successful work, and his run at Hi lasted until the onset of disco. Clay remained true to his gospel and deep soul roots. His refusal to compromise his music paid off when his voice was heard by soul/blues fans overseas. Tours of Europe followed in the late 1970s and early 1980s, and Clay was able to establish himself solidly in Japan. In 1985 Clay returned to popularity in the U.S. Clay remains one of Chicago's strongest and most moving vocalists, performing around the world in a variety of settings, including blues festivals, clubs and churches.

what to buy: In recent years, Cream/Hi Records issued several magnificent compilations of Clay's early-1970s work for Hi. Among the best of these is *The 45's* 𝄫𝄫𝄫𝄫 (Cream/Hi, 1993, prod. Willie Mitchell), which captures Clay in the years 1971–74, backed by Hi luminaries Charles, Teenie and Leroy Hodges and Howard Grimes. Few recorded offerings of Memphis soul are more powerful. Included are "Brand New Thing," "I Didn't Know the Meaning of Pain" and "If I Could Reach Out." Another sterling collection of Clay's Hi work is found on *The Best of Otis Clay—The Hi Records Years* 𝄫𝄫𝄫𝄫 (The Right Stuff, 1996, prod. Willie Mitchell). *Soul Man—Live in Japan* 𝄫𝄫𝄫𝄫 (Bullseye Blues, 1991, prod. Hiroshi Asada) captures Clay onstage backed again by ace session men from Hi. Clay and crew work their way expertly through classics, including Al Green's "Here I Am (Come Take Me)," "A Nickel and a Nail," "Precious Precious" and the gospel "His Precious Love."

what to buy next: Although there is considerable duplication among the current bumper crop of Clay reissues on Cream/Hi, almost all of the material is stunning. Also among the better of these packages is *That's How It Is* 𝄫𝄫𝄫𝄪 (Cream/Hi, 1994, prod. Willie Mitchell) and *Willie Clayton and Otis Clay* 𝄫𝄫𝄫𝄪 (Cream/Hi, 1995, prod. Willie Mitchell). Clay's versatility as a singer is best displayed on his studio debut for the Bullseye Blues label, *I'll Treat You Right* 𝄫𝄫𝄫𝄫 (Bullseye Blues, 1992, prod. Ron Levy). Clay and several of his colleagues from the Hi period (Grimes and Leroy and Charles Hodges) work through the solid soul of "I'll Take You to Heaven Tonight" as well as the bluesy, Lowell Fulson composition "Thanks a Lot" before hitting the gospel of "Children Gone Astray." The listener can hear

Clay indulging his gospel leanings more thoroughly on *The Gospel Truth* 𝄫𝄫𝄫𝄫 (Blind Pig, 1993, prod. Otis Clay).

what to avoid: Mediocre material and poor production can hobble even a master like Clay, and that's what happened on *You Are My Life* 𝄫𝄫 (Waylo/MMS, 1995, prod. Willie Mitchell). Released originally on Waylo in 1989 under the title *Watch Me Now*, Mitchell presents Clay in an urban contemporary format. As a result, Clay's gifts as a vocalist—sensitivity and soulfulness—are blunted by the concussion of drum machines and the mechanized whirl of synthesizers.

worth searching for: Originally released in Japan on vinyl, *The Only Way Is Up* 𝄫𝄫𝄫 (B.L.U.E.S. R&B, 1985, prod. Otis Clay, Benjamin Wright, Troy Thompson) finds Clay in a funky, hard-driving session. Hardcore collectors will also want to seek Clay's single gems for the One-der-ful label, *I'm Satisfied* (One-der-ful, 1963, prod. Maurice Dollison) and *That's How It Is (When You're in Love)* (One-der-ful, 1963, prod. Eddie Silvers).

influences:

◀◀ O.V. Wright

▶▶ Robert Cray

Steven Sharp

Eddy Clearwater

Born Edward Harrington, January 10, 1935, in Macon, MS.

Eddy Clearwater has been active on the Chicago blues scene since the early 1950s and, along with Magic Sam and Otis Rush, was one of the architects of the so-called West Side sound. In contrast to his B.B. King-inspired contemporaries, Clearwater's style relies more heavily on country and western-derived rhythm guitar patterns and phrasing. His is a unique amalgamation of country, deep Delta blues, gospel, R&B and pop influences—a sound Clearwater himself refers to as "rock-a-blues." A survey of a few song titles, "Hill Billy Blues," "A Minor Cha-cha," "Twist Like This," "A Little Bit of Blues, a Little Bit of Rock and Roll," hints at the multi-dimensional nature of his varied repertoire. Many of his recordings reveal a strong Chuck Berry influence. Like Berry, Clearwater has always been adept at generating the kind of excitement craved by young rock and rollers. Unlike Berry, however, Clearwater is also a master of dark, brooding blues such as "I Came up the Hard Way" and "Bad Dream." This wide range of sensitive expression sets him apart from almost any other blues singer in Chicago and has secured him a loyal following of many different kinds of listeners.

what to buy: *The Chief* 🎵🎵🎵 (Rooster Blues, 1980, prod. Jim O'Neal) is his strong debut, also the first for *Living Blues* founder Jim O'Neal's Rooster Blues label. The songs, mostly originals, are an assortment of Chuck Berry-styled rockers ("I Wouldn't Lay My Guitar Down"), harrowing blues ("Bad Dream," "Blues for Breakfast") and soul-blues hybrids ("Lazy Woman"). *Real Good Time-Live!* 🎵🎵🎵 (Rooster Blues, 1991, prod. Jim O'Neal) is as passionate and intense a live recording as you're likely to hear. Accompanied by a stellar band of Chicago-based musicians, Clearwater turns in superb versions of original songs, like "Real Good Time"/"Cool Water" and "Party at My House" to the delight of a crowd of 600 yelping college students.

what to buy next: *Blues Hang Out* 🎵🎵🎵 (Evidence, 1989, prod. Disques Black & Blue) is another strong set of sharp-edged shuffles ("Blues Hang Out," "Mayor Daley Blues"), minor-key blues ballads (the autobiographical "I Came up the Hard Way"), and pumping rockers ("Boogie Woogie Baby"). Big Time Sarah is a featured vocalist on three of the songs. *Help Yourself* 🎵🎵🎵 (Blind Pig, 1992, prod. Jerry Del Giudice, Michael Freeman) covers much of the same ground, with cousin Carey Bell lending harmonica support on several tracks.

what to avoid: *Boogie My Blues Away* 🎵🎵 (Delmark, 1995, prod. Ralph Bass) is a reissue of a 1977 session with Bass originally intended for release on T.K. Records as one of 10 albums for a proposed Chicago blues series. The album was recorded in one day without playbacks. Need I say more?

the rest:
Flimdoozie 🎵🎵🎵 (Rooster Blues, 1986)
2x9 🎵🎵🎵 (Fan Club, 1992)
Chicago Blues Session Vol. 23 🎵🎵🎵 (Wolf, 1992)
Live at the Kingston Mines 1978 🎵🎵🎵 (Fan Club, 1992)
Black Night 🎵🎵🎵 (Storyville, 1995)
Mean Case of the Blues 🎵🎵🎵 (Cleartone, 1996)

worth searching for: His earliest singles (made for his uncle, the Rev. Houston Harrington, on his Atomic-H label) are on *Chicago Ain't Nothin' but a Blues Band* 🎵🎵🎵🎵 (Delmark, 1972, prod. Robert Koester), along with other fine cuts from Sunnyland Slim, J.T. Brown, Jo Jo Williams, Harmonica George and Morris Pejoe. Other early singles, including the original version of "Cool Water," are gathered up on *LaSalle Chicago Blues Recordings, Vol. 2* 🎵🎵🎵 (Wolf, 1991, prod. Jump Jackson).

Otis Clay (© Linda Vartoogian)

influences:
◀◀ Chuck Berry, Muddy Waters, Otis Rush
▶▶ Will Crosby, Lurrie Bell

D. Thomas Moon

Albert Clemens
See: Cripple Clarence Lofton

Willie Cobbs
Born July 15, 1932, in Monroe, AR.

Cobbs' story began with one song, "You Don't Love Me," and appears to be heading toward a happy ending. The harpist is one of many blues (also pop, R&B and soul) songwriters to pen a bona-fide classic, then essentially vanish for years from the music industry. Many bigger names have recorded his song, including the Allman Brothers Band, Junior Wells and John Hammond Jr., but Cobbs channeled all his royalty payments back into studio sessions. Plagued by an early Vee-Jay executive's mean-spirited comment that Cobbs sounded too much like the label's hitmaker Jimmy Reed, he drifted in and out of blues. He recorded singles on obscure labels, opened a club and a barbecue joint but didn't really become a concert draw until his early-1990s resurgence— his more recent albums have a jump in their step, and Cobbs (who had roles in the movies *Mississippi Masala* and *Memphis*) is happy to finally be heard.

what to buy: *Down to Earth* 🎵🎵🎵 (Rooster Blues, 1994, prod. Willie Cobbs, Jim O'Neal, Patty Johnson) is Cobbs' nice comeback album, finding the singer in excellent voice and including, of course, a re-reading of "You Don't Love Me."

the rest:
Hey Little Girl 🎵🎵 (Wilco, 1991)

worth searching for: If you come across Cobbs' original 1960 version of "You Don't Love Me," by all means, buy it. Cobbs himself compiled his early singles on a tape released in the early 1990s. A more realistic bet is finding *Mr. C's Blues in the Groove!* 🎵🎵🎵🎵 (Mina, 1986), which collects Cobbs' singles on the obscure Bracob, Record Gallery and Wilco labels.

influences:
◀◀ Jimmy Reed, Little Walter, Sonny Boy Williamson I, Rufus Thomas
▶▶ Junior Wells, Allman Brothers Band, John Hammond Jr., Charlie Musselwhite, Slim Harpo

Steve Knopper

Deborah Coleman

Born in Portsmouth, VA.

In a genre whose biggest shadows belong to Bessie Smith, Billie Holiday, Etta James and Koko Taylor, it's astounding that so few young African-American women are willing to front their own blues bands. Coleman is even more rare—she's a guitarslinger in the style of Buddy Guy, Jimi Hendrix and Stevie Ray Vaughan, and her solid vocals come across almost as an afterthought. An excellent songwriter whose musical style is similar to Paul Shaffer's bouncy jazz on *The Late Show with David Letterman,* this mother and former nurse and electrician seems destined to break blues guitar's inexplicable gender barrier.

what to buy: *I Can't Lose* ♫♫♫ (Blind Pig, 1997, prod. Michael Freeman) contains the requisite Billie Holiday song ("Fine and Mellow") and seven originals dealing with love, relationships and, of course, the blues. The man-hungry rap trio Salt-N-Pepa (not to mention Bessie Smith) would be happy with the salacious "Roll with Me" and the admiring "The Man Is Mine."

what to buy next: Coleman's debut, *Takin' a Stand* ♫♫♫ (New Moon, 1994), gave her performing credibility, which led to on-stage performances with Delbert McClinton, Lonnie Brooks and others. Her distinct style, which comes across so clearly on *I Can't Lose,* hadn't yet emerged on the debut.

influences:

◀◀ Jimi Hendrix, Albert Collins, Buddy Guy, Paul Shaffer, James Brown

Steve Knopper

Albert Collins

Born October 3, 1932, in Leona, TX. Died November 24, 1993, in Las Vegas, NV.

It's cool to like Texas now, but not long ago much of the U.S. regarded it as a boondock too full of trailer trash and chainsaw murderers to warrant visiting. This, in spite of its being turf to a bluesman the caliber of Albert Collins, who first came to light with "Frosty" (Kangaroo, 1958), a regional hit that established the "cool sound" he got from his Telecaster. He did some more obscure 45s and cut LPs for Imperial and Blue Thumb but didn't really hit his stride until he signed with Alligator in 1978. Collins got most of his press for his shrill, icy guitar tactics, but he also sang well, was a tremendous showman and wrote some brilliant (and often brilliantly witty) material. Collins and his Icebreakers (who at various times included A.C. Reed, Aron Burton and Debbie Davies) toured relentlessly, bowling over nation after nation and developing a rep as a bitch to have to play after on a show. Few artists as prolific as Collins have anywhere near his consistency of high quality on their recordings; he simply never recorded a dud. Even on the inevitable live CDs on which his band members were all Euros he'd probably never rehearsed with, he himself sounded great. His death (from cancer) was shockingly premature, but toast his life in the time-honored Texas way: pound down a couple cold ones, give the volume knob an injudicious crank and groove to his indomitable music.

what to buy: *Frostbite* ♫♫♫♫ (Alligator, 1980, prod. Bruce Iglauer, Dick Shurman, Casey Jones) has tons of all the elements that made Collins great: heaps of his vaunted guitar intensity, cool covers (Johnnie Taylor's "If You Love Me Like You Say," which he often performed live, and a killing rendition of Johnny Morissette's "Brick") and humor ("Don't Go Reaching across My Plate"). There's also an absolute masterpiece called "Snowed In," wherein the Texan describes trying to start his car in an icy Chicago winter. He creates guitar sound effects with jaw-dropping accuracy, particularly that suspenseful grinding you hear when you crank your engine and it sounds like it'll be a no-go. This goes on for 9:12. When Collins finally gets "the car" started, it's an almost orgiastic liftoff—and one of the best items in the Alligator catalog. Blues pundits of yore dissed Collins' Imperial output, which is now universally respected for its concise but magnificent instrumentals and sly vocal performances. Beginning in 1969 he cut three LPs for the label, and *Complete Imperial Recordings* ♫♫♫♫ (EMI, 1991, prod. Bill Hall), a 100-minute, two-disc set with extensive liner notes and photos, comprises them all. Quintessential Collins in concert is *Frozen Alive* ♫♫♫♫ (Alligator, 1981, prod. Bruce Iglauer, Dick Shurman), on which he is backed by a kick-butt fivesome that includes wallpaper-peeling saxophonist A.C. Reed.

what to buy next: Three of the same Icebreakers present on *Frozen Alive* (Reed, drummer Casey Jones, bassist J.B. Gayten) were on board when Collins cut the torrid Tokyo outing *Live in Japan* ♫♫♫♫ (Alligator, 1984, prod. Bruce Iglauer). "Tired Man" is a standout, and there's a 9:10 "Stormy Monday" that's so forceful you forget how shop-worn the song is.

the rest:

Truckin' with Albert Collins ♫♫♫♫ (Blue Thumb, 1969/MCA, 1991)

Albert Collins (© Jack Vartoogian)

Ice Pickin' ♪♪♪ (Alligator, 1978)

Don't Lose Your Cool ♪♪♪♪ (Alligator, 1983)

Cold Snap ♪♪♪♪ (Alligator, 1986)

(With Robert Cray and Johnny Copeland) *Showdown* ♪♪♪ (Alligator, 1986)

Molten Ice ♪♪♪ (Red Lightnin', 1992)

Collins Mix (The Best of Albert Collins) ♪♪♪♪ (Point Blank, 1993)

Albert Collins & Barrelhouse Live ♪♪♪♪ (Munich, 1995)

Live '92–93 ♪♪♪♪ (Pointblank, 1996)

influences:

◀◀ Willow Brown, Clarence "Gatemouth" Brown, T-Bone Walker

▶▶ Mark May, Anson Funderburgh

Tim Schuller

Sam Collins

Born August 11, 1887, near Kentwood, LA. Died October 20, 1949, in Chicago, IL.

Known as "Crying Sam Collins" for the pitiful wailing voice he used, Sam Collins was one of the earliest blues slide guitar practitioners and among the first Mississippi Delta artists to record. Playing in slide style so crude he sometimes sounded out of tune, Collins' Delta pedigree was unmistakable. Some of his 22 tunes seemed to hearken back to the post-Civil War era. "Riverside Blues" sounds like it could have been played in a Matthew Brady landscape. Like many of the earliest bluesmen, the details of Collins' life are sparse. Collins roamed for a spell with McComb bluesman Joe Holmes, who recorded under the alias King Solomon Hill. Blues researchers once thought the two men were the same—largely because both employed an eerie falsetto. But Collins recorded first, waxing the first version of "The Midnight Special" in 1927, preceding Leadbelly's better-known rendition by several years. Almost all of Collins' recordings were made in Richmond, Indiana, or Chicago. By 1931, his recording career was over, and he soon moved to Chicago, where he finished out his days in silence.

what to buy: All of Collins' moaned recordings are on *Sam Collins 1927–31* ♪♪♪♪ (Document, 1991, prod. Johnny Parth), some in clear pressings, some clouded by worn 78 vinyl.

the rest:

Jailhouse Blues ♪♪♪ (Yazoo, 1990)

influences:

◀◀ King Solomon Hill

Steve Braun

Joanna Connor

Born August 31, 1962, in Brooklyn, NY.

Joanna Connor is part of that elite group of female guitarists playing in a blues-based vein which includes Bonnie Raitt, Rory Block, Deborah Coleman, Debbie Davies and Sue Foley. Of these, Connor rocks the hardest and is the most muscular and heavy player. Connor plays blues-based rock with an aggressive slide style, finely-honed chops and a sultry, husky, singing voice. Raised in central Massachusetts by her bohemian mother (who exposed her daughter to many different types of music), she recalls seeing Bonnie Raitt in a coffee house at age 7. Originally a saxophonist, her developing style incorporated multiple influences—Chicago blues a la Buddy Guy and Luther Allison, the Texas blues of Freddie King, funky, energetic R&B and late-1960s, early-1970s rock. She moved to Chicago, backing other players before putting together her own band.

what to buy: *Big Girl Blues* ♪♪♪♪ (Blind Pig, 1996, prod. Joanna Connor) is the fully realized effort of an outspoken, self-assured woman. It showcases her affinity for late-1960s southern blues-rock on songs like the title track, and for *Let It Bleed*-era Stones, on the simply terrific ode to her son, "Sweet Baby." But Connor does more than merely imitate, bringing a convincing fire and power to these borrowed styles that claim them as her own while updating them.

what to buy next: *Believe It!* ♪♪♪♪ (Blind Pig, 1989, prod. Joanna Connor, Jerry Del Giudice, Michael Rasfeld) finds her playing for keeps mostly on well-chosen covers. Connor does fiery Texas-style blues (Freddie King's "Texas Flyer" and her own "He's Mine") and hard-edged remakes of soul and R&B classics like Aretha Franklin's "Dr. Feelgood" and Ann Peeble's "Somebody's on Your Case." A strong first effort.

the rest:

Fight ♪♪♪ (Blind Pig, 1992)

influences:

◀◀ Bonnie Raitt, Freddie King, Luther Allison, Allman Brothers Band, Rolling Stones

▶▶ Deborah Coleman

Michael Dixon

Ry Cooder

Born Ryland Peter Cooder, March 15, 1947, in Los Angeles, CA.

Like so many of his guitar-playing contemporaries—Jimmy Page, Jeff Beck and Eric Clapton among them—Cooder started his career playing blues and folk songs in the early 1960s. Instead of becoming a rock 'n' roll superstar, though, he slowly developed his skills and built his reputation as a thorough musicologist and reputable session musician. He was in a few bands early in his career, including one with soul singer Jackie DeShannon, another with fellow blues fanatic Taj Mahal, in the short-lived-but-influential Rising Sons, and one with the musically complex lunatic Captain Beefheart's band c. 1967. Cooder's many solo albums, particularly 1976's *Chicken Skin Music* and 1974's *Paradise and Lunch*, have a raw, refreshing sense of humor, and they're almost always rooted in 1950s rockabilly and harder-than-they-sound guitar licks. Possibly because Cooder has never been willing to stick to one style for very long, even his beloved blues and rockabilly, he has stretched out much more on movie soundtracks than he ever did with consistency on his solo recordings. Master of slide guitar, mandolin, banjo and plenty of other, more exotic instruments, Cooder's interests lurched from American rockabilly to Tex-Mex to Hawaiian "snap-key" guitar music, and he expanded his breadth with each new style. Beginning with the Rolling Stones' landmark *Let It Bleed* album—Cooder claims to have come up with the "Honky Tonk Women" riff—he became a prolific sideman, working on albums by Little Feat, Randy Newman, John Hiatt, Arlo Guthrie and Van Dyke Parks. He delved into soundtrack albums, most notably *Paris, Texas*, *The Long Riders* and *Trespass* (in which he plays behind Ice Cube and Ice-T in what could be the first example of rap-blues fusion). He served dutifully in Little Village, a quick-lived supergroup featuring fellow session musician extraordinaire Jim Keltner, bassist Nick Lowe and Hiatt, and he collaborated with West African guitarist Ali Farka Toure on 1993's superb *A Meeting by the River*. The Rising Sons never led to superstardom like the Yardbirds did for Jimmy Page and the Rolling Stones did for Keith Richards, but Cooder has managed to build a career with longevity and the respect of his peers.

what to buy: *Paradise and Lunch* 𝄢𝄢𝄢𝄢 (Reprise, 1974, prod. Lenny Waronker, Russ Titelman) includes the heart warming "Mexican Divorce" and a fun, definitive version of "Ditty Wa Ditty." *Chicken Skin Music* 𝄢𝄢𝄢𝄢 (Reprise, 1976, prod. Ry Cooder) predated Paul Simon's *Graceland* by incorporating Tex-Mex accordion hero Flaco Jiminez (who helps with a killer "Stand by Me") and Hawaiian slack-key guitarist Gabby Pahinui into Cooder's more American-sounding rock 'n' roll. Both *Into the Purple Valley* 𝄢𝄢𝄢 (Reprise, 1972, prod. Lenny Waronker, Jim Dickinson), with its Johnny Cash, Woody Guthrie and Jackie Wilson songs, and *Bop Till You Drop* 𝄢𝄢𝄢 (Warner Bros., 1979,

Albert Collins

song
T-Bone Shuffle

album
(with Robert Cray &
Johnny Copeland) Showdown! (Alligator)

instrument
Guitar

monster solo

prod. Ry Cooder), with "Down in Hollywood," showcase Cooder's fun-loving history-of-rock side. Finally, his collaborations with world-music heavies V.M. Bhatt on *A Meeting by the River* 𝄢𝄢𝄢𝄢 (Water Lily Acoustics, 1993, prod. Kavichandran Alexander) and with Ali Fark Toure on *Talking Timbuktu* 𝄢𝄢𝄢𝄢 (Hannibal, 1994), round out any full Cooder collection.

what to buy next: The two-disc *Music by Ry Cooder* 𝄢𝄢𝄢𝄢 (Warner Bros., 1995, prod. Ry Cooder, Joachim Cooder) is such a thorough collection of Cooder's movie music it saves you the trouble of combing through his uneven soundtrack albums. Individually, his better soundtracks are *Paris, Texas* 𝄢𝄢𝄢 (Warner Bros., 1984, prod. Ry Cooder), *Johnny Handsome* 𝄢𝄢𝄢 (Warner Bros., 1989, prod. Ry Cooder), *The Long Riders* 𝄢𝄢𝄢 (Warner Bros., 1980, prod. Ry Cooder), *The Border* 𝄢𝄢𝄢𝄢 (Backstreet, 1981), with interesting collaborations with Hiatt, Freddie Fender and the long-lost Sam Samudio, and the much-maligned *Crossroads* 𝄢𝄢𝄢 (Warner Bros., 1986, prod. Ry Cooder), a terrible

movie which features great Cooder pure-blues slide work with fellow string enthusiast David Lindley.

what to avoid: Cooder's experiments and ambitions occasionally backfire, especially on the tedious *Jazz* ♫♫ (Warner Bros., 1978, prod. Ry Cooder, Joseph Byrd), which has interesting ideas, like a cover of the 1880 folk song "The Dream," but nothing else to recommend. He sounds plain bored on *Get Rhythm* ♫♫ (Warner Bros., 1987, prod. Ry Cooder), despite the presence of old friend Jiminez and the always-unusual Van Dyke Parks. Also not up to snuff is his solo debut, *Ry Cooder* ♫ (Reprise, 1970, prod. Van Dyke Parks, Ry Cooder).

the rest:

Boomer's Story ♫♫♫ (Reprise, 1972)
Show Time ♫♫♫ (Warner Bros., 1977)
Borderline ♫♫ (Warner Bros., 1980)
The Slide Area ♫♫ (Warner Bros., 1982)
Alamo Bay ♫♫ (Slash, 1985)
Blue City ♫♫ (Warner Bros., 1986)
Geronimo: An American Legend ♫♫♫ (Warner Bros., 1993)
Trespass ♫♫♫ (Sire, 1994)

worth searching for: The Little Village debut, *Little Village* ♫♫♫ (Reprise, 1992, prod. Little Village), contained a few funny, rocking moments, including the nice "Solar Sex Panel" and the John Hiatt vehicle "She Runs Hot"—but it didn't come close to matching the Hiatt-Cooder-Lowe-Keltner inspiration on Hiatt's *Bring the Family* album. And the long-collected rarity *Rising Sons* ♫♫♫ (Columbia/Legacy, 1992, prod. Terry Melcher) puts Cooder's legendary band with Taj Mahal in a nice historical light, with some great blues-rock cuts, like "Statesboro Blues" but also a lot of unfocused messy stuff.

influences:

◀◀ Elmore James, Charlie Christian, Mississippi Fred McDowell, Tampa Red, Rolling Stones, Jimi Hendrix, Buddy Guy, Taj Mahal

▶▶ Sonny Landreth, Bonnie Raitt, Rory Block, Daniel Lanois, Robbie Robertson

Steve Knopper

Johnny Copeland

Born March 27, 1937, in Haynesville, LA. Died July 3, 1997, in New York, NY.

Johnny Copeland's career was marked by joyous, high energy

Ry Cooder (© Jack Vartoogian)

Ry Cooder
song
Get Rhythm
album
Get Rhythm (Warner Bros.)
instrument
Slide guitar

monster solo

performances, which earned him the nickname the "Texas Twister," and a restless musical spirit, which led him to record with everyone from West African musicians to jazz explorers like Byard Lancaster, Arthur Blythe and Randy Weston and fellow guitarslingers Albert Collins and Robert Cray. Though Copeland began recording as early as 1958, his career didn't really start moving until 1981, when the by then-New York-based Texas native began recording for Rounder. Over the next 15 years he cut a series of fine albums featuring his superb songwriting, deep soul singing and melodic, in-the-groove guitar playing. He began suffering from heart problems in 1994 and continued performing and even recording, even as he underwent numerous surgeries, first having an LVAD, a mechanical heart of sorts, installed, and later undergoing a heart transplant. He seemed to make a remarkable recovery from that operation, resumed touring, but died during follow-up surgery some seven months later.

what to buy: Copeland was already ailing when he recorded his last album, *Jungle Swing* 𝄞𝄞𝄞𝄞 (Verve, 1995, prod. John Snyder). Compensating for a decrease in his whirlwind energy with an increased emotional depth and resonant serenity, he cut a great, groove-oriented album featuring several acoustic songs and some blues enriched by doses of African polyrhythms. That's a hybrid he worked on since *Bringin' It All Home* 𝄞𝄞𝄞𝄞 (Rounder, 1985), an album recorded with local musicians in Africa's Ivory Coast and a fascinating experiment which worked beautifully. Copeland's collaboration with Cray and Collins, *Showdown!* 𝄞𝄞𝄞𝄞 (Alligator, 1985, prod. Bruce Iglauer, Dick Shurman) is a modern blues guitar classic.

what to buy next: *Texas Twister* 𝄞𝄞𝄞𝄞 (Rounder, 1986, prod. Dan Doyle) and *When the Rain Starts Fallin'* 𝄞𝄞𝄞𝄞 (Rounder, 1987, prod. Dan Doyle) both collect material from Copeland's first four Rounder albums with great success.

what to avoid: The material on *Boom Boom* 𝄞𝄞 (Rounder, 1989) is largely subpar, though it does include three or four very strong tracks. It would have been a better choice to excerpt from and delete than other Rounder Copeland catalog albums that were treated this way.

the rest:

Live in Australia 1990 𝄞𝄞𝄞𝄞 (Black Top)
Copeland Special 𝄞𝄞𝄞𝄞 (Rounder, 1981)
I Make My Home Where I Hang My Hat 𝄞𝄞𝄞 (Rounder, 1982)
Ain't Nothin' but a Party 𝄞𝄞𝄞𝄞 (Rounder, 1988)
Collection, Volume One 𝄞𝄞𝄞𝄞 (Collectables, 1988)
Flyin' High 𝄞𝄞𝄞𝄞 (Verve, 1992)
Catch up with the Blues 𝄞𝄞𝄞𝄞 (Verve, 1993)

influences:

◀◀ T-Bone Walker, Albert Collins, Clarence "Gatemouth" Brown, Guitar Slim, Otis Redding, Johnny "Guitar" Watson

▶▶ Robert Cray, Jimmie Vaughan, Stevie Ray Vaughan, Joe Louis Walker, Johnny Winter

Alan Paul

Aaron Corthen

See: A.C. Reed

James Cotton

Born July 1, 1935, in Tunica, MS.

Though Cotton's mentors Muddy Waters and Sonny Boy Williamson were the primary inspirations for rockers in the 1960s, this Chicago-style harpist forged much more direct links between the two communities. Cotton, who had tracked down Williamson after listening to his *King Biscuit Time* radio show in the 1940s, traveled with the harp master and proved a quick learner. He recorded a few singles around 1953, but his most significant work was with other people; he and Junior Parker were Howlin' Wolf's main harmonicists, and those are Cotton's precise tones in the background of Wolf's Sun singles. Waters invited Cotton to replace George "Harmonica" Smith in his band in 1955, and the partnership lasted through 1966, when Cotton left to form his own band, frequently working with rock performers, including Steve Miller, Paul Butterfield, Johnny Winter, Elvin Bishop and many others, and opening for them at San Francisco's Fillmore auditoriums. A master showman who pranced around the stage and worked his harps to the limit, he built a minor audience in the 1970s, but his rough voice (especially after severe throat problems) was never a match for his fantastic harmonica playing. But as the blues cult audience began to grow into a significant fraction of the music industry, Cotton became one of the club circuit's shining lights. Of all the living bluesmen who served in Muddy Waters' bands, Cotton summons his former boss' spirit with the most reverence and credibility.

what to buy: Though Cotton has been recording for almost three decades, his best work came after the blues labels started picking him up again in the mid-1980s. *High Compression* 𝄞𝄞𝄞𝄞 (Alligator, 1984, prod. Bruce Iglauer, James Cotton) includes two backup combos, the best of which features Pinetop Perkins on piano and Magic Slim on guitar. *Harp Attack!* 𝄞𝄞𝄞 (Alligator, 1990, prod. Bruce Iglauer) unites Cotton with fellow blues harp greats Junior Wells, Billy Branch and Carey Bell. *Mighty Long Time* 𝄞𝄞𝄞 (Antone's, 1991, prod. Clifford Antone) spotlights the bandleader on "Baby Please" and "Call It Stormy Monday" despite the presence of Perkins, guitarist Matt Murphy and (on one track) ex-Fabulous Thunderbird Jimmie Vaughan.

what to buy next: The early solo material is uneven, but the next best is clearly the rock 'n' roll-heavy *100% Cotton* 𝄞𝄞𝄞 (One Way, 1974), with explosive versions of "Boogie Thing" and "Rocket 88."

what to avoid: Sadly, Cotton's voice has deteriorated, and it shows on *Living the Blues* 𝄞𝄞 (Verve, 1994, prod. John Snyder), which is overloaded with guests.

James Cotton (© Linda Vartoogian)

best of the rest:

Chicago/the Blues/Today!, Vol. 2 🎵🎵🎵 (Vanguard, 1964)
Live & on the Move 🎵🎵 (One Way, 1966)
94Cut You Loose! 🎵🎵🎵 (Vanguard, 1967)
The James Cotton Blues Band 🎵🎵🎵 (Verve, 1967)
Cotton in Your Ears 🎵🎵🎵 (Verve, 1968)
Take Me Back 🎵🎵🎵 (Blind Pig, 1980)
Best of the Verve Years 🎵🎵🎵 (Verve, 1995)
Deep in the Blues 🎵🎵🎵🎵 (Verve, 1997)

influences:

⏪ Muddy Waters, Sonny Boy Williamson I, Little Walter, Sonny Boy Williamson II

⏩ Junior Wells, Billy Branch, Charlie Musselwhite, Paul Butterfield, Sugar Blue, Rolling Stones

Steve Knopper

Robert Covington

Born Robert Lee Travis, December 13, 1941, in Yazoo City, MS. Died January 17, 1996, in Chicago, IL.

Nicknamed "the Golden Voice of the Blues" for his rich baritone, Robert Covington studied singing and drums in high school. He practiced as early as 1961 in Big Joe Turner's touring band and was influenced by Turner as a singer and performer. Covington amassed a huge experience in various styles, leading a R&B band and touring with Ernie K. Doe and Ted Taylor from 1962–65. When he moved to Chicago in 1965, he worked with Junior Wells, Buddy Guy, Fenton Robinson, Lonnie Brooks and Sunnyland Slim, developing his own style of drumming—and singing, when he could—and building a laudatory reputation of a bluesman with soul. He played more and more with Sunnyland, becoming a full-time mainstay of the Big Four from 1983–94. Covington's deep voice, sexy charm and smooth delivery made him a favorite of Chicago audiences with Sunnyland and with his own band. He'll always be the singer with the golden voice, a big, backbeat drummer and a reliable timekeeper in the Fred Below school.

what to buy: *Blues in the Night* 🎵🎵🎵🎵 (Red Beans, 1988/Evidence, 1995, prod. Peter Crawford) includes his complete output under his own name, with Carl Weathersby on guitar, recorded in 1983 and 1987–88.

what to buy next: *Chicago Jump* 🎵🎵🎵🎵 (Red Beans, 1983/Evidence, 1995, prod. Samuel Burckhardt) is a Sunnyland Slim album recorded in 1985 with The Big Four and the solid drumming of Covington.

influences:

⏪ Big Joe Turner, Fred Below

Robert Sacré

Ida Cox

Born Ida Prather, February 25, 1896, in Toccoa, GA. Died November 10, 1967, in Knoxville, TN.

Aside from being a well-known classic blues singer in the style of Bessie Smith and Ma Rainey, Cox was an influential early-century African-American businesswoman. She owned and managed a touring company, produced stage shows and wrote songs—decades before Berry Gordy Jr. built his Motown Records empire and Sam Cooke started his own record label. A singer and comic at vaudeville shows, Cox befriended Jelly Roll Morton and signed with Paramount, which called her the "Uncrowned Queen of the Blues." Her songwriting endures more than her singing—Cox classics include "Bone Orchard Blues," "Pink Slip Blues" and, perhaps her trademark, "Wild Women Don't Have the Blues." A coveted slot on John Hammond's 1939 From Spirituals to Swing concert at New York City's Carnegie Hall led to important recording dates with Lionel Hampton, Charlie Christian and others. But she retired in the 1950s, despite a final 1961 session (with Coleman Hawkins) before her death.

what to buy: *Wild Women Don't Have the Blues* 🎵🎵🎵🎵 (Rosetta, 1961), her final album, links her still-strong voice with bandleader Coleman Hawkins' swinging jazz.

best of the rest:

Ida Cox 🎵🎵🎵 (Riverside, 1954)
Blues for Rampart Street 🎵🎵🎵 (Riverside, 1961)
The Moanin' Groanin' Blues 🎵🎵🎵 (Riverside, 1961)

influences:

⏪ Bessie Smith, Ma Rainey, Memphis Minnie, Erskine Hawkins

⏩ Sippie Wallace, Billie Holiday, Hadda Brooks, Bonnie Raitt, Rory Block

Steve Knopper

Davell Crawford

Born September 3, 1975, in New Orleans, LA.

Davell Crawford is the grandson of the great New Orleans R&B vocalist and pianist Sugar Boy Crawford. Since his early teens he's been touted as New Orleans' next great keyboardist. One can detect any number of styles in his playing and singing, but

New Orleans R&B is a heavy influence. However, his versatility is such that his career could turn toward gospel, jazz, hip-hop, pop or all of the above. Let's hope he doesn't forget his roots.

what to buy: Not only was *Let Them Talk* ♪♪♪♪ (Rounder, 1995, prod. Scott Billington) a fine debut, but it included a surprise guest appearance by his grandfather. *Live on Bourbon Street* (Bourbon Street Music Club, 1995) was actually recorded in Brazil, but it's a satisfying taste of Crawford's treatment of rhythm and blues.

what to avoid: *Davell Crawford* ♪♪♪♪ (Her, 1996) is perhaps a little too jazzy for blues listeners.

influences:

◀◀ Sugarboy Crawford, Little Richard, James Booker, Professor Longhair, Allen Toussaint, Sammy Berfect, Fats Domino, Isidore "Tuts" Washington, Ray Charles

Jeff Hannusch

Robert Cray

Born August 1, 1953, in Columbus, GA.

In the mid-1980s, when the hits were full of synthesizers and Stevie Ray Vaughan hadn't yet come around to revitalize the business, the blues needed a young new hero. Cray, a superb songwriter and distinctive electric guitarist with a passion for tradition and a look for pop stardom, was the right man in the right place. His breakthrough album, 1986's Grammy-winning *Strong Persuader*, told excellent stories about, for example, stealing a man's wife and feeling guilty afterwards. After that, Cray became a minor celebrity, appearing in the Chuck Berry film *Hail! Hail! Rock 'n' Roll* and co-headlining at star-studded concerts, such as the one just before his friend Vaughan's death. But Cray's inclination towards old-fashioned Stax-style soul, while creatively lucrative, ended his flirtation with the commercial mainstream. He continued to record many fine horn-heavy albums—including a detour into pure blues with 1995's *Some Rainy Morning*—but has settled comfortably into the blues-circuit celebrity status afforded Buddy Guy, Otis Rush, Keb' Mo' and Luther Allison.

what to buy: Among the impeccably written songs on *Strong Persuader* ♪♪♪♪ (Mercury, 1986, prod. Bruce Bromberg, Dennis Walker) are "Right Next Door (Because of Me)," "Smoking Gun" and "I Wonder." *Bad Influence* ♪♪♪♪ (HighTone, 1983, prod. Bruce Bromberg, Dennis Walker) is more of a venue for Cray's fine soul voice and nicely juxtaposed sharp electric-guitar tones. Though he hired the Memphis Horns early on and al-

ways dabbled in soul, Cray's soul obsession comes across best on *Midnight Stroll* ♪♪♪ (Mercury, 1990, prod. Dennis Walker).

what to buy next: *Don't Be Afraid of the Dark* ♪♪♪ (Mercury, 1988) is sort of a Strong Persuader Part II, with the title track sneaking deservedly onto the pop charts. You can gauge Cray's direction from the cover of *Some Rainy Morning* ♪♪♪ (Mercury, 1995, prod. Robert Cray), which features a painting of the singer, posing like an old bluesman, with his skin tinted blue—lately, Cray's central focus has been guitar playing above songwriting.

what to avoid: Two of Cray's soul workouts, *Shame + Sin* ♪♪♪ (Mercury, 1994, prod. Robert Cray) and *Sweet Potato Pie* ♪♪♪ (Mercury, 1997, prod. Robert Cray), find the bandleader operating on autopilot.

the rest:

Who's Been Talking ♪♪♪ (Tomato, 1980/Atlantic, 1986)
False Accusations ♪♪♪♪ (HighTone, 1985)
I Was Warned ♪♪♪ (Mercury, 1992)

worth searching for: Rarely will you find three better guitarists—and a better blues team—than on *Showdown!* ♪♪♪♪ (Alligator, 1985, prod. Bruce Iglauer, Dick Shurman), which features Cray, Albert Collins and Johnny "Clyde" Copeland on Cray's story/song "The Dream" and such blues classics as "T-Bone Shuffle" and "Black Cat Bone."

influences:

◀◀ B.B. King, Albert King, Buddy Guy, Jimi Hendrix, T-Bone Walker, Albert Collins, Freddie King, Otis Rush, Eric Clapton, Bonnie Raitt, Steve Cropper, Chuck Berry

▶▶ Keb' Mo', Stevie Ray Vaughan, Kenny Wayne Shepherd, Johnny "Clyde" Copeland

Steve Knopper

Connie Curtis "Pee Wee" Crayton

Born December 18, 1914, in Rockdale, TX. Died June 25, 1985, in Los Angeles, CA.

Texas guitarist Pee Wee Crayton was a prominent member of the first generation of electric guitarists whose music has mostly been lost in the mists of modern blues history. As Crayton put it in 1982, "A lot of people don't understand how this blues bit got started. The first man to walk out onstage with a guitar in front of a band was T-Bone Walker. After T-Bone, it was me. After Pee Wee Crayton it was Lowell Fulson. Then it was B.B. King and Gatemouth Brown." Pee Wee started late; he got

interested in playing guitar when he heard Charlie Christian, then flipped when he saw Walker in action. While staying in Oakland, California, Pee Wee persuaded Walker to give him lessons and spent a month of intensive study with the master of the electric guitar. Thus armed, Pee Wee soon garnered a record contract with Modern and enjoyed a big hit with "Blues After Hours," the first electric blues guitar instrumental to go to the top of the R&B charts. In 1951 he moved to Imperial and scored with singles like "When It Rains It Pours," the surreal "Win-O," "Runnin' Wild" (recorded with Dave Bartholomew in New Orleans) and "Yours Truly." Pee Wee turned up on Vee-Jay in the mid-1950s, where he cut the magnificent "Telephone Is Ringing" and "I Love Her Still," among other tasty sides. His star was eclipsed for several years before he returned with a fine album, *Things I Used to Do*, for Vanguard in the late 1960s. Crayton joined the Johnny Otis Show for several years, playing the Monterey Festival in 1970 and the Ann Arbor Blues & Jazz Festival in 1973. His final years were spent in musical obscurity, and most of his classic recordings are still not available on compact disc. Justice will be served when Crayton is recognized as one of the finest guitarists, singers and recording artists of the early days of rhythm & blues.

what to buy: Crayton's Imperial recordings were finally collected on *Pee Wee's Blues* ♫♫♫♫ (Capitol, 1996, prod. Pete Welding), and *Things I Used to Do* ♫♫♫♫ (Vanguard, 1990) has been issued on CD, but the need for an overview of Crayton's career—and a collection of all his extant recordings—remains pressing. His Modern recordings turn up now and then on English anthologies, but a comprehensive presentation is desperately needed. He can be also heard onstage with the Johnny Otis Show on *Live at Monterey* ♫♫♫♫ (Sony, 1993).

what to buy next: A scattering of Pee Wee's singles for Modern, Recorded in Hollywood, Vee-Jay, and other labels can be heard on some hard-to-find anthologies. *The Real Blues Brothers* ♫♫♫♫ (Dunhill, 1986) includes "The Telephone Is Ringing" and "I Love Her Still"; *Blues from Dolphin's of Hollywood* ♫♫♫♫ (Specialty, 1991) has issued singles like "Baby, Pat the Floor" and "Crying and Walking," plus several unreleased RIH masters, including the very fine "Fillmore Street Blues," all from 1953.

worth searching for: I wish I knew where to find Pee Wee's Flair singles, but if you see them anywhere, don't hesitate to cop.

Robert Cray (© Jack Vartoogian)

influences:

◀◀ T-Bone Walker, Charlie Christian

▶▶ Snooks Eaglin, Ronnie Earl, Duke Robillard

John Sinclair

Arthur "Big Boy" Crudup

Born August 24, 1905, in Forest, MS. Died March 28, 1974, in Nassawadox, VA.

Arthur Crudup was a 30-year-old farm worker in rural Mississippi when he learned to play guitar in an effort to pick up some extra money playing house parties. Near poverty, he was forced to learn on a guitar with a broken neck bound together with wire. As a result, he learned only a few basic chords and riffs. By 1940 Crudup headed north, spurred by the stories of good jobs in the big cities, and he signed to Bluebird Records, where he made a modest living after selling away the rights to his music. Eventually, he moved back to the South, returning only for an annual recording session. This went on until 1954, when a discouraged Crudup gave up in despair. (He had recorded under pseudonyms for the Chess and Trumpet labels.) In 1960, he was coaxed back into recording for Fire Records, and from the late 1960s until his death recorded for Delmark. Although Crudup seemed hampered by stage fright during the first phase of his career, the Delmark years found him an enthusiastic performer. None of it would have mattered if he hadn't created such evocative images and if his high, clean voice didn't sound so forlorn in songs of lost love. Crudup also indirectly changed the course of pop music as a major influence on Elvis Presley. Presley's hopped-up version of "That's All Right, Mama" was his first regional hit on Sun Records and the catalyst of the rock 'n' roll explosion of the 1950s.

what to buy: *That's All Right Mama* ♫♫♫♫ (Bluebird, 1992, prod. Billy Altman) is the definitive collection, hitting the major highlights from his Bluebird years (1941–54), starting with the rural Delta sound of "If I Get Lucky" and ending with the proto-rock 'n' roll of "She's Got No Hair." Listen to him croon, "She cries, 'Ooo-wee, I believe I'll change my mind'" on "So Glad You're Mine" or hear the smile in his voice in "Shout, Sister, Shout" for a heaping serving of Crudup's charms. Another *That's All Right Mama* ♫♫♫♫ (Relic, 1992) documents Crudup's return from retirement for the Fire label in the early 1960s. His remakes of many of his classic tunes have much of the power of the originals, and there are a few new tunes as well. The collection supplants *Mean Ol' Frisco* ♫♫♫♫ (Collectables, 1988), which contains fewer songs from the same sessions.

what to buy next: *Arthur Crudup Meets the Master Blues Bassists* &&&& (Delmark, 1994), recorded with long-time bass collaborator Ransom Knowling and Willie Dixon, is the only reissue on compact disc from Crudup's late-1960s Delmark years. Crudup seemed virtually unchanged nearly 30 years after starting his career.

what to avoid: It's not hard to avoid some bad Crudup releases since they haven't made it to CD yet, but leave *Roebuck Man* && (Liberty, 1974) and *Star Bootlegger* && (Krazy Kat, 1983) alone if they ever come out in a jewel box. They're not all right, mama!

the rest:

Complete Recorded Works, Vols. 1–4 &&& (Document, 1994)

worth searching for: *Crudup's Mood* &&& (Delmark, 1969) and *Look on Yonder's Wall* &&& (Delmark, 1969) might still be around on crackling vinyl. Crudup proved he was a sturdy soul in these late-1960s recordings.

influences:

◀◀ Robert Johnson, Big Bill Broonzy

▶▶ Elvis Presley, Bob Dylan

Salvatore Caputo

Maria D'Amato

See: Maria Muldaur

Billy Davenport

See: Paul Butterfield Blues Band

Charles "Cow Cow" Davenport

Born Charles Edwards Davenport, April 23, 1894, in Anniston, AL. Died December 3, 1955, in Cleveland, OH.

Scott Joplin's early-century ragtime instrumentals slowly transmuted into boogie-woogie piano blues, and it didn't happen by coincidence. Obscure players like Davenport, who in the 1920s was actually one of the first pianists to play in the two-fisted boogie style, had a lot to do with it. He began as a vaudeville performer with traveling carnivals and wrote "Cow Cow Blues"—which Ella Mae Morse recorded in 1942, when boogie-

woogie had its first major commercial explosion—considered by many an early example of rock 'n' roll. Davenport wasn't a huge talent, so it's not surprising that he remains a relatively obscure figure, but he was an important pianist who helped usher a key historical shift in blues styles.

what to buy: Davenport's solo work, including "Cow Cow Blues," "New Cow Cow Blues," "Jeep Boogie" and "Jump Little Jitterbug," is gathered on *Complete Recorded Works in Chronological Order, Vol. 1–2, 1925–45* &&&& (Document). He backs singers Dora Carr and Hound Head Henry, among others on *The Accompanist* &&& (Document) and plays with Ivy Smith on *Ivy Smith and Cow Cow Davenport* &&& (Document).

the rest:

Charles "Cow Cow" Davenport 1926–38 &&&& (Best of Blues)
Alabama Strut &&& (Magpie, 1979)

influences:

◀◀ Scott Joplin, Victoria Spivey

▶▶ Jimmy Yancey, Ray Charles, Charles Brown, Professor Longhair

Steve Knopper

Lester Davenport

Born January 16, 1932, in Tchula, MS.

Lucky bluesmen toil for years in bar bands, get their big break by chance, then ride it to national success. This singer and harpist's break came in 1955, when rocker Bo Diddley's regular harpist, Billy Boy Arnold, quit and Diddley asked Davenport to join his band. Unfortunately, Davenport was never able to make much of the break, and despite a few amazing gigs backing Diddley and, later, Muddy Waters and Howlin' Wolf and the Kinsey Report, he faded. (This sad story illustrates his luck: Once, better-known harpist Junior Wells hired Davenport's entire band an hour before Davenport was scheduled to perform.) In 1991, though, the singer managed to use his Kinsey Report connection to finally record an album.

what's available: What's missing from *When the Blues Hit You* &&& (Earwig, 1992, prod. Michael Robert Frank), despite Davenport's terrific harp playing and Sunnyland Slim's perfect piano, is a swinging rhythm section; the straightforward blues rarely catch fire.

influences:

◀◀ Bo Diddley, Little Walter, Sonny Boy Williamson I, Muddy Waters

Steve Knopper

Debbie Davies

Born August 22, 1952, in Los Angeles, CA.

Bandleader and Stratocaster-slinger Debbie Davies is an alumnus of a three-year stint as a member of Albert Collins' Icebreakers. She has since toured relentlessly while recording three albums on Blind Pig Records. Raised in Los Angeles, Davies has established her niche as one of the top white female blues artists working today, standing alongside the likes of Marcia Ball and Sue Foley. Her most recent recording reflects the sort of reach (her grasp remains to be seen) that could catapult her alongside legitimate "crossover" artists like Bonnie Raitt.

what to buy: Davies' latest, *I Got That Feeling* ♫♫♫ (Blind Pig, 1997, prod. Jim Gaines) puts her in a softer, less guitar-oriented light. It works well, although hard-core blues guitar fans might prefer her earlier work.

what to buy next: *Loose Tonight* ♫♫♫ (Blind Pig, 1994, prod. Billy Rush, Debbie Davies) features tasteful, traditional Fender-tone riffing a la Ronnie Earl or her Telecaster daddy, Albert Collins. It draws from the same well of influences as its predecessor, *Picture This* ♫♫♫ (Blind Pig, 1993, prod. Edward Chmelewski, Debbie Davies).

influences:

◀◀ Albert Collins, Freddie King, Magic Sam

Bryan Powell

CeDell Davis

Born Ellis Davis, June 9, 1927, in Helena, AR.

By the time CeDell Davis reached age 10, his body had been ravaged by polio. Before the onset of the disease, however, Davis had begun to develop a guitar style based on that of his neighborhood friend, Isaiah Ross (later known to blues fans around the world as Dr. Ross). Despite living a childhood nightmare, the young Davis refused to allow paralysis to curtail his pursuit of blues guitar. His hands might have been mangled and virtually useless, but CeDell had feelings to express, so he stole a butter knife from his mother's silverware drawer and slid it up and down the fretboard of his guitar. In the ensuing years, Davis refined his slide style into one of the most chilling and distinctive in blues. From 1953 to 1963 he traded licks nightly with slide master Robert Nighthawk at clubs in the Mississippi Delta and Arkansas. From his wheelchair these days, Davis continues to cast his spells. With what his former producer Robert Palmer has called the gift of "instant composition," Davis can create beautiful songs on the spot. Critics have stated that

Davis plays out of tune. That's not true: he hears, interprets and manipulates blues in his own creative way. In doing so, he pushes the limits of the genre to mind-bending extremes.

what to buy: Snippets of Davis' work have appeared on the Rooster and L+R labels. Few blues albums released in the past decade are as poignant as his first full-length recording, the brilliant *Feel Like Doin' Something Wrong* ♫♫♫♫ (Fat Possum, 1994, prod. Robert Palmer). For those who have not heard Davis, many of the 14 songs will be downright shocking. For the most part, it captures CeDell in a solo setting. But when the band comes in, the players, seasoned veterans of punk and free jazz, are able to follow Davis on his twisted, butter-knife slide adventures.

what to avoid: As astonishing as his Fat Possum debut was, Davis' follow-up, ironically titled *The Best of CeDell Davis* ♫♫ (Fat Possum, 1995, prod. CeDell Davis), is a disaster. Davis is allowed to shine midway through on "Laura Mae," "Get to Steppin'" and "Baby, Don't Do It," but much of the rest is ruined by a plodding backing band and an obnoxious, clueless side guitarist. Missing is the insightful production of Palmer, who has been a boon to 1990s recordings of Mississippi and Arkansas artists, including Junior Kimbrough and R.L. Burnside.

influences:

◀◀ Dr. Isaiah Ross, Robert Nighthawk, Big Joe Turner, John Lee Hooker

▶▶ Diamanda Galas, Fruteland Jackson

Steven Sharp

Guy Davis

Born May 12, 1952, in New York, NY.

Guitarist/songwriter/singer Guy Davis has exploded onto the blues scene as one of the most captivating performers of pre-World War II blues. As an African-American, he brings a sense of cultural heritage to his recordings that white artists can only aspire to. His commitment to the acoustic tradition, realized via 6- and 12-string guitar, slide guitar, harmonica and washboard, creates a "time-capsule" feel to his recordings, even on his original material.

what to buy: Davis, son of actor Ossie Davis, has recorded twice. *Call Down the Thunder* ♫♫♫♫ (Red House, 1996, prod. Joe Ferry, Guy Davis) blends classic Piedmont hokum stomp, old-time gospel, deft fingerpicking and straight-up blues for a unique, original recording.

what to buy next: *Stomp Down Rider* ♫♫♫ (Red House, 1995, prod. Thom Wolke), a live recording, is enjoyable, but less intriguing than *Call Down the Thunder*, relying too heavily on the familiar legacy of Robert Johnson.

influences:

◀◀ Big Bill Broonzy, Rev. Gary Davis, Robert Johnson, Mance Lipscomb, Blind Willie McTell

Bryan Powell

James "Thunderbird" Davis

Born November 10, 1938, in Mobile, AL. Died January 24, 1992, in St. Paul, MN.

One of the great but lesser-known artists to record for Duke was James Davis. He broke into show business in 1957 when he joined Guitar Slim's band as valet and opening act and eventually moved to Thibodeaux, Louisiana, Slim's adopted home town, remaining there until the guitarist's untimely death in 1959. In 1961 his first Duke single, "What Else Is There to Do," caught the ear of Duke prexy Don Robey, who convinced Davis to move to Houston to be closer to the studio. Duke continued to release Davis singles, but Robey also used Davis in another capacity—cutting demos for Bobby Bland. Davis left Duke after five singles in 1966 to join Joe Tex's revue. By 1974 he was back in Louisiana and out of the music business. His luck changed in 1988 when Black Top found him working in a dog pound. Davis briefly had a second career, but he died of a heart attack onstage just before recording his second album.

what to buy: Davis' forte was slow, minor-keyed blues, as amplified by his versions of "Your Turn to Cry" and "Blue Monday," reissued on *Angels in Houston* ♫♫♫♫ (Rounder, 1982, prod. Scott Billington, Peter Guralnick). *Check Out Time* ♫♫♫♫ (Black Top, 1988, prod. Lloyd Lambert, Hammond Scott) uses seasoned back-up musicians like Clarence Hollimon, Grady Gaines and Lloyd Lambert.

worth searching for: All the Duke singles Davis cut—not all of them reissued on CD—are worth the search.

influences:

◀◀ Brother Joe May, Guitar Slim, Roy Brown, Wynonie Harris

▶▶ Joe Tex, Little Milton, Z.Z. Hill, Earl King, Ernie K-Doe, Albert Collins, Otis Rush

Jeff Hannusch

Guy Davis (© Linda Vartoogian)

Larry Davis

Born December 4, 1936, in Kansas City, MO. Died 1994.

It is inevitable that Larry Davis will be best known for penning "Texas Flood," the song which launched Stevie Ray Vaughan's career; it is, after all, a modern blues classic. But Davis was much more than just a one-hit songwriting wonder, and his own recordings deserve more attention than they ever received during his lifetime. Davis was not a flashy guitarist, but he was effective and lyrical, and he was among blues' most emotive singers, delivering big soul ballads as well as anyone.

what to buy: Davis' last recording, *Sooner or Later* ♫♫♫♫ (Bullseye Blues, 1992, prod. Ron Levy) is also his best and most consistent. The whole album moves with a sensuous, sinewy energy and drips with true blues feeling. An under-appreciated classic.

what to buy next: *I Ain't Begging Nobody* ♫♫♫ (Evidence, 1987/1993) is solid, and "Giving up on Love" is absolutely devastating, as fine a blues vocal performance as you'll ever hear. *Blues Knights* ♫♫♫ (Evidence, 1986/1994) is also top-notch but only contains four Davis tracks; it's split with Byther Smith, another under-appreciated blues artist.

worth searching for: *Funny Stuff* ♫♫♫ (Rooster Blues, 1982) helped Davis re-launch a dormant career. It has yet to make it to compact disc.

influences:

◀◀ Albert King, Bobby "Blue" Bland, T-Bone Walker, Clarence "Gatemouth" Brown

▶▶ Robert Cray, Stevie Ray Vaughan, Jimmie Vaughan

Alan Paul

Maxwell Davis

Born Thomas Maxwell Davis, 1916, in Independence, KS. Died September 18, 1970, in Los Angeles, CA.

An important behind-the-scenes character, this Kansas-to-Los Angeles transplant helped create an entire era of the West Coast R&B big-band sound, but aside from the minor 1956 hit "Slow Walk," he faded into obscurity after his work was done. The saxophonist was a sideman, performer, arranger, producer and talent scout for record labels, working closely with Amos Milburn, Johnny "Guitar" Watson, Etta James, Big Joe Turner, Percy Mayfield, Clarence "Gatemouth" Brown and B.B. King, to name a few. In a not-unfamiliar story, the rise of rock 'n' roll gutted his career, but the prolific performer continued to put out albums through the 1950s and 1960s.

what to buy: The primary available Davis collection, *Father of West Coast R&B* ♫♫♫♫ (Ace), contains his best work with Modern, Aladdin and several other labels.

influences:

⏮ Louis Jordan, Benny Goodman, Charlie Christian

⏭ Etta James, Grady Gaines, Clarence "Gatemouth" Brown, Big Joe Turner, Jimmy Witherspoon, Floyd Dixon

Steve Knopper

Maxwell Street Jimmy Davis

Born Charles W. Thompson, March 2, 1925, in Tippo, MS. Died December 28, 1995, in Chicago, IL.

Charles Thompson (a.k.a. "Maxwell Street Jimmy Davis" or "Jewtown Jimmy") was a regular fixture on Chicago's funky near West Side marketplace. Beginning in the early 1950s he could be found there amidst vendors of second-hand merchandise, snake oils and southern home-cooking belting out the blues in a style reminiscent of older Mississippi blues artists. His urgent singing and rhythmically incisive single-chord guitar technique owe a debt to his mentor, John Lee Hooker, from whom he learned to play as a teenager. In fact, Thompson and Hooker were both regularly gigging in Detroit throughout the 1940s, helping to usher in an era of uninhibited energetic and penetrating electric blues. Unlike Hooker, Thompson did not gain national recognition during the folk-blues revival of the early 1960s. Nevertheless, he recorded a fine album for Elektra in 1965 that showcases his powerful vocals and his primal guitar style. Nearly 30 years and several sporadic recordings later, Thompson was still in command of his musical faculties. Thompson died of a heart attack the following year, but he lived long enough to inaugurate Chicago's New Maxwell Street Market, where his presence will be sorely missed.

what to buy: *Modern Chicago Blues* ♫♫♫♫ (Testament, 1994, prod. Pete Welding) contains a sampling of prime Maxwell Street Jimmy cuts and provides the perfect context for appreciating his artistry. In addition to his "Hanging around My Door" and "Crying Won't Make Me Stay," we are treated to marvelous recordings by other Maxwell Street regulars, guitarist/mandolin player Johnny Young, slide wizard Robert Nighthawk and the talented and under-recorded harmonica player John Wrencher.

the rest:

Maxwell Street Jimmy Davis: Chicago Blues Session, Vol. 11 ♫♫♫ (Wolf, 1994)

worth searching for: His single best recording as a solo artist is *Maxwell Street Jimmy Davis* ♫♫♫♫ (Elektra, 1965, prod. Norman Dayron, Pete Welding), which is sadly unavailable on compact disc. He can also be found in fine form on the compilations *Chicago Breakdown* ♫♫♫♫ (Takoma, 1980, prod. Norman Dayron) and *Rare Blues* ♫♫♫♫ (Takoma, 1980, prod. Norman Dayron), the latter sporting a cover photo of an apron-clad Thompson playing on Maxwell Street in front of the Knotty Pine Grill, where he once worked as a short-order cook.

influences:

⏮ Tony Hollins, John Lee Hooker

⏭ Willie James

D. Thomas Moon

The Rev. Gary Davis

Born April 30, 1896, in Laurens, SC. Died May 5, 1972, in Hammonton, NJ.

When it comes to blues guitarists who have demonstrated virtuosity on the instrument and whose influence is still felt today, the Reverend Gary Davis is at the top of the list. His ability to be inventive on 6- and 12-string guitars, using complex patterns, incredible runs and different keys, not only influenced the likes of Blind Boy Fuller but reaches contemporary audiences through the work of Taj Mahal, Dave Van Ronk, Jackson Browne, Bob Dylan, Jorma Kaukonen, David Bromberg and Ry Cooder, the latter four having studied guitar with him. One of the best Piedmont blues stylists, Davis launched his career playing the streets of Durham, North Carolina, in the 1920s. Prior to that, as a teenager, he came under the tutelage of Willie Walker in Greenville, South Carolina, playing in a string band and developing his guitar playing. Although sources differ as to when his blindness occurred, it appears that it was during his teens, and he became a prototype for blind street singers. Businessman J.B. Long recorded Davis in 1935, but after a couple blues numbers, Davis became adamant about playing religious songs. He was ordained in 1937 and added "Reverend" before his name. He moved to New York in 1944, preaching and singing on the streets of Harlem before resuming his recording career, which stalled until the 1960s, when his appearances at Newport and other folk festivals revived interest, eventually leading to two documentaries on his life. He continued to perform until his death in 1972, leaving behind a legacy that still resonates.

what to buy: Of the early recordings that are available, *The Complete Early Recordings of the Reverend Gary Davis* ♫♫♫♫ (Yazoo, 1994) best captures Davis from those J.B. Long sessions and a couple of cuts from 1949. Songs such as "I'm Throwin' up My Hand" demonstrate guitar playing that sounds like an end run on a piano. His religious fervor is captured on cuts such as "The Great Change in Me," where he sounds like he is preaching to the flock, "I Saw the Light," convincing proof that God and religious faith have transformed him, and the slow country blues of "O Lord, Search My Heart," which has a country/western feel. This remastered set has eliminated some of the tape hiss from those early sessions without compromising the rest of the sound. *Pure Religion and Bad Company* 𝄢𝄢𝄢𝄢 (Smithsonian/Folkways, 1991) features material recorded in 1957. Still strongly religious and fervid as ever, Davis' fiery guitar skills are highlighted on instrumental tracks like "Mountain Jack," the deliberate "Cocaine Blues," his fast finger picking on "Evening Sun" and the progressions of "Hesitation Blues." His proselytizing is forceful in "Right Now," just as his voice is on "Crucifixion."

what to buy next: *Say No to the Devil* 𝄢𝄢𝄢𝄢 (Bluesville, 1961, prod. Kenneth Goldstein) highlights Davis' religious zeal, but what makes it more interesting for collectors is the haunting harmonica work. On "No One Can Do Me Like Jesus," his voice echoes the sound of his harp. But it is still the combination of finger picking and scorching vocals on the title cut as well as "Lord, I Looked down the Road" and "Tryin' to Get to Heaven in Due Time" that remind us how masterfully Davis blended blues and gospel. *Blues & Ragtime* 𝄢𝄢𝄢𝄢 (Shanachie, 1993, prod. Stefan Grossman) is the most interesting disc of his later work (between 1962–66) because of the inclusion of longer tracks such as the almost rambling "Hesitation Blues," which clocks in at nearly 12 minutes. It best captures how Davis abandoned some of his religious fervor in the 1960s and returned to some early roots with ragtime pieces such as "Cincinnati Flow Rag" (which he had learned back in the Willie Walker days) and "Cocaine Blues," and it even displays his sense of humor on a seven-minute "She's Funny That Way." *Live at Newport* 𝄢𝄢𝄢𝄢 (Vanguard, 1967) is a must for anyone who wants the *live* Davis experience, with a short but effective and fast-fingered turn on "Buck Dance" and great vocals that demonstrate his range on the gospel-tinged "You Got to Move," "I've Done All My Singing for My Lord" and the country blues of "Lovin' Spoonful."

what to avoid: *At the Sign of the Sun* 𝄢𝄢𝄢 (Gospel/Heritage, 1962) is not particularly bad, but the recording quality for this period is better represented on other discs.

the rest:

Gospel Blues & Street Songs 𝄢𝄢𝄢𝄢 (Original Blues Classics, 1961)

From Blues to Gospel 𝄢𝄢𝄢 (Biograph, 1992)
Harlem Street Singer 𝄢𝄢𝄢 (Prestige/Bluesville, 1992)
Complete Recorded Works 1935–49 𝄢𝄢𝄢𝄢 (Document, 1994)
O Glory—The Apolostic Studio Sessions 𝄢𝄢𝄢 (Genes, 1995)

influences:

◀◀ Willie Walker, Blind Boy Fuller, Blind Lemon Jefferson

▶▶ Bob Dylan, Ry Cooder, Taj Mahal, Jorma Kaukonen, Dave Van Ronk, Peter, Paul & Mary

John Koetzner

Walter Davis

Born March 1, 1912, in Grenada, MS. Died October 22, 1963, in St. Louis, MO.

Neither hugely successful nor tragically unsuccessful, this singer and pianist, better known for his singing than his piano playing, recorded hundreds of singles in the 1930s and 1940s. He figured out the piano, moved to St. Louis and earned a reputation among brighter lights such as Peetie Wheatstraw and Roosevelt Sykes. A stroke spurred his career switch from blues to preaching, which is what he was doing when he died in 1963.

what to buy: There are seven volumes in *Complete Recorded Works in Chronological Order 1933–52* 𝄢𝄢𝄢𝄢 (Document), more than enough to keep you occupied. Three hard-to-find collections, *Walter Davis/Cripple Clarence Lofton* 𝄢𝄢𝄢𝄢 (Yazoo), *Walter Davis, 1930–33* 𝄢𝄢𝄢 (Old Tramp) and *Walter Davis, Vol. 1* 𝄢𝄢𝄢 (Blues Documents) are handy for a mix-and-match set of Davis' most essential recordings. Though Davis' performing career never made him a huge star, he was prolific, releasing more than 150 sides.

influences:

◀◀ Peetie Wheatstraw, Charles "Cow Cow" Davenport, Victoria Spivey, Speckled Red, Scott Joplin

▶▶ Professor Longhair, Jimmy Witherspoon, Memphis Slim, Otis Spann

Steve Knopper

Jimmy Dawkins

Born James Henry Dawkins, October 24, 1936, in Tchula, MS.

Few blues performers communicate with the painful honesty and immediacy of Jimmy Dawkins. Through his howling guitar and often anguished vocals, Dawkins projects the sorrow and fury that grip his soul, discussing social, economic and political topics in his compositions. Of course he also addresses love and lust but does even that with remarkable passion and intensity. Controversy and adversity have always dogged Dawkins, and today, perhaps more than ever in his 40-year career, he is an enigma in the Chicago blues world. Dawkins' life in Chicago began in 1955. Still in his teens, he stepped from a train and quickly found employment in a box factory. At night he played backing guitar for harmonica player Lester Hinton. Dawkins quit his job at the factory in 1957 to pursue music full-time. He honed his guitar skills playing West Side Chicago clubs with Magic Sam and Left Hand Frank, and with these and other players developed a fresh sound that was dubbed the "West Side style." By the mid-1970s Dawkins was a master of controlled tension—suspending painfully long segments of feedback and sustain over the top of a faithfully chugging blues/funk rhythm section. Dawkins spent the 1970s and 1980s establishing himself as a recording and touring artist, enjoying peaks in each decade on both record and stage.

what to buy: Blues fans talk of desert island discs? Don't get stranded without *Hot Wire 81* ✍✍✍ (Evidence, 1994, prod. Didier Tricard, Jerry Gordon), an album that Dawkins, in mid-1997, still called his favorite. With one of his greatest backing bands Dawkins works through seven originals, including a touching remake of "Welfare Line." *Blisterstring* ✍✍✍ (Delmark, 1976, prod. Steve Tomashefsky, Jimmy Dawkins Band) finds Dawkins at his menacing best with a solid band featuring Jimmy Johnson on second guitar. Also from the *Blisterstring* era, recorded live on Chicago's West Side, is *Come Back Baby* ✍✍✍ (Storyville, 1995, prod. Marcelle Morgantini). Dawkins entered the 1990s with his bold declaration *Kant Sheck Dees Bluze* ✍✍✍✍ (Earwig, 1991, prod. Jimmy Dawkins, Michael Frank), retaining his great bass anchor, the late Sylvester "Porky Pig" Boines, who supports Dawkins through "Wes Cide Bluze" and a remake of "Luv Somebody."

what to buy next: Touring Europe in 1971, Dawkins entered Cordorcet Studio in Tolouse with an unusual but ultimately effective backing unit that included Clarence "Gatemouth" Brown, Cousin Joe and Ted Harvey. They recorded the tracks for what became Dawkins' Black & Blue release, *Tribute to Orange* ✍✍✍ (Evidence Music, 1993, prod. Jerry Gordon), on which Dawkins is found in a particularly serious mood. Collectors note that the Evidence CD re-issue of this album contains five bonus tracks from 1974 with Otis Rush on backing guitar. Dawkins' exploration of human emotion continued in the mid-1980s on the aptly titled *Feel the Blues* ✍✍✍ (JSP, 1985/1997, prod. Jimmy Dawkins). Like *Kant Scheck Dees Bluze*, it also features the vocals of the great but obscure Nora Jean Wallace on

several tracks. Compared to his Ichiban debut, a warmer, fuller sound pervades Dawkins' second effort for the label, *B Phur Real* ✍✍✍ (Ichiban, 1995, prod. Bryan Cole).

the rest:
Love Me Mama ✍✍✍ (Delmark, 1969)
All for Business ✍✍✍✍ (Delmark, 1971)
Chicago Blues ✍✍✍✍✍ (Arhoolie, 1990)
Blues and Pain ✍✍✍✍ (Ichiban, 1994)
Chicago Blues Nights Vol. 1 ✍✍✍✍ (Storyville, 1994)

worth searching for: To this day, many of Dawkins' vinyl albums have not been re-issued on CD. These include, amazingly, *Fast Fingers* ✍✍✍✍ (Delmark, 1969, prod. Robert Koester), as well as *Transatlantic 770* ✍✍✍ (Excello, 1972, prod. Mike Vernon), *Jimmy Dawkins* ✍✍✍ (Vogue, 1972, prod. Charles Delaney), the live *Jimmy Dawkins: I Want to Know* ✍✍✍✍ (MCM, 1975, prod. Marcelle Morgantini) and *All Blues* ✍✍✍ (JSP, 1986, prod. John Stedman). Dawkins also appears on the vinyl compilations *Montreux Blues Festival* ✍✍✍ (Excello, 1972, prod. Mike Vernon) and *American Blues Festival* ✍✍✍✍ (Paris, 1982, prod. Sylvain Mustaki).

influences:
◀◀ Magic Sam, Smiley Lewis, John Lee Hooker
▶▶ Keith Scott, Vance Kelly

Steven Sharp

Paul DeLay
Born January 31, 1952, in Portland, OR.

A popular regional act in the Pacific Northwest for more than 25 years, Paul DeLay has in recent years begun to attract national and international acclaim for his brilliant harp work. DeLay embraces the fat, amplified Chicago style and the sweet, upper register chromatic harp. He is also a big man with a big voice, handling vocals with a gruff authority. He's earned a reputation as a tough and exciting regional act since forming the Paul DeLay Band about 1980. (Occasional double billing with the early Robert Cray Band resulted in some heated and memorable nights of harp showdowns between DeLay and Cray harp blower Curtis Salgado.) DeLay calls his style a "combination of Big Walter, George Smith, Sonny Boy II and Toots Thielmans." A 1990 arrest on controlled substance charges sidetracked his performing career for three years, but he emerged from his prison stint re-energized and more focused than ever.

what to buy: A heartfelt and well done set of originals penned by DeLay during his prison stay, *Ocean of Tears* ✍✍✍ (Evidence,

1996, prod. Paul DeLay Band, Craig Brock) perfectly showcases the massive talent of DeLay's harp abilities. From the exuberance of the wildly uptempo "I Won" to the bluest moments, DeLay and band are in great form. *Take It from the Turnaround* 𝄞𝄞𝄞𝄞 (Evidence, 1996, prod. Paul DeLay, Peter Dammann, Louis Pain) brings together *Just This One* and *Paulzilla* , both originally on the Criminal label. A prolific songwriter, DeLay ranges lyrically from moody and introspective to tongue-in-cheek casual with more of that fat and fiery harpwork.

worth searching for: *Burnin'* 𝄞𝄞𝄞𝄆 (Criminal, 1988, prod. Paul Jones) marks the debut of fine blues guitarist Peter Dammann, who has become an essential member of the Paul DeLay Band.

influences:

◀◀ Paul Butterfield, George "Harmonica" Smith, Jean "Toots" Thielemans

▶▶ Norton Buffalo, Little John Crisley, John Paris

Tali Madden

Bernardo Dennis

See: Big Three Trio

Derek & the Dominos

Formed 1970, in New York, NY.

Eric Clapton, vocals, guitar; Bobby Whitlock, organ, vocals, guitar; Jim Gordon, drums; Carl Radle, bass; Duane Allman, guitars.

Eric Clapton's earlier bands, the Yardbirds and Cream, borrowed sloppy passion and classic guitar riffs from the blues. Derek & the Dominos only made one album as a group, and it's a monster, the unmistakable sound of talented craftsmen meticulously creating new blues rules. With guitarist Allman's death in late 1971, the group never got the chance to break them.

what to buy: The most familiar legacy of *Layla and Other Assorted Love Songs* 𝄞𝄞𝄞𝄞𝄞 (Polydor, 1970, prod. Tom Dowd, the Dominos) is the smash FM radio hits, including the enduring "Layla" and "Bell Bottom Blues," but it also changed the way musicians and fans thought about blues. A transition from Clapton's sloppy-young-rocker phase to his much longer professional-pop-hitmaker phase, *Layla* collides soaring guitar solos by Allman against Clapton's more down-to-earth riffs. The songwriting is also impeccable, capturing a loose, relaxed jamming style without ever sounding meandering or ostentatious. The cover of Jimi Hendrix's "Little Wing" is appropriate because

Eric Clapton & Duane Allman (of Derek & the Dominos)

song
Why Does Love Got to Be So Sad

album
Layla and Other Assorted Love Songs (Polydor)

instruments
Guitars

monster solo

Hendrix was the first to successfully "psychedelicize" the blues the way Clapton and Allman do on *Layla*. But even more important, where Cream and Led Zeppelin transformed blues into heavy metal, *Layla* turns it into pop. Even today, songs like "Why Does Love Got to Be So Sad?" sound remarkably fresh, and it's because nobody—including Clapton—could capture the same mix of talent, love of American music history, jamming ability and uncanny pop/blues sense.

the rest:

Derek & the Dominos in Concert 𝄞𝄞𝄆 (RSO, 1973)
The Layla Sessions—20th Anniversary Edition 𝄞𝄞𝄆 (Polydor, 1990)
Live at the Fillmore 𝄞𝄞𝄆 (Polydor, 1994)

influences:

◀◀ Albert King, Freddie King, Jimi Hendrix

▶▶ Stevie Ray Vaughan, Allman Brothers Band

Steve Knopper

Bo Diddley

Born Ellas McDaniel, December 30, 1928, in Macomb, MS.

Bo Diddley certainly belongs in a book about blues. He should also be in books about rock 'n' roll—and surrealism. He didn't just do songs; he performed mini-operas of urban weirdness set to a primal beat. While Mud and Wolf and B.B. haunted the outskirts of white America, Bo kicked open the door to Dagwoodland and stormed on in, backed by thundering tom-toms and custom-made guitars. His first band was called the Hipsters. By the 1950s he, drummer Clifton James, harpblower Billy Boy Arnold and maracas-shakin' Jerome Green were working the clubs. In 1955 he cut a double-sided hit, "Bo Diddley"/"I'm a Man," that ranks as a landmark in American music history. The "shave-and-a-haircut—two-bits" beat of the former stirred loins throughout the land and filled squares with woe as they saw their peers succumbing to its carnality. Other Chess 45s followed, as Bo bloomed as a songwriter, guitarist and personality. One year he'd be in cowboy garb, chanting "Bo Diddley's a gunslinger," then his axe would be suckin' wind as he proclaimed, "Bo's a lumberjack." He would tromp on his amplifier's vibrato button and flail away, his ululating chords melding with drubbing drums on tunes that'll symbolize the sound of revelry as long as revelry exists. Certainly it existed in the 1960s, when Quicksilver Messenger Service did a version of his "Who Do You Love" that filled a whole LP side and was ranked as one of the era's best works to groove to while plowed on LSD. The Stones did "Mona," the Yardbirds did "I'm a Man" and the sinister crow in *Fritz the Cat* finger-popped to the tune of "Bo Diddley." Later, the image of a "rock 'n' roll nurse" cramming drugs into beleaguered Bo in the hospital proved irresistible to the New York Dolls, who credibly did Bo's "Pills." Lester Davenport, Little Walter, Lafayette Leake and other Chess mainstays played on Bo's myriad Chess outings. (Even the Moonglows got into the act, singing background on 1955's "Diddley Daddy.") In the late 1970s he opened shows on a Clash tour, and has since recorded for Triple X and Code Blue/Atlantic. He has never neared the popularity he had in the 1950s and, surprisingly, has not loomed large on the bluesfest circuit. But his legacy is unshakable: every single, solitary night in America, bands play and people dance to the Bo Diddley beat.

what to buy: Even Bo loyalists would admit that most of his LPs had one great song (or two), a cool novelty song (or two), and the rest filler. Hence for years the Bo LP to have was *Bo Diddley's 16 All Time Greatest Hits* . The 20-cut *Bo Diddley: His Best* ♫♫♫♫♫ (MCA/Chess, 1997, prod. Leonard Chess, Phil Chess, Bo Diddley) has 12 of said hits, plus the hilarious "Pills,"

the mantric "Mona," the bio-epic "Story of Bo Diddley" and other items missing from the LP. The terminally weird "Who Do You Love" is there, as is "Road Runner," on which Bo pioneered the scraping of one's guitar pick lengthwise against round-wound strings, creating a sonic whoosh Jeff Beck would popularize years later. "Say Man," his biggest hit (on which he and Jerome Green trade such insults as "you look like you been whupped wid a ugly stick!") is there, as is "You Can't Judge a Book by Its Cover," one of Willie Dixon's greatest compositions. All in all, this is a great collection, and it won't be unseemly if you do what it says on all those rock albums—play it loud!

what to buy next: *His Best* doesn't include the immortal "Bo Diddley's a Gunslinger," but the way-cheap *Bo Knows Bo* ♫♫♫ (MCA Special Products, 1995) does, along with the skanky, rarely heard "Diddy Wah Diddy" as well as more well-known selections. Ideal for the CD stash you keep in your car.

best of the rest:

London Sessions ♫♫♫ (MCA/Chess, 1989)
Bo Diddley Is a Gunslinger ♫♫♫♫ (MCA/Chess, 1990)
The EP Collection ♫♫♫♫ (See for Miles, 1991)
Rare and Well Done ♫♫♫♫♫ (MCA/Chess, 1991)
(With Chuck Berry) *Two Great Guitars* ♫♫♫ (MCA/Chess, 1993)
Mighty Bo Diddley ♫♫♫ (Triple X, 1995)
Bo Diddley/Go Bo Diddley ♫♫♫♫ (Chess/MCA, 1996)
A Man Amongst Men ♫♫♫ (Code Blue/Atlantic, 1996)

influences:

◀◀ Cab Calloway, Louis Jordan

▶▶ Rolling Stones, Yardbirds, Animals, George Thorogood

Tim Schuller

Floyd Dixon

Born February 8, 1928, in Marshall, TX.

Floyd Dixon's place in musical history would be assured if the only song he'd ever written was "Hey, Bartender." Dixon is a prolific songwriter who's authored scores of tunes during a 50-year career. He has sometimes been a smooth balladeer in the mold of Nat "King" Cole and Charles Brown and has been equally effective mining the gritty, jump R&B territory staked out by Amos Milburn and Louis Jordan. A crack pianist who melds elements of barrelhouse, boogie and stride in his playing, he's frequently found in the company of first-rate musicians, such as guitarists Johnny and Oscar Moore, bassist Eddie Williams and saxophonist Maxwell Davis in his 1950s work or saxophonists Eddie Synigal and Charlie Owens currently, and he

Bo Diddley (© Jack Vartoogian)

even backed Lionel Hampton on some sides. Dixon was a mentor to younger, less-well-established artists who became superstars, namely Ray Charles in the early 1950s, and Robert Cray in the late 1970s. Dixon's own career has been one of fits and starts. As a youngster in Texas he came under the sway of house-party piano players, notably an unrecorded legend named "Road Master," and showed his own natural talent for the instrument. In his teens he relocated to Los Angeles, where he attended Thomas Jefferson High School and continued to develop his musical skills under the tutelage of Sammy Brown. Dixon went on to become an important contributor to the smooth, urbanized California blues typified by artists like Cole and Brown. Dixon's strength, however, was his ability to integrate the house-party rawness of the Southwest into this mellower, more urbane form of blues. In 1949 he enjoyed R&B chart success with the songs "Dallas Blues" and "Mississippi Blues" on the Modern label. He had R&B Top 5 chart action with both "Telephone Blues" and "Operator 210" for Aladdin. He did sessions for Specialty, Checker, Cat (for whom he cut "Hey, Bar-

tender") and Dolphin. By 1957 his golden period was over. Dixon enjoyed a resurgence during the 1970s blues revival, after he heard one of his early songs playing on the radio and went to introduce himself to the disc jockey, Tom Mazzolini, who connected him to the festival and European tour scene, where he was greeted with enthusiasm. In the late 1980s, aided by Southern California Blues Society members Kathleen Cherrier and Port Barlow, Dixon has rejuvenated his career again.

what to buy: Two compilations capture Dixon's early glories. The two-CD set *His Complete Aladdin Recordings* 🎵🎵🎵🎵 (Capitol, 1996, prod. Eddie Mesner) collects all of Dixon's Aladdin sessions, both under his own name and with Johnny Moore's Three Blazers. While there's some chaff among the 48 tunes presented—even a few songs on which Dixon was once thought to have played but didn't—there's plenty of seminal work and informative liner notes by Billy Vera. *Marshall Texas Is My Home* 🎵🎵🎵🎵 (Specialty, 1991, prod. Art Rupe, Ahmet Ertegun, Jerry Wexler, John Dolphin, Leona Rupp) collects post-Aladdin output from the mid-1950s. Dixon's versatility and songcraft are obvious on this varied collection, which includes the original and definitive version of "Hey, Bartender," with its big, fat baritone sax bridge. *Wake Up and Live* ♪♪♪♪ (Alligator, 1996, prod. Port Barlow) is a strong outing featuring many great Dixon songs, like the slow swing "Don't Send Me No Flowers in the Graveyard" or the jumping "450 Pound Woman." The performances are quite jazzy, featuring an excellent horn section. Dixon's voice has deepened and thickened as he's aged, but is still in fine form, and his playing is as limber as ever. The disc won a W.C. Handy Award for Comeback Blues Album of 1996.

what to avoid: *Hitsville Look Out: Here's Mr. Magnificent* ♪♪ (Cottontail Music West, 1985, prod. Floyd Dixon) is a somewhat ragged effort that introduces Dixon as "Mr. Magnificent." It has its moments, like the instrumental "I Can Blues" with Dixon on organ, but this vinyl release is best left to completists.

worth searching for: *Mr. Magnificent Strikes Again* ♪♪♪ (Cottontail West Music, 1992, prod. Floyd Dixon) is basically a homemade, self-bootlegged album that was mostly recorded in Cherrier and Barlow's living room. The immediacy of the performances and the naturalness of the sound make this well worth seeking. It includes a jazzy updating of "Call Operator 210" done in a radio station that is just superb. *Live at Monterey with Port Barlow & the Full House* ♪♪♪ (Right Time, 1992, prod. Port Barlow) is a cassette release which includes both a festival and a club date from a few years ago. Dixon's performance is a little uneven, but when he catches a groove, look out. Also contains the updated "Call Operator 210."

influences:

◄◄ Amos Milburn, Louis Jordan, Charles Brown, Nat "King" Cole

►► Ray Charles, Curtis Salgado

Michael Dixon

Willie Dixon

Born July 1, 1915, in Vicksburg, MS. Died January 29, 1992, in Burbank, CA.

At the risk of getting carried away, it's safe to say Dixon's name belongs in the same "Great American Writers" chapter as William Faulkner, Flannery O'Connor, F. Scott Fitzgerald, Cole Porter and the Gershwins. His blues songs are among the greatest ever recorded: "Spoonful," a deliberately cryptic metaphor for people fighting over drugs and money; "Back Door Man," a jarring song about anal sex with the oft-repeated line "the men don't know, but the little girls understand"; "You

Shook Me," which is both raucously sexy and cold-sweat frightening; and "Hoochie Coochie Man," a playful expression of extreme macho. As the house producer, band leader, bassist and songwriter for Chess Records in the 1940s and 1950s, Dixon penned these instant classics for some of the best voices in blues history, including Muddy Waters, Howlin' Wolf, Sonny Boy Williamson and Little Walter. (Later the reverential Rolling Stones and the Doors and the decidedly unreverential Led Zeppelin—Dixon sued the band successfully for using parts of "I Can't Quit You Baby"—learned the blues from these Chess sides.) Dixon's rumbling bass lines became the standard in the blues and R&B worlds, and he was a primary link between raw, electric Chicago blues and both of the first waves of rock 'n' roll. Dixon learned music early in life from his poetry-writing mother, but his career detoured into boxing (he was a heavyweight champion in Illinois who once fought Joe Louis) and prison (as a conscientious objector, he refused to be drafted) delayed his success. With guitarist Bernardo Dennis and Leonard "Baby Doo" Caston, the bassist formed the Big Three Trio, which recorded several singles before breaking up in 1952. Through various connections, he met Chicago blues club owners Leonard and Phil Chess, who gave him a part-time job; the rest ranks with Robert Johnson's tragic life story among the most beloved lore in blues history. After Chess' glory days faded and rock 'n' roll took over the pop charts, Dixon started touring with his Chicago Blues All-Stars in Europe and released several albums with—shockingly—his own lead vocals. He also formed the Blues Heaven Foundation in 1982, using money from his substantial royalties to help keep the blues going through school programs, financial aid and scholarships. It's hard to think of any blues, R&B or even rock 'n' roll musician who hasn't somehow been touched by Dixon's work.

what to buy: The songs on *The Chess Box* ♪♪♪♪♪ (MCA/Chess, 1988, prod. Willie Dixon) will sound familiar no matter how much previous knowledge a listener has of Dixon or his work. It includes Williamson's "Bring It on Home," Waters' "Hoochie Coochie Man," Wolf's astounding "Little Red Rooster," "Spoonful" and "Back Door Man" and Koko Taylor's brilliant "Wang Dang Doodle," among cuts by Lowell Fulson, Bo Diddley and many others. But be sure to sample Dixon's own voice, a smooth, deep growl that quickly grows on you: *I Am the Blues* ♪♪♪ (Mobile Fidelity, 1970/Columbia/Legacy, 1993, prod. Abner Spector) contains his playful versions of "Back Door

Willie Dixon (© Jack Vartoogian)

Man," "I Can't Quit You Baby," "Little Red Rooster" and several others, which are fun and interesting even if Dixon's Chicago Blues All-Stars aren't quite the Muddy Waters Band.

what to buy next: *The Big Three Trio* 𝄞𝄞𝄞 (Columbia/Legacy, 1990) contains such early boogies as "Hard Notch Boogie Beat" and "Big 3 Stomp."

what to avoid: His comeback attempt, *Hidden Charms* 𝄞𝄞 (Bug/Capitol), isn't as playful and fresh as *I Am the Blues*, but it's still worth owning as the last significant Dixon album before his death.

the rest:

Willie Dixon—Catalyst 𝄞𝄞𝄞 (Ovation, 1973)

worth searching for: Dixon recorded a few wonderful but largely unrecognized tracks late in his life, and they're all surprisingly great: Los Lobos' Cesar Rosas co-wrote "I Can't Understand" with Dixon for *The Neighborhood* 𝄞𝄞𝄞𝄞 (Slash/Warner Bros., 1990, prod. Larry Hirsch, Los Lobos); an obscure singer, Willie Jones, did a raunchy, wonderful blues duet, "Long Legged Goddess," with Dixon on her *Willie Jones* 𝄞𝄞𝄞 (Geffen, 1990, prod. Niko Bolas); and old pal Bo Diddley proved Dixon still had his producer's chops on a new version of "Who Do You Love," still available on *La Bamba Original Motion Picture Soundtrack* 𝄞𝄞𝄞𝄞 (Slash/Warner Bros., 1987, prod. various).

influences:

◀◀ Robert Johnson, Son House, Charley Patton

▶▶ Muddy Waters, Howlin' Wolf, Sonny Boy Williamson II, Little Walter, Buddy Guy, Otis Rush, Los Lobos, Bo Diddley, Rolling Stones, Led Zeppelin, Eric Clapton, Stevie Ray Vaughan, Jimi Hendrix

Steve Knopper

Lefty Dizz

Born Walter Williams, 1937, in AR. Died September 7, 1993, in Chicago, IL.

Lefty Dizz was prone to wildly physical performances. At times his theatrics, which included splits while playing his guitar behind his back, threatened to eclipse the fact he was one of the most formidable guitarists on the Chicago scene. Dizz's guitar style was one of wild abandon, and he had a reputation as a "head cutter," shutting down many an onstage challenger. Self taught, Dizz began playing as a teenager. His talent led to membership in the Junior Wells band for most of the 1960s. As leader of his own band, Shock Treatment, Dizz became leg-

endary in Chicago for his kinetic, antic-filled performances and knockout guitar work. For whatever reason, this energy was never captured satisfactorily on record. Active into the 1990s, Dizz died of cancer, an overlooked and unique artist.

what to buy: Dizz's records are in woefully short supply. His best recorded work surfaced recently on a remarkable, rediscovered Louisiana Red session. On *Walked All Night Long* 𝄞𝄞𝄞𝄞 (Blues Alliance, 1997, prod. Kent Cooper, Heiner Stadler), originally recorded in 1975 for the tiny Blue Labor label, Dizz accompanies Red's country-with-an-urban-edge blues—Red on vocals and acoustic slide, Dizz on phenomenal electric guitar—through an intimate set, as if the listener lucked out and sat down in the right room at the right time. An informal yet charged set, it perfectly combines the dark lyricism of the enigmatic Louisiana Red and the remarkably deft and unique guitar work of Lefty Dizz.

the rest:

Ain't It Nice to Be Loved 𝄞 (JSP, 1995)

worth searching for: On *Somebody Stole My Christmas* 𝄞𝄞𝄞 (Isabel, 1993, prod. Didier Tricard) Dizz blusters and smolders through a set of originals and blues standards, and provides sturdy vocals as well. His own title tune is one of the better blues Christmas themes on record.

influences:

◀◀ Hound Dog Taylor, Guitar Slim

▶▶ Lil' Ed Williams

Tali Madden

Dr. John

Born Malcolm John "Mac" Rebennack Jr., November 21, 1940, in New Orleans, LA.

With his spooky, voodoo-drenched debut as the Night Tripper in 1967 and his guided tour of New Orleans roots music on *Gumbo* in 1972, Dr. John paved the way for America's rediscovery of the Crescent City's rich musical heritage. It was Dr. John who led listeners to legendary New Orleans artists such as Professor Longhair and Huey (Piano) Smith. And his 1973 hits "Right Place, Wrong Time" and "Such a Night" helped bring national attention to regional stars such as the Meters and Allen Toussaint. Born and raised in New Orleans, Rebennack already was performing and recording in his teens, mainly as a guitarist. But it was his funky piano and distinctive, gravelly drawl that made him a star with the release of the *In the Right Place* album in 1973. Financial and drug problems plagued him well into the 1980s, but the growing popularity of New Orleans music helped him regain his stride. He reigns as the acknowledged master of the New Orleans sound; no one has done more to popularize it.

what to buy: *Mos' Scocious* 𝄢𝄢𝄢𝄢 (Rhino, 1993, prod. various) is the definitive Dr. John anthology—a two-CD set that begins with rare early sides cut with local bands such as Ronnie and the Delinquents, then marches on through more than 30 years of the doctor's finest remedies. A virtual encyclopedia of the New Orleans sound. The one-disc *The Very Best of Dr. John* 𝄢𝄢𝄢𝄢 (Rhino, 1995, prod. various) skims the cream of *Mos' Scocious*. *Dr. John's Gumbo* 𝄢𝄢𝄢𝄢 (Atlantic, 1972, prod. Jerry Wexler, Harold Battiste) is Rebennack's landmark tribute to the Crescent City's R&B roots—while, a year later, *In the Right Place* 𝄢𝄢𝄢𝄢 (Atco, 1973, prod. Allen Toussaint) gave him a hit. (Both *Gumbo* and *In the Right Place* are combined on a Mobile Fidelity Sound Lab 24K disc.)

what to buy next: *Goin' Back to New Orleans* 𝄢𝄢𝄢𝄢 (Warner Bros., 1992, prod. Stewart Levine) is another fine reflection of his early influences, with lots of stellar guest artists. *In a Sentimental Mood* 𝄢𝄢𝄢𝄢 (Warner Bros., 1989, prod. Tommy LiPuma) is Rebennack's career-reviving take on standards such as "Makin' Whoopee" (a Grammy-winning duet with Rickie Lee Jones) and "Accentuate the Positive." And have your mojo hand ready should you fall under the hoodoo incantations of the Night Tripper on *Gris Gris* 𝄢𝄢𝄢 (Atco, 1968, prod. Harold Battiste). His first in-concert set, *Trippin' Live* 𝄢𝄢𝄢𝄢 (Surefire, 1997, prod. Mac Rebennack), is worth the wait, especially for the long-anticipated "Renegade," a staple of his stage shows.

what to avoid: *At His Best* 𝄢𝄢 (Special Music Company, 1989) has been rendered redundant by the several more complete best-ofs.

best of the rest:

Gumbo 𝄢𝄢𝄢𝄢 (Atco, 1972/1990)
Dr. John Plays Mac Rebbenack 𝄢𝄢𝄢𝄢 (Clean Cuts, 1981)
The Ultimate Dr. John 𝄢𝄢𝄢 (Warner Bros., 1987)
Such a Night 𝄢𝄢𝄢 (Makin' Waves, 1988/1992)
The Brightest Smile in Town 𝄢𝄢𝄢 (Clean Cuts, 1989)
Goin' Back to New Orleans 𝄢𝄢𝄢𝄢 (Warner Bros., 1992)
Gumbo/In the Right Place 𝄢𝄢𝄢𝄢 (Ultradisc Gold Disc, 1994)
Television 𝄢𝄢𝄢 (GRP, 1994)
Afterglow 𝄢𝄢𝄢 (Blue Thumb, 1995)

worth searching for: Listen for that famous voice on any number of television commercials. And if you're in a used store, an import CD of formative, loose-limbed 1960s sessions, *Cut Me*

While I'm Hot 𝄢𝄢𝄢𝄢 (Magnum America) would make a nice collector's trophy.

influences:

◀◀ Professor Longhair, James Booker, Isidore "Tuts" Washington, Joe Liggins, Huey "Piano" Smith

▶▶ Neville Brothers, Marcia Ball, Radiators

Doug Pippin and Leland Rucker

Morris Dollison Jr.

See: Cash McCall

Fats Domino

Born Antoine Domino, February 26, 1928, in New Orleans, LA.

Not only is Domino responsible for 63 charted singles and astounding record sales, he did it with nothing more than pure musical charm. A short-statured man of ample girth, Domino possessed none of the titillating antics or wild personality traits of contemporaries such as Little Richard and Chuck Berry. Instead, he smiled and let the rolling triplets of his piano and his warm New Orleans drawl steer his never-ending string of self-penned hits. Nearly everything the man recorded has a rollicking charm and gentleness, and the hits retain their impact and innocence to this day. He cut his first hit, "The Fat Man," in 1949, predating both Bill Haley and Elvis Presley by several years and therefore making it arguably the first rock 'n' roll song. From that point on, Domino's influence and importance as a musical force cannot be overstated.

what to buy: The four-disc boxed set *They Call Me the Fat Man* 𝄢𝄢𝄢𝄢 (EMI, 1991, prod. Dave Bartholomew) chronicles his stay at Imperial and renders almost every other release redundant with hits such as "Blueberry Hill," "Ain't That a Shame" "Walkin' to New Orleans," "I'm Walkin'" and "Whole Lotta Lovin'." *My Blue Heaven* 𝄢𝄢𝄢𝄢 (EMI, 1990, prod. Dave Bartholomew) is a fine introductory single-disc sampler to the warm Creole sound of the Fat Man.

what to buy next: *Antoine "Fats" Domino* 𝄢𝄢𝄢𝄢 (Tomato, 1992, prod. Kevin Eggers, Robert G. Vernon) is a vivacious live document, recorded when Domino was 61 and still in full possession of all his friendly energy. Plus, it offers a good version of "Red Sails in the Sunset."

what to avoid: Yes, *Christmas Is a Special Day* 𝄢𝄢 (The Right Stuff/EMI, 1993), so buy the boxed set and leave the caroling to Perry Como.

the rest:

The Best of Fats ♫♫♥ (Pair, 1990)
All-Time Greatest Hits ♫♫♥ (Curb, 1991)
Best of Fats Domino Live Vol. 1 ♫♫♥ (Curb, 1992)
Best of Fats Domino Live Vol. 2 ♫♫♥ (Curb, 1992)
Fats Domino: The Fat Man—25 Classics ♫♫♫♫ (EMI, 1996)
That's Fats! A Tribute to Fats Domino ♫♫♫ (EMI, 1996)

worth searching for: Find *Out of New Orleans* ♫♫♫♫♫ (Bear Family, 1993), an eight-disc import set that presents the complete Imperial recordings along with unedited alternate takes and a 72-page book containing extensive liner notes and a complete sessionography.

influences:

◄◄ Big Joe Turner, Louis Jordan, Professor Longhair

►► Van Morrison, Paul Simon, Billy Joel, Bruce Hornsby, Neville Brothers, Allen Toussaint

Allan Orski

Thomas A. Dorsey

Born July 1, 1899, in Villa Rica, GA. Died January 23, 1993, in Chicago, IL.

Thomas Dorsey will stay in blues history as the composer of more than 100 suggestive and low-moaning tunes and as the gifted partner of the blues who's-who of the 1920s and early 1930s. He also made his mark in gospel music as the most prolific composer of all time, as well as a talent scout with the magic touch. Dorsey lived some time in Atlanta, where as a teenager he developed a piano style influenced by ragtime, early jazz, blues and gospel. He moved to Chicago in 1916, where as Barrelhouse Tom he went on playing ragtime and vaudeville music, learning to read and arrange music and to write lead sheets with Richard M. Jones. In the early 1920s he started a successful career in secular music as singer/composer/pianist in jazz groups and with classic blues singers, touring with Ma Rainey, recording with Kansas City Kitty and writing songs for Monette Moore, Trixie Smith and Alberta Hunter, among others. At the same time, as Georgia Tom, he teamed with Hudson Whittaker (Tampa Red) for a remarkable series of conventional blues ("M&O Blues") and hokum extravaganzas (the superhit "Tight Like That" and "You Ain't Living Right") with risqué lyrics and infectious rhythms. Their success was tremendous, and he performed with the Hokum

Boys (with Bob Robinson) and the Famous Hokum Boys (with Big Bill Broonzy) to record more of it. Dorsey also worked with other artists like Scrapper Blackwell ("Six Shorter Blues") under various pseudonyms and as session pianist with Half Pint Jaxon, Memphis Minnie and Jim Jackson. Very influential in his time, Dorsey was a serene singer with a soft voice, a piano player with a gently rocking style, introverted but highly effective, and a great, prolific composer. In the early 1930s, he felt that the future of the blues and hokum music was hazardous, and in 1932 he abandoned secular music to become the "father of modern gospel music," composing hundreds of songs with religious lyrics backed by jazzy blues music, most of which are still performed today ("Precious Lord," "Peace in the Valley"). A profoundly religious man, he had composed and performed hymns and spirituals before, but after 1932 he worked full time in his "gospel blues" business, forming his own publishing company, selling his songs and scouting gospel talents with partner Sallie Martin (Mahalia Jackson and the Ward Singers among them). He was appointed choir director at the Pilgrim Baptist Church in Chicago, a life-long job, but stayed loyal to his former blues acolytes, since unlike many religious people, he never rejected the secular music. He recorded little as a gospel artist, prioritizing his composing and publishing business, his work with choirs and solo artists and the organization of his annual gospel conventions. He stayed active until the early 1980s and even starred in a film, *Say Amen Somebody*, in 1983.

what to buy: *Come on Mama Do That Dance* ♫♫♫♫ (Yazoo, prod. Nick Perls, Stephen Calt) offers blues and hokum numbers with a variety of partners; *Georgia Tom 1928–34, Vols. 1–2* ♫♫♫♫ (Document, 1992, prod. Johnny Parth) adds even more blues and hokum sides. *Say Amen Somebody* ♫♫♫♫ (DRG, 1983, prod. George T. Nierenberg) is the soundtrack of the film with Dorsey, the Barrett Sisters, O'Neal Twins, Sallie Martin and Mother Smith. *Thomas A. Dorsey—Precious Lord* ♫♫♫♫ (Columbia, 1973/1994, prod. Tony Heilbut) is a collection of the best gospel compositions of Dorsey sung by Marion Williams, Dixie Humming Birds and other groups or soloists.

the rest:

Famous Hokum Boys 1930–31, Vols. 1–2 ♫♫♫♫ (Wolf, 1991)
Kansas City Kitty & Georgia Tom ♫♫♫♫ (Document, 1992)

worth searching for: There is an excellent book on Dorsey's contributions by author Michael W. Harris: *The Rise of Gospel Blues—The Music of Thomas A. Dorsey in the Urban Church,* (Oxford University Press, 1992).

Dr. John (© Linda Vartoogian)

thomas a. dorsey

influences:

◀◀ Jimmy Blythe, Dave Peyton, Richard M. Jones, Rev. W.W. Nix

▶▶ Sallie Martin, James Cleveland, Mahalia Jackson, Clara Ward

Robert Sacré

influences:

◀◀ Tommy Johnson, Charley Patton

▶▶ Taj Mahal, Keb' Mo'

Tali Madden

K.C. Douglas

Born November 21, 1913, in Sharon, MS. Died October 18, 1975, in Berkeley, CA.

K.C. Douglas grew up in rural Mississippi, absorbing the rich blues traditions of the region. An uncle, Smith Douglas, introduced him to guitar. He was inspired by local area musicians and the early Victor blues recordings of Tommy Johnson. Douglas was busking on the street corners of Jackson, Mississippi, by his early twenties, where he met and played with Johnson. Unlike many of his Mississippi blues contemporaries, he chose not to relocate to Chicago. Availing himself of a government work-force recruitment program, Douglas moved to the San Francisco Bay area to work at the naval shipyards. He formed a band and in 1948 recorded his "Mercury Boogie" for Bob Geddins' Down Town label, which enjoyed some success commercially. His down-home, rural, electric blues style set him apart from most of the Oakland blues scene, which tended toward a modern urban style. Douglas held his day job for the Department of Public Works, turning to music full-time upon his retirement. "Mercury Boogie" gained international notoriety via a hit cover by blues/rock star Steve Miller. Not quite as captivating as other artists of the genre, such as Jesse Fuller or Brownie McGhee, Douglas was nonetheless a fine and original country blues performer.

what to buy: A few of Douglas' recordings have made the transition to disc. *K.C. Douglas: The Country Boy* 🎵🎵🎵 (Arhoolie, 1981, prod. Chris Strachwitz) is a good example of his rustic Delta stylings with sparse but effective accompaniment on harp, bass and drums. Originally recorded in 1973 and issued on vinyl in 1974, *The Country Boy* includes "Mercury Boogie." Douglas' stringy, metallic slide guitar takes the listener back to where it all began, his Delta home turf. *K.C.'s Blues* 🎵🎵🎵 (Bluesville, 1990, prod. Chris Strachwitz, Kenneth Goldstein) is also a traditional Mississippi Delta blues outing. Originally released in 1961, *Big Road Blues* 🎵🎵🎵 (Ace, 1988, prod. Chris Strachwitz) is more of the same cotton-picking blues, as Douglas called it.

Lizzie Douglas

See: Memphis Minnie

Chris Duarte

Born February 16, 1963, in San Antonio, TX.

If anyone deserves to called the "next Stevie Ray Vaughan," it's Chris Duarte. Fortunately, it's a title he neither pursues nor rejects. Like Vaughan, Duarte prefers a vintage Stratocaster, leans toward raw, intense blues and worships Jimi Hendrix. He's also a road warrior, rarely putting in fewer than 300 gigs a year. If there's a fat Harley-Davidson in front of a club, Duarte's probably played there—at least twice. A San Antonio native, Duarte dropped out of high school (as did Vaughan) in 1979, moved to Austin (as did Vaughan) and started hanging out, eventually fronting the Bad Boys, a loosely focused fusion-blues band. After almost 15 years on the road, he landed a record deal with Silvertone. *Guitar Player* magazine readers named Duarte "Best New Talent" in 1995 and a *Guitar World* readers' poll pegged him fourth among Best Blues Guitarists behind Eric Clapton, Buddy Guy and B.B. King. Like Vaughan, Duarte's followers are loyal. Deservedly so.

what to buy: *Texas Sugar/Strat Magic* 🎵🎵🎵🎵 (Silvertone, 1994, prod. Dennis Herring) is a dazzling collection of spontaneous, hard-rockin' blues that won immediate airplay among the nation's hard-rock radio stations. Three years later, they're still playing "Big Legged Woman," "Just Kissed My Baby" and "Letter to My Girlfriend."

what to avoid: Only 1,000 copies of *Chris Duarte and the Bad Boys* **woof!** (1986) were pressed. Thank God.

influences:

◀◀ John McLaughlin, Jimi Hendrix, Stevie Ray Vaughan

Dave Ranney

Champion Jack Dupree

Born July 23, 1909, in New Orleans, LA. Died January 21, 1992, in Hanover, Germany.

Champion Jack Dupree liked to refer to himself as "last of the barrelhouse piano players," and he may have been right. Or-

Chris Duarte (© Ken Settle)

phaned as a child, Dupree was raised in the Colored Waifs' Home for Boys, the same orphanage that reared Louis Armstrong, and he learned to play as a teenager in brothels and speakeasies. At age 20 or so he headed north, and in Detroit met Joe Louis, who got him started as a boxer. He fought 107 bouts, and the pugilistic nickname "Champion Jack" stuck. By 1940, he commenced recording for a series of independent labels. From the beginning he displayed an unflashy, bass-heavy piano style, a deep blues singing voice and a penchant for penning cutting social commentary and songs that captured the lifestyle of the poor and infamous: prostitutes, junkies and gamblers. In 1958, he moved to London and remained in Europe for most of the next 32 years, amongst the first black bluesmen to make that move. In 1990, he returned to his hometown for the first time, making a triumphant appearance at the New Orleans Jazz & Heritage Festival.

what to buy: *Blues from the Gutter* 𝄢𝄢𝄢𝄢 (Atlantic, 1958, prod. Jerry Wexler) is not only Dupree's best work, but a blues masterpiece that belongs in any respectable collection. It retains a certain elegant dignity even while songs like "T.B. Blues," "Junker's Blues," "Evil Woman" and "Can't Kick the Habit" are about as down and dirty as music can get. Dupree was in a much more upbeat mood when he cut his last album, *One Last Time* 𝄢𝄢𝄢𝄢 (Bullseye Blues, 1993, prod. Ron Levy). Spontaneously done in one day after Dupree finished the less exciting *Forever and Ever* 𝄢𝄢𝄢 (Bullseye Blues, 1991, prod. Ron Levy) ahead of schedule, it's a low-key delight. An all-star band of New Orleans players, most notably saxist Earl Turbinton, play off the grand old man with joyous energy. The fact that it was released posthumously lent songs like "Bring Me Flowers While I'm Livin'" a special poignancy.

what to buy next: *New Orleans Barrelhouse Boogie* 𝄢𝄢𝄢𝄢 (Columbia Legacy, 1993, prod. Lawrence Cohn, Gary Pacheco) collects Dupree's OKeh sides from 1940–41. Not as essential or modern-sounding as *Blues from the Gutter* but pretty damned moving nonetheless. *Back Home in New Orleans* 𝄢𝄢𝄢 (Bullseye Blues/Rounder, 1990) captures Dupree's return to his hometown after a 36-year absence.

influences:

◄◄ Isidore "Tuts" Washington, Fats Waller

►► Professor Longhair, Fats Domino, Allen Touissant

Alan Paul

Bob Dylan (© Ken Settle)

Garrett Dutton

See: G. Love & Special Sauce

Omar Dykes

Born Kent Dykes, 1950, in McComb, MS.

Hailing from the same birthplace as that of Bo Diddley, guitarist Kent "Omar" Dykes could best be described as blue-eyed Cajun with gritty blues and rock 'n' roll overtones. With tunes frequently built around the infectious Diddley beat, Omar and the Howlers meld southern-fried, Chicago blues and swampy rock 'n' roll—packaged in Dykes' growling, wailing vocal attack. As a youngster in Mississippi, Dykes grew up listening to his mother's diverse collection of country and western, rock 'n' roll and soul records. Oblivious to the racially polarized atmosphere in the Deep South during the late 1960s, he was one of the few white teenagers in his community to venture into black juke joints—not just to hear the music but to play it. After a few years on the Mississippi club circuit, he relocated to Austin in 1976.

what to buy: With a powerful title track and additional instruments augmenting Omar's trio, *Hard Times in the Land of Plenty* 𝄢𝄢𝄢𝄢 (Austin, 1987, prod. Richard Mullen) offers a slightly more sophisticated sound than its predecessors. *World Wide Open* 𝄢𝄢𝄢 (Watermelon, 1996, prod. Omar Dykes, Kevin Wommack, James Tuttle) shows a maturity in songwriting and arranging, without sacrificing the basic swampy rhythms.

what to buy next: *Blues Bag* 𝄢𝄢𝄢 (Bullseye Blues/Rounder, 1991) is Omar's return to the trio format—and his personal tribute to the blues. *Courts of Lulu* 𝄢𝄢𝄢 (Bullseye Blues, 1992, prod. Omar Dykes, Kevin Wommack) features occasional accordion work by Ponty Bone that further enhances the bayou flavor. Omar's most pop-rock influenced work, *Southern Style* 𝄢𝄢𝄢 (Watermelon, 1997, prod. Omar Dykes, Richard Mullen) takes the Howlers a few steps beyond a twangy guitar band and explores a variety of atmospheres.

the rest:

I Told You So 𝄢𝄢𝄢 (Austin, 1984)
Monkey Land 𝄢𝄢𝄢 (Antone's, 1990)
Live at Paradiso 𝄢𝄢𝄢𝄢 (Bullseye Blues, 1993)
Muddy Springs Road 𝄢𝄢𝄢 (Watermelon, 1995)

worth searching for: *Big Leg Beat* 𝄢𝄢𝄢 (Amazing, 1980) is a solid, confident first outing for this young trio new to the big city. *Wall of Pride* 𝄢𝄢𝄢 (CBS, 1988) features more of the big sound characteristic of the band's CBS period.

influences:

 Jimmy Reed, Howlin' Wolf, J.J. Cale

John C. Bruening

Bob Dylan

Born Robert Allen Zimmerman, May 24, 1941, in Duluth, MN.

The standard rap on Bob Dylan is that he's a folkie who later became a rocker. To think of him as a Woody Guthrie clone who suddenly got electric religion misses the point of Dylan as an artist. Besides the Guthrie tribute, his 1961 debut album was an exploration of black styles with a preoccupation with death and a gnarled, hardscrabble voice trying to sound like a blues singer three times his age. On his second album, *Freewheelin'*, he was already using a backup band. *Highway 61 Revisited* was, courtesy of young guitar gun Michael Bloomfield, his 1965 version of urban Chicago blues filtered through his own adrenaline-rushed lyrics, and his appearance with the Paul Butterfield Blues Band at Newport that year was one of the pivotal events in American popular music. Though he prefers emotion over technology in most of his recordings and uses blues forms in many of his compositions, Dylan hasn't tried consciously to be a bluesman—his songs and albums have reached far beyond any single genre—but there is considerable evidence of his love for the music throughout his lengthy career.

what to buy: On *Highway 61 Revisited* 🎵🎵🎵🎵 (Columbia, 1965, prod. Bob Johnston), Dylan's on a roll, echoing Muddy Waters' electric Chicago blues and the Paul Butterfield Band but adding a new lexicon to blues lyricism. "Tombstone Blues," "It Takes a Lot to Laugh, It Takes a Train to Cry," "From a Buick 6," and "Highway 61 Revisited" are blues without barriers. Dylan takes material from the 1920s and 1930s by the Mississippi Sheiks and Blind Willie McTell and interprets them for the present on *World Gone Wrong* 🎵🎵🎵 (Columbia, 1993), and to a lesser degree on *Good As I Been to Ya* 🎵🎵🎵 (Columbia, 1992).

what to buy next: There is plenty of evidence of Dylan's blues leanings on *The Bootleg Series Vols. 1–3* 🎵🎵🎵🎵 (Columbia, 1991), especially on Volume 3, which includes "Blind Willie McTell," Dylan's haunting landscape of the land where the blues came from. Despite its Old Testament theology, *Slow Train Coming* 🎵🎵🎵 (Columbia, 1979, prod. Barry Beckett) is one of Dylan's bluesiest efforts. Later versions of *Shot of Love* 🎵🎵🎵 (Columbia, 1981, prod. Chuck Plotkin, Bob Dylan) include the rollicking "Groom's Still Waiting at the Altar."

best of the rest:

Bob Dylan 🎵🎵🎵 (Columbia, 1961)

The Freewheelin' Bob Dylan 🎵🎵🎵🎵 (Columbia, 1962)
Bringing It All Back Home 🎵🎵🎵🎵 (Columbia, 1965)
Blonde on Blonde 🎵🎵🎵🎵 (Columbia, 1966)
Blood on the Tracks 🎵🎵🎵🎵 (Columbia, 1975)
Infidels 🎵🎵🎵🎵 (Columbia, 1983)
Oh Mercy 🎵🎵🎵🎵 (Columbia, 1989)

worth searching for: Dylan and Tom Petty & the Heartbreakers collaborated on the title track for the film soundtrack *Band of the Hand* (MCA, 1986, prod. Tom Petty), a romping, stomping blues number (not on any official Dylan album) that's worth finding.

influences:

 Mance Lipscomb, Muddy Waters, Dock Boggs, Harmonica Frank Floyd, Woody Guthrie, Mississippi Sheiks, Blind Willie McTell, Jimmie Rodgers

▶▶ Byrds, Tom Petty, Bruce Springsteen, John Mellencamp

Leland Rucker

E

Fird Eaglin Jr.

See: Snooks Eaglin

Snooks Eaglin

Born Fird Eaglin Jr., January 21, 1936, in New Orleans, LA.

"Snooks" Eaglin, named for radio character Baby Snooks, is one of New Orleans' greatest guitar players and singers. In a recording career spanning 40 years, he has played everything from acoustic folk songs to powerhouse funk to delicate jazz instrumentals. Playing without a pick, he combines jazz-styled single-note runs with muddy chords straight from the Mississippi. When Eaglin was 19-months-old he was diagnosed with glaucoma and a brain tumor, resulting in blindness. At age six he began playing guitar and by 11 was winning talent contests. Eaglin was a member of the legendary R&B group the Flamingos, featuring Allen Toussaint on piano. When the band broke up, he worked anywhere he could, including on the streets of the French Quarter playing for tourists. In 1958 he recorded his first sides for Harry Oster as a street musician playing folk music and blues. He signed with Imperial and recorded for Dave Bartholomew, and over the next 25 years he played every style and venue possible, though he recorded very rarely. The

New Orleans Jazz and Heritage Festival brought Eaglin to the attention of a much wider audience. Today he is acknowledged as one of New Orleans' musical treasures and known throughout the world as a stellar performer.

what to buy: At age 23, Eaglin began recording for Dave Bartholomew, the legendary trumpeter-composer-producer for Fats Domino. All 26 of their collaborations over a three-year period are collected for the first time on *The Complete Imperial Recordings* ✍✍✍✍ (Capitol, 1995, prod. Pete Welding), which restores Eaglin to his proper place in the history of New Orleans music. Eaglin's singing is particularly strong on these early cuts, which range from the bouncy New Orleans R&B of "Yours Truly" to the sorrowful blues of "By the Water," on which Eaglin sings and shouts like Ray Charles. In the later sessions, his guitar playing comes to the fore and hints at the pleasures to come. While all the Black Top discs are worthwhile, *Out of Nowhere* ✍✍✍ (Black Top, 1989, prod. Hammond Scott) is the best of the lot, a glorious romp through New Orleans funk and pop. Eaglin and the powerhouse Black Top band rock from start ("Oh Lawdy My Baby," with Eaglin and Anson Funderburgh trading licks) to finish (the novelty "Cheeta," about a chimp and his underwear). Two beautiful instrumentals are included: the jazz standard "Out of Nowhere" and the Spanish-tinged "Kiss of Fire." It's hard to imagine any other guitarist tackling this variety of music and succeeding so well. *Teasin' You* ✍✍✍ (Black Top, 1992, prod. Hammond Scott) is a great collection of material from Snooks' voluminous songbook. The stripped-down arrangements leave plenty of room for him to strut his stuff vocally and instrumentally. Earl King contributes three songs of classic Crescent City roll, while Grady Gaines is the sole guest and makes himself right at home. Eaglin plays lead *and* rhythm on the instrumental "Sleepwalk." *Live in Japan* ✍✍✍ (Black Top, 1997, prod. Snooks Eaglin), Eaglin's first stage recording, is a completely enjoyable set of blues, R&B and jazz with the guitarist at the top of his form and a sharp band of George Porter on bass, John Autin on keyboards and Jeffrey "Jellybean" Alexander on drums pushing things along nicely. Snooks shines on Bill Doggett's "Quaker City," a bright, bouncy swing tune, and the second-line "Lillie Mae." The band gets *really* funky on songs like "I Went to the Mardi Gras," "Josephine" and a thoroughly Snookified "It's Your Thing."

what to buy next: *Soul's Edge* ✍✍✍ (Black Top, 1995, prod. Hammond Scott) is another fine outing. Eaglin plays great solos on the pretty soul ballad "Nine Pound Steel" and the goofy "Skinny Minnie." "I Went to the Mardi Gras" is a New Or-

leans rhumboogie Carnival classic. The only negatives are three rather lengthy instrumentals. Three dozen years after the last of Eaglin's Imperial sessions, Black Top honcho Hammond Scott brought him back to the studio for *Baby, You Can Get Your Gun!* ✍✍✍ (Black Top, 1987, prod. Hammond Scott). The band leans more toward jazz—David Lastie on sax, Erving Charles (bass) and Smokey Johnson (drums) from Fats' band, plus Ron Levy on keyboards and Ronnie Earl on rhythm guitar. Snooks works his way through bar blues songs like "You Give Me Nothing but the Blues" with Levy on B-3 organ to the pleading "Baby Please," and smokes on the flamenco-surf instrumental "Perfidia." *Country Boy Down in New Orleans* ✍✍✍ (Arhoolie, 1991, prod. Chris Strachwitz) and *That's All Right* ✍✍✍ (Original Blues Classics, 1994, prod. Kenneth Goldstein) are both based on the same original recordings by Harry Oster in 1958. Oster presented Eaglin as a folk musician accompanying himself on 6- and 12-string guitar, Crescent City's answer to Leadbelly. The Arhoolie set gets the nod because of its far greater length (68 minutes to 38) and inclusion of additional material featuring Percy Randolph on harmonica and washboard. There's even a rare acoustic version of the New Orleans party favorite, "Mardi Gras Mambo."

worth searching for: Eaglin has served as studio musician on dozens of New Orleans R&B sessions. Look for him backing up James "Sugar Boy" Crawford on the 1954 release "Jockomo" (the first recording of the New Orleans anthem "Iko Iko"), the Wild Magnolias black Indian group and several dates with his good friend Professor Longhair.

influences:

◄◄ Leadbelly, Fats Domino, Ray Charles

►► Dr. John, Earl King, Leo Nocentelli

David Feld

Ronnie Earl

Born Ronnie Horvath, 1951, in Queens, NY.

Ronnie Earl didn't fully find his voice as a guitarist until it came to dominate his music; when he quit using a vocalist and went to an all-instrumental approach he blossomed from a quality journeyman to a major artist. After honing his chops in clubs for years, first as a member of Roomful of Blues, then as a solo artist, around 1990, Earl quit drinking and drugging—then stopped relying on mediocre vocalists to express his muse. The results have been nothing less than revelatory, one stunning all-instrumental album after another, each fusing jazz and blues with equal parts skill, verve and soul, and each displaying continued growth and maturity.

what to buy: *Blues Guitar Virtuoso Live in Europe* ♪♪♪♪ (Bullseye Blues, 1995, prod. Ronnie Earl) lives up to its rather pompous title, singeing eardrums from the first notes of Freddie King's "San-Ho-Zay" to the fade-out on the very original "Rego Park Blues." Earl followed this blast of sheer in-your-face intensity with something completely different; *Grateful Heart: Blues and Ballads* ♪♪♪♪ (Bullseye Blues, 1996, prod. Neil Ward) also lacks words, but it is a mellow, late-night blend of jazz and blues featuring tenor sax master David "Fathead" Newman and displaying Earl's continued development as a composer.

what to buy next: *Language of the Soul* ♪♪♪♪ (Bullseye Blues, 1994, prod. Ronnie Earl) and *The Colour of Love* ♪♪♪♪ (Verve, 1997, prod. Tom Dowd) are also excellent instrumental offerings, paying tribute to Earl heroes from Anne Frank to Otis Rush, and from Martin Luther King to Carlos Santana. *The Colour of Love* does feature one vocal track, by Gregg Allman.

best of the rest:

I Like It When ♪♪♪ (Antone's)
Plays Big Blues ♪♪♪ (Black Top)
They Call Me Mr. Earl ♪♪♪ (Black Top)
Peace of Mind ♪♪♪♪ (Black Top, 1990)
Surrounded by Love ♪♪♪♪ (Black Top, 1991)
Test of Time ♪♪♪ (Black Top, 1992)
Still River ♪♪♪ (Audioquest, 1994)

influences:

◄◄ Earl Hooker, T-Bone Walker, Robert Junior Lockwood, Robert Nighthawk, Freddie King, Carlos Santana, Duane Allman, Ray Charles, John Coltrane, Jimmie Vaughan, Duke Robillard, Dickey Betts

►► Kenny Wayne Shepherd, Jonny Lang

Alan Paul

Amos Easton
See: Bumble Bee Slim

David "Honeyboy" Edwards
Born June 28, 1915, in Shaw, MS.

Along with Robert Junior Lockwood, Honeyboy Edwards is one of the last surviving members of the first rank of 1930s Delta bluesmen. He and Lockwood are the only musicians who can talk intimately about Robert Johnson—his wanderings, his

music and his last days of life. In August 1938, Edwards had teamed up with Johnson for a trip through Greenwood, Mississippi, where Johnson was poisoned and died of pneumonia several days later. "At 2 a.m., he got so sick," Edwards told researcher Pete Welding, "they had to bring him back to town." But Edwards is more than a witness with a good memory. He recorded a series of impressive Library of Congress cuts for folklorist Alan Lomax during a trip through the Delta in 1942, the same trip that netted ground-breaking performances by Son House and Muddy Waters. He recorded briefly in the early 1950s for the Sun and Chess labels. And more than a half-century later, Edwards still mesmerizes audiences in Chicago, delivering the deep blues as if he was stretched out on a Mississippi front porch. He can be erratic and his droning chords sometimes numb, but there is no more authentic purveyor of the music's most basic roots.

what to buy: *Delta Bluesman* ♪♪♪♪ (Earwig, 1992, prod. Michael Frank, Mike Vernon) is slightly schizophrenic, stretching from 1942 material to 1991 workouts. But due to the presence of all 13 of Edwards' Library of Congress classics, it is Edwards' signature recording. The 1991 items are more sketchy, but a sympathetic backup band with the late Sunnyland Slim and harpist Carey Bell helps out nicely.

what to buy next: *White Windows* ♪♪♪♪ (Evidence, 1993, prod. Gregory Oatis, John Gibbs Rockwood, Robert Seeman) is Edwards in his best setting, alone. There are some old regulars here, "Goin' Down Slow" and "Roll and Tumble Blues" the most obvious, but Edwards reaches deeper into his bag and provides subtle versions of "Drop Down Mama" and Robert Johnson's unrecorded "Take a Walk with Me." *I've Been Around* ♪♪♪♪ (Trix, 1995, prod. Honeyboy Edwards, Pete Lowry) is another mixed bag featuring cuts from 1974 to 1977. The most effective are the solos. Edwards nimbly refurbishes Charley Patton's "Pony Blues" and "Banty Rooster" and mixes it up well with the late Big Walter Horton for the balance of the album—a sad reminder of what might have been an inspired partnership. On *Drop Down Mama* ♪♪♪♪ (Chess, 1990), only the title song is Edwards'—bruising as it is. The rest are top-notch takes by Johnny Shines, Robert Nighthawk and Floyd Jones, and all worth owning.

influences:

◄◄ Charley Patton, Robert Petway, Robert Johnson, Sunnyland Slim

►► Little Walter, Big Walter Horton

Steve Braun

David "Honeyboy" Edwards (© Jack Vartoogian)

Robert "Big Mojo" Elem

Born January 22, 1928, in Ita Bena, MS. Died February 5, 1997.

Bass player, guitarist and vocalist Robert Elem got his first job in Chicago in 1951 playing guitar behind Arthur "Big Boy" Spires. In 1953 he played briefly with Otis Rush before forming his own band with a young Freddie King on lead guitar; Elem was present on King's debut recording in 1956 on El Bee. By this time Elem had switched to electric bass because there was more work for bass players in Chicago than guitarists. Elem spent eight years playing bass behind King. In the 1960s he backed Jimmy Dawkins, Smokey Smothers and G.L. Crockett, and first recorded as a vocalist on Delmark's 1967 anthology *Sweet Home Chicago*. In 1979 he was part of a "Chicago Blues" package tour through Europe.

what to buy: Elem's only solo CD, *Mojo Boogie* 🎵🎵🎵 (St. George, 1994, prod. George Paulus) features driving bass and effective vocals.

worth searching for: Elem played on all three CDs recorded by Austria's Mojo Blues Band. The *Sweet Home Chicago* 🎵🎵🎵 (Delmark, 1967) anthology is also worth a listen.

influences:

◀◀ J.B. Lenoir, Elmore James, Robert Nighthawk

▶▶ Freddie King, Magic Slim

Jeff Hannusch

Big Chief Ellis

Born Wilbert Thirkield Ellis, November 10, 1914, in Birmingham, AL. Died December 20, 1977, in Birmingham, AL.

Big Chief Ellis began playing piano at his great-aunt's house because his parents were religious and wouldn't indulge his fascination with the blues. He became a professional gambler, traveling the country and honing his slowed-down, moaning, 12-bar piano songs by learning from the people he met. His travels took him to New York City, where he ran nightclubs, and to Ft. McClellan, Alabama, where he served in the Army and composed Stick McGhee's eventual R&B hit, "Drinking Wine Spo-Dee-O-Dee." He recorded for several record companies in the 1940s and 1950s with such artists as Sonny Terry, Brownie McGhee, John Cephas and Tarheel Slim. Despite late-career activity—he recorded for Trix and played festivals—he didn't get to touch many people beyond the musicians he played with.

what to buy: *Big Chief Ellis Featuring Tarheel Slim* ♫♫♫ (Trix, 1977, prod. Big Chief Ellis, Pete Lowry, Richard Spottswood), with guitar help from McGhee, Cephas and Tarheel Slim, is one of the few albums you can find by this unfortunately forgotten talent; his soft-spoken voice is a perfect fit for the blues, and he channels a tangible sadness into standards like "Sweet Home Chicago" and the originals "All Down Blues," "Rocky Mountain Blues" and "Prison Bound."

influences:

◀◀ Jimmy Yancey, Otis Spann, Charles Brown, Ray Charles

▶▶ Stick McGhee, Sonny Terry, Brownie McGhee, Cephas & Wiggins, Dr. John

Steve Knopper

Emmit Ellis Jr.

See: Bobby Rush

Tinsley Ellis

Born June 4, 1957, in Atlanta, GA.

What sets Ellis apart from all the other flashy blues guitarists— and there are a lot of them—is his ability to recreate old-fashioned southern soul grooves. Though the heavy-touring Ellis uses songs loosely in concert, as structures for jamming, his albums emphasize funk, rock and songwriting craft. He borrows just as much from 1970s hard-rock bands Bachman-Turner Overdrive and Foghat as he does from heroes Muddy Waters, John Lee Hooker and Chuck Berry. After moving from southern Florida back to his native Atlanta in 1975, he played in various bar bands, including the Alley Cats and the Heartfixers; eventually, he earned a reputation as one of the city's best-known guitar hotshots. That gave him momentum for a solo career and five solid Alligator albums.

what to buy: *Storm Warning* ♫♫♫ (Alligator, 1994, prod. Eddy Offord) is full of typically solid guitar jams and strong rock power chords, but Ellis' songwriting on the reflective "To the Devil for a Dime" and "A Quitter Never Wins" distinguishes him.

what to buy next: *Fire It Up* ♫♫ (Alligator, 1997, prod. Tom Dowd) suffers from a humorless cover of the cringe-inducing Kenny Rogers psychedelic hit "Just Dropped In," but the rest is solid rock 'n' blues.

what to avoid: *Georgia Blue* ♫♫ (Alligator, 1988, prod. Ricky Keller), Ellis' solo debut, is all show-offy guitar solos and little else.

the rest:

Fanning the Flames ♫♫ (Alligator, 1989)
Trouble Time ♫♫♫ (Alligator, 1992)

worth searching for: Two of the Heartfixers' early albums, *Cool on It* ♫♫♫ (Landslide, 1986/Alligator, 1993, prod. Eddy Offord) and *Tore Up* ♫♫ (Landslide, 1984), have been released by Alligator.

influences:

◀◀ Buddy Guy, Kenny Rogers, Bachman-Turner Overdrive, Eric Clapton, Muddy Waters, Howlin' Wolf, Fleetwood Mac, John Mayall

▶▶ Kenny Wayne Shepherd, Stevie Ray Vaughan, Jonny Lang, Eric Johnson

Steve Knopper

John Ellison

Born Willie John Ellison, in Montgomery, WV.

What makes a pop-music hit more than just a pop hit? What gives it soul? For an answer, you might want to listen to "Some Kind of Wonderful," a 1967 hit by the Soul Brothers Six. Neither the lyrics nor the title are exceptional or original—the Drifters had a hit of the same name back in 1961. But the record stomps with the fervor of a gospel-singing elephant. There's not a second of contrivance or artifice in it. It is transcendent, yet also deeply and raucously earthy. John Ellison was the lead singer/songwriter on that hit. The group consisted of Ellison, who also played guitar; bass player Vonell Benjamin; and four brothers who Ellison met while living in Rochester, New York, in the early 1960s—Sam, Charles, Harry and Moses Armstrong. Sam and Ellison had played together in a group called, oddly, the Satans Four. (The name came from their manager.) The four others were in the Brothers Four. Ellison, one of six sons of a West Virginia coal miner, sang gospel as a boy and learned guitar at age 12. He moved to Rochester at age 18 to play music. "Some Kind of Wonderful" was recorded in 1967 and the group signed with Atlantic Records. Subsequent Atlantic singles failed, however, and the members disbanded in 1969. Ellison recorded solo on the Phil-L.A. of Soul label and organized a new Soul Brothers Six II band that recorded and toured in the mid-1970s. During that time, Grand Funk Railroad had a hit with "Wonderful," sparking European interest in Ellison. His new Soul Brothers Six toured extensively and even did a European TV show with Abba. In 1992, after too many years of obscurity, Ellison was "rediscovered" at a Rochester club where he was a guest performer and started touring again. Meanwhile, Buddy Guy and Huey Lewis have cut popular versions of "Wonderful" in the 1990s. It may be Ellison's one hit, but it's an enduring one.

what to buy: *The Very Best of John Ellison & the Soul Brothers Six* 𝄢𝄢𝄢 (Forevermore, 1995, prod. Chris Biehler, Steve Brodie) is frustrating because it's all that's out there. Forevermore didn't get the Atlantic singles; the version of "Wonderful" included is from Ellison's 1993 comeback album. But it does have six good early singles, nine mid-1970s cuts derivative of the Isley Brothers and the Temptations and five songs from the 1990s.

the rest:
Welcome Back 𝄢𝄢𝄢 (After Hours, 1993)

influences:
◀◀ James Brown, Gene Chandler

▶▶ Grand Funk Railroad, Buddy Guy

Steven Rosen

Billy "The Kid" Emerson

Born December 21, 1929, in Tarpon Springs, FL.

Billy Emerson's claim to fame is his authorship of "When It Rains It Pours," a tuneful blues that was one of Elvis Presley's first recordings for Sun, and the cackling "Red Hot," converted by Billy Lee Riley into a rockabilly standard. But aside from playing organ vamps behind Chuck Berry on some of the duck-walker's mid-1960s sessions, Emerson failed to make a dent as a singer in his own right. More than anything else, it may have been bad timing. Unlike Howlin' Wolf, Junior Parker and James Cotton, all who recorded with Sam Phillips in the early 1950s, Emerson began his association with Phillips several years later, when the fabled producer was already focusing on making a star out of Presley. After a stint in the Air Force, Emerson had relocated to Greenville, Mississippi, where he joined Ike Turner's Kings of Rhythm as a vocalist and guitar player. From 1954 to 1955 Emerson recorded frequently but never seemed to find a niche either as an R&B singer or a rock 'n' roll man. Whatever the reasons, Emerson moved north in 1955 to

Chicago, where stints with Vee-Jay and Chess failed to spark. He continued to play and tour with blues revues into the late 1970s but in recent years is reported to have returned to Florida and taken up gospel singing.

what to buy: Billy Emerson's Memphis recordings can be found on almost any Sun compilation, but the massive eight-disc *Sun Records: The Blues Years 1950–58* 𝄢𝄢𝄢𝄢 (Charly, 1996, prod. Sam Phillips) contains the most on record. There are seven tracks here, including "Rain" and "Red Hot," along with romping takes like "Little Fine Healthy Thing" and "Shim Sham Shimmy." There are enough fine unavailable Sun tracks to warrant an entire disc devoted to Emerson.

influences:
◀◀ Ike Turner

▶▶ Elvis Presley, Billy Lee Riley

Steve Braun

Sleepy John Estes

Born John Adam Estes, January 25, 1899, in Ripley, TN. Died June 5, 1977, in Brownsville, TN.

Some blues artists earned repute for hooking up with the right people, or recording in the right studio, at the right time. A select few—Robert Johnson, Muddy Waters, Howlin' Wolf, Buddy Guy—became famous because they're just drop-dead talented. You can hear from the first notes of Estes' classic "The Girl I Love, She Got Long, Curly Hair" a natural high-pitch tremolo, an instinctive yodel that communicates heartbreak without much effort. Estes' father was a guitar picker, and John—who later earned the nickname "Sleepy" because he could supposedly sleep standing up—fashioned his own guitar from a cigar box. He led a work gang for a railroad maintenance crew, singing to keep everybody else alert. Through his travels he met musicians like Jab Jones and James "Yank" Rachell, and they wound up auditioning for the Victor company in 1929. Though he never made enough money to exist above the poverty line, he sustained an amazingly prolific career, recording for almost a dozen record companies until his death.

what to buy: Estes' songwriting talent—on the detail-rich "Broken-Hearted, Ragged and Dirty Too" and "Fire Department Blues (Martha Hardin)"—comes across just as well as his teary singing style and excellent small-combo arrangements in the almost-definitive *I Ain't Gonna Be Worried No More 1929–41* 𝄢𝄢𝄢𝄢 (Yazoo, 1992, prod. Richard Nevins, Don Kent, Stefan Grossman). It's all traditional blues, but Estes takes the lyrics a step further than most performers; "Floating Bridge" describes in astounding detail a near-drowning incident Estes endured in Kentucky, and the frustrated "Who's Been Telling You Buddy Brown" asks, "Have you ever tried lovin', when you can't get it in your mind?"

what to buy next: In the 1960s Estes was a prime subject for revivalists and historians, not to mention admiring musicians. *Electric Sleep* ♫♫♫ (Delmark, 1964/1991, prod. Robert Koester) matches the singer with an electric Chicago blues combo, including pianist Sunnyland Slim, harpist Carey Bell and bassist Earl Hooker. *Broke and Hungry* ♫♫♫ (Delmark, 1964/1995, prod. Robert Koester) is a collaboration with blues upstart Michael Bloomfield and Estes' old stomping partner Yank Rachell.

the rest:
In Europe ♫♫ (Delmark)
The Legend of Sleepy John Estes ♫♫♫ (Delmark, 1962)
Brownsville Blues ♫♫♫ (Delmark, 1965)
1929–40 ♫♫♫ (Smithsonian Folkways, 1967)
Complete Works, Vols. 1–2 ♫♫♫ (Document, 1991)

worth searching for: *First Recordings* ♫♫♫ (JSP) collects Estes' earliest recordings, his 1929 sessions with troubled harpist Noah Lewis and guitarist Yank Rachell.

influences:
◀◀ Robert Johnson, Son House, Tommy Johnson, Willie Brown, Blind Boy Fuller

▶▶ Jackie Wilson, Jimmie Dale Gilmore, Eric Clapton, Paul Butterfield Blues Band, Otis Redding, Sam Cooke

Steve Knopper

Terry Evans

Born in Vicksburg, MS.

An incredibly gifted vocalist whose warm and sometimes gruff bass-baritone has been heard often, Terry Evans has a list of recording and performing credits that many session singers would kill for. He teamed with fellow vocalist Bobby King in the 1970s, and the pair worked the Los Angeles club and studio scene. Eventually they hooked up with Ry Cooder, and their astounding tandem vocals became a featured part of Cooder's albums *Chicken Skin Music*, *Show Time*, *The Slide Area* and *Get Rhythm*. Evans also has worked on albums by Boz Scaggs, Maria Muldaur, John Fogerty and John Lee Hooker. As a leader he's just as versatile, getting down and dirty on a rough roadhouse blues one minute and crooning a smooth soul ballad the next. Whether on his own, with King, or working behind others, Evans' is a voice worth hearing.

what to buy: The musical centerpiece of *Puttin' It Down* ♫♫♫ (AudioQuest, 1995, prod. Joe Harley, Terry Evans, Jorge Calderon) is a scary, otherworldly reading of J.B. Lenoir's backwoods blues "Down in Mississippi." But the album has its lighter moments, too, like the smart "In This Day and Time" and Evans' own simmering "One Sided Love Affair."

the rest:
Blues for Thought ♫♫♫ (Pointblank/Charisma Records America, 1993)

worth searching for: Evans and his one-time partner, Bobby King, were a murderously good soul duo, laying down old-school Stax/Volt grooves that were certainly in a league with Sam & Dave. Both *Live and Let Live!* ♫♫♫ (Rounder, 1988) and *Rhythm, Blues, Soul and Grooves* ♫♫♫ (Rounder, 1990) are treasures and still in the catalogs.

influences:
◀◀ Otis Redding, Sam & Dave, Solomon Burke

Daniel Durchholz

Fabulous Thunderbirds

Formed 1974, in Austin, TX.

Kim Wilson, vocals, harmonica; Jimmie Vaughan, guitar, vocals (1974–90); Michael "Duke" Robillard, guitar (1990–93); Doug "The Kid" Bangham, guitar (1990–93); Kid Ramos, guitar (1994–present); Keith Ferguson, bass (1974–86); Preston Hubbard, bass (1986–93); Harvey Brooks, bass (1994–95); Willie J. Campbell, bass (1996–present); Mike Buck, drums (1974–80); Fran Christina, drums (1980–95); Jimmy Bott, drums (1995–present); Gene Taylor, keyboards (1994–present).

Bringing hard rock muscle to Chicago blues, the Fabulous Thunderbirds were the hottest band on Texas' spicy rock 'n' blues bar circuit in the 1970s, when disco was king and nobody in Texas thought they had a snowball's chance in hell to make it big. But word spread, and the band got a deal with the independent label Takoma (home to John Fahey and Leo Kottke) before Chrysalis signed them a year later. Their hit "Tuff Enuff" brought the group mainstream success—it was a Top 10 hit and was featured on several movie soundtracks. All the years of hard work that founders Kim Wilson and Jimmie Vaughan (Stevie Ray Vaughan's older brother) had put into it began to take their toll, and the group started repeating itself. Vaughan lost interest and left to pursue a solo career; personnel changes persisted. Wilson, an expert harmonica player, put the band on hold to cut a couple of overlooked solo albums, then put together a new version of the band in 1995. He reformed the band a year later with a new line-up (Wilson, Kid Ramos, Gene Taylor, Willie J. Campbell and drummer Jimmy Bott) and a new album in 1997.

what to buy: While many critics and fans point to the Dave Edmunds-produced *Tuff Enuff* as *the* T-birds album to own, *The Essential Fabulous Thunderbirds Collection* 🎵🎵🎵 (Chrysalis, 1991, prod. Denny Bruce, Nick Lowe) is prime stuff from the band's early days, when it still played smoky bars and wasn't thinking about writing a hit song. The collection is drawn from its first four albums, including the Takoma debut, all of which are now out of print.

the rest:
Tuff Enuff 🎵🎵 (CBS, 1986)
Hot Number 🎵🎵 (Epic/Associated, 1987)
Powerful Stuff 🎵🎵 (Epic, 1989)
Walk That Walk, Talk That Talk 🎵🎵 (Epic, 1991)
Hot Stuff: The Greatest Hits 🎵🎵 (Epic, 1992)
Roll the Dice 🎵🎵🎵 (Private Music, 1995)
High Water 🎵🎵🎵 (High Street, 1997)

solo outings:
Kim Wilson:
Tigerman 🎵🎵 (Antone's, 1993)
That's Life 🎵🎵 (Antone's, 1994)

influences:
◀◀ Muddy Waters, Bo Diddley, Slim Harpo, Freddie King
▶▶ Stevie Ray Vaughan, Roomful of Blues, Red Devils

see also: *Jimmie Vaughan*

Doug Pullen

Jerome Felder

See: Doc Pomus

H-Bomb Ferguson

Born c. 1931, in Charleston, SC.

No one who has seen him will ever forget the flamboyant H-Bomb Ferguson. The son of a Baptist minister, he started playing piano in his father's storefront church at age six. Discovered at 18 in a Charleston club by Cat Anderson, Ferguson went out

on the road with Joe Liggins & His Honeydrippers and settled in New York City around 1950. As a teenaged blues shouter modeled after his idol, Wynonie "Mr. Blues" Harris, Ferguson became known as "the Cobra Kid" for his slinky moves behind the keyboard. He made a series of obscure 78s for Derby ("Wine Head," "Jumpin' and Shoutin'"), Atlas (Ferguson's signature number, "Rock H-Bomb Rock"), Prestige ("Feel Like I Do"), Decca ("Hole in the Wall Tonight" with the Andy Kirk Orchestra) and Savoy ("Slowly Going Crazy", "My Brown Frame Baby"). By the mid-1950s the R&B era was over as far as record sales were concerned, and Ferguson resettled in Cincinnati, Ohio, where he worked the local clubs and cut singles to little avail. James Brown picked up on a couple of his local hits, "Spaghetti and Meatballs" and "Little Tiger," and took him into the King studios, but nothing happened there either. When H-Bomb reappeared several years later he was pumping an electric piano, leading his own band and sporting an incredible collection of wigs of every description—"one for every day of the month," he once bragged to a reporter. He staked out a regular gig in a Cincinnati nightclub and began recording for the local Radiation label, winning W.C. Handy Awards for the album *Shake and Bake* (1986) and the song "Medicine Man."

what to buy: Ferguson finally burst into the digital era with the fantastic *Wiggin' Out* 🎵🎵🎵🎵 (Earwig, 1994, prod. Michael Frank), a funky, hip-shaking tour-de-force by the venerable bluesman. "Shake Your Apple Tree" and "Meatloaf" are beautifully bawdy and rough, while "Love Her, Don't Shove Her" is a rare blues diatribe against domestic violence. Unhappily, the H-Bomb Ferguson CD discography begins and ends with *Wiggin' Out*.

worth searching for: One of H-Bomb's obscure Specialty sides, "She's Been Gone," can be found on disc three of *The Specialty Records Story* 🎵🎵🎵 (Specialty, 1994), and his Savoy singles—including the magnificent "Slowly Going Crazy"—are collected on an out-of-print LP, *Life Is Hard* 🎵🎵🎵 (Savoy, 1986).

influences:
◀◀ Buddy Johnson, Wynonie Harris, Eddie "Cleanhead" Vinson

John Sinclair

Fleetwood Mac

Formed 1967, in London, England.

Mick Fleetwood, drums; John McVie, bass; Peter Green, guitar, vocals (1967–69); Jeremy Spencer, guitar, vocals, piano (1967–70); Danny Kirwan, guitar, vocals (1968–72); Christine McVie, piano, vocals (1970–present); Bob Welch, guitar, vocals (1971–74); Dave Walker,

guitar, vocals, harmonica (1972–73); Bob Weston, guitar, banjo, harmonica (1972–73); Lindsay Buckingham, guitar, vocals (1975–87); Stevie Nicks, vocals (1975–90); Billy Burnette, guitar, vocals (1987–present); Rick Vito, guitar (1987–91); Bekka Bramlett, vocals (1993–present); Dave Mason, guitar, vocals (1994–present).

From 1975 to 1982, a band that started out playing pure blues had 12 consecutive Top 20 singles, and overall has totaled 18 Top 40 hits despite personnel turmoil and turnover that make Spinal Tap seem stable. Fleetwood Mac went from being the Green-founded blues group—which was very popular in the British blues scene—to a bland, West Coast pop outfit under the lead of guitarist Welch. The crucial evolution came when Welch was replaced in 1975 by two fellow Californians, Buckingham and Nicks, and Fleetwood Mac became one of pop's hottest groups during the 1970s. Sadly, except in reissue, they never returned to their blues roots.

what to buy: Fleetwood Mac's blues period can be comfortably sampled on *English Rose* 𝄞𝄞𝄞 (Blue Horizon, 1969, prod. Mike Vernon) known in the U.K. in somewhat different form as *Mr. Wonderful.* If Green and Spencer weren't always convincing blues singers, they were gifted guitarists. The double album *Fleetwood Mac in Chicago 1969* 𝄞𝄞𝄞 (Blue Horizon/Sire, 1975, prod. Mike Vernon, Marshall Chess), with guests Otis Spann, Willie Dixon, Shakey Horton, Honeyboy Edwards, Buddy Guy and other bluesmen, is also a good context in which to hear the Brits' 6-string blues expertise with more competent singers to the fore.

what to buy next: Recorded with special guest Eddie Boyd, *Live at the BBC* 𝄞𝄞𝄞𝄞 (Griffin, 1996) offers up generous slices of Brit blues at its best.

the rest:
Mystery to Me 𝄞𝄞𝄞 (Reprise, 1973)
Fleetwood Mac 𝄞𝄞𝄞𝄞 (Reprise, 1975)
Rumours 𝄞𝄞𝄞𝄞 (Warner Bros., 1977)
Tusk 𝄞𝄞𝄞𝄞 (Warner Bros., 1979)
Peter Green's Fleetwood Mac Live at the BBC 𝄞𝄞𝄞 (Castle, 1995)

worth searching for: An import, *London Live 68* 𝄞𝄞𝄞𝄞 (Thunderbolt, 1995) is a good session with Peter Green.

solo outings:
Peter Green:
Green and Guitar: The Very Best of Peter Green 1977–81 𝄞𝄞𝄞 (Music Club, 1996)

Kim Wilson of the Fabulous Thunderbirds (© Ken Settle)

Christine McVie:
The Legendary Christine Perfect Album 𝄞𝄞𝄞 (Blue Horizon, 1969/Sire, 1976)
Christine McVie 𝄞𝄞 (Warner Bros., 1984)

influences:
◀◀ Elmore James, Etta James, John Mayall

Steve Holtje

Eddie Floyd

Born June 25, 1935, in Montgomery, AL.

One of soul music's most underrated vocalists and composer of some of the genre's timeless classics, Eddie Floyd is still going strong, a Stax survivor. Floyd has been performing since 1955, when he and three Detroit friends began crooning together in a group they named the Falcons. The group permutated over several years, adding Joe Stubbs—brother of Levi, the Four Tops shouter—and Mack Rice, who later wrote "Mustang Sally." They first scored with "You're So Fine," with Stubbs on lead. Three years later, with a new vocalist, Wilson Pickett, they hit again, with the scorching "I Found a Love." When the volatile Pickett went solo, Floyd was brought down to Memphis by future Stax executive Al Bell. Soon enough, Floyd and Pickett were back in the studio—and sometimes trading punches—as Stax grew into a southern soul powerhouse. Writing with Pickett, Otis Redding and guitarist Steve Cropper, Floyd's output was phenomenal: "99 and 1/2 Won't Do," "634-5789," "Don't Fight It." The songs he kept himself—"Knock on Wood" and "Raise Your Hand"—proved just as big. But as Stax began to implode with bad management in the mid-1970s, artists like Floyd suffered. After a last gasp produced the bluesy "I've Never Found a Girl" and "Soul Street," Floyd signed with the deep soul Malaco label and has since toured fitfully with former Stax mates Carla and Rufus Thomas and members of Booker T. and the MGs. He still goes out on the road several times a year, exhorting gleeful audiences to raise their hands.

what to buy: *Knock on Wood* 𝄞𝄞𝄞𝄞 (Atlantic/Rhino, 1967, prod. Jim Stewart) is Floyd in his prime, singing "Knock on Wood," "Raise Your Hand," the downcast "Got to Make a Comeback" and other soul standards. Some of the rawest soul group singing ever to send volume meters into the red, *I Found a Love* 𝄞𝄞𝄞𝄞 (Relic, 1986, prod. Robert West) captures the Falcons at their most explosive in the early 1960s. With a shifting vocal line-up of Floyd, Pickett, Stubbs and Rice and gut-bucket guitar by Robert Ward and his Ohio Untouchables, the Falcons were a super-group who split apart much too soon. Recorded for the Detroit-based Lupine and a gaggle of other firms, one shudders to think what they could have done for Motown.

what to buy next: *Chronicle* 🎵🎵🎵 (Stax, 1979) contains "Knock on Wood" and the cream of Floyd's later Stax hits, including "I've Never Found a Girl" and "Soul Street." Since most of his later albums were uneven affairs sandwiched around hits, this collection does nicely.

what to avoid: *California Girl/Down to Earth* 🎵🎵 (Stax, 1970/1971) is a rare two-fer set, but beyond minor singles like "California Girl" and "My Girl," the pickings are slim.

worth searching for: *Rare Stamps* 🎵🎵🎵 (Stax, 1993), a 25-cut set, is prized for its inclusion of 1968's "Big Bird," an account of a frightening plane trip to Redding's funeral.

influences:

◀◀ Hank Ballard, Nolan Strong

▶▶ Al Green, Bruce Springsteen, Southside Johnny

Steve Braun

Sue Foley

Born March 29, 1968, in Ottawa, Ontario, Canada.

Musician magazine made a good call when it cited Sue Foley's "little girl nudge that draws the ear in a crowded genre." Not that she's light on musicianship. She's an engaging singer not afraid to take chances with material, and with her trademark paisley Telecaster she's a whip-snap guitarist. Foley lived a while in Vancouver before moving to Austin, Texas. The toothsome redhead could've quintupled her press by tarting it up even a little, but she stuck to business and always fronted good, no-shuck bands. (Her drummers have been S.P. Leary-influenced Jason Moeller and the undisputed king of the Texas shuffle beat, Freddy "Pharoah" Walden.) Foley has toured France, Holland, Sweden, Norway and Japan and has done big-time TV shows in her native Canada. Critics who compare her to Bonnie Raitt are blues-clueless; Foley has better material and plays more guitar than Raitt has since the 1970s.

what to buy: *Young Girl Blues* 🎵🎵🎵♪ (Antone's, 1992, prod. Derek O'Brien, George Rains) was a lauded debut that featured a winsome "(Me & My) Chauffeur Blues" that does Memphis Minnie proud and an infectious cover of Betty James' "Little Mixed Up."

what to buy next: The 1990s most upbeat bluesgrrl surprises with two well-done Dylan covers on *Big City Blues* 🎵🎵🎵 (Antone's, 1995, prod. Stephen Bruton) and doesn't disappoint

with straight-on "Howlin' for My Darlin'" and "One Hundred Dollar Bill" (originally by Howlin' Wolf and Buddy Guy, respectively). A guilty pleasure is the instrumental "Girl's Night Out" with the Antone's Fun Girls (Toni Price, Sarah Brown, etc.) whooping and yipping in the background.

the rest:

Without a Warning 🎵🎵 (Antone's, 1993)

influences:

◀◀ Memphis Minnie, Earl Hooker

▶▶ Debbie Babcock, Cricket Taylor

Tim Schuller

Aleck Ford

See: Sonny Boy Williamson I

Robben Ford

See: Charles Ford Band

Charles Ford Band /Ford Blues Band /Robben Ford

Formed 1971, in San Francisco, CA.

Mark Ford (born October 21, 1953, in Ukiah, CA), harmonica; Patrick Ford (born February 19, 1949, in Woodlake, CA), drums; Robben Ford (born December 16, 1951, in Woodlake, CA), guitar, vocals; Stanley Poplin, bass.

The Charles Ford Band was one of the best of the blue-eyed blues bands to emerge from the weirdness of the late 1960s and early 1970s. Unfortunately, the band recorded only one album. If they'd stayed together—who knows, could they have given Paul Butterfield a serious run for his money? Where Butterfield's early bands were anchored by guitarists Mike Bloomfield and Elvin Bishop, the Charles Ford Band had wunderkind guitarist Robben Ford and two of his brothers. Robben and Pat Ford moved to San Francisco in the late 1960s, joining Charlie Musslewhite's band and appearing on his *Taking My Time* album. After almost two years, they started the Charles Ford Band, naming it after their father. The group broke up before being able to take advantage of a signed offer from Chess to record two songs with Muddy Waters. Mark left the business. Robben split for Los Angeles, releasing several jazz-oriented albums and scoring much-praised stints behind Jimmy Witherspoon and Joni Mitchell. He's since formed Robben Ford & the Blue Line, a guitar-fronted trio that mixes blues, rock and jazz, and he remains a tasty, in-demand session guitarist. Pat Ford returned to Musslewhite's band before dropping out to raise a family. He's since started Blue Rock'It Records, which specializes in recording Bay Area blues bands, and formed the Ford Blues Band.

what to buy: Delightfully reckless, *The Charles Ford Band* ♫♫♫♫ (Arhoolie, 1972, prod. Chris Strachwitz) is what happens when a still-pink-in-the-cheeks garage band—the Ford brothers are barely in their twenties—discover the blues.

what to buy next: The woefully under-recorded Luther Tucker turns up the heat on *Luther Tucker and the Ford Blues Band* ♫♫♫♪ (Blue Rock'It, 1995, prod. Pat Ford). *Ford and Friends* ♫♫♫♫ (Blue Rock'It, 1996, prod. Pat Ford) is a slightly uneven but enjoyable collection of sit-ins with friends Charlie Musslewhite, Chris Cain, Lowell Fulson, Luther Tucker and Robben Ford.

the rest:
A Reunion Live ♫♫♫ (Blue Rock'It, 1983)
As Real As It Gets ♫♫♫ (Blue Rock'It, 1996)

solo outings:
Robben Ford and the Blue Line:
Robben Ford and the Blue Line ♫♫♫♫ (Stretch, 1992)
Mystic Mile ♫♫♫♪ (Stretch, 1993)
Handful of Blues ♫♫♫♫ (Blue Thumb, 1995)
Discovering the Blues ♫♫♫♫ (Avenue Jazz, 1997)

Ford Blues Band:
Ford Blues Band ♫♫♫ (Blue Rock'It, 1988)
Breminale '92—Live in Europe ♫♫♫ (Blue Rock'It, 1992)
Ford Blues Band ♫♫♫ (Crosscut, 1994)
Hotshots ♫♫♫ (Blue Rock'It, 1994)

influences:
◀◀ Paul Butterfield Blues Band, Lowell Fulson, Michael Bloomfield

Dave Ranney

Ford Blues Band
See: Charles Ford Band

Jesse Fortune
Born February 28, 1930, in Macon, MS.

Even his own album liner notes refer to Fortune as an "obscure blues figure." His primary claim to fame was a 1963 single "Too Many Cooks" (later recorded by Robert Cray). A barber since the late 1960s, he sang with Otis Rush and Buddy Guy—before

Robben Ford

song
Ain't Got Nothin' but the Blues

album
Talk to Your Daughter (Warner Bros.)

instrument
Guitar

monster solo

Willie Dixon—then with the USA label he was convinced to cut several sides of his own. (Guy played guitar and Lafayette Leake played piano on most of them.) Despite his made-for-fame name, Fortune seems destined for cult fandom.

what to buy: *Fortune Tellin' Man* ♫♫♪ (Delmark, 1993, prod. Robert Koester) has some nice soul singing and, of course, an updated version of "Too Many Cooks," but it's easy to see why Fortune never rose to the level of his 1960s star contemporaries.

influences:
◀◀ Willie Dixon, Ray Charles, T-Bone Walker, B.B. King
▶▶ Buddy Guy, Otis Rush, Otis Clay, Robert Cray

Steve Knopper

James Founty
See: Dan Pickett

Carol Fran & Clarence Hollimon

Carol Fran born October 23, 1933, in Lafayette, LA. Clarence Hollimon born October 24, 1937, in Houston, TX.

Both Fran and Hollimon had lengthy solo careers before they teamed up in the late 1980s. Fran, a pianist, was playing in Joe Lutcher's band at the age of 15. In 1958 she cut "Emmitt Lee" for Excello, a strong seller in Louisiana. Other regional hits followed, and Fran became a session piano player at J.D. Miller's studio in Crowley. Fran split from Miller and Excello in 1962, cut two singles for Khoury's, and then moved to New Orleans, where she became a regular attraction at the Dew Drop Inn. In the late 1960s she joined Joe Tex's revue. In 1983 she and Hollimon struck out as a duo. One of the most dynamic blues guitarists of the modern era, Clarence Hollimon has an impressive blues pedigree. At the age of 16, he was playing sessions for Duke in Houston with Bobby "Blue" Bland. When he graduated high school he went on the road with Big Mama Thornton and later Charles Brown. After leaving Brown in 1960, Hollimon became the premier session guitarist at Duke, recording with O.V. Wright, Junior Parker, Buddy Ace, Miss Lavelle and James Davis, among others. Hollimon stayed with Duke until 1973, when the company was sold. Recording work slowed, but he managed to stay busy playing with various R&B combos around Houston. Since becoming a duo, Fran and Hollimon's schedule includes foreign tours, U.S. blues festivals and engagements on Houston's society circuit. Most recently they've recorded for Black Top.

what to buy: Both *Soul Sensation!* ♫♫♫♫ (Black Top, 1992, prod. Hammond Scott) and *See There!* (Black Top, 1995, prod. Hammond Scott) feature plenty of Hollimon's inventive Texas guitar and Fran's brilliant singing and piano.

what to buy next: Fran and Hollimon are included on the anthology *Gulf Coast Blues* ♫♫♫♫ (Black Top, 1989, prod. Hammond Scott).

worth searching for: In addition to the dozen or so singles Fran had, Hollimon's group the Hawks cut an instrumental single, "The Grissle," for ABC in 1960.

influences:

◀◀ Johnny Moore, Oscar Moore, T-Bone Walker, Clarence "Gatemouth" Brown, Guitar Slim, Charlie Christian, Roy Gaines

▶▶ Cal Green, Johnny Brown, Johnny Winter, Joe Hughes, Johnny Copeland, Pete Mayes, Derek O'Brien

Jeff Hannusch

Calvin Frazier

Born February 16, 1915, in Osceola, AR. Died September 23, 1972, in Detroit, MI.

Like Robert Junior Lockwood, Johnny Shines and Honeyboy Edwards, Calvin Frazier was a running partner of Robert Johnson. And like the others, Frazier came away from his brief union with Robert Dusty a changed man, his music stamped with the unmistakable imprint of Johnson's influence. Johnson's bad luck must have rubbed off as well, embroiling Frazier in a still-mysterious murder that forced him to flee north to Detroit, where he jobbed in virtual anonymity for the rest of his life. Frazier left behind a few scant recordings, among them a glorious 1938 solo session cut for folklorist Alan Lomax two months after Johnson died. Frazier was a lazy-voiced singer who swallowed words like horse pills, at times indecipherable. Yet like Robert Nighthawk's doomy vocals, Frazier's sound worked, in counterpoint to exquisite slide and bass guitar work. Frazier's lyrics were a mix of his own and Johnson's images. The tune of "Lily Mae" is a direct lift from Johnson's "Honeymoon Blues," but the surrealistic, violent lyrics ("I'm gonna step on your nipples and tear your heart to pieces") are all his own. "Highway 51" is even more astonishing, a "Dust My Broom" facsimile in which Frazier baldly admits: "I was once accused of murderin', and I had to clear up my name." According to Julie Ann Schwartz, who interviewed Frazier family members, Calvin Frazier played music with his brothers and had traveled with Shines to Helena, Arkansas, where he met Johnson in 1930. The trio roamed as far north as Detroit, where they sang hymns on a gospel radio program. Frazier also played rhythm guitar in a string band with Johnson and drummer Peck Curtis, who would later play with Rice Miller. But Frazier had to flee in 1935 after he was wounded in a shoot-out that left one man dead in Memphis. Hiding in Detroit, Frazier married a cousin of Shines and settled down to an uneventful life of odd jobs and occasional blues gigs with musicians such as Big Maceo Merriweather, Rice Miller and Baby Boy Warren. After the 1938 session for the Library of Congress, Frazier appeared on several 1951 cuts with T.J. Fowler's jump band and in 1954 in a tough combo with Miller and Warren. He continued playing without much reward until his death in 1972.

what to buy: Even plagued by loud scratches and muffled sound, the 10 songs gathered on *This Old World's in a Tangle* ♫♫♫♫ (Laurie, 1993, prod. Alan Lomax) are crucial evidence of the power Robert Johnson worked on his contemporaries when he was alive. It is accompanied by a 40-page booklet that con-

Carol Fran (© Jack Vartoogian)

tains Frazier's history and the lyrics to his songs—at times a necessity because of his mumbled delivery.

what to buy next: *Blues Hangover* &&&& (AVI/Excello, 1995) is a two-CD survey of Excello's fine Louisiana swamp boogie appended oddly by four 1954 tracks cut by Frazier with Sonny Boy Williamson II and Baby Boy Warren. Recorded for Detroit producer Jon Van Battle and leased to Excello, Warren sings likes a banshee, and Williamson provides some of his most puckish harp on record. Frazier stays silent, but backs up Warren with gritty guitar fills that Robert Junior Lockwood might envy.

influences:

◀◀ Robert Johnson, Johnny Shines

Steve Braun

Henry St. Claire Fredericks

See: Taj Mahal

Frank Frost & Sam Carr

Frank Frost born April 15, 1936, in Augusta, AR. Sam Carr born April 17, 1926, in Friars Point, MS.

Singer-harpist-pianist Frost and his long-time drummer and friend, Sam Carr, never did make the trip to Chicago that so many of their contemporaries made in the 1930s, 1940s and 1950s. They stayed around the Mississippi Delta, content with their fishing holes and reputation as two of the best bluesmen in the South, emerging to the rest of the world in gigs with the late Rice "Sonny Boy Williamson" Miller and Robert Nighthawk or on obscure but invariably great albums. (In recent years, Frost has played piano behind Little Milton, Albert King, Bobby Rush and O.V. Wright on their Mississippi club swings.) Frost started as Williamson's guitar player, then learned the master's licks and became a harpist himself. They didn't make many waves until guitarist Jack Johnson made them a trio; Sun Records impresario Sam Phillips produced them in one of his last blues recordings. (Scotty Moore, Elvis Presley's guitarist, produced a later album, and Michael Frank formed his Earwig label to record the trio.) Frost frequently puts out albums without Carr, an incredibly precise and powerful drummer, even though the two continue to tour together. Along with fellow Mississippians R.L. Burnside and Junior Kimbrough, Frost reached a wider audience when critic Robert Palmer stuck him, with a band called Freddie and the Screamers, on his *Deep Blues* movie soundtrack.

what to buy: *Hey Boss Man* ♪♪♪♪ (Phillips International, 1963, prod. Sam Phillips) is the ultimate document of the tragically underrecognized trio. *Midnight Prowler* ♪♪♪♪ (Earwig, 1989, prod. Michael Robert Frank, Frank Frost), more than anything else, has incredible chemistry: Carr, Johnson and Frost have played together for so long that, like Booker T. and the MGs, they know exactly when to fill each others' spaces. Johnson's high-pitched plucking evokes Muddy Waters on "Gonna Put Her Down" and there are nice versions of Slim Harpo's "Scratch My Back" and Wilson Pickett's "Mustang Sally."

what to buy next: *Jelly Roll Blues* ♪♪♪ (Paula, 1966/1991, prod. Scotty Moore) isn't quite as raw and powerful, but it makes up for it with sexy humor ("Feel Good Babe"), freshly interpreted classics ("Got My Mojo Workin'") and subtle Slim Harpo parody ("My Back Scratcher").

what to avoid: *Deep Blues* ♪♪ (Appaloosa, 1992, prod. Fred James), not to be confused with Palmer's soundtrack of the same name and year, relies on a fairly conventional blues band led by long-time producer James; Frost is solid but rarely spectacular, like on his stuff with Carr and Johnson.

the rest:
Frank Frost ♪♪ (Paula, 1973)
Ride with Your Daddy Tonight ♪♪♪ (Charly, 1985)
(With the Jelly Roll Kings) *Rockin the Juke Joint Down* ♪♪♪♪ (Earwig, 1993)
Keep Yourself Together ♪♪♪ (Evidence, 1996)

worth searching for: The Palmer soundtrack, *Deep Blues* ♪♪♪♪♪ (Atlantic, 1992, prod. Robert Palmer), unearths obscure southern blues heroes in a way that hasn't been this fresh since the 1960s; Frost, Burnside and Kimbrough are among the many discoveries.

influences:

◀◀ Sonny Boy Williamson II, Little Walter, Leadbelly, Sonny Terry, Brownie McGhee

▶▶ Junior Kimbrough, Sugar Blue, Charlie Musselwhite, R.L. Burnside

Steve Knopper

Blind Boy Fuller

Born Fulton Allen, July 10, 1907, in Wadesboro, NC. Died February 13, 1941, in Durham, NC.

Blind Boy Fuller was one of the most inventive and successful blues guitarists of the late 1930s. Stylistically, he is most often placed in the Piedmont blues school, though Fuller's complex, hard-driving rhythms and assured vocal delivery contrast sharply with the light touch and whispering vocals of, say, Mississippi John Hurt or other fingerpickers from the Southeast. Among the first bluesmen to tap the wealth of source material available on the popular race records of the day, his repertoire consisted of numerous adaptations of others' songs, deriving inspiration from Blind Blake, Blind Willie McTell and Carl Martin, among others. Nevertheless, even these reinterpretations bore his distinctive mark, many only remotely bearing any similarity to the original source. Most of his best-selling records were lively rags, such as the marvelous "Piccolo Rag," "Jitterbug Rag" and "Rag, Mama, Rag." The highly influential "Step It Up and Go" and "Trucking My Blues Away" are among his best-known compositions of this ilk, the latter immortalized by underground cartoonist Robert Crumb as a popular logo in the 1970s. But Fuller's legacy does not end with his finger-picked ragtime guitar compositions. "Homesick and Lonesome" showcases his skillful slide playing in a straight blues context, "Red River Blues" is proof of his mastery of traditional ballads and his recording of the Rev. Gary Davis' "Twelve Gates to the City" illustrates that he was no slouch as a gospel singer. Lyrically, as well as musically, one never knew quite what to expect from Fuller. He could come across as a gentle and compassionate soul, as on "Weeping Willow" or "Little Woman You're So Sweet," or as a humorously indecent character, as demonstrated by the numerous hokum songs he recorded bearing pornographic titles like "What's That Smells Like Fish?" or "I Want Some of Your Pie." Such diversification undoubtedly had much to do with his unmitigated success and mass appeal. The void created by his premature death was so great, record company moguls even went as far as to cast others in the role of the "second" Blind Boy Fuller, as was the case of Brownie McGhee ("Blind Boy Fuller #2"), and Richard Trice ("Little Boy Fuller"). Fuller's shoes have yet to be filled.

what to buy: *East Coast Piedmont Style* ♪♪♪♪♪ (Columbia/ Legacy, 1991, prod. Lawrence Cohn) is a 20-track collection of some of Fuller's best sides, many previously unissued alternate takes. Included is a rare slide performance ("I'm a Stranger Here"), some powerful slow blues numbers with accompaniment from Gary Davis ("My Brownskin Sugarplum," "Keep Away from

My Woman") and the inventive "Cat Man Blues," his variation of a century-old folk song. Along the way, there are plenty of his trademark rags, most notably the rhythmically complex "Big Leg Woman Gets My Pay." *Truckin' My Blues Away* 𝄢𝄢𝄢𝄢 (Yazoo, 1990, prod. Nick Perls) is equally fine, with more of his superb slide work ("Homesick and Lonesome"), rag tunes ("Truckin' My Blues Away," "I Crave My Pigmeat"), deep blues ("Mamie") and openly suggestive hokum ("Sweet Honey Hole").

what to buy next: Can't get enough? *Complete Chronological Recordings, Vols. 1–6* 𝄢𝄢𝄢 (Document, prod. Johnny Parth) is a sure cure for those smitten by Blind Boy Fuller's boogie bug. Essential listening for anyone seriously interested in Piedmont blues.

what to avoid: While it is not particularly bad, *Blind Boy Fuller 1935–40* 𝄢𝄢𝄢 (Travelin' Man, 1994) is a varied collection heavily weighted with tunes from his last and least inspired session. Sound quality generally pales in comparison to the more sonically pristine Yazoo and Columbia sets.

the rest:

The Remaining Titles 1935–40 𝄢𝄢𝄢 (Best of Blues)
Get Your Yas Yas Out: The Essential Blind Boy Fuller 𝄢𝄢𝄢𝄢 (Indigo, 1996)

influences:

◀◀ Blind Blake, Rev. Gary Davis, Blind Willie McTell, Carl Martin

▶▶ Floyd Council, Brownie McGhee, Richard Trice, Carolina Slim, Ralph Willis, Curley Weaver

D. Thomas Moon

Jesse Fuller

Born March 12, 1896, in Jonesboro, GA. Died January 29, 1976, in Oakland, CA.

Jesse Fuller, who sang and played such instruments as guitar, harp, kazoo and "fotdella," a stove-shaped percussive device made of foot pedals and padded hammers, was the living bridge between two eras. He grew up under grim, tough conditions, having been "smoked over a fire in a gunnysack, not even told of his mother's death in 1903 until a month after the event," according to 1958 liner notes. He lived long enough, though, to wander the country, settle in Los Angeles, become a musician in the 1950s and record several albums. Many of his songs, including "San Francisco Bay Blues" and "Beat It on down the Line," inspired such Bay Area rockers as the Grateful Dead and Janis Joplin. He took advantage of the 1960s folk and blues revival, performing at coffee houses and festivals throughout Europe and the U.S. until his death.

what to buy: With yodeling and moaning reminiscent of both Leadbelly and country singer Merle Travis, Fuller's classic *Jazz, Folk Songs, Spirituals & Blues* 𝄢𝄢𝄢𝄢 (Good Time Jazz, 1958/Original Blues Classics, 1993, prod. Lester Koenig) is full of astounding guitar picking and a rhythmic style that unquestionably influenced rock 'n' roll; the instrumental "Tiger Rag" and Fuller's spooky, lively take on "Stagolee" are among the many highlights.

what to buy next: *San Francisco Bay Blues* 𝄢𝄢𝄢 (Contemporary/Fantasy, 1963, prod. Lester Koenig), a clear influence on country-leaning 1960s rock bands, contains Fuller's happy-but-sad take on the classic "John Henry" and his own title track.

the rest:

The Lone Cat Sings and Plays Jazz, Folk Songs, Spirituals and Blues 𝄢𝄢𝄢 (Good Time Jazz, 1961)
Favorites 𝄢𝄢𝄢 (Prestige, 1965)

worth searching for: Where "Take This Hammer" opens *Jazz, Folk Songs . . .* on an immediately familiar note, *Frisco Bound* 𝄢𝄢𝄢𝄢 (Arhoolie, 1993), a collection of recordings from 1955 and 1967, focuses on more obscure but just as wonderful acoustic blues and country songs. Standouts are the previously unreleased "I'm Going to Sit down at the Welcome Table" and the recollection of wandering the U.S., "Leaving Memphis, 'Frisco Bound.'"

influences:

◀◀ Merle Travis, Jimmie Rodgers, Leadbelly, Bukka White, Son House, Charley Patton, Emmett Miller, Mississippi Sheiks

▶▶ Grateful Dead, Janis Joplin, Bob Dylan, Screamin' Jay Hawkins, Hank Williams, Rev. Gary Davis

Steve Knopper

Lowell Fulson

Born March 31, 1921, in Tulsa, OK.

Lowell Fulson applied his incisive lead guitar and unaffected vocalizing to as many styles of blues as have come and gone in the five decades of his career—acoustic country, jump, Chicago style, southern style, rhythm & blues, soul and funk, to name a few. Fulson began playing at age 12 and left home in the late 1930s to play in Dan Wright's String Band, a gig that included country and western numbers. He played guitar for Texas Alexander in 1940 and then shipped out to the Navy. Discharged in 1945, he settled in Oakland, California, and began recording for Big Town. By 1948, he'd had an important hit in "Three O'-Clock Blues" and signed on with Swing Time, where he recorded the durable "Everyday I Have the Blues." Fulson kept the blues fresh by incorporating the styles of the day into his music. Even his classic "Reconsider Baby"—propelled by his brittle lead guitar—featured a driving saxophone section, instrumentation associated at the time more with R&B than blues. Fulson kept recording even though he faded from the charts during his productive tenure with Chess Records (1954–62), and he enjoyed a return to hitmaking with the soul-infused sounds of "Black Nights" and "Tramp" in 1965. Although the hits again diminished, Fulson has continued recording and performing, even showing up in 1993 as a guest on B.B. King's *Blues Summit*.

what to buy: *Hung Down Head* ♫♫♫♫ (MCA/Chess, 1991, prod. Lowell Fulson) remains the heavyweight champ, capturing Fulson's classic mid-1950s output, including "Reconsider Baby" and "Do Me Right." *Tramp/Soul* ♫♫♫♫ (Flair, 1991) showcases Fulson's soul-flavored blues of the 1960s by teaming up his two top vinyl LPs on one disc.

what to buy next: *Reconsider Baby* ♫♫♫ (Charly, 1993) includes many of the same songs as *Hung Down Head*, with some choice differences, including "Lonely Hours." *Sinner's Prayer* ♫♫♫♫ (Night Train, 1995) and *Everyday I Have the Blues* ♫♫♫♫ (Night Train, 1995) cover Fulson's tenure on Swing Time in the late 1940s and early 1950s with a collection of stellar songs, including "Lonesome Christmas." *San Francisco Blues* ♫♫♫♫ (Black Lion, 1992, prod. Jack Lauderdale) is another solid collection of Swing Time numbers.

what to avoid: There's a reason that *In a Heavy Bag* ♫ (Jewel, 1970) has not been released on CD yet: it's easily the worst album Fulson recorded. Imagine him taking on the Beatles' trash-rock ditty "Why Don't We Do It in the Road?" 'Nuff said?

the rest:

Think Twice before You Speak ♫♫♫ (JSP, 1984/1997)
It's a Good Day ♫♫♫ (Rounder, 1988)
Hold On ♫♫♫♫ (Bullseye Blues, 1992)
One More Blues ♫♫♫ (Evidence, 1993)
Swingin' Party ♫♫♫ (New Rose, 1993)
Them Update Blues ♫♫♫♫ (Bullseye Blues, 1995)

worth searching for: *Lowell Fulson (Early Recordings)* ♫♫♫♫ (Arhoolie, 1975) fills in the Fulson picture; he's a country-blues player in sessions with his brother, Martin, on acoustic guitar, originally recorded for the Big Town label.

influences:

◄◄ Texas Alexander, T-Bone Walker, Blind Lemon Jefferson

►► Ray Charles, Otis Redding, Eric Clapton

Salvatore Caputo

John Funchess
See: Johnny Littlejohn

Anson Funderburgh & the Rockets Featuring Sam Myers
Formed 1978, in Dallas, TX.

Anson Funderburgh, guitar (1978–present); Sam Myers, vocals, harmonica (1986–present); Darrell Nulisch, vocals, harmonica (1981–86); Jim Milan, bass (1990–92); Rhandy Simmons, bass (1987, 1989); Mike Judge, bass (1989); Rory MacLeod, bass (1984); Jack Newhouse, bass (1981–82); Carl "Sonny" Leyland, piano (1995); Craig Semechek, organ (1995); Matt McCabe, piano (1987–92); Marc Wilson, drums (1987–89); Wes Starr, drums (1984); Freddie "Pharoah" Walden, drums (1981–82); Danny Cochran, drums (1990–present); Doug Rynack, piano (1981–84, 1997–present); Pat Whitefield, bass (1995–present).

Anson Funderburgh grew up in the suburban Dallas neighborhoods that produced Jimmie and Stevie Ray Vaughan. His crisp, stinging Texas guitar style is economical, well-articulated and rooted in the Texas blues guitar heritage, particularly the Houston slick-picking tradition of players like Albert Collins, Johnny "Guitar" Watson and Clarence "Gatemouth" Brown. As a teenager, Funderburgh was already playing in black and white clubs around Dallas. The band's early recordings with Darrell Nulisch are reminiscent of the Fabulous Thunderbirds. But the addition of Sam Myers' classic blues harp and vocals in 1986 added the element that set this band apart from other young bands recreating old blues. Myers started playing professionally in the mid-1950s. A harmonica player and drummer as well as a vocalist, Myers also played with Elmore James and Robert Junior Lockwood. His harmonica melds the influences of Delta blues with urban Chicago sounds, and his deep, resonant, honeyed vocals bring back "chitlin' circuit" juke joints.

what to buy: *Live at the Grand Emporium* ♫♫♫♫ (Black Top, 1995, prod. Hammond Scott) captures the magical chemistry and excitement of Funderburgh and Myers, with the latter in top form in the Kansas City club. *That's What They Want* ♫♫♫♫ (Black Top, 1997, prod. Hammond Scott, Anson Funderburgh) commemorates Myers' decade with Funderburgh in an upbeat and engaging showcase. Not officially a Rockets CD, *My Love Is Here to Stay* ♫♫♫♫ (Black Top, 1985, prod. Hammond Scott, Anson Funderburgh) was intended to be a forum for Myers' talents with Funderburgh's band backing up and takes its name from Myers' 1957 Ace single. *Through the Years: A Retrospective, 1981–92* ♫♫♫♫ (Black Top, 1985, prod. Hammond Scott,

Anson Funderburgh), an overview of Funderburgh's career through 1992, is a good sampler of the remaining recordings in the Rockets' discography.

what to buy next: Check out Funderburgh's guitar solos on "Changing Neighborhoods" and "Chill Out" (an instrumental nod to Albert Collins) or his stinging slide on "Can't Stop Loving" on *Sins* ✸✸✸✸ (Black Top, 1988, prod. Hammond Scott, Anson Funderburgh). *Rack 'Em Up* ✸✸✸✸ (Black Top, 1989, prod. Hammond Scott, Anson Funderburgh) is, all in all, a very good recording which often gets underrated in the band's large discography. The bass player on this one, Mike Judge, went on to create the animated *Beavis and Butt-Head* characters.

the rest:

Talk to You by Hand ✸✸✸✸ (Black Top, 1981/1990)
She Knocks Me Out! ✸✸✸✸ (Black Top, 1982/1989)
Tell Me What I Want to Hear ✸✸✸✸ (Black Top, 1991)

worth searching for: The Rockets perform in the Kevin Costner-produced film *China Moon* (Orion, 1990), featuring tunes included on *Tell Me What I Want to Hear*.

influences:

◀◀ Albert Collins, Freddie King, Jimmy Reed, Clarence "Gatemouth" Brown, Johnny "Guitar" Watson, Otis Rush, Magic Sam, Howlin' Wolf, Little Walter, Sonny Boy Williamson II

▶▶ R.J. Mischo, Mike Morgan & the Crawl, Smokin' Joe Kubek Band with Bnois King

B.J. Huchtemann

Earl Gaines

Born August 19, 1935, in Decatur, AL.

A self-described innocent in 1955, Earl Gaines, then only 20, went right to the top of the R&B charts with "It's Love Baby (24 Hours a Day)," recorded for Excello with Louis Brooks and the Hightoppers. Listeners took to his sweet tenor backed in this bouncy version by Brooks' robust sax. Gaines had started singing in church and was bitten early by the music bug. He moved to Nashville when he was just 16 to take advantage of the booming blues scene, fueled largely by radio station WLAC's interest in the music. Gaines hooked up with local im-

presario Ted Jarrett, singing with him in clubs and then doing demo tapes before he got the chance to record with Brooks. The success of "24 Hours" turned Gaines into a featured singer with Brooks and the Hightoppers, and they made a number of other well-received singles for Excello (including a new and more mature version of "24 Hours"). Gaines moved on to other labels, including DeLuxe/King, Hanna Barbera, (recording "24 Hours" for each) and Sound Stage 7, but he always maintained a close relationship with WLAC, where two of the disc jockeys served as his managers. When the station stopped playing blues and R&B—and with the market drying up—record companies producing this music went out of business. Gaines found other work as the driver of a cross-country big rig through the 1970s and 1980s. His re-emergence in 1993 suggests that maybe you *can* go home after all. Out of the studio more than 20 years, he and two other Excello singers, Roscoe Shelton and Clifford Curry, started recording again thanks to Fred James, a young, energetic Nashville musician with a deep fondness for blues.

what to buy: *I Believe in Your Love* ✸✸✸ (Appaloosa, 1995, prod. Fred James) opens with "24 Hours," and it's as full-bodied a version as Gaines ever did. His voice is a little huskier than it was at 32 or 22, but the thoughtful phrasing and respect for melody are still there. "Part Time Love" is good, affecting blues. The ballad-like title cut shows off Gaines's still-pleasing tenor.

the rest:

Tennesse R&B: The Excello Legends—Earl Gaines, Rosco Shelton, Clifford Curry ✸✸✸ (Magnum Music Group, 1994)
Earl Gaines/Roscoe Shelton/Clifford Curry Live ✸✸✸ (Appaloosa, 1997)

influences:

◀◀ Big Joe Turner

▶▶ Mighty Sam McLain

Nadine Cohodas

Grady Gaines

Born May 14, 1934, in Houston, TX.

One of the great unknown rock 'n' roll sidemen, energetic and charismatic saxophonist Gaines was the first bandleader of Little Richard's original Upsetters beginning in 1955. (He shows up prominently in the classic rock films *Don't Knock the Rock, Mr. Rock and Roll* and *The Girl Can't Help It*.) And that was just the beginning—the Upsetters played behind Jackie Wilson, Sam Cooke and Little Willie John, and Gaines went on to back Millie Jackson, Curtis Mayfield, Joe Tex and Johnnie Taylor. His 1980 re-

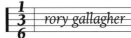
tirement didn't last very long, and Gaines began a solo career, playing live shows worthy of 1950s-era Little Richard and just about capturing that explosion on two extremely fun albums.

what to buy: Lots of bluesmen hop up the tempo and try rocking, but Gaines puts on a clinic on *Horn of Plenty* ♪♪♪♪ (Black Top, 1992, prod. Hammond Scott). His band, featuring guitarists Anson Funderburgh and Clarence Holliman and singers Teddy Reynolds and Carol Fran, sets a terrific playground for Gaines' lively sax to frolic on.

what to buy next: *Full Gain* ♪♪♪ (Black Top, 1988) is Gaines' first all-star Texas album, and it's a superb, raucous introduction of the saxman as a solo artist.

influences:

Little Richard, Louis Jordan, Clarence "Gatemouth" Brown, Curtis Mayfield

Clarence Clemons, Dire Straits, Memphis Horns, Clarence Holliman, Carol Fran

Steve Knopper

Rory Gallagher

Born March 2, 1949, in Ballyshannon, Ireland. Died June 14, 1995, in London, England.

A blues-rock guitarist and singer, Rory Gallagher had a lengthy career beginning with his trio Taste—something of an Irish response to the success of England's Cream—in 1969. Gallagher became a solo artist and fronted bands under his own name for the rest of his career. One of the most aggressive guitarists in this genre, his style wasn't diluted by changing musical tastes and attitudes. Given some of the experimentation he had done with Taste, it's a pity that Gallagher didn't spread his creative wings further; while his recordings were accomplished, there is a strong similarity to them. He penned most of the blues songs, which tended to be lengthy with increasingly dynamic improvisations. Unlike contemporaries Eric Clapton, Jeff Beck, Jimmy Page and Jimi Hendrix, Gallagher experimented little and always stayed close to his blues roots. If nothing else, with Gallagher you always knew what to expect.

what to buy: *The Best of Taste Featuring Rory Gallagher* ♪♪♪♪♪ (Polydor, 1994) is a solid sampling of his earlier, raw-boned blues guitar and vocal attack. Long out of print, these recordings are a welcome return and the linchpin to Gallagher's career.

what to buy next: Gallagher's fifth solo album, *Tattoo* ♪♪♪♪ (Polydor/Griffin, 1973), contains a number of strong songs, in-

cluding "Cat Cradle," "Living Like a Trucker" and "They Don't Make It Like That Anymore."

what to avoid: *Blueprint* ♪♪ (Polydor/Griffin, 1973/1995) is one of those moribund, same-sounding collections.

the rest:

Irish Tour '74 ♪♪♪ (Polydor/I.R.S., 1974)
Against the Grain ♪♪♪♪ (Chrysalis/Griffin, 1975)
Calling Card ♪♪♪♪ (Chrysalis/I.R.S., 1976)
Top Priority ♪♪♪ (Chrysalis/I.R.S., 1979)
Defender ♪♪♪ (I.R.S., 1987)
Fresh Evidence ♪♪♪ (I.R.S., 1991)
Live in Europe/Stage Struck ♪♪♪ (I.R.S., 1991)

influences:

Albert King, Freddie King, Muddy Waters, Bo Diddley

Gary Moore, George Thorogood & the Destroyers

Patrick McCarty

Cecil Gant

Born April 6, 1913, in Nashville, TN. Died February 4, 1951, in Nashville, TN.

Cecil Gant was one of the great one-hit wonders of 1940s rhythm and blues, a singer who riveted the entire blues-buying public with his 1944 smash, "I Wonder," but was unable to repeat his phenomenal success. "I Wonder" stayed on the R&B charts for 28 weeks, turning Gant, an Army private who had sung at Los Angeles war bond rallies, into the "G.I. Sing-Sation." Gant's mellow blues and laid-back boogie hearkened back to Leroy Carr, and though Gant couldn't keep his own fortunes afloat, his brief fame influenced the early careers of cocktail-and-riff pianists like Charles Brown and Amos Milburn. Gant followed the melancholy "I Wonder" with a string of lesser hits, but he disappeared from the charts after 1949.

what to buy: Neither "I Wonder" nor the rest of Gant's Gilt-Edge recordings are on *Cecil Gant* ♪♪♪ (Krazy Kat, 1989), but the 20 cuts from the late 1940s that do appear are pretty representative of Gant's talents, divided almost evenly between mopey ballads and light boogies.

what to buy next: Buying *Mean Old World: The Blues from 1940 to 1994* ♪♪♪♪ (Smithsonian, 1996, prod. Bruce Talbot, Lawrence Hoffman), a costly, well-annotated four-CD survey of American blues, is the only way to find "I Wonder" in the digital realm. Worth getting if you want the rest of the set's expansive blues view (Billie Holiday to Tutu Jones), but otherwise "I Wonder" is at best a historical curiosity.

influences:

Grady Gaines

song
Soul Twist

album
Full Gain (Black Top)

instrument
Saxophone

monster solo

influences:

◀◀ Leroy Carr

▶▶ Charles Brown, Amos Milburn, Ray Charles

Steve Braun

Larry Garner

Born 1952, in New Orleans, LA.

Baton Rouge's Larry Garner is heartening proof that undeniable talent can't be suppressed for too long. After decades of itinerant playing (and working in a chemical plant), Garner asserted his gifts in Baton Rouge's thriving blues scene in the 1980s, playing and hanging out with the likes of Raful Neal, Lonesome Sundown and ex-Howlin' Wolf and Little Walter pianist Henry Gray. A self-produced cassette made the industry rounds and opened the doors for Garner's first record contract in 1991, after his song "Dog House Blues" won the B.B. King Lucille Award for Blues Song of the Year in 1990. His no-frills guitar style echoes King's concise single-note precision, but it's Garner's fresh songwriting that makes him a major creative force.

what to buy: *You Need to Live a Little* ♪♪♪♪ (Verve, 1994, prod. John Snyder), Garner's third album, benefits from a major-label recording budget and presents his impeccably crafted songs in the sonic glory they deserve. "Another Bad Day," "Nobody's Special" and the title track are moody, minor-key masterpieces, while "Miracles of Time"'s unabashed sentiment sparkles with touches of chimes and percussion. A keen sense of humor surfaces also, with Garner telling the tale of a tough female in "Shak Bully" and sharing the all-consuming task of raising multiple teenagers in the hilarious "Four Cars Running." The one cover version is a barnburner, with guest Sonny Landreth's riveting low-down slide guitar hammering home the squalor of Silas Hogan's "Rats and Roaches in My Kitchen."

what to buy next: *Double Dues* ♪♪♪ (JSP, 1991, prod. Larry Garner) and *Too Blues* ♪♪♪ (JSP, 1993, prod. Larry Garner) both boast strong performances and respectively contain more winning original Garner compositions like "Tale Spreaders" and "Kleptomaniac." However, listeners who start off their Garner collection with *You Need to Live a Little* may be disappointed with the average production quality of these two releases.

worth searching for: *Baton Rouge* ♪♪♪♪ (Gitanes Jazz, 1995, prod. John Snyder) is another gem that picks up where *You Need to Live a Little* left off , but the termination of Garner's U.S. deal with Verve scuttled the record's domestic release. The

original import copies are still lurking in a few American bins, and are well worth their heftier price tags.

influences:

◀◀ T-Bone Walker, Louis Jordan, Slim Harpo

▶▶ John Weston, Lonnie Shields

Scott Jordan

J. Geils Band /Bluestime

Formed 1967, in Boston, MA. Disbanded 1985.

J. (Jerome) Geils, guitars; Peter Wolf, vocals (1967–83); Magic Dick, harmonica, saxophone; Danny Klein, bass; Stephen Jo Bladd, drums; Seth Justman, keyboards (1968–85).

Pure blues was so serious in the 1960s, when historians rediscovered old Mississippi legends and dragged them to festivals alongside young, studious heroes like Paul Butterfield. Setting the stage for the "The Blues Brothers" a decade later, the J. Geils Band viewed the blues as good-time party music, barely a step removed from 1950s-style rock 'n' roll. The band began when singer Peter Wolf, a fast-talking painter, energetic rock singer and DJ who moved from the Bronx to Boston, joined an acoustic blues trio called the J. Geils Blues Band. He immediately injected a party touch, with rambling speeches by his split personality, the Woobah Goobah with Green Teeth. The band's horn-heavy boogie-rock concerts, documented to great effect on *Blow Your Face Out*, became legendary. Throughout the 1970s, thanks to such hits as the slow "Looking for a Love" and the funky "Give It to Me," the J. Geils Band dominated metropolitan rock radio. It wasn't until the band quit its long-time record label, Atlantic, and found MTV, that it became a household name. *Freeze-Frame* netted several smash singles, including the title track and the #1 hit, "Centerfold." After personal problems splintered the band in the mid-1980s, the remaining members quickly faded from the public eye; Wolf put out a few uneven solo albums and mostly backed away from touring, and co-founders J. Geils and Magic Dick went full circle as an acoustic blues duo called Bluestime.

what to buy: The J. Geils Band *Anthology: Houseparty* 𝅘𝅥𝅮𝅘𝅥𝅮𝅘𝅥𝅮𝅘𝅥𝅮 (Rhino, 1993, prod. various) saves you the trouble of navigating the various greatest-hits collections from Atlantic and EMI-America; it has "Must of Got Lost," "Centerfold," good Woobah Goobah concert speeches and everything else. *Freeze-Frame* 𝅘𝅥𝅮𝅘𝅥𝅮𝅘𝅥𝅮𝅗𝅥 (EMI America, 1981, prod. Seth Justman) creates a fun, upbeat party atmosphere and collects the great 1980s singles "Freeze-Frame" and "Centerfold" along with the hilariously vulgar "Piss on the Wall."

what to buy next: The title track of *Love Stinks* 𝅘𝅥𝅮𝅘𝅥𝅮𝅘𝅥𝅮 (EMI America, 1980, prod. Seth Justman) is a perfect counterpart to Roy Orbison's classic "Love Hurts." The band's best concert document is *Blow Your Face Out* 𝅘𝅥𝅮𝅘𝅥𝅮𝅘𝅥𝅮 (Atlantic, 1976, prod. Allan Blazek, Bill Szymczyk, J. Geils Band), with a terrific Wolf monologue about "Reputah the Beautah" and all kinds of nonsensical house-partyisms. For Bluestime fans, both *Bluestime* 𝅘𝅥𝅮𝅘𝅥𝅮𝅘𝅥𝅮𝅗𝅥 (Rounder, 1995, prod. Magic Dick, J. Geils) and *Little Car Blues* 𝅘𝅥𝅮𝅘𝅥𝅮𝅘𝅥𝅮𝅗𝅥 (Rounder, 1996, prod. Magic Dick, J. Geils) capture the essence of the Chess 1950s blues classics.

what to avoid: The band, for whatever reason, insisted on making an album or two every year in the early 1970s, and many are rushed and forgettable, including *Bloodshot* 𝅘𝅥𝅮𝅗𝅥 (Atlantic, 1973, prod. Bill Szymczyk), *Nightmares . . . and Other Tales from the Vinyl Jungle* 𝅘𝅥𝅮𝅗𝅥 (Atlantic, 1974, prod. Bill Szymczyk)

and *Hotline* 𝅘𝅥𝅮 (Atlantic, 1975, prod. Bill Szymczyk, Allan Blazek). Also, if you have the Rhino anthology, there's no need to track down *The Best of the J. Geils Band* 𝅘𝅥𝅮𝅘𝅥𝅮𝅘𝅥𝅮 (Atlantic, 1979), *Best of the J. Geils Band, Vol. 2* 𝅘𝅥𝅮𝅘𝅥𝅮 (Atlantic, 1982, prod. various) or even *Flashback: The Best of the J. Geils Band* 𝅘𝅥𝅮𝅘𝅥𝅮 (EMI America, 1985, prod. Seth Justman, Joe Wissert).

the rest:
The J. Geils Band 𝅘𝅥𝅮𝅘𝅥𝅮𝅘𝅥𝅮 (Atlantic, 1970)
The Morning After 𝅘𝅥𝅮𝅘𝅥𝅮𝅘𝅥𝅮 (Atlantic, 1971)
"Live" Full House 𝅘𝅥𝅮𝅘𝅥𝅮𝅗𝅥 (Atlantic, 1972)
Ladies Invited 𝅘𝅥𝅮𝅘𝅥𝅮𝅗𝅥 (Atlantic, 1973)
Monkey Island 𝅘𝅥𝅮𝅘𝅥𝅮𝅘𝅥𝅮 (Atlantic, 1977)
Sanctuary 𝅘𝅥𝅮𝅘𝅥𝅮𝅘𝅥𝅮 (EMI America, 1978)
You're Getting Even While I'm Getting Odd 𝅘𝅥𝅮𝅘𝅥𝅮 (EMI America, 1984)

worth searching for: Though tensions were rising and Wolf was about to leave the band, one of the last tours produced *Showtime!* 𝅘𝅥𝅮𝅘𝅥𝅮𝅘𝅥𝅮 (EMI America, 1982, prod. Seth Justman), in which the singer tells a 10-minute, worthy-of-memorization story about Adam and Eve, ending with a screamed "Love! . . . Stinks!"

solo outings:
Peter Wolf:
Lights Out 𝅘𝅥𝅮𝅘𝅥𝅮𝅘𝅥𝅮 (EMI America, 1984)
Come As You Are 𝅘𝅥𝅮𝅘𝅥𝅮 (EMI America, 1987)
Up to No Good 𝅘𝅥𝅮𝅘𝅥𝅮 (MCA, 1990)
Long Line 𝅘𝅥𝅮𝅘𝅥𝅮𝅘𝅥𝅮 (Reprise, 1996)

influences:
◀◀ Muddy Waters, Rolling Stones, Elvis Presley, Screamin' Jay Hawkins, Beach Boys, Smiley Lewis

▶▶ Mojo Nixon, Blues Brothers, Van Halen, Rockpile, Squirrel Nut Zippers

Steve Knopper

Clifford Gibson

Born April 17, 1901, in Louisville, KY. Died December 21, 1963, in St. Louis, MO.

A lesser-known contemporary of guitarist Lonnie Johnson—himself a lesser-known contemporary of Robert Johnson and Son House—Clifford Gibson moved from Louisville to St. Louis to record in the early 1920s. He recorded for several labels beginning in 1929 and collaborated with the great country singer Jimmie Rodgers in 1931, but the Depression destroyed his liveli-

J. Geils (© Ken Settle)

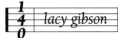

hood, and he wound up performing mostly on the streets. Though he had a small flurry of recording activity in the early 1960s, he died before gaining any new momentum.

what to buy: The 23-song *Complete Recorded Works in Chronological Order 1929–31* 𝄢𝄢𝄢 (Document, 1991, prod. various), with superb guitar work but not much on the singing side, offers the basics for a Gibson catalog.

what to buy next: *Beat You Doing It* 𝄢𝄢𝄢 (Yazoo, 1972) is less thorough than the Document set, but the packaging is more user-friendly.

influences:

◀◀ Lonnie Johnson, Charley Patton, Son House, Willie Brown

▶▶ Muddy Waters, Big Bill Broonzy, Elmore James, Tampa Red

Steve Knopper

Lacy Gibson

Born May 1, 1936, in Salisbury, NC.

By the time this singer-guitarist was in a position to take over the spotlight, his health deteriorated and he had to have major surgery. But for years the Chicago transplant showed up on records by many of his era's best-known musicians—he backed Duke Ellington, Count Basie, Buddy Guy (he's on "No Lie") and Junior Wells ("Messing with the Kid") and wound up in the early 1970s in Son Seals' band (for *Live and Burning*). Billy Boy Arnold has hired him several times, putting Gibson before the public as late as 1994's Chicago Blues Festival. Because of his health, the Albert King-style funky guitarist has recorded only a few albums, which is disproportionate given the number of fellow musicians' lives he has touched. Fortunately, Gibson seems to have recovered from his illness.

what to buy: *Switchy Titchy* 𝄢𝄢𝄢 (Black Magic, 1982/1995, prod. Dick Shurman) is like Albert King without the surging power. Gibson's band, including pianist Sunnyland Slim, sets down laid-back grooves and lets the leader casually pluck his licks.

what to buy next: Gibson's only other album, *Crying for My Baby* 𝄢𝄢𝄢 (Delmark, 1996, prod. Robert Koester), comes from a 1977 Chicago session, and its songs about Chicago women and CB radios have real lyrical personality to go with Gibson's always-consistent playing and fragile soul singing.

influences:

◀◀ Albert King, Buddy Guy, Duke Ellington, Junior Wells, Ray Charles

▶▶ Billy Branch, Willie Kent, Eddy Clearwater, Son Seals

Steve Knopper

Bill "Jazz" Gillum

Born William McKinley Gillum, September 11, 1904, in Indianola, MS. Died March 29, 1966, in Chicago, IL.

A victim of bad timing, Gillum was a contemporary of John Lee "Sonny Boy" Williamson and a prolific session harpist in the 1930s. But he hooked up with unsupportive record company executives, including one who, according to liner notes, wanted him to record surefire pop songs like "The Music Goes Round and Around." RCA Victor's Bluebird label wound up recording him anyway, but he tried too hard to determine what would sell—including the hillbilly song "Sarah Jane"—and never found the right commercial outlet for his considerable talent. Gillum moved to Chicago in 1923 and hooked up with guitarist Big Bill Broonzy. But Williamson had redefined harmonica playing, making Gillum's style obsolete, and his career trailed off when Bluebird folded. Like fellow harpists Williamson and, later, Little Walter, Gillum died violently, of a gunshot wound to the head in Chicago. Though Muddy Waters and the other rocking electric bluesmen dated Gillum's old-school style in the 1950s, he was poised for rediscovery at the time of his death. Like so many bluesmen, his influence was more direct on other musicians of the time rather than on the record-buying public.

what to buy: Regardless of what would or wouldn't sell at the time, the singles on *The Bluebird Recordings 1934–38* 𝄢𝄢𝄢𝄢 (RCA, 1997, prod. Vince Caro) have a jaunty, persistent rhythm and thin, simple harmonica lines. Gillum wasn't an obvious talent like the flashier Williamson, but songs like "Just Like Jesse James" and "Don't Scandalize My Name" are filled with a riveting sadness.

what to buy next: Without historical context, it's actually easier to appreciate Gillum's surprisingly large recorded output collected on *Complete Recorded Works in Chronological Order 1936–49, Vols. 1–4* 𝄢𝄢𝄢𝄢 (Document, prod. Johnny Parth). His style wasn't as ear-catching as Williamson's, but "The Devil Blues" has plenty of genuine devil in it.

worth searching for: *Roll Dem Bones 1938–49* 𝄢𝄢𝄢𝄢 (Wolf) is an import containing some of Gillum's last recorded material.

influences:

◀◀ Sonny Boy Williamson I, Son House, Tampa Red, Big Bill Broonzy

▶▶ Sonny Boy Williamson II, Little Walter, Charlie Musselwhite, Sugar Blue

Steve Knopper

Barry Goldberg

Born 1941, in Chicago, IL.

An expert jazz-blues fusion organist, Goldberg played with many of the leading performers who interpreted blues as a framework for showing off their technical instrumental skills. He was a sideman for harpist Charlie Musselwhite, guitarists Harvey Mandel and Mike Bloomfield and many others. Many of his contemporaries, including Al Kooper, gained more repute as solo artists, but Goldberg helped define the stretched-out psychedelic sound that characterized much white blues in the late 1960s.

what's available: *Two Jews Blues* ♪♪♫ (One Way, 1969), a collaboration between Goldberg and Bloomfield, is slow, spacey blues more like Muddy Waters' unfortunate *Electric Mud* album than any short, tight Chess Records single. It has its high points, especially for fusion fans, but it isn't particularly essential.

influences:

◀◀ Booker T. & the MG's, Mike Bloomfield, Al Kooper, Jeff Beck, Eric Clapton, Love, Doors, Miles Davis, Grateful Dead

▶▶ Ron Levy, Joey DeFrancesco, Wallflowers, Kenny Wayne Shepherd, Harvey Mandel

Steve Knopper

Blind Roosevelt Graves

Like many roaming Mississippi artists who drifted into recording studios in the late 1920s and 1930s, Blind Roosevelt Graves did not impart much more than the rag and Dixieland-inflected blues and spirituals he played. His origins, according to Delta legend Ishmon Bracey, were in the south-central part of Mississippi, likely Hattiesburg, where he and his brother, Uaroy, emerged in 1929 to record for Paramount. Despite Graves' complete sightlessness and Uaroy's blindness in one eye, both men were equally adept at duets or keeping up with barrelhouse piano wizard Will Exell and clarinetist Baby Jay. Roosevelt Graves sang in the typical laconic, nasal drawl favored by 1920s blues singers—shedding it for a more fervent interpretation only when singing the gospel numbers he clearly loved. After cutting 16 tracks in an Indianapolis studio in 1929, the Graves brothers returned once more in 1936, joined by veteran pianist Cooney Vaughn, then fell silent. Roosevelt Graves reportedly settled in Gulfport, Mississippi, where he is said to have remained until his death sometime in the 1960s.

what to buy: The patchily recorded 21 tracks on *Complete Recorded Works 1929–36* ♪♪♫ (Document, 1992, prod. Johnny Parth) is highlighted by the Graves brothers' somber delivery of gospel standards. The most stunning is their version of "Telephone to Glory," an absurdly-serious hymn that could easily have been authored by one of the demented characters in Flannery O'Connor's fiction.

influences:

◀◀ Will Ezell

Steve Braun

Henry Gray

Born January 19, 1925, in Kenner, LA.

Influenced by spirituals, black religious music and boogie woogie heard on the radio and inspired by Roosevelt Sykes, Henry Gray learned to tickle the ivories all by himself. He moved to Chicago just after World War II and was trained in the Big Maceo classic Chicago school of piano. He played in Little Hudson's Red Devil Trio in the early 1950s before joining Howlin' Wolf, with whom he stayed from 1956–68. At the same time, through his pounding piano playing and his lowdown, rocking style, he became a highly praised session pianist for Vee-Jay and Chess stars Bo Diddley, B.B. Arnold, Little Walter and Jimmy Rogers. In 1968 he came back to Baton Rouge and started a new career as a swamp/blues artist, combining his Big Maceo/Otis Spann influences with Fats Domino triplets and recording with Whispering Smith, Silas Hogan, Raful and Kenny Neal, Tabby Thomas and others, his nice smoky voice gracing his own and his partners' records. Some of his songs—"Blues Won't Let Me Take My Rest," "Lucky Lucky Man," "Cold Chills," "You're My Midnight Dream," "Gray's Bounce"—have become blues standards, and Gray is still very active on the Louisiana scene.

what to buy: A solid, rocking collection, *Lucky Man* ♪♪♪♫ (Blind Pig, 1988, prod. Steve Freund), includes Gray's compositions and other Chicago/New Orleans classics. *They Call Me Little Henry* ♪♪♪♫ (Bluebeat, 1977, prod. Hans W. Ewert) is a solo session recorded in Europe. *Howlin' Wolf—The Genuine Article* ♪♪♪♫ (MCA/Chess, 1997, prod. Leonard Chess, Phil Chess, Willie Dixon) and *Howlin' Wolf—Ain't Gonna Be Your Dog* ♪♪♪♫ (MCA/Chess, 1994, prod. Leonard Chess, Phil Chess, Willie Dixon) both offer glorious classics of electric Chicago blues and most of Gray's collaborations with the Wolf.

what to buy next: *Louisiana Blues Album* 🎵🎵🎵🎵 (Arhoolie, 1970, prod. Chris Strachwitz) and *Swamp Blues* 🎵🎵🎵🎵 (Excello, 1970) are splendid swamp/blues performances, including Gray's. *Don't Start That Stuff* 🎵🎵🎵 (Last Call/Sidetrack, 1996, prod. Steve Coleridge) offers up Gray in the 1990s, with more southern flavor.

influences:

◄◄ Roosevelt Sykes, Big Maceo Merriweather, Otis Spann

Robert Sacré

Al Green

Born April 13, 1946, in Forest City, AR.

Al Green stands in the soul pantheon with Sam Cooke and Otis Redding, performers who moved their music forward and transfixed audiences by creating a legacy of soul classics and turning in otherwordly performances time after time. Cooke and Redding flared out quickly, as Green almost did in mid-career. But 20 years since his last bona-fide R&B hit, Green is still at the top of his class, able to whip audiences into a secular frenzy and then cool them out in the name of the Lord. Even at times without a record contract, the Reverend remains such a force that he performed at recent presidential inaugurals and at the opening of the Rock 'n' Roll Hall of Fame, where his heart-stopping rendition of Cooke's "A Change Is Gonna Come" tore down the house. Green's mastery extends not only to archetypal soul and gospel but also to the blues. "Take Me to the River" and "Love and Happiness" are just two of the definitive blues performances that studded his classic albums for the Hi label in the 1970s. After waxing the lower-chart hit "Back Up Train" in 1967, Green seemed fated to a minor career on the southern club circuit when he bumped into Hi producer Willie Mitchell in Texas. When Green dropped in on Mitchell again in Memphis, the producer took the young singer under his wing. Mitchell urged Green to tame his raw-voiced Redding imitation and broaden his range from hoarse grunts to falsetto flights. Green eagerly complied, and, backed by a crackerjack band that emphasized guitar filagrees and fatback drums, he pumped out hit after hit in the early 1970s. From "Tired of Being Alone" to "Let's Stay Together" to "Call Me" to "Take Me to the River," Green's songs throbbed out of ghetto jukeboxes for nearly a decade. His concerts were exercises in hysteria. Outfitted in garish, checked leisure suits, Green showered roses on swooning women, goosed them with fast-paced hits and vanished, often without encores. The pace almost

killed him when a demented fan scalded him with a pot of hot grits and then shot herself. Roiling with doubt, Green began making albums dominated by conversations with God. By 1980, he became the Rev. Al Green, who rushed back from shows to lead Sunday services at his church in Memphis. Since then, Green has flitted back and forth between gospel and soul-pop, producing schizophrenic records that have yet to match his volcanic output of the 1970s. But in person, Al Green is still unmatched, one of only a handful of artists who can be transported by their own music and then transport those listening.

what to buy: The album that every proper inner-city bar owner still keeps on the jukebox, *Let's Stay Together* 🎵🎵🎵🎵 (The Right Stuff, 1972, prod. Willie Mitchell) is the equal of Redding's *Otis Blue*. Every song is soul perfect, especially the title monster and the stomping soul-blues vamps, "Ain't No Fun for Me" and "So You're Leaving." Green showed his range on *Call Me* 🎵🎵🎵🎵🎵 (The Right Stuff, 1972, prod. Willie Mitchell), mixing the prophetic gospel ("Jesus Is Waiting") and country ("I'm So Lonesome I Could Cry") with the title gem and "Here I Am (Come and Take Me)." For tighter budgets, The Right Stuff took the original Hi collection and added some later period hits for *Greatest Hits* 🎵🎵🎵🎵 (Right Stuff, 1996). All of it is essential.

what to buy next: *Gets Next to You* 🎵🎵🎵 (The Right Stuff, 1971, prod. Willie Mitchell) is Green on the verge. "Tired of Being Alone" is the best-known, but "I'm a Ram" and Junior Parker's "Driving Wheel" burn like cinders. *I'm Still in Love with You* 🎵🎵🎵🎵 (The Right Stuff, 1972, prod. Willie Mitchell) is slighter than its predecessor, *Let's Stay Together*, but boasts the thundering "Love and Happiness" among other chart-toppers. Green's return after recovering from the grits incident, the skeletal *Explores Your Mind* 🎵🎵🎵 (The Right Stuff, 1974, prod. Willie Mitchell) was long on fine songs. The standout track was "Take Me to the River," Green's insistent tribute to cousin Junior Parker that was later strip-mined by the Talking Heads. Green's voice is a bit distant and the Hodges brothers' backing is clearly missed, but *Tokyo Live* 🎵🎵🎵 (The Right Stuff, 1981, prod. Al Green) distills the thrill of watching the Reverend get to work.

what to avoid: Green's soul fans have ached for a full-scale secular return since the mid-1970s, but *Love Is Reality* 🎵🎵 (Word, 1992, prod. Tim Miner), a formulaic R&B dance record, wasn't the moment. We're still waiting.

Al Green (© Jack Vartoogian)

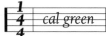

the rest:

Green Is Blues 𝄢𝄢 (The Right Stuff, 1970)

Livin' for You 𝄢𝄢𝄢 (The Right Stuff, 1973)

Al Green Is Love 𝄢𝄢𝄢𝄢 (The Right Stuff, 1975)

Full of Fire 𝄢𝄢𝄢𝄢 (The Right Stuff, 1976)

The Belle Album 𝄢𝄢𝄢 (The Right Stuff, 1977)

Your Heart's In Good Hands 𝄢𝄢𝄢 (MCA, 1995)

Anthology 𝄢𝄢𝄢𝄢 (The Right Stuff, 1997)

influences:

◀◀ Sam Cooke, Otis Redding, Junior Parker, Willie Mitchell

▶▶ Prince, Seal

Steve Braun

Cal Green

Born June 22, 1937, in Dayton, TX.

Cal Green is one of the unsung heroes who created the distinctive sound behind one of R&B's founding groups, Hank Ballard and the Midnighters. Like Wayne Bennett's work behind Bobby "Blue" Bland or Jimmy "Chank" Nolen's for James Brown, Green's string-bending was a crucial part of Ballard's success. His signatures were lightning-stroke riffs, blasted over Ballard's ecstatic moans on rave-ups like "Tore up over You" and "The Twist." Green's hot-wire sound showed up years later in the playing of admirers like Lonnie Mack and Stevie Ray Vaughan.

what to buy: Green isn't always behind Ballard, but shows up on every great cut from 1955 to 1959 on *Sexy Ways (The Best of Hank Ballard and the Midnighters)* 𝄢𝄢𝄢𝄢 (Rhino, 1993, prod. Syd Nathan). His rumble on "Open up Your Back Door" would make Link Wray weep in admiration.

what to buy next: *Greatest Juke Box Hits* 𝄢𝄢𝄢𝄢 (King, 1957, prod. Syd Nathan) is an exact reproduction of the classic 1950s King LP. There is some duplication with the Rhino anthology, but it's still worth searching out for Green-backed rarities like the insane "Henry's Got Flat Feet" and "Switchie, Witchie, Titchie." *Scratchin'* 𝄢𝄢𝄢 (Charly, 1991, prod. Syd Nathan) is an assortment of King guitar instrumentals featuring T-Bone Walker-influenced guitarists Pete Lewis, Chank Nolen and, on two plangent cuts, Green.

influences:

◀◀ T-Bone Walker

▶▶ Lonnie Mack, Stevie Ray Vaughan

Steve Braun

Cornelius Green

See: Lonesome Sundown

Peter Green

See: Fleetwood Mac

John Grimaldi

See: Studebaker John

Guitar Gabriel

Born Robert Lewis Jones, October 12, 1925, in Atlanta, GA. Died April 2, 1996, in Winston-Salem, NC.

Guitar Gabriel, a.k.a. Nyles Jones and Bobby Jones, was the son of recording bluesman Sonny Jones, a partner of Blind Boy Fuller and Sonny Terry. He was influenced by early blues, spirituals and country dance music and began an itinerant musician's life as a teenager playing Dixieland music, blues and marches in old-time medicine shows. A living encyclopedia of blues and gospel songs, he settled down in Winston-Salem and played in the streets and drink houses as well as performing religious songs in churches. Rediscovered in 1991 by Tim Duffy, he was soon back in show business recording new albums, touring Europe and playing festivals either solo or with small groups. His music—he called it "toot blues"—was an eclectic mixture of East Coast blues, Piedmont traditions, jump blues with Chicago and Texas influences and gospel, with every style being a source of inspiration for him. A popular poet and troubadour, he was a gifted and prolific writer of lyrics adapted to his relaxed guitar style.

what to buy: In 1971 he recorded a memorable session in Pittsburgh showing the strong, rural influence of Lightnin' Hopkins. *My South, My Blues* 𝄢𝄢𝄢𝄢𝄢 (Gemini, 1970/Jambalaya, 1988, prod. Bill Lawrence) includes "Welfare Blues," *the* master blues piece of 1970. *Guitar Gabriel, Vol. 1* 𝄢𝄢𝄢𝄢𝄢 (Music Maker, 1994, prod. Tim Duffy) is a moving collection with reminiscences of the days passed and the life of a country bluesman.

what to buy next: *Do You Know What It Means to Have a Friend—Toot Blues* 𝄢𝄢𝄢𝄢 (Karibu, 1991, prod. Tim Duffy) is the rediscovery session of an original, unpolished talent. An anthology of little-known or obscure Carolina artists, *A Living Past* 𝄢𝄢𝄢𝄢 (Music Maker, 1995, prod. Tim Duffy), includes four tracks by Guitar Gabriel. *Deep in the South* 𝄢𝄢𝄢 (Karibu, 1992, prod. Tim Duffy) includes 1991 recordings in the same vein as *Toot Blues*.

influences:

◀◀ Blind Boy Fuller, Rev. Gary Davis, Sonny Jones

Robert Sacré

Guitar Shorty

Born William David Kearney, September 8, 1939, in Houston, TX.

Guitar Shorty's live shows are likely to find him cranking out searing guitar solos while standing on his head, turning flips or working all kinds of gymnastics. But this on-stage athleticism, inspired by Guitar Slim, only augments the core of Shorty's musical talents: blazing guitar work and soulful vocals. Shorty first started performing as a teenager and cut his first single for Cobra in 1957. After a few more singles in the late 1950s, Shorty virtually disappeared from the recording world for 30 years while he continued to work clubs and polish his frenetic live act. Shorty's guitar can roar and weep, and he is credited with teaching Jimi Hendrix a few tricks after marrying his stepsister in the 1960s. In recent years, Shorty has resurfaced in the studio and proven that his boundless energy and passion transfer quite nicely onto tape.

what to buy: *Get Wise to Yourself* 🎵🎵🎵 (Black Top, 1995, prod. Hammond Scott) incorporates Shorty's stellar guitar work with a talented backing band that adds a funky, New Orleans flavor. Shorty's playing adds sensitive layers of emotion to full-band jams and slower, stripped-down tunes without ever letting his axe overpower the moment. Pleasures here include a sharp horn section anchored by sax player Kaz Kazanoff and two covers of songs by infamous R&B legend Swamp Dogg.

what to buy next: Shorty's debut on Black Top, *Topsy Turvy* 🎵🎵🎵 (Black Top, 1993, prod. Hammond Scott) is filled with his raucous enthusiasm on guitar and vibrant, soulful singing sharpened from years on the road.

the rest:

My Way on the Highway 🎵🎵🎵 (JSP, 1991)

influences:

◀◀ Albert King, Guitar Slim, Willie Dixon

▶▶ Larry Garner

Matt Pensinger

Guitar Slim

Born Edward Jones, December 10, 1926, in Greenwood, MS. Died February 7, 1959, in New York, NY.

New Orleans guitarist and singer Earl King refers to his mentor Guitar Slim as "the performanist man I ever seen." Aside from his flamboyance—Slim occasionally played solos perched on the shoulders of a valet or in a club's parking lot—he was a noteworthy blues singer and one of the first electric guitarists

Buddy Guy

song
Are You Losing Your Mind?

album
Stone Crazy (Alligator)

instrument
Guitar

monster solo

to employ distorted melodic overtones. Slim grew up in rural Mississippi and migrated to New Orleans after learning the rudiments of the guitar. By 1950, his dynamic live performances were causing a sensation in clubs like the Dew Drop and the Tijuana. Imperial and Bullet recorded him with little success, but Slim's luck changed when he signed with Specialty in 1953, where his first single, "The Things I Used to Do," became one of the most influential blues records of all time. Slim waxed other classics for Specialty—including "Well I Done Got Over It," "Bad Luck Blues," "Certainly All" and "Something to Remember You By"—but they didn't have the commercial impact of his debut. Atco signed Slim in 1956, where he added to his legacy with "Down through the Years" and "It Hurts to Love Someone," before he died prematurely at the age of 32, robbing the blues world of one of its most talented and colorful stars.

what to buy: No blues CD collection is complete unless it contains *Sufferin' Mind* 🎵🎵🎵🎵 (Specialty, 1969), which includes

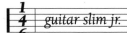

guitar slim jr.

most of Slim's devastating Specialty material. *The Atco Sessions* 🎸🎸🎸🎸 (Atlantic, 1987, prod. Bob Porter) is an excellent companion; the only drawback is its sparse playing time.

influences:

◀◀ Clarence "Gatemouth" Brown, T-Bone Walker, B.B. King, Willie Warren, Clarence Hollimon, Fats Domino

▶▶ Earl King, Guitar Ray, Eddie Lang, Ray Charles, James "Thunderbird" Davis, Ike Turner, Dr. John, Guitar Slim Jr., Phillip Walker, Lonnie Brooks, Buddy Guy, Jimi Hendrix, Stevie Ray Vaughan

Jeff Hannusch

Guitar Slim Jr.

Born Rodney Armstrong, 1954, in New Orleans, LA.

The son of one of the fathers of electric blues, Eddie Jones (a.k.a. Guitar Slim), Slim Jr. quite naturally picked up the guitar at an early age—by the time he was in his twenties he was playing blues and soul in the tiny blues taverns around New Orleans. Slim Jr. plays a full repertoire of his father's material, which keeps the older folks happy, but he can also cover the latest urban radio hits, which holds the younger audience. Despite a Grammy nomination for his debut, *The Story of My Life*, personal problems have hamstrung his career.

what to buy: *The Story of My Life* 🎸🎸🎸 (Orleans, 1988, prod. Carlo Ditta) and *Nothing Nice* 🎸🎸🎸 (Warehouse Creek, 1996) have their moments, but one can't help but feel Slim Jr.'s talent hasn't yet been fully tapped.

influences:

◀◀ Guitar Slim, Earl King, Rockie Charles, Tyrone Davis, Otis Redding, B.B. King

Jeff Hannusch

Adam Gussow

See: Satan & Adam

Buddy Guy

Born George Guy, July 30, 1936, in Lettsworth, LA.

With a gigantic grin and inventive electric guitar riffs played so fast you can barely focus on one at a time, Buddy Guy has come to symbolize traditional Chicago blues. Until 1991, he was, amazingly, still an undiscovered talent by most of the world; he ran his downtown Chicago nightclub, Buddy Guy's Legends, and showed off his immense charisma and talent on

the national blues circuit. But despite opening gigs for the Rolling Stones and other blues-rock performers in the early 1970s, few outside Chicago and the national blues community had really heard of him. Then came a marketing break: his comeback album, *Damn Right, I've Got the Blues*—with a new version of the old standard "Mustang Sally" and guest cameos by Mark Knopfler and Eric Clapton—worked like a charm. It sold well, earned a Grammy, established Guy as a blues celebrity along with B.B. King and John Lee Hooker and eventually opened the doors for a lucrative Reebok television commercial with White Sox slugger Frank Thomas. Guy's career beginnings paralleled those of many other bluesmen, from mentors Muddy Waters and King to contemporaries Otis Rush and Junior Wells. Born to a sharecropping family, Guy picked cotton until blues songs on the radio inspired him to pick up a guitar. After playing local roadhouses, he moved to Chicago's thriving, blues-friendly South Side and, despite his young age, gained renown in "head-cutting" competitions against Rush and Magic Sam. Following Howlin' Wolf, Little Walter, Waters and so many others to the legendary Chess Records, Guy recorded his trademark songs, including 1960 versions of Eurreal Montgomery's "First Time I Met the Blues" and Willie Dixon's "Let Me Love You Baby." In the 1960s he was one of the few nationally recognized bluesmen who wasn't old enough to be a rock 'n' roller's father so he started to cross over into the rock audience. The blues revival died down in the 1970s, and despite a creatively rich partnership with harpist Junior Wells, Guy had trouble translating the energy of his long, heavy-jamming songs to record. He eked out a living in Chicago as owner of the Checkerboard Lounge before opening Legends, befriending the hero-worshiping Stevie Ray Vaughan (he played at the guitarist's final show before his death) and recording. He continues to tour, play festivals, sell out 20 or 30 consecutive Legends appearances every January and serve as Chicago's reigning blues hero.

what to buy: True to its reputation, *Damn Right, I've Got the Blues* 🎸🎸🎸 (Silvertone, 1991, prod. John Porter) pretty much captures Guy's fiery performances, although you miss things like watching him walk from the stage to the bathroom while continuing to play the guitar. Despite an overwillingness to please non-blues fans—"Mustang Sally" is included just for familiarity, not because it adds anything to the original, and the guest stars sometimes crowd the singer—Guy's voice is at top soul power. His best album is *Stone Crazy* 🎸🎸🎸🎸 (Alligator, 1981, prod. Didier Tricard), with a hot Chicago four-piece rhythm section and Guy's soaring-and-smashing electric riffs. Before that, the closest Guy came to matching his live power was his debut, *A Man and the Blues* 🎵🎵🎵🎵 (Vanguard, 1968/1987, prod. Samuel Charters), with killer versions of "Mary Had a Little Lamb" and "Money (That's What I Want)." To complete the set, you'll need one of several Chess compilations, such as *Buddy's Blues* 🎵🎵🎵🎵 (Chess/MCA, 1997), and at least one Junior Wells collaboration, most notably *Alone and Acoustic* 🎵🎵🎵🎵 (Alligator, 1991, prod. Didier Tricard), a spontaneous 1981 Paris session including Hooker's "I'm in the Mood," Guy's "Sweet Black Girl" and the rock classic "High Heel Sneakers."

what to buy next: An early linking with Clapton, who once called Guy the world's greatest living guitar player, produced the nice but not-so-explosive *Buddy Guy & Junior Wells Play the Blues* 🎵🎵🎵 (Atlantic, 1972/Rhino, 1992, prod. Eric Clapton, Ahmet Ertegun, Tom Dowd, Michael Cuscuna). While Chess/MCA has mined Guy's early hits on many indistinguishable compilations, it's always worth tracking down the original LP of Chess singles, *I Was Walkin' through the Woods* 🎵🎵🎵🎵 (Chess, 1970). *Feels Like Rain* 🎵🎵🎵 (Silvertone, 1993, prod. John Porter), the slower follow-up to *Damn Right*, is especially worth buying for Guy's soulful vocals, but not for the Travis Tritt and Paul Rodgers cameos.

what to avoid: Chess Records has driven a long way on the strength of its classic 1950s and 1960s singles; if you buy the newer *Buddy's Blues*, you won't need the more thorough but redundant *The Complete Chess Studio Recordings* 🎵🎵🎵 (Chess/MCA, 1992). *Live! The Real Deal* 🎵🎵🎵 (Silvertone, 1996, prod. Buddy Guy, Eddie Kramer), with the pompous pony-tailed guitarist G.E. Smith and his *Saturday Night Live* band, captures a lackluster performance, with typically good Guy solos but very little else.

the rest:

I Left My Blues in San Francisco 🎵🎵🎵 (Chess, 1967/MCA, 1987)
This Is Buddy Guy 🎵🎵🎵 (Vanguard, 1968)
(With Junior Wells and Junior Mance) *Buddy and the Juniors* 🎵🎵🎵 (MCA, 1970)
Hold That Plane! 🎵🎵🎵 (Vanguard, 1972)
(With Junior Wells) *Live in Montreux* 🎵🎵🎵 (Evidence, 1977/1992)
(With Junior Wells) *Drinkin' TNT and Smokin' Dynamite* 🎵🎵🎵 (Blind Pig, 1982)
The Best of Buddy Guy 🎵🎵🎵 (Rhino, 1992)
My Time After Awhile 🎵🎵🎵 (Vanguard, 1992)
Slippin' In 🎵🎵🎵 (Silvertone, 1994)
Southern Blues 1957–63 🎵🎵🎵 (Paula, 1994)

worth searching for: The import-only JSP series captures Guy smoking, with his great 1970s band (including brother Phil on

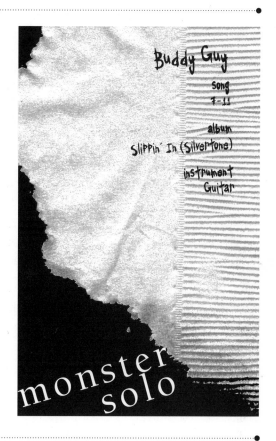

rhythm guitar); best of the hard-to-find CDs are *D.J. Play My Blues* 🎵🎵🎵 (JSP, 1994), *Breaking Out* 🎵🎵🎵🎵 (JSP, 1993) and *Live at the Checkerboard Lounge* 🎵🎵🎵 (JSP, 1979/1995).

influences:

⏮ Muddy Waters, Magic Sam, Otis Rush, Junior Wells, T-Bone Walker, Guitar Slim, B.B. King, Albert King

⏭ Eric Clapton, Stevie Ray Vaughan, Son Seals, Jonny Lang, Kenny Wayne Shepherd, Tinsley Ellis, Luther Allison, Rolling Stones, Jeff Beck

Steve Knopper

Phil Guy

Born April 28, 1940, in Lettsworth, LA.

A Chicago favorite, guitarist Phil Guy is four years younger than his better-known brother, Buddy. The Guys began their profes-

Buddy Guy (© Jack Vartoogian)

sional playing careers in Louisiana, Phil following literally in his brother's footsteps. Phil replaced Buddy in a succession of bands as Buddy moved on, including Raful Neal's hot, Baton Rouge-based group after Buddy split for Chicago. Eventually Phil quit his day job and followed him, becoming a local Windy City fixture with his funky hybrid of Louisiana blues and the modern urban styles of his newer surroundings. He was featured on many of Buddy's recordings of the 1970s and 1980s as part of a dense layer of rhythm guitars over which Buddy would soar. Phil also led his own band, the Chicago Machine, demonstrating his tough, amplified leads and powerful vocals. A regular at blues festivals throughout the world, Phil continues to pursue his music and emerge from the looming shadow of his sibling.

what to buy: Recordings under Guy's own name are imports and tend not to fully capture his power and skill. *Tina Nu* 𝄞𝄞𝄞𝄞 (JSP, 1988, prod. John Stedman) is a short but relentless set of tunes with a funky vigor. Phil's angular leads are rich yet edgy

in style, his vocals strong, and the band includes Chicago keyboard genius Eddie Lusk.

what to avoid: The uneven *Breaking out on Top* 𝄞𝄞 (JSP, 1993, prod. John Stedman), a compilation of selections from the LP *Bad Luck Boy* and other sessions, is more indicative of JSP's penchant for cashing in than any concern for the genre.

worth searching for: Brother Buddy is aboard adding some tasty ax, and premier Chicago drummer Ray Allison is also present for *Bad Luck Boy* 𝄞𝄞𝄞𝄞 (JSP, 1983, prod. Phil Guy), a competent set of blues with some great moments. The high-energy instrumental "Breaking out on Top" features good interplay from the Guy brothers and an opportunity to discern their different guitar styles.

influences:

◀◀ T-Bone Walker, Earl King, Buddy Guy

▶▶ Joe Louis Walker, Tab Benoit

Tali Madden

Jimmy Hall

Born in Mobile, AL.

Best known as the former lead singer of southern-boogie outfit Wet Willie, Jimmy Hall is a triple threat: he's a singer/songwriter, plays a mean harmonica and can even throw in some saxophone when called upon to do so. As you might expect, Hall is a student of the blues and R&B and his music is a gumbo of many worthwhile influences. But when blues come to the fore as his chosen metier, Hall seems not quite up to the task of carrying on the legacies of Muddy, Albert and so many others. Perhaps the kid shoulda just kept on smilin'. Interestingly, his current day job is that of musical director for country renegade Hank Williams Jr. Go figure.

what's available: Hall's solo debut, *Rendezvous with the Blues* ♫ is a bit of a letdown. He has the skills, but the song selection is poor—do we really need another rendition of Sam Cooke's "A Change Is Gonna Come?"—and the execution often pedestrian: Hall's take on Albert King's "The Hunter" is as toothless a version as can be recalled. The rest of it is like walking into a blues club on a slightly off night. You could be spending your time in worse ways, but the band is neither so hot that you want to dance, nor bad enough to make you leave. Ho hum.

worth searching for: Hear what Hall does best on either of two Wet Willie collections, *Greatest Hits* ♫♫♫ (Rebound, 1994) or *The Best of Wet Willie* ♫♫♫♫ (Polydor, 1994).

influences:
◀◀ Otis Redding, Muddy Waters

Daniel Durchholz

John Hammond Jr.

Born John Paul Hammond, November 13, 1942, in New York, NY.

John Hammond has created his own niche as a solo blues performer armed with only his guitar, a harmonica and a rich singing voice that forages through historic explorations of country blues. Emerging out of the American folk movement of the 1960s, Hammond first brought his rich sense of blues history and adept musicianship to the coffeehouse circuit in California and later to the burgeoning Greenwich Village scene in New York. The son of noted Columbia Records executive John

Hammond, Hammond grew up with his mother. After a short stint at Antioch College in Ohio, Hammond hitched his way to Los Angeles. At the age of 20, he inked his first record deal and began an impressive recording career that spans 25 years and more than 30 albums. Hammond is not a songwriter but has dedicated his life to re-interpreting blues classics, and in doing so, he has resurrected tunes that might have disappeared. And while he continues to tour as a solo act, Hammond's recording career has featured a wider range of material, including magical full-band sessions.

what to buy: Released when Hammond was only 24, *Big City Blues* ♫♫♫ (Vanguard, 1964/1995) was his second album and one of the first electric blues recordings by a white artist. Hammond gives a fresh, electric guitar twist to older classics, including several Chess hits. The only full-length live set Hammond has released in the U.S., *John Hammond Live* ♫♫♫ (Rounder, 1983/1992, prod. John Nagy), captures the immense power and depth of emotion he can extract from guitar, harmonica, plaintive vocals and a stomping foot onstage. Recorded at McCabe's in Los Angeles, it is the highlight of his Rounder stint. In between labels, Hammond financed *Nobody but You* ♫♫♫ (Flying Fish, 1988/Pointblank, 1996, prod. Ken Whiteley). He is joined by a tight, five-piece band that provides restrained, backing fill behind Hammond's emotive singing, nimble guitar picking and some of his best harmonica work on songs by John Lee Hooker, Muddy Waters and Little Walter. *Trouble No More* ♫♫♫♫ (Pointblank, 1994, prod. J.J. Cale, Mike Kappus) finds Hammond switching between solo Delta blues standards and raucous full-band workouts featuring Little Charlie & the Nightcats. Hammond also pulls in other guests for jaunts into western swing jazz fare, but the spunky, electric jams are the real treats.

what to buy next: *I Can Tell* ♫♫♫ (Atlantic, 1967) is one of Hammond's hottest collaborations, a loose session teamed with the Rolling Stones' Bill Wyman on bass, Robbie Robertson on lead guitar, Charles Otis on drums and Artie Butler on piano. *The Best of John Hammond* ♫♫♫♫ (Vanguard, 1970/1989, prod. Maynard Solomon) is a strong collection of Hammond's most alluring early work. On *Found True Love* ♫♫♫♫ (Pointblank, 1996, prod. John Hammond, Duke Robillard) the power of Hammond's vocals really come to the front in duets with singer Soozie Tyrell and several Howlin' Wolf tunes. Other highlights include the punch/counterpunch of Hammond's acoustic playing jousting with Robillard's piercing electric guitar.

the rest:

John Hammond 🎝🎝🎝 (Vanguard, 1962/1992)
Country Blues 🎝🎝🎝 (Vanguard, 1964/1995)
So Many Roads 🎝🎝🎝 (Vanguard, 1965/1993)
Mirrors 🎝🎝 (Vanguard, 1967)
Sooner or Later 🎝🎝🎝 (Atlantic, 1968)
Encore 🎝🎝🎝 (Spivey, 1969)
Southern Fried 🎝🎝🎝 (Atlantic, 1969)
Source Point 🎝🎝🎝🎝 (Columbia, 1970)
I'm Satisfied 🎝🎝🎝 (Columbia, 1972)
Triumvirate 🎝🎝🎝 (Columbia, 1973)
Can't Beat the Kid 🎝🎝🎝 (Capricorn, 1975)
John Hammond Solo 🎝🎝🎝 (Vanguard, 1976/1992)
Footwork 🎝🎝🎝 (Vanguard, 1978)
Hot Tracks 🎝🎝🎝 (Vanguard, 1979)
Mileage 🎝🎝 (Rounder, 1980/1995)
Frogs for Snakes 🎝🎝🎝 (Rounder, 1982/1994)
John Hammond Live in Greece 🎝🎝🎝 (Lyra, 1984)
John Hammond 🎝🎝🎝🎝 (Rounder, 1987)
Got Love If You Want It 🎝🎝🎝🎝 (Pointblank/Charisma, 1992)
I Can Tell 🎝🎝🎝🎝 (Atlantic, 1992)
You Can't Judge a Book by Its Cover 🎝🎝🎝🎝 (Vanguard, 1993)

worth searching for: Hammond composed and performed all of the music for the movie soundtrack *Little Big Man* 🎝🎝🎝 (Columbia, 1971). Spivey issued an impressive compilation, *Kings & the Queen* 🎝🎝🎝🎝 (Spivey, 1970) that includes a Hammond duet with Roosevelt Sykes and harmonica accompaniment on a couple of tracks from a very young Bob Dylan.

influences:

◀◀ Robert Johnson, Jimmy Reed, Lightnin' Hopkins

▶▶ Corey Harris, Rory Block

Matt Pensinger

Beck Hansen
See: Beck

Tre Hardiman
See: Tre

James Harman
Born June 8, 1946, in Anniston, AL.

James Harman was the top-selling artist on New Orleans' Black Top label during a five-year stint beginning in 1991. The California-based bandleader/vocalist/harmonica player writes original music that clearly reflects his blues roots, but stands out as unique, personal and memorable.

what to buy: *Do Not Disturb* 🎝🎝🎝🎝 (Black Top, 1991, prod. Hammond Scott, James Harman, Jerry Hall) is superb, cataloging life on the road with wit, insight and not a small measure of humor. Fifty years from now, it will likely be recognized as one of the classic blues recordings. *Two Sides to Every Story* 🎝🎝🎝🎝 (Black Top, 1993, prod. Hammond Scott, James Harman, Jerry Hall) is more of the same, only a bit more raw in its instrumental tones and overall feel. *Black & White* 🎝🎝🎝🎝 (Black Top, 1995, prod. James Harman, Jerry Hall) captures Harman at his most diverse.

what to buy next: *Cards on the Table* 🎝🎝🎝🎝 (Black Top, 1994, prod. Hammond Scott, James Harman, Jerry Hall) is a successful offering, but not as essential as those listed above.

the rest:

Icepick's Story 🎝🎝🎝🎝 (Me and My Blues Records/Continental Record Service, 1997)

worth searching for: Harman's recordings for the independent Rivera/Icepick label are set for reissue on Ron Levy's new Cannonball label. Among them: *Extra Napkins: Strictly the Blues* 🎝🎝🎝🎝 (Rivera/Icepick, 1988, prod. James Harman, Jerry Hall), previously released only on vinyl, featuring Harman in his most exclusively blues-focused setting; and *Strictly Live . . . in '85* 🎝🎝🎝 (Rivera/Icepick, 1990, prod. James Harman, Jerry Hall), a live date with guitarist Kid Ramos and the late Hollywood Fats, then members of Harman's ensemble. Also worth finding: *Thank You Baby* 🎝🎝🎝 (Enigma, 1983), long out of print. Good luck.

influences:

◀◀ Big Walter Horton, Sonny Boy Williamson II

▶▶ Gary Primich

Bryan Powell

Harmonica Fats & Bernie Pearl
Formed mid-1980s, in Los Angeles, CA.

Harmonica Fats (born Harvey Blackston, September 8, 1927, in McDade, LA), harmonica, vocals; Bernie Pearl, guitar.

Incorpating nearly every style of blues from swing to country blues, Harmonica Fats and Bernie Pearl have created a great contemporary stage act. Why not? Harvey Blackston started his career in the early 1950s as "Harmonica Fats—320 Pounds of Rhythm and Blues" and toured with Bill Cosby, Sam Cooke and Ringo Starr before things dried up in the 1970s. He hooked with Pearl's band and they've been together ever since, finally evolving from an electric band into an acoustic duo, delighting audiences and releasing albums on a regular basis.

what to buy: *I Had to Get Nasty* ♪♪♪⁷ (Bee Bump, 1991, prod. Harmonica Fats, Bernie Pearl, Cash McCall) is a full-band effort that shows off Fats' deep, booming vocals and Pearl's varied bag of guitar tricks. *Two Heads Are Better Than One* ♪♪♪⁷ (Bee Bump, 1994, prod. Harmonica Fats, Bernie Pearl) is a good document of their acoustic evolution with witty songs like "Just Like Richard Nixon."

the rest:
Blow Fat Daddy Blow! ♪♪♪ (Bee Bump, 1995)

influences:

◀◀ Blind Lemon Jefferson, Peetie Wheatstraw, Lightnin' Hopkins, Mance Lipscomb, Fred McDowell, Sonny Terry & Brownie McGhee

Leland Rucker

Harmonica Slim

Born Richard Riggins, July 1, 1921, in Tupelo, MS.

Pay close attention, because this gets confusing: Richard Riggins became the second Harmonica Slim after Muddy Waters, in 1955, pointed out his resemblance to Travis "Harmonica Slim" Blaylock. Waters married this Slim's sister, Lily Riggins, in 1932, and taught him how to play the harmonica. After that, Slim worked as a railroad man, which gave him the opportunity to travel and learn technique by jamming with B.B. King, Lightnin' Hopkins and many others. Little Walter, in Detroit, also gave him tips. In the early 1970s, Slim hooked up with the Blues Connoisseur label, which released some of his singles; he moved to Fresno, California, played the occasional festival and drifted out of music until he began recording again for Trix in the mid-1990s.

what to buy: The great harpists know exactly how to complement their riffs with their singing style; on *Black Bottom Blues* ♪♪♪⁷ (Trix, 1995, prod. Chris Millar) both Slim's harp and his deep, tough voice combine short, quick bursts of power. On traditional songs like Elmore James' "Dust My Broom" and Slim's own "Gonna Move Back to Town" and "Stoop Down," the singer taps into his railroad background, approximating the sounds of heavy trains chugging near your ear.

Slim Harpo

song
Baby Scratch My Back

album
Hip Shakin': The Excello Collection
(AVI/Excello)

instrument
Harmonica

monster solo

influences:

◀◀ Muddy Waters, Travis "Harmonica Slim" Blaylock, Little Walter, B.B. King, John Lee Hooker

▶▶ Slim Harpo, Junior Wells, R.L. Burnside, A.C. Reed

Steve Knopper

Slim Harpo

Born James Moore, January 11, 1924, in Baton Rouge, LA. Died January 31, 1970, in Baton Rouge, LA.

Slim Harpo is the architect of the swamp blues Baton Rouge sound perfected in producer Jay Miller's Crowley, Louisiana-based studio. Harpo's sensuous, relaxed adenoidal singing delivery, slinky harmonica playing and R&B guitar style found a ready audience (including the young Rolling Stones, who made his "King Bee" a staple of their early repertoire, as well as many other rock bands). After a decade as Harmonica Slim on the southern bar circuit, he began recording with Miller in 1955. "King Bee" was followed by "Rainin' in My Heart" in 1961 and the salacious, delightful "Baby Scratch My Back" five years later. The success of the latter brought Harpo into the rock realm, where he remained until his death of a heart attack.

what to buy: *Hip Shakin': The Excello Collection* ♫♫♫♫ (AVI/Excello, prod. various) has all the hits and more, 44 tracks that cover the bases. It's all there on "King Bee," the dense bass sound, sneering voice, slippery harp and the "sting" of his guitar. *The Scratch* ♫♫♫ (AVI/Excello, 1996, prod. various) could have been added as a third disc to *Hip Shakin'*, with many interesting outtakes from the Miller vaults. The last third comes from a live, one-microphone tape made by some teenagers at a Harpo dance concert in June 1961, in Mobile, Alabama. It might bother audiophiles' sensitive ears, but if you want to hear what Mick Jagger and Keith Richards were trying to sound like when they started the Stones, you can't get much closer.

influences:

◀◀ Muddy Waters, Little Walter, Jimmy Reed

▶▶ Rolling Stones, Kinks, Van Morrison, Dave Edmunds, the Band, Yardbirds, Moody Blues

Leland Rucker

Edward Harrington

See: Eddie Clearwater

Corey Harris

Born February 21, 1969, in Denver, CO.

Still in his twenties, acoustic bluesman Corey Harris has turned his fascination with country blues into a full-fledged career. He's a performing and recording artist whose first CD garnered rave reviews, the front cover of *Living Blues* and opening spots on tours with Buddy Guy, B.B. King and other established stars. Corey grew up in Denver, went to college in Maine, traveled in Africa and came to Louisiana as part of the Teach America program. He started playing and singing on the streets of New Orleans during weekends off from his work as a schoolteacher, made several "live" broadcasts from the studios of WWOZ-FM and recorded an album with blues producer Larry Hoffman, which was picked up by Alligator and released in 1995 as *Between Midnight and Day*. Harris is one of several young African-American bluesmen who have reached back to the pre-war blues era for their primary inspiration,

learning the styles and drawing on the emotive force of musicians like Charly Patton, Son House, Tommy Johnson, Bukka White, Robert Johnson and their contemporaries. Harris' immersion in the music of his idols and mentors is total; he's stripped everything back to a man of feeling and intelligence and his guitar, working in tandem to express the burning issues of daily life in song and verse. While his repertoire is largely drawn from the classics and appealing obscurities of the idiom, he has already started forming his own material in the traditional mode, and as he develops as a performer and composer Corey Harris is bound to make his own personal extension of acoustic blues.

what to buy: Harris' first album, *Between Midnight and Day* ♫♫♫♫ (Alligator, 1995, prod. Larry Hoffman) investigates songs by bluesmen as diverse as Charly Patton, Sleepy John Estes, Blind Boy Fuller, Bukka White, Mississippi Fred McDowell, Tampa Red, Robert Petway, Muddy Waters and Louis Jordan. His three originals—"Roots Woman," "Between Midnight and Day" and "Bound to Miss Me"—are thoroughly rooted in the tradition and boast occasional flashes of a personal style. He followed with a strong second album, *Fish Ain't Bitin'* ♫♫♫♫ (Alligator, 1997, prod. Larry Hoffman, Corey Harris), again drawing his repertoire from across the pre-war blues spectrum and infusing it with an increasingly personal sound and style. Highly recommended.

worth searching for: Club members of WWOZ Radio in New Orleans who joined in the spring of 1997 received a CD of "live" music by Crescent City artists. *Guardians of the Groove—WWOZ on CD, Vol. 7* ♫♫♫♫ includes a moving Corey Harris performance of "Sweet Black Angel" at the Funky Butt club in January 1997, where he was backed by bassist Chris Severin. Harris also appears as a guest on Junior Wells' *Come on in This House* ♫♫♫ (Telarc, 1996).

influences:

◀◀ Charley Patton, Bukka White, Muddy Waters, Sleepy John Estes, Mississippi Fred McDowell, Tampa Red, Louis Jordan

John Sinclair

Eleanora Harris

See: Billie Holiday

Corey Harris (© Jack Vartoogian)

Shakey Jake Harris

Born James D. Harris, April 12, 1921, in Earle, AR. Died March 2, 1990, in Forrest City, AR.

One of the more colorful figures associated with Chicago blues was harmonica man Shakey Jake. A gambler by trade, Jake played music in order to make a name for himself. To further his reputation as a crap shooter he cut "Roll Your Money Maker" in 1958 for Artistic with Magic Sam backing on guitar. In 1959 Harris cut the first of two albums issued on Bluesville, which led to his invitation to join the 1961 American Folk Blues Festival caravan that toured Europe. In 1968 he moved to Los Angeles and later ran a blues club and continued to record sporadically. Unfortunately, most of the news concerning Jake in the 1980s concentrated on his ill health.

what to buy: *Mouth Harp Blues* ♪♪♪♪ (Original Blues Classics, 1959) and *Good Times* ♪♪♪♪ (Original Blues Classics, 1960) are reissues of the original Bluesville LPs. Low-key affairs, the original LPs were aimed at the folk market.

worth searching for: Of his handful of LPs, *Further on up the Road* ♪♪♪♪ (World Pacific, 1968, prod. Stephen LaVere) is excellent and featured a band that included Luther Allison on guitar and Robert "Mojo" Elem on bass.

influences:

◄◄ Sonny Boy Williamson I, Sonny Boy Williamson II, Little Walter, Big Walter Horton, Junior Wells, George "Harmonica" Smith

►► Magic Sam, Johnny Dyer, Rod Piazza, William Clarke

Jeff Hannusch

William Harris

Born near Glendora, MS. Died reportedly in Chicago, IL.

A cipher in a pre-war blues world populated by phantoms, William Harris left 10 known recordings, sung and played in a vein reminiscent of the Jackson, Mississippi, school of Tommy Johnson. Harris' entire legacy was delivered in 1927 and 1928 in studios in Birmingham, Alabama, and Richmond, Indiana. A minstrel-show performer and dancer, Harris evidently found steady work in juke joints until a reported move to Chicago around 1929. Then he disappeared.

what to buy: Almost all of Harris' rhythmic, delicate work, including versions of Jim Jackson's "Kansas City Blues" and Blind Lemon Jefferson's "Electric Chair Blues," are included on *William Harris and Buddy Boy Hawkins: 1927–29* ♪♪♪♪ (Docu-

ment, 1991, prod. Johnny Parth). Beware: several tracks are cloaked in the tell-tale scratches that often obscure worn 78s.

what to buy next: Smaller helpings of Harris, along with seminal recordings by Garfield Akers, King Solomon Hill and Geeshie Wiley, are included on *Mississippi Masters* ♪♪♪♪ (Yazoo, 1994).

the rest:

Too Late, Too Late Vol. 3 ♪♪♪ (Document, 1994)

influences:

◄◄ Tommy Johnson, Jim Jackson

►► Tommy McClennan

Steve Braun

Wynonie Harris

Born August 24, 1915, in Omaha, NE. Died June 14, 1969, in Los Angeles, CA.

One of the greatest stars of the Golden Age of Rhythm & Blues (1945–55), Wynonie "Mr. Blues" Harris broke into the limelight as singer with the Jimmy Lunceford Orchestra in 1944 when he hit with "Hurry Hurry" and "Who Threw the Whiskey in the Well" for Decca. This revolutionary jump-blues and Harris' subsequent small-group recordings for Apollo in 1945 helped pioneer the idiom which would dominate African-American popular music for the next ten years. Harris signed with King in 1947 and made a series of all-time classics for the Cincinnati label. His recording of Roy Brown's epochal "Good Rocking Tonight" in 1948 was the biggest hit of his career, covered to good effect six years later by Elvis Presley, but lesser-known masterpieces like "Bloodshot Eyes," "Good Morning Judge," "Grandma Plays the Numbers," "I Love My Baby's Pudding" and "All She Wants to Do Is Rock" are among the best rhythm & blues singles ever recorded. He covered Louis Prima's "Oh Babe!" with the Lucky Millinder Orchestra in 1950 and continued to cut for King until the fall of 1954, always using topnotch bands and outstanding saxophonists like Red Prysock, Big John Greer, John Hardee, Louis Stephens, Hal Singer, Tommy Archia, Johnny Griffin and Rufus Gore. Chess sponsored a comeback attempt 10 years later, including a great version of Memphis Slim's "The Comeback," but Wynonie Harris' day had come and gone. The availability of his Apollo and King singles on CD has reintroduced the erstwhile "Mr. Blues" to modern audiences, but the size and scope of his achievement has yet to be properly assessed.

what to buy: *Bloodshot Eyes: The Best of Wynonie Harris* 🎵🎵🎵🎵 (Rhino, 1994, prod. James Austin) provides a brilliant introduction to the great blues shouter in his prime. All his King hits are included, along with salacious gems like "Keep on Churnin'" ("'til the butter flows"), "Lovin' Machine," "Luscious Woman" and "Sittin' on It All the Time." *Bloodshot Eyes* will literally show you where rock 'n' roll came from and how it got its name. *Everybody Boogie* 🎵🎵🎵🎵 (Delmark, 1996) collects Harris' four 1945 Apollo sessions. Standout tracks include "Wynonie's Blues" and "Here Comes the Blues" with Illinois Jacquet, "Somebody Changed the Lock" and "That's the Stuff You Gotta Watch" with Jack McVea, "Everybody Boogie" with Oscar Pettiford and the sizzling "Young and Wild." These recordings were immensely influential on the development of small-band R&B. Wynonie's King singles can also be found on three King replica CDs: *Battle of the Blues, Volume One* 🎵🎵🎵🎵 (King, 1988) and *Battle of the Blues, Volume Two* 🎵🎵🎵🎵 (King, 1988) with Roy Brown, and *Battle of the Blues, Volume Four* 🎵🎵🎵🎵 (King, 1988) with Roy Brown and Eddie "Cleanhead" Vinson, where they share space with an equal number of sides by Brown and Vinson.

the rest:

Women Whiskey & Fish Tails 🎵🎵🎵🎶 (Ace, 1993)
Wynonie Harris 1944–45 🎵🎵🎵🎶 (Jazz Chronological Classics, 1996)

worth searching for: The 1964 Chess session is worth finding, not only for Harris' aprocryphal sides but also for rare cuts by Jimmy Witherspoon, Jimmy Rushing and Al Hibbler, on *Shoutin', Swingin' & Makin' Love* 🎵🎵🎵🎶 (MCA/Chess, 1964). Harris' original "Battle of the Blues (Parts 1 & 2)" with Big Joe Turner, recorded in concert in 1950, can be heard on *Jumpin' with Joe: The Complete Aladdin and Imperial Recordings* 🎵🎵🎵🎵 (EMI, 1993, prod. Ron Furmanek), another painstakingly produced R&B reissue package.

influences:

◄◄ Jimmy Rushing, Louis Jordan, T-Bone Walker, Big Joe Turner

►► Chuck Berry, Little Richard, Elvis Presley

John Sinclair

Wilbert Harrison

Born January 6, 1929, in Charlotte, NC. Died October 26, 1994, in Spencer, NC.

Wilbert Harrison's 1959 recording of "Kansas City" was one of rock 'n' roll's greatest hits. Harrison's country approach to R&B, his rolling Fats Domino-style piano and Jimmy Sprull's wild lead guitar ("Mustard!") should have been the formula for many hits to come. Reality was different. Harrison signed with DeLuxe in 1953, where he recorded odd blends of R&B and old-time country that failed to sell. The following year he latched on to New Jersey-based Savoy, where his bouncy reworking of Terry Fell's country hit, "Don't Drop It," was a fair seller. Four more singles flopped. When he inquired about future recording time, label owner Herman Lubinsky literally chased Harrison out of his office, telling him to never return. After he signed with Bobby Robinson's Fury and scored the million-selling smash "Kansas City" (#1 on both the pop and R&B charts), Lubinsky claimed to still have Harrison under contract. Robinson settled out of court for $13,500, but by the time the legal smoke had cleared, the momentum of Harrison's recording career had been stopped cold. Good records such as "Don't Wreck My Life," "Goodbye Kansas City" (a catchy sound-alike sequel), "Why Did You Leave" and others did not even chart. Harrison kept at it, and at Sue in 1969 turned one of his old love songs from the Fury era into a bluesy plea for racial tolerance. "Let's Work Together" was a Top 40 pop hit, and Canned Heat scored a Top 20 hit with a 1971 remake. With no further hit records to fuel it, Harrison's comeback couldn't last, but his music has endured; "Kansas City" is still a staple of oldies radio and "Let's Work Together" transformed into an extremely popular jingle for a national chain of auto parts stores.

what to buy: All of Harrison's 1959–61 Fury sides are on *Kansas City* 🎵🎵🎵🎵 (Relic, 1992, prod. Bobby Robinson). For a broader view of Harrison's career, you might prefer *Kansas City: His Legendary Golden Classics* 🎵🎵🎵🎵 (Collectables, 1994), with material from the Savoy, Fury and Sue eras.

what to avoid: Be aware that *Greatest Classic R&B Hits* 🎵🎵🎶 (Grudge, 1992, compilation prod. Juggy Murray) is a deceptively titled repackaging of Harrison's 1969 Sue album comprising late-1960s remakes of Harrison's own hits as well as cover versions of "Stand by Me," "Stagger Lee," "What Am I Living For," "C.C. Rider" and others. Harrison does some of these well, but they aren't his originals.

the rest:

Wilbert Harrison 🎵🎵🎶 (Ace, 1989)

worth searching for: Some import shops and catalogs list *Da-De-Ya-Da* 🎵🎵🎶 (P-Vine, 1990, compilation prod. Cliff White), with the original "Kansas City" and "Goodbye Kansas City" as well as some great, little-known material such as "Lovin' Operator," "Tell on Yourself" and a weird cover of "On Top of Old Smoky."

influences:

◀◀ Little Willie Littlefield, Chuck Willis, Fats Domino

▶▶ Canned Heat, Creedence Clearwater Revival, Roy Clark

Ken Burke

Alvin Youngblood Hart

Born Gregory Edward Hart, March 2, 1963, in Oakland, CA.

Alvin Youngblood Hart is part of a revival of rural blues among young African-American guitarists. Born in Oakland, he lived in Los Angeles, Ohio and Chicago while growing up, but his musical and psychological roots are in Carroll County, Mississippi, where his family is from. Equally skilled at 6- and 12-string, tenor and steel-bodied guitars, Hart is a repository of ancient black storytelling and a gifted contemporary composer. His repertoire includes the music of early-twentieth-century black string bands and Mexican waltzes, but his primary area of expertise is Mississippi blues of the Son House and Robert Johnson variety. Hart is a gifted guitarist and powerful performer with a bright future ahead of him.

what to buy: "Big Mama" is Hart's Mississippi-based grandmother, and *Big Mama's Door* ♪♪♪ (Columbia/OKeh, 1996, prod. Michael Nash, Carey Williams) wears like a warm evening on the front porch. It opens with the title tune, on which Hart thumps and plucks his way back to the country. He sounds most like Delta icon Robert Johnson on "Joe Friday," the slide matching his vocal: "I got to call up Joe Friday and put him on my baby's trail." Covers include Charley Patton's "Pony Blues" and Willie McTell's "Hillbilly Willie's Blues." His guitar playing, all fingerpicked, conveys the sense of a lost treasure rediscovered. Nominated for five W.C. Handy Awards, this is country blues storytelling at its best.

worth searching for: Hart is one of six guest slide guitarists on the Junior Wells sessions that produced *Come on in This House* ♪♪♪♪ (Telarc, 1996, prod. John Snyder). Hart performs on 12-string dobro and National steel guitar.

influences:

◀◀ Mississippi Sheiks, Charley Patton

David Feld

Buddy Boy Hawkins

Birth and death dates unknown.

A Mississippi singer who came out either from the northern Delta or Alabama, Hawkins sang achingly slow rags and dirges featuring fillagreed finger-picking that sounded like a plucked harpsichord. In 12 songs for the defunct Paramount label, he sang often about trains. One tune, "Workin' on the Railroad," suggests he may have laid track. The melody to his "Number Three Blues" was borrowed years later by British guitarist Peter Green to grace Fleetwood Mac's *Then Play On*.

what to buy: Growling and crooning, Hawkins sounds like a voice from the 1800s on *William Harris and Buddy Boy Hawkins: 1927–29* ♪♪♪♪ (Document, 1991, prod. Johnny Parth). He is paired with the equally-mysterious William Harris—two men whose history could fit in a thimble but whose music still mesmerizes 70 years on.

influences:

▶▶ Fleetwood Mac

Steve Braun

Jamesetta Hawkins

See: Etta James

Screamin' Jay Hawkins

Born Jalacy Hawkins, July 18, 1929, in Cleveland, OH.

Primarily known as one of early rock's great showmen, Hawkins found fame promoting himself as a rock 'n' roll lunatic—appropriate for both Wolfman Jack and Dr. Demento. A former Golden Gloves boxing champion, he embarked on a musical career working small clubs with an energetic R&B revue show that often found him carried onstage in a flaming coffin, using flash powder or waving spears with skulls on them at the audience. His work was attacked by the usual authorities; early singles, particularly the classic "I Put a Spell on You" (reportedly cut by a dead-drunk Hawkins), featured so much of his wild moaning and vocal thrashing that they were banned from some radio stations and therefore, sold little. A surprising cameo in Jim Jarmusch's 1989 *Mystery Train*—as well as a song for *The X-Files'* album project *Songs in the Key of X* (Warner Bros., 1996) were enthusiastically received and led to a minor resurgence of interest in his career.

what to buy: *Portrait of a Man* ♪♪♪ (Demon, 1995, prod. various) compiles his crucial tracks, with all the great histrionics of

Screamin' Jay Hawkins (© Jack Vartoogian)

near-misses and should've-beens such as "The Whammy" and "Little Demon."

the rest:

Voodoo Jive: The Best of Screamin' Jay Hawkins 🎜🎜🎜 (Rhino, 1990)
Cow Fingers and Mosquito Pie 🎜🎜🎜 (Epic/Legacy, 1991)

influences:

⏮ Howlin' Wolf, Muddy Waters

⏭ Bobby Boris Pickett

Todd Wicks

Ted Hawkins

Born 1936, in Lakeshore, MS. Died January 1, 1995, in Los Angeles, CA.

If Sam Cooke's voice makes you want to fall in love, Ted Hawkins' makes you scared to death of losing it. Blessed with a voice from the heavens but cursed with a life of homelessness and incarceration, he died months after he signed to a major label and seemed poised to become a star. The singer-songwriter was at a disadvantage from the beginning: For shoplifting and other minor crimes, he was sent to a reform school before he hit his teens. He was switched to Parchman Farm prison, where he endured pistol-beatings (and heard Sam Cooke for the first time), and later rode the rails as a hobo before landing in a California medical facility. "The uvular blends of his vocal style were similar to those of Sam Cooke and Otis Redding," Francis Davis wrote in the *Oxford American* magazine, "but his solitary presentation and vagabond life gave him more in common with Robert Johnson, Blind Lemon Jefferson or Blind Willie McTell." After singing on the Los Angeles streets, a local DJ heard him and set him up with producer Bruce Bromberg. From there, Hawkins' superb recordings gained him a loyal cult following, especially in Europe, but his life continued to run an unsteady course. He drifted, putting out a record every now and then, but mostly trying to fill his tip jar while singing on an old milk crate propped against a wall on some beach-front street. Knowing Hawkins' background sometimes makes listening to his music a painful, or at least difficult, experience: though he consistently denied the charge, he served a final term at the California Medical Facility for allegedly molesting a 13-year-old girl. His long-deserved break came in 1994, when he signed to Geffen and started to play for ticket-buying audiences at clubs around the country before his untimely death.

what to buy: It's chilling to hear Hawkins sing the sad part in "I Got What I Wanted," from *Songs from Venice Beach* 🎜🎜🎜🎜 (Evi-

dence, 1995, prod. H. Thorp Minister III), about walking on the beach alone, knowing everybody's used to seeing him with his woman. On this reissued album, culled from the hard-to-find *On the Boardwalk: The Venice Beach Tapes*, Hawkins can express loneliness as well as Roy Orbison and can even hit the same high (and low) notes.

what to buy next: Though the writing isn't as strong as his best material, Hawkins' first official recordings—*Watch Your Step* 🎜🎜🎜 (Rounder, 1982/1993, prod. Bruce Bromberg, Dennis Walker) and *Happy Hour* 🎜🎜🎜 (Rounder, 1986/1993, prod. Bruce Bromberg, Dennis Walker, Dale Wilson) share an amazing street-bred talent with the rest of the world. Parts of *The Next Hundred Years* 🎜🎜🎜 (Geffen, 1994, prod. Tony Berg), such as the heartbreaking "The Good and the Bad" and the high notes in the soul-pop classic "There Stands the Glass," will make your hair stand up and bring tears involuntarily to your eyes, but some of the production drowns the voice.

worth searching for: *On the Boardwalk: The Venice Beach Tapes* 🎜🎜🎜🎜 (1986, prod. H. Thorp Minister III) and *Dock of the Bay: The Venice Beach Tapes* 🎜🎜🎜🎜 (1987, prod. H. Thorp Minister III) were recorded by a young fan in Nashville and made their way to Europe without a label, helping boost Hawkins' huge following abroad. If they're virtually impossible to find, try digging up his first single, "Baby"/"Whole Lotta Women," recorded for Money Records in 1966.

influences:

⏮ Sam Cooke, Otis Redding, Robert Johnson, Wilson Pickett, Blind Lemon Jefferson, Curtis Mayfield, Roy Orbison

⏭ Chris Isaak, Satan & Adam, Robert Cray

Steve Knopper

Johnny Heartsman

Born February 9, 1937, in San Fernando, CA. Died December 27, 1996, in Sacramento, CA.

The closest this singer-keyboardist-pianist-flutist-you-name-it-ist ever got to being a star was his 1957 R&B hit instrumental "Johnny's House Party." Yet his influence has touched a wide range of talented musicians—his "hammer on" technique, which involved bending the guitar strings with the left hand while plucking *and* twiddling the volume knob with his right

Ted Hawkins (© Jack Vartoogian)

hand, has been adopted by many guitarists, from Jimi Hendrix (on "Red House") to Ronnie Earl. Beyond that production trick, Heartsman was responsible for the original guitar licks in Tiny Powell's "My Time after Awhile," which Buddy Guy copied in his own trademark version. He had serious studio work in the 1960s, as Lou Rawls and LaVern Baker dropped in to work with him, but disco's popularity quickly dated his jazz-and-blues style. For years, in Sacramento, he worked as a cocktail pianist, but he returned to the blues, playing festivals throughout the U.S. and Europe. It took him 30 years to venture out as a solo recording artist, but his diverse, upbeat debut was worth the wait.

what to buy: *The Touch* ♫♫♫ (Alligator, 1991, prod. Dick Shurman) lurches from pure blues ("Paint My Mailbox Blue") to staccato, bouncy funk-jazz ("You're So Fine"). The textures keep listeners on their toes, especially when Heartsman unleashes the flute on "Tongue."

what to buy next: Heartsman's first two albums similarly mix blues, R&B, jazz and funk, and he plays all kinds of instruments—*Sacramento* ♫♫♫ (Crosscut, 1987) and the live-from-Germany *Still Shinin'* ♫♫♫ (Have Mercy, 1994, prod. Big Mike Balma) have more energy than *Music of My Heart* ♫♫♫ (Cat 'n' Hat, 1989).

influences:

◄◄ Lafayette "Thing" Thomas, Lowell Fulson, Jimmy McCracklin, T-Bone Walker, Charlie Christian

►► Jimi Hendrix, Jethro Tull, Ronnie Earl, Buddy Guy, Dire Straits

Steve Knopper

Jessie Mae Hemphill

Born 1940, near Como, MS.

Jessie Mae Hemphill is among the few women blues singers playing her own guitar and singing mostly her own compositions. Unlike many contemporary singers, she doesn't shout the blues; her mellow voice has a melismatic quality that reinforces the hypnotic guitar runs and chords in the open tunings she favors, with repetitive riffs. Raised in a musical family, she started the guitar at age eight and played bass and snare drum in fife and drum bands in the Como/Senatobia area. She played and sang for her family and friends before 1979, then began an international career that led her in the largest festivals all over the world, earning Handy awards in 1987 and 1988 as Best Traditional Female Blues Artist. She is deeply rooted in the Mississippi traditions but chose to play an electric guitar, keeping the fife and drum band sound (with leg

bells and tambourine attached to one foot) and snare drum overdubbed on some records. Her signature songs include "Feeling Good," "Streamline Train," "Go Back to Your Used to Be," "She-Wolf," "Black Cat Bone" and "Jessie's Boogie," and she presents one of the most unusual and original sounds in the blues world today: the traditional Mississippi blues brought up to date.

what to buy: *Feelin' Good* ♫♫♫♫ (High Water, 1990, prod. David Evans) is the definitive collection, 12 tracks recorded in 1984 and 1988 with Evans on second guitar and R.L. Boyce on drums on six tracks. The tracks for *She-Wolf* ♫♫♫♫ (Vogue, 1981, prod. David Evans) were done in 1979 and 1980.

influences:

◄◄ Sid Hemphill, Rosa Lee Hill, Fred McDowell

Robert Sacré

John William Henderson

See: Homesick James

Mike Henderson

Born July 7, 1951, in Yazoo City, MS.

Mississippi-born, Missouri-raised, Mike Henderson's music is a high-octane mix of country, blues and rock 'n' roll. A former member of the Missouri blues-rock outfit the Bel-Airs, Henderson kicked around Nashville doing session work for Kevin Welch and Tracy Nelson and writing songs (including the Fabulous Thunderbirds' "Powerful Stuff"). After an abortive run with RCA's Nashville branch, Henderson signed with Dead Reckoning, an artist-run label where he's clearly more at home.

what to buy: The bluesiest of Henderson's albums, *First Blood* ♫♫♫♫ (Dead Reckoning, 1996, prod. Peter Coleman), recorded with the Bluebloods, is a scorcher, but it shares a roadhouse mentality with the best honky-tonk country music. And besides, a song titled "When I Get Drunk" can surely fit in either genre.

the rest:

Edge of Night ♫♫♫ (Dead Reckoning, 1996)

worth searching for: The unjustifiably deleted *Country Music Made Me Do It* ♫♫♫ (RCA, 1994) confounded Henderson's label, which didn't know how to market his renegade sound.

Jessie Mae Hemphill (© Jack Vartoogian)

influences:

◄◄ Jerry Lee Lewis, Merle Haggard, Dave Alvin

Daniel Durchholz

Jimi Hendrix

Born November 27, 1942, in Seattle, WA. Died September 18, 1970, in London, England.

It's amazing to look back and list all the things Hendrix did in his short life: he was arguably rock 'n' roll's greatest guitarist and one of the most enduring icons of the 1960s, and he released a string of singles and three albums with the Experience that changed pop music almost as much as Bob Dylan and the Beatles before him. But before doing all of this, he mastered the blues. He's best known, still, for "Purple Haze" and "Foxy Lady," but blues guitarists continue to pay close attention to Hendrix's takes on "Red House," "Catfish Blues" and "Hey Joe."

Like his British peers Keith Richards, Eric Clapton and Jimmy Page, Hendrix learned the guitar from old Muddy Waters and B.B. King records. As Jimmy James, he moved to New York City and paid his dues as a backup guitarist for many rock 'n' roll and R&B luminaries, from Little Richard to Sam Cooke. After a brief stint in his own band, Jimmy James and the Blue Flames, he hooked up with the Animals' Chas Chandler—who later became Hendrix's manager and Svengali figure—and formed the Jimi Hendrix Experience. That's when the fun started. The band's first single, "Hey Joe," a cover of an old wife-beating folk song, might be a classic-rock song today, but it sounded like blues in the mid-1960s.

As Hendrix's talent quickly grew, he started doing things to rock and blues songs (not to mention "The Star-Spangled Banner" at Woodstock) that nobody had ever done before. He strained every note with feedback, simulated skyscraper-sized bonfires, produced every single the way he heard it in his head and stole the show by burning his guitar at the Monterey Pop Festival. Though his tales of backstage excess became legendary, he came to symbolize freedom from conventions, politics and sexual constraints and earned a huge following. But for all the histrionics, innovative guitar-playing and iconoclasm, one of Hendrix's central legacies was his advancement of the blues. Nobody played them quite the same after him. Hendrix's death in 1970, coming around the same time as the deaths of Janis Joplin and the Doors' Jim Morrison, dealt a blow to the free-love generation. Oddly (and cynically) enough, many, many more Hendrix albums have been released after his death than during his life.

what to buy: The first shot, *Are You Experienced?* 𝄢𝄢𝄢𝄢 (MCA, 1967/1993, prod. Chas Chandler), is a collection of exploding, guitar-driven pop songs, including "Hey Joe," "Purple Haze," the under appreciated "The Wind Cries Mary," "Manic Depression" and on the CD reissue, "Red House." *Axis: Bold As Love* 𝄢𝄢𝄢𝄢 (MCA, 1967/1993, prod. Chas Chandler) contains some of Hendrix's most heartwarming songwriting, from the freak-flag-flying "If 6 Was 9" to the beautiful "Little Wing" and moving story/song "Castles Made of Sand." *Electric Ladyland* 𝄢𝄢𝄢𝄢 (MCA, 1968/1993, prod. Jimi Hendrix) is a concept album with a few tremendous songs—"Burning of the Midnight Lamp," "Crosstown Traffic" and the enduring riffs in "Voodoo Child (Slight Return)"—but is most notable for its overall sound, which Hendrix heard in his head as "blue water."

what to buy next: Beware: It's hard to figure out which post-Hendrix collections are dogs and which contain manna from heaven. Start with the rarities collection *Radio One* 𝄢𝄢𝄢 (Rykodisc, 1988) and the incendiary *Live at Winterland* 𝄢𝄢𝄢 (Rykodisc, 1987). A collection, *Blues* 𝄢𝄢𝄢 (MCA, 1994), has a repetitive, almost droning quality, but it directly shows the extent to which Hendrix influenced Vaughan and almost every younger-than-Jimi blues guitarist performing today. *Band of Gypsys* 𝄢𝄢𝄢𝄢 (Capitol, 1970, prod. Heaven Research) is less focused, more like a live concert, but it's a stellar document of Hendrix's nearing-end-of-life direction, with bassist Billy Cox and drummer Buddy Miles.

what to avoid: Unless you're a personal family friend who wants to see Hendrix's father, Al, make money off his son's estate, the Experience Hendrix reissue packages of *Are You Experienced?* 𝄢𝄢𝄢 (Experience Hendrix/MCA, 1997), *Electric Ladyland* 𝄢𝄢𝄢 (Experience Hendrix/MCA, 1997) and *Axis: Bold As Love* 𝄢𝄢𝄢 (Experience Hendrix/MCA, 1997) are totally redundant versions of the previous MCA packages—without the extra tracks. Hendrix's catalog resembles many jazz artists' cumbersome chronologies; it's tough to find the diamonds in the coal. In particular, stay away from *Voodoo Soup* 𝄢 (MCA, 1994, prod. Alan Douglas) and *Isle of Wight* 𝄢𝄢 (Polydor, 1971, prod. Michael Jeffery).

the rest:

Otis Redding/Jimi Hendrix Experience: Historic Performances Recorded at the Monterey International Pop Festival 𝄢𝄢𝄢 (Reprise, 1970)
The Cry of Love 𝄢𝄢 (Reprise, 1971)
Rainbow Bridge 𝄢𝄢 (Reprise, 1971)
Hendrix in the West 𝄢𝄢𝄢 (Reprise, 1972)
War Heroes 𝄢𝄢𝄢 (Reprise, 1972)
Soundtrack from the film "Jimi Hendrix" 𝄢𝄢𝄢 (Reprise, 1973)
Crash Landing 𝄢𝄢𝄢 (Reprise, 1975)

Midnight Lightnin' 🐊🐊 (Reprise, 1976)

The Essential Jimi Hendrix, Vols. 1 and 2 🐊🐊🐊 (Reprise/Warner Bros., 1979)

Nine to the Universe 🐊🐊🐊 (Reprise, 1980)

The Jimi Hendrix Concerts 🐊🐊🐊 (Warner Bros., 1982)

Band of Gypsys 2 🐊🐊 (Capitol, 1986)

Jimi Plays Monterey 🐊🐊🐊 (Reprise, 1986)

Johnny B. Goode: Original Video Soundtrack 🐊🐊🐊 (Capitol, 1986)

Lifelines (The Jimi Hendrix Story) 🐊🐊 (Reprise, 1990)

Stages 1967–70 🐊🐊🐊🐊 (Reprise, 1991)

Woodstock 🐊🐊🐊 (MCA, 1994)

First Rays of the New Rising Sun 🐊🐊🐊 (Experience Hendrix/MCA, 1997)

worth searching for: *Stone Free: A Tribute to Jimi Hendrix* 🐊🐊 (Reprise/Warner Bros., 1993, prod. Jeff Gold, Eddie Kramer, John McDermott, Michael Ostin) is uneven—program the player to skip the Spin Doctors' forgettable version of "Spanish Castle Magic"—but P.M. Dawn's fiddly take on "You Got Me Floatin'" and Buddy Guy's made-for-himself "Red House" do Hendrix's ghost justice.

influences:

◀◀ Little Richard, Buddy Guy, Muddy Waters, T-Bone Walker, Charlie Christian, Albert King, B.B. King, Eric Clapton, Beatles, Bob Dylan, Rolling Stones, Steve Cropper

▶▶ Stevie Ray Vaughan, Led Zeppelin, Luther Allison, Son Seals, Neil Young, Van Halen, Prince, George Clinton, Frank Zappa, Kenny Wayne Shepherd

Steve Knopper

Jimi Hendrix
song
Red House
album
Are You Experienced? (MCA)
instrument
Guitar

monster solo

Clarence "Frogman" Henry

Born March 19, 1937, in Algiers, LA.

Clarence "Frogman" Henry was hired by Leonard and Phil Chess as a way to cash in on the profitable New Orleans sound of the 1950s. They got an entertaining character and surprisingly effective interpreter of standards in the bargain. Proficient on both the trombone and piano, Henry worked the early 1950s with Bobby Mitchell's and later, Eddie Smith's popular bands. In 1956 he signed with Argo (a Chess subsidiary) and recorded "Ain't Got No Home," a wonderfully weird novelty with Henry singing in a shrill girl voice, a croaking frog voice (hence the nickname "Frogman"), and the intense, nonsensical hook: "Ooh ooh, ooh ooh, ooh ooh, ooh ooh ooh." It was a solid hit on the R&B and pop charts. Subsequent records ("It Won't Be Long" and "I'm in Love") made much less impact, and "I Found a Home" (a belated follow-up to "Ain't Got No Home") proved that the multi-voice gimmick had already grown stale. Henry's most successful year was 1961, when he recorded Bobby Charles' "I Don't Know Why, but I Do" and up-

dated the old Mills Brothers hit, "You Always Hurt the One You Love." Sung in a playful, Fats-Domino style, complete with stride piano and punchy New Orleans brass, these singles were huge hits, appealing to teenagers and adults alike. Henry hit the charts a few more times with a neat cover of "Lonely Street," as well as "On Bended Knee" and "A Little Too Much," but by 1962, his days as a hitmaker were over. The oldies craze of the late 1960s brought Henry back temporarily with plentiful tour work and an LP on Roulette that says it all even now: *Alive and Well and Living in New Orleans.*

what to buy: All of Henry's Argo hits are included on the 18-track compilation *Ain't Got No Home: The Best of Clarence "Frogman" Henry* 🐊🐊🐊🐊 (MCA, 1992, prod. Paul Gayten), capable of inciting a full scale Mardi Gras in your home.

worth searching for: If you're digging through the import bins, *But I Do* 🐊🐊🐊 (Charly, 1994, prod. Paul Gayten) features essentially the same tunes as the compilation, but with two extra tracks.

influences:

◀◀ Fats Domino, Professor Longhair, Huey "Piano" Smith

▶▶ Jimmy Jones, Dr. John

Ken Burke

Otis Hicks

See: Lightnin' Slim

Robert Hicks

See: Barbecue Bob

King Solomon Hill

Born Joe Holmes, 1897, in Sibley, LA. Died 1949, in Sibley, LA.

Hill recorded four strange, dramatic blues recitations at Paramount's Grafton, Wisconsin, studio in January 1932. Alternating between an otherworldly falsetto and an apocalyptic tenor, Hill reportedly strung out his guitar notes with a cow bone. The title of his "Gone Dead Train," a creepy narrative about a tramp's life, was later resurrected by rock producer Jack Nietzsche in romping versions by Randy Newman and Neil Young's backup band, Crazy Horse. Hill roamed with fellow bluesmen Sam Collins and Oscar "Lone Wolf" Woods through the Delta, Arkansas, Texas and Louisiana. Said to drink heavily, he died of a hemorrhage at the age of 52.

what to buy: All six known Hill cuts, including two alternate versions of "Whoopee Blues" and "Down on Bended Knee," are on *Backwoods Blues 1926–35* 𝄞𝄞𝄞𝄞 (Document, 1991, prod. Johnny Parth), which also features work by obscure Mississippi Delta talent Lane Hardin and southern neighbors Bo Weavil Jackson and Bobby Grant.

what to buy next: Hill's "Gone Dead Train" and "Whoopee Blues," accompanied by William Harris, Otto Virgial and Joe Callicott, can be found on *Mississippi Masters* 𝄞𝄞𝄞𝄞 (Yazoo, 1994).

influences:

◀◀ Rambling Thomas, Lone Wolf Woods, Sam Collins

▶▶ Jack Nietzsche, Crazy Horse

Steve Braun

Lester (or Leslie) Hill

See: Joe Hill Louis

Michael Hill

Born in New York, NY.

In some ways, this young singer-guitarist is doing for blues what Living Colour's Vernon Reid did for hard rock. He keeps enough traditional elements to make the music fit blues conventions, but he twists it around, adding elements of reggae, country-style storytelling and, most notably, an eloquent, up-to-date social conscience. Hill has a terrific voice and a clear Robert Cray enunciation, and he isn't afraid to go off on a long guitar-solo tangent. But his songwriting sets him apart from his contemporaries: the Blues Mob's update of "Stagolee" isn't quite up there with the Geto Boys' hip-hop street drama "Mind Playin' Tricks on Me," but it's the same idea. Hill also salutes Africa and women, and tells Curtis Mayfield-like stories about poverty, drugs and the streets.

what to buy: Hill's band, the Blues Mob, hasn't yet mixed all its elements—jazz, reggae, stories and blues guitar solos—seamlessly into one album, but *Have Mercy!* 𝄞𝄞𝄞 (Alligator, 1996, prod. Michael Hill, Bruce Iglauer, Brian Young, Kevin Hill) comes the closest. Standout songs are the soft, jazzy "Bluestime in America," the "Stagolee" update, the R&B tribute "Women Make the World Go 'Round" (which quotes Sonny Boy Williamson) and the story-songs "Grandmother's Blues" and "Backyard in Brooklyn."

what to buy next: *Bloodlines* 𝄞𝄞 (Alligator, 1993) is more notable in theory than in practice—it's a long walk from the typical Alligator guitarslingers and traditionalists, and Hill sings in a refreshingly crisp pop voice.

influences:

◀◀ Living Colour, Robert Cray, Buddy Guy, Luther Allison, Bob Marley, Stevie Wonder, Sonny Boy Williamson II

Steve Knopper

Z.Z. Hill

Born Arzell Hill, September 29, 1936, in Naples, TX. Died April 27, 1984, in Dallas, TX.

Z.Z. Hill is credited with helping repopularize the blues in black America in the early 1980s. His 1981 *Down Home Blues* spent over 100 weeks on the charts and is one of the top-selling blues albums of all time. Hill started singing blues and soul in Dallas clubs in the early 1960s. In 1964, he moved to the West Coast

Clarence "Frogman" Henry (© Jack Vartoogian)

and had a minor hit with his first single, "You Were Wrong." Hill spent nearly two decades bouncing from label to label, occasionally reaching the lower depths of the R&B charts. He had some fine blues releases—"Don't Make Me Pay for His Mistakes" and "It Ain't No Use" stand out—but his soul and disco efforts were forgettable. In 1980, he found a home at the Jackson, Mississippi-based Malaco label. Hill's second Malaco album, *Down Home*, contained "Down Home Blues," a natural hit if there ever was one. The LP spent nearly one year in the R&B Top 10 and helped persuade radio programmers to add more blues to the mix. Hill followed with several successful singles and albums; he died when his career was at its apex.

what to buy: *In Memorium* 𝅘𝅥𝅮𝅘𝅥𝅮𝅘𝅥𝅮𝅘𝅥𝅮 (Malaco, 1986, prod. Tommy Couch, Wolf Stephenson) chronicles Hill's success on Malaco. Besides "Down Home Blues," classics like "Cheatin' in the Next Room" and "Shade Tree Mechanic" are included. Malaco productions can be rigid and technical, but they certainly have a pulse on their followers. Take *Down Home Blues* 𝅘𝅥𝅮𝅘𝅥𝅮𝅘𝅥𝅮𝅘𝅥𝅮 (Malaco, 1982, prod. Tommy Couch, Wolf Stephenson), a classic by anyone's standards. An inventive reissue, *The Brand New Z.Z. Hill* 𝅘𝅥𝅮𝅘𝅥𝅮𝅘𝅥𝅮𝅘𝅥𝅮 (Aim, 1996, prod. Jerry Williams) is a good blend of soul and blues. The double-disc *The Complete Hill/United Artist Record Collection* 𝅘𝅥𝅮𝅘𝅥𝅮𝅘𝅥𝅮𝅘𝅥𝅮 (EMI, 1996) includes a little bit of pop and disco fodder, but lots of great Hill blues material.

what to buy next: *Turn Back the Hands of Time* 𝅘𝅥𝅮𝅘𝅥𝅮𝅘𝅥𝅮 (Night Train, 1994) offers more soul than blues. *Blues Master* 𝅘𝅥𝅮𝅘𝅥𝅮𝅘𝅥𝅮𝅘𝅥𝅮 (Malaco, 1983, prod. Wolf Stephenson, Tommy Couch) is worthwhile but unnecessary if you've already got *In Memorium*.

what to avoid: Outside of the title track, *Love Is So Good When You're Stealin' It* **woof!** (Ichiban, 1994) is comprised of bad pop and disco.

worth searching for: Hill cut so many 45s and LPs that sooner or later you'll turn one or more up in a thrift store. Look for the ones on the independent labels. All of the Malaco LPs are also available on cassette.

influences:

◀◀ Bobby "Blue" Bland, Roscoe Gordon, B.B. King, Little Richard, Otis Redding, James Davis, Little Johnny Taylor, Sam Cooke

Jeff Hannusch

Silas Hogan

Born September 15, 1911, in Westover, LA. Died February 1994, near Baton Rouge, LA.

Silas Hogan was one of the second-tier group of bayou bluesmen who recorded for producer Jay Miller throughout the 1950s and 1960s. Not as commercially bent as Slim Harpo or Lazy Lester or as drenched in the deep blues as Lightnin' Slim or Lonesome Sundown, Hogan was still able to deliver powerful vocal performances on demand. Taught by two uncles who later played a role in the career of prison bluesman Robert Pete Williams, Hogan was a journeyman who spent the 1950s in anonymity, toiling in Baton Rouge's insular blues scene. After cutting one unsuccessful single, he began recording at the age of 52 on Harpo's recommendation. Some of his tracks aped Lightnin' Slim's slow-motion voodoo boasts, but Hogan found his own voice on brooding lopes like "Dark Clouds Rollin'" and "Early One Morning." Dropped by the label in the late 1960s, Hogan worked at a gas refinery and stuck to the bayous, venturing out of Baton Rouge only for occasional appearances at the New Orleans Jazz and Heritage Festival. Brief stints with the Arhoolie and Blue Horizon labels did little to raise his profile before his death at age 82.

what to buy: Every master and alternate take known—26 cuts worth—of Hogan's swamp boogie offerings are included on *Trouble: The Best of the Excello Masters* 𝅘𝅥𝅮𝅘𝅥𝅮𝅘𝅥𝅮𝅘𝅥𝅮 (AVI-Excello, 1995, prod. J.D. Miller). He is best when he keeps it simple, wallowing in the deep blues like a pig in slop. His organ-flecked soul attempts are throwaways at best. AVI's sound runs rings around earlier, out-of-print collections.

influences:

◀◀ Robert Murphy, Frank Murphy, Lightnin' Slim

Steve Braun

Dave Hole

Born March 30, 1948, in Heswall, Cheshire, England.

Dave Hole, who has called Australia home since he was four, is one of the contemporary masters of blues slide guitar. An adequate singer and good songwriter, Hole's albums with his small, tight, homegrown quartet are must haves for slide aficionados.

what to buy: Hole's third album, *Steel on Steel* 𝅘𝅥𝅮𝅘𝅥𝅮𝅘𝅥𝅮𝅘𝅥𝅮 (Alligator, 1995, prod. Jim Gaines), benefits greatly from the clearer sound and better mixing not present on his earlier offerings.

the rest:

Short Fuse Blues 𝅘𝅥𝅮𝅘𝅥𝅮𝅘𝅥𝅮𝅘𝅥𝅮 (Alligator, 1992)
Working Overtime 𝅘𝅥𝅮𝅘𝅥𝅮𝅘𝅥𝅮𝅘𝅥𝅮 (Alligator, 1993)

influences:

◀◀ Blind Lemon Jefferson, Muddy Waters, Elmore James, Mississippi Fred McDowell, Robert Johnson

Jennifer Zogott

Billie Holiday

Born Eleanora Harris, April 7, 1915, in Baltimore, MD. Died July 17, 1959, in New York, NY.

Billie Holiday's voice—sweet, sexy and pulsing with blues feeling—could chill a soul or warm it like a fireplace of emotion. Born to teenage parents Sadie Harris and Clarence Holiday, the singer was raped at the age of 10 and, thanks to the sexual double standard of the day, was sent to a home for wayward girls as a result. Her father, a jazz guitarist with Fletcher Henderson, abandoned her. Today, mental-health professionals believe such abuse will shape and shadow the rest of a victim's life, and Holiday's life did seem to play out with the predestination of a Greek tragedy.

Music was Holiday's rescue from early careers as a house servant and hooker, but it did not stop her from ravaging herself with drugs, which in her final years took away all but a remnant of her voice. Known affectionately as "Lady Day," a name she was given by Lester Young, she brought the breadth of her worldly experience to the stage and recording studio with a vulnerability that—like all the best blues—didn't just speak of being a victim but of self-worth betrayed—by the world, a lover or the singer herself. That's not to say that all her songs were sad, but that even her happy tunes had an edge. She seemed in those happier songs to want to overindulge in every appetite to gird herself for the hard times. Offstage, she was dependent on a succession of not-quite-Svengalis who acted as lovers and father figures. In "God Bless the Child," she sings what one reviewer called a whiny lyric (her own) about how people court a person who's successful but ignore the same person when "money's gone." Yet she doesn't sound whiny at all; she's having a gentle laugh at the weakness of human nature.

Talent scout John Hammond found Holiday all but irresistible in live performance, so he brought her to the top people in jazz. Benny Goodman led her first session in 1933. Teddy Wilson followed. When she hit the peak of her form in the late 1930s, the presence of and her interplay with Buck Clayton and Lester Young underscored just how much her singing resembled the playing of an instrument. She sang slowly and "behind the beat" and trailed off her voice for emotional punctuation. (Her influence shows up in the work of many singers who followed, possibly most notably in Frank Sinatra.) The fluid phrasing and the rasp in her voice were reminiscent of Louis Armstrong. Although she sang very few actual blues tunes, the blue feeling in her voice descended directly from Bessie Smith. Holiday melded these influences into a completely distinctive sound.

Despite her submissiveness to her lovers, Holiday was strong-willed and moody, which often hindered her career. Yet her landmark 1939 recording, "Strange Fruit," a disturbing protest against lynchings, was a triumph of determination. Columbia, to which she was signed for the bulk of the 1930s, would not record the tune, so she secured a contract that put her on loan to Milt Gabler's Commodore for a single session. Gabler later signed her to Decca. In this period of the late 1930s and early 1940s, she gradually abandoned the jazz settings of her earlier recordings for grander, pop orchestrations. The voice at its peak, her version of "Lover Man" defines her style. By the 1950s, when she signed up with Norman Granz after serving a prison term for heroin possession, she was on a downward spiral. Although her voice faded in the late stages of her life, she retained her expressive capabilities, so nearly all of her recordings are of interest.

what to buy: Holiday's work is documented on more than 80 discs and collections, but thanks to the archival genius of the digital age, it's very easy to reduce that number to a core, must-have collection. First of all, the title of Columbia's nine-volume retrospective series, *The Quintessential Billie Holiday* 𝄞𝄞𝄞𝄞𝄞 (Columbia, 1987–91, prod. John Hammond, Bernie Hanighen), is not far off the mark. A chronological series of her work for Columbia, Brunswick and Vocalion, even the most dispensable disc, *Volume 1, 1933–35* , contains great performances—"Miss Brown to You," "If You Were Mine"—as the new recording artist finds her sea legs. By *Volume 9, 1940–42* , Holiday's character and style are completely formed, and she sings with absolute certainty on such definitive numbers as "God Bless the Child," "Solitude" and "Gloomy Sunday." For listeners who want to delve deeply into her creative process in the studio, *The Complete Commodore Recordings* 𝄞𝄞𝄞𝄞𝄞 (GRP, 1997, prod. Orrin Keepnews, Joel Dorn) is a two-disc set full of alternate takes (including a second one of "Strange Fruit") that gives insight into her evolution from the jazz-band-oriented style to full-blown pop. *The Complete Decca Recordings* 𝄞𝄞𝄞𝄞𝄞 (GRP, 1991, prod. Milt Gabler) covers Holiday's best performing period in only two CDs. She recorded only 36 sides for the label, and the definitive "Lover Man" sets the collection's tone, which includes a number of alternate takes but isn't as heavy with them as the Commodore collection. This is the most satisfying and consistent listening experience in Holiday's catalog. After her vacation in the reformatory, Norman Granz returned her to jazz-oriented sessions. Her voice was raspier, and sometimes you can hear her struggle for the breath to finish a phrase, but there's a soulfulness that the ravages of abuse bring out in her voice that makes her stint with Granz nearly as memorable as her Decca years. Hence, the 10-CD *The Complete Billie Holiday on Verve 1945–49* ♫♫♫♫ (Verve, 1995, prod. Norman Granz) is an indispensable collection of the work she did as she collapsed upon herself, including "Lady Sings the Blues," the tune written to capitalize on the title of her autobiography.

what to buy next: *Lady in Satin* ♫♫♫ (Columbia, 1986, prod. Ray Ellis) is based on the template of the original 1958 album that paired Holiday, at her request, with the easy-listening orchestral sounds of Ray Ellis. Technical wizardry creates a stereo take of "The End of a Love Affair," which previously existed only in a mono master. The juxtaposition of her soulful but nearly shot voice and Ellis' extremely sweet strings gives the project a character it couldn't have had when she was younger. *Billie's Blues* ♫♫♫ (Blue Note, 1988) features Holiday's top concert recording, from a 1954 date in Europe.

what to avoid: *Last Recordings* ♫ (Verve, 1988, prod. Ray Ellis), recorded early in 1959, is another date with Ellis, absent the triumph of *Lady in Satin*. Besides, you have the complete Verve set already, don't you?

best of the rest:

Live and Private Recordings in Chronological Order ♫♫♫ (New Sound Planet Jazz Up)
Solitude ♫♫♫ (Verve, 1952)
All or Nothing at All ♫♫♫ (Verve, 1955)
The Essential Billie Holiday: Carnegie Hall Concert ♫♫♫ (Verve, 1956)
Lady Sings the Blues ♫♫♫ (Verve, 1956)
Songs for Distinguished Lovers ♫♫♫ (Verve, 1957)
Masters of Jazz, Vol. 3 ♫♫♫ (Storyville, 1987)
At Storyville ♫♫♫ (Black Lion, 1988)
Fine and Mellow ♫♫♫ (Collectables, 1990)
Lady in Autumn: The Best of the Verve Years ♫♫♫ (Verve, 1991)

worth searching for: The good stuff that's left is concert recordings: *At Storyville* ♫♫♫ (Black Lion, 1988) and *Fine and Mellow* ♫♫♫ (Collectables).

influences:
◀◀ Bessie Smith, Louis Armstrong
▶▶ Frank Sinatra, Betty Carter

Salvatore Caputo

Clarence Hollimon

See: Carol Fran & Clarence Hollimon

Tony Hollins

Born c. 1900, in Clarksdale, MS. Died 1959, in Chicago, IL.

With his easy, liquid voice and his lightly-propulsive guitar,

Tony Hollins might not seem like an obvious influence on the tortured blues of John Lee Hooker. But the Hook has cited Hollins as a musical ancestor and appropriated Hollins' "Crawlin' King Snake"—recorded around the same time by Big Joe Williams—for his own. Hollins often sounded like Delta master Robert Petway and such lazy-voiced disciples as Jimmy Rogers and Eddie Taylor. Hollins also refined Tommy McClennan's "Crosscut Saw," and his "Traveling Man Blues" was transformed by Hooker into "When My First Wife Quit Me." After sessions in 1941 and 1951, Hollins kept his day gig as a barber and was last heard of in the late 1950s.

what to buy: Hollins' 11 Chicago recordings for OKeh and Decca are supplemented by workmanlike sessions by Alfred Fields and essential 1950s-vintage efforts for Columbia and Chess by Robert Johnson's running partner, Johnny Shines, on *Chicago Blues 1939–51* ♫♫♫ (Document, 1994, prod. Johnny Parth). The Hollins cuts are as pristine as 1940 technology could deliver.

influences:
◀◀ Robert Petway, Tommy McClennan
▶▶ John Lee Hooker, Jimmy Rogers

Steve Braun

Joe Holmes

See: King Solomon Hill

The Holmes Brothers

Formed 1980, in New York, NY.

Sherman Holmes, bass; Wendell Holmes, guitar; Popsy Dixon, drums.

Soul, R&B, blues, gospel, country, funk—no one mixes it up and delivers it quite like the Holmes Brothers. Brothers Sherman and Wendell Holmes and drummer Popsy Dixon, all originally from Virginia, blend their rough and sweet voices into harmonies that could wring tears from a stone. Dixon has one of the best falsettos in the business, and their live act is something not to be missed.

what to buy: *Promised Land* ♫♫♫♫ (Rounder, 1997, prod. Scott Billington, Andy Breslau) presents the most adventurous mix of music the band has recorded so far, including Dixon's wonderful reads of Tom Waits' "Train Song" and the Beatles' "And I Love Her," a couple of beautiful spirituals penned by Sherman Holmes and the tight and funky "Got Myself Together," long a staple of their live performances.

The Holmes Brothers (from left): Popsy Dixon, Wendell Holmes and Sherman Holmes (© Jack Vartoogian)

what to buy next: Their debut, *In the Spirit* ♫♫♫ (Rounder, 1989, prod. Scott Billington, Andy Breslau) boasts a super selection of characteristic Holmes material, including Wendell's rocking composition, "Squeal Like an Eel" and the band's show-stopping version of "When Something Is Wrong with My Baby."

the rest:

Where It's At ♫♫♫ (Rounder, 1991)
Jubilation ♫♫♫ (Real World, 1992)
Soul Street ♫♫♫ (Rounder, 1993)

worth searching for: *Lotto Land* ♫♫♫ (Stony Plain, 1995, prod. Andy Breslau) is the soundtrack for the indie film in which Wendell acted and the full band performed. The film's writer-director John Rubino wrote most of the lyrics, which makes it a kind of Holmes Brothers Lite, but well worth having for fans.

influences:

◄◄ Muddy Waters, Robert Johnson, Hank Williams, Charley

Pride, Jimmy Jones, Shep & the Limelighters, John Lee Hooker, Jerry Butler, Impressions, Inez & Charlie Foxx

Jennifer Zogott

Morris Holt

See: Magic Slim

Homesick James

Born John William Henderson, April 30, 1910, in Somerville, TN.

Homesick James is the last of the uncompromised blues itinerants, most associated with Chicago but apt to turn up in this town or that just like the folk troubadours of old. He played Tennessee with Yank Rachell and John Estes during the Depression and was in Chicago by the mid-1930s, updating his sound with an electric Gibson guitar. By the early 1950s he was making records; in 1951 he cut his trademark "Homesick" (with its landmark slide playing) for Chance. He gigged and recorded extensively with Elmore James. Fast forward to the 1970s, when he had an apartment on the North Side and was playing weekly at Elsewhere on Lincoln Street in Chicago. He looked amazingly young, could out-party Hunter Thompson on a good night, and had a lot of good nights. The city's blues intelligentsia regarded him as an outlaw, too crazed and set in his ways to record or book into mainstream clubs. Not that Homesick gave a damn. He stayed busy, cutting LPs and doing European dates with Snooky Pryor. To his naysayers Homesick can extend his middle digit, as he's still active and productive, cutting good music and enjoying his life and debauchery.

what to buy: *Blues on the South Side* 𝄞𝄞𝄞𝄞 (Original Blues Classics, 1990, prod. Sam Charters) is the quintessential Homesick band album, his biting slide guitar and moanin' vocals supported by Clifton James on drums and Lafayette Leake on piano. (Liner credits say Eddie Taylor played bass, but it was really Lee Jackson.) Every cut is great but prime is "Goin' Down Swingin'," because if Homesick ever does go down, that's just the way it'll be.

what to buy next: *Words of Wisdom* 𝄞𝄞𝄞𝄞 (Icehouse, 1997, prod. Fred James) has the energetic octogenarian in a more countrified vein, with old-time selections on an acoustic guitar (though the lengthy "Pock Me Baby" is thoroughly electrified). Homesick's in fine fettle but really steps into "12 Year Old Boy," a tale of the aging process he so joyously defies. Sound quality's A-plus, and his backup musicians support him ably.

the rest:
Goin' Sack in the Times 𝄞𝄞𝄞 (Earwig, 1994)
Got to Move 𝄞𝄞𝄞𝄞 (Trix, 1995)
Sweet Home Tennessee 𝄞𝄞𝄞 (Appaloosa, 1995)
Juanita 𝄞𝄞𝄞 (Appaloosa, 1997)

influences:
◀◀ Blind Boy Fuller
▶▶ Johnny Long

Tim Schuller

Earl Hooker

Born January 15, 1930, in Clarksdale, MS. Died April 21, 1970, in Chicago, IL.

John Lee's cousin, Earl Hooker is a true unsung genius of the blues, beloved and revered by countless peers but still largely unknown to most listeners. A groundbreaking slide player, Hooker was also a wide-ranging guitarist who dabbled in jazz, country and rock, working primarily as a sideman for the likes of Junior Wells, Muddy Waters, Ike Turner, Jimmy Witherspoon and many others. On his own, partly because he unnecessarily

lacked confidence in his singing voice, Hooker excelled at penning memorable, deeply moving instrumentals like "Blue Guitar" and "Wah Wah Blues." As the latter title illustrates, he was also one of the first bluesman to successfully incorporate wah wah pedals and other contemporary guitar effects. Hooker was a true modernist, with a thin but very satisfying catalog.

what to buy: *Blue Guitar* 𝄞𝄞𝄞𝄞 (Jewel/Paula, 1981) collects Hooker's excellent early-1960s sides, including a host of masterful instrumentals, most notably the title track. An oft-overlooked gem. *Two Bugs and a Roach* 𝄞𝄞𝄞𝄞 (Arhoolie, 1968, prod. Chris Strachwitz) is almost as good.

the rest:
Sweet Black Angel 𝄞𝄞𝄞 (One Way, 1970)
Play Your Guitar Mr. Hooker 𝄞𝄞𝄞 (Black Top, 1985)

influences:
◀◀ Robert Nighthawk, T-Bone Walker
▶▶ Buddy Guy, Joe Louis Walker, Luther Allison

Alan Paul

John Lee Hooker

Born August 22, 1920, in Clarksdale, MS.

When the words Delta blues are whispered like holy script, there are but a few names that accurately embody the weight associated with the term. Hooker, certainly the last of the living greats, is one. His looming presence in the last 40-plus years bears a stamp over not only the blues itself, but R&B, early rock 'n' roll and musicians ranging from Carlos Santana to Bonnie Raitt. Emerging from the tutelage of his stepfather and church gospel, Hooker begat his recorded legacy at age 31 with an arrestingly unorthodox approach of feral, six-string blues singles, including "Boogie Chillun" and "I'm in the Mood." The style he came to epitomize was a bone-spare, snake-like groove (often just one chord) supplanted only by the clicking of bottle caps under his stamping feet. The booming low growl emanating from his throat was unhinged animal strength, equal parts menace, barking bravado and morose longing. Eventually he did weld his open tunings and strange chording to a band format (after all, Mayall's Bluesbreakers and Clapton provided live back up in the 1960s), although most U.S. audiences didn't get wind of it until his recorded union with blues disciples Canned Heat in the 1970s. Strangely quiet throughout the latter part of that decade and most of the 1980s, Hooker (at age 72) roared back in 1989 with *The Healer*, winning universal acclaim and a Grammy in the process. Since then, he's recorded at a rate of men half his age, reworking his classics alongside Van Morrison, Keith Richards, Ry Cooder, Carlos Santana and Robert Cray, to name a few. As one of the few legends to enjoy the fruits of his work during his lifetime, Hooker has since retired from live performance but promises to keep recording until he's taken his last breath.

what to buy: The staggering number of Hooker albums available can make for a maddening selection process, but the uninitiated will be served well with *The Ultimate Collection* ♫♫♫♫ (Rhino, 1991, compilation prod. James Austin), a two-disc set that provides an ample overview for further inquiries, from brutal original versions of "Crawlin' King Snake," "Boogie Chillun" and "House Rent Boogie," in all their unsophisticated raw power, to his Canned Heat stew and late-1980s recordings. For a quick dive into the Delta swamps, *The Real Folk Blues* ♫♫♫♫ (Chess, 1966, prod. Ralph Bass) showcases Hooker manhandling a spare band while flashing uncontrollable lust ("You Know, I Know") and the oft-covered classic drinker's call to arms, "One Bourbon, One Scotch, One Beer."

what to buy next: Time may have diminished his growl a bit, but Hooker can still summon more danger than a teenager with an unlicensed pistol, as *The Healer* ♫♫♫♫ (Chameleon, 1989, prod. Roy Rogers) demonstrates. A celebratory outing with a star-studded guest list offering inspired performances at the feet of the master, the most welcome aspect of his comeback is that the record's most powerful moments occur when Hooker is unaccompanied.

what to avoid: There are far too many compilations glutting his oeuvre, and *Boogie Chillun* ♫♫ (Charly) is one of the unnecessary stops.

best of the rest:
Plays and Sings the Blues ♫♫♫♫ (Chess, 1961/1989)
Boogie Chillun ♫♫♫♫ (Fantasy, 1962/1989)
Urban Blues ♫♫♫♫♫ (MCA, 1967/1993)
Hooker 'n' Heat ♫♫♫♫ (EMI, 1970/1991)
Alone ♫♫♫♫ (Tomato, 1991)
The Cream ♫♫♫♫ (Tomato, 1991)
More Real Folk Blues: The Missing Album ♫♫♫♫♪ (Chess, 1991)
The Best of John Lee Hooker (1965 to 1974) ♫♫♫♫♪ (MCA, 1992)
Chill Out ♫♫♫♫ (Point Blank, 1995)
Don't Look Back ♫♫♫♫ (Point Blank, 1997)

worth searching for: If you thought Tom Jones bellowing "Tennessee Waltz" with the Chieftains was a goofy hoot, Hooker growling lines like "I eat heavy metal/locomotive pies" alongside Pete Townshend on the former Who guitarist's *The Iron Man* ♫♫ (Atlantic, 1989, prod. Pete Townshend) is a gas.

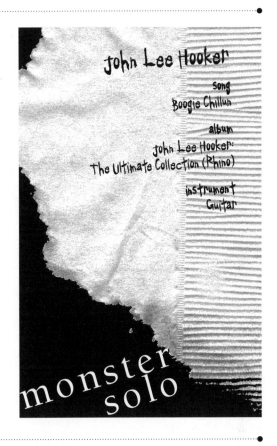

John Lee Hooker

song
Boogie Chillun

album
John Lee Hooker:
The Ultimate Collection (Rhino)

instrument
Guitar

monster solo

influences:

◀◀ Tony Hollins, Blind Lemon Jefferson, Robert Johnson, Willie Dixon

▶▶ Animals, Van Morrison, George Thorogood, Canned Heat, Johnny Winter, Rolling Stones, John Mayall, Eric Clapton

Allan Orski

Hadda Hopgood
See: Hadda Brooks

Lightnin' Hopkins
Born Sam Hopkins, March 15, 1912, in Centerville, TX. Died January 30, 1982, in Houston, TX.

Lightnin' Hopkins was one of the most prolific and frequently recorded bluesmen in history. His recordings span nearly four decades and encompass almost every imaginable style, from re-

laxed down-home acoustic blues to no-holds-barred proto-rock. His sound, while drawing on older influences, was uniquely his own and had a pervasive influence on a multitude of post-war musicians. His rough-hewn vocal delivery could be both mild-mannered and urgent, while his repertoire of guitar licks was always effortlessly adapted to the ever-changing currents of popular musical tastes. Though primarily a country bluesman, Hopkins was a master of electric guitar boogie and even scored an R&B hit or two. Hopkins is often thought of as a link between country blues and the urban electric blues it spawned. He was also an inventive songwriter and a consummate folk poet with the uncanny ability to compose tunes on the spot that artfully summarized his life experiences while at the same time striking a common chord with his listeners. He tackled war, natural disasters and the conquest of inner and outer space, often in an inimitable half-sung, half-spoken singing style tastefully punctuated by trademark bends, pull-offs and single-string runs. His raw blues songs and storytelling talents made him the darling of the folk-blues revival of the early 1960s, while his utterly hip attitude opened doors with the West Coast rock fraternity—he headlined on bills with the Jefferson Airplane and the Grateful Dead, among others. He died two years after being inducted into the Blues Foundation's Hall of Fame.

what to buy: *The Complete Aladdin Sessions* ✞✞✞✞ (EMI, 1991, prod. Pete Welding) is a collection of his earliest recordings, made for Aladdin in the late 1940s. He is joined on the first 13 songs by "Thunder" Smith, the dynamic pianist and vocalist responsible for Hopkins' "Lightnin'" moniker, but the rest is all Hopkins at his creative zenith. Stand-outs include the classic blues numbers "Katie May" and "Short Haired Woman," and the pre-rock-and-roll rocker "Play with Your Poodle." Whenever there was up-front cash on the table, he could also be found in Houston's Gold Star studios. There he recorded landmark songs like the plaintive "Going Home Blues" and "Unsuccessful Blues," inspired by a misunderstanding over payment for a session, and "Tim Moore's Farm," an explicit commentary on the sociological conditions faced by southern blacks. His complete Gold Star output can be found on *The Gold Star Sessions, Vol. 1* ✞✞✞✞ (Arhoolie, 1990, prod. Bill Quinn, Chris Strachwitz) and *The Gold Star Sessions, Vol. 2* ✞✞✞✞ (Arhoolie, 1990, prod. Bill Quinn, Chris Strachwitz). Fifteen years after the aforementioned sessions, Hopkins was a blues-revival icon, regularly touring from coast to coast on the circuit and making television

and documentary film appearances. Fortunately for blues fans, he also spent time recording some of his songs, the best of which are collected on *Texas Blues* ✞✞✞✞ (Arhoolie, 1994, prod. Chris Strachwitz). These tunes nearly equal the power and blues presence of his earlier recordings and explain in no uncertain terms what all of the fuss was about. Still unconvinced? Give a listen to *Swarthmore Concert* ✞✞✞✞ (Bluesville Prestige/Fantasy, 1993, prod. Shel Kagen), an outstanding concert appearance from the same period.

what to buy next: *The Herald Recordings* ✞✞✞✞ (Collectables, 1989) and *The Herald Recordings, Vol. 2* ✞✞✞✞ (Collectables, 1993) are two collections of small group recordings Hopkins made for the Herald label in the early 1950s, the hardest-driving, raunchiest records Hopkins ever cut. *Blues Train* ✞✞✞✞ (Mainstream, 1991, prod. Bob Shad) is another outstanding assortment of songs recorded in the early 1950s, this time for the Sitting In With and Jax labels. "Coffee Blues" and "Hello Central" both charted, and numerous others on this set should have. *Lightnin' in New York* ✞✞✞✞ (Candid, 1988, prod. Nat Hentoff) was recorded in 1960, just as Hopkins was coming into prominence on the folk-blues circuit. Highlights include several magnificent slow blues numbers ("Take It Easy," "Wonder Why") and the lengthy folk-tale "Mister Charlie."

what to avoid: For a guy as prolific as Hopkins, it comes as quite a surprise to find so few stinkers in the body of his recorded work. *Free Form Patterns* ✞✞ (International Artists, 1968/Charly 1991, prod. Lelan Rogers), however, is one to steer clear of. If you are looking for a record that captures what Hopkins would sound like on the other side of a thick wall backed by a bewildered band intent on a 12-bar groove that never materializes, this one's for you!

best of the rest:

Houston Bound ✞✞✞✞ (Relic, 1960/1994)
Last Night Blues ✞✞✞ (Original Blues Classics, 1960/Fantasy, 1992)
Smokes Like Lightning ✞✞✞ (Original Blues Classics, 1962/Fantasy, 1992)
Soul Blues ✞✞✞ (Original Blues Classics, 1964/Fantasy, 1991)
Lightnin' Hopkins ✞✞✞✞ (Smithsonian/Folkways, 1990)
The Complete Prestige/Bluesville Records ✞✞✞✞ (Prestige/Fantasy, 1991)
The Hopkins Brothers: Joel, Lightnin' & John Henry ✞✞✞ (Arhoolie, 1991)
Sittin' in with Lightnin' Hopkins ✞✞✞✞ (Mainstream, 1991)
Lightnin' ✞✞✞✞ (Arhoolie, 1993)
Mojo Hand: The Lightnin' Hopkins Anthology ✞✞✞✞ (Rhino, 1993)
Po' Lightnin' ✞✞✞✞ (Arhoolie, 1995)
Barbara Dane and Lightnin' Hopkins ✞✞✞ (Arhoolie, 1996)

John Lee Hooker (© Jack Vartoogian)

worth searching for: The Houston-based Gold Star label once boasted a stable of some of the finest post-war country blues artists, which included Lil Son Jackson and L.C. Williams, among others. On *Texas Blues* 🎸🎸🎸🎸 (Arhoolie, 1992, prod. Bill Quinn, Chris Strachwitz) Hopkins stretches out as an accompanist, laying down some of his finest instrumental work on record. On Williams' "Trying, Trying," he even turns out some terrific boogie-woogie piano!

influences:

◄◄ Texas Alexander, Blind Lemon Jefferson, Lonnie Johnson, Joel Hopkins

►► Carolina Slim, Robert Pete Williams, Hound Dog Taylor, Buddy Guy, Albert Collins, Lonnie Brooks, Bob Dylan

D. Thomas Moon

Sam Hopkins
See: Lightnin' Hopkins

Ted Horowitz
See: Popa Chubby

Big Walter Horton
Born April 6, 1917, in Horn Lake, MS. Died December 8, 1981, in Chicago, IL.

When blues followers list the greatest harp players of all time, "Shakey" Horton's name usually trails Little Walter and both Sonny Boy Williamsons. It's unfair, because Horton spent most of his career—including a long stint with Chess Records, which landed him on classics like Otis Rush's "I Can't Quit You Baby," Muddy Waters' "40 Days and 40 Nights" and Jimmy Rogers' "I Can't Believe"—as the consummate role-playing professional. He soloed frequently, of course, but his smooth, soothing tones were just as effective in the background, propping up Waters' guitar or Otis Spann's piano. At age 5, Horton taught himself the harp, and worked in the late 1920s with the Memphis Jug Band, in southern juke joints and on the Memphis streets. Though details are hazy, it's possible that Horton predated his better-known contemporaries—"Sonny Boy" Williamson II may have learned the amplified harp style from him, and he may have been the original Little Walter before agreeing to give up the name to Walter Jacobs. ("Big" Walter Horton fit him better anyhow.) His major career work came in the 1950s, when he moved to Chicago and replaced Junior Wells in Muddy Waters' band. That connection led to much work with Chicago stars such as Rogers, Rush and Johnny

Shines. In the 1960s, he backed Tampa Red, Big Mama Thornton and many others, before winding up as a member of Willie Dixon's touring Blues All-Stars. Horton put out several solo albums in the 1970s and 1980s, but his most amazing work was as a back-up musician.

what to buy: Horton's early material was his best, and it's collected on the mostly electric *Memphis Recordings 1951* 🎸🎸🎸🎸 (Kent, 1991, prod. Sam Phillips) and the mostly acoustic *Mouth Harp Maestro* 🎸🎸🎸 (Ace, 1988, prod. Sam Phillips)—both sessions produced by Sun Records head Phillips in the 1950s.

what to buy next: Horton performs his trademark songs, including "La Cucaracha," on *Fine Cuts* 🎸🎸🎸 (Blind Pig, 1979), one of the best albums of his late solo career.

the rest:
The Soul of Blues Harmonica 🎸🎸🎸 (MCA/Chess, 1964)
Offer You Can't Refuse 🎸🎸🎸 (Red Lightnin', 1972)
Big Walter Horton with Carey Bell 🎸🎸🎸 (Alligator, 1973)
Live at the El Mocambo 🎸🎸 (Red Lightnin', 1973)
Little Boy Blue 🎸🎸🎸 (JSP, 1980)
Harmonica Blues Kings 🎸🎸🎸 (Pearl Flapper, 1987)
Can't Keep Lovin' You 🎸🎸🎸 (Blind Pig, 1989)

worth searching for: Horton plays with several combos, including the Johnny Shines Blues Band and Horton's Blues Harp Band, on *Chicago/The Blues/Today!, Vol. 3* 🎸🎸🎸🎸 (Vanguard, 1967), an important document of 1960s Chicago blues and Horton's career.

influences:

◄◄ Sonny Boy Williamson I

►► Little Walter, Sonny Boy Williamson II, Billy Boy Arnold, Charlie Musselwhite, William Clarke

Steve Knopper

Ronnie Horvath
See: Ronnie Earl

Hot Tuna
Formed 1969, in San Francisco, CA.

Jorma Kaukonen, guitar, vocals; Jack Casady, bass; Will Scarlet, harmonica (1970–71); Papa John Creach, violin (1971–72); Sammy Piazza, drums (1971–74); Bob Steeler, drums (1974–77); Michael Falzarano, guitar, mandolin, harmonica, vocals (1990–present).

Formed in hotel rooms across the country after Jefferson Airplane concerts when guitarist Kaukonen and bassist Casady couldn't stop playing, Hot Tuna slowly emerged into the public, first as an acoustic duo and then as an electric quartet appearing often as a support act for the mothership. Essentially a vehicle for Kaukonen's remarkable skills as a country blues guitarist, Tuna specialized in lengthy improvisations in which Casady's fluid, inventive bass figures would wrap around Kaukonen's Delta blues lines almost endlessly. The band, on one occasion at least, performed for eight hours straight. Friends since childhood, Kaukonen and Casady split in the late 1970s and reformed about 10 years later. The original unplugged band, Tuna remains the sole surviving unit of the San Francisco psychedelic scene's heyday.

what to buy: Either *First Pull Up—Then Pull Down* ♫♫♫♫ (RCA, 1971, prod. Jorma Kaukonen) or *Burgers* ♫♫♫♫ (RCA, 1972, prod. Jorma Kaukonen) will provide the quintessential Tuna experience, mixing the Rev. Gary Davis/Mississippi John Hurt fingerpicking nobody does any better than Kaukonen with Casady's imaginative bass playing.

what to buy next: The duo's quiet acoustic debut, *Hot Tuna* ♫♫♫ (RCA, 1970, prod. Al Schmitt) captured the lads, fresh out of the hotel rooms, in a small Berkeley nightclub playing relatively straight-ahead elaborations on traditional country blues, unplugged before its time.

what to avoid: The sound quality on *Classic Hot Tuna Acoustic* ♫♫ (Relix, 1996, prod. Michael Falzarano), taken from a radio broadcast, leaves much to be desired, although the companion piece, *Classic Hot Tuna Electric* ♫♫♫ (Relix, 1996, prod. Michael Falzarano), fared better since it was taken from multi-track recordings made during the 1971 final week at the Fillmore West.

the rest:
The Phosphorescent Rat ♫♫ (RCA, 1973)
America's Choice ♫♫ (RCA, 1975)
Yellow Fever ♫♫ (RCA, 1975)
Hoppkorv ♫♫ (RCA, 1976)
Double Dose ♫♫♫ (RCA, 1977)
Pair a Dice Found ♫♫♫ (Epic, 1991)
Live at Sweetwater ♫♫♫ (Relix, 1992)
Live at Sweetwater Two ♫♫ (Relix, 1993)

worth searching for: Fans take note: packaged in a snazzy tin can in an individually numbered, limited-edition release and remastered for compact disc, *Hot Tuna in a Can* ♫♫♫♫ (RCA, 1996) pulls together *Hot Tuna*, *First Pull Up—Then Pull Down*, *Burgers*, *Hoppkorv* and *America's Choice*, with extensive liner notes and histories.

Lighthin' Hopkins
song
Baby Please Don't Go
album
Mojo Hand:
The Lighthin' Hopkins Anthology (Rhino)
instrument
Guitar

monster solo

solo outings:
Jorma Kaukonen:
Quah ♫♫♫♪ (Relix, 1974)
Magic ♫♫♫ (Relix, 1985)
Too Hot to Handle ♫♫♫ (Relix, 1986)
Land of Heroes ♫♫♫♪ (American Heritage, 1995)

influences:
◄◄ Rev. Gary Davis, Mississippi John Hurt, Scott LeFaro
►► Keb' Mo', Jeff Buckley, Chris Whitley, Jeff Healey

Joel Selvin

Son House

Born Eddie James House Jr., March 21, 1902, in Clarksdale, MS. Died October 19, 1988, in Detroit, MI.

One of the greatest exponents of Mississippi Delta blues was Son House. A sharecropper, House taught himself to play guitar, developing a highly dramatic slide guitar style. He traveled to Grafton, Wisconsin, in May 1930 with his partner, Willie Brown, and recorded for Paramount. Three 78s were issued, which featured slashing slide guitar, dark, moaning vocals and walking bass lines. House would become an early inspiration to Robert Johnson. Although he was one of the most popular bluesmen in the Delta, House wouldn't record again until 1942 when Alan Lomax taped him for the Library of Congress. Around this time, House took a job as a railway porter, moved to Rochester, New York, and forgot about music. However, House's rediscovery in 1964 helped fuel the first blues boom, and he made a courageous comeback. Although he hadn't picked up the guitar in nearly two decades, House quickly re-developed his technique. Throughout the 1960s and 1970s, he recorded and toured extensively, entertaining audiences with his music and stories.

what to buy: *Son House and the Great Delta Blues Singers 1928–30* 𝄞𝄞𝄞𝄞𝄞 (Document, 1994) includes the haunting Paramount sides as well as tracks by Willie Brown and Rube Lacey, among others. House rarely sounded better than on *Delta Blues* 𝄞𝄞𝄞𝄞𝄞 (Biograph, 1991, prod. Alan Caplin), which includes the Library of Congress field recordings from 1941 and 1942. Although House hadn't been in a recording studio in 35 years, he mustered all of his power on *Death Letter Blues* 𝄞𝄞𝄞𝄞𝄞 (Edsel, 1965, prod. Alan Wilson), proving he was still a master of the Delta blues. Consisting of 1970 recordings, *Delta Blues and Spirituals* 𝄞𝄞𝄞𝄞 (Capitol, 1995) has House accompanied by Alan Wilson on guitar and harmonica.

what to buy next: *At Home 1969* 𝄞𝄞𝄞𝄞𝄞 (Document) contains several of the songs, monologues and a cappella vocals House used in his performances.

influences:

◀◀ Charley Patton, Willie Brown, Willie Wilson

▶▶ Skip James, Robert Johnson, Muddy Waters, Howlin' Wolf, Elmore James, Alan Wilson, John Mooney

Jeff Hannusch

Peg Leg Howell

Born Joshua Barnes Howell, March 5, 1888, in Eatonton, GA.

Peg Leg Howell was one of the first and most extensively recorded Georgia bluesmen. He embodies the evolution of the blues from country dance and folk idioms to conventional 12-bar stylings. His recordings illustrate the richness of African-American rural folk music, and are among the most under-represented and least frequently savored flavors of the blues.

Though he began playing the guitar as a young man to amuse himself while working the fields in rural Georgia, an argument with a shotgun wielding brother-in-law resulted in the loss of a leg and necessitated his migration to the city, where playing music became more a matter of survival. Beginning in the early 1920s, he was pulling in sizable chunks of change on Atlanta's Decater Street, while supplementing his income as a bootlegger. In 1925, he was arrested for selling liquor and served a one year prison term, which is alluded to in his "Ball and Chain Blues." Shortly after his release from prison, a talent scout from Columbia heard him and signed him to the label, marking Columbia's entry into the down-home blues market. Howell was nearly 40 years old at the time and had amassed a vast repertoire of songs derived from multiple sources. He recorded traditional ballads ("Skin Game Blues"), dance tunes ("Beaver Slide Rag," "Peg Leg Stomp"), penitentiary songs ("New Prison Blues") and even covers of popular jazz and blues recordings. ("Hobo Blues" bears a striking resemblance to "Cow Cow" Davenport's "Cow Cow Blues," while "New Jelly Roll Blues" is roughly based on the Jelly Roll Morton original.) Howell was also joined in the studio on many occasions by his street band, the "Gang," which featured country fiddle player Eddie Anthony and guitarist Henry Williams. Most of these recordings are boisterous string-band pieces, and afford us a rare glimpse of a once wide-spread style of dance and party music.

what to buy: All of Howell's pre-war recordings are contained on *Complete Recorded Works Vol. 1: 1926–28* 𝄞𝄞𝄞𝄞 (Document, prod. Johnny Parth) and *Complete Recorded Works Vol. 2: 1928–30* 𝄞𝄞𝄞𝄞 (Document, prod. Johnny Parth). *Volume 1* highlights include the chilling "New Prison Blues," which contains the lyric "I'll cut your throat, mama, drink your blood like wine," the autobiographical "Low Down Rounder Blues," the Coon-Can gambler's moan, "Skin Game Blues" and the magnificent "Coal Man Blues," in which Howell effortlessly combines a ballad fragment, a coal vendor's song, and a handful of standard blues verses to great effect. *Volume 2* is more heavily weighted with string-band material, including "Turkey Buzzard Blues" (derived from the popular country dance tune "Turkey in the Straw"), the comic, medicine show styled "Monkey Man Blues" and a number of interesting . . . er, uhm, titles ("Tantalizing Bootblack," "Warm Wipe Stomp") from Macon Ed and Tampa Joe.

worth searching for: *The Black Country Music of Georgia 1927–36* 𝄞𝄞𝄞𝄞 (Origin Jazz Library, prod. Don Kent) is a terrific assortment of tunes that does justice to the great variety of musical styles prevalent in pre-war Georgia. *The Georgia Blues*

𝄞𝄞𝄞𝄞 (Yazoo, 1991) is another fine, and more readily available, collection of recordings by many of the same artists.

influences:

⏮ Blind Lemon Jefferson, Tampa Red, Blind Blake, Lonnie Johnson

⏭ Robin Williamson, Mike Heron

D. Thomas Moon

Howlin' Wolf

Born Chester Arthur Burnett, June 10, 1910, in Aberdeen, MS. Died January 10, 1976, in Hines, IL.

Bow at the very mention of his name. Wolf was the ultimate caldera of blues, a singer/persona whose ferocity has never been equalled and rarely even approached. He, Mud, Walter, and Sonny Boy were the Big Four of Chess, but his story starts long before he cut for the Chicago label.

Wolf was schooled down South by Charley Patton and by 1949 fronted a band that included pagan-toned guitarist Willie Johnson and a pianist called Destruction. In 1949 he started broadcasting on KWEM in West Memphis, alternating between musical performances and pitches for farm goods. He commenced recording, and even the baldest summary of this is complicated. He cut for Sam Phillips' Memphis Recording Service (Phillips had yet to form Sun); tapes were sent to the Biharis (of Modern in Los Angeles) and to Chess in Chicago. The Biharis were PO'ed that tapes were being sent to their rivals, all the more so when said rivals released Phillips' recording of Wolf's "How Many More Years" on a 78 in August 1951. So the Biharis got Ike Turner to cut Wolf for their RPM imprint, with the result that Wolf material started coming out on both RPM and Chess. To court went the record men, their legal slugfest colorful enough for *Billboard* magazine to give intermittent coverage. All the while Wolf played—in a band called the House Rockers with Johnson and prison-bound Pat Hare on guitar. The Chess/Bihari feud ceased when Modern swapped its claim on Wolf for Chess' Rosco Gordon, and Wolf moved to Chicago.

Discussion of Wolf's Chess output could fill volumes. His old henchman Johnson was on some of his sessions, as were a raft of dreadnought sidemen that included Hubert Sumlin, Jody Williams, Lee Cooper, Jimmy Rogers, Sam Lay and the ubiquitous Otis Spann. The drubbing mantra of "Smokestack Lightning," the blast-off dynamics of "Killing Floor," the evil of "Evil" and much more represent the zenith of power in recorded blues. Wolf was no slouch in live performance, either. He

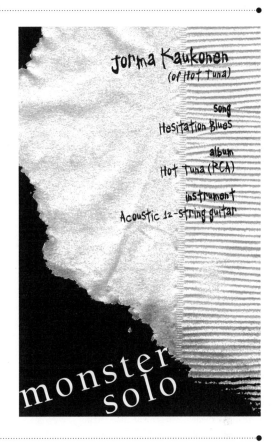

Jorma Kaukonen (of Hot Tuna)

song
Hesitation Blues

album
Hot Tuna (RCA)

instrument
Acoustic 12-string guitar

monster solo

stopped making truly great recordings around 1965, but tales abound of his magnificent showmanship until bare months before his death a decade later. Loremakers who would tell of Wolf must strain their vocabularies to even hint at how his music could thrill and chill. Better to recount the famous profundity of Sam Phillips, who said of Wolf: "This is where the soul of man never dies."

what to buy: Though Wolf's best-known material was on Chess, the sides on *Howlin' Wolf Rides Again* 𝄞𝄞𝄞𝄞 (Flair/Virgin, 1991, prod. Ike Turner) have a rawness and ferocity that must be heard to be believed. The disc opens fittingly with "House Rockin' Boogie," four minutes of hell-bent mania taken at breakneck pace, with Turner moshing a gloriously out-of-tune piano. As for Willie Johnson—mall rockers spend fortunes on special FX devices for their guitars and still can't get tones as leprous and depraved as his! For proof that Wolf was a naturally prescient proto-rocker, consult this cut and the comparably frenzied "Keep What You Got." "Moaning at Midnight" and "Crying at Daybreak" are moody, primal and downright scary. Essential! Scarcely less so is *Howlin' Wolf: His Best* ♫♫♫♫ (MCA/Chess, 1997, prod. Leonard Chess, Phil Chess, Sam Phillips, Willie Dixon), a 20-cut anthology that presents most of his prime work for Chess. "I Asked for Water" and "Sitting on Top of the World" he derived from old-time Delta sources. "Three Hundred Pounds of Heavenly Joy" is a Dixon ditty often derided as lyrically less grand than Wolf deserved, but he's in fine voice as he lows over the beery horn section. "Little Red Rooster," "Spoonful" and "Back Door Man" became staples for rock bands. Sound quality's good, and an informative booklet is enclosed.

what to buy next: Wolf was an artist of such high merit even his second string stuff rewards attention. Some of the material on the two-disc *Ain't Gonna Be Your Dog* ♫♫♫♪ (MCA/Chess, 1994, prod. Leonard Chess, Phil Chess, Sam Phillips, Willie Dixon) saw release, as did 1952's rousing "Oh Red" (which was updated by Long John Hunter on the 1996 Alligator release, *Border Town Legend*) and the snake-hipped "Come to Me Baby," from 1955. Rounding out the set are unreleased gems, arguably not of commercial quality in their day but revealing treasures to students of Wolf's body of work. Know how certain irretrievably bad movies have a perverse appeal to them? Same story with *Super Super Blues* ♫♪ (MCA/Chess, 1991, prod. Marshall Chess). Wolf, Mud and Bo were grouped in a studio for the purpose of achieving competitive and hopefully comedic badinage on jivey versions of their standards, awash in wah-wah guitar and trillings from a remarkably tasteless trio of chick singers. Despite the utterly bogus setting, our three heroes are in very good voice, and on occasion the hoped-for repartee even developed. Given the nature of the material he specialized in, Bo is unsurprisingly the peppiest, though he falls prey to a precious zinger from Wolf. While the band plows on, Wolf gruffly asks Bo, "You know dat bran new car you bought yo' girl?" Bo, hip to comic uptakes from his own "Say, Man", drawls, "yeahh...?" Wolf's response: "I'm drivin' it."

what to avoid: *Howlin' Wolf: The Chess Box* ♫♪ (MCA/Chess, 1992) has great material and a very informative booklet, but the CDs in my copy are tonally so harsh and toppy that they're a good argument for searching out the rare, five-LP set. Bypass unless you see it used for a greatly reduced price. Likely, you will. Also avoid the Brit-infested *London Sessions* **woof!** (MCA/Chess, 1971/1989).

best of the rest:
The Real Folk Blues ♫♫♫ (MCA/Chess, 1966/1987)

More Real Folk Blues ♫♫♫ (MCA/Chess, 1967/1988)
Cadillac Daddy ♫♫♫♫ (Rounder, 1989)
Moaning at Midnight ♫♫♫♫♫ (MCA/Chess, 1989)
Change My Way ♫♫♫♫♫ (MCA/Chess, 1990)

worth searching for: Aficionados might want to seek out *Memphis Days: Definitive Edition* ♫♫♫♪ (Bear Family, 1989, prod. Sam Phillips), two volumes of Sun recordings.

influences:

◄◄ Charley Patton, Tommy Johnson, Mississippi Sheiks, Sonny Boy Williamson II, Jimmy Rogers

►► Tail Dragger, Smokey Wilson, Captain Beefheart, Jimmy Morello

Tim Schuller

Joe "Guitar" Hughes

Born 1938, in Houston, TX.

Joe Hughes has been lucky and talented enough to revive his career after an almost 20-year recording and performing gap. A Texas flashy-guitar colleague of Albert Collins and Johnny Copeland, Hughes' heavily plucked tone is clean and fast, and his 1996 album *Texas Guitar Slinger* set him up as, at the very least, the standard-bearer to Albert King. He scored several interesting late-1950s and early-1960s singles, including "Ants in My Pants," and wound up touring with Little Richard, Sam & Dave, Jerry Butler and Bobby "Blue" Bland. After his comeback in 1985, he put out a few excellent guitar-lovers' albums. In 1997 Hughes, along with 13 other Houston blues artists, won a $260,000 judgment against producer Roy Ames and Collectables Records for copyright infringement over recordings released without the artists' consent.

what to buy: *Texas Guitar Slinger* ♫♫♫ (Bullseye Blues/Rounder, 1996, prod. Joe "Guitar" Hughes, Jerry Jenkins) is full of solos, of course, but what Hughes does with the quiet spaces is almost more interesting; frequently he'll stop, let a harpist or horn player do something, then resume playing when you least expect it.

what to buy next: *If You Want to See These Blues* ♫♫♫ (Black Top, 1989) captures Hughes before he really warmed up into his distinctive guitar sound; some of the songs are powerful, but some start to go on and on with the soloing.

the rest:
Texas Guitar Master Craftsman ♫♫♪ (Double Trouble, 1988)

influences:

◀◀ Albert King, Son Seals, Buddy Guy, Otis Rush, Albert Collins, Johnny Copeland

Steve Knopper

Helen Humes

Born June 23, 1913, in Louisville, KY. Died September 9, 1981, in Santa Monica, CA.

Guaranteed a footnote in jazz history for replacing Billie Holiday in Count Basie's band, Humes cut such classics as "Be-ba-ba-le-ba" and "Million Dollar Secret" and was one of this century's great underrecognized pop and blues singers. Humes' performing career began when she was 14, when blues guitarist Sylvester Weaver discovered her and escorted her to St. Louis recording sessions in the late 1920s. She drifted to New York City, working in cabarets, when John Hammond stuck her in his influential 1938 From Spirituals to Swing concert line-up. Hammond was so impressed that he offered her the singing job in Basie's band—Basie apparently offered her the same job a year earlier, but she inexplicably turned it down. She recorded and performed a whirlwind of gigs and studio sessions with Basie from 1938 to 1942 before striking out on her own. As a solo performer, she headlined several prominent New York and California clubs and did the soundtracks for films such as *My Blue Heaven*. Rock 'n' roll helped cut short her career and she had almost completely stopped performing by the 1960s; a revival helped bring her back to the studio and to European tours.

what to buy: *E-Baba-Le-Ba: The Rhythm and Blues Years* 𝄢𝄢𝄢𝄢 (Savoy, 1986) collects Humes' sessions from 1944 through 1950, in which she leaps out of her constrictions as a pop singer and belts in a deep sexy voice.

what to buy next: *Helen Humes and the Muse All Stars* 𝄢𝄢𝄢𝄢 (Muse, 1979) is the best album of the singer's jazzy comeback years, which yielded several new studio albums and world tours. Highlights include the bluesy "Loud Talking Woman" and a duet with Eddie "Cleanhead" Vinson on "I'm Gonna Move to the Outskirts of Town."

the rest:

Tain't Nobody's Biz-Ness If I Do 𝄢𝄢𝄢𝄢 (Original Jazz Classics, 1959)
Songs I Like to Sing 𝄢𝄢𝄢𝄢 (Original Jazz Classics, 1960)
Swingin' with Humes 𝄢𝄢𝄢𝄢 (Original Jazz Classics, 1961)
On the Sunny Side of the Street 𝄢𝄢𝄢 (Black Lion, 1974)
Sneakin' Around 𝄢𝄢𝄢 (Classic Jazz, 1974)
Helen Humes: Talk of the Town 𝄢𝄢𝄢 (Columbia, 1975)

Helen Humes with Red Norvo and His Orchestra 𝄢𝄢𝄢 (RCA, 1975)
Helen 𝄢𝄢𝄢 (Muse, 1980)
Let the Good Times Roll 𝄢𝄢𝄢 (Classic Jazz, 1981)

influences:

◀◀ Billie Holiday, Bessie Smith, Ma Rainey, Doris Day, Victoria Spivey

▶▶ Hadda Brooks, Bonnie Raitt, Etta James, Aretha Franklin, Saffire—The Uppity Blues Women

Steve Knopper

Alberta Hunter

Born April 1, 1895, in Memphis, TN. Died October 17, 1984, in New York, NY.

An encounter with Bessie Smith—who wound up recording her "Down Hearted Blues" in 1923—gave Alberta Hunter enough clout to sustain a career worthy of her songwriting and performing talent. A singer since she ran away from home at age 12, Hunter started playing racy Chicago joints and worked her way up to prominent cabarets. She signed first with Black Swan, then the more powerful Paramount, writing and recording her own songs, often with prominent back-up musicians such as Fletcher Henderson, Sidney Bechet, Fats Waller and Louis Armstrong. Hunter wound up starring in *Showboat* with Paul Robeson in London in the late 1920s and she recorded with orchestras in Paris before returning to the U.S. to sing for military troops during World War II and the Korean War. She retired in 1956 and worked as a non-musical nurse until she made a jazz comeback in the mid-1970s—at age 82. Like her contemporaries, Sippie Wallace and Big Mama Thornton, Hunter was a key link from the old (mostly women) "classic blues" singers to such belting rock and R&B queens as Etta James, Aretha Franklin and Janis Joplin.

what to buy: One of the few documents of Hunter's early material is *Young Alberta Hunter* 𝄢𝄢𝄢𝄢 (Vintage Jazz), 23 raucously sung tunes and a swing bottom provided by such well-known backup musicians as Fletcher Henderson.

best of the rest:

Chicago: The Living Legends 𝄢𝄢𝄢 (Riverside, 1961)
Songs We Taught 𝄢𝄢𝄢 (Original Blues Classics, 1961)
Amtrack Blues 𝄢𝄢𝄢 (CBS, 1988)

influences:

◀◀ Victoria Spivey, Bessie Smith, Sippie Wallace, Ma Rainey, Memphis Minnie, Fletcher Henderson, Sidney Bechet

▶▶ Bonnie Raitt, Saffire—The Uppity Blueswomen, Rory Block, Charles Brown, Hadda Brooks

Steve Knopper

Ivory Joe Hunter

Born October 10, 1914, in Weirgate, TX. Died November 8, 1974, in Memphis, TN.

This singer-pianist had all the right skills and was willing to try anything, but he just wasn't born in the right era to be a star. An R&B man at heart, he began recording cylinders for the Library of Congress in the 1930s—as Ivory Joe White. After moving to California in 1942, he started to merge his growing business acumen with his performing talent, opening the short-lived Ivory Records and co-founding Pacific Records. And he did wind up with smash hits, including 1950's "I Almost Lost My Mind" and "I Need You So," 1956's "Since I Met You Baby" and 1957's "Empty Arms." But R&B quickly gave way to rock 'n' roll, and Hunter was unable or unwilling to ride with the wave, so he switched to country music in the early 1960s. He tried to use his superb songwriting skills to eke out a behind-the-scenes Nashville career, then made an excellent comeback attempt with *The Return of Ivory Hunter*. But when he died of lung cancer in 1974, his career, sadly, had stalled.

what to buy: *Since I Met You Baby: The Best of Ivory Joe Hunter* ♪♪♪♪ (Razor & Tie, 1994) reminds us how important this sadly overlooked R&B star was at his peak. The material, recorded from 1949 to 1958 is nicely diverse: rockers like "Rockin' Chair Boogie" change the pace effectively amid slower ballads like "I Almost Lost My Mind."

what to buy next: *The Return of Ivory Joe Hunter* ♪♪♪ (Epic, 1970) is a weird-sounding album, an amalgam of jumping 1940s R&B, workmanlike 1960s country and the psychedelic stretched-out soul that sidemen Isaac Hayes (on organ) and Charlie Chalmers (on sax) brought to the mix.

the rest:
Sixteen of His Greatest Hits ♪♪♪ (King, 1988)

influences:
◀◀ Big Joe Turner, Charles Brown, Louis Jordan, Fats Domino, Louis Armstrong, T-Bone Walker

▶▶ Albert Collins, Clarence "Gatemouth" Brown, Hop Wilson, Robert Cray, Jerry Lee Lewis, Chuck Berry, Otis Rush

Steve Knopper

Long John Hunter

Born 1931, in LA.

Success has come late to Long John Hunter, but after decades honing his act in Mexican border bars, he has broken into the U.S. blues circuit with a vengeance. His trademark is his glassy guitar playing, spitting out shards of notes like the late Albert Collins, and before him, the manic Guitar Slim. Hunter has a fluid, if thin, voice that makes itself known just enough to keep listeners interested until the next ropy solo. After a few little-noticed singles for Yucca (out of the former nuclear test grounds of Alamogordo, New Mexico) Hunter cut two albums that sold poorly but managed to catapult him into southern festivals and catch the attention of Alligator. His 1996 *Border Town Legend* didn't quite roar out of Texas like Albert Collins did in the 1980s, but it is a solid effort with one soon-to-be-standard, the chilly "Ice Cold." In an industry overpopulated with lethargic copycats, Hunter is one to watch.

what to buy: Like Texas masters Gatemouth Brown and T-Bone Walker, Hunter takes his time building up the momentum on a slow blues, teasing out his guitar notes and singing lazily, as if he had just wakened. Backed by a spit-and-polish horn section, Hunter showed that all those years ducking beer bottles in border bars can come to something on *Border Town Legend* ♪♪♪♪ (Alligator, 1996, prod. Tary Owens, Jon Foose).

influences:
◀◀ Clarence "Gatemouth" Brown, T-Bone Walker, Albert Collins, Guitar Slim

Steve Braun

Mississippi John Hurt

Born John Smith Hurt, July 3, 1893, in Teoc, MS. Died November 2, 1966, in Grenada, MS.

It reads like a fairy tale or a Hollywood script: "Ardent blues lover uses a song lyric to track down long-lost, thought-to-be-dead musician whose only recordings were 35 years past and who had been working as a farm laborer ever since. 'Rediscovered' musician takes folk world by storm." Truth is indeed stranger than fiction. It happened in 1963 when young blues enthusiast Tom Hoskins found Mississippi John Hurt in Avalon, Mississippi, a city Hurt had immortalized in "Avalon Blues," one of 13 songs Hurt recorded in 1928 for the OKeh label. Singer/songwriter/guitarist Hurt's return was marked by a tri-

Long John Hunter (© Linda Vartoogian)

umphant appearance at the 1963 Newport Jazz Festival. He went on to become the most celebrated of the rediscovered 1960s folk artists and a star at age 71, when he moved his family from Mississippi to Washington, DC, to take advantage of opportunities to play festivals and coffeehouses across the U.S. and Canada. Hurt moved back to Mississippi shortly before his death in 1966. Hurt played gentle, folksy ballads and blues tunes with an even fingerpicking style and a friendly, front-porch demeanor. His guitar technique sounds deceptively simple, but Hurt possessed a smooth, rolling style characterized by a challenging combination of "constant bass" work with his thumb and an ever-present melodic line on top. His work remains a litmus test for fingerpicking acoustic guitar players and a unique pleasure for blues fans.

what to buy: There are no bad John Hurt albums, not a clunker out of the lot. If you're starting from scratch, here's a recommended order: *Avalon Blues: The Complete 1928 OKeh Recordings* 𝄢𝄢𝄢𝄢 (Columbia/Legacy, 1996, prod. Lawrence Cohn) includes the definitive, essential 1928 material mentioned above, packaged with tender-loving care and attention to detail, including excellent liner notes and a reproduction of the OKeh label on the CD itself. Well done. *The Best of Mississippi John Hurt* 𝄢𝄢𝄢𝄢 (Vanguard, 1987, prod. Bob Scherl) captures Hurt in an hour of 1965 live performance, demonstrating his affable command of enraptured folk audiences. *Avalon Blues 1963* 𝄢𝄢𝄢𝄢 (Rounder, 1991, prod. Richard Spottswood, Thomas Hoskins) and *Worried Blues* 𝄢𝄢𝄢𝄢 (Rounder, 1991, prod. Richard Spottswood, Thomas Hoskins) present Hurt's first recordings after rediscovery. The liner notes, duplicated on both CDs, are the best available for purposes of historical reference. One gripe: *Avalon Blues* is barely 30 minutes long; *Worried Blues* 40 minutes. Why aren't they on one CD?

what to buy next: *Memorial Anthology* 𝄢𝄢𝄢𝄢 (Genes, 1993, prod. Gene Rosenthal) is a two-CD live set that clocks in at more than two hours. Most of the performances come from the Ontario Place coffeehouse in Washington in 1964, but the release also includes a 30-minute Hurt interview conducted by Pete Seeger followed by Hurt performing a handful of songs for Seeger. All the performances are solid, well-recorded and nicely packaged with a 16-page booklet. *Today!* 𝄢𝄢𝄢𝄢 (Vanguard, 1987, prod. Patrick Sky) covers much of the same turf as the 1963 sessions released on Rounder, but the sound is not quite as crisp as the Rounder material.

the rest:

The Immortal Mississippi John Hurt 𝄢𝄢𝄢𝄢 (Vanguard, 1967)
Last Sessions 𝄢𝄢𝄢𝄢 (Vanguard, 1972)

worth searching for: The Canadian LP *Mississippi John Hurt: Volume One of a Legacy* 𝄢𝄢𝄢𝄢 (Rebel Records) features excellent studio performances of tunes unavailable on the CDs listed, such as "See See Rider" and "Do Lord Remember Me."

influences:

▷▷ Chris Smither, John Fahey, Leo Kottke, Bob Dylan, Fred Neil, Dave Van Ronk

Bryan Powell

J.B. Hutto

Born April 29, 1926, in Blackville, SC. Died June 12, 1983, in Harvey, IL.

Originally a gospel singer and drummer, J.B. Hutto, along with contemporary Hound Dog Taylor, became one of Chicago's best-known practitioners of down-home electric slide guitar. He was a member of the Golden Crown Gospel Singers in the early 1950s, then moved to Johnny Ferguson & the Twisters before plunging into the art of slide guitar and forming his own band, the Hawks. He left the business for awhile—even was a janitor at a funeral home at one point—before coming back as a heavy blues honcho. Hutto will always be known for a rasping, hypnotic playing style and an ever-changing array of on-stage headware. His nephew, Lil' Ed Williams, carries on the tradition.

what to buy: From the first stammering slide lick, you can't go wrong with *Hawk Squat* 𝄢𝄢𝄢𝄢 (Delmark, 1968, prod. Robert Koester), a romping, stomping, bass-slapping, boogie-woogieing, juke joint party that stays up past dawn. Producer Pete Welding caught an equally raucous Hawks for the smokin' *Masters of Modern Blues* 𝄢𝄢𝄢𝄢 (Testament, 1966/1994, prod. Pete Welding).

what to buy next: There's a jagged symmetry to *And the Houserockers Live 1977* 𝄢𝄢𝄢𝄢 (Wolf, 1991), which catches Hutto and Brewer Phillips tossing fireballs back and forth at each other in a Boston bar.

the rest:

Slidewinder 𝄢𝄢𝄢 (Delmark, 1973)
Keeper of the Flame 𝄢𝄢𝄢 (Wolf, 1991)
Slideslinger 𝄢𝄢𝄢 (Evidence, 1992)

worth searching for: Other harder-to-find titles include *High and Lonesome* 𝄢𝄢𝄢𝄢 (New Rose, 1993), *Live at Shaboo Inn—Connecticut 1979* 𝄢𝄢𝄢𝄢 (New Rose, 1993) and the cassette-only *Slippin' and Slidin'* 𝄢𝄢𝄢𝄢 (Varrick).

influences:
◀◀ Elmore James, Muddy Waters

▶▶ Jimmy Dawkins, Buddy Guy, Lil' Ed Williams

Leland Rucker

J

Arthur Jackson

See: Peg Leg Sam

Bullmoose Jackson

Born Benjamin Jackson, April 22, 1919, in Cleveland, OH. Died July 31, 1989, in Cleveland, OH.

To look at Bullmoose Jackson, you'd hardly peg him for a sex symbol. A lantern-jawed, bulbous-nosed giant, Jackson appealed to the ladies with his bellows voice, his ease with a tenor sax and some of the most salacious songs ever written. His "Nosey Joe" still outdoes "The Humpty Dance" for nasal nookie, and "Big Ten Inch Record" has yet to be surpassed for the sheer audacity of its virile boast. Bullmoose indeed. Jackson came to the fore as a vocalist during a sax stint with the Lucky Millinder big band. Hired to replace jazz ace Lucky Thompson, Jackson's booming vocals turned "I Love You, Yes I Do" into a dreamy national ballad hit. From there, King owner Syd Nathan tried Jackson on uptempo and torch blues, striking gold until old-style R&B grew stale in the mid-1950s. Jackson lit out with a few small West Coast labels and took a job as a janitor until a Pittsburgh-based roots revival band discovered him in the late 1970s. Jackson toured as far as Los Angeles, his voice still plummy enough to chant the old hits. But the novelty wore off quickly before he died of lung cancer in a Cleveland hospital.

what to buy: *Badman Jackson, That's Me* 𝄞𝄞𝄞𝄞 (Charly, 1991, prod. Syd Nathan) is non-stop booting by Jackson, with only a pause for a few slower shuffles. Jackson was a prime vehicle for scuffling blues writers like Jerry Leiber, Mike Stoller and Henry Glover. All his double-entendre hits are here—"Ten Inch," "I Want a Bowlegged Woman" and "Big Fat Mamas Are Back in Style Again." Not for kids or apostles of virtue.

influences:
◀◀ Wynonie Harris, Trevor Bacon

Steve Braun

Jim Jackson

Born 1884, in Hernando, MS. Died 1937, in Hernando, MS.

A medicine-show entertainer whose stately rags and simple blues pieces won a wide following in the north Mississippi and Memphis region, Jim Jackson gave the world the first version of "Kansas City." Although the song was almost certainly widespread in the blues repertoire by then, Jackson made sure that it was titled "Jim Jackson's Kansas City Blues"—a proprietary claim that Little Willie Littlefield, Wilbert Harrison, Hank Ballard, James Brown and dozens of other singers easily ignored. Jackson also was the first to record the folk standard "Old Dog Blue," picked up years later by the Byrds. Jackson, a stout, 235-pound minstrel, was a familiar figure on Memphis street corners, sparring with Furry Lewis, Gus Cannon, Will Shade and Robert Wilkins. Recording with Victor in 1928 and Vocalion in 1929, Jackson appeared in the all-black cast of King Vidor's 1929 film classic, *Hallelujah,* and he recorded at least 31 cuts before returning to the streets of Memphis.

what to buy: Of the two separate discs that contain all of Jackson's work, *Jim Jackson Complete Recorded Works 1927–30* 𝄞𝄞𝄞𝄞 (Document, 1992, prod. Johnny Parth), the first is indispensable and the second unnecessary. All of Jackson's important recordings are on the first volume, in surprisingly good sound for late-1920s sessions.

influences:
▶▶ Robert Wilkins

Steve Braun

John Jackson

Born February 25, 1924, in Woodville, VA.

A talented singer and guitarist who playfully and lovingly reproduces bouncy classics like "The Midnight Special," Jackson continues to show Washington, DC, audiences why the music of Blind Blake and Blind Boy Fuller is so timeless. He performs (frequently with James, his son) in the traditional rickety rhythms and sing-song vocals of the East Coast Piedmont style. Jackson learned guitar and banjo as a child in Virginia by listening to 78s and paying attention when guitarists like Willie Walker visited his father's house. Though a popular performer at house parties in Rappahannock County, in 1951 he started work as a gravedigger to pay the bills. The 1960s folk revival gave him more clout as a performer, which he continues to use to this day, nailing down European festivals, album deals and, of course, continuous nightclub bookings in the DC area.

what to buy: Jackson's folk music, by turns serious and goofy, comes across in a warm, friendly style on *Blues and Country Dance Tunes from Virginia* 𝄞𝄞𝄞 (Arhoolie, 1965), an excellent document of the Piedmont tradition played by a surviving master.

what to buy next: *Step It Up & Go* 𝄞𝄞𝄞 (Rounder, 1979) is more ragtime than blues, and also includes lots of hillbilly and folk tunes.

the rest:

John Jackson in Europe 𝄞𝄞𝄞 (Arhoolie, 1969)
Don't Let Your Deal Go Down 𝄞𝄞𝄞 (Arhoolie, 1970)
More Blues and Country Dance Songs 𝄞𝄞𝄞 (Arhoolie, 1971)

influences:

◀◀ Willie Walker, Blind Blake, Blind Boy Fuller, Leadbelly, Jesse Fuller

▶▶ Cephas & Wiggins, Keb' Mo'

Steve Knopper

Marion Walter Jacobs

See: Little Walter

Colin James

Born August 17, 1964, in Regina, Saskatchewan, Canada.

To listen to Colin James sing and play the blues on his guitar, you'd think the guy was from Austin, but James cut his teeth on blues, rock, funk, jazz and even bluegrass as a kid on the Canadian prairie. He even backed Billy Cowsill of the Cowsills (who returned the favor on James' first album). He dropped out of high school at age 16 to play music full-time, and within 10 years he had jammed with Stevie Ray Vaughan, Buddy Guy and Keith Richards, launched a solo career and won two Junos, the Canadian equivalent of the Grammy, in 1991. James' matinee-idol good looks, soulful cool-guy voice and expressive, root-conscious electric guitar stylings make him one of the few young blues guys today who can appeal to rock and pop audiences. He remains obscure largely because his record companies, radio programmers and music fans don't know what to make of a good looking white blues-rocker who's too bluesy for the rockers and too rock for the blues traditionalists.

what to buy: James gets better with age, and his most recent album, *Bad Habits* 𝄞𝄞𝄞 (Elektra Entertainment, 1995, prod. Chris Kimsey), is his best. Recorded in the Bahamas with former Rolling Stones producer Kimsey, it's a crisp, moody excursion into slick, urbane blues with side trips into soul, funk and

gospel and includes some of James' most expressive vocals and precise playing. Mavis Staples, Sarah Dash, Lenny Kravitz and Kim Wilson chip in with key contributions.

what to buy next: *Sudden Stop* 𝄞𝄞𝄞 (Virgin, 1990, prod. Joe Hardy) was a quantum leap from James' formulaic debut, with stronger songwriting, more of a band feel, tasty guest shots (like Bonnie Raitt's vocal on the sexy "Give It Up") and Hardy's gritty production.

the rest:

Colin James 𝄞𝄞 (Virgin, 1988)
Colin James and the Little Big Band 𝄞𝄞𝄞 (Virgin, 1993)

influences:

◀◀ Jimi Hendrix, John Lee Hooker, Rolling Stones, Stevie Ray Vaughan

▶▶ Chris Duarte, Kenny Wayne Shepherd, Ian Moore

Doug Pullen

Elmore James

Born Elmore Brooks, January 27, 1918, in MS. Died May 24, 1963, in Chicago, IL.

In Elmore James' raunchy voice and buzzing, electric slide-guitar riffs, you can hear the Chicago blues dissolving into early rock 'n' roll. Best known for "Dust My Broom" (which he borrowed from Robert Johnson and souped up), "Shake Your Money Maker" and "Madison Blues," James' licks became as much part of blues and rock standard practice as Bo Diddley's beat and Chuck Berry's lyrics. James, who like Muddy Waters was born in Mississippi and moved to Chicago to make his name, built his entire career on the electric boogie riff that pulses through his best hits. He also had the Broomdusters, the smokingest band this side of Waters' legendary combo in the early 1950s. James influenced generations of bluesmen and rockers, from B.B. King and Jimmy Reed to the Rolling Stones, Jimi Hendrix, George Thorogood, Stevie Ray Vaughan and every band that picked up guitars and cranked up the amp volume.

what to buy: James recorded so many sessions with so many different record labels—he put out countless versions of "Dust My Broom," for example—that until 1992 it was tough to compile a definitive collection. *The Sky Is Crying: The History of Elmore James* 𝄞𝄞𝄞𝄞𝄞 (Rhino, 1993, prod. Robert Palmer, James

John Jackson (© Jack Vartoogian)

Colin James (© **Ken Settle**)

Austin) solved that problem, collecting the best versions of "Dust My Broom," "The Sky Is Crying," "Shake Your Money-maker" and the explosive "Rollin' and Tumblin'." Song completists will probably want *The Complete Elmore James Story* 🎵🎵🎵 (Capricorn/Warner Bros., 1992), which has many more songs but starts to drown you with slide after a while.

what to buy next: *The Complete Fire and Enjoy Sessions, Parts 1–4* 🎵🎵🎵 (Collectables, 1989, prod. Bobby Robinson) are overwhelming but establish James as a crucial guitar pioneer whose wailing slide was as powerful as Howlin' Wolf, the Rolling Stones or anybody who has dabbled in the blues. *Street Talkin'* 🎵🎵🎵 (Muse, 1975/1988) also features bluesman Eddie Taylor.

what to avoid: Some of the early compilations—*Anthology of the Blues: Legend of Elmore James* 🎵🎵 (Kent, 1976), *Anthology of the Blues: Resurrection of Elmore James* 🎵🎵 (Kent, 1976), *Red Hot Blues* 🎵🎵 (Quicksilver, 1982), *The Classic Early Recordings, 1951–56* 🎵🎵 (Atomic Beat, 1994)—are solid but have been trumped by the superior Rhino and Capricorn collections,

so they're recommended to blues completists and James aficionados only.

the rest:

Blues Masters, Vol. 1 🎵🎵 (Blues Horizon, 1966)
Tough 🎵🎵 (Blues Horizon, 1970)
I Need You 🎵🎵 (Sphere Sound, 1971)
The Sky Is Crying 🎵🎵 (Sphere Sound, 1971)

worth searching for: *Whose Muddy Shoes* 🎵🎵🎵 (Chess, 1969/Chess/MCA, 1991) contains songs by James and the obscure-but-great Chicago bluesman John Brim.

influences:

◀◀ Robert Johnson, Sonny Boy Williamson II, Muddy Waters, Robert Nighthawk

▶▶ Rolling Stones, B.B. King, Jimi Hendrix, Stevie Ray Vaughan, George Thorogood, Allman Brothers Band, Johnny Winter

Steve Knopper

Etta James

Born Jamesetta Hawkins, January 25, 1938, in Los Angeles, CA.

Is it heresy to suggest that it is Etta James—not schmaltzy, Vegasified Aretha Franklin—who rules as Queen of Soul these days? Not only does she have the lineage—from her days as a 1950s R&B teen queen through her time as a 1960s soul shouter—but James has matured into one of the grand dames of R&B. She's always sung with a great, intense passion, but the years only seem to have added depth of character and subtle, rich color and emotion. Her first record was a simple answer to a popular Hank Ballard cut, "Roll with Me Henry," that landed James on the road in 1954, where she has stayed for the rest of her life. She made one of the great gospel soul records, "Something's Got a Hold on Me," in 1961, and by 1967 she could be found putting the fiery lead vocals on one of the landmarks of southern soul, "Tell Mama." By 1994, she could assay material some thought indelibly linked with Billie Holiday for *Mystery Lady*, an album that was at once a tribute to her earliest source of inspiration and a personal liberation. Through her own relentless determination and stubborn artistic strength, Etta James steered her own course through the rapid waters of the music's ever changing path, relying always on instincts and bald-faced honesty. And the years have apparently only strengthened her resolve.

what to buy: A double-disc retrospective of her 1960–74 tenure at Chess, *The Essential Etta James* ✺✺✺✺ (Chess/MCA, 1993, prod. various) collects the backbone of her illustrious career.

what to buy next: *Mystery Lady* ✺✺✺✺ (Private, 1994, prod. John Snyder) is a leap from her vernacular soul and blues into a realm of pure personal expression. With jazz pianist Cedar Walton at the bandstand, the resulting work defies easy categorization and gave James a platform to just be herself in a stunning triumph that finally earned her a Grammy.

what to avoid: Even her most paltry recent effort, *Stickin' to My Guns* ✺✺ (Island, 1990, prod. Etta James), a largely unsuccessful attempt to incorporate rap and hip-hop into a more traditional R&B context, is more of an aberration than an artistic misstep.

the rest:

The Second Time Around ✺✺✺✺ (Chess, 1961)
Tell Mama ✺✺✺✺ (Chess, 1968)
Come a Little Closer ✺✺ (Chess, 1974)
Deep in the Night ✺✺✺ (Bullseye Blues, 1978)
R&B Dynamite ✺✺✺✺ (Flair, 1986)
(With Eddie "Cleanhead" Vinson) *Blues in the Night* ✺✺ (Fantasy, 1986)

Elmore James
song
Dust My Broom
album
The Sky Is Crying: The History of Elmore James (Rhino)
instrument
Slide guitar

monster solo

(With Eddie "Cleanhead" Vinson) *The Late Show* ✺✺ (Fantasy, 1987)
Seven Year Itch ✺✺✺ (Island, 1989)
The Right Time ✺✺✺✺ (Elektra, 1992)
How Strong Is a Woman: The Island Sessions ✺✺✺ (Polydor, 1993)
Live in San Francisco ✺✺✺ (On the Spot, 1994)
Time after Time ✺✺ (Private, 1994)
These Foolish Things: The Classic Balladry of Etta James ✺✺✺ (MCA, 1995)
Her Best ✺✺✺✺ (MCA/Chess, 1997)
Love's Been Rough on Me ✺✺✺ (Private, 1997)

worth searching for: *Etta James Rocks the House* ✺✺✺✺ (Chess, 1964), an early album, more than lives up to its title.

influences:

◀◀ Billie Holiday, Hank Ballard, Big Mama Thornton, Bessie Smith

▶▶ Tina Turner, Janis Joplin

Joel Selvin

Skip James

Born Nehemiah Curtis James, June 9, 1902, in Bentonia, MS. Died October 3, 1969, in Philadelphia, PA.

It's an incredible American tragedy that Skip James did not play blues concerts or make recordings from 1931 to 1964. But there's not much point in once again ripping early-century racism or the music industry for derailing James' career after Paramount put out 18 of his eerie, wonderfully sung and subtly played country-blues songs. James, a major talent, grew frustrated with music and became a gospel singer, touring with his father's revival show throughout the south and eventually becoming a minister. The often ill-tempered James, who did not suffer fools, had been in a Tunica, Mississippi, hospital in 1964 when John Fahey and two other blues historians tracked him down and persuaded him back into blues. (It should be noted that James was not always in a bad mood; he welcomed reverential young musicians and fans backstage and thrilled them by introducing them to friends such as Son House and Bukka White.) That was when James' career, 30 years too late, began to take off—his high-pitched, effortlessly lonesome vocals and haunting, textured acoustic guitar playing established him as one of the most reliable festival performers throughout the 1960s. Eric Clapton, among many others, took notice and stuck a bombastic version of "I'm So Glad" on one of Cream's million-selling classic rock albums, giving James serious royalty payments just before he died. James was responsible for some of this century's best popular songs—"Drunken Spree," "Devil Got My Woman," "Worried Blues," "Catfish" and, of course, "I'm So Glad." More important, like the more posthumously heralded Robert Johnson, James contributed a key haunting, moaning soul to American music. We're lucky James, unlike Johnson, hung around long enough so he could receive at least a fraction of his deserved popularity.

what to buy: Of 26 Paramount sides James was said to have recorded in 1929, 18 survive—and they're compiled on the absolutely essential *Complete Early Recordings* ♫♫♫♫ (Yazoo, 1994). James' guitar-plucking style is more enthusiastic and pronounced than his 1960s recordings, but his voice is the main attraction; he sings like nobody else, smoother than Robert Johnson and grittier than Sam Cooke, but the direct or indirect inspiration behind them both. This collection includes definitive versions of "Drunken Spree," "22-20 Blues," "I'm So Glad" and "Devil Got My Woman."

what to buy next: There are many 1960s James recordings to choose from, so we recommend going with an original, *Today!*

♫♫♫♫ (Vanguard, 1965/1988), in which James' guitar playing has slowed down but his voice seems richer and more textured. Another excellent document is *Greatest of the Delta Blues Singers* ♫♫♫♫ (Biograph, 1992, prod. Arnold S. Caplin), James' first studio sessions after his legendary 1964 Newport Folk Festival appearance.

what to avoid: It's hard to go wrong with James' albums, but after the essential stuff his 1960s material gets somewhat repetitive; *Devil Got My Woman* ♫♫♫ (Vanguard, 1968/1988) is the least important. Also, the great *Complete 1931 Session* ♫♫♫♫ (Yazoo, 1986) has been displaced on the market by the better *Complete Early Recordings*.

the rest:

Skip's Piano Blues ♫♫♫♫ (Genes, 1996)

worth searching for: *She Lyin'* ♫♫♫♫ (Genes, 1964/1993, prod. John Fahey, Ed Denson, Bill Barth) was once hard to find, sitting explicably in the vaults for years until its recent reissue.

influences:

◄◄ Tommy Johnson, Charley Patton, Son House

►► Robert Johnson, Muddy Waters, Sam Cooke, Eric Clapton, Charles Brown, Art Tatum, Charlie Parker, B.B. King

Steve Knopper

Steve James

Born July 15, 1950, in New York, NY.

Acoustic guitarist/singer/songwriter Steve James blends all manners of America's musical roots, including blues, folk and old-time hokum and ragtime, and does it as well as anyone alive. His range of influence reflects his travels, which include time in Memphis in the 1970s, learning the blues from Furry Lewis and Lum Guffin and soaking up the style of hillbilly guitar originator Sam McGee. As a songwriter, James has learned his lessons well: He avoids familiar cliches, populating his tunes with stories of memorable characters that he puts forth with clarity and invention. As a player, he moves fluently from guitar to slide guitar to mandolin, always with taste and fine technique.

what to buy: On *American Primitive* ♫♫♫♫ (Antone's, 1994, prod. Steve James), James' convincing originals are right at home among covers of Bumble Bee Slim, Willie Brown, Memphis Minnie, Tampa Red and Uncle Dave Mason.

Etta James (© Ken Settle)

the rest:

Two Track Mind ♪♪♪♪ (Antone's, 1993)

Art and Grit ♪♪♪♪ (Antone's, 1995)

influences:

◄◄ Bumble Bee Slim, Willie Brown, Memphis Minnie, Tampa Red, Uncle Dave Mason, Furry Lewis, Big Bill Broonzy, Mance Lipscomb, Curley Weaver

►► Bad Livers

Bryan Powell

Blind Lemon Jefferson

Born reportedly as Lemon Jefferson, July 11, 1897, in Couchman, TX. Died December 1929, in Chicago, IL.

Blind Lemon Jefferson roamed thousands of miles and packed 100 recordings into his abbreviated 32 years, enough to establish himself as the first great male blues star of the 1920s and a man whose success set the standard for generations who followed. Corpulent, blinking out at the world through wire-rimmed spectacles, Jefferson's unmistakable keening voice and odd, stop/start strumming reportedly sold thousands of copies of Paramount 78s. The record company issued 43 records, rare for a blues artist of that time. Jefferson was such an admired figure among his peers that blues titans like Leadbelly and T-Bone Walker talked reverently about leading Jefferson around Dallas for street performances. Titles and stanzas from his songs have found their way into the blues lexicon for decades. Among the most familiar: "That Black Snake Moan"; "Matchbox Blues" (later a standard for Albert King and Carl Perkins); "Easy Rider Blues"; and the solemn "See That My Grave Is Kept Clean" (adapted by Bob Dylan).

Little is known about Jefferson's early years; he seemed to have appeared out of nowhere, a fully-formed bluesman, on the streets of Dallas. Described by other musicians as an independent sort who equipped himself with both a cane and a gun, Jefferson could reportedly identify paper bills by feeling them in his hands. Brought to Paramount's attention by a Dallas retailer in 1925, Jefferson was an overnight success. Paramount treated him the way big labels now pamper gangster rappers, buying him a new Ford equipped with a chauffeur. Jefferson had the repertoire to back up their confidence in him, able to trot out Texas specialties like "Mean Jumper Blues" or cover Leroy Carr's "How Long How Long." Commuting between Dallas and Chicago, where he recorded, Jefferson apparently found work as a porter during lean times. He was in Chicago for the harsh winter of 1929, dying under mysterious circumstances in

the middle of a snowstorm. Some accounts maintain he froze to death; others insist he collapsed of a heart attack in his car and was abandoned there by his chauffeur. However he died, Jefferson left a motherlode of recordings and some of the most influential songs ever pressed.

what to buy: The four discs of *Blind Lemon Jefferson: Complete Works 1926–29* ♪♪♪♪ (Document, 1991, prod. Johnny Parth) contain all of Jefferson's known efforts. Most are surprisingly clear-sounding, considering the fact that the Paramount 78s tended to scratch and wear out quickly. It is hard to choose a favorite among the four, but the third disc, which covers 1928, has better sound than the earlier volumes and a wide variety of fine performances, including "Grave." *Blind Lemon Jefferson* ♪♪♪♪♪ (Milestone, 1992, prod. Orrin Keepnews) is the best single-disc representation of Jefferson's work, ranging from 1926 to 1929 and including "Black Snake Moan," "Matchbox Blues" and 23 other cuts. The sound is as good as early-1990s technology can provide.

what to avoid: *Penitentiary Blues* ♪♪ (Collectables, 1994) offers a stingy sampling of Jefferson with mushy sound and haphazard notes. An afterthought.

the rest:

King of the Country Blues ♪♪♪♪ (Yazoo, 1990)

influences:

◄◄ Mamie Smith, Bessie Smith

►► T-Bone Walker, Lightnin' Hopkins, Albert King, B.B King, Carl Perkins, Bob Dylan

Steve Braun

Big Jack Johnson

Born July 30, 1940, in Lambert, MS.

On Big Jack Johnson's 1987 version of the Howlin' Wolf-by-way-of-Jimi Hendrix classic "Killing Floor," you can hear his confident, rhythmic guitar practically dragging the rest of the band from blues to rock 'n' roll. His playing isn't flashy, but he has a devastating melodic sense, breaking spontaneously into choruses when you least expect it. Best of all, he has impeccable taste in sidemen, touring frequently with the rock-solid Mississippi duo Frank Frost and Sam Carr. (The ex-oil truck driver known as "The Oil Man" became a reputable performer after sitting in with Frost and Carr at the Clarksdale Savoy Theatre in the early 1960s.) He tries to keep his songs topical—1989's "Mr. U.S. AIDS" was not only one of the few blues songs to address the AIDS crisis, but one of the first songs in any genre to do so—but rhythm is really the bottom line. Critics have compared his style to Albert King's late-1960s work with Stax and Booker T. and the MGs, which is appropriate, because the worst thing you can say about Johnson's music is it keeps you dancing so intently you stop paying attention to the wonderful guitar playing. Along with Frost, Carr, R.L. Burnside and Junior Kimbrough, Johnson was one of the long-time traditional Mississippi bluesmen who got a boost from critic Robert Palmer's *Deep Blues* documentary and soundtrack.

what to buy: Despite a too-easy rip on disco, *The Oil Man* 𝄞𝄞𝄞𝄞 (Earwig, 1987/1993, prod. Michael Robert Frank, Big Jack Johnson) is really a rock 'n' roll record; the versions of "Killing Floor" and "Catfish Blues" recall Jimi Hendrix, and Johnson's no-frills quartet (including Frost on piano) simply works on propelling the rhythm along. You can also hear Johnson's country influence on Merle Travis' "Steel Guitar Rag (Going Bass Fishing)."

what to buy next: *Daddy, When Is Mama Comin' Home?* 𝄞𝄞𝄞𝄞 (Earwig, 1989, prod. Michael Robert Frank, Big Jack Johnson) has more frills—Frost actually plays a synthesizer!—but it works extremely well as a protest album, taking on domestic abuse in "I Slapped My Wife in the Face," the economy in "United States Got Us in a Bad Shape" and AIDS in "Mr. U.S. AIDS."

the rest:

We Got to Stop This Killin' 𝄞𝄞𝄞 (M.C., 1996, prod. Mark Carpentieri, Catherine Carpentieri)

worth searching for: The soundtrack *Deep Blues* 𝄞𝄞𝄞𝄞 (Atlantic, 1992, prod. Robert Palmer) gave R.L. Burnside a national reputation, and while it hasn't generated the same level of exposure for Johnson or Frost, it contains two of their great tracks.

influences:

◀◀ B.B. King, Albert King, Frank Frost & Sam Carr, Jimi Hendrix, Booker T. & the MGs

▶▶ R.L. Burnside, Son Seals, Junior Kimbrough

Steve Knopper

Blind Willie Johnson

Born 1902 or 1903, reportedly in Temple, TX. Died December 1949, in Beaumont, TX.

Although he recorded only religious music, Blind Willie Johnson was influential in the blues world as one of the great purveyors of the bottleneck style of guitar. A guitar evangelist also known as Blind Texas Marian, the adolescent Johnson was taken by his father to the small towns between Houston and Dallas, where he played on the streets. While the lyrics to his songs were religious, his relentless guitar rhythms and harsh, growling vocals were as intense as that of any blues singer. Johnson recorded extensively for Columbia, but the Depression eliminated the demand for his recordings. Some were later re-released on Vocalion, but Johnson never recorded again after 1930. Eventually Johnson moved to Beaumont, where he earned a meager living singing on street corners and at church benefits.

what to buy: An intense two-CD set, *The Complete Willie Johnson* 𝄞𝄞𝄞𝄞 (Legacy, 1993, prod. Lawrence Cohn) contains all of the known sides recorded by the great guitar evangelist.

what to buy next: All of the tracks contained on *Praise God I'm Satisfied* 𝄞𝄞𝄞𝄞 (Yazoo, 1991) and *Sweeter As the Years Go By* 𝄞𝄞𝄞𝄞 (Yazoo, 1991) are contained on *The Complete Willie Johnson.*

influences:

▶▶ Leadbelly, Texas Alexander, Blind Lemon Jefferson, Black Ace, Mississippi Fred McDowell, Lightnin' Hopkins, Bob Dylan

Jeff Hannusch

Buddy Johnson

Born Woodrow Wilson Johnson, January 10, 1915, in Darlington, SC. Died February 9, 1977, in New York, NY.

A few years ago, the only Buddy Johnson records available were hidden in obscure 1950s R&B compilations. But lately much of Johnson's vast catalog has been issued, befitting the man who led the only full-fledged blues big band and composed "Since I Fell for You," "Please Mr. Johnson" and "That's the Stuff You Gotta Watch." There were times in the 1950s when Johnson's streamliner of a band outplayed and outsold Count Basie and Duke Ellington. But while his rivals thrived by returning to their jazz roots, Johnson's brassy R&B withered as rock 'n' roll took over. Johnson played with combos and bands in New York and Europe in the 1930s until he joined Decca Records, trolling for dance bands in the hothouse swing atmosphere then in New York. Johnson quickly built a band and hired his sister, Ella, to sing out front. In the war years, they hit with "When My Man Comes Home" and "Stuff You Gotta Watch," later cribbed by Wynonie Harris and Muddy Waters. After "Since I Fell for You" enshrined itself as a pop ballad standard, Johnson moved toward more gutbucket rhythm style. Tough tunes like "Upside Your Head" and "Hittin' on Me" could have

been theme songs for the film noir era. But Johnson's hard-boiled R&B soon lost favor, and he softened his approach to win over a teenaged audience that had no time for him. An astute businessman, Johnson's tight control over his song rights kept him in the money until he died of a brain tumor.

what to buy: *Walk 'Em* 𝄞𝄞𝄞𝄞 (Ace, 1996, prod. Richard Topp, John Broven) is a swinging compilation that gleans 24 of the best of Johnson's late-1940s sessions with Decca. The band is seamless, and sister Ella sounds either like an angel or a vamp. Ace's mastering is impeccable—especially for 50-year-old masters.

what to buy next: A reprint of Johnson's old Mercury album from the 1950s, *Rockin' and Rollin'* 𝄞𝄞𝄞 (Collectables, 1995) offers tight dynamics and a wall of honking saxes, a solid taste of what Johnson was putting down until he strayed in the rock 'n' roll wilderness. *Buddy and Ella Johnson 1953–64* 𝄞𝄞𝄞 (Bear Family, 1995) is a sprawling four-volume set that covers everything the Johnsons recorded for Mercury and Roulette after leaving Decca in the early 1950s. There are 104 cuts, and the best are no-nonsense R&B stompers and sultry ballads that define what jump blues was all about. But as sparkling as the transfers are—par for the course for the German label—there is plenty of dross here, too, usually when Buddy tried too hard at hooking the kids. Only for blues fanatics and cyber millionaires at a loss for ways to spend their cabbage.

influences:

◀◀ Jimmy Lunceford, Lucky Millinder, Count Basie, Lionel Hampton

▶▶ Muddy Waters, Little Walter, Ruth Brown, Roomful of Blues

Steve Braun

Earl Silas Johnson IV

See: Earl King

James "Super Chikan" Johnson

Born James Johnson, February 16, 1951, in Darling, MS.

James "Super Chikan" Johnson has called the Mississippi Delta home since his birth, and his unusual music is a direct and heart-warming reflection of his daily life in that region. Johnson's sound can be laid-back and funky, his lyrics humorous. He can also be quirky, with a frequently befuddling sense of timing.

Big Jack Johnson (© Jack Vartoogian)

The honesty with which Johnson presents his thoughts and feelings makes him one of the genre's least self-conscious artists. Johnson squawks like a chicken being boiled alive and bellows like an old woman. Guitarist, vocalist, pianist, harp player, Super Chikan spells things—and does things—his own way.

what to buy: An insightful man, Super Chikan possesses the ability to notice and savor the beauty of life even in the bleakest of times. He exhibits this winning trait on "Down in the Delta," which opens his debut, *Blues Come Home to Roost* 𝄞𝄞𝄞 (Rooster Blues, 1997, prod. James Johnson, Jim O'Neal, Patty Johnson), with Johnny Rawls and L.C. Luckett providing accompaniment and all compositions on this refreshingly strange effort credited to Johnson.

influences:

◀◀ Roosevelt "Booba" Barnes, Big Jack Johnson

▶▶ Wesley Jefferson Band

Steven Sharp

Jimmy Johnson

Born Jimmy Thompson, November 25, 1928, in Holly Springs, MS.

Why Jimmy Thompson and his brother, Syl Thompson, both changed their names to "Johnson" remains unclear, but Johnson's alliterative stage name eventually paid dividends in 1978. The singer-guitarist was one of the first relatively obscure artists to earn an audience with the Alligator collection *Living Chicago Blues*, and though he has never become a major blues superstar, he continues to sell out shows all over Chicago. Born to a musical family—Syl Johnson, of course, had a huge hit with "Take Me to the River," and brother Mack Thompson played bass for Magic Sam—Johnson switched from blues to R&B in the 1960s. (He played behind Otis Clay, Denise LaSalle, Jimmy Dawkins and, on a prominent Japanese tour, Otis Rush.) An Indiana car accident killed his keyboardist and bassist and injured Johnson, threatening to derail his career in late 1988, but he came back in 1994 with an album and renewed touring and Chicago-area playing.

what to buy: Johnson proves he's as noticeable a Chicago-style player as bigger stars Son Seals and Buddy Guy on his landmark *Bar Room Preacher* 𝄞𝄞𝄞 (Alligator, 1983, prod. Disques Black and Blue). His solo style is much more laid-back and subtle than typical Chicago guitarists, sometimes to the point that you can't hear him amid the swinging, funky rhythm section; but he communicates power without knocking you over the head with his guitar.

what to buy next: The funny, playful *Johnson's Whacks* ♫♫♫ (Delmark, 1979/1991, prod. Steve Tomashefsky, Jimmy Johnson Band) contains a front-cover photo of Johnson solemnly wielding an axe and a rear-cover photo of a smashed red guitar. "Take Five" is a jaunty R&B solo, almost a subversive joke version of the "beautiful music" so prominent on radio stations in the late 1970s, and Johnson's voice is consistently high and soulful.

the rest:

North/South ♫♫♫ (Delmark, 1982)
I'm a Jockey ♫♫♫ (Verve, 1995)

influences:

◀◀ Buddy Guy, Little Milton, Syl Johnson, Otis Clay, Otis Rush, Son Seals

▶▶ Willie Kent, Billy Branch, Stevie Ray Vaughan, Robert Cray

Steve Knopper

Johnnie Johnson

Born July 8, 1924, in Fairmont, WV.

Turnabout, as they say, is fair play, and it is sweet irony to note that the career of rock 'n' roll piano legend Johnnie Johnson is flourishing these days, and he is receiving the recognition he so richly deserves, while his former employer, Chuck Berry, can't get arrested (figuratively speaking, that is). For if Berry is the father of rock 'n' roll, then Johnson should be accorded credit as its stepfather. Berry may have been the crucible in which the blues, rhythm & blues and country gave birth to a new form further shaped by his wit and poetic sense, but it was Johnson who led his band and who contributed, uncredited, the music for some of the songs that are the very cornerstone of rock. Gracious to a fault, Johnson is willing to let bygones be bygones and his music—more blues-oriented than his work with Berry—to speak for itself. In recent years, Johnson has recorded with Eric Clapton, Buddy Guy and Bo Diddley and played the summer-tour circuit with ex-Grateful Dead guitarist Bob Weir's band, Ratdog.

what to buy: *Johnnie B. Bad* ♫♫♫ (Elektra Nonesuch American Explorer Series, 1991, prod. Terry Adams, Keith Richards) is Johnson's best album overall, thanks in part to an all-star cast that includes Richards, Eric Clapton and members of NRBQ. "Tanqueray" and "Stepped in What!?" are Johnson's first vocal performances ever, and while far from spectacular, capture perfectly his gentle, self-effacing personality.

what to buy next: *Johnnie Be Back* ♫♫♫ (Musicmasters, 1995, prod. Jimmy Vivino) is another all-star affair, with Phoebe Snow, Buddy Guy, Al Kooper, John Sebastian and Max Weinberg all lending a hand. There's still plenty of room for Johnson to shine, though. *Rockin' Eighty-Eights* ♫♫♫ (Modern Blues, 1991, prod. Daniel Jacoubovitch) teams Johnson with two other St. Louis piano greats, Clayton Love, who played with Ike Turner in the 1950s, and Jimmy Vaughn, who played with Albert King, Little Milton Campbell and Ike Turner, among others. It's an interesting compendium of midwestern post-war blues styles. Of special note is Johnson's smoking take on "Frances," an instrumental track named for his wife.

the rest:

Blue Hand Johnnie ♫♫♫ (Pulsar, 1988/Evidence, 1993)
(With the Kentucky Headhunters) *That'll Work* ♫♫♫ (Elektra Nonesuch American Explorer Series, 1993)

influences:

◀◀ Earl "Fatha" Hines, Count Basie, Bud Powell

▶▶ Ian McLagen, Ian Stewart, Long John Baldry

Daniel Durchholz

Larry Johnson

Georgia-born Larry Johnson can truly be called a practitioner of the country blues guitar, not just an interpreter or recreator. Building on his studies with the Rev. Gary Davis, he developed a style he called "stride guitar," with the loping bass lines and ornate treble of the great stride pianists like Fats Waller.

what to buy: Johnson's rich voice and clean, speedy, melodic picking were captured beautifully on the recently re-released 1971 Blue Goose album *Fast and Funky* ♫♫♫♫ (Blue Goose, 1971/Baltimore Blues Society, 1996).

what to buy next: *Midnight Hour Blues* ♫♫♫♫ (Biograph, 1995) is another 1970s re-release. John Hammond sits in on harp and National steel guitar, though his embellishments are hardly necessary. Technically brilliant, but a bit less warm than *Fast and Funky*.

influences:

◀◀ Rev. Gary Davis, Fats Waller

Jennifer Zogott

Larry Johnson (© Jack Vartoogian)

Leslie Johnson

See: Lazy Lester

Lonnie Johnson

Born Alonzo Johnson, February 8, 1889, in New Orleans, LA. Died June 16, 1970, in Toronto, Ontario, Canada.

To credit Lonnie Johnson as "the originator of modern guitar blues" (which is, in fact, the title of one of his best CDs) is to inadvertently sell him short. Not only was Johnson one of the most accomplished bluesmen of his day, but he was also of monumental importance in the development of jazz. As early as 1927, when he recorded "6/88 Glide," he was already wowing audiences with his innovative bent notes and remarkable vibrato. Not surprisingly, by 1928 he was in great demand as a studio musician, laying down amazing solos while in the service of the likes of Louis Armstrong ("Hotter than That"), Duke Ellington ("The Mooch"), and the Chocolate Dandies ("Puducah"). His pioneering duets with Eddie Lang are especially revered by fans of early jazz guitar. Johnson's career met with hard times during the Depression. But in the 1940s, after nearly 20 years in and out of the music business, Johnson re-emerged to become, of all things, a pop commodity, racking up a string of hits for King, including "Pleasing You," "So Tired" and the acoustic pop ballad, "Tomorrow Night." Meanwhile, he was setting the music world on its ear with his innovative experiments on the electric guitar, as evidenced by his 1948 recording of "I Know It's Love." In spite of his success, Johnson once again floundered throughout the 1950s, unable to keep in synch with changing musical trends. When he resurfaced in 1960, he cut a series of "rediscovery" recordings for Prestige-Bluesville, which were especially popular with young, white audiences and helped to secure his place on the folk/blues circuit, where he remained until his death in 1970.

what to buy: Johnson's early work is best represented on *Steppin' on the Blues* ♫♫♫♫ (Columbia/Legacy, 1991, prod. Lawrence Cohn), which features some outstanding guitar instrumentals, incendiary duets with Eddie Lang and a couple of double-entendre vocal duets with Victoria Spivey. A good sampling of his post-Depression Bluebird recordings are gathered on *He's a Jelly Roll Baker* ♫♫♫♫ (Bluebird, 1992, prod. Billy Altman), which presents Johnson in a relaxed, jazzy blues setting. *Me and My Crazy Self* ♫♫♫♫♫ (Charly, 1991, prod. Syd Nathan) showcases his pop-ish R&B repertoire, including the magnificent "You Can't Buy Love," "I Can't Sleep Anymore," "Nothing but Trouble," and "Friendless Blues." *The Originator of Modern Guitar Blues* ♫♫♫♫♫ (Blues Boy,

1980, prod. Per Notini) contains more of the same pop-blues and R&B, with fine accompaniment from Blind John Davis, Red Prysock and Todd Rhodes.

what to buy next: While his rediscovery recordings generally pale in comparison, *Blues and Ballads* ♫♫♫♫ (Original Blues Classics, 1960/Fantasy, 1990, prod. Chris Albertson) and *Blues, Ballads & Jumpin' Jazz* ♫♫♫♫ (Original Blues Classics, 1960/Fantasy 1994, prod. Chris Albertson) contain tunes from a 1960 session that paired Johnson with jazz guitar legend Elmer Snowden. For fans of up-tempo jazz, these are not to be missed.

what to avoid: Despite the title, the 1965 recordings on *Stompin' at the Penny* ♫♫ (Columbia/Legacy, 1990, prod. Lawrence Cohn) were *not* made at Toronto's Penny Farthing coffee house, but rather originate from a lackluster studio outing with the Metro Stompers, a Canadian Dixieland band. Johnson is kept in the background and does not even appear on much of the recording. For completists only.

best of the rest:

Blues by Lonnie Johnson ♫♫♫♫ (Original Blues Classics, 1960/Fantasy, 1992)
Losing Game ♫♫♫♫ (Original Blues Classics, 1960/Fantasy, 1991)
Idle Hours ♫♫♫ (Original Blues Classics, 1961/Fantasy 1992)
The Complete Folkways Recordings ♫♫♫♫ (Folkways, 1967/Smithsonian 1993)
Complete Recorded Works in Chronological Order 1925–32, Vols. 1–7 ♫♫♫♫ (Document, 1992)
Complete 1937–June 1947 Recordings in Chronological Order Vols. 1–3 ♫♫♫♫ (Document, 1992)

worth searching for: *Giants of Jazz: The Guitarists* (Time-Life, 1980, prod. Michael Brooks) collects some of Johnson's best moments as a jazz guitarist and provides the context needed to appreciate his inclusion in the pantheon of jazz giants. The accompanying booklet contains some terrific photos in addition to thumbnail biographical sketches of famed jazz guitar players.

influences:

◀◀ Punch Miller, New Orleans jazz

▶▶ Big Bill Broonzy, Robert Johnson, Charlie Christian, T-Bone Walker, Albert King, B.B. King, Lowell Fulson

D. Thomas Moon

Luther "Georgia Boy" Johnson

Born Lucius Johnson, August 30, 1934, in Davisboro, GA. Died March 18, 1976, in Boston, MA.

So many Luther Johnsons, so little time. This LJ, nicknamed "Georgia Boy" for his native state and "Snake Boy" for less obvious reasons, was a Muddy Waters Band guitarist and bassist in the late 1960s. After learning the guitar at a young age, he joined the Army and performed at officer clubs during the Korean War. Upon his return, he sang in gospel groups, moved to Chicago and collaborated frequently with pianist Otis Spann and guitarist Elmore James before joining Waters' band. He hired his own band in 1970, performing solo shows in Europe and recording for a French record label before he died.

what to buy: Johnson worked best as a role player, but his solo career contained frequent glimmers of talent and inspiration; he peaked with *Lonesome in My Bedroom* ♫♫♫ (Disques Black & Blue, 1976/Evidence, 1992), a pure Chicago electric blues album that features backing guitarists Lonnie Brooks and Hubert Sumlin and three bonus tracks on the Evidence version.

what to buy next: An unabashed tribute to Muddy Waters, *Get down to the Nitty Gritty* ♫♫♫ (New Rose, 1976) contains "Hoochie Coochie Man" and rocks reasonably hard despite horrible sound quality and overlong guitar solos.

the rest:
Come on Home ♫♫♪ (Douglas, 1969)
The Muddy Waters Blues Band ♫♫ (Douglas, 1970)
Born in Georgia ♫♫♫ (Disques Black & Blue, 1972)
On the Road Again ♫♫♫ (Disques Black & Blue, 1976)

influences:
◀◀ Muddy Waters, Elmore James, Buddy Guy, Otis Rush

▶▶ Son Seals, Eddy Clearwater, Stevie Ray Vaughan, Jonny Lang

Steve Knopper

Luther "Guitar Junior" Johnson
Born April 11, 1939, in Itta Bena, MS.

As the third and youngest of the unrelated bluesmen Luther Johnson, you'd think this LJ would have avoided confusion with the others and called himself "Sonny Boy Williamson" or something. A few years after Luther "Georgia Boy" Johnson left Muddy Waters Band in 1970, Luther "Guitar Junior" joined up for more than seven years. "I just naturally got that West Side style," he said in 1980 liner notes; like his inspirations Otis Rush and Magic Sam, Johnson developed a single-note-and-distorted-chord approach specific to certain parts of Chicago. In Mississippi he got his first guitar from his mother before moving to Chicago in 1955. After playing with Bobby Rush, Jimmy Dawkins, Willie Kent and many others, he cut his first single in 1972, then joined Waters' band. That connection gave him a credible solo career after the band broke up in 1980.

what to buy: *I Want to Groove with You* ♫♫♫ (Bullseye Blues/Rounder, 1990, prod. Ron Levy) was the first Johnson album to get the production right, showing off his Magic Sam obsession, charismatic slurred voice and excellent single-note solos.

what to buy next: Though Johnson moved to Boston, *Slammin' on the West Side* ♫♫♫ (Telarc, 1996, prod. Bob Basili) has a stylistically accurate title—founding Meters bassist George Porter Jr. adds an important funk to enliven all the guitar solos.

the rest:
Luther's Blues ♫♫♪ (Evidence, 1977)
Doin' the Sugar Too ♫♫♪ (Rooster Blues, 1984)
It's Good to Me ♫♫♪ (Bullseye Blues/Rounder, 1992)
Country Sugar Papa ♫♫♪ (Bullseye Blues/Rounder, 1994)

worth searching for: Johnson's four tracks on *Living Chicago Blues Vol. IV* ♫♫♫ (Alligator, 1980/1991, prod. various)—which includes Sam Cooke's "Somebody Have Mercy"—are textbook examples of the West Side style, electric 12-bar blues with lots of backing harmonica and chiming, fuzzy guitar solos.

influences:
◀◀ Magic Sam, Otis Rush, Muddy Waters, Little Milton

▶▶ Willie Kent, Son Seals, Stevie Ray Vaughan, Kenny Wayne Shepherd

Steve Knopper

Luther "Houserocker" Johnson
Born July 15, 1939, in Atlanta, GA.

Not to be confused with Luther "Georgia Boy" Johnson or Luther "Guitar Junior" Johnson, Atlanta native Luther "Houserocker" Johnson has been a fixture of that city's blues scene since the 1960s. Since 1984 Johnson has been a regular performer—probably the most popular—in the rotation of premier Atlanta blues venue Blind Willie's. Johnson is a vigorous, charismatic, affable live performer who anchors his show with 1950s and 1960s blues, rock 'n' roll and R&B and a "watch me play it with my teeth, y'all" shtick made possible by a decidedly snaggle-tooth smile.

what to buy: Johnson recorded two albums on the Marietta, Georgia, Ichiban label in the early 1990s. The better of the two is *Takin' a Bite Outta the Blues* ♫♫♫♫ (Ichiban, 1990, prod. Bryan Cole), which is highlighted by a take-your-time version of Willie Love's double entendre classic "Little Car Blues," Ray

Charles' "What'd I Say" and heaping helpings of Jimmy Reed (as well as two fine Johnson originals).

the rest:

Houserockin' Daddy 🎵🎵🎵 (Ichiban, 1991)

influences:

◀◀ Jimmy Reed, Charles Brown, Wilson Pickett, B.B. King, Chuck Berry

▶▶ Shadows

Bryan Powell

Pete Johnson

Born Peter Johnson, 1904, in Kansas City, MO. Died May 23, 1967, in Buffalo, NY.

Considered one of the most brilliant boogie-woogie players of all time, Pete Johnson started his career as a drummer. He had a small band that played at the Sunset Crystal Palace on Kansas City's 12th Street, where a powerfully built bartender named Joe Turner worked. The two became friends and made a sensational team with Turner's booming vocals supported by Johnson's rolling piano. The duo was invited to New York to play on Benny Goodman's radio show. Johnson returned that same year to play John Hammond's From Spirituals to Swing concert at Carnegie Hall. The Carnegie appearance helped him break into New York's cafe society, where he played alongside Albert Ammons and Meade Lux Lewis. This brought popularity that stretched well beyond the realm of jazz and created a craze for boogie-woogie. Johnson and Turner reunited, playing and recording on the West Coast between 1947 and 1950. By the mid-1950s, the boogie-woogie craze had ended, and Johnson settled in Buffalo where he led a small group. In 1958 he toured Europe and appeared at the Newport Jazz Festival, but a stroke that year cut short his comeback and he never was able to play again.

what to buy: *Joe Turner with Pete Johnson's Orchestra* 🎵🎵🎵🎵 (Arhoolie, 1990, prod. Chris Strachwitz) features Turner's booming voice and some mind-boggling two-fisted piano from Johnson. *Pete's Blues* 🎵🎵🎵🎵 (Savoy) contains more of Johnson's pounding rhythm and a churning right hand.

what to buy next: Consisting of Apollo material, *Central Avenue Boogie* 🎵🎵🎵 (Delmark, 1992, prod. Robert Koester, Steve Wagner) is a mite short, and there are a lot of retakes. *Vol. 1, the Boogie Woogie Trio* 🎵🎵🎵 (Storyville, 1990) and *Boogie Woogie Boys, 1938–44* 🎵🎵🎵 (Magpie, 1992, prod. Bruce

Bastin) finds Johnson in the company of the two other boogie-woogie masters, Lewis and Ammons.

influences:

◀◀ Udell Wilson, Nero Edgar, Stacey La Guardia, Good Booty Johnson, Slam Foot Brown, Charles Johnson

▶▶ Saunders King, Crown Prince Waterford, Albert Ammons, Sammy Price, Meade Lux Lewis, Fats Domino, Roosevelt Sykes, Paul Gayten, Charles "Cow Cow" Davenport

Jeff Hannusch

Robert Johnson

Born May 8, 1911, in Hazlehurst, MS. Died August 16, 1938, in Greenwood, MS.

More has been made about the 29 songs Robert Johnson recorded during three sessions 60 years ago than any other blues music, or almost any other music, for that matter. That thin, smoldering sheaf of songs, his edgy, high moaning voice, cryptic life and the unusual circumstances of his death (apparently poisoned by a jealous husband at a country roadhouse gig), compounded by rumours of Johnson's pact with the devil, have made him much larger than whatever he could have become on his own. Despite the deluge of hype over the last few years, really listening to *King of the Delta Blues Singers* is still the next scariest thing to spending the night alone at a crossroads in Coahoma County under a full moon. The ironies have proliferated: one of the youngest of a generation of Delta acoustic bluesmen, Johnson was nearly an anachronism by the time he was recorded (although who knows what he could have done with electricity coursing through his guitar?); producer John Hammond came looking for Johnson for his From Spirituals to Swing black revue—several months after his death; he didn't make the *Billboard* charts until a half century after he died; though no one is sure where he's buried, at least two cemeteries have markers for him. Except for those fortunate enough to buy the few 78s distributed during his lifetime and a ever-growing list of tape collectors, Johnson's music was pretty much unavailable until more than 20 years after his death. Research has lifted some of the clouds from his life just as it seemingly has obscured others. But beyond the myth, it's those existential songs—"Hellhound on My Trail," "Stones in My Passway," "Love in Vain," "32-20 Blues"—and that tightly strung, slightly scared, tormented voice—all frozen in time—that burn right through the decades and the scratches, pointing the way to the future. Recent advances in studio technology have attempted to make those scratchy recordings more clear. But no matter how remastered a version of "Hellhound on My

Trail" you wind up with, you'll still have to squint a little to see that big devil dog in the shadows behind paranoid Bob's hunched back.

what to buy: There is no let-up on _King of the Delta Blues Singers_ ✍✍✍✍ (Columbia, 1961, prod. Don Law, Frank Driggs), which introduced Johnson to the world at large, heavily influencing a generation of superstars, including Keith Richards and Eric Clapton. Johnson sometimes sounds like a band, and the connection between his voice and guitar is complete—they sound like one instrument. (There's even a gold disc version of this one available.) And it's an album, not a greatest-hits collection. If you're interested in hearing the full sessions in chronological order, pick up _Robert Johnson: The Complete Recordings_ ✍✍✍✍ (Columbia, 1990, prod. Don Law, Frank Driggs, Stephen LaVere), the two-disc set which landed old Bob in the pop charts and on _Entertainment Tonight._

what to avoid: For some inexplicable reason, there's a "new" compilation, _Robert Johnson: King of the Delta_ ✍✍✍ (Columbia/Legacy, 1997), which, since all tracks have been released before—most of them twice—there is no reason to own.

the rest:

King of the Delta Blues Singers Vol. 2 ✍✍✍✍ (Columbia, 1970)

worth searching for: For more on Johnson's life, we heartily recommend _Deep Blues_ (Viking, 1981), Robert Palmer's groundbreaking book that makes the connection between the acoustic Delta blues of Johnson and the electric version that Muddy Waters conceived in Chicago. Also worth watching is _The Search for Robert Johnson_ (Sony Video, 1992), with narrater John Hammond traveling the Delta in a convertible, stopping to talk to historians and scholars, former Johnson girlfriends and contemporaries (including Honeyboy Edwards, who was there the night Johnson was poisoned). On the flip side, except for a short, sepia-toned opening segment, steer way clear of Walter Hill's totally inept 1986 film, _Crossroads_, which stars Ralph Macchio as a blues kid who winds up in a guitar "duel" with a heavy-metal devil played by Steve Vai. Really!

influences:

◀◀ Lonnie Johnson, Tommy Johnson, Charley Patton, Willie Brown, Son House

▶▶ Muddy Waters, Eric Clapton, Keith Richards, Robert Junior Lockwood

Leland Rucker

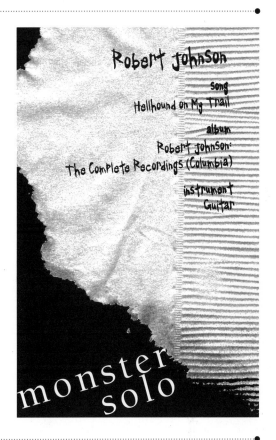

Robert Johnson
song
Hellhound on My Trail
album
Robert Johnson: The Complete Recordings (Columbia)
instrument
Guitar

monster solo

Syl Johnson

Born Sylvester Thompson, July 1, 1936, in Holly Springs, MS.

The versatile Syl Johnson has enjoyed a career which has spanned nearly four decades and several styles of music. He started out in the late 1950s, playing guitar with Magic Sam, Eddie Boyd, Jimmy Reed, Junior Wells and Billy Boy Arnold. He was signed by King Records in 1959 but his six singles were quite uninspiring R&B. Johnson didn't hit paydirt until he cut the punchy "Come on Sock It to Me," which came out on Twinight in 1967. He followed with a string of Windy City soul classics like "Different Strokes," "Dresses Too Short" and "Concrete Reservation." However, Johnson's most successful period—1971 to 1975—was when he recorded for the Memphis-based Hi label and was produced by Willie Mitchell. Johnson made three great albums for Hi—_Back for a Taste of Your Love_ (1973), _Diamond in the Rough_ (1974) and _Total Explosion_ (1975)—which included several great singles, including his version of Al Green's "Take

Me to the River." After Hi was sold, Johnson started his own label, Shamma, and had local hits with "Goodie Goodie Good Times" and the inventive 1982 single, "Ms. Fine Brown Frame," which married rap to the blues. In the late 1980s, Johnson stepped back from the music business briefly but got his creative juices flowing again when he heard rappers sampling his old hits. By the mid-1990s he was performing and recording again, often with his daughter Syleena in tow.

what to buy: Collecting 22 tracks, *The Best of Hi* 𝒜𝒜𝒜𝒜 (Demon, 1996, prod. Willie Mitchell) is a potent blend of Johnson's melodic soul. *Music to My Ears—The A-Sides* 𝒜𝒜𝒜 (Demon, 1995) also offers Johnson's great Hi material, some of which didn't make it to LP. *Twilight & Twinight—Masters Collection* 𝒜𝒜𝒜 (Collectables, 1995) is a solid collection of Johnson's harder soul material from the late 1960s and includes several hits. On *Back in the Game* 𝒜𝒜𝒜 (Delmark, 1994, prod. Pete Nathan), Johnson fronts the Hi rhythm section. While they sound great together, the spark of the original Hi sides isn't achieved.

what to buy next: All the Hi LPs have been reissued on CD, but if you've got *The Best of Hi*, they are unnecessary. *This Time Together* 𝒜𝒜𝒜 (Twinight, 1995) pairs Johnson with his daughter. Her material and the duets don't do much, but the CD is filled out with some of Johnson's great Shamma material.

what to avoid: The one poor Johnson CD is *Uptown Shakedown* 𝒜𝒜 (Demon, 1995, prod. Syl Johnson), which Johnson himself produced before leaving Hi.

worth searching for: P-Vine released the LP *Goodie, Goodie Good Times* 𝒜𝒜𝒜 (P-Vine, 1979), which included unreleased Shamma and Twinight material. The original Twinight LP and the Hi LPs are a nice addition to any soul/blues record collection.

influences:

◀◀ Jimmy Johnson, Matt Murphy, Al Green

▶▶ Magic Sam, Luther Allison, Tyrone Davis

Jeff Hannusch

Tommy Johnson

Born c. 1896, in Terry, MS. Died November 1, 1956, in Crystal Springs, MS.

Tommy Johnson was a powerful singer and inventive guitarist. A contemporary of Charley Patton, Son House and Ishmon Bracey—the seminal figures of early Mississippi blues—his

recorded output consists of 17 songs recorded between 1928 and 1929 for Victor and Paramount, hardly in itself an appropriate legacy for such an important and influential musician. Fortunately, the legacy has been bolstered significantly by the enduring blues standards he penned; his "Canned Heat Blues" supplied Bob Hite and Al Wilson a name for their pioneering blues-rock band, and other Johnson songs have been covered by Howlin' Wolf, Houston Stackhouse, Robert Nighthawk and Floyd Jones.

what to buy: The obvious choice is *Tommy Johnson Complete Recorded Works in Chronological Order 1928–29* 𝒜𝒜𝒜𝒜 (Document, 1994, prod. Johnny Parth), which gives you everything.

what to buy next: If you're still dabbling in early blues and aren't ready to go the completist route with the Document disc, you'll be pleased to know that there are a number of good compilation discs out there with samplings of Johnson's recordings. Two worth mentioning are *Masters of the Delta Blues: The Friends of Charley Patton* 𝒜𝒜𝒜𝒜 (Yazoo), with five Tommy Johnson songs, plus others by Son House, Kid Bailey, Ishmon Bracey, Bukka White, Louise Johnson and Bertha Lee, and *Canned Heat Blues: Masters of the Delta Blues* 𝒜𝒜𝒜𝒜 (RCA/Bluebird, 1992), with seven from Johnson, eight from Furry Lewis and six from Ishmon Bracey and a great introduction to these three important artists.

influences:

▶▶ Howlin' Wolf, Houston Stackhouse, Robert Nighthawk, Floyd Jones, Canned Heat

Rob Hutten

Casey Jones

Born July 26, 1939, in Nitta Yuma, MS.

You never know when you're going to come across one of the best living blues back-up musicians by random chance in Chicago. Jones, a wonderful, time-keeping drummer who has performed regularly at the Kingston Mines nightclub for more than a decade, honed his style with prominent session work (behind Earl Hooker and Muddy Waters, among others) in the 1960s and with Albert Collins' Icebreakers beginning in 1978. His rhythm is so steady it swings, much like a jazz player or the Rolling Stones' Charlie Watts. The classically named Jones is less effective as a singer, however, even though being a frontman is the easiest way to get along in the blues world.

what to buy: *(I-94) On My Way to Chicago* 𝒜𝒜𝒜 (Airwax, 1995) grabs you as soon as you start paying close attention to the drumming; it's rarely flashy, but it drives the music as insistently as the great drummer Sam Carr.

the rest:

Crowd Pleaser 𝄢𝄢𝄢 (Airwax, 1993)

worth searching for: The out-of-print *Solid Blue* 𝄢𝄢𝄢 (Rooster Blues, 1988) includes harpist Billy Branch and guitarist Maurice Vaughn and relies on Jones' steady rhythm and original songs (such as "Hip Hip Hooray" and "Mr. Blues").

influences:

◀◀ Sam Carr, Rolling Stones, Muddy Waters, Little Milton, Otis Rush, Son Seals

▶▶ Willie Kent, Billy Branch

Steve Knopper

Curtis Jones

Born August 18, 1906, in Naples, TX. Died September 11, 1971, in Munich, Germany.

Author of one classic 1930s blues song, the piano-based "Lonesome Bedroom Blues," Curtis Jones effectively had two careers. The first came after he moved to Chicago, when the song about a breakup with his wife became a 1937 hit for the Vocalion label; the second after years of on-and-off (mostly off) recording, when he walked into a studio in 1960 to record his first album, *Trouble Blues*. He took advantage of the 1960s blues revival, becoming a popular festival performer, then moved to Germany in 1962 and continued to tour Europe until he died. His largely unknown singles touched blues performers who were carefully paying attention, such as Jimmy McCracklin, but he managed to reach a wide swath of the blues audience through his late-career touring.

what to buy: Jones makes a case for including his name among the blues piano greats—Otis Spann, Floyd Dixon, Jimmy Yancey and, of course, Ray Charles—on *Trouble Blues* 𝄢𝄢𝄢𝄢 (Original Blues Classics, 1960/Prestige, 1993, prod. Rudy Van Gelder), which opens with "Lonesome Bedroom Blues" and touches on Charles Brown-style cocktail jazz ("Please Say Yes") and down-and-dirty boogie (the bonus track "Pinetop Boogie").

what to buy next: *Lonesome Bedroom Blues* 𝄢𝄢𝄢 (Delmark, 1962, prod. Robert Koester) (which contains a great version of Jones' "Tin Pan Alley") and *Curtis Jones: 1937–40* 𝄢𝄢𝄢 (Document, 1995, prod. various), are excellent supplements to the essential *Trouble Blues*.

influences:

◀◀ Charles Brown, Jimmy Yancey, Walter Davis, Blind Lemon Jefferson

▶▶ Jimmy McCracklin, Dr. John, Sunnyland Slim, Pinetop Perkins

Steve Knopper

Eddie Lee Jones

Born March 1929, near Ephram, GA.

Nicknamed "Mustright," Eddie Lee Jones was discovered by accident and recorded by Bill Koon in Lexington, Georgia, in August 1965. His music represents a pre-blues form preserved by his isolation in a rural area and influenced by old Anglo-American fiddle pieces. His playing reflects also an atmosphere of conviviality: when Jones played, everyone in the neighborhood gathered around him and started a joyous party. His music is simple, happy and sincere, and a mutual affection between the player and his audience is perceptible.

what to buy: His only known album, *Yonder Go That Old Black Dog* 𝄢𝄢𝄢𝄢 (Testament, 1974/1995, prod. Pete Welding) is a unique document of a past era, a mixture of pre-blues, archaic blues and spirituals. It offers Jones' complete output; this artist should have been recorded again.

Robert Sacré

Edward Jones

See: Guitar Slim

Floyd Jones

Born July 21, 1917, in Marianna, AR. Died December 19, 1989, in Chicago, IL.

Part of the mass exodus of bluesmen from the Mississippi Delta to Chicago in the 1940s, this moaning, downbeat guitarist was an important behind-the-scenes figure in creating the electric Chicago style. He grew up learning from Charley Patton (who worked with Jones' father), Tommy Johnson and other legendary Delta figures, then took his skills to Chicago, specifically the active Maxwell Street area, in 1945. There he hooked up with Sunnyland Slim and Little Walter, recording solo songs such as the spooky classic "Dark Road," but more frequently augmenting other people's sessions. Though he recorded briefly for both Chess and Vee-Jay and took up bass to become more marketable, he had to work most of his later years as a fork-lift operator and embark on other career paths to support his family. When he died of a heart attack, he left behind a tragically sparse catalog.

what to buy: One of the few documents of Jones' career, *Masters of Modern Blues* ♪♪♪♪ (Testament, 1994, prod. Pete Welding) includes "Dark Road," "Stockyard Blues" and other 1966 masterpieces of loneliness and frustration; pianist Otis Spann and harpist Big Walter Horton are among the sidemen, who also play on guitarist Eddie Taylor's sides on the same disc.

worth searching for: While Jones was an active sideman on the Chicago blues circuit, he recorded *Old Friends* ♪♪♪ (Earwig, 1979) with Sunnyland Slim, Horton and Honeyboy Edwards, among others.

influences:

◀◀ Muddy Waters, Eddie Taylor, Tommy Johnson, Charley Patton, Willie Dixon

▶▶ Willie Kent, Son Seals, Jimmy Reed, Buddy Guy, Etta James, Koko Taylor

Steve Knopper

Johnny Jones

See: Little Sonny Jones

Johnny Jones

Born November 1, 1924, in Jackson, MS. Died November 19, 1964, in Chicago, IL.

Every retrospective of this well-connected and hugely talented artist takes on a sad "if only . . ." tone. "Little Johnny" Jones, the piano-playing equal of Otis Spann (who was possibly his cousin), Floyd Dixon and Charles Brown, moved from Mississippi to Chicago in 1946 and almost immediately found work in the guitarist Tampa Red's band. (As a footnote, during the four years he played with Red, he also backed Muddy Waters and Howlin' Wolf on important blues singles.) What made him famous, though, was the octane he added to Elmore James' legendary band and classic 1950s singles; he had powerful fingers and could quickly bring a lackluster song to life. If he had lived, he could have been one of the most famous backup pianists in blues history; but he died far too young of lung cancer.

what to buy: There are a few essential boogie-woogie piano records, and the underheralded *Johnny Jones with Billy Boy Arnold* ♪♪♪♪ (Alligator, 1979, prod. Norman Dayron) is clearly one of them; recorded at Chicago's Fickle Pickle club in 1963,

Casey Jones (© Jack Vartoogian)

it's a terrific document of Jones' deceptively smooth piano style (backed sparsely by harpist Arnold). At first, on Lowell Fulson's straightforward two-fister "I Believe I'll Give It Up," Jones sounds too clunky, like he's trying to bash his way through the song, but when the rhythm clicks it's as smooth as anything Nat King Cole has ever done.

influences:

◀◀ Charles Brown, Jimmy Yancey, Otis Spann, Ray Charles, Professor Longhair

▶▶ Dr. John, Little Richard, Jerry Lee Lewis

Steve Knopper

Little "Sonny" Jones

Born Johnny Jones, April 15, 1931, in New Orleans, LA. Died December 17, 1989, in New Orleans, LA.

Jones was an engaging journeyman vocalist who got his start with the Fats Domino band in the early 1950s. He made isolated, but excellent, R&B singles on Imperial, Specialty and Chart but didn't do much commercially. Jones toured with Domino until 1961, when he started his own band with the Lastie Brothers. His only recording during the 1960s appeared as a single on Scram. Jones quit playing music in 1968, but the Danish label C.S.A. coaxed him out of retirement seven years later. The record helped him get hired at the New Orleans Jazz and Heritage Festival, where he appeared each year until his death.

what to buy: The Danish album has been reissued as *New Orleans Jems* ♪♪♪♪ (Black Top, 1975, prod. Lars Edegran). Truly a renaissance effort, it features brilliant accompaniment by Clarence Ford, Justin Adams, Fatman Williams, David Lastie and Frank Fields, among others.

worth searching for: Watch for Jones' singles on a variety of vinyl and compact disc anthologies over the years.

influences:

◀◀ Fats Domino, Roscoe Gordon, Junior Parker, Big Joe Turner, Smiley Lewis, Guitar Slim

▶▶ Jessie Hill, Prince La La, Dr. John

Jeff Hannusch

Paul "Wine" Jones

Paul "Wine" Jones emerged out of nowhere with *Mule* ♪♪♪ (Fat Possum/Capricorn, 1995), a refreshingly raw slab of electrified country blues. Nothing about it, or him, is extraordinary or particularly important. It's just liquor-soaked roadhouse fun, with slurred vocals, raggedy-ass guitars and a relentless beat that moves with the straight-ahead kick of the titular animal. This is late-night, get-down Mississippi moonshine music. About 80 proof.

Alan Paul

Robert Lewis Jones

See: Guitar Gabriel

Ruth Lee Jones

See: Dinah Washington

Tutu Jones

Born John Jones Jr., September 9, 1966, in Dallas, TX.

To personify the phrase "grew up with the blues," use Tutu Jones. His dad was a South Dallas R&B guitarist, so throughout Tutu's life his family's house guests included Freddie King, Little Joe Blue and Ernie Johnson. Tutu was a pro drummer when still in his teens, playing dates behind Curly "Barefoot" Miller and L.C. Clark (both uncles) and soon graduated to gig with Z.Z. Hill, R.L. Griffin, Al "TNT" Braggs and other southwestern soul-circuit stalwarts. All the while he was honing his skill on guitar, and at the advice of Little Joe Blue started fronting bands of his own. Guitar-wise Tutu is Albert King mixed with Magic Sam. As singer and songwriter he's the sum of the myriad parts of the passionate Texas soul-blues styles he spent so many years providing the backbeat for.

what to buy: Too bad more products aren't labeled as accurately as *Blue Texas Soul* 🎵🎵🎵🎵 (Bullseye Blues, 1996, prod. Ron Levy). Scalding, straight-on blues team with Jones' own hard soul compositions for a well-rounded set steeped in regional textures. A hat-tip to producer Levy and the Memphis Horns.

what to buy next: *I'm for Real* 🎵🎵🎵 (JSP, 1994, prod. Tutu Jones) mixes tense, hardball blues with Tutu's trademark soul-blues (exemplified by his thrilling "Do You Love Steppin' on Me"), and has a sparseness that seems to spur Tutu's busy guitar work and fiery singing.

influences:

◀◀ Freddie King, Albert King, Z.Z. Hill

Tim Schuller

Janis Joplin /Big Brother & the Holding Company

Janis Joplin born January 19, 1943, in Port Arthur, TX. Died October 4, 1970, in Hollywood, CA.

Sam Andrew, vocals, guitar; James Gurley, guitars; Peter Albin, bass; David Getz, drums.

When Janis Joplin left the nurturing fold of Big Brother & the Holding Company, she turned into a commodity. Her early recordings with the San Francisco ballroom band capture a raw Joplin enmeshed in the passionate throes of an equally untamed band. Ambition was her true weapon of self-destruction, not the drugs and ill-fated romances. But she left behind a frustrating glimpse of something powerful enough to ignite her enduring legend. Joplin exploded all over the crowd at the historic 1967 Monterey Pop Festival; in a single show she established her reputation. At that very moment, she also sowed the seeds of eventual departure from her helpless communal colleagues in Big Brother. The very week their *Cheap Thrills* album hit #1, Joplin announced her intention to go solo to her unsurprised bandmates. As a solo artist, she was a disaster. Joplin made her debut performance after a mere two days rehearsal, headlining an authentic soul show to an indifferent audience at an annual Memphis black fundraiser. Her first band, the Kozmik Blues Band, never gelled, and although its successor, the Full Tilt Boogie Band, represented a substantial improvement, she didn't have time to build up a substantial enough body of work to support her looming posthumous stature. She was dead at age 28 before even finishing that final, second solo album.

what to buy: Even more than a quarter-century later, *Cheap Thrills* 🎵🎵🎵🎵 (Columbia, 1968, prod. John Simon) stills sounds nervy, rich and radical. The album rips along, high-voltage electricity charging every number, until it reaches its climax, "Ball and Chain," which Joplin turns into one of the high points of personal expression in rock history.

what to buy next: Although the band's debut album, *Big Brother & the Holding Company* 🎵🎵🎵🎵 (Mainstream, 1967, prod. Bob Shad) was a shoddy and hasty affair made in a few days, the record captured nevertheless the warm, sloppy atmosphere of the band and some precious Joplin vocals. And if you're enamored enough, find *Janis* 🎵🎵🎵🎵 (Columbia/Legacy, 1993, prod. Bob Irwin) for three discs filled with stuff you got, plus lots of outtakes, home recordings and other et cetera.

what to avoid: *I Got Dem Ol' Kozmic Blues Again Mama!* 🎸 (Columbia, 1970, prod. Gabriel Meckler) is a sprawling, awful mess of a pseudo-soul album that sounded forced and shrill at the time and has not held up well over the years.

the rest:

Pearl 🎸🎸🎸 (Columbia, 1971)
Joplin in Concert 🎸🎸🎸 (Columbia, 1972)
Farewell Song 🎸🎸🎸 (Columbia, 1982)
Janis Joplin 🎸🎸🎸 (Columbia, 1993)
18 Essential Songs 🎸🎸🎸🎸 (Columbia, 1995)

worth searching for: Big Brother drummer David Getz released a particularly raw early live performance of this unruly and exciting young band on an album, *Cheaper Thrills* 🎸🎸🎸 (Made to Last, 1982, prod. David Getz) that has been released on CD in England.

influences:

◀◀ Memphis Minnie, John Coltrane, Lightnin' Hopkins

▶▶ Melissa Etheridge, Mariah Carey

Joel Selvin

Charley Jordan

Born c. 1890, in Mabelville, AR. Died November 15, 1954, in St. Louis, MO.

The guitar-playing partner of well-known guitarist Peetie Wheatstraw, Jordan was a minor figure who persevered through personal hardship and changing musical trends. After a brief stint in the Army during World War I, he performed cheap for parties and clubs around the South. Then he moved to St. Louis and became a bootlegger but was shot in 1928 and lived with a resulting spine injury. In St. Louis, he hooked up with Wheatstraw, Roosevelt Sykes and Memphis Minnie, among others, and recorded for a few labels in the 1930s. Though he also worked as a label talent scout, and performed regularly with Big Joe Williams late in his career, Jordan was effectively washed up in the 1940s.

what to buy: Though the sound quality is wildly uneven, the collections *Charley Jordan Vol. 1, 1930–31* 🎸🎸🎸 (Document), *Charley Jordan Vol. 2, 1931–34* 🎸🎸🎸 (Document) and *Charlie Jordan Vol. 3, 1935–37* 🎸🎸🎸 (Document) capture Jordan's excellent singing and guitar-playing skills on 1930s recordings.

influences:

◀◀ Peetie Wheatstraw, Big Joe Williams, Robert Johnson, Son House, Charley Patton

▶▶ Muddy Waters, Curley Weaver, Tampa Red, Otis Rush, Buddy Guy

Steve Knopper

Louis Jordan

Born July 8, 1908, in Brinkley, AR. Died February 4, 1975, in Los Angeles, CA.

Countless blues and R&B pioneers have been offered up as fathers (and, on the distaff side, mothers) of rock 'n' roll. Louis Jordan, the inventor of jump blues, may have had the strongest case of all. Jordan's unparalleled success as the first major star of the fledgling urban rhythm and blues movement during the war years showed the way for tougher acts like Wynonie Harris and Roy Brown. Early R&B's direct bloodline to rock is reason enough to give Jordan the nod, but he had even more direct influence. Jordan's sly wit and unerring satirical digs at the foibles of American life were reborn in the speeded-up, blues- and hillbilly-drenched inventions of Chuck Berry—inspiration that even the proud Berry is quick to admit. And Jordan was equally important in the development of Ray Charles, one of the key architects of soul music. Jordan owned the R&B charts for nearly a decade, through the lean years of World War II and up until the dawn of the rock era. A half-century after his glory years, Jordan's 54 Top 10 R&B hits still rank second only to James Brown's 57.

Like Joe Turner and other peers in early R&B, Jordan got his start in the big-band era. An alto sax player in the early 1930s with the Charlie Gaines Orchestra, Jordan gained renown as a blower and vocalist with Chick Webb, who commanded New York's Savoy Ballroom. Jordan sometimes dueted with Webb's other powerhouse vocalist, Ella Fitzgerald, but as her star rose, Jordan's role diminished. Dissatisfied, he took off with a small band. Between 1938 and 1941, Jordan scuffled, but in 1941 he struck gold with his own "Knock Me a Kiss" and a strong version of Big Bill Broonzy's "I'm Gonna Move to the Outskirts of Town." Suddenly, the hits seemed to come by the month. The topical war songs "G.I. Jive" and "Ration Blues" hit big, but peace did nothing to tame Jordan's chart assault. "Caldonia," "Buzz Me," "Choo Choo Ch'Boogie," "Run Joe," "Jack, You're Dead" and "Saturday Night Fish Fry" all reached #1. Jordan's range was encyclopedic; he was as much the experimenter in the R&B field as Charlie Parker and Dizzy Gillespie were in bop, absorbing Latin and Caribbean rhythms. Jordan's natural clowning found him roles on more than a dozen "soundies," short musical films that were the direct ancestors of today's MTV videos; his barbed wit could skewer American social inanities as savagely as W.C. Fields' films. In Jordan's 219 Decca recordings between 1938 and 1954, railroad bums, pompous politicians, battling newlyweds, marriage-obsessed spinsters and dim-witted partiers all got their comeuppance. Bigoted whites were carefully needled, but black society, too, was lovingly ribbed. Jordan's career seemed unending, but he failed to adapt to R&B's toughened beat in the early 1950s. Jordan and his sound were simply too old for the rock 'n' roll era. After false starts for Aladdin and RCA, Jordan lived off his royalties and played clubs in the Los Angeles area in his final years, returning for several nostalgic albums before he died of a heart attack in 1975.

what to buy: Cash in your stocks. Pawn your toaster. Sell your Wang Chung albums. Hire out as a soldier of fortune. Do whatever it takes to buy *Let the Good Times Roll* ♫♫♫♫♫ (Bear Family, 1992, prod. Richard Weize), an eight-disc Jordania treasury containing every one of his Decca sides. The sound of these original Milt Gabler and Mayo Williams sessions is impeccable for that era, par for the course for the German label. A history-laden booklet pulses with obscure photos and facts, including Jordan's stabbing by an avenging mistress. Get it. Before the Jordan explosion of the late 1980s and early 1990s, *The Best of Louis Jordan* ♫♫♫♫♫ (MCA, 1989, prod. Milt Gabler, Mayo Williams) was the only collection out there. It's still the best place for Jordan novices to start—crammed with undying offerings like "Caldonia," "Don't Let the Sun Catch You Crying" and "Ain't Nobody Here but Us Chickens."

what to buy next: *5 Guys Named Moe* ♫♫♫♫ (MCA, 1992) is as entertaining as MCA's first volume of hits, only strewn with Jordan's second-tier classics; a list that includes "Jack, You're Dead" and "Is You Is or Is You Ain't My Baby?" ain't chicken feed. Not to be mistaken for the MCA hits sequel, *Five Guys Named Moe* ♫♫♫♫ (Vintage Jazz Classics, 1991) is worth getting in its own right. Jordan was a mainstay of 1940s radio, and there are apparently dozens of transcriptions out there. This VJC collection has 27 up-tempo jumpers and plenty of rarities, the most startling being Jordan's "Ofay and Oxford Grey," a less-than-subtle meditation on race relations that somehow sneaked derogatory black slang for "white people" onto the airwaves. *Live Jive* ♫♫♫♫ (A Touch of Magic, 1989) offers more Jordan radio transcriptions, as clean-sounding as VJC's and with no duplication.

what to avoid: *One Guy Named Louis: The Complete Aladdin Sessions* ♫♫ (Blue Note, 1992) should have worked. Even though Jordan was past his prime, Aladdin was adept at pump-

ing out great R&B. Instead, these 21 cuts are dated. And watch for the muffled-sounding *Louis Jordan 1934-43* ♫♫♫ (Classics, 1993), an alternative to the Bear Family completist approach; where Jordan's occasional clinkers are overwhelmed by his vast repertoire on the former, they stick out on these individual four CDs.

the rest:
Rock 'n' Roll Call ♫♫♫ (RCA/Bluebird, 1955/1993)
At the Cat's Ball—The Early Years (1937–39) ♫♫♫♫ (JSP, 1991)
Louis Jordan & Chris Barber ♫♫♫ (Black Lion, 1991)
I Believe in Music ♫♫♫ (Evidence, 1992)
Just Say Moe! Mo' Best of Louis ♫♫♫ (Rhino, 1992)
No Moe: Louis Jordan's Greatest Hits ♫♫♫ (Verve, 1992)
Elks Rendezvous Band and Tympany Five ♫♫♫ (Affinity, 1994)
On Film 1942 ♫♫♫ (Krazy Kat, 1996)

worth searching for: Jordan appears with Woody Herman, Stan Kenton, Dinah Washington, Jo Stafford and Charlie Barnet on *The Swingin' Singin' Years* ♫♫♫ (Vintage Jazz Classics, 1992), which contains footage from a 1960 show hosted by Ronald Reagan.

influences:

◄◄ Louis Armstrong, Cab Calloway

►► Wynonie Harris, Roy Brown, B.B. King, Chuck Berry, Ray Charles

Steve Braun

Pleasant "Cousin Joe" Joseph

Born December 20, 1907, in Wallace, LA. Death date unknown.

New Orleans vocalist and composer Pleasant Joseph appeared on record under several names—Smilin' Joe, Joseph Pleasant, Brother Joshua, even Pleasant Joseph—but it was as Cousin Joe that he made his mark on the music world of the mid-1940s. Cousin Joe was a popular New Orleans nightclub attraction by the mid-1930s and moved to New York City in 1942, where he recorded a string of 78 rpm singles before returning to New Orleans in 1947. He cut with Paul Gayten for DeLuxe and Dave Bartholomew for Imperial and signed a five-year contract with Decca. Joseph then saw his career as a recording artist eclipsed for many years while he learned the piano and kept working clubs and nightspots in New Orleans as a solo performer and re-surfacing on record from time to time.

what to buy: The contribution to the music made by Cousin Joe can be examined in unprecedented depth on *Pleasant Joseph: The Complete Recordings, 1945–47* ♫♫♫♫ (Blue Moon, 1995, prod. Mezz Mezzrow, Leonard Feather, Teddy Reig, Earl Bostic,

Paul Gayten). Cousin Joe straddled the thin line between blues and jazz, shouting and singing his imaginative, frequently bawdy lyrics to the accompaniment of jazz greats like Sidney Bechet, Al Sears, Earl Bostic, Hot Lips Page and Dickie Wells. Gathered here are long-lost classics like "Post War Future Blues," "Desperate G.I. Blues," "You Ain't So Such a Much," "Lightning Struck the Poorhouse" and the original "Box Car Shorty and Peter Blue." After a painfully long recording drought, Cousin Joe was finally captured on tape at an impromptu late 1971 French session now available as *Bad Luck Blues* (Disques Black and Blue, 1971/Evidence, 1994, prod. Jacques Morgantini). Joe's undeservedly obscure masterworks like "Life Is a One-Way Ticket," "I'm Living on Borrowed Time," "Bad Luck Blues" and "Boxcar Shorty" are treated to spirited performances, and his genius, humor, warmth and strength of character are beautifully showcased.

worth searching for: Anything you can find by Cousin Joe. You might look for an album that's not yet on disc, *Cousin Joe from New Orleans* ♪♪♪♪ (ABC-Bluesway, 1973, prod. Al Smith), recorded in New Orleans. Be sure to check out his autobiography, written with Harriet J. Ottenheimer, *Cousin Joe: Blues from New Orleans* (University of Chicago Press, 1987), which remains a classic of the genre.

influences:

◀◀ Jelly Roll Morton, Clarence Williams

▶▶ Professor Longhair, Paul Gayten, Edward Frank, Fats Domino, Allen Toussaint, Dr. John

John Sinclair

Candye Kane

Born in Los Angeles, CA.

Bad girls and the blues have gone together since the time of Ma Rainey, and so it is today with Candye Kane, a former stripper who's not ashamed of her past and whose, um, assets should afford her a worthwhile future. Vocally, Kane is a belter, which suits her predominately bluesy style, but she can take it sweet and soft for one of her folkier numbers or add some Patsy Cline twang for some country honk—she's extremely versatile, even if her voice isn't the first thing you notice about her.

She's also a songwriter of note, whose work often carries a none-too-subtle political or social commentary. Kane is an outspoken supporter of feminist issues and organizations from NOW to COYOTE. But the music still comes first: she's anything but a one-dimensional performer.

what to buy: "Play to your strengths" is advice artists don't take nearly enough. On *Diva la Grande* ♪♪♪ (Antone's/Discovery, 1997, prod. Dave Alvin, Derek O'Brien, Candye Kane) Kane embraces her role as a blues-belting hefty mama intent on shaking her moneymaker, consequences be damned. Randy and raucous, Kane is sexy and assertive on the originals "You Need a Great Big Woman," "The Lord Was a Woman," and "All You Can Eat (and You Can Eat It All Night Long)." There's also a spicy Cajun-flavored version of Nancy Sinatra's hit "These Boots Are Made for Walkin'."

the rest:

Home Cookin' ♪♪♪♪ (Antone's, 1994)
Knockout ♪♪♪ (Antone's, 1995)

influences:

◀◀ Big Mama Thornton, Patsy Cline, Mae West

Daniel Durchholz

William David Kearney

See: Guitar Shorty

Jack Kelly

Birth date unknown. Died 1960, in Memphis, TN.

Jack Kelly and violinist Will Batts led the South Memphis Jug Band, one of the most blues-inflected of the string bands that were popular in the city's parks and bars from the early 1900s until the 1950s. Kelly was the band's lead vocalist and guitarist, able to draw on a deep reservoir of minstrel tunes, rags, vaudeville numbers, reels and blues sketches. His hoarse medicine show shout kept the band going in various incarnations as late as the mid-1950s. Touring through Mississippi, Arkansas and Indiana, the band was known for its signature tune, "Highway #61 Blues."

what to buy: Batt's violin and Kelly's rhythmic guitar lead the way through 10 out of the band's 14 performances from 1933 and 1939 on *The Sounds of Memphis* ♪♪♪♪ (Story of Blues, 1987, prod. Johnny Parth), along with some odd numbers by Little Buddy Doyle, a street-singing dwarf, and Tennessee musician Charlie Pickett.

influences:

◀◀ Jim Jackson

▶▶ Martin, Bogan and Armstrong, Jim Kweskin Jug Band

Steve Braun

Vance Kelly

Born January 24, 1954, in Chicago, IL.

Until 1992 ace guitarist and human juke box Vance Kelly was one of the best-kept of Chicago blues secrets. Kelly, then only 39 years old, had been playing South Side clubs as a solo artist and with A.C. Reed and Little Johnny Christian for almost 25 years. Still, no record company had bothered to make him a priority. Then, along came Wolf. Kelly builds his guitar sound on what he calls "riffling." Melting from his strings are bright, shimmering runs that ride over the solid funk of his band. Kelly served in Reed's Sparkplugs from 1987–90 and learned his "lumps" style of blues from that master of the form. His supple voice and versatility as a guitarist make him sound as good interpreting a Johnnie Taylor classic as he does remaking Magic Sam's "All Your Love." Kelly is a young blues man to watch.

what to buy: Wolf rushed Kelly and his Backstreet Blues Band into the studio for his debut, *Call Me* ✍✍✍✍ (Wolf, 1994, prod. Vance Kelly), and came away with a release good enough to warrant the *Living Blues* award for Best New Recording. Kelly does it all, full of fresh songs and ideas—funk, soul, traditional Chicago blues—and he delivers his energetic and creative musical mix with a confidence usually reserved for studio veterans. *Joyriding on the Subway* ✍✍✍✍✍ (Wolf, 1995, prod. Vance Kelly, John Primer) is equally varied and more impressive. With a better mix, Kelly's guitar and more adventuresome vocals can be fully heard and enjoyed, and it's a treat to finally hear the soulful keyboards of Erskine Johnson, whose sympathetic accompaniment was lost in the mix of *Call Me*.

worth searching for: Kelly can be heard providing backing guitar on portions of Lovie Lee's *Good Candy* ✍✍✍✍ (Earwig, 1994, prod. Eddie "Lovie" Lee Watson, Michael Frank).

influences:

◀◀ Buddy Scott, Mary Lane, Little Johnny Christian, A.C. Reed, B.B. King, Muddy Waters

▶▶ Tre

Steven Sharp

Willie Kent

Born February 24, 1936, in Inverness, MS.

This singer-bassist has been one of Chicago's most reliable performers—first as a backup bassist, then as a solo performer—since he moved from his home town in 1950. He started playing bass as a $250 one-night replacement for a band's drunken bassist and was soon playing with literally everybody in town at Chicago's thriving nightclubs. He became an in-demand touring musician, too, with Junior Parker and, on fill-in dates, Muddy Waters and Howlin' Wolf. Kent's recording career has been spotty, beginning with European releases in the late 1970s, and finally gaining steam with Delmark beginning in 1991. He's a solid singer and bassist and continues to sell out regular shows on the Chicago blues circuit with his band, the Gents.

what to buy: Obviously a bassist's album, *Ain't It Nice* ✍✍✍ (Delmark, 1991, prod. Robert Koester, Steve Wagner) is more notable for its tough, swinging funk rhythm than Kent's unremarkable voice; still, there's a friendliness to everything, especially the romping "What You're Doing to Me" and "Ma Bea's."

what to buy next: *Long Way to Ol' Miss* ✍✍✍ (Delmark, 1996, prod. Robert Koester) has an even more pronounced funk, especially on the title track and "Extension 309." Best of all, the central concept is soul power, not flashy solos.

the rest:

Too Hurt to Cry ✍✍ (Delmark, 1994)

worth searching for: A blues singer hasn't arrived until one of his Chicago concerts winds up on a CD released by an Austrian company; *Live at B.L.U.E.S.* ✍✍✍ (Wolf, 1994, prod. Willie Kent, Hannes Folterbauer) has an excellent song selection, including Kent's "All My Life," Little Milton's "Tin Pan Alley," Lowell Fulson's "Black Night" and Magic Sam's "Looking Good."

influences:

◀◀ B.B. King, Albert King, Lowell Fulson, Wilson Pickett, Robert Nighthawk, Otis Clay

▶▶ Billy Branch, Eddy Clearwater

Steve Knopper

Junior Kimbrough

Born David Kimbrough, July 28, 1930, in Hudsonville, MS.

Music as singular and intense as Junior Kimbrough's may be bound to pick up devotees and force its way out to a broader audience. Yet few outside of Mississippi had heard of Kimbrough before critic Robert Palmer's film *Deep Blues* and its parallel soundtrack exposed the insular contemporary hill country blues scene of rural northern Mississippi, and Fat Possum, a label Palmer has been heavily involved with, documented this scene on compact disc. Marshall County, where Kimbrough and other musicians such as R.L. Burnside and Jessie Mae Hemphill resided, became isolated when the railroads contracted, making the wide-ranging travel that characterized Mississippi musicians in the 1920s and 1930s less easy. Though radio and cars have loosened that isolation somewhat, the scene continues in a highly distinctive vein, unlike the more formulaic and standardized blues styles.

Kimbrough grew up not far from the Tennessee state line and was playing at house parties when his age was still in the single digits. For more than 30 years he's owned and run juke joints (most recently just outside Holly Springs) that have been a focal point of the scene. Rockabilly legend Charlie Feathers, in the liner notes of *Deep Blues*, calls Kimbrough "the beginning and the end of music," which conveys a sense of the primal materials and urgency of Kimbrough's style, a droning, spontaneous flow of simple patterns ornamented and varied with rhythmic subtlety. Kimbrough's music can easily be accused of "all sounding the same," but its trance-like power is considerable nonetheless. It's made for live performance, stretched out and aimed at juke-joint dancers. Before Palmer came along, Kimbrough had recorded a grand total of five songs: the 45 singles "Tramp"/"You Can't Leave Me" for Philwood in 1968 and the later "Keep Your Hands Off Her"/"Good Little Girl" for High Water, and one track on a Southland Records anthology. Since then, he's made three albums for Fat Possum, and if they tend to be similar overall, on a song-to-song basis he changes his style and settings enough to keep them far from monotony. With bass and drums accompaniment, his music becomes insistent and driving; when he plays alone, his style becomes freer and more ornamented. Kimbrough's sons, Kenny Malone (drums) and David Malone (vocals/guitar), are also blues musicians; Kenny plays in R.L. Burnside's group, and David has also recorded for Fat Possum.

what to buy: *Sad Days, Lonely Nights* ♪♪♪♪ (Fat Possum/Capricorn, 1994, prod. Robert Palmer) is the best way for new listeners to approach Kimbrough's music, as it contains covers of "Crawling King Snake" and "Old Black Mattie," both obviously indicative of his early influences.

what to buy next: *All Night Long* ♪♪♪♪ (Fat Possum/Capricorn, 1995, prod. Robert Palmer) is a family affair, with Kenny Malone on drums and R.L. Burnside's son, Garry Burnside, on bass. Its loose structures capture the hypnotic feeling of a juke joint gig.

the rest:

Most Things Haven't Worked Out ♪♪♪ (Fat Possum/Capricorn, 1997)

worth searching for: *National Downhome Blues Festival, Vol. 2* ♪♪♪ (Southland, 1986) contains Kimbrough's "All Night Long" in a different recording than on the Fat Possum album of the same title. *Deep Blues* ♪♪♪♪ (Anxious/Atlantic, 1992, prod. Robert Palmer) includes the otherwise unreleased "Jr. Blues" amongst its many fine tracks.

influences:
◀◀ Mississippi Fred McDowell
▶▶ David Malone

Steve Holtje

Albert King

Born April 25, 1923, in Indianola, MS. Died December 21, 1992, in Memphis, TN.

Never as well-known as his like-named contemporary B.B., Albert King was nonetheless almost as big an influence. More rock guitarists, notably Jimi Hendrix, Cream-era Eric Clapton and Stevie Ray Vaughan, have copped directly from Albert more than any other bluesman. Standing an imposing 6 feet 5 inches and weighing in at 250 pounds, the left-handed, former bulldozer driver played with brute force, bending the strings on his upside-down Gibson Flying V with a ferocity that could be downright frightening. King made his first recordings in the early 1950s and cut some fantastic sides for Bobbin and King from 1959–63, but he really hit his stride when he signed with Stax in 1966 and began working with Booker T. and the MGs and the Memphis Horns. His collaborations with them worked as well as they did because for all his toughness, King's music swung, a fact well-documented on the excellent live albums, where he recaptures the Stax albums' drive backed by a horn-less quartet. He was also a fantastic, if not particularly flexible, singer.

what to buy: King's Stax debut, *Born Under a Bad Sign* ♪♪♪♪♪ (Atlantic, 1967, prod. Al Jackson), is an undisputed classic. The two-disc compilation, *The Ultimate Collection* ♪♪♪♪ (Rhino, 1992) offers a fine career overview. Any of the three live albums recorded at San Francisco's Fillmore West Auditorium in 1968 capture the full power of Albert King onstage: *Live Wire/Blues Power* ♪♪♪♪ (Stax, 1968, prod. Al Jackson); *Wednesday Night in San Francisco* ♪♪♪♪ (Stax, 1990, prod. Al Jackson); and *Thursday Night in San Francisco* ♪♪♪♪ (Stax, 1990, prod. Al Jackson).

what to buy next: *Let's Have a Natural Ball* ♪♪♪♪ (Modern Blues, 1989) collects King's late-1950s/early-1960s sides backed

Albert King (© Jack Vartoogian)

by a hard-charging horn section. *I'll Play the Blues for You* 🎸🎸🎸🎸 (Stax, 1972, prod. Allen Jones, Henry Bush) includes the killer title track as well as "Little Brother," perhaps King's most tender moment. Soul-blues never got much better than this.

what to avoid: *Red House* 🎸🎸 (Castle, 1991, prod. Joe Walsh, Alan Douglas) is a misguided, probably well-intentioned attempt to help the great bluesman by modernizing his sound. Ugh. Somebody got really excited when they discovered long-missing tapes of King jamming with John Mayall. Then Fantasy released *The Lost Session* 🎸🎸 (Stax, 1986), and it became painfully clear why the tapes got shoved into the warehouse in the first place.

the rest:

Jammed Together: Albert King, Steve Cropper, Pops Staples 🎸🎸🎸 (Stax, 1969)

Years Gone By 🎸🎸🎸🎸 (Stax, 1969)

Lovejoy 🎸🎸🎸🎸 (Stax, 1970)

I Wanna Get Funky 🎸🎸🎸 (Stax, 1973)

The Pinch 🎸🎸🎸 (Stax, 1977)

Montreux Festival 🎸🎸🎸 (Stax, 1979)

New Orleans Heat 🎸🎸🎸🎸 (Tomato, 1979)

Blues for Elvis 🎸🎸 (Stax, 1981)

Crosscut Saw: Albert King in San Francisco 🎸🎸🎸🎸 (Stax, 1983/1992)

I'm in a Phone Booth Baby 🎸🎸🎸 (Stax, 1984)

Blues at Sunrise 🎸🎸🎸🎸 (Stax, 1988)

influences:

◀◀ B.B. King, Jimmy Reed, T-Bone Walker

▶▶ Otis Rush, Eric Clapton, Jimi Hendrix, Stevie Ray Vaughan, Buddy Guy, Billy Gibbons, Joe Louis Walker, Kenny Wayne Shepherd

Alan Paul

B.B. King

Born September 16, 1925, near Itta Bena, MS.

No other blues artist has ever entered mainstream American

culture quite like B.B. King. He is the only one to step inside from the commercial cold that has long been the bluesman's fate, to receive presidential citations and honorary degrees and star in commercials for the likes of Wendy's and Northwest Airlines. He has become so omnipresent that it's easy to forget *why* he's so revered: he fundamentally changed the way the electric guitar is played. The roots of any blues-based electric guitarist can be traced back to B.B. King, whether they know it or not. King took single-string electric lead guitar playing, pioneered by Charlie Christian and T-Bone Walker, and coated it with Mississippi grit. The result was a highly personalized style—marked by stinging finger vibrato, incredible economy and uncanny vocal-like phrasing—which had tremendous impact on virtually every electric blues guitarist to follow, including Buddy Guy, Albert King, Freddie King and Otis Rush. These players, in turn, inspired countless rock guitarists, notably Jimi Hendrix, Eric Clapton and Stevie Ray Vaughan.

what to buy: The emergence of King's groundbreaking style can be heard on *The Best of B.B. King, Vol. One* ♪♪♪♪ (Flair/Virgin, 1991), an essential collection of 1950s recordings which includes his original versions of standard-bearers like "Three O'Clock Blues," "You Upset Me Baby" and "Every Day I Have the Blues." B.B.'s vocal-like guitar playing is part and parcel of his rare ability to communicate intimately with an audience, a powerful rapport which is perfectly captured on *Live at the Regal* ♪♪♪♪ (MCA, 1971, prod. Johnny Pate), a 1964 performance considered by many to be not only his finest recording but the greatest album in all modern blues. This treasure-trove of sophisticated-yet-down-home music includes such staples as "It's My Own Fault," "Every Day I Have the Blues" and "Sweet Little Angel." *Completely Well* ♪♪♪♪ (MCA, 1969, prod. Bill Szymczyk) contains King's only Top-20 hit, "The Thrill Is Gone," and is solid through and through.

what to buy next: Sooner or later, you'll probably want the four-CD boxed set, *King of the Blues* ♪♪♪♪ (MCA, 1992, prod. Andy McKaie), an excellent summary of King's career. *Live at San Quentin* ♪♪♪♪ (MCA, 1990) and *Blues Summit* ♪♪♪♪ (MCA, 1993), which features a host of guest stars, are King's best recent efforts, both showing that he still has plenty of both sting in his vibrato and ideas in his head.

what to avoid: *B.B. King in London* ♪♪ (MCA, 1971) is the usual pointless hook-the-blues-guy-up-with-well-meaning-rockers-who-love-him-but-can't-play-his-stuff-half-as-well-as-his-own-band exercise. Also, his 1970s and 1980s records are virtually all burdened by over-production. Tread carefully.

Albert King

song
Crosscut Saw

album
Born Under a Bad Sign (Atlantic)

instrument
Guitar

monster solo

the rest:

Blues Is King ♪♪♪ (MCA, 1967)
The Electric B.B. King—His Best ♪♪♪♪ (MCA, 1968)
Lucille ♪♪♪♪ (MCA, 1968)
Live & Well ♪♪♪♪ (MCA, 1969)
Incredible Soul of B.B. King ♪♪♪ (MCA, 1970)
Indianola Mississippi Seeds ♪♪♪♪ (MCA, 1970)
Live in Cook County Jail ♪♪♪♪ (MCA, 1970)
Back in the Alley: The Classic Blues of B.B. King ♪♪♪♪ (MCA, 1973)
The Best of B.B. King ♪♪♪♪ (MCA, 1973)
To Know You Is to Love You ♪♪♪ (MCA, 1973)
B.B. King and Bobby Bland: Together for the First Time Live ♪♪♪♪ (MCA, 1974)
Friends ♪♪♪ (MCA, 1974)
Lucille Talks Back ♪♪♪♪ (MCA, 1975)
B.B. King & Bobby Bland: Together Again . . . Live ♪♪ (MCA, 1976)
King Size ♪♪♪♪ (MCA, 1977)
Midnight Believer ♪♪ (MCA, 1978)
Take It Home ♪♪ (MCA, 1979)

B.B. King (© Jack Vartoogian)

Live at Ole Miss 🎧🎧🎧♪ (MCA, 1980)
Great Moments with B.B. King 🎧🎧🎧 (MCA, 1981)
There Must Be a Better World Somewhere 🎧🎧🎧♪ (MCA, 1981)
Love Me Tender 🎧🎧♪ (MCA, 1982)
Blues 'N' Jazz 🎧🎧🎧 (MCA, 1983)
Six Silver Strings 🎧🎧 (MCA, 1985)
Do the Boogie: Early 50's Classics 🎧🎧🎧🎧 (Flair/Virgin, 1988)
King of the Blues 1989 🎧🎧🎧 (MCA, 1989)
The Fabulous B.B. King 🎧🎧🎧🎧 (Flair/Virgin, 1991)
Live at the Apollo 🎧🎧🎧♪ (GRP, 1991)
Singin' the Blues/The Blues 🎧🎧🎧🎧 (Flair/Virgin, 1991)
There Is Always One More Time 🎧🎧🎧 (MCA, 1991)
Sweet Little Angel 🎧🎧🎧🎧 (Flair/Virgin, 1992)

influences:

⏮ Blind Lemon Jefferson, T-Bone Walker, Django Reinhardt, Lonnie Johnson, Clarence "Gatemouth" Brown

⏭ Buddy Guy, Eric Clapton, David Gilmour, Albert King, Otis Rush, Albert Collins

Alan Paul

Earl King

Born Earl Silas Johnson IV, February 7, 1934, in New Orleans, LA.

The magnificent Earl King has been a major force on the New Orleans music scene since the early 1950s. A prolific composer, brilliant guitarist and distinctive vocalist, King has been around since the beginning of the modern era and is a walking repository of historic—and scandalously personal—information on his colorful peers. Enormously popular in his home town and among R&B fanatics everywhere, King began his recording career around 1954, cutting singles for Specialty ("A Mother's Love"), Ace ("Those Lonely, Lonely Nights"), Imperial ("Come On," "Trick Bag," "Mama and Papa"), Watch ("Big Chief" with Professor Longhair), Chess ("Feeling My Way Around"), Kansu ("Street Parade") and Motown, among many others. His songs have been covered by Jimi Hendrix, Dr. John, Fats Domino, Lee Dorsey, Johnny "Guitar" Watson and many others, and King has continued to write and perform all through the many ups and downs of his recording career. Producer Hammond Scott recorded King's first full-scale album, *Glazed*, in 1987. The ensuing critical acclaim and blues radio play helped create a vast new market for King's exciting live performances. Now he's rarely seen in New Orleans, but his many fans continue to ask, in the words of esteemed colleague Geraldine Wyckoff, "Why isn't this man president?"

what to buy: King is at his very best on *Hard River to Cross* ♪♪♪♪ (Black Top, 1993, prod. Hammond Scott). Backed by a crack New Orleans band featuring Snooks Eaglin, David Torkanowsky, Sammy Berfect, George Porter Jr. and Herman V. Ernest III, it offers a healthy round of terrific original works. His previous Black Top albums deliver plenty of Earl's ambitious compositions, first-rate playing, massive wit and sly sense of humor. *Glazed* ♪♪♪♪ (Black Top, 1987) finds Earl in the adoring company of Ronnie Earl and Roomful of Blues with a scintillating repertoire. *Sexual Telepathy* ♪♪♪♪ (Black Top, 1990) has backing by the Black Top All Stars—Snooks Eaglin, George Porter Jr., Kenny Blevins, Ron Levy—and the Kamikaze Horns, alternating with Ronnie Earl & the Broadcasters. All these albums provide indispensible listening.

what to buy next: In 1990 Charly Records obtained an album's worth of Earl King material recorded in 1972 and rejected for release at the time by Atlantic. These masters were issued as *Street Parade* ♪♪♪ (Charly, 1990, prod. Allen Toussaint, Marshall Sehorn) and add considerably to the Earl King discography, especially the irrepressible title track and other gems like "You Make Me Feel Good," "I'm Gonna Keep on Trying" and "This Is What I Call Living." Hearing Earl King live is always an exhilarating experience, and his Tipitina's performances captured on *Black Top Blues-A-Rama Volume Two* ♪♪♪ (Black Top, 1988) and *Volume Five* ♪♪♪ (Black Top, 1991)—especially his moving reading of "Night Time Is the Right Time"—are no exception.

worth searching for: Shards of King's enormous catalog can be found on several anthologies, usually one or two cuts each. His great Imperial recordings can be found on *The Best of New Orleans Rhythm & Blues, Volume One* ♪♪♪ (Rhino, 1988); his Ace singles (including "Those Lonely Lonely Nights" and "Packin' Up") on *The Best of Ace Records: The R&B Hits* ♪♪♪ (Ace/Scotti Brothers, 1993); and his two immortal Carnival songs—"Big Chief" and "Street Parade"—on the essential compilation, *Mardi Gras in New Orleans* ♪♪♪♪ (Mardi Gras). The Earl King Christmas tune, "Santa, Don't Let Me Down," on *Blues, Mistletoe & Santa's Little Helper* ♪♪♪ (Black Top, 1995) is a real holiday treat.

B.B. King

song
The Thrill Is Gone

album
Live in Cook County Jail (MCA)

instrument
Guitar

monster solo

influences:

◄◄ Guitar Slim, Professor Longhair, Dave Bartholomew

►► Snooks Eaglin, Walter "Wolfman" Washington, Dr. John

John Sinclair

Freddie King

Born September 30, 1934, in Gilmer, TX. Died December 28, 1976, in Dallas, TX.

Serious discussion of Freddie King brings to light dichotomy and factionalism. He was born in Texas but came up in Chicago, where he counted as influences Robert Lockwood, Jimmy Rogers and Eddie Taylor (not that he ever sounded like any of them). He knew Magic Sam, and it's a wonder guitar pundits haven't written dissertations on their stylistic similarities. Some say his only great work was for King-Federal from 1960–66, when he did 45s that were often scorching vocal performances like "Now I've Got a Woman" (Federal) backed with instrumentals brilliant in their succinctness ("Onion Rings," the flip of the aforementioned). Others stump for his rock-oriented Shelter output. Yet a third faction reveres King less for his recordings than for his live shows. A King band in full cry was unforgettably forceful. King himself was an enormous man with a powerful onstage persona; he played at room-rattling volume, and his accompanists were strongmen like Andrew "Jr. Boy" Jones (guitar), Benny Turner (bass) and Charles Myers (drums). Curiously, there are no great discs of King live (though there are, thankfully, wonderful videos of him in concert). King moved to Dallas in 1963, and held forth with equal aplomb at black joints like Delmonico's (stronghold of Al "TNT" Braggs and Big Bo Thomas) and hippie joints like Mother Blues. His renown increased in 1970 when he signed with Leon Russell's Shelter, and though some slag the rock-style work he did there it was better than what was to come on RSO, for whom he cut LPs in 1974 and 1975. There's a photo of King standing in conversation with Peter Frampton in the 1970s. He looks to be four, maybe five feet taller, and even though you know he can't really be that much bigger, you can stare at the picture hard and try as you might, not dispel the impression. That's the way it was with Freddie, who was truly larger than life.

what to buy: The definitive Freddie King compilation would be more comprehensive than *Hideaway: The Best of Freddie King* 𝄞𝄞𝄞𝄞𝄞 (Rhino, 1993, reissue prod. James Austin), but this one is cost effective, and most of its 20 cuts are excellent King-Federal sides from the early 1960s. Included are instrumentals ("Hideaway," "Stumble," "Sen-Sa-Shun") that became rites of passage for upcoming guitarists and classic vocal performances ("I'm Tore Down," "It's Too Bad Things Are Going So Tough"). There are also two Shelter cuts, enough to give you an idea what the Leon Russell period was all about. Unrepresented in this collection is anything from King's mid-period at Atlantic-Cotillion. Forget the long-held critical tack that this output was no good. *Freddie King Is a Bluesmaster* 𝄞𝄞𝄞𝄞 (Atlantic, 1992, prod. King Curtis) is quite good, far less compromised than what was to come. King's guitar is too far down in the mix, but the performances are still concise and soulful. If there were a contest for Best Live CD by King, the winner by default would be *Live at the Electric Ballroom* 𝄞𝄞𝄞𝄞 (Black Top, 1994) because most of the other posthumous in-concert releases are of little better than bootleg quality. You need to know what this power hitter was about onstage, and *Electric Ballroom*'s best cuts (including "Big Legged Woman" and "Woman across the River") fill the bill. There are two, rare

acoustic cuts, and Black Top retained most of the excellent liner note/photo inclusion on its original release on the Dallas label Topcat.

what to buy next: *King of the Blues* 𝄞𝄞𝄞𝄞 (EMI, 1996) is a two-CD overview that comprises all three of his Shelter LPs plus some unissued items. Pricey but nice. *Just Pickin'* 𝄞𝄞𝄞𝄞 (Modern) gathers the contents of two all-instrumental LPs King did for King-Federal. *My Feeling for the Blues* 𝄞𝄞𝄞𝄞 (Atlantic, 1992, prod. King Curtis) is King's other under-appreciated Cotillion album originally released in 1969. Toss a coin over *Getting Ready* 𝄞𝄞𝄞𝄞 (Shelter, 1971/The Right Stuff, 1991, prod. Leon Russell) and *Woman across the River* 𝄞𝄞𝄞𝄞 (Shelter, 1973/The Right Stuff, 1996, prod. Leon Russell). The former has the potent "Goin' Down," which became his signature song; the latter includes some dreck ("Help Me through the Night," "Boogie Man"), but also some fine straight-on blues ("I'm Ready," "Yonder's Wall," "You Don't Have to Go") and enough hot guitar to burn out a rain forest.

the rest:
1934–76 𝄞𝄞 (Polydor, 1977)
Blues Guitar Hits 𝄞𝄞𝄞𝄞 (Ace, 1993)
Live at Liberty Hall 𝄞𝄞𝄞 (Blue Moon, 1993)
Let the Good Times Roll 𝄞𝄞𝄞 (Wolf, 1994)
Live in Germany 𝄞𝄞𝄞 (King Biscuit, 1994)
Key to the Highway 𝄞𝄞𝄞 (Wolf, 1995)
All His Hits 𝄞𝄞𝄞𝄞 (King, 1996)
Texas Cannonball 𝄞𝄞𝄞 (The Right Stuff, 1996)

influences:
◀◀ Robert Junior Lockwood, Jimmy Rogers, B.B. King

▶▶ Eric Clapton, Jimmie Vaughan, Stan Webb, Bugs Henderson, Tutu Jones

Tim Schuller

Little Jimmy King

Born Manuel Gales, December 4, 1968, in Memphis, TN.

One of the last pieces of business Albert King attended to before his death was getting his predecessor, guitarist Little Jimmy King, signed to a record deal. They're not technically related, although the elder King "adopted" his fellow left-handed, upside-down playing guitarist and singer. Musically Little Jimmy is clearly an Albert acolyte, using funky rhythm as the launching pad for fast, fluid, wah-wah solos. What separates him from his mentor is an affinity for blues-rock fusion; he likes to show off like Jimi Hendrix or Stevie Ray Vaughan rather than playing with subtlety, as Albert King did on his Stax soul classics. Still, he's a young guitarist to watch, and if he's not prepared to step directly into King's shoes, he'll certainly be ready when Son Seals steps out of them.

what to buy: King's fiery debut, *Little Jimmy King and the Memphis Soul Survivors* 𝄢𝄢𝄢 (Bullseye Blues/Rounder, 1991, prod. Ron Levy), is the sound of a new hot-shot flexing his talent with as much speed and originality as he can muster; King just hasn't learned when it's best to stop playing.

what to buy next: On *Something Inside of Me* 𝄢𝄢𝄢 (Bullseye Blues/Rounder, 1994, prod. Ron Levy), King's funk side begins to come across, especially on the fast-paced opening track, "Under Pressure."

the rest:
Soldier for the Blues 𝄢𝄢𝄢 (Bullseye Blues/Rounder, 1997)

influences:
◄◄ Albert King, Albert Collins, Buddy Guy, Jimi Hendrix, Luther Allison

Steve Knopper

Shirley King

Born October 26, 1949, near West Memphis, AR.

Shirley King, daughter of B.B., began singing professionally in 1991. By the spring of 1992 she was already in the studio recording her debut with harp player Chicago Beau. A former exotic dancer on the chitlin' circuit, King can be an electrifying live performer. She prides herself on being an all-around entertainer. Her stage antics and husky vocals have made her a hit in Chicago's North Side clubs. Although she's still a bit rough around the edges as a vocalist, King shows promise.

what to buy: *Jump through My Keyhole* 𝄢𝄢𝄢 (GBW, 1992, prod. L. McGraw-Beauchamp), King's first and only CD, captures her in a formative stage in her vocal career backed by Jimmy Dawkins and his band. To her credit, King remakes only one of her father's numbers, "Three O'Clock Blues." She contributes one original, "Pass It On."

influences:
◄◄ B.B. King, Ruth Brown, Etta James
►► Melviena Allen

Steven Sharp

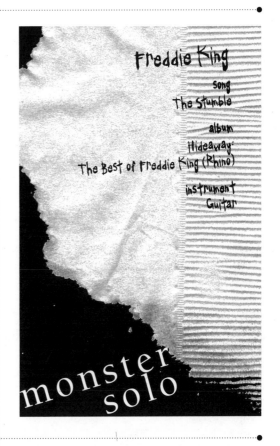

Freddie King
song
The Stumble
album
Hideaway:
The Best of Freddie King (Rhino)
instrument
Guitar

monster solo

Lester "Big Daddy" Kinsey

Born March 18, 1927, in Pleasant Grove, MS.

Southeast of Chicago and just across the state line into Indiana lies the town of Gary, where Big Daddy Kinsey became a local blues legend by combining the best of the Chicago blues with his deep roots in the Mississippi Delta. Big Daddy passed on his talents as a slide guitarist and harmonica player to his sons, who formed the Kinsey Report, but he has always stayed true to the blues while his offspring have opted to give hard rock and reggae spins to the music. Instead of pushing his own career, Big Daddy spent decades working in the Gary steel mills, and unfortunately that's why his catalog of recordings is so small, despite many years of playing. And while Kinsey has always felt it was more important to support his children, first as a provider and later as a backing musician to several Kinsey Report projects, his own work is dazzling.

what to buy: *Can't Let Go* ♫♫♫ (Blind Pig, 1990, prod. Bob Greenlee, Kinsey Family) shows off Big Daddy's power as an elder statesman of the blues who can still crank out rocking grooves, here with the help of his talented sons Donald (electric guitar), Kenneth (bass) and Ralph (drums). Hearing recordings like this make you regret there isn't more out there from Big Daddy.

what to buy next: *I Am the Blues* ♫♫♫ (Verve, 1993) is a tribute album dedicated to Muddy Waters and features artists that played with Waters at some point during his career. While it's pure bliss to hear this legendary group go off on these solid tunes, the set comes across with a bravado that's out of character for Big Daddy.

the rest:
Bad Situation ♫♫♫ (Rooster Blues, 1985)

worth searching for: Kinsey collaborated with Little Mike & the Tornadoes for *Heart Attack* ♫♫♫ (Blind Pig, 1990, prod. Mike Markowitz, Jerry Del Giudice), a stellar up-tempo, blues jam session that also features Pinetop Perkins, Ronnie Earl and Paul Butterfield. Big Daddy also has guest shots on numerous Kinsey Report releases, including *Edge of the City* ♫♫♫ (Alligator, 1987, prod. Bruce Iglauer, Donald Kinsey).

influences:
◀◀ Elmore James, Muddy Waters, Little Walter
▶▶ William Clarke, Sonny Landreth

Matt Pensinger

Kinsey Report
Formed 1984, in Gary, IN.

Donald Kinsey, guitar, vocals; Kenneth Kinsey, bass; Ralph "Woody" Kinsey, drums, percussion; Ron Prince, guitar.

This family band cut its teeth on the blues while watching Dad become a guitar/harmonica legend in their hometown. The offspring added rock, funk, soul and reggae to create a unique hybrid. Frontman Donald also worked with Bob Marley and Albert King, and you can hear both legends in the Kinsey Report's recordings.

what to buy: *Edge of the City* ♫♫♫ (Alligator, 1987, prod. Bruce Iglauer, Donald Kinsey) shows the boundless possibili-

ties of splicing contemporary rock and funk with Chicago blues traditions. The guitar work is solid and sharp, but it's the added dimensions of the rhythm section that makes this an infectious release.

what to buy next: *Midnight Drive* ♫♫♫ (Alligator, 1989, prod. Bruce Iglauer, Donald Kinsey, Kinsey Family) digs deeper into the generational pastiche and includes straight, rocking blues numbers along with politically-charged reggae and rock rants.

the rest:
Powerhouse ♫♫♫ (Charisma, 1991)
Crossing Bridges ♫♫♫ (Pointblank, 1993)

worth searching for: The group has backed Dad, Big Daddy Kinsey, on numerous releases, and *Can't Let Go* ♫♫♫ (Blind Pig, 1990, prod. Bob Greenlee, Kinsey Family) is a gem of their collaboration.

influences:
◀◀ Big Daddy Kinsey, Muddy Waters, Percy Mayfield
▶▶ Living Colour

Matt Pensinger

Eddie Kirkland
Born August 16, 1928, in Jamaica.

This veteran singer-songwriter is sort of a living cross between Otis Redding (with whom he played guitar in the early 1960s), Albert Collins (whose straightforward electric guitar sound he emulates) and Bob Marley (with whom he shares a homeland and an obvious rhythmic quality, even though he doesn't play any reggae). After moving to the U.S. as a teenager, he spent time in Dothan, Alabama; Detroit, Michigan; Macon, Georgia, and many other places—thus he injected his anything-goes performing approach into several different music scenes. He has tried many different styles, from the spare acoustic Delta ambience that opens *Front and Center* to the energetic jump blues of *Where You Get Your Sugar?*. Though he's hardly a household name, even in the blues world, Kirkland has been present at many of blues' important intersections with other genres. His determination to play pure blues, and his long-time visibility in the music industry, helps keep the tradition from collapsing under its innovations.

what to buy: Kirkland's debut, *It's the Blues Man!* ♫♫♫ (Original Blues Classics, 1961/Fantasy, 1993, prod. Esmond Edwards), is raw like an early Howlin' Wolf record, beginning with the pleading "Down on My Knees"; King Curtis' tenor sax blends sloppily with Kirkland's deep fuzztones.

Eddie Kirkland (© Jack Vartoogian)

what to buy next: Kirkland's best recent album, *Where You Get Your Sugar?* 𝄞𝄞𝄞 (Deluge, 1995, prod. Randy Labbe), uses familiar 12-bar grooves to showcase Kirkland's considerable guitar-playing skills on "Pity on Me" and "Sugar Mama."

what to avoid: The live *All around the World* 𝄞 (Deluge, 1992, prod. Randy Labbe, Eddie Kirkland) was the wrong concert to record; Kirkland has played many, many more energetic dates than this.

the rest:

Three Shades of the Blues 𝄞𝄞𝄞 (Relic)
The Devil & Other Blues Demons 𝄞𝄞 (Trix, 1975)
Have Mercy 𝄞𝄞𝄞 (Evidence, 1993)
Some Like It Raw 𝄞𝄞𝄞 (Deluge, 1993)

worth searching for: *Front and Center* 𝄞𝄞𝄞 (Trix, 1995, prod. Eddie Kirkland, Pete Lowry) is just two guitars and drums, beginning with the slow, acoustic "When I First Started Hoboing" and building noisily to "Detroit Rock Island"; the sessions, from 1971 and 1972 in Macon, captured a hungry and talented Kirkland with the right band.

influences:

◄◄ John Lee Hooker, Otis Redding, B.B. King, Albert King, Albert Collins, Buddy Guy

►► Son Seals, Stevie Ray Vaughan, Johnny Copeland, Luther Allison

Steve Knopper

Bob Kirkpatrick

Born January 1, 1934, in Haynesville, LA.

After seeing combat in the Korean conflict, Bob Kirkpatrick settled in Dallas and has been one of the city's best kept music secrets ever since. He did a few Newport fests in the early 1970s, and in 1973 recorded *Feeling the Blues* for Folkway, but most of his work has been, and is, in neighborhood bars in Big D.

what to buy: Big-voiced Bob puts a jazzy spin to his guitar work on *Going Back to Texas* 𝄞𝄞𝄞 (JSP, 1996, prod. Paul Osborne), a swinging, dance-friendly disc cut with his working band.

Tim Schuller

Mark Knopfler

Born August 12, 1949, in Glasgow, Scotland.

It was 1978, and young upstarts punk and disco were laughing in the face of grandfather rock 'n' roll and the musical tradition it represented. Then, out of the English fog, came the distant sound of a Fender Stratocaster reverberating with the echoes of American blues. The Strat belonged to Mark Knopfler, singer/songwriter/guitarist with Dire Straits, and the song was "Sultans of Swing," a semi-autobiographical sketch of musical traditionalists being scoffed at by young know-nothings. In Knopfler's case, he got the last laugh as Dire Straits became one of the world's best-selling bands in the 1980s and early 1990s with a blues-based sound.

Raised in Newcastle, England, Knopfler organized bands for school dances, but it wasn't until much later—after becoming a reporter and then a college lecturer—that he pursued music seriously. Cafe Racers, an early band of his that covered blues and R&B standards, became a club favorite in London in 1976. The next year Dire Straits came together; its 1978 debut, totally out of step with what was happening at the time, flew to #2 on the *Billboard* charts, while "Sultans of Swing" became a top five single. The group, propelled by Knopfler's lean, nimble electric blues sound that's often compared to Eric Clapton and J.J. Cale, leapt from strength to strength, crafting a series of moody yet accessible albums such as *Communique*, *Making Movies* and *Love Over Gold*. Dire Straits subsequently moved in a more adult contemporary direction and scored a big hit with the superfluous anti-MTV jibe "Money for Nothing," while Knopfler's attentions drifted to soundtracks and country. Now settled into a solo career, Knopfler is once again demonstrating his unique style that fuses his interests in rock, blues, country and Irish folk. Over the years, Knopfler also has been a star session player, guesting on and producing albums by Bob Dylan, Steely Dan, Van Morrison and Kate & Anna McGarrigle, among others, and playing second guitar in Clapton's band on an American tour.

what to buy: Dire Straits' first three albums are indispensable. The lean and hungry *Dire Straits* 𝄞𝄞𝄞𝄞 (Warner Bros., 1978, prod. Muff Winwood), the dark and dramatic *Communique* 𝄞𝄞𝄞𝄞𝄞 (Warner Bros., 1979, prod. Jerry Wexler, Barry Beckett) and the more lushly romantic *Making Movies* 𝄞𝄞𝄞𝄞𝄞 (Warner Bros., 1980, prod. Jimmy Iovine, Mark Knopfler)—featuring the hit "Skateaway" and the set pieces "Romeo and Juliet" and "Tunnel of Love"—show off some of Knopfler's most heartfelt and soulful playing. *Golden Heart* 𝄞𝄞𝄞𝄞 (Warner Bros., 1996, prod. Mark Knopfler, Chuck Ainlay), the performer's first non-soundtrack solo effort, is a solid move away from the overproduction and sterility of Dire Straits' later days and a return to evocative simplicity.

what to buy next: Knopfler's film scoring work generally abandons rock 'n' roll in favor of low-key, mood-setting instrumentals, but the composer's dusky emotionalism remains. For an overview, *Screenplaying* ♫♫♫ (Warner Bros., 1993, prod. Mark Knopfler) is best, featuring tracks from *Cal*, *Last Exit to Brooklyn*, *The Princess Bride* and *Local Hero*. A short but worthwhile live album, *Live at the BBC* ♫♫♫ (Warner Bros., 1995, prod. Jeff Griffin, Michael Appleton), documents Dire Straits' early, pre-stardom days, while a duo session with Chet Atkins, *Neck and Neck* ♫♫♫ (Columbia, 1990, prod. Mark Knopfler), features impressive playing from two masters.

what to avoid: *Alchemy* ♫♫ (Warner Bros., 1984, prod. Mark Knopfler), easily Dire Straits' worst album, boasts some tasty Knopfler solos, but much of it is bloated and dull. For live sets, try *On the Night* ♫♫♫ (Warner Bros., 1993, prod. Guy Fletcher, Neil Dorfsman, Mark Knopfler, Chuck Ainlay, Steven Jackson) or, better yet, *Live at the BBC* instead.

the rest:

(With Dire Straits) *Love Over Gold* ♫♫♫♫ (Warner Bros., 1982)
Local Hero ♫♫♫♫ (Warner Bros., 1983)
(With Dire Straits) *Twisting by the Pool* ♫♫♫ (Warner Bros., 1983)
Cal ♫♫♫♫ (Mercury, 1984)
(With Dire Straits) *Brothers in Arms* ♫♫ (Warner Bros., 1985)
Princess Bride ♫♫♫ (Warner Bros., 1987)
(With Dire Straits) *Money for Nothing* ♫♫♫ (Warner Bros., 1988)
Last Exit to Brooklyn ♫♫ (Warner Bros., 1989)
(With Dire Straits) *On Every Street* ♫♫♫ (Warner Bros., 1991)

worth searching for: Knopfler regrouped with some of his pre-Dire Straits homies for *Missing . . . Presumed Having a Good Time* ♫♫♫♫ (Warner Bros., 1990, prod. Mark Knopfler, Guy Fletcher), released under the name of the Notting Hillbillies.

influences:

◀◀ Albert King, B.B. King, Eric Clapton, J.J. Cale, Richard Thompson

▶▶ Mavericks

Cary Darling

Koerner, Ray & Glover

Formed early 1960s, in Minneapolis, MN.

"Spider" John Koerner, vocals; "Snaker" Dave Ray, vocals, guitar; Tony "Little Sun" Glover, harmonica.

Like Dave Van Ronk and Keith Richards, these three white University of Minneapolis college students fell in love with the blues and set out to stamp their slightly fun-loving take on traditional music. But instead of hopping up the old styles into rock 'n' roll, they stuck to the folk crowds, becoming a popular festival act and releasing a string of well-written, respectful albums throughout the 1960s. They have much more in common with the Kingston Trio than the Rolling Stones, or even Howlin' Wolf, but Koerner's impeccable songwriting (including "I Ain't Blue" and "Boys Were Shooting It Out"), Ray's warm guitar licks and Glover's "Blues Harp" instructional book and liner notes for John Lee Hooker and Jayhawks albums have had lasting influence. Koerner and Ray continue to perform regularly, but the full trio gets together only on special occasions.

what to buy: *Blues, Rags and Hollers* ♫♫♫♫ (Elektra, 1963/Red House, 1995) and *Lots More Blues, Rags and Hollers* ♫♫♫ (Elektra, 1964) are similar to Peter, Paul & Mary's material from that era; but this trio is more talented and understands and uses the soul and blues idioms better than their more hit-loving counterparts.

what to buy next: *Good Old Koerner, Ray & Glover* ♫♫♫ (Mill City, 1972) is a nice comeback record, although the trio's time had clearly come and gone. The live reunion album, *One Foot in the Groove* ♫♫♫ (Tim Kerr, 1996, prod. Mark Trehus), is an even better one, with fun songs like the traditional "Dodger" and more solemn takes on Bill Monroe's "With Body and Soul" and the classics "Black Jack Davy" and "Deliah's Gone."

the rest:

Return of Koerner, Ray & Glover ♫♫ (Elektra, 1966)
Blues Rags and Hollers ♫♫ (Audiophile, 1995)

worth searching for: They're out of print, but Glover and Ray's two duet albums *Ashes in My Whiskey* ♫♫♫♫ (Rough Trade, 1990) and *Picture Has Faded* ♫♫♫ (Tim Kerr, 1992) are powerful, often harrowing, mostly blues sets. Glover's career as a producer and music writer has been occasionally more interesting than his career as a performer: he has worked on albums by punk singer Patti Smith and an excellent documentary film, *Blues, Rags and Hollers: The Koerner, Ray & Glover Story* (Latch Lake, 1996).

influences:

◀◀ Pete Seeger, Joan Baez, Bob Dylan, Dave Van Ronk, Mississippi Fred McDowell, Sonny Terry & Brownie McGhee, Son House, Skip James, Doc Watson, Big Joe Williams, James Cotton

▶▶ Taj Mahal, Ry Cooder, John Hammond Jr., Keb' Mo'

Steve Knopper

Al Kooper

Born February 5, 1944, in Brooklyn, NY.

Kooper is one of those great rock 'n' roll stars many have never heard of. Consider the list of accomplishments: joining the Royal Teens ("Short Shorts") at age 15; co-writing Gary Lewis and the Playboys' #1 hit "This Diamond Ring;" playing the organ hook on Bob Dylan's "Like a Rolling Stone" and the French horn lick for the Rolling Stones' "You Can't Always Get What You Want"; forming the Blues Project and Blood, Sweat & Tears; and producing acts such as Lynyrd Skynyrd, the Tubes, Nils Lofgren and many others. He loves to play, write and sing, period, and the only thing that's kept Kooper from mass recognition is his own eclecticism and a reedy singing voice that's not quite the stuff of Top 40 hits. Still active today, Kooper remains an estimable talent and also a fine rock 'n' roll historian—as anyone who can scare up a copy of his 1976 memoir, *Backstage Passes* can attest.

what to buy: Getting him on record isn't much easier. The best buy at the moment is *Super Session* ♫♫♫♫ (Columbia, 1968, prod. Al Kooper) a lively project that features guitar whiz Michael Bloomfield on half and Stephen Stills on the other half, subbing after the mercurial Bloomfield disappeared. *Live Adventures of Michael Bloomfield and Al Kooper* ♫♫♫♫ (Columbia, 1968/Columbia/Legacy, 1997), groovy enough to include songs by Paul Simon and Sonny Boy Williamson, sounds pretty good 30 years later.

what to buy next: *Rekooperation—A Nonverbal Scenic Selection of Soul Souvenirs* ♫♫♫ (MusicMasters, 1994, prod. Al Kooper) is enjoyable but a little stiff; the concept really comes to life on *Soul of a Man: Al Kooper Live* ♫♫♫ (MusicMasters, 1995, prod. Al Kooper), an electric performance with guest appearances by the Blues Project, John Sebastian and former BS&T trumpeter Michael Brecker.

influences:

◀◀ Muddy Waters, Willie Dixon, Bob Dylan, Rolling Stones, Blues Project

Gary Graff

Smokin' Joe Kubek Band with Bnois King

Joe Kubek born November 30, 1956, in Grove City, PA. Bnois King born 1943, in Delhi, LA.

Kubek and King were each seasoned members of the Texas music community before they were a team. King had concen-trated on solo gigs, playing Grant Green-style jazz but invariably tearing into a mournful blues (or two) a night; Kubek gigged and recorded with South Dallas soul-blues luminaries Al "TNT" Braggs, Ernie Johnson and Charlie Roberson and had done some shows with Freddie King. They teamed, honing their act with a series of Monday night gigs at Poor David's Pub, and soon had become an almost dauntingly powerful blues force. They tour relentlessly and are one of the best-selling acts on the Bullseye roster.

what to buy: King sings and does about half the lead guitar work on the hard-driving *Chain Smokin' Texas Style* ♫♫♫♫ (Bullseye Blues, 1992, prod. Ron Levy), on which Levy's B-3 juices the sizzling opener, "Way Down There." Just as tough is *Texas Cadillac* ♫♫♫♫ (Bullseye Blues, 1994, prod. Ron Levy), with the snake-hipped title cut and "Mellow Down Easy" as feisty as pit bulls on caffeine. "No Time" is timely indeed, with King addressing how hard it is for a working couple to stay together when they're on different shifts. The slide work on "Little Red Rooster" is hot enough to weld with.

what to buy next: *Axe Man* ♫♫♫ (Double Trouble, 1991, prod. P. Whittacker, Marc Benno) is a pre-Bullseye quickie one-off of covers—but not bad at all!

the rest:

Steppin' out Texas Style ♫♫♫♫ (Bullseye Blues, 1991)
Cryin' for the Moon ♫♫♫ (Bullseye Blues, 1995)
Got My Mind Back ♫♫♫ (Bullseye Blues, 1996)

influences:

◀◀ Roger Boykin, Grant Green, Tal Farlow, Freddie King, Jimi Hendrix, B.B. King

Tim Schuller

Rube Lacy

Born Rubin Lacy, January 2, 1901, in Pelahatchie, MS. Died c. 1972, in Bakersfield, CA.

Rube Lacy produced only two known recordings, both of them classics. But he was equally important as an influence on Delta master Son House, who also collaborated with blues patriarchs Charley Patton and Willie Brown. Little is known about Lacy beyond his appearance in the Lamar Life Insurance Building in

March 1928, to record the droning "Mississippi Jail House Groan" and "Ham Hound Crave" for Paramount. Both featured simple guitar strums and the wordless moans that Son House later incorporated into his own repertoire. Lacy is reported to have recorded another four cuts for Paramount, but those have yet to be found. He worked as a preacher from 1932 through the 1950s.

what to buy: Lacy's two known songs have shown up on Yazoo and several other blues compilations, but are in no better company than on *Son House and the Great Delta Blues Singers 1928–29* &⅃⅃⅃⅃ (Document, 1990, prod. Johnny Parth), which includes seminal 1920s tracks by pupil Son House, Willie Brown, Garfield Akers and Joe Callicott. These cuts, along with Charley Patton's, are the wellspring of Mississippi and Chicago blues.

influences:

▶▶ Son House, Ishman Bracey, Charlie McCoy, Joe McCoy

Steve Braun

Lady Bianca

Born Bianca Thornton, August 8, 1953, in Kansas City, MO.

Lady Bianca grew up in San Francisco, California, where she studied music theory at the San Francisco Conservatory of Music after high school. It was in the early 1970s, while performing as Bessie Smith in Jon Hendrick's *Evolution of the Blues,* that her contralto voice drew critical acclaim. By the early 1980s, she was doing background vocals for Van Morrison's *Beautiful Vision* and *Inarticulate Speech of the Heart,* and she has performed with Morrison, John Lee Hooker, Willie Dixon, Sylvester, Frank Zappa and Merle Haggard over the years. She hooked up with her current songwriting partner, Stanley Lippitt, in the late 1980s. They produced and recorded some songs together that drew the attention of Joe Louis Walker, which in turn led to a record deal.

what to buy: Her debut, *Best Kept Secret* &⅃⅃⅃⅃ (Telarc, 1995, prod. John Snyder), demonstrates how Lady Bianca's past has contributed to her artistic expression through the range of styles she embraces. The title track has especially strong piano work from Bianca, and her voice smokes with passion.

influences:

◀◀ Mahalia Jackson, Mavis Staples, Five Blind Boys of Alabama, Sam Cooke

John Koetzner

Sonny Landreth

Born 1951, in Caton, MS.

Sonny Landreth has kept alive a guitar form thought by some to have died with Duane Allman, the art of slide guitar as a lead instrument. Landreth first got attention as the leader of the Goners, the swampy-sounding trio that backed John Hiatt on his *Slow Dancing* record and tour. Now based in Lafayette, Louisiana, Landreth is steeped in the region's indigenous music, and though he has absorbed something of the rhythmic accents of the area, he found his own voice as a guitarist, with a sound distinct in its thick, saturated electricity, as if the notes are always about to shriek into feedback. He is also a nimble player, creating interesting textures with a flurry of fingers and treating his instrument, in the grand tradition of all bluesy slide masters, as a voice. He writes songs that serve his warm and evocative but not exactly bluesy vocal range.

what to buy: Both his major-label albums are worth owning not just for the six-string pyrotechnics but for the depth of the material. Of the two, pick *Outward Bound* &⅃⅃⅃ (Zoo/Praxis, 1992, prod. R.S. Field, Sonny Landreth) first, a great find that includes his signature tune, "Back to Bayou Têche." If you like Landreth's style, add *South of I-10* &⅃⅃⅃⅊ (Zoo/Praxis, 1995, prod. R.S. Field, Sonny Landreth), with sketchier songs but great guitar.

the rest:

Blues Attack &⅃ (Audio-Visual International, 1996)

worth searching for: Completists might keep an eye out for the out-of-print *Down in Louisiana* &⅃⅊ (Epic, 1993, prod. Sonny Landreth, Bayou Rhythm).

influences:

◀◀ Robert Johnson, Mississippi John Hurt, Elmore James, Duane Allman, Tommy Bolin, David Lindley, Ry Cooder

▶▶ Kelly Joe Phelps

Gil Asakawa

James A. Lane

See: Jimmy Rogers

Mary Lane

Born November 23, 1935, in Clarendon, AR.

Mary Lane possesses one of the sweetest and most interesting voices in Chicago. Until recently she had never been heard outside the gritty clubs of the city's West Side. She cut her teeth

singing in Arkansas juke joints with Robert Nighthawk, Howlin' Wolf, Little Junior Parker and James Cotton. Lane arrived in Chicago in 1957 and with the help of the great bluesman Morris Pejoe recorded her first single, "You Don't Want My Lovin' No More," for Friendly Five. Years of intermittent gigging followed, but Lane couldn't seem to get a break. Then, a few years ago, her spirit virtually broken after so many years on the grueling West Side scene, Lane was invited to record three songs for Wolf. Shortly thereafter came her full-length debut.

what to buy: *Appointment with the Blues* 𝄢𝄢𝄢 (Noir, 1997, prod. Kirk Whiting) is that long-overdue debut. Her talents as a vocalist and songwriter are displayed on traditional blues outings, as well as soul blues, supported by a virtual Who's Who of West and South Side blues talent, including Johnny B. Moore, Bald Head Pete Williams and soulful keyboardist Erskine Johnson. A highlight is Lane's duet with the legendary Detroit Jr. on "Three-Six-Nine Blues."

influences:

◀◀ Robert Nighthawk, Howlin' Wolf, James Cotton

▶▶ Vance Kelly, Gloria Thompson Rogers

Steven Sharp

Jonny Lang

Born Jon Langseth, January 29, 1981, in Fargo, ND.

Can a boy from the Great White North sing the blues? He can if he's Kid Jonny Lang, who hails from Minneapolis by way of Fargo, but who plays and sings like he was raised on catfish and collard greens, not lutefisk. Lang played saxophone in his junior high band until he took an interest in guitar. A few perfunctory lessons and a year or so of intense practice on his own, and the then-barely teenaged prodigy was leading his guitar teacher's band and hitting the club circuit. Lang's guitar skills are indeed impressive, though he's still copping others' styles at this point—a little Stevie Ray and Eric here, a little Albert and Buddy there. But what makes Lang a well-rounded performer (and a serious contender for long-time stardom) is his equally impressive vocal skill: he convincingly gets across lyrical situations likely out of the bounds of his actual experience. And while that may seem disingenuous, a mere *Star-Search* freak show to some, a little time spent with Lang suggests he will eventually come into his own. After all, how can

you live through 16 winters on the northern plains and not come down with a serious case of the blues?

what to buy: You could hardly ask for a sharper contemporary blues debut—regardless of the performers' age—than *Lie to Me* 𝄢𝄢𝄢𝄢 (A&M, 1996, prod. David Z). Kicking off with the clavinet-driven title track, an honest-to-goodness hit single, the disc starts at a startlingly high level and pretty much stays there for its entire length. There's also a decent song about playing pool, the strutting "Rack 'Em Up," a couple of credible Lang originals and a nimble take on Sonny Boy Williamson's "Good Morning Little School Girl," perhaps the first version where the singer is not singing *about* jailbait, but rather *is* himself jailbait. Disconcerting perhaps, but as with most things concerning Lang, his talent just makes you smile and accept it.

worth searching for: To hear the young guitar hero's not-so-humble beginnings, look for the self-released *Smokin'* 𝄢𝄢 (1995, prod. Mike Bullock), which shows his guitar chops already in place, though his vocal skill and blues sensibility were still works in progress. It contains a cover of Robert Johnson's "Malted Milk," apparently as strong a curative for the blues as a teenager can score in these days of enforced temperence.

influences:

◀◀ Stevie Ray Vaughan, Eric Clapton, Luther Allison, Albert Collins

Daniel Durchholz

Johnny Laws

Born July 12, 1943, in Chicago, IL.

Johnny Laws has been a beloved figure on Chicago's South Side blues scene since the mid-1960s but has broken through to an international audience only a few years ago with his first recordings. Singer/guitarist Laws prides himself on his versatility as a performer; he is as comfortable presenting a tune by Marty Robbins as one by McKinley Mitchell. But when Laws sings a song—no matter who did it originally—he makes it his own. His voice, prone to moving bursts of falsetto, is like no other. Although best-known for his vocal abilities, Laws' Buster Benton-influenced guitar style can be as interesting and refined as his voice.

what to buy: The subtle artistry of Johnny Laws in a studio is documented beautifully on his debut, *My Little Girl* 𝄢𝄢𝄢𝄢 (Wolf, 1995, prod. John Primer), where his voice soars over support provided by Nick Holt of Magic Slim's Teardrops, John

Sonny Landreth (© Jack Vartoogian)

Jonny Lang (© Jack Vartoogian)

Primer and Little Mack Simmons. The choice of backing musicians for Laws on this outing is somewhat curious: the eclectic Laws with this relatively traditional crew? But it works.

influences:

⏪ Jimmy Reed, Buster Benton, Little Johnny Christian, McKinley Mitchell, Brook Benton, Jimmy Dawkins, Marty Robbins

⏩ John Primer

Steven Sharp

Lazy Lester

Born Leslie Johnson, June 20, 1933, in Torras, LA.

A self-taught harmonica player at age 19, influenced by Little Walter and Jimmy Reed, Lazy Lester came in touch with producer-record man Jay Miller in Crowley, Louisiana, in 1956 through Lightnin' Slim. He was nicknamed "Lazy" after Miller noticed the "lazy like manner in which he handled himself and acted" and immediately included him in his Excello team

of swamp blues masters for the great musicality of his sharp harmonica riffs. Endowed with fantasy and a wacky sense of humor, he wrote great lyrics ("Man, that fits like a saddle fits a pig . . . ") and catchy songs like "I'm a Lover, Not a Fighter," "Sugar Coated Love," "Lester's Stomp," " They Call Me Lazy" and "I Hear You Knockin'." A limited vocalist, his slightly harsh voice often enhanced his singing and others', because if he was a talented solo artist himself, he was at his best as session musician, giving wonderful support to partners like Lightnin' Slim, Lonesome Sundown, Katie Webster, Tabby Thomas and others. Occasionally, he also played guitar, washboard and percussion (rolled-up newspapers, cardboard boxes, etc.). He remains a leading exponent of the swamp blues, that unique blend of southern blues, Cajun, rockabilly and country music. He recorded again with Lightnin' Slim in 1972 and was "rediscovered" in 1987; with a deeper voice and an unaltered talent as harmonicist he toured Europe and recorded a couple of nice albums, demonstrating he was still a master of harp, with verve.

what to buy: *I'm a Lover, Not a Fighter* ♫♫♫♫ (Excello/AVI, 1994, prod. Jay Miller) includes the cream of the crop, with 24 Excello sides, alternate takes and rarities. *Harp and Soul* ♫♫♫♫ (Alligator/King Snake, 1988, prod. Bob Greenlee) is 10 tracks that show the comeback of a great artist.

what to buy next: *Lazy Lester* ♫♫♫ (Flyright, 1989, prod. Jay Miller), 20 Excello sides, complements *I'm a Lover*, with some duplication. *Lazy Lester Rides Again* ♫♫♫ (Blue Horizon, 1987, prod. Mike Vernon) was recorded in the U.K. in 1987 with Bob Hall and a British band.

influences:

◀◀ Jimmy Reed, Little Walter

Robert Sacré

Leadbelly

Born Huddie Ledbetter, January 15, 1888, in Mooringsport, LA. Died December 6, 1949, in New York, NY.

While he is recognized as a seminal blues artist, Leadbelly was also one of the greatest repositories of American folk music. Many of his trademark songs—"Goodnight Irene," "Rock Island Line," "Take This Hammer" and "The Midnight Special"—are considered classics in any genre. Proficient on several instruments, he is generally associated with the 12-string guitar. Leadbelly grew up a farmer and a songster, playing reels and traditional songs at country suppers. He didn't add blues to his repertoire until he visited Shreveport in 1906. In 1912 Leadbelly moved to Dallas and befriended Blind Lemon Jefferson, who taught the youngster more about the blues and the bottleneck guitar technique. Leadbelly was imprisoned three times. In 1934, while at the Louisiana State Prison, he recorded for folklorist Alan Lomax, who was collecting songs for the Library of Congress. After his parole, Leadbelly, who was also known as Walter Boyd, helped Lomax search for blues and folk singers to record, and accompanied him on a lecture tour. While in New York on the tour he performed over national radio and soon became quite popular within Manhattan society. Leadbelly's commercial recordings on Arc sold poorly, but Lomax continued to record him for the Library of Congress. In the 1940s Leadbelly recorded prolifically for RCA and Folkways. When folk music became popular later in the decade, the demand for Leadbelly recordings and appearances soared. Unfortunately, during a 1949 tour of France, Leadbelly was diagnosed with amyotrophic lateral sclerosis—Lou Gehrig's disease. He died before the year was

out, but not before leaving an important body of American blues and folk music.

what to buy: The selection of Leadbelly CDs is daunting. A good start is choosing at least one of the six *The Library of Congress Recordings* ♫♫♫♫ (Rounder, 1995, prod. Alan Lomax). All are filled with timeless music and stories. *The Original Asch Recordings* ♫♫♫♫ (Folkways, 1993, prod. Moses Asch) is just as enjoyable and important as *Last Sessions* ♫♫♫♫ (Folkways, 1994, prod. Anthony Seeger, Matt Walters).

best of the rest:

Alabama Bound ♫♫♫♫ (RCA Bluebird, 1989)
Sings Folk Songs ♫♫♫ (Folkways/Smithsonian, 1989)
Storyteller Blues ♫♫♫ (Drive Archive, 1994)
Goodnight Irene ♫♫♫ (Tradition/Rykodisc, 1996)
In the Shadow of the Gallows Pole ♫♫♫ (Tradition/Rykodisc, 1996)
Where Did You Sleep Last Night? ♫♫♫ (Smithsonian, 1996)
Bourgeois Blues: Lead Belly Legacy Vol. 2 ♫♫♫ (Folkways/Smithsonian, 1997)

worth searching for: The excellent book *The Life and Legacy of Leadbelly*, by Charles Wolfe and Kip Lornell, is a great read. So, too is the *Lead Belly Letter* (PO Box 6678, Ithaca, NY, 14851).

influences:

◀◀ Blind Lemon Jefferson

▶▶ Lightnin' Hopkins, Pete Seeger, Woody Guthrie, Burl Ives, Josh White

Jeff Hannusch

Led Zeppelin

Formed 1968, in London, England. Disbanded 1980.

Jimmy Page, guitars; John Paul Jones, bass; Robert Plant, vocals; John Bonham, drums.

Rock fans continue to revere this British quartet, which virtually invented heavy metal and built FM rock radio, but its reputation is more controversial in blues circles. Led Zeppelin formed after guitarist Jimmy Page's previous band, the Yardbirds, broke up, out of a shared love for the blues and Page's ability to reproduce great old licks from Muddy Waters and Howlin' Wolf records. Zep's early songs, in fact, applied the band's heavy-guitar, thudding-drum, shrieking-voice treatment to classic blues arrangements: the debut *Led Zeppelin* contained reworked versions of "You Shook Me" and Willie Dixon's "I Can't Quit You Baby." By *Led Zeppelin II*, released a year later, the band had mostly shed its cover songs, but the influence was obvious on the harp-heavy "Bring It on Home,"

which shared a title and harmonica riffs with the Sonny Boy Williamson classic. Many purists, even today, deride Led Zeppelin for transforming Chess Records' roster of 1940s and 1950s hits from blues into what would become hard rock and heavy metal. Willie Dixon, Chess' principal songwriter in those days, was consistently critical of Plant and Page for building their FM staple "Whole Lotta Love" out of his "You Need Love" riffs; the band settled with Dixon in 1987 for a substantial payment. Legal issues aside, the band's pillaging of old blues records wasn't particularly evil. The Rolling Stones, Elvis Presley, Beatles, Yardbirds, Derek & the Dominos and the Allman Brothers Band were among the many young musicians who "borrowed" from blues and R&B to advance rock 'n' roll.

As Led Zeppelin progressed, its blues roots became an anchor, but the music moved far beyond "You Shook Me." "Stairway to Heaven" and "Kashmir," to name a couple of Zep's radio-dominating songs, were epic stories full of dense "Lord of the Rings"-derived imagery and poetic lyrics. Though the songs never became hit singles, the band grew a massive, black-shirted, long-haired audience and responded to the fame by taking it to the extreme. Tales of the band's groupie trysts, not to mention dropping grand pianos from the balconies of tall hotels, have become part of rock lore. As solo artists, Plant fared the best commercially, fronting a heavier, Sha Na Na-style 1950s revival group called the Honeydrippers and releasing several blues-influenced albums. Page, battling drug problems and high-profile arrests, drifted towards contemporary heavy-metal, forming the Firm with ex-Bad Company singer Paul Rodgers and Coverdale/Page with ex-Deep Purple-Whitesnake singer David Coverdale. The 1995 Plant-Page reunion tour was an unqualified commercial success.

what to buy: If you can afford it, *Led Zeppelin: The Complete Studio Recordings* (Atlantic, 1993) has everything you need; it packages all 10 of the band's self-released albums, from *Led Zeppelin* to the post-breakup *Coda*. Most fans didn't get into Zep via such a fancy route, however: they probably bought the untitled fourth album, nicknamed *Led Zeppelin IV* (Atlantic, 1971, prod. Jimmy Page), or *Zoso* for its distinctive medieval hieroglyphics, which has "Stairway to Heaven" and the intense rockers "Black Dog" and "Rock and Roll."

Robert Plant of Led Zeppelin **(© Ken Settle)**

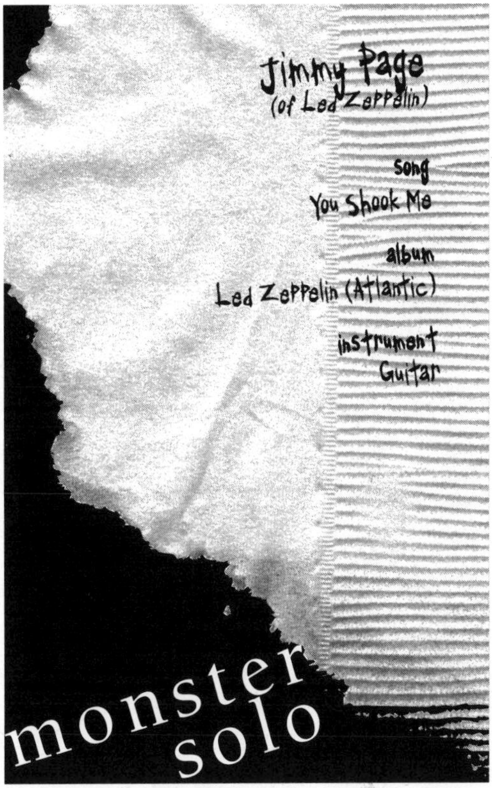
Jimmy Page
(of Led Zeppelin)
song
You Shook Me
album
Led Zeppelin (Atlantic)
instrument
Guitar
monster
solo

Houses of the Holy (Atlantic, 1973, prod. Jimmy Page) is more funky, converting James Brown's "take me to the bridge" workouts into spooky, spiritual metal funk on "The Crunge" and the unusually punctuated "D'Yer Mak'er." Zepheads sick of all the talk about "Stairway" will steer you to the double-album *Physical Graffiti* (Atlantic, 1975, prod. Jimmy Page) for its original version of the classic "Kashmir." Rounding out the roster of must-haves are the first three albums, *Led Zeppelin* (Atlantic, 1969, prod. Jimmy Page), *Led Zeppelin II* (Atlantic, 1969, prod. Jimmy Page) and *Led Zeppelin III* (Atlantic, 1970, prod. Jimmy Page).

what to buy next: *Presence* (Atlantic, 1976, prod. Jimmy Page) and *In through the Out Door* (Atlantic, 1979, prod. Jimmy Page) have their moments—such as the latter's prototypical metal ballad "All My Love" and the former's bizarre pictures of "2001"-style black obelisks—but they're weak compared to the first four albums. *No Quarter: Jimmy Page and*

Robert Plant Unledded 🎝🎝🎝 (Atlantic, 1994, prod. Jimmy Page), which isn't technically Led Zeppelin because bassist Jones wasn't invited to attend the reunion and tour, is a crucial epilogue for fans and collectors; novices should start with the first four studio albums.

what to avoid: *Coda* 🎝🎝 (Atlantic, 1982, prod. Jimmy Page) got a lot of attention for being the band's first post-Bonham project, but it's just a bunch of odds and sods, including the interminable drum solo "Bonzo's Montreaux" and a not-so-interesting alternate version of "I Can't Quit You Baby." The soundtrack to a live Zep movie, *The Song Remains the Same* 🎝🎝 (Atlantic, 1976, prod. Jimmy Page) contains an even longer version of "Stairway to Heaven," believe it or not, plus overdramatic Plant shrieking and overplayed Page riffs.

the rest:
Remasters 🎝🎝🎝 (Atlantic, 1992)
Led Zeppelin—Boxed Set 2 🎝🎝🎝 (Atlantic, 1993)

solo outings:
Coverdale/Page:
Coverdale/Page 🎝 (Geffen, 1993)

The Firm:
The Firm 🎝🎝 (Atlantic, 1985)
Mean Business 🎝 (Atlantic, 1986)

The Honeydrippers:
Volume One 🎝🎝🎝 (Es Paranza/Atlantic, 1984)

Jimmy Page:
Death Wish II 🎝 (Swan Song, 1982)
Outrider 🎝🎝 (Geffen, 1988)

Robert Plant:
Pictures at 11 🎝🎝 (Swan Song, 1982)
The Principle of Moments 🎝🎝🎝 (Es Paranza/Atlantic, 1983)
Shaken 'n' Stirred 🎝🎝🎝 (Es Paranza/Atlantic, 1985)
Now and Zen 🎝🎝🎝 (Es Paranza/Atlantic, 1988)
Manic Nirvana 🎝🎝🎝 (Es Paranza/Atlantic, 1990)
Fate of Nations 🎝🎝🎝 (Es Paranza/Atlantic, 1993)

influences:
◀◀ Chuck Berry, Willie Dixon, Muddy Waters, Sonny Boy Williamson II, Eric Clapton, Yardbirds, Rolling Stones, Beatles, Kinks, Jimi Hendrix

▶▶ Aerosmith, Guns N' Roses, Pearl Jam, Motley Crue, Nirvana, Black Sabbath, Lenny Kravitz, Embarrassment, G. Love & Special Sauce

Steve Knopper

Bryan Lee

Born 1945, in rural WI.

A talented guitarist, Bryan Lee has been a fixture in New Orleans on Bourbon Street since 1983. One of the few alternatives to strip clubs and dixieland music in the French Quarter, Lee, as "The Braille Blues Daddy" and "The Blind Blues Daddy" packs in the tourists six days a week. A disciple of the Kings—as in B.B., Albert, Freddie and Earl—Lee has also absorbed a lot of Chicago stylings.

what to buy: His albums have a sameness to them, but *The Blues Is* 🎝🎝🎝 (Justin Time, 1991, prod. Bryan Lee) is the best of Lee's lot.

the rest:
Memphis Bound 🎝🎝🎝 (Justin Time, 1993)
Braille Blues Daddy 🎝🎝🎝 (Justin Time, 1994)
Heat Seeking Missile 🎝🎝🎝 (Justin Time, 1995)

influences:
◀◀ Magic Sam, Earl King, B.B. King, Albert King, Freddie King

Jeff Hannusch

Frankie Lee

Born April 29, 1941, in Mart, TX.

Blues performers know this soulful singer better than the general record-buying public—though his first single came out in 1963, he didn't record a full album until 1984. But he has played with an incredible all-star roster of singers, including Big Mama Thornton, Junior Parker, Clarence "Gatemouth" Brown, the Ike and Tina Turner Revue and Albert Collins. He has a strong R&B voice, but you can tell from his albums that he lacks the charisma to be a major star. Robert Cray played guitar with his band before Cray became a household name.

what to buy: His debut, *Ladies and the Babies* 🎝🎝🎝 (HighTone, 1984), is the best document of Lee's gospel-and-soul voice.

the rest:
Going Back Home 🎝🎝🎝 (Blind Pig, 1994)

worth searching for: *Sooner or Later* 🎝🎝🎝 (Flying Fish, 1992) was recorded with Doug Newby and the Bluzblasters.

influences:
◀◀ Bobby "Blue" Bland, James Carr, Otis Redding, Joe Tex, Sam Cooke

▶▶ Robert Cray, Otis Clay, Johnny "Guitar" Watson, Albert Collins

Steve Knopper

Irma Lee

See: Irma Thomas

Lovie Lee

Born Eddie Lee Watson, March 17, 1909, in Chattanooga, TN. Died May 23, 1997, in Chicago, IL.

Lee's two major blues claims to fame are his piano-playing stint in Muddy Waters' last band and his better-known, adoptive son, harpist Carey Bell. On his own, though, Lee's career has been underrecognized; he bangs the piano with the powerful glee of Professor Longhair and slows it down to the mournful tempo of Otis Spann. By the time his solo material was put to vinyl in 1992, Lee was 69 years old, and he didn't have the hunger to prove himself the way he did in Chicago neighborhood bars throughout the 1950s, 1960s and 1970s. The one-time factory wood-worker and upholsterer is one of the many life-long blues performers who built an amazing local reputation but never had the resources to parlay that into stardom.

what to buy: *Good Candy* ♫♫♫ (Earwig, 1994, prod. Lovie Lee) contains remastered versions of Lee's 1984 and 1989 recordings—aptly titled *Lovie's Music Part I* and *Lovie's Music Part II*—and new songs recorded with stepson Bell on harmonica and a tight, driving band.

worth searching for: The *Lovie's Music* installments are impossible to find; more realistically, chase down his section of *Living Chicago Blues* ♫♫♫ (Alligator, 1978).

influences:

◀◀ Charles Brown, Muddy Waters, Otis Spann, Professor Longhair, Howlin' Wolf

▶▶ Carey Bell

Steve Knopper

Legendary Blues Band

Formed 1980, in Chicago, IL.

Calvin Jones (born 1926, in Greenwood, MS), vocals, bass, violin; Willie Smith (born 1935, in Helena, AR), drums; Pinetop Perkins (born July 13, 1913, in Belzoni, MS), piano (1980–85); Jerry Portnoy (born November 25, 1943, in Evanston, IL), harmonica (1980–86); Smokey Smothers (born March 21, 1929, in Lexington, MI), guitar (1989); Billy Flynn, guitar (1989); Mark Koenig, harmonica (1989).

They were unquestionably legendary at first, when some of the best bluesmen in the country quit Muddy Waters' band in 1980 and formed this unit. Their early albums easily matched Wa-

ters' fire and innovation, especially when Perkins sang powerful lead vocals. Then he, and all the original members save Smith and Jones, left the band, and it dwindled into a professional but hardly ground-breaking Chicago blues unit. Though Jones and Smith have always constituted one of the most solid rhythm sections in contemporary blues, Smith's lead singing is merely adequate, and few of the temporary musicians enter the revolving personnel door to distinguish themselves.

what to buy: Anything with Pinetop Perkins' name, meaning the first two albums, *Life of Ease* ♫♫♫ (Rounder, 1981) and *Red Hot 'n' Blue* ♫♫♫ (Rounder, 1983), which are literally like Muddy Waters' band without Waters.

what to buy next: After Perkins, it's a crap shoot, but *Keepin' the Blues Alive* ♫♫♫ (Ichiban, 1990) has Jones and Smith still trying to prove themselves as reliable frontmen to go with their unquestionable rhythm expertise.

what to avoid: *U B Da Judge* ♫♫ (Ichiban, 1991, prod. Willie Smith, Legendary Blues Band) erred in issuing the challenge of its title; the energy dwindles by the end of "Got Love If You Want It" and never fully returns.

the rest:

Woke up with the Blues ♫♫ (Ichiban, 1989)
Prime Time Blues ♫♫ (Ichiban, 1992)
Money Talks ♫♫♫ (Ichiban, 1993)

influences:

◀◀ Muddy Waters, Otis Spann, Jimmy Rogers, Elmore James, Buddy Guy

▶▶ Omar & the Howlers, Red Devils, Kinsey Report

Steve Knopper

Keri Leigh

Born April 21, 1969, in Birmingham, AL.

Since her late teens, Keri Leigh has followed the dual career track of blues singer and music journalist, making a name for herself in both disciplines. In the process she has developed a vocal style that follows in the footsteps of Koko Taylor and Janis Joplin. With vocal prowess that belies her diminutive stature, Leigh covers a range of styles rooted in Delta blues, yet encompassing R&B and blues-based rock. Sharing a strong songwriting and performing chemistry with her guitarist/collaborator husband, Mark Lyon, she defined herself early on as a traditionalist. She has since broadened her sensibilities to embrace more contemporary blues styles, and even touches of R&B and rock, both in her own songs and those she covers. Still, her live show frequently includes a brief, Delta-blues duo interlude with Lyon. Leigh's dedication to the blues extends far beyond that of a performer and recording artist. By age 18 she had founded the Oklahoma Blues Society and had established herself as a music writer and radio host in Oklahoma City. She is the author of *Soul to Soul* (Taylor, 1993), a biography of Stevie Ray Vaughan.

what to buy: Leigh's ambitious debut, *Blue Devil Blues* 🎸🎸🎸🎸 (Amazing, 1991, prod. Keri Leigh, Mark Lyon, Andy Murphy, Daiv Richardson), was originally intended as a demo, but Amazing picked it up and ran with it. The album is firmly rooted in the Delta tradition via the thickly textured guitar chops of Lyon, who excels on both acoustic and electric. Leigh has no trouble putting a sassy feminine spin on male-oriented standards like Willie Dixon's "I'm Ready" and John Lee Hooker's "I'm in the Mood."

what to buy next: Leigh and Lyon stretch out a little on *No Beginner* 🎸🎸🎸 (Amazing, 1993, prod. Keri Leigh, Mark Lyon, Tom Malone) and embrace Chicago blues and R&B without sacrificing their Delta roots. The arrangements get a little more elaborate with piano, Hammond B-3 and horns.

the rest:
Arrival 🎸🎸🎸 (Waldoxy, 1995)

influences:
⏪ Bessie Smith, Koko Taylor, Janis Joplin

John C. Bruening

Overton Lemons
See: Smiley Lewis

J.B. Lenoir
Born March 5, 1929, in Monticello, MS. Died April 29, 1967, in Urbana, IL.

J.B. Lenoir's high-pitched vocals, hook-laden songwriting and high-energy boogie guitar made him a popular attraction on the Chicago club scene of the 1950s. His music appeared on various Chicago-based labels, including JOB, Chess and Parrot. To this day, no other artist has even attempted to sound like him. Lenoir was raised in rural Mississippi on the blues of Arthur "Big Boy" Crudup, Lightnin' Hopkins and Blind Lemon Jefferson. He began learning guitar from his father at age eight. The young Lenoir found that he liked plucking strings considerably more than farm work, and he drifted down to New Orleans in his mid-teens. By 1944, Lenoir was playing in the company of

Sonny Boy Williamson II and Elmore James on Rampart Street. After hearing of the artistic and economic opportunities offered in the North, Lenoir relocated to Chicago in 1949. He found work at a meat-packing plant; at night he was taken around to the clubs by Big Bill Broonzy and Memphis Minnie. It didn't take long for Lenoir's talent to be recognized in the blues recording hotbed of 1950s Chicago, and he entered the studio in 1951 backed by Sunnyland Slim, Leroy Foster and Alfred Wallace. The four sides were sold to Chess. Lenoir attracted a bit too much attention in 1954 with his politically charged, outspoken "Eisenhower Blues." The popular single attracted heat from the U.S. government, and Lenoir was quickly and not-so-subtly coerced into remaking the tune under the title "Tax Paying Blues." Lenoir spent a substantial portion of the 1950s and 1960s delivering his topical, melodic blues for various labels. After a brief stint with Vee-Jay in the early 1960s, Lenoir made some of his last recordings for Horst Lippmann's Europe-based L+R in 1965 and 1966. In this overseas outlet, Lenoir turned his political spirit lose, recording some of his most stark, poignant work, including "Born Dead" and "Vietnam Blues."

what to buy: A fine sampling of Lenoir's well-known work for Parrot and Chess is found on *Charly Blues Masterworks, Vol. 47, Mama Watch Your Daughter* 🎸🎸🎸🎸 (Charly, 1993). In the absence of that one, couple *Natural Man* 🎸🎸🎸🎸 (Chess/MCA, 1990, prod. Leonard Chess) with *I Don't Know* 🎸🎸🎸🎸 (Chess, 1969/Vogue, 1989). Most of Lenoir's recordings for JOB, with backing from Sunnyland Slim, are included on *J.B. Lenoir 1951–54: His JOB Recordings* 🎸🎸🎸🎸 (Flyright, 1989), reissued recently in the U.S. on Paula. Two of Lenoir's albums for L+R are captured on *Vietnam Blues* 🎸🎸🎸🎸 (Evidence, 1995, prod. Horst Lippmann, Jerry Gordon), with Lenoir working his magic on acoustic guitar—a real treat. Willie Dixon provides occasional accompaniment.

what to buy next: *Fine Blues* 🎸🎸🎸🎸 (Official, 1989) is a collection of Lenoir's obscure work for Chess, Parrot, Checker, Shad and Vee-Jay spanning 1951 through 1960, including Lenoir's first recordings in Chicago and two extremely rare tracks—"In the Evening" and "Please Don't Go Away"—from 1952, with Snooky Pryor.

influences:
⏪ Big Bill Broonzy, Lightnin' Hopkins, Arthur "Big Boy" Crudup, Blind Lemon Jefferson

⏩ Robert "Bilbo" Walker, John Brim, Bobby Rush

Steven Sharp

Ron Levy

Born Reuvin Zev ben Yehoshua Ha Levi, May 29, 1951, in Cambridge, MA.

Ron Levy's solo albums, full of organ-heavy jazz improvisation, are interesting but not the reason he's so well-respected in the blues world. As the musical director for Rounder Records' Bullseye Blues label, he has produced or sat in with many of the country's best-known blues musicians. He also worked with Albert King, B.B. King and Luther "Guitar Junior" Johnson in the 1970s and 1980s and was a Roomful of Blues member for three years. As an organist, he has an impeccable sense for blues grooves and, even on the heavy-soloing *Zim Zam Zoom: Acid Blues on B-3*, never strays from the 12-bar bottom line. He's an excellent soloist, but his true talent is in bringing out the best from other artists.

what to buy: *B-3 Blues and Grooves* ♫♫♫ (Bullseye Blues/Rounder, 1993, prod. Ron Levy) pays attention to a long-underrated blues and soul instrument, the Hammond B-3 organ (with guest guitar bits by Albert Collins); Levy's fingers are fast and confident, although he doesn't have nearly the soul of his forebear Booker T. Jones.

what to buy next: *Zim Zam Zoom: Acid Blues on B-3* ♫♫♫ (Bullseye Blues/Rounder, 1996, prod. Ron Levy, Bob Porter) is a spacier take on Levy's basic organ-dominated concept that never gets as inspired as the funny baseball-stadium quotes of *B-3 Blues and Grooves*.

the rest:

Paving the Way ♫♫♫ (Black Top)
Ron Levy's Wild Kingdom ♫♫ (Black Top, 1987)
Safari to New Orleans ♫♫♫ (Black Top, 1988)

influences:

◄◄ Booker T. & the MGs, Doors, Thelonious Monk, Billy Preston

►► Medeski, Martin & Wood

Steve Knopper

Furry Lewis

Born Walter Lewis, March 6, 1893, in Greenwood, MS. Died September 14, 1981, in Memphis, TN.

Although his recorded legacy lacks quantity, Furry Lewis has had a major impact on the Memphis blues scene and the rest of the blues world still felt today. An original in the way he improvised his own lyrics in traditional songs, as well as showing an incredible sense of humor about human relationships, Lewis, who was also a presence playing slide guitar, should be best remembered for linking the nineteenth century traditional and ragtime pieces to the world of blues. One of the early country blues artists to garner attention for his fiery interpretations of traditional and ragtime pieces, Lewis got his first opportunity to record in 1927, and most of his reputation is built on this early period's recordings for Vocalion and Victor. This followed years of traveling in medicine and minstrel shows, where he developed a knack for showmanship such as tossing his guitar in the air and playing while holding his guitar behind his head. During this early period he performed for a time with the W.C. Handy Orchestra. Lewis was a storyteller, and his wit is yet another facet of his performance that helped sustain his popularity with audiences. Never able to fully support himself by his music, Lewis took a job with the city of Memphis in the 1920s, staying employed for more than 40 years as a way to protect himself financially because he had lost a leg in a train accident sometime in 1917. However, it was not until the middle of the Depression that Lewis abandoned music as a profession, playing primarily for friends at parties and other social functions. In 1959 Samuel Charters, having rediscovered him as part of the blues revival of that period, got Lewis back in the studio again, first for Folkways and then Prestige. Lewis found even greater popularity in the 1970s as a result of an appearance on *The Tonight Show*, a *Playboy* magazine interview and a small role playing himself in a Burt Reynolds movie, *W.W. and the Dixie Dance Kings*. In 1976, Joni Mitchell recorded "Furry Sings the Blues," a song that characterized the aging bluesman as cantankerous, living in poverty and surrounded by people fascinated by the blues. Even though he had little activity after this period, he still played blues until the end of his life. He left behind a humble but significant body of work.

what to buy: The single best collection of Lewis' early period, *Furry Lewis—1927–29* ♫♫♫♫ (Document, 1990, prod. Johnny Parth), shows off his wit for lyrics that bemoan relationships, as in "Mr. Furry's Blues" and some great slide work on "Falling Down Blues," and it contains both versions of "Kassie Jones." It also offers an alternate take for "I Will Make Your Money Green," showing off how Lewis would often alternate the pattern for singing lines and change his playing patterns.

what to buy next: *Shake 'Em on Down* ♫♫♫♫♫ (Fantasy, 1972, prod. Samuel Charters) is a compilation of two albums from 1961, *Back on My Feet Again* and *Done Changed My Mind*. These twenty tracks find Lewis in good playing form, showing off his improvisational skills, slipping in lines like "I will turn your money green" into "John Henry" and telling a story about his showmanship in the medicine shows during "Old Blue."

"Baby You Don't Want Me" and "Goin' to Kansas City" are another couple cuts that return to his popular themes of failed relationships and moving on. *In His Prime, 1927–28 𝄢𝄢𝄢𝄢* (Yazoo, 1991) has some cleaner sounding tracks than the Document collection, but at 14 cuts, it misses a couple significant sides such as "Mr. Furry's Blues" and "John Henry," one of his performance staples. While it does include both parts of "Kassie Jones," it only offers one take of "Judge Harsh Blues." *Mississippi Delta Blues Jam, Vol. 1 𝄢𝄢𝄢* (Arhoolie, 1981, prod. Chris Strachwitz) includes three cuts that last 20 minutes and captures Lewis on "Furry's Blues" and a great version of "Judge Bushay Blues," performed during the Memphis Blues Festival in June 1969. His singing and playing are coherent compared to a session recorded a few months earlier. *When I Lay My Burden Down 𝄢𝄢𝄢* (Biograph, 1994, prod. Arnold S. Caplin) contains sets by Fred McDowell and Robert Wilkins, but clocks in 18 minutes of Lewis' music. The six songs show how easily Lewis was able to blend a variety of styles—traditional, gospel and his original lyrics. "When I Lay My Burden Down" stands out as well as a modified "Casey Jones (Ramblin' Mind)."

what to avoid: *Fourth and Beale 𝄢𝄢𝄢* (Lucky Seven, 1992, prod. Terry Manning) is worth hearing, but it has much sloppier playing and singing. The liner notes state that the tracks were recorded in Lewis' home while Lewis was "in bed, with his leg off." For whatever reason, they lack the fire that sets apart his early work, and even the level of playing that other sessions from the same period in the late 1960s exhibit.

the rest:

Canned Heat Masters 𝄢𝄢𝄢 (BMG, 1992)

influences:

◄◄ W.C. Handy, Gus Cannon

John Koetzner

Smiley Lewis

Born Overton Lemons, July 5, 1920, in Union, LA. Died October 7, 1966, in New Orleans, LA.

Smiley Lewis is one of the finest singers ever produced by the great musical city of New Orleans. His long string of Imperial recordings produced by Dave Bartholomew between 1949 and 1961 contain an incredible body of work and stand as a tremendous achievement, even though none of his releases made much of an impression on the charts. The closest he came was with the magnificent "I Hear You Knocking" from 1955, which was bumped off the radio by the cover version cut by TV star Gale Storm, heroine of the weekly program *My Little Margie*.

Smiley's next session produced the majestic "One Night (of Sin)," later covered by Elvis Presley once the lyrics had been bowdlerized for popular airplay. Irrespective of the machinations of the record business, however, Smiley Lewis contributed an amazing body of music which is ours to hear and enjoy, from the early (1949–52) classics like "Tee Nah Nah," "Growing Old," "Dirty People," "Don't Jive Me," "Gumbo Blues" and "The Bells Are Ringing" through his mid-period (1953–56) masterworks like "It's Music," "The Rocks," "That Certain Door," "Too Many Drivers," "Lost Weekend," "Real Gone Lover," "Queen of Hearts," "Nothing but the Blues," "Hook Line and Sinker," "Rootin' and Tootin'," the Crescent City favorite "Someday" and the first recording of Bartholomew's "Blue Monday," a monster hit for labelmate Fats Domino. Smiley's final four years (1957–60) with Imperial produced yet more timeless sides like "Go on Fool," "I Wake Up Screaming," "Going to Jump and Shout" and the ballad "I Want to Be with Her." Each can be listened to again and again and again with no fear of boredom. Smiley Lewis ranks with Fats Domino, Professor Longhair, Champion Jack Dupree, Roy Brown and Dave Bartholomew as one of the all-time giants of New Orleans rhythm & blues.

what to buy: Work, rob, steal or otherwise get your little money together to cop *Shame Shame Shame—Complete Smiley Lewis 𝄢𝄢𝄢𝄢* (Bear Family, 1993), a four-disc set containing everything ever recorded by Lewis, including his initial DeLuxe single, "Turn on Your Volume" and "Here Comes Smiley"; "Tore Up" and "I'm Coming down with the Blues," his OKeh pairing from December 1961; and his final sessions for Dot and Loma. There's so much great music in this collection you'll feel like it would be cheap at twice the price. If you want to test the waters first, pick up *I Hear You Knocking: The Best of Smiley Lewis 𝄢𝄢𝄢𝄢* (Collectables, 1995), a single-disc distillation of Smiley's greatness.

influences:

◄◄ Pleasant "Cousin Joe" Joseph, Champion Jack Dupree, Professor Longhair

►► Chris Kenner, Jessie Hill, Ernie K-Doe

John Sinclair

Walter Lewis

See: Furry Lewis

Jimmy Liggins

Born October 14, 1922, in Newby, OK. Died July 18, 1983, in Durham, NC.

Though Jimmy Liggins briefly tried to make it as a boxer and a disc jockey, his lineage made it impossible for him to stay away from the R&B world for very long. His older brother, Joe Liggins, bandleader and singer of the well-known R&B group the Honey-drippers, hired Jimmy as his chauffeur—and before long Jimmy was fronting his own band, the Drops of Joy. Liggins' subsequent string of hits, including 1948's "Tear Drop Blues" and 1953's hi-lariously blunt "Drunk," just barely predated rock 'n' roll. Later hits by Little Richard, Elvis Presley and Ike Turner drew heavily from jumping R&B sides by both Liggins brothers—as well as Big Joe Turner, Ivory Joe Hunter and Elmore James.

what to buy: Both collections of Liggins' 1940s and 1950s sides are excellent (they include "Drunk," of course): *And His Drops of Joy* ♫♫♫♫ (Specialty, 1989) and the slightly jazzier *Rough Weather Blues, Vol. 2* ♫♫♫♫ (Specialty, 1992) are important transitional documents of the years between jumping blues and swinging rock 'n' roll.

influences:

◀◀ Louis Jordan, Joe Liggins, Ivory Joe Hunter, Big Mama Thornton, Lloyd Price, Ruth Brown, Ray Charles, Johnny Otis, Stick McGhee

▶▶ Little Richard, Chuck Berry, Albert King, Booker T. and the MGs, Bill Haley, Buddy Holly, Elvis Presley

Steve Knopper

Joe Liggins

Born 1915, in Guthrie, OK. Died July 26, 1987, in Los Angeles, CA.

Joe Liggins was the living image of smooth, mid-century R&B, so staid that he could easily have been mistaken for an avuncu-lar professor while leading one of the West Coast's finest bands. Liggins was Mr. Dependable compared to his guitar-stroking brother, Jimmy, who led a steroid-pumped band across the country until he was sidelined by a demented fan who shot him in the face. Yet for all of Joe's milquetoast tendencies, he was a chart monster, racking up 13 Top-10 hits on Exclusive and Specialty from 1945 until 1951. His sound almost never varied between his two #1 hits: "The Honeydripper" in 1945 and "Pink Champagne" in 1950. Liggins refined Louis Jordan's airy combo sound—arcing, rubbery horns over a light back beat—and topped them with his offhandedly pleasant vocals. Liggins be-came a full-fledged musician soon after his family moved to San Diego in 1932, joining tenor sax honker Illinois Jacquet in Los Angeles in 1939. Liggins, who played alto and tenor, started up his own band and joined Exclusive, which was mak-ing its mark with crooners like Charles Brown, Nat Cole and

Herb Jeffries. "The Honeydripper" helped jump-start the post-war R&B craze, selling 2 million copies. When the label began to falter with the introduction of the 45 rpm disc, Liggins bolted to Specialty and continued his winning ways. Liggins' easy-going ditties were soon lost in the mid-1950s crest of rock 'n' roll, and Liggins found himself label-hopping without success. Scuffling to find work in the 1960s and 1970s, Liggins benefited from a renewed interest in post-war R&B in the mid-1980s, be-coming a fixture on Los Angeles' club scene and showing up at West Coast blues festivals until his untimely death.

what to buy: As popular as Liggins' mid-1940s Exclusive sides were, his Specialty sessions, *Joe Liggins and the Honeydrip-pers* ♫♫♫♫ (Specialty, 1990, prod. Art Rupe), featured a more driving band attuned to the toughening R&B feel of the early 1950s. This 25-track survey includes Liggins' best for the label, including "Pink Champagne," the weird "Rhythm in the Barn-yard" and re-recordings of "The Honeydripper" and "Tanya." Sound is as punchy and clear as any on Specialty.

what to buy next: The cream of Liggins' Exclusive repertoire, including 10 Top-10 charters, is included on *The Honeydripper* ♫♫♫ (Night Train, 1996, prod. Leon Rene), but there is teeth-gritting fluff here too, like the obnoxious "Darktown Strutters Ball."

what to avoid: *Darktown Strutters Ball* ♫ (Jukebox Lil, 1990) of-fers a few hits, but mostly dregs from Liggins' Exclusive era. "Spooks Holiday" is grotesque enough to plead for Bill Haley. The leftovers of Liggins' Specialty years, further diluted by sev-eral mawkish ballads, can be found on *Dripper's Boogie* ♫♫ (Specialty, 1992, prod. Art Rupe).

influences:

◀◀ Illinois Jacquet, Louis Jordan

▶▶ Jimmy Liggins, Little Willie Jackson

Steve Braun

Lightnin' Slim

Born Otis Hicks, March 13, 1913, in St. Louis, MO. Died July 24, 1974, in Detroit, MI.

The brooding, skeletal croak of Lightnin' Slim was the deepest, starkest product that came out of producer Jay Miller's Crowley, Louisiana, studio, the purest distillation of bayou blues. There was nothing soft or forgiving about Slim's music. Even his rare, wry gusts of humor were as cold as the grave; his resigned laughter could spook horses. Slim dominated the swamp cir-cuit the way Muddy Waters ran Chicago. He was not as popular as Excello labelmate Slim Harpo, but he was the uncontested master of the minor-key backwoods style. Slim unabashedly rifled others' material, cadging Big Boy Crudup for "Rock Me Mama," Muddy Waters for "I'm Grown" and Sonny Boy Williamson for "Too Close Blues." But Slim made everything his own, stretching his verses out into plodding dirges, never failing to add an inevitable "Play yo' harmonica, son." Son of a Missouri sharecropper, Slim took up the guitar after his family moved to St. Francisville, Louisiana. Graduating from rural parties to Baton Rouge clubs, Slim joined the stable of musicians who hung around Miller's Crowley studio. "Bad Luck," his first minor hit, came out on Miller's Feature label in 1954. Miller's distribution deal with the Nashville-based Excello label gave Slim more national exposure, but savage numbers like "G.I. Slim" and "It's Mighty Crazy" won only regional success. Slim broke into the national charts just once, with 1959's "Rooster Blues." By the mid-1960s, when the popular Harpo had become a favorite of soul tours, Slim had tapped out. Only in the early 1970s did Slim's star rise again. He played blues festivals in Ann Arbor, Michigan, and Montreux, Switzerland, recorded with British blues bands and chucked his old suits for bell-bottoms and a pillow-sized beret. Returning to the U.S., he was diagnosed with stomach cancer, which snuffed out his second wind in mid-year 1974.

what to buy: Slim's two original Excello albums are melded in bruising sound into *Rooster Blues/Bell Ringer* ♫♫♫♫ (Ace, 1996, prod. J.D. Miller), more than 70 minutes of early Slim material, from Rooster's "Long Leanie Mama" to Bell Ringer's "Wintertime Blues." Dig it out. Some of the same songs can be found on *I'm Evil* ♫♫♫♫ (AVI/Excello, 1994, prod. J.D. Miller), but in alternate versions, along with several unreleased treasures. AVI's remastering adds timbre to the flat echo of earlier compilations.

what to buy next: *Nothin' but the Devil* ♫♫♫♫ (Ace, 1996), a potpourri of original releases and alternate versions, includes 24 cuts that feature Slim's usual guttural vocals and harp flourishes by Slim's harmonica son, Lazy Lester. *Rooster Blues* ♫♫♫♫ (El Diablo, 1993), a domestic reissue of one of Slim's two Excello albums, is augmented by six bonus tracks. If the Ace twofer is unavailable, snap this one up.

the rest:

Rollin' Stone ♫♫♫ (Flyright, 1989)
King of the Swamp Blues ♫♫♫ (Flyright, 1992)

worth searching for: A real rarity—Slim live in 1972 backed by a workmanlike British blues group—can be found on *Blue Lightning* ♫♫♫ (Indigo, 1992, prod. Mike Vernon). Slim snarls through

his own classics ("G.I. Slim" and "Might Crazy") and standards like "The Sky Is Crying." Slim goes at his own funereal pace, mostly ignoring the pedestrian efforts of the other musicians. Worth it if only to hear what Slim was like in a club setting.

influences:

◀◀ Lightnin' Hopkins, Muddy Waters

▶▶ Lonesome Sundown, Silas Hogan

Steve Braun

Lil' Ed & the Blues Imperials

Born Little Ed Williams, April 8, 1955, in Chicago, IL.

What Lil' Ed Williams may lack in highly refined guitar chops he makes up for with truckloads of enthusiasm and spontaneity. Throughout two decades in the local and national club circuit, he and his Imperials maintained a simple approach to traditional Chicago blues via squealing, unpolished slide guitar licks backed by a raw but house-rocking rhythm section. Nephew and protégé of slide guitarist J.B. Hutto, Lil' Ed (he stands just over five feet tall) was washing cars by day and playing in Chicago clubs by night when Alligator released *The New Bluebloods*, a 1986 compilation of local talent that led to a contract. The Imperials disbanded after a falling out between Williams and Alligator president Bruce Iglauer that led to Williams' departure from the label in the mid-1990s. Williams has since reunited with original rhythm guitarist Dave Weld.

what to buy: *Roughhousin'* ♫♫♫♫ (Alligator, 1986, prod. Lil' Ed & the Blues Imperials, Bruce Iglauer) is a roller-coaster ride of highly-charged one-take wonders—the best 10 of 30 tracks recorded in one night. In addition to Williams' crisp, gutsy shuffles, it includes plenty of driving boogie tracks like "Mean Old Frisco" and "Walkin' the Dog."

what to buy next: Although not quite as spontaneous and freewheeling as its predecessor, *Chicken, Gravy & Biscuits* ♫♫♫♫ (Alligator, 1989, prod. Lil' Ed & the Blues Imperials, Bruce Iglauer) includes plenty of houserocking boogie, and flirts with the R&B and jump-blues styles of Louis Jordan.

the rest:

What You See Is What You Get ♫♫♫ (Alligator, 1992)
(With Dave Weld and the Imperial Flames) *Keep on Walkin'* ♫♫♫♫ (Earwig, 1997)

Lil' Ed (© Ken Settle)

influences:

◀◀ J.B. Hutto, Elmore James, Louis Jordan

John C. Bruening

Hip Linkchain

Born Willie Richard, November 10, 1936, in Jackson, MS. Died 1989.

Born to a guitar-playing family—Richard's father, a logger, was the first to be called "Linkchain"—Willie and his brother, Jesse James, performed at house parties and fish fries all over the Jackson area. He learned electric guitar after moving to Louise, in the Delta, and would hitchhike to Midwestern cities to hear Sonny Boy Williamson, Elmore James and many others play. He moved to Chicago in the 1950s, worked as a paint sprayer, bought a guitar and began to make connections—he recorded with Little Walter and Lester Davenport, and played in house bands behind Howlin' Wolf, Muddy Waters and Williamson. He recorded several singles, none of which made much chart impact, but they were enough to give him a credible career touring, playing Chicago clubs and making occasional albums.

what to buy: The only sad thing about *Airbusters* ♫♫♫ (Evidence, 1993, prod. Hip Linkchain, Dick Shurman) is its timing; Linkchain died of cancer two years after it was recorded. It's standard 12-bar blues, but Linkchain's snappy guitar pushes everything faster—even though his voice isn't particularly distinctive.

what to avoid: Linkchain's debut, *Change My Blues* ♫♫ (Teardrop, 1983), is misnamed—he doesn't try to change much of anything, and the singing and playing drastically needs a kick in the rear.

worth searching for: It's tough to find Linkchain's late-1950s singles, but if you come across compilation albums like *Fishin' in My Pond* ♫♫♫ (JSP) and *Confusion Blues* ♫♫♫ (Blues King), for heaven's sake, buy them.

influences:

◀◀ Elmore James, Little Milton, Sonny Boy Williamson II, Lester Davenport, Jimmy Reed

▶▶ Otis Rush, Buddy Guy, Son Seals, Lonnie Brooks, Luther Allison

Steve Knopper

Little Charlie & the Nightcats

Formed 1976, in San Francisco, CA.

Charlie Baty (born July 10, 1953, in Birmingham, AL), guitar; Rick Estrin (born October 5, 1950, in San Francisco, CA), vocals, harmonica;

Jay Peterson, bass (1976–90); Brad Lee Sexton, bass (1990–94); Ronnie James Weber, bass (1994–present); Dobie Strange, drums (1976–96); June Core, drums (1996–present).

If they weren't such high-caliber musicians, one might mistake Little Charlie & the Nightcats for a musical comedy act. A fixture in the Bay Area club circuit since the mid-1970s, this blues/R&B/swing quartet's records mix traditional Chicago blues, jazz-flavored West Coast sounds and occasional shades of rockabilly and surf rock. At the core are Charlie Baty, originally a harmonica player who later switched to guitar (with a vengeance!) and vocalist/harpist/songwriter Rick Estrin, who careens through recordings and live performances with a combination of silky vocals and loads of sarcastic, self-deprecating wit in the tradition of Louis Jordan and the Coasters.

what to buy: Tight and well-defined, *The Big Break* ♫♫♫♫ (Alligator, 1989, prod. Bruce Iglauer, Charles Baty, Rick Estrin) balances Chicago blues, R&B and jazz in a sound that is classic and contemporary at the same time. Keyboardist Jimmy Pugh, in his pre-Robert Cray days, makes fine contributions on three of the 12 tracks. *Night Vision* ♫♫♫♫ (Alligator, 1993, prod. Joe Louis Walker) beefs up the Nightcats sound via producer Joe Louis Walker on guitar, Pugh on keyboards and a two-man trumpet team of Jeff Lewis and Tim Divine.

what to buy next: Keyboardist Pugh and occasional saxman John Firman make *Straight Up* ♫♫♫ (Alligator, 1995, prod. Charles Baty, Rick Estrin) the Nightcats' jazziest effort—without sacrificing the band's light-hearted swing.

the rest:

All the Way Crazy ♫♫♫ (Alligator, 1987)
Disturbing the Peace ♫♫ (Alligator, 1988)
Captured Live ♫♫♫ (Alligator, 1991)

influences:

◀◀ Louis Jordan, Little Walter, Coasters

▶▶ Mighty Blue Kings

John C. Bruening

Little Milton

Born Milton James Campbell, September 7, 1934, in Inverness, MS.

Though he never quite amassed the fame and marketability of his colleagues, Muddy Waters and B.B. King, Little Milton re-

Little Milton (© Ken Settle)

mains one of the most influential blues musicians in the world. He has an excellent charismatic voice that fits perfectly with straightforward blues and romantic 1970s-style soul, and he's an underated, fine guitarist even if his style isn't as identifiable as King's or Waters'. Almost more importantly, though, he was present during some of the most significant periods in blues, R&B and rock 'n' roll history. In the late 1940s he became a sideman for Trumpet Records performer Willie Love; he caught the ear of rock pioneer Ike Turner, who helped snag him a contract with Memphis' Sun Records. In Sun's pre-Elvis Presley blues years Little Milton made "Beggin' My Baby" and "Homesick for My Baby," but he hadn't yet developed the distinct personality that gave his labelmates Junior Parker, Howlin' Wolf and Turner such notoriety. It wasn't until he hooked up with Chicago's Chess, though, that he became one of the best-selling 1960s blues artists and an important force in the blues world. He started singing as powerfully as soul man Bobby "Blue" Bland and notched several important hits, including "More and More" and "Grits Ain't Groceries (All around the World)." He then switched to Stax just as the label was shifting from straightforward soul to stretched-out funk-and-croon music. Now with Malaco, he continues to draw big crowds in clubs across the South.

what to buy: A thorough Little Milton collection will sample his stints at all the big labels: the two-disc *Welcome to the Club: The Essential Chess Recordings* 𝄞𝄞𝄞𝄞 (Chess/MCA, 1994, prod. various) lived up to its name briefly, until the more compact update, *Greatest Hits* 𝄞𝄞𝄞𝄞 (Chess/MCA, 1997, prod. various), came along. Both will get you "Grits Ain't Groceries" and "If Walls Could Talk." His original releases are both surprisingly easy to find and surprisingly cohesive for such a long-time, singles-oriented artist. The best are *We're Gonna Make It/Little Milton Sings Big Blues* 𝄞𝄞𝄞𝄞 (Chess/MCA, 1965/1986, prod. Billy Davis, Gene Barge), *If Walls Could Talk* 𝄞𝄞𝄞𝄞 (Chess/MCA, 1970), *Grits Ain't Groceries* 𝄞𝄞𝄞 (Checker, 1970) and the soulful, not-so-bluesy *Age Ain't Nothin' but a Number* 𝄞𝄞𝄞 (MCA, 1983, prod. Al Perkins).

what to buy next: "Back then, I didn't know who Little Milton was," he says in liner notes to *The Sun Masters* 𝄞𝄞𝄞 (Rounder, 1990, prod. Sam Phillips). "I was just doing whoever came out with a hit record." Still, they capture an excited, hungry Milton and set his great voice in the context of Sun's magical old country train-driving sounds. The singer's best contemporary album is *I'm a Gambler* 𝄞𝄞𝄞𝄞 (Malaco, 1994, prod. Wolf Stephenson, Tommy Couch), which is back to blues and has funny covers of Eddie Rollins' "Casino Blues" (complete with ringing slot ma-

chines in the background) and Tony Joe White's "Polk Salad Annie" (in which Milton, unlike White, carefully enunciates all the words).

what to avoid: The more recent Chess/MCA CD collections have rendered the long-important greatest-hits LP *Chess Blues Master Series* 𝄞𝄞𝄞𝄞 (Chess/MCA, 1976, prod. various) unnecessary. Ditto *Greatest Hits* 𝄞𝄞𝄞 (Chess/MCA, 1972, prod. various), *Greatest Sides* 𝄞𝄞𝄞𝄞 (Chess/MCA, 1984, prod. various) and *Raise a Little Sand* 𝄞𝄞𝄞 (Red Lightnin', 1982, prod. Sam Phillips), an early Sun retrospective.

the rest:
Waiting for Little Milton 𝄞𝄞 (Stax, 1973)
Blues 'n' Soul 𝄞𝄞 (Stax, 1974)
Tin Pan Alley 𝄞𝄞𝄞 (Stax, 1975)
(With Albert King) *Chronicle* 𝄞𝄞 (Stax, 1979)
Playing for Keeps 𝄞𝄞𝄞 (Malaco, 1984)
Annie Mae's Cafe 𝄞𝄞𝄞 (Malaco, 1987)
The Blues Is Alright! 𝄞𝄞𝄞 (Evidence, 1993)
Greatest Hits 𝄞𝄞𝄞 (Malaco, 1995)
Live at Westville Prison 𝄞𝄞𝄞 (Delmark, 1995)

worth searching for: Atlantic hasn't gotten around to remastering and updating all the great old records from its catalog on CD; one that deserves the revisionist treatment is the live *What It Is* 𝄞𝄞𝄞𝄞 (Stax, 1989, prod. Henry Bush), a swinging, stretched-out Montreux Festival recording that's up there—almost—with James Brown's *Live at the Apollo* and Otis Redding's *Live at Monterey*.

influences:

◀◀ Bobby "Blue" Bland, B.B. King, Albert King, Willie Love, Elmore James, Fats Domino, Guitar Slim, Ike Turner, John Lee Hooker

▶▶ Otis Redding, Wilson Pickett, Johnnie Taylor, Bruce Springsteen, John Hiatt, Willie Kent, Buddy Guy, Otis Rush

Steve Knopper

Little Sonny

Born Aaron Willis, October 6, 1932, in Greensboro, AL.

Little Sonny moved to Detroit in the early 1950s to pursue a career as a baseball player. Eventually he forgot about sports and began playing harp after being inspired by Little Walter and Sonny Boy Williamson. After a stint with Washboard Willie, he formed his own combo and became a fixture on the Motor City blues scene. His first single, "I Got to Find My Baby," was leased to Duke in 1958. His next record, "Love Shock," was recorded for JVB and leased to Excello. In the 1960s he had several singles, including "The Mix Up," which was released on his own Speedway label. Later he recorded several albums that were an innovative blend of hard Detroit blues and Memphis funk for Stax/Enterprise. A favorite at the Ann Arbor Blues Festival, Sonny also appeared in the movie *Wattstax*.

what to buy: *Hard Goin' Up* ♬♬♬ (Stax, 1973) is the best of the Stax CDs. Recorded at the 1972 Ann Arbor Blues & Jazz Festival, *Blues with a Feeling* ♬♬♬ (Schoolkids, 1995, prod. John Sinclair) captures one of Sonny's high-energy sets and also contains an interesting interview. *Sonny Side Up* ♬♬♬ (Glynn, 1991, prod. Little Sonny) was originally released in Japan on P-Vine and displays Sonny's contemporary sound and includes some of his early 1960s singles.

the rest:

New King of the Blues Harmonica ♬♬♬ (Stax)
Black and Blue ♬♬♬ (Stax, 1992)

influences:

◀◀ Little Walter, Sonny Boy Williamson II, Jimmy Reed, King Curtis, Booker T. & the MGs

Jeff Hannusch

Little Walter

Born Marion Walter Jacobs, May 1, 1930, in Marksville, LA. Died February 1, 1968, in Chicago, IL.

Harmonica before Little Walter was totally 1940s. Like a big, honking, fin-heavy automobile, he came roaring onto the postwar scene, his harp amped to the guts. In his wake saxophonists despaired, their gigs taken by harp blowers as the Chicago blues world jumped on his bandwagon. Because of him, harmonica came to define the sound of Chicago blues. Walter flamed out with his era; by the 1960s he was a wreck and he died from physical violence in 1968. Nonetheless, examination of his body of work results in thrills at its brilliance. If he'd never made a record of his own he'd have fame for his fiery harp work on the Chess recordings of Muddy Waters and Jimmy Rogers. But make records of his own he did, on Chess and in the company of Chess stalwarts Robert Junior Lockwood and Luther Tucker on guitars and Fred Below, a drummer whose work behind Walter was busier than the drumming on most Chicago blues records, surefire testimony to the restlessness and vigor Walter put into his work. The harpmaster was a good songwriter, and when he performed standards he was convincing—just check his 1958 version of the chestnut "Key to the Highway." His records ran the gamut: jaunty instrumentals ("Juke"), hell raisers ("Boom Boom Out Go the Lights"), and lowdown laments ("Blue Midnight"). So

pervasive has been his influence in blues harmonica that those who have taken up the instrument of late sometimes endeavor *not* to be influenced by him. Nothing wrong with a diversity of inspirations, but anyone who takes up a harp and blows it through a mike on this sphere blows in the shadow of Little Walter.

what to buy: Unless you opt for the more comprehensive but pricey two-CD *Essential Little Walter* ♬♬♬♬ (MCA/Chess, 1993, prod. Leonard Chess, Phil Chess, Willie Dixon), the best overview of the harpmaster's Chess work is on *Little Walter: His Best* ♬♬♬♬ (MCA/Chess, 1997, prod. Leonard Chess). Both include examples of primal harmonica from whence it came.

what to buy next: *The Blues World of Little Walter* ♬♬♬♬ (Delmark, prod. Monroe Passis, reissue prod. Robert Koester) includes eight cuts Walter did pre-Chess for Parkway (plus two by Walter and Baby Face Leroy). It's hyper and raucous music, highlighted by "Rollin' & Tumblin'," a two-parter with Walter pouring it on while none other than Muddy Waters tears it up on bottleneck guitar.

best of the rest:

Hate to See You Go ♬♬♬♬ (MCA/Chess, 1968/1990)
Confessin' the Blues ♬♬♬♬ (MCA/Chess, 1974/1996)
Best of Little Walter Vol. 2 ♬♬♬♬ (MCA/Chess, 1989)
Blues with a Feeling Vol. 3 ♬♬♬ (MCA/Chess, 1995)

influences:

◀◀ Sonny Boy Williamson II

▶▶ Rod Piazza, Good Rockin' Charles, Paul Butterfield

Tim Schuller

Johnny Littlejohn

Born John Funchess, April 16, 1931, in Lake, MS. Died February 1, 1994, in Chicago, IL.

Chicago has been home to a stunning array of slide guitar players. Few, however, have displayed the ethereal musical beauty of Johnny Littlejohn. Littlejohn recalled hearing blues for the first time when he was about 12 years old at a country fish fry. Not long after his father won a guitar in a card game, and with his dad's victory came Littlejohn's vehicle of expression. After working a series of day jobs, including gas-station attendant, bulldozer driver, ice carrier and automobile mechanic in Mississippi, Arkansas and New York, Littlejohn hit Chicago in 1953 and spent most weekends performing in the clubs of the city's West Side. Despite hard work and immense talent, Littlejohn never gained much recognition beyond his neighborhood friends, a handful of blues lovers in Europe and scholars in the

U.S. The sounds created by Littlejohn's picking and slide are often delicate, but he could make them turn caustic in a heartbeat. Littlejohn's vocals—and his bands—usually provided rough-hewn foils for his soaring guitar work.

what to buy: A throbbing horn section provides support for Littlejohn's slashing guitar on his bold debut, *Chicago Blues Stars* ἀἀἀ (Arhoolie, 1968/1991, prod. Willie Dixon, Chris Strachwitz), a classic of post-war Chicago blues. Despite over-the-top production, *Johnny Littlejohn's Blues Party* ἀἀ (Wolf, 1989, prod. Hannes Folterbauer, Willie Kent, Daniel Gugolz) contains some fine displays of Littlejohn's slide work and vocals, including moving versions of the classic "29 Ways," "Dream" and the positively scary "Bloody Tears." *When Your Best Friends Turn Their Back on You* ἀἀ (JSP, 1992, prod. John Stedman) finds Littlejohn sounding tired or, perhaps by this time, ill, with moments of beauty. Especially worthwhile are "Slidin' Home," a swaying version of "Driftin'" and "Feel like Choppin'."

worth searching for: An all-star cast of Alabama Jr. Pettis, Lafayette Leake, Nick Holt and Fred Below backs Littlejohn on *Sweet Little Angel* ἀἀ (Black and Blue, 1978, prod. Disques Black and Blue), still only found on vinyl. Although they nap through a pair of B.B. King classics, things heat up on side two. Littlejohn's lilting slide has rarely sounded better than it does on his "Burro Beat." Littlejohn entered the studio in 1984 and 1985 to record tracks for *So-Called Friends* ἀἀἀ (Rooster Blues, 1985, prod. Jim O'Neal, Tom Radai, Johnny Littlejohn). Another impressive cast supports Littlejohn on this horn-laden affair. Littlejohn also makes an appearance on Buster Benton's *Blues at the Top* ἀἀἀἀ (Blue Phoenix, 1988, prod. Disques Black and Blue). Once a hard-to-get import, it's now available on Evidence.

influences:

◀◀ Henry Martin, Elmore James

▶▶ Little Ed

Steven Sharp

Robert Junior Lockwood

Born Robert Lockwood, March 27, 1915, in Marvel, AR.

The bit about Lockwood being Robert Johnson's son-in-law stems from Johnson's living with Lockwood's mother (at times). Johnson was only a few years older than Lockwood and was certainly his main influence. While still in his teens, Lockwood took to the road with Sonny Boy Williamson, playing gambling houses and juke joints in Mississippi and Arkansas. He was in Chicago by the 1940s and cut some sides for Bluebird, but went back down South for two years to broadcast on KFFA. It was upon his return to the Windy City that he gained fame as a guitarist for his session work, which was often brilliant, particularly on myriad sides by Little Walter and Sonny Boy Williamson. (Lockwood has also been on records by John Brim, Sunnyland Slim, Roosevelt Sykes and more.) In the early 1960s he moved to Cleveland, where he and Sonny Boy held forth at Loving's Bar in the Ohio city's tough Hough district.

Lockwood is a vexing artist to discuss discographically, as to comprehend the scope of his work you have to examine it from a couple of viewpoints: his records—and his work on other peoples' records. No student of electric blues guitar can overlook his classic, jazz-tinged backings of Walter and Sonny Boy on their Chess outings. No fan of blues, period, should overlook *Otis Spann Is the Blues*, wherein he duets with the great pianist Spann (who himself never sounded better) and is featured on two cuts, "Take a Little Walk with Me" and "My Daily Wish," that are among the greatest gems in his entire body of work. Discussion of his own works must also be split into before and after he got his Guild 12-string. He started using the instrument at the Grapes of Wrath club in Cleveland in the early 1970s, and agreeable as his work with it is, it's hard to emote on a 12-string, and those who remember him when he used a Gretsch 6-string to kick ass all over Cleveland may regard his present work as less passionate. Still, a bluesman of Lockwood's talent and seniority has the artistic license to do as he damned well pleases.

what to buy: *Contrasts* ἀἀἀἀ (Trix, 1991, prod. Robert Junior Lockwood, Pete Lowry) is Lockwood with his 6-string Gretsch tearing into a jazzy blues-blend, with lean and mean Cleveland sidemen, including his long-time henchmen Maurice Reedus and Gene Schwartz on sax and bass, respectively.

what to buy next: . . . *Does Twelve* ἀἀἀ (Trix, 1991, prod. Robert Lockwood, Pete Lowry, reissue prod. J. Gordon) is the best of his 12-string albums and certainly the most driven, with an absolutely kickin' instrumental "Red Top," a compelling "This Is the Blues" and a blistering "Terraplane Blues," the latter played solo and one of history's best-ever takes on a Robert Johnson song.

the rest:
(With Johnny Shines) *Hangin' On* ἀἀἀ (Rounder, 1980)
Robert Lockwood ἀἀἀ (Paula, 1991)
Steady Rollin' Man ἀἀἀ (Delmark, 1992)
Plays Robert & Robert ἀἀἀ (Evidence, 1993)

Robert Junior Lockwood (© Jack Vartoogian)

worth searching for: Produced by Trio Records of Japan, *Blues Live in Japan: Robert Lockwood and the Aces* 🎵🎵🎵 (Advent LP, 1976) is the Lockwood fans of his pre-12 string reign want to hear. It's the Baldster blasting loose backed ably by the Aces and bolstered by a wildly appreciative audience. Dig that steamin' "Honky Tonk"! *Robert Junior Lockwood & Chicago Gangs: The Baddest New Guitar* 🎵🎵🎵 (P-Vine) is an LP Japanese P-Vine got via Jewel in Shreveport (odd provenance) that is a bit uneven but has plenty of nice guitar from Robert. A couple selections feature vocals by Sunnyland Slim and Fat Man Wallace. From the title to its being in mono, it has the oddly skewed feel common to imports, but it's a good'un for Lockwood completists.

influences:

◀◀ Robert Johnson

▶▶ Byther Smith, Cleveland Fats, Anson Funderburgh, Freddie King, Steve Freund

Tim Schuller

Cripple Clarence Lofton

Born Albert Clemens, March 28, 1887, in Kingsport, TN. Died January 9, 1957, in Chicago, IL.

A birth defect affected his walking ability (thus the nickname), but clearly had no impact on his fingers. With the more obscure "Cow Cow" Davenport, this barrelhouse pianist helped create the enduring boogie-woogie style from the ragtime tradition. An incredible showman by all accounts, Clarence Lofton tap-danced, whistled, scatted and otherwise dressed up his shows so it wasn't just a guy sitting on a piano bench. He taught himself to play as a child, moved to Chicago in 1917 and was such a popular house-party attraction that he became one of the city's best-known performing pianists. His career petered out when the boogie-woogie craze of the 1930s and early 1940s gave way to more textured R&B.

what to buy: *Cripple Clarence Lofton & Walter Davis* 🎵🎵🎵 (Yazoo) is an excellent document of two great boogie-woogie pianists, but Lofton's theatrics and enthusiasm clearly steal the show.

what to buy next: *Complete Recorded Works in Chronological Order Vol. 1 and 2* 𝅘𝅥𝅘𝅥𝅘𝅥 (Document) contain every song a Lofton fan could ever want, including "Streamline Train" and "Brown Skin Girls."

the rest:

Cripple Clarence Lofton and Meade Lux Lewis 𝅘𝅥𝅘𝅥𝅘𝅥 (Euphonic)
Cripple Clarence Lofton 𝅘𝅥𝅘𝅥 (Riverside, 1954)
Honky-Tonk and Boogie-Woogie Piano 𝅘𝅥𝅘𝅥 (Riverside, 1954)

influences:

◄◄ Scott Joplin, Charles "Cow Cow" Davenport, Victoria Spivey

►► Professor Longhair, Ray Charles, Jerry Lee Lewis, Little Richard, Jimmy Yancey

Steve Knopper

Lonesome Sundown

Born Cornelius Green, December 12,1928, in Donaldsonville, LA. Died April 23, 1995, in Gonzales, LA.

Cornelius Green started to play piano at an early age and took up guitar around 1950, influenced by Eddie "Guitar Slim" Jones. In 1953 he had become proficient enough to be noticed and hired as second guitarist by Clifton Chenier (with Philip Walker as first guitarist). He settled down in Opelousas, Lousiana, in 1956 and came to the attention of Jay Miller, for whom he recorded until 1965. His guitar style, original and melodious, combined with his dark, warm and expressive vocals, epitomized the swamp blues style, even if he was equally at ease in the straight country blues idiom, pop ballads and rock 'n' roll. His creativity as a songwriter was amazing, and he wrote a thrilling row of catchy signature songs like "Mojo Man," "I Stood By," "Lonesome Whistler," "Lost without Love," "Sundown Blues," "Don't Say a Word," "My Home Ain't Here" and "I'm a Samplin' Man." His signature guitar riffs (already on his first recorded song, "Lost without Love," and reproduced many times later) are a trademark that make him recognizable. After leaving blues in 1965 for religion, he returned in 1976. He retired for good, unhappily for collectors, moved to Baton Rouge in 1980 and stayed there until his death.

what to buy: *I'm a Mojo Man* 𝅘𝅥𝅘𝅥𝅘𝅥𝅘𝅥 (Excello/AVI, 1994, prod. Jay Miller) is a swamp blues feast with all the fixin's, 24 Excello sides from 1956–65 and every Lonesome Sundown classic. For *From La. to L.A.* 𝅘𝅥𝅘𝅥𝅘𝅥 (Rounder, 1979, prod. Bruce Bromberg) Philip Walker and Green come together again in a nice session.

what to buy next: *Lonesome Sundown* 𝅘𝅥𝅘𝅥𝅘𝅥 (Flyright, 1990, prod. Jay Miller) includes more Excello sides with alternate

takes compiled from three other Flyright LPs. *Been Gone Too Long* 𝅘𝅥𝅘𝅥𝅘𝅥 (Joliet, 1976/HighTone, 1991, prod. Bruce Bromberg) is the 1976 "comeback" session.

influences:

◄◄ Guitar Slim

Robert Sacré

Joe Hill Louis

Born Lester (or Leslie) Hill, September 23, 1921, in Froggy Bottom, TN. Died August 5, 1957, in Memphis, TN.

If Joe Hill Louis' backing band sometimes sounded a little rough or out-of-tune playing behind him, there was good reason. Louis *was* his own backup band, able to bash on drums, slash at his guitar and wail on his harmonica with a fury surpassed only by Howlin' Wolf in his early prime. And just to let people know that he could take on all comers, Louis was capable of a Wolf impersonation that could have fooled the Chess brothers. Like Wolf, Louis took advantage of the sniping between the Chesses and their recording rivals, the Bihari brothers, to record for both the Chess and RPM labels through much of the early 1950s. Playing in roadhouses and in Memphis' Handy Park, Louis had become popular after appearing on radio station WDIA in a daily 15-minute show sponsored by Pepticon, a southern elixir. He was soon recording for Sun records owner Sam Phillips, who also supplied both the Chess brothers and the Biharis with early Louis cuts. Almost everything Louis did was raw, but the most unvarnished of all was "Tigerman," a savage boast that echoed Rufus Thomas' "Bearcat" and Big Mama Thornton's version of Leiber and Stoller's "Hound Dog." Louis recorded for several other small Memphis-based labels and was a fixture on the local juke-joint scene until he cut his thumb while doing yard work. Infected by fertilizer, the wound worsened and Louis contracted a fatal case of tetanus.

what to buy: *The Be-Bop Boy* 𝅘𝅥𝅘𝅥𝅘𝅥𝅘𝅥 (Bear Family, 1992, prod. Sam Phillips), a hard-to-find German import, boasts superb sound and bonus 1950s-era tracks by Memphis regulars Big Walter Horton and Mose Vinson. Louis' 15 tracks are all rip-snorters, as mellifluous as a chainsaw.

what to buy next: Another import, *Sun Records: The Blues Years* 𝅘𝅥𝅘𝅥𝅘𝅥𝅘𝅥 (Charly, 1996, prod. Sam Phillips), is only for the well-heeled or the blues-crazy. At eight discs, this set crams in 202 Sun blues stars—including 10 cuts by Louis, all found on the Bear Family disc.

worth searching for: *Memphis Blues* ♫♫♫ (Blues Interactions, 1994) is another expensive and spottily-found import, worth searching for only because it contains three Louis cuts not found elsewhere, along with coarse Memphis blues by Howlin' Wolf, Willie Nix, Bobby Bland and the late great Johnny Ace. Oh, mama . . . .

influences:
◄◄ Howlin' Wolf

Steve Braun

Louisiana Red

Born Iverson Minter, March 23, 1936, in Vicksburg, MS.

Self-taught guitar and harmonica player, Louisiana Red (a.k.a. Playboy Fuller, Rocky Fuller, Guitar Red and Elmore James Jr.) started imitating his idols (Muddy Waters, Lightnin' Hopkins, Earl Hooker, Elmore James, Jimmy Reed, Little Walter) before developing a more personal, instinctive style. Quickly, he showed a rare talent to build and write sarcastic stories well served by his scorched voice, stories often autobiographical ("I Am Louisiana Red," "Story of La Red," "Sweet Alesse," "Death of Elesse," "Valerie," "Starving in Detroit," "When My Mama Was Living"), and sometimes topical ("Red's Dream," "Antinuclear Blues," "Reagan Is for the Rich Man," "Gasoline Blues"). He is a specialist of introverted, intense performance, living his sad stories again and crying in true despair over emotionally charged guitar licks, well served by his great slide playing. Some of his blues are happy, though, and his heavily rhythmic style does wonders.

what to buy: *The Low Down Back Porch Blues* ♫♫♫♫ (Roulette, 1962/1964/Sequel, 1992, prod. Henry Glover) is a collection of his best early 1960s sides in New York with Tommy Tucker. *Louisiana Red Sings the Blues* ♫♫♫♫ (Atco, 1971/Blue Sting, 1994, prod. Herb Abramson) offers up more from the period 1965–71 with Tucker on piano and Bill Dicey on harp and great songs like "Red's New Dream" and "Country Playboy." *The Blues Purity of Louisiana Red* ♫♫♫♫ (Blue Labor, 1975, prod. Kent Cooper, Heiner Stadler) is two volumes of acoustic blues, Red at his best.

what to buy next: *My Life* ♫♫♫ (L&R, 1979, prod. Horst Lippmann), *New York Blues* ♫♫♫ (L&R, 1979, prod. Horst Lippmann) and *Boy from Black Bayou* ♫♫♫ (L&R, 1983, prod. Horst Lippmann) are the European sessions in various settings with the same unique talent. *King Bee* ♫♫♫ (JSP, 1979, prod. John Stedman) is a duo with harmonica player Sugar Blue.

the rest:

Midnight Rambler ♫♫♫ (Tomato, 1992)

Best of Louisiana Red ♫♫♫♫ (Evidence, 1995)
Sittin' Here Wonderin' ♫♫♫ (Earwig, 1995)
(With Lefty Dizz) *Walked All Night Alone* ♫♫♫♫ (Blues Alliance, 1997)

influences:
◄◄ Guitar Slim, Fred McDowell

Robert Sacré

G. Love & Special Sauce

Formed 1993, in Boston, MA.

G. Love (born Garrett Dutton, October 3, 1972, in Philadelphia, PA), vocals, guitar; Jeffrey Clemens, drums; Jimmy Prescott, bass (1993–96); King Kane, bass (1996–present).

A contemporary update of Jimmy Page, Keith Richards, Eric Clapton and all the young British 1960s musicians who scavenged old blues records, G. Love is a surprisingly successful merger of hip-hop and traditional styles. But while Love's stylish sideburns help draw the teenage girls to his shows, he's no sarcastic hipster. Like the Rolling Stones and Yardbirds before him, he makes a point of honoring his influences, from Bob Dylan to Professor Longhair.

what to buy: The young singer-songwriter's style, especially on his debut, *G. Love & Special Sauce* ♫♫♫ (OKeh/Epic, 1994, prod. Stiff Johnson, Special Sauce), mimics the Beastie Boys' bratty rap. Still, if anything, his music is too tradition-conscious; he titles his first single, "The Things That I Used to Do," closely after the Guitar Slim classic "The Things I Used to Do."

what to buy next: Love uses classic old instruments and amps to impeccably reproduce classic New Orleans rhythms on *Coast to Coast Motel* ♫♫♫ (OKeh/Epic, 1995, prod. Jim Dickinson, Special Sauce). If there was an "alternative blues" niche, like the recent no-depression movement in country music, Love's Special Sauce, along with Jon Spencer, Doo Rag and PJ Harvey, would be the figurehead.

influences:
◄◄ Guitar Slim, Professor Longhair, Bob Dylan, Eric Clapton

Steve Knopper

Willie Love

Born Willie Love Jr., November 4, 1906, in Duncan, MS. Died August 1, 1953, in Jackson, MS.

Willie Love was a talented pianist who specialized in midtempo blues numbers. In addition to working solo in juke joints, in the 1940s he was a member of the Tunica, Mississippi-based Silver Kings. In 1946 he moved to Greenville, Mississippi, where he was considered the town's leading blues pianist, appearing in jukes and on several radio stations. A contemporary of Sonny Boy Williamson II—Sonny Boy introduced him to Trumpet Records' Lillian McMurray—Love accompanied Miller on several Trumpet sessions before cutting his first single in 1951, the attractive "Take It Easy Baby"/"Little Car Blues." Of his seven Trumpet releases, the most popular was "Nelson Street Blues," which paid tribute to his Greenville home.

what to buy: Alligator—which has reissued the Trumpet catalog—chose to spread Love's material over three CDs. Investigate *Clownin' with the World* 𝄢𝄢𝄢𝄢 (Alligator, 1993)—a CD he shares with Sonny Boy; *Delta Blues—1951* 𝄢𝄢𝄢𝄢 (Alligator, 1993); and *Shout Brother Shout* 𝄢𝄢𝄢𝄢 (Alligator, 1993).

worth searching for: If you'd like all your Willie Love material in one place and you still own a turntable, Oldie Blues collected all of the Love 78s on one LP back in 1983.

influences:

 Leroy Carr, Roosevelt Sykes, Little Brother Montgomery

▶▶ Otis Spann, Little Milton

Jeff Hannusch

Albert Luandrew

See: Sunnyland Slim

Willie Mabon

Born October 24, 1925, in Memphis, TN. Died April 19, 1985, in Paris, France.

"I Don't Know" paid this singer-pianist-harpist's rent for a long time after it became a top R&B hit in 1952. But beyond that and the original Chess version of Willie Dixon's "The Seventh Son," Mabon lived a hard-luck life of obscurity. It's uncanny how much like Dixon he sounds on his solo albums, which undoubtedly helped establish him as a viable touring act in Europe. (He moved to Paris, after a long escape from the music industry, in 1972.) That quality never helped him get to the right record company at the right time—save for his brief stay at Chess—and, like so many of his contemporaries, his big breaks never quite lived up to his big talent.

what to buy: *Chicago 63* 𝄢𝄢𝄢 (America, 1974) and the 1979 studio document *Chicago Blues Session!* 𝄢𝄢𝄢 (Evidence, 1995, prod. Horst Lippmann) are solid but unspectacular albums, with Mabon making like Dixon on the master's "Little Red Rooster" and "Seventh Son" but hitting the high notes with much more soulful frequency.

what to buy next: *I Don't Know: The Best of Willie Mabon* 𝄢𝄢𝄢 (Wolf, 1995) includes Mabon's post-Chess 1960s songs and some live European recordings from the 1970s.

the rest:

Original USA Recordings 𝄢𝄢𝄢 (Flyright, 1981)

worth searching for: Preoccupied with its never-ending compilations of Muddy Waters, Howlin' Wolf and Buddy Guy, Chess has never reissued Mabon's underrecognized hits, so until then the import LP *The Seventh Son* 𝄢𝄢𝄢𝄢 (Crown Prince, 1991) and *Seventh Son* 𝄢𝄢𝄢 (Charly, 1993) will have to do—they contain "Got to Have It," "Knock on Wood" and, of course, "Seventh Son."

influences:

 Willie Dixon

Steve Knopper

Samuel Maghett

See: Magic Sam

Magic Sam

Born Samuel Maghett, February 14, 1937, in Grenada, MS. Died December 1, 1969, in Chicago, IL.

Unlike his Chicago blues contemporaries, Otis Rush and Buddy Guy, Magic Sam's explosive 1950s and 1960s music is frozen in time. The tragic character never got the chance to grow old with the blues, record albums, make a comeback or tape a commercial for Reebok, because he died of a heart attack at age 32. But his many singles, all cut with the explosive single-guitar solos that defined Chicago's West Side style at the time, have a screaming, lurching power that even Guy and Rush have had trouble maintaining. Born in the Mississippi Delta, Maghett built his own guitar and copied the players he heard at parties and picnics; he was eventually good enough to join Homesick James' band. (The Army drafted him in 1959; he deserted, got caught and served in jail until 1961.) After that, he became one of the West Side's most popular club performers and recorded several excellent sides for, most prominently, Cobra. His career was about to take off after an astounding performance at the

1969 Ann Arbor Blues Festival, but he died before he could embark upon planned European tours.

what to buy: *Magic Sam 1957–66 West Side Guitar* 🎸🎸🎸🎸 (Paula, 1991, prod. various), the most complete CD document of Sam's Cobra sides, captures the young guitarist at his hungriest; on "Everything Gonna Be Alright" and "Roll Your Money Maker," the singer's moaning voice and sharp, fast and perfectly timed solos sound like they could explode any second.

what to buy next: *West Side Soul* 🎸🎸🎸 (Delmark, 1968) is one of those astounding Chicago blues albums—with "Sweet Home Chicago," of course—that makes so many other Chicago blues albums sound stale and redundant. Sam pulls off soul ("That's All I Need") and flashy guitar instrumentals ("Lookin' Good") with equal poise and power.

the rest:

Black Magic 🎸🎸🎸 (Delmark, 1969)
Late Great Magic Sam 🎸🎸🎸 (Evidence, 1984)
Magic Sam Legacy 🎸🎸🎸 (Delmark, 1989)
Live at Ann Arbor & in Chicago 🎸🎸🎸 (Delmark, 1990)
Give Me Time 🎸🎸🎸 (Delmark, 1991)
Otis Rush & Magic Sam 🎸🎸🎸 (Paul, 1991)

influences:

⏪ Muddy Waters, Otis Rush, Buddy Guy, Freddie King, Albert King

⏩ Son Seals, Stevie Ray Vaughan, Jimi Hendrix, Eric Clapton, Magic Slim

Steve Knopper

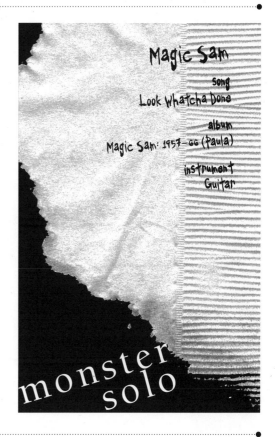

Magic Sam

song
Look Whatcha Done

album
Magic Sam: 1957–66 (Paula)

instrument
Guitar

monster solo

Magic Slim

Born Morris Holt, August 7, 1937, in Grenada, MS.

You can't hear the best parts of a Magic Slim and the Teardrops concert on any CD. The singer-guitarist stalks the stage, even tiny ones like his venerable Chicago nightclub haunts B.L.U.E.S. and B.L.U.E.S. Etc., wanders into the audience to march around and dance and frequently winds up sitting at the bar. Slim's an excellent guitarist, but his Jackie Wilson-like voice doesn't get nearly enough attention—sometimes he seems overly goofy, singing barely disguised sex-frustration songs like "Can't Get No Grindin'," but it all makes him a more fun and charismatic performer. Born in Mississippi, Holt lost his little finger in an accident with a cotton gin, so he had to stop playing the piano and take up guitar. His friend Magic Sam gave him his name, but he quickly became frustrated when his talent didn't live up to the highly competitive Chicago scene.

After returning to Mississippi to practice and perform, Holt, with guitarist John Primer at his side for 13 years, came back and very slowly built a reputation as one of Chicago's most reliable blues showmen.

what to buy: The title track of *Scufflin'* 🎸🎸🎸 (Blind Pig, 1996, prod. Jerry Del Giudice, Michael Freeman) is one of Slim's raunchy trademarks, and while the album occasionally slows down to conventional 12-bar blues, its playful highlights include "Room 109" and "Hole in the Wall."

what to buy next: It's difficult to truly capture the charisma and visual energy of Slim's Teardrops, but *Live at B.L.U.E.S.* 🎸🎸🎸 (B.L.U.E.S. R&B, 1987), comes close. Standouts include the long, stretched-out "Mother Fuyer" and "Help Yourself."

what to avoid: Slim's timing, as far as figuring out which performances to record when, has always been a little off; *Live at the Zoo Bar* 🎸🎸 (Candy Apple, 1980), a Nebraska concert docu-

ment, seems even more off than usual, barely hinting at the Teardrops' still-maturing talent.

the rest:

Highway Is My Home ♫♫♪ (Evidence, 1979)
Raw Magic ♫♫♪ (Alligator, 1982)
Gravel Road ♫♫♪ (Blind Pig, 1990)

worth searching for: Slim, who had just taken over for Hound Dog Taylor at the popular South Side club Florence's, acquits himself well on "Stranded on the Highway," the playful "Spider in My Stew" and four other heavy-soloing tracks on *Living Chicago Blues, Vol. II* ♫♫♪ (Alligator, 1978/1991, prod. various). Also, his excellent LP *Grand Slam* ♫♫♪ (Rooster Blues, 1982) has never been reissued on CD and is very hard to track down.

influences:

◀◀ Magic Sam, Otis Rush, Buddy Guy, Freddie King, Albert King, Muddy Waters

▶▶ Luther Allison, Stevie Ray Vaughan, Kenny Wayne Shepherd

Steve Knopper

Taj Mahal

Born Henry St. Claire Fredericks, May 17, 1942, in New York, NY.

Although he grew up in Brooklyn and went to college in Massachusetts, Taj Mahal extends his hands to other musical cultures and soaks them up like a sponge. His father was a jazz musician, his mother a gospel singer, and his 30-plus years of exploring the blues, ragtime and Caribbean rhythms show those and many other influences. If his music seems like a history lesson at times, those didactic leanings are matched by his boundless enthusiasm and a formidable instrumental versatility. Mahal's journey began during the mid-1960s with the equally eclectic Ry Cooder in a short-lived assemblage called the Rising Sons. Mahal's first albums dug into standard blues in a manner that presented him as a guardian of tradition, then abruptly veered toward African rhythms, Caribbean reggae and even children's music before venturing into the then-untested waters of world music. Uncharacteristically quiet during the 1980s, Taj has returned to a blues approach since the turn of the decade. Whether he's with a full band playing pop arrangements or stripped-down roots, Mahal has asserted himself yet

again as a keeper of the faith and a still vital force that continues to roam past musical boundaries.

what to buy: Two albums on one disc, *Giant Step/De Old Folks at Home* ♫♫♫♫ (Columbia, 1969, prod. David Rubinson) tosses up distinctively different sides of the blues coin, the former lightly rocking with a down-home band while the rural solo blues of the latter reveal a surprisingly adept multi-instrumentalist and vocalist. For a harder-edged entry into his early work, *Taj's Blues* ♫♫♫♫ (Columbia Legacy, 1992, prod. David Rubinson, Taj Mahal) is a handy sampler of some of his more celebrated moments, such as the classic stomper "Statesboro Blues" and "Dust My Broom."

what to buy next: The ease at which Mahal slips into third-world rhythms is disarming, as the easy-fitting reggae beats of *World Music* ♫♫♫♫ (Columbia Legacy, 1993, prod. Lawrence Cohn) demonstrate. Since it contains nearly all of *Mo' Roots* plus other tracks in remastered form, it gets the slight edge over *Mo' Roots* itself. In a welcome paradoxical twist, the Grammy-winning *Phantom Blues* ♫♫♫♫ (Private Music, 1996, prod. John Porter) deserves the attention it received. Save for the rolling, country soul of the opening cut, he didn't pen a single tune, instead paying a charging homage to mentors like Fats Domino and Ray Charles, his vocals as muscular as ever. His clear love for the material gives an extra shot of energy.

what to avoid: If you have kids, by all means go for *Shake Sugaree—Taj Mahal Sings and Plays for Children* ♫♫♪ (Music for Little People, 1988, prod. Taj Mahal). If your largest responsibility is a goldfish, there are plenty of others to get first.

the rest:

Mo' Roots ♫♫♪ (Columbia, 1974)
Best of Taj Mahal, Vol. 1 ♫♫♪ (Columbia, 1981)
Like Never Before ♫♫♪ (Private Music, 1991)
Mule Bone ♫♫♪ (Gramavision, 1991)
Dancing the Blues ♫♫♪ (Private Music, 1993)
The Rising Sun Collection ♫♫♪ (Just a Memory, 1994)
Taj ♫♫♪ (Gramavision, 1994)
An Evening of Acoustic Music ♫♫♪ (Ruf, 1996)
Live at Ronnie Scott's, London ♫♫♪ (DRG, 1996)
Senor Blues ♫♫♪ (Private Music, 1997)

worth searching for: The divergence that led to the band's split is spelled out on *Rising Sons Featuring Taj Mahal and Ry Cooder* ♫♫♪ (Legacy, 1992, prod. Amy Herot, Bob Irwin), a collection of the fledgling group's only recordings. Half the time is devoted to Mahal and Cooder's raw-boned blues temperament,

Magic Slim (© Linda Vartoogian)

Taj Mahal (© Jack Vartoogian)

while a good portion contains pop and folk sunshine brought by the group's other half. And *Mumtaz Mahal* 🎸🎸🎸 (Water Lilly Acoustics, 1995, prod. Kavichandran Alexander), a jam session with master Indian string musicians V.M. Bhatt and Narasimhan Ravikiran, offers strong evidence that all blues didn't come from the Delta.

influences:

◀◀ Robert Johnson, Fats Domino, Howlin' Wolf, Ray Charles

▶▶ Robert Cray, Eric Clapton, Ry Cooder

Allan Orski

Harvey Mandel

Born March 11, 1945, in Detroit, MI.

Though he got his start in the blues—specifically, as a Chicago guitarist among other young white hotshots such as Steve Miller and Mike Bloomfield—Mandel has spent most of his career mak-

ing jazz-rock fusion albums. In Chicago, he played in harpist Charlie Musselwhite's bands, went solo, served briefly as Canned Heat's guitarist in 1969 and 1970 and did three separate stints with John Mayall's Bluesbreakers. He never became a huge star, even losing a Rolling Stones audition to Ron Wood in the mid-1970s, but young guitarists were paying attention. Future metal and jazz guitar virtuosos borrowed regularly from his techniques.

what to buy: You'll need to love flashy guitar jams and appreciate technical fingerwork to enjoy Mandel's albums. (Or, as critic Robert Christgau once remarked: "Ron Wood made better solo albums. And Bill Wyman came close.") The double-disc *Mercury Years* 🎸🎸🎸 (Mercury, 1995, prod. various) includes Mandel's first three solo albums, and it's a nice batch of jazz-blues-Latin-rock fusion guitar showmanship for people who appreciate Jeff Beck, Carlos Santana and Eric Clapton's more show-offy jams.

what to buy next: *Baby Batter* 🎸🎸 (Janus, 1971) is probably Mandel's most successful instrumental album.

the rest:

Cristo Redentor ♫♫ (EG, 1968)
Righteous ♫♫♫ (Philips, 1969)
Games Guitars Play ♫♫♫ (Philips, 1970)
Get Off in Chicago ♫♫ (Ovation, 1972)
The Snake ♫♫♫ (Janus, 1972)

influences:

◀◀ Jeff Beck, Eric Clapton, Mike Bloomfield, Steve Miller, Carlos Santana, Jimi Hendrix

▶▶ Steve Vai, Kenny Wayne Shepherd, Chick Corea, Eddie Van Halen, Stanley Jordan

Steve Knopper

Bob Margolin

Born May 9, 1949, in Boston, MA.

Steady Rollin' Bob Margolin very self-consciously bears the stamp of Muddy Waters—that nickname, for example—but Margolin has a better claim to the legacy than most. He spent seven years as a sideman in Waters' band, appearing on nine of his albums as well as alongside him in the Band's 1978 concert movie *The Last Waltz*. He has since parlayed that into a decent journeyman's career, seemingly content to keep Muddy's memory alive. And if Margolin ain't gonna make anybody forget Muddy, that seems perfectly OK by him.

what to buy: While Margolin has always been a fine guitarist, his first two albums suffer from vocals too similar to old mentor Muddy—and they can't help but pale by comparison. His more recent work is vastly better, especially *My Blues & My Guitar* ♫♫♫ (Alligator, 1995, prod. Bob Margolin, Mark "Kaz" Kazanoff). He's not much of a roarer, but he can croon just fine. On the instrumental side, *My Blues & My Guitar* shows some unexpected range with the jazzy overtones of the amusing original "Maybe the Hippies Were Right."

what to buy next: *Down in the Alley* ♫♫♫ (Alligator, 1993, prod. Bob Margolin, Mark "Kaz" Kazanoff) isn't far behind *My Blues & My Guitar*, a solid meat-and-potatoes effort and also Margolin's first real attempt to get beyond Waters' daunting shadow, with seven originals among its 15 songs.

the rest:

The Old School ♫♫♫ (Powerhouse, 1989)
Chicago Blues ♫♫♫ (Powerhouse, 1991)

influences:

◀◀ Muddy Waters, Eric Clapton, Freddie King

David Menconi

Johnny Mars

Born December 7, 1942, in Laurens, SC.

Inspired by Little Walter, Jimmy Reed and Muddy Waters, Johnny Mars was a child growing up in Florida when he began playing harmonica. While still a teenager, he lived briefly in New York state, where he started his first blues band. After moving to California in the mid-1960s, he continued playing, often working with blues artists that toured the area like Magic Sam. Mars moved to England in the early 1970s and joined the Sunflower Blues Band. The band got good ink in the English blues magazines and made an LP on Big Bear. Mars took ill in 1975 and returned to the U.S. His whereabouts are currently unknown.

worth searching for: *The Big Bear LP* ♫♫♫ (Blues on Mars) is comprised of mostly covers.

influences:

◀◀ Muddy Waters, Little Walter, Sonny Boy Williamson II

Jeff Hannusch

David Maxwell

Born March 10, 1950, in Waltham, MA.

David Maxwell is an accomplished pianist who is equally at home in both blues and jazz idioms. During his 25-year career he has played on upwards of 20 albums and been a touring band member with Freddie King, Bonnie Raitt, Buddy Guy, Junior Wells and James Cotton. Maxwell began taking piano lessons at age eight, first from various neighborhood teachers, then from the Boston area's top piano instructors, as a teen studying with Saul Skersey and Charlie Banacos. In the late 1960s, Maxwell became involved in the local Boston club scene at such places as the Jazz Workshop, Paul's Mall, Club 47, the Catacombs and the Unicorn—where blues was often the featured music—sitting in with Muddy Waters, John Lee Hooker and Big Mama Thornton as well as forming his own Boston Blues Band with Bob Margolin. In 1972, Freddie King invited Maxwell to join his road band, and during the 1970s and 1980s Maxwell often could be found backing visiting blues dignitaries Albert Collins, Big Walter Horton, Otis Rush, Lowell Fulson, Hubert Sumlin, Johnny Shines or Eddie Vinson at Boston area clubs or playing behind one major artist or another at the big festivals. In the early 1990s, Maxwell spent three years as one of Ronnie Earl's Broadcasters.

what to buy: *Maximum Blues Piano* ♫♫♫♫ (Tone-Cool, 1997, prod. Bob Kempf, David Maxwell) is Maxwell's only official release as a leader. The mostly instrumental album effectively shows off Maxwell's feel and technical proficiency, demonstrating why he's become such a popular session musician, with contributions from guitarist Ronnie Earl and hornmen Gordon Beadle and Mark Kazanoff. Its only fault may be dabbling in too many styles.

worth searching for: Maxwell has appeared on many albums, including James Cotton's Grammy-winner, *Deep in the Blues* ♪♪♪♪ (Verve, 1997).

influences:

◄◄ Otis Spann, Pinetop Perkins, Johnny Johnson, Sunnyland Slim, Big Maceo Merriweather, Meade Lux Lewis, Albert Ammons, Pete Johnson

►► Anthony Gerassi, Teo Layesmeyer, Barrelhouse Chuck

Michael Dixon

John Mayall

Born November 29, 1933, in Macclesfield, England.

Two truths about John Mayall: he's a survivor, and he's got a keen ear for talent. Mayall was a seminal force in the early British blues scene that produced so many great and influential artists, most notably Eric Clapton. Slow Hand was working construction after leaving the Yardbirds, then a relatively unknown young British rock band, when Mayall made him one of his Bluesbreakers, the band he fronted until the 1980s and revived in the 1990s. The roster of artists who've worked with the venerable singer and harmonica player is a who's who of British blues-rock: Mick Taylor, John McVie, Mick Fleetwood, Colin Allen, Jimmy McCulloch, Peter Green, Jack Bruce, Aynsley Dunbar, Chris Mercer, Jon Mark and Johnny Almond, to name several. Mayall is considered one of the fathers of the 1960s British blues movement, but, unlike his peer, the late Alexis Korner, he was able to make it beyond the small clubs to become a star in his own right, releasing some of the most consistent, faithful blues records on either side of the Atlantic. Mayall's longevity—he's still recording and touring and discovering new talent well into his sixties—is attributable largely to his ability to redefine the blues, finding new and challenging ways to interpret and expand the American music he loves so dearly.

what to buy: If ever an artist cried out for a boxed set, Mayall is it. But there is no such thing, so you're better off checking out a few albums that represent important phases in Mayall's career. *Bluesbreakers—John Mayall with Eric Clapton* ♪♪♪ (Deram, 1966, prod. Mike Vernon) captures the legendary singer and guitarist in one of their earliest and grittiest phases (there's a

more expensive, Mobile Fidelity gold-disc version that offers improved sound; the recordings are pretty raw). *The Turning Point* ♪♪♪ (Deram, 1969, prod. John Mayall) is an all-acoustic affair (no drums, even) that includes his harmonica showcase, "Room to Move." *Archives to Eighties* ♪♪♪ (Deram, 1988, prod. John Mayall) is an unusual and successful late-1980s restoration of his 1971 *Back to the Roots* album which featured Clapton and Mick Taylor. Mayall spruced up the drums, added some new material and essentially came up with a new and fresh-sounding record.

what to buy next: The mid-1970s to 1980s were mostly fallow for Mayall, who had fallen out of favor with blues and rock fans. But he hung in there and in 1990 came up with one of the most assured and eloquent sets of blues-rock in his career. *A Sense of Place* ♪♪♪ (Island, 1990, prod. R.S. Field) is a little more slick than his fans are used to, but Mayall's wisened vocals and smart song selection prove that the blues don't have to be raw or formulaic.

what to avoid: *Behind the Iron Curtain* ♪♪ (GNP/Crescendo, 1985) is a good idea—it was recorded in Hungary—but not a particularly thrilling or memorable live album.

the rest:

A Hard Road ♪♪♪ (Deram, 1967)
Diary of a Band, Vol. 1 ♪♪♪ (London, 1968)
Diary of a Band, Vol. 2 ♪♪♪ (London, 1968)
Bare Wires ♪♪♪ (Rebound, 1968)
Blues Alone ♪♪♪ (Deram, 1968)
Blues from Laurel Canyon ♪♪♪ (Deram, 1968)
Looking Back ♪♪♪ (Deram, 1968)
Empty Rooms ♪♪♪ (Polydor, 1969)
USA Union ♪♪♪ (Polydor, 1970)
Jazz Blues Fusion ♪♪♪ (Polydor, 1972)
Primal Solos ♪♪♪ (Deram, 1988)
John Mayall: London Blues, 1964–69 ♪♪♪ (Polydor, 1992)
John Mayall: Room to Move, 1969–74 ♪♪♪ (Polydor, 1992)
Wake Up Call ♪♪♪ (Silvertone, 1993)
Spinning Coin ♪♪♪ (Silvertone, 1995)
Blues for the Lost Days ♪♪♪ (Silvertone, 1997)

worth searching for: Mayall's first album, *John Mayall Plays John Mayall* ♪♪♪♪ (1965) was released in his native England, but never made it to these shores.

influences:

◄◄ Muddy Waters, Little Walter, Howlin' Wolf

►► Rolling Stones, Blues Traveler

Doug Pullen

Percy Mayfield

Born August 12, 1920, in Minden, LA. Died August 11, 1984, in Los Angeles, CA.

Percy Mayfield lived two blues careers, the first as a singing heartthrob, the second as the author of such Ray Charles classics as "Hit the Road Jack," "At the Club" and "Danger Zone." What separated Mayfield's two lives was a car wreck in 1952 that left him disfigured with a dented skull. Unable to woo audiences in person, Mayfield drew on the songwriting talent that had already produced a formidable catalog, including the tortured "Please Send Me Someone to Love" and "Strange Things Happening." A young poet who learned musical composition in a parish school in Louisiana, Mayfield hit the ground running when he arrived in Los Angeles in the early 1940s. Balancing singing jobs with work as a taxi driver and presser, Mayfield first recorded for Exclusive. He had written "Two Years of Torture" for Jimmy Witherspoon, but his own version marked him as an up-and-comer. Picked up by Art Rupe for Specialty, Mayfield's first session in 1950 launched "Someone to Love" to the top of the charts. Riding high for two years on the strength of his introspective ballads and loping, slang-hopped blues, Mayfield was devastated by the car crash that sent him into seclusion. Not confident enough to perform, Mayfield recorded fitfully with Chess and Imperial. But mostly he sharpened his writing talents, becoming a key player in Charles' growing stable of talents and even recording two albums for the Genius' Tangerine label in the 1960s. Relations between the two men grew frosty late in the decade, but by then, Mayfield had finally begun to appear in public again. Before his 1984 death, Mayfield had returned to prominence on the L.A. blues scene, a respected figure no matter what he looked like.

what to buy: From the opening of 1950's pleading "Please Send Me Someone to Love," the compilation *Poet of the Blues* ♪♪♪♪♪ (Specialty, 1990, prod. Art Rupe) never flags. There are 25 artfully-penned blues finds here, all piloted by an expert L.A. band led by the king of session men, Maxwell Davis. Highlights are the dark "Life Is Suicide" and "Get Way Back," a swinging caution to a clinging woman that has Brother Ray written all over it.

what to buy next: Leavened by several alternate takes of Mayfield's biggest hits, the 25-song *Memory Pain* ♪♪♪♪ (Specialty, 1992, prod. Art Rupe) is nearly as accomplished as the first Specialty volume. Mayfield rarely repeated himself, avoiding the trap that snared many R&B performers. The most fascinating tidbit here is a demo version of "Hit the Road, Jack" that shows how Mayfield tailored his songs for the Genius.

John Mayall
song
Room to Move
album
The Turning Point (Deram)
instrument
Harmonica/mouth percussion

monster solo

the rest:

Hit the Road Again ♪♪♪ (Timeless, 1989)
Percy Mayfield Live ♪♪♪ (Winner, 1992)

influences:

◀◀ Jimmy Witherspoon, Walter Brown

▶▶ Ray Charles, Lou Rawls, B.B. King

Steve Braun

Jerry McCain

Born June 18, 1930, in Gadsden, AL.

For every Chuck Berry and Bo Diddley, there was a 1950s R&B singer who could rock just as well as anybody but never quite got the fame. This singer-songwriter-harpist's earliest singles, from "East of the Sun" on Trumpet to a wonderful string of late-1950s Excello non-hits, had the same explosive quality as

"School Days" and "I'm a Man." His songs were harmonica-driven, obviously, but what continues to stand out is the sly romanticism of the lyrics and the tightness of McCain's early bands. It's unclear why even the beautiful 1960 Rex single "She's Tough" never became a hit, but shortly after that McCain drifted below even his cult audience's radar screen. He resurfaced with Ichiban in 1989 and has been recording and touring ever since.

what to buy: The uncanny resemblance to Chuck Berry comes across on *That's What They Want: The Best of Jerry McCain* 🎵🎵🎵 (Excello, 1995, prod. Ernie Young), but McCain is a true original, writing such terrific blues lines as "you get paid on Saturday, but Saturday never come" on "Bad Credit"; it's amazing that this crucial supplement to better-known 1950s rock hasn't earned a larger audience.

what to buy next: *Strange Kind of Feelin'* 🎵🎵🎵 (Acoustic Archives, 1990), his 1953–54 Trumpet 78s, includes the funny "Stay out of Automobiles" and "Middle of the Night." The best of his contemporary blues albums is *Struttin' My Stuff* 🎵🎵🎵 (Wild Dog/Ichiban, 1992, prod. Bryan Cole).

what to avoid: Possibly disgusted by his failed efforts at rock notoriety, McCain coasted through *Blues 'n' Stuff* 🎵🎵 (Ichiban, 1967).

the rest:
Love Desperado 🎵🎵 (Ichiban, 1992)
I've Got the Blues All Over Me 🎵🎵 (Wild Dog/Ichiban, 1993)

influences:
◀◀ Chuck Berry, Elmore James, Bo Diddley, Muddy Waters, Ike Turner, Louis Jordan, Screamin' Jay Hawkins

▶▶ Elvis Presley, Beatles, Rolling Stones, John Hiatt, Blasters

Steve Knopper

Cash McCall

Born Morris Dollison Jr., January 28, 1941, in New Madrid, MO.

Though his voice is rich with charisma and he has tried his best to become a blues singing star, McCall is best known as a behind-the-scenes writer and producer. After a stint in the Army's 82nd Airborne Division, he started out playing guitar with Chicago gospel bands, including Otis Clay's Gospel Songbirds. He recorded various R&B singles, including 1963's "Earth Worm" and more successfully, 1966's "When You Wake Up," which hit #19 on the R&B charts and earned him a slot on a national Dick Clark tour with rock singer Mitch Ryder. He wound up as a Chess Records session guitarist, where he befriended Willie Dixon (whose 1988 *Hidden Charms* he co-produced). Mc-

Call's early albums, on labels from Checker to Paula, are difficult to find; easier are his conventional 1980s blues albums.

what to buy: *No More Doggin'* 🎵🎵 (Evidence, 1983/1995, prod. Horst Lippmann) shows McCall as a nice, personable singer and decent, understated guitarist; he has the same kind of goofy gravel in his voice as Rufus Thomas, but he insists on singing predictable 12-bar blues like "Mojo Woman" and "Southern Woman." *Cash Up Front* 🎵🎵 (Stony Plain, 1987) is even more professionally produced and, in the end, unoriginal.

worth searching for: *Omega Man* 🎵🎵🎵 (Paula, 1973, prod. Cash McCall, Chuck Colbert Jr.) shows McCall drifting from his familiar R&B and, possibly because of Dixon's influence, heading toward straightforward blues.

influences:
◀◀ Willie Dixon, Ray Charles, Rufus Thomas, Otis Redding

Steve Knopper

Mighty Sam McClain

Born 1943, in Monroe, LA.

Back in the 1960s, when people fretted that electric blues was losing its commercial appeal, gospel-derived secular soul music was seen as the culprit. The voices of Otis Redding, Solomon Burke and Wilson Pickett were more exciting—and more relevant—than the instrumental prowess of Muddy, Sonny Boy or Little Walter. In the years since blues has experienced a resurgence as soul has become passe. But a hybrid—soul-blues—has allowed some great 1960s vocalists to find a new audience. The man who perhaps has gained the most from this, Mighty Sam McClain, was a virtual unknown in the 1960s. At age five he started singing with his mother's gospel group; by 13 he left home to escape his stepfather. Working as a musician throughout the South, first with Monroe guitarist Little Marvin Underwood and then with the Alabama-based Dothan Sextet, he finally got a chance to cut a record in 1966. Under the stewardship of manager Papa Don Schroeder, his version of Patsy Cline's "Sweet Dreams," recorded in Muscle Shoals, Alabama, became a regional hit, although a rival version by Tommy McClain (no relation) went nationwide. His follow-ups went nowhere, and he even spent time homeless in New Orleans, selling plasma to survive. But he did get support from friends in the Crescent City's music community. Finally, signed to California-based Audioquest, his first disc—*Give It up to Love*—was astonishingly accomplished. It was as if he'd spent the last 20 years playing the finest clubs and blues festivals with the best-rehearsed players, not just scraping to survive.

McClain is making better music in this important genre as any comeback-minded 1960s-era soul singer, including many who were much more famous than he ever became.

what to buy: *Keep on Movin'* ♫♫♫ (Audioquest, 1995, prod. Joe Harley, Mighty Sam McClain) is the best of his three 1990s albums to date. A suave horn section and his tight, groovin' combo allow his voice to go deep and emerge with strongly felt resonance on ballads and mid-tempo numbers like his own "Can You Stand the Test of Love" and Ronnie Earl's "A Soul That's Been Abused."

what to buy next: *Sledgehammer Soul & Down Home Blues* ♫♫♫ (Audioquest, 1996, prod. Joe Harley, Mighty Sam McClain) stresses straightforward blues a bit more than his previous discs. *Give It up to Love* ♫♫♫ is available in two versions; the regular-priced Audioquest release and a deluxe, remastered reissue from JVC Records. With an expressive baritone voice not unlike Bobby "Blue" Bland and a fine band featuring Kevin Barry's stinging B.B. King-style guitar and Bruce Katz's jazzy Hammond B-3 organ, it's a template for what's come to be called soul-blues.

the rest:

Your Perfect Companion ♫♫♫ (Orleans, 1995)

worth searching for: Charly Records in England collected Mc-Clain's early singles on a 1988 LP, *Nothing but the Truth* ♫♫♫ (Charly, 1988).

influences:

◀◀ Bobby "Blue" Bland, Solomon Burke, B.B. King, Al Kooper

▶▶ Ronnie Earl & the Broadcasters

Steven Rosen

Tommy McClennan

Born April 8, 1908, in Yazoo City, MS. Died c. 1960, in Chicago, IL.

Tommy McClennan's glory was his froggish, hoarse voice, reminiscent of Charley Patton's throaty growl. His spare guitar work was acceptable for time keeping, but McClennan was steeped in deep blues tunings, adept enough to win him popularity as a Mississippi house-party favorite. A prolific adapter who joined Lester Melrose's Bluebird gang, McClennan had none of their subtlety or finesse. Instead, he pounded away like a jackhammer, striking paydirt with the lasting "Bottle It Up and Go" and "Whiskey Head Woman." McClennan's "Cross Cut Saw Blues" influenced Albert King years later, and his boastful "I'm a Guitar King" is as succinct and ebullient a description of a bluesman's reason for keeping on as any has offered. A slightly-built man whose figure belied his hellhound voice, McClennan came on

the Delta scene in the late 1920s. He tramped through Greenwood, Indianola and Itta Bena, sometimes with his stylistic partner, Robert Petway, author of the timeless "Catfish Blues" (later adapted by McClennan as "Deep Sea Blues"). Summoned to Chicago by Bluebird in late 1939, McClennan recorded 41 tracks over the next three years until the start of World War II silenced his gravelly roar. Reportedly a heavy drinker, McClennan is said to have continued playing in Chicago clubs until the early 1950s. He died destitute, according to guitarist Mike Bloomfield, in Chicago sometime in the early 1960s.

what to buy: *The Bluebird Recordings 1941–42* ♫♫♫ (BMG, 1997, prod. Michael Omansky) is the complete McClennan, every track a yowling classic. BMG's sure-footed mastering puts McClennan right in your living room—a voice certain to give your landlady a stroke. The two-disc set also includes an excellent bio and rare photos of the Guitar King.

what to buy next: *Travelin' Highway Man* ♫♫♫ (Travelin' Man, 1990) includes half of McClennan's Bluebird sides, now rendered vestigial by BMG's two-disc set. *Tommy McClennan 1939–42* ♫♫♫ (Wolf, 1990) is a companion to the Travelin' Man set, worth hunting for only to satisfy your McClennan fix. Sound, like on the Travelin' Man set, is decent, but not up to the level of the BMG release.

influences:

◀◀ Charley Patton, Willie Brown, Robert Petway

▶▶ Albert King, Howlin' Wolf

Steve Braun

Delbert McClinton

Born November 4, 1940, in Lubbock, TX.

Delbert McClinton has been kicking around for years, playing a decidedly unfashionable mix of blues, rock, country and R&B that has rarely dented the charts. Highly regarded as a raspy, southern-fried vocalist, an adroit songwriter and harmonica player and performer par excellence, McClinton got his start on the Texas honky-tonk circuit, where he is still a fixture today. His early years were filled playing blues and breaking racial barriers—one of his bands, the Straitjackets, crossed the color line on a Ft. Worth black station in 1960 with a cover of Sonny Boy Williamson's "Wake Up Baby." He played harmonica on Bruce Channel's 1962 hit, "Hey Baby," and taught a then-unknown John Lennon a few licks while on tour in England. After fronting the Ron Dels in the 1960s, he formed a duo with Glen Clark, with whom he released two acclaimed albums in the early 1970s. The label-jumping, style-bending singer has been plugging ever since; his songs have been covered by artists as diverse as Emmylou Harris ("Two More Bottles of Wine") and the Blues Brothers ("B Movie Boxcar Blues").

what to buy: Few of McClinton's studio albums have done him justice, because it's onstage where he excels. His *Live from Austin* 𝄞𝄞𝄞 (Alligator, 1989, prod. Delbert McClinton), taped during an *Austin City Limits* appearance, is a rock-solid example of what this guy can do.

what to buy next: McClinton, no doubt frustrated at his lack of commercial success, called in the big guns for *Never Been Rocked Enough* 𝄞𝄞𝄞 (Curb, 1992, prod. Don Was, Jim Horn, Delbert McClinton, Bonnie Raitt), which includes his Grammy-winning version of "Good Man, Good Woman" (sung with Raitt) and guest shots from Melissa Etheridge, Tom Petty, Paul Shaffer and members of David Letterman's house band.

what to avoid: *Honky Tonk 'n' Blues* 𝄞𝄞 (MCA, 1994) sounds tired and uninspired.

the rest:
Second Wind 𝄞𝄞𝄞 (Mercury, 1978)
I'm with You 𝄞𝄞 (Curb, 1990)
The Best of Delbert McClinton 𝄞𝄞𝄞 (Curb, 1991)
Delbert McClinton 𝄞𝄞 (Curb, 1993)
Classics Vol. 1: The Jealous Kind 𝄞𝄞 (Curb, 1994)
Classics Vol. 2: Plain from the Heart 𝄞𝄞 (Curb, 1994)
The Great Songs: Come Together 𝄞𝄞 (Curb, 1995)

worth searching for: The two Delbert & Glen albums, *Delbert & Glen* 𝄞𝄞 (Clean, 1972, prod. Daniel J. Moore, J. Henry (T-Bone) Burnett) and *Subject to Change* 𝄞𝄞𝄞 (Clean, 1973, prod. Geoffrey Haslam), foresaw the fusion of country, rock and blues and hold up well today. They're long out of print and pressings are rare, but they're worth the trouble for completists.

influences:
◀◀ Jimmy Reed, Sonny Boy Williamson I, Bobby "Blue" Bland
▶▶ Lonnie Mack, Fabulous Thunderbirds

Doug Pullen

The McCoy Brothers

Charlie McCoy born May 26, 1909, in Jackson, MS; died July 26, 1950, in Chicago, IL. Joe McCoy born 1905, in Jackson, MS; died January 28, 1950, in Chicago, IL.

Like Charley Patton's sidekick, Willie Brown, the immensely creative McCoy brothers felt most at ease when they backed up other talented blues musicians. Charlie McCoy provided supple, sensitive guitar backing to Delta giants Tommy Johnson and Ishmon Bracey, while brother Joe backed up and was married (for six years) to the no-nonsense Memphis Minnie. Joe McCoy was the brasher of the two brothers. With Memphis Minnie, he was known as Kansas Joe McCoy, but he packed more sobriquets than Saddam Hussein has titles. Joe was known alternately as Mud Dauber Joe, the Georgia Pine Boy, Hamfoot Ham, the Hillbilly Plowboy, Hallelujah Joe and Wilbur McCoy. While Joe's voice was slightly plummy and deep, Charlie sang in a higher tenor. Charlie also was the first to record the standard that eventually became known as "Sweet Home Chicago." Charlie recorded his "Baltimore Blues" four weeks before Kokomo Arnold set his "Old Original Kokomo Blues" to wax, but both could be looked on as precursors to Robert Johnson's oft-played standard. Given a decent push at stardom, the McCoys, who were expert guitar players and rarely repeated themselves, might have gone further. Instead, they settled into long careers as backup men, making their way to Chicago, where they died six months apart.

what to buy: The blues contained on the two discs of *The McCoy Brothers, 1934–44* 𝄞𝄞𝄞𝄞 (RST, 1992, prod. Johnny Parth) often approaches the sublime playing and singing of Tommy Johnson, Ishmon Bracey and other bluesmen who frequented the Jackson area in the 1920s and 1930s. While Charlie McCoy's guitar on cuts like "Candy Man Blues" and "Baltimore Blues" is as inventive and nimble as any Delta blues on record, Joe McCoy often favors the spare slide-guitar style popularized by Kokomo Arnold and Casey Bill Weldon. Joe McCoy unleashes a bombastic religious streak on several spiritual and blues cuts, including a raucous "Highway 61." This is as good as Mississippi country blues gets.

what to buy next: More near-perfect blues from an often-overlooked master, Charlie McCoy steps out as a front man on many of the tracks of *Charlie McCoy, 1928–32* 𝄞𝄞𝄞𝄞 (Document, 1992, prod. Johnny Parth), playing mandolin almost as subtly as he plays guitar. The stars who retreated to become the ultimate sideman's backup include Bo Chatmon, Walter Vincson, Tampa Red and Georgia Tom Dorsey. The stand-out track here is the melancholic "That Lonesome Train Took My Baby Away."

worth searching for: The swaggering Memphis Minnie is the hands-down star of *Memphis Minnie and Kansas Joe McCoy,*

Delbert McClinton (© Ken Settle)

1929–34 ✍✍✍ (Document, 1991, prod. Johnny Parth), but Joe McCoy got his licks in too, often dueting with his wife on some of her most memorable classics and stealing the spotlight whenever she was out of the studio.

influences:

◄◄ Tommy Johnson, Ishmon Bracey

►► Robert Johnson, Memphis Minnie

Steve Braun

Jimmy McCracklin

Born August 13, 1921, in St. Louis, MO.

Jimmy McCracklin is one of the most prolific R&B singers and composers of all time. Still active after more than a half-century of recording, he has worked his way through just about every popular form of R&B. He accompanied himself on piano or harmonica and sang and led popular bands that played jump music, blues, R&B, rock 'n' roll and soul. McCracklin moved to California after serving in World War II and became a boxer. A car wreck curtailed his career in the ring, and he eventually got interested in singing and writing songs. His first recordings came in 1945, but it wasn't until 13 years later—after experimenting with several music forms and being associated with nearly a dozen labels—that he gained much commercial success. In 1957 he recorded "The Walk," which reached #7 on the pop charts and became a rock 'n' roll classic. In 1961 McCracklin started his own label, Art Tone, and had the successive hits "Just Got to Know" and "Shame Shame." Not only did these sides display the maturation of McCracklin's vocals and piano playing, but he found an effective song formula. By the mid-1960s McCracklin signed with Liberty, scoring more hits and recording prolifically. Things fell off in the early 1970s, but he salvaged his career with a brilliant album, *Yesterday Is Gone*. McCracklin continued to tour but wouldn't record again until 1989 when "Same Lovin'" came out on Evejam. Most recently McCracklin has recorded for Bullseye.

what to buy: Spanning several portions of McCracklin's career, *The Walk* ✍✍✍✍ (Razor & Tie, 1997) includes most of his hits. Containing dance records and ballads, *The Mercury Recordings* ✍✍✍✍ (Bear Family, 1992) puts McCracklin's versatility on display. Check out "Georgia Slop," which is excellent rockabilly. *High on the Blues* ✍✍✍ (Stax, 1972, prod. Al Jackson, Willie Mitchell) is a reissue of the brilliant Stax album with some extra sides. *My Story* ✍✍✍ (Bullseye Blues, 1991, prod. Jimmy McCracklin, Ron Levy) has a few low points but overall shows McCracklin in good form.

what to buy next: *A Taste of the Blues* ✍✍✍ (Bullseye Blues, 1994, prod. Ron Levy) finds McCracklin in the company of West Coast blues legends Johnny Otis and Lowell Fulson.

worth searching for: Not unexpectedly, there were a lot of McCracklin 45s, 78s and LPs pressed. The early Imperial/Liberty LPs *I Just Got to Know* ✍✍✍✍, *Think* ✍✍✍✍ and *Everynight, Everyday* ✍✍✍✍ all showed up in Woolworth's 99-cent bins but are prized collectors' items today. Collecting his earliest sides, *Rockin' Man* ✍✍✍✍ and *You Deceived Me* ✍✍✍✍ were solid LP reissues on Route 66, also now out of print.

influences:

◄◄ Walter Davis, Memphis Slim, Roy Milton, Erskine Hawkins, Ray Charles, Charles Brown

►► Magic Sam, Lowell Fulson, Johnny Otis

Jeff Hannusch

Larry McCray

Born April 5, 1960, in Magnolia, AR.

It's hard to find new young heroes in a genre that's so obsessed with tradition and who played with whom in 1929 or 1942, so it's twice as refreshing when contemporary talent finally arrives. This young singer-guitarist, who learned his licks from his band-leading sister, worked on a Detroit General Motors assembly line before he cobbled together his debut album. He has all the right moves—an excellent smooth soul voice, a superb sense of rhythm and where to stick the piano and horns and a refreshingly understated guitar style.

what to buy: McCray covers Otis Spann's "Country Girl" and Albert King's "The Sun Rises in the East," but his debut, *Ambition* ✍✍✍ (Pointblank/Charisma, 1990, prod. Bobby Hankins, David Robinson), is unquestionably a soul record. McCray sounds like he wouldn't do anything else but this if given the chance.

what to buy next: *Delta Hurricane* ✍✍ (Pointblank/Charisma, 1993, prod. Mike Vernon) is the slightly disappointing follow-up, in which McCray sounds like he's trying too hard to prove his "bluesness." He still sings just fine, like a soul man, but he overdoes the guitar bits and emphasizes conventional blues like "Within' Moon," "Blue River" and the title track.

influences:

◄◄ Bobby "Blue" Bland, Albert King, Son Seals, Rufus Thomas, B.B. King, Muddy Waters

Steve Knopper

Robert Lee McCullum

See: Robert Nighthawk

Ellas McDaniel

See: Bo Diddley

Mississippi Fred McDowell

Born January 12, 1904, in Rossville, TN. Died July 3, 1972, in Memphis, TN.

One of the last of the great Mississippi Delta bluesmen, McDowell's moaning vocals were the perfect companion to his eerie bottleneck slide guitar. McDowell grew up a sharecropper, toiling in various parts of the Delta. In 1928 he was at a work camp near Cleveland, Mississippi, where he saw Charley Patton perform and was impressed by what he heard. He began to learn how to play the guitar, but was too poor to afford his own until his boss gave him an instrument in 1941. McDowell continued to work in the fields, but on weekends he played dances and country suppers near his Como, Mississippi, home for a few dollars and a bottle. In 1959 folklorist Alan Lomax "discovered" McDowell and he recorded several of his songs, which were released on the Southern Folk Heritage LP series. These recordings installed McDowell on the folk circuit and led to mid-1960s recordings on Arhoolie and Testament. Unaffected by his fame, by the early 1970s McDowell had visited Europe several times and had recorded extensively, playing the same blues he heard as a youth in the Delta.

what to buy: Straight-up blues recorded in 1964 and 1965, *Mississippi Delta Blues* ♳♳♳♳ (Arhoolie, 1989, prod. Chris Strachwitz) also includes two tracks from McDowell's mentor, Eli Green. *I Do Not Play No Rock 'n' Roll* ♳♳♳♳ (Capitol, 1996, prod. Tommy Couch) won a Grammy in 1971 and features McDowell on electric guitar with a small band. *Amazing Grace* ♳♳♳♳ (Testament, 1995, prod. Pete Welding) features the Hunter's Chapel Singers and presents the spiritual side of McDowell's repertoire. *Mississippi Fred McDowell* ♳♳♳♳♳ (Rounder, 1984) consists of some of the earliest McDowell recordings.

what to buy next: *My Home Is in the Delta* ♳♳♳♳ (Testament, 1995, prod. Pete Welding) includes some vocals by McDowell's wife Annie Mae. *Good Morning Little School Girl* ♳♳♳♳ (Arhoolie, 1994, prod. Chris Strachwitz) and *This Ain't No Rock 'n' Roll* ♳♳♳♳ (Arhoolie, 1995, prod. Chris Strachwitz) consist of mid-1960s recordings. *Standing at the Burying Ground* (Se-

quel, 1996, prod. Pete Gibson, Alex Hooper) is a live recording of McDowell in London dating from 1969. Never one to slack on stage or in the studio, other interesting McDowell CD releases include *Steakbone Slide Guitar* ♳♳♳♳ (Rykodisc, 1996), *Long Way from Home* ♳♳♳♳ (Original Blues Classics, 1968) and *Mississippi Fred McDowell* ♳♳♳♳ (Flyright, 1990).

worth searching for: The original "Southern Folk Heritage Series" LP anthologies, *The Blues Roll On* ♳♳♳♳ (Atlantic, 1959, prod. Alan Lomax) and *Roots of the Blues* ♳♳♳♳ (Atlantic, 1959, prod. Alan Lomax), introduced McDowell to the masses. McDowell can be heard on several blues anthologies.

influences:

⏪ Charley Patton, Eli Green, Sid Hemphill, Blind Lemon Jefferson, Robert Johnson, John Lee Hooker

⏩ R.L. Burnside, Bonnie Raitt, Jo Ann Kelly, Junior Kimbrough

Jeff Hannusch

Sterling McGee

See: Satan & Adam

Brownie McGhee

See: Sonny Terry & Brownie McGhee

Stick McGhee

Born Granville McGhee, March 23, 1917, in Kingsport, TN. Died August 15, 1961, in New York, NY.

He's still primarily known as "Brownie McGhee's brother," but his secondary nickname is much more interesting: "The 'Drinkin' Wine Spo-Dee-O-Dee' Guy." Stick (sometimes Sticks) McGhee's buoyant 1949 drinking hit was on the surface a novelty number, but McGhee sang it so fast and with such alcoholic relish that it became a classic R&B song, up there with "Mother-in-Law" and "Get a Job." McGhee, who wrote the song during World War II, recorded several others for Atlantic, including the 1951 hit "Tennessee Waltz Blues." His fun, enthusiastic songs directly inspired later rock pioneers like Jerry Lee Lewis and Johnny Burnette, both of whom covered "Wine."

what to buy: For comic relief and pure Screamin' Jay Hawkins-style fun, stick *Stick McGhee and His Spo-Dee-O-Dee Buddies* ♫♫♫♫ (Ace) on the wall next to your Robert Johnson and Lightnin' Hopkins. It contains most of his 1953–55 drinking singles, plus a few (shudder) more serious blues and country/blues.

what to buy next: *Highway of Blues* ♫♫♫ (DeLuxe, 1959) is another good collection of 1950s singles.

worth searching for: The *Atlantic Rhythm and Blues* ♫♫♫♫ (Atlantic, 1986, prod. various) boxed set puts "Drinkin' Wine Spo-Dee-O-Dee" in historical context; it provides comic relief amid the more serious soul crooning and moaning blues songs.

influences:

◄◄ Brownie McGhee, Screamin' Jay Hawkins, Emmett Miller, Louis Jordan

►► Jerry Lee Lewis, Little Richard, Bill Haley, Mojo Nixon, Beat Farmers

Steve Knopper

Big Jay McNeely

Born Cecil McNeely, April 29, 1927, in Los Angeles, CA.

Jay McNeely has never been shy about his claim to fame; he simply will not be blown off the stage. Neither a disciplined stylist like King Curtis nor a revolutionary like Charlie Parker, McNeely became a legend for his ability to deliver a never-ending spray of honks, squawks, bleats and squeals. He blew on his knees, on his back, standing on his head. (One story has it that during one lengthy solo, McNeely left the stage, went to the men's room, relieved himself, zipped up and returned to the stage, blowing all the while.) A fan of Earl Hines and Jack McVea, McNeely caught McVea whenever he played the clubs on Los Angeles' jazz-heavy Central Avenue and later claimed to have played briefly during an appearance by Parker. Brought to Savoy by legendary talent scout Ralph Bass, McNeely's second go-round for the New York firm produced "Deacon's Hop," a sax-and-handclap classic that set the pace for the rest of McNeely's career. Taking his cue from audience pleasers like Illinois Jacquet and Arnett Cobb, McNeely barnstormed through the chitlin' circuit, becoming famous for his stage antics. Through the 1950s he took his act to Exclusive, then Aladdin, Federal and Atlantic. The dawn of soul music in the late 1950s did nothing to dim his nuclear energy. McNeely's soulful take on "There Is Something on Your Mind" in 1959 landed up in the Top 10 again. McNeely cut down on his touring from the 1960s through the 1980s, but the growing fascination with the heroes of early R&B drew him back out again. He has even found work on several television series, playing—what else?—the leader of a hard-blowing blues combo.

what to buy: The packaging on *Swingin'-Golden Classics* ♫♫♫♫ (Collectables, 1990) is as sparse as a wish sandwich, but all you need is on the front cover—a grainy shot of Big Jay contorted on his back, blowing to the heavens. It contains 16 late-1950s steamers, not only "Something on Your Mind," but the wild "Back . . . Shack . . . Track" and the wilder "Psycho Serenade." More honks than a runaway tugboat.

what to buy next: An amalgam of Big Jay in the 1950s wouldn't be complete without the giddy "Nervous, Man Nervous," a Federal smash that featured a wigged-out chorus chanting the title behind Big Jay's wails. It's included on *Nervous* ♫♫♫♫ (Saxophile, 1995), which also includes several takes from a pristine recording of a 1957 concert. *Live at Birdland: 1957* ♫♫♫♫ (Collectables, 1990) is the complete version of a 1957 McNeely set at the Seattle Birdland show. Big Jay vaults into the stratosphere on churners like "Insect Ball" and the old Illinois Jacquet favorite, "Flying Home."

the rest:

Big Jay in 3-D ♫♫♫ (King)
Az Bootin' ♫♫♫ (Big J, 1993)

influences:

◀◀ Earl Hines, Illinois Jacquet, Jack McVea, Arnett Cobb, Charlie Parker

▶▶ King Curtis, Gene Barge

Steve Braun

Jay McShann

Born January 12, 1916, in Muskogee, OK.

One of the last living survivors of the swing era, Jay McShann's musical journey continues unabated; the same "Hootie" McShann who hired an embryonic teenager, Charlie Parker, as his saxophonist in 1939 fronted the Duke Robillard Band at the 1997 Kansas City Blues and Jazz Fest. McShann, who began playing the piano as a child, had his own band in Kansas City by 1938, and by the early 1940s his enlarged group, fronted by singer Walter Brown, greased by cocky saxman Parker and catapulted by a huge hit called "Confessin' the Blues," could hold its ground against any big band of the period. Led by McShann's powerful piano pumping, his bands always struck a balance between blues and jazz—and they swung like crazy. After he got out of the service and the Basie and Andy Kirk bands went nationwide, McShann recorded in Hollywood with singer Julia Lee before returning to Kansas City, still his base of operations. Whether big band or the smaller groups he used in the 1940s, including a nascent R&B combo that included singer Crown Prince Waterford, Numa Lee Davis and, in his debut recording, Jimmy Witherspoon, McShann is still a powerful pianist and vocalist who performs a couple times a month and obviously is not yet content to rest on his considerable laurels.

what to buy: *Hootie's Jumpin' Blues* ♫♫♫♫♫ (Stony Plain, 1997, prod. Duke Robillard, Holger Peterson) pits the eightyish pianist with a hard-swinging contemporary group. *The Early Bird Charlie Parker* ♫♫♫♫♫ (MCA, 1982) has the studio recordings of the early McShann powerhouse, including "Swingmatism," "Hootie Blues," and "Confessin' the Blues." McShann is the main force behind *Kansas City Blues 1944–49* ♫♫♫♫♫ (Capitol, 1997, prod. Billy Vera), an exhaustive three-disc look at post-World War II KC line-ups. Besides introducing Witherspoon, he sings up a storm of his own—you wonder why McShann let other singers front the band—alongside equally noteworthy tracks by Julia Lee & Her Boyfriends, Bus Moten & His Men, Tiny Kennedy and Walter Brown.

what to buy next: The historical "Wichita transcriptions" and live performances on *Early Bird* ♫♫♫♫♫ (Stash, 1991) capture

young gun Charlie Parker at a significant moment in his development and offer more proof that the McShann band could kick anybody's ass off any stage. The much more recent *Swingmatism* ♫♫♫♫ (Sackville, 1990) offers a tasty choice of material, including the gems "Night in Tunisia" and "The Mooche."

the rest:

Goin to Kansas City ♫♫♫ (New World, 1972/1987)
Hootie's Vine Street Blues ♫♫♫ (Black Lion, 1974/1994)
Solo at Cafe Copains ♫♫♫ (Sackville, 1980)
Air Mail Special ♫♫♫ (Sackville, 1990)
Some Blues ♫♫♫♫ (Chiaroscuro, 1993)
(With John Hicks) *Hootie and Hicks: The Missouri Connection* ♫♫♫ (Reservoir, 1993)
Just a Lucky So and So ♫♫♫ (Sackville, 1996)
Piano Playhouse ♫♫♫ (Night Train, 1996)
(With Al Casey) *Best of Friends* ♫♫♫ (JSP, 1997)

worth searching for: Jazz giants Herbie Mann, Gerry Mulligan and John Scofield get down to late-night jazz business on *The Big Apple Bash* ♫♫♫♫ (Atlantic, 1979, prod. Ilhan Mimaroglu), still only available on vinyl.

influences:

◀◀ Bennie Moten

▶▶ Louis Jordan, Tommy Douglas, Wynonie Harris, Roy Brown

Leland Rucker

Blind Willie McTell

Born William Samuel McTell, May 5, 1901, in Thomson, GA. Died April 19, 1959, in Milledgeville, GA.

A pathetic figure to strangers who listened to him sing for coins on the streets of Atlanta, Blind Willie McTell was a blues giant—a stirring guitarist, a composer of stunningly moving songs and an interpreter of the first rank. Like John Lee Hooker, he blithely moved from label to label, scattering gems everywhere he recorded. He was Blind Sammie for Columbia, Georgia Bill on OKeh, Barrelhouse Sammy for Atlantic and Pig 'n Whistle Red on Regal. Whatever McTell's aliases, the snapping of his 12-string guitar and his sly voice were unmistakable. No song was out of his range. His repertoire included his own classic songs, obscure folk performances, sprightly rags and dignified gospel laments. He was capable of launching off on a rollicking version of "Pinetop's Boogie Woogie" one moment, then stepping back with a haunting reading of the folk ballad "Delia." McTell's rolling "Statesboro Blues" became fodder for both the Allman Brothers Band and Taj Mahal. But he alone performed his vast arsenal of songs best, and it is hardly surprising that 40 years after McTell's death, few artists have tried to adapt him.

McTell was born in deep Georgia cotton country, about 30 miles west of Augusta. His last name at birth was reportedly McTear or McTier. How it became corrupted to McTell is unknown. Blinded soon after birth, he compensated by relying on his memory and his acutely-developed senses of hearing and touch. Legends grew around his exploits: McTell reportedly was able to lead sighted people around Atlanta's streets and even navigated New York's subway system; friends said he once picked off a threatening dog with a handgun. But McTell was most at home as a singer, often accompanied by his Atlanta colleague Curley Weaver. After performing with traveling shows, McTell enrolled in the state's school for the blind in Macon. There he learned Braille and obscure crafts like broom making and leather work. He attended blind academies in New York and Michigan before returning to Atlanta in 1927, where his long recording career started. His first nine sessions for Victor were among his most lasting, producing "Statesboro Blues" and the powerful "Dark Night Blues." He moved to Columbia, an association that lasted four years before McTell moved on in 1933. On more than 40 recordings McTell gave the widest view of his talents, from the jaunty "Razor Ball" to the chilling "You Was Born to Die." He recorded briefly with Decca, then dropped from sight until 1940, when archivist John Lomax recorded him for the Library of Congress. The heyday of urban R&B should have spelled the end for McTell's lonely minstrelsy, yet he was recording again stunningly in 1949 for Atlantic Records, despite its emphasis on brass-driven R&B. He and Weaver followed up with sessions for Regal beginning in 1950. Drinking heavily, McTell still had enough verve left for one last session with Prestige in 1956. His death of a brain hemorrhage in 1959 was so ignored that blues researchers were still trying to find him a decade later. Their obsession was understandable. "Nobody," Bob Dylan sings in his barren tribute to the blind street performer, "sings the blues like Blind Willie McTell."

what to buy: The title *The Definitive Blind Willie McTell* 🎜🎜🎜🎜🎜 (Columbia Legacy, 1994, prod. Lawrence Cohn) exaggerates only slightly. This two-CD set omits only McTell's Victor sides in its comprehensive culling of his classic early work. It is still indispensable, both for its respectful mastering and top-notch research by blues historian David Evans. Tipped off by a distributor that McTell was alive and well in Atlanta, record mogul Ahmet Ertegun lost no time in recording the street singer on *Atlanta Twelve String* 🎜🎜🎜🎜 (Atlantic, 1991, prod. Ahmet Ertegun, Herb Abramson). Even if the released single sank like a stone,

McTell's performance is a tour de force, ranging from the dooming "On the Cooling Board" to the infectious "Kill It Kid."

what to buy next: For those who have to have everything, there is *Blind Willie McTell: Complete Recorded Works 1927–35, Vols. 1–3* 🎜🎜🎜🎜 (Document, 1990, prod. Johnny Parth). Among Austrian archivist Parth's finest sets, these three separate CDs will not lose their luster until BMG and MCA put out their own McTell on disc. *Complete Library of Congress Recordings* 🎜🎜🎜🎜 (Document, 1990) includes songs and recorded monologues, including a wary McTell's careful discourse on race relations in the South, but for some reason, the four songs seem just a cut below his 1930s works. On *Last Session* 🎜🎜🎜 (Original Blues Classics, 1991), McTell's voice is frayed and his fingers have lost some of their dexterity, but there is still haunted dignity in these final works. Not to be overlooked, either, is *Blind Willie McTell, 1927–35* 🎜🎜🎜 (Yazoo, 1990), a decent primer for those new to McTell but overshadowed in recent years by the Columbia and Document sets. The Victor classics included here complement the Columbia set nicely.

worth searching for: *Pig 'n Whistle Red* 🎜🎜🎜🎜 (Biograph, 1993) is a delicately-remastered reissue of McTell's 1950 flirtation with Regal. The 20 tracks are a mixed bag, including a revamped "Savannah Mama" and a reprise of 1933's "Good Little Thing." The session is watered down by some weak hokum and three throwaways by McTell's running buddy, Curley Weaver.

influences:

◀◀ Blind Blake, Curley Weaver

▶▶ Taj Mahal, Allman Brothers Band, Bob Dylan

Steve Braun

Memphis Jug Band

Formed late 1920s, in Memphis, TN.

A rollicking collection of street musicians led by the irrepressible Will Shade, the Memphis Jug Band dominated the town's blues culture in the 1930s with their jazzed-up version of country standards. Some of Memphis' most creative blues players shuffled in and out of Shade's group, among them harmonica maestro Walter Horton, mandolinist Charley Burse, slide guitar ace Will Weldon, jug popper and comic Charlie Polk and vocalist Hattie Hart. And always close at hand was kazoo man Ben Ramey, whose nattering instrument at times leavened—and other times marred—the group's fluid picking and singing. The group's almost-instant success among blues buyers in 1927 paved the way for similar jug groups led by Gus Cannon and Jack Kelly. The rolling "Memphis Jug-Blues" and "Sometimes I

Think I Love You" set the pattern for the band's easy-paced, humorous efforts. Sweet-natured, romantic rags alternated with tough-minded tracks that played off the violent, comic nature of Memphis life. The most sardonic titles included "I Whipped My Woman with a Single-Tree" and "I Can Beat You Plenty"; their most enduring recording is "Stealing, Stealing," decades later a favorite in the jug band revival that swept through the folk community in the 1960s. The prolific band recorded nearly 70 songs for Victor and OKeh between 1927 and 1934, dropped only after their quaint country stylings fell out of favor with record buyers who preferred more urbane musicians such as Leroy Carr and Walter Davis. Undaunted, Will Shade kept putting together new versions of the Jug Band as late as the 1960s. Only his death in 1966 ended the long-running group.

what to buy: The 18 tracks that comprise *State of Tennessee Blues* 🎵🎵🎵🎵 (Memphis Archives, 1995, prod. Richard James Hite) aren't quite a greatest-hits collection, but it makes up in its sonic qualities what it lacks in comprehension. The sound is surprisingly lifelike compared to other available Jug Band discs and likely might only be surpassed by metal parts or discs presumably owned by those who now retain Victor's original recordings.

what to buy next: The best single-disc selection of Jug Band performances, the 28-song *Memphis Jug Band* 🎵🎵🎵🎵 (Yazoo, 1990) includes "Stealin'" and other essential sides, mostly from the band's Victor studio sessions. The R. Crumb cover alone is worth half the price of admission. The Jug Band's 60 recordings for Victor are spread out over the three discs of *Memphis Jug Band, Complete Recorded Works, 1927–30* 🎵🎵🎵 (Document, 1991, prod. Johnny Parth). Many feature thin, one-dimensional sound and the grating kazoo work of Ben Ramey, but there are dozens of fine blues recordings that overpower the group's occasional lame efforts.

the rest:

Memphis Jug Band, 1932–34 🎵🎵🎵 (RST, 1990)
Associates and Alternate Takes, 1927–30 🎵🎵🎵 (Wolf, 1991)

influences:

◀◀ Clifford Hayes, Jim Jackson

▶▶ Jack Kelly, Gus Cannon, Jed Davenport

Steve Braun

Memphis Minnie

Born Lizzie Douglas, June 3, 1897, in Algiers, LA. Died August 6, 1973, in Memphis, TN.

A tough lady, Memphis Minnie had to fight vigorously to make her niche in a men's world and establish herself as one of the greatest blues artists of all times. Raised in Walls, Mississippi, she learned to play banjo and guitar and moved, alone, to Memphis in 1910 (at age 13!). She played on the streets and toured the South with medicine shows and circuses and lived with Casey Bill Weldon, who tutored her. In 1929, she married guitarist "Kansas" Joe McCoy, with whom she formed a marvelous, inventive duo with a rural flavor. She recorded some masterpieces of guitar playing ("Hoodoo Lady"), and her style became more urbanized. She kept evolving, and in 1938 formed a duo with her new lover, guitarist Ernest "Little Son Joe" Lawlars, whose compositions ("Digging My Potatoes," "Me and My Chauffeur," "I'm So Glad") and delicate accompaniment combined with stunning guitar interplay helped to increase Minnie's popularity and success ("In My Girlish Days"). In the late 1940s and early 1950s she tried several come-backs, but asthma and new trends in African-American music forced her to retire in Memphis in 1957. Memphis Minnie will remain one of the most influential blues personalities, a powerful vocalist, prolific composer and outstanding guitar stylist with a legacy of more than 250 recordings, some of which are still widely performed by contemporary artists.

what to buy: *Hoodoo Lady (1933–37)* 🎵🎵🎵🎵 (Columbia/Roots 'n' Blues, 1991, prod. Lawrence Cohn) is an 18-track collection of the best songs recorded in that period—"Hoodoo Lady," "If You See My Rooster," "Black Cat Blues" and "Good Morning" among them. *Me and My Chauffeur 1935–46* 🎵🎵🎵🎵 (E.P.M. Blues Collection, 1997, prod. Jean Buzelin), a 20-track collection, includes "Diggin My Potatoes," "I'm So Glad," "Down in New Orleans" and other masterpieces with some overlap from *Hoodoo Lady*. Minnie's electric guitar work combines nicely with Joe's acoustic playing on *I Ain't No Bad Gal 1941* 🎵🎵🎵🎵 (CBS/Portrait Masters, 1988, prod. Bob Thiele), containing 12 tracks from two 1941 sessions, including four previously unissued selections.

what to buy next: *Memphis Minnie & Kansas Joe—1929–34 Recordings in Chronological Order, Vols. 1–4* 🎵🎵🎵🎵 (Document, 1991, prod. Johnny Parth) is for completists but highly recommended.

the rest:

Memphis Minnie: Complete Recorded Works 1935–41, Vols. 1–5 🎵🎵🎵🎵 (RST, 1991)
Memphis Minnie: The Complete Post-War Recordings in Chronological Order 1944–53, Vols. 1–3 🎵🎵🎵🎵 (Wolf, 1991)

worth searching for: *Memphis Minnie's Blues—Woman with Guitar* (Da Capo Press, 1992) offers a fascinating read and look at Minnie's importance. Written by Paul and Beth Garon, the first part, a biography with selected lyrics, is essential reading. Part two, a surrealistic analysis of Minnie's personality and lyrics, is more controversial.

influences:

◀◀ Frank Stokes, Furry Lewis, Beale Street Sheiks, Robert Wilkins, Jim Jackson, Casey B. Weldon

▶▶ Baby Boy Warren, Johnny Shines, J.B. Hutto, J.B. Lenoir

Robert Sacré

Memphis Slim

Born John Len "Peter" Chatman, September 3, 1915, in Memphis, TN. Died February 24, 1988, in Paris, France.

One of the funniest men ever to sing serious blues songs, Memphis Slim began his career as a hobo, juke-joint owner and whiskey maker before his encounter with Big Bill Broonzy changed his life. Slim had been playing piano casually to entertain his guests and customers, but Broonzy convinced him to take the music more seriously. After a few years backing Broonzy, his solo career began in 1944, when the singer-pianist formed the Houserockers and commenced pioneering the boogie-woogie, or barrelhouse, blues style. What distinguishes Slim from his forebears, such as Speckled Red or Victoria Spivey, is a goofy voice and a hilarious sense of humor—in "Beer Drinking Woman" and others of his sexy, teasing songs, he spent as much time rambling stories as singing choruses. And, oh yes, the piano: his left hand walks like a panther on "John Henry," and his right hand is all over the place, pounding chords one second and flitting tremolos the next. Though the spread of electric blues (and, later, rock 'n' roll) threatened to blunt his old-school boogie-woogie career, Slim managed to stay commercially soluble. He reeled off an amazing amount of great singles—"Boogie Woogie Memphis," "Sassy Mae," "Rockin' the House," "Nobody Loves Me," "Lend Me Your Love" and "Bye Bye Baby," to name a few—before leaving a United States that didn't appreciate its black artists in 1962. Inspired by the attention he received on a European tour with Willie Dixon, he moved to Paris, where he lived like an expatriate rock star before dying in 1988.

what to buy: Slim recorded for so many record labels, it's difficult to come up with the definitive collection, but here's a suggestion of how to start: though he shares top billing, *Chicago Blues Masters, Vol. 1: Muddy Waters and Memphis Slim* ♪♪♪♪ (Capitol, 1995, prod. Pete Welding) is Slim-dominated, with a terrific take on the piano-heavy "John Henry" and lots of impeccable boogie, with a few Waters sides enclosed for historical context. After

that, proceed to *Memphis Slim at the Gate of Horn* ♪♪♪♪ (Vee-Jay, 1959/1993, prod. Billy Vera), a short but fiercely rocking document of Slim's Vee-Jay period, with Matt "Guitar" Murphy and the pianist trading incredible licks on the instrumental "Steppin' Out." A longer, more definitive sampling of the same 1958–59 period is *Rockin' the Blues* ♪♪♪♪ (Charly, 1981, prod. various).

what to buy next: Though Slim did his best work for other record companies, his ultimate Chess compilations include *The Real Folk Blues* ♪♪♪ (Chess/MCA, 1966) and *Memphis Slim* ♪♪♪♪ (Chess/MCA, 1961/1986), the latter containing Studs Terkel liner notes and definitive versions of "Mother Earth" and the Latin-spiced "Tia Juana."

what to avoid: Late in life, Slim's instincts had dulled, and he allows himself to be presented with a mediocre band on the 1980 Paris concert document *Live at the Hot Club* ♪♪ (Milan, 1994, prod. Emmanuel Chamboredon, Toby Pieniek).

best of the rest:

Alone with My Friends ♪♪♪ (Original Blues Classics, 1961/Fantasy, 1996)
Baby Please Come Home: Memphis Slim and Willie Dixon in Paris ♪♪♪ (Original Blues Classics, 1962/Fantasy, 1996)
U.S.A. ♪♪♪ (Candid, 1962)
Steady Rollin' Blues ♪♪♪ (Bluesville, 1964)
Mother Earth ♪♪♪ (Buddah, 1969)
Messin' around with the Blues ♪♪♪ (King, 1970)
Raining the Blues ♪♪♪ (Fantasy, 1989)
Memphis Slim/Matt Murphy/Eddie Taylor ♪♪♪ (Antone's, 1990)

worth searching for: Slim's last American session, in 1962, before he moved to Europe, is contained on *Lonesome* ♪♪♪ (Drive Archive, 1994), including the playful "Big Bertha" and the dancey "Good Time Roll Creole" and "What Is the Mare-Back."

influences:

◀◀ Speckled Red, Big Bill Broonzy, Art Tatum, Professor Longhair

▶▶ Charles Brown, B.B. King, Jimmy Witherspoon, Dr. John, Ray Charles, Matt "Guitar" Murphy

Steve Knopper

Charles Merick

See: Rockie Charles

Big Maceo Merriweather

Born Major Merriweather, March 31, 1905. Died February 26, 1953, in Chicago, IL.

Big Maceo was the link between the hammer-fisted barrelhouse piano players of the 1930s and modern Chicago blues keyboard stalwarts like Otis Spann and Johnny Jones. Maceo's rasping, plummy voice was the perfect complement to a piano style that alternated delicate fills with a thundering walking bass. Unlike so many of his keyboard rivals, Maceo was adept with both hands, capable of powerful left-handed runs and intricate right-handed fills that left their mark on Spann and even Ray Charles. Quickly establishing himself as a regular in Bluebird producer Lester Melrose's stable of stars—Big Bill Broonzy, Sonny Boy Williamson, Tampa Red and Big Boy Crudup were among them—Maceo thrived during in the months leading up to World War II and in the recording rush that came with peacetime. His compositions were often as memorable as his mastery of the 88s. "Worried Life Blues" is a chestnut later adopted by Little Walter, and Muddy Waters appropriated "County Jail Blues." An impressive figure even in his youth—growing to six-foot-four and topping 250 pounds—Maceo first began polishing the ivories on Atlanta's Harvard Street, finding work at house parties and bars. He moved to Detroit, working in Ford plants and the rent-party circuit. Hattie Spruel, an employer who later became his wife, recommended him to Melrose. The veteran producer was impressed, bringing Maceo to Chicago in June 1941 for his first session. Melrose backed Maceo with Tampa Red, a pairing that lasted through 1947. When recording was halted because of the war effort, Maceo remained a powerful draw in Chicago clubs, and he was sent back into Bluebird's studio as soon as the war ended. It took a sudden stroke to slow Maceo down in 1946. He kept recording, but his illness took a devastating toll. His voice was slurry, and paralysis of the right side made piano playing almost impossible. In his final session in Detroit, Maceo played a sad duet, working the left side of the keyboards with his functional left hand while another pianist played the right. A fatal heart attack stilled his talented hands for good in 1953.

what to buy: The bulk of Maceo's best cuts have been crammed onto *The King of Chicago Blues Piano* ♪♪♪♪ (Arhoolie, 1992, prod. Chris Strachwitz). Rarely one to race off into the boogie stratosphere as Amos Milburn and even Johnny Jones would later do, Maceo was built for comfort, and his relaxed songs showed it. These 25 cuts wear like vintage brandy.

what to buy next: The rest of Maceo's recordings are on *Charlie Spand: The Complete 1940 Recordings/Big Maceo: The Remaining Titles 1941–52* ♪♪♪ (Old Tramp, 1993, prod. Johnny Parth), and that is both treasure and curse. Five tracks show Maceo in his prime, including the romping "Macy Special." But 12 ago-

nizing cuts follow, charting Maceo's decaying health and fading power. It is saved by the inclusion of eight rare 1940 recordings by Detroit piano master Charlie Spand, one of the giants of 1920s-era barrelhouse. After a long wait, *Big Maceo 1941–42* ♪♪♪ (BMG, 1997) is the official release of the Bluebird archives. The crisp sound trumps all other sets, but the selection is skimpy. *Victor/Bluebird Recordings 1945–47* ♪♪♪ (BMG, 1997), the second expertly mastered volume of Maceo's Bluebird tracks, suffers the same flaw as the first—a skimpy collection compared to the expansive, judiciously-selected Arhoolie set.

influences:

◀◀ Charlie Spand, Will Ezell

▶▶ Johnny Jones, Henry Gray, Otis Spann, Ray Charles

Steve Braun

Amos Milburn

Born April 1, 1927, in Houston, TX. Died January 3, 1980, in Houston, TX.

Pianist, vocalist and composer Amos Milburn was one of the brightest stars in the post-World War II rhythm & blues firmament. A Texas native who came to fame on the West Coast in the late 1940s with a series of hit singles for Aladdin, Milburn was a great songwriter as well as a fine blues & boogie pianist and a smooth, expressive vocalist with a sly, insinuating sound all his own. The artist's early works ("After Midnite," "In the Middle of the Night," "Let's Rock Awhile" and "Let's Have a Party") and a string of drinking songs, including "Good Good Whiskey," "One Scotch, One Bourbon, One Beer" and "Let Me Go Home Whiskey" helped set the standard for the Golden Age of rhythm & blues. His holiday anthem, "Let's Make Christmas, Merry Baby," remains a perennial favorite. Milburn's best-known tune, "Chicken Shack Boogie," was twice a hit for Aladdin, but the 1956 remake marked the end of his R&B chart success. He cut some 45s for Ace and King around the turn of the decade, and Motown attempted to revive Milburn's career in the early 1960s with little impact. But during his heyday, Amos Milburn made a series of immortal rhythm & blues recordings that can be played over and over again, in sequence of release or at random, and never fail to entertain and delight.

what to buy: *Blues Barrelhouse and Boogie Woogie* ♪♪♪♪♪ (Capitol, 1996, prod. Pete Welding) is a comprehensive three-disc collection of Milburn's Aladdin masters originally produced by Maxwell Davis and the Aladdin staff between 1946–57. While not complete—you have to find the Mosaic boxed set, *The Complete Aladdin Recordings of Amos Milburn* ♪♪♪♪ (Mosaic, 1993) to get it all—this tasty package presents the full range of the artist's achievement and provides thrill after musical thrill for modern listeners. A slew of unissued sides adds to the excitement, with standouts from Milburn's 1947 sessions like "Mean Woman," "Aladdin Boogie," "Nickel Plated Baby," "My Tortured Mind" and two takes of "Rocky Road Blues." A pair of single-disc anthologies, *Blues & Boogie: His Greatest Hits* ♫♫♫♫ (Sequel, 1990) and *Down the Road Apiece: The Best of Amos Milburn* ♫♫♫♫ (EMI, 1993) collect his best-known Aladdin singles with quite a bit of overlap. A recent repackage, also called *Down the Road Apiece* ♫♫♫♫ (Alliance, 1997) keeps Milburn's classic works available in the present and belongs in every serious rhythm & blues collection. It doesn't get any better than this.

what to buy next: Berry Gordy's attempt to rekindle Milburn's recording career is documented on *The Motown Years 1962–64* ♫♫♫ (Motown, 1996). Most of these Motown sides went unheard for more than 30 years, and though they don't measure up to the Aladdin recordings, even second-rate Milburn efforts are worth our attention. For completists and serious students of the idiom only.

worth searching for: "Famous" Amos Milburn and Aladdin labelmate Charles Brown toured together for many years and once cut an amusing duet on Huey "Piano" Smith's "Educated Fool" for Ace, now to be found on *The Ace Story, Volume Two* (Ace).

influences:

◄◄ T-Bone Walker, Charles Brown, Clarence "Gatemouth" Brown, Jimmy Rushing, Jay McShann

►► Wynonie Harris, Bull Moose Jackson, Louis Jordan, Roy Milton, Joe Liggins, Jimmy Liggins

John Sinclair

Rice Miller

See: Sonny Boy Williamson II

Steve Miller

Born October 5, 1943, in Milwaukee, WI.

Throughout his prolific and protean journeyman career, Steve Miller has braided together polished pop-rock, straight-ahead blues and acoustic-flavored pop. Widely regarded as a Top 40 stooge whose 1970s hits remain a staple of classic rock radio 20 years later, Miller—usually performing under the Steve Miller Band moniker—has actually made rewarding forays into a broad array of musical styles, displaying a depth and

prowess often nothing short of astonishing. His father was a fanatical music buff with a tape recorder, and Les Paul, T-Bone Walker and Charles Mingus all held sessions in the Miller living room. His first high school band in Dallas also included schoolmate Boz Scaggs and backed up visiting R&B stars like Jimmy Reed at local clubs. He found his real starting place several years later in the burgeoning San Francisco rock scene. His band appeared at the historic 1967 Monterey Pop Festival and signed to Capitol, an association that lasted more than a quarter-century. While Miller's early albums made him an underground radio favorite, he finally found the pop chart stroke in 1973 with *The Joker*; subsequent albums *Fly Like an Eagle* and *Book of Dreams* made Miller one of the top attractions of the day. Although the gleaming hits gave Miller his Top 40 hack reputation, he was still capable of turning out a soulful jazz experiment like *Born 2B Blue* or a solid blues outing like *Living in the Twentieth Century*. He *is* Maurice, the Gangster, the Space Cowboy, Stevie "Guitar" Miller—the musician of many faces.

what to buy: His second greatest hits album, *The Best of the Steve Miller Band 1974–78* ♫♫♫♫ (Capitol, 1978, prod. Steve Miller), has stayed on the best-seller lists since its release. But *Fly Like an Eagle* ♫♫♫♫ (Capitol, 1976, prod. Steve Miller) contains the best single all-around look at his great gifts.

what to buy next: Samples of his first six albums cover a broad territory, but *Best of 1968–73* ♫♫♫ (Capitol, 1990, prod. various) provides a quick, albeit spotty retrospective of his development. *Living in the Twentieth Century* ♫♫♫ (Capitol, 1986) is his only real blues album with a heavy Jimmy Reed emphasis. He practically turns the guitar off for the high-tech *Born 2B Blue* ♫♫♫ (Capitol, 1988), which includes jazzy versions of "Ya, Ya," "Willow Weep for Me," "When Sonny Gets Blue" and, gasp!—"Zip-A-Dee-Do-Dah."

what to avoid: Miller remixed and edited many of the tracks on the three-CD collection, *Box Set* ♫♫ (Capitol, 1994, prod. various), without broadening the set's viewpoint beyond much more than a greatest hits on steroids.

best of the rest:

Sailor ♫♫♫ (Capitol, 1969)
Wide River ♫♫♪ (Polydor, 1993)

worth searching for: Collectors will want the *Musical Miller Moments Interview* that was created as a radio promotion for *Born 2B Blues*, with interview bits about Les Paul and Mary Ford visiting his home when he was a child.

influences:

◄◄ Jimmy Reed, Beatles, Cream, Les Paul

►► Omar & the Howlers, Blues Traveler, Spin Doctors, Big Head Todd & the Monsters

see also: *Boz Scaggs*

Joel Selvin

Roy Milton

Born July 31, 1907, in Wynnewood, OK. Died September 18, 1983, in Los Angeles, CA.

Drummer Roy Milton emerged from the rich Oklahoma music community that produced Charlie Christian, Jay McShann, Jimmy Rushing, Oscar Pettiford and other pioneers of modern music. Indeed, it may well be that the idiom was created by Rushing with the Count Basie Orchestra and advanced by Jay McShann and his Kansas City combo, featuring vocalist Walter Brown and saxophonist Charlie Parker. Milton worked with the Ernie Fields Orchestra, a popular territory band, and migrated to Los Angeles in the 1930s. He was first recorded by Lionel Hampton and then signed with producer Art Rupe, who was starting up JukeBox records in 1945. Milton's second release for Rupe, "R.M. Blues," was a smash R&B hit and put both the bandleader and the fledgling label (soon to become Specialty Records) on the musical map. Milton and his band, the Solid Senders, featuring pianist Camille Howard, contributed an unending stream of great singles to the Specialty catalog over the next 10 years. Milton helped define the small-band rhythm & blues idiom with records like "Milton's Boogie," "True Blues," "Keep a Dollar in Your Pocket," "Hop, Skip & Jump" and "Information Blues." Howard was featured on a series of singles issued under her own name, including the classic "X-Temperaneous Boogie," recorded in the waning moments of New Year's Eve 1947, just before the recording ban of 1948 took effect. Roy Milton was a fine drummer, an excellent composer, and a first-rate band leader whose gigantic contribution to the development of modern music—like so many of his contemporaries—has been all but relegated to the dustbin of history.

what to buy: Roy Milton & His Solid Senders can be heard in all their glory in the "Legends of Specialty Records" series, meticulously produced and annotated by Billy Vera. *Volume One* ♫♫♫♫ (Specialty, 1990) reprises most of *R.M. Blues* ♫♫♫♫ (Specialty, 1988)—from the first batch of Specialty CDs before the catalog was purchased by Fantasy—and contains the hits cited above plus things like Brown's version of "The Huckle-buck," "Porter's Love Song," "Bartender's Boogie," "The Numbers Blues," "Christmas Time Blues" and his cover of Louis Prima's "Oh Babe!" *Volume Two: Groovy Blues* ♫♫♫♫ (Specialty, 1992) continues to mine the vaults, turning up seven unissued sides and excellent singles like "Groovy Blues," "Pack Your Sack, Jack," "Cryin' and Singin' the Blues," "Playboy Blues" and "Short, Sweet and Snappy." *Volume Three: Blowin' with Roy* ♫♫♫♫ (Specialty, 1994) continues with another dozen unissued sides and more fine singles: "Train Blues," "New Year's Resolution," "Everything I Do Is Wrong" and more. The Swedish collection, *Grandfather of R&B* ♫♫♫♫ (Mr. R&B, 1994), samples Roy's Specialty hits in a one-disc set. You can't get too much of Roy Milton & His Solid Senders.

what to buy next: Milton can be heard in concert with the Johnny Otis Show on *Live at Monterey* ♫♫♫♫ (Sony, 1993), a 1970 performance that also featured Esther Phillips, Roy Brown and other R&B pioneers reassembled by Otis for modern listeners.

worth searching for: A recent Billy Vera-produced sampler is a fantastic collection of jump blues and jazz from the Golden Age. *Jumpin' and Jivin'* ♫♫♫♫ (Specialty, 1997), digs out another five Roy Milton Specialty singles—including "Tell It Like It Is" and "Baby Don't Do That to Me"—and another unissued side to tantalize Milton completists.

influences:

◄◄ Jay McShann, Count Basie

►► Johnny Otis, Ray Charles, Dave Bartholomew

John Sinclair

Iverson Minter

See: Louisiana Red

Mississippi Heat

Formed 1992, in Chicago, IL.

Pierre Lacocque, harmonica; Bob Stroger, bass; Billy Flynn, guitar; Robert Covington, vocals, drums (1992–93); James Wheeler, guitar (1992–96); Deitra Farr, vocals (1993–96); Allen Kirk, drums (1993–96); Barrelhouse Chuck, piano (1997–present); Kenny Smith, drums (1997–present); Mary Lane, vocals (1997–present); Zora Young, vocals (1997–present).

Mississippi Heat has been one of the most original of the bands that consistently perpetuate the Chicago blues sounds of the 1950s and 1960s with gusto and creativity. The band's repertoire consists mainly of Lacocque's original compositions and also benefits from the skills of Billy Flynn and Deitra Farr's writing ability during her stay. Lacocque came to blues via Walter Horton and Junior Wells, who along with Jimmy Reed remain his principal influences, while Flynn's slide guitar work is reminiscent of Elmore James.

what to buy: *Straight from the Heart* 🎵🎵🎵🎵 (Van der Linden, 1993/1996, prod. Michel Lacocque, Pierre Lacocque) includes a couple of harmonica tours-de-force ("She Knows What Love Is All About" and "Heartbroken," a moving tribute to Lawrence "Sonny" Wimberley) and the jazzy instrumental named after the group. *Learned the Hard Way* 🎵🎵🎵🎵 (Van der Linden, 1994, prod. Michel Lacocque, Pierre Lacocque) includes ten Pierre Lacocque compositions, with a great "Je me Souviens" sung by Farr; slow, down-home blues ("Moanin' and Cryin'"), a nice cover of Little Walter's "Mean Old World" and "Bull Frog Hop," a stunning Billy Flynn guitar lesson. *Thunder in My Heart* 🎵🎵🎵 (Van der Linden, 1995, prod. Michel Lacocque, Pierre Lacocque) has excellent harmonica work throughout, a lovely blues ballad by Farr ("You Gave Nothing") and great band cohesion on "Nothing but Trouble" and "Better Days."

influences:

◀◀ Big Walter Horton, Junior Wells, Little Walter, Elmore James

Robert Sacré

Mississippi Sheiks

Formed late 1920s.

Walter Vincson (born February 2, 1901, in Bolton, MS; died April 22, 1975, in Chicago, IL), guitar, vocals; Lonnie Chatmon (born early 1880s, in Bolton, MS; died 1942 or 1943, in Bolton, MS), fiddle, vocals.

Playing the simple tandem of acoustic guitar and fiddle, the Mississippi Sheiks were an anachronism almost from the moment they began recording in 1930. But guitarist and singer Walter Vincson (also given as Vinson and even Vincent) and violinist Lonnie Chatmon (of the prolific Chatmon family that also produced brothers Bo and Sam) had a prodigious repertoire, and their willingness to try almost any string-based music won them audiences and influenced bluesmen wherever they roamed. Their most popular song, "Sitting on Top of the World," became a standard years later for Chicago kingpin Howlin' Wolf. And Wolf also copped a Sheiks' verse about "smokestack lightnin'" for his own song of the same name—borrowed as well by Wolf's rival, Muddy Waters. And through those Chicago blues titans, the Sheiks also have lived on in electric-juiced versions by Cream and respectful acoustic replays by Bob Dylan.

The reasons for the pairing of Vincson and Chatmon were never clear. Chatmon apparently fought with his brothers in an early fraternal group over who sang lead. And Vincson later told interviewers he took up playing in the string band and abandoned farming because he was "tired of smellin' mule farts." The two men grew so close they took to calling each other "Bruno" and locked so tightly as musicians that they could anticipate each other's solos. A 1930 recording session in Shreveport produced the first version of "Sitting on Top of the World," a song so popular that several other groups claiming to be the Sheiks soon began stealing gigs on the Delta. The real Sheiks paid regular visits to studios in San Antonio and Jackson, Mississippi, scoring nearly 70 tracks between 1930 and 1936. They ranged from Tommy Johnson-influenced blues like "Stop and Listen" and "Blood in My Eyes for You" to hokum social commentaries like "Sales Tax" and "The World Is Going Wrong." At times, Vincson and Chatmon augmented their sound by adding Bo and Sam Chatmon. But the two original Sheiks stayed together as the heart of the group until the late 1930s, when their recording career ebbed. The pair's break-up is as mysterious as their coming together, attributed at various times by Vincson and Chatmon to either racism, a stroke or the urgent need to flee an angry husband. Vincson recorded on his own but was unable to duplicate the Sheiks' early success.

what to buy: There could be no more perfect cross-section of the Sheiks' bountiful talents than *Stop and Listen* 🎵🎵🎵🎵 (Yazoo, 1992, prod. Richard Nevins, Don Kent, Stefan Grossman), a well-chosen 20 selections. All of the above-mentioned Sheiks classics are included, as are the unissued "Livin' in a Strain" and the sardonic "He Calls That Religion." The sound is surprisingly clean for 1930s-era 78s.

what to buy next: The four discs of *Complete Recorded Works Vols. 1–4* 🎵🎵🎵 (Document, 1991, prod. Johnny Parth) (sold separately) contain all of the Sheiks' recordings, and what surprises most is how rarely Chatmon and Vincson duplicated themselves. Like most bluesmen of that era they knew enough to harp on a good thing, and were quick to remake "Sitting on Top of the World" and "Stop and Listen." But the Sheiks' dexterity and open minds kept the records sounding fresh even as many of their peers' music palled.

influences:

◀◀ Henderson Chatmon, Neil Winston, Bo Chatmon, Sam Chatmon, Tommy Johnson

▶▶ Howlin' Wolf, Muddy Waters, Cream, Bob Dylan

Steve Braun

McKinley Mitchell

Born December 25, 1934, in Jackson, MS. Died January 18, 1984, in Jackson, MS.

McKinley Mitchell was a journeyman vocalist who recorded for several Chicago and southern labels. Gospel trained, he moved to Chicago and recorded with the Howlin' Wolf band on the Boxer label in 1959. He hit the charts in 1961 with the distinctive "The Town I Live In," issued on One-derful. Other singles on that label failed to find a market but Mitchell became a regular in Chicago clubs. Mitchell began recording with Willie Dixon in 1968, but the mediocre singles did nothing to enhance his career. Finally, in 1976, Mitchell's "Trouble Blues" made noise in the South, and he returned to Jackson. Further recordings for Malaco and later Retta continued to exploit the blues side of Mitchell. Sadly, Mitchell died when his career was still in full swing.

what to buy: *The Complete Malaco Recordings* ♫♫♫ (Waldoxy, 1992, prod. Tommy Couch, Wolf Stephenson) contains all of Mitchell's slicker Malaco, Chimneyville and Southern Biscuit sides.

influences:

◀◀ Sam Cooke, Bobby "Blue" Bland, Harold Burrage

▶▶ Z.Z. Hill, Tyrone Davis, Geater Davis

Jeff Hannusch

Keb' Mo'

Born Kevin Moore, 1952, in Compton, CA.

Once a journeyman backup guitarist who played with Buddy Guy, Joe Cocker and Santana, this soft-spoken singer-songwriter picked up an acoustic guitar in the early 1990s and set out to be one of the rare blues superstars. His debut album emphasized his worship of Robert Johnson and Taj Mahal, the follow-up leaned on Bonnie Raitt-style adult-contemporary pop, but his live shows showcase his smiling charisma and electric-band passion. *Just Like You* was one of 1996's best-selling blues albums, and in a time when so many bluesmen play the same classics and guitar solos in an endless loop, Keb' Mo' may just have the talent and personality for mainstream success.

what to buy: *Keb' Mo'* ♫♫♫ (OKeh/Epic, 1994, prod. John Porter) isn't revolutionary—John Hammond Jr., Rory Block, Buddy Guy, Junior Wells and Taj Mahal are among the many revivalists who have tried to rejuvenate Robert Johnson-style acoustic blues—but it announces a nice, smooth voice and a potential for greatness.

what to buy next: *Just Like You* ♫♫♫ (OKeh/Epic, 1996, prod. John Porter) is a well-crafted pop album, with decent songwriting, a sense of humor and cameos from Bonnie Raitt and Jackson Browne, but it's so nice, friendly and calm you just can't believe Moore is a follower of the devil-plagued Robert Johnson.

worth searching for: The soundtrack CD, *Tin Cup* ♫♫ (Epic, 1996), contains a new Keb' Mo' song, "Crapped Out Again."

influences:

◀◀ Robert Johnson, Bonnie Raitt, Taj Mahal, John Hammond Jr., Rory Block, Buddy Guy, Shawn Colvin, Papa John Creach, Tracy Chapman

▶▶ Jonny Lang, Corey Harris

Steve Knopper

Eurreal Wilford Montgomery

See: Little Brother Montgomery

Little Brother Montgomery

Born Eurreal Wilford Montgomery, April 18, 1906, in Kentwood, LA. Died September 6, 1985, in Champaign, IL.

Little Brother Montgomery is easily the most talented and stylistically versatile blues pianist on record. Not only was he a master of blues, boogie woogie and ragtime-inflected stride, but he was an equally capable performer of Irish tunes, hymns and pop standards. Montgomery grew up listening to ragtime pianists in his father's honky tonk and began his career on the southern barrelhouse circuit during World War I. At age 18 he enlisted with a traditional jazz ensemble and was soon picked up by the New Orleans-based Joyland Revelers. Frustrated with life on the road, he settled in Chicago in 1928 and found steady work playing rent parties with Blind Blake, Charlie Spand and others. During his tenure in the Windy City, Little Brother Montgomery helped to usher in The Golden Age of blues piano. His exceptional 1930 Paramount recordings, "No Special Rider" and "Vicksburg Blues," are genre classics, a testament to his pioneering genius. As interest in piano blues began to wane during the late 1930s, Montgomery resumed mixing his blues with traditional jazz, which began making a comeback in the 1940s. By the late 1950s, his solid blues presence was once again strongly felt in Chicago. It is his piano playing that one hears on Otis Rush's legendary Cobra sides, to name but one high-profile session appearance. Little Brother recorded (often to great effect, as on the Original Blues Classics sessions) throughout the 1960s and 1970s and enjoyed widespread

recognition during the folk and electric blues revivals. He remained active in many musical settings until his death in 1985.

what to buy: *Complete Recorded Works 1930–36* ✍✍✍✍ (Document, 1992, prod. Johnny Parth) conveniently gathers up all of his Paramount and Bluebird recordings on one disc. All of the classics are here: "No Special Rider," the much-imitated, double-rhythm marvel "Vicksburg Blues," the rag-like "Crescent City Blues" and the bouncy, boogie-woogie show-stopper "Farish Street Jive." Also here, for those who care, is the 1936 recording of "The First Time I Met You," a huge hit for Buddy Guy when he covered it as "The First Time I Met the Blues" in 1960. *Vocal Accompaniments and Post-War Recordings, 1930–54* ✍✍✍✍ (Document, 1993, prod. Johnny Parth) is a varied collection of pre-war vocal accompaniments and post-war piano solos, along with a handful of quintet numbers. The 1940s piano solos are absolutely beautiful and not to be missed.

what to buy next: The appropriately titled *Blues Piano Orgy* ✍✍✍✍ (Delmark, 1996, prod. Robert Koester) has more of Little Brother's classic 1940s sides, along with stellar performances by Speckled Red, Roosevelt Sykes, Memphis Slim, Curtis Jones and Otis Spann. Whew! *Tasty Blues* ✍✍✍ (Original Blues Classics, 1960/Fantasy, 1992, prod. Esmond Edwards) and *Chicago's Living Legends—Piano, Vocal & Band* ✍✍✍ (Original Blues Classics, 1961/Fantasy, 1993, prod. Chris Albertson) are his best recordings from the 1960s.

what to avoid: *At Home* ✍✍ (Earwig, 1990, prod. Michael Frank, Janet Montgomery) is made up of informal recordings that date from 1967 to 1982. Though Montgomery's vocals are good throughout, his piano playing is a bit lack-luster. His wife's dreadful singing does not help matters much. For fans only.

the rest:

Little Brother Montgomery/Sunnyland Slim: The LaSalle Chicago Blues Recordings Vol. 1 ✍✍✍ (Wolf)

Blues Masters ✍✍✍ (Storyville, 1992)

(With State Street Swingers) *Goodbye Mister Blues* ✍✍✍ (Delmark, 1993)

worth searching for: *Unissued Chicago Blues of the 1950s from Cobra and JOB* ✍✍✍✍ (Flyright, 1981, prod. Joe Brown, Eli Toscano) contains a couple of tunes Montgomery recorded (with electric guitar backing) for Joe Brown's JOB label in 1953, along with a pair from Memphis Slim and nine from Big Joe Williams,

Keb' Mo' (© Jack Vartoogian)

who is accompanied on piano by Little Brother's protégé, Erwin Helfer. Country meets barrelhouse meets big-city blues!

influences:

◀◀ Jelly Roll Morton, Rip Top, Loomis Gibson, Leon Brumfield

▶▶ Lee Green, Sunnyland Slim, Roosevelt Sykes, Otis Spann, Erwin Helfer

D. Thomas Moon

Coco Montoya

Born 1951, in Santa Monica, CA.

Singer, songwriter and guitarist, this Albert Collins protégé spent 10 years in one of the most important guitar chairs in bluesdom: with John Mayall's Bluesbreakers. On his own in the 1990s, Montoya demonstrates great skill in all areas, with a particularly beautiful singing voice that he uses to great effect.

what to buy: *Gotta Mind to Travel* ✍✍✍✍ (Blind Pig, 1995, prod. Albert Molinaro) boasts first-rate material and arrangements and guest appearances by Collins, Debbie Davies, Mayall and Al Kooper. The original "Too Much Water" and a great version of "Someday after Awhile" are particular standouts.

what to buy next: *Ya Think I'd Know Better* ✍✍✍ (Blind Pig, 1996, prod. Jim Gaines) has only one Montoya original, and while the energy and the chops are there, the material is less strong than on his debut.

influences:

◀◀ Stevie Ray Vaughan, Eric Clapton

Jennifer Zogott

John Mooney

Born April 3, 1955, in East Orange, NJ.

John Mooney has forged a unique musical niche through the ingenious marriage of two disparate blues traditions: Mississippi Delta country blues and the distinctive rhythms of New Orleans. Mooney comes by both honestly, having spent many of his teenage years as a friend and musical protégé of seminal Delta bluesman Son House, who then lived in Mooney's hometown, Rochester, New York. In the early 1970s Mooney spent several years as a traveling street singer, traversing the country while based mostly in California and Arizona. He settled in New Orleans in 1976, absorbing the unique percussive flavor and rhythmic character of the Crescent City's music, and gradually evolved from an acoustic musician to an electric bandleader. In either setting, he is a gifted performer with a memorable personal style.

what to buy: *Late Last Night* 🎵🎵🎵🎵 (Bullseye Blues/Rounder, 1990, prod. Mark Bingham, John Mooney) defined Mooney's Delta/New Orleans fusion for the first time in an electric band setting. It's a powerful, energetic effort that at the same time captures the laggard, steamy atmosphere of the Deep South. *Telephone King* 🎵🎵🎵🎵 (Blind Pig, 1983/Powerhouse, 1991, prod. John Mooney) is a banner showcase for Mooney's acoustic wizardry. Recorded with Jimmy Thackery, *Sideways in Paradise* 🎵🎵🎵🎵 (Blind Pig, 1993, prod. John Mooney, Jimmy Thackery) is an acoustic duo effort recorded poolside at a Jamaican villa in 1985 and first released as an LP on Thackery's Seymour label. Mooney's devastating bottleneck rendition of Bukka White's "Jitterbug Swing" is worth the purchase price alone. *Against the Wall* 🎵🎵🎵🎵 (House of Blues, 1996, prod. Rob Fraboni), Mooney's latest studio effort, is rock-solid, stripped to the core elements of the trio format Mooney uses most often in live gigs.

what to buy next: *Dealing with the Devil* 🎵🎵🎵🎵 (Ruf, 1997) is unique among Mooney's catalog—a live solo recording. It's an intense, very electric effort, and Mooney is fully up to the task. *Comin' Your Way* 🎵🎵🎵🎵 (Blind Pig, 1979, prod. Edward Chmelewski, Jerry Del Giudice), Mooney's debut release, is acoustic, steeped in the flavor of musical influences such as House, Leroy Carr and Arthur Crudup.

the rest:
Testimony 🎵🎵🎵🎶 (Domino, 1992)
Travellin' On 🎵🎵🎵🎶 (Crosscut, 1993)

worth searching for: Mooney has made guest appearances on numerous recordings, including Junior Wells' *Come on in This House* (Telarc, 1996); Spencer Bohren's *Vintage* (Zephyr, 1994) —including cuts produced by Mooney in 1984; Paula & The Pontiacs' *Cadillac Love* (Pontiac, 1994); *The Mardi Gras Indians Super Sunday Showdown* (Rounder, 1992); and Champion Jack Dupree's *Forever and Ever* (Bullseye Blues, 1991).

influences:
◀◀ Son House, Professor Longhair

Bryan Powell

Gary Moore
Born April 4, 1952, in Belfast, Ireland.

A lively, energetic guitar player, Moore served stints in Coliseum and Thin Lizzy—during the latter's mid-1970s *Jailbreak*

peak—before following his own path. He stumbled at first, chasing rock radio with a series of plodding, occasionally contrived albums. But during the late 1980s Moore got the blues, and since then, all has been well. Moore isn't necessarily about flash, so you have to pay attention to hear his subtle mix of rhythm and lead elements. He's also good for a few hot guests on each album, ranging from blues heroes such as B.B. King and Albert Collins to heavy metal icon Ozzy Osbourne.

what to buy: *Still Got the Blues* 🎵🎵🎵🎶 (Charisma, 1990, prod. Gary Moore) commands an immediate re-assessment of Moore's place in the rock pantheon, with guest appearances by Albert King and Albert Collins and Moore's best-known track, "Oh Pretty Woman." He also helmed *Blues for Greeny* 🎵🎵🎵🎵 (Charisma, 1996, prod. Gary Moore, Ian Taylor), an album of deftly played early Fleetwood Mac covers in tribute to that band's troubled founder Peter Green.

what to buy next: Moore can cut a commanding live figure, though that aspect of his talents has never been captured adequately on record. *Blues Alive* 🎵🎵🎵 (Virgin, 1993, prod. Gary Moore, Ian Taylor) is the best of his concert albums, with estimable—though not quite transcendent—versions of blues staples such as "The Sky Is Crying," "Further on up the Road" and "Walking by Myself."

what to avoid: *Wild Frontier* 🎵🎶 (Virgin, 1987), one of those early albums that show for a hard rocker, Moore is a pretty good blues player.

best of the rest:
After the War 🎵🎵🎵 (Virgin, 1989)
Live at the Marquee 🎵🎵🎵 (Griffin, 1994)
Ballads + Blues 1982–94 🎵🎵🎵 (Charisma, 1995)

worth searching for: There's a plethora of Moore guest appearances in the record racks. Check out his licks on "If Trouble Was Money" from the Albert Collins best-of *Collins Mix* 🎵🎵🎵🎶 (Pointblank, 1993) or his solo on "She's My Baby" from the Traveling Wilburys' *Vol. III* 🎵🎵 (Warner Bros., 1990).

influences:
◀◀ Fleetwood Mac, John Mayall's Bluesbreakers, Elmore James, B.B. King, Albert Collins, Hubert Sumlin

▶▶ Stevie Ray Vaughan, Randy Rhoads, Metallica, Colin James, Kenny Wayne Shepherd

Gary Graff

James Moore
See: Slim Harpo

Johnny B. Moore

Born January 24, 1950, in Clarksdale, MS.

This long-time Chicago guitarist met Jimmy Reed at an early age and later, as a teenager, performed with him. That connection—along with encouragement from pianist Johnny Jones' widow—pushed Johnny B. Moore into the blues world. But he didn't make guitar playing a full-time job until Koko Taylor made him her Blues Machine's lead man in 1975. After that and tours with Willie Dixon, Moore finally embarked on a solo career (which he continues to supplement with high-profile Chicago session work), and released several solid albums.

what to buy: *Hard Times* 🎵🎵🎵 (B.L.U.E.S. R&B, 1987), Moore's first solo album, updates traditional Chicago electric-guitar blues with several fresh sonic twists.

the rest:

Johnny B. Moore 🎵🎵🎵 (Delmark, 1996)
Live at Blue Chicago 🎵🎵🎵 (Delmark, 1997)

influences:

◀◀ Jimmy Reed, Elmore James, Chuck Berry, Muddy Waters, Buddy Guy

▶▶ Koko Taylor, Son Seals, Stevie Ray Vaughan

Steve Knopper

Kevin Moore

See: Keb' Mo'

Whistlin' Alex Moore

Born November 22, 1899, in Dallas, TX. Died January 20, 1989, in Dallas, TX.

Alex Moore was the barrelhouse piano patriarch of Texas. When he reminisced, it was of a Dallas hoary and violent, rife with characters like Bobby Cadillac, Blind Norris MacHenry, Whistlin' Billiken Johnson and Blind Benny—all friends of his. His scant discography included six sides for Columbia in 1929, and a few more for Decca and RPM in 1937 and 1951, respectively. Moore was an exponent of a choppy, tangential piano style that probably was common in the saloons and road houses in the Texas of yore. (Robert Shaw of Austin played comparably, though he developed independently of Moore.) The style had virtually died out but was at least put to wax by Chris Strachwitz for his fledgling Arhoolie label in 1960. The label's eighth release was Alex Moore; a bit less than a decade later came Moore's *In Europe,* cut live during the pianist's first

and only tour overseas. Moore continued to play in night clubs all and sundry in Dallas, occasionally venturing into Austin, until his heart gave out and he died in 1989. He hadn't driven a car since 1927 (though he kept his license up to date) and meandered all over Dallas' 375 square miles by bus, cab and foot. The city is poorer, since its great piano patriarch will stride its streets no more.

what to buy: The first 13 cuts on *From North Dallas to the East Side* 🎵🎵🎵 (Arhoolie, prod. Chris Strachwitz) comprised Moore's 1960 LP, among them poignant, time-warp Texas travelogues ("Going to Froggy Bottom," "West Texas Woman") and the title cut. Moore was a disjointed pianist compared to, say, Roosevelt Sykes, but his raucous and sometimes plain weird playing was never less than intriguing. His voice was gruff, his drawl thick as mud. There are also recordings from 1947 disinterred by the Dallas Blues Society in the 1980s and two selections culled from Moore's lone Euro-tour. "Boogiein' in Strasburg" is a gem, a thundergust of old-time, Texas barrelhouse piano from a man who personified the genre.

the rest:

Wiggle Tail 🎵🎵🎵 (Rounder, 1988)
Whistlin' Alex Moore: 1929–51 🎵🎵🎵 (Document, 1993)

influences:

◀◀ Nathaniel "Squadlow" Washington, Mary Wright, Chummy Dougherty, Blind Bobby Bryant

Tim Schuller

Teddy Morgan

Born July 8, 1971, in Minneapolis, MN.

Despite his relative youth, Teddy Morgan is already a veteran guitarist, vocalist and frontman for his own swing-style blues trio, the Sevilles. Morgan has absorbed all the old-school traditions, finessing swing-inflected licks, rhythmic roots grooves, traditional blues and even New Orleans rhythms. A professional guitarist since age 17 when he was known as "Kid" Morgan, he's played in the bands of James Harman, R.J. Mischo and Lamont Cranston. Mentor Kim Wilson transplanted Morgan to Austin and Antone's Records.

what to buy: *Louisiana Rain* 🎵🎵🎵 (Antone's/Discovery, 1996, prod. Teddy Morgan, Steve Mugalian, Jerry Hall) is a rave-up of high-spirited roots-blues, swingin' jump-blues and a couple of sweet ballads with Kim Wilson on harp, Derek O'Brien on rhythm guitar, Gene Taylor on piano and Jeff Turmes on bass.

what to buy next: On *Ridin' in Style* 🎵🎵🎵, (Antone's, 1994, prod. Derek O'Brien) the Sevilles get equal billing. Morgan's vocals aren't quite as polished, but overall it's still mighty fine, especially the guitar work. Morgan is the sideman and gets a couple of featured instrumentals ("Kidstuff," "Lightnin' Blues") that point toward his later work on R.J. Mischo & the Teddy Morgan Blues Band's *Ready to Go* 🎵🎵🎵 (Atomic Theory/Blue Loon Records, 1992).

influences:

◄◄ Connie Curtis "Pee Wee" Crayton, Charlie Christian, T-Bone Walker, Jimmie Vaughan, Dave Gonzales

B.J. Huchtemann

McKinley Morganfield

See: Muddy Waters

Maria Muldaur

Born Maria D'Amato, September 12, 1943, in New York, NY.

When Maria Muldaur started her solo career, she rode her distinctive, sweet voice to the pop stratosphere with the single "Midnight at the Oasis." As usual with overnight successes, she had worked a long time to get there. Through the 1960s she was part of the Even Dozen Jug Band and then the Jim Kweskin Jug Band (with whom she recorded a great early version of her solo hit, "I'm a Woman"). After the Kweskin band broke up, she and bandmate/husband Geoff Muldaur recorded before they divorced in 1972. She released her self-titled solo debut in 1973 and enjoyed a quick rise and fall on the pop charts. In the 1980s she became a born-again Christian and recorded some gospel and contemporary Christian albums. Muldaur has enjoyed good success on the blues and roots circuit in the 1990s.

what to buy: There's no question that Muldaur's best album is her first. *Maria Muldaur* 🎵🎵🎵🎵 (Reprise, 1973/Warner Archives, 1993, prod. Lenny Waronker, Joe Boyd) came out at a time when the pop scene was ready to enjoy the eclecticism of American music. She hit swing with "Walking One and Only" and sexy radio pop with "Midnight at the Oasis"—a song that, for good or ill, set a standard for come-on pop songs of the 1970s. The follow-up, *Waitress in a Donut Shop* 🎵🎵🎵🎵 (Reprise, 1974/Warner Archives, 1993, prod. Lenny Waronker, Joe Boyd), was just as broad and excellently performed but didn't hang to-

gether as well. It featured her rock 'n' rolling "I'm a Woman" (her second and last chart hit) as well as two cuts led by jazz great Benny Carter—"Sweetheart" and "It Ain't the Meat (It's the Motion)."

what to buy next: On *Sweet and Slow* 🎵🎵🎵 (Tudor, 1983/Stony Plain, 1993, prod. David Nichtern) Muldaur sings with her old fire for Nichtern, who wrote "Midnight at the Oasis," with bands led by Dr. John and Kenny Barron. *Jazzabelle* 🎵🎵🎵 (Stony Plain, 1995, prod. Maria Muldaur), recorded a decade later, is a jazz effort that finds Muldaur just as sharp with a huskier voice. *Louisiana Love Call* 🎵🎵🎵 (Black Top, 1992, prod. Hammond Scott) and *Fanning the Flames* 🎵🎵🎵 (Telarc, 1996, prod. John Snyder, Maria Muldaur, Elaine Martone) don't capture the pop moment the way her earlier albums did, but in terms of performance, Muldaur certainly gives her all vocally.

what to avoid: Generally speaking, you can't go wrong with a Muldaur album, but if you're rummaging through remainder bins of old vinyl, avert your eyes and close your wallet for *Southern Winds* 🎵🎵 (Reprise, 1978) and *Open Your Eyes* 🎵 (Reprise, 1979, prod. Patrick Henderson), which sound totally tired.

the rest:

There Is a Love 🎵🎵🎵 (Myrrh, 1982)
On the Sunny Side 🎵🎵🎵 (Music for Little People, 1992)
Meet Me at Midnite 🎵🎵🎵 (Black Top, 1994)

worth searching for: Geoff and Maria Muldaur's fine *Pottery Pie* 🎵🎵🎵 (Reprise, 1967/Hannibal, 1993, prod. Joe Boyd) points the way toward Maria's first solo outing. Out of print, Muldaur's third solo outing—*Sweet Harmony* 🎵🎵🎵 (Reprise, 1976, prod. Lenny Waronker)—was just a tad less interesting than her first two.

influences:

◄◄ Billie Holiday, Bessie Smith, Dolly Parton

►► Wendy Waldman, Linda Ronstadt

Salvatore Caputo

Matt "Guitar" Murphy

Born December 29, 1937, in Sunflower, MS.

A player since he was a child, Matt Murphy possesses a dynamic and sophisticated range. Many blues artists have benefited from collaborative partnerships with him. He has left a strong and indelible mark on blues—from his days with Memphis Slim in the 1950s to a remarkable barn-burning stint with James Cotton in the 1970s. As a child Murphy would listen to his aunt's extensive collection of jazz and blues. The resulting dual influence is evident in Murphy's fluid jazzy work and hard

Johnny B. Moore (© Jack Vartoogian)

Matt "Guitar" Murphy (© Jack Vartoogian)

but sweet blues playing. He is also a masterful rhythm guitarist, capable of deft, rich chording. After decades of busying himself as an asset to other bandleaders, Matt Murphy has finally begun to record under his own name.

what to buy: *Way Down South* 𝄞𝄞𝄞𝄞 (Antone's, 1990, prod. Matt Murphy) Murphy's debut disc, is a strong and confident set of tunes, sheer joy for lovers of electric guitar blues. The plentiful grooves build on each other, and Murphy handles the vocals with a husky, commanding style. He teams up with guitarist and brother Floyd Murphy on a few selections.

what to buy next: *The Blues Don't Bother Me* 𝄞𝄞𝄞 (Roesch, 1996, prod. Joe Roesch) isn't quite as focused but is still an enjoyable and adventurous outing with more funky, swaggering, southern fried blues and guitar finesse.

the rest:

Memphis Slim with Matt Murphy Together Again One More Time 𝄞𝄞𝄞 (Antone's, 1985)

worth searching for: *Live at Electric Lady: The James Cotton Band Featuring Matt "Guitar" Murphy* 𝄞𝄞𝄞𝄞 (Sequel, 1992), a British disc of a live performance of the Cotton band from the mid-1970s, is a must-have. Excellent recording quality on the digital re-master captures the high-energy antics of one of the most amazing live blues acts. Cotton is at his performing zenith, and Murphy's solos are captivating, especially on "Stormy Monday."

influences:

◄◄ Charlie Christian, Charles Brown, Blind Boy Fuller

►► Lurrie Bell, Ronnie Earl, Robben Ford

Tali Madden

Charlie Musselwhite

Born January 31, 1944, in Kosciusko, MS.

Part of the first wave of white blues performers, Charlie Musselwhite learned the blues first-hand playing harmonica behind

Homesick James, Robert Nighthawk and Johnny Young on Maxwell Street in Chicago. In the mid-1960s he formed his own band and began recording for Vanguard and later Arhoolie. Unlike some players of his generation, Musselwhite avoided the temptation to over play. By 1970 he'd moved to the West Coast, where his popularity increased via recordings and a busy touring schedule that included jaunts overseas. By the mid-1990s, Musselwhite had earned a spot as one of the top names in the blues. He continues to win over new fans with his warm vocals and melodic harmonica work.

what to buy: *Memphis Charlie* ♫♫♫♪ (Arhoolie, 1989, prod. Chris Strachwitz) is the CD reissue of Musselwhite's two Arhoolie LPs, featuring fine Chicago backing. *The Blues Never Die* ♫♫♫ (Vanguard, 1994, prod. Barry Goldberg, Pete Welding, Charlie Musselwhite) includes Musselwhite's first solo material recorded between 1966 and 1969. *Rough News* ♫♫♫ (Point Blank, 1997) confirms Musselwhite as a front-line blues player. *In My Time* ♫♫♫ (Alligator, 1994, prod. Kevin Morrow) is one of Musselwhite's more energetic releases.

what to buy next: There are plenty of enjoyable releases from this prolific artist, including *Ace of Harps* ♫♫♫ (Alligator, 1990, prod. Pat Ford), *Signature* ♫♫♫ (Alligator, 1990, prod. Charlie Musselwhite), *Louisiana Fog* ♫♫♫ (LaserLight, 1995) and *The Harmonica According To* ♫♫♫ (Blind Pig, 1995, prod. Charlie Musselwhite). The original Vanguard LPs *Stand Back* ♫♫♫♪ and *Tennessee Woman* ♫♫♫♪ have also been reissued on CD.

influences:

⏮ Big Walter Horton, Little Walter, Carey Bell, Junior Wells, Big John Wrencher, Muddy Waters, Fenton Robinson

⏭ Paul Butterfield, William Clarke, James Harman, Rod Piazza

Jeff Hannusch

Dave Myers
See: The Aces

Louis Myers
See: The Aces

Mark Naftalin
See: Paul Butterfield Blues Band

Kenny Neal
Born October 14, 1957, in Baton Rouge, LA.

Guitarist, singer, harmonica player, and songwriter Kenny Neal is one of the most consistent, and criminally under-recognized, talents in contemporary blues. Kenny is the son of Baton Rouge, Louisiana's legendary harmonica player Raful Neal, and the oldest in a musical family that also includes Noel and Ray Neal, bandmates of James Cotton and Bobby "Blue" Bland. After an apprenticeship in his father's band as a teenager, Neal went out on the road playing bass with Buddy Guy. He's never strayed far from those early inspirations, remaining steeped in swamp blues and dramatic Chicago-informed guitar solos. Blessed with a booming voice and impeccable chops, Neal's greatest asset is his economic delivery. The current crop of teenaged guitar phenoms should take a lesson from Neal's unwavering commitment to the heart of his songs; he lets his lyrics guide his on-the-money harp and 6-string accompaniment, and he's liable to play almost anything onstage.

what to buy: Neal's multiple talents shine brightest through *Hoodoo Moon* ♫♫♫♪ (Alligator, 1995, prod. Kenny Neal, Bob Greenlee, Bruce Iglauer), which features the syncopated funk of "Don't Fix Our Love," the brilliantly arranged slow-blues lament "If Heartaches Were Nickels" and "Carrying the Torch," a moving statement of Neal's mission that steers clear of maudlin territory. *Hoodoo Moon* strikes a perfect balance between classic and contemporary styles, nimbly moving from powerful readings of "I'm a Blues Man" and "It Hurts Me Too" to "Money Don't Make the Man," a poignant chronicle of the guns, gangs and drugs that tempt today's youth.

what to buy next: *Bayou Blood* ♫♫♫♪ (Alligator, 1992, prod. Kenny Neal, Bob Greenlee, Bruce Iglauer) strips away the horn section for a fierce collection of raw-bones blues featuring Neal with a rhythm section and keyboardist Lucky Peterson; "You Ain't Foolin' Me," "Lightning's Gonna Strike" and "That Knife Don't Cut No More" sum up the album's tenacious vibe. *Walking on Fire* ♫♫♫ (Alligator, 1991, prod. Kenny Neal, Bob Greenlee) is notable for the brass grooves supplied by James Brown alumni Fred Wesley and Maceo Parker.

what to avoid: *Big News from Baton Rouge* ♫♫ (Alligator, 1988, prod. Kenny Neal, Bob Greenlee) is a reissue of Neal's first independently-released effort, and while it contains some great playing, the production values and songwriting haven't aged well compared with the rest of his catalog.

the rest:
Devil Child ♫♫♫ (Alligator, 1989)

Raful (l) and Kenny Neal (© Jack Vartoogian)

influences:

◄◄ Slim Harpo, Buddy Guy, Lazy Lester

►► Larry Garner, Tab Benoit

Scott Jordan

Raful Neal

Born Raful Neal Jr., June 1936, in Erwinville, LA.

Neal is perhaps better known for siring a family of blues musicians than he is for his own recordings. Inspired to play harmonica in 1954 after seeing Little Walter at the Temple Roof in Baton Rouge, Neal formed a trio and began playing throughout a three-state area. One of the few Baton Rouge-based blues artists not to record for J.D. Miller, Neal first got on disc with Peacock in 1958 with "The Sunny Side of Love." Despite his local popularity, he wouldn't record again until 1968, when he cut "I'm Gonna Change My Way of Living," a regional hit. After Slim Harpo's death in 1970, Neal took over his friend's band.

Local success followed with his cover of "Let's Work Together" on Whit that same year. By the early 1980s, Neal was being backed by his sons Kenny, Noel and "Little" Ray and recordings followed on Fantastic. Ill health slowed Neal briefly in the mid-1990s, but he's made a comeback. Blues festivals keep him busy, and he often works with Tab Benoit.

what's available: Unfortunately, Neal's CDs just don't do his talent justice. As a result, *Louisiana Legend* ♪♪♪ (Fantastic/Alligator, 1987, prod. Bob Greenlee, Kenny Neal) and *I've Been Mistreated* ♪♪♪ (Wilddog, 1991) can't be wholeheartedly recommended.

worth searching for: Neal's great swamp blues single "Gonna Change My Way of Living"/"Getting Late in the Evening" is included on *Lafayette Soul Show* ♪♪♪♪ (Kent, 1992).

influences:

◄◄ Little Walter, Jimmy Reed, Slim Harpo, Whispering Smith, Lightnin' Slim, Wilbert Harrison, Silas Hogan

▶▶ The entire Neal clan, Tab Benoit, Tabby Thomas

Jeff Hannusch

L.F. Nelson

See: Jack Owens

Tracy Nelson

Born December 27, 1944, in French Camp, CA.

Tracy Nelson has spent much of her career listening to people wonder why it wasn't a bigger one. With good reason. Nelson has one of the most commanding and rich voices around, big but not brassy, full of emotion but devoid of the the tricks common to singers of lesser talent. Despite 17 albums over 30 years and plenty of critical acclaim, she has never had the commercial success to go with the good reviews, so she is something of a treasure to those who know her music and appreciate her fealty to blues. Nelson is very much her own person, singing only what and when she wants and eschewing the big city and bright lights for life in rural Tennessee outside of Nashville. By her own admission she has not always been the easiest person to work with, and she developed a reputation among some club owners for being difficult. But after three decades in the business, she does not apologize for calling things as she sees them. Nelson landed in Nashville in 1969 with Mother Earth, the country blues band she had put together the previous year, when it came to the city to record its second album. Nelson has never strayed too far from the music of her debut, *Deep are the Roots*, made when she was 20, produced by the legendary Sam Charters and backed by another 20-year-old, Charlie Musselwhite. It was spare and basic blues—several Ma Rainey tunes—sung sweetly and honestly. After Mother Earth disbanded in the mid-1970s, Nelson went out on her own with a mixed bag of records. She always sounded good, but some of the material was ponderous and overdone. Through the 1980s she remained in recording Siberia, unable to get any kind of record deal. Then in 1992 Rounder asked her to do a blues album, and her career was revived.

what to buy: The quintessential Nelson are the three Rounder records. *In the Here and Now* ♫♫♫♫ (Rounder, 1993, prod. Tommy Goldsmith) includes Nelson's own "Living the Blues," a basic blues with witty lyrics, a roaring duet with Irma Thomas on Percy Mayfield's "Please Send Me Someone to Love" and a haunting rendition of Elvie Thomas' "Motherless Child," which Nelson had first recorded on *Deep are the Roots. I Feel So Good*

♫♫♫♫ (Rounder, 1995, prod. Tommy Goldsmith) opens with "I Want to Know." Sugar Pie DeSanto put this one on the map, but when Nelson sings, "please don't start no stuff 'cause I don't wanna get rough," she makes it her own, not exactly threatening, but serious. Nelson's "Words Unspoken" isn't a typical blues tune, but the theme of romance gone awry fits the subject, and she mines it for all it is worth. A highlight is her dead-on take of Bessie Smith's "Send Me to the 'Lectric Chair," a grim tale but a toe-tapper nonetheless. *Move On* ♫♫♫♫ (Rounder, 1996, prod. C. Michael Dysinger) is more eclectic.

what to buy next: Her one major detour from blues was *Tracy Nelson Country* ♫♫♫ (Mercury, 1969/Reprise, 1996, prod. Pete Drake, Scotty Moore), and it's a gem. Nelson's voice is clear, sweet and haunting. Listen to "Stand by Your Man" and you'll forget about Tammy Wynette. Her version of "That's All Right Mama" is every bit as good as Elvis', and the opening track, "Sad Situation," is a poignant, understated heartbreaker. The same direct, no-frills approach that marks her blues and R&B work is present: country without gimmicks. *The Best of Tracy Nelson/Mother Earth* ♫♫♫ (Reprise, 1996, prod. Gregg Geller) is a sampling of Nelson's early career with Mother Earth. It includes the first recording of Nelson's signature song, the torchy "Down So Low." Also included is Allen Toussaint's "Cry On," affecting in its maturity and given a little more emotional heft than the Irma Thomas original.

what to avoid: On *Sweet Soul Music* ♫♫♫ (MCA, 1975/One Way, 1995, prod. Bob Johnston), Nelson sings fine, and while there are a number of good moments, some songs feel like they try too hard. If you're interested in full-throttle Nelson applied to Bob Dylan, you'll find it on "I'll Be Your Baby Tonight."

the rest:

Time Is on My Side ♫♫♫ (MCA, 1976/One Way, 1995)
Homemade Songs/Come See about Me ♫♫♫ (Flying Fish, 1992)

worth searching for: You can hear some of the very earliest Nelson recordings from *Deep are the Roots* on *Prestige/Folk Years Vol. II* ♫♫♫♫ (Fantasy, 1994). A spare but good version of "Move On" and another sturdy performance of the blues classic "It Hurts Me Too" are available on *Mountain Stage Vol. IV* ♫♫♫♫ (Blue Plate Music, 1992) and *Blues Live from Mountain Stage* ♫♫♫♫ (Blue Plate Music, 1995). A tribute recording to Janis Joplin, *Blues Down Deep—Songs of Janis Joplin* ♫♫♫♫ (House of Blues, 1996, prod. Steve Levick, Thomas R. Leavens), features Nelson giving a nice, honky-tonk twist to a little-known Joplin song appropriate to her troubled life: "What Good Can Drinkin' Do."

influences:

◀◀ Ma Rainey, Bessie Smith, Irma Thomas

▶▶ Michelle Willson, Jonelle Moeser, Rory Block

Nadine Cohodas

Hambone Willie Newbern

Born Willie Newbern, reportedly 1899. Died reportedly 1947.

Another blues cipher, Hambone Willie Newbern is known for six tracks recorded in 1929 in Atlanta and is truly significant for one of them: the first waxing of the immortal blues standard, "Roll and Tumble Blues." The demarcations of this songster's life are so blurred that the few facts known about him were provided by one of his pupils, the Tennessee bluesman Sleepy John Estes, who met Newbern while working in medicine shows in Mississippi. Despite the old-fashioned rag influences on Newbern's blues style, he was apparently an ornery sort who, Estes said, "wouldn't work for nowhere." His disposition led him to jail, where Estes reported he died after a savage beating in 1947.

what to buy: Newbern's six Atlanta sides are joined by all of Mississippi John Hurt's early recordings and New Orleans singer Richard "Rabbit" Brown's dramatic works on *The Greatest Songsters 1927–29* ♫♫♫♫ (Document, 1990, prod. Johnny Parth). Newbern's rag influences on "She Could Toodle-Oo" might seem slight, but his masterful blues performances on "Roll and Tumble" and "Hambone Willie's Dreamy-Eyed Woman's Blues" offer clear evidence of his importance as an early blues influence.

influences:

▶▶ Robert Johnson, Elmore James, Muddy Waters

Steve Braun

Robert Nighthawk

Born Robert Lee McCullum, November 30, 1909, in Helena, AR. Died November 5, 1967, in Helena, AR.

Robert Nighthawk is one of the most violent, dark, enigmatic and talented artists in blues history. Muddy Waters called him the finest slide guitarist in the Mississippi Delta; B.B. King has also placed Nighthawk near the top of his list. Nighthawk's influence can be heard in the playing of both legends. The boy who would become Robert Nighthawk developed a talent for the harmonica when he was in his teens and by 1930 was recording behind pianist Peetie Wheatstraw. At the age of 21 McCullum was taught guitar by his cousin, Houston Stackhouse, and they toured Arkansas and the Mississippi Delta in the early 1930s, playing together at parties and fish fries until McCullum was involved in a shooting. After the incident he moved to St. Louis, adopting his mother's maiden name: McCoy. He waxed his first sides as a guitarist in the late 1930s as Robert Lee McCoy for Victor's Bluebird label, and he worked extensively as a session man for Bluebird on guitar and harmonica. From the early 1940s on, McCoy frequently was on the move, relocating to Chicago and then, in 1943, back to Helena, where he worked for radio station KFFA. Around this time McCoy began calling himself Robert Nighthawk, taking the name from his popular tune, "Prowling Night-Hawk." His slide style having congealed under the tutelage of Tampa Red, Nighthawk returned to Chicago, where Muddy Waters introduced him to Phil and Leonard Chess. The sides that resulted, including "Annie Lee Blues," "Jackson Town Gal" and "Return Mail Blues," cry and ring with pain. But they didn't sell, so Nighthawk headed to the United label in the early 1950s, and later, to States. Nighthawk was not heard from again until 1964, when he reappeared on Testament. He returned to Helena in the mid-1960s.

what to buy: Much of Nighthawk's work for the Bluebird label from 1937 to 1940 is captured on *Robert Lee McCoy (Robert Nighthawk) Complete Recorded Works in Chronological Order* ♫♫♫♫ (Wolf, 1990), an astonishing, earthy and beautiful collection with Nighthawk accompanied by Speckled Red and Henry Townsend, among others. Nighthawk splits *Black Angel Blues* ♫♫♫♫ (Charly, 1990) with harp player Forest City Joe, a fellow Arkansan. Nighthawk's tracks are sprinkled with vocal accompaniment from his long-time girlfriend, Ethel Mae. Eerily, Nighthawk's slide takes on the stark, pleading tones of a human voice on his interpretation of his mentor Tampa Red's "Annie Lee Blues." By this time Nighthawk's guitar style had become deliberate, yet it remained fluid and natural-sounding. Collector Norman Dayron had the foresight to record Nighthawk on Maxwell Street in 1964, and these tapes surfaced on *Robert Nighthawk—Live on Maxwell Street* ♫♫♫♫ (Rounder, 1980/1991, prod. Norman Dayron). Nighthawk is accompanied by Johnny Young on rhythm guitar and Carey Bell on harp, and his brutally sweet slide cuts across the dirt and grit of Maxwell Street to touch the souls of the partiers and dancers heard cavorting in the background. Nighthawk's last recordings are captured on *Masters of Modern Blues—Robert Nighthawk and Houston Stackhouse* ♫♫♫♫ (Testament, 1967, prod. Norman Dayron, Pete Welding). Welding himself writes in the liner notes that, although the album was meant to be a showcase for Nighthawk's "uncommon, under-appreciated gifts as one of the most imaginative and distinctive interpreters of the blues, it has wound up, sadly, as a memorial." The subtle, laid-back yet volatile beauty of Nighthawk is captured from three different sessions: October 1964 with John Wrencher on harp; May 1964 with Little Walter and Johnny Young; and late August 1967—just two months before his death from heart disease.

what to buy next: *Drop Down Mama* 𝄢𝄢𝄢𝄢 (MCA/Chess, 1970/1990, prod. Leonard Chess, Phil Chess) finds Nighthawk delivering slick versions of "Sweet Black Angel," "Anna Lee," and "Return Mail Blues" with Sunnyland Slim and Willie Dixon in 1949. A version of "Jackson Town Gal" is taken from a session in 1950, with backing from Dixon and Pinetop Perkins. Much of Nighthawk's work for the United label, recorded in 1951 and 1952, is gathered on *Bricks in My Pillow* 𝄢𝄢𝄢 (Pearl/Delmark, 1978, prod. Lew Simpkins, Leonard Allen, Robert Koester).

influences:

◀◀ Peetie Wheatstraw, Houston Stackhouse, Tampa Red

▶▶ Muddy Waters, Earl Hooker, B.B. King

Steven Sharp

Darrell Nulisch

Born 1953, in Dallas, TX.

An early singer-harpist with Anson Funderburgh's Rockets and Ronnie Earl's Broadcasters, Nulisch has a deep, subtly powerful voice that fits straightforward Chicago-style blues just fine. Frustrated with his frontman role in other people's bands, Nulisch started singing solo in the early 1990s. His desire for freedom makes sense, but a listener can't help wishing he'd have made more of the solo opportunity. As it is, his albums are like lots of other contemporary blues albums.

what to buy: There's some nice guitar work by Jon Moeller and, of course, solid vocal-harp interplay by Nulisch on the debut *Business As Usual* 𝄢𝄢𝄥 (Black Top, 1991, prod. Hammond Scott), but too many songs, like "Count on Me" and "Orange Soda," just kind of lay there.

what to buy next: *Bluesoul* 𝄢𝄢𝄥 (Higher Plane, 1996, prod. Bobby Hankins), true to the title, puts Nulisch in a more soulful context, and the singer is starting to write some excellent blues songs, such as "Crime of Passion" and "Worried," but again, there's just not much of a spark here.

influences:

◀◀ Anson Funderburgh, Little Walter, Sonny Boy Williamson II, Jerry Portnoy

Steve Knopper

Robert Nighthawk

song
Nighthawk Shuffle

album
Live on Maxwell Street (Rounder)

instrument
Guitar

monster solo

St. Louis Jimmy Oden

Born James Burke Oden, June 26, 1903, in Nashville, TN. Died December 30, 1977, in Chicago, IL.

Though this singer-pianist recorded singles for many different record labels in the 1930s and 1940s, he's remembered more for his songwriting. Specifically, he's remembered for "Goin' Down Slow," which Oden cut in several different versions, and which countless bluesmen, most notably Howlin' Wolf with Willie Dixon spooking up the spoken verses in 1961, have performed since. In the 1920s, Oden and Roosevelt Sykes were among the most prominent piano players at Chicago house parties; the repute kick-started his recording career, which continued sporadically until the 1960s.

what to buy: The two primary Oden collections, *St. Louis Jimmy Oden, 1932–48* ✒✒✒ (Blues Documents) and *St. Louis Jimmy Oden, 1932–38* ✒✒✒ (Story of Blues), occasionally overlap. But, of course, they include "Goin' Down Slow."

influences:

◀◀ Roosevelt Sykes, Art Tatum, Victoria Spivey, Speckled Red, Jimmy Yancey

▶▶ Little Richard, Jerry Lee Lewis, Muddy Waters, Howlin' Wolf, Dr. John, Professor Longhair

Steve Knopper

Andrew "B.B." Odom

Born December 15, 1936, in Denham Springs, LA. Died December 23, 1991, in Chicago, IL.

Andrew "Big Voice" Odom was a fairly popular Chicago club vocalist for three decades. He worked with Earl Hooker's group for 10 years until the guitarist's death in 1970. Later he often worked with Jimmy Dawkins and did spot gigs on the South Side with other artists. Odom recorded infrequently and died just before the release of his first CD.

what to buy: *Feel So Good* ✒✒✒ (Black & Blue, 1973/Evidence, 1993) features Magic Slim on guitar. He lives up to his "Big Voice" nickname on *Goin' to California* ✒✒✒ (Flying Fish, 1992, prod. Steve Freund), which pairs Odom with an efficient band from Canada, the Gold Tops.

worth searching for: Check the used singles bins for Odom's singles on small Chicago labels. His work can also be heard on Earl Hooker's Arhoolie sides. If you can find *Further on down the Road* ✒✒✒✒ (Bluesway, 1973, prod. Ed Michel), you've got a classic, one of Earl Hooker's last sessions before his death.

influences:

▶▶ B.B. King, Little Milton, Bobby "Blue" Bland, Junior Parker

Jeff Hannusch

Omar & the Howlers

See: Omar Dykes

Paul Oscher

Born April 5, 1950, in Brooklyn, NY.

Paul Oscher is a fine player whose membership in Muddy Waters' band challenged a color barrier. Though not by a long shot the first white guy to be in an integrated band, Oscher did it as a sideman, rather than as a leader, and toured the Deep South with Waters during a murderous period in America's racial politics. Bitten by the the blues bug at an early age, Oscher practiced his harmonica until he was proficient enough to be playing in black clubs by age 15. One night he got to sit in with Waters, long one of his heroes. Three years later, in 1967, a second club encounter with Waters, then on a road trip without a harpist, resulted in an invitation to the 18-year-old Oscher to join the band. During the next six years Oscher was a Waters' regular, playing on several of his albums (including the Chess sets *Live at Mr. Kelly's* and *Unk in Funk*). Oscher later put out a couple of singles under the moniker "Brooklyn Slim" but dropped out of sight. Years later, driven by the pain of a failed relationship, Oscher became visible again in the mid-1990s, recording new albums and looking to put together a touring band.

what to buy: *Knockin' on the Devil's Door* ✒✒✒ (Viceroots, 1996, prod. Lonesome Dave Peverett) finds Oscher playing as much guitar as harmonica with help from David Maxwell on piano, Steve Guyger on harmonica, Mudcat Ward on bass and Big Eyes Smith on drums. This album of mostly Oscher originals achieves a classic Chicago blues feel and features good performances and sound in a very worthy effort. On *The Deep Blues of Paul Oscher* ✒✒✒ (Blues Planet, 1996, prod. Jeff "Red" Alperin), Oscher stretches out some, incorporating 1950s R&B and gospel elements into his blues mix and rounding out the sound with sax and a female chorus.

influences:

◀◀ Little Walter, Big Walter Horton, James Cotton

▶▶ Jerry Portnoy, Steve Guyger

Michael Dixon

Johnny Otis

Born John Veliotes, December 28, 1921, in Vallejo, CA.

Truly a renaissance man, Johnny Otis has not only been a prominent figure in R&B, blues and rock, but he is also a gifted author, minister, bandleader, composer, vocalist, singer and artist who has continued to perform on a weekly basis in Sonoma County, California, where he currently makes his home. His career started in 1939 as a drummer in a boogie woogie blues band called Count Otis Matthews' West Oakland House Rockers. After years on the road and in the Midwest, Otis settled in Los Angeles, starting his own band in 1943 and trimming it down to a nine-piece R&B band in 1947. His groups featured vocalists such as Little Esther Phillips, Mel Walker and the Robins (later called the Coasters). At the same time, Otis was a disc jockey in Los Angeles, helping discover and promote different artists. Another avenue Otis explored was opening the Barrel House Club in Watts in 1948. He recorded West Coast jump blues on a variety of labels, including Savoy, Peacock, Federal and Mercury. Developing his own record company, Dig, in 1955, Otis recorded himself and moved into production, helping Johnny Ace and Big Mama Thornton. He is also credited with discovering and promoting Etta James, Jackie Wilson and Hank Ballard. His own records often demonstrated the influences between blues, R&B and rock. He recorded on Captiol at the end of the 1950s, but it was really the 1970s when his career took off again. A performance at the Monterey Jazz Festival in 1970 with a slew of veteran vocalists that included Big Joe Turner, Eddie Vinson, Roy Milton, Ivory Joe Hunter and Little Esther Phillips helped reignite his live performances. As a songwriter Otis has his signature "Willie and the Hand Jive," which has appeared on numerous recordings over the years, as well as "Every Beat of My Heart," which launched Etta James and graces a number of his recordings with male as well as female vocalists. Yet, one finds a real pop sensibility to his songwriting, especially in the pieces he composed for his own Dig label. In the 1970s Otis was ordained as a minister, and his career continued with live shows. He moved to northern California by the early 1990s and opened a deli that also became the location for his weekly shows, drawing crowds with a new generation of vocalists. He has resumed preaching in Santa Rosa, California, while still performing live shows, doing radio broadcasts for KPFA in Berkeley, California, and recording discs. Otis is definitely responsible for helping shape and define much of the R&B world that developed in the 1950s, but he continues the legacy of West Coast blues in his performances and recordings.

what to buy: The definitive set to know Otis' early work is *The Original Johnny Otis Show* ♫♫♫♫♫ (Savoy, 1994, prod. Ralph Bass), highlighted by vocal turns on "Mistrustin' Blues" between Little Esther and Mel Walker that capture a playfulness that reminds us that the blues are about good times as well as bad. "I Found out My Troubles," with the Robins on vocals, is a stunning example of West Coast blues. Instrumental tracks like "Harlem Nocturne" show how the whole band could flex its muscle, while the guitar and sax work on "Hangover Blues" create a throb that lingers as the cut ends.

what to buy next: The set to understand Johnny Otis as a musician who moved across genres, *Creepin' with the Cats* ♫♫♫♫♫ (Ace, 1991, prod. Johnny Otis) features Otis' skill at crafting pop songs that could be radio friendly. Whether the rocking instrumental "Dog Face Boy Part 1," the fast rockers with Otis on vocals or the slower, R&B styled "My Eyes Are Full of Tears," this captures the Otis who was all of it—songwriter, performer and promoter. To capture the influences, try *Spirit of the Black Territory Bands* ♫♫♫♫ (Arhoolie, 1992, prod. Johnny Otis, Tom Morgan), a series of mostly instrumental covers of material by Count Basie, Duke Ellington and Lionel Hampton. From the opening cut, Basie's "Swinging the Blues," to a smoky version of Earl Hagen's "Harlem Nocturne," you feel transported to some late-1940s club. Otis does a great vocal turn on "Margie" and plays some mean vibes on "Flying Home" and "Jumping the Blues." For live performance and a line-up of classic vocal talent, *The Johnny Otis Show Live at Monterey* ♫♫♫♫ (Epic, 1993, prod. Johnny Otis) highlights a revue performance from the 1970 Monterey Jazz Festival. Just hearing the soaring sax work of Eddie "Cleanhead" Vinson and his vocals on "Cleanhead's Blues" is worth the price of admission, but his later turn on his own "Kidney Stew" is an even meatier performance. Ivory Joe Hunter's "Since I Met You Baby" captures yearning and heartache, while Johnny's son, Shuggie Otis, evokes the Delta and the past on "The Time Machine," with some great harp accompaniment by Jim Bradshaw. Even the stage patter between Otis and Pee Wee Crayton before Crayton launches into "The Things I Used to Do" is delightful. The generations come together on *The New Johnny Otis Show* ♫♫♫♫ (Alligator, 1981, prod. Johnny Otis).

what to avoid: *L.A. 1970—Live* ♫♫ (Wolf, 1991, prod. Ron Bartolucci) includes some of the same great performers that appear on the Monterey disc—Big Joe Turner, Roy Milton and Little Esther Phillips, but the recording quality is inferior to the point of disappointment.

the rest:
Too Late to Holler ♫♫♫ (Night Train, 1994)
Billy Eckstine/Big Joe Turner/Johnny Otis ♫♫♫ (Savoy, 1995)
Nothin' but the Blues ♫♫♫ (Delta, 1995)
Otisology ♫♫♫ (Kent, 1995)
R&B Dance Party ♫♫♫ (J&T, 1997)

worth searching for: *The Capitol Years* ♫♫♫♫ (Capitol, 1988) pulls together some of his best from his days with the label.

influences:
◄◄ T-Bone Walker

►► Shuggie Otis, Mitch Woods

John Koetzner

Jack Owens

Born L.F. Nelson, November 17, 1904, in Bentonia, MS. Died February 9, 1997, in Bentonia, MS.

Jack Owens was a farmer, bootlegger, blues player and jukehouse operator who lived out his 92 years in the small town of Bentonia, Mississippi. An active performer in his own and other local jukes since before 1920, Owens was unrecorded until his discovery by musicologist David Evans in 1966. Owens' reluctance to travel ruled out much of a touring career, although he did play a number of festivals in America and abroad after his wife died in the 1980s. This lack of exposure could explain Jack's status as a relative unknown among blues fans; certainly there was no lack of talent holding him back. His obscurity might also be explained by the frequent comparisons to fellow Bentonian Skip James, whose 1931 recordings established his near-legendary status long before his rediscovery in 1965. However, Jack was a powerful singer and a brilliant guitarist in his own right, and it's unfortunate that his music is not better represented on compact disc.

what to buy: Other than a few tracks scattered on various compilations, the only Jack Owens recordings currently available are found on *It Must Have Been the Devil* 🎜🎜🎜🎜 (Testament, 1995), sessions he made with his harmonica-playing friend Bud Spires, recorded by David Evans in 1970.

influences:
◀◀ Skip James

Rob Hutten

Jay Owens

Born Isaac Jerome Owens, September 6, 1947, in Lake City, FL.

Writer of more than 100 songs, Owens began performing in high school, then earned enough of a local reputation to back such soul stars as O.V. Wright, Stevie Wonder, Donny Hathaway and Al Green. (He and his friend, Johnny Kay, led premier Tampa-St. Petersburg-area backup bands such as the Barons, the Dynamites and the Funk Bunch.) He put his own group together in the late 1980s, backed Etta James, and performed solo on several swings through Europe. He's a decent soul singer, but he's most significant as a songwriter and a backup musician.

what to buy: You can tell *Movin' On* 🎜🎜✓ (Code Blue/Atlantic, 1995, prod. Mike Vernon) is a veteran session musician's album, because it's so perfectly crafted it almost takes some of the soul away from Owens' straightforward, slightly gritty

voice. Some songs, such as "Workin' Man," have a certain enthusiastic bounce, but it quickly lapses into workmanship.

what to buy next: Owens' debut, *The Blues Soul of Jay Owens* 🎜🎜 (Code Blue/Atlantic, 1993, prod. Mike Vernon), is even less spontaneous, although "Come on to My House" and "Back Row" have a nice soul touch.

influences:
◀◀ Stevie Wonder, O.V. Wright, Bobby "Blue" Bland, Rufus Thomas, Elmore James

Steve Knopper

Bobby Parker

Born c. 1939, in Lafayette, LA.

Bobby Parker grew up in Los Angeles and began playing guitar at the age of nine. While still in high school he won a talent show at Johnny Otis' Barrelhouse club. He parlayed his ability into stints backing Don and Dewey, Otis Williams and the Charms and Bo Diddley. After moving to Washington, DC, Parker cut "Watch Your Step" in 1961, a hit on the short-lived V-Tone label. In 1969 he toured England and recorded "It's Hard but It's Fair" for Blue Horizon. Parker returned home and for the next two decades eked out an existence playing clubs and Army bases, mixing blues with radio hits. Little was heard from Parker simply because the Washington area didn't afford many recording opportunities for blues artists. After signing with Black Top in 1993 he was able to rejoin the front line of the blues world.

what to buy: Granted, *Bent out of Shape* 🎜🎜🎜🎜 (Black Top, 1993, prod. Hammond Scott) is busy and occasionally overproduced, but Parker's talent overrides most of the distractions. *Shine Me Up* 🎜🎜🎜🎜 (Black Top, 1995, prod. Hammond Scott) includes lots of "go-go guitar"—Washington's indigenous funk style.

worth searching for: Parker's Vee-Jay, Blue Horizon and V-Tone 45s are all worth inclusion in a blues 45 collection.

Jack Owens (© Jack Vartoogian)

influences:

◀◀ T-Bone Walker, Jimmy Nolen, James Brown, Bo Diddley, Ray Charles

▶▶ Little Milton, Bobby Radcliff, Ronnie Earl

Jeff Hannusch

Junior Parker

Born Herman Parker, March 27, 1932, in West Memphis, AR. Died November 18, 1971, in Chicago, IL.

Plump-faced Junior Parker never won the loyalty of blues audiences the way Muddy Waters and Howlin' Wolf commanded their followings through the 1960s and 1970s. But Parker had his own successes to comfort him—steady work in the blues revues that criss-crossed the U.S. and a string of hit singles that kept him in pocket change. Parker's early Sun sides "Mystery Train" and "Feelin' Good" were Memphis blues giants, and though he cocooned himself in slicker big-band backings on Duke, Parker's dry, country harmonica always stood out, a reminder of his days as a sideman for Howlin' Wolf's original band of Delta house rockers. A young acolyte of Sonny Boy Williamson II, Parker joined Wolf in 1949, blowing with harpmate James Cotton and guitar legend Matt Murphy. Early 1950s sides for Modern went unreleased, but Parker's Sun classics gave him instant name recognition. "Feelin' Good" was the hit; "Mystery Train" stiffed in 1953, but gained mythic status when Elvis Presley tried his own version. Parker had a last gasp of sides with Sun, then slipped off to Duke. From 1953 to the late 1960s, Parker toured with label sidekick Bobby "Blue" Bland and churned out horn-blaring blues-and-soul mixtures such as "Driving Wheel," "Next Time You See Me" and "Man or a Mouse." The power of his workouts was not lost on those who came after him. Soon after Parker died of a brain tumor, his cousin, Al Green, opened a smoking 1972 blues shuffle by saying: "I'd like to dedicate this song to Little Junior Parker, a cousin of mine who's gone, but we'd like to carry on in his name." The song was "Take It to the River."

what to buy: The early country Junior, crooning over Memphis shuffles like he had just come out of the fields can be heard on *Mystery Train* ♫♫♫♫ (Rounder, 1990, prod. Sam Phillips). "Mystery Train" and "Feelin' Good" are here, as is the resentful "Sittin' at the Bar" and equally knocked-kneed cuts by James Cotton and the doomed Pat Hare, who later went on to play guitar with Muddy Waters and fulfill the baleful threat of one of the songs he sings here: "I'm Gonna Murder My Baby."

what to buy next: The subtitle of *Junior's Blues* ♫♫♫♫ (MCA, 1992, prod. Andy McKaie) is "The Duke Recordings Vol. One," and there ought to be more soon. Some of Parker's most well-known Duke records are part of this disc. But as nice as it is to have "I Wanna Ramble" and "Driving Wheel" available again, there are dozens more still out of reach, like "Man or a Mouse." These are the hits that taught men like Little Milton and Z.Z. Hill how to sing down-home soul-blues.

influences:

◀◀ Howlin' Wolf, Sonny Boy Williamson I

▶▶ Al Green, Little Milton, Z.Z. Hill

Steve Braun

Charley Patton

Born April 1891, in Bolton, MS. Died April 28, 1934, in Indianola, MS.

Thanks to Eric Clapton and the marketing power of Sony Records, the great Delta bluesman Robert Johnson has become an American icon. Patton, whose dark and occasionally frightening delivery influenced Johnson, Son House and Howlin' Wolf, to name a few, is still known mainly to historians and hard-core blues fans. After he started playing guitar in 1907, his talent made him a celebrity in his native Mississippi, where he drew unprecedented, large crowds to hear him sing. Like his successors Johnson and Lightnin' Hopkins, Patton's songs were obsessed with death: "Oh Death," "Prayer of Death," "Jesus Is a Dying-Bed Maker" and "Poor Me" were among his better-known titles. What's really jarring, even upon hearing the static-filled 1929 recordings that constitute his legacy, is the emotional desperation in his deep voice and the urgent one-*two* rhythm of his acoustic guitar. Just five years after record-store owner H.C. Speir tracked him down and took him into the studio, Patton died of a chronic heart condition.

what to buy: Unlike Johnson, Patton was a prolific studio musician, recording 43 sides in his first year and continuing through his death. The two collections of this output, *King of the Delta Blues* ♫♫♫♫ (Yazoo/Shanachie, 1991) and *Founder of the Delta Blues* ♫♫♫♫ (Yazoo/Shanachie, 1989), have been impeccably transferred to compact disc with thorough accompanying liner notes and an R. Crumb portrait.

worth searching for: The multi-volume *Complete Recorded Works* ♫♫♫ (Document) has absolutely everything, but it's hard tracking down all the volumes. *Masters of the Delta Blues: The Friends of Charley Patton* ♫♫♫ (Yazoo/Shanachie) has excellent performances by Patton followers Willie Brown, Son House, Bukka White and several others.

influences:

◀◀ Blind Lemon Jefferson, Earl Harris, Jim Jackson

▶▶ Robert Johnson, Willie Brown, Booker Miller, Lightnin' Hopkins, Howlin' Wolf, Skip James, Eric Clapton, John Hammond Jr.

Steve Knopper

Peg Leg Sam

Born Arthur Jackson, December 18, 1911, in Jonesville, SC. Died November 27, 1977, in Jonesville, SC.

Not so much a blues musician as a medicine-show comedian who happened to have mastered the harp, Jackson lost his leg in a 1930 accident. Though he was a terrific player, he wasn't as influential a harpist as he was a performer; his jokes, monologues and fake toasts provided a shtick that many bluesmen—like their country ilk—gradually incorporated into their own performances.

what to buy: Sam's two known albums, *Joshua* ♫♫♫ (Tomato, 1990) and *Peg Leg Sam* ♫♫♫ (Tomato), are filled with funny, rickety old-school blues—again, the medicine-show spirit is more interesting than the actual harmonica licks.

influences:

◀◀ Emmett Miller, Jimmie Rodgers, Al Jolson, Sonny Boy Williamson II, Little Walter

▶▶ Hank Williams, B.B. King, Harmonica Frank

Steve Knopper

Pinetop Perkins

Born July 13, 1913, in Belzoni, MS.

Pinetop Perkins was almost 60 years old when he replaced the legendary Otis Spann as resident pianist with the Muddy Waters Band. Late starts were not unusual for Perkins, who didn't begin playing piano until he was in his thirties after an injury left him unable to play guitar. In his younger days Perkins was based out of Helena, Arkansas, where he appeared regularly on Robert Nighthawk's blues radio show and Sonny Boy Williamson's *King Biscuit Time* broadcast. An early 1950s stint with guitarist Earl Hooker produced "Pinetop's Boogie Woogie," his first recording. Joining with the Waters band, however, was a decisive turning point in Perkins' career. His style doesn't plumb the pathos laden

depths Spann visited, but is brilliant nonetheless. Rich vocals and rolling keyboard work are Perkins' mainstay. A decade with Muddy ended with Pinetop and bandmates splitting to form the Legendary Blues Band, where Perkins presided as an elder blues spokesman. He is considered the premiere living blues pianist and has appeared on many blues artist's recordings. Slowed a trifle by age, Perkins remains active on the blues scene.

what to buy: *Eye to Eye* ♫♫♫ (AudioQuest, 1997, prod. Joe Harley) is a solid back-to-basics blues set with Legendary Blues Band/Muddy Waters alumni Calvin Jones and Willie Smith aboard and featuring guitarist Ronnie Earl. *Portrait of a Delta Bluesman* ♫♫♫♫ (Omega, 1993, prod. George Kilby Jr., Bob Ward) offers pure, unadulterated Perkins on a solo outing and excerpts from interviews that give it an autobiographical tone.

what to buy next: *Boogie Woogie King* ♫♫♫ (Evidence, 1992, prod. Jerry Gordon), originally recorded in 1976 for the French Black and Blue label, is a lively disc with great support from Luther Johnson, Jones and Smith. A host of big names, including Kim Wilson, Matt Murphy, Jimmy Rogers and Duke Robillard, turn out for *Pinetop's Boogie Woogie* ♫♫♫♫ (Antone's, 1992, prod. Clifford Antone), a live and kicking set from the legendary Austin blues club.

what to avoid: Perkins is backed by an Icelandic group, the Blue Ice Band, for *After Hours* ♫♫ (Blind Pig, 1989, prod. Edward Chmelewski), with less than memorable results.

the rest:

On Top ♫♫♫ (Deluge, 1992)
Live Top ♫♫♫♫ (Deluge, 1995)

Tali Madden

Rufus Perryman

See: Speckled Red

William Perryman

See: Piano Red

James Peterson

Born November 4, 1937, in Russell County, AL.

Peterson's blues story reads like many others: he grew up singing gospel music in a church, learned the blues from hanging out at his father's juke joint, met some important people and struck out on his own. Peterson had automatic influence,

though: his son, Lucky, made his recorded debut at age five on James' first album in 1970. A club operator in Florida, New York and Alabama and a frequent performer in his one-time East Chicago, Indiana, hometown, Peterson has scored gigs backing such luminaries as Jimmy Reed, Koko Taylor and Freddie King.

what to buy: Peterson's conventional style, a bit of Howlin' Wolf grit in his voice and a laid-back moan in his guitar playing, comes across best on *Rough and Ready* 𝄢𝄢𝄢 (Kingsnake, 1977), which has his son Lucky backing him on solid but hardly ground-breaking blues tracks.

what to buy next: *Preachin' the Blues* 𝄢𝄢 (Malaco, 1996, prod. Tommy Couch Jr., Paul "Heavy" Lee), true to its title, has a much more pronounced gospel strain than Peterson's previous albums. "Who Shot John?" owes its catchy chorus to the church-like harmonies.

the rest:

Too Many Knots 𝄢𝄢 (Ichiban, 1995)

worth searching for: Peterson's early albums, including the debut *The Father, Son and the Blues* 𝄢𝄢𝄢 (Perception/Today, 1970) and *Tryin' to Keep the Blues Alive* 𝄢𝄢𝄢 (Perception/Today, 1971), are much tougher to track down than his recent stuff for more CD-oriented labels.

influences:

◀◀ Howlin' Wolf, Ray Charles, Rufus Thomas, Muddy Waters, Son Seals

▶▶ Lucky Peterson, Willie Kent, Billy Branch

Steve Knopper

Judge Kenneth Peterson

See: Lucky Peterson

Lucky Peterson

Born Judge Kenneth Peterson, December 13, 1963, in Buffalo, NY.

After Little Stevie Wonder but before Little Michael Jackson, there was Little Lucky Peterson, who at six years old had a hit on the national R&B charts. Peterson's "1-2-3-4," produced by Willie Dixon, wasn't exactly the second coming of "Fingertips" or the precursor to "ABC," but it got the young singer on *The Tonight Show* and established him as a significant talent who

Pinetop Perkins (© Linda Vartoogian)

clearly knew his way around the music business. Peterson, son of singer-guitarist James Peterson, grew up to become a well-known session musician, backing Etta James and Otis Rush before starting a blues solo career that has shown him to be a straightforward and reliable blues singer-guitarist-songwriter with an affinity for fusion.

what to buy: The title *Triple Play* 𝄢𝄢𝄢 (Alligator, 1990, prod. Bob Greenlee) refers to Peterson's versatility; he sings and plays guitar and piano on almost all the tracks, most notably "Repo Man" and the soulful update of Wilson Pickett's "I Found a Love."

what to buy next: Peterson was just 21 when he put out his debut *Ridin'* 𝄢𝄢𝄢 (Evidence, 1984/1993, prod. Didier Tricard), an enthusiastic mix of R&B and pure blues that recalls the singer's influences, Little Milton and Bobby "Blue" Bland. The best tracks are the most soul-oriented; Peterson, with Melvin Taylor on guitar and a strong rhythm section, tackles Booker T. and the MG's "Green Onions" and "Kinda Easy Like."

what to avoid: *I'm Ready* 𝄢𝄢 (Verve, 1992, prod. John Snyder) is the beginning of Peterson's "cool" phase, in which he wears snazzy sunglasses on album covers and slides much more bland, meandering jazz-rock-gospel-blues fusion into the songs.

the rest:

Lucky Strikes 𝄢𝄢𝄢 (Alligator, 1989)
Beyond Cool 𝄢𝄢 (Verve, 1993)
Lifetime 𝄢𝄢𝄢 (Verve, 1996)

influences:

◀◀ James Peterson, Willie Dixon, Little Milton, Eddie Taylor, Buddy Guy, Bobby "Blue" Bland, Stevie Wonder

▶▶ Michael Hill's Blues Mob, Michael Jackson, Robert Cray, Jonny Lang

Steve Knopper

Robert Petway

Birth and death dates unknown.

As mysterious as Robert Johnson once was, Robert Petway has long failed to get his due from music scholars as the major figure he deserves to be in the blues firmament. Petway was the first to record the undying "Catfish Blues," refashioned by Muddy Waters into his own signature classic, "Rollin' Stone." A gravel-voiced disciple of the equally-raspy Tommy McClennan, Petway rarely lapsed into the chaotic flailing and repetitious formulas that captured McClennan. Though McClennan fancied

himself the Guitar King, it was Petway who was string royalty, nimbly churning out infectious rhythms and fills. Petway also paved the way for the rhythm guitar wizard Eddie Taylor, who copped two of his tunes, "Stroll out West" (another "Catfish" imitation) and "Ride 'Em on Down." Petway appeared for two sessions in Chicago in 1941 and 1942—perhaps joined on one cut by McClennan—before he dropped out of sight, never to be heard from again.

what to buy: All 14 of Petway's Bluebird cuts are on *Mississippi Blues: The Complete Recorded Works of Otto Virgial, Robert Petway and Robert Lockwood 1935–51* ♪♪♪♪ (Wolf, 1991, prod. Johnny Parth), mastered as well as old 78s can be, in all their stomping glory. Petway was not subtle, but neither were Charley Patton or Howlin' Wolf. Besides Petway's tough tunes, this contains four slices of the equally-unknown Otto Virgial and six early efforts by Robert Junior Lockwood, including four stunning 1941 tunes associated with his oft-purported stepfather, Robert Johnson.

influences:

◀◀ Tommy McClennan

▶▶ Muddy Waters, Bo Bo Thomas, Eddie Taylor, Little Feat

Steve Braun

Arthur Phelps
See: Blind Blake

Brewer Phillips
Born November 16, 1924 or 1925, in Ciola, MS.

Brewer Phillips is best known for his years of service (1958 to 1975) as Hound Dog Taylor's rhythm guitarist. Like Taylor, his playing never displayed urban stylings; it remained rooted in the primitive blues he heard in the juke joints of Mississippi. Phillips' biting tone is accentuated by his choice of instruments—vintage Fender Telecasters. After Taylor's death, Phillips played briefly with J.B. Hutto and made a couple of solo albums for European labels in the early 1980s. Apart from some travel, mostly to Europe, Phillips continues to play in tiny Chicago clubs.

James Peterson (© Jack Vartoogian)

what to buy: *Homebrew* ♪♪♪♪ (Delmark, 1995, prod. Pete Nathan) has some rough edges, but Phillips' singing and his raw playing are outstanding.

worth searching for: Phillips' playing embellishes all of Hound Dog Taylor's Alligator CDs. Another good representation of Phillips' magnificent style can be heard on *J.B. Hutto & the Houserockers Live 1977* ♪♪♪♪ (Wolf, 1992, prod. Ron Bartolucci).

influences:

◀◀ Willie Johnson, Pat Hare, Jimmy Reed, Hound Dog Taylor, Memphis Minnie

Jeff Hannusch

Piano Red
Born Willie Perryman, October 19, 1913, in Hampton, GA. Died July 25, 1985, in Decatur, GA.

Perryman was rewarded for his fine piano skills with a 1961 R&B hit, "Dr. Feelgood." The boogie-woogie house fixture at Atlanta's Magnolia Ballroom for years and the brother of Rufus "Speckled Red" Perryman, Red had been an active southern performer for more than two decades before his hit. (He also scored with 1950's "Red's Boogie.") Blues didn't always pay his bills; he often worked as an upholsterer in the Atlanta area. The blues revival gave him slightly renewed popularity, and he played the Montreux Festival in Switzerland in 1974.

what to buy: The best thing about the solo *Atlanta Bounce* ♪♪♪♪ (Arhoolie, 1972/1992, prod. Chris Strachwitz) is Red's rambling and storytelling, which comes across much more frequently above the piano than the actual singing of choruses.

influences:

◀◀ Speckled Red, Fats Waller, Art Tatum, Victoria Spivey, Scott Joplin

▶▶ Ray Charles, Memphis Slim, Dr. John, Professor Longhair

Steve Knopper

Piano C. Red
Born James Wheeler, September 14, 1933, in Montevallo, AL.

A consummate showman, Piano C. Red has been a part of Chicago's blues scene since his arrival in 1956. He has shared stages with Elmore James, Muddy Waters and Memphis Slim and waxed a single for Checker. Yet today Red still works in relative obscurity, scuffling for gigs at clubs while holding down his day job as a cab driver. For years Red has been a mainstay at the historic Maxwell Street Market. With his Flat Foot Boogie Blues Band, Piano C. Red is one of a handful of blues artists keeping the spirit of the old street blues alive.

what to buy: Originally released on Big Boy Records, *Cab Drivin' Man* ♪♪♪♪ (Fan Club, 1992) is Red's only compact disc. The churning Flat Foot Boogie Blues Band lays down solid, Maxwell Street boogie to accompany Red's piano and humorous storylines. Highlights are Red's signature tune, "Cab Drivin' Man," as well as "Flat Foot Boogie," "Disable Man" and "Hobo Sam." Red's keyboards and vocals are as raw on this disc as they are at the market. This is one spirited performance.

influences:

◀◀ Ray Charles, Little Richard, T-Bone Walker, Sugar Chile Robinson

▶▶ Johnny Dollar, David Lindsey, Byther Smith

Steven Sharp

Rod Piazza

Born December 18, 1947, in Riverside, CA.

Rod Piazza has become well known for making straightforward, harmonica-dominated 12-bar blues music for more than three decades. Like many young blues fans who grew up in the 1960s, Piazza was inspired to form a group, the Dirty Blues Band in his case—and even put out a few albums. An opportunity to collaborate with his hero, occasional Muddy Waters sideman George "Harmonica" Smith, came up in the mid-1960s, and the student-and-teacher harp duo formed Bacon Fat before forming the Mighty Flyers, which includes the pulsing piano work of his wife, Honey Piazza, a performer in her own right, and which has become a top touring act.

what to buy: Piazza was really hitting his stride in the early 1990s, tossing off earnest, playful boogies, fast rockers and instrumental harp ballads with equal enthusiasm: document this period with *Alphabet Blues* ♪♪♪♪ (Black Top, 1992, prod. Hammond Scott) and *The Essential Collection* ♪♪♪ (HighTone, 1992), the latter of which samples material from Piazza's more recent albums.

what to avoid: Eventually, it becomes obvious that Piazza is starting to put out the same CD again and again; it may work for John Lee Hooker and Bo Diddley, but it gets stale on *Tough and Tender* ♪♪ (Tone-Cool, 1997, prod. Rod Piazza, Rick Holmstrom).

best of the rest:

Rod Piazza Blues Man ♪♪♪ (LMI, 1973)

Chicago Flying Saucer Band ♪♪ (Gangster, 1979)
Harp Burn ♪♪♪ (Black Top, 1986)
So Glad to Have the Blues ♪♪♪ (Murray Brothers/Black Top, 1988)
Blues in the Dark ♪♪♪ (Black Top, 1991)
Live at B.B. King's Blues Club ♪♪♪ (Big Mo, 1994)

worth searching for: The Dirty Blues Band's early albums, *Stone Dirty* ♪♪♪ (ABC/Bluesway, 1968) and *The Dirty Blues Band* ♪♪ (ABC/Bluesway, 1967), weren't exactly the Yardbirds, but they had a certain youthful energy.

influences:

◀◀ George "Harmonica" Smith, Little Walter, Sonny Boy Williamson II, Junior Wells

▶▶ Omar & the Howlers, Gary Primich

Steve Knopper

Greg Piccolo

Born May 10, 1951, in Westerly, RI.

Rooted in post-World War II blues and R&B, saxophonist Greg Piccolo established a reputation as a powerful sax player and equally gifted vocalist during his 20-plus-year tenure with Roomful of Blues. His subsequent solo career, launched in 1995, has afforded him more room to explore jazz, Latin and pop sensibilities. Piccolo and guitarist Duke Robillard played together as teens in the mid-1960s, then reunited in 1970 when Piccolo joined Robillard's fledgling Roomful of Blues. Piccolo became frontman and primary songwriter when Robillard departed in 1979, continuing to produce original material within Roomful's big-band context throughout the 1980s, but he found his personal tastes straying from those of the band. He left Roomful for good in 1994.

what to buy: *Heavy Juice* ♪♪♪♪ (Black Top, 1990) is a satisfying mix of rhythm and blues covers featuring Robillard and a handful of other Roomful players and alums.

what to buy next: Pic's first post-Roomful solo effort, *Acid Blue* ♪♪♪ (Fantasy, 1995), fuses jazz and Latin styles into a more pop-oriented package with the help of Ron Levy behind the keyboards.

influences:

◀◀ Gene Ammons, Lester Young, Coleman Hawkins

John C. Bruening

Dan Pickett

Birth and death dates unknown.

It is frustrating enough for the lives of pre-war blues musicians to slip through the cracks of history, but the case of Dan Pickett is even more agonizing. He walked into Gotham Records' Philadelphia studio in 1949, laid down 14 powerful tracks—some of the most stunning post-war acoustic blues on record—and then disappeared back into the mists of time. Some blues researchers insist Pickett is a Texan; others say he is from Alabama. Blues academic Paul Oliver has suggested he might be Tennessee master Charlie Pickett, whose career seemed abruptly finished by the World War II recording ban. He may well be one James Founty, a Tennessee musician who may have settled in Alabama. Whoever Pickett is, he displayed eyebrow-raising talent. Sounding like a slightly hipper Blind Willie McTell, he was capable of arch digs at American life like "Number Writer" and "Ride to a Funeral in a V-8." And he could turn around and produce a soulful gospel version of "99 and 1/2 Won't Do" that would make Wilson Pickett (no relation) stand up and squawk. Dan Pickett didn't produce much, but when he did, he always gave a hundred.

what to buy: Often a slapdash presenter of blues, Collectables manages to exceed expectations on *1949 Country Blues* ♫♫♫♫ (Collectables, 1987), a collection of 14 Pickett songs that includes decent notes and adequate sound. Save for a rare British CD, this is the only way to find Pickett's work in the U.S.

influences:
◀◀ Leroy Carr, Robert Johnson, Peetie Wheatstraw, Sleepy John Estes

Steve Braun

Lonnie Pitchford

Born October 8, 1955, in Lexington, MS.

Lonnie Pitchford, who grew up listening to his father play blues on the porch, joined a swing band in high school and learned classics by Tyrone Davis, Little Milton, James Brown and Howlin' Wolf. The understated singer and guitarist played blues, soul and—the horror!—disco in little joints around the South, then moved around the country, doing odd jobs—peeling potatoes and mopping floors—before being introduced to men with blues connections. After meeting Peg Leg Sam, Honeyboy Edwards and, most signficantly, Robert Junior Lockwood, Pitchford struck out on his own. He played on Robert Palmer's 1992 *Deep Blues* documentary soundtrack and appears at U.S. and European clubs and festivals.

what to buy: *All Around Man* ♫♫♫ (Rooster Blues, 1994, prod. Lonnie Pitchford, Patty Johnson, Duncan Hudson) is refresh-

ingly subtle, with Pitchford communicating a lot of emotions without even raising his voice and using his pinpricking guitar licks to overcome the silence.

influences:
◀◀ Honeyboy Edwards, Howlin' Wolf, Robert Junior Lockwood, Peg Leg Sam, James Brown, R.L. Burnside

Steve Knopper

Doc Pomus

Born Jerome Felder, 1925, in New York, NY.

"If the music industry had a heart," Atlantic Records' Jerry Wexler told *Rolling Stone* in 1991, "it would be Doc Pomus." The large, bearded man, wheelchair-bound since he was 40, was the superstar songwriter behind Elvis Presley ("Little Sister" and "Viva Las Vegas," among others), the Drifters ("Save the Last Dance for Me" and "This Magic Moment"), Ray Charles ("Lonely Avenue"), Big Joe Turner ("Boogie Woogie Country Girl") and many, many others. But despite his songs' popularity among pop, R&B and rock 'n' roll singers, Pomus began his career as a blues singer and was always a bluesman at heart. His songs were impeccably crafted, perfect for the three-minutes-or-less constraints of pop singles, and whether they were about losing money at the roulette wheel or a girlfriend dancing with another man, they always contained a tinge of bluesy sadness. Going against his parents' wishes for a lawyer or an accountant, he began singing as a teenager (despite his painful struggle with polio) with Big Joe Turner's band in New York City. Because a white blues singer was unheard of in the 1950s—and Elvis Presley hadn't been invented yet—Pomus gravitated to songwriting. It proved a lucrative career, and his string of hits never really ended, even in the 1970s, when he mostly wrote with his friend Mac "Dr. John" Rebennack. (B.B. King won a Grammy with Pomus' "There Must Be a Better World Somewhere" in 1982.) Despite Pomus' success, he was always on the lookout to help wronged artists—he helped Turner's next of kin receive their rightful royalty payments after the singer died, and he fought vigilantly to get R&B songwriters their due. The many luminaries who turned out at his Manhattan funeral included Lou Reed (who dedicated an album, *Magic and Loss*, to Pomus), Dr. John, Phil Spector and Ben E. King.

what to buy: You probably own much of Pomus' best work already—just check the songwriting credits on some of the biggest pop and R&B hits of all time. But *Till the Night Is Gone: A Tribute to Doc Pomus* ♫♫♫♫ (Forward/Rhino, 1995, prod. various)—the proceeds of which go to the R&B Foundation that Pomus helped create—is a fun and solemn revelation. It lurches from B.B. King's slow, soft version of "Blinded by Love" to Bob Dylan's rickety acoustic-blues take on "Boogie Woogie Country Girl" to Lou Reed's bombastic-metal-guitar transformation of the love song "This Magic Moment."

influences:

◄◄ Big Joe Turner, Louis Jordan, B.B. King, George & Ira Gershwin, Cole Porter, Nat "King" Cole, Charles Brown

▶▶ Lou Reed, Bob Dylan, Drifters, Ben E. King, Ray Charles, Kris Kristofferson, Otis Blackwell, Ruth Brown, Dion & the Belmonts, Elvis Presley, Phil Spector

Steve Knopper

Popa Chubby
Born Ted Horowitz, in Bronx, NY.

With a name that only Beavis and Butt-head could find endearing, Popa Chubby (huh-huh, huh-huh) is a New York-based blues-rock combo and also the moniker of the estimably sized Ted Horowitz. A veteran of the local club circuit along the eastern seaboard that also gave us Blues Traveler, Spin Doctors, and Joan Osborne, Chubby (heh-heh, heh-heh) earned his following the way they did—slogging it out, night after night, with albums that were not so much ends in themselves as they were calling cards for scoring the next gig. It's a serviceable act; Horowitz is a rapid-fire, heavy riffing guitarist, an able vocalist, and, with his girth, tattoos and a single tendril of hair dangling down his forehead, quite a sight. Still—are you sure Willie Dixon did it this way?

what to buy: The sentence "you gotta see him live" comes up enough in reference to Chubby that *Hit the High Hard One: Popa Chubby Live* ♫♫♫ (1-800-PRIME CD, 1996, prod. Ted Horowitz) is probably the best way to check him out on record. He earns some points for song selection (covers of Tom Waits' "Heart Attack and Vine" and Dylan's "Isis" are interesting, but who needs another "Wild Thing?"), and his own compositions are only so much blooze.

the rest:

It's Chubby Time ♫♫ (Laughing Bear, 1991)
Gas Money ♫♫ (Laughing Bear, 1993)
Booty and the Beast ♫♫♫ (OKeh/550 Music, 1995)

influences:

◄◄ Chuck Berry, Rolling Stones, Willie Dixon

Daniel Durchholz

Jerry Portnoy
Born November 25, 1943, in Evanston, IL.

Playing in Muddy Waters' band, it turned out, could set a musician up for his entire career. Portnoy, a harpist who played on *Muddy "Mississippi" Waters Live* and more of his late-1970s output with Johnny Winter, eventually quit and went with Pinetop Perkins and others to form the Legendary Blues Band. The talented, supremely professional harmonica expert used these impeccable credentials to score a later gig in Eric Clapton's band. As a solo artist, he's full of clever tricks, such as titling an album *Home Run Hitter* and starting it with a baseball stadium-style harp version of "The Star Spangled Banner."

what to buy: *Poison Kisses* ♫♫♫ (Modern Blues, 1991) is a fine harp album, worth collecting for harpists who like to study the masters' licks, but as an overall Chicago electric blues albums, you'd best collect *Muddy "Mississippi" Waters Live* instead.

what to buy next: *Home Run Hitter* ♫♫♫ (Indigo, 1995, prod. Kim Wilson, Jerry Portnoy) has a couple of spooky changes of pace, such as the title track, and a couple of funny tricks, (like the anti-credit card novelty "Charge It"), but Portnoy's band isn't particularly explosive and he's just not the greatest singer.

influences:

◄◄ Sonny Boy Williamson II, Harmonica Slim, Little Walter, Muddy Waters, Eric Clapton

▶▶ Charlie Musselwhite, Sugar Blue

Steve Knopper

Preacher Boy
Born Chris Watkins, 1968, in Iowa City, IA.

Young white bluesmen have traditionally tried to become fast, flashy guitar players or harpists. Chris Watkins and his four-man band go instead for feeling—they're sloppy and raw, just like they perceive early Bukka White and Lightnin' Hopkins singles to be, and saxes and harps don't so much jam as add honking textures. Though Watkins tries a little too hard for hipness with his slick shades—a goofy goatee and snazzy leather jackets on sleeve photos—slow-groove songs like "Catfish" and "Ugly" are stellar, and the band's energy makes them combust. While Kenny Wayne Shepherd and Jonny Lang appeal to blues fans who love fast fingers, artists like Preacher Boy and Popa Chubby have started taking the gargle-to-sound-like Tom Waits approach. Who knows? Maybe they're the future of blues.

what to buy: *Gutters and Pews* 🎵🎵🎵 (Blind Pig, 1996, prod. Bryan Zee), Preacher Boy's second album, came out around the same time as Popa Chubby's first live album. Songs like "Back Then We Only Cared for Hell" and "Cold Mountain Music" sound like drunk guys who just might be waiting for the devil to show up at the party.

what to buy next: Watkins introduces his improbable jugband style on *Preacher Boy & the Natural Blues* 🎵🎵🎵 (Blind Pig, 1995, prod. Chris Watkins, Bryan Zee).

influences:

◀◀ Tom Waits, Son House, Bukka White, Robert Johnson, Muddy Waters, Howlin' Wolf, Captain Beefheart, Yardbirds, Red Devils, Jon Spencer Blues Explosion

▶▶ Popa Chubby

Steve Knopper

Elvis Presley

Born Elvis Aron Presley, January 8, 1935, in East Tupelo, MS. Died August 16, 1977, in Memphis, TN.

People sometimes forget that Elvis Presley—King of Rock 'n' Roll, movie star, tragic symbol of garish excess, paragon of moral decay, one of the best-selling pop artists of all time, even a pop-culture Jesus Christ figure—was actually talented. Whether or not he invented rock 'n' roll by linking, as myth recalls, white country music and black blues, he had an innate command of stage and audience and was a terrific singer and interpreter. Presley, born to a poor southern couple, Vernon and Gladys, has always been known (sometimes proudly) as a hillbilly who made it big. His blues background, learned mostly from radio stations he picked up in Mississippi and Tennessee, usually gets lost in his life history. Presley's first hit, "That's All Right (Mama)," was originally recorded by bluesman Arthur "Big Boy" Crudup, and all the way through Big Mama Thornton's "Hound Dog" he continued to mine the blues for inspiration. He earned harsh criticism throughout his career, and even after his death, for changing black music into a commercial product for whites while the original musicians rarely received adequate compensation. But in Presley's defense, the financial disparity wasn't his fault, and he sang the older songs with reverence, passion and, above all, talent.

Presley's career effectively began after a year of persistent hanging around the downtown Sun Records studio, when confident entrepreneur and record producer Sam Phillips saw an intangible quality in Presley and set him up for a session.

(Phillips, a longtime recorder of black bluesmen and minor R&B stars, from Junior Parker to Rufus Thomas, had long predicted that if he could get a white boy with "the Negro look and the Negro feel" to sing black music, he would make a million dollars. That turned out to be a major understatement.) With hungry sessionmen Scotty Moore on guitar and Bill Black on upright bass, the trio performed take after take until, while fooling around, they came up with reworked versions of "That's All Right (Mama)" and Bill Monroe's "Blue Moon of Kentucky." They were fast, and smooth, and they sounded like nothing anybody had ever heard. An excited Phillips dropped the cuts off to famous Memphis DJ Dewey Phillips, who played "That's All Right" countless times in a row, thus creating Presley's first official buzz. For the subsequent two decades, Presley's career moved so fast he—and his friends and family, who were simultaneously excited and suspicious—could barely keep up. "The Colonel," brilliant opportunist and Hank Snow manager Tom Parker, took the young singer under his wing and autocratically began navigating Presley's career trajectory. Parker immediately negotiated a deal with RCA, with whom Presley remained for the rest of his recording career.

As Presley began performing more and more unprecedentedly great concerts, attracting teenage girls by the truckload to scream their heads off, his legend started to grow well beyond one-hit wonder level. Over at Sun, Phillips trotted out Carl Perkins, Roy Orbison and Johnny Cash in Presley's huge rockabilly wake. Gene Vincent, Eddie Cochran, Buddy Holly and Richie Valens were waiting in the wings. The King bought a pink Cadillac for his mother, many more Cadillacs for himself and, in 1957, Graceland, a former Memphis church he converted into a massive mansion. Everything was going perfectly, until Presley was inducted into the Army in 1958; shortly after that, a plane carrying Holly and Valens crashed, which became, as Don McLean later lamented cryptically, the "day the music died." But despite all this and the eventual onslaught of Bob Dylan, the Beach Boys and the Beatles, Presley never went away. He was rock's first "careerist," continuing to release hits through the 1960s. In the decade of hippies, the Vietnam War and baby-boom counterculture, Presley focused on innocent movies and soundtracks. By the 1970s Graceland was becoming famous for its lavish Jungle Room and Presley for creating an isolationist world for himself and a close circle of family, friends and hangers-on. He became a Las Vegas star and an almost total parody of himself, though some of his later hits—"In the Ghetto," "Suspicious Minds," "Burning Love"—were explosive and funky. Wracked with fear and insecurity and nearly broke despite his fame and success, Presley died alone in his Graceland bathroom at age 42, leading to Colonel Parker's famous statement that he "would go right on managing him." A fascinating and lucrative cottage industry has grown up around his image and Graceland in the two decades since his death.

what to buy: The three five-disc boxed sets were a godsend, because without them it was impossible to navigate the record store binfuls of studio albums and greatest-hits collections for the essential stuff. Start with *Elvis—The King of Rock 'n' Roll—The Complete '50s Masters ♫♫♫♫♫* (RCA, 1992, prod. Ernst Mikael Jorgensen, Roger Semon), and hear the young truck driver transform from raw talent in the early hits "Blue Moon of Kentucky" and "That's All Right" to accomplished showman in "Jailhouse Rock" and "Love Me Tender." Next stop: *From Nashville to Memphis: The Essential '60s Masters I ♫♫♫♫♫* (RCA, 1994, prod. Ernst Mikael Jorgensen, Roger Semon) proves that despite the Beatles and his late-1950s stint in the Army, Presley was still a vital performer; "Little Sister," "Suspicious Minds," "In the Ghetto" and "Fever" are among the transcendental tracks. *Walk a Mile in My Shoes: The Essential '70s Masters ♫♫♫♫♫* (RCA, 1995, prod. Ernst Mikael Jorgensen, Roger Semon) and *Command Performances: The Essential '60s Masters II ♫♫♫♫* (RCA, 1995, prod. Ernst Mikael Jorgensen, Roger Semon), compile the best live tracks and soundtrack songs and eliminate most of the chaff. There's much, much more: *The Complete Sun Sessions ♫♫♫♫♫* (RCA, 1987, original prod. Sam Phillips) is mostly revisited on the first boxed set, but it contains the fascinating sound of Elvis, guitarist Scotty Moore, bassist Bill Black and producer Phillips inventing rock 'n' roll in the Sun Records studio; "Milcow Blues Boogie" has Elvis stopping a slow blues song, announcing "that don't MOVE me" and proceeding to change it before our ears into something completely different.

what to buy next: The three boxed sets render many of the previous greatest-hits sets redundant, but these are some of the best: *Elvis' Golden Records, Vol. I ♫♫♫♫♫* (RCA, 1958, prod. various); *50,000,000 Elvis Fans Can't Be Wrong: Elvis' Golden Records, Vol. 2 ♫♫♫♫♫* (RCA, 1960, prod. various), with the classic and much-parodied cover of many leering Elvises in shiny gold suits; *Elvis' Golden Records, Vol. 3 ♫♫♫♫* (RCA, 1963, prod. various); *Elvis' Golden Records, Vol. 4 ♫♫♫♫* (RCA, 1968, prod. various); *Elvis' Gold Records, Vol. 5 ♫♫♫* (RCA, 1984, prod. various); and many more.

what to avoid: Most of Presley's schlock, which became almost as famous as his great stuff, was in either the bad-live-performance or icky-movie-soundtrack categories. His bad live al-

bums were most prominent in the 1970s, including *As Recorded at Madison Square Garden ♫♫* (RCA, 1972, prod. Felton Jarvis), *Recorded Live on Stage in Memphis ♫♫* (RCA, 1974, prod. Felton Jarvis), *Having Fun with Elvis on Stage* **woof!** (RCA, 1974) (just the King making bad jokes), *Elvis in Concert* **woof!** (RCA, 1977, digital prod. Don Wardell) and *Elvis on Stage ♫* (RCA, 1977). His icky movie soundtracks were most prominent in the 1960s, with *Fun in Acapulco ♫♫* (RCA, 1963, prod. Elvis Presley), *Live a Little, Love a Little/Charro!/The Trouble with Girls/Change of Habit ♫♫* (RCA, 1995, reissue prod. Ernst Mikael Jorgensen, Roger Semon) and several others.

best of the rest:

Elvis ♫♫♫♫ (RCA, 1956)
Elvis Presley ♫♫♫♫ (RCA, 1956)
Elvis' Christmas Album ♫♫♫♫♫ (RCA, 1957)
Loving You ♫♫♫♫ (RCA, 1957)
King Creole ♫♫♫♫ (RCA, 1958)
A Date with Elvis ♫♫♫♫ (RCA, 1959)
For LP Fans Only ♫♫♫♫ (RCA, 1959)
Elvis Is Back! ♫♫♫♫ (RCA, 1960)
His Hand in Mine ♫♫♫♫ (RCA, 1960)
Spinout ♫♫♫♫ (RCA, 1966)
How Great Thou Art ♫♫♫♫ (RCA, 1967)
Elvis NBC-TV Special ♫♫♫♫♫ (RCA, 1968)
From Elvis in Memphis ♫♫♫♫♫ (RCA, 1969)
Kissin' Cousins/Clambake/Stay Away, Joe ♫♫♫♫ (RCA, 1994)

worth searching for: Great songs about Elvis: "Elvis Is Dead," by Living Colour; "Elvis Is Everywhere," by Mojo Nixon; "My Boy Elvis," by Janis Martin; "Galway to Graceland," by Richard Thompson; "Elvis Ate America," by U2/Brian Eno as the Passengers; "Little Sister," by Dwight Yoakam; "Johnny Bye Bye," by Bruce Springsteen. Great versions of songs Elvis did: "Hound Dog," by Big Mama Thornton; "That's All Right (Mama)," by Arthur "Big Boy" Crudup; "Good Rockin' Tonight," by Roy Brown; "Burning Love," by Arthur Alexander; "Burning Love," by Grant Lee Buffalo; "Jailhouse Rock," by the Cramps; "Mystery Train," by Junior Parker's Blue Flames; and the entire soundtrack of *Honeymoon in Vegas ♫♫* (Epic, 1992, prod. Peter Afterman, Glen Brunman), despite the lifeless carbon-copy Billy Joel versions of "All Shook Up" and "Heartbreak Hotel."

influences:

◀◀ Bill Monroe, Hank Snow, Arthur "Big Boy" Crudup, Little Richard, Chuck Berry, Lowell Fulson, Big Mama Thornton, Frank Sinatra, Hank Williams, Roy Brown, Carter Family, Jimmie Rodgers, Ink Spots, Eddy Arnold

▶▶ Buddy Holly, Carl Perkins, Roy Orbison, Beatles, Johnny

Cash, Bob Dylan, Beach Boys, Janis Martin, Bruce Springsteen, Billy Joel, Mojo Nixon, Dwight Yoakam, the Band, Blasters, Elvis Hitler, Elvis Costello, U2, Stray Cats, Living Colour, Public Enemy

Steve Knopper

Lloyd Price

Born March 9, 1933, in Kenner, LA.

When Lloyd Price made his recording debut in 1952, the musical cards were definitely stacked in his favor. With pumping piano support from Fats Domino and a second-line horn arrangement courtesy of Dave Bartholomew, "Lawdy Miss Clawdy" was practically guaranteed a spot on the top of the charts. Price's first record did that and then some; it was named *Billboard*'s R&B Record of the Year and bears the distinction of being one of the first black records to catch the ears of white teenagers (or, as legend has it, adult women, who would scour the New Orleans record stores in order to secure a copy "for their black maids or housekeepers"). A string of hits followed on Specialty, including "Restless Heart," "Ooh, Ooh, Ooh," and "Ain't It a Shame," but by 1958 Price was seeking "greener" pastures, which resulted in a contract with ABC-Paramount. When he and producer Don Costa set their sights on the crossover market, they substituted slick arrangements for the gritty New Orleans rhythms that characterized his Specialty recordings, resulting in a catchy, R&B-based pop sound. The formula apparently worked well enough for Price to score with hits like "Stagger Lee" (a re-write of an old folk-blues tune), "Where Were You (on Our Wedding Day)," "Personality," "I'm Gonna Get Married," "Come into My Heart," and "Lady Luck," but by the mid-1960s he was out of gas. The hits became fewer and fewer as musical tastes shifted away from lavishly produced, commercial pop. Curiously, instead of pulling the plug on the intrusive choruses and orchestral backing, Price dove headlong into Tin Pan Alley, further sealing his fate with younger listeners. Still, his prominent place in the annals of R&B history is well deserved. Few artists have been able to weave divergent elements of blues shouting and pop crooning into one seamless fabric of sound as effortlessly as he did. In many ways, Price set the stage for the soul revolution of the 1960s.

what to buy: The cream of Price's Specialty material is gathered up on two discs, *Lawdy!* 𝄢𝄢𝄢𝄢 (Specialty, 1991, prod. Billy Vera) and *Vol. 2: Heavy Dreams* 𝄢𝄢𝄢𝄢 (Specialty, 1993, prod. Billy Vera). The former has the #1 R&B hit "Lawdy Miss Clawdy," in addition to other prime cuts such as "If Crying Was Murder,"

"Mailman Blues" and "Carry Me Home." Volume Two has the Top Ten R&B numbers "Ooh, Ooh, Ooh," "Restless Heart" and "Ain't It a Shame" and a great assortment of b-sides and previously unissued tracks. On both sets, Price is backed by New Orleans' heaviest session men: Dave Bartholomew, Herb Hardesty, Lee Allen, Earl Palmer, Ernest McLean, Frank Fields and Fats Domino. Crescent City R&B of the highest order.

what to buy next: *Greatest Hits* 𝄢𝄢𝄢 (MCA, 1994, prod. Bill Inglot) is a fine collection of material originally released on the ABC Paramount label. All of the hits are here ("Just Because," "Where Were You (on Our Wedding Day)," "Personality," "I'm Gonna Get Married"), along with the innocuous "Bandstand" version of "Stagger Lee," in which Stagger and Billy end their dispute amicably, proof that the ABC make-over could be both sonically and lyrically emasculating.

what to avoid: *16 Hits of Lloyd Price* **woof!** (Phoenix Entertainment, 1981) is one of those exploitation packages that the unwary public must steer clear of at all costs. It is safe to say that Price was as far afield singing tunes like "Me and You and a Dog Named Boo" and "Hooked on a Feeling" as Bing Crosby was singing "Hey Jude."

the rest:
Greatest Hits 𝄢𝄢𝄿 (Curb, 1990)
Sings His Big Ten 𝄢𝄢𝄢 (Curb, 1994)

worth searching for: *Mr. Personality Sings the Blues* 𝄢𝄢𝄢𝄢 (ABC Paramount, 1960) finds Mr. Split Personality reverting back to his unexpurgated self just long enough to belt out soulful covers of Eddie Vinson's "Kidney Stew," Paul Perryman's "Just to Hold My Hand" and other blues-inflected R&B numbers. Great stuff if you can find it.

influences:
◀◀ Big Joe Turner, Fats Domino, Tommy Ridgley
▶▶ Otis Redding

D. Thomas Moon

Sammy Price

Born October 6, 1908, in Honey Grove, TX. Died April 14, 1992, in New York, NY.

A consummate professional who impressed his early colleagues with an ability to play easily in any piano key, Price for years occupied the same jazz-blues intersection as Jimmy Witherspoon. He also lived a colorful life. His secret, he wrote in 1975 liner notes, was "there are only two things in my life: jazz and women. Boogie woogie never changes; women can change. Eleven wives; I must be the Casanova of the century." After studying piano in Dallas, he performed and recorded there, as well as Kansas City, Chicago and Detroit, putting out a 1929 single with a band called the Four Quarters. A boogie-woogie pianist who played primarily in horn-heavy jazz bands, he was more famous as a studio musician and live performer than a solo artist. As a Decca studio musician in Harlem, he backed Sister Rosetta Tharpe and Trixie Smith, then worked jazz festivals and occasional 1950s rock 'n' roll sessions.

what to buy: Two discs sample the most prolific points of Price's career: *Sam Price 1929–41* ⚜⚜⚜ (Classics) tours his early output, when he was a barrelhouse bluesman with traces of jazz influence, and the compilation LP *Rib Joint/Roots of Rock & Roll* ⚜⚜⚜ (Savoy) samples his much more rocking 1950s phase, when he played in R&B and barrelhouse-dominated blues bands.

what to buy next: *King of Boogie Woogie* ⚜⚜⚜ (Storyville, 1992, prod. Henri Dufresne), in addition to the hilarious boastful liner notes, is an accessible pop album with such standards as "Making Whoopie" and "My Blue Heaven."

the rest:

And the Blues Singers ⚜⚜⚜ (Wolf)
Blues and Boogies ⚜⚜⚜ (Black and Blue, 1969)

worth searching for: *Barrelhouse and Blues* ⚜⚜⚜ (Black Lion, 1991, prod. Terry Brown, Alan Bates), a 1969 session reissued on a German record label, is a straightforward sampling of Price's solo walking piano style and his much jazzier work with big, horny bands.

influences:

◄◄ Scott Joplin, Charles Brown, Louis Armstrong, Duke Ellington, Jimmy Witherspoon, T-Bone Walker, Art Tatum, Louis Jordan

►► Ray Charles, Little Richard, Jerry Lee Lewis, Jimmy Yancey, Otis Spann, Pinetop Perkins

Steve Knopper

Gertrude Pridgett

See: Ma Rainey

John Primer

Born Alfonzo Primer, March 3, 1945, in Camden, MS.

The Chicago blues scene has always needed talented role players like Primer to play on everybody's albums and fill the clubs

when Buddy Guy or Otis Rush is on tour someplace else. He's an excellent guitarist who played for 13 years with the Chicago fixture Magic Slim and the Teardrops—that was essentially an extension of his long gig as house guitarist at the South Side's Theresa's Lounge. He recorded his solo debut, *Stuff You Got to Watch*, in 1993, which began a career of solid, credible Chicago blues with few twists or distinctive ideas.

what to buy: *Stuff You Got to Watch* ⚜⚜ (Earwig, 1992, prod. Michael Robert Frank) is a nice introduction to Primer, and an excellent reward for a musician so important for so long in the Chicago blues scene. But it rarely catches fire, even on Primer's well-written "I'm Gonna Ride until I Get Satisfied" or Otis Rush's standard "Double Trouble."

what to buy next: *Poor Man Blues: Chicago Blues Session Volume 6* ⚜⚜ (Wolf, 1991, prod. John Primer, Hannes Folterbauer) is a nice document of 1987 and 1991 sessions with Magic Slim, Billy Branch and other local luminaries.

the rest:

Blues Behind Closed Doors: Chicago Blues Session Volume 29 ⚜⚜⚜ (Wolf, 1994)
The Real Deal ⚜⚜ (Code Blue, 1995)

influences:

◄◄ Muddy Waters, Buddy Guy, Otis Rush, Magic Slim, Little Milton, Elmore James

►► Willie Kent, Billy Branch, Son Seals

Steve Knopper

Gary Primich

Born April 20, 1958, in Chicago, IL.

A cross between traditional harpists like Little Walter and Sonny Boy Williamson and contemporary white blues singers like Stevie Ray Vaughan and Kim Wilson, Primich keeps his name prominent in the blues world by putting out an album every year or so. He's an excellent harpist, handling intimidating classics like John Lee "Sonny Boy" Williamson's "She Was a Dreamer" and "Shake the Boogie" without much trouble. Primich takes the right approach to his instrument, aiming for melodic lines instead of fast, show-off solos—he once said he wanted to emulate the country steel guitarist Jerry Byrd. His

Sammy Price (© Jack Vartoogian)

problem is in the singing, which sounds like lukewarm Fabulous Thunderbirds.

what to buy: Refreshingly referential—the second track is a funny phone message from blues singer Jerry McCain, giving a blessing to use his classic "Ding Dong Daddy"—*Travelin' Mood* 𝄢𝄢𝄢 (Flying Fish, 1994, prod. Gary Primich) has a bouncy upbeat style that works great with the harp riffs.

what to buy next: *Mr. Freeze* 𝄢𝄢 (Flying Fish, 1995, prod. Gary Primich) is most notable for its blues history, covering obscure songs like Washboard Sam's "Easy Ridin' Mama" and Dave Bartholomew's "Go on Fool"; Primich's songwriting is becoming more solid, especially with jumping blues like the opening "Bad Poker Hand" and "Jenny Brown."

what to avoid: Primich is starting to put the same album out over and over; *Company Man* 𝄢𝄢 (Black Top, 1996) makes you wonder if he has any other tricks to occasionally change the pace.

the rest:

Gary Primich 𝄢𝄢 (Amazing, 1991)
My Pleasure 𝄢𝄢𝄢 (Amazing, 1992)
Hot Harp Blues 𝄢𝄢 (Amazing, 1993)

worth searching for: Primich and his longtime collaborator, ex-Frank Zappa drummer Jimmy Carl Black, formed a band called the Mannish Boys (yes, they played blues) and put out a solid one-off, *A L'il Dab'll Do Ya* 𝄢𝄢𝄢 (Amazing, 1988).

influences:

◄◄ Charlie Musselwhite, Sonny Boy Williamson II, Little Walter, Sugar Blue, Harmonica Slim, Washboard Sam

Steve Knopper

Professor Longhair

Born Henry Roeland Byrd, December 19, 1918, in Bougalusa, LA. Died January 30, 1980, in New Orleans, LA.

Considered by many the father of New Orleans rhythm and blues, Professor Longhair was an unorthodox pianist and singer who has been an inspiration for three generations of New Orleans musicians. Born in rural northern Louisiana, his family moved to New Orleans in the 1920s. As a youth, Longhair tap-danced for tips on the streets, which partially accounts for his unique sense of rhythm. Later, Longhair listened and sought out instruction from many of the blues, stride and Dixieland pianists that played on Rampart Street in the 1930s. In 1948 Longhair broke into the music business at the Caldonia Inn, where he caused a sensation. It was his un-

cropped hair which attracted his unique appellation. The following year he made his first recordings for the Star Talent label. Although they sold poorly, his Calypso-influenced blues attracted feelers from other labels. By 1953 he'd recorded for Mercury, Atlantic, Wasco and King. In the mid-1950s, a mild stroke interrupted his career, but in 1957, he waxed three singles for Ebb. Between 1958 and 1964, he recorded for the Ron label—where he cut "Mardi Gras in New Orleans"—and Watch—where he recorded "Big Chief"—both songs which are now indelibly associated with the city's Mardi Gras celebration. But by the mid-1960s Longhair had sunk into obscurity and had left music behind. His musical reincarnation took place at the 1971 New Orleans Jazz & Heritage Festival, where he stole the show. Several recording sessions followed—although none would be issued until after his death. However, his career began to slowly gain momentum, and his travels took him to Europe and several major American cities. Finally Barclay, a French label, recorded *Rock 'n' Roll Gumbo*, which teamed Longhair with Gatemouth Brown. In 1977, Longhair's music inspired a group of young New Orleans fans to open a music club so their hero would have a place to perform. Naturally it was called Tipitina's, after one of his signature compositions. More recordings followed, and in 1979, Dr. John helped out on the excellent Alligator LP *Crawfish Fiesta*. Considered one of his best contemporary recordings, it wasn't issued until after Longhair died.

what to buy: A comprehensive two-CD set, *The Professor Longhair Anthology* 𝄢𝄢𝄢𝄢 (Rhino, 1993, prod. James Austin) includes material from each portion of Longhair's storied career. *Rock 'n' Roll Gumbo* (Dancing Cat, 1985, prod. Philippe Rault) was the result of a swinging session Longhair cut with Gatemouth Brown and Julius Farmer in the early 1970s. Recorded shortly before his death, *Fess' Gumbo* 𝄢𝄢𝄢𝄢 (Stoney Plain, 1996, prod. Holger Peterson) includes an accomplished solo set and an informative Longhair interview. *Crawfish Fiesta* 𝄢𝄢𝄢𝄢 (Alligator, 1980, prod. Bruce Iglauer) teams Dr. John up with Fess and his fiery band the Blues Scholars.

what to buy next: Unnecessary if you possess *The Professor Longhair Anthology, New Orleans Piano* 𝄢𝄢𝄢𝄢 (Atlantic, 1972, prod. Jerry Wexler, Ahmet Ertegun, Herb Abramson) consists of early 1950s recordings and was the Holy Grail for blues fans introduced to Longhair in the 1970s. *House Party New Orleans Style* 𝄢𝄢𝄢 (Rounder, 1987, prod. Quint Davis) includes choice material cut with Snooks Eaglin and the Meters. *Mardi Gras in Baton Rouge* 𝄢𝄢𝄢 (Rhino, 1993, prod. Quint Davis) reissues the rest of the Longhair/Eaglin session. There are also plenty of live Professor Longhair recordings from the second stage of his career, including *Live on the Queen Mary* ♫♫♫ (One Way, 1975), *Rum and Cola* ♫♫♫ (Rhino, 1993), *Live in Germany* ♫♫♫ (New Rose), *Live Like You Like Him* ♫♫♫ (Collectables, 1995) and *The London Concert* ♫♫♫ (JSP, 1978).

worth searching for: Stephenson Palfi made an interesting film documentary, *Piano Players Rarely Play Together* (Stephenson Productions, 1980), which includes Longhair alongside his teacher, Tuts Washington, and his pupil, Allen Toussaint.

influences:

◀◀ Isidore "Tuts" Washington, Champion Jack Dupree, Robert Bertrand, Sullivan Rock, Kid Stormy Weather, Mardi Gras Indian tribes and parade bands

▶▶ Fats Domino, Allen Toussaint, Paul Gayten, Huey Smith, James Booker, Earl King, Dr. John, Art Neville, Davell Crawford, Mardi Gras Indian tribes and parade bands

Jeff Hannusch

Snooky Pryor

Born James Pryor, September 15, 1921, in Lambert, MS.

Influenced by Sonny Boy Williamson I, Snooky Pryor moved to Chicago in 1940 and began playing on Maxwell Street. By 1948 he had begun recording with his circle of Maxwell Street musicians. Compared to his contemporary, Little Walter, Pryor's playing was more traditional. He had fleeting success with "Telephone Blues" and "Judgment Day," but his career might well have advanced had he been able to catch on with Chess, just as Walter did. Pryor quit the music business in 1962 and stayed retired for a decade. In the 1970s he began touring Europe and has been recording ever since, most recently for Antone's.

what to buy: *Snooky Pryor* ♫♫♫♫ (Paula/Flyright, 1990), with Floyd Jones, Moody Jones and Johnny Young, is a collection of spectacular, rough-and-tumble early Chicago blues. *Snooky Pryor* ♫♫♫ (Blind Pig, 1987, prod. Steve Freund) contains mostly traditional material, but Pryor's engaging style is inviting. *Too Cool to Move* ♫♫♫ (Antone's, 1992, prod. Snooky Pryor, Derek O'Brien) displays Pryor's ageless energy and includes a band made up of Chicago veterans and younger Austin, Texas, musicians.

what to buy next: *Mind Your Own Business* ♫♫♫ (Antone's, 1996, prod. Derek O'Brien) picks up where *Too Cool to Move* finished off.

Professor Longhair

song
Big Chief (live version)

album
'Fess: The Professor Longhair Anthology (Rhino)

instrument
piano

monster solo

influences:

◀◀ Sonny Boy Williamson I, Sonny Boy Williamson II, Little Walter

▶▶ Billy Boy Arnold, Junior Wells, Kim Wilson

Jeff Hannusch

Yank Rachell

Born March 16, 1910, near Brownsville, TN. Died April 9, 1997, in Indianapolis, IN.

But for James "Yank" Rachell (which he pronounced "ray-shell"), the mandolin, common in early string bands, nearly died out as a blues instrument. While a few others were recorded playing blues mandolin, Rachell not only recorded prolifically but brought the instrument into new contexts. He also played rhythmically interesting guitar. In later years he electrified his instruments at times, but his mandolin sound, characterized by biting fills and swirling lines, ever remained haunting. Over his nearly 70-year recording career he left a deep musical mark on sides under his own name and in accompanying Sleepy John Estes, John Lee "Sonny Boy" Williamson I and Big Joe Williams, among others. Coming out of the musical scene around Brownsville, Tennessee, Rachell made his first records in Memphis in 1929 with Estes, including "Divin' Duck Blues." Together they played in jug bands, backing Noah Lewis in 1930 on "New Minglewood Blues" (covered by the Grateful Dead). Rachell left Tennessee and worked variously in Chicago, St. Louis and Indianapolis, where he settled in 1958, raising a large family. In the blues revival of the 1960s he reunited with Estes and Hammie Nixon, another of his jug band cronies, for recordings and European festivals. Of his compositions, the best known is "She Caught the Katy," popularized by Taj Mahal as well as the Blues Brothers in their movie. One of Rachell's last associations was with John Sebastian and the J-Band, getting together for recordings and concerts even to the final weeks of his life. (Sebastian's band, the Lovin' Spoonful, was the most jug-band influenced of the popular 1960s rock groups). As a gracious, kind-hearted, and charming man, Rachell left a deep personal mark on those who knew him.

what to buy: The 24 tracks of *Sleepy John Estes: Complete Recorded Works in Chronological Order Vol. 1, 1929–37* &&&& (Document, 1990) contain a famous partnership in its first go around. Rachell sings on four and backs Estes on 10 more tracks, including "Diving Duck" and "Broken-Hearted, Ragged and Dirty Too." Accompanied by Washboard Sam and Sonny Boy, *James "Yank" Rachell Vol. 2 (1938–41)* &&&& (Wolf) contains Rachell's compositions "Hobo Blues" (covered by John Lee Hooker), "Loudella" (covered and claimed by Jimmie Rodgers), and "Army Man Blues" (covered by Big Joe Williams).

what to buy next: *Yank Rachell* &&&& (Blue Goose) is all acoustic and lovely. *James "Yank" Rachell Vol. 1 (1934–38)* &&&& (Wolf) offers mostly duets with guitarists Dan Smith or Elijah Jones, sometimes joined by Sonny Boy Williamson. The all-acoustic *Pig Trader Blues* &&&& (Slippery Noodle Sound, 1995) was recorded with long-time Indianapolis playing partner Dave Morgan. A bonus is Rachell telling the classic story of how as a boy he obtained his first mandolin by trading a pig.

the rest:
Blues Mandolin Man &&& (Blind Pig)
Mandolin Blues &&& (Delmark)
Chicago Style &&& (Delmark, 1979)

influences:
◀◀ Hambone Willie Newbern, Peetie Wheatstraw
▶▶ Ry Cooder, Rich DelGrosso

Craig Morrison

Bobby Radcliff

Born Robert Radcliff, 1950, in Washington, DC.

A scrappy singer and explosive guitarist, Bobby Radcliff was 17 years old when he made a pilgrimage to Chicago to see the legendary Magic Sam. After a few lessons and some encouragement, Radcliff returned to his hometown and began playing blues gigs. He cut a single for the Washington-based Aladdin label in 1974 and an LP on A-Okay in the early 1980s. Not long after, he moved to New York and in 1988 signed with Black Top.

what to buy: *Dresses Too Short* &&&& (Black Top, 1989, prod. Hammond Scott) displays lots of extroverted playing and singing. Just slightly less blues oriented were *Universal Blues* &&&& (Black Top, 1991, prod. Hammond Scott) and *There's a Cold Grave in Your Way* &&&& (Black Top, 1994, prod. Hammond Scott).

what to buy next: Several live Radcliff tracks are found on *Black Top Bluesarama* &&& (Black Top, 1989, prod. Hammond Scott).

influences:
◀◀ Magic Sam, Freddie King, Buddy Guy, Albert Collins, Jimmy Nolen, Otis Rush, Earl Hooker, Syl Johnson
▶▶ Ronnie Earl

Jeff Hannusch

Radio Kings

Formed 1991, in Boston, MA.

Brian Templeton, vocals, harmonica, accordion; Michael Dinallo, guitar.

Their recordings have been described as "the best Fabulous Thunderbirds albums the Texas band never made," and the similarity to the T-Birds is downright eerie at times, but this is no lame sound-alike, tribute band. The Radio Kings just might

Yank Rachell (© Jack Vartoogian)

have that wicked sound because they're drawing it from the same old blues classics. They've discovered the gritty, authentic music that turned on the likes of Vaughan and Wilson to the blues in the first place and dialed into the same frequency with genuine, inspired heart and skill.

what to buy: The majority of the 15 cuts on *It Ain't Easy* ✸✸✸ (Icehouse/Priority, 1996, prod. Rusty McFarland, Jay Sheffield) are originals so shrewdly and soulfully executed they sound like revived classics.

what to buy next: *Live at B.B. Kings* ✸✸✸ (Icehouse/Priority, 1995, prod. Rusty McFarland, Jay Sheffield), is mostly covers, and it's equal parts fine musicianship and tantalizing, dance-floor motivation.

influences:

◀◀ Little Walter, Howlin' Wolf, Slim Harpo, James Harman, Kim Wilson, Freddie King, Jimmie Vaughan, Ronnie Earl, Elvis Presley, Blasters, Roomful of Blues, Fabulous Thunderbirds

B.J. Huchtemann

Ma Rainey

Born Gertrude Pridgett, April 26, 1886, in Columbus, GA. Died December 22, 1939, in Columbus, GA.

As much as anyone Ma Rainey was responsible for popularizing the blues when she made the music a part of her traveling tent shows in the early 1900s. Rainey first put a blues tune in her show, probably around 1905, after hearing a young girl sing plaintively about the man who had left her. Rainey was so struck by the song that she learned it to use as an encore. The song was immediately popular with audiences, and the legend was built from there. Rainey's claim to be "Mother of the Blues" is an appropriate one; she inspired generations of singers who came after her, and she played the part of blues queen to the hilt, traveling from show to show in railroad cars emblazoned with her name and hauling four trunks of scenery. On stage she wore sequined dresses, festive headbands, fancy jewelry—one necklace was made of gold coins—and her megawatt, gold-toothed smile. She had a great capacity to touch the audience with a deep contralto presented effortlessly but with unmistakable emotion.

Gertrude Pridgett became "Ma" Rainey after she married song-and-dance man William "Pa" Rainey in 1904, when she was barely 18. Sometimes they called themselves "Rainey and Rainey, Assassinators of the Blues," and they traveled the South with established tent-show groups. It was during these book-

ings that Rainey was thought to have coached an even younger Bessie Smith, though this has never been completely documented. That she influenced Smith artistically, however, is not in doubt. Rainey's blues were not just about infidelity and other domestic maladies but also about poor southern blacks trying to make a living. It endeared her to her regional audience well before she got her first recording contract in 1923, at age 37. The noted black poet Sterling Brown alluded to her impact in a poem about the singer: "O Ma Rainey, Sing yo' song. Now you's back Whah you belong, Git way inside us, Keep us strong." Rainey's recording contract with Paramount, a small record company in Wisconsin, lasted six years. During that time she recorded roughly 100 songs, among them such classics as "See See Rider," "Bo-weevil Blues" and the slightly ribald "Ma Rainey's Black Bottom." While Rainey often played with her rough-house Georgia Tub Jug Washboard band, from time to time she was backed by such noted musicians as Louis Armstrong on cornet, Fletcher Henderson or Jimmy Blythe on piano and Coleman Hawkins on the saxophone. Rainey stopped performing in 1933 at a time when the careers of other female blues singers came to a halt. Always a good businesswoman, she had earned enough money to return home to Georgia to operate two theaters she owned until she died of a heart attack in 1939.

what to buy: The best buy is *Ma Rainey* ✸✸✸ (Milestone, 1992, prod. Orrin Keepnews), a compilation of 32 songs Rainey recorded between 1923 and 1928. It is a varied lot—the earlier recordings feature a young Armstrong on cornet and Henderson on piano. The group is billed as the "Georgia Jazz Band," and there is a kind of sophistication to the arrangements behind Rainey's straightforward but affecting presentation. The later recordings have a rootsier feel, with Rainey accompanied by the Tub Jug Washboard band, which featured two of her favorite sidemen, Georgia Tom Dorsey on piano and Tampa Red on the guitar, and rudimentary instruments—a wash tub and broom-handle for a one-string bass, a seven-gallon jug for a tuba and a "jazzhorn," a kazoo with a trombone bell attached. There's a good natured sensuality to many of the songs, particularly on "Hear Me Talking You" when Rainey sings, "you want to be my man you got to fetch it with you when you come" or "Eve and Adam in the garden, takin' a chance; Adam didn't take time to get his pants." The liner notes, written by Dan Morgenstern, are thorough, informative and interesting.

what to buy next: For those who want it all, the way to go is *The Complete Madam Gertrude "Ma" Rainey Mastertake's Collection 1923–28, Vols. 1–4* ✸✸✸ (King Jazz, prod. George Avakian).

Ma Rainey—The Complete 1928 Sessions in Chronological Order 𝄞𝄞𝄞 (Document, 1993)

Ma Rainey, The Paramount Recordings in Chronological Order Vol. 5 𝄞𝄞𝄞 (GHB)

influences:

▶▶ Bessie Smith, Etta James, Big Mama Thornton, Tracy Nelson, Koko Taylor, Katie Webster, Big Time Sarah, Bonnie Lee, Karen Carroll

Nadine Cohodas

Bonnie Raitt

Born November 8, 1949, in Los Angeles, CA.

There are two Raitt stories—one in the bottle and one out. From the late 1960s to the early 1980s, the Quaker-raised, Radcliffe-educated daughter of Broadway star John Raitt was a blues mama who learned her craft at the feet of John Lee Hooker, Mississippi Fred McDowell and Sippie Wallace. They taught her to play hard and true—and to party hard, too. Raitt made good on their lessons, turning out songs that mined blues, pop and folk while developing a distinctive, stinging slide guitar style and an aching, honest vocal delivery. An exceptional cover of Del Shannon's "Runaway" unjustly defined the first phase of her career, though Raitt also proved herself a performer of rare conscious, joining kindred spirits such as Jackson Browne and James Taylor at various benefits and rallies. It was after being dropped by Warner Brothers in 1983 that Raitt decide to clean up, dry out and, essentially, start over again. Her 1989 release, *Nick of Time*, revealed a smoother pop style that retained just enough blues touches to make it work; it sold more than four million copies and started a string of Grammy victories that made Raitt—who married actor Michael O'Keefe in 1991—the darling of her peers as well as the mainstream audience. She's explored other styles on subsequent releases, though never straying too far from the proven sound. And in 1995, Fender made her the first female guitarist to have an instrument named after her, with royalties funding a program to provide guitars and music lessons to inner city youths.

what to buy: Smooth, assured and forthright, *Nick of Time* 𝄞𝄞𝄞𝄞 (Capitol, 1989, prod. Don Was) is a mature and celebratory effort in which Raitt unveils her new sound and sings with depth and feeling about the tribulations of the past; she even makes Jerry Williams' "I Will Not Be Denied" sound like one of her own songs. *The Bonnie Raitt Collection* 𝄞𝄞𝄞𝄞 (Warner

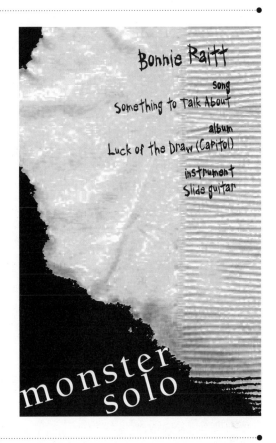

Bonnie Raitt

song
Something to Talk About

album
Luck of the Draw (Capitol)

instrument
Slide guitar

monster solo

Bros., 1990, prod. various) is her old label's cash-in on *Nick of Time*'s success, but it's a terrific overview anyway, featuring previously unreleased live duets with Wallace ("Woman Be Wise") and John Prine ("Angel from Montgomery").

what to buy next: *Give It Up* 𝄞𝄞𝄞 (Warner Bros., 1973, prod. Michael Cuscuna) is the best of Raitt's Warner albums, a corker that blasts open with her own "Give It Up or Let Me Go" and continues through an inspired collection of originals and covers. *Luck of the Draw* 𝄞𝄞𝄞𝄞 (Capitol, 1991, prod. Don Was, Bonnie Raitt) finds the Raitt of *Nick of Time* exuberantly in love and ready to tell the world about it on "Something to Talk About" and her burning duet with Delbert McClinton, "Good Man, Good Woman."

what to avoid: *Home Plate* 𝄞 (Warner Bros., 1975, prod. Paul D. Rothchild) is a weak and ill-conceived attempt to take Raitt in a country direction–and it strikes out.

the rest:

Bonnie Raitt 🎜🎜🎜 (Warner Bros., 1971)
Takin' My Time 🎜🎜🎜🎜 (Warner Bros., 1973)
Streetlights 🎜🎜 (Warner Bros., 1974)
Sweet Forgiveness 🎜🎜 (Warner Bros., 1977)
The Glow 🎜🎜 (Warner Bros., 1979)
Green Light 🎜🎜🎜 (Warner Bros., 1982)
Nine Lives 🎜🎜🎜 (Warner Bros., 1986)
Longing in Their Hearts 🎜🎜🎜🎜 (Capitol, 1994)
Road Tested 🎜🎜🎜 (Capitol, 1995)

worth searching for: Raitt's ubiquitous guest shots on her friends albums have resulted in some fine music. Her Grammy winning duet with Hooker on "In the Mood" from his album *The Healer* 🎜🎜🎜🎜🎜 (Chameleon, 1989, prod. Roy Rogers) is definitive, while her contributions to her father's *Broadway Legend* 🎜🎜🎜 (Angel, 1995) are sweet.

influences:

◀◀ Howlin' Wolf, Muddy Waters, Sippie Wallace, Mississippi Fred McDowell, John Lee Hooker, Odetta, Joan Baez

▶▶ Pat Benatar, Melissa Etheridge, Melissa Ferrick, Sheryl Crow, Joan Osborne

Gary Graff

Moses Rascoe

Born 1917, in Windsor, NC. Died March 6, 1994, in Lebanon, PA.

This singer-guitarist spent his whole life pursuing blues as a hobby, learning it from Brownie McGhee records and Jimmy Reed jukebox hits while he worked as a day laborer and truck driver. When he retired in 1982, he started to play music full-time and became a folkie, playing folk festivals around the world and recording a live album full of Reed and Reed-like blues songs.

what to buy: Rascoe's only album, *Blues* 🎜🎜🎜 (Flying Fish, 1987), is more of a reverential document than a declaration of his own style—he's obsessed with Jimmy Reed, and it shows, although there are traces of old Sonny Terry-Brownie McGhee techniques in his style.

influences:

◀◀ Jimmy Reed, Elmore James, Sonny Terry & Brownie McGhee, Leadbelly, Muddy Waters

Steve Knopper

Bonnie Raitt (© Ken Settle)

Kenny "Blue" Ray

Born Kenny Ray Ladner, 1950, in Lodi, CA.

Kenny is a reassuring reminder that there are still great "unknowns" out there chugging away in the blues landscape. Well, not a complete unknown: he was a member of Little Charlie & the Nightcats in the mid-1970s, backed and recorded with William Clarke and Marcia Ball and appeared on recording sessions with Mitch Woods, Charlie Musselwhite, Ronnie Earl and numerous Bay Area artists. Stevie Ray Vaughan, whom he met and befriended, is an obvious influence, but he draws equally as much from Albert Collins and other Texas guitar greats. Since 1994 he has released five CDs on his own label, all discs that stand head and shoulders above the normal run of home-made blues products.

what to buy: On his first "major label" release *In All of My Life* 🎜🎜🎜🎜 (JSP, 1997, prod. Kenny "Blue" Ray, Jimmy Morello), Ray gets the kind of production he deserves, with appropriate vocals by Jimmy Morello (formerly of Pat Boyack & the Prowlers) and Jackie Payne. The guitar work is tough and always in a blue, not rock, pocket. *Fired Up!* 🎜🎜🎜 (Blue Ray, 1994, prod. Kenny "Blue" Ray) and *Pull the Strings* 🎜🎜🎜 (Tone King, 1996, prod. Kenny "Blue" Ray) are standouts among his self-produced discs, each featuring 13 tunes with plenty of meat on their bones.

the rest:

Cadillac Tone 🎜🎜🎜 (Blue Ray, 1995)
Strat Daddy 🎜🎜🎜 (Blue Ray, 1995)
Git It! 🎜🎜🎜 (Tone King, 1996)

influences:

◀◀ Albert Collins, Stevie Ray Vaughan, Albert King, Freddie King, Magic Sam

Cary Wolfson

Mac Rebennack

See: Dr. John

A.C. Reed

Born Aaron Corthen, May 9, 1926, in Wardell, MO.

If songs like "I Can't Go on This Way" and "I Am Fed Up with This Music" are any indication, this fun-loving saxophonist apparently has the blues because he plays the blues. In concert the showman plays up the crotchety shtick, pretending he'd rather be doing anything else, while simultaneously delivering enthusiastic rock-and-blues concerts full of big saxo-

A.C. Reed (© Jack Vartoogian)

phone tones. Classically trained (at the Chicago Conservatory of Music), the Missouri native befriended Jimmy Reed (thus A.C.'s last name) and became an in-demand back-up saxman for many R&B and blues artists in the 1950s and 1960s. He gained notoriety in the Buddy Guy-Junior Wells band for 10 years beginning in 1967 and wound up touring with the Rolling Stones, Son Seals and Albert Collins. More a live attraction than a recording artist, Reed's solo album career began in 1978 with a few tracks on Alligator's *Living Chicago Blues* collection. Though his band, the Spark Plugs, regularly tour blues clubs around the world, Reed has only released two solo albums.

what to buy: The guest stars—Stevie Ray Vaughan, Bonnie Raitt, Maurice John Vaughn—are impressive on *I'm in the Wrong Business!* ✺✺✺ (Alligator, 1987), but Reed rarely relinquishes his hold on the spotlight. He's playful, in fine Bobby Rush and Screamin' Jay Hawkins style on the title track, and

occasionally proselytizing, on the closing "Don't Drive Drunk."

what to buy next: Reed's debut, *Take These Blues and Shove 'Em* ✺✺✺ (Rooster Blues, 1982) began Reed's "I-hate-the-blues-ha-ha" era; but fortunately, Reed's naturally funky sax bails out the album when the concept wears thin.

worth searching for: With Buddy Guy's brother, Phil, on guitar and Chicago stalwart Casey Jones on drums, Reed's Spark Plugs contribute four brassy, upbeat tracks to *Living Chicago Blues, Vol. III* ✺✺✺ (Alligator, 1978/1991), including "Hard Times" and "Going to New York."

influences:

◀◀ Jimmy Reed, Grady Gaines, Buddy Guy, Otis Rush, Junior Wells, Muddy Waters, Screamin' Jay Hawkins

▶▶ Clarence Clemons, Son Seals, Bobby Rush, Mojo Nixon

Steve Knopper

Dalton Reed

Born 1952, in Cade, LA. Died September 23, 1994, in Minneapolis, MN.

Dalton Reed seemed like a major new voice—whatever he sang sprouted roots. He died young, from heart problems while in Minneapolis to perform, at the point where his career was starting to take off. The loss was great—he was a gifted singer drawn to lilting, stylish soul-blues not as time-capsule music but as something dynamic for the 1990s. His vocals sounded naturally wedded to the material; he made his songs exciting and contemporary. Raised in Lafayette, the heart of Louisiana's Cajun-zydeco territory, he began singing in the choir of his family's local Catholic church. In high school he discovered soul music and started to sing it, as well as play it on trumpet, trombone and piano with several bands. Although not a Cajun-zydeco performer, he later formed a group that toured with Rockin' Sidney of "Toot Toot" fame. Reed and brother Johnny became popular in Lafayette, and Bullseye Blues producer Scott Billington liked Reed's songs enough to sign him when he heard them on a Lafayette club's jukebox in 1990.

what to buy: *Willing & Able* ♫♫♫ (Bullseye Blues, 1994, prod. Scott Billington) is the better of Reed's two albums. The material is consistently punchy and the variety impressive. There's a rollicking, New Orleans-style R&B influence on "The One Thing" and "Ophelia." The title tune is an effectively sinewy and romantic ballad, and his more straightforward blues tunes are suitably earnest. His baritone voice can glide or probe.

what to buy next: While *Louisiana Soul Man* ♫♫♫ (Bullseye Blues, 1992, prod. Scott Billington, Lee Allen Zeno) is more tentative, it includes excellent material and good arrangements. In particular, Reed performs Gary Nicholson and Dan Penn's "Blues of the Month Club," later recorded by Joe Louis Walker, as well as Delbert McClinton's rockin' good "Read Me My Rights." His own "Party on the Farm" has a polite yet irresistible funk quality.

influences:
◀◀ Ray Charles, Johnny Adams, Otis Redding

Steven Rosen

Francine Reed

Born July 11, 1947, in Kankakee, IL.

Born in Chicago but reared in Phoenix, where she began her singing career with her family, Reed gained prominence as a member of Lyle Lovett's Large Band, in which her role was that of "foreground singer." Reed dueted memorably with the gangly bandleader on unconventional, hilarious, blues-tinged numbers such as "Here I Am" and "She's Hot to Go." Lovett was not shy in turning the spotlight over to Reed, who flourished in its glow. As a solo artist she has yet to hit it big, but her work is impressive and stylistically adventurous. Unfortunately, aside from her gig with Lovett, Reed has most widely been heard singing James Brown's "I Feel Good" for a laxative commercial. But, as they say, given time and a little luck, this too shall pass.

what to buy: There's no point in ignoring the Lovett connection in Reed's career, so *I Want You to Love Me* ♫♫♫ (Ichiban International, 1995, prod. Bryan Cole) kicks off with a duet between the two, "Why I Don't Know." There's also a steamy take on Muddy Waters' "I Want You to Love Me," some fine southern soul in Marvin Taylor's "What Is That Light" and a soaring version of Jerry Butler's "For Your Precious Love." Reed seldom falters, her performance is assured, and her voice rich and brassy. She's hardly a rookie, but this is an impressive debut.

the rest:
Can't Make It on My Own ♫♫♫ (Ichiban International, 1996)

influences:
◀◀ Etta James, Aretha Franklin, Lyle Lovett

Daniel Durchholz

Jimmy Reed

Born September 9, 1925, in Leland, MS. Died August 29, 1976, in Oakland, CA.

One of the most easily recognizable blues sounds is that of Jimmy Reed: his lazy, loping lead guitar, inseparable from his aching, plaintive, dust-choked, alcohol-soaked voice, the piercing moan of his soulful harmonica. The plodding yet insistent boogie back beat, walking bass, laid-back drumming and sawing rhythm is provided for the most part by the same small handful of musicians. Reed never strayed far from his trademark sound, and that can be problematic for listeners: there is a definite sameness to much of his work. A little Reed goes a long way. On the bright side, you don't have to own a lot of Jimmy Reed music to be very familiar with all of it. And you'll definitely want to own *some*, because Reed's distinctive country blues sound, in measured doses, is perfect for many moods and much pleasure. Most of Reed's success, which was considerable, came during his years with Vee-Jay from 1953 to 1959, beginning with the hit single "You Don't Have to Go," which hit #5 on the *Billboard* R&B charts. Thirteen others followed, and even more amazingly, Reed crossed over 11 times on *Billboard*'s Hot 100, an unparalleled feat for a bluesman. One of 10 children born about a dozen miles from the river and well within its Delta plain, Reed was learning the basics of guitar on a cigar-box version supplied by one of his life-long partners, Eddie Taylor, who also taught him harmonica. Heavily influenced by Sonny Boy Williamson (Rice Miller)—"He was the man I got my ideas from," Reed once said—the duo left home when Reed was 15, eventually landing in the Chicago/Gary area by 1943. His lyric themes are summed up wonderfully in the 1967 record, "Cousin Peaches" (his nickname down South): "I'm just a poor country boy/Trying to find a home/While I may look like I'm happy/Everything I do is wrong." Almost all of Reed's records are produced by his manager Al Smith. Lefty Bates or Eddie Taylor always play rhythm guitar, sometimes joined by Jimmy Reed Jr. Earl Phillips usually can be found on drums. Reed's material was written with Smith and Reed's long-suffering wife Mary, known widely as "Mama" Reed, a feature of most recording sessions, seated on a piano bench and whispering lyrics to her forgetful mate. The sameness of sound has led to criticism over the years, much of it valid. "Jimmy's style is so peculiar and so different from anybody else that he never fitted in with other musicians," Smith says. Reed was an inveterate boozehound, and his stage antics, when he appeared at all, were every bit as boorish as those of George Jones or Warren Zevon.

what to buy: *The Best of Jimmy Reed* ♪♪♪♪ (GNP/Crescendo, 1974) includes the cream of Reed's crop among its 20 cuts. Huge hits like "Honest I Do" (a version appears on the first Rolling Stones album), "Take Out Some Insurance," "Big Boss Man," "Baby What You Want Me to Do" (covered by Elvis Presley, among innumerable others), "Goin' to New York" and especially "Bright Lights Big City" ("Bright lights/Big city/ Goin' to my baby's head") chronicled the trials of a country boy confronted with urban madness.

what to buy next: *Jimmy Reed* ♪♪♪♪ (Paula, prod. Al Smith) was originally recorded sometime between 1967–71 and offers Reed backed by the best band he assembled on record, with Eddie Taylor on second guitar and Phil Upchurch on electric bass. This is the Reed sound at its fullest; his sometimes thin and tinny sound is augmented by a hard-driving, simpatico group.

what to avoid: There are three reasons to avoid *Jimmy Reed at Carnegie Hall* ♪♪ (Vee-Jay, 1961, prod. Al Smith): more than half the cuts end in a jarring, abrupt manner, as if someone pulled the plug in the middle of a riff; half the record is yet another studio greatest-hits compilation (which you probably already have); and the other half is a studio "recreation" of a concert held several days earlier. Contractual and technical difficulties supposedly prevented the recording of the actual event.

the rest:
Bright Lights/Big City: Charly Blues Masterwork ♪♪♪ (Charly, 1992)
Greatest Hits ♪♪♪ (Charly, 1992)
Greatest Hits ♪♪♪ (Hollywood/Rounder, 1992)
Johnny Winter, Jimmy Reed Live at Liberty Hall Houston 1972 ♪♪♪♪ (New Rose, 1993)
Speak the Lyrics to Me, Mama Reed ♪♪♪♪ (Vee-Jay, 1993)
Jimmy Reed ♪♪♪♪ (Paula, 1994)
Cry before I Go ♪♪ (Drive Archive, 1995)
Jimmy Reed: Classic Recordings ♪♪♪ (Tomato, 1995)
Rockin' with Reed ♪♪♪♪ (Eclipse, 1996)

worth searching for: Reed and Eddie Taylor guest on John Lee Hooker's *The Early Years* ♪♪♪ (Tomato, 1994), a two-disc monaural recording made sometime between 1955 and 1964. Reed's mentor and long-time sideman teams up with Hubert Sumlin, Carey Bell and Sunnyland Slim on *The Eddie Taylor Blues Band: My Heart Is Bleeding* ♪♪♪ (Evidence, 1994, prod. Horst Lippmann).

influences:

◀◀ Sonny Boy Williamson I, Eddie Taylor

▶▶ Bob Dylan, Slim Harpo, Rolling Stones, Animals, Yardbirds

Rob Reuteman

Johnny Reno
Born in AR.

Sax man Johnny Reno was honkin' and barwalkin' throughout the 1980s with the Sax Maniacs, fusing swing, jump-blues, rockabilly and jazz with impeccable sax and showmanship. Along with Roomful of Blues, the Maniacs were one of the few touring bands keeping the horn-heavy, swingin' jump-blues traditions alive. Reno's early credits include a stint (1978–80) with Stevie Ray Vaughan's Triple Threat Revue (alongside W.C. Clark and Lou Ann Barton) that became the first incarnation of Double Trouble after Clark left the band. Reno played sax in the Ft. Worth-based Juke Jumpers from 1980–83. He fronted a stripped-down, more rock 'n' roll-influenced band, the Johnny Reno Band, later in the 1980s, but the emphasis was still on his remarkable command of the Texas tenor style and tone. Reno spent the early 1990s touring with rockabilly-pop crooner Chris Isaak. In 1997, Reno was invited to record some tracks for a forthcoming set in the Capitol Ultra-Lounge series, the first to feature contemporary players.

what to buy: Reno's latest project is the Lounge Kings, a swing-influenced band focusing on jumpin' sax-fueled instrumentals and smoky torch songs. On *Swinging & Singing* 𝄢𝄢𝄢 (Menthol, 1997, prod. Johnny Reno), Reno lays down the vocals in the cool and bittersweet tradition of Chet Baker and Frank Sinatra. For a touch of be-bop, beatnik, bachelor pad cool, Alan Pollard adds groovy bongos.

what to buy next: The Johnny Reno Band performs a potent, mixed bag of scorchin' rockabilly and mainstream pop on *Third Degree* 𝄢𝄢𝄢 (Wildcat, 1990, prod. Johnny Reno).

worth searching for: Available only on vinyl and cassette, *Full Blown* 𝄢𝄢𝄢 (Rounder, 1985/1993) includes some swingabilly classics. Reno's vocals on "Thrill Me" and "Feels So Good" are barn-burnin' screamers. The Sax Maniac's EP, *Born to Blow* 𝄢𝄢𝄢𝄢 (Black Top, 1983, prod. Hammond Scott, Johnny Reno), still in the catalog but only on vinyl, is worth it for "Mellow Saxophone," the only recording of one of Reno's signature performance tunes, and a dynamite version of "Harlem Nocturne."

influences:

◀◀ Illinois Jacquet, Arnett Cobb, King Curtis, Red Prysock, Louis Prima, Sam Butera, Elvis Presley, Frank Sinatra, Chet Baker

▶▶ Mighty Blue Kings, Naughty Ones, Royal Crown Revue, Big Bad Voodoo Daddy, Brian Setzer Orchestra

B.J. Huchtemann

Sonny Rhodes

Born Clarence Edward Smith, November 3, 1940, in Smithville, TX.

An energetic, flashy showman—he once opened for Bruce Springsteen in Asbury Park, New Jersey, and actually managed to quiet the fans shouting "Broooce!"—Rhodes went from good to great after playing behind Freddie King and Albert Collins in the 1950s. After recording several solo singles throughout the 1960s and failing to get adequate record deals, he put out his own singles beginning in 1978—a European tour led to overseas recording deals, but that never made him much money. He toiled for years in frustrating obscurity, then started signing contracts with better companies in the mid-1980s. Rhodes' albums are fine outlets for his fast guitar-playing touch, but the turbaned singer-songwriter's charismatic presence translates better to the stage than the studio.

what to buy: Rhodes wrote all the songs on *Livin' Too Close to the Edge* 𝄢𝄢𝄢 (Wild Dog/Ichiban, 1992, prod. Bob Greenlee), which features Lucky Peterson on keyboards, Noble "Thin Man" Watts on tenor sax and, of course, great whining guitar licks by Rhodes.

what to buy next: His guitar is solid as usual, but what comes across best on *Out of Control* 𝄢𝄢𝄢 (King Snake, 1996, prod. Bob Greenlee) is the soul singing; Rhodes' voice softly testifies, then builds to a Bobby "Blue" Bland explosion of high-pitched crooning.

what to avoid: *Just Blues* 𝄢𝄢 (Rhodesway, 1985/1993/Evidence, 1995, prod. Sonny Rhodes, Steve Gannon) sounds a little too desperate to get attention, despite nice versions of Jimmy McCracklin's "Think" and Percy Mayfield's "Strange Things Happening."

the rest:

In Europe 𝄢𝄢 (Appaloosa)
Disciple of the Blues 𝄢𝄢𝄢 (Ichiban, 1991)
The Blues Is My Best Friend 𝄢𝄢𝄢 (King Snake, 1994)

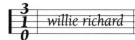
worth searching for: With Jimi Hendrix-level versions of Howlin' Wolf's "Killing Floor" and Rhodes' own "All Night Long They Play the Blues," Rhodes first attracted significant attention in the blues world with his European debut, *I Don't Want My Blues Colored Bright* ✍✍✍ (Black Magic, 1994, prod. Sonny Rhodes, J.J. Malone, Gary Smith).

influences:

◄◄ Albert Collins, Freddie King, Buddy Guy, Elmore James, Albert King, Son Seals

►► Bruce Springsteen, Lucky Peterson, Kenny Wayne Shepherd, Robert Cray

Steve Knopper

Willie Richard

See: Hip Linkchain

Tommy Ridgley

Born October 30, 1925, in Shrewsbury, LA.

One of New Orleans' most prolific musical artists, Ridgley has been recording for nearly half a century. His first break came in 1949 when Dave Bartholomew hired him as his band's vocalist. At the time, Bartholomew had begun producing records for Imperial, and Ridgley became one of the early foundations for the label. He started his own band in 1953 and jumped to Decca, Atlantic—just missing the charts with the instrumental "Jam Up"—and Herald before the decade was out. Ridgley started out the 1960s on Ric, where he scored several regional hits, including "Double Eyed Whammy" and "Should I Ever Love Again." After Ric folded, Ridgley continued to label hop, waxing dozens of singles over the next 25 years. Although he never had a national hit, his reputation in New Orleans is solid. Even into the 1990s, he continued to record for various labels.

what to buy: Ridgley fans and New Orleans R&B buffs will find *The New Orleans King of the Stroll* ✍✍✍✍ (Rounder, 1986) indispensable, as it collects most of the Ric material. Almost as enjoyable is *The Herald Recordings* ✍✍✍✍ (Collectables, 1992). *Since the Blues Began* (Black Top, 1995, prod. Hammond Scott) surrounds Ridgley with a marquee New Orleans band which includes Snooks Eaglin and George Porter.

what to buy next: *She Turns Me On* ✍✍✍✍ (Modern Blues, 1992, prod. Daniel Jacoubovitch) and *How Long* ✍✍✍✍ (Sound of New Orleans, 1990, prod. Gary Edwards) showcase Ridgley's contemporary R&B sound.

worth searching for: Ridgley recorded scores of singles; many have never been released. His work often pops up on New Orleans R&B anthologies.

influences:

◄◄ Paul Gayten, Ivory Joe Hunter, Chuck Willis, Roy Brown, Isidore "Tuts" Washington, Dave Bartholomew, Fats Domino

►► King Floyd, Larry Hamilton, Snooks Eaglin, Lloyd Price, Irma Thomas, Rose Davis

Jeff Hannusch

Richard Riggins

See: Harmonica Slim

Paul Rishell

Birth information unavailable.

A revivalist like John Hammond Jr., Rory Block, Keb' Mo' and Taj Mahal, Boston singer-guitarist Rishell plays mostly country blues in the style of Lightnin' Hopkins and Brownie McGhee. (His longtime partner, Little Annie Raines, supplies the Sonny Terry harp role.) Rishell is certainly not the first to take this solemn preservational approach to the blues, but the soft-spoken singer and excellent guitarist does it extremely well—among his impeccable cover choices are Robert Johnson's "32-20 Blues," Blind Boy Fuller's "Mamie," Skip James' "Devil Got My Woman" and Blind Blake's "Too Tight." The blues needs people like Rishell and Hammond to deliberately point listeners back to the originals.

what to buy: *Blues on a Holiday* ✍✍✍ (Tone-Cool, 1990, prod. Ron Levy) begins with an acoustic set (with covers of Blind Willie McTell, Scrapper Blackwell, Son House and others) and shifts halfway through to a horn-heavy big-band arrangement (on Willie Dixon, Billy Boy Arnold and Tabby Thomas songs).

what to buy next: *Swear to Tell the Truth* ✍✍✍ (Tone-Cool, 1993, prod. Paul Rishell, Richard Rosenblatt) has Rishell stretching farther into the electric band style; he's backed by Raines and the tight band Ronnie Earl & the Broadcasters on concise, reverential originals and classic covers.

the rest:

(With Annie Raines) *I Want You to Know* ✍✍✍ (Tone-Cool, 1996)

influences:

◄◄ John Hammond Jr., Blind Boy Fuller, Robert Johnson, Taj Mahal, Rory Block

►► Keb' Mo', Corey Harris

Steve Knopper

Duke Robillard

Born October 4, 1948, in Woonsocket, RI.

There are certainly tons of phenomenal guitarists dotting the history of the blues, but few have ever managed to display a dazzling proficiency in as many diverse styles as Duke Robillard. He founded Roomful of Blues in 1967 and worked with the seminal outfit until 1979. Along the way he caught the eye of Muddy Waters and jammed onstage with his idol repeatedly for several years. Robillard later signed on with rockabilly singer Robert Gordon's group before founding his own band in 1981. As songwriter, bandleader and torrid guitarist, Robillard has expanded his exploration of music through forays into rockabilly, jazz, R&B and rock that build upon his blues roots. Constantly re-inventing himself, Robillard has delved into everything from jazzy horn sections and old-time rock to understated swing and rough, guitar-powered blues standards. In between projects, Robillard also replaced Jimmie Vaughan in the Fabulous Thunderbirds from 1990–92 and recently has produced albums for other top blues acts, including John Hammond and Jay McShann.

what to buy: *Duke Robillard and the Pleasure Kings* ♪♪♪♪ (Rounder, 1984, prod. Scott Billington, Duke Robillard), Robillard's debut as bandleader, is filled with tight, polished arrangements from his trio. These stripped-down tunes, mostly originals, connect early electric blues with Robillard's updated vision and edge. *After Hours Swing Session* ♪♪♪♪ (Rounder, 1992, prod. Duke Robillard) is an absolute treat, showing off Robillard's crisp journey into swinging jazz, including tunes plucked from Nat "King" Cole, Billie Holiday and Tiny Grimes along with a few originals. His band (consisting of several Roomful of Blues pals) provides shimmering lead work on clarinet, sax and piano while Robillard's guitar rings straight and true. Tribute albums too often pay boring homages to an artist's influences, but *Duke's Blues* ♪♪♪♪ (Pointblank, 1996, prod. Duke Robillard) is an exciting blend of Robillard originals and covers that bow to his idols while also giving them a kick in the pants. Robillard's guitar effortlessly darts between scorching assaults and restrained, jazzy fills while his vocals are scuffed or smooth depending on the moment.

what to buy next: *Turn It Around* ♪♪♪♪ (Rounder, 1991, prod. Duke Robillard, John Paul Gauthier) is a modern, rock-oriented set that features vocalist Susann Forrest. While Robillard lets his guitar ramble and roar more than on previous albums, Forrest's singing adds a sultry flare that provides a vibrant dimension to Duke's ensemble. *Dangerous Place* ♪♪♪ (Pointblank, 1997, prod. Duke Robillard) takes Robillard's adventures in

swing, including an exceptional horn section, and melds them together with a fuzzed-out, hard-driving guitar. The full-band jams are hard-driving explosions, and the softer stuff displays some towering jazz constructions on saxophone.

the rest:
Too Hot to Handle ♪♪♪ (Rounder, 1985)
Swing ♪♪♪♪ (Rounder, 1987)
Rockin' Blues ♪♪♪ (Rounder, 1988)
You Got Me ♪♪♪ (Rounder, 1988)
Temptation ♪♪♪♪ (Pointblank, 1994)

worth searching for: Robillard and band revisit some of Jay McShann's classic tunes for *Hootie's Jumpin' Blues* ♪♪♪♪ (Stony Plain, 1997, prod. Duke Robillard, Holger Peterson).

influences:
◀◀ T-Bone Walker, B.B. King, Lowell Fulson
▶▶ Chris Duarte, Kenny Wayne Shepherd

Matt Pensinger

Fenton Robinson

Born September 23, 1935, in Greenwood, MS.

Despite formidable talents as a singer, songwriter and guitarist, Fenton Robinson has remained a truly unsung hero of Chicago blues. The subtlety and jazz inflections of both his guitar work and his distinctly soaring voice have probably hindered his acceptance in the Windy City, which tends to favor rougher-edged practitioners. Though Robinson hails from Mississippi, his music bears little of his home state's stamp, having more in common with swinging Texans like T-Bone Walker and Gatemouth Brown than his Delta peers. He is a major artist whose work should be better documented. Many pleasures await the listener unfamiliar with Robinson's recordings.

what to buy: *Somebody Loan Me a Dime* ♪♪♪♪ (Alligator, 1974, prod. Fenton Robinson, Bruce Iglauer) is a great album through and through, and the title track is a bona fide masterpiece. Also included is a great take on "Texas Flood"—Robinson played guitar on Larry Davis' original version. *I Hear Some Blues Downstairs* ♪♪♪♪ (Alligator, 1977, prod. Fenton Robinson, Bruce Iglauer, Richard McCleese) is an extremely able follow-up. *Nightflight* ♪♪♪♪ (Alligator, 1984, prod. Fenton Robinson, Dick Shurman) is every bit as good.

what to buy next: *Special Road* ♪♪♪, (Evidence, 1993, prod. Fenton Robinson, Gerard Robs, Kees Van Wijngaarden), which

collects European sides cut in 1989, is rougher and more inconsistent, but strong nonetheless.

influences:

◀◀ T-Bone Walker, B.B. King, Grant Green, Kenny Burrell

▶▶ Stevie Ray Vaughan, Jimmie Vaughan, Ronnie Earl, Joe Louis Walker

Alan Paul

Ikey Robinson

Born July 28, 1904, in Dublin, VA. Died October 25, 1990, in Chicago, IL.

Singer-guitarist-banjoist Ikey Robinson undoubtedly would have been a much bigger star had his studio dates not become so inconsistent after his beloved swing era died out. His connections were impeccable: he played with the great Jelly Roll Morton, plus Clarence Williams and Jabbo Smith, in the late 1920s—then did solo recordings for the next several years. Robinson played off and on with some big names, including Erskine Tate and Franz Jackson, before blues revivalists rediscovered him in the 1970s.

what to buy: The Australian import *"Banjo" Ikey Robinson* ♪♪♪ (RST) is the most thorough document you'll find of Robinson's 1920s and 1930s swing work, and it includes collaborations with his cornetist pal Jabbo Smith (with whom he reunited in Europe in the 1970s), and singers Charlie Slocum and Half Pint Jackson.

influences:

◀◀ Duke Ellington, Jelly Roll Morton, Louis Armstrong, Coleman Hawkins, Benny Goodman

▶▶ T-Bone Walker, Louis Jordan, Charlie Christian, Lionel Hampton

Steve Knopper

Jimmie Lee Robinson

Born April 30, 1931, in Chicago, IL.

Veteran blues guitarist Jimmie Lee Robinson grew up a stone's throw away from the musically bountiful Maxwell Street Market and began playing with a miscellany of street musicians as a youth in the early 1940s. He joined forces with Eddie Taylor in 1948 and soon thereafter became a regular performer on Chicago's thriving club circuit. Through the years he has enlisted with innumerable blues titans, including Freddie King, Elmore James, Little Walter and Magic Sam. His virtuoso guitar work graces many of their seminal recordings. Nevertheless, his firm foundation in Chicago's urban blues is betrayed by his low-topped and wide-brimmed, western-style hat, string tie and spurs. Fans of early rockabilly will remember Robinson as "Lonesome Lee," the creator of a string of quirky Bandera singles replete with piercing falsetto wails and snappy guitar lines. Robinson continues to straddle this line between mainstream Chicago blues and country-tinged folk music. While neither his technical skill nor his eclecticism really set him apart, the intimacy and unexaggerated expressiveness that Robinson brings to his broad musical repertoire is a rare pleasure.

what to buy: Are you looking for blues or something stylistically adventurous? If blues is your bag, check out *Lonely Traveller* ♪♪♪ (Delmark, 1994, prod. Steve Cushing). The trademark turnarounds and timing nuances that characterize Robinson's best blues guitar work from the 1950s and 1960s are wondrously present on such tunes as "Easy Baby," "Triflin' on You" and "All My Life." Though some of the music on this recording blurs the boundaries a bit, the stylistically hybrid songs, such as "Robinson's Rang Tangle," add a vivacity of character that is sometimes lacking in the straight blues numbers. For those who prefer their blues with a few ballads and a homily or two on the side, look no further than *Guns, Gangs and Drugs* ♪♪♪ (Amina, 1996, prod. Jimmie Lee Robinson).

the rest:

Chicago Blues Legends ♪♪♪ (Wolf, 1996)

worth searching for: Robinson's best records to date are the three 45s made for Bandera in the late 1950s and early 1960s. Those six songs are scattered over two out-of-print vinyl LPs, *Chicago Jump* ♪♪♪♪ (JSP, 1979, prod. John Stedman) and *Bandera Rockabillies* ♪♪ (JSP, 1979, prod. John Stedman). The former has the bluesiest numbers, among them the original recording of "All My Life," which was covered by John Mayall in the 1960s.

influences:

◀◀ Blind Percy, Daddy Stovepipe, Moody Jones

▶▶ Eddie Taylor, Freddy King

D. Thomas Moon

Fenton Robinson (© Jack Vartoogian)

Ray Charles Robinson

See: Ray Charles

Tad Robinson

Born June 24, 1956, in New York, NY.

Tad Robinson is an enormous talent. He sings with the depth and breadth of, say, a Johnny Adams, plays major-league harmonica and writes much of his own material. But Robinson has been—will always be—hampered by a single shortcoming: he doesn't *look* like a bluesman. A short, balding Caucasian, he looks more like the guy in Manhattan Transfer. But if you can get past the appearance thing, you're in for a treat; Robinson, an off-and-on member of Dave Specter's Bluebirds, is never afraid to take chances. Robinson also recorded one song ("Move Over") and produced *Songs of Janis Joplin: Blues Down Deep* (House of Blues, 1997).

what to buy: *One to Infinity* ♫♫♫♫ (Delmark, 1994, prod. Steve Wagner) is a wonderful mix of ballads, killer blues and harmonica-driven shuffles. There's even an R&B version of the Beatles "Eight Days a Week" that works amazingly well. *Blueplicity* ♫♫♫♫ (Delmark, 1994, prod. Dave Specter) and *Live in Europe* ♫♫♫♫ (Delmark, 1995, prod. Dave Specter) are only slightly less spectacular.

what to buy next: *Midnight Blues* ♫♫♫ (Delmark, 1994) includes various artists with Magic Sam, Junior Wells, Little Walter, Dave Specter (with Robinson), Luther Allison and Louis Myers.

worth searching for: Look for Robinson with Barkin' Bill Smith on *Gotcha!* ♫♫♫♫ (Delmark, 1994, prod. Steve Wagner).

influences:

◄◄ Johnny Adams, Ray Charles, Bobby "Blue" Bland, Arthur Alexander, Otis Redding, Joe Cocker, Eric Burdon

Dave Ranney

Jimmy Rogers

Born James A. Lane, June 13, 1924, in Ruleville, MS.

When guitarists want to learn rhythm, they lend an ear to Jimmy Rogers, whose propulsive chords and bass lines were integral to the genre-defining Muddy Waters band of the 1950s and Rogers' own classic Chess records. He may have derived "Walkin' by Myself" from T-Bone Walker's "Why Not" and "Back Door Friend" from Tommy Hollins' "Married Woman Blues," but by and large his vintage work was hallmarked by outstanding songwriting and singing. His best-known numbers had an insouciance that set them apart from the splashy passion of his peers (though delve in his discography and you'll find plenty that's satisfyingly low-down). Eddie Ware, J.T. Brown, S.P. Leary and other notables played on Rogers' Chess records; even if Little Walter had never made a record of his own he would be renowned for the magnificence of his playing with Jimmy. Classics like "Money, Marbles and Chalk," "That's Alright," "You're the One" and "Chicago Bound" should have set Rogers up for life, but by the mid-1960s he was fed up with music's scant rewards and acquired a clothing store. It gave him a good living until 1968, when the fires from the riots that followed the Martin Luther King killing burned his store and set him on the comeback trail. He hooked up with Robert Reidy, then an energetic young pianist on the scene and upped his visibility with gigs on Chicago's emerging North Side milieu. Rogers has made his share of albums, usually replicating the approach he took with Chess. One could argue that he's exhibited little creativity since the 1950s, but this doesn't diminish the fact that in his art, he's as Cezanne or Hemingway were in theirs.

what to buy: The title is right for *Jimmy Rogers: The Complete Chess Reissue* ♫♫♫♫ (MCA/Chess, 1997, prod. Leonard Chess, Phil Chess), which reminds us that other than his most famous songs—which are all right here—Rogers used similar tempos more often than not. But within this admittedly limited rhythmic template, genre fans will find much to admire, as Rogers guns for Reds ("World's in a Tangle") and plays crunching, evil guitar ("Chance to Love" and "My Little Machine"). With grabby, shocking lyrics ("I forsook my mother!") and the coyote sax of J.T. Brown, "Crying Shame" is a standout, as is "Blues All Day Long," with Odie Payne's mantric tap-tap-booin! on drums. Sound quality's nice and warm, and there's a well-written booklet enclosed, with print that's actually big enough to read.

what to buy next: In all of Rogers post-1950s records he's willfully stepping in his own tracks, but on *Feelin' Good* ♫♫♫♫ (Blind Pig, 1995, prod. Rob Murray, Rod Piazza) it's with a vigor he's rarely otherwise approached.

the rest:

Chicago Bound ♫♫♫♫ (MCA/Chess 1990)
Ludella ♫♫♫♫ (Antone's, 1990)
Sloppy Drunk ♫♫♫ (Evidence, 1993)
The Complete Shelter Recordings ♫♫♫ (Gold Rush, 1996)

Jimmy Rogers (© Jack Vartoogian)

worth searching for: Rogers' old bud Freddie King cut him into a deal with Leon Russell, and *Gold Tailed Bird* ♫♫♫ (Shelter, 1971) was the result. Rogers got a good payday, but Shelter went belly-up, which makes all their albums fairly coveted collectables.

influences:

◀◀ Big Bill Broonzy, Robert Junior Lockwood, Joe Willie Wilkens

▶▶ Anson Funderburgh, Ted Morgan, Junior Watson, Derek O'Brien

Tim Schuller

Roy Rogers

Born July 28, 1950, in Redding, CA.

Although originally from the San Francisco Bay Area, Roy Rogers derives his slide guitar sound from Misssissippi Delta blues roots, in the tradition of Earl Hooker and Robert Nighthawk. In addition to pursuing a solo career since the 1970s, Rogers also did some road and studio time with John Lee Hooker in the 1980s and produced four highly successful Hooker albums—*The Healer, Mr. Lucky, Boom Boom* and *Chill Out*. Rogers' music has assumed increasing dimensions of rhythm and blues, country and rock with each successive album, but the frequent covers of Delta and early-Chicago slide masters—Robert Johnson and Elmore James, especially—always serve to reaffirm his deep blues roots.

what to buy: Rogers' ambitious solo debut, *Chops Not Chaps* ♫♫♫♫ (Blind Pig, 1986, prod. Roy Rogers), mixes four original tunes with covers of classics by Robert Johnson, Elmore James and Skip James. *Travellin' Tracks* ♫♫♫ (Blind Pig, 1992, prod. Norton Buffalo, Roy Rogers), recorded with harpist Norton Buffalo, is a country blues mix of live duet recordings with more orchestrated studio tracks.

what to buy next: *Slide Zone* ♫♫♫ (Liberty, 1994, prod. Roy Rogers) is a highly textured recording that includes appearances by harpist Charlie Musselwhite, Windham Hill pianist Philip Aaburg and Euro-folk banjoist Bela Fleck. *Rhythm and Groove* ♫♫♫ (Pointblank, 1996, prod. Roy Rogers) re-employs Musselwhite and Aaburg and incorporates shades of Latin music.

the rest:

Slidewinder ♫♫♫ (Blind Pig, 1988)
Blues on the Range ♫♫♫ (Blind Pig, 1989)
R&B ♫♫♫ (Blind Pig , 1991)
Slide of Hand ♫♫♫ (Liberty, 1993)

worth searching for: *A Foot in the Door* ♫♫♫ (Waterhouse, 1976), recorded with harpist Dave Brugin prior to the launch of Rogers' solo career, gives a clear, early indication of his versatility and virtuosity on guitar.

influences:

◀◀ Earl Hooker, Robert Nighthawk

▶▶ Keb' Mo'

John C. Bruening

Rolling Stones

Formed 1962, in London, England.

Mick Jagger (born Michael Phillip Jagger), vocals, guitar; Keith Richards, guitar, vocals; Brian Jones (born Lewis Brian Hopkins-Jones; died 1969), guitar (1962–69); Bill Wyman (born William Perks), bass (1962–94); Charlie Watts, drums; Mick Taylor, guitar (1969–74); Ronnie Wood, guitar (1974–present); Daryl Jones, bass (1994–present).

In its first decade, the Stones defined the classic rock lineup—two guitars, bass, drums and a little red rooster crowing out front—and created the enduring standard for how it should sound. The Stones never were much for innovation; the group's more experimental tracks and albums sounded instantly contrived and dated. Instead they were expert at synthesis: Chicago blues, hard country music, a bit of Motown (and later, Stax), played with a raw sexuality that freely appropriated from black performers such as James Brown and Tina Turner. They affirmed the primacy of the electric guitar as Richards succeeded Chuck Berry as rock's primary riff-meister. Richards and Jagger (a.k.a. The Glimmer Twins) wrote classic melodies and pithy, unsentimental and frequently just plain cruel lyrics that were the equal of their 1960s rivals Bob Dylan and the Beatles. And the group's rhythm section, anchored by the peerless Watts, made it all swing like nobody's business. Only problem is, the Stones kept the money machine in motion long after their artistic drive waned. Like their blues heroes, the Stones entered their fifties still singing about their overworked mojos and cranking out competent product that bespoke professionalism rather than inspiration.

what to buy: The weakest cuts on *Beggars Banquet* ♫♫♫♫ (Abkco, 1968, prod. Jimmy Miller) are its best known: "Street

Keith Richards of the Rolling Stones (© Ken Settle)

Fighting Man" offers a rare political commentary that is musically stirring but lyrically ambivalent; and "Sympathy for the Devil" finds Jagger pandering to the group's bad-boy image. Otherwise, *Banquet* is a tour de force of acoustic-tinged savagery and slumming sexuality, particularly the gleefully flippant "Stray Cat Blues." *Let It Bleed* ♫♫♫♫ (Abkco, 1969, prod. Jimmy Miller) slams the door on the 1960s with such harrowing anthems as "Gimme Shelter" and "You Can't Always Get What You Want." *Exile on Main Street* ♫♫♫♫♫ (Virgin, 1972, prod. Jimmy Miller) got some bum reviews when first issued for its muddy sound and decadent atmospherics. It's now rightly hailed as a masterpiece, and from the passionate yearning of the gospel-tinged "Let It Loose" to the demon fury of "Rip This Joint," it remains a towering survey of the Stones as they reinvent their influences.

what to buy next: *Aftermath* ♫♫♫♫ (Abkco, 1966, prod. Andrew Loog Oldham) marked the entry of these erstwhile blues traditionalists into the album-rock pantheon alongside Dylan and the Beatles, with its canny use of sitar, marimba and dulcimer (all performed by Brian Jones) to augment Jagger's multifaceted star turn as a vocalist on "Paint It Black," "Lady Jane" and "Under My Thumb." *Big Hits/High Tide and Green Grass* ♫♫♫♫♫ (Abkco, 1966, prod. Andrew Loog Oldham) is an impeccable 12-cut summary of the Stones' pre-*Aftermath* singles; of the hits collections, it's surpassed only by the pricey but worth-it boxed set, *The Singles Collection* ♫♫♫♫♫ (Abkco, 1989, prod. various), which documents the band's first and best decade of music-making. *Sticky Fingers* ♫♫♫♫♫ (Virgin, 1971, prod. Jimmy Miller) has the most famous cover art of any Stones album (Andy Warhol's zippered crotch shot) and—"Brown Sugar" excepted—among the most darkly weary music. But amid the druggy drama, the luminous beauty of "Sway" and "Moonlight Mile" is redemptive. *Some Girls* ♫♫♫♫ (Virgin, 1978, prod. Glimmer Twins) is the last gasp of greatness, with Richards' "Before They Make Me Run" serving as what should have been a fitting epitaph: "See my tail lights fading/Not a dry eye in the house." Those who insist on owning something from the latter-day, Steel Wheelchairs-era Stones should head straight for *Stripped* ♫♫♫ (Virgin, 1995, prod. Don Was, Glimmer Twins), the first live album by the group that isn't superfluous, with its revelatory "unplugged" treatment of several classic tracks compensating for a tepid cover of Dylan's "Like a Rolling Stone."

what to avoid: Before *Stripped*, the Stones released five live albums, all of them stiffs. None offer tracks that improve upon the studio originals, including: *Got Live If You Want It* **woof!**

(Abkco, 1966, prod. Andrew Loog Oldham); the overrated *Get Yer Ya-Ya's Out* ♫♫ (Abkco, 1970, prod. Glyn Johns, Rolling Stones); *Love You Live* **woof!** (Rolling Stones, 1977, prod. Glimmer Twins); *Still Life* **woof!** (Rolling Stones, 1982, prod. Glimmer Twins); and *Flashpoint* **woof!** (Rolling Stones, 1991, prod. Chris Kimsey, Glimmer Twins).

best of the rest:

12 X 5 ♫♫♫♫ (Abkco, 1964)
The Rolling Stones: England's Newest Hit Makers ♫♫♫♫ (Abkco, 1964)
December's Children ♫♫♫♫ (Abkco, 1965)
Out of Our Heads ♫♫♫ (Abkco, 1965)
The Rolling Stones, Now! ♫♫♫♫ (Abkco, 1965)
Between the Buttons ♫♫♫♫ (Abkco, 1967)
Flowers ♫♫♫ (Abkco, 1967)
Through the Past Darkly (Big Hits, Vol. 2) ♫♫♫♫ (Abkco, 1968)
Hot Rocks 1964–71 ♫♫♫♫ (Abkco, 1972)
More Hot Rocks: Big Hits and Fazed Cookies ♫♫♫♫ (Abkco, 1973)
Black and Blue ♫♫♫ (Virgin, 1976)
Sucking in the Seventies ♫♫♫ (Rolling Stones, 1981)
Tattoo You ♫♫♫ (Virgin, 1981)
Voodoo Lounge ♫♫♫ (Virgin, 1994)

worth searching for: *Jump Back: The Best of the Rolling Stones* ♫♫♫♫ (Virgin, 1993, prod. various), a sparkling sounding (20-bit mastered) U.K. compilation spanning 1971–93, with exceptional liner notes, is a great find.

influences:

◀◀ Willie Dixon, Muddy Waters, Chuck Berry, Buddy Holly, Sam Cooke, Beatles

▶▶ New York Dolls, Aerosmith, Guns N' Roses, Black Crowes

Greg Kot

Roomful of Blues

Formed 1968, in RI.

Rich Lataille, alto sax, tenor sax (1970–present); Doug James, baritone sax (1971–present); Bob Enos, trumpet (1981–present); John Rossi, drums (1970–present); Matt McCabe, piano (1993–present); Carl Querfurth, trombone (1978, 1987–present); Ken "Doc" Grace, bass (1992–present); Chris Vachon, guitar (1990–present); Sugar Ray Norcia, vocals, harmonica (1990–present); Duke Robillard, guitar (1968–79); Al Copley, piano (1968–84); Larry Peduzzi, bass (1968–early 1970s, 1990–93); Chuck Riggs, drums (1968); Fran Christina, drums (1968–70); Greg Piccolo, tenor sax, vocals (1970–94); Preston Hubbard, bass (1970s, 1982–84); Jimmy Wimpfheimer, bass (1979–82); Rory MacLeod, bass (1984–86); Ronnie Earl, guitar (1979–88); Tommy K, guitar (1988–90); Danny Motta,

trumpet (1979–81); Porky Cohen, trombone (1979–87); Lou Ann Barton, vocals (1979–80); Curtis Salgado, vocals (1984–86); Ron Levy, piano, organ (1984–88); Jr. Brantley, piano (1988–93); Paul Tomasello, bass (late 1980s); Rhandy Simmons, bass (mid- to late 1980s).

Roomful of Blues is one of the few bands preserving and promoting the horn-based jump blues and swing sounds of the old 1930s and 1940s territory bands. The band members are not historic archivists; for them the music is a living, breathing, swingin' thing. Founded by Duke Robillard, the Roomful concept gelled in 1971 after the guitarist was inspired by classic old swing orchestra recordings to add horns. Despite many line-up changes, a consistent core group, especially the horn section, has remained through most of the band's history. With a focus on live performances, their recordings have been intermittent but consistently excellent. The Roomful horn section, often with drummer Rossi, has been an in-demand unit for other artists' recordings.

what to buy: *Turn It On! Turn It Up!* ✍✍✍✍ (Bullseye Blues/Rounder, 1995, prod. Carl Querfurth) stomps, swaggers and smokes. "I Left My Baby" is a vibrant and gleaming tribute to the swinging Count Basie Orchestra and vocalist Jimmy Rushing, while the title track is a razor sharp original by guitarist Vachon. On *Dressed Up to Get Messed Up* ✍✍✍✍ (Varrick, 1984/Rounder, 1996, prod. Greg Piccolo), Piccolo's vocals exude an in-your-face confidence, swing vet Porky Cohen cooks and Kim Wilson offers low-down lead vocals on "The Last Time." The only in-concert Roomful recording, *Live at Lupo's Heartbreak Hotel* ✍✍✍✍ (Varrick/Rounder, 1987, prod. Greg Piccolo, Doug James, Roomful of Blues), is also the only one to include the extraordinary vocalist and harpist Curtis Salgado on three tracks. Listening to Sugar Ray fronting Roomful on his first CD with the band, *Dance All Night* ✍✍✍✍ (Bullseye Blues/Rounder, 1994, prod. Carl Querfurth), it's hard to believe he wasn't part of the line-up from the start. (He had, in fact, been a long-time fan.) His versatile, emotive vocals and harp are a perfect match for the band's big, rich sound.

what to buy next: Originally released on the Muse label in 1982 and 1983, *Two Classic Albums: Roomful of Blues with Joe Turner/with Eddie "Cleanhead" Vinson* ✍✍✍✍ (32 Blues, 1997, prod. Doc Pomus, Bob Porter, Joel Dorn) is as good as you'd expect from this brilliant pairing. Most of the tracks with Vinson were first or second takes. The selection of material isn't quite as engaging as on *Turn It On! Turn It Up!*, but *Under One Roof*

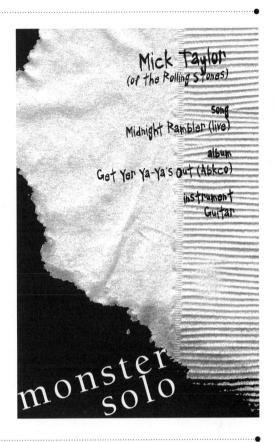

Mick Taylor (of the Rolling Stones)

song
Midnight Rambler (live)

album
Get Yer Ya-Ya's Out (Abkco)

instrument
Guitar

monster solo

✍✍✍✍ (Bullseye Blues/Rounder, 1997, prod. Carl Querfurth) is swingin', rock-solid and in command of a thrilling sound. Despite being its founder and mainstay for 12 years, *First Album* ✍✍✍✍ (32 Blues, 1996, prod. Joel Dorn, Doc Pomus) is the only available Roomful recording with Duke Robillard. A must for hard-core fans.

the rest:

Hot Little Mama ✍✍✍ (Blue Flame, 1981/Varrick/Rounder, 1989)

influences:

◀◀ Eddie "Cleanhead" Vinson, Count Basie, T-Bone Walker, Big Joe Turner, Wynonie Harris, Jimmy Rushing, Big Joe Williams, Jay McShann, Bennie Moten

▶▶ Big Swing, Mighty Blue Kings, Indigo Swing, Big Bad Voodoo Daddy, Royal Crown Revue, Brian Setzer Orchestra

B.J. Huchtemann

Isaiah "Doc" Ross

Born Charles Isaiah Ross, October 21, 1925, in Tunica, MS. Died May 28, 1993, in Flint, MI.

Doc Ross was an anachronism in the era of electric blues. A virtual one-man band, he played harmonica (thus the nickname "the Harmonica Boss"), acoustic guitar (left-handed), bass drum and high-hat. It was less an homage to the itinerant country blues players of his native Mississippi Delta than a necessity—Ross was a harmonica player who added the other instruments for a USO show after he joined the Army during World War II. The "Doctor" was attached to his name because he carried his harmonicas in a doctor's bag. His music was raw and emotive, inspired by the Delta blues of forebears Sonny Boy Williamson I, Robert Johnson and Blind Boy Fuller. After the Army stint, he became a popular fixture in the Memphis area, hosting his own show on WDIA. He claimed to have seen several killings during those days, which is why he swore off clubs later in his life. Ross cut his first sides, including "Chicago Breakdown," for Chess and Sun. He settled in Flint in 1954 and worked as a janitor for General Motors most of his adult life, excepting the occasional tour, before retiring in 1990. He didn't tour much (his first European trek was in 1965) and was known to cancel gigs to watch his beloved Detroit Tigers on television. Ross claimed that Muddy Waters stole "Rollin' Stone" from him, and that Cream lifted his "Cat Squirrel," though he never sought legal compensation. Recognition came late for the enigmatic bluesman, including a 1981 Grammy Award for his *Rare Blues* Takoma album (sadly, like most of his records, now out of print). A resurgence of interest capped his final years, including festival appearances and a live radio broadcast in his adopted home town. A scholarship fund has been established in his name at Flint's Mott Community College.

what to buy: Ross had a sporadic recording career. Even though he started in the early 1950s, he didn't cut his first album until 1965. His unadulterated, cut-to-the-bone style is very much in evidence on *Call the Doctor* ✍✍✍ (Testament, 1965/1995, prod. Pete Welding), from the moaning harmonica breaks to his muffled down-home vocals and wiry acoustic guitar.

worth searching for: Many of Ross' signature tunes, including "Chicago Breakdown," "Good Morning, Little Schoolgirl" and "G.M. Blues," can be found on the hard-to-find British import *I Want All My Friends to Know* ✍✍✍ (JSP, 1993, prod. John Stedman), recorded live at the Burnley Blues Festival in 1991. *Doc Ross in Concert* (Foundation for Mott Community College, 1994) is an independently released video of the Doctor's penultimate performance, a January 1993 concert at the Flint Public Library.

influences:

◀◀ Blind Boy Fuller, Sonny Boy Williamson I, Blind Lemon Jefferson

▶▶ Eric Clapton, John Hammond Jr., Ben Harper

Doug Pullen

Bobby Rush

Born Emmit Ellis Jr., November 10, 1940, in Homer, LA.

Bobby Rush has spent 40 years creating one of the chitlin' circuit's most beloved characters. A great multi-instrumentalist, Rush is one of the hardest-working and talented people in show business. His music, usually classified in record stores as blues, defies description. The charmingly cocky, self-deprecating Rush claims he has developed what he calls "folk-funk," and whatever you call it, his unique sound is an amalgamation of blues, soul and funk grooves that he sprinkles liberally with sexual innuendo and good-natured humor. Rush moved to Chicago with his family in 1953 and began his life as a blues musician as a member of some of the 1960s most prominent West Side blues bands. After drastically changing his style, he made the chitlin' circuit his target market. Rush had his first hit, "Chicken Heads," on Galaxy in 1971, and he scored with "Bow-Legged Woman" for Jewel. Rush worked tirelessly in the 1970s with various labels, closing the decade by teaming with the legendary Kenny Gamble and Leon Huff at Philadelphia International. In the early 1980s Rush developed a long-lived and productive relationship with LaJam. His most recent releases for Waldoxy have allowed Rush deeper penetration into the world's blues markets.

what to buy: *Gotta Have Money* ✍✍✍ (LaJam, 1984, prod. James Bennett) is a cleanly produced, over-the-top, folk-funk extravaganza. Rush struts his stuff on "Buttermilk Kid," "She Caught Me with My Pants Down" and "She's So Fine." "Mojo Boogie," a bizarre take on the J.B. Lenoir number and a highlight of Rush's recording career, is also included. The song might sound out-of-place on *Gotta Have Money*, but it would fit perfectly on his next release, the suggestive *What's Good for the Goose Is Good for the Gander* ✍✍✍✍ (LaJam, 1985, prod. James Bennett), with songs so lascivious that, to this day, even Rush won't touch them live: "Dr. Funk," "Let's Get It On," "Poor Tang" and the classic "Bull Manure." Rush has remained prolific in the mid-1990s; his Waldoxy debut, *One Monkey Don't Stop No Show* ✍✍✍✍ (Waldoxy, 1995, prod. Bobby Rush), is a mature, varied and consistently solid disc, one of the most enjoyable soul blues efforts of this decade.

Rush incorporates each of the artistic styles in which he has worked over the course of his career. There's funk, blues, reggae and humor, but it's more focused. *Sue ♫♫♫* (LaJam, 1982, prod. James Bennett) marked the beginning of Rush's funky, prolific period for LaJam.

what to buy next: *A Man Can Give It, but He Can't Take It ♫♫♫* (LaJam, 1988) followed *What's Good for the Goose Is Good for the Gander* but is tame by comparison. Rush conjures a tasty and casual groove on the highlight, "I Am Tired" before moving to solid, propulsive funk on "Nine Below Zero." In his own way, Rush solidifies his connection to the Delta blues of Sonny Boy Williamson II with the album's closing number, "Playin' Me Crazy." Despite master tape anomalies and tinny harshness, the fairly comprehensive *It's Alright ♫♫♫* (Jewel/Paula/Ronn, 1995, prod. Bobby Rush) documents Rush's 1970s work for Jewel. Highlights include "Get It on with Me," "Bow-Legged Woman, Knock-Kneed Man—Part 1," "Niki Hoeky," and Rush's rare straight-blues presentation of "Dust My Broom/Baby What You Want Me to Do." *Rush Hour ♫♫♫* (Philadelphia International, 1979, prod. Leon Huff) includes the Gamble and Huff collaboration; a highlight is "Evil Is," a great song Rush still presents live.

the rest:

Wearing It Out ♫♫♫ (LaJam, 1983)
I Ain't Studdin' You ♫♫♫ (Urgent/Ichiban, 1991)
Handy Man ♫♫♫ (Urgent/Ichiban, 1992)
Instant Replays: The Hits ♫♫♫ (Urgent/Ichiban, 1992)
Lovin' a Big Fat Woman ♫♫♫ (Waldoxy, 1997)

influences:

◄◄ Sonny Boy Williamson II, Muddy Waters, J.B. Lenoir, Howlin' Wolf, Redd Foxx

►► Vance Kelly

Steven Sharp

Otis Rush

Born April 29, 1934, in Philadelphia, MS.

Otis Rush is arguably the greatest living bluesman, with only John Lee Hooker and B.B. King at his level as distinctive and innovative stylists both on guitar and vocally. Hooker and King have had long, continuously productive recording careers, however, whereas Rush's discography is shockingly thin (and erratic) for a blues legend in his mid-sixties. From 1956–58, his string of truly great singles for Cobra, a Chicago blues label, revealed an amazingly expressive, intense electric guitarist and powerful singer. Playing lefthanded and upside down, with a distinctive

picking style, Rush sounded—and still sounds—utterly unique. Those sides—"I Can't Quit You Baby," "All Your Love (I Miss Loving)" and others—not only formed, with the contemporaneous work of Magic Sam and Buddy Guy, the basis of the West Side style of Chicago blues, but also inspired several generations of guitarists to favor Fender Stratocasters and cover tunes associated with Rush (Led Zeppelin and Eric Clapton played Rush songs, and Stevie Ray Vaughan named his band Double Trouble after a Cobra title). His slow minor blues started a much-imitated trend, and his band was the first to use electric bass.

Growing up in the country in Mississippi, Rush had sung in church choirs and played guitar casually, but had learned mostly from his two older brothers and from records, lacking access to a live scene. When he moved to Chicago in 1948 at age 14, he started listening to more blues records, mostly the Delta performers popular in Chicago's largely transplanted black community. Within a few years he was playing covers of such material in small clubs, but the influences of more guitar-solo-oriented performers—the epitome of whom was B.B. King—began to influence his thinking, and he also took lessons from a local jazz session guitarist, Reggie Boyd, and learned from Kenny Burrell and George Benson records. The West Side style, so-called because its practitioners played in clubs in the western part of Chicago, was built of these materials, and it was from those clubs that Cobra owner Eli Toscano drew his talent. But Toscano was a gambler, and after he lost all his money (which included money owed to his artists), Cobra went out of business and Toscano died mysteriously (if, considering whom he owed his debts to, unsurprisingly). Subsequently, circumstances were less kind to Rush himself than to his legacy. He joined his Cobra producer, Willie Dixon (who had written much of Rush's material), at Chess for two years but had only one single released ("So Many Roads, So Many Trains"); moving to Duke for five years, he again put out only one single (1962's "Homework"). Rush's fortunes changed somewhat after he recorded five songs for Vanguard's *Chicago/The Blues/Today!* series in 1966, as that helped expose him to the burgeoning white audience for the blues. But when Rush finally got to record some albums, the results were disastrous. His first album, recorded for a subsidiary of Atlantic Records, was a totally botched production by two white blues scene admirers (Paul Butterfield guitarist Mike Bloomfield and Electric Flag vocalist/keyboardist Nick Gravenites). His second album had no such production problems, but for some reason (perhaps poor sales of other blues titles on the label) Capitol refused to release *Right Place, Wrong Time* after having put a lot of money into it, granting its title a hideous irony. Rush was finally able to buy back the tapes five years later and release it on an indie label. At one point he was semi-retired, playing occasional gigs to pay the rent but mostly, he says, shooting pool. He fortunately found a sympathetic label, Delmark (in conjuction with the Japanese label Trio), for a few albums, while also recording for European labels. In yet another bizarre development, when Alligator reissued the 1977 Sonet album *Troubles, Troubles*, retitling it *Lost in the Blues*, Lucky Peterson was brought in to overdub organ and piano, much to Rush's disdain. Some of his guitar solos were even edited out. Rush's suspicion of record companies, however justified, has clearly interfered with his productivity; he even blew off a session that Rooster Blues had set up, with many top sidemen hired, because he didn't like his amplifier. Perhaps as a result, most of his albums since then have been live recordings, but finally, more than two decades after *Right Place, Wrong Time*, he received another major-label studio production of equal care and love thanks to John Porter, and this time it came out right away. It also marked his return to using the solid-body Strat after a long period of favoring a bright red hollowbody Gibson Epiphone. But whatever momentum he might have gathered from the Mercury album was lost to the nebulous career malady "personal problems," though now he's been signed to the new House of Blues label and may once again revive his career. Though Rush has often been an erratic performer, at his peak he remains capable of vocals packing stunning emotional intensity and highly individual guitar solos of shocking impact and originality.

what to buy: Rush's Cobra material is required for every blues and R&B lover's collection. At the moment there are two main options. *1956–58 Cobra Recordings* 𝄞𝄞𝄞𝄞 (Paula, 1991, prod. various) has all the Cobra material—16 songs and four alternate takes. "I Can't Quit You Baby," "Groaning the Blues," "Double Trouble" and "All Your Love (I Miss Loving)" have to be heard to be believed; that some of the Willie Dixon-penned songs are trivial doesn't matter a bit once Rush unleashes his guitar fury on them. *The Cobra Records Story: Chicago Rock and Blues 1957–58* 𝄞𝄞𝄞𝄞𝄞 (Capricorn, 1993, prod. various) is a two-CD set with not only all the Rush tracks but also a healthy sampling of Cobra's other singles, including everyone from Sunnyland Slim, Magic Sam and Buddy Guy to Harold Burrage, Betty Everett and Ike Turner's Kings of Rhythm (Turner also plays, magnificently, with Rush on "Double Trouble"). The enclosed booklet (which includes Rush's memories of the period) is well-done, and those interested in Chicago blues can have

not only the crucial Rush sides but also a fine cross-section of the milieu in which he was operating. *Right Place, Wrong Time* 𝄞𝄞𝄞𝄞 (Bullfrog/HighTone, 1976, prod. Nick Gravenites, Otis Rush) has plenty of intense slow blues tracks, always Rush's most reliably awe-inspiring material, but also sounds good on the soul and uptempo numbers, which are so often his downfall. Production-wise, the guitar and vocals are recorded and mixed well, and Rush sings and plays as though his life depends on it.

what to buy next: *So Many Roads* 𝄞𝄞𝄞𝄞 (Delmark, 1978, prod. Steve Tomashefsky) is his best live recording and offers an unbeatable combination of classic songs in a stretched-out format allowing maximum expression of his guitar prowess. *Ain't Enough Comin' In* 𝄞𝄞𝄞𝄞 (This Way Up/Mercury, 1994, prod. John Porter) has the best sound of any Rush album. The production is elaborate without being busy or distracting from Rush's generally excellent performance, and rock fans will note that Billy Payne of Little Feat and Ian McLagan of the Rolling Stones add spicy piano and organ. The album lacks only the manic edge that Rush sometimes summons, but he's hardly coasting.

what to avoid: Don't be tempted by a personnel list that includes Duane Allman (strictly rhythm guitar) and Jerry Jemmott (bass); *Mourning in the Morning* 𝄞𝄞 (Cotillion/Atlantic, 1969, prod. Mike Bloomfield, Nick Gravenites) is a production nightmare, with Rush's vocals (poorly recorded) and guitar buried under overdubbed horns, female backing vocals and lots of other bad ideas, including tacky electric piano.

the rest:
Cold Day in Hell 𝄞𝄞𝄞 (Delmark, 1975)
Screamin' and Cryin' 𝄞𝄞𝄞𝄞 (Disques Black and Blue, 1975/Evidence, 1992)
Tops 𝄞𝄞𝄞𝄞 (Blind Pig, 1988)
Lost in the Blues 𝄞𝄞𝄞𝄞 (Alligator, 1991)
Live in Europe 𝄞𝄞𝄞𝄞 (Evidence, 1993)
Blues Interaction: Live in Japan with Break Down 1986 𝄞𝄞 (Castle, 1996)

worth searching for: Rush has five tracks on *Chicago/The Blues/Today! Vol. 2* 𝄞𝄞𝄞 (Vanguard, 1966, prod. Sam Charters), with James Cotton and Homesick James filling out the other two-thirds of the album.

influences:

◀◀ John Lee Hooker, Muddy Waters, T-Bone Walker, B.B. King, Kenny Burrell

▶▶ Bobby "Blue" Bland, Eric Clapton, Rolling Stones, Jimi Hen-

Otis Rush (© Linda Vartoogian)

drix, Led Zeppelin, Duane Allman, Mike Bloomfield, Lurrie Bell, Stevie Ray Vaughan

Steve Holtje

Jimmy Rushing

Born August 26, 1903, in Oklahoma City, OK. Died June 8, 1972, in New York, NY.

Jimmy Rushing was not only the singer and primary frontman of Count Basie's orchestra but the glue that held the band together in rough times. (It was big glue, too: Rushing was known as "Mr. Five by Five" for his intimidating physique.) From 1935 to 1950 Rushing sang on Basie swing classics like "Boogie-Woogie," "Evenin'" and even "Did You See Jackie Robinson Hit That Ball." As a teenager, he lived the prototypical bluesman's life, hoboing through the Midwest and singing at occasional parties and churches. He wound up in California and quickly started making connections: Jelly Roll Morton em-

ployed him as a singer; Walter Page's Blue Devils, the famous Kansas City band of the late 1920s, made him its vocalist; and he toured with Bennie Moten's Kansas City Orchestra. He met Basie in 1936 and frequently sang duets with Billie Holiday. The orchestra disbanded in 1950, and Rushing just couldn't stay retired; he wound up working with Dave Brubeck, Earl Hines and other sidemen and made small acting appearances in several movies. He and Basie reunited just once—at the 1957 Newport Jazz Festival—but after 1950 neither performer was able to recreate the old orchestra's success.

what to buy: Though the most essential Rushing collection will extensively sample the singer's years with the Count Basie Orchestra, *The Essential Jimmy Rushing* ♪♪♪♪ (Vanguard, 1978) is a fine document of Rushing's mid-1950s solo material. He recreates a number of Basie standards, including "Going to Chicago," often with old Basie friends and sidemen.

what to buy next: Filled with late material, *The You and Me That Used to Be* ♪♪♪ (RCA/Bluebird, 1971/1988) is more slick and pop-oriented and doesn't have quite the same sparkle as the mid-1950s stuff. Still, Rushing's booming voice is nice to hear in many different contexts.

the rest:

Dave Brubeck and Jimmy Rushing 𝅘𝅥𝅘𝅥𝅘𝅥 (Columbia, 1960)
Gee, Baby, Ain't I Good to You 𝅘𝅥𝅘𝅥𝅗𝅥 (Master Jazz, 1968)
Mister Five by Five 𝅘𝅥𝅘𝅥𝅘𝅥 (Columbia, 1980)

influences:

◀◀ Count Basie, Duke Ellington, Louis Armstrong, Billie Holiday, Bessie Smith

▶▶ Jimmy Witherspoon, Big Joe Turner, Charlie Parker, Louis Jordan, Dinah Washington

Steve Knopper

Saffire—
The Uppity Blues Women

Formed 1988, in Fredericksburg, VA.

Ann Rabson, vocals, piano; Gaye Adegbalola, vocals, guitar; Earlene Lewis, vocals, bass (1989–92); Andra Faye McIntosh, vocals, bass (1994–present).

With a great sense of humor and a refreshingly playful approach to classic boogie-woogie blues, these southern women have slowly built their classy nightclub act into a significant recording career. Their album covers might initially make them look like low-key mothers and grandmothers. But upon listening to innuendo-laced songs like "Two in the Bush Is Better Than One in the Hand" and lyrics like "I need a young, young man to drive away my middle age blues," you begin to notice the sly winks in their eyes. Saffire is almost as obsessed with sex as the 2 Live Crew's Luther Campbell (not to mention Bessie Smith and John Lee Hooker), only they sing about it with such creativity and subtlety they can make listeners do double-takes. Rabson's knowledge of blues history and the ability to borrow riffs from such legends as Sunnyland Slim and Jimmy Yancey is at least as developed as Taj Mahal's. Plus they're terrific players—Rabson's blues-guitar career lasted in nightclubs for 20 years (with an office job by day) before she formed the band. Adegbalola, a biochemist

and teacher, took guitar lessons from Rabson before they performed together for the first time at a Fredericksburg Unitarian Fellowship hall.

what to buy: The band's debut, *Saffire—The Uppity Blues Women* 𝅘𝅥𝅘𝅥𝅘𝅥 (Alligator, 1990, prod. Saffire, Bruce Iglauer), was a fresh alternative to the flashy guitarists and macho men dominating the blues industry; it also contains some of their best writing, and earned Adegbalola a W.C. Handy award for "Middle Aged Blues."

what to buy next: Though *Broadcasting* 𝅘𝅥𝅘𝅥𝅘𝅥 (Alligator, 1992, prod. Saffire, Bruce Iglauer) relies on guest musicians to cover for the departed Lewis, the album showcases Rabson and Adegbalola in a warmer, more give-and-take context.

what to avoid: Rabson's solo debut, *Music Makin' Mama* 𝅘𝅥𝅘𝅥𝅗𝅥 (Alligator, 1997, prod. Ann Rabson, Bruce Iglauer) is solid because of Rabson's always-impeccable piano playing, but it lacks the devilish glee Adegbalola brought to the table and leans on more conventional blues sidemen Bob Margolin and Cephas & Wiggins.

the rest:

Hot Flash 𝅘𝅥𝅘𝅥𝅘𝅥 (Alligator, 1991)
Old, New, Borrowed and Blue 𝅘𝅥𝅘𝅥𝅗𝅥 (Alligator, 1994)
Cleaning House 𝅘𝅥𝅘𝅥𝅗𝅥 (Alligator, 1996)

influences:

◀◀ Ray Charles, Bessie Smith, Mose Allison Jr., Jimmy Yancey, Sunnyland Slim, Willie Dixon, Billie Holiday, Hadda Brooks, Charles Brown, Dr. John

▶▶ Keb' Mo', Cephas & Wiggins, Rory Block

Steve Knopper

Doug Sahm

Born November 6, 1941, in San Antonio, TX.

A guitar prodigy—he was placed on Hank Williams Sr.'s lap just before the country legend died—Doug Sahm has spent his life onstage, beginning his career as Little Doug Sahm at age six. In 1964, after moving to California and recruiting keyboardist Augie Meyers, Sahm started the Sir Douglas Quintet. Though the music of their first big single, "She's about a Mover," produced by Cajun wildman Huey Meaux, was a mixed bag of border conjunto and San Francisco psychedelia (especially Meyer's primal organ licks), their long hair and quasi-royal name had many thinking they were from England! The band had one more hit, 1969's "Mendocino," before Sahm began a fascinating, checkered solo career that has included recordings with Bob Dylan, Dr. John, Flaco Jimenez, David "Fathead" Newman, Yusef Lateef and most recently with Freddy Fender, Jimenez and Meyer as the Texas Tornados. Sahm's wry blend of blues, country, conjunto, soul and horn-based R&B has grown even better with age, and he remains an understated master of stringed instruments. In whatever incarnation, Sahm represents Texas music at its finest.

what to buy: Two recent solo albums capture the heady ambience of Sahm's bluesy side. *Juke Box Music* &&&&" (Antone's, 1988, prod. Doug Sahm) offers a danceable set of pure Texas soul, including Sahm's unforgettably tasty cover of Little Sunny's "Talk to Me." *The Last Real Texas Blues Band* &&&&" (Antone's, 1994, prod. Doug Sahm, Derek O'Brien) forms a perfect bookend, reprising the R&B of the big horn bands that Sahm chewed on in San Antonio in the 1950s, recorded very live with a fine big band.

what to avoid: *Daydreaming at Midnight* && (Elektra, 1994, prod. Doug Sahm, Doug Clifford), a heavy-metal version of the Quintet with Sahm's son Shawn on second guitar.

the rest:
Live &&& (Bear Family, 1988)
Amos Garrett, Doug Sahm, Gene Taylor &&& (Ryko, 1989)
Best of Doug Sahm and the Sir Douglas Quintet &&&& (Mercury, 1990)
Best of Doug Sahm and Friends: Atlantic Sessions &&&" (Rhino, 1992)

worth searching for: You can't go wrong with most of the Quintet's long-out-of-print vinyl albums, especially *Honkey Blues* &&&& (Smash, 1968), *Mendocino* &&&& (Smash, 1969) or *1+1+1=4* &&&&" (Philips, 1970). Back then they sounded like they came from a planet somewhere near Texas and Mars. Today they sound better. The exceptional *Border Wave* &&&& (Takoma, 1981) gathers some of the old Quintet back. Another period piece worth seeking out is *Groover's Paradise* &&&& (Warner Bros., 1974), a hilarious, stoned Tex-Mex trip through the mid-1970s.

influences:
◀◀ Hank Williams, Freddy Fender, Santiago Jimenez Sr., Little Sunny & the Skyliners, T-Bone Walker, Junior Parker, Bobby "Blue" Bland, Howlin' Wolf, Jimmy Reed

▶▶ Sam the Sham & the Pharoahs, ? & the Mysterians, Mouse & the Traps, Joe "King" Carrasco & the Crowns, Elvis Costello & the Attractions, Uncle Tupelo, Wilco, Son Volt

Leland Rucker

Curtis Salgado

Born February 4, 1954, in Everett, WA.

With his limited discography, Curtis Salgado could be one of the most over-looked of contemporary blues artists, and he certainly deserves a bigger niche in blues history than the customary footnote he gets as the man who introduced John Belushi to the blues and inspired the Blues Brothers' shtick. Salgado's broad vocal range and aching emotional depth mix and match stylistic influences from old blues to R&B, soul and gospel, and he's a harp player with dazzling technique and extraordinary soulfulness. Salgado was the lead singer/harp man for the Robert Cray Band from 1976 to 1982, fronted Roomful of Blues from 1984 to 1986 and continues to be an active force on the Pacific Northwest blues scene.

what to buy: *Hit It 'N Quit It* &&&& (Lucky, 1996, prod. Curtis Salgado, Terry Robb), a mix of classic blues tunes and traditional originals done in one or two takes, documents the long-standing collaboration between Salgado and guitarist Terry Robb. *More Than You Can Chew* &&&& (Rhythm Safari Records/Priority, 1995, prod. Marlon McClain) offers a good mix of what Salgado calls "Pentecostal Delta Funk Punk" or "Sly Stone meets Muddy Waters."

worth searching for: Unfortunately, *Curtis Salgado & the Stilettos* &&&& (JRS/BFE, 1991), Salgado's first, very fine, full-length recording, is currently hard to locate. The Robert Cray Band's *Who's Been Talkin'* &&& (Atlantic, 1978), includes a limited record (4 tracks) of Salgado's contributions.

influences:
◀◀ Little Walter, Howlin' Wolf, Muddy Waters, James Brown, George Clinton, Sly Stone, O.V. Wright, Prince

▶▶ Gary Primich, Brian Templeton

B.J. Huchtemann

Satan & Adam

Formed 1986, in Harlem, NY.

Sterling McGee (born May 20, 1936, in Mount Olive, MS), guitar, vocals; Adam Gussow (born April 13, 1958, in New York, NY), harmonica, vocals.

No contemporary blues duo is more street savvy than Satan and Adam. That's because for five years the pair plied their trade as street musicians at 7th Avenue and 125th Street in Harlem, playing their gritty brand of funkified urban blues for passersby on their way home from work. Mr. Satan, as virtual one-man-band and former session musician Sterling McGee prefers to be called, plays nimble-fingered guitar and thumps a jury-rigged trap set while singing in a gravelly roar. The Ivy-League educated Adam, who once played harmonica in a national touring company of *Big River* and busked his way across Europe, affords a foil for Satan's stripped-down sound, filling it out and occasionally driving their more frenzied jams to heights of ecstasy. When rock superstars U2 were canvassing America to find its musical soul, they stopped by Satan & Adam's corner to soak up some blues, an encounter captured in their film/attempted hagiography *Rattle & Hum.*

what to buy: Alas, over the course of three albums, Satan and Adam have grown progressively slick—although with them that's a relative term—making their debut, *Harlem Blues* ♫♫♫♫ (Flying Fish, 1991, prod. Rachel Faro), their rawest and also their best. A joyous, foot-stomping street-corner throwdown, McGee and Gussow mix covers such as "C.C. Rider" and Duke Ellington's "Don't Get around Much Anymore" with originals such as "I Want You" and "Sunshine in the Shade" that sound like they come straight from the Delta—the East River Delta, that is.

the rest:

Mother Mojo ♫♫♫ (Flying Fish, 1993)
Living on the River ♫♫♫ (Rave On, 1996)

influences:

◄◄ Robert Johnson, James Brown, Sonny Terry & Brownie McGhee

Daniel Durchholz

Savoy Brown

Formed 1966, in London, England.

Kim Simmonds (born December 5, 1947, in Wales, Great Britain), guitar, vocals; Bryce Portius, vocals (1966–68); Martin Stone, guitar (1966–68); Ray Chappell, bass (1966–68): Leo Mannings, drums (1966–68); Bob Hall, keyboards (1966–70); Chris Youlden, vocals (1968–70); Lonesome Dave Peverett, guitar, vocals (1968–70); Rivers Job, bass (1968); Tone Stevens, bass (1968–70); Roger Earl, drums (1968–70); Dave Walker, vocals (1971–72, 1988–90); Paul Raymond, keyboards (1971–74); Andy Pyle, bass (1971, 1972–74); Andy Sylvester, bass (1971–72); Dave Bidwell, drums (1971–72); Jackie Lynton, vocals (1972–74); Ron Berg, drums (1972–74); Stan Webb, guitar, vocals (1974); Miller Anderson, guitar, vocals (1974); Jimmy Leverton, bass (1974); Eric Dillon, drums (1974); Andy Rae, bass, vocals (1975); Ian Ellis, bass, vocals (1976–78); Tom Farnell, drums (1975–78); Jim

Dagnesi, bass (1988–89); Al Macomber, drums (1988–89); Rick Jewett, keyboards, vocals (1990); Lou Kaplan, bass, vocals (1990); Pete Mendillo, drums (1990); Pete McMahon, vocals, harmonica (1994–95); Jim Heyl, bass (1994–96); Dave Olson, drums (1994–95); Nathaniel, bass, vocals (1996–present).

Kim Simmonds might just be the Rodney Dangerfield of the blues world. It's not that there's anything comedic about his music, but who could blame him for pulling nervously at the neck of his guitar and complaining that he gets "no respect." Simmonds is no whiner, but the fact is he's been dealt with dismissively, if at all, in blues guides, and frequently has fared only marginally better in rock guides, this despite his having stayed relatively true to his (admittedly imported) blues roots through a career that has spanned 30-plus years and more than 20 albums. He keeps the Savoy Brown logo active, continuing to make new music, while pleasing old fans through regular touring on the club circuit. At its inception, Savoy Brown was part of an important if imitative British blues movment that helped popularize blues in America by introducing the music in an acceptable boogie and rock fusion setting. Always more pleasing to American than British audiences, Savoy Brown first appeared in 1966 with the long out-of-print *Shake Down.* In a move that signalled a career pattern of constantly changing line-ups, Simmonds was soon found playing with a whole new group of musicians. Lacking a particularly strong voice, Simmonds usually opted to front the vocals to someone more capable. During Savoy's salad days in the late 1960s, Simmonds found two truly exceptional vocalists in Chris Youlden and Dave Peverett.

what to buy: In a six-month period in 1970 the band released two outstanding albums. *Raw Sienna* ♫♫♫♫ (Deram, 1970, prod. Kim Simmonds, Chris Youlden) features Youlden's world-weary, sometimes anguished, always satisfying croak and a full horn section that gives it a hard-edged R&B feel. *Looking In* ♫♫♫♫ (Deram, 1970, prod. Kim Simmonds) is a more stripped-down, hard-rocking affair with Peverett rising to the occasion. *The Savoy Brown Collection* ♫♫♫♫ (Deram/Chronicles, 1993, prod. various) is a well-chosen, nicely-annotated, chronologically-arranged two-disc overview that starts at the earliest days of the band and ends two-and-a-half hours later with material recorded in the late 1970s, including more than a half-hour of material from *Raw Sienna* and *Lookin' In*. A return to roots, *Bring It Home* ♫♫♫♫ (Viceroy, 1995, prod. Kim Simmonds) is straight-ahead rocking blues.

what to buy next: *Getting to the Point* ♫♫♫ (Deram, 1968, prod. Mike Vernon), *Blue Matter* ♫♫♫♫ (Deram, 1968, prod. Mike Vernon) and *A Step Further* ♫♫♫♫ (Deram, 1969, prod.

Mike Vernon), Savoy's second, third and fourth albums respectively, are all worthwhile, showing a band gaining in skill and confidence and developing the group voice that came to fruition on *Raw Sienna* and *Lookin' In*. *Street Corner Talking* ♫♫♫ (Deram, 1971, prod. Neil Slaven) seems a boogie-based step in the direction of commerciality and mainstream acceptance with some memorable original songs like "Tell Mama," and "All I Can Do (Is Cry)."

what to avoid: In the late 1980s, Simmonds reunited with Walker. The two resulting studio efforts, *Make Me Sweat* **woof!** (GNP Crescendo, 1988) and *Kings of Boogies* **woof!** (GNP Crescendo, 1989) have a high boogie-bombast quotient, hoarsely brayed vocal histrionics by Walker and period arena rock trappings like the annoying and pointless synthesizer washes on the latter.

the rest:

Hellbound Train ♫♫♫ (Deram, 1972)
Lion's Share ♫♫♫ (Deram, 1972)
Jack the Toad ♫♫♫ (Deram, 1973)
Live and Kickin' ♫♫♪ (GNP Crescendo, 1990)

worth searching for: One of the biggest reasons for Simmonds' longevity has been his willingness to tour and perform live. Thus, it's fitting that there are several live albums worth hearing. The concert recorded for *Live in Central Park* ♫♫♫♪ (Relix, 1989) was voted the best of New York's 1972 summer concert series by the *Village Voice*, and mostly features material from *Street Corner Talking* and *Lion's Share*. *Slow Train* ♫♫♫ (Relix, 1987), an all-acoustic set, includes solo studio recordings by Simmonds and several live numbers recorded with harmonica and bass backing in 1986 at New York City's Lone Star Cafe.

solo outings:
Kim Simmonds:
Solitaire ♫♫♫ (Blue Wave, 1997)

influences:

◄◄ Freddie King, Howlin' Wolf, Hubert Sumlin, Willie Dixon, Earl King, Eric Clapton, Peter Green

►► Foghat, Allman Brothers Band, Cactus, George Thorogood & the Destroyers

Michael Dixon

Boz Scaggs

Born June 8, 1944, in OH.

The cool, urbane sounds of Boz Scaggs' brand of white soul were more than just the soundtrack to singles bars of the

Kim Simmonds (of Savoy Brown)

song
Louisiana Blues

album
Blue Matter (Deram)

instrument
Guitar

monster solo

1970s. His R&B blood runs a tad deeper. Prior to his emergence as a sophisticated soulful crooner, he was Steve Miller's cohort in a Dallas prep school during the late 1950s. After their shared college years in Wisconsin, they made some blues-based R&B, culminating in Scaggs' appearances on the first two Steve Miller albums. Fueled to go the solo route, Scaggs' debut was earthy blues with some stellar slide guitar from the late Duane Allman. Gradually eschewing rockers for ballads while picking up top Los Angeles studio pros along the way, he created the slick adult soul that hit its peak with *Silk Degrees*. That urban pop became a five-million seller and set the course for all his later recordings, although he has never reached that level of success since. Recently he's spent more time nurturing his Bay Area club, Slim's, than as a recording artist, although he records sporadically.

what to buy: *Silk Degrees* ♫♫♫♫ (Columbia, 1976, prod. Joe Wissert) represents an obvious creative and commercial peak, with the laid-back, cool elegance of "Lowdown" and the chugging "Lido Shuffle," both FM staples. *Boz Scaggs* ♫♫♫ (Atlantic, 1969/1988, prod. Jann Wenner, Marlin Greene) is highlighted by the Muscle Shoals house band, which provides hot backing on his rootsy debut, and also a fiery Duane Allman tearing up "Loan Me a Dime."

what to buy next: For latter-day Scaggs, *Some Change* ♫♫♫ (Virgin, 1994, prod. Boz Scaggs, Ricky Fataar) is a sincere comeback that has a down-home comfort. Scaggs sounds assured and inspired, and Booker T. Jones on the organ doesn't hurt either.

what to avoid: His first release after an eight-year hiatus, *Other Roads* ♫♫ (Columbia, 1988, prod. Bill Schnee, Stewart Levine) is so anti-climactic, it makes you wonder if he shouldn't stick to running his restaurant. Scaggs' voice is in fine form, but the material is unchallenging, and the wimp-chops of backing band Toto squash out any remaining life.

the rest:

Slow Dancer ♫♫♫ (Columbia, 1974)
Down Two Then Left ♫♫♫ (Columbia, 1977)
Hits ♫♫♫ (Columbia, 1980)
Come on Home ♫♫♫ (Virgin, 1997)

worth searching for: *My Time* ♫♫♫ (Columbia, 1972) has the last of the rockers, "Full-Lock Power Slide" and "Dinah Flo." Pretty charged-up stuff, considering what the next 20 years would hold.

influences:

◄◄ Lou Rawls, Dan Penn, Steve Miller Band

►► Phil Collins, Huey Lewis & the News, Michael Bolton

Allan Orski

Buddy Scott

Born Kenneth Scott, January 9, 1935, in Jackson, MS. Died February 1994, in Chicago, IL.

Many of today's prominent South Side musicians—Vance Kelly, Gloria Thompson Rogers, Melviena Allen—call Buddy Scott their musical godfather. Scott, whose mother was guitarist Ida Scott, became a mentor to many budding musicians in Chicago right up to the time of his death from cancer. Scott served as a session man from the 1950s through the 1970s, doubling on guitar and bass for Syl and Jimmy Johnson, McKinley Mitchell, Lee Shot Williams and others. He also backed Muddy Waters and Howlin' Wolf. After a series of singles for Biscayne, PM,

I.C.T. and Capri, Scott gained international notoriety in the early 1980s when Alligator included four tracks from Scott and his band, the Rib Tips, on its *Living Chicago Blues* series. Scott was heard from again in 1993, when Verve released what would be his final work.

what to buy: Scott demonstrates his versatility as a performer on the four tracks he recorded for *Living Chicago Blues, Vol. III* ♫♫♫♫ (Alligator, 1991, prod. Bruce Iglauer), delivering fine renditions of "Big Leg Woman," "Careless with Our Love," "Road Block" and "Poison Ivy." Also included in this lengthy survey of then somewhat obscure Chicago talent are A.C. Reed & the Spark Plugs, Lovie Lee, Lacy Gibson and the Sons of Blues. On the full-length *Bad Avenue* ♫♫♫ (Verve, 1993, prod. Jay Newland, Joe Lopes, Suzy Fink) Scott's T-Bone Walker-influenced guitar still stings, and his vocals remain strong.

influences:

◄◄ Ida Scott, T-Bone Walker, Charlie Parker, Kenny Burrell, Phil Upchurch

►► Vance Kelly, Gloria Thompson Rogers, Kenneth "Hollywood" Scott

Steven Sharp

Son Seals

Born August 13, 1942, in Osceola, AR.

Frank "Son" Seals was literally born into the blues. His father Jim owned the Dipsy Doodle club, an Osceola roadhouse which featured Albert King and Sonny Boy Williamson. By age 13, he was playing drums behind Delta great Robert Nighthawk, among others, displaying a rhythmic drive which informed his music when he picked up a guitar and became a front man. Though both his guitar playing and singing have a somewhat limited range, Seals isn't afraid to play around with different grooves and settings, and everything he touches smolders with a slow burn. For more than 20 years, he has been one of Chicago's leading contemporary lights, consistently performing with a gritty intensity and deeply rooted sense of groove and fronting tough, hard-driving outfits while brooking nary a wasted note.

what to buy: *Live and Burning* ♫♫♫♫ (Alligator, 1978, prod. Son Seals, Bruce Iglauer, Richard McCleese) is not only Son's best work, but a modern Chicago classic. *Live: Spontaneous Com-*

Son Seals (© Jack Vartoogian)

bustion ♫♫♫♫ (Alligator, 1996, prod. Son Seals, Bruce Iglauer) shows that nearly 20 years later, Seals has lost none of his fire while gaining a little more breadth and versatility, working out some of the funk grooves which first began to surface on the excellent *Chicago Fire* ♫♫♫♫ (Alligator, 1980, prod. Son Seals, Bruce Iglauer).

what to avoid: Seals is a master of consistency. *Nothing but the Truth* ♫♫♫ (Alligator, 1994, prod. Son Seals, Bruce Iglauer) is the only album where he lacks his usual intensity and at times seems to be going through the motions.

the rest:

The Son Seals Blues Band ♫♫♫ (Alligator, 1973)
Midnight Son ♫♫♫♫ (Alligator, 1976)
Bad Axe ♫♫♫♫ (Alligator, 1984)
Living in the Danger Zone ♫♫♫ (Alligator, 1991)

influences:

◀◀ Albert King, Robert Nighthawk, Otis Rush

▶▶ Kinsey Report, Michael Coleman, Kenny Neal

Alan Paul

Mem Shannon

Born December 21, 1959, in New Orleans, LA.

"If my luck ever changes, I'm gonna quit this cab business someday," vows New Orleans taxi driver and part-time blues-man Shannon on "Taxicab Driver," a cut on his debut album. And what do you know? Circumstances have smiled on Shannon enough to allow that particular dream to come true. With the release of his second disc, Shannon hung up his beaded seat cover and hit the road in a much broader sense than ever before. But he should be thankful for those 15 years of hack driving. The stories he's heard, the people he's met and the perspective on life he's gained from experience inform nearly every song he has written. Though he's from New Orleans, Shannon avoids the standard Crescent City Chamber of Commerce BS for a plainspoken, working-class version of the blues that is unspectacular but full of the truth and humor of every-day life. His baritone voice is warm, and his guitar playing, though occasionally flashy, takes a back seat to his songwriting. Altogether, Shannon's is a low-key approach to the blues that's too often overlooked in favor of shouters and guitar he-roes who are talking loud and saying nothing.

what to buy: Shannon's debut, *A Cab Driver's Blues* ♫♫♫♫ (Han-nibal, 1995, prod. Mark Bingham) is full of wit and wisdom, the kind that only can come from facing down hard times and per-severing. "Play the Guitar Son" is perhaps the first recollection a musician has had of his father in which he is advised to be-come a musician, not get a real job. "My Baby's Been Watching TV" is a hilarious set of anecdotes about dealing with his woman, who tries everything she's seen on the daytime talk shows. What makes the album really special, though, is the in-clusion of real conversations with passengers Shannon surrep-titiously recorded in his cab. They feature horny businessmen, prostitutes, drunk rowdies and others. They're as funny, as tragic, and as real as Shannon's music.

the rest:

2nd Blues Album ♫♫♫ (Hannibal, 1997)

influences:

◀◀ B.B. King, Walter "Wolfman" Washington, Snooks Eaglin

Daniel Durchholz

Eddie Shaw

Born March 20, 1937, in Stringtown, MS.

With more than 40 years of heavy horn honking behind him, Eddie Shaw is one of the most renowned saxophonists in blues. By the mid-1950s, the teenaged hornsman was already a favorite on the southern circuit, regularly backing Little Milton, Ike Turner and other blues icons. Equally competent with every-thing from swing to blues to rock 'n' roll, it is not surprising that he was snatched up without hesitation by Muddy Waters dur-ing one of his whirlwind tours through the Delta. Shaw moved to the Windy City permanently in 1957 to play with Muddy but soon settled into what became a near 20-year term as Howlin' Wolf's right-hand man. Meanwhile, he gained great notoriety for his session work (Wolf's 1965–67 Chess sides, Magic Sam's classic Delmark recordings), his arrangements and his song-writing skills (Shaw penned numerous tunes for Howlin' Wolf, Willie Dixon and Magic Sam, among others). In spite of his ac-complishments, his career as a solo artist didn't take off until the late 1970s. By the 1980s, dues fully paid, Shaw was one of the most visible blues artists on the Chicago scene, distin-guished by his formidable technical skill and ability to keep one step ahead of the pack creatively. (Who else has come up with anything that remotely resembles "Dunkin' Donut Woman" or the lodging-house endorsement, "Motel Six.") Taken together, his recent recordings constitute one of the most satisfying bodies of work in modern blues.

what to buy: *King of the Road* ♫♫♫♫ (Rooster Blues, 1985, prod. Jim O'Neal) is an excellent survey of Shaw's career, from his first 1966 single, "Blues for the West Side," to his mid-1980s sessions. The sides from the 1960s and 1970s present him at his best, though the more recent tunes are well worth a listen. *In the Land of the Crossroads* 🎵🎵🎵🎵 (Rooster Blues, 1992, prod. Jim O'Neal) is a terrific set of lively, no-nonsense blues recorded with the Wolf Gang, featuring Shaw's extraordinary, flowing horn lines and endlessly inventive song lyrics ("She Didn't Tell Me Everything," "Dunkin' Donut Woman," "Wine Head Hole").

the rest:

Movin' and Groovin' Man 🎵🎵🎵 (Isabel, 1984/Evidence, 1993)
The Blues Is Good News 🎵🎵🎵 (Wolf, 1990)
Home Alone 🎵🎵🎵 (Wolf, 1994)

worth searching for: Shaw's first solo release, *Have Blues Will Travel* 🎵🎵🎵 (Simmons, 1977, prod. Eddie Shaw, Lillian Burnett), was recorded with the Wolf Gang immediately after the death of Howlin' Wolf. Interestingly, Wolf's widow, Lillian Burnett, was co-producer.

influences:

◀◀ Winchester "Little Wynn" Davis

▶▶ Eddie "Vaan" Shaw Jr.

D. Thomas Moon

Robert Shaw

Born August 9, 1908, in Stafford, TX. Died May 18, 1985, in Austin, TX.

Possibly because he was such a smart businessman—he was proprietor of Shaw's Market and Barbecue in Austin in the 1960s—Shaw never seemed to worry much about hit records or the music industry. He was a mean barrelhouse pianist, though, with a rhythmic walking style and a clean tone to match his moaning voice. As a youth he drifted along the Santa Fe railroad with labor gangs, playing at whorehouses, joints and clubs where he could find the biggest potential audience. In the mid-1930s, he slowed down his public appearances to concentrate on running the store, playing mostly at home. He didn't come out much again until 1963, when Arhoolie's Mack McCormick encouraged him to hit the studio; his only album, *The Ma Grinder*, was the resulting barrelhouse piano classic.

what to buy: *The Ma Grinder* 🎵🎵🎵🎵 (Arhoolie, 1963/1992, prod. Chris Strachwitz, Mack McCormick) is a wonderfully complex document of Texas piano blues, from the impossible-to-reproduce "The Cows" to the funny, partying "Whores Is Funky" and "Here I Come with My Dirty, Dirty Duckings On." It sounds like

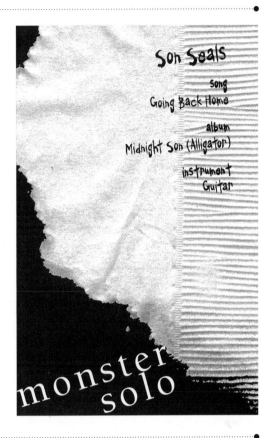

Son Seals
song
Going Back Home
album
Midnight Son (Alligator)
instrument
Guitar

monster solo

Shaw is tickled to be playing before an appreciative audience again—on the cover, Shaw beams and laughs as he prepares to launch his hands onto the keyboard.

influences:

◀◀ Victoria Spivey, Speckled Red, Art Tatum, Scott Joplin, Jelly Roll Morton

▶▶ Little Richard, Jerry Lee Lewis, Professor Longhair, Pinetop Perkins, Otis Spann

Steve Knopper

Kenny Wayne Shepherd

Born June 12, 1977, in Shreveport, LA.

Just as the mantle of "next Dylan" has been placed on the shoulders of countless unlucky folksingers, the term "next Stevie Ray" has been thrown around carelessly in blues circles, most recently in the direction of young gun Kenny Wayne Shepherd. Maybe it's their use of middle names, or the nearly complete shadow Vaughan's ghost casts over Shepherd's playing, in terms of tone, feel, phrasing—you name it. But there is more than a little spark of originality in his playing, and hell, he's young. Chances are he'll grow out of it and into his own style like every guitarist of note before him. Shepherd is not a vocalist, however, and must rely on his guitar to do his talking for him. So far, it's doing just fine.

what to buy: An unexpected hit, *Ledbetter Heights* ♫♫♫ (Giant, 1995, prod. David Z) caught on with blues fans looking for a Stevie Ray fix and rock fans seeking out a bluesier alternative. Both sides can be sated with this impressive debut, featuring "Born with a Broken Heart," which pays tribute to Vaughan without mentioning his name, and the rock steady "Deja Voodoo." Shepherd tackles country-style blues on "Aberdeen" and shines on the live instrumental "While We Cry." He even takes tentative steps toward becoming a vocalist on "Riverside." Altogether an impressive outing.

influences:

◀◀ Stevie Ray Vaughan, Albert King

Daniel Durchholz

Lonnie Shields

Born April 17, 1956, in West Helena, AR.

Even the Pillsbury Dough Boy would sound like an amazing guitarist if he managed to hire the rock-solid backing trio of drummer Sam Carr, keyboardist Frank Frost and rhythm guitarist Big Jack Johnson. Fortunately, Lonnie Shields has not only guitar-playing talent but fine instincts for all kinds of rhythm, from funk to R&B to conventional blues. The young singer started out playing Al Green songs in his high school band, the Shades of Black. He was playing one night in a club when Carr stopped in, liked what he heard, introduced Shields to Frost and helped get Shields into a studio. His debut, *Portrait*, is solid enough to make any blues fan wonder where the next one's coming from.

what to buy: Shields' soft-spoken style of singing and playing is a nice match for Carr's strong, solid drumming, even though he, Frost and Jackson play on just a few tracks of *Portrait* ♫♫♫ (Rooster Blues, 1992, prod. Jim O'Neal, Patty Johnson, Lonnie Shields).

influences:

◀◀ Frank Frost & Sam Carr, Big Jack Johnson, Al Green, Stevie Wonder, Buddy Guy

Steve Knopper

Johnny Shines

Born April 26, 1915, in Frazier, TN. Died April 20, 1992, in Tuscaloosa, AL.

Johnny Shines perhaps was best known—along with Robert Junior Lockwood—as the musical heir to the legacy of Robert Johnson, with whom Shines traveled off-and-on in the 1930s. It was an association Shines embraced proudly, and one which anchored a recording career of more than 40 years. Along the way, Shines recorded an outstanding, diverse body of blues material in both acoustic and electric settings. His early 1950s sessions for JOB bridge the gap between Mississippi Delta country blues and its modern Chicago counterpart no less effectively than did Muddy Waters' work of the same period. However, it is Shines' acoustic Delta blues work, in the Johnson tradition, for which he will most be remembered. Although a stroke in 1980 greatly diminished his guitar technique, Shines toured regularly as an acoustic performer until shortly before his death.

what to buy: The essential Shines acoustic release, *Traditional Delta Blues* ♫♫♫♫ (Biograph, 1991, prod. Arnold S. Caplin), was recorded in 1972 and 1974 and features potent solo Delta blues performances captured with a warm, clean guitar tone. Look for the original LP release of this material, titled *Sitting on Top of the World* (Biograph, 1972), for an outstanding cover photo! *Hey Ba-Ba-Re-Bop* ♫♫♫♫ (Rounder, 1992, prod. Peter Guralnick, Scott Billington) captures Shines' solo Delta material in an energetic, commanding live performance from 1971. Another acoustic set, *Standing at the Crossroads* ♫♫♫♫ (Testament, 1995, prod. Pete Welding) from 1970, is close behind. On the electric side, Shines' superb JOB sessions are collected on *Johnny Shines and Robert Lockwood* ♫♫♫♫ (Paula, 1991, prod. Stan Lewis), which includes 10 cuts from each artist. The Shines' sessions, from 1952 and 1953, include Big Walter Horton on harmonica. Utterly essential and guaranteed to turn your head.

what to buy next: *Mr. Cover Shaker* ♫♫♫♫ (Biograph, 1992, prod. Arnold S. Caplin) includes six additional cuts from the *Traditional Delta Blues* sessions plus seven numbers recorded with Dave Bromberg and his band in 1974. The latter feature cornet, trumpet and other horns plus backing vocals, offering an enticing peak at what Shines may have been able to do with the right kind of ensemble support. Although only available on

Kenny Wayne Shepherd (© Ken Settle)

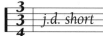
cassette, *Hangin' On* 𝄆𝄆𝄆 (Rounder, 1980, prod. Robert Junior Lockwood, Johnny Shines) is a wonderful 1980 collaboration by the two artists—playing together, not just appearing on the same record—that begs for CD release. *Masters of Modern Blues* 𝄆𝄆𝄆 (Testament, 1966/1994, prod. Frank Scott), which casts Shines in an electric setting with pianist Otis Spann and Walter Horton, works most of the time.

what to avoid: *Johnny Shines 1915–92* 𝄆𝄆 (Wolf, 1993) packages a 1974 acoustic show and a 1970 studio session. Neither reflects Shines' best work, although completists may find some interesting spoken asides in the acoustic set.

the rest:
Back to the Country 𝄆𝄆𝄆𝄆 (Blind Pig, 1991)
Johnny Shines 𝄆𝄆𝄆 (HighTone, 1991)

worth searching for: A reissue of a 1975 acoustic session that included Louisiana Red on guitar and Sugar Blue on harp, *Too Wet to Plow* 𝄆𝄆𝄆𝄆 (Tomato/Rhino, 1988), is worth finding. It also appeared on vinyl on the Blue Labor label in the 1970s.

influences:
◀◀ Robert Johnson, Charley Patton, Howlin' Wolf

▶▶ Muddy Waters, Elmore James, Eric Clapton

Bryan Powell

J.D. Short

Born December 26, 1902, in Port Gibson, MS. Died October 21, 1962, in St. Louis, MO.

A wandering harpist, Short met bigger names like Honeyboy Edwards, Big Joe Williams and Henry Spaulding as he toured southern house parties. The superb singer, who grew up playing many different instruments, used these connections to score several recording sessions with various record companies, including Delmark and Folkways. He also appeared in the 1963 documentary film, *The Blues.*

what to buy: It's tough to find evidence of Short's singles, but *Stavin' Chain Blues* 𝄆𝄆𝄆 (Delmark, 1965) is more than anything else a singing display; Short's voice conveys all kinds of emotion, and his harp slips nicely into the empty spaces.

influences:
◀◀ Honeyboy Edwards, Willie Brown, Robert Johnson

▶▶ Sonny Boy Williamson I, Little Walter, Sonny Boy Williamson II, Junior Wells

Steve Knopper

Frankie Lee Sims

Born 1906, in New Orleans, LA. Died May 10, 1970, in Dallas, TX.

As dedicated as Frankie Lee Sims was in trying to fashion himself into a Lightnin' Hopkins clone, he never quite succeeded, and a good thing it was. Sims could just not get that bayou sludge out of his blood, and it made for an irresistible permutation—arid Texas country blues laced with Louisiana vodun magic. Sims recorded little, mostly for Art Rupe's Specialty label between 1953 and 1954, but what he put down rivaled Hopkins' torrid Herald recordings of the same period and Lightnin' Slim's early Jay Miller sides for out-and-out nastiness. His "Lucy Mae Blues," a 1953 regional hit in the South, took off from Jim Jackson's old "My Monday Woman Blues," but added an infectious cow lope of a beat, stingy guitar, Sims' parched voice and a taste of the surreal ("My Saturday woman bought a Gatling gun, cut you if you stand, shoot you if you run"). Sims began playing guitar at age 12 with encouragement from his cousin, Hopkins. Sims, too, became a wandering Texas bluesman but never won his cousin's folk following. After finishing with Specialty and then flirting with Ace in the mid-1950s, he settled briefly in Chicago and found sporadic session work, even backing King Curtis on his "Soul Twist." Returning to Dallas, Sims died of pneumonia, leaving behind a blues-singing son, Little Frankie Lee.

what to buy: No matter how low Sims got, he never forgot to add a dirty swamp shuffle to spice things up. On *Lucy Mae Blues* 𝄆𝄆𝄆𝄆 (Specialty, 1992, prod. Art Rupe) he had enough orneriness inside to record two versions of "Lucy Mae" and add several other brutal cuts with titles odd enough to provoke double-takes: "Wine and Gin Bounce," "Rhumba My Boogie," and the lowdown "I Done Talked and I Done Talked."

influences:
◀◀ Lightnin' Hopkins

▶▶ Little Frankie Lee

Steve Braun

Percy Sledge

Born November 25, 1941, in Leighton, AL.

The remarkable thing about Percy Sledge's landmark 1966 hit, "When a Man Loves a Woman," is that it wasn't his only one. "It Tears Me Up," "Warm and Tender Love" and "Take Time to Know Her" weren't the songs that his biggest hit was, but the fact that they did some business is testimony to the charms of Sledge's vocals—full of country tearfulness on a soulful bed of blues. Sledge learned to sing in church and was a hospital orderly when he shopped the idea for "When a Man Loves a Woman" to Quin Ivey, a disc jockey who became the producer of all of Sledge's 1960s recordings. Since the end of the 1960s, when the hits ran out, Sledge has continued to perform. He recorded for Capricorn Records in the mid-1970s, had a period where he re-recorded his hits and came back in 1994 with his best album in 20 years.

what to buy: One might quibble over the exclusion of a song here or there, but it's difficult to think of a record that does a better job of capsulating a career than *It Tears Me Up* 🎸🎸🎸🎸 (Rhino/Atlantic, 1992, prod. Quin Ivey, Marlin Greene). The 23 tracks include his hits and an array of sad, cautionary tunes such as "Dark End of the Street," "Sudden Stop" and "Drown in My Own Tears" that let Sledge "preach" about the woes of emotional treachery.

what to buy next: *Blue Night* 🎸🎸🎸 (Pointblank, 1994, prod. Barry Goldberg) is a sentimental favorite, but Sledge doesn't rest on his laurels, giving everything with that remarkable voice of his.

what to avoid: As with many performers who were primarily singles artists, there are a myriad of Sledge collections. Avoid everything that isn't listed here, and you'll miss a bum steer.

best of the rest:
Percy Sledge Way 🎸🎸🎸 (Atlantic, 1967)
Take Time to Know Her 🎸🎸🎸 (Atlantic, 1968)
Golden Voice of Soul 🎸🎸🎸 (Atlantic, 1974)
I'll Be Your Everything 🎸🎸🎸 (Capricorn, 1974)
Any Day Now 🎸🎸🎸 (Charly, 1984)
Percy! 🎸🎸🎸 (Charly, 1987)

worth searching for: The original vinyl of Sledge's first works, *When a Man Loves a Woman* 🎸🎸🎸🎸 (Atlantic, 1966, prod. Quin Ivey, Marlin Greene) and *Warm and Tender Soul* 🎸🎸🎸🎸 (Atlantic, 1966, prod. Quin Ivey, Marlin Greene), are both above average albums from the age when singles ruled.

influences:
◀◀ Ray Charles
▶▶ Levon Helm

Salvatore Caputo

Drink Small

Born January 28, 1933, in Bishopville, SC.

Drink Small—the name he was given at birth, not a stage name, by the way—possesses a deep, gruff, and richly expres-

sive voice, and an eclectic, dynamic guitar style that even at its most citified retains an authentic country rawness. While not a particularly memorable songwriter, he is nonetheless a skilled and demonstrative interpreter whose playing convincingly incorporates Piedmont, Delta, Texas and Chicago mannerisms applied to blues and soulful R&B styles. Born into a musical family in small-town South Carolina, Small became fascinated with the sound of the plucked string, fashioning his own instruments out of sticks, string, wire and rubber bands and using an uncle's real guitar at every chance. As a teen, he was drawn to whatever musical outlets were available to him, playing with spiritual fervor (on piano) in church, but equally comfortable playing the "devil's music" at house parties. He quickly became the best guitarist around. After several years of leading his own gospel groups, in 1955 he came to the attention of Charles Derrick, leader of the Columbia, South Carolina-based gospel act, the Spiritualaires. Small was much better than the group's then-guitarist and soon gained recognition as a top gospel guitarist. In 1959 Small christened himself the Blues Doctor—because of his facility with different playing styles—and pursued a career as a bluesman, touring mostly in the South to college audiences but making little real impact, although he enjoyed a flurry of activity beginning in the late 1980s. Small has enjoyed neither the widespread exposure nor financial success that he would have liked, a sore spot that shows up often in his music, where his disappointment and frustration are at times palpable. "If I don't soon make it, I'm going back to South Carolina, and sit down on my behind," he sighs in "I'm Tired Now." And maybe Small's gripe is legitimate; in a fair world he would at least be able to make a living off his not-inconsiderable talent.

what to buy: All three of Small's readily available albums have points to recommend them. *Round Two* 🎸🎸🎸🎸 (Ichiban, 1991, prod. Bryan Cole) frequently veers heavily into R&B territory, like on the sax-drenched reworking of the soul ballad "Steal Away," the funky "Don't Let Nobody Else" and the pop "Can I Come Over Tonight," but contains its share of finger-picked country blues, such as the ode to his hometown gals, "Bishopville Women" and "Widow Woman." *The Blues Doctor* 🎸🎸🎸🎸 (1990, Ichiban, prod. Charles Derrick) isn't a live recording but includes Small's between-song, sometimes boastful, jiving patter as if it were. Small churns out cutting, driving versions, sometimes featuring piano and organ, of "Little Red Rooster," "Stormy Monday" and Leadbelly's fine "I'm Going to Move to the Outskirts of Town." Docked style points for racy numbers ("Tittie Man," "Rub My Belly") that seem more silly than salacious.

what to buy next: *Electric Blues Doctor Live* ✽✽✽ (Mapleshade Productions, 1994, prod. Pierre M. Sprey) is a high-quality recording of a 1988 date at a school in Washington, DC. After Small introduces us to his guitar, Geraldine—his good-natured banter with the audience includes the assertion, "I ain't scared of B.B. King, and Geraldine ain't scared of Lucille"—he performs a few originals and extended covers of King's "Three O'-Clock in the Morning," Guitar Slim's "The Things I Used to Do" and The Isley Brothers "Shout," among others. Tasty enough but sometimes a little low-key.

influences:

◀◀ Blind Boy Fuller, T-Bone Walker, Lightnin' Hopkins, Brownie McGhee

▶▶ John Cephas, Taj Mahal

Michael Dixon

Barkin' Bill Smith

Born August 14, 1928, in Cleveland, MS.

Barkin' Bill Smith is one of the last of a dying breed in Chicago—the blues singer. He began his life of singing as a member of the Glory Bound Quartet, a gospel group in his hometown, and in his late teens began performing blues in juke joints throughout the Delta. He arrived in Chicago in 1958 and has been singing in the city's clubs on and off ever since, working with such greats as Willie Kent, Lonnie Brooks and Sam Lay. Although Smith still presents his blues in the ghetto clubs of Chicago's West Side, his recorded work for Delmark has allowed him to make inroads recently on the moneyed North Side. His vocal acrobatics are a welcome respite from the blare of the many guitar-driven bands now dominating the scene. Barkin' Bill Smith is one of Chicago's greatest, yet most under appreciated blues singers.

what to buy: Smith's smooth, supple baritone, reminiscent of Joe Williams, was heard by scouts from Chicago's Delmark Records in the late 1980s. They promptly invited him into the studio to record his hard-driving debut *Bluebird Blues* ✽✽✽✽ (Delmark, 1991, prod. Robert Koester, Steve Wagner) with guitarist Dave Specter and his Bluebirds. Included here are uplifting renditions of "Tell Me What's the Reason," "Buzz Me," "Railroad Station Blues" and Bill's own "Get Me While I'm Free." Smith's dignified demeanor and jazzy phrasing made him a natural for the label, and he was invited back by Delmark to record the satisfying follow-up, *Gotcha!* ✽✽✽✽ (Delmark, 1994, prod. Steve Wagner).

influences:

◀◀ Big Joe Williams, Jimmy Witherspoon, Brook Benton, Wynonie Harris

▶▶ Big Bill Hickey, Dave Specter

Steven Sharp

Bessie Smith

Born April 15, 1894, in Chattanooga, TN. Died September 26, 1936, in Clarksdale, MS.

Bessie Smith is without question the greatest of all "classic blues" performers. She began her career as a vaudeville dancer while still in her teens, but her potential as a singer sparked Ma Rainey's interest early on. She established herself while touring with Rainey's Rabbit Foot Minstrels, and by the end of World War I was a bona fide star on the T.O.B.A. (Theatre Owners Booking Association) circuit. Her first record, the straight, round-toned "Down Hearted Blues," was made in 1923 and sold 780,000 copies in less than six months. A slew of hit records followed, each more remarkable than its predecessor in terms of intonation and inflection.

Smith's voice has withstood the test of time. "Jailhouse Blues" is an early example of her mastery of slides, "drop-offs" and other melismatic embellishments, fully realized on later recordings such as "Careless Love" and "Whip It to a Jelly." Her judicious use of guttural inflections on tunes like "Cemetery Blues" and "Dirty No-Gooder's Blues" further illustrates her artistry. Through careful employment of these and other vocal devices, Smith convincingly conveyed many moods on record. In somber and wistful songs like "Nobody Knows When You're Down and Out" or the amazing "St. Louis Blues," she brought an uncanny sense of loss and melancholy by a simple turn of phrase or lightening of tone. By contrast, the exuberance she created in tunes like "Alexander's Ragtime Band" frequently sent listeners into finger-popping, toe-tapping frenzies. In fact, just about everything she sang was warmly received by an admiring, record-buying public. Smith put her unique spin on popular songs ("I Ain't Got Nobody"), hokum pieces ("I Want Every Bit of It," "I Need a Little Sugar in My Bowl") and even gospel ("On Revival Day"), in addition to straightforward blues numbers. She was an anomalous success, every bit deserving of the title "Empress of the Blues." No star shone brighter than

Drink Small (© Jack Vartoogian)

Bessie's throughout the "classic blues" heyday. However, by the early 1930s, at the onset of the Depression, even Smith's popularity was waning. She died tragically in an automobile accident in 1937, just as she was beginning to make in-roads with a new, decidedly more contemporary, swing-oriented style.

what to buy: *The Complete Recordings, Vol. 2* 𝄞𝄞𝄞𝄞 (Columbia/Legacy, 1991, prod. Lawrence Cohn) contains sides recorded between April 1924 and November 1925, in a well-suited, small-group setting. (Louis Armstrong is one of the most notable accompanists.) In contrast to earlier recordings, Smith's vocal delivery is markedly more authoritative at this juncture in her career, as evidenced by the plaintive numbers "Reckless Blues" and "Careless Love Blues." The highlight is "St. Louis Blues," a masterpiece of controlled tension. *The Complete Recordings, Vol. 3* 𝄞𝄞𝄞𝄞 (Columbia/Legacy, 1992, prod. Lawrence Cohn) contains more recordings from Smith's artistic zenith (late November 1925 to mid-February 1928). Highlights include the magnificent "Back Water Blues," "After You've Gone," "Muddy Water," "Trombone Cholly," "Lock and Key" and "A Good Man Is Hard to Find." For those wanting but one representative set.

what to buy next: *The Complete Recordings, Vol. 1* 𝄞𝄞𝄞𝄞 (Columbia/Legacy, 1991, prod. Lawrence Cohn) contains Smith's first 38 recordings, among them the magnificent debut, "Down Hearted Blues," the blues-inflected pop tune "Baby Won't You Please Come Home" and her mesmerizing rendition of "T'aint Nobody's Bizness If I Do." Most sides feature her with sparse and rather pedestrian piano accompaniment. *The Complete Recordings, Vol. 4* 𝄞𝄞𝄞𝄞 (Columbia/Legacy, 1993, prod. Lawrence Cohn) showcases Smith's late 1920s and early 1930s recordings. As the Depression hit America, vaudeville was on the decline and fewer people were listening to the blues. Sadly, by July of 1930, Smith could do no better than bottom billing at Harlem's Apollo Theater. Understandably, her voice had begun to show signs of wear by the time of these sessions, yet recordings like "Empty Bed Blues" and "Nobody Knows When You're Down and Out" are nevertheless powerful.

what to avoid: *The Complete Recordings, Vol. 5: The Final Chapter* 𝄞𝄞𝄞 (Columbia/Legacy, 1996, prod. Lawrence Cohn) contains the rest of Smith's 1931 recordings and a 1933 session for OKeh, along with alternate takes, the *St. Louis Blues* soundtrack and a 72-minute interview with Smith's niece, Rudy Smith. The 1933 session is especially fine and hints at the new musical directions Smith was exploring at the time of her death. The rest of this set will find more favor with collectors and serious fans.

the rest:

Bessie Smith 1925–33 𝄞𝄞𝄞𝄞 (Nimbus, 1987)
The Collection 𝄞𝄞𝄞𝄞 (Columbia, 1989)
Empress of the Blues 𝄞𝄞𝄞 (Charly, 1992)
Alexander's Ragtime Band 𝄞𝄞𝄞 (Four Star, 1994)
Bessie Smith 1923 𝄞𝄞𝄞 (Classics, 1994)
Bessie Smith 1923–24 𝄞𝄞𝄞 (Classics, 1994)
Mama's Got the Blues 𝄞𝄞𝄞 (Pearl, 1994)

worth searching for: *Bessie Smith* 𝄞𝄞𝄞𝄞𝄞 (Time-Life, 1982, prod. Michael Brooks) is the best single-package overview of Smith's recorded legacy. The accompanying 46-page booklet written by Bessie Smith biographer Chris Albertson is packed with rare photos, anecdotes and informed musical commentary.

influences:

◀◀ Ma Rainey

▶▶ Mahalia Jackson, Odetta, Jimmy Rushing, Ella Fitzgerald, Billie Holiday

D. Thomas Moon

Byther Smith

Born Byther Claude Earl John Smith, April 17, 1933, in Monticello, MS.

Byther Smith is a West Side artist with a bitter, stinging guitar style and a bullmoose voice. After coming to Chicago in 1958, he picked up guitar tips from Hubert Sumlin and Robert Lockwood, and according to B.L. Pearson's *Sounds So Good to Me*, took lessons at the Lyon & Healy music company from Roy Buchanan. Though talented and individualistic, Smith always seemed to fly under the radar of Windy City blues cognoscenti; he has made his records for little labels like BeBe and CJ and to this day plays less in the tourist's clubs on the North Side than he does in workingman's bars in the rowdier parts of town. In this age when some Chicago mainstays sound like imitations of their imitators, the uncompromising music of Smith is more vital than ever.

what to buy: *Addressing the Nation with the Blues* 𝄞𝄞𝄞𝄞 (JSP, 1994, prod. John Stedman) is a typically high-tensile Smith set. From the drop-dead lyrics of "I Wish My Mother Was Here" to the carnality of the J.B. Lenoir-derived "You Should Be Proud of Your Daughter," this is hard-bitten stuff, full of stringent guitar and more than a jolt of anger. There are lurid rhythms ("Hello Mrs. Brown"), skanky slide ("I Was Coming Home") and "Play the Blues on the Moon," which conjures an image of Smitty (as

Byther's pals call him) in space gear, playing his guitar in lunar climes.

what to buy next: *I'm a Mad Man* 🎵🎵🎵 (Bullseye Blues, 1993, prod. Ron Levy) is fiery stuff. The kickoff cut is "I Got So Much Love," and maybe Byther does, but with that he-man voice he's surely no softy. The title cut is the most macho take *ever* on the "Mannish Boy" theme; Byther's mad at being called "boy" and determines to "'stroy the world" while the Memphis Horns provide backup for his assault. The production here is smoother, but as befits Smith, it's far from slick!

the rest:
Housefire 🎵🎵🎵 (Bullseye Blues, 1991)
Mississippi Kid 🎵🎵 (Delmark, 1997)

influences:
◀◀ J.B. Lenoir, Robert Junior Lockwood, Hubert Sumlin

Tim Schuller

Clarence Smith
See: Pine Top Smith

Clarence Edward Smith
See: Sonny Rhodes

George "Harmonica" Smith
Born April 22, 1924, in Helena, AR. Died October 2, 1983, in Los Angeles, CA.

This reliable and talented harpist never became as famous as his inspiration, Little Walter, or even his student and protégé, Rod Piazza, but he's an important transitional figure in blues history. He joined Muddy Waters' influential band in 1954—replacing the recently murdered Henry Strong—which began an on-again-off-again partnership that lasted through the 1970s. It also gave Smith even more visibility, which he used to hook up with Little Willie John, Champion Jack Dupree and many others. Smith grew up in Cairo, Illinois, and may have been the first bluesman to amplify his harp, using a speaker he pulled from the moviehouse where he worked. In the late 1960s he joined a group called Bacon Fat with Piazza and toured occasionally with Waters' later bands. Smith's recordings with Waters were primary study material for generations of harpists, including Charlie Musselwhite and William Clarke.

what to buy: Smith, who once toured under nicknames like "Little Walter Junior" and "Big Walter," covers his hero's well-known songs impeccably on *Tribute to Little Walter* 🎵🎵🎵 (World Pacific, 1968).

best of the rest:
Oopin' Doopin' Doopin' 🎵🎵🎵 (Ace)
No Time to Jive 🎵🎵🎵 (Blue Horizon, 1970)
George Smith of the Blues 🎵🎵 (Bluesway, 1973)

influences:
◀◀ Little Walter, Larry Adler, Sonny Boy Williamson II

▶▶ William Clarke, Rod Piazza, Junior Wells, Sugar Blue, Charlie Musselwhite, Paul Butterfield

Steve Knopper

J.T. "Funny Paper" Smith
Born John T. Smith, c. 1890, in TX. Death date unknown (last seen c. 1939).

Another minstrel who wandered the expanse of Texas like fellow drifter Texas Alexander, "Funny Paper" Smith stayed in place long enough to record two dozen simple blues in the 1930s before vanishing. Also known as "Funny Papa," Smith cut an outlandish figure, wearing a battered top hat as he sang on street corners and at country dances. He also took a second nickname from the country boast he recorded in four different versions, "Howling Wolf," some two decades before Chester Burnett—a.k.a. "Big Foot Chester"—appropriated the name for himself. Smith dueted with Texas barrelhouse pianist Tom Shaw in the 1920s and accompanied both Texas Alexander and singer Bernice Edwards. His spare guitar accompaniment made its mark on more popular players like Josh White before he vanished from the Texas blues scene in the early 1940s.

what to buy: *Texas Blues Guitar (1929–35)* 🎵🎵🎵 (Story of Blues, 1987, prod. Johnny Parth) is a fine sampling of Smith, 10 songs worth, balanced with 10 more by the early folk blues of Dennis "Little Hat" Jones. Only two versions of Smith's "Howling Wolf Blues" are here, more than enough for a single sitting. The bathetic "Heart Bleeding Blues" and Smith's back-country "Bantam Rooster Blues" highlight the set.

the rest:
J.T. "Funny Paper" Smith (The Howling Wolf) 1930–31 🎵🎵🎵 (RST, 1992)

influences:
◀◀ Texas Alexander

▶▶ Tom Shaw, J.D. Short, Josh White

Steve Braun

Pine Top Smith

Born Clarence Smith, January 11, 1904, in Orion, AL. Died March 15, 1929, in Chicago, IL.

Besides bequeathing his unusual nickname to a generation of younger blues piano players like Pine Top Perkins, the original Pine Top is the man who kicked off the boogie woogie craze of the 1920s with his driving "Pine Top's Boogie Woogie." The true author of boogie woogie—the music and the phrase—has long been a sure route to an argument. "Cow Cow" Davenport, for instance, long claimed that he coined the term. But Smith's use of the term was the first on record, and his shouted lyrics—"Hold it now . . . Stop . . . Boogie Woogie!"—was the blueprint for dozens of later piano-based classics. Ray Charles took Smith's shout, "Mess Around," for one of his early classics, and used another Smith aside—"See that girl with the red dress on"—to anchor his immortal "What'd I Say?" Pine Top Smith never lived to see his drawled narration repeated again and again in modern R&B hits. He took to the road in 1920 as a dancer and pianist. It was Davenport who recommended Smith to talent scout J. Mayo Williams. Smith's first records for Brunswick and Vocalion in 1928 included his "Boogie Woogie" and "Pine Top Blues." Return Chicago sessions in 1929 produced several lesser numbers, but among the dross was a hilarious, complaining version of the blues standard, "Nobody Knows You When You're Down and Out." Smith had no time to show how deep his talent lay; he was killed by a stray bullet fired during a dance hall melee.

what to buy: Not all of Pine Top Smith's 11 tracks are blues masterworks, but there are two versions each of his "Pine Top Blues" and "Pine Top's Boogie Woogie," all of them the giddy essence of early boogie woogie, on *Boogie Woogie and Barrelhouse Piano 1928–32* ♪♪♪♪♪ (Document, 1992, prod. Johnny Parth). Even if Smith's cuts are not uniformly perfect, most of the rest is filled with the complete recordings of piano legends Charles Avery, Freddie "Redd" Nicholson and "Jabo" Williams.

influences:

◀◀ Charles "Cow Cow" Davenport

▶▶ Blind Willie McTell, Ray Charles, Pine Top Perkins

Steve Braun

Chris Smither

Born in New Orleans, LA.

Chris Smither performs solo on acoustic guitar, but his music is equally informed by elements of folk, blues and rock 'n' roll. Instrumentally, he features an astonishing fingerpicking technique that melds a variety of styles, while vocally, Smither's world-weary voice conveys a wealth of emotion. A performer who first came to prominence in the coffeehouse circuit of Boston in the late 1960s, Smither recorded a pair of albums in the early 1970s before drifting away from music and then back again. He's best known for his songs "Love You Like a Man" and "I Feel the Same," both of which have been recorded by his old friend, Bonnie Raitt, but he's also an excellent interpreter of others' material—indeed, Smither may be the only performer who, at this late date, can make a Chuck Berry song sound fresh. Often accompanied by nothing but his loudly tapping foot, Smither stomps the terra in more ways than one.

what to buy: As unadulterated an approximation of what Smither does as is possible on record, *Another Way to Find You* ♪♪♪♪ (Flying Fish, 1991) features Smither in front of a small audience of guests in the friendly confines of a recording studio. The material, which includes interpretations of Chuck Berry ("Tulane"), Bob Dylan ("Down in the Flood"), the Grateful Dead ("Friend of the Devil") and Blind Willie McTell ("Statesboro Blues"), plus some of Smither's finest originals, is all over the musical map, amounting to an impressive show of Smither's wide-ranging prowess. The setting and performances are so intimate, you can't help but be drawn in.

what to buy next: For a switch, Smither is placed in a band context on *Happier Blue* ♪♪♪♪ (Flying Fish, 1993, prod. John Nagy), though the other instruments are unobtrusive and Smither's guitar, voice and tapping foot are allowed to dominate. The songs, mostly originals, are of uniformly high quality, though the deeply conflicted title track stands out. For covers, there's a lickety-split version of John Hiatt's "Memphis in the Meantime" and a lovely, mournful take on Rolly Sally's "Killing the Blues."

the rest:

I'm a Stranger Too/Don't It Drag On ♪♪♪ (Poppy, 1970/Collectables, 1997)
It Ain't Easy ♪♪♪♪ (Adelphi, 1984/Genes, 1989)
Up on the Lowdown ♪♪♪♪ (HighTone, 1995)
Small Revelations ♪♪♪♪ (HighTone, 1997)

influences:

◀◀ Lightnin' Hopkins, Mississippi John Hurt, Chuck Berry, Bob Dylan

Daniel Durchholz

James Solberg

Birth information unavailable.

Wisconsin native James Solberg has been something of a "man-behind-the-man" until recently, best known for his long-time association with Luther Allison as co-songwriter and leader of Allison's American band. Solberg doesn't have a great voice but he's a good singer and an excellent songwriter, guitarist and arranger. If you're a fan of Allison's recent albums, you'll enjoy Solberg.

what to buy: *One of These Days* ♫♫♫ (Atomic Theory, 1996, prod. James Solberg, Jim Gaines) is a good sampling of the kind of style, taste and skill Solberg brings to the table. Strong originals and interesting covers—plus guest appearances by the Memphis Horns and some nice palm-pedal slide by Jon Paris—make for a good listen.

what to buy next: *See That My Grave Is Kept Clean* ♫♫♫ (Atomic Theory, 1994, prod. James Solberg) features the spooky Solberg-Allison composition "Bad Love" and a wonderful "St. James Infirmary Blues."

Jennifer Zogott

Clarence Spady

Born 1961, in Paterson, NJ.

Clarence Spady emerged out of nowhere (Scranton, Pennsylvania, to be specific) with *Nature of the Beast* ♫♫♫ (Evidence, 1996, Scott Goldman), one the more promising blues debuts of recent years. Blending gospel and R&B into his blues, Spady produced a distinct, highly satisfying contemporary sound, with a band featuring tenor sax and organ, and no second guitar or bass. It's a unique sound, and Spady is a fine, driving guitarist possessing a raspy, soulful voice, but what really made the album stand out is that it is blessed with that special spark of life which separates great music from the pack. Remember the name.

Alan Paul

Charlie Spand

Birth and death dates unknown.

Charlie Spand came and went like a warm wind, staying still just long enough between 1929 and 1931 and again in 1940 to scatter a small treasure of barrelhouse piano masterpieces. There is not enough biographical material for even a sketch. Spand is known only by his pleasant, husky voice and his sublime bluesy dominance of the keys. His origins are uncertain. In a rolling 1940 number, "Alabama Blues," he sings of his birth in Alabama. Two earlier songs, "Mississippi Blues" and "Levee Camp Man," suggest links to the Delta. Spand emerged from Detroit's fertile boogie-woogie piano culture of the 1920s, singing about its rollicking "Hasting Street," years later immortalized in John Lee Hooker's "Boogie Chillun." Spand dueted with ragtime picker Blind Blake on "Moanin' the Blues," a perfect realization of early barrelhouse. In all, Spand put down at least 25 takes for Paramount by 1931. He picked up where he left off in June 1940, this time in Chicago, backed by Little Son Joe and Bill Broonzy. His eight final tracks are as entrancing as his first 25.

what to buy: When Charlie Spand hunched over the piano, he could do no wrong. There are 25 recordings on *Charlie Spand: The Complete Paramounts in Chronological Order, 1929–31* ♫♫♫♫ (Document, 1992, prod. Johnny Parth), each of them a relaxed, masterful example of how boogie-woogie replaced ragtime as the cutting edge of 1920s piano playing.

what to buy next: Spand's power was undiminished on the 1940 recordings, *Charlie Spand (1940)/Big Maceo (1941–52)* ♫♫♫ (Old Tramp, 1992, prod. Johnny Parth, Paul Duvive). Eight tracks, featuring a tough "Rock and Rye" and the evocative "Alabama Blues," are followed by the last of Big Maceo Merriweather's 1941 sessions, and the Detroit influence is unmistakable. What follows are Maceo's painful late-1940s works, marred by a crippling stroke.

influences:
▶▶ Big Maceo Merriweather

Steve Braun

Otis Spann

Born March 21, 1930, in Jackson, MS. Died April 24, 1970, in Chicago, IL.

Otis Spann possessed an alarming piano virtuosity. Sometimes his right hand did so much it sounded like a whole 'nother sideman had incarnated right before your ears. Robert Lockwood said Spann played *too* busily and that he liked Curtis Jones and Sunnyland Slim better, but Lockwood made the best recordings of his life with Spann. At age 17, Spann left Mississippi and joined Muddy Waters' band. By 30 he had recorded with Sonny Boy Williamson, Howlin' Wolf, Chuck Berry and more. Though young, he seemed as seasoned a pianist as Big Maceo but with even greater technical facility. He had a smoker's singing voice and often did wistful, melodic blues that are in sharp contrast to the screamin' stuff that's the coin of the realm today. Personable and friendly, he opened the way to numerous wide-eyed acolytes. Mike Bloomfield told hilarious stories about copping weed from Spann, and Fleetwood Mac members cut LPs with him in Chicago and New York. In his latter days, Spann, James Cotton and Sam Lay grouped to play dates at The Green in Youngstown, Ohio, and were great. After their last gig they went to a nearby house and partied until 10 a.m.; much drink was taken. At the house dwelt this writer, who remembers the experience with glee, but was saddened only a few months afterward to learn that Spann had died, at only 40 years of age. Thankfully, his genius is still here for us.

what to buy: *Otis Spann Is the Blues* 𝄢𝄢𝄢𝄢 (Candid, 1960, prod. Nat Hentoff) contains the legendary Spann/Lockwood duo sessions, rare and only on vinyl for decades. Included are four Spann vocals, four by the guitarists and two Spann solo outings, all rife with great pianistics and Lockwood's Delta-jazz hybrid style at its best. The instrumental "Great Northern Stomp" is hell-bent, bawdy house piano so evocative it gives rise to suspicion that Spann was an avatar from the Cripple Clarence Lofton age. *The Blues Never Die* 𝄢𝄢𝄢𝄢 (Original Blues Classics, 1990, prod. Sam Charters) arguably features less virtuosity from Spann than some records, but it's a quintessential band record of the era (1965), with Spann and James Cotton sharing vocals on rousing fare like "I'm Ready," "Dust My Broom" and Spann's patented "Must Have Been the Devil."

what to buy next: A Spann banquet, previously unissued and mighty welcome, is *Live the Life* 𝄢𝄢𝄢𝄢 (Testament, 1997, prod. Pete Welding). Five cuts are Spann live and intimate at a Martin Luther King tribute; six have Mud cohorts providing backup and there are quirky gems like Spann joining old-time mandolinist Johnny Young on "Mean Old Train." Though much of the ABC/Bluesway series met with slipshod production by Al Smith, Bob Thiele's firmer hand wrought two crackling, street-wise LPs with Spann backed by S.P. Leary, Sam Lawhorn, Mojo Buford and even Mud himself. Both are gathered now as *Down to Earth: The Bluesway Recordings* 𝄢𝄢𝄢𝄢 (MCA, 1995, prod. Bob Thiele). Highlights? The irrepressible "Popcorn Man," "Nobody Knows Chicago Like I Do" and "Brand New House." *Otis Spann* 𝄢𝄢𝄢𝄢 (Storyville, 1992) is mostly solo tracks with sublime, billowing piano and compelling vocals. "T.B. Blues" and "Goin' Down Slow" are heart-grindingly lonely, testament to how Spann could bring passion to a song without even raising his voice. A couple cuts feature Lonnie Johnson on subtle, wispy guitar. *Cryin' Time* 𝄢𝄢𝄢𝄢 (Vanguard, 1989, prod. Sam Charters) was cut in Chicago in 1968

and has guitarists Luther Johnson and Barry Melton, the latter of Country Joe & the Fish. It's a good session, with Spann on organ—hey come back here; it's only on a couple cuts—and then he's back on his native piano. While you're in a Vanguard frame of mind, Spann does good work on *Chicago/The Blues/Today Vol. 1* (Vanguard, 1989, prod. Sam Charters), as do J.B. Hutto and Junior Wells.

the rest:
Walking the Blues 𝄢𝄢𝄢 (Candid, 1989)
Otis Spann's Chicago Blues 𝄢𝄢𝄢𝄢 (Testament, 1997)

influences:
◀◀ Cripple Clarence Lofton, Big Maceo Merriweather, Little Brother Montgomery

▶▶ Johnny Jones, Honey Alexander, David Maxwell

Tim Schuller

Speckled Red

Born Rufus Perryman, October 23, 1892, in Monroe, LA. Died January 2, 1973, in St. Louis, MO.

After he moved with his mother to Detroit, this young church-trained organist heard Paul Seminole's ragtime piano playing and determined to play just like him. He simplified the style, though, to the kind of 16-bar blues he heard at burlesque shows, and the switch helped his career, giving him gigs at medicine shows, lumber camps and levee camps. After he built a buzz playing house parties in Detroit and Memphis, he recorded for Brunswick and had a 1929 hit with "The Dirty Dozens." He never got a major break, though, and by the time the blues revival helped him play American and European festivals instead of his fall-back Memphis clubs, he was too old to make much of it. Still, Speckled Red was an important link between Scott Joplin's early-century ragtime and the barrelhouse style that later begat Professor Longhair and Ray Charles.

what to buy: *Complete Recorded Works 1929–38* 𝄢𝄢𝄢 (Document, 1993, prod. Johnny Parth) contains two versions of Red's trademark "The Dirty Dozen," plus "St. Louis Stomp," "The Right String—but the Wrong Yo Yo" and other stop-and-start classics in his thumping barrelhouse style.

what to buy next: *Dirty Dozens* 𝄢𝄢𝄢 (Delmark, 1996, prod. Robert Koester) and *Barrelhouse Piano 1929–38* 𝄢𝄢𝄢 (Wolf) are excellent supplements to the *Complete Recorded Works*—the latter, recorded with guitarist Robert Lee McCoy and a guest spot by harpist John Lee "Sonny Boy" Williamson, includes an excellent Paul Oliver essay.

influences:

◄◄ Scott Joplin, Art Tatum, Paul Seminole, Eubie Blake

▶▶ Professor Longhair, Ray Charles, Charles Brown, Floyd Dixon, Jimmy Yancey

Steve Knopper

Dave Specter

Born May 21, 1963, in Chicago, IL.

These days, power-blues guitarists are a dime a dozen. Everybody, it seems, is ready to get in your face. Clearly, this is not what the founding fathers had in mind: they knew that while brawn has its place, so does beauty, and one was not meant to replace the other. Dave Specter is a perfect example of a blues musician who moves his listeners with subtlety and finesse. He rocks the way Magic Sam and T-Bone Walker rocked. More than any other contemporary bluesman (except, of course, Duke Robillard), Specter has been willing to mix cool blues with vintage jazz. To his ears, the blues credentials of Charlie Parker, John Coltrane, Wes Montgomery and Kenny Burrell are every bit as legitimate as, say, those of Otis Rush or Muddy Waters. Specter, who grew up on Chicago's North Side, didn't start playing guitar until his freshman year at the University of Illinois–Champaign. He later worked as a doorman at Chicago's North Side B.L.U.E.S. club, where he heard Junior Wells, Magic Slim, Buddy Guy and Pinetop Perkins. From there, he toured with Sam Lay, Hubert Sumlin and Son Seals. He also been in the Legendary Blues Band and in groups with Jimmy Johnson, Johnny Littlejohn and Valerie Wellington. Specter started his own band, the Bluebirds, in 1989. Since then, he's either produced or appeared on 12 other Delmark projects. With each, his sound has become more precise, more distinct, until today, Specter's shimmering tone is like no one else's.

what to buy: In 1996, Specter took his blues in a slightly different direction, recording the soothing *Left Turn on Blue* 🎵🎵🎵🎵 (Delmark, 1996, prod. Dave Specter) with Hammond B-3 master Jack McDuff. Since then, he's been exploring ways for injecting blues guitar into a traditional, jazz-organ trio setting. *Bluebird Blues* 🎵🎵🎵🎵 (Delmark, 1994, prod. Dave Specter) features Ronnie Earl and Barkin' Bill Smith.

what to buy next: The only problem with *Blueplicity* 🎵🎵🎵 (Delmark, 1994, prod. Dave Specter) is that vocalist Tad Robinson's reach exceeds his grasp on a couple tunes, something he cor-

rected by *Live in Europe* 🎵🎵🎵🎵 (Delmark, 1995, prod. Dave Specter).

the rest:

(With Barkin' Bill Smith) *Gotcha!* 🎵🎵🎵 (Delmark, 1994)
(With Barkin' Bill Smith) *Wild Cards* 🎵🎵🎵 (Delmark, 1995)

worth searching for: You can find Specter in the distinguished company of Magic Sam, Junior Wells, Little Walter, Luther Allison and Louis Myers on the collection *Midnight Blues* 🎵🎵🎵🎵 (Delmark, 1994).

influences:

◄◄ Muddy Waters, Howlin' Wolf, Otis Rush, Magic Sam, Wes Montgomery, Kenny Burrell, Grant Green, Charlie Parker, John Coltrane, Jack McDuff, Jimmy Smith

▶▶ Duke Robillard, Ronnie Earl, Anson Funderburgh

Dave Ranney

Jon Spencer Blues Explosion

Formed 1990, in New York, NY.

Jon Spencer (born 1965, in Hanover, NH), vocals, guitar; Russell Simins, drums; Judah Bauer, guitars.

Are they making fun of the blues? Or honoring the music by turning it into punk rock? Spencer doesn't like to answer those kinds of questions, and nobody else seems to know for sure. In fact, he clouds the issue by collaborating with bluesman R.L. Burnside and sticking the word "blues" in his band's name even more pointedly than Blues Traveler but insisting in interviews that he doesn't play the blues. Rarely does Spencer, who used to front the equally sloppy punk band Pussy Galore, provide song structures resembling 12-bar blues, and except for persistent Who-like guitar chords, the solos are few. The lyrics are rarely cohesive and sometimes devolve into shouts of "Bell bottoms!" or "Blues explosion!" Critics cite songs like 1994's "Cowboy," in which Spencer affects an exaggerated yodel and seems to poke fun at country music. More likely, the Explosion is living up to rock 'n' roll tradition: they often sound like the Stooges, who didn't admit it but were clearly influenced by the blues, or the early Rolling Stones, who loudly proclaimed their love for Muddy Waters and Howlin' Wolf. If the music's inherent sarcasm bothers you, well, that's the price of paying attention to rock in the 1990s.

what to buy: *Now I Got Worry* 🎵🎵🎵 (Matador, 1996, prod. Jon Spencer, Jim Waters) is the first significantly cohesive Blues Explosion album; it doesn't rely on repetitive shouting (for the most part) and its good ideas include enlisting (for $300) Memphis soul legend Rufus Thomas on "Chicken Dog."

what to buy next: Spencer's fuzzy experiments with the theremin pay off on the raw and repetitive *Orange* ♫♫♫ (Matador, 1995, prod. Jon Spencer, Jim Waters), a must for punks but negligible for traditional blues types.

what to avoid: *Extra Width* ♫♫ (Matador, 1993) is mostly unfocused noise, trying to fit into boring-white-guy-soul territory at best and hard-to-follow blues mocking at worst.

the rest:

Crypt Style ♫♫ (Crypt, 1992)
The Jon Spencer Blues Explosion ♫♫♫ (Caroline, 1992)
A Reverse Willie Horton ♫♫♥ (Pubic Pop Can, 1992)
Experimental Remixes ♫♥ (Matador, 1995)

worth searching for: Aside from Spencer's excellent collaboration with Mississippi bluesman R.L. Burnside—*A Ass Pocket of Whiskey* ♫♫♫ (Matador, 1996, prod. Matthew Johnson)—a thorough Blues Explosion collection should include a few of Pussy Galore's 10-plus records. Best are *Exile on Main Street* ♫♫♫ (Shove, 1986), a disgusting but cathartic rewriting of the classic Rolling Stones album, and *Historia De La Musica Rock* ♫♫♫ (Caroline, 1990, prod. Pussy Galore).

influences:

◀◀ Stooges, Rolling Stones, Sonic Youth, Howlin' Wolf, R.L. Burnside, Sex Pistols, Minutemen, Screamin' Jay Hawkins, James Brown

▶▶ PJ Harvey, Beastie Boys, Chemical Brothers, Moby, Beck

Steve Knopper

Victoria Spivey

Born October 15, 1906, in Houston, TX. Died October 3, 1976, in New York, NY.

You can hear Victoria Spivey winking along to her powerful, deceptively agile piano-pounding as she sings songs like "Let's Ride Tonight," "I Got Men All Over This Town" and "I'm a Red Hot Mama." Borrowing innuendo from Bessie Smith and a ragtime piano style from Scott Joplin himself, Spivey was a popular Texas performer in the late 1920s and a pal of well-known guitarist Lonnie Johnson, with whom she recorded several duets. The singer-songwriter spent most of the 1930s in films like *Hallelujah* and clubs, where she was band leader of the Omaha-based Hunters Serenaders, among many others. She continued to perform for a while after moving to Harlem, but

retired in 1952 to take care of her family; in the early 1960s, she reunited with Johnson, recorded a few albums and became a reasonably popular personality in guest radio and club appearances.

what to buy: *Woman Blues!* ♫♫♫♫ (Original Blues Classics, 1961, prod. Kenneth Goldstein, Len Kunstadt) is her reunion album with Lonnie Johnson, and it's really fun; Spivey seems delighted to be recording, her piano dances eloquently with Johnson's smooth guitar, and despite the presence of the festive "Christmas without Santa Claus," the songs are subtly (and not-so-subtly, as in the blatantly man-trapping "I Got Men All Over This Town") sexy.

what to buy next: *And Her Blues, Vol. 2* ♫♫♫ (Spivey, 1972), recorded on Spivey's own label, is a tour of her jazz material from 1961 to 1972; it's not as energetic as *Woman Blues!* but still a nice document of a great singer and pianist.

the rest:

Complete Recorded Works—1926–41, Vols. 1–5 ♫♫♫ (Document)

worth searching for: Spivey's first two "comeback" albums, *Idle Hours* ♫♫♫ (Bluesville, 1961), with Johnson, and *Songs We Taught Your Mother* ♫♫♫♥ (Bluesville, 1961), with fellow blueswomen Alberta Hunter and Lucille Hagamin and a big jazz band, are tough to find but important documents of her career progression.

influences:

◀◀ Bessie Smith, Scott Joplin, Art Tatum, Lonnie Johnson

▶▶ Katie Webster, Saffire—The Uppity Blues Women, Koko Taylor, Ray Charles, Sippie Wallace, Hadda Brooks, Alberta Hunter

Steve Knopper

Houston Stackhouse

Born September 28, 1910, in Wesson, MS. Died 1980, in Houston, TX.

Stackhouse was a devotee of Tommy Johnson, whose claim to fame was tutoring the brooding Delta slide master Robert Nighthawk. A lugubrious singer who specialized in Johnson standards like "Big Road Blues" and "Cool Water Blues," Stackhouse gained more renown as a genial interview subject than performer. He rarely recorded, and what was released did not help his reputation much. He toured Europe on occasion but stuck mostly to the Delta border towns between Mississippi and Arkansas, playing with musicians who had long associated with Sonny Boy Williamson II.

what to buy: *Masters of Modern Blues* ♫♫♫ (Testament, 1994, prod. Pete Welding) includes 1964 and 1967 sessions that feature both Stackhouse and his student, the great Robert Nighthawk. The nine Nighthawk cuts from 1964 are sublime, contrasting his grim vocal shadings and eerie guitar work against the stringent harp-blowing of John Wrencher and Little Walter. Nighthawk also joined Stackhouse for an eight-song session from 1968. Saved from mediocrity by Nighthawk's backing, Stackhouse offers the usual Tommy Johnson versions and a decent reading of Robert Johnson's unrecorded "Take a Little Walk with Me."

the rest:

Cryin' Won't Help You ♫♫♫ (Genes, 1996)

influences:

◀◀ Tommy Johnson

▶▶ Robert Nighthawk

Steve Braun

Pops Staples

Born December 2, 1915, in Winona, MS.

Roebuck "Pops" Staples made his name while transforming his clan of siblings from southern-bred gospel singers (reflecting his own church-reared youth) to soul-pop hit makers that rose to prominence with Stax in the late 1960s. Pops himself didn't go the solo route until late in life.

what to buy: Released at age 77, *Peace to the Neighborhood* ♫♫♫ (Pointblank, 1992, prod. Roebuck Staples), is a startlingly vibrant and seer-like distillation of blues and gospel. Portraits of a troubled homeland fraught with violence, addiction and spiritual decay drift across the album as if seeking Staples' own visions of peace and healing. Staples' firm but ultimately gentle stance and delivery win out (no doubt assisted by a crack guest list and daughter Mavis' able pipes). Staples followed up with the equally strong *Father Father* ♫♫♫♫ (Pointblank, 1994), which earned him a Grammy for Best Contemporary Blues Album.

Allan Orski

Billy Stewart

Born March 24, 1937, in Washington, DC. Died January 17, 1970, in NC.

A singer whose vocal eccentricities rivaled those of cartoon voice-over whiz Mel Blanc, the amazing Billy Stewart could simply never sing a song straight. Whether raver or ballad, Stewart peppered everything he sung with sudden burps, trills and hiccup-mannerisms that somehow always seemed to work. A walrus of a man, Stewart even managed to turn his nickname, "Fat Boy," into a chart hit. He emerged from a Washington doo-wop group, the Rainbows, who also claimed soul tunesmith Don Covay as a member. Stewart toured with Bo Diddley, who backed him on the 1956 effort, "Billy's Blues," then floundered in chitlin' circuit clubs for several years, eventually growing close to producer Billy Davis, who prodded him to write his own material after he joined Chess. "Reap What You Sew" was his first minor R&B hit in 1962. Two years later, Stewart scored with the lushly-arranged soul bonanzas "I Do Love You" and "Sitting in the Park." It was on George Gershwin's "Summertime," released in 1966, that Stewart's histrionics really soared. But that was his high point. Stewart continued recording and touring, but he was hampered by diabetes and a 1969 motorcycle crash. Another road disaster ended it for him in January 1970, when a car carrying Stewart and his band skidded into a North Carolina river, killing him and three musicians.

what to buy: All of the "Fat Boy's" crucial hits are on *One More Time* ♫♫♫♫ (Chess/MCA, 1988, prod. Adam White, Andy Mc-Kaie), and without a single breep, chuck chuck or brrrrrrip removed. The mastering is on par with MCA's other Chess vault offerings.

influences:

◀◀ Bo Diddley

Steve Braun

Frank Stokes

Born January 1, 1888, in Whitehaven, TN. Died September 12, 1955, in Memphis, TN.

Frank Stokes and guitar wizard Dan Sain made up the Beale Street Sheiks, a two-man string band that roamed the streets of Memphis in the 1920s and 1930s, taking on the rest of the town's jug-poppers and kazoo blowers. Stokes and Sain were a good decade older than many of their rivals, well-versed in the minstrelsy and ragtime standards popular among Beale Street and Handy Park habitués. Raised in Tutwiler, Mississippi, by an uncle, Stokes absorbed the gentle guitar patterns of ragtime as a kid, replaying them time and again as a dancer and shill for the Doc Watts Medicine Show. By the late 1920s, Stokes and Sain were popular enough to find recording work with Paramount and Victor. The tune and some of the lyrics of Stokes' jaunty "I Shall" were durable enough to be resurrected by Bob Dylan as "I Shall

Be Free" on his *Freewheelin'* album. Stokes, backed by Sain and fiddler Will Batts, also recorded other lasting sides like the nutty barnhouse lament, "Chicken, You Can Roost behind the Moon" and the sly attack on segregationist pol E.H. Crump on "Mr. Crump Don't Like It," set to the tune of "Mama Don't Allow." The Sheiks fell apart in the 1930s, but Stokes continued to play with Batts on and off until his death in 1955.

what to buy: The 19 songs Stokes and Sain performed for Paramount, marred by that company's infamous poor recording and flimsy vinyl 78s are now on *The Beale Street Sheiks* 𝄞𝄞𝄞 (Document, 1990, prod. Johnny Parth). "Crump" and "You Shall" are perfect string-band efforts, even through the rain of surface noise.

what to buy next: *Frank Stokes, The Victor Recordings 1928–29* 𝄞𝄞𝄞𝄞 (Document, 1990, prod. Johnny Parth) contains Stokes' remaining efforts for Victor, better recorded and perked up by the fluid fiddle of Will Batts. The title is debatable, but the selection of Stokes' Paramount and Victor sides on *Creator of the Memphis Blues* 𝄞𝄞𝄞𝄞 (Yazoo, 1990) can't be challenged. Biographical notes outshine the typically spare Document discs.

influences:

▶▶ Furry Lewis, Big Walter Horton, Bob Dylan

Steve Braun

Sarah Streeter

See: Big Time Sarah

Percy Strother

Born July 23, 1946, in Vicksburg, MS.

There's a certain outrage in Strother's booming soul voice, which probably still owes to his father's violent death when he was a child. That incident destroyed his youth—Strother's mother died not long after, he lost the family farm and, instead of succumbing to a life at an orphanage, he fled to Jackson, Mississippi. After drifting between jobs and battling the bottle he discovered the blues, took up guitar and turned out to be quite the self-taught soul singer. He didn't release an album until 1992, and there's a devastating sad look in his eyes on all the album pictures, but it's nice to hear Strother sound like he's where he's supposed to be.

what to buy: Strother's first release, *A Good Woman Is Hard to Find* 𝄞𝄞𝄞 (Blue Moon, 1992, prod. Percy Strother, Pat Dawson), is a terrific R&B album with a big horn sound to play against the singer's sad, explosive voice; most of the songs are about love and loss, such as "I'm Falling in Love with You, Baby" and "Someday I Will Be Over You," but Strother gives the conventions renewed energy.

worth searching for: *The Highway Is My Home* 𝄞𝄞𝄞 (Black Magic, 1995, prod. Percy Strother) came out in Holland, and it's another excellent document of the singer's natural strength and depth.

influences:

◀◀ Wilson Pickett, Willie Dixon, Muddy Waters, Albert King, Son Seals

▶▶ Fabulous Thunderbirds, Robert Cray, Johnny Copeland, Roomful of Blues

Steve Knopper

Studebaker John

Born John Grimaldi, November 5, 1952, in Chicago, IL.

Multi-instrumentalist and songwriter extraordinaire Grimaldi, whose stage name is from a car he once owned, came of age at a vibrant time for Chicago blues: real-deal street performers busked at open air flea markets on Chicago's Maxwell Street and the blues clubs were always hopping. As a youngster, Grimaldi learned to play his father's musical instruments, including harmonica, but it was hearing performances by giants like Big and Little Walter, Sonny Boy Williamson and One-Armed John Wrencher that hipped Grimaldi to the real potentialities of the instrument. Seeing Hound Dog Taylor play one night in a club was also a "eureka" experience, inspiring him to focus his guitar playing on the fiery slide style of Taylor, Elmore James, Johnny Littlejohn and J.B. Hutto. Grimaldi pursued his taste for blues-infused rock, and for a quarter of a century now Grimaldi has led one version or another of the Hawks. Until recently, economic reality usually required that he hold a day job, often in some aspect of construction. Grimaldi has proven himself to be a rock solid player with a raw amplified harp sound and stinging slide hand. An emotive singer with a reedy voice, he's an exciting live performer who alternates between harmonica and slide guitar (one of his collection of sweet-toned Danelectros) onstage. He is also an exceptional songwriter with a hook-laden melodic sense and an ability to compose lyrics that convey the emotional complexities of life with conviction and freshness, never sounding maudlin or bathetic.

what to buy: A gem, though a little-known one, *Too Tough* 𝄞𝄞𝄞𝄞 (Blind Pig, 1994, prod. Jerry Del Giudice, John Grimaldi) covers lots of electric blues bases, from jump to slow to rock, with tight playing, an electrified ambience to the sound, and plenty of insights.

what to buy next: If Grimaldi's other two readily available releases, *Outside Lookin' In* 𝄞𝄞𝄞𝄞 (Blind Pig, 1995, prod. John Grimaldi) and *Tremoluxe* 𝄞𝄞𝄞𝄞 (Blind Pig, 1996, prod. Jim Gaines) aren't quite up to the standard set by *Too Tough*, it's only because he gave himself such a hard act to follow. Actually, *Outside* was largely recorded prior to *Too Tough* in 1990, released in Europe, and then put out as Grimaldi's second Blind Pig album. Grimaldi borrows a page from Bo Diddley's book on "She's a Rocker" and generally shows his developing songcraft. *Tremoluxe* finds Grimaldi in a boogie mood and includes many more fine numbers, like "Voodoo Woman" with its otherworldly harmonica skronk.

worth searching for: *Rockin' the Blues '85* 𝄞𝄞𝄞 (Double Trouble, 1992) is a reissue of a 1985 album recorded in the Netherlands that presents Grimaldi at an earlier stage of his development and features all harmonica numbers, some of which are still part of Grimaldi's live repertoire.

influences:

◀◀ Little Walter, Big Walter Horton, Elmore James, Hound Dog Taylor, Paul Butterfield Blues Band

▶▶ Lil' Ed & the Blues Imperials, Mississippi Heat, Gary Primich

Michael Dixon

Sugar Blue

Born James Whiting, 1950, in New York, NY.

One of the most unique blues harmonica stylists, Sugar Blue has one foot in the present and the other in its fertile past. He grew up in Harlem in a musical environment. His mother, a singer/dancer who performed at the legendary Apollo Theatre, frowned on young James pursuing a life as a musician. An avid, self-taught student, he received his first harmonica at the age of 10 from a relative. Sitting in as a teenager with Muddy Waters during one of the blues giant's visits to New York was a turning point and solidified the decision to become a musician. He dubbed himself Sugar Blue and by the early 1970s was recording with artists like Johnny Shines, Louisiana Red and others. He relocated to Paris in 1976 and via introductions from his friend Memphis Slim moved from street-corner jamming to recording with the Rolling Stones (*Some Girls*, *Emotional Rescue*, *Tattoo You*). His funky, skulking harp was widely heard on "Miss You" as well as a diverse range of recordings by other artists, including jazz players Stan Getz and Paul Horn. By 1982 he was firmly established as a harp player to be reckoned with amongst musicians but not very well known outside that community. He moved to Chicago and within a few years had a Grammy and a recording contract with Alligator. Sugar Blue is a modern blues player, playing his Huang harmonica through a Mesa Boogie amplifier and going for a totally electric approach. His incendiary, mercurial, upper-register harmonica riffing has led to comparisons with Jimi Hendrix and Charlie Parker.

what to buy: Blue cuts a fiery swath through modern and traditional blues on *Blue Blazes* 𝄞𝄞𝄞𝄞 (Alligator, 1994, prod. Fred Breitberg). His excursions into multi-note, upper-register harmonica solos are unleashed as if they'd been held inside too long. The ultra-melodic jazzy tilt manages not to compromise any of his blues edge. His treatment of "Miss You" has a strong funk/rock undercurrent and pugnacious harmonica soloing, and he proves to be a smooth and capable vocalist as well.

what to buy next: Continuing in the same vein, *In Your Eyes* 𝄞𝄞𝄞 (Alligator, 1995, prod. Fred Breitberg, John Zwierzko) consists primarily of original selections with one cover, Willie Dixon's "Little Red Rooster."

worth searching for: *Crossroads* (Blue Silver/Europa, 1980, prod. Dominique Buscail), recorded in France in 1979, is an interesting set of very urban cool blues with horn arrangements and Blue's inimitable harp, and Sonny Boy Williamson II's "Pontiac" and "Another Man Done Gone" acting as traditional bookends to the more modern pieces in between. The original tunes, co-written by Blue and bassist Cecile Savage, are polished and jazzy, with a bit of grit thrown in at either end. *Too Wet to Plow* 𝄞𝄞𝄞𝄞 (Tomato, 1989, prod. Kent Cooper, Heiner Stadler), originally recorded on the defunct Blue Labor in 1975, is a Johnny Shines Delta acoustic blues project that includes Louisiana Red and a young Sugar Blue. A truly exemplary traditional blues recording with very appealing Blue harmonica accompaniment on five of the 12 selections. There are none of the latter-day harp acrobatics; he is playing closer to the bone on this one.

influences:

◀◀ Carey Bell, Jean "Toots" Thielemans

▶▶ Norton Buffalo, Lee Oskar, John Popper

Tali Madden

Hubert Sumlin

Born November 16, 1931, near Greenwood, MS.

There is no better, more distinctive or more influential blues guitarist than Hubert Sumlin. The quirky fury of his guitar solos was a powerful influence on Eric Clapton, Keith Richards, Jimi Hendrix and Stevie Ray Vaughan. Sumlin's recorded work as Howlin' Wolf's lead guitarist from 1956 until Wolf's death in 1976 is clearly his best. Producer Dick Shurman, in extensive liner notes for *Howlin' Wolf: The Chess Box*, pays homage to "Sumlin's imaginative angular, taut attack, frequent glissandi, maniacally wide vibrato and percussive chords, all drawn with an exaggerated brush." Comparing him with other Wolf guitarists, Shurman writes, "Sumlin was more like a whip, playing his leads in almost totally unconventional bursts and his chords in choppy patterns." The Wolf/Sumlin musical collaboration became one of blues' most productive and enduring. "I got to where I knew what he wanted before he asked for it, because I could feel the man," Sumlin has said. Unfortunately, when Wolf died in 1976, Sumlin had the musical rug pulled out from under him. Devastated, he reportedly didn't play for several years afterwards. Though he has recorded steadily in the past two decades, his efforts are hit-and-miss, mostly the latter. Put simply, his records are good if he has a good singer, and he usually has a different one each time. Unfortunately, he shares the vocal duties rather than give them up completely; it as if the problem is fully recognized but not fully solved. The power and imagination of his guitar work remain, but while they were once driven by a singular blues powerhouse, they are now more evocative than anything else.

what to buy: *Hubert Sumlin's Blues Party* 𝄢𝄢𝄢𝄢 (Black Top, 1987, prod. Ronnie Earl, Hammond Scott) is Sumlin's strongest solo effort. He shares guitar duties with a clearly inspired Ronnie Earl, and the best (but not all) vocals are handled by Mighty Sam McClain. A powerful rendition of Wolf's "Hidden Charms" is highlighted by an updated version of what has been called Sumlin's most powerful guitar solo. A Ronnie Earl tune, "Soul That's Been Abused," is maybe the best single cut, a mourner paced by Sumlin's sizzling, crackling notes and sinuous horn support.

what to buy next: *My Guitar and Me* 𝄢𝄢𝄢 (Evidence, 1994, prod. Disques Black and Blue, reissue prod. Jerry Gordon) was recorded in Paris in 1976 during Sumlin's first solo tour, weeks before Wolf's death, and features a feisty Lonnie Brooks on rhythm guitar. "Broke and Hungry" is perhaps Hubert's best vocal performance. The record happily is largely instrumental and features four solo acoustic tracks that both reveal and re-

flect Sumlin's Delta roots. Recorded in East Berlin in 1964 with Willie Dixon and Sunnyland Slim, *Blues Anytime* 𝄢𝄢𝄢𝄢 (Evidence, 1994, prod. Horst Lippmann) is a minor treasure trove that features some of Dixon's finest bass playing on record. Dixon and Slim handle most of the vocal chores. Four acoustic numbers are penned by Sumlin, and his solo work propels a remake of Dixon's "My Babe."

what to avoid: It's a shame *Heart and Soul* 𝄢𝄢 (Blind Pig, 1989, prod. Jerry Del Giudice, Mike Markowitz), a reunion with Sumlin's childhood friend James Cotton, is not better. There are few magic moments. Take "No Time for Me," where the duo build up a haunting blues melody, then Sumlin starts to sing and the mood is shattered, leaving the listener hungry for the nearest solo break. Sumlin's vocal work on covers of Wolf classics "Little Red Rooster" and "Sitting on Top of the World" is lifeless and largely unaided by the backup of Little Mike & the Tornadoes. The instrumental "Chunk" is a slowed-down, watered-down version of "Killing Floor."

the rest:

Blues Guitar Boss 𝄢𝄢𝄢 (JSP, 1990)
Healing Feeling 𝄢𝄢𝄢 (Black Top, 1990)

worth searching for: Sumlin has guest-starred on several fine records. Jimmy Rogers' *Ludella* (Antone's, 1991) features several great live cuts with Sumlin joined by Pinetop Perkins on piano and Kim Wilson on harmonica. The Eddie Taylor Blues Band's *My Heart Is Bleeding* (Evidence, 1994) features the long-time Jimmy Reed sideman leading Sumlin, Sunnyland Slim, Carey Bell and Odie Payne through "Dust My Broom." Buddy Guy and Junior Wells' *Live in Montreux* (Evidence, 1977/1992) features Sumlin as a guest star.

influences:

◀◀ Charley Patton, Robert Johnson

▶▶ Jimi Hendrix, Eric Clapton, Keith Richards

Rob Reuteman

Sunnyland Slim

Born Albert Luandrew, September 5, 1907, in Vance, MS. Died March 17, 1995, in Chicago, IL.

Sunnyland Slim was ten feet tall. He strode into bluesdom like some mythic man out of folklore, having played piano in the

Hubert Sumlin (© **Jack Vartoogian**)

lumber camps, mining towns and roadhouses on every highway and byway of America. He was in Chicago by 1933, years before any of those who became the city's most famed blues stars. It was Sunnyland who expedited Mud's signing with Chess; J.B. Lenoir, Little Walter, Snooky Pryor, Bonnie Lee and Big Time Sarah are a few others whose careers he goosed. Piano-wise he wasn't as florid as Otis Spann, and he wasn't a flamboyant stage personality like Roosevelt Sykes. His was the old-style barrelhouse blues, and being a true man of the people he slathered his talents over many labels. This had its good points. A thrilling blues memory would be of a windswept Chicago eve when Sunnyland reached into the trunk of one of his famous cars to get, and give you, a copy of one of his LPs on his own Airway label. That side two of the vinyl slab was found to have a pressing defect that renders it unlistenable does not by a whit diminish its holiness as a keepsake. Such things do, however, vex the discographer, who is supposed to have more objective reasons for touting a record. Sunnyland cut for Victor, JOB, World Pacific, Jewel, Spivey, Storyville, ABC/Bluesway and more. Some of this is on vinyl and hard to get, but there is much on CD that's good by Sunnyland, who was, by the way, ten feet tall.

what to buy: Pricey but worth every penny, *Rediscovered Blues* ✺✺✺✺✺ (Capitol, 1996, prod. Pete Welding) offers a whopping 19 vintage cuts (some previously unissued) by Sunnyland. The rest is by Arthur Crudup, Bumble Bee Slim and Sunnyland's piano pal, Roosevelt Sykes. *Chicago Jump* ✺✺✺✺ (Evidence, 1995, prod. Sam Burckhardt) is a cookin' session from 1985 with Sunnyland and his working band, a great unit featuring long-term Sunnyland loyalist Steve Freund on guitar.

what to buy next: The maestro was getting old (he was 80 when this was cut in 1987) but *Live at the D.C. Blues Society* ✺✺✺✺ (Mapleshade, 1995, prod. Pierre M. Sprey) shows him still adept at swingin' jump blues ("Get to My Baby"), deep-dish laments ("She Don't Love Me No More," spiked with his trademark Woody Woodpecker laugh) and his standard, "When I Gets to Drinkin'." A compelling, latter-day aural document from an irreplaceable man. The LP version of *Blues Piano Orgy* ✺✺✺✺ (Delmark, 1996, prod. Robert Koester) that came out in 1972 had two cuts by Sunnyland. This one has four, and they're all great! The other keypounders on this collection include Roosevelt Sykes, Little Brother Montgomery and Otis Spann.

the rest:

Chicago Piano from Cobra & Jewel ✺✺✺ (Paula)
Sad & Lonesome ✺✺✺ (Jewel, 1992)
Slim's Shout ✺✺ (Original Blues Classics, 1993)

Decoration Day ✺✺✺ (Evidence, 1995)
Sunnyland Train ✺✺✺✺ (Evidence, 1995)

worth searching for: *Sunnyland Slim/Bluesmasters Vol. 8* ✺✺✺✺✺ (Blue Horizon LP, 1969, prod. Mike Vernon), cut in Chicago in 1968, has Sunnyland in the stellar company of Johnny Shines, Willie Dixon, Walter Horton and Clifton James. Blue Horizon was a short lived blues wing of Polydor; the *Bluesmasters* series comprised eight LPs. Of the spate of Sunnyland LPs in the era, this one is the best.

influences:

◀◀ Little Brother Montgomery

▶▶ Barrelhouse Chuck, Big Moose Walker

Tim Schuller

Super Chikan

See: James "Super Chikan" Johnson

Roosevelt Sykes

Born January 31, 1906, in West Memphis, AR. Died July 17, 1983, in New Orleans, LA.

One of the most prolific and important blues artists of all time was Roosevelt Sykes. A strong singer and powerful pianist, Sykes, also known as "The Honeydripper," "Dobby Bragg," "Willie Kelly" and "Easy Papa Johnson," has had a profound influence on blues performers from several generations. Signature compositions like "Sweet Home Chicago," "The Honeydripper" and "Driving Wheel" have become blues standards. Sykes was playing piano at the age of 12. His family moved to St. Louis in the early 1920s where Sykes became the city's top blues attraction. In 1929 he recorded "44 Blues" for OKeh which became quite popular. This led to other recordings (occasionally using an alias) for Victor, Paramount, Brunswick, Decca, Bluebird and Champion. Although he often played solo in lumber camps and barrelhouses, by the late 1930s he was touring with a 10-piece band. Such was his popularity that Sykes was one of the few blues artists to have recorded during World War II, when there was shellac rationing. By the 1950s Sykes had moved to Chicago, and in 1961 became one of the first blues artists to visit Europe. Eventually he moved to New Orleans, recording in between European concert tours and his regular piano bar gigs in the French Quarter. Later in life he became a deacon at his Baptist church and played only occasionally.

what to buy: The amount of Roosevelt Sykes material available on CD is extremely large. *Roosevelt Sykes, Volumes 1–10* ✺✺✺✺ (Document, 1995) presents all of Sykes' recordings in chronological order from 1929 to the mid-1950s. Any one would be a good Sykes primer. Containing lesser-known classics like "Date Bait," "This Tavern Boogie" and the title track, *West Helena Blues* ♬♬♬ (Wolf, 1993) has a nice understated Chicago sound. *The Honeydripper* ♬♬♬ (Original Blues Classics, 1960) includes some of Sykes' more humorous material, and saxophonist King Curtis helps give it a contemporary swing. Sykes' roguish personality is especially evident on *Hard Drivin' Blues* ♬♬♬ (Delmark, 1995, prod. Robert Koester), which is comprised of 1963 solo recordings.

what to buy next: *Raining in My Heart* ♬♬♬ (Delmark, prod. Robert Koester) consists of Sykes' swinging United material waxed in the early 1950s in Chicago. Recorded in Europe in 1966, Sykes reprises several songs from his first recording session for *Gold Mine* ♬♬♬ (Delmark, 1992, prod. Robert Koester). *Blues Boy* ♬♬♬ (Folkways, 1991) is another fine effort.

worth searching for: Sykes' LP, *Sings the Blues* ♬♬♬ (Crown, 1962) is worth obtaining just for the cover, which pictures Beale Street at night. *Dirty Double Mother* ♬♬♬♬ (Bluesway, 1973, prod. Al Smith) features an all-star New Orleans band that includes Clarence Ford and Justin Adams. *The Original Honeydripper* ♬♬♬ (Blind Pig, 1978, prod. Jerry Del Giudice, Edward Chmelewski) catches an especially energetic live performance.

influences:

◀◀ Pine Top Smith, Lee Green, Charles "Cow Cow" Davenport, Fats Waller, Little Brother Montgomery

▶▶ Curtis Jones, Sunnyland Slim, Paul Gayten, Fats Domino, Little Johnny Jones, Jack DuPree, Pinetop Perkins, Willie Love, Professor Longhair, Ray Charles, Otis Spann

Jeff Hannusch

Tampa Red

Born Hudson Whittaker, January 8, 1904, in Smithville, GA. Died March 19, 1981, in Chicago, IL.

If anyone embodied the prolific, workmanlike and restrained nature of Chicago's blues scene in the 1930s and early 1940s, it was Tampa Red. No one was more likely to pop up at one of producer Lester Melrose's seemingly endless studio sessions than Red, who backed up scores of vocalists with his tasteful slide guitar work—and sometimes scarred their efforts with his grating kazoo styles. The affable "Guitar Wizard" was equally able to shine on his own, racking up more than 335 recording spots with OKeh and Bluebird in 20 years work—still saving inspiration for a late-age return to blues records in the late 1950s and early 1960s. Early on, he was a frequent partner with Thomas A. "Georgia Tom" Dorsey, who ultimately left a surefire blues career to become known as the "Father of Modern Gospel." Red and Dorsey collaborated on the raunchy "It's Tight Like That" and other late 1920s risqué hokum songs. By the 1940s, Red had become a tunesmith in his own right, author of the seminal "Black Angel Blues," "Anna Lou Blues" and "It Hurts Me Too," songs adopted by hotter 1950s slide masters Robert Nighthawk and Elmore James.

Red won one part of his nickname from his childhood town of Tampa, where he started his guitar education, picking up tips from his brother, Eddie, and a friend known as "Piccolo Pete." The "Red" came from his light-skinned complexion. Traveling through Mississippi and the Deep South, he mastered the famous National metal guitar, known for its acoustic resonance, then joined the migration to Chicago. Once there he settled in as an accompanist to such Chicago stalwarts at Big Bill Broonzy, Frankie "Half-Pint" Jaxon, Big Maceo Merriwether, Sonny Boy Williamson I, Memphis Minnie and Big Joe Williams. His traveling days over, Red turned his sprawling South Side home into a way-station for bluesmen passing through town. The rise in the late 1940s of rawer, less urbane Delta bluesmen like Muddy Waters, Howlin' Wolf and Elmore James eclipsed the Bluebird studio's interchangeable session men. With them went Tampa Red, who could not match the ferocity of artists like James—even though he was borrowing Red's own classics.

what to buy: The material on *Tampa Red, 1938–40* ♬♬♬♬ (BMG/Bluebird, 1997, prod. Michael Omansky) are from Red's finest years, just before World War II and the birth of electric Chicago blues put him out to pasture. His downcast "Anna Lee Blues" later became a perfect vehicle for mournful Robert Nighthawk. "Don't You Lie to Me" was pop fodder for Fats Domino and Chuck Berry. And here is the timeless "It Hurts Me Too," adopted by artists as varied as Elmore James and John Lee Hooker. BMG's resurrection of the original Bluebird masters is cause for celebration.

what to buy next: Red was willing to try almost anything and most of it is on *Tampa Red, 1934-36* ♬♬♬ (BMG/Bluebird, 1997, prod. Michael Omansky): gut-clenching blues, silly hokum, restrained slide guitar instrumentals and, at times, life-less efforts that showed Red marking time. Above all else, "Black Angel Blues" is as sure a love song as the blues has ever produced. With enough money to burn, you could pick up the entire, 15-CD set of Tampa Red's OKeh and Bluebird recordings, *Tampa Red Complete Works in Chronological Order 1928–53* 𝄢𝄢𝄢 (Document, 1991, prod. Johnny Parth). There are hours of Red here, enough to program into your CD for a week to keep away prowlers while you winter in, say, Tampa. For the truly addled, imagine how many hours of mind-altering kazoo can be found here. And, more often than it sounds, there are also some top-notch blues performances, particularly in Red's early years and at his peak in the early 1940s.

the rest:

Don't Tampa with the Blues 𝄢𝄢𝄢 (Original Blues Classics, 1982)
Bottleneck Guitar, 1928–37 𝄢𝄢𝄢 (Yazoo, 1990)
Tampa Red: The Story of the Guitar Wizard 𝄢𝄢𝄢𝄢 (EPM, 1992)
The Guitar Wizard 𝄢𝄢𝄢𝄢 (Columbia/Legacy, 1994)

influences:

◀◀ Eddie Whitaker, Piccolo Pete, Thomas A. Dorsey

▶▶ Robert Nighthawk, Elmore James, Fats Domino, B.B. King, John Lee Hooker, Chuck Berry

Steve Braun

Tarheel Slim

Born Alden Bunn, September 24, 1924, in Wilson, NC. Died August 21, 1977, in New York, NY.

Long before Ray Charles and Sam Cooke sparked national controversies by crossing over from God's music to Satan's, Alden Bunn and his cohorts switched from gospel to R&B. He started as a singer and guitarist in various gospel bands, including the Gospel Four and the Selah Jubilee Singers; eventually, a record label with dollar signs in its eyes convinced Bunn's band to go secular. They became the Larks, an R&B vocal group that sang Sonny Boy Williamson's "Eyesight to the Blind" and many other songs God would, in theory, not be pleased with. Bunn continued to sing for many vocal groups, including the Wheels, whose best-known hit was 1957's "Darling It's Wonderful." Bunn dubbed himself Tarheel Slim and made several explosive blues and rockabilly singles before rock 'n' roll put him out of business for good—excepting a minor comeback in the early 1970s.

what to buy: Sharing billing with Little Ann, *Red Robin & Fire Years* 𝄢𝄢𝄢𝄢 (Collectables, 1993, prod. various) is a sharp docu-

ment of Alden Bunn's amazing versatility; he lurches on these 1950s singles from blues to pop to R&B to rockabilly, all with rock 'n' roll-level stamina. Another excellent collection: *#9 Train* 𝄢𝄢𝄢 (Charly, 1980).

influences:

◀◀ Sonny Boy Williamson II, Elmore James, Fairfield Four, Soul Stirrers

▶▶ Sam Cooke, Ray Charles, Little Richard, Chuck Berry, Aretha Franklin

Steve Knopper

Baby Tate

Born January 28, 1916, in Elberton, GA. Died August 17, 1972, in Columbia, SC.

Baby Tate joined the Army during World War II, rendering a promising blues career a footnote instead. An acoustic guitarist who adapted much of his style from his mentor Blind Boy Fuller, Tate became a solid draw at local clubs, recorded for Decca and did shows with the Carolina Blackbirds for the radio station WFBC. But after he returned from the Army in 1946, his window of opportunity had closed. He recorded again in 1950 for Kapp, released his only album in 1962 and earned enough 1960s festival repute to land in the documentary *The Blues*. He was a minor historical figure kind enough to leave behind recorded evidence of his broad talent.

what to buy: *See What You Done Done* 𝄢𝄢𝄢𝄢 (Original Blues Classics, 1962/Fantasy, 1994, prod. Kenneth Goldstein) is an impeccably written acoustic blues album in the style of Lightnin' Hopkins and, of course, Blind Boy Fuller.

influences:

◀◀ Blind Boy Fuller, Lightnin' Hopkins, Jesse Fuller, Brownie McGhee, Leadbelly

▶▶ Buddy Guy, Junior Wells, John Hammond Jr., Taj Mahal, Keb' Mo'

Steve Knopper

Eddie Taylor

Born January 29, 1923, in Benoit, MS. Died December 25, 1985, in Chicago, IL.

"A guitar in the country don't sound good 'till late at night," it says in liner notes to his *I Feel So Bad* album, and you couldn't invent a more descriptive sentence for his music. Best known for his explosive guitar sound behind Jimmy Reed's string of

1950s classics—not to mention his own solid sides for Vee-Jay—Eddie Taylor grew up learning from Delta legends the likes of Robert Johnson. After that, like Muddy Waters and so many others, he brought his skills with him to Chicago. He wound up playing the Maxwell Street Market, where he met bassist Jimmy Lee Robinson and guitarist Honeyboy Edwards and was re-united with his Mississippi friend Reed. Taylor isn't the most original electric guitarist ever to play the Chicago blues—his slowed-down tones directly recall both Charley Patton and Waters—but he stamps his own laid-back feeling and deceptively speedy rhythm on everything he does. After playing on most of Reed's Vee-Jay classics from 1953 to 1955, Taylor worked with Elmore James, John Lee Hooker and Waters, but his career slowed down when blues gave way to rock 'n' roll. The 1960s blues revival gave Taylor a renewed career at festivals, and he continued to perform at mainstay clubs in Austin, Texas, and Chicago until his death.

what to buy: Two essential collections capture the most important peaks of Taylor's career: *Ride 'Em on Down* 𝄢𝄢𝄢𝄢 (Charly, prod. various) is 24 of the singer-guitarist's wonderful solo Vee-Jay tracks, including "Bad Boy," "Find My Baby" and the title track; *I Feel So Bad* 𝄢𝄢𝄢𝄢 (HighTone, 1972, prod. Frank Scott) is a perfect Chicago blues prototype, as solid as Buddy Guy's *Stone Crazy* even though it was (the horror!) recorded live in Los Angeles in 1972.

what to buy next: There's too much tribute going around on *My Heart Is Bleeding* 𝄢𝄢𝄢 (Evidence, 1994, prod. Horst Lippmann). We get the point—Taylor likes Waters and Reed—but pianist Sunnyland Slim and harpist Carey Bell help turn this 1980 session into a decent Taylor document.

what to avoid: For years, *Bad Boy* 𝄢𝄢𝄢𝄢 (Charly, 1993, prod. various) was the definitive collection of Taylor's Vee-Jay sides—but *Ride 'Em on Down* rendered it redundant and incomplete.

the rest:

Still Not Ready for Eddie 𝄢𝄢𝄢 (Antone's, 1988)
Bad Boy 𝄢𝄢𝄢 (Wolf, 1993)
Long Way from Home 𝄢𝄢𝄢 (Blind Pig, 1995)

influences:

◀◀ Jimmy Reed, Robert Johnson, Muddy Waters, Albert King, Charley Patton, Memphis Minnie

▶▶ Buddy Guy, Son Seals, Otis Rush, Etta James, Eric Clapton, Rolling Stones

Steve Knopper

Tampa Red
song
Reckless Man Blues
album
The Guitar Wizard (Columbia/Legacy)
instrument
Guitar

monster solo

Hound Dog Taylor

Born Theodore Roosevelt Taylor, April 12, 1915, in Natchez, MS. Died December 17, 1975, in Chicago, IL.

Hound Dog Taylor was electric, slide guitar-dominated Chicago blues honed to its most raw, essential ingredients. Accompanied only by guitarist Brewer Phillips and drummer Ted Harvey, Taylor's South Side blues oozed spontaneous energy and good vibes. It was Hound Dog's music that inspired Alligator's Bruce Iglauer to launch the label in 1971.

what to buy: Every blues collection should have at least one Hound Dog Taylor album, but you don't need them all. The best, *Beware of the Dog!* 𝄢𝄢𝄢𝄢 (Alligator, 1976, prod. Bruce Iglauer), captures lively performances and entertaining crowd interaction. Taylor's debut, *Hound Dog Taylor and the House-rockers* 𝄢𝄢𝄢 (Alligator, 1971, prod. Hound Dog Taylor, Bruce Iglauer, Wesley Race), is raw, raw, raw, unleashing a lifetime of blues power from Hound Dog.

the rest:

Natural Boogie 𝄢𝄢𝄢 (Alligator, 1974)

Genuine Houserocking Music 𝄢𝄢𝄢 (Alligator, 1982)

influences:

◀◀ Elmore James

▶▶ George Thorogood

Bryan Powell

Koko Taylor

Born Cora Walton, c. 1938, in Memphis, TN.

Best-known for her growling belt of a voice, heavy night-club touring and facial features so distinctive and charismatic she earned a cameo in David Lynch's film, *Wild at Heart,* Koko Taylor began her singing career after she moved to Chicago in 1953. It was just soon enough; by the early 1960s, just before Chicago's famed Chess Records lost momentum to rock 'n' roll, she hooked up with songwriter-producer Willie Dixon and squeezed out the terrific blues anthem "Wang Dang Doodle." Though that 1965 hit, a stomping, funky description of an all-night house party, continues to be the Queen of the Blues' main show-stopper, Taylor has released nine straightforward blues albums since then and continues to be one of the most reliable and consistent performers on the blues circuit. Some blues heroes and heroines, like Taylor's immediate predecessor Etta James, have experimented with different sounds to reach a broader audience. Not Taylor. You can count on her traveling through your town with a band of hot instrumentalists playing no-frills, 12-bar electric blues songs, before the year is out.

what to buy: Because Taylor has such a visual presence, her ferocious onstage energy rarely comes across on record. On *I Got What It Takes* 𝄢𝄢𝄢𝄢 (Alligator, 1975, prod. Koko Taylor, Mighty Joe Young, Bruce Iglauer) she's hungry to make an impact, with hot guitarist Mighty Joe Young, great songs by Willie Dixon and Otis Spann and a pure-blues cover of the R&B classic "Mama, He Treats Your Daughter Mean." She basically put out the same album every few years after that. *Force of Nature* 𝄢𝄢𝄢 (Alligator, 1993, prod. Criss Johnson, Koko Taylor, Bruce Iglauer), her best recent album, gets a boost from guest guitarist Buddy Guy and explosive readings of "Born under a Bad Sign" and "Hound Dog."

what to buy next: Especially on the fast stuff, *The Earthshaker* 𝄢𝄢𝄢 (Alligator, 1978) shows Taylor using her big voice to great effect. The pre-Alligator album you want, with frequently funny collaborations from creative partner Willie Dixon, is *Koko Taylor* 𝄢𝄢𝄢 (Chess, 1972, prod. Willie Dixon). *Queen of the Blues* 𝄢𝄢𝄢

(Alligator, 1985, prod. Koko Taylor, Bruce Iglauer, Criss Johnson) features guest guitarists Albert Collins, Son Seals and Lonnie Brooks.

what to avoid: Taylor's one-dimensional blues approach sometimes lodges her in a rut, which is the case on *From the Heart of a Woman* 𝄢𝄢 (Alligator, 1989) and *Jump for Joy* 𝄢𝄢 (Alligator, 1990).

the rest:

Basic Soul 𝄢𝄢 (Chess, 1972)

Live from Chicago—An Audience with the Queen 𝄢𝄢𝄢 (Alligator, 1987)

What It Takes 𝄢𝄢𝄢 (Chess/MCA, 1991)

worth searching for: Her first album, *Koko Taylor* 𝄢𝄢𝄢 (USA, 1963, prod. Big Bill Hill) doesn't use Taylor's still-maturing voice to great effect, but it's a nice historical document of her early career. Because Taylor has her record company's consummate sound—straight-ahead blues with big vocals and lots of guitar solos—devotees will want to try *The Alligator Records 20th Anniversary Collection* 𝄢𝄢𝄢 (Alligator, 1991) and the *Alligator Records 25th Anniversary Collection* 𝄢𝄢𝄢 (Alligator, 1996).

influences:

◀◀ Muddy Waters, Bessie Smith, Etta James, Willie Dixon, B.B. King, Big Mama Thornton, Buddy Guy

▶▶ Katie Webster, Son Seals, Big Time Sarah, PJ Harvey, Janis Joplin, Melissa Etheridge

Steve Knopper

Little Johnny Taylor

Born Johnny Lamar Young, February 11, 1943, in Memphis, TN.

One of the greatest blues singers of all time, Little Johnny Taylor grew up in Los Angeles, where he sang gospel and was a member of the Mighty Clouds of Joy. In 1959 he joined Johnny Otis' revue. "You'll Need Another Favor," his debut on Galaxy in 1963, met with modest success, but the follow-up, "Part Time Love," a lazy blues shuffle with effective lyrics, shot to the top of the R&B charts. "Since I Found a New Love," "Somebody's Got to Pay" and "Zig Zag Lightning" were additional examples of soul blues and displayed his gospel roots. In the early 1970s, Taylor switched to Ronn and was a frequent visitor to the R&B charts. Songs like "Everybody Knows about My Good Thing" and "Open House at My House" were especially popular in the Deep South. Taylor still occasionally plays dates in the South, but he hasn't recorded since the late 1980s.

what to buy: Collecting most of his Galaxy sides, *Greatest Hits* 𝄢𝄢𝄢𝄢𝄢 (Fantasy, 1982, prod. Ray Shanklin, Cliff Goldstein) simply ranks as one of the best blues CDs of all time. Interestingly,

Part Time Love ✍✍✍✍ (Paula, 1997, prod. Bobby Patterson, Miles Grayson) doesn't include the original hit, but it *does* include his excellent Ronn sides.

what to buy next: Available only in Europe, *The Galaxy Years* ✍✍✍✍ (Ace, 1992) contains all of the material contained on *Greatest Hits* plus five extra tracks. Taylor shares *The Super Taylors* ✍✍✍ (Paula, 1991, prod. Bobby Patterson) with Ted Taylor on this enjoyable but nonessential CD.

what to avoid: Unfortunately, *Stuck in the Mud* ✍✍ (Ichiban, 1988) includes too many dispirited covers to make it worth obtaining.

worth searching for: Galaxy issued two outstanding LPs, *Part Time Love* and *Soul Full of Blues* , as did Ronn with *Open House at My House* and *Everybody Knows about My Good Thing* ✍✍✍ (Ronn). The singles released on these labels normally hit the mark, but the latter is the only one available on compact disc.

influences:

◀◀ Julius Cheeks, Bobby "Blue" Bland, Junior Parker, Solomon Burke, Sam Cooke

Jeff Hannusch

Melvin Taylor

Born March 13, 1959, in Chicago, IL.

A Chicago guitarslinger with impeccable credentials—he played with the Legendary Blues Band, where pianist Pinetop Perkins took him under his wing and convinced him to start singing—Taylor knocks rock and blues against each other with force and speed. After hearing both Jimi Hendrix's *Electric Lady-land* and Muddy Waters, he started guitar as a teenager (you thought maybe Kenny Wayne Shepherd and Jonny Lang were the first blues prodigies?) and joined an R&B band called the Transistors. He frequently works with jazz artists, so many of his 1980s albums have a heavy-jamming, fusion feel, and he continues to play Chicago blues clubs with regularity.

what to buy: *Blues on the Run* ✍✍✍ (Evidence, 1982/1994, prod. Didier Tricard) contains only six songs, including the 10-minute finale "Chitlins Con Carne," so you know this isn't a man who values conciseness. But he's a fine jazz-influenced guitarist and occasionally reaches the Buddy Guy improvisational level.

what to buy next: *Melvin Taylor and the Slack Band* ✍✍✍ (Evidence, 1995, prod. John Snyder) is an accessible blues-pop album with covers of Jimi Hendrix's "Voodoo Chile (Slight Re-

turn)," Larry Flood's popularized-by-you-know-who "Texas Flood" and the goofy instrumental rock classic "Tequila."

the rest:

Plays the Blues for You ✍✍ (Isabel, 1984/Evidence, 1993)

influences:

◀◀ Jimi Hendrix, Muddy Waters, Buddy Guy, Pinetop Perkins, Son Seals, Eric Clapton, Stevie Ray Vaughan

▶▶ Kenny Wayne Shepherd, Jonny Lang, Sammy Mayfield

Steve Knopper

Johnnie "Geechie" Temple

Born October 18, 1906, in Canton, MS. Died November 22, 1968, in Jackson, MS.

Though he never attained stardom or even major hit singles, Johnny Temple was an incredibly influential singer and guitarist

from the Mississippi Delta. His trademark boogie style—the bottom-string bass—caught on with countless successors, from Elmore James to Buddy Guy. He began recording in 1935, and had some popularity throughout the late 1940s and 1950s. Until electric blues made him a relic, he toured with Big Walter Horton and Billy Boy Arnold, then moved back from Chicago to Mississippi to play random juke joints and clubs before retreating into obscurity.

what to buy: One of the few Temple collections, *1935–39* 𝄞𝄞𝄞𝄞 (Document, prod. various) includes "Lead Pencil Blues" and other singles he recorded during his prolific studio period.

influences:

◄◄ Robert Johnson, Son House, Tommy Johnson, Skip James, Tampa Red

►► Elmore James, Buddy Guy, Otis Rush, John Lee Hooker, Taj Mahal

Steve Knopper

Ten Years After

Formed 1967, in Nottingham, England. Disbanded 1974. Reunited 1989.

Alvin Lee, guitar, vocals; Chick Churchill, keyboards; Leo Lyons, bass; Ric Lee, drums.

Before there was "Stairway to Heaven" or "Free Bird," Ten Years After held the Bic lighter-inducing crown for "I'm Going Home," a crunching, bruising blues-rocker that lit up the Woodstock festival in a 13-minute version that featured seemingly endless (and if you were on acid, it probably was) improvised riffing by Alvin Lee. Playing electrifying blues at a peace 'n' love gathering is kind of the way TYA does things; it'll crank up the volume with something like "Baby Let Me Rock 'n' Roll You," but then the group will glide into something fuzzy and trippy like its biggest hit, "I'd Love to Change the World." Always a workhorse, Lee has kept playing with his own band, though he did bring TYA together for an album and tour in 1989.

what to buy: *Cricklewood Green* 𝄞𝄞𝄞𝄞 (Deram, 1970, prod. Ten Years After) is the group's most mature and varied effort, striding from the bravado of "Love Like a Man" through the psychedilia of "50,000 Miles beneath My Brain" to the almost jazzy swing of "Me and My Baby."

Koko Taylor (© Jack Vartoogian)

what to buy next: *Essential Ten Years After* 𝄞𝄞𝄞 (Chrysalis, 1991, prod. various) gets you most of what you'd want—with a nicely annotated booklet, too—although it leaves some good tracks off and includes a live rendition of "I'm Going Home" recorded somewhere other than Woodstock.

what to avoid: Take your pick of a fair share of leaden, same-sounding albums—a category that holds both *Stonehenge* 𝄞𝄞 (Deram, 1969, prod. Mike Vernon) and *Watt* 𝄞𝄞 (Deram/Chrysalis, 1970, prod. Chris Wright).

best of the rest:

Greatest Hits 𝄞𝄞𝄞 (Deram)
Rock and Roll Music to the World 𝄞𝄞𝄞 (Columbia, 1972/Chrysalis, 1989)
Recorded Live 𝄞𝄞𝄞 (Columbia, 1973/Chrysalis, 1989)
Live at Reading 𝄞𝄞𝄞 (Dutch East India, 1983)
Collection 𝄞𝄞𝄞 (Griffin, 1994)

worth searching for: What else—"I'm Going Home" live at Woodstock, either via one of the Woodstock albums or on the out-of-print TYA collection *Universal* 𝄞𝄞𝄞 (Chrysalis, 1987).

solo outings:

Alvin Lee:

Zoom 𝄞𝄞𝄞 (Viceroy, 1992)
Nineteen Ninety Four 𝄞𝄞 (Thunderbolt, 1993)
I Hear You Rockin' 𝄞𝄞 (Viceroy, 1994)
Pure Blues 𝄞𝄞𝄞 (EMI, 1995)
Live in Vienna 𝄞𝄞𝄞 (Viceroy, 1996)

influences:

◄◄ John Lee Hooker, John Mayall's Bluesbreakers, Jimi Hendrix

►► George Thorogood & the Destroyers, Molly Hatchet, Stevie Ray Vaughan

Gary Graff

Sonny Terry & Brownie McGhee

Sonny Terry born Saunders Teddell, October 24, 1911, in Durham, NC; died March 11, 1986, in Mineola, NY. Brownie McGhee born Walter Brown McGhee, November 30, 1915, in Knoxville, TN; died February 23, 1996, in Oakland, CA.

As important a team in blues as Lennon and McCartney were in rock 'n' roll or Ruth and Gehrig in baseball, harpist Terry and guitarist McGhee had several significant bonds that created a prolific and influential life-long partnership. McGhee overcame polio as a child, though he had to walk on crutches for years; Terry lost almost all his eyesight in two separate childhood acci-

dents. They met in 1939, after Terry had recorded with Blind Boy Fuller and McGhee hadn't yet recorded his influential Columbia recordings as "Blind Boy Fuller #2." (Terry found himself on-stage at Carnegie Hall, as one of many performers in John Hammond's important From Spirituals to Swing concert, in 1939.) They hooked up in the early 1940s, and it was immediately obvious that Terry's enthusiastically squawking harp lines fit nicely above McGhee's understated guitar strumming—and their folksy harmonies (punctuated with Terry's occasional trademark whoops) were just perfect for McGhee's singalong songwriting style. After World War II, when they had business problems with record companies, they took to the streets and made occasional Broadway appearances in such plays as *Cat on a Hot Tin Roof* and Langston Hughes' *Simply Heavenly.* Soon they were swept up in the American folk movement, performing with Leadbelly, Woody Guthrie, Josh White, Pete Seeger and other leftists who believed traditional music could be used to effect important societal change. (Bob Dylan and Joan Baez were among the 1960s artists to build effectively on this approach.) Where rock 'n' roll destroyed the careers of many popular bluesmen, especially traditional acoustic ones, Terry and McGhee timed everything just right. They caught on in Europe in the late 1950s, while Elvis Presley and Jerry Lee Lewis were exploding in the States, and returned just in time for the 1960s blues revival. Their European tours and American festival work gave them extraordinary career longevity, although there was reported friction which slowed down the partnership in the 1970s. McGhee was always the more prolific solo artist, although Terry made several excellent R&B singles for various record labels in the 1950s. But they're the most influential duo in blues history and one of a select few in popular music in general.

what to buy: Start with two important solo collections: Terry's *Whoopin' the Blues: The Capitol Recordings, 1947–50* ♫♫♫♫ (Capitol, 1995, prod. Pete Welding) collects all 16 of his Capitol blues combo sides, some with McGhee on guitar and some with his guitarist brother, "Drinking Wine Spo-Dee-O-Dee" hitmaker Stick McGhee; the two-disc *The Complete Brownie McGhee* ♫♫♫♫ (Columbia/Legacy, 1994, prod. various) includes many soft-spoken, occasionally spooky and depressing, solo sides as Blind Boy Fuller #2, but despite the eloquence of "Death of Blind Boy Fuller" and "Back Door Stranger" it's clearly lacking Terry's playful harp element. Among the best of many duo compilations are *Brownie McGhee and Sonny Terry Sing* ♫♫♫♫

(Smithsonian Folkways, 1958/Rounder, 1990), *Back to New Orleans* ♫♫♫♫ (Bluesville, 1961/Fantasy, 1989) and the 1948–51 recordings *Hometown Blues* ♫♫♫♫ (Mainstream/Legacy, 1993, prod. Bob Shad).

what to buy next: McGhee and Terry recorded six and eight albums for Folkways between 1944 and 1963, and although they got separate star billing, most of the songs were basically Terry-McGhee duo recordings. The original albums are hard to find, but the best available collections are McGhee's *The Folkways Years 1945–59* ♫♫♫♫ (Smithsonian Folkways/Rounder, 1991, prod. various), which includes the solemn "Grievin' Hearted Blues" and the lecherous "'Fore Day Creep"; and Terry's *The Folkways Years 1944–63* ♫♫♫♫ (Smithsonian Folkways/Rounder, 1991, prod. various), with "Going Down Slow," "Custard Pie Blues" and "Harmonica with Slaps."

what to avoid: On Terry's *Whoopin'* ♫♫ (Alligator, 1984, prod. Johnny Winter), the harpist sounds like he's coasting, and the

Alvin Lee of Ten Years After (© Ken Settle)

Alvin Lee
(of Ten Years After)

song
Woodchopper's Ball

album
Undead (Deram)

instrument
Guitar

monster solo

presence of the great bassist Willie Dixon and ex-Muddy Waters guitarist Johnny Winter only works to twist the sound in an unfocused direction.

the rest:

Back Country Blues ♫♫♫ (Savoy, 1958)
Sonny's Story ♫♫♫ (Original Blues Classics, 1960)
At Sugar Hill ♫♫♫ (Original Blues Classics, 1961/Fantasy, 1991)
At the 2nd Fret ♫♫♫ (Original Blues Classics, 1962/Fantasy, 1993)
The Best of Brownie McGhee ♫♫♫ (Storyville, 1971)
Sonny & Brownie ♫♫♫ (A&M, 1973)
Sonny Terry ♫♫♫ (Collectables, 1987)
Blowin' the Fuses: Golden Classics ♫♫♫ (Collectables, 1989)
California Blues ♫♫♫ (Fantasy, 1990)
Po' Boys ♫♫♫ (Drive Archive, 1994)

worth searching for: The original Folkways albums, including *Sonny Terry's Washboard Band* ♫♫♫♫ (Smithsonian Folkways) and *Sonny Terry, Harmonica* ♫♫♫♫ (Smithsonian Folkways), have long since been trumped by the 1991 CD collections, but they're excellent holy grails for collectors.

influences:

◄◄ Sonny Boy Williamson I, Josh White, Leadbelly, Blind Boy Fuller

►► Woody Guthrie, Bob Dylan, Joan Baez, Buddy Guy, Junior Wells, Charlie Musselwhite

Steve Knopper

Jimmy Thackery

Born May 19, 1953, in Pittsburgh, PA.

Backed by a simple two-man bass-and-drum crew, Nighthawks alumnus Jimmy Thackery has developed a rich, multi-textured guitar style that mixes traditional electric blues with twangy West Coast surf and gritty hard rock. After 13 years and a dozen albums with the Washington, DC-based Nighthawks—and another half-dozen years as frontman for the Assassins—Thackery assembled the Drivers in the early 1990s. A growler more than a singer, Thackery's greater strength has been his guitar virtuosity and frequently cynical, tongue-in-cheek songwriting. His live shows feature lengthy Hendrix-style guitar jams that get plenty of mileage out of fuzz and distortion—effects that have also become prominent on his more recent studio recordings.

what to buy: Thackery's first studio outing with the Drivers, *Empty Arms Motel* ♫♫♫♫ (Blind Pig, 1992, prod. Jimmy Thackery, Jerry Del Giudice) is a taste of Thackery before his head-long plunge into heavy distortion and pyrotechnics, and includes

several covers of familar tunes by blues and blues rock giants like B.B. King, Hendrix and SRV, plus a couple solid originals. *Drive to Survive* ♫♫♫♫ (Blind Pig, 1996, prod. Jim Gaines) features strong songwriting, solid arrangements and Thackery's strongest, most melodic vocal work to date.

what to buy next: *Trouble Man* ♫♫♫ (Blind Pig, 1994, prod. Jim Gaines) again showcases a range of styles yet holds together well. It's all here—blues, rock, surf, and even touches of country and swing.

the rest:

Wild Night Out ♫♫♫ (Blind Pig, 1995)

influences:

◄◄ Duane Eddy, Jimi Hendrix, Albert Collins

John C. Bruening

Rosetta Tharpe

Born Rosetta Nubin, March 20, 1915, in Cotton Plant, AR. Died October 9, 1973, in Philadelphia, PA.

Rosetta Tharpe was the most well-known of the guitar playing female gospel singers, her high-pitched rough voice enhanced by an exuberant and dynamic guitar style inspired by jazz, early rock 'n' roll and most of all, the blues. She had a forceful presence on stage and exuded happiness and delight. Tharpe started singing in church and playing guitar at a very early age with her mother, an itinerant evangelist. Her experience on the road with her mother led to torrid sessions in Chicago's Church of God in Christ in the early 1930s. In 1934 she married Pastor Thorpe, and the trio had success in the storefront churches of Florida before settling down in New York in 1936. In 1938 she made her first gospel records as Sister Rosetta Tharpe (from Thorpe), "Rock Me" and "That's All," and the same year, as star attraction, she played the Cotton Club in Harlem, fronting Cab Calloway's band and recording with Lucky Millinder and his orchestra, Louis Jordan and Noble Sissle. The sides she recorded for Decca between 1944 and 1954 with the Sammy Price Trio and her duos with Marie Knight ("Didn't It Rain?"), graced by her biting guitar and strong voice, are masterpieces of swing, dripping with rejoicing and contagious joy. In 1950 she recorded a moving album for Verve with her mother, Katie Bell Nubin, and the ceremony of her second marriage in 1951 was recorded and issued on Decca. She was busy from the late 1950s on. A colorful artist, she was the flamboyant gospel counterpart to Memphis Minnie, and she deserves the strong following of collectors and specialists.

what to buy: _Sister Rosetta Tharpe_ 🎵🎵🎵🎵 (Frèmeaux & Associates, 1994, prod. Jean Buzelin) offers the best sides from the period 1938–43. _Live at the Hot Club de France_ 🎵🎵🎵🎵 (Flame, 1966/Milan, 1992, prod. Jacques Morgantini), a solo, live session, is the best of the gospel evergreens. _Sister R. Tharpe_ 🎵🎵🎵🎵 (Rosetta, 1988, prod. Rosetta Reitz) offers a nice selection of 1941–69 sides. _Sister R. Tharpe_ 🎵🎵🎵🎵 (MCA, 1975) is a multi-volume series with the best sides recorded between 1944–56 with the Sammy Price Trio, Marie Knight and various groups.

what to buy next: The two-volume _Sister Rosetta Tharpe Complete Recorded Works_ 🎵🎵🎵🎵 (Document, 1995, prod. Johnny Parth) includes 53 tracks, her complete output from 1938–44, and is worthwhile not only for completists. Not to be overlooked is _Live in Paris—1964_ 🎵🎵🎵🎵 (France's Concerts, 1988), which includes two live shows; one with Otis Spann, Ransom Knowling and Willie Smith and a second with the Original Tuxedo Jazz Band.

influences:

◀◀ Big Bill Broonzy, Memphis Minnie

▶▶ Sister O.M. Terrell, Dinah Washington

Robert Sacré

Beulah Thomas

See: Sippie Wallace

Henry "Ragtime Texas" Thomas

Born reportedly 1874, in TX. Death date unknown.

When the Los Angeles blues-rock group Canned Heat hit with "Going up the Country" in December 1968, the song charted at #11 on its eerie pan-pipe backing. If the ethereal tune seemed transported from another time, it was. The pipes and the song's lilting melody were lifted from Texas drifter Henry Thomas, the oldest known singer to record the blues at the start of its recorded history in the late 1920s—likely the clearest link to the birth of the blues. Thomas' delicate ragtime and ballad-influenced blues, sung in a rasping baritone, seem born of the nineteenth century, more naturally sung around a wagon train campfire than in a juke joint. Thomas was a one-man-band of sorts who could dive off into a rapid reel, backing himself both on the pan pipes—an instrument of several reeds also called "quills"—and guitar. His "Run, Mollie, Run" speeds along at a dizzying clip, sounding like a drunk band of hornpipe-blowing seadogs. His version of black composer Irving

Jones' "Honey Won't You Allow Me One More Chance?" was definitive, appropriated years later by a young Bob Dylan on _Freewheelin'_, and his "Fishing Blues" has become a folk standard. A traveling minstrel who likely roamed with medicine shows, Thomas reportedly rode the boxcars as far as St. Louis and Chicago. He made repeated trips to Chicago, showing up twice in 1927 and again in 1928 and 1929, recording 23 sides for Vocalion, ranging from songster classics like "John Henry" to spirituals like "Joshua in the Wilderness." Unlike fellow Texans Leadbelly and Texas Alexander, Henry Thomas could not be tamed. He hit the rails and disappeared, leaving only his ageless music as his legacy.

what to buy: The first comprehensive release of Thomas' stirring sides is _Texas Worried Blues_ 🎵🎵🎵🎵 (Yazoo, 1990, prod. Richard Nevins), accompanied by as definitive a history of his life as can be gleaned by the scant details turned up by researchers. The Austrian version, _Henry Thomas 1927–29_ 🎵🎵🎵🎵

Irma Thomas (© Jack Vartoogian)

(Document, 1991, prod. Johnny Parth), has the same exquisite 23 songs but fewer scholarly notes.

influences:

▶▶ Leadbelly, Bob Dylan, Taj Mahal, Canned Heat

Steve Braun

Irma Thomas

Born Irma Lee, February 18, 1941 in Ponchatoula, LA.

If the lovely "Soul Queen of New Orleans" has never reached the kind of mass audience enjoyed by contemporaries Aretha Franklin and Etta James, it certainly has nothing to do with her voice—or her soul. Maybe she's never had the right promotional machinery or perhaps it's just that New Orleans musicians don't travel well. But those who know . . . really know. Not much of what Thomas has recorded would be considered "straight-ahead" blues. She says that she always thought she was a rock 'n' roll singer, but if blues people like it, that's just

fine. But behind her disarming smile, that voice more than hints at the hurt suffered by a woman who was pregnant at age 14 and endured a series of disastrous relationships and career setbacks.

what to buy: Her first single on Ron Records, "Don't Mess with My Man," made the national R&B charts in 1959. She had strong regional hits for Minit with "Cry On," "It's Raining" and "Ruler of My Heart"—the latter quickly reworked into the huge national hit "Pain in My Heart" by Otis Redding. Her "Wish Someone Would Care" made it to #17 on the *Billboard* Hot 100 in 1964. These and more of her early singles (including her original of "Time Is on My Side," which smokes the Rolling Stones' hit version) are collected on *Sweet Soul Queen of New Orleans: The Irma Thomas Collection* ♪♪♪♪ (Razor & Tie).

what to buy next: In recent years, she has put out a series of solid discs for Rounder under the guiding hand of producer Scott Billington. The most consistently rootsy of these is *The*

Way I Feel ✻✻✻✻ (Rounder, 1988, prod. Scott Billington), with three great Jerry Ragovoy-penned tunes and a cover of "Sit Down and Cry" that can stand next to Aretha's original. *The New Rules* ✻✻✻ (Rounder, 1986, prod. Scott Billington) has its share of body heat, but it's also saddled with bombastic crapola like "The Wind beneath My Wings (Hero)." The real sleeper, though, is *Something Good: The Muscle Shoals Sessions* ✻✻✻✻ (Chess, 1967). Figuring they might catch lightning with what worked for Otis and Aretha, Chess shipped its new signee down to Fame Studios in Muscle Shoals, Alabama. But only one of the 13 titles recorded there even dented the R&B charts, and they were soon consigned to some shelf in a warehouse. Thirty years on, their raw emotion reminds us of what soul was all about.

what to avoid: While it's hard to recommend avoiding anything recorded by such a talented artist, her *Walk around Heaven: New Orleans Gospel Soul* ✻✻ (Rounder, 1994) is well-sung but a bit too controlled.

the rest:

Live: Simply the Best ✻✻✻ (Rounder, 1991)
True Believer ✻✻✻ (Rounder, 1992)
Turn My World Around ✻✻ (Shanachie, 1993)
The Story of My Life ✻✻✻ (Rounder, 1997)

worth searching for: For contrast, check out her megawatt rendition of "O Holy Night" on the compilation *A Creole Christmas* (Epic, 1990). It features a run down the scale on the word "holy" that's guaranteed to rattle whatever cage your spirit is kept in.

influences:

◀◀ Lavelle White

▶▶ Tracy Nelson

Cary Wolfson

James "Son" Thomas

Born October 14, 1926, in Eden, MS. Died June 26, 1993, in Greenville, MS.

Compared to his forebears, Robert Johnson and Son House, this singer-guitarist's brand of Delta country-blues lacked anything more than regional influence. But he was extremely talented, and he developed some notoriety at festivals and in films, including a 1970 documentary, *Delta Blues Singer: James "Sonny Ford" Thomas*, about his work. Though he didn't start his recording career until the late 1960s, he regularly toured the festival circuit and wound up making records for several different labels up through the 1980s.

Henry "Ragtime Texas" Thomas

song
Bull Doze Blues

album
Roots of Rock (Yazoo)

instrument
Pennywhistle

monster solo

what to buy: *Son Down on the Delta* ✻✻✻ (Flying High, 1981) is a good introduction to his mature guitar style.

influences:

◀◀ Arthur "Big Boy" Crudup, Elmore James, Robert Johnson, Son House, Willie Brown, Tommy Johnson, Charley Patton

▶▶ Muddy Waters, Elmore James, Buddy Guy, Eric Clapton, Rolling Stones, John Hammond Jr.

Steve Knopper

Jesse Thomas

Born reportedly 1908, in Logansport, LA. Died reportedly 1995.

Louisiana man Jesse Thomas had three careers as a blues singer. He won a modicum of early fame in his home state and Texas as the singing brother of slide guitar troubador Willard "Rambling" Thomas. He returned as a Texas-based shouter in the late 1940s

and early 1950s. And he surfaced again in the early 1990s as a wise old veteran who mixed old-style country blues with electrified jump band music. He rarely relied on old blues standards, even if his own smooth, urbane music was not always inspired. Ironically, the rediscovery of Thomas' early work by some blues scholars prompted claims that his voice eerily mirrored Robert Johnson's muted vocals. In fact, Thomas' singing was chameleon-like, sometimes laden with vibrato like Johnny Shines, sometimes keening like Big Boy Crudup, sometimes even blasting like Joe Turner. The nearest he got to a full-fledged hit came during his 1951 stint with the Oakland-based Swingtime label, cranking out several R&B efforts backed by pianist Lloyd Glenn. Returning to the Shreveport area and the Louisiana club scene, Thomas won a last round of attention, recording a 1995 disc, *Looking for That Woman*, issued the year he died.

what to buy: Thomas' middle career was his most productive, a decade over which he cut 28 songs in Los Angeles, Houston and Shreveport, chronicled on *Jesse Thomas 1948–58* ♪♪♪♪ (Document, 1993, prod. Johnny Parth). Thomas could throttle up on boogies like "Let's Have Some Fun," then turn right around and retreat into the brooding "Gonna Write You a Letter." Not everything he tried worked, but Thomas rarely lapsed into formula.

what to buy next: "Blue Goose Blues," one of four rare sides Thomas recorded in 1929 under the nickname of "Babyface," is included on *Looking for That Woman* ♪♪♪ (Black Top, 1995, prod. Hammond Scott, Nauman Scott) along with 15 tracks from 1995 played with a band of studio sidemen. Nearly 90, Thomas still sounded vibrant, even if a remake of "Blue Goose" and most of his other cuts are hardly revelatory.

influences:
◀◀ Willard "Rambling" Thomas, Blind Lemon Jefferson, Blind Blake

Steve Braun

Tabby Thomas

Born January 5, 1929, in Baton Rouge, LA.

Swamp bluesman and elder statesman Rockin' Tabby Thomas is largely responsible for helping keep the fertile blues scene of Baton Rouge, Louisiana, alive. In 1979, four decades after his talent took him to the finals of a singing contest alongside Etta

James "Son" Thomas (© Jack Vartoogian)

James and Johnny Mathis, Thomas opened Tabby's Blues Box and Heritage Hall, a club that finally gave the area's legends and up-and-comers a regular place to play. Guitarist, singer and songwriter Thomas presides over the action, jamming with compatriots like Raful and Kenny Neal and Tab Benoit.

what to buy: *Rockin' Tabby Thomas Greatest Hits Volume 1* ♪♪♪ (Blues Beat, 1996, prod. Tabby Thomas) is the only collection available of the vital sides that Thomas cut for Excello Records in the 1960s. It's filled with classic swamp blues, propelled by Thomas' fuzzy guitar licks, a muddy Louisiana beat, and rollicking tracks like "Hoodoo Party," "Roll on Old Mule" and "My Baby's Got It."

what to avoid: Watch out for any imports featuring Thomas' material—he isn't receiving royalties from these unauthorized releases.

influences:
◀◀ Arthur "Big Boy" Crudup, Peetie Wheatstraw, Slim Harpo
▶▶ Larry Garner, Bluebirds

Scott Jordan

Charles W. Thompson

See: Maxwell Street Jimmy Davis

Dave Thompson

Born 1971.

Critic Robert Palmer almost singlehandedly created the blues' future—at least, to the general record-buying public—when he ventured down South for his 1992 documentary, *Deep Blues*. He found Mississippi mainstays such as R.L. Burnside and Junior Kimbrough, who had been playing juke joints for years and wound up, through Palmer's connections, with national album distribution. Palmer bestowed this opportunity on Thompson, a terrific young guitarist who has had to contend with the death of his father and mother from cancer. Unlike the barrier-breaking Burnside, Thompson's style fits more squarely with the showoffy Chicago-style blues practiced by Buddy Guy and Otis Rush. But he sings and plays with excellent soul, and his venerable band, Big Love, keeps the tiger-tattooed guitarist from going so far into a solo that he can't come back. He's already a consistent sellout at joints all over the South, and with the right record label he's poised to become, if not the next Buddy Guy, certainly somebody who can stomp all over Kenny Wayne Shepherd and Jonny Lang.

what to buy: In producer's notes for Thompson's debut, Palmer writes that "Dave is already his own man musically, his inspirations and role models entirely absorbed into his own highly personal style." He channels Son Seals, Muddy Waters and Jimi Hendrix throughout the all-original *Little Dave and Big Love* 𝄢𝄢𝄢𝄢 (Fat Possum/Capricorn, 1995, prod. Robert Palmer), which is full of guitar solos but the effect is surprisingly low-key and subtle.

influences:

◄◄ Buddy Guy, Son Seals, R.L. Burnside, Jimi Hendrix, Otis Rush, Big Jack Johnson, Junior Kimbrough

Steve Knopper

Jimmy Thompson

See: Jimmy Johnson

Sylvester Thompson

See: Syl Johnson

Kathryn Jewel Thorne

See: Katie Webster

Bianca Thornton

See: Lady Bianca

Big Mama Thornton

Born Willie Mae Thornton, December 11, 1926, in Montgomery, AL. Died July 25, 1984, in Los Angeles, CA.

Nothing against Elvis Presley, but Willie Mae Thornton's original version of "Hound Dog" communicates much more power and emotion than the King's million-selling rock classic. Her 1953 #1 R&B hit (written by Jerry Leiber and Mike Stoller) is filled with playful howling noises and a certain bottom-line funk that Presley, despite his controversial hip-shaking, smoothed out. It's too bad Thornton's great career has been, because of that song, relegated to a rock footnote: her explosive singing bridged the gap between Bessie Smith's no-nonsense proto-feminism and later soul and rock heroes such as Etta James, Aretha Franklin, Janis Joplin and even Alanis Morissette. Thornton, whose mother sang in church, joined a traveling revue in 1941 before moving to Houston and becoming a solo singer (and drummer and harpist). There she hooked up with Johnny Otis, the great R&B bandleader, and Peacock Records' Don Robey; the connections led to some phenomenal, hard-hitting R&B songs, including "Ball and Chain," "Yes Baby," "The Fish," "They Call Me Big Mama" and, of course, "Hound Dog." Like many other blues originals who were pushed aside for rock 'n' roll, her career slipped in the 1960s. The blues revival gave her some touring clout in Europe, and she continued to record and play international festivals.

what to buy: *Hound Dog: The Peacock Recordings* 𝄢𝄢𝄢𝄢 (MCA, 1992, prod. various) includes all of Thornton's most famous material; the most welcome revelation is how wonderful Otis' jump and swing bands sound underneath the singer's booming voice.

what to buy next: Thornton's career as an album artist began in the 1960s, and it has excellent moments, but it's not nearly as consistent as her old singles. Still, *Jail* 𝄢𝄢𝄢 (Vanguard, 1975) contains fun new versions of "Ball and Chain," Willie Dixon's "Little Red Rooster" and "Hound Dog."

the rest:

In Europe 𝄢𝄢𝄢 (Arhoolie, 1966)
Chicago Blues 𝄢𝄢𝄢 (Arhoolie, 1967)
Ball and Chain 𝄢𝄢𝄢 (Arhoolie, 1968)
Stronger Than Dirt 𝄢𝄢 (Mercury, 1969)
She's Back 𝄢𝄢 (Backbeat, 1971)
Sassy Mama 𝄢𝄢𝄢 (Vanguard, 1975)
Mama's Pride 𝄢𝄢𝄢 (Vanguard, 1978)

worth searching for: Thornton's best-known song drops into *Blues Masters, Vol. 5: Jump Blues Classics* 𝄢𝄢𝄢𝄢 (Rhino, 1992, prod. various), landing comfortably among Wynonie Harris' "Good Rockin' Tonight" and Big Jay McNeely's "Deacon's Hop." She even blows away the disc's closer, Ruth Brown.

influences:

◄◄ Memphis Minnie, Ma Rainey, Bessie Smith, Billie Holiday, Johnny Otis

►► Janis Joplin, Etta James, Aretha Franklin, Elvis Presley, Koko Taylor

Steve Knopper

George Thorogood & the Destroyers

Formed 1973, in Wilmington, DE.

George Thorogood, guitar, vocals; Michael Lenn, bass (1973–75); Jeff Simon, drums; Billy Blough, bass (1975–present); Hank Carter, saxophone (1980–present).

George Thorogood (© Ken Settle)

Thorogood blew a breath of fresh air into the studied poses of the New Wave era with a blast of unexpurgated, unrepentant blues and boogie on a series of albums for the tiny independent label, Rounder Records of Boston. His faithful, frankly derivative attack on blues classics made up in splashy conviction and hard-wrought passion what it lacked in originality. As Thorogood caught fire with radio and the public, he honed his approach, supplying himself with effective originals alongside the vintage R&B numbers, and emphasized the boogie side of his mix somewhat more heavily. But in general, Thorogood has remained true to his initial vision after more than 20 years of recording.

what to buy: His breathtaking debut, *George Thorogood & the Destroyers* 𝄢𝄢𝄢𝄢 (Rounder, 1975, prod. John Nagy), retains its fresh, ferocious feel as Thorogood introduces a style that would remain constant—blues, boogie and lots of slashing slide guitar.

what to buy next: *The Baddest of George Thorogood & the Destroyers* 𝄢𝄢𝄢 (EMI, 1992, prod. Terry Manning, Delaware Destroyers) contains only one track from that original release and collects the highlights of his dozen subsequent albums.

what to avoid: His 1974 demo recordings, when the band was unformed and Thorogood himself rather green, found their way into release as *Better Than the Rest* 𝄢𝄢 (MCA, 1979, prod. Danny Lipman), without any hint that these were early experiments by the then-popular guitarist. Tsk, tsk.

the rest:

Move It on Over 𝄢𝄢𝄢 (Rounder, 1978)
More George Thorogood & the Destroyers 𝄢𝄢𝄢 (Rounder, 1980)
Bad to the Bone 𝄢𝄢𝄢 (EMI, 1982)
Maverick 𝄢𝄢 (EMI, 1985)
Live 𝄢𝄢 (EMI, 1986)
Born to Be Bad 𝄢𝄢 (EMI, 1988)
Boogie People 𝄢𝄢 (EMI, 1991)
Haircut 𝄢𝄢𝄢 (EMI, 1993)

worth searching for: *Greatest Hits* 𝄢𝄢𝄢𝄢 (Rounder, 1988, prod. various) is a Japanese import that provides a good summation of his Rounder years.

influences:

◀◀ John Lee Hooker, Bo Diddley, Chuck Berry, Duane Eddy

▶▶ Nighthawks, Fabulous Thunderbirds, Black Crowes

Joel Selvin

Henry Townsend

Born October 27, 1909, in Shelby, MS.

Among the last of the great country bluesmen, Henry Townsend has never really gotten his due. Born in Mississippi and raised in southern Illinois, Townsend left home at age nine and made his way to St. Louis, where he began playing guitar at 15. He accompanied artists such as Walter Davis and Roosevelt Sykes and recorded some sessions as a leader, though some of these have been lost to the ages. A versatile guitarist, Townsend added piano to his instrumental arsenal, and though he never achieved the widespread acclaim of peers Sonny Boy Williamson I, Robert Nighthawk and others, he helped establish St. Louis as a major blues center. Townsend gave up on music in the 1950s and worked for years in a series of day jobs, only to be periodically rediscovered by various blues scholars.

what to buy: Perhaps the first album on which Townsend is able to show the full range of his skills, *Mule* 𝄢𝄢𝄢𝄢𝄢 (Nighthawk, 1980, prod. Bob Schoenfeld, Leroy Pierson) is solid evidence of how the blues is a continuing evolution of styles and themes. Most of the songs were improvised in the studio, capturing snippets of various tunes along the way and turning them into something original. Townsend plays piano and a little guitar, and is joined by his wife Vernell on two cuts and by Yank Rachell on three.

worth searching for: Townsend's sides for Adelphi in the 1960s and Wolf in the 1980s are out of print, but all worth seeking in the used bin.

influences:

◀◀ Lonnie Johnson, Clifford Gibson, Roosevelt Sykes

▶▶ Sonny Boy Williamson I, Robert Nighthawk

Daniel Durchholz

Tre

Born Tre Hardiman, in Grenada, MS.

Chicago singer/guitarist Tre, the son of L.V. Banks, is a head strong young man who began playing R&B and rock 'n' roll on Chicago's South Side as a teenager. Now in his 30s, he is intent on keeping the blues of his father's generation alive. Tre has the talent and respect for 1950s-era Chicago blues to be a torch-bearer for the genre, and he has paid some blues dues, backing his father from 1981–87. A guitarist with the ability to produce clean, shimmering runs, he's also an interesting, though sometimes wordy, lyricist. Tre shows promise, but it's too early to tell just where the "blues road" he speaks of in the liner notes to his debut CD will lead him.

what to buy: *Delivered for Glory—Reclaiming the Blues* ♪♪♪ (JSP, 1996, prod. Tre) is that debut. Traces of L.V. Bank's guitar picking can be heard in his style.

influences:

◄◄ L.V. Banks, B.B. King, Howlin' Wolf, Jimmy Reed

►► Michael Coleman, Vance Kelly

Steven Sharp

Bessie Tucker

Birth and death dates unknown.

This mysterious figure's powerful (and frequently raunchy) "classic blues" singing voice stuck around long enough to grace a few singles. She seems to have learned her style from field hollers and early-century Texas blues, and she may have done prison time. But she worked with pianist K.D. Johnson in Memphis, recording such singles as "Penitentiary" for the Victor label.

what to buy: Two recordings in Tucker's sparse catalog exist: *Complete Works 1928–29* ♪♪♪ (Document, 1991) and *Bessie Tucker and Ida May Mack: The Texas Moaners* ♪♪♪ (Magpie).

influences:

◄◄ Bessie Smith, Charley Patton, Robert Johnson

►► Victoria Spivey, Sippie Wallace, Billie Holiday, Ma Rainey, Bonnie Raitt

Steve Knopper

Luther Tucker

Born January 20, 1936, in Memphis, TN. Died June 18, 1983, in San Francisco, CA.

A prolific guitarist who occasionally played bass, Tucker replaced David Myers in Little Walter's band in the late 1950s. Besides recording and working with Walter, he also had stints with Howlin' Wolf, Muddy Waters, Sunnyland Slim, Otis Rush and Willie Mabon. Tucker was working with James Cotton's band in the late 1960s when he resettled in San Francisco to be near the spawning hippie culture; he then started his own band and worked with other artists like Charlie Musselwhite. Tucker lived in Austin off-and-on during the last decade of his life in order to be near Antone's blues club. His last recordings were made on the Antone's label.

what to buy: Tucker didn't stand in the spotlight much, but on *Sad Hours* ♪♪♪♪ (Antone's, 1991, prod. Derek O'Brien) he got a

chance to pay tribute to many of the artists who influenced him.

what to avoid: *Luther Tucker & the Ford Blues Band* ♪ (Blue Rocket, 1995) suffers from too much rock.

worth searching for: Tucker's work as a sideman can be heard on any number of recordings by Chicago artists.

influences:

◄◄ Dave Myers, Louis Myers, Robert Junior Lockwood, Jimmy Rogers, Otis Rush

►► Derek O'Brien

Jeff Hannusch

Babe Karo Lemon Turner

See: Black Ace

Big Joe Turner

Born May 18, 1911, in Kansas City, MO. Died November 24, 1985, in Inglewood, CA.

Big Joe Turner was singing rock 'n' roll long before there was a name for it; he was its founding father. Turner was a bartender in prohibition-era Kansas City when he first began shouting the blues. His work with pianist Pete Johnson in the 1930s and 1940s helped popularize boogie woogie and laid the groundwork for the rhythm & blues revolution of the 1950s. Turner's first records, "Roll 'Em Pete" and "Cherry Red," were made for Vocalion in 1939. Through the 1940s he recorded swing, jazz and some pretty raw blues with some of the hottest players of that period (Johnson, Meade Lux Lewis and Freddie Slack, to name a few). Many of Turner's sides were strong regional sellers, but his first national R&B hit was 1947's "My Gal's a Jockey," one of the most lascivious records of that era. Always prolific in the studio, he shouted about the joys of sex, sin and boogie. In 1951, he signed with Atlantic and was suddenly at the forefront of a hot new trend called rhythm & blues. Atlantic's musicians played a little sweeter, and their engineering was a helluva lot better, but Turner's approach ("Get it going in C, boys, and keep rollin'") hadn't changed a bit. "Chains of Love," "Sweet Sixteen," "Honey Hush," "TV Mama" and "Don't You Cry" were major R&B hits, but biggest of all was 1954's "Shake, Rattle, and Roll," which leered almost as much as it rocked. Bill Haley and Elvis Presley would cut later versions, but they couldn't match the stomp and sass of Big Joe's original. "Flip, Flop & Fly," "The Chicken & the Hawk" and the dual market smash "Corrine, Corinna" extended his hit streak. At his commercial peak, Turner appeared in two motion pictures, *Rhythm and Blues Revue* (1955) and *Shake, Rattle and Rock* (1956). When rock 'n' roll became the province of white teenagers, Turner's days as a hitmaker came to an end, though he made many superb recordings for Atlantic until 1959. Turner churned out records for Savoy, RCA/Bluebird, Bluesway and Blues Time, among others, but didn't find another long-term deal until he signed with Norman Granz'ablo in the 1970s. Though he recorded many well-regarded jazz LPs with Dizzy Gillespie, Milt Jackson, Roy Eldridge and Eddie "Cleanhead" Vinson, Joe Turner never really stopped rocking. Even when old age, obesity and diabetes forced him to sit while singing, he would pound out the beat with his cane and sing with impressive power until the day he died.

what to buy: You can get your feet wet with *Rhythm & Blues Years* ✍✍✍ (Rhino, 1986, reissue prod. Bob Porter) or *Greatest Hits* ✍✍✍✍ (Rhino, 1987, reissue prod. Bob Porter), which feature the best from his Atlantic Records era. If you want to indulge yourself, get *Big, Bad and Blue: The Big Joe Turner Anthology* ✍✍✍✍ (Rhino, 1994, prod. James Austin), a 61-song, three-disc set comprising Turner's best sides for several labels from the 1930s through the 1950s. An instant history lesson and lots of cool boogie as well. To hear Turner onstage in his rockin' prime, there is *Big Joe Rides Again* ✍✍✍✍ (Rhino, 1987, prod. Nesuhi Ertegun), containing 10 songs from his 1959 Carnegie Hall appearance.

what to buy next: *The Boss of the Blues* ✍✍✍✍ (Rhino, 1981, prod. Nesuhi Ertegun) is a 10-track reproduction of Turner's 1956 Atlantic LP that still cooks today. *Tell Me Pretty Baby* ✍✍✍✍ (Arhoolie, 1992, prod. Jack Lauderdale) features many of Turner's great sides with Pete Johnson and his orchestra from the 1940s. Despite an ugly cover, *Shake, Rattle & Roll* ✍✍✍✍ (Tomato, 1994, prod. various) is a really good budget compilation with many strong Atlantic sides and great notes by Pete Welding. *Blues Train* ✍✍✍✍ (Muse, 1995, prod. Doc Pomus, Bob Porter) is a reissue of Turner's 1983 LP with Roomful of Blues, and *Jumpin' with Joe: The Complete Aladdin & Imperial Recordings* ✍✍✍ (ERG, 1996) has a couple of hot duets with Turner rival Wynonie Harris.

what to avoid: Turner re-recorded his big hits several times, some of which pop up on *The Best of Joe Turner* ✍✍✍ (Pablo, 1987, prod. Norman Granz), which is mostly material from the 1970s, not his all-time classics. And beware *Stormy Monday* ✍✍ (Pablo, 1991, prod. Norman Granz), a reissue of one of Turner's lesser LPs from 1976.

the rest:
The Midnight Special ✍✍✍ (Pablo, 1987)
Bosses of the Blues ✍✍✍ (RCA Bluebird, 1989)
Flip, Flop, and Fly ✍✍✍ (Pablo, 1989)
I've Been to Kansas City, Vol. 1 ✍✍✍✍ (MCA Special Products, 1990)
Singing the Blues ✍✍✍✍ (Mobile Fidelity, 1990)
The Trumpet Kings Meet Joe Turner ✍✍✍✍ (Original Jazz Classics, 1990)
Everyday I Have the Blues ✍✍✍ (Original Jazz Classics, 1991)
Kansas City Here I Come ✍✍✍✍ (Original Jazz Classics, 1992)
Let's Boogie: The Freedom Story 1959–64 ✍✍✍ (Collectables, 1992)
Texas Style ✍✍✍ (Evidence, 1992)
Every Day in the Week ✍✍✍ (Decca Jazz, 1993)
Life Ain't Easy ✍✍✍ (Original Jazz Classics, 1994)
Have No Fear, Big Joe Turner Is Here ✍✍✍✍ (Savoy, 1995)
In the Evening ✍✍✍ (Original Jazz Classics, 1995)
Things That I Used to Do ✍✍✍ (Original Jazz Classics, 1995)
Honey Hush ✍✍✍ (Jewel, 1996)
Patcha, Patcha All Night Long ✍✍✍ (Original Jazz Classics, 1996)
Shouting the Blues ✍✍✍ (Eclipse, 1996)

worth searching for: If you dig the great boogie and jazz pianists, Pete Johnson, Freddie Slack, Willie "The Lion" Smith and Art Tatum back up Turner with gusto on *The Complete 1940–44* ✍✍✍✍ (Official, 1991), which features 25 tracks from his Decca days. *Early Big Joe 1940–44* ✍✍✍ (MCA Special Products, 1980) is easier to track down, but has only 14 cuts.

influences:

◀◀ Pete Johnson, Jimmy Rushing

▶▶ Wynonie Harris, Roy Brown, Bill Haley, B.B. King

Ken Burke

Buck Turner

See: Black Ace

Ike Turner

Born Izear Luster Turner, November 5, 1931, in Clarksdale, MS.

Most of the moviegoing public now knows Ike Turner as the butthead who savagely abused his wife, Tina Turner, in the autobiographical film *What's Love Got to Do with It*. But without Turner's excellent guitar playing, important bandleading and presence at exactly the right time in American music history, rock 'n' roll may have progressed in a very different way. Turner was such a behind-the-scenes character that his biggest solo hit—1951's "Rocket 88," often cited as the first true rock 'n' roll single—was credited not to Turner but to Jackie Brensten & the Delta Cats. Turner listened attentively to 1940s and 1950s electric-guitar blues by Elmore James, Muddy Waters and Jimmy

Reed (and horn solos in older Louis Jordan records), then transferred those styles into jumping R&B music. The combination, as discovered later by Elvis Presley and Chuck Berry, among others, effectively became rock 'n' roll. Turner began his career as leader of a high school group, the Top Hatters, who eventually became his Kings of Rhythm and played jukejoints around the Mississippi Delta. After "Rocket 88," as a session guitarist, producer and talent scout, he recorded with an amazing all-star roster of blues artists, including Howlin' Wolf, B.B. King, Bobby "Blue" Bland, Otis Rush and Willie Dixon. But it wasn't until 1956, when a hotshot singer named Annie Mae Bullock finally leaped on stage to sing with Turner's band, that Turner's true fame (and infamy) began. Bullock, who changed her name to Tina, married Turner, which inaugurated a creatively and financially lucrative performing career and a frequently stormy relationship. Tina Turner, according to her biography, escaped from her abusive husband's hotel room in 1976 with exactly 36 cents to her name. Her amazing solo comeback and tell-all autobiography, perhaps deservedly, further destroyed Turner's long-sagging career.

what to buy: Until the Turner boxed-set comes along, *I Like Ike! The Best of Ike Turner* &&&& (Rhino, 1994, prod. Bill Greensmith) will have to do. It dodges the better-known Ike and Tina hits for 18 of Turner's R&B churners. Whether the rubbed-raw "Hoo-Doo Say," the heavy blues of "Consider Yourself" or the country twang of "Steel Guitar Rag," as a guitarist Turner can do it all.

what to buy next: *1958–59* &&& (Paula, 1991, prod. various) opens appropriately with Turner's methodical chiming guitar, then lurches into the sloppy, slurred "Matchbox." Most of this generous sampling of Turner's early session work—with his Kings of Rhythm, plus a few tracks with Otis Rush and Willie Dixon—has that raw R&B quality, like somebody stuck microphones in a juke joint.

the rest:
Rhythm Rockin' Blues && (Ace, 1995)

worth searching for: Though their duo work was hardly pure blues, *Proud Mary—The Best of Ike and Tina Turner* &&&& (Sue/EMI, 1991, prod. various) contains some of the best soul interpretations ever recorded, including the Phil Spector-produced "River Deep, Mountain High," Creedence Clearwater Revival's "Proud Mary," Bob Seger's "Nutbush City Limits" and the Who's "Acid Queen." You can also find a generous selection of Turner classics on *The Cobra Records Story: Chicago Rock and Blues* &&&& (Capricorn, 1993, prod. Diana Reid Haig),

alongside seminal, smokin' sides by Louis Myers, Otis Rush, Magic Sam and Buddy Guy.

influences:

◀◀ Louis Jordan, Elmore James, Muddy Waters, Jimmy Reed, Willie Dixon, Otis Rush

▶▶ Bill Haley, Elvis Presley, Chuck Berry, Little Richard, Janis Joplin, Booker T. and the MGs, Jackie Wilson, Wilson Pickett, Otis Redding

see also: *Jackie Brenston*

Steve Knopper

U–V

Upsetters
See: Grady Gaines

Dave Van Ronk
Born June 30, 1936, in Brooklyn, NY.

Dave Van Ronk was one of the leading figures in the early 1960s folk-music revival centered in Greenwich Village. Performing alongside Bob Dylan, Odetta and Phil Ochs, Van Ronk was known for his growling vocals and unmatched repertoire of obscure blues, folk and jug-band tunes. In the early 1960s he recorded several classic albums for Prestige and Folkways. While recording sporadically over the next several decades for a series of small labels, Van Ronk has continued to perform at small clubs and festivals. A big bear of a man sporting a gravelly voice tinged with honey, he can sing the most wretched blues and "Teddy Bears' Picnic" with equal conviction. It's easy to imagine him singing drinking songs hour after hour with a group of Dutch sailors just arrived in port. Hunched over his guitar with a shock of greasy hair falling in his face, he exhibits a complete commitment to his music. His acoustic guitar playing is heavily influenced by Piedmont-area pickers like the Rev. Gary Davis and Brownie McGhee.

what to buy: *Inside Dave Van Ronk* &&&& (Fantasy, 1989) combines two separate releases recorded in April 1962. The first, comprising 13 selections, was originally titled *Folksinger* and is Van Ronk's crowning achievement. Passionate singing and instrumental mastery distinguish these songs, which sound

like they're forcing their way out to be heard. The fearsome visions of "Samson and Delilah" start things off with a wallop, while "Motherless Children" looks unblinkingly at absolute despair and loneliness. On each song, his guitar work, whether intricate or spare, reinforces the mood and propels the story. The second half was the original release of *Inside Dave Van Ronk* , and it's a different kettle of fish—a pleasant album of British- and Appalachian-style folk songs with Van Ronk on 12-string guitar, autoharp and dulcimer. *From . . . Another Time & Place* ♪♪♪ (Alcazar, 1995) is an excellent set of acoustic blues and folk songs, with Van Ronk covering old favorites of his like "Lovin' Spoonful," Gary Davis' humorous look at sex, and Carr & Blackwell's "Down South Blues." Several original compositions, including the gorgeous "Honey Hair," first recorded three decades ago, add a gentler, folk-music element. His Southeast-style finger picking is as good as ever. Van Ronk has made his career by playing other people's music. In a well-deserved tribute to himself, *Going Back to Brooklyn* ♪♪♪ (Gazell, 1991), he recorded 14 of his own compositions accompanied only by his guitar. Included are the anti-war diatribe "Luang Prabang," a hilarious song made up entirely of the names of New Jersey cities, and Van Ronk's terrific, after-hours "Last Call," with the great line: "If I'd been drunk when I was born, I'd be ignorant of sorrow."

what to buy next: *The Folkways Years: 1959–61* ♪♪♪♪ (Smithsonian/Folkways, 1991) is a compilation of Van Ronk's Folkways recordings at the height of the "folk revival." It includes great story-songs like "Duncan and Brady" and "Gambler's Blues," classic rag-style guitar picking on "Hesitation Blues" and the spare emotion of "Please See That My Grave Is Kept Clean." *A Chrestomathy* ♪♪♪♪ (Gazell, 1992) is the only Van Ronk retrospective covering his entire career and wisely includes five cuts from *Folksinger*. Other songs showcase him with various groups including the Red Onion Jazz Band, the Hudson Dusters and the Ragtime Jug Stompers. As might be expected, the stylistic range is enormous—from the novelty pop of "Alley Oop" and "My Little Grass Shack" to the heartfelt tribute of "John Hurt." *Hummin' to Myself* ♪♪♪♪ (Gazell, 1990, prod. Sam Charters) offers a charming set of jazz standards on which Van Ronk is backed by an excellent combo, including John Pizzarelli on guitar and Harry Allen on tenor sax. Van Ronk sounds perfectly at home swinging his way through "Making

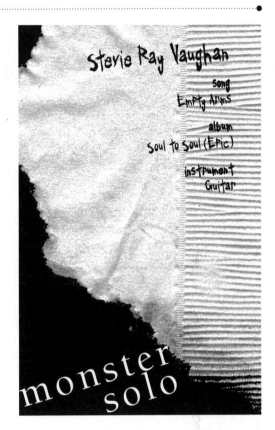

Whoopie," "Jack You're Dead," and Hoagy Carmichael's classic "Hong Kong Blues."

the rest:
Let No One Deceive You ♪♪♪♪ (Flying Fish, 1990)
Peter and the Wolf ♪♪♪ (Alacazam, 1990)
To All My Friends in Far-Flung Places ♪♪♪ (Gazell, 1994)

worth searching for: *Sunday Street* ♪♪♪♪ (Philo, 1976, prod. Dave Van Ronk) and *Songs for Aging Children* ♪♪♪ (Cadet, 1973, prod. Michael Brovsky) are out-of-print vinyl releases from the 1970s that reveal Van Ronk's varied interests. *Sunday Street* is all acoustic, a collection of blues, rags and jive, while *Songs for Aging Children* mixes blues, rock and Brecht. Several of the songs show up on *A Chrestomathy*, but it's worth having both entire sessions.

influences:
◄◄ Rev. Gary Davis, Brownie McGhee, Mississippi John Hurt

Jimmie Vaughan (© Jack Vartoogian)

Stevie Ray Vaughan (© Ken Settle)

▶▶ David Bromberg, Bob Dylan

David Feld

Jimmie Vaughan

Born March 20, 1951, in Dallas, TX.

The older sibling of the more famous Stevie Ray, Jimmie Vaughan kicked around Texas blues and rock bands the Chessmen and the Swinging Pendulums during his teen years, eventually forming the Fabulous Thunderbirds in the early 1970s. With vocalist/harmonica player Kim Wilson, the Thunderbirds developed a reputation as a road-ready rockin' blues unit that was as palatable to purists as it was to new wave fans (the group toured with Rockpile, and Nick Lowe produced one of the group's albums). Wilson may have been the frontman, but Vaughan's lean, loud guitar lines were the band's defining characteristic. The group topped out in 1986 with the hit "Tuff Enuff," which broke the blues-rock scene wide open in the mid-

to late 1980s. But as the Thunderbirds struggled to repeat that success, Vaughan grew restless and left the band in 1990. Jimmie and Stevie Ray recorded *Family Style*, a long awaited collaboration whose joyous tunes are tempered by Stevie Ray's death in a helicopter accident. In 1996, Jimmie and a wide array of guests, including Eric Clapton, Bonnie Raitt, Buddy Guy, and Robert Cray recorded a moving tribute album to the late guitarist. On his own, Jimmie is a less-than-spectacular vocalist, but as long as the focus is kept on the grooves and the guitar, everything's cool.

what to buy: Vaughan came into his own with *Strange Pleasure* ♫♫♫♫ (Epic, 1994, prod. Nile Rodgers), an impressive solo bow that featured hard-charging rave-ups ("Boom-Bapa-Boom"), strutting instrumentals ("Tilt a Whirl") and smoky blues ("Love the World"). But the album's emotional centerpiece is "Six Strings Down," a harrowing acoustic number that envisions Stevie Ray as the newest member of an all-star blues band jamming in the hereafter.

the rest:

(With Stevie Ray Vaughan) *Family Style* 🎸🎸🎸🎸 (Epic/Associated, 1990)
A Tribute to Stevie Ray Vaughan 🎸🎸🎸🎸 (Epic, 1996)

influences:

◀◀ Eric Clapton, Jimi Hendrix, B.B. King, Freddie King, Albert King

▶▶ Stevie Ray Vaughan

Daniel Durchholz

Stevie Ray Vaughan

Born October 3, 1954, in Dallas, TX. Died August 26, 1990, in East Troy, WI.

Stevie Ray Vaughan burst onto the national scene in 1983 with *Texas Flood*, a scorching, overdriven blues tornado that blew down the doors of popular music and proclaimed loud and clear that blues could actually be a potent force in the marketplace. Playing with deep blues feeling and a roof-shaking rock energy and virtuosity—and matching volume—Stevie Ray became a certified guitar hero and shone a light on many of his own heroes, notably Buddy Guy and Albert King. His rise also paved the way for the return of blues-based rockers like the Allman Brothers Band. One thing that separated Vaughan from other earnest young bluesmen was that he also worshipped at the House of Jimi, and while his attempts at slavish Hendrix imitation were destined to fall flat, his understanding of Hendrix's more subtle, chordal elements informed all of his playing, allowing him to write gorgeous instrumentals like "Lenny" and "Riviera Paradise." Vaughan's career shot like a skyrocket before hitting some seriously rocky roads as he wrestled with drug and alcohol abuse. In 1989 a new, clean SRV came out swinging for the fences, and his last two albums were by far his most focused, hinting that he was on the verge of reaching a whole new level of greatness when he died in a 1990 helicopter crash.

what to buy: Though at times it's downright jittery, Vaughan's debut, *Texas Flood* 🎸🎸🎸🎸 (Epic, 1983, prod. Stevie Ray Vaughan, Richard Mullen, Double Trouble) remains a gritty summation of his strengths: hard-rocking shuffles ("Pride and Joy," "Love Struck Baby"); slow, nasty blues ("Texas Flood," "Dirty Pool"); overdriven guitar workouts ("Rude Mood," "Testify"); and shimmeringly gorgeous instrumental masterpieces ("Lenny"). His last solo album, *In Step* 🎸🎸🎸🎸 (Epic, 1989, prod. Jim Gaines, Stevie Ray Vaughan, Double Trouble) is just as passionate while reflecting a new-found lyrical maturity as well as a musical and vocal confidence highlighted by "Riviera Par-

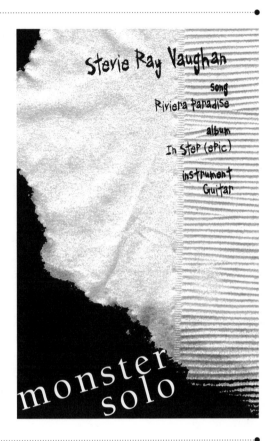

Stevie Ray Vaughan
song
Riviera Paradise
album
In Step (ePic)
instrument
Guitar

monster solo

adise," probably Vaughan's most serene recording. *Family Style* 🎸🎸🎸🎸 (Epic, 1990, prod. Nile Rodgers) is as much brother Jimmie's album as Stevie's—which doesn't make it any less great. Quite the contrary; it contains some of the Vaughans' finest songs, more of *In Step*'s maturity and confidence and, of course, lots of serious guitar slinging. The posthumous *The Sky Is Crying* 🎸🎸🎸🎸 (Epic, 1991, prod. various) sketches out the contours of Stevie's talents and influences, including Hubert Sumlin, Albert King, jazzman Kenny Burrell and, of course, Hendrix. Stevie's breathtaking instrumental, "Little Wing," is here, as is his first recorded slide ("Boot Hill") and acoustic ("Life by the Drop") playing.

what to buy next: *Soul to Soul* 🎸🎸🎸🎸 (Epic, 1985, prod. Stevie Ray Vaughan, Double Trouble, Richard Mullen) is a fine, relatively relaxed outing. Once you're hooked, you'll want to own *In the Beginning* 🎸🎸🎸🎸 (Epic, 1992, prod. Wayne Bell), a rough, ragged, thoroughly intense 1980 live performance. The packaging even includes a rare photo of a bare-headed Stevie.

what to avoid: *Live Alive* 🎵🎵 (Epic, 1986, prod. Stevie Ray Vaughan, Double Trouble) is, at times, downright painful to listen to, reflecting as it does a great artist's deterioration. Vaughan was a mess, strung out on drugs and alcohol, necessitating more overdubs than is proper for a live album, particularly for this caliber of performer. Only his resurgence prevents this from being a tragic album.

the rest:

Couldn't Stand the Weather 🎵🎵🎵 (Epic, 1984)
Greatest Hits 🎵🎵🎵 (Epic, 1995)
Live at Carnegie Hall 🎵🎵🎵 (Epic, 1997)

worth searching for: *Interchords* (Epic, 1992), a promotional CD released with *The Sky Is Crying*, features interviews with Jimmie Vaughan and the members of Double Trouble, as well as snippets of songs and a few quotes from older SRV interviews.

influences:

◀◀ Albert King, Otis Rush, Buddy Guy, Jimi Hendrix, Lonnie Mack, Cream, Kenny Burrell, Jimmie Vaughan, W.C. Clark

▶▶ Kenny Wayne Shepherd, Big Head Todd & the Monsters, Blues Traveler, Jonny Lang, Monster Mike Welch

Alan Paul

John Veliotes

See: Johnny Otis

Walter Vincson

Born February 2, 1901, in Bolton, MS. Died 1975, in Chicago, IL.

The singing and guitar-playing half of the fabled Mississippi Sheiks, Walter Vincson managed to work on several side projects through most of the 1920s and 1930s. Vincson (also known at times as Vinson or Vincent) rarely played alone and was most comfortable in duets and trio settings. He would join the revolving pack of musicians who filtered in and out of the Sheiks, among them his long-time partner Lonnie Chatmon, brother Bo Chatmon, studio stalwart Charlie McCoy and even (the unrelated) Robert Lee McCoy (later known as Robert Nighthawk). A somewhat vain man who held his own with such Delta legends as Tommy Johnson, Ishmon Bracey and Rube Lacy, Vincson rarely deviated from the sweet rags and hokum nonsense that he often played in the Sheiks. After Vincson and Lonnie Chatmon disbanded the Sheiks in 1933, Vincson recorded with new partners in Jackson, Mississippi, New Orleans and Chicago, but was unable to duplicate his earlier success. He moved to Chicago, organizing several Sheik reunions and recording in 1961 and 1972 before hardened arteries idled him for good.

what to buy: Despite the able accompaniment of blues veterans Bo and Lonnie Chatmon and Robert Nighthawk, the 24 sides of *Walter Vincson, 1928–41* 🎵🎵🎵 (RST, 1991, prod. Johnny Parth) are at best a hodge-podge of Vincson's talent. Many of the tracks could have been performed with more life by the Mississippi Sheiks. Only the startling "Mississippi Yodelin' Blues" is a distinct departure, with its obvious nod to hillbilly minstrel Jimmie Rodgers.

influences:

◀◀ Lonnie Chatmon, Tommy Johnson, Charlie McCoy, Rube Lacy

▶▶ Howlin' Wolf, Muddy Waters, Bob Dylan, Eric Clapton

Steve Braun

Eddie "Cleanhead" Vinson

Born December 19, 1917, in Houston, TX. Died July 2, 1988, in Los Angeles, CA.

"Cleanhead" Vinson's voice cracked as badly as that of a 12-year-old boy with his first chin hairs, but adoring female fans had no complaints about the man's macho swagger. Though Eddie Vinson was a horn man first and an R&B crooner later, it was his earthy, ribald singing that sold records. Called "Cleanhead" after he became bald as a result of an accident with a lye hair straightener, Vinson took off in the late 1930s with the Milt Larkin band, blowing tenor sax with fellow Texans Illinois Jacquet and Arnett Cobb. He detoured to play behind Big Bill Broonzy for a year, then found his home as a saxophonist and vocalist with Cootie Williams. It was with Williams that Vinson hit with his monster blues squeal, "Cherry Red Blues," which he would record repeatedly over his 50-year career. Going it alone, Vinson churned out three dozen tough R&B sides for Mercury and a lesser number of gutbucket recordings for King. Vinson's 1950s band included a young John Coltrane, and he loved to prove his mettle with the top sax aces of his day, blowing with everyone from Cannonball Adderley to Ben Webster. Vinson joined fellow blues shouter Joe Turner in churning out sessions for the Pablo label in the 1960s and 1970s, then toured regularly with Etta James until his death by a heart attack in 1988.

what to buy: *Battle of the Blues Vol. 3* 🎵🎵🎵🎵 (King, 1988, prod. Syd Nathan), a reproduction of the 1950s-vintage King album, splits 16 cuts evenly between Vinson and fellow lungsman Jimmy Witherspoon. Vinson goes over the top on "Person to Person" and "Ashes on My Pillow" and hauls out a Cherry Red soundalike on "Somebody Done Stole My Cherry Red." Witherspoon's no-nonsense, Kansas City shouting is a fine complement to Cleanhead's Texas twisters. *Blues, Boogie and Bop: The 1940s Mercury Sessions* 🎵🎵🎵🎵 (Verve, 1995, prod. Richard Seidel, Kazu Yanagida), a prohibitively-expensive, limited-edition, seven-CD boxed set, contains nearly three dozen Vinson sides from the late 1940s. They're all booting R&B with hard-boiled titles like "Juice Head Baby," "Luxury Tax Blues" and "Shavetail." Packaged in a plastic copy of a postwar-era radio, it contains exhaustive notes and superbly-reproduced jazz and blues winners by Witherspoon, Albert Ammons, Professor Longhair, Jay McShann and Helen Humes.

what to buy next: There are only five Vinson tracks on *Cootie Williams and His Orchestra 1941–44* 🎵🎵🎵🎵 (Classics, 1995), but they include his historic 1944 version of "Cherry Red." The rest are uptempo, big-band instrumentals verging on R&B, with some of bop pianist Bud Powell's earliest performances.

the rest:

Kidney Stew Is Fine 🎵🎵🎵 (Delmark, 1969)
I Want a Little Girl 🎵🎵🎵 (Pablo, 1981)
Blues in the Night Vol. 1: The Early Show 🎵🎵🎵 (Fantasy, 1992)
The Late Show 🎵🎵🎵 (Fantasy, 1992)
Back in Town 🎵🎵🎵 (Bethlehem, 1996)
Cherry Red 🎵🎵🎵 (One Way, 1996)

influences:

◀◀ Louis Jordan

▶▶ Nappy Brown, Big Joe Williams

Steve Braun

W

Joe Louis Walker

Born December 25, 1949, in San Francisco, CA.

Variety is Joe Louis Walker's calling card. Each of his albums feature gospel-drenched ballads, down-and-dirty acoustic Delta blues, uptempo, rock-tinged R&B and painfully slow,

over-driven Chicago-style blues. His distinctively staccato lead work, in-the-pocket rhythm playing, intelligent songwriting and gutsy, soulful singing mark him as one of the music's true artists and justify his standing amongst its finest contemporary practitioners.

what to buy: *Blue Soul* 🎵🎵🎵🎵 (HighTone, 1989, prod. Joe Louis Walker) is an impeccable collection of songs, highlighting all the above-mentioned diversity. Either *Live at Slim's, Vol. One* 🎵🎵🎵🎵 (HighTone, 1991, prod. Joe Louis Walker, Bruce Bromberg) or *Volume Two* 🎵🎵🎵 (HighTone, 1992, prod. Joe Louis Walker, Bruce Bromberg) would make for a fine introduction, serving as veritable greatest-hits compilations of his first three albums and displaying the full range of Walker's talents.

what to buy next: *Blues of the Month Club* 🎵🎵🎵 (Verve, 1995, prod. Joe Louis Walker, Steve Cropper) is prime Walker, even if he and Cropper lay on a fairly slick sheen. The title track is a witty pop-blues, while "Lost Heart" sounds like a long-lost Stax nugget. "Your Lyin' Eyes" is a bone-cutting acoustic blues and "Second Street" a grinding mid-tempo rocker with jazz changes powered by a fluid Delta-style slide line.

the rest:

Cold Is the Night 🎵🎵🎵 (HighTone, 1986)
The Gift 🎵🎵🎵 (HighTone, 1988)
Blues Survivor 🎵🎵🎵 (Verve, 1993)
JLW 🎵🎵🎵 (Verve, 1994)
Great Guitars 🎵🎵🎵 (Verve, 1997)

influences:

◀◀ Mississippi Fred McDowell, Earl Hooker, Buddy Guy, B.B. King, Freddie King, Magic Sam

▶▶ Robert Cray, Sherman Robertson, Clarence Spady

Alan Paul

Phillip Walker

Born February 11, 1937, in Welsh, LA.

Born in Louisiana, raised in Texas and now living in California, Phillip Walker has blended the influences from these areas into his own style. Walker joined Clifton Chenier's band on guitar in 1955, recording and touring extensively with the accordionist for the next three and a half years. When he left Chenier, Walker settled in El Paso and formed the Blue Eagle Band, which played opposite Long John Hunter. He continued moving West and in 1959 found himself in Los Angeles, where he began to establish a reputation as one of the West Coast's finest blues guitarists. Walker cut several singles, recorded

with his wife, Bea Bopp, and met producer Bruce Bromberg, with whom he's collaborated often since. In 1988 Bromberg and Walker teamed up for *Blues for HighTone*, which contained "Don't Be Afraid of the Dark," the title track of a million-selling Robert Cray CD.

what to buy: Both *Someday You'll Have These Blues* ✍✍✍ (Joliet, 1969/HighTone, 1991, prod. Bruce Bromberg) and *The Bottom of the Top* ✍✍✍ (Playboy, 1973/HighTone, 1990, prod. Bruce Bromberg) are reissues of Walker's first two LPs and feature lots of his busy guitar. *Big Blues from Texas* ✍✍✍ (JSP, 1992, prod. Phillip Walker, Otis Grand, John Stedman) is a surprisingly strong and entertaining CD with lots of shuffles. *Working Girl Blues* ✍✍✍ (Black Top, 1995, prod. Hammond Scott) is a reminder that even after four decades of playing, Walker is still capable of adding some new twists to the blues.

worth searching for: Watch West Coast blues anthologies for Walker singles. Originally on P-Vine, 1983's *From La. to L.A.* — shared with Lonesome Sundown—and 1984's *Tough As I Want to Be* are available on cassette on the Rounder label.

influences:

◀◀ T-Bone Walker, Clarence "Gatemouth" Brown, Lowell Fulson, B.B. King, Guitar Junior, Long John Hunter, Lonesome Sundown

▶▶ Rick Holmstrom, Hollywood Fats, Robert Cray, Otis Grand

Jeff Hannusch

Robert "Bilbo" Walker

Born February 19, 1937, in Clarksdale, MS.

The blues of the Mississippi Delta and Chicago as well as the country and western of Bakersfield, California, can be heard in the music of Robert "Bilbo" Walker. He has lived in all three of the regions and soaked up the sounds of each locale. What makes Walker truly interesting, however, is his spirited interpretation of what he has heard over the years. Walker's raw, ringing, whammy-bar guitar and urgent vocals make the music of Chuck Berry (a principal influence), J.B. Lenoir and Muddy Waters, uniquely Bilbo-esque. And although Walker denies being influenced by Ike Turner, his guitar style bears close resemblance to that of the Clarksdale legend. Walker operates a cotton plantation in Bakersfield but still finds time to make fre-

quent appearances on the Mississippi Delta juke scene. Nearing 60, Walker is hoping to finally break into blues full time.

what to buy: After finally catching up with the itinerant Walker, Jim O'Neal recorded *Promised Land* ✍✍✍ (Rooster Blues, 1997, prod. Jim O'Neal, Patty Johnson, Robert Walker), a raw, beautiful, 14-song extravaganza—with backing from Sam Carr and Frank Frost—that sounds as if it is recorded in a juke joint. Walker yodels a version of "The Wild Side of Life/It Wasn't God Who Made Honky Tonk Angels" before moving north to Chicago's West Side to sample a portion of Magic Sam's "Easy Baby" for use on "Everything Gonna Be Alright." Walker then heads to the South Side—and back a decade—to grab J.B. Lenoir's "Mama, Talk to Your Daughter." A highlight is Walker's extra-dark and brooding version of Muddy Water's "Still a Fool."

influences:

◀◀ Chuck Berry, Muddy Waters, Ike Turner, Jimmy Reed, Little Walter

▶▶ Lonnie Shields

Steven Sharp

T-Bone Walker

Born Aaron Thibeaux Walker, May 28, 1910, in Linden, TX. Died March 16, 1975, in Los Angeles, CA.

Undisputed cornerstone of the modern electric blues guitar movement, T-Bone Walker single-handedly revolutionized the blues. With elegant fluidity and a unique gritty sophistication, Walker triumphed throughout the 1940s and 1950s as the pathfinder of the modern electric guitar movement; every blues guitarist after him bears his influence. He was the original link between the rural blues of singers like Blind Lemon Jefferson and the contemporary blues of the electric combos he pioneered. His fascination with electrified guitar led him to experiment with amplification, an interest that had to do with his crossing paths earlier with another electrified guitar proponent, Charlie Christian. First to record electric blues, Walker was a commanding guitarist, excellent vocalist and author of numerous blues classics.

Smitten by wanderlust and a love of the entertainment world while still in grade school, Walker ran off with a medicine show. His insatiable thirst for learning instrumental and performing skills led him to a week's membership in the Cab Calloway Band. After he took a solo in Houston, playing banjo and doing splits and dance moves, Walker was a hit, and by the early

Joe Louis Walker (© Jack Vartoogian)

1930s had logged numerous miles on the road and was already beginning to fall victim to health and drinking problems. Walker found a new audience in the European tour circuit during the 1960s, when a new generation discovered the magic of his anthem, "Stormy Monday," through its considerable exposure by the Allman Brothers Band. Despite declining health and a car accident, Walker mounted a domestic comeback of sorts in the early 1970s. Health and financial setbacks got the best of him, and he never fully recovered after being sidelined by a stroke in 1974. Walker's overwhelming contributions virtually define what the blues is today.

what to buy: The vast and rich Walker discography is complete enough to satisfy the most avid collector or casual listener. Must-haves for collectors include *The Complete Capitol/Black and White Recordings* ♪♪♪♪ (Capitol, 1995, prod. Pete Welding), 75 tracks on three CDs that chronicle the 1940s phase, with extensive notes and many alternate takes. Another collector's dream set is the specially priced, two-disc *The Complete Imperial Recordings* ♪♪♪♪ (EMI America, 1991), which covers his prolific early 1950s stint with Imperial. Among the 52 selections are the stellar instrumental "Strollin' with Bones." For those who are not ready to invest as heavily, try the single-disc *T-Bone Blues* ♪♪♪♪ (Atlantic Jazz, 1989, prod. Bob Porter), a solid collection of some better known Walker compositions, including the classic "Stormy Monday." Originally recorded in the late 1960s for the Black and Blue label, *I Want a Little Girl* ♪♪♪♪ (Delmark, 1973, prod. Robert Koester) is another winner. Backed by a polished and empathetic band, T-Bone radiates all that he is legendary for—from uptempo jazz/blues grooves to smoldering slow blues.

what to buy next: Another outing originally recorded in France in 1969, *Good Feelin'* ♪♪♪ (Verve, 1993), is rather uneven instrumentally, with the French back-up band not quite meshing as well as others have with T-Bone. Oddly, this effort won Walker a Grammy, belatedly, toward the end of his life.

what to avoid: Unless you just want another version of "Stormy Monday," steer clear of *Rare T-Bone Walker* ♪♪ (Offbeat, 1996).

the rest:

Rare and Well Done ♪♪♪♪ (Magnum)
Inventor of the Electric Blues Guitar ♪♪♪ (Blues Collection, 1991)
T-Bone Shuffle: Charly Masterworks Vol. 14 ♪♪♪♪ (Charly, 1992)
Legendary T-Bone Walker ♪♪♪ (Brunswick, 1996)
Stormy Monday ♪♪♪ (Laserlight, 1996)
(With Eddie Vinson) *Blues Collective* ♪♪♪ (Laserlight, 1997)

worth searching for: Another compelling six-disc collection, *The Complete Recordings of T-Bone Walker 1940–52* ♪♪♪♪♪

(Mosaic, 1990), again demonstrates Walker's remarkable impact.

influences:

◄◄ Blind Lemon Jefferson, Charlie Christian

►► Freddie King, B.B. King, Albert Collins, Eric Clapton, Robert Cray, Stevie Ray Vaughan

Tali Madden

Sippie Wallace

Born Beulah Thomas, November 1, 1898, in Houston, TX. Died November 1, 1986, in Detroit, MI.

One of the original "classic blues" singers—a slightly ambiguous label meaning she sang in a raw, boisterous voice while a slick, upscale jazz band played behind her—Wallace is most famous for her take-no-crap standard "Women Be Wise." ("Don't advertise your man," goes the song's conclusion.) After she learned singing and piano playing in church and the blues from her older brother, she began performing with her younger brother around Texas. She then moved to New Orleans, married Matt Wallace, headed straight for the city's jumping jazz scene and recorded several not-so-subtle compositions, including "Special Delivery Blues" and "I'm a Mighty Tight Woman." Among her friends were Louis Armstrong, who played cornet on "Special Delivery Blues," Sidney Bechet and Johnny Dodds. This explosive recording career, which made her regionally famous throughout most of the 1920s, quickly ground to a halt. Her husband and brother died in 1936, and she moved to Detroit and became a church singer and organist for 40 years. Two comebacks followed: first, her old friend and fellow classic blues singer Victoria Spivey coaxed Wallace into the 1960s blues revival; second, her unknown protégé, Bonnie Raitt, used her connections to land Wallace an Atlantic Records contract in 1982. In 1983, Wallace's Atlantic album *Sippie* won a prestigious W.C. Handy award; it was, sadly, Wallace's last major accomplishment.

what to buy: Given the predominant prudeness of the era, *Complete Recorded Works in Chronological Order 1923–29* ♪♪♪♪ (Document) is a thorough and extremely sexual collection of Wallace's major glory years, including songs like "I'm a Mighty Tight Woman" and "Can Anybody Take Sweet Mama's Place?"

what to buy next: Her voice is croakier on *Women Be Wise* ♪♪♪ (Storyville, 1966/Alligator, 1992, prod. Karl Emil Knudsen), a 1966 Denmark concert originally titled *Sippie Wallace*

Sings the Blues , but her winking in the background is so pronounced it's practically another percussion instrument.

the rest:

Sippie ✍✍✍ (Atlantic, 1983)

influences:

T-Bone Walker

song
She's My Old Time Used to Be

album
The Complete Capitol/Black and White Recordings (Capitol)

instrument
Guitar

monster solo

◄◄ Victoria Spivey, Ma Rainey, Memphis Minnie, Louis Armstrong, Sidney Bechet, Bessie Smith

►► Bonnie Raitt, Saffire—The Uppity Blues Women, Etta James, Hadda Brooks, Charles Brown

Steve Knopper

Vann "Piano Man" Walls

Born Harry Eugene Vann, August 24, 1918, in Middlesboro, KY.

Walls' dynamic and expressive piano playing made him an important part of early rhythm & blues as developed in New York City on the Atlantic label. A few records came out under the name Harry Van Walls, but he's famous for his work as a session musician, from 1949 to 1955. Many of the songs he played on are classics, including Ruth Brown's "5-10-15 Hours" and "Mama He Treats Your Daughter Mean," the Drifters' "Such a Night" (featuring Clyde McPhatter), the Clovers' "One Mint Julep" and Big Joe Turner's "Boogie Woogie Country Girl," in which Turner calls out "swing it Vann!" (All are readily available on Atlantic anthologies.) Walls was much in demand, recording for dozens of other labels and touring, where he developed his flamboyant showmanship. His contributions were recognized in 1997, when he was awarded a Rhythm & Blues Foundation Pioneer Award.

what to buy: *In the Evening* ✍✍✍✍ (Bros, 1997, prod. René Moisan, Steven Morris) shows Walls is still in great form even if he is nearly 80. Tastefully accompanied by the Stephen Barry Band from Montreal (where Walls has resided since 1963), it contains recent compositions and choice covers, including Big Joe Turner's "Chains of Love," which Walls wrote.

worth searching for: *They Call Me Piano Man* ✍✍✍ (Whiskey, Women, and . . . , 1987, prod. Dan Kochakian, George A. Moonoogian) is a vinyl-only record. One side is Walls playing solo in 1987; the flip contains rare early 1950s tracks of him with Brownie McGhee and others.

influences:

◄◄ Art Tatum, Earl "Fatha" Hines, Count Basie, Jay McShann

►► Dr. John

Craig Morrison

Cora Walton

See: Koko Taylor

Mercy Dee Walton

Born August 13, 1915, in Waco, TX. Died December 2, 1962, in Stockton, CA.

This rich barrelhouse pianist's best-known song, the 1950 hit "One Room Country Shack," wasn't nearly as memorable as his spooky, melodic style. He plays familiar licks—at least, they've become familiar in many successors' hands over the last four decades—but infuses them with a certain sadness, like the piano's trying to say something different than Dee's straightforward voice. Walton moved from Texas to California just before World War II and worked in the fields to supplement his night job as a bar pianist. "One Room Country Shack" gave him a national audience, and through touring he hooked up with Big Jay McNeely, Smokey Hogg and T-Bone Walker. Like Speckled Red

and Little Johnny Jones, he was an obscure pianist who, directly and indirectly, contributed important styles to help shift the course of blues piano forever.

what to buy: "One Room Country Shack" winds up on *Troublesome Mind* ♫♫♫ (Arhoolie, 1961/1991, prod. Chris Strachwitz), in which Walton flicks the keys so hard and fast his piano sounds like an entire orchestra. Walton's 1950s Specialty sides, including "Lonesome Cabin Blues," "The Drifter," "My Woman Knows the Score" and the title track, highlight the compilation *One Room Country Shack* ♫♫♫ (Specialty, 1993, prod. Billy Vera).

what to buy next: *Mercy Dee Walton & His Piano* ♫♫♫ (Arhoolie, 1961) and *Mercy Dee* ♫♫♫ (Original Blues Classics, 1962) collect Walton's 1960s material.

influences:

◀◀ Victoria Spivey, Speckled Red, Scott Joplin, Art Tatum, Maxey Delois

▶▶ Professor Longhair, Ray Charles, Jimmy Yancey, Floyd Dixon

Steve Knopper

Robert Ward

Born October 15, 1938, in Luthersville, GA.

Known for his vibrato-drenched guitar sound, Robert Ward might well owe his career to his choice of a Magnatone amplifier when he went to buy equipment so many years ago. Not that his playing's not stellar—it is!—but that wet, organ-like sound became a trademark, at least until Lonnie Mack appropriated the sound, and the amp, for his hits "Wham!" and "Memphis." Ward moved from Georgia to Ohio, where he started the Ohio Untouchables, a band that would, after his departure, morph into the Ohio Players. Years of obscurity and even prison followed, before Ward was rediscovered by Black Top owner Hammond Scott, who released the classic comeback *Fear No Evil*. Reunited with his Magnatone amp, Ward is recording and touring regularly, seeking the much-deserved fame and fortune that eluded him the first time around.

what to buy: An amazing and richly deserved comeback effort, *Fear No Evil* ♫♫♫♫ (Black Top, 1990, prod. Hammond Scott) introduced Ward's unique guitar sound and soulful vocals to a

new generation. *Fear* contains supercharged remakes of some of the material he cut years before with the Ohio Untouchables, including "Your Love Is Amazing," "Forgive Me Darling," "Something for Nothing" and the title track. He may be covering old territory, but with a newfound energy and determination. Long may he run.

what to buy next: A budget-priced release, *Twiggs County Soul Man* ♫♫♫♫ (Black Top, 1997, prod. Hammond Scott) contains selections from each of his three albums for the label. For a taste of his earlier work, there's *Hot Stuff* ♫♫♫♫ (Relic, 1995, prod. Don Davis, Robert West), which surveys his work with the Ohio Untouchables and includes sessions the band did behind Wilson Pickett's group, the Falcons.

the rest:

Rhythm of the People ♫♫♫ (Black Top, 1993)
Black Bottom ♫♫♫♫ (Black Top, 1995)

influences:

◀◀ B.B. King, John Lee Hooker, Wilson Pickett

▶▶ Lonnie Mack, Ohio Players

Daniel Durchholz

Baby Boy Warren

Born Robert Henry Warren, August 13, 1919, in Lake Providence, LA. Died July 1, 1977, in Detroit, MI.

Baby Boy Warren was raised in Memphis and learned to play guitar at age 12 with his brothers and Little Buddy Doyle. In the late 1930s he had plenty of gigs in and around West Helena, Arkansas, and he developed his own style with partners like Howlin' Wolf, Johnny Shines, Robert Junior Lockwood, Rice Miller, Willie Love and others. In 1944, he made Detroit his home, and he became a pioneer of the Motown post-war blues scene, leading his own band in 1949 and recording. He was very popular on the local scene, but after 1961 he remained in semi-retirement, making a comeback in 1971 and touring Europe and appearing at festivals. Curiously, he never had an opportunity to make a complete album under his own name. Warren's guitar style is direct and sharp, with sober chords based on boogie riffs producing a lot of swing and a solid rhythm. If suggestive and well fitted to his singing, his voice is unexceptional, but he was a major songwriter and he produced well-thought out lyrics with much sense and humor. Many of his stories, ("Taxi Driver,""Nervy Woman Blues," "Mattie Mae") are vivid paintings of life in Detroit's ghetto in the 1950s and 1960s.

Robert Ward (© Linda Vartoogian)

what to buy: Several high quality anthologies offer a couple of Warren sides each, including *Deep Harmonica Blues* ♫♫♫ (Ace, 1997), with two tracks of Sonny Boy Williamson II with B.B. Warren, and *Ann Arbor Festival* ♫♫♫ (Sequel, 1996).

worth searching for: *Baby Boy Warren—Detroit Blues 1949–54* ♫♫♫♫ (Kingfish), a bootleg recording from the late-1970s, has 14 tracks out of 20 recorded in that period that are essential but hard to find. *Baby Boy Warren* ♫♫♫♫ (B.B.W.) is a must, collecting the complete 20 sides recorded by Warren. Very rare.

influences:

◀◀ Little Buddy Doyle, Willie Blackwell

Robert Sacré

Robert Henry Warren

See: Baby Boy Warren

Washboard Sam

Born Robert Brown, July 15, 1910, in Walnut Ridge, AR. Died November 13, 1966, in Chicago, IL.

One of the blues most prolific role players, Washboard Sam was a master percussionist, excellent singer and solid songwriter. After moving to Memphis to play music, Sam began the process of making good blues artists' songs better—he performed on the streets with Sleepy John Estes, hooked up in a lucrative connection with his half-brother (they shared the same father), Big Bill Broonzy, and later played on some of Memphis Slim's Bluebird sessions. Sam's solo career began in earnest around 1935, when he started making singles for Bluebird and Vocalion. When electric blues took hold after World War II, Sam's career was all but over—although he recorded a Chess session in 1953 and reluctantly started performing in clubs and at European festivals in the 1960s. Two years after his 1964 final sessions, he died of heart disease.

what to buy: Building a comprehensive Washboard Sam collection involves the difficult task of fitting all the pieces together. *Washboard Sam 1936–47* ♫♫♫ (Best of Blues/Wolf, 1991) captures him and his small piano-bass-percussion combo when they really click; the washboard adds just the right playful quality to complement Sam's low, moaning voice on "Mixed Up Blues" and others.

what to buy next: *Blues Classics by Washboard Sam 1935–41* ♫♫♫♫ (Blues Classics) collects all his singles. And if you're really interested, his entire works are contained on seven discs titled *Washboard Sam—1935–49* ♫♫♫ (Document, 1993). Volume 1

includes tracks with Big Bill Broonzy, and who could resist "Who Pumped the Wind in My Doughnut?"

the rest:

Feeling Lowdown ♫♫♫ (RCA Victor, 1971)
Washboard Sam 1935–47 ♫♫♫ (RCA Victor, 1991)
Rockin' My Blues Away ♫♫♫ (Bluebird, 1992)

worth searching for: Sam sits in with Bukka White on a few tracks of the import-only *Complete Sessions* ♫♫♫♫ (Travelin' Man, 1976).

influences:

◀◀ Big Bill Broonzy, Memphis Slim, Bukka White, Jazz Gillum

▶▶ Bleecker Street, Taj Mahal, Willie Dixon

Steve Knopper

Dinah Washington

Born Ruth Lee Jones, August 29, 1924, in Tuscaloosa, AL. Died December 14, 1963, in Detroit, MI.

Honored with a postage stamp by the U.S. Postal Service in 1993, 30 years after her death, Dinah Washington's popularity as a blues, gospel, jazz and pop singer has continued to swell as we move into the new millenium. Bouyed by the success of "Soft Winds" and "Blue Gardenia" in the film *The Bridges of Madison County,* Mercury has continued to release new compilations of her work and reissue older releases, allowing new generations to discover her artistry as a vocalist and performer. Born in Alabama, Washington moved to Chicago at age three. She played piano at church, won a talent contest for singing "I Can't Face the Music" at age 15, and had joined Lionel Hampton's band as a singer by 18. However, Decca, the label Hampton was signed with, was not interested in Washington, so she began recording with Hampton backing her up on some of her early sides with songs penned by jazz critic Leonard Feather, who had been impressed by her debut at the Apollo. These were blues songs that led to more associations with great players such as Milt Jackson and Charles Mingus in 1945. Known to be volatile, Washington finally left Hampton's band in 1946, the same year she was signed with the newly formed Mercury Records, an association that would last 15 years.

As Washington's career progressed, she drifted further away from the blues, although she did pen and record "Long John Blues," a tantalizing double entendre about a dentist, in 1947. Her singing became more jazz influenced throughout the remainder of the 1940s, and she eventually became a leading stylist who was able to become a successful crossover artist in the 1950s. Washington's vocals on love songs touched audiences, and her personal life was as tumultuous as the emotions she sang, as she married nine different times. Eventually, she began incorporating more popular standards by the likes of Irving Berlin, Cole Porter, and the Gershwins, finally scoring a pop song hit with "What a Diff'rence a Day Made," but she sang the lyrics as "makes," leading to some collections using the wrong title for the song. From this point on, Washington used lush orchestras to back her up, and she sang mostly slow ballads, trying to repeat the formula. One way that she continued to follow that popular vein was by teaming up with Brook Benton for duets such as "Baby, You've Got What It Takes." She signed with Roulette in 1961, but her music was not as compelling. However, she did make *Back to the Blues* in 1962, and demonstrated what she still could do vocally on blues songs. Dead at 39 from an overdose of alcohol and diet pills, Washington's catalog continues to grow, and her influence on blues, jazz and pop music is steady as ever.

what to buy: The import *Dinah Washington—The Complete Volume 1* 𝄞𝄞𝄞𝄞 (Official, 1988) is definitive for the early blues sides that Washington cut between 1943–45. It opens with "Evil Gal Blues," penned by Leonard Feather specifically for her, as well as three other cuts he wrote, including "Salty Papa Blues," which opens with some muted trumpet while Washington's voice sounds seductive and tough at the same time, a trick she uses on Charles Mingus' "Pacific Coast Blues," too. These 17 tracks alone would be enough to secure Washington's place in the blues. The two discs of *First Issue: The Dinah Washington Story (The Original Recordings)* 𝄞𝄞𝄞𝄞 (Mercury, 1993, prod. Michael Lang, Richard Seidel) offer a great overview of Washington's career on Mercury, and also include two of the early sides from Keynote. Disc one is the better, and it includes Washington compositions such as "Postman Blues," which sounds like a personal letter to an old lover, and "Record Ban Blues," which captured the woes of artists like Washington for the upcoming record ban of 1947. Disc two has its highlights: "Blue Gardenia," "Lover, Come Back to Me" and a cover of Bessie Smith's "Back Water Blues." *The Complete Dinah Washington on Mercury, Vol. 1 (1946–49)* 𝄞𝄞𝄞𝄞 (Mercury, 1987, prod. Kiyoshi Koyama) is the first of seven boxed sets that Mercury did in the late 1980s covering the nearly 500 sides she recorded for the label. The set contains some tasty selections spread across the three discs, including alternate takes and previously unavailable material. While a bit much, it does capture that peak early period when Washington first got signed by Mercury.

what to buy next: *What a Diff'rence a Day Makes* 𝄞𝄞𝄞𝄞 (Mobile Fidelity Sound Lab, 1997) is the way to really hear Washington's vocals; her voice is as close, intimate and crisp as being in the front row—the best of her pop music releases. Her ease at making us feel the nostalgia in "I Remember You," or her conviction that she has "locked her heart" in "I'm Thru with Love" are only the appetizers for the velvety and dreamy "What a Diff'rence a Day Made." While most critics write off her late 1950s and early 1960s releases, *Back to the Blues* 𝄞𝄞𝄞𝄞 (Roulette, 1997, prod. Henry Glover) captures that moment when Washington made an effort to return to her roots, and while it might not quite get there, she handles the material in such a way that it recalls her best singing on those early records. Recorded only a year before her death, Washington, who co-wrote six of the tracks, sings with a conviction about relationships that rings quite true for the road she had traveled. She closes the album with "Me and My Gin," and there's a ominous sense that she's long been living the song.

what to avoid: *Dinah 63* 𝄞𝄞 (Roulette, 1990, prod. Henry Glover) is a return to the pop material that Washington was mining over those last years, but this set is especially pallid. She covers such tunes as "I Left My Heart in San Francisco" and "Bill," but they are pedestrian compared to her earlier work in popular tunes.

the rest:
The Bessie Smith Songbook 𝄞𝄞𝄞 (EmArcy, 1986)
Compact Jazz 𝄞𝄞𝄞 (Mercury, 1986)
The Complete Dinah Washington on Mercury, Vol. 2 (1950–52) 𝄞𝄞𝄞𝄞 (Mercury, 1987)
The Complete Dinah Washington on Mercury, Vol. 3 (1952–54) 𝄞𝄞𝄞𝄞 (Mercury, 1988)
The Complete Dinah Washington on Mercury, Vol. 4 (1954–56) 𝄞𝄞𝄞𝄞 (Mercury, 1988)
The Complete Dinah Washington on Mercury, Vol. 5 (1956–58) 𝄞𝄞𝄞𝄞 (Mercury, 1989)
Verve Jazz Masters 19 𝄞𝄞𝄞𝄞 (Verve, 1994)
Blue Gardenia 𝄞𝄞𝄞𝄞 (EmArcy, 1995)

influences:
◀◀ Bessie Smith

▶▶ Etta James, Natalie Cole, Rachelle Ferrell

John Koetzner

Isidore "Tuts" Washington

Born January 24, 1907, in New Orleans, LA. Died August 16, 1984, in New Orleans, LA.

Despite a minicular body of recorded work, "Tuts" Washington became one of New Orleans' most influential pianists. Considered a child prodigy, by the time he was in his teens he was able to outplay blues pianists in barrelhouses as well as accompany established Dixieland and society bands. In the late 1940s Washington teamed with guitarist and singer Smiley Lewis; together they recorded some of the best New Orleans rhythm and blues of the era. Washington and Lewis parted ways in 1952, but not before classic tracks like "Tee-Nah-Nah-Nah," "The Bells" and "Dirty People" were waxed. While Washington could have enjoyed a prolific recording career, he felt making records wasn't the earmark of success; Washington felt confident in the fact that every other pianist in the city knew that he was the best player in New Orleans. He wouldn't enter a studio to make solo recordings until he was 76, once his talent had begun to erode.

what to buy: Washington's piano is the springboard on the early tracks contained on *The Best of Smiley Lewis, I Hear You Knockin'* ♪♪♪♪ (Collectables, 1994, prod. Ron Ferminack). Completists might also consider the four-CD set *Shame, Shame, Shame* ♪♪♪♪ (Bear Family, 1995, prod. Richard Weiser). Recorded just a year before his death, *New Orleans Piano Professor* ♪♪♪♪ (Rounder, 1983, prod. Jeff Hannusch) proved Washington was still a master instrumentalist. Washington also appears in the video *Piano Players Rarely Play Together* (Stephenson Prod., 1980) along with Allen Toussaint and Professor Longhair.

what to avoid: The playing on *The Larry Borenstein Collection—Vol. 3* ♪♪♪ (1994, prod. Larry Borenstein) isn't bad, but the "live" sound quality is low-fi, as Washington is forced to compete with conversation from the audience and a telephone.

worth searching for: Washington also recorded with Big Joe Turner on Imperial. Some of these recordings have been reissued on now long out-of-print LPs and CDs over the years that would only show up in used bins.

influences:

◀◀ Jimmy Yancey, Pine Top Smith, Red Cayou, Jelly Roll Morton, Art Tatum, Fats Pichon, Little Brother Montgomery, Jeanette Kimble, Burnell Santiago

▶▶ Professor Longhair, Roosevelt Sykes, Allen Toussaint, James Booker, Dr. John, Jack Dupree, Fats Domino, Paul Gayten, Edward Frank, Salvador Doucet, Harry Connick Jr.

Jeff Hannusch

Walter "Wolfman" Washington

Born December 21, 1943, in New Orleans, LA.

New Orleans guitarist/vocalist/composer/bandleader Walter "Wolfman" Washington is one of the most underrated talents on the modern music scene. Backed by his super-tight band, the Roadmasters, featuring the powerful drums of Wilbert "Junk Yard Dog" Arnold, the Wolfman in performance lays down an evening's worth of high-intensity music night after night, featuring his highly personal mixture of original songs, urban blues classics by Ray Charles, Chuck Willis and Bobby "Blue" Bland, R&B obscurities like "Steal Away," the old Ohio Players number, "Skintight" and Tyrone Davis' "Can I Change My Mind." The product of a vast musical family—he's related to the legendary Nelsons and grew up in the same Central City household as his cousin, Ernie Kdoe—Wolfman apprenticed himself to the great singer Lee Dorsey while still in his teens, backing Dorsey on his tours and playing on records like "Get out of My Life Woman." He spent years as bandleader, accompanist and musical foil to Johnny Adams before making his own records. Wolfman's next recording will be for Rounder once again. While his recordings don't do full justice to the power and precision of the band's live performances, they are full of great songs delivered with joy and excitement and the wonderful sound of the Wolfman's voice and guitar.

what to buy: Wolfman's most recent release, *Blue Moon Rising* ♪♪♪♪ (4-Tune, 1994), features the Roadmasters and the J.B. Horns in a program of originals and classics including "Drown in My Own Tears," Little Willie John's "Fever" and "Use Me," the Bill Withers anthem. Wolf cooks on "Stop and Think," "Can't Stop Lovin' You" and "Cadillac Woman" and gets deep and soulful on "Blues Has Got to Go," "I Had a Dream" and the title track. *Wolf at the Door* ♪♪♪♪ (Rounder, 1991, prod. Scott Billington) is probably the best of his three Rounder albums, with original numbers like "At Night in the City," "Don't Say Goodbye," and "I Want to Know," plus the Doc Pomus-Mac Rebennack chiller "Hello Stranger" and an exuberant medley of "Is It Something You Got"/"I Had It All the Time." *Sada* ♪♪♪♪ (Pointblank, 1991, prod. Craig Wroten) is more of the same from 1991, with "Ain't No Love in the Heart of the City" from the Bobby Bland songbook, "I Got a Woman" from Ray Charles and Johnny "Guitar" Watson's "Nothing Left to Be Desired," plus a set of originals by keyboardist/producer Wroten and Wolfman's touching tribute to his daughter, Sada.

what to buy next: Backed by a New Orleans studio band, Wolfman introduces the results of his songwriting collabora-

Walter "Wolfman" Washington (© Jack Vartoogian)

tion with Timothea Beckerman on *Wolf Tracks* ♪♪♪♪ (Rounder, 1986, prod. Scott Billington). On the follow-up, *Out of the Dark* ♪♪♪♪ (Rounder, 1988, prod. Scott Billington), the opening cut, "You Can Stay but the Music Must Go," remains one of Wolf's finest recorded efforts, and he shines on "Nobody's Fault but Mine" and Bobby Bland's "Ain't That Loving You." Wolfman's first album for Hep' Me, now available as *Best of New Orleans Rhythm & Blues, Volume Two* ♪♪♪♪ (Mardi Gras, 1995), has also been issued as *Get on Up* (Charly, 1994) and *Rainin' in My Life* (Maison de Soul, 1994), but the excellence of the sides remains the same: "Get on Up," "Sure Enough It's You," "Good & Juicy" and a raucous reading of "Honky Tonk" head up a program of funky, tasty, sure-nuff rhythm & blues from the old school.

worth searching for: Wolfman and the Roadmasters work out on a 10-minute-plus version of "Skintight," recorded live at the New Orleans Jazz & Heritage Festival in 1995 and heard on *WWOZ on CD: Sounds of New Orleans, Volume 4* ♪♪♪♪ (WWOZ,

1995). A European project, *Blue Moon Rising* ♪♪♪♪ (1994), featuring the Maceo Parker/Fred Wesley/Pee Wee Ellis horn section on top of the mighty Roadmasters, was released in 1994 but has still to find a home in the U.S.

influences:

◄◄ Bobby "Blue" Bland, Ray Charles, Lee Dorsey, Earl King, Walter "Papoose" Nelson, Lawrence "Prince La-La" Nelson

►► Kapori "Li' Wolf" Woods

John Sinclair

Ethel Waters

Born October 31, 1896, in Chester, PA. Died September 1, 1977, in Chatsworth, CA.

She wasn't famous for blues singing, but Ethel Waters used her blues foundation to become a great jazz, vaudeville and pop artist, a movie star and a best-selling writer. After singing and dancing on the vaudeville circuit, she moved to New York City in

1919 and immediately cut several pure-blues singles, including "Down Home Blues" and "Oh Daddy." She then drifted into up-scale jazz and pop, using her polished singing approach not for Bessie Smith-style blues but for show tunes—Waters' revues, including "Africana" and "Paris Bound," led to a lucrative acting career. She landed parts in *On with the Show* and (with both Duke Ellington and Amos 'n' Andy) *Check and Double Check*. She wrote two autobiographies, including 1951's best-selling *His Eye Is on the Sparrow* and 1972's *To Me It's Wonderful*. Although she ended her career singing spirituals for evangelist Billy Graham for almost 20 years, she was an important historical figure who brought blues styles into the pop mainstream.

what to buy: Completists will want each of the six volumes in the Classics series, because they document Waters' fascinating progression from "Down Home Blues" to "Sweet Georgia Brown" to "Someday Sweetheart" to "Porgy." The best individual volumes are *1925–26* 𝅘𝅥𝅘𝅥𝅘𝅥𝅘𝅥 (Classics), a selection of Bessie Smith singing styles adapted to more playful, slick pop tunes, and *1926–29* 𝅘𝅥𝅘𝅥𝅘𝅥𝅘𝅥 (Classics), with pianist James P. Johnson and an obvious turn towards showtunes. Other volumes include sides with Jack Teagarden, Fletcher Henderson, Benny Goodman and the Dorsey brothers, and versions of "Dinah" and "Stormy Weather."

what to buy next: *Ethel Waters on Stage/Screen (1925–40)* 𝅘𝅥𝅘𝅥𝅘𝅥 (Columbia) has nice singing, but it's less for blues fans than for nostalgists who (like most listeners of that era) remember Waters as a star actress and pop singer.

what to avoid: *Ethel Waters' Greatest Years* 𝅘𝅥𝅘𝅥𝅘𝅥 (Columbia) was an essential two-album LP set until the Classics CDs trumped it.

the rest:
Foremothers, Vol. 6 𝅘𝅥𝅘𝅥𝅘𝅥 (Rosetta)

influences:
◀◀ Bessie Smith, Memphis Minnie, Ma Rainey, Victoria Spivey, Louis Armstrong, Benny Goodman

▶▶ Billie Holiday, Mildred Bailey, Billy Graham, Aretha Franklin, Dinah Washington, Mahalia Jackson

Steve Knopper

Muddy Waters
Born McKinley Morganfield, April 4, 1915, in Rolling Fork, MS. Died April 30, 1983, in Chicago, IL.

Mud was and ever will be the grand overlord of blues. Of regal mien, with voice deep and commanding, his body of work is a fundament of the idiom. Though mentored by an archetype—Delta patriarch Son House—he was a stone revolutionary when he hit Chicago, his music slamming the coffin lid on the waning wartime old guard with ruthless finality.

Waters' first city recordings were surprisingly subtle and countrified, but soon he was cutting with his kick-ass band, issuing classic after intense classic for Chess. In the ranks of his band James Cotton, Little Walter, Peewee Madison, Otis Spann, Jimmy Rogers, Junior Wells, Buddy Guy and others served formative stints. Incredible as it seems, by the mid-1960s he was on lean times. The Texas singer Angela Strehli met him in Chicago around that time and recalls that he felt strapped enough to ask her for a loan. Chess' answer to the slump was to jump on the hippie bandwagon with the famously ill-contrived *Electric Mud*, which came replete with a booklet that (God only knows why) included snapshots of Mud getting his hair conked. Though this LP stiffed decisively, Chess issued yet another attempt at psychedelizing Mud, the obscure *After the Rain*, the cover of which inexplicably showed Mud clutching a frog, and against all odds, has some—not many—good bits. (On the closing cut, "Bottom of the Sea," Mud gets really revved; his voice and the fuzz-toned guitars start sounding eerily alike, and the song achieves an incantatory power that makes it the most unlikely gem in the Great One's canon.)

By the 1970s Waters was doing well again, not because of Chess (far from it, actually) but by fielding bands of such excellence that he was in constant demand on bluesfests and in clubs. Example: In 1972 he took to the road with Louis Myers, Peewee Madison, Mojo Buford, Pinetop Perkins and the drum/bass team of Fuzz Jones and Willie Smith, a unit as highly charged as even those he led in the 1950s. He continued cranking out LPs for Chess, and though he was generally in good voice himself, the projects were usually scuttled by lame sidemen (like the execrable rhythm guitarist whose unvarying skank-space-skank ruined *Can't Get No Grinding*) or gratuitous rock stars (*London Sessions*). In the mid-1970s Chess was inoperable, and there was an ominous window of time when Mud's music for the label was out of print. Which made it all the more welcome for him to reprise some of it for Blue Sky, a CBS-distributed label for which Johnny Winter sat at the soundboard. With Winter as his producer, Mud sounded more exciting than he had on any LP he'd done for Chess since the underrated *Fathers and Sons* of 1969. It was an impressive career revival, expedited by the Texan eschewing celebrity sessions and/or other crap, and just letting Mud be Mud, backed by his working bands and old buds like James Cotton and Jimmy

Rogers. In his latter years Mud was revered throughout the world. His road bands were still strong, his voice majestic, and when he played a slide solo on his trademark red Telecaster, the sound chilled your nape and rippled your blood. In 1983 he took leave of us, but his music and personality will forever be the bedrock of blues.

what to buy: "Long Distance Call," "I Just Want to Make Love to You," "I'm Ready," "She Moves Me" and other history-makers comprise *His Best 1947–55* (MCA/Chess, 1997, prod. Leonard Chess). *Fathers & Sons* (MCA/Chess, 1989), initially released as a two-LP set, has been long undervalued despite an entirely credible studio "side" and a devastating live set on which Mud's henchmen include Paul Butterfield, Mike Bloomfield, "Duck" Dunn, Otis Spann and the deadly drummer Sam Lay. "Same Thing" is one of the most darkly passionate readings ever of a Willie Dixon tune (and check Mud's poison slide!), while the two-part "Mojo" fairly explodes from one's speakers in what may well be the most frantic, hell-bent, rip-roaring blues performance ever recorded. Made on Stovall's Plantation in Mississippi, *Complete Plantation Recordings: The Historic 1941–42 Library of Congress Field Recordings* (MCA/Chess, 1993, prod. Alan Lomax, John Work) shows Muddy's debt to Delta masters Son House and Robert Johnson while still evincing his nascent mojo. Fine music from before he hit the city.

what to buy next: Anyone who thought Mud's latter-day dross on Chess meant he was past it gets comeuppance on *Muddy "Mississippi" Waters Live* (CBS/Blue Sky, 1989, prod. Johnny Winter), as the Great One goes ballistic. Accompanied by Winter, Cotton, Bob Margolin and other seasoned cronies, Mud pounds out a relentless "Mannish Boy," glorious in its vigor and braggadocio. On his patented "She's Nineteen Years Ago" he plays a vicious slide solo, and other cuts similarly threaten the rafters. Pinetop Perkins shouldn't be so low in the mix but otherwise this is an exemplary recording of Mud tearing a place up good. *They Call Me Muddy Waters* (MCA/Chess, 1990) comprises two early 1950s obscurities ("Howling Wolf" and "They Call Me Muddy Waters") and some little-known, mid-period Chess work. Dixon's rollicking paean to payday, "When the Eagle Flies," is a highlight, as are the woebegone "County Jail" and a very low-down "Crawling Kingsnake." Some very fine stuff here.

what to avoid: Save your pennies for the above and pass these up even if they're in cheapo bins: *Super Blues* (MCA/Chess), *Muddy—Brass & the Blues* (MCA/Chess, 1966/1989), *Can't Get No Grinding* (MCA/Chess, 1973), *The Muddy Waters Woodstock Album* **woof!** (MCA/Chess, 1975), *London Sessions* **woof!** (MCA/Chess, 1972/1989) and *Electric Mud* **woof!** (MCA/Chess, 1968/1996). See above for just a few of the reasons.

Muddy Waters
song
Honey Bee
album
More Real Folk Blues (MCA/Chess)
instrument
Guitar
monster solo

best of the rest:

Muddy Waters at Newport (MCA/Chess, 1960/1986)
Sings Big Bill Broonzy (MCA/Chess, 1960/1986)
Folk Singer (MCA/Chess, 1964/1987)
The Real Folk Blues (MCA/Chess, 1966/1987)
The Real Folk Blues Vol. 2 (MCA/Chess, 1967/1988)
Live at Mr. Kelly's (MCA/Chess, 1971)
The Chess Box (MCA/Chess, 1989)
Hard Again (CBS/Blue Sky, 1989)
I'm Ready (CBS/Blue Sky, 1989)
King Bee (CBS/Blue Sky, 1989)
His Best 1956–64 (MCA/Chess, 1997)

influences:

◀◀ Son House, Robert Johnson, Scott Bohanna

Johnny "Guitar" Watson (© Jack Vartoogian)

▶▶ Rolling Stones, Big Daddy Kinsey, Bob Margolin, Eric Clapton, Stevie Ray Vaughan

Tim Schuller

Johnny "Guitar" Watson

Born February 3, 1935, in Houston, TX. Died May 17, 1996, in Yokohama, Japan.

As a young Texas blues player in the early 1950s, Johnny "Guitar" Watson shared the stage with Albert Collins and Johnny Copeland. In his early days as a musician his primary instrument was piano. (That's him on keys and vocals on Chuck Higgins' 1952 "Motorhead Baby.") Watson relocated to Los Angeles when he was 15 years old, switched to guitar and immediately revealed himself to be a most unique player, with cool vocals and cutting guitar; his signature soloing, cold and angular with rapid-fire bursts of notes was contemporary and trend-set-

ting. Recorded in 1953, the classic instrumental "Space Guitar" was ahead of its time, and another of Watson's most enduring songs, 1957's "Gangster of Love," would appear in different versions over the years and was widely popularized by rock/blues star Steve Miller, who successfully usurped the "Gangster" persona for awhile. Watson resurfaced in the 1970s with a complete musical makeover as a soul/funk artist, and kept fairly eclectic company for a blues/funkster, recording as a guest with Frank Zappa (*Them or Us* and *Thingfish*, both Rykodisc, 1995) and George Duke. The latter collaboration produced the exceptional title track on Duke's first solo record, *I Love the Blues, She Heard My Cry*. Watson had great success with DJM from a string of well-produced, deeply funky albums with irresistible hooks, clever lyrics and a scattering of blues tunes, often with the multi-talented Watson featured on all of the instruments. He emerged again in 1994 with another funk smash, "Bow Wow," and was in the midst of a successful comeback tour in 1996 when he collapsed onstage.

what to buy: Though hard-to-find, perhaps the most complete retrospective of Watson's early years, *Gonna Hit That Highway: The Complete RPM Recordings* ♫♫♫ (P-Vine, 1992), includes his mid-1950s definitive burners—"Too Tired," "Oh Baby" and "Hot Little Mama"—rarities and alternate takes. Another compilation from the same period is *Three Hours Past Midnight* ♫♫♫ (Flair, 1991), which also contains the above-mentioned hot tunes on *Gonna Hit That Highway*. The title song, a stunning slow blues, strengthens this uneven collection.

what to buy next: *Ain't That a Bitch* ♫♫♫ (Collectables, 1976, prod. Johnny "Guitar" Watson) is the first of a string of successful funk outings. Bedecked in pimp-chic garb and pumping up the bass, Watson's new persona was a far cry from his 1950s days, yet he still found time for close-to-the-bone slow blues, as on "I Want to Ta-Ta You Baby." *Real Mother* ♫♫♫ (Collectables, 1994, prod. Johnny "Guitar" Watson) is his big-selling 1977 DJM release, *A Real Mother for Ya* , a nonstop funkathon with blues undertones. Impeccable production values give aural gloss to Watson's spiky funk guitar leads.

the rest:
Johnny "Guitar" Watson ♫♫♫ (King, 1963)
Blues Soul ♫♫♫ (MCA/Chess, 1965)
Love Jones ♫♫ (Collectables, 1980)
Johnny "Guitar" Watson and the Family Clone ♫♫♫ (DJM, 1981)
Strike on Computers ♫♫♫ (Valley Vue, 1984)
Listen/I Don't Want to Be Alone Stranger ♫♫♫ (Ace, 1992)
Bow Wow ♫♫♫♫ (Wilma, 1994)
Lone Ranger ♫♫♫ (Fantasy, 1995)
Best of ♫♫♫ (Collectables, 1996)
Giant ♫♫♫ (Collectables, 1996)
What the Hell Is This ♫♫♫ (Collectables, 1996)
Funk beyond the Call of Duty ♫♫♫ (Collectables, 1997)

worth searching for: *Gangster of Love* ♫♫♫♫ (Charly) tastes his King and Federal periods in the 1950s and 1960s. *I Heard That* ♫♫♫♫ (Charly, 1985) includes the above-mentioned "Space Guitar."

influences:
◀◀ Albert Collins
▶▶ Robert Cray, Steve Miller

Tali Madden

Noble "Thin Man" Watts
Born February 17, 1926, in DeLand, FL.

Watts' life in the music industry has criss-crossed many im-

Muddy Waters & Johnny Winter

song
Mannish Boy

album
Muddy "Mississippi" Waters Live
(CBS/Blue Sky)

instruments
Guitars

monster solo

portant artists in various genres. As a Florida A&M student in 1942, he joined the marching band—fellow members included eventual jazzmen Nat and Cannonball Adderley—then joined the Griffin Brothers. He played with prolific backup saxman Paul "Hucklebuck" Williams and found himself in bands behind Amos Milburn, Dinah Washington, Lionel Hampton, Chuck Berry, Jerry Lee Lewis, Fats Domino and Jackie Wilson. He's not nearly as well known as a solo artist, but his 1950s instrumental R&B tracks—especially 1957's "Hard Times (the Slop)," later covered by Duane Eddy—are up there with Booker T. and the MGs and the JBs. He lost his audience, for the most part, for several decades, but he returned with less explosive but still fun sax-heavy music with albums beginning in 1987.

what to buy: With appreciative liner notes and guest guitar playing by fan Taj Mahal, *Return of the Thin Man* ♫♫♫ (Alligator, 1987, prod. Bob Greenlee) has a surprisingly mellow feeling.

Watts' voice is friendly and subtle, like he's talking to you from the next bar stool, but it doesn't match the sharp power of his sax tones on "Slop Bucket" and "Blow Your Horn."

what to buy next: *King of the Boogie Sax* 𝄞𝄞𝄡 (Wild Dog/Ichiban, 1993, prod. Bob Greenlee) is more of the same, and without Watts' earlier hunger and excitement, some of the instrumentals just lay there.

the rest:

Noble & Nat 𝄞𝄞𝄞𝄡 (King Snake, 1990)

influences:

◀◀ John Coltrane, Cannonball Adderley, Grady Gaines, Duke Ellington, Fats Domino

▶▶ Booker T. and the MGs, Taj Mahal, Duane Eddy, Roomful of Blues

Steve Knopper

Carl Weathersby

Born 1955, in Jackson, MS.

This Chicago singer-guitarist emerged from Billy Branch's band in 1996 with his debut album. He grew up in Mississippi, and his family moved to northwest Indiana, just between Chicago and Gary, when he was a kid. Weathersby worked in steel mills, as a police officer and a prison guard, then joined Branch's band in 1982. He plays a fine guitar, but still hasn't reached his goal of distinguishing himself like his hero, Albert King (a friend of his father's).

what to buy: Weathersby has released just one album, *Don't Lay Your Blues on Me* 𝄞𝄞𝄡 (Evidence, 1996, prod. John Snyder), in which he shows off obvious guitar talent but does nothing to make himself stand out from all the other Chicago guitarslingers out there. He writes his own songs, which are almost as predictable as the covers (including Willie Dixon's "Same Thing" and Howlin' Wolf's "Killing Floor").

influences:

◀◀ Albert King, Willie Dixon, Howlin' Wolf, Muddy Waters, Buddy Guy, Billy Branch

Steve Knopper

Curley Weaver

Born March 26, 1906, in Covington, GA. Died September 20, 1962, in Covington, GA.

Long before Keith Richards and Jimmy Page, this "Georgia Gui-

tar Wizard" was the talented role player who made the lead singer look even better. He sang and recorded his own songs, but Weaver remains best known as the fast, inventive player behind Blind Willie McTell, Barbecue Bob and other Atlanta-based bluesmen in the 1920s and 1930s. Son of a gospel-singing and guitar-playing mother, Weaver and his frequent partner, harpist Eddie Mapp, moved to Atlanta when they were young. They met Barbecue Bob, who helped Weaver snag a 1928 Columbia Records recording session; the trio also formed a band called the Georgia Cotton Pickers. The 1930s proved depressing for Weaver, as Barbecue Bob and Mapp died suddenly and fellow bluesman Buddy Moss went to prison. But he hooked up with McTell, an excellent 12-string guitarist in his own right, and their collaborations through 1949 led some of the most important blues recordings ever made. In the end, Weaver's tragic life even overwhelmed his blues career: he began to lose his sight in the 1950s, which forced him to retire. When he died in 1962, he hadn't played in years.

what to buy: The two primary Weaver collections, which focus on his solo material, are *Georgia Guitar Wizard (1928–35)* 𝄞𝄞𝄞𝄞 (Story of Blues, 1987) and *Complete Studio Recordings* 𝄞𝄞𝄞𝄡 (Document, 1990). The former contains several influential blues songs, including "Down in the Bottom" and "Oh Lawdy Mama," altered and taken up later by Willie Dixon and the Rolling Stones.

worth searching for: Though Blind Willie McTell got all the accolades, Weaver was his steady right-hand man: two of the tracks on *The Definitive Blind Willie McTell* 𝄞𝄞𝄞𝄞 (Columbia/Legacy, 1994) are Weaver solo tracks, and most of the rest are two of the best guitarists ever to play the blues perfectly filling each others' spaces.

influences:

◀◀ Blind Willie McTell, Barbecue Bob, Buddy Moss, Charley Patton, Robert Johnson, Son House

▶▶ Muddy Waters, Willie Dixon, Buddy Guy, Otis Rush, Rolling Stones, Bob Dylan, Eric Clapton, Taj Mahal, John Hammond Jr., Keb' Mo'

Steve Knopper

"Boogie" Bill Webb

Born 1924, in Jackson, MS. Died August 23, 1990, in New Orleans, LA.

Raised in New Orleans' rural Ninth Ward, Webb's early inspiration was Mississippi bluesman Tommy Johnson, who played at his mother's fish fries. A man with a keen ear, he often sought out other guitarists for pointers, and he copied many of the blues hits he heard on the radio. Webb's neighbor Fats Domino brought him to Imperial in 1953, where he cut the raucous "Bad Dog"/"I Ain't for It," fine examples of country blues. A stevedore by day, Webb worked neighborhood joints occasionally but wouldn't record again until Dr. David Evans found him in the late 1960s. In the 1980s, Webb got exposure via appearances at the New Orleans Jazz & Heritage Festival and from sporadic trips to Europe. He made only one full length album shortly before his death.

what to buy: Although it's an uneven effort, on *Drinkin' and Stinkin'* 𝄫𝄫𝄫 (Flying Fish, 1989, prod. Ben Sandmel), Webb performs many traditional blues numbers with a small band. It also includes some baudy "toasts."

worth searching for: The ultra-rare Imperial 78, and two unreleased tracks, were reissued on Liberty's Legendary Masters series in the early 1970s. The Evans field recordings tracks appeared on LP anthologies on Arhoolie, L&R and Roots.

influences:

◀◀ Tommy Johnson, Roosevelt Holts, Jimmy Reed, Muddy Waters, Chuck Berry

Jeff Hannusch

Katie Webster

Born Kathryn Jewel Thorne, January 9, 1939, in Houston, TX.

An innuendo-laced barrelhouse pianist in the tradition of Victoria Spivey and Sippie Wallace—not to mention Pinetop Perkins—Webster hooked up with Otis Redding early and used the connection to build a successful touring career. She's incredibly charismatic, smiling constantly and telling energetic stories to the audience, and her "two-fisted mama" piano style is, as advertised, powerful and direct. The daughter of religious parents, Kathryn Thorne couldn't resist the allure of Fats Domino, and she became an R&B singer, recording her debut single "Baby Baby" in 1958. After that, she was a prolific session musician, helping Lonnie Brooks, Lazy Lester and Phil Phillips (on his enduring hit "Sea of Love"). Meanwhile, her solo career was doing fine, as she won the ear of Redding, who booked her as his opening act three straight years. She also played keyboards in his bands, backing him on the *Live at the Whiskey a Go Go* album and dueting with him on live versions of "Tramp." Since then, she has developed a fun-loving persona as the "Swamp Boogie Queen," a blueswoman with an irresistible style, rambling story-speeches on her albums and an

endless collection of bright-colored and spangly performing outfits.

what to buy: Webster's Alligator albums are her best, including the definitive *The Swamp Boogie Queen* 𝄫𝄫𝄫 (Alligator, 1988, prod. Bruce Iglauer, Ice Cube Slim), which has high-profile guest appearances by Robert Cray, Bonnie Raitt and the Memphis Horns, and the less star-studded but still solid followup *Two-Fisted Mama!* 𝄫𝄫𝄫 (Alligator, 1989, prod. Katie Webster, Bruce Iglauer, Vasti Jackson, Ice Cube Slim). *Katie Webster* 𝄫𝄫𝄫 (Paula, 1991) collects her 1950s and 1960s singles, including her own version of "Sea of Love."

what to buy next: Webster suffered a stroke after *No Foolin'!* 𝄫𝄫𝄫 (Alligator, 1991, prod. Katie Webster, Bruce Iglauer, Vasti Jackson, Ice Cube Slim), so here's hoping these nice boogie-woogie songs, including "I'm Bad" and the unexpected crossover "Zydeco Shoes and California Blues," don't constitute her last album.

what to avoid: Before she hit Alligator, Webster recorded several albums, including the bland *I Know That's Right* 𝄫𝄫 (Arhoolie, 1987/1993, prod. Chris Strachwitz, John Lumsdaine), which is full of rock and boogie-woogie but never really clicks like her later material.

influences:

◀◀ Otis Redding, Victoria Spivey, Sippie Wallace, Bessie Smith, Koko Taylor, Jimmy Yancey

▶▶ Saffire—The Uppity Blues Women, Ann Rabson, A.J. Croce, Deborah Coleman, Debbie Davies

Steve Knopper

Gillian Welch

Born 1968, in West Los Angeles, CA.

Revival, this young Nashville-based singer-songwriter's debut album, is technically closer to country and western music but aims for a swooping, spiritual feeling that recalls gospel, soul and blues. Welch, daughter of songwriters for "The Carol Burnett Show," grew up learning basic, reliable pop songwriting skills. As a student at the University of California–Santa Cruz and Boston's Berklee School of Music she merged her love for country music with a new found appreciation for the Pixies, Velvet Underground and other punk bands. Her songs are slow and hypnotic, occasionally reminiscent of the Cowboy Junkies, but she accelerates to honky-tonk on "Tear My Stillhouse Down." The stark production and dramatic soft guitar-playing,

which seems like the backdrop to *The Grapes of Wrath* or an old western, perfectly fits Welch's smooth, strong twang.

what to buy: *Revival* 🎵🎵🎵 (Almo Sounds, 1996, prod. T-Bone Burnett), is just a little too polished and slick, like both Welch and Burnett are trying really, really hard to achieve a haunting type of sound. Still, the songwriting is stellar, and "Tear My Stillhouse Down" is as cathartic as Bruce Springsteen's "Open All Night."

influences:

◀◀ Emmylou Harris, Cowboy Junkies, Pixies, Velvet Underground, Richard Buckner, Rosanne Cash, Mekons, James Taylor

Steve Knopper

Casey Bill Weldon

Born Will Weldon, July 10, 1909 in Pine Bluff, AR. Died reportedly 1960s, in Detroit, MI.

An adherent of the wavy "Hawaiian" slide guitar style, Will Weldon came to the fore as a member of the Memphis Jug Band, married the roistering Memphis Minnie and cut several dozen spritely blues numbers for Vocalion and Bluebird in the 1930s. Weldon was a frequent collaborator with Peetie Wheatstraw, the self-styled "High Sheriff from Hell," playing a role similar to Scapper Blackwell's with Leroy Carr. After a brief early stop with Will Shade's Memphis Jug Band aggregation, Weldon became Memphis Minnie's first husband and backed her up until she took up with Man Number Two, Kansas Joe McCoy. Weldon moved on to put out an early version of "Somebody Changed the Lock on That Door," later a hit for Louis Jordan. Weldon's "W.P.A. Blues" satirized the heavy-handedness of Franklin Roosevelt's vaunted Depression aid program. He reportedly headed out to the West Coast and found soundtrack work. His last known whereabouts were in Detroit in the mid-1960s.

what to buy: Of the three volumes of Weldon's work put out by this Austrian label, the strongest is the first set, *Casey Bill Weldon, 1935–38* 🎵🎵🎵 (Document, 1993, prod. Johnny Parth). Weldon did most of his solo work between 1935 and 1936, featuring his slide guitar's unique island sound. The later discs are weighted down by Weldon's backing work for several undistinguished vocalists.

Katie Webster (© Ken Settle)

influences:

◀◀ Kokomo Arnold, Peetie Wheatstraw

▶▶ Louis Jordan

Steve Braun

Valerie Wellington

Born November 14, 1959, in Chicago, IL. Died January 4, 1993, in Chicago, IL.

This talented singer had her toes dipped in many different pools, and she may have become a star had she not died so young of a heart attack. She was a talented Chicago club singer, equally adept at blues, soul, R&B (with the Chi-Town Instamatics) and classical (she studied at the American Conservatory of Music). She also parlayed her reverence for old-school "classic blues" singers into an acting career, portraying Ma Rainey in the Chicago musical *The Little Dreamer* and Big Maybelle in the film *Great Balls of Fire*.

what to buy: Backed by Chicago fixtures Magic Slim and the Teardrops (plus Sunnyland Slim, Billy Branch and Casey Jones), Wellington proves she can belt worthy of Etta James and Aretha Franklin on *Million Dollar $ecret* 🎵🎵🎵 (Flying Fish, 1984).

the rest:

Life in the Big City 🎵🎵🎵 (GBW, 1982)

influences:

◀◀ Etta James, Ma Rainey, Bessie Smith, Aretha Franklin, Koko Taylor, Katie Webster

▶▶ E.C. Scott, Big Time Sarah

Steve Knopper

Junior Wells

Born Amos Blackmore, December 9, 1934, in Memphis, TN.

Blues lore has it that a 12-year-old Junior Wells worked for a week to buy a harmonica he had seen at a pawnshop. Upon being told that it cost two dollars, he threw down his weeks' wages of $1.50 and ran out with the harp. When a judge asked why he had done this, Junior replied that he just had to have it. The judge asked him to play it, and upon hearing the precocious kid, gave the complainant 50 cents and dismissed the case. It's probably an apocryphal tale, but some things are true even if they never happened. Wells is one of a handful of people, along with Little Walter, the two Sonny Boy Williamsons and James Cotton, who wrote the book on Mississippi Delta/Chicago-style harmonica playing. Wells replaced Walter in Muddy Waters' seminal band in 1952. He began making solo recordings the following year while AWOL from the Army. In 1966, Wells began a lengthy partnership with Buddy Guy which resulted in some of the guitarist's finest recorded work.

what to buy: Years of playing South Side blues clubs, often backed by Guy, honed Wells' chops as he developed an expansive, new, hardened style, adding heavy dollops of urban menace and James Brown-style proto-funk to his traditional Chicago blues. The result, *Hoodoo Man Blues* ♫♫♫♫ (Delmark, 1965, prod. Robert Koester) is not only Wells' finest moment, but a modern blues masterpiece that leaps out of the gate with "Snatch It Back and Hold It," a burst of funky R&B fun, and never looks back, with Wells and Guy constantly prodding each other to new heights. *It's My Life, Baby!* ♫♫♫♫ (Vanguard, 1966, prod. Samuel Charters) is almost as strong. Of his co-headlining albums with Guy, *Drinkin TNT 'N' Smokin' Dynamite* ♫♫♫♫ (Blind Pig, 1974/1988, prod. Bill Wyman) is by far the best, documenting a fiery 1974 live performance with a band including pianist Pinetop Perkins and Rolling Stones bassist Wyman.

what to buy next: *On Tap* ♫♫♫♫ (Delmark, prod. Robert Koester) is a laid-back treat, capturing the feel of a typical Wells South Side performance. The mostly acoustic *Come on in This House* ♫♫♫♫ (Telarc, 1996, prod. John Snyder), on which Wells is joined by young guitarists including Corey Harris, Sonny Landreth and John Mooney, is a remarkable achievement: a top-notch album cut years after Wells was written off as a creative force.

what to avoid: On *Coming at You* ♫♫♫ (Vanguard, 1969), Wells and Guy are weighed down by a superfluous horn section. Wells' first album in years was the lifeless *Better off with the Blues* ♫♫ (Telarc, 1993).

the rest:
Blues Hit Big Town ♫♫♫♫ (Delmark, 1954/1967)
Southside Blues Jam ♫♫♫♫ (Delmark, 1970)
(With Buddy Guy) *Play the Blues* ♫♫♫♫ (Atco, 1972/1992)
(With Buddy Guy) *Live in Montreaux* ♫♫♫ (Evidence, 1977/1991)
Pleading the Blues ♫♫♫♫ (Evidence, 1979/1993)
(With Buddy Guy) *Alone & Acoustic* ♫♫ (Alligator, 1981/1991)
(With Carey Bell, James Cotton and Billy Branch) *Harp Attack* ♫♫♫♫ (Alligator, 1990)
1957–63: Messin' with the Kid ♫♫♫♫ (Paula, 1991)
Everybody's Gettin' Some ♫♫♫ (Telarc, 1995)

influences:
◀◀ Sonny Boy Williamson II, James Cotton, Little Walter, Big Walter Horton

▶▶ Carey Bell, Billy Branch, Sugar Blue, John Popper

Alan Paul

Peetie Wheatstraw
Born William Bunch, December 21, 1902, in Ripley, TN.

In Ralph Ellison's novel *Invisible Man*, the narrator encounters a jive-talking character while wandering the streets of Harlem. He introduces himself as "Peter Wheatstraw . . . the devil's only son-in-law . . . a piano player and a rounder, a whiskey drinker and a pavement pounder." This semi-accurate description was inspired by none other than William Bunch (a.k.a. Peetie Wheatstraw), one of the most popular and prolific bluesmen of the 1930s. Recording under such imposing identities as "The Devil's Son-in-Law" or "The High Sheriff from Hell," he recorded more than 160 songs and provided instrumental accompaniment to countless others, including Charlie Jordan, Kokomo Arnold, Casey Bill Weldon and Alice Moore. While adept at both guitar and piano, Wheatstraw's legacy owes more to his imaginative lyrics and his rich, emotive vocal delivery than his musicianship. His relaxed singing style, characterized by his slurred lyrics and the trademark phrase "oooh, well, well," had a profound influence on the blues singers of his day. Nevertheless, his individualistic piano stomps are exceptional and are well worth a listen.

what to buy: *Complete Recorded Works in Chronological Order, Vol. 4* ♫♫♫♫ (Document, 1994, prod. Johnny Parth) and *Complete Recorded Works in Chronological Order, Vol. 5* ♫♫♫♫ (Document, 1994, prod. Johnny Parth) contain the best recordings made by this prolific bluesman. The former has the lyrically startling "Drinking Man Blues," in which the singer is driven by drink to kill his father, brutalize an infant and assault a police officer, resulting in a six-month sentence. Also noteworthy is Wheatstraw's grim depiction of the homeless in "Jungle Man Blues." Musical highlights include the boisterous, self-assured piano workouts "Peetie Wheatstraw Stomp" and "Peetie Wheatstraw Stomp #2." *Volume 5* has more swinging piano ("Shack Bully Stomp") in addition to some fine collaborations with guitar virtuoso Lonnie Johnson, including the wonderful "What More Can a Man Do?" His famous red-light-district lament, "Third Street's Going Down," is also included in this set, along with the "project" songs "Working on the Project,"

Junior Wells (© Linda Vartoogian)

"New Working on the Project," and "304 Blues (Lost My Job on the Project)," each rife with rare social commentary.

what to buy next: *Complete Recorded Works in Chronological Order, Vol. 3* 🎵🎵🎵 (Document, 1994, prod. Johnny Parth) has fewer highlights than the other recommended volumes, but it does contain the superb fast-tempo stomp "Johnnie Blues," the plaintive "Kidnapper's Blues" and a few metaphorically unique hokum pieces ("Cocktail Man Blues," "King Spider Blues").

what to avoid: *The Devil's Son-in-Law* 🎵🎵🎵 (Story of Blues, 1988, prod. Johnny Parth) is not a bad collection, but features neither Wheatstraw's jerky guitar nor his most incendiary piano workouts.

worth searching for: *Kokomo Arnold/Peetie Wheatstraw* (Original Blues Classics, prod. Chris Strachwitz) is a beautiful collection of Arnold's best sides ("Milk Cow Blues," "Old Original Kokomo Blues") together with standout Wheatstraw numbers "Peetie Wheatstraw Stomp," "Peetie Wheatstraw Stomp #2" and "Shack Bully Stomp." A great place to whet your appetite for more from either artist.

influences:

◄◄ Leroy Carr, Scrapper Blackwell

►► Muddy Waters, Robert Johnson, Smokey Hogg, Harmon Ray

D. Thomas Moon

James Wheeler

See: Piano C. Red

Bukka White

Born Booker T. Washington White, November 12, 1906, in Houston, MS. Died February 26, 1977, in Memphis, TN.

Let Bukka White tell you he was "Fixin' to Die" (or anything else, for that matter) and you'd be likely to believe him. A big man, White always sang about the big things in life—sex, doing time (in prison and on earth), trains and good gin—with a searing intensity. Somewhere in all that is a hint that a rambling life might make the rambler sing a worried blues. White belted the blues and literally belted his steel-body guitar in his idiosyncratic, rhythmically jagged style. Over that quirky guitar he sang his moody, plain blues melodies. Legends surround his first recording session for Vocalion because he was supposed to be doing time at Parchman Farm for a shooting. Did someone secure his release for the session? Or did he jump bail? Regardless, he

recorded more when the prison sentence was up, but the blues world that had made a hit of "Shake 'Em on Down" in 1937 had changed. Despite the brilliance of his 1940 recordings, White's fortunes faded. A boxer and baseball player before he settled into the blues, White began working in a defense plant to avoid combat during World War II. Music gigs were something he did on the side. Life was still like that for White when folkies Ed Denson and John Fahey found and recorded him in 1963. White played with as much fire as he had two decades earlier and recorded more tunes in his second career than he had in the period when he established himself as a major voice.

what to buy: As if White's emotional directness wasn't scary enough, the sonic clean-up on *The Complete Bukka White* 🎵🎵🎵🎵 (Columbia Legacy, 1994, prod. Frank Briggs), which collects all 14 sides White recorded for Vocalion and OKeh, puts White in the room with you; it supplants a number of other collections, even the vinyl-only *Parchman Farm* 🎵🎵🎵🎵 (Columbia, 1970). This is as deep and personal as Robert Johnson's recordings.

what to buy next: Chris Strachwitz says in his liner notes to *Sky Songs* 🎵🎵🎵🎵 (Arhoolie, 1963, prod. Chris Strachwitz) that White improvised all of these songs for him. It's an impressive, energetic collection that touches all his usual bases and includes the improbably touching "Jesus Died on the Cross to Save the World," which has a "skip" in it. (Did they record the CD master from a turntable?)

what to avoid: *1963 Isn't 1962* 🎵🎵 (Genes, 1994, prod. John Fahey, Ed Denson) features White recorded live in 1963 in another fine sonic cleanup, but the producers should have listened a little harder to the way they put it together. The pacing drags, and no Bukka White album should DRAG! Even so, many individual cuts, such as "1963 Isn't 1962 Blues," are worthwhile.

the rest:

Memphis Hot Shots 🎵🎵🎵 (Blue Horizon, 1968)
Baton Rouge Mosby Street 🎵🎵🎵 (Blues Beacon, 1972)
Big Daddy 🎵🎵🎵 (Biograph, 1974)
Shake 'Em on Down 🎵🎵🎵 (ROIR, 1993)

worth searching for: *Legacy of the Blues* 🎵🎵🎵🎵 (Sonet, 1969, prod. Ed Denson, John Fahey) features White's energetic return to the recording studio. *The Complete Sessions* 🎵🎵🎵 (Travelin' Man, 1976) is an import that features all the Vocalion and OKeh sessions and White's earliest, religious recordings.

influences:

◄◄ Charley Patton, Big Bill Broonzy, Tampa Red

►► Bob Dylan, Captain Beefheart

Salvatore Caputo

Josh White

Born February 11, 1908, in Greenville, MS. Died September 5, 1969, in Manhasset, NY.

Though White's influence never took on the stature of, say, Muddy Waters or Sonny Boy Williamson, he was present at two distinct key periods of blues development. At the beginning of his career, the singer-guitarist befriended Blind Blake, Blind Lemon Jefferson and other important proponents of the rhythmic, playful East Coast "Piedmont" blues style; his songs, from religious hymns to pre-rock standards like "Milk Cow Blues," were excellent supplements to the sound. He outlasted blues' popularity, fronting the Josh White Singers and the Carolinans, but, like his peers Sonny Terry and Brownie McGhee, found new life in the 1960s folk revival. With Terry, McGhee, Leadbelly, Woody Guthrie and others, he changed his image to a folkie showman and played lucrative gigs at coffeehouses and festivals and appeared in films. White was a major player in both phases: other acoustic bluesmen learned from his early songs, and young 1960s folk musicians, such as Bob Dylan and Joan Baez, helped transfer his ideas to modern-day folk and rock 'n' roll. His son, Josh White Jr., keeps his father's tradition alive by performing his songs.

what to buy: *Blues Singer 1932–36* 🐾🐾🐾🐾 (Columbia/Legacy, 1996, prod. various) thoroughly samples White's "first career" as he shifts easily between hymns and playful Piedmont blues numbers.

what to buy next: *Complete Recorded Works, Vols. 1–4* 🐾🐾🐾 (Document, 1993, prod. various) fills in the gaps from the Legacy set; it includes absolutely everything White recorded between 1929 and 1941, and if anything it's far too thorough.

the rest:
The Legendary Josh White 🐾🐾🐾 (MCA)
Plays the Blues & Sings 🐾🐾🐾 (Collectables, 1995)

worth searching for: Josh White Jr. leads a trio through his father's standards (including "House of the Rising Sun") on *Jazz, Ballads & Blues* 🐾🐾🐾 (Rykodisc, 1986).

influences:
◀◀ Blind Blake, Blind Lemon Jefferson, Leadbelly, Woody Guthrie

▶▶ Sonny Terry & Brownie McGhee, Bob Dylan, Joan Baez, Pete Seeger, Cephas & Wiggins, Washboard Sam

Steve Knopper

Lavelle White

Born c. 1930, in Hollandale, MS.

"Miss Lavelle" has been singing straight-ahead soul and blues since the 1950s, when she got her first professional opportunity with Johnny Copeland. Copeland introduced her to Don Robey of Houston's Duke Records, for whom she cut several strong (if not strong-selling) singles, including "Yes, I've Been Crying," "Stop These Teardrops" (both re-recorded on her debut CD) and "If I Could Be with You." She is also an accomplished songwriter. Although White toured throughout the 1960s with the likes of B.B. King, the Drifters, Gene Chandler, Gladys Knight, the Isley Brothers, Bobby Womack and Sam Cooke, her recording career stalled and it wasn't until the release of 1994's *Miss Lavelle* that she was able to revive it.

what to buy: *Miss Lavelle* 🐾🐾🐾🐾 (Antone's, 1994, prod. Derek O'Brien, Sarah Brown) showcases a soulful voice in full display, one that the passing years have not diminished a whit. Her delivery is reminiscent of Irma Thomas (no faint praise!) on eight originals and emotive covers that include "Tin Pan Alley" and O.V. Wright's "You're Gonna Make Me Cry." *It Haven't Been Easy* 🐾🐾🐾 (Antone's/Discovery, 1997, prod. Derek O'Brien) eschews some of the slow scorchers for a more uptempo soul sound that is still plenty effective.

influences:
◀◀ Johnny Copeland, Big Mama Thornton

▶▶ Irma Thomas, Lou Ann Barton, Marcia Ball, Sarah Brown

Cary Wolfson

Lynn White

Born August 6, 1953, in Mobile, AL.

Lynn White's sweet voice is a gospel-tinged breath of fresh air in a blues world dominated by gravelly-voiced female belters. That's not to say that the sexy Memphis diva can't summon a blood-curdling howl or two, but the true beauty of White's voice is in its subtlety and control. White began singing in church at age six and has been a staple on the chitlin' circuit since the late 1970s, when she began her recording career at the behest of late producer Ike Darby. White recorded several singles for the Mobile-based Darby before her first album, *Am I Too Much Woman for You*, in 1981. White's single, "I Don't Ever Want to See Your Face Again," for Sho Me, followed in 1982. It was heard by producer Willie Mitchell, who, in the 1970s, was a driving force at Hi. Mitchell re-issued the song on his then-new

Waylo and quickly brought White to his studio to record. White's career blossomed with Waylo through 1990, when she formed her own label, Chelsea Avenue. White's voice continues to be a popular attraction on the black club circuit of the South and Midwest, and one that should be heard by all who enjoy great soul/blues.

what to buy: Some of White's best work for Waylo in the 1980s is documented on *Take Your Time* ✍✍✍✍ (Waylo/MMS, 1995, prod. Willie Mitchell). White wraps her vocal chords around beautiful numbers, including "Don't Let Success (Turn Our Love Around)," "Sorry," "Take Your Time" and "Slow and Easy." For fans of sensuous Memphis soul, this 70-minute monster is a must. Skipping ahead, White created the infectiously funky *Home Girl* ✍✍✍ (Chelsea Avenue, 1991, prod. Willie Bean, Lynn White). Examples of White's work with Darby, as well as tracks from her current Chelsea period are included on *At Her Best* ✍✍✍✍ (Blues Works, 1996, prod. Milton Price, William Brown, Homer Banks, Lester Snell, Lynn White, Ike Darby), which contains such rarities as White's "Blues in My Bedroom" and great tracks like her remake of "Slow and Easy."

what to buy next: *The New Me* ✍✍✍ (Chelsea Avenue, 1990, prod. Homer Banks, Lester Snell), White's debut on her own label, attempted to reinvent herself after a troubling period in her personal life. She is heard edging closer to a punchy, urban contemporary sound, but strong, soulful material—including a duet with J. Blackfoot—makes this title an asset to her discography. There are worthwhile moments on White's third and most recent disc, *Cheatin'* ✍✍✍ (Chelsea Avenue, 1993, prod. Willie Bean, Lynn White), but with this one, over-production becomes an annoyance.

worth searching for: *Love and Happiness* ✍✍✍ (Waylo, 1987, prod. Willie Mitchell) contains highlights such as "Love Me Like You Do" and White's version of Bobby Womack's "If You Think You're Lonely Now."

influences:

◀◀ Aretha Franklin, Bessie Smith, Nina Simone, B.B. King

▶▶ Shirley Brown, Denise LaSalle, Nancy Wilson, J. Blackfoot, Lee "Shot" Williams.

Steven Sharp

James Whiting

See: Sugar Blue

Chris Whitley

Born August 31, 1960, in Houston, TX.

Listening to Chris Whitley is like opening a vein. The slide guitarist and songwriter deals with topics drenched in the blues—prison, life on the street, addictions of various stripes—and his playing, on a National steel guitar on the quieter numbers and a loud, heavily distorted electric on the rockers, falls like acid rain across the ruined landscapes of his characters' lives. A foot-loose dropout who moved to New York City and busked in parks and on streetcorners, Whitley moved to Europe for a time and became something of a success in Belgium, where he recorded a funk-oriented album before coming back to the States. A somewhat troubled soul who knows of what he writes, Whitley's postcards from the edge have arrived sporadically, but are worth frequent and intent perusal.

what to buy: Whitley's debut album, *Living with the Law* ✍✍✍✍ (Columbia, 1991, prod. Malcolm Burn) is a stunner. Stark, subtle and atmospheric, Whitley's sound is rock 'n' roll, but his stance and attitude are pure blues. Harrowing tracks are included, such as the title cut, on which Whitley calmly declaims such lines as "I do my dreaming with a gun," and "Poison Girl," one of many drug-crazed tales the singer has to tell. Whitley's nimble National steel playing and his haunted voice make *Living with the Law* quite unforgettable.

the rest:

Din of Ecstasy ✍✍✍ (Work, 1995)
Terra Incognita ✍✍✍ (Work, 1996)

influences:

◀◀ Johnny Winter, Jimi Hendrix, Muddy Waters, Bob Dylan

Daniel Durchholz

Hudson Whittaker

See: Tampa Red

Phil Wiggins

See: Cephas & Wiggins

Robert Wilkins

Born January 16, 1896, in Hernando, MS. Died May 26, 1987, in Memphis, TN.

His blues life was a nearly-forgotten phase when the Rev. Robert Wilkins learned in 1968 that one of his old tunes had found new life. His 1929 dirge, "That's No Way to Get Along," had been resurrected by the Rolling Stones as "Prodigal Son" for *Beggars Banquet*. What Mick Jagger and Keith Richards may have seen as a tribute, Wilkins bitterly perceived as a suspicious entreaty from the secular world he had rejected years earlier. Like Ishmon Bracey and other Delta singers who turned away from the earthly pursuit of the blues to join the church, Wilkins came to see his early career as a wayward path—even if, like Bracey, he remained proud of his accomplishments. Because of the many years he spent in Hernando, a Mississippi town just south of Memphis (for many years home to Jerry Lee Lewis), Wilkins' work bore traces both of the rhythmic Delta style and the more rag-tinged urban path of Frank Stokes. But Wilkins was his own man, as his dark one-chord moan, "Rollin' Stone," showed. After his rediscovery in the mid-1960s Wilkins told interviewers that he was steeped in the blues from infancy. The legendary Jim Jackson, author of "Kansas City Blues," is said to have often cradled the young Wilkins. After serving with the American Expeditionary Force in World War I, Wilkins started up his blues around Memphis, for a time rivaling Stokes, Jackson and the young Memphis Minnie. Known for awhile as "Tim Wilkins" (using his middle name), he did some rambling, as far as Chicago for the World's Fair in 1933, but always returned to the Memphis area. Recording between 1928 and 1935, he explained years later, he quit the blues after a bloody brawl interrupted a Hernando performance. He became a gospel singer and minister with the Church of God in Christ, dabbling in extracurricular work as a root doctor. His life remained suspended in time until 1964, when he was found by a new generation of blues researchers. Wilkins refused to play the blues again, but he grudgingly overhauled several of his blues tunes into gospel pieces, including "Prodigal Son." Hurt when the Rolling Stones did not accord him the royalties he thought he deserved from their use of his song, Wilkins withdrew back into the spiritual world. Yet even long after his death in 1987, Robert Wilkins is still being rediscovered by Stones fans intrigued by the band's influences.

what to buy: *The Original Rolling Stone* ♫♫♫♫ (Yazoo, 1989, prod. Richard Nevins) includes Yazoo's masters of these 14 Wilkins classics and a superbly-researched history by blues writer Steve Calt that fleshes out Wilkins' melancholy tale.

what to buy next: A 1971 concert recording, *Remember Me* ♫♫♫♫ (Genes, 1971, prod. David Evans), displays Wilkins in the service of the Lord, his guitar mastery slightly frayed but still suffused with the scent of the Delta. Wilkins would not play the blues, but in a way, it played him—or through him. *Memphis Blues 1929–35* ♫♫♫♫ (Document, 1991) has all 14 of Wilkins'

sides, along with tracks by Memphis figures Allen Shaw and Tom Dickinson, but the liner notes are sketchy.

influences:

◄◄ Jim Jackson, Garfield Akers, Buddy Taylor

►► Little Son Joe, Rolling Stones

Steve Braun

Big Joe Williams

Born October 16, 1903, in Crawford, MS. Died December 17, 1982, in Macon, GA.

Playing a nine-string guitar that "looked like somebody had hit him over the head with it," according to his ex-producer Bob Koester in 1996 liner notes, Williams and his impeccably played Delta blues endured long enough to influence just about everybody. (It helped that he wrote "Baby Please Don't Go," later recorded by Van Morrison, Muddy Waters and who-knows-how-many others.) After leaving his home state to hobo around the South, Williams gained notoriety by playing at lumber camps; his work with the Birmingham Jug Band led to several high-profile recording situations. His style proved fluid enough to hang on even when musical trends threatened to make him obsolete. Through the 1950s and 1960s, when his rough, old-school rural blues had given way first to electric Chicago blues and R&B, then to rock 'n' roll, the folk movement latched onto his Charley Patton-inspired songs. He played concerts, coffeehouses, European festivals and, in the early 1970s, memorable installments of the Ann Arbor Blues and New Orleans Jazz & Heritage festivals. As one of the few original Delta performers to live through rock 'n' roll, he was able to touch artists in many different genres, from John Hammond Jr. to Bob Dylan to Beck.

what to buy: Williams was a prolific recording artist for almost four decades, so it's tough to choose which phase of his career to sample. Try beginning with the 1930s material (most of the best compilations contain "Baby Please Don't Go"), on *Early Recordings 1935–41* ♫♫♫♫ (Mamlish, 1965), then leaping to his rediscovery period, on *Shake Your Boogie* ♫♫♫♫ (Arhoolie, 1990), a reissue of two excellent 1960s albums.

what to buy next: *Have Mercy!* ♫♫♫♫ (Tradition/Rykodisc, 1996) gathers eight dramatic c. 1960 blues songs, including "Brand New Car" and "Chain Gang Blues," all backed with the great Lightnin' Hopkins, Brownie McGhee and Sonny Terry. And of course, aficionados can drown themselves in *Complete Works, Vol. 1 (1935–41)* ♫♫♫ (Document, 1991) and *Complete Works*

Vol. 2 (1945–49) 𝄢𝄢𝄢 (Document, 1991) if they're looking for more than a few trademark songs.

the rest:

Blues for 9 Strings 𝄢𝄢𝄢 (Bluesville)
Piney Woods Blues 𝄢𝄢𝄢 (Delmark, 1958)
Blues on Highway 49 𝄢𝄢𝄢 (Delmark, 1961)
Nine String Guitar Blues 𝄢𝄢𝄢 (Delmark, 1961)
Walking Blues 𝄢𝄢𝄢 (Fantasy, 1961)
Back to the Country 𝄢𝄢𝄢 (Testament, 1964)
Classic Delta Blues 𝄢𝄢𝄢 (Milestone, 1966)
Stavin' Chain Blues 𝄢𝄢𝄢 (Delmark, 1966)
Delta Blues—1951 𝄢𝄢𝄢 (Trumpet/Alligator, 1993)

worth searching for: Williams cut several albums in the 1960s; many of them have been reissued in various CD packages, but the original LPs have become serious collectors' items.

influences:

◀◀ Charley Patton, Mississippi Fred McDowell, Robert Johnson, Son House, Blind Lemon Jefferson

▶▶ Honeyboy Edwards, Bob Dylan, John Hammond Jr., Sonny Terry & Brownie McGhee

Steve Knopper

Lee "Shot" Williams

Born Henry Lee Williams, May 21, 1938, in Lexington, MS.

Lee "Shot" Williams, cousin of Chicago guitarist Little Smokey Smothers, has been singing in soul blues clubs since the early 1960s. Along the way he recorded beautiful singles for Federal, 4-Way, Tchula and Chelsea Avenue. Until 1995, however, Williams' honest, soulful and frequently lustful presentation of blues has been largely unknown outside the chitlin' circuit. Though it has seemed at times that his music would cross over to a white audience, Williams seems content to re-focus on the chitlin' circuit, and it is in that market that he continues to produce remarkable work and remain an icon.

what to buy: Williams' output on compact disc is limited, but the strength of his tortured voice and artistic approach is apparent. Williams made new friends in the blues world with the relatively widely distributed *Lee "Shot" Williams Sings Big Time Blues* 𝄢𝄢𝄢𝄢 (Black Magic, 1995, prod. Dick Shurman), which won *Living Blues'* Album of the Year with its well-done remakes, including "Drop Your Laundry," Gene Barge's "I Feel an Urge Coming On" and Ike Turner's "I'm Tore Up" (which Williams re-made in the early 1960s for Federal). Williams' voice is encumbered by a powerful horn section that doesn't

know when enough is enough, but his choice of songs and vocal delivery save this good but sometimes stiff-sounding effort. Although marred by overly slick production, *Hot Shot* 𝄢𝄢𝄢𝄢 (Ecko, 1996, prod. John Ward, Lee "Shot" Williams) remains the most natural-sounding of Williams' work, a chitlin' circuit, juke-box favorite. Williams re-makes his old 45s, including the incredible "Make Me Holler," "Times Are Tough" and his own compositions "I Like Your Style" and "You've Got to Try Me."

worth searching for: Williams' singles for various labels, as well as *I Like Your Style* 𝄢𝄢𝄢𝄢 (4-Way, prod. Otis Clay, Dedrick Blanchard), available only on cassette, are treasures worth seeking.

influences:

◀◀ Magic Sam, Earl Hooker, Bobby "Blue" Bland

▶▶ Lynn White, Johnny Rawls, L.C. Luckett

Steven Sharp

Robert Pete Williams

Born March 14, 1914, in Zachary, LA. Died December 31, 1980, in Rosedale, LA.

Set apart by his unconventional tunings, song structures and technique, Robert Pete Williams was a truly great blues original, one of the most exciting discoveries of the folk blues revival of the early 1960s. Unlike other country blues bards of that period, Williams' treatment of the classical blues form was astonishingly fluid and malleable. His improvised, free-verse lyrics and African-sounding harmonies, drones and single-chord guitar patterns are so unusual that he literally defies any attempt at categorization. He is both musically and lyrically peerless. No other performer has captured the emotional effect of a desperate situation quite like Williams, whose moving "Prisoner's Talking Blues" is an autobiographical account of the dilemmas he faced while serving a life sentence for killing a man in a barroom brawl. (Many of his best songs were, in fact, recorded over a two-year period beginning in January 1959 in the older section of Angola Prison, where laundry and tool rooms were used as makeshift studios.) Legend has it that blues great Big Joe Williams was so taken by Robert Pete's recording of "Pardon Denied Again" that he personally composed a passionate letter urging Gov. Earl Long to free his confrere. Upon his release from prison, Williams immediately began performing publicly and by the mid-1960s had become a regular fixture on the folk/blues circuit. In ensuing years, in addition to high-profile concert appearances at home and abroad, he made a series of fine recordings for a number of record labels, including Takoma, Storyville and Fortune.

what to buy: *I'm As Blue As a Man Can Be—Vol. 1* 🎵🎵🎵 (Arhoolie, 1994, prod. Chris Strachwitz, Harry Oster) and *When a Man Takes the Blues—Vol. 2* 🎵🎵🎵 (Arhoolie, 1994, prod. Chris Strachwitz, Harry Oster) each contain 70 minutes of vital field recordings made in 1959 and 1960 by folklorist Dr. Harry Oster at Angola State Penitentiary. Most of the tunes are impromptu compositions about prison life ("Pardon Denied Again," "Levee Camp Blues"), though there are numerous traditional and gospel songs here as well. While definitely not for the faint of heart, both discs deserve a place in every blues lover's library.

what to buy next: *Free Again* 🎵🎵🎵 (Prestige, 1960/Fantasy, 1992, prod. Kenneth Goldstein) was recorded shortly after the aforementioned sessions and coincides with his release from prison. On the chilling "I've Grown So Ugly," he sings "I'm goin' to town, have some pictures made, I'm gonna bring 'em back, put 'em side by side, I'm gonna take a good look, see if they's the same as me." Williams' total emotional investment in his material is apparent on every track. *Angola Prisoner's Blues* 🎵🎵🎵 (Arhoolie, 1996, prod. Chris Strachwitz, Harry Oster) is a monumental collection of blues, stories and traditionals performed by Angola Prison inmates Robert Pete Williams, Guitar Welch, Hogman Maxey and Otis Webster among others. Absolutely spellbinding! Williams' "Prisoner's Talking Blues" alone is well worth the price of admission.

what to avoid: *Blues Masters Vol. 1* 🎵🎵 (Storyville, 1991, prod. Karl Emil Knudsen) is his least-inspired set. Recorded in Denmark in 1972, Williams' 12-string and bottleneck guitar work lack some of the intensity of his earliest performances. It does, however, contain the charming "Talking Blues," in which he comments frankly about prison, religion and folklorist Dr. Harry Oster.

the rest:
Legacy of the Blues, Vol. 9 🎵🎵🎵 (GNP/Crescendo)
Santa Fe Blues 🎵🎵🎵 (EPM, 1996)

worth searching for: *Louisiana Blues* 🎵🎵🎵 (Takoma, 1980, prod. Norman Dayron) is an excellent LP which features William's re-working of traditional themes, such as "Freight Train Blues" and "Going Down Slow," along with superb originals like "High As I Want to Be." Keep an eye out for the inevitable CD reissue.

influences:
◀◀ Blind Lemon Jefferson, Peetie Wheatstraw, Walker Green, Willie Hudson, Dan Jackson

▶▶ Ry Cooder, Captain Beefheart, Miroslav Tadic

D. Thomas Moon

Walter Williams
See: Lefty Dizz

Homesick James Williamson
See: Homesick James

Sonny Boy Williamson I
Born John Lee Williamson, March 30, 1914, in Jackson, TN. Died June 1, 1948, in Chicago, IL.

By the time Rice Miller, a.k.a. Sonny Boy Williamson II, was roaming around Europe in the early 1960s insisting he was the first and only Sonny Boy, the original Sonny Boy was in no condition to argue. Bludgeoned to death on his way home from a Chicago bar in 1948, one can only guess how important John Lee Williamson might have become during the birth of electric Chicago blues several years later. But this much is clear: Sonny Boy I was the most influential harp blower of the pre-war blues era, whose fluid, swinging style showed up repeatedly in the amplified harmonica attack of Little Walter Jacobs, Big Walter Horton, Junior Wells and scores of lesser imitators. Williamson was a prolific songwriter as well, and an easy, buttery-voiced singer who rarely repeated himself over 125-plus tracks for Bluebird. In the years after his death, Chicago blues' royalty picked over Sonny Boy I's repertoire like greedy crows. Wells nicked "Hoodoo Hoodoo." Dr. Ross lifted "Polly Put the Kettle On." Jimmy Rogers rifled "Bring Another Half a Pint." Floyd Jones took "Drink On, Little Girl." Muddy Waters snatched "Train Fare Blues." Howlin' Wolf grabbed "Blue Bird Blues" and "Sugar Mama." And even that rounder, Rice Miller, changed Williamson's "Apple Tree Swing" to his own "Peach Tree."

Like the young Little Walter, Sonny Boy I was a teenage prodigy, cribbing licks from Tennesseans Hammie Nixon and Sleepy John Estes before heading north. Apparently recommended to Bluebird producer by pianist-singer Walter Davis, Williamson first surfaced on 1937 cuts with Mississippi wanderers Big Joe Williams and Robert Lee McCoy, who later gained blues fame as Robert Nighthawk. That May, Williamson headed his own sessions, starting out with a track copied by artists ranging from Muddy to the Yardbirds. The sales figures for "Good Morning, School Girl" are unknown, but the song did well enough to become a blues staple. For the next decade, Williamson was the king of Chicago's blues scene, playing with a revolving band of titans: Nighthawk, Williams, Davis, Tampa Red, Bill Broonzy and Eddie Boyd. Williamson seemed perfectly positioned for the electric blues revolution that Muddy Waters began pioneering in 1948. The very last track of his last session, "Better Cut That Out," would be revived only a few years later by Wells. But Williamson took the wrong route home from the Plantation Club on the morning of June 1, 1948. Robbed and beaten by a gang of thugs who were never identified, Williamson staggered to his house. Before collapsing into a coma, he gasped a phrase he sometimes used as a blues refrain: "Lord have mercy."

what to buy: The five separate discs of *Sonny Boy Williamson Complete Recorded Works 1937–47* 𝄞𝄞𝄞𝄞 (Document, 1991,

prod. Johnny Parth) each contain at least 25 sides of prime Sonny Boy—more than 125 classics in all. The sound is surprisingly good, even for well-recorded 1940s Bluebird 78s. One caveat: This top-notch series is slowly being supplanted by BMG's cheaper and slightly stingier CDs. On *The Bluebird Recordings 1938* 𝄞𝄞𝄞𝄞 (BMG, 1997, prod. Michael Omansky), the sound from the original Bluebird masters seems even sharper than the clean old 78s used by Johnny Parth. If you are a patient sort, it may be worth waiting over the next several years while BMG dribbles out all of Sonny Boy's takes. If not, pony up for the Document releases.

what to buy next: When folklorist Lomax produced *Blues in the Mississippi Night* 𝄞𝄞𝄞𝄞 (Rykodisc, 1991, prod. Alan Lomax), a candid, scabrous look at how racism dogged the lives of blues musicians and their audiences, it was simply too hot to handle for the record-buying public of 1946 America. It was too hot as well for the three anonymous blues singers who played and provided grim, sometimes macabre and funny tales of staying a step ahead of the Man. Nearly 50 years later, Rykodisc finally revealed the identity of the three bluesmen, all now dead: Sonny Boy Williamson I, Bill Broonzy and Memphis Slim.

what to avoid: Nice try, nice selection, studious notes, but *Sonny Boy Williamson Vol. 1, 1937–39* 𝄞𝄞 (EPM, 1992) sounds like it was recorded in a hollow log. Fine, if you're into audio lichen.

worth searching for: A hard-to-find RCA compilation of Sonny Boy and Big Joe, *Throw a Boogie Woogie* 𝄞𝄞𝄞𝄞 (RCA Bluebird, 1990), has been replaced by the new BMG series. But for those who want to get a taste of Sonny Boy, this one holds up well. Transfers sound as clean as the BMG versions.

influences:

◀◀ Hammie Nixon, Noah Lewis, Sleepy John Estes

▶▶ Little Walter, Big Walter Horton, Junior Wells, Muddy Waters, Howlin' Wolf, Jimmy Rogers, Johnny Shines, Floyd Jones, Billy Boy Arnold, John Lee Hooker, Yardbirds

Steve Braun

Sonny Boy Williamson II

Born Aleck Ford, December 5, 1899, in Glendora, MS. Died May 25, 1965, in Helena, AR.

For the Sonny Boy Williamson story, consult the literature of the blues. There's only enough room here for a thumbnail sketch. No character out of American folklore is more colorful; even his name is suspect—he was also known as Rice Miller.

He wandered the South with Robert Johnson, taught Howlin' Wolf how to play harmonica and was the star of *King Biscuit Time,* history's first live blues radio show. He made classic recordings for Checker and Trumpet, and with guitarists Robert Lockwood, Joe Willie Wilkens and Houston Stackhouse, he helped electrify the Delta blues. He nicked the Sonny Boy so-briquet from a 1940s recording artist so named but was the older of the two and had such talent and panache that he's by far the most well-remembered and influential. Artistically he's three-ply; he blew dry, piquant harmonica, sang with sly and brilliant phrasing and wrote some of the coolest lyrics in the history of speech. A session of really listening to Sonny Boy lyrics is a stroll through the Louvre of blues.

From 1950–54 Sonny Boy recorded for the Mississippi label Trumpet, and though much of this work is exquisite, it was overshadowed by what was to come. In 1955, Sonny Boy cut "Don't Start Me Talkin'," a jumpin', stop-time blues with street-smart lyrics for Checker. With top-shelf Chicago sidemen (often including his old pal Lockwood), he recorded for the label until 1960, with masterpieces "Help Me" (with its greasy, backlit beat), "Fattening Frogs for Snakes" and "I Don't Know" among those that hallmarked his tenure. In 1960 he moved to Cleveland for a while. Lockwood followed, stayed put and established a blues outpost in the Ohio city. Sonny Boy's influence continued as he cropped up in Europe, still spry enough to rock with the Animals and cut records with the Yardbirds. Sonny Boy went back to the South to visit old haunts and died there. His like will never be seen again.

what to buy: The classics are all on the 20-cut *Sonny Boy Williamson: His Best* 𝄞𝄞𝄞𝄞𝄞 (MCA/Chess, 1997, prod. Leonard Chess, Phil Chess, Willie Dixon) from the Chess 50th Anniversary Collection series. Had Robert Lockwood never played on another session, he'd have rank for his excellent, Delta-jazz guitar work here. Other accompanists, luminaries all, include Otis Spann, Lafayette Leake, Luther Tucker and Fred Below. Highlights include a lively commentary on risk-taking ("One Way Out") and the ornery "Your Funeral and My Trial" and "Sad to Be Alone," the latter with a prime Sonny Boy malapropism, "so sad to be lonesome, too much *unconvinion* to be alone." This is masterpiece stuff; for a blues buff to be without it is worse than unthinkable—it's too much unconvinion.

what to buy next: *King Biscuit Time* 𝄞𝄞𝄞𝄞 (Arhoolie, 1990, prod. Bill Holford, reissue prod. Chris Strachwitz) has some Sonny Boy live, on-the-air KFFA tunes but is mostly material from his Trumpet stint. Far more rustically produced than his

Sonny Boy Williamson II
(a.k.a. Rice Miller)

song
Eyesight to the Blind

album
King Biscuit Time (Arhoolie)

instrument
Harmonica

monster solo

Checker output, this is still exquisite, essential material. Harpwork is abundantly showcased and ranges from vibrato-laced flutters to feline yowls, as on "Sonny Boy's Christmas Blues," wherein our cranky protagonist promises to get drunk on Xmas. "Pontiac Blues" is a hard hitter in the car-blues genre, and "Mighty Long Time" is a gentle gem. *Bummer Road* 𝄞𝄞𝄞𝄞 (MCA/Chess, 1990, prod. Leonard Chess, Phil Chess) includes more great Checker material and more of Sonny Boy's trademark, mordant wit. On "Santa Claus" he conjures an hysterical image of himself ransacking the house, trying to find stashed gifts. *Bummer Road* first came out on LP in 1969 and was probably the most talked-about blues release of that year thanks to Sonny Boy's profanity to producer Len Chess on the now famous "Little Village." Sonny Boy was an artist of such creativity even his minutia rewards scrutiny. *Goin' in Your Direction* 𝄞𝄞𝄞𝄞 (Alligator, 1994, prod. Lillian McMurray) is comprised of Trumpet recordings, and though some founder, Sonny Boy

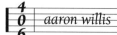

surges on indomitably. Standouts include the delightfully titled "Cat Hop" and "Red Hot Kisses" and the infectious "From the Bottom" (the latter with a young B.B. King on guitar). The booklet enclosed is both entertaining and informative.

the rest:

One Way Out 🎵🎵🎵 (MCA/Chess, 1990)
Clownin' with the World 🎵🎵🎵 (Alligator, 1993)
In Europe 🎵🎵🎵 (Evidence, 1995)

influences:

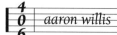 Howlin' Wolf, Junior Parker, James Cotton, Frank Frost, Little Walter, Willie Cobbs

Tim Schuller

Aaron Willis

See: Little Sonny

Chick Willis

Born Robert Willis, September 29, 1934, in Atlanta, GA.

Not to be confused with his cousin, the heralded blues and R&B singer Chuck Willis, Chick is yet another unheralded blues figure who cut one hit single and built a decent career out of it. Willis has a friendly voice (and a friendly cowboy hat, which he wears consistently) and with a nice, unflashy guitar style, he knows exactly what has to go into a great R&B song. His best-known singles were 1972's "Stoop Down Baby" and 1956's "You're Mine." He has long outlasted his cousin, who died in 1958, and he catches your attention with sexy songs like the title track to *I Got a Big Fat Woman*.

what to buy: Despite his recent efforts, Willis' best stuff was clearly made in the 1970s—*Stoop Down Baby . . . Let Your Daddy See* 🎵🎵🎵 (Collectables, 1972, prod. various), despite the incestuous title, is a fun collection of the title track, goofy sex-obsessed novelty songs and serious blues covers.

what to buy next: Willis' contemporary career has been less distinctive, although both *Back to the Blues* 🎵🎵🎵 (Ichiban, 1991, prod. Buzz Amato, Bryan Cole) and *I Got a Big Fat Woman* 🎵🎵🎵 (Ichiban, 1994, prod. Chick Willis) are full of solid guitar solos and fun-loving singing.

the rest:

Now! 🎵🎵 (Ichiban, 1988)
Footprints in My Bed 🎵🎵 (Ichiban, 1990)

influences:

Chuck Willis, Guitar Slim, Elmore James, Screamin' Jay Hawkins

Willie Kent, Otis Clay, Otis Rush, Buddy Guy, Sir Mix-A-Lot

Steve Knopper

Chuck Willis

Born Harold Willis, January 31, 1928, in Atlanta, GA. Died April 10, 1958, in Atlanta, GA.

Chuck Willis was one of the first crossover successes in black music, moving from a promising gig as a turbanned blues shouter to an even more lucrative career as a songwriter and pop crooner for Atlantic Records. But like Jesse Belvin and Otis Redding after him, Willis' flirtation with white record buyers was aborted by an early death. Willis' tough early 1950s sessions with OKeh were among that label's finest blues entrees, capturing the attention of a young Elvis Presley. Wooed away by Atlantic's Ahmet Ertegun in 1956, Willis showed an effortless knack for penning pop hits, blossoming with "It's Too Late," "Hang up My Rock and Roll Shoes" and the spookily-prophetic "What Am I Living For?" Willis came of age as a singer just as jump blues took off in the early 1950s. Sounding like a peppier Roy Brown, Willis sang with several local bands, impressing influential disc jockey Zenas "Daddy" Sears enough to tout him to Columbia and OKeh, the label's revived "race" subsidiary. Willis, as adept with mournful ballads like "My Story" as he was with booters like "Loud Mouth Lucy," wasted no time. Much of his output was in the standard Roy Brown mold, but Willis' sharp baseball metaphors on "Feel So Bad" prompted a 1961 Presley rendition and later attempts by Little Milton and Otis Rush. Hopping over to Atlantic, Willis kept up his blistering songwriting pace. The label's producers began sweetening his performances with strings and choruses, as they would try with the Drifters soon after. The touches found Willis a new teen audience. Wearing his trademark turban more often to hide thinning hair, Willis began complaining of stomach ulcers. His ailment worsened into peritonitis, which laid him out fatally in April 1958; he had just turned 30.

what to buy: Judiciously cherry-picked from Willis' five years with OKeh, the 26 cuts on *Let's Jump Tonight! The Best of Chuck Willis 1951–56* 🎵🎵🎵🎵 (Columbia Legacy, 1994, prod. Bob Irwin) show his prowess with both torch songs and flag-wavers. Among them are tracks that inspired Elvis Presley and Otis Redding.

what to buy next: *Stroll On: The Chuck Willis Collection* 🎵🎵🎵 (Razor and Tie, 1994) has sweeter stuff than the sax-pumped OKeh sides, but still displays Willis' blues power. Most affecting is Willis' version of the standard, "C.C. Rider." Slowed to the pace of an ad jingle with a bouncy chorus and goosey vibes, it was somehow still infectious—the perfectly irresistible hit.

the rest:

My Story ☟☟☟ (Columbia, 1990)

influences:

◀◀ Roy Brown, Lloyd Price, Charles Brown

▶▶ Jesse Belvin, Chick Willis, Otis Redding, Elvis Presley, Derek & the Dominos

Steve Braun

Little Sonny Willis

Born Aaron Willis, October 6, 1932, in Greensboro, AL.

Little Sonny Willis, who moved to Detroit as a youth, was a minor link between straightforward 1950s blues and R&B and 1960s southern soul. The harpist built a following on Detroit's club scene, then recorded "Love Shock" and other singles in the 1950s and 1960s before winding up with Memphis' influential Stax Records. He recorded several sweet soul songs, including "Where Women Got Meat on Their Bones," before fading into obscurity.

what to buy: Willis' main Stax album, *New King of Blues Harmonica* ☟☟☟☟ (Stax, 1970), is an excellent mixture of soul vocals and pure blues harp. He employed the same formula on *Hard Goin' Up* ☟☟☟ (Enterprise, 1974) and *Black & Blue* ☟☟☟ (Enterprise, 1989).

influences:

◀◀ Little Walter, Sonny Boy Williamson II, Junior Wells, Ray Charles, Otis Redding

▶▶ Charlie Musselwhite, Sugar Blue, Carey Bell

Steve Knopper

Michelle Willson

Born in Boston, MA.

An excellent R&B singer who squeaks her high notes in just the right way, Willson switched as a teenager from actress in musicals to singer with a strange affinity for naming her bands after nonexistent characters (Alex Clayton and Mimi Jones, for instance). After she organized a tribute to her favorite singers—such as Dinah Washington and Ruth Brown—she wound up in a band (Evil Gal) and won several local and national awards.

what to buy: Willson's thing is jump and swing blues, and she belts energetically and playfully throughout both *Evil Gal Blues*

☟☟☟ (Bullseye Blues/Rounder, 1994) and *So Emotional* ☟☟☟ (Bullseye Blues/Rounder, 1996).

influences:

◀◀ Dinah Washington, Ruth Brown, Bessie Smith, Etta James, Big Maybelle, Aretha Franklin, Marcia Ball

Steve Knopper

Hop Wilson

Born Harding Wilson, April 27, 1921, in Grapeland, TX. Died August 27, 1975, in Houston, TX.

Hop Wilson was one of the few blues artists to employ the Hawaiian-style electric steel guitar. A regular attraction in Houston blues clubs, he cut his first single, the bizarre instrumental "Chicken Stuff," for Goldband in 1958. His second release, *Broke and Hungry*, had a traditional theme, but Wilson's steel playing set it apart. His next stop was Ivory, operated by his drummer, Ivory Lee Semien, which issued his best known song, "My Woman Has a Black Cat Bone," in 1960. Wilson's innovative sound sparked the interest of European blues listeners, but his career didn't benefit much from the attention. He never recorded after 1961 and almost never performed outside of Houston's Third Ward.

what to buy: Collecting Wilson's solo Ivory material and some sessions he worked on as a sideman, *Houston Ghetto Blues* ☟☟☟☟ (Ace/Bullseye Blues, 1993, prod. Ivory Lee Semien) is one of the most low-down blues CDs of all time. Wilson's steel playing really sears.

worth searching for: Wilson's 45s are rarities market material; however, "Rockin' in the Coconut Top" would be the centerpiece of any blues 45 collection. The LPs *Blues with Friends* ☟☟☟☟ (Goldband, 1975) and *Rockin Blues Party* ☟☟☟☟ (Charly, 1987) collected Wilson's Goldband singles.

influences:

◀◀ Black Ace, Elmore James, Lightnin' Hopkins

▶▶ Jimmie Vaughan, Albert Collins, Johnny Copeland

Jeff Hannusch

Smokey Wilson

Born July 11, 1936, in Glen Allan, MS.

After years on the Los Angeles blues scene, where he ran the famed Pioneer Club, a 60-something Smokey Wilson made a dynamic national debut with 1993's *Smoke n' Fire*, which revealed him to be a fantastic singer with a gravelly, *smoky* voice and a dynamic, high-energy guitarist with a rough-edged yet fluent style. He also performs with so much enthusiasm that it feels like he might jump out of the speakers any minute.

what to buy: Wilson kicks off *Smoke n' Fire* ♫♫♫♫ (Bullseye Blues, 1993, prod. Ron Levy) by shouting, "Here I go." Then he takes off and never looks back. The whole affair is good, high-octane fun highlighted by the topical blues "Don't Burn Down L.A.," cut in the midst of the city's riots.

what to buy next: The material on *The Real Deal* ♫♫♫♫ (Bullseye Blues, 1995, prod. Ron Levy) isn't as consistently strong as its predecessor, but its high points are just as high, most notably the joyous, defiant "Not Picking Your Cotton," where Wilson digs into the tune's funky syncopated groove with sly gusto.

what to avoid: *88th Street Blues* ♫♫♫ (1983/Blind Pig, 1995, prod. Rod Piazza) isn't really bad at all. It's just sort of generic, not nearly as distinct—or fun—as either of the Bullseye sessions.

the rest:
The Man from Mars ♫♫♫ (Bullseye Blues, 1997)

influences:
◀◀ Howlin' Wolf, Albert King, Elmore James
▶▶ Ray Bailey

Alan Paul

U.P. Wilson

Born Huary Wilson, September 4, 1935, in Shreveport, LA.

Wilson is a Ft. Worth blues badman with a shrill, piercing guitar sound not drastically unlike that of Albert Collins. After leaving Shreveport he moved to West Dallas, where he hung with (and learned from) Zuzu Bollin, Frankie Lee Sims and the obscure Nappy Chin Evans. When he moved to Ft. Worth (where he was an acknowledged influence on Cornell Dupree), he was in a two-man group, the Boogie Chillun, with singing drummer Robert Ealey. Though once considered too wild for non-Texas climes, Wilson has been active in the 1990s, recording and touring overseas.

what to buy: *Whirlwind* ♫♫♫ (JSP, 1996, prod. John Stedman) is Wilson's third and best JSP outing, with scads of his trademark guitar stridency and a greater diversity of material than his other work offers.

what to buy next: *The Texas Tornado* ♫♫♫ (Wolf, 1994, prod. Richard Chalk, Tom Loughborough) is Wilson live, raucous and loud at the East Dallas beer joint Schooner's with Tutu Jones on rhythm guitar.

the rest:
Boogie Boy: The Texas Tornado Returns ♫♫♫ (JSP, 1995)
This Is U.P. Wilson ♫♫♫ (JSP, 1996)

influences:
◀◀ Zuzu Bollin, Clarence "Nappy Chin" Evans
▶▶ Cornell Dupree, Texas Slim Sullivan

Tim Schuller

Johnny Winter

Born February 23, 1944, in Leland, MS.

Albino blues guitarist Johnny Winter was already a journeyman by 1968, when fame beckoned from the rock 'n' roll crowd via a feature in *Rolling Stone* magazine. Raised in Texas, Winter helped familiarize white rock audiences with traditional blues by incorporating rock into his music. Winter's first few rock recordings made him a top draw, and he played at the Woodstock festival and other high-profile gigs. While Winter semi-retired in 1972 to recover from heroin addiction, his brother Edgar formed White Trash with the rest of Johnny's band; they had a bright but brief rock career that actually eclipsed Johnny's fame, and Johnny didn't repeat his early success until he started working with Muddy Waters in 1977 as a sideman and producer. Two Winter-produced Waters albums won Grammys, and Winter stayed with the elder bluesman until his death in 1983. Winter has continued touring and recording for various labels with varying degrees of success. Not a prolific writer, Winter's skill lies most in putting his stamp on other people's tunes. In 1986, he became the first white artist inducted into the Blues Foundation's Hall of Fame.

what to buy: *Johnny Winter and . . . Live* ♫♫♫♫ (Columbia, 1970, prod. Johnny Winter, Rick Derringer) busted him out as big as he would get. With the help of backup guitar ace Derringer, Winter rips through "Jumping Jack Flash" and rocks out the blues on "Good Morning Little Schoolgirl." *Guitar Slinger* ♫♫♫♫ (Alligator, 1983, prod. Bruce Iglauer, Dick Shurman) avoids the rock pyrotechnics as a group of veteran blues side-

Johnny Winter (© Jack Vartoogian)

men give full support to Winter's rootsier side. Check out his slide guitar on "It's My Life, Baby" and "Iodine in My Coffee."

what to buy next: After laying off to kick heroin, Winter sent a message with *Still Alive and Well* 🐾🐾🐾 (Columbia, 1973, prod. Rick Derringer). He rocks hard, and even though "Too Much Seconal" and "Cheap Tequila" warn against substance abuse, it doesn't preach. *Serious Business* 🐾🐾🐾🐾 (Alligator, 1985/1993, prod. various) is solid Texas roadhouse music. "Master Mechanic" proves Winter a master guitarist.

what to avoid: *Captured Live* 🐾🐾 (Blue Sky, 1976, prod. Johnny Winter) finds Winter still trying to climb the rock mountain before turning back to the blues. It's journeyman work, and unexciting.

the rest:

Johnny Winter 🐾🐾🐾 (Columbia, 1969)
Second Winter 🐾🐾🐾 (Columbia, 1970)
Johnny Winter And 🐾🐾🐾 (Columbia, 1971)
Nothin' but the Blues 🐾🐾🐾 (Blue Sky, 1977)
Third Degree 🐾🐾🐾 (Alligator, 1986)
The Winter of '88 🐾🐾🐾 (MCA, 1988)
Let Me In 🐾🐾🐾 (Charisma, 1991)
Hey, Where's Your Brother 🐾🐾🐾 (Pointblank, 1992)
Scorchin' Blues 🐾🐾🐾 (Legacy, 1992)
A Rock 'n' Roll Collection 🐾🐾🐾 (Columbia Legacy, 1994)

worth searching for: The bootleg *Texas International Pop Festival* 🐾🐾🐾 (Oh Boy) captures a seminal Winter performance on home turf highlighted by a burning, nearly 13-minute take of "Mean Mistreater."

influences:

◀◀ T-Bone Walker, Albert Collins, Chuck Berry, Muddy Waters, Keith Richards

▶▶ Stevie Ray Vaughan, Jimmie Vaughan, Eric Johnson, Edgar Winter

Lawrence Gabriel

Jimmy Witherspoon

Born August 8, 1923, in Gurdon, AR. Died September 18, 1997, in Los Angeles, CA.

Instead of following the exodus of southern bluesmen to Chicago, Jimmy "Spoon" Witherspoon turned in the opposite direction, both geographically and musically: Los Angeles. So instead of discovering the raw, dirty, electric blues that later influenced so many British rock 'n' rollers, Witherspoon downshifted into a slick, jazzy cocktail style that recalled Duke Ellington and T-Bone Walker as much as it did Muddy Waters and Charley Patton. Witherspoon started out singing in his church but didn't get his first real professional opportunity until Walker asked Witherspoon, who had been washing dishes at a drugstore, to sing with him during a Little Harlem nightclub show in Watts. After that, Spoon became a cook in the Merchant Marine and earned opportunities to sing on Armed Forces Radio; in 1945, after his discharge, he hooked up with band leader Jay McShann, and the two recorded the classic "Confessin' the Blues" and spent four years together. When Spoon left the band he was primed for a solo career, which began lucratively with the hits "Ain't Nobody's Business, Parts 1 & 2," and later "No Rollin' Blues" and "Wind Is Blowing." After several more hits, rock 'n' roll destroyed his R&B career, but the irrepressible Witherspoon re-emerged as a jazz singer, playing festivals, touring the world, appearing on the Steve Allen and Johnny Carson shows, recording for many influential labels and even notching the minor 1975 hit "Love Is a Five Letter Word." (He also hooked up with jazzmen Roy Eldridge, Coleman Hawkins and Earl Hines.) When throat cancer threatened to kill his career in the early 1980s, Witherspoon overcame it with radiation treatments and returned to singing. Where his friend Muddy Waters transformed Delta juke-joint blues into rocking electric Chicago blues, Witherspoon's slicker direction continued to remind people where jazz came from. His 1993 version of "Kansas City" opens with pure jazz, then detours into Waters' trademark "Got My Mojo Workin'." Very few musicians have combined blues and jazz with as much musical success.

what to buy: Witherspoon had an amazingly consistent, prolific career, so it's tough to pick a starting point: *Blowin' in from Kansas City* 🐾🐾🐾🐾 (Flair/Virgin, 1991, prod. various) not only is an essential historic document of the singer's jazzy jump blues, but it swings wonderfully, with a horn section and the presence of arrangers Jay McShann and Tiny Webb; *'Spoon and Groove* 🐾🐾🐾🐾 (Tradition/Rykodisc, 1996, prod. various) tours his 1960s material with organist Richard Arnold "Groove" Holmes; *Call My Baby* 🐾🐾🐾🐾 (Night Train, 1991, prod. Dan Nooger) reissues his 1940s classics for Supreme and Swing Time, including both versions of "Ain't Nobody's Business" and "Hey Mr. Landlord."

what to buy next: *Evenin' Blues* 🐾🐾🐾 (Original Blues Classics, 1964/Fantasy, 1993) operates in that gray zone between rock 'n' roll (a version of "Good Rockin' Tonight"), jazz ("Kansas City") and pure blues ("How Long Blues"). The compilation *Ain't Nobody's Business* 🐾🐾🐾 (Polydor, 1967/Drive, 1994) is somewhat mysterious because the liner notes don't refer specifically to the performances on this disc; they're from 1948, 1949 and 1950, and these versions of "Ain't Nobody's Business" and "New Orleans Woman" are among the best Witherspoon recorded.

what to avoid: Even Spoon made missteps, including *Midnight Lady Called the Blues* 🐕🐕 (Muse, 1986, prod. Doc Pomus, Mac Rebennack), in which Witherspoon sings bland, uninspired versions of songs written by Pomus and Dr. John. (Note ridiculous cover photo of babe in blue sequins.)

the rest:

Jays Blues 🐕🐕🐕 (Charly)
Mean Old Frisco 🐕🐕🐕 (Prestige)
Jimmy Witherspoon and Jay McShann 🐕🐕🐕 (DA, 1949)
Goin' to Kansas City Blues 🐕🐕🐕 (RCA, 1958)
The 'Spoon Concerts 🐕🐕🐕 (Fantasy, 1959)
Roots 🐕🐕 (Reprise, 1962)
Baby Baby Baby 🐕🐕🐕 (Original Blues Classics, 1963/Fantasy, 1993)
Blues around the Clock 🐕🐕🐕 (Original Blues Classics, 1963/Fantasy)
Some of My Best Friends Are the Blues 🐕🐕🐕 (Original Blues Classics, 1964/Fantasy, 1994)
Hey Mr. Landlord 🐕🐕🐕🐕 (Route 66, 1965)
Blues for Easy Livers 🐕🐕🐕 (Original Blues Classics, 1966/Fantasy, 1996)
The Spoon Concerts 🐕🐕🐕 (Fantasy, 1972)
Spoonful 🐕🐕🐕 (Avenue Jazz, 1975/Rhino, 1994)
Live 🐕🐕🐕 (Avenue Jazz/Rhino, 1976)
Rockin' L.A. 🐕🐕 (Fantasy, 1988)
Spoon Go East 🐕🐕🐕🐕 (Chess/MCA, 1990)
Spoon So Easy: The Chess Years 🐕🐕🐕🐕 (Chess/MCA, 1990)
Call Me Baby 🐕🐕🐕 (Night Train, 1991)
Ain't Nothin' New about the Blues 🐕🐕 (Aim, 1994)
Spoon's Life 🐕🐕🐕 (Evidence, 1994)
Spoon's Blues 🐕🐕🐕 (Stony Plain, 1995)
(With Robben Ford) *Live at the Mint* 🐕🐕🐕 (On the Spot/Private, 1996)

worth searching for: *Jimmy Witherspoon Sings the Blues* 🐕🐕🐕🐕 (Aim, 1993, prod. Peter Noble) comes from 1980 studio sessions with a Melbourne, Australia, band. Witherspoon is in powerful, happy voice in relaxed versions of "C.C. Rider," "Kansas City" and his hero Joe Turner's song, "Roll 'Em Pete."

influences:

◀◀ Louis Jordan, T-Bone Walker, Jay McShann, Muddy Waters, Big Joe Turner, Charles Brown

▶▶ Robben Ford, Animals, B.B. King, Roy Eldridge, Chris Daniels & the Kings, Phil Alvin

Steve Knopper

johnny Winter

song
Good Morning Little Schoolgirl

album
johnny Winter and . . . Live (Columbia)

instrument
Guitar

monster solo

Mitch Woods

Born April 3, 1951, in Brooklyn, NY.

Mitch Woods has continued to carry the mantle for jump-blues, boogie woogie, Chicago blues and New Orleans second-line playing. Originally trained in classical music, Woods blossomed at the University of Buffalo, where his interest in the boogie-woogie style of Pete Johnson and the Chicago blues styles of Otis Spann eventually led him to explore a variety of blues, R&B and rock techniques. Moving to San Francisco in 1970, he formed a duo, Mitch Woods & His Red Hot Mama, and later formed a band, the Rocket 88s (named after the Jackie Brenston song) and began a career of playing boogie-woogie and jump-blues that he dubs "rock-a-boogie." While his early albums highlight energetic covers of songs from the likes of Louis Jordan, Roy Milton, Joe Liggins and others, Woods has become a songwriter whose songs continue to build on his roots, demonstrating a keen ability to blend lyrics and music that pay homage to the traditions he admires while establishing himself as a contemporary stylist in a similar vein.

what to buy: The essential disc is *Solid Gold Cadillac* 𝄞𝄞𝄞𝄞 (Blind Pig, 1991, prod. Mitch Woods), which features Woods playing Hammond organ on a cover of Albert Collins' "Frosty" as well as Ronnie Earl adding a tasty guitar solo on that track and on a slow blues composition by Woods, "10th & Parker Blues." "Blues Hangover" features Charlie Musselwhite on harp and some great boogie-woogie riffing by Woods. Other tracks that stand out are the covers of Joe Liggins' "Pink Champagne," which features the Roomful of Blues horn section and shows how comfortable Woods is straddling different musical genres, as well as the cover of Little Milton's "That Will Never Do." These 11 tracks help define Woods' style.

what to buy next: Woods stepped back in time to trace some of his roots on *Keeper of the Flame* 𝄞𝄞𝄞𝄞 (Viceroots, 1996, prod. Mitch Woods), which finds him performing duets with John Lee Hooker, James Cotton, Earl King and Johnnie Johnson and reinterpreting three of his earlier original songs. The interplay between Johnnie Johnson and Woods on "Blues Ya 'fore I Lose Ya" and "Full Tilt Boogie" is like stepping into a smoky club late at night. *Mr. Boogie's back in Town* 𝄞𝄞𝄞𝄞 (Blind Pig, 1988, prod. Mitch Woods) crosses jump-blues, rockabilly and boogie-woogie.

what to avoid: *Steady Date* 𝄞𝄞 (Blind Pig, 1984, prod. Mitch Woods) lacks the depth or production qualities that make its successors worthy of collecting.

the rest:

Shakin' the Shack 𝄞𝄞𝄞 (Blind Pig, 1993)

influences:

◀◀ Roy Milton, Louis Jordan, Pete Johnson, Otis Spann, Professor Longhair

John Koetzner

Big John Wrencher

Born February 12, 1924, in Sunflower, MS. Died July 15, 1977, in Clarksdale, MS.

A self-taught harmonica player at age 12, John left Mississippi in 1947 for Chicago, where he played on Maxwell Street for dimes. In 1956 he moved to Detroit but on a trip back to Mississippi in 1958 he lost his arm in a car wreck; in 1960 he settled down in St. Louis but moved to Chicago for good in 1962. Technically limited after the accident, he managed to become a virtuoso of the harmonica, succeeding in getting a spectacular command of the instrument and developing rich and beautiful tones as his trademark. A mellow vocalist, keen on falsetto effects, he composed ear-catching songs and will stay in blues history as the harpist with the raw delivery, tense playing and strong rural influences.

what to buy: *Big John Wrencher & His Maxwell Street Blues Boys* 𝄞𝄞𝄞𝄞 (Barrelhouse, 1974/Blue Sting, 1995, prod. George Paulus) is a very rough, down-home session with splendid warhorses "Maxwell Street Alley Blues," "John's Moonshine Blues" and "Rubbin' My Root." A 1974 London concert with Eddie Taylor in top form, *B.J. Wrencher with Eddie Taylor & Bluehounds* 𝄞𝄞𝄞𝄞 (Bear, 1975, prod. Jim Simpson) includes his own "Troublemakin' Woman," "Telephone Blues" and "Lonesome in My Cabin."

what to buy next: *The Chicago String Band* 𝄞𝄞𝄞𝄞𝄞 (Testament, 1970/1994, prod. Pete Welding) is recorded with a string band that includes Johnny Young, John Lee Granderson and Carl Martin.

influences:

◀◀ Sonny Boy Williamson II, Big Walter Horton

Robert Sacré

Billy Wright

Born May 21, 1932, in Atlanta, GA. Died October 27, 1991, in Atlanta, GA.

Trained on vaudeville shows, R&B singer Billy Wright was called "Prince of the Blues" when he first started performing as a teen at the 81 Theatre in Atlanta. By all accounts he was a terrific singer and fun, energetic performer, but his biggest gigs came maybe five or six years too early. Instead of becoming an R&B legend, he sired Little Richard, a huge fan and imitator, to a record deal. Richard, of course, became a rock 'n' roll pioneer while Wright recorded singles—and occasional R&B hits, such as "Stacked Deck"—for Savoy, Peacock and Carrollton before settling into a career as an Atlanta concert emcee. A stroke in the mid-1970s ended his recording activity.

what to buy: It's uncanny how much Wright sounds like Little Richard, or vice versa, on his 1949–54 Savoy sessions, collected on *Billy Wright* 𝄞𝄞𝄞𝄞 (Savoy Jazz, 1994, prod. various), which includes "Billy's Boogie Blues" and other upbeat pre–rock 'n' roll classics.

what to buy next: *Goin' Down Slow (Blues, Soul and Early R 'n' R, Vol. 1)* 𝄞𝄞𝄞 (Savoy, 1984, prod. various) is an important pre-rock document, capturing Wright as a key link between late-1940s jump blues and R&B and mid-1950s rock 'n' roll.

influences:

◀◀ Louis Jordan, Wynonie Harris, Amos Milburn, Elmore James, Charles Brown

▶▶ Little Richard, Paul "Hucklebuck" Williams, Bill Haley, Elvis Presley, Chuck Berry

Steve Knopper

O.V. Wright

Born Overton Vertis Wright, October 9, 1939, in Leno, TN. Died November 16, 1980, in Birmingham, AL.

The sad case of O.V. Wright is another soul tragedy, his breakdown and death as senseless and heartbreaking as the eerie self-isolation of James Carr. Wright's glory was his howling, ragged voice, a brutal force of nature that propelled a brace of late-1960s soul classics like the desert wind. Recording for Houston record czar Don Robey's Back Beat label, Wright powered a string of minor-key soul storms: "You're Gonna Make Me Cry," "Eight Men, Four Women," "Ace of Spades," and the hopeless "A Nickel and a Nail." Even in decline, Wright continued to work wonders for Memphis production wizard Willie Mitchell, still capable of vocal flights that even Hi label colleague Al Green might envy. Like Sam Cooke, Wright abandoned the safety of the gospel world for the hectic pace of R&B clubs. A lead singer with famed Highway QCs and Sunset Travelers, Wright strayed to the soul life after meeting Roosevelt Jamison, author of the Otis Redding classic, "That's How Strong My Love Is." Wright was the first to record Jamison's song for Goldwax (also Carr's label), but it was pulled after Robey insisted Wright was still under contract to him from his stint with the Sunset Travelers. While Redding's version became the hit, Wright soldiered on, finally charting with the moody "Make Me Cry." From 1965 to 1972, Wright surfaced with three albums and a handful of singles, all of them near-perfect crystallizations of Memphis soul. After some late 1960s productions with Mitchell, Wright joined the producer at Hi. Their soulful combination lasted a few more years, including a powerful Tokyo concert. But Wright was reportedly gripped by heavy drug use, said to be a factor in his sudden death at the age of 41.

what to buy: There are 18 stone soul classics on *The Soul of O.V. Wright* ⅊⅊⅊⅊ (MCA, 1992, prod. Andy McKaie). But as fine a compilation as this is, MCA should do the right thing and make all of Wright's 1960s sessions available. Both of his super albums, *Eight Men, Four Women* and *A Nickel and a Nail and Ace of Spades* deserve to see the light of day.

what to buy next: At first glance, *The Wright Stuff/Live* ⅊⅊⅊⅊⅊ (Hi/Demon, 1990, prod. Willie Mitchell) might seem second-rate stuff, O.V. almost on his deathbed. Although there are no bona-fide hits here, Wright still wields his voice like a voodoo totem. The Demon label combines a late 1970s album with a magisterial live show Wright put on in Tokyo in 1979. Wright rips through several of his 1960s hits—and even cuts Al Green on the Reverend's own "Love and Happiness."

influences:

◀◀ Archie Brownlee

▶▶ Al Green

Steve Braun

The Yardbirds

Formed 1963, in London, England. Disbanded 1968.

Keith Relf (died May 14, 1976), vocals, harmonica (1963–68); Anthony "Top" Topham, guitar (1963); Eric Clapton, guitar (1963–65); Jeff Beck, guitar (1965–66); Jimmy Page, guitar (1966–68); Chris Dreja, guitar (1963–66), bass (1966–68); Paul Samwell-Smith, bass (1963–66); Jim McCarty, drums (1963–68).

The Yardbirds were among the wave of 1960s U.K. bands—the Animals, Them, the Rolling Stones—that tipped their hats more toward the blues and rhythm & blues side than the pop and country side of rock 'n' roll. Even so, guitarist Eric Clapton left the group complaining of commercialism after recording its first hit "For Your Love." The band virtually invented the concept of the rock guitar god and filled the Clapton void with Jeff Beck, whose experimentalism—feedback, Eastern tonalities—fit right into the mood of the times. Toward the end of his tenure, he shared guitar duties with Jimmy Page, who was heading in a similar direction with his playing. Unfortunately Beck left, and the Yardbirds' new producer wasted the potential of Page and the band. The Yardbirds weren't as big as the Rolling Stones, but they were just as influential. Young guitarists still practice those licks by the torrid trio that held the lead-guitar chair, which is why the 1983 Box of Frogs regrouping (featuring Samwell-Smith, Dreja and McCarty) and the

1990s revival of the Yardbirds (featuring Dreja and McCarty) enjoyed some success on the touring circuit.

what to buy: *Greatest Hits, Vol. 1: 1964–66* ♫♫♫♫ (Rhino, 1986, prod. Giorgio Gomelsky) is the place to start a Yardbirds collection on compact disc. The 18 well-chosen tracks include the real hits, such as "For Your Love," and the band's signature blues takes, such as "Train Kept a-Rollin'." *Vol. 1: Smokestack Lightning* ♫♫♫♫ (Sony Legacy, 1991) and *Vol. 2: Blues, Backtracks and Shapes of Things* ♫♫♫♫ (Sony/Legacy, 1991) expand on what the Rhino set includes with rarities and live cuts.

what to buy next: *Five Live Yardbirds* ♫♫♫ (Rhino, 1988, prod. Giorgio Gomelsky) is a reissue of the original live debut album recorded in 1964 at the Marquee Club in London. It's a dynamic record that, despite Clapton's later protests about commercialism, shows the band was already pretty far from blues purism in its "rave up" approach. Next comes a tough choice, *Little Games* ♫♫♫ (EMI, 1996, prod. Mickie Most, Paul Samwell-Smith) or *Little Games Sessions & More* ♫♫♫ (EMI, 1992, prod. Mickie Most, Paul Samwell-Smith). The latter is a two-CD set that contains 10 more tracks than the former, and both feature the entirety of the band's original *Little Games* album, one of the weakest in the catalog. Both are of interest because they display Page's work as the band's solo lead guitarist. The single-disc set is a tad more listenable, so it depends on whether you think getting rarities, like the mono mix of the title cut, is worth paying twice the price. Getting both is completist overkill.

what to avoid: Despite the allure of Mr. Page, the original vinyl or bootlegged versions of *Live Yardbirds Featuring Jimmy Page* ♫ (Epic, 1971) stink. Page himself had the thing pulled off the market. Also, the band is over-anthologized. Stick with the listings here and you'll avoid many ugly rip-offs.

the rest:
On Air ♫♫♫ (Band of Joy, 1991)

worth searching for: *Roger the Engineer* ♫♫♫♫ (Edsel, 1966, prod. Paul Samwell-Smith, Simon Napier Bell) is the cream of the band's original album output with the dream team of Beck and Page on board and such key cuts as "Over, Under, Sideways, Down" and "Happenings 10 Years Time Ago." Thanks to a legal wrangle, it is the only album made from the original master tapes and therefore has a more brilliant sound than any other Yardbirds record. For blues content, check out *With Sonny Boy Williamson* ♫♫♫ (Mercury, 1966). The band was new and played tentatively behind their hero in a live recording from before the band's own debut album. Williamson carries the day. It's interesting to hear embryonic Clapton when there was little hint of impending godhood.

influences:

◀◀ Sonny Boy Williamson II, John Lee Hooker, Howlin' Wolf

▶▶ Cream, Led Zeppelin

Salvatore Caputo

Johnny Young

Born January 1, 1917, in Vicksburg, MS . Died April 18, 1974, in Chicago, IL.

When he was 12, Johnny Young's family moved to Rolling Fork, Mississippi, and Johnny started on harmonica before learning guitar and mandolin. Influenced by a multi-instrumentalist uncle, he taught himself to play and mandolin became his main instrument. He performed at picnics and home parties in his area and played the clubs with his cousin, Henry Williams (also a guitarist/mandolinist). He moved to Chicago in 1940 and became part of the Mississippi-born musicians that gave shape to the modern electric blues there. Teaming with Muddy Waters in 1945 and later with Snooky Pryor, Moody Jones and Floyd Jones, he regularly played the Maxwell Street flea market. Young already had developed a personal style as a fine, if rugged, and expressive singer, a wizard on the electrified mandolin and a talented guitarist. Commercial success eluded him until the 1960s, when he was finally recognized as a master of the blues. His spontaneity, good humor and sense of rhythm led to new recordings under his own name and as rhythm guitarist for a lot of artists who appreciated his true worth. His place in blues history is secure as an expressive, traditional artist with a large repertoire that combined southern evergreens and strong modern Chicago blues songs. Young's mandolin playing remains one of the most original and exciting sounds of any style of blues.

what to buy: *Chicago Blues* ♫♫♫♫ (Arhoolie, 1966/1968/1990, prod. Chris Strachwitz, Willie Dixon) includes the 12 sides recorded in 1965 with Otis Spann, James Cotton and S.P. Leary and eight sides (out of 10) recorded in 1967 with Walter Horton, Jimmy Dawkins and Lafayette Leake. Good to the last note. The compact disc version of *Johnny Young & His Friends* ♫♫♫♫ (Testament 1975/1994, prod. Pete Welding) gathers the album's 18 tracks in various settings and adds four unissued

Mighty Joe Young (© Jack Vartoogian)

tracks alongside immortal warhorses like "Meet Me in the Bottom," "Prison Bound" and "Humpty Dumpty." Young sings on two tracks of *Lake Michigan Ain't No River* ♫♫♫♫ (Rounder, 1973, prod. Bob Riedy, Bruce Kaplan) and plays a fierce mandolin, but what a treat! "Mandolin Boogie" and "Johnnie's Jump" particularly stand out.

what to buy next: On *I Can't Keep My Foot from Jumping* ♫♫♫ (Bluesway/ABC, 1973, prod. Al Smith) Young is joined by Louis Myers, Bill Warren and Richard Evans; on *Fat Mandolin* ♫♫♫ (Blue Horizon, 1970, prod. Bart Friedman, Otis Spann) he teams with Spann, Paul Oscher, Sammy Lawhorn and S.P. Leary.

worth searching for: *Johnny Young Plays and Sings the Blues with His Gut Bucket Mandolin* ♫♫♫ (Blues on Blues, 1971, prod. Al Smith), a hard to find album with Riedy, Mac Simmons, Louis Myers, Fred Below and Dave Myers, is well worth the search.

influences:

◀◀ Mississippi Sheiks, Lonnie Chatmon, Sam Chatmon, Charlie McCoy

Robert Sacré

Johnny Lamar Young

See: Little Johnny Taylor

Mighty Joe Young

Born September 23, 1927, in Shreveport, LA.

Mighty Joe Young was one of the first blues artists to break through into the clubs on the North Side of Chicago. For nearly three decades he had a reputation as one of the city's steadiest blues guitarists; besides his own recordings, his prolific work as a session man makes it almost impossible not to have heard him at some time. His rhythm guitar was especially effective on Magic Sam and Jimmy Dawkins' debut albums on Delmark. Earlier sessions were as varied as "Trace of You" by Jimmy Rogers and "Can I Change My Mind" by Tyrone Davis. Tragedy struck Young in 1986 when an operation for a pinched nerve resulted in the loss of feeling in his hands and vertigo. Today he hopes to fully recover and play as he once did.

Billy Gibbons
(of ZZ Top)

song
Blue Jean Blues

album
Fandango! (London)

instrument
guitar

monster solo

Billy Gibbons of ZZ Top (© Ken Settle)

what to buy: The title of *A Touch of Soul* ♫♫♫ (Delmark, 1972, prod. Robert Koester) pretty much sums up its contents. *Mighty Man* ♫♫♫ (Blind Pig, 1997, prod. Mighty Joe Young) contains some tracks recorded before Young's operation that weren't completed for nearly a decade.

worth searching for: Young's *Chickenheads* ♫♫♫ (Ovation, 1974, prod. Willie Dixon) was one of the few blues albums ever recorded in quadrophonic (remember that configuration?). Vinyl albums on Sonet and Blues on Blues were standard stereo but still good. All of his 45 singles are worth seeking, but "Guitar Star" on the Jacklyn label is especially effective.

influences:

◀◀ T-Bone Walker, Lowell Fulson, Jimmy Rogers, Otis Rush, Freddie King, Magic Sam, Muddy Waters

▶▶ Luther Allison, Lefty Dizz, Jimmy Dawkins

Jeff Hannusch

Rusty Zinn

Born April 3, 1970, in Long Beach, CA.

Growing up in the laid-back college town of Santa Cruz, California, Rusty Zinn was introduced to the blues through his older brother's record collection. He began teaching himself guitar by playing along with recordings of Chicago blues musicians. Eventually, he met Luther Tucker, who became a close friend and mentor. The youngster was soon performing with James Cotton, Mark Hummel and Snooky Pryor. Kim Wilson of the Fabulous Thunderbirds took Zinn out on the road and into the recording studio, co-producing Zinn's debut recording. His proficient guitar style, mixing fast runs with sustained single notes, means that his career won't be sittin' and waitin' for anyone.

what to buy: *Sittin' and Waitin'* ♫♫♫ (Black Top, 1996, prod. Kim Wilson, Hammond Scott) showcases his playing and singing in a number of styles. In addition to Howlin' Wolf's "Moanin' for My Baby," he performs New Orleans-style R&B on "Don't Let Daddy Slow Walk You Down" and swings madly on the title tune. Zinn's vocals are an added pleasure; he sounds like a mix between the hep cat vocals of Wynonie Harris and swamp pop stylist Frankie Ford.

worth searching for: Zinn is one of several guitarists on Kim Wilson's *That's Life* (Antone's, 1994 , prod. Kim Wilson) and *Tigerman* (Antone's, 1993, prod. Kim Wilson), both enjoyable outings in Wilson's tough blues mode.

influences:

◀◀ Jimmy Rogers, Luther Tucker

David Feld

ZZ Top

Formed 1969, in Houston, TX.

Billy Gibbons Jr., guitar, vocals; Frank Beard, drums; Dusty Hill, bass, vocals.

Few bands have enjoyed the longevity and steady personnel of Texas blues/rock/pop band ZZ Top. And working together has paid off, as the trio has improved over the years rather than faded away. Its psychedelic blues-rock led it to national stardom with 1973's *Tres Hombres,* and it stayed on the charts until 1976 when, due to label problems, the group stopped playing and even jamming together. After changing labels, it tossed off a killer blues rock album, *Deguello,* then recreated itself; Gibbons' trademark licks were still in there, but the sound embraced synthesizers while the band adapted to the MTV gener-

ation with its huge beards and humorous videos filled with leggy models. The resultant *Eliminator* in 1983 pumped the trio to superstar status with the hits "Legs," "Sharp Dressed Man" and "Gimme All Your Lovin'." ZZ Top rode that formula until it sputtered out during the early 1990s, at which point it began reverting back to its blues-rock roots.

what to buy: Coming off a two-year layoff, the guys laid it on the line for *Deguello* ♫♫♫♫ (Warner Bros., 1979, prod. Bill Ham), showcasing deep blues like "Dust My Broom" and funky fun on "Cheap Sunglasses"—kink, kitsch and some searing guitar riffs. They had gone nationwide, and *Eliminator* ♫♫♫♫ (Warner Bros., 1983, prod. Bill Ham) let anybody who hadn't heard of them yet in on the secret.

what to buy next: *Tres Hombres* ♫♫♫♫ (London, 1973/Warner Bros., 1987, prod. Bill Ham) catches the band as it was coming into the spotlight, when its idea of a jam was "Beer Drinkers and Hell Raisers." If you just want to skim the hits, *ZZ Top's Greatest Hits* ♫♫♫♫ (Warner Bros., 1992, prod. Bill Ham) covers all the bases and adds a cover of Elvis Presley's "Viva Las Vegas." And *One Foot in the Blues* ♫♫♫♫ (Warner Bros., 1994) gathers some of their better blues numbers in one place.

what to avoid: The only questionable product is *Six Pack* ♫♫ (Warner Bros., 1987, prod. Bill Ham), a CD compilation of the first six albums remixed with drum samples that lost some of the earthiness of their sound.

the rest:

ZZ Top ♫♫♫ (London, 1970/Warner Bros., 1987)
Rio Grande Mud ♫♫♫♫ (London, 1972/Warner Bros., 1987)
Fandango! ♫♫♫♫ (London, 1975/Warner Bros., 1987)
Tejas ♫♫♫ (London, 1976/Warner Bros., 1987)
The Best of ZZ Top ♫♫♫♫ (London, 1977/Warner Bros., 1987)
El Loco ♫♫♫ (Warner Bros., 1981)
Afterburner ♫♫♫♫ (Warner Bros., 1985)
Recycler ♫♫♫ (Warner Bros., 1990)
Antenna ♫♫♫ (RCA, 1994)
Rhythmeen ♫♫♫ (RCA, 1996)

worth searching for: *A Taste of the ZZ Top Six Pack* ♫♫♫♫ (Warner Bros., 1987, prod. Bill Ham), a lively 13-song promotional sampler from the first six albums, is a good find.

influences:

◀◀ Johnny Winter, Lightnin' Hopkins, T-Bone Walker, Cream

▶▶ Stevie Ray Vaughan, Big Head Todd & the Monsters

Lawrence Gabriel

musicHound blues

Resources and Other Information

Books, Magazines, and Newspapers

Web Pages

Music Festivals

Radio Stations

Record Labels

Five-Bone Albums

Compilation Albums

Can't get enough blues? Here are some books, magazines, and newspapers you can check out for further information. Happy reading!

Books

BIOGRAPHIES

The Arrival of B.B. King
Charles Sawyer (Da Capo Press, 1980)

The B.B. King Companion: Five Decades of Commentary
Richard Kostelanetz and Anson John Pope, ed. (Schirmer Books, 1997)

Bessie
Chris Albertson (Stein and Day, 1972)

Big Bill Blues
Yannick Bruynoghe and Big Bill Broonzy (Cassell and Company, 1955)

Blues All Around Me: The Autobiography of B.B. King
B.B. King, with David Ritz (Avon Books, 1996)

Born with the Blues: His Own Story
Perry Bradford (Oak Publications, 1965)

Bossmen: Bill Monroe and Muddy Waters
James Rooney (Da Capo Press, 1971)

Charley Patton
John Fahey (Studio Vista, 1970)

Dan Emmett and the Rise of Early Negro Minstrelsy
Hans Nathan (University of Oklahoma Press, 1962)

The Devil's Son-in-Law: The Story of Peetie Wheatstraw and His Songs
Paul Garon (Studio Vista, 1971)

Elvis: The Illustrated Record
Roy Carr and Mick Farren (Harmony, 1982)

Eric Clapton: Lost in the Blues
Harry Shapiro (Da Capo Press, 1992)

Everyday I Sing the Blues: The Story of B.B. King
David Shirley (Franklin Watts, 1995)

I Am the Blues: The Willie Dixon Story
Willie Dixon, with Don Snowden (Da Capo Press, 1990)

Jimi Hendrix: Electric Gypsy
Harry Shapiro and Caesar Glebbeek (St. Martin's, 1991)

Jimi Hendrix: The Final Days
Tony Brown (Omnibus Press, 1997)

Jimi Hendrix: Inside the Experience
Mitch Mitchell, with John Platt (Harmony, 1990)

King of the Delta Blues
Stephen Calt and Gayle Wardlow (Rock Chapel Press, 1988)

Last Train to Memphis: The Rise of Elvis Presley
Peter Guralnick (Little, Brown & Co., 1994)

Let the Good Times Roll: The Story of Louis Jordan and His Music
John Chilton (University of Michigan Press, 1994)

The Life and Legend of Leadbelly
Charles Wolfe and Kip Lornell (Harper Collins, 1992)

The Life and Times of Little Richard
Charles White (Harmony Books, 1984)

Love in Vain: The Life and Legend of Robert Johnson
Alan Greenberg (Doubleday, 1983)

Mother of the Blues: A Study of Ma Rainey
Sandra Lieb (University of Massachusetts, 1981)

Peter Green: Founder of Fleetwood Mac
Martin Celmins (Castle Communications, 1995)

The Rolling Stones: An Illustrated Record
Roy Carr (Crown, 1976)

Searching for Robert Johnson
Peter Guralnick (E.P. Dutton, 1989)

Slowhand: The Life and Music of Eric Clapton
Marc Roberty (Harmony, 1991)

Stevie Ray: Soul to Soul
Keri Leigh (Taylor, 1993)

Stevie Ray Vaughan: Caught in the Crossfire
Joe Nick Patoski and Bill Crawford (Little, Brown and Company, 1993)

Stormy Monday: The T-Bone Walker Story
Helen Oakley Dance (Louisiana State University Press, 1987)

Tommy Johnson
David Evans (Studio Vista, 1971)

The True Adventures of the Rolling Stones
Stanley Booth (Vintage, 1984)

The Voice of the Delta: Charley Patton and the Mississippi Blues Traditions
Robert Sacré, ed. (Presses Universitaires de Liege, 1987)

The World Don't Owe Me Nothing: The Life and Times of Delta Bluesman Honeyboy Edwards
David Honeyboy Edwards, with Janis Martinson and Michael Robert Frank (Chicago Review Press, 1997)

GENERAL INTEREST

All Music Guide to the Blues
Michael Erlewine, Vladimir Bogdanov, Chris Woodstra, and Cub Koda, ed. (Miller Freeman, 1996)

Beale Black and Blue: Life and Music on Black America's Main Street
Margaret McKee and Fred Chisenhall (Louisiana State University Press, 1981)

Been Here and Gone
Frederic Ramsey (Rutgers University Press, 1960

The Best of the Blues: The 101 Essential Blues Albums
Robert Santelli (Penguin, 1997)

The Big Band Years
Bruce Crowther and Mike Pinfold (Facts on File, 1988)

The Big Book of Blues: A Biographical Encyclopedia
Robert Santelli (Penguin, 1993)

Big Road Blues: Tradition and Creativity in the Folk Blues
David Evans (University of California Press, 1982)

The Blackwell Guide to Recorded Blues
Paul Oliver, ed. (Blackwell, 1993)

Black Pearls: Blues Queens of the 1920s
Daphne Duval Harrison (Rutgers University Press, 1988)

Blacks, Whites, and Blues
Tony Russell (Studio Vista, 1970)

Blues and Gospel Records, 1902–1943
John Godrich and R.M.W. Dixon (Storyville Publications, 1982)

Blues and the Poetic Spirit
Paul Garon (Eddison, 1975)

Blues Fell This Morning: The Meaning of the Blues
Paul Oliver (Cassell and Company, 1960)

Blues from the Delta
William Ferris (Da Capo Press, 1978)

Blues Guitar: The Men Who Made the Music
Jas Obrecht, ed. (Miller Freeman, 1993)

Blues Legends
Charles K. Cowdery (Gibbs Smith, 1995)

Blues Lyric Poetry: A Concordance
Michael Taft (Garland, 1984)

The Blues Makers
Sam Charters (Da Capo Press, 1991)

Blues Records, 1944–1970
Mike Leadbitter and Neil Slaven (Record Information Services, 1987)

The Blues Revival
Bob Groom (Studio Vista, 1971)

The Blues Route
Hugh Merrill (William Morrow, 1990)

Blues: The British Connection
Bob Brunning (Blanford Press, 1986)

The Blues Tradition
Paul Oliver (Oak Publications, 1970)

Blues Who's Who: A Biographical Dictionary of Blues Singers
Sheldon Harris (Da Capo Press, 1988)

Bluesland
Pete Welding and Toby Byron, ed. (Dutton, 1991)

The Bluesman
Julio Finn (Interlink, 1992)

The Bluesmen
Samuel B. Charters (Oak Publications, 1967)

Boogie Lightning
Michael Lydon (Dial Press, 1974)

Chicago Blues
Mike Rowe (Da Capo Press, 1973)

The Country Blues
Samuel Charters (Da Capo Press, 1959)

Crying for the Carolines
Bruce Bastin (Studio Vista, 1971)

Deep Blues
Robert Palmer (Viking Press, 1981)

The Devil's Music: A History of the Blues
Giles Oakley (British Broadcasting Corporation, 1976)

The Down Home Guide to the Blues
Frank Scott (A Cappella books, 1991)

Early Downhome Blues: A Musical and Cultural Analysis
Jeff Todd Titon (University of Illinois Press, 1977)

The Early History of Rhythm and Blues
Alan Govenar (Rice University Press, 1990)

Encyclopedia of the Blues
Gerard Herzhaft (University of Arkansas Press, 1992)

Feel Like Going Home
Peter Guralnick (First Perennial Library (Harper & Row), 1989)

Goin' Back to Memphis: A Century of Blues, Rock 'n' Roll, and Glorious Soul
James Dickerson (Simon & Schuster, 1996)

Good Rockin' Tonight: Sun Records and the Birth of Rock 'n' Roll
Colin Escott with Martin Hawkins (St. Martin's Press, 1991)

Great Guitarists
Rich Kienzle (Facts on File, 1985)

The Grove Press Guide to the Blues on CD
Frank John Hadley, ed. (Grove Press, 1993)

The History of the Blues
Francis Davis (Hyperion, 1995)

Honkers and Shouters: The Golden Years of Rhythm and Blues
Arnold Shaw (Macmillan, 1978)

I Hear You Knockin': The Sound of New Orleans Rhythm and Blues
Jeff Hannusch (Swallow, 1985)

It Came from Memphis
Robert Gordon (Faber & Faber, 1995)

The Land Where the Blues Began
Alan Lomax (Delta, 1995)

The Legacy of the Blues
Samuel Charters (Da Capo Press, 1975)

Living Country Blues
Harry Oster (Folklore Associates, 1969)

Lost Highway
Peter Guralnick (Vintage, 1979)

Making Tracks
Charlie Gillett (Souvenir Press, 1974)

Meeting the Blues: The Rise of the Texas Sound
Alan Govenar (Da Capo Press, 1995)

Memphis Blues and Jug Bands
Bengt Olsson (Studio Vista, 1970)

MusicHound Rock: The Essential Album Guide
Gary Graff, ed. (Visible Ink Press, 1996)

Nighthawk Blues
Peter Guralnick (Thunder's Mouth Press, 1988)

Nothing But the Blues
Mike Leadbitter, ed. (Hanover Books, 1971)

Nothing But the Blues: The Music and the Musicians
Lawrence Cohn, Mary Katherine Aldin and Bruce Bastin (Abbeville Press, 1993)

Portrait of the Blues: America's Blues Musicians in Their Own Words
Paul Trynka (Da Capo Press, 1997)

The Promised Land: The Great Black Migration and How It Changed America
Nicholas Leman (Vintage, 1991)

Red River Blues: The Blues Tradition in the Southeast
Bruce Bastin (University of Illinois Press, 1986)

Rhythm and Blues in New Orleans
John Broven (Blues Unlimited, 1978)

Rhythm and the Blues: A Life in American Music
Jerry Wexler, with David Ritz (St. Martin's, 1994)

Rhythm Oil
Stanley Booth (Pantheon, 1991)

Roll, Jordan, Roll: The World the Slaves Made
Eugene D. Genovese (Pantheon Books, 1974)

The Roots of the Blues
Samuel Charters (Da Capo Press, 1981)

Saints and Sinners: Religion, Blues, and Evil in African-American Music and Literature
Robert Sacré (Presses Universitaires de Liege, 1996)

Savannah Syncopators: African Retentions in the Blues
Paul Oliver (Studio Vista, 1970)

Screening the Blues: Aspects of the Blues Tradition
Paul Oliver (Cassell and Company, 1968; Da Capo Press, 1988)

Sinful Tunes and Spirituals: Black Folk Music to the Civil War
Dena J. Epstein (University of Illinois Press, 1977)

Songsters and Saints: Vocal Traditions on Race Records
Paul Oliver (Cambridge University Press, 1984)

The Sound of the City
Charlie Gillett (Da Capo Press, 1970)

South to Louisiana: The Music of the Cajun Bayous
John Broven (Pelican, 1988)

The Spirituals and the Blues: An Interpretaion
James Cone (Seabury Press, 1972)

Stomping the Blues
Albert Murray (Da Capo Press, 1989)

Sweet Soul Music: Rhythm and Blues and the Southern Dream of Freedom
Peter Guralnick (Harper & Row, 1986)

Unsung Heroes of Rock 'n' Roll
Nick Tosches (Charles Scribner's Sons, 1984)

Urban Blues
Charles Keil (University of Chicago Press, 1966)

Wake Up Dead Man: Afro-American Worksongs from Texas Prisons
Bruce Jackson (Harvard University Press, 1972)

What Was the First Rock 'n' Roll Record?
Jim Dawson and Steve Propers (Faber & Faber, 1992)

Magazines and Newspapers

Austin Blues Monthly
PO Box 91491
Austin, TX 78709
(512) 462-0364

Big City Blues
PO Box 1805
Royal Oak, MI 48068
(313) 872-BLUES

Billboard
1515 Broadway
New York, NY 10036
(212) 764-7300

Blue Suede News
PO Box 25
Duvall, WA 98019

Blues Access
1455 Chestnut Pl.
Boulder, CO 80304
(303) 443-7245

Blues & Rhythm
1 Cliffe Ln.
Thornton, Bradford, BD13 3DX, U.K.
+44 (0) 1234 826158

Blues Audience
104 Old Nelson Rd.
Marlborough, NH 03455
(603) 827-3952

Blues Revue
916 Douglas Dr.
Suite 101

Endwell, NY 13760
(607) 786-3622

Cadence
Cadence Building
Redwood, NY 13679
(315) 287-2852

Down Beat
102 N. Haven Rd.
Elmhurst, IL 60126
(800) 535-7496

Goldmine
700 E. State St.
Jola, WI 54990
(715) 445-4612

ICE
PO Box 3043
Santa Monica, CA 90408
(800) 647-4ICE

Juke Blues
PO Box 148
London, W9 IDY, England

Living Blues
Hill Hall
Room 301
University of Mississippi
University, MS 38677
(800) 390-3527

Musician
1515 Broadway
New York, NY 10036
(212) 536-5208

Rolling Stone
1290 Avenue of the Americas
2nd Floor
New York, NY 10104
(212) 484-1616

Texas Blues
PO Box 540365
Houston, TX 77520
(713) 420-1677

The blues is everywhere, even out in cyberspace. Point your Web browser to these pages for more information on your favorite artists or the blues in general.

Artists

Johnny Adams
http://www.rounder.com/rounder/catalog/byartist/a/adams_johnny/

Luther Allison
http://www.rosebudus.com/allison/

Mose Allison
http://www.mcs.net/~modika/mose.html

Allman Brothers Band
http://www.netspace.org/allmans/

Little Willie Anderson
http://www.rounder.com/rounder/catalog/byartist/a/anderson_little_willie/

Pink Anderson
http://www.rounder.com/rounder/catalog/byartist/a/anderson_pink_others/

The Animals
http://www.rockhall.com/induct/animals.html

Billy Boy Arnold
http://centerstage.net/chicago/music/whoswho/BillyBoyArnold.html

Kokomo Arnold
http://www.surfin.com/TheBlueFlameCafe/Kokomo_Arnold.html

Etta Baker
http://www.rounder.com/rounder/catalog/byartist/b/baker_etta/

LaVern Baker
http://www.rockhall.com/induct/bakelave.html

Marcia Ball
http://www.rounder.com/rounder/catalog/byartist/b/ball_marcia/

L.V. Banks
http://centerstage.net/chicago/music/whoswho/L.V.Banks.html

Lou Ann Barton
http://www.ddg.com/AMW///Labels/Antones/labarton.old.index.html

Barbeque Bob
http://www.surfin.com/TheBlueFlameCafe/Barbeque_Bob.html

Roosevelt "Booba" Barnes
http://www.rounder.com/rounder/catalog/byartist/b/barnes_roosevelt_booba_/

Beck
http://www.rain.org/~truck/beck/
http://www.voyageronline.net/~debber/
http://pages.infinit.net/zmehari/

Jeff Beck
http://www.wsvn.com/~staff/beck/

Carey Bell
http://centerstage.net/chicago/music/whoswho/CareyBell.html

Lurrie Bell
http://centerstage.net/chicago/music/whoswho/LurrieBell.html

Big Time Sarah
http://centerstage.net/chicago/music/whoswho/BigTimeSarah.html

Big Twist & the Mellow Fellows
http://www.rounder.com/rounder/catalog/byartist/b/big_twist_the_mellow_fellows/

Elvin Bishop
http://www.alligator.com/artists/21/index.html

Scrapper Blackwell
http://www.surfin.com/TheBlueFlameCafe/Scrapper_Blackwell.html

Blind Blake
http://www.surfin.com/TheBlueFlameCafe/Blind_Blake.html

Bobby "Blue" Bland
http://malaco.com/blues/bbb/
http://www.surfin.com/TheBlueFlameCafe/Bobby_Blue_Bland.html

Rory Block
http://www.rounder.com/rounder/catalog/byartist/b/block_rory/

Michael Bloomfield
http://www.bluespower.com/a-mb.htm

Deanna Bogart
http://www.rounder.com/rounder/catalog/byartist/b/bogart_deanna/

James Booker
http://www.rounder.com/rounder/catalog/byartist/b/booker_james/

Pat Boyack & the Prowlers
http://www.rounder.com/rounder/catalog/byartist/b/boyack_pat_the_prowlers/

Ishman Bracey
http://www.surfin.com/TheBlueFlameCafe/Ishman_Bracey.html

Billy Branch
http://centerstage.net/chicago/music/whoswho/BillyBranch.html

Jackie Brenston
http://www.surfin.com/TheBlueFlameCafe/Jackie_Brenston.html

John Brim
http://centerstage.net/chicago/music/whoswho/JohnBrim.html

Hadda Brooks
http://www.virginrecords.com/artists/PB.cgi?ARTIST_NAME=Hadda Brooks

Lonnie Brooks
http://www.rounder.com/rounder/catalog/byartist/b/brooks_lonnie/

Big Bill Broonzy
http://www.surfin.com/TheBlueFlameCafe/Big_Bill_Broonzy.html
http://www.rounder.com/rounder/catalog/byartist/b/broonzy_big_bill_others/

Charles Brown
http://www.rounder.com/rounder/catalog/byartist/b/brown_charles/

Clarence "Gatemouth" Brown
http://www.rounder.com/rounder/catalog/byartist/b/brown_clarence_gatemouth_/

Nappy Brown
http://www.rounder.com/rounder/catalog/byartist/b/brown_nappy/

James Brown
http://pages.prodigy.com/funk/father.htm
http://www.geocities.com/SunsetStrip/5689/jb.html
http://web3.starwave.com/showbiz/memorybank/starbios/james brown/a.html

Roy Buchanan
http://www.home.ch/~spaw1203/Music/rbuch.html

George "Wild Child" Butler
http://www.rounder.com/rounder/catalog/byartist/b/butler_george_wild_child_/

Paul Butterfield Blues Band
http://www.island.net/~blues/butter.html

Chris Cain
http://members.aol.com/bluesagent/index.html

Eddie C. Campbell
http://www.rounder.com/rounder/catalog/byartist/c/campbell_eddie_c_/

Leroy Carr
http://www.io.com/~tbone1/blues/bios/carr.html

Chuck Carbo
http://www.rounder.com/rounder/catalog/byartist/c/carbo_chuck/

Karen Carroll
http://centerstage.net/chicago/music/whoswho/KarenCarroll.html

Tommy Castro
http://www.tcband.com/

John Cephas & Phil Wiggins
http://www.rounder.com/rounder/catalog/byartist/c/cephas_john_phil_wiggins/

Ray Charles
http://www.raycharles.com/
http://www.mrshowbiz.com/starbios/raycharles/index.html
http://www.surfin.com/TheBlueFlameCafe/Ray_Charles.html

Sam Chatmon
http://www.surfin.com/TheBlueFlameCafe/Sam_Chatmon.html

Clifton Chenier
http://www.surfin.com/TheBlueFlameCafe/Clifton_Chenier.html

Eric Clapton
http://www.kiss.uni-lj.si/~k4mf0026/eric_frame_index.html
http://www.geocities.com/SunsetStrip/Towers/8488/
http://www.surfin.com/TheBlueFlameCafe/Eric_Clapton.html

W.C. Clark
http://www.rounder.com/rounder/catalog/byartist/c/clark_w_c_/

Otis Clay
http://www.rounder.com/rounder/catalog/byartist/c/clay_otis/

Eddy Clearwater
http://www.rounder.com/rounder/catalog/byartist/c/clearwater_eddy/

Willie Cobbs
http://www.rounder.com/rounder/catalog/byartist/c/cobbs_willie/

Albert Collins
http://dragon.acadiau.ca/~rob/blues/artists/albert.collins.html

Joanna Connor
http://centerstage.net/chicago/music/whoswho/JoannaConnor.html

Johnny Copeland
http://www.rounder.com/rounder/catalog/byartist/c/copeland_johnny/

James Cotton
http://www.rounder.com/rounder/catalog/byartist/c/cotton_james_others/

Ida Cox
http://www.surfin.com/TheBlueFlameCafe/Ida_Cox.html

Robert Cray
http://www.surfin.com/TheBlueFlameCafe/Robert_Cray.html

Arthur Crudup
http://centerstage.net/chicago/music/whoswho/ArthurCrudup.html

http://www.surfin.com/TheBlue
FlameCafe/Arthur_Big_Boy_Crud
up.html

Debbie Davies
http://www.island.net/~blues/deb.
html

Guy Davis
http://www.island.net/~blues/guy
davis.htm

James "Thunderbird" Davis
http://www.rounder.com/rounder/
catalog/byartist/d/davis_james_
thunderbird_/

Larry Davis
http://www.rounder.com/rounder/
catalog/byartist/d/davis_larry/

Rev. Gary Davis
http://www.camsco.com/artists/
davis.html

Jimmy Dawkins
http://www.geocities.com/Bourbon
Street/Delta/1225/dawhem.html

Paul DeLay
http://www.europa.com/~damray/

Bo Diddley
http://www.codeblue-records.com/
diddley.html

Willie Dixon
http://www.vivanet.com/~blues/
tbh3.html

Lefty Dizz
http://anansi.panix.com/~bsco/jsp/
259.html

Fats Domino
http://www.crl.com/www/users/ts/
tsimon/domino.htm

Dr. John
http://www.rounder.com/rounder/
catalog/byartist/d/dr_john/

Chris Duarte
http://www.hyperweb.com/duarte/
duarte.html

Champion Jack Dupree
http://www.rounder.com/rounder/
catalog/byartist/d/dupree_
champion_jack/

Bob Dylan
http://www.dreammusic.com/artists/
d/dylan.htm
http://metaverse.com/woodstock/
artists/bobdylan/index.html
http://orad.dent.kyushu-u.ac.jp/
dylan/bd.html

Snooks Eaglin
http://www.rounder.com/rounder/
catalog/byartist/e/eaglin_snooks/

Ronnie Earl & the Broadcasters
http://www.wcnet.org/~kjenkins/DIR
_ronnieearl/pg_RonnieEarl.html

Tinsley Ellis
http://www.thefuturenow.com/ce/
ellis/biography.html

Sleepy John Estes
http://www.surfin.com/TheBlueFlame
Cafe/Sleepy_John_Estes.html

Fabulous Thunderbirds
http://www.awpi.com/TBirds/

H-Bomb Ferguson
http://www.rounder.com/rounder/
catalog/byartist/f/ferguson_h_
bomb/

Sue Foley
http://www.antones.com/label/
artists/Foley.html

Robben Ford
http://www.shayes.com/Robben_
Ford.html

Carol Fran
http://www.rounder.com/rounder/
catalog/byartist/f/fran_carol_
clarence_hollimon_other/

Frank Frost
http://www.wrldcon.com/frost/

Jesse Fuller
http://www.rounder.com/rounder/
catalog/byartist/f/fuller_jesse_
others/

Lowell Fulson
http://www.rounder.com/rounder/
catalog/byartist/f/fulson_lowell/

Anson Funderburgh & the Rockets
http://www.rounder.com/rounder/
catalog/byartist/f/funderburgh_
anson/

Grady Gaines
http://www.rounder.com/rounder/
catalog/byartist/g/gaines_grady/

Guitar Shorty
http://www.rounder.com/rounder/
catalog/byartist/g/guitar_shorty/

Guitar Slim Jr.
http://www.esva.net/~warehouse/

Buddy Guy
http://www.buddyguy.com/index_2.
html
http://www.surfin.com/TheBlueFlame
Cafe/Buddy_Guy.html

John Hammond
http://www.vivanet.com/~catbauer/
bio/hammond.html

James Harman
http://www.rounder.com/rounder/
catalog/byartist/h/harman_
james/

Harmonica Fats & Bernie Pearl
http://www.island.net/~blues/bpfat.
htm

Ted Hawkins
http://www.rounder.com/rounder/
catalog/byartist/h/hawkins_ted/

Mike Henderson & the Bluebloods
http://songs.com/deadreck/blue
bloods.html

Jimi Hendrix
http://www.jimi-hendrix.com/
http://www.inconnect.com/~hendrix/
http://www.geocities.com/Sunset
Strip/Stage/4863/

Michael Hill Blues Mob
http://www.alligator.com/artists/37/
index.html

Z.Z. Hill
http://malaco.com/blues/zzhill/

Silas Hogan
http://www.cnotes.com/cnotes.
artists/hogan.html

Billie Holiday
http://users.bart.nl/~ecduzit/billy/
index.html/album36.html
http://www.teleport.com/~boydroid/
blues/bill-bio.htm

Holmes Brothers
http://www.rounder.com/rounder/
artists/holmes_brothers/profile.
html

John Lee Hooker
http://www.virginrecords.com/jl
hooker/home.html
http://www.teleport.com/~boydroid/
blues/jhooker.htm

Big Walter Horton
http://www.island.net/~blues/big_
walt.html

Son House
http://www.en.utexas.edu/~sbowen/
314spring/tom/index.html

Howlin' Wolf
http://hob.com/essential/howl.html
http://www.rockhall.com/induct/wolf
howl.html

Alberta Hunter
http://www.acommonreader.com/wu
/V/V112.html
http://www.surfin.com/TheBlueFlame
Cafe/Alberta_Hunter.html

Long John Hunter
http://www.geocities.com/Bourbon
Street/2690/
http://www.alligator.com/artists/32/
index.html

Mississippi John Hurt
http://www.vivanet.com/~blues/tbh1
.html

Colin James
http://www.canoe.com/JamMusicPop
EncycloPages/james.html
http://www.canoe.com/JamMusic
ArtistsE2K/james_colin.html

Elmore James
http://hob.com/essential/ejames.
html
http://mathrisc1.lunet.edu/blues/
Elmore_James.html

Skip James
http://www.eyeneer.com/America/
Genre/Blues/Profiles/skip.james.
html
http://www.island.net/~blues/skip.
html

Blind Lemon Jefferson
http://www.vivanet.com/~blues/
tbh2.html

Big Jack Johnson
http://www.vicjazz.bc.ca/Jazzfest96/
profiles/1115.html

Jimmy Johnson
http://www.jimmyjohnson-swamper.
com/

Larry Johnson
http://www.clark.net/pub/mgantt/
bbs/larry.html

Luther "Guitar Jr." Johnson
http://www.thefuturenow.com/
dinosaur/luther.html
http://www.rounder.com/rounder/
catalog/byartist/j/johnson_luther
_guitar_junior_/

Robert Johnson
http://www.london-
calling.co.uk/musrjohn.html
http://www.navicom.com/~ericj/
blues/
http://www.island.net/~blues/
johnson.html

Tommy Johnson
http://www.surfin.com/TheBlueFlame
Cafe/Tommy_Johnson.html
http://www.london-calling.co.uk/
rjtommy.html#top

Little Sonny Jones
http://www.rounder.com/rounder/
catalog/byartist/j/jones_little_
sonny/

Tutu Jones
http://www.rounder.com/rounder/
catalog/byartist/j/jones_tutu/

Louis Jordan
http://www.surfin.com/TheBlueFlame
Cafe/Louis_Jordan.html

Willie Kent
http://centerstage.net/chicago/
music/whoswho/WillieKent.html

Junior Kimbrough
http://www.metroactive.com/papers/
metro/11.22.95/jrkim.html

Albert King
http://centerstage.net/chicago/music
/whoswho/AlbertKing.html

B.B. King
http://www.worldblues.com/bbking/
default.asp
http://bbking.mca.com/
http://www.teleport.com/~boydroid/
blues/bbking.htm
http://Prairie.Lakes.com/~jkerekes/

Earl King
http://www.rounder.com/rounder/
catalog/byartist/k/king_earl/

Freddie King
http://www.mazeppa.com/fking.html

Little Jimmy King
http://www.rounder.com/rounder/
catalog/byartist/k/king_little_
jimmy/

Kinsey Report
http://centerstage.net/chicago/music
/whoswho/KinseyReport.html

Smokin' Joe Kubek Band
http://www.rounder.com/rounder/
catalog/byartist/k/kubek_smokin
_joe_band_feat_bnois_king/

Lady Bianca
http://www.big2resorts.com/blues/
bianca.html

Lazy Lester
http://www.island.net/~blues/lester.
html

Jonny Lang
http://www.amrecords.com/current/
jonnylang/index.html
http://204.254.123.80/jonny/

Leadbelly
http://www.surfin.com/TheBlueFlame
Cafe/Leadbelly.html
http://www.island.net/~blues/huddy.
html

Bryan Lee
http://www.justin-
time.com/hiband/bio/lee_brian.
html

Frankie Lee & the Bluzblasters
http://www.rounder.com/rounder/
catalog/byartist/l/lee_frankie_
the_bluzblasters_w_doug/

Legendary Blues Band
http://www.rounder.com/rounder/
catalog/byartist/l/legendary_
blues_band/

Keri Leigh
http://malaco.com/blues/kleigh/

Ron Levy
http://www.rounder.com/rounder/
catalog/byartist/l/levy_ron/

Furry Lewis
http://www.rounder.com/rounder/
catalog/byartist/l/lewis_furry/

Lightnin' Hopkins
http://www.vivanet.com/~blues/
tbh3.html

Lil' Ed & the Blues Imperials
http://www.alligator.com/artists/13/
index.html

Little Charlie & the Nightcats
http://www.alligator.com/artists/14/
index.html

Little Milton
http://www.teleport.com/~luckylg/
sirius/little_milton.html
http://malaco.com/blues/littlem/

Little Walter
http://www.island.net/~blues/
little_w.html

Robert Junior Lockwood
http://www.london-calling.co.uk/
rjlock.html

Lonesome Sundown
http://www.cnotes.com/cnotes.artists
/lonesome.html

Joe Hill Louis
http://www.surfin.com/TheBlueFlame
Cafe/Joe_Hill_Louis.html

Louisiana Red
http://www.vicjazz.bc.ca/Blues96/
Profile/1005.html

Magic Slim
http://www.surfin.com/TheBlueFlame
Cafe/Magic_Sam.html

Taj Mahal
http://www.hawaiian.net/~sparrow/
taj.htm

Harvey Mandel
http://www.punmaster.com/mandel/

Bob Margolin
http://www.alligator.com/artists/30/
index.html

John Mayall
http://www.teleport.com/~boydroid/
blues/mayall.htm
http://www.surfin.com/TheBlueFlame
Cafe/John_Mayall.html

Jerry McCain
http://www.cnotes.com/cnotes.artists
/mccain.html

Delbert McClinton
http://www.ao.net:80/~sound/
delbert.html
http://home.idgonline.no/~tom/
tom&co/artists/delbert_mcclinton.
html

Larry McCray
http://www.digitalmen.com.au/blues
/perform.htm#4

Mississippi Fred McDowell
http://www.surfin.com/TheBlueFlame
Cafe/Mississippi_Fred_Mcdowell.
html

Brownie McGhee
http://www.island.net/~blues/
brownie.html
http://www.surfin.com/TheBlueFlame
Cafe/Brownie_McGhee.html

Blind Willie McTell
http://www.surfin.com/TheBlueFlame
Cafe/Blind_Willie_Mctell.html

Memphis Minnie
http://www.surfin.com/TheBlueFlame
Cafe/Memphis_Minnie.html

Memphis Slim
http://www.surfin.com/TheBlueFlame
Cafe/Memphis_Slim.html

Amos Milburn
http://www.algonet.se/~freguz/amos.
htm

Steve Miller Band
http://www.serve.com/joker/index.
html

Keb' Mo'
http://web.syr.edu/~jcolasan/keb.
html

John Mooney
http://hobmusic.com/mooney2.html

Gary Moore
http://www.bourgoin.holowww.com/
GM/

Charlie Musselwhite
http://www.rosebudus.com/mussel
white/
http://www.surfin.com/TheBlueFlame
Cafe/Charlie_Musselwhite.html
http://www.alligator.com/artists/23/
index.html

Mark Naftalin
http://www.bluespower.com/a-mn.
htm

Kenny Neal
http://www.alligator.com/artists/18/
index.html

Tracy Nelson
http://www.island.net/~blues/tracy.
htm

Robert Nighthawk
http://www.surfin.com/TheBlueFlame
Cafe/Robert_Nighthawk.html

Darrell Nulisch
http://www.rounder.com/rounder/
catalog/bylabel/btop/1070/1070.
html

Paul Oscher
http://www.echonyc.com/~louisx/
rough.html

Jay Owens
http://www.codeblue-records.com/
jay.html

Junior Parker
http://hob.com/essential/jrparker.
html

Charley Patton
http://www.surfin.com/TheBlueFlame
Cafe/Charley_Patton.html

James Peterson
http://malaco.com/blues/jpeterson/

Lucky Peterson
http://www.alligator.com/artists/25/
index.html

Piano Red
http://www.vivanet.com/~blues/red.
html

Greg Piccolo
http://www.gregpiccolo.com/

Elvis Presley
http://www.elvis-presley.com/
http://www.elvispresleyonline.com/
html/elvis_presley_online.htm
http://sunsite.unc.edu/elvis/elvis
hom.html

Lloyd Price
http://www.crl.com/www/users/ts/
tsimon/price.htm

John Primer
http://www.codeblue-records.com/
primtrd.html

Gary Primich
http://www.yami.com/primich/

Professor Longhair
http://www.surfin.com/TheBlueFlame
Cafe/Professor_Longhair.html
http://www.island.net/~blues/fess.
html

Snooky Pryor
http://discoveryrec.com/artists/pryor
/bio.html

Yank Rachell
http://www.io.com/~tbone1/blues/
bios/yank.html

Bobby Radcliff
http://webcom.com/~inotes/artist/r
/bobby_radcliff.html

Ma Rainey
http://www.surfin.com/TheBlueFlame
Cafe/Ma_Rainey.html
http://www.rockhall.com/induct/
rainma.html

Bonnie Raitt
http://hollywoodandvine.com/
brokenspoke/bonnieweb.html
http://www.surfin.com/TheBlueFlame
Cafe/Bonnie_Raitt.html

Kenny "Blue" Ray
http://home.earthlink.net/~blueray/

A.C. Reed
http://centerstage.net/chicago/
music/whoswho/A.C.Reed.html

Jimmy Reed
http://www.surfin.com/TheBlueFlame
Cafe/Jimmy_Reed.html
http://www.island.net/~blues/reed.
html

Sonny Rhodes
http://www.metroactive.com/papers/
metro/07.11.96/rhodes-9628.
html

Paul Rishell
http://www.nxi.com/WWW/rishell/
homepage.html

Duke Robillard
http://www.rosebudus.com/robillard
/bio.html

Fenton Robinson
http://www.alligator.com/artists/03/
index.html

Roy Rogers
http://www.vivanet.com/~blues/roy/
rogers.html
http://www.royrogers.com/

Rolling Stones
http://www.stones.com/
http://www.stonesworld.com/2.0/
http://galaxy.einet.net/editors/
douglas-bell/rock/stones.html

Otis Rush
http://www.surfin.com/TheBlueFlame
Cafe/Otis_Rush.html

Jimmy Rushing
http://www.surfin.com/TheBlueFlame
Cafe/Jimmy_Rushing.html

Saffire
http://www.onewdesign.com/saffire/
http://www.alligator.com/artists/22/
index.html

Satan & Adam
http://hob.com/bn/960923/feature1.
html
http://www.akula.com/~rbu/satana
dam.htm

Boz Scaggs
http://bspaa.com/Artist/boz/boz.
html

Son Seals
http://www.alligator.com/artists/02/
index.html

http://centerstage.net/chicago/
music/whoswho/SonSeals.html

Kenny Wayne Shepherd
http://www.albino.com/hrbjr/kws.htm
http://ugalumni.uoguelph.ca/~
bswitzer/kws/index.html

Johnny Shines
http://www.island.net/~blues/
johnnys.htm

Bessie Smith
http://mathrisc1.lunet.edu/blues/
Bessie_Smith.html
http://www.surfin.com/TheBlueFlame
Cafe/Bessie_Smith.html

Byther Smith
http://www.vivanet.com/~blues/
byther.html

George "Harmonica" Smith
http://www.kachinatech.com/~hjjou
/hpp/g_smith.html

Chris Smither
http://www.intermarket.net/~stessa/
smither/welcome.html

Otis Spann
http://www.surfin.com/TheBlueFlame
Cafe/Otis_Spann.html

Victoria Spivey
http://www.surfin.com/TheBlueFlame
Cafe/Victoria_Spivey.html

Frank Stokes
http://www.surfin.com/TheBlueFlame
Cafe/Frank_Stokes.html

Hubert Sumlin
http://www.surfin.com/TheBlueFlame
Cafe/Hubert_Sumlin.html

Roosevelt Sykes
http://www.surfin.com/TheBlueFlame
Cafe/Roosevelt_Sykes.html

Tampa Red
http://www.surfin.com/TheBlueFlame
Cafe/Tampa_Red.html

Hound Dog Taylor
http://www.alligator.com/artists/01/
index.html

KoKo Taylor
http://www.teleport.com/~boydroid/
blues/kokotay.htm

http://www.alligator.com/artists/04/
index.html

Ten Years After/Alvin Lee
http://www.webcom.com/leerocks/
live.html

Sonny Terry
http://www.surfin.com/TheBlueFlame
Cafe/Sonny_Terry.html

Irma Thomas
http://www.helsinki.fi/~ilva/irma.
html

Tabby Thomas
http://members.aol.com/adamsmus/
tabby.htm

Big Mama Thornton
http://www.surfin.com/TheBlueFlame
Cafe/Big_Mama_Thornton.html

George Thorogood & the Destroyers
http://qlink.queensu.ca/~4bgs/

Big Joe Turner
http://dspace.dial.pipex.com/town/
square/e035/index.htm

Ike Turner
http://www.rockhall.com/induct/
turnike.html

Dave Van Ronk
http://www.rootsworld.com/folklore/
vanronk.html

Jimmie Vaughan
http://www.surfin.com/TheBlueFlame
Cafe/Jimmie_Vaughan.html
http://www.music.sony.com/Music/
ArtistInfo/JimmieVaughan.html

Stevie Ray Vaughan
http://www.prism.gatech.edu/
~gt1325a/SRV.html
http://www.geocities.com/Bourbon
Street/2461/srv.htm

Eddie "Cleanhead" Vinson
http://www.surfin.com/TheBlueFlame
Cafe/Eddie_Cleanhead_Vinson.
html

Joe Louis Walker
http://www.teleport.com/~boydroid/
blues/jlwalker.htm

Sippie Wallace
http://www.surfin.com/TheBlueFlame
Cafe/Sippie_Wallace.html

T-Bone Walker
http://www.io.com/~tbone1/blues/
bios/tbone.html
http://www.island.net/~blues/tbone.
html

Robert Ward
http://dspace.dial.pipex.com/town/
square/e035/index.htm

Washboard Sam
http://www.surfin.com/TheBlueFlame
Cafe/Sam_Washboard.html

Ethel Waters
http://www.surfin.com/TheBlueFlame
Cafe/Ethel_Waters.html

Muddy Waters
http://www.surfin.com/TheBlueFlame
Cafe/Muddy_Waters.html

Carl Weathersby
http://members.aol.com/jlemko/carl/
nfmenucw.htm

Katie Webster
http://www.teleport.com/~boydroid/
blues/katiew.htm
http://www.alligator.com/artists/20/
index.html

Gillian Welch
http://geffen.com/almo/gillian/bio.
html

Junior Wells
http://www.island.net/~blues/junior.
html
http://www.surfin.com/TheBlueFlame
Cafe/Junior_Wells.html

Peetie Wheatstraw
http://www.surfin.com/TheBlueFlame
Cafe/Peetie_Wheatstraw.html

Bukka White
http://www.surfin.com/TheBlueFlame
Cafe/Bukka_White.html

Lavelle White
http://www.island.net/~blues/lavelle.
html
http://discoveryrec.com/artists/
white/index.html

Big Joe Williams
http://www.surfin.com/TheBlueFlame
Cafe/Big_Joe_Williams.html
http://www.island.net/~blues/bigjoe.
htm

Robert Pete Williams
http://www.surfin.com/TheBlueFlame
Cafe/Robert_Pete_Williams.html

Sonny Boy Williamson I
http://www.surfin.com/TheBlueFlame
Cafe/John_Lee_Sonny_Boy_
Williamson.html
http://www.island.net/~blues/
johnlee.html

Sonny Boy Williamson II
http://www.surfin.com/TheBlueFlame
Cafe/Sonny_Boy_Williamson.
html

Robert Wilkins
http://home1.gte.net/deltakit/robert
wilkins.htm

Smoky Wilson
http://webcom.com/~inotes/artist/w
/smokey_wilson.html

Johnny Winter
http://sicel-home-2-
19.urbanet.ch:8080/Music/winter
.html
http://www.seachange.com:8010/
jwinter/
http://www.island.net/~blues/
winters.html

Jimmy Witherspoon
http://www.uel.ac.uk/pers/K.Eley/
jimmywit.htm

Yardbirds
http://www.idsonline.com/yardbirds/

Rusty Zinn
http://www.panix.com/~bsco/bios/
rustyzinnonblacktop.html

ZZ Top
http://www.cen.uiuc.edu/~pzurich/
zztop.html

Other Blues and Music-Related Sites

Alligator Records
http://www.alligator.com/index.html

Beef Stew's Blues Playground
http://www.neca.com/~bfstew/index
.htm

Billboard Magazine
http://www.billboard.com/

The Blue Flame Cafe
http://www.surfin.com/TheBlueFlame
Cafe/

The Blue Highway
http://www.vivanet.com/~blues/

Blues Access Online
http://www.bluesaccess.com/

Blues and Soul Magazine
http://www.bluesandsoul.co.uk/

Blues Bytes
http://www.bluenight.com/Blues
Bytes/index.html

The Blues Channel
http://www.realblues.com/

The Blues Foundation
http://www.blues.org/explore.htm

The Blues Harp Page
http://www.axionet.com/bluesharp/

Blues-Links
http://transport.com/~firm/bluzlink.
html

BluesNet
http://www.hub.org/bluesnet/

BluesWEB
http://www.island.net/~blues/

Blues World
http://www.bluesworld.com/

BMG Music Service
http://www.bmgmusicservice.com/

Columbia House Music Club
http://www.columbiahouse.com

Delta Blues Museum
http://www.clarksdale.com/dbm/

ICE Magazine
http://www.icemagazine.com/

King Biscuit Times
http://www.kingbiscuit.com/

Peter's Blues and Soul Music Primer
http://dspace.dial.pipex.com/town/
square/e035/

Scottyboy's Blues Au Go Go
http://www.geocities.com/Sunset
Strip/4466/

Scotty's Place for Blues
http://www.geocities.com/Bourbon
Street/5346/

That Blues Music Page
http://www.fred.net/turtle/blues.
shtml

USA TODAY (Music Page)
http://www.usatoday.com/life/enter/
music/lem99.htm

Wall of Sound
http://www.wallofsound.com/

Ziggy's Blues
http://www.city-net.com/~davidsr/
ziggy.htm

If you want to see the blues performed live, we suggest you check out some of these North American music festivals. (For more information on these and other music festivals, consult Visible Ink Press' Music Festivals from Bach to Blues.)

UNITED STATES

Alabama

Birmingham
Birmingham Jam
Columbus Day weekend, Friday–Sunday
(205) 323-0569
WWW: http://www.bhm.tis.
net/bhmjam/

City Stages
Father's Day weekend, Friday–Sunday
(800) 277-1700
(205) 715-6000
WWW: http://www.citystages.
org/1996

Fairhope, Gulf Shores, Orange Beach
Frank Brown International
Songwriters Festival
First Thursday–second Sunday in November

(334) 981-5678
(904) 492-7664
E-mail: songfest@amaranth.
com
WWW: http://www.amaranth.
com/~ken/fbrown.html

Florence (and nearby towns)
W.C. Handy Music Festival
First Sunday in August through the following Saturday
(800) 472-5837
(205) 766-7642

Alaska

Homer
Concert on the Lawn
Second weekend in August, Saturday or Sunday
(907) 235-7721
E-mail: IZKBBI@tundra.alaska.
edu
WWW: http://www.tundra.
alaska.edu/~izkbbi/

Arizona

Flagstaff
Arizona Jazz, Rhythm & Blues
Festival
A weekend in late June or early July
(800) 520-1646
(520) 744-9675

Phoenix
Black & White & Blues
Sunday of Memorial Day weekend
(602) 274-0552

Blues Blast
A Saturday and Sunday in early February
(602) 252-0599
E-mail: phxblues@aztec.asu.
edu

Tucson
Tucson Blues Festival
Third weekend in October
(520) 325-9192

Arkansas

Eureka Springs
Eureka Springs Blues Festival
Weekend after Memorial Day, Thursday–Sunday
(501) 253-5366

Fort Smith
Fort Smith Riverfront Blues
Festival
A weekend in early September, Thursday–Saturday
(501) 783-6353

Helena
King Biscuit Blues Festival
Second weekend in October, Friday–Sunday
(501) 338-9798

Jacksonport
Port Fest
Last full weekend in June
(501) 523-3618

California

Monterey
Monterey Bay Blues Festival
Fourth weekend in June, Friday–Sunday
(416) 649-6544

San Francisco
San Francisco Blues Festival
Second or third weekend in September, Friday–Sunday
(415) 979-5588

Colorado

Central City
Central City Jazz Fest
Third weekend in August
(800) 542-2999

Snowmass
Jazz Aspen Snowmass
Third or fourth weekend in June, Wednesday–Sunday, and Labor Day Weekend, Friday–Monday
(970) 920-5770
(970) 920-4996

4
3   *music festivals*
4

Connecticut

Woodbury
Taylormade Blues Fest
Third Sunday in September
(203) 263-2203

District of Columbia

Washington
D.C. Blues Festival
Saturday after Labor Day
(202) 828-3028
E-mail: gray@mrcwdc.com
WWW: http://intelus.com/
dcblues/

Florida

Perdido Key, Pensacola, Pensacola Beach
Frank Brown International
Songwriters Festival
*First Thursday through second
Sunday in November*
(334) 981-5678
(904) 492-7664
E-mail: songfest@amaranth.
com
WWW: http://www.amaranth.
com/ken/fbrown.html

Sarasota
Sarasota/Bradenton Blues
Festival
*A weekend in late September
or early October*
(941) 377-3279

Tallahassee
Jazz & Blues Festival
Third weekend in March
(904) 575-8684

West Palm Beach
Sunfest
First weekend in May
(407) 659-5980
WWW: http://www.emi.net/
sunfest/

Georgia

Atlanta
Montreux Atlanta Interna-
tional Music Festival

*One week ending the first
Monday in September*
(404) 378-2525

Villa Rica
Thomas Dorsey Gospel Festival
Saturday before July 4
(770) 459-7019

Illinois

Berwyn
American Music Festival
*Weekend closest to July 4,
Thursday–Sunday*
(708) 788-2118
E-mail: FitzMail@aol.com

Chicago
Chicago Blues Festival
First weekend in June
(312) 744-3370
(312) 744-3315
WWW: http://www.ci.chi.il.us

Murphysboro
Riverside Blues Fest
Third Saturday in July
(618) 684-3333

Quincy
Mid-Mississippi Muddy Water
Blues Bash
*Second weekend in July,
Friday–Sunday*
(314) 393-2011

Iowa

Davenport
Mississippi Valley Blues Festival
First full weekend in July
(515) 838-2311

Keokuk
Rollin' on the River Blues Fes-
tival
*Third weekend in August,
Friday–Sunday*
(800) 383-1219

Kentucky

Carrollton
Blues to the Point—Two
Rivers Blues Festival
*Friday and Saturday after
Labor Day*
(800) 325-4290

Henderson
W.C. Handy Blues & Barbecue
Festival
*One full week starting the sec-
ond Sunday in June*
(502) 826-3128

Kenlake State Resort Park
Kenlake's Hot August Blues
Festival
*Weekend prior to Labor Day
weekend, Friday–Sunday*
(800) 325-0143

Louisville
Garvin Gate Blues Festival
*Second full weekend in Octo-
ber, Friday–Sunday*
(502) 495-9089

Somerset
Master Musicians Festival
First week after Labor Day
(606) 678-2225

Louisiana

Baton Rouge
Baton Rouge Blues Festival
*A Saturday and Sunday in
early or mid-October*
(800) 527-6843
(504) 383-1825

Covington
Bluesberry Festival
A Saturday in mid-June
(504) 892-8650

Lafayette
Festival International de
Louisiane
*Last week in April,
Tuesday–Sunday*
(318) 232-8086
WWW: http://www.usl.edu/
Regional/ Festival/

Monroe
Louisiana Folklife Festival

*Second full weekend in Sep-
tember, Saturday*
(318) 329-2375

New Orleans
French Quarter Festival
*Second full weekend in April,
Friday–Sunday*
(504) 522-5730

New Orleans Jazz and Her-
itage Festival
*Last weekend in April (Fri-
day–Sunday) and first
weekend in May (Thurs-
day–Sunday)*
(504) 522-4786

Shreveport
Red River Revel Arts Festival
*Last Saturday in September
through the first Saturday
in October*
(318) 424-4000

Massachusetts

Quincy
City of Presidents Blues Festival
Last Sunday in June
(617) 472-9383

Michigan

Ann Arbor
Ann Arbor Blues & Jazz Festival
*Second weekend in Septem-
ber, Friday–Sunday*
(313) 747-9955

Kalamazoo
Kalamazoo Blues Festival
*A weekend in mid-July,
Thursday–Sunday*
(616) 381-6514

Ypsilanti
Frog Island Festival
*Fourth weekend in June,
Friday–Sunday*
(313) 487-2229

Minnesota

Duluth
Bayfront Blues Festival

Second or third weekend in August
(800) 369-4123

Mississippi

Canton
Elmore James Hickory Street Festival
First Saturday in September
(601) 859-5703

Drew
Pops Staples Blues and Gospel Heritage Festival
First Saturday in June
(601) 745-6576

Greenville
Mississippi Delta Blues Festival
Third weekend in September
(601) 335-3523
(800) 467-3582

Hattiesburg
Zoo Blues
Last Saturday in August
(601) 545-4576
E-mail: hattzoo@aol.com

Indianola
B. B. King Homecoming and Indian Bayou Festival
Last weekend in May or first weekend in June
(601) 887-4454

Jackson
Farish Street Heritage Festival
Fourth weekend in September, Friday and Saturday
(601) 960-1891

Meridian
Main Street Salutes the Blues
Third weekend in July, Friday and Saturday
(601) 485-1996

Missouri

Kansas City
Kansas City Blues and Jazz Festival
Third weekend in July, Friday–Sunday
(816) 753-3378

St. Louis
St. Louis Blues Heritage Festival
Labor Day weekend, Saturday and Sunday
(314) 241-2583
(800) 325-7962
(314) 534-1111

New Jersey

Elmer
Appel Farm Arts and Music Festival
First Saturday in June
(800) 394-1211
E-mail: appelarts@aol.com
WWW: http://www.rowan.edu/-appel

Montclair
Montclair Blues & Jazz Festival
Weekend closest to July 4
(201) 509-4910
E-mail: kshane@intac.com
WWW: http://www.intac.com/mbjf

New Hampshire

Portsmouth
Portsmouth Blues Festival
Labor Day weekend, Saturday and Sunday
(603) 929-0654
E-mail: Bluesbank@aol.com

North Carolina

Durham
Bull Durham Blues Festival
First weekend in September, Friday and Saturday
(919) 683-1709

Raleigh
Spring Jazz and Art Festival
Weekend before Memorial Day
(919)832-8699

Wilkesboro
Merle Watson Festival
Last full weekend in April
(800) 343-7857
(800) 666-1920
(910) 838-6291

Wilmington
Cape Fear Blues Festival
Last weekend in July, Wednesday–Sunday
(910) 313-2612

Ohio

Cincinnati
Pepsi Jammin' on Main
Second weekend in May, Friday and Saturday nights
(513) 744-8820

Cleveland
Emerald City Folk Festival
Last Sunday in August
(216) 351-6300

Columbus
Big Bear Rhythm & Food Festival
Memorial Day weekend, Friday–Sunday
(614) 645-7995

Toledo
Toledo Rock, Rhythm and Blues Festival
Memorial Day Weekend, Friday–Sunday
(419) 243-8024

Oklahoma

Rentiesville
Dusk 'Til Dawn Blues Festival
Labor Day weekend, Friday–Sunday
(918) 473-2411

Oregon

Coos Bay and nearby communities
Jazz at the Lake—the Wallowa Lake Festival of Music
Third full weekend in July, Friday and Saturday
(541) 963-8530

Corvallis
Red, White, and Blues
July 4
(541) 754-6624

Gresham
Mount Hood Festival of Jazz
First full weekend in August
(503) 231-0160

Portland
Waterfront Blues Festival
Weekend closest to July 4
(503) 733-5466
WWW: http://www.teleport.com/-kgon

Pennsylvania

Lake Harmony
Pocono Blues Festival
Fourth weekend in July
(717) 722-0100

Rhode Island

Escoheag
Big Easy Bash
Last weekend in June
(401) 351-6312
(800) 738-9808

South Dakota

Deadwood
Deadwood Jam
Second Saturday after Labor Day
(605) 578-1102

Rockerville
Black Hills Jazz and Blues Festival
Last full weekend in June (Friday evening–Sunday morning)
(605) 394-4101

Tennessee

Chattanooga
Riverbend Festival and Bessie Smith Strut
Nine days ending the last Saturday in June
(423) 756-8687

Memphis
Beale Street Music Festival
First weekend in May
(901) 525-4611

Memphis Blues Festival
A weekend in August
(901) 525-1515
(901) 398-6655
(800) 332-1991

Memphis Music & Heritage
Festival
Second weekend in July
(901) 525-3945

Texas

Austin
Antone's Anniversary Party
*Ten days, usually ending July
15 (Antone's anniversary)*
(512) 474-5314

Houston
Bayou Bash
A Saturday in late June
(713) 799-9791

Juneteenth Blues Festival
*A weekend in early or mid-
June*
(713) 667-8000

Meridian
John A. Lomax Gathering
Fourth Saturday in April
(817) 435-2966

Port Arthur
Gulf Coast Jam
*Last weekend in July or first
weekend in August*
(409) 722-3699

Janis Joplin's Birthday Bash
Second Saturday in January
(409) 722-3699

Utah

Snowbird
Utah Jazz & Blues Festival
*Last weekend in July, Friday
and Saturday*
(801) 742-2222
(801) 233-2787
E-mail: 75407.3034@com-
puserve.com

Vermont

Middlebury
Summer Festival on the Green

*Week after July 4,
Sunday–Saturday*
(802) 388-0216

Warren
Ben & Jerry's One World One
Heart Festival
Fourth weekend in June
(800) 253-3787
(802) 244-6959
WWW: http://www.benjerry.
com

Virginia

Virginia Beach
Blues at the Beach Festival
Second weekend in October
(804) 456-1675

Wolf Trap Farm/Vienna
Wolf Trap's Jazz and Blues Festival
*A weekend in late June,
Friday–Sunday*
(703) 218-6500
(703) 255-1860
WWW: http://www.wolf.trap.
org/

Washington

La Conner
Swinomish Blues Festival
*Third full weekend in August,
Saturday and Sunday*
(360) 466-3052

Port Townsend
Port Townsend Country Blues
Festival
*Second or third weekend in
June, Friday and Saturday*
(800) 733-3608
(360) 385-3102

Ritzville
Ritzville Blues, Brews and Bar-
becues
Third Saturday in July
(509) 659-1936

Wisconsin

Beloit
Beloit Riverfest

*First or second weekend in
July*
(800) 423-5648

Glendale
Sprecherfest
*Labor Day weekend, Friday
and Saturday*
(414) 964-2739

Wyoming

**Alta (Grand Targhee Ski and
Summer Resort)**
Rockin' the Tetons Music Festival
A weekend in mid-July
(800) 827-4433
(307) 353-2300

Cody
Yellowstone Jazz Festival
*Second or third Saturday in
July*
(307) 587-3898
(307) 587-2777

CANADA

Alberta

Calgary
Afrikadey
Third week in August
(403) 282-7119
(403) 284-3674
E-mail: edm.folkfest@ccinet.
ab.ca

British Columbia

Whistler
Whistler Country, Roots &
Blues Festival
*Third or fourth weekend in
July, Friday–Sunday*
(800) 944-7853
(604) 644-5625
(604) 932-4222

New Brunswick

Fredericton
Harvest Jazz & Blues Festival

*Second week in September,
Tuesday–Sunday*
(506) 454-2583
(800) 320-3988

Lam̈que
Lam̈que International
Baroque Music Festival
*Second and third weekends in
July*
(506) 344-5846

Shediac
Festival Baie Jazz & Blues
*A weekend in mid-July,
Wednesday–Sunday*
(506) 858-0571

Newfoundland

St. John's
George Street Festival
*Five days before the first
Wednesday in August*
(709) 642-5254

Ontario

Ottawa
Ottawa International Jazz Festival
Ten days in mid- or late July
(613) 594-3580

Quebec

Mont-Tremblant
Tremblant Blues Festival
First weekend in August
(800) 461-8711
(819) 681-3000

Saskatchewan

Saskatoon
Sasktel Saskatchewan Jazz
Festival
*Last weekend in June through
the first weekend in July*
(306) 652-1421
(800) 638-1211
E-mail: sask.jazz@sasknet.
sk.ca
WWW: http://www.sasknet.
sk.ca/jazz/

These are just some of the radio stations in the United States and Canada that carry some sort of blues programming. Please be advised that the blues may make up only a small portion of the station's program schedule, and that radio formats often change like the weather. Your best bet would be to check the local radio listings in the cities below.

UNITED STATES

Alabama

Atmore
WYDH (105.9 FM)

Auburn
WEGL (91.1 FM)

Huntsville
WJAB (90.9 FM)
WLRH (89.3 FM)

Mobile
WGOK (900 AM)

Montgomery
WXVI (1600 AM)

Tuscaloosa
WUAL (91.5 FM)
WQPR (88.7 FM)
WVUA (90.7 FM)

Alaska

Anchorage
KSKA (91.1 FM)

Homer
KBBI (890 AM)

Juneau
KTOO-FM (various)

Ketchikan
KRBD (105.9 FM)

Kodiak
KMXT (100.1 FM)

Arizona

Mesa
KDKB (93.3 FM)
KJZZ (91.5 FM)

Phoenix
KZON (101.5 FM)

Tucson
KEKO (92.1 FM/106.3 FM)
KLPX (96.1 FM)
KXCI (91.3 FM)

Arkansas

Arkadelphia
KSWH (91.1 FM)

Helena
KFFA (1360 AM)
KCRI (103.1 FM)

Fayetteville
KUAF (91.3 FM)

Hope
KXAR (101.7 FM)

Jonesboro
KASU (91.9 FM)

Little Rock
KABF (88.3 FM)

Lonoke
KWTD (106.3 FM)

California

Alameda
KJAZ (92.7 FM)

Arcata
KHSU (90.5 FM)

Arroyo Grande
KWBR (95.3 FM)

Berkeley
KPFA (94.1 FM)

Cambria
KOTR (94.9 FM)

Chico
KCHO (91.7 FM)
KZFR (90.1 FM/107.1 FM)

Claremont
KSPC (88.7 FM)

Cupertino
KKUP (91.5 FM)

Davis
KDVS (90.3 FM)

Eureka
KXGO (93.1 FM)

Gualala
KWAN (100.5 FM)

Hollywood
KPFK (90.7 FM)

Long Beach
KLON (88.1 FM)

Los Altos Hills
KFJC (89.7 FM)

Los Angeles
KXLU (88.9 FM)

Mission Viejo
KSBR (88.5 FM)

Modesto
KVFX (96.7 FM)

Nevada City
KVMR (89.5 FM/99.3 FM)

Northridge
KCSN (88.5 FM)

Pacific Grove
KAZU (90.3 FM)

Pasadena
KPCC (89.3 FM)

Philo
KZYX (90.7 FM)

Redlands
KUOR (89.1 FM)

Redway
KMUD (91.1 FM)

Sacramento
KCBL (88.7 FM)

San Diego
KSDS (88.3 FM)

San Francisco
KALW (91.7 FM)
KFOG (104.5 FM)
KPOO (89.5 FM)
KUSF (90.3 FM)

San Jose
KOME (98.5 FM)

San Mateo
KCSM (91.1 FM)

Santa Clara
KSCU (103.3 FM)
KTYD (99.9 FM)

Santa Cruz
KUSP (88.9 FM/90.3 FM)
KZSC (88.1 FM)

Santa Monica
KCBX (89.9 FM)

Santa Rosa
KBBF (89.1 FM)
KRCB (91.1 FM)
KRSH (98.7 FM)

Stanford
KZSU (90.1 FM)

Stockton
KUOP (91.3 FM)

Turlock
KCSS (91.9 FM)

Visalia
KIOO (99.7 FM)

Colorado

Aspen/Redstone
KDNK (88.3 FM)

Boulder
KGNU (88.5 FM)
KUCB (530 AM)

Carbondale
KDNK (90.5 FM)

Colorado Springs
KRCC (91.1 FM)

Durango
KDUR (91.9 FM)

Glenwood Springs
KDNK (91.3 FM)

Grand Junction
KMSA (91.3 FM)

Gunnison
KWSB (91.1 FM)

Telluride
KOTO (91.7 FM)

Connecticut

Bridgeport
WPKN (89.5 FM)

Greenwich
WGCH (1490 AM)

Middletown
WESU (88.1 FM)

New Britain
WFCS (107.7 FM)

New Haven
WYBC (94.3 FM)

New London
WCNB (91.1 FM)

Storrs
WHUS (91.7 FM)

West Hartford
WWUH (91.3 FM)

West Haven
WNHU (88.7 FM)

Delaware

Claymont
WJBR (1290 AM)

District of Columbia

Washington
WAMU (88.5 FM)
WDCU (90.1 FM)
WGTB (690 AM)
WPFW (89.3 FM)

Florida

Boca Raton
WYFX (1040 AM)

Charlotte Harbor
WEEJ (100.1 FM)

Cocoa
WXXU (1300 AM)

Ft. Myers
WJBX (99.3 FM)

Key West
WOZN (98.7 FM)

Melbourne
WFZT (89.5 FM)

Miami
WDHA (88.9 FM)

Orlando
WUCF (89.9 FM)

Pensacola
WUWF (88.1 FM)

Tampa
WMNF (88.5 FM)

Winter Park
WLOQ (103.1 FM)

Georgia

Atlanta
WRAS (88.5 FM)
WREK (91.1 FM)
WRFG (89.3 FM)

Idaho

Boise
KBSU (91.3 FM)

Moscow
KUOI (89.3 FM)

Illinois

Champaign
WEFT (90.1 FM)

Charleston
WEIU (88.9 FM)

Chicago
WBEZ (91.5 FM)
WHPK (88.5 FM)
WKKC (89.3 FM)

WSSD (88.1 FM)
WVON (1450 AM)
WXRT (93.1 FM)
WZRD (88.3 FM)

Evanston
WNUR (89.3 FM)

Macomb
WZUS (88.3 FM)

Normal
WGLT (89.1 FM)

Peoria
WCBU (89.9 FM)

Peru
WLRZ (100.9 FM)

Rockford
WNIJ (90.5 FM)
WXRX (104.9 FM)

Springfield
WSSR (91.9 FM)

Wilmington
WKBM (100.7 FM)

Indiana

Bloomington
WFHB (91.3 FM)
WTTS (92.3 FM)

Elkhart
WVPE (88.1 FM)

Indianapolis
WFYI (90.1 FM)
WLTC (1310 AM)

Richmond
WSND (88.9 FM)

Terre Haute
WISU (89.7 FM)

Iowa

Ames
KUSR (91.5 FM)

Davenport
KALA (88.5 FM/105.5 FM)

Decorah
KDEC (1240 AM/100.5 FM)

Sioux City
KWIT (90.3 FM)

Kansas

Lawrence
KANU (91.5 FM)

Overland Park
KCFX (100.7 FM)

Pittsburg
KRPS (89.9 FM)

Wichita
KMUW (89.1 FM)

Kentucky

Highland Heights
WNKU (89.7 FM)

Louisville
WFPK (91.9 FM)

Morehead
WMKY (90.3 FM)

Whitesburg
WMMT (88.7 FM)

Louisiana

Angola
KLSP (91.7 FM)

Baton Rouge
KLSU (91.1 FM)
WXOX (1460 AM)

Lafayette
KRVX (88.7 FM)

Monroe
KEDM (90.3 FM)

New Orleans
WWNO (89.9 FM)
KTLN (90.5 FM)
WYLD (940 AM)
WWOZ (90.7 FM)

Shreveport
KDAQ (89.9 FM)
KOKA (1550 AM)

Maine

Blue Hill Falls
WERU (89.9 FM)

Portland
WMPG (90.9 FM)

Skowhegan
WTOS (105.1 FM)

Waterville
WMHB (90.5 FM)

Maryland

Annapolis
WAHW (1190 AM)

College Park
WMUC (88.9 FM)

Frostburg
WFWM (91.7 FM)

Landover
WHFS (99.1 FM)

Princess Anne
WESM (91.3 FM)

Massachusetts

Amherst
WFCR (88.5 FM)
WMUA (91.1 FM)

Boston
WGBH (89.7 FM)

Cambridge
WHRB (95.3 FM)

Fitchburg
WXPL (91.3 FM)

Greenfield
WRSI (95.3 FM)

Lowell
WJUL (91.5 FM)

Marlboro
WSRO (1470 AM)

Medford
WMFO (91.5 FM)

North Dartmouth
WSMU (91.1 FM)

Provincetown
WOMR (92.1 FM)

Salem
WMWM (91.7 FM)

South Hadley
WMHC (91.5 FM)

Springfield
WSCB (89.1 FM)

Vineyard Haven
WMVY (92.7 FM)

Waltham
WBRS (100.1 FM)

Michigan

Ann Arbor
WCBN (88.3 FM)

Detroit
CIDR (93.9 FM)
WCSX (94.7 FM)
WDET (101.9 FM)

Flint
WFBE (95.1 FM)

Grand Rapids
WGVU (88.5 FM)

Kalamazoo
WIOR (89.1 FM)

Lansing
WJXQ (106.1 FM)

Mt. Pleasant
WCML (91.7 FM)
WCMU (89.5 FM)
WCMW (103.9 FM)
WCMZ (98.3 FM)
WUCX (90.1 FM)

Traverse City
WNMC (90.9 FM)

Ypsilanti
WEMU (89.1 FM)

Minnesota

Mankato
KMSU (89.7 FM/91.3 FM)

Minneapolis
KFAI (90.3 FM)
KMOJ (89.9 FM)

St. Paul
WMCN (91.7 FM)

Mississippi

Canton
WONG (1150 AM)

Clarksdale
WQMA (1520 AM)
WWUN (101.7 FM)

Columbus
WMUW (88.5 FM)

Greenwood
WKXG (1540 AM)
WYMX (99.1 FM)

Hattiesburg
WMSU (88.5 FM)

Holly Springs
WKRA (92.7 FM)
WURC (88.1 FM)

Jackson
WJSU (88.5 FM)
WKXI (1300 AM)

McComb
WAKK (1140 AM)

Oxford
WUMS (92.1 FM)

Senatobia
WSAO (1140 AM)

Missouri

Liberty
KCLX (1140 AM)

Kansas City
KCUR (89.3 FM)
KKFI (90.1 FM)

Point Lookout
KCOZ (91.7 FM)

St. Charles
KCLC (89.1 FM)

St. Louis
KDHX (88.1 FM)
KWMU (90.1 FM)

West Plains
KSPQ (93.9 FM)

Montana

Missoula
KUFM (89.1 FM)

Nebraska

Lincoln
KTGL (92.9 FM)

KZUM (89.3 FM)

Omaha
KIOS (91.5 FM)

Nevada

Las Vegas
KKLZ (96.3 FM)
KUNV (91.5 FM)

Reno
KUNR (88.7 FM)

New Hampshire

Henniker
WNEC (91.7 FM)

Keene
WKNH (91.3 FM)

Plymouth
WPCR (91.7 FM)

New Jersey

Hackettstown
WNTI (91.9 FM)

Newark
WBGO (88.3 FM)

Spotswood
WRSU (88.7 FM)

Stone Harbor
WLFR (91.7 FM)

Teaneck
WFDU (89.1 FM)

Trenton
WTSR (91.3 FM)
WWFM (89.1 FM)

Upper Mountain
WMSC (101.5 FM)

New Mexico

Albuquerque
KUNM (90.1 FM)

Las Cruces
KRWG (90.7 FM)

Portales
KENW (89.5 FM)
KMTH (98.7 FM)

New York

Binghamton
WHRW (90.5 FM)

Brookville
WCWP (88.1 FM)

Buffalo
WBFO (88.7 FM)
WVFO (1080 AM)

Canton
WSLU (89.5 FM)

Fredonia
WCVF (88.9 FM)

Geneva
WEOS (89.7 FM)

Ithaca
WVBR (93.5 FM)

New Rochelle
WRTN (93.5 FM)

New York
WBAI (99.5 FM)
WKCR (89.9 FM)

Oswego
WNYO (88.9 FM)

Plattsburg
WPLT (93.9 FM)

Rochester
WGMC (90.1 FM)
WITR (89.7 FM)
WXXI (1370 AM)

Staten Island
WSIA (88.9 FM)

Stony Brook
WUSB (90.1 FM)

Syracuse
WAER (88.3 FM)
WOLF (1490 AM)

Watertown
WCIZ (97.5 FM)

Woodstock
WDST (100.1 FM)

North Carolina

Chapel Hill
WXYC (89.3 FM)

Durham
WXDU (88.7 FM)

Greensboro
WNAA (90.1 FM)
WQFS (90.9 FM)

Raleigh
WLLE (570 AM)
WSHA (89.1 FM)

Salisbury
WRDX (106.5 FM)

Spindale
WNCW (88.7 FM)

Wilmington
WHQR (91.3 FM)
WSFM (107.5 FM)

North Dakota

Fargo
KDSU (91.9 FM)

Grand Forks
KFJM (1370 AM/89.3 FM)

Ohio

Berea
WBWC (88.3 FM)

Cincinnati
WAIF (88.3 FM)
WVXU (91.7 FM)

Cleveland
WCPN (90.3 FM)
WCSB (89.3 FM)
WNCX (98.5 FM)

Columbus
WCBE (90.5 FM)

Kent
WKSU (89.7 FM)

Millbury
WJZE (97.3 FM)

Oberlin
WOBC (91.5 FM)

Oxford
WMUB (88.5 FM)

Toledo
WXUT (88.3 FM)

Yellow Springs
WYSO (91.3 FM)

Oklahoma

Claremore
KRSC (91.3 FM)

Norman
KGOU (106.3 FM)
KROU (105.7 FM)

Oklahoma City
KALU (90.7 FM)

Sand Springs
KTOW (1340 AM)

Tulsa
KMOD (97.5 FM)
KAKC (970 AM)

Oregon

Ashland
KSMF (89.1 FM)
KSBA (88.5 FM)
KSKF (90.9 FM)
KAGI (930 AM)

Astoria
KMUN (91.9 FM)

Corvallis
KBVR (88.7 FM)

Eugene
KRVM (91.9 FM)

Gresham
KMHD (89.1 FM)

Hood River
KMCQ (104.5 FM)

Portland
KBOO (90.7 FM)

Salem
KBZY (1490 AM)

Pennsylvania

Allentown
WMUH (91.7 FM)

California
WVCS (91.9 FM)

Carlisle
WDCV (88.3 FM)

Erie
WMCE (880 AM/88.5 FM)

Hughesville
WUNS (96.3 FM)

Lancaster
WFNM (89.1 FM)

Philadelphia
WRTI (90.1 FM)
WXPN (88.5 FM)

Pittsburgh
WRCT (88.3 FM)
WYEP (91.3 FM)

Schnecksville
WXLV (90.3 FM)

State College
WPSU (91.5 FM)

Swarthmore
WSRN (91.5 FM)

South Carolina

Clemson
WSBF (88.1 FM)

Mt. Pleasant
WSCI (89.3 FM)

South Dakota

Rapid City
KTEQ (91.3 FM)

Spearfish
KBHU (89.1 FM)

Tennessee

Chattanooga
WNOO (1260 AM)
WUTC (88.1 FM)

Franklin
WYOR (560 AM)

Johnson City
WETS (89.5 FM)

Lebanon
WFMQ (91.5 FM)

Memphis
WAVN (1240 AM)
WDIA (1070 AM)
WEVL (89.9 FM)

Nashville
WFSK (88.1 FM)
WQQK (92.1 FM)
WRLT (100.1 FM)
WRVU (91.1 FM)

Texas

Austin
KUUT (90.5 FM)

Corpus Christi
KNCN (101.3 FM)

Dallas
KNON (89.3 FM)

El Paso
KTEP (88.5 FM)

Grand Prairie
KKDA (730 AM)

Houston
KPFT (90.1 FM)
KTRU (91.7 FM)
KTSU (90.9 FM)

Utah

Salt Lake City
KRCL (90.9 FM)

Vermont

Burlington
WIZN (106.7 FM)
WRUV (90.1 FM)

Middlebury
WRMC (91.1 FM)

Virginia

Alexandria
WCXR (105.9 FM)

Charlottesville
WTJU (91.1 FM)

Hampton
WHOV (88.1 FM)

Harrisonburg
WMRA (90.7 FM)
WMRL (89.9 FM)

Norfolk
WHRV (89.5 FM)
WNSB (91.1 FM)

Richmond
WCVE (88.9 FM)

Washington

Bellevue
KBCS (91.3 FM)

Bellingham
KUGS (91.3 FM)
KZAZ (91.7 FM)

Olympia
KAOS (89.3 FM)

Spokane
KPBX (91.1 FM)

Tacoma
KPLU (88.5 FM)

Wisconsin

Green Bay
WPNE (89.3 FM)

La Crosse
WLSU (88.9 FM)

Madison
WORT (89.9 FM)

Milwaukee
WMSE (91.7 FM)
WYMS (88.9 FM)

Oshkosh
WRST (90.3 FM)

Stevens Point
WWSP (89.9 FM)

CANADA

Alberta

Edmonton
CJSR (88.5 FM)

British Columbia

New Westminster
CFMI (101.1 FM)

Vancouver
CFRO (102.7 FM)

Ontario

Brampton
CFNY (102.1 FM)

Hamilton
CFMU (93.3 FM)

London
CHRW (94.7 FM)

North York
CHRY (105.5 FM)

Ottawa
CHUO (99.3 FM)
CKCU (93.1 FM)

Sudbury
CJMX (105.3 FM)

Toronto
CBL (740 AM)
CIUT (89.5 FM)
CJRT (91.1 FM)

Windsor
CIDR (93.9 FM)

Quebec

Montreal
CIBL (104.5 FM)

The following record labels are just some of the labels that have substantial blues catalogs. You may want to contact them if you have questions regarding specific releases.

Ace Records
PO Box 5982
Pearl, MS 39208
(601) 939-6868
Fax: (601) 932-3038

Acoustic Music Records
PO Box 1945
49009 Osnabruck, Germany
0541 70205
Fax: 0541 708667

Acoustic Sounds
PO Box 2043
Salina, KS 67402-2043
(913) 825-8609
Fax: (913) 825-0156

Adelphi Records
PO Box 7778/7688
Silver Spring, MD 20907
(301) 434-6958
Fax: (301) 434-3056

ADP Records and Tapes
237 E. 26 St., Ste. 5H
New York, NY 10010
(212) 725-1853

Airwax Records
PO Box 288291
Chicago, IL 60628
(312) 779-2384

Alcazar/Alcazam! Records
PO Box 429
Waterbury, VT 05676
(802) 244-7845
Fax: (802) 244-6128

Alley Way Records
PO Box 728
Anniston, AL 36202-0728

Alligator Records
PO Box 60234
Chicago, IL 60660
(312) 973-7736
Fax: (312) 973-2088

Amblin Records
PO Box 15960
Lenexa, KS 66215
(913) 888-6774
(913) 541-1216

Antone's Records
500 San Marcos, Ste. 200
Austin, TX 78702
(512) 322-0617

Appaloosa Records
4, Via San G. B. De La Salle
20132 Milano, Italy
39 225 91700
Fax: 39 225 920664

Arhoolie Records
10341 San Pablo Ave.

El Cerrito, CA 94530
(415) 525-7471
(510) 525-7471
Fax: (510) 525-1204

Ascending Productions
PO Box 688
Point Lookout, NY 11569
(516) 897-7532

Atlantic Recording Corporation
75 Rockefeller Plaza
New York, NY 10019
(212) 275-2000

Atomic Beat
10390 Santa Monica Blvd.,
  Ste. 210
Los Angeles, CA 90025-5058
(617) 661-0401
Fax: (617) 661-6349

Atomic Theory
2217 Nicolett Ave. S.
Minneapolis, MN 55404
(612) 874-2431
Fax: (612) 874-2472
E-mail: atomic@tt.net

AudioQuest Music
PO Box 6040
San Clemente, CA 92674
(714) 498-1977
Fax: (714) 498-6223

AVI Entertainment
10390 Santa Monica Blvd.,
  Ste. 210
Los Angeles, CA 90025

(310) 556-7744
Fax: (310) 556-1299

Bahoomba Music
847A Second Ave., Ste. 294
New York, NY 10017
(718) 591-4382
E-mail: bahoomba@aol.com

Barfly Records
906 Date St.
Las Vegas, NV 89108
(702) 646-4865
Fax: (702) 648-5135

Bear Family Records
PO Box 1154
Hambergen, Germany D
  27727
04794-93000
Fax: 04794-930020

Bee Bump Records
2256 Magnolia Ave.
Long Beach, CA 90806
(310) 426-0761

Big Boss Records
RR 1, Box 389-C
Thetford Center, VT 05075
(802) 785-4225
Fax: (802) 785-4221
E-mail: big.mo.records@
  valley.net

Biograph Records
PO Box 369
Canaan, NY 12029
(518) 781-3711
Fax: (518) 781-3715

Bizarre/Planet
740 N. LaBrea Ave., 2nd fl.
Los Angeles, CA 90038
(213) 935-4444

Black Magic Records
Balladelaan 262, 3813 CG
Amersfoort, The Netherlands
31 (0) 33 4808075

Black Top Records
PO Box 56691
New Orleans, LA 70156
(800) 833-9872
Fax: (504) 891-1510

Blind Pig Records
PO Box 2344
San Francisco, CA 94126
(415) 550-6484
Fax: (415) 550-6485
E-mail: piggies@aol.com

Blue Plate Music
33 Music Square W., Ste. 102-A
Nashville, TN 37203
(615) 742-1250

Blue Rock'It Records
PO Box 85
Palo Alto, CA 94302
(415) 424-9850
Fax: (415) 856-2583

Blue Suit Records
304 N. Westwood Ave.
Toledo, OH 43607
(419) 531-2811

Blue Wave Records
3221 Perryville Rd.
Baldwinsville, NY 13027
(315) 638-4286
Fax: (315) 635-4757

Blues Factory, Inc.
2911 Elmhurst Blvd.
Royal Oak, MI 48073
(810) 280-0363
Fax: (810) 588-4491

Blues Over Blues Records
PO Box 218
Tempe, AZ 85280
(602) 994-1234

Blues Street
R133 N. Washington Ave.
Scranton, PA 18503
(717) 341-19122

Bluesberry Records
7 E. 14th St., Ste. 919
New York, NY 10003
(212) 989-0021
Fax: (212) 727-3808

BlueSong Records
17216 Saticoy St., #233
Van Nuys, CA 91406
(818) 773-3731
Fax: (818) 774-9149
E-mail: nothin_but_the_blues
   @msn.com

BluesTime Records
PO Box 3920
San Rafael, CA 94912
(415) 454-4308
Fax: (415) 756-4731

BMG Entertainment
8750 Wilshire Boulevard
Beverly Hills, CA 90211
(310) 358-4067

Bowers Dance
PO Box 224144
Dallas, TX 75222-4144
(214) 291-2294

Buffalo Fish Records
1301 W. Jefferson, #6A
Morton, IL 61550
(309) 263-2788

Bullseye Blues Records
1 Camp St.
Cambridge, M 02140
(617) 354-0700
Fax: (617) 491-1970
Info@rounder.com

Burnside Records
3158 E. Burnside
Portland, OR 97214
(503) 231-0876

Cadence Blues
Cadence Bldg.
Redwood, Ny 13679
(315) 287-2852
Fax: (315) 287-2860

Capitol-EMI
17750 N. Vine St.
Nashville, TN 37203
(615) 320-8470
Fax: (615) 320-8479

Castle Records
239 Ethan Allen Hwy.
Ridgefield, CT 06877
(203) 438-7070

Catfish Records
PO Box 2761
Austin, TX 78768
(512) 385-5852
Fax: (512) 385-5877
reddrum@bga.com

Centrum Records
PO Box 1158
Port Townsend, WA 98368
(206) 385-2470

Charly Distribution Ltd.
156-166 Ilderton Rd.
London, England SE15 1NT
0171 639 8603
Fax: 0171 639 2532

Chesky Records
355 W. 52nd St.
New York, NY 10019-6239
(212) 586-7799
Fax: (212) 262-0814

Chess Records
70 Universal City Plaza
Universal City, CA 91608
(818) 777-4000

Choctaw Records
PO Box 764
Ardmore, PA 19003
(215) 844-7797

Clarity Recordings
PO Box 411407
San Francisco, CA 94141-1401
(415) 626-7540

CMA Music Productions
Behringstr. 3
63812 Mainaschaff, Germany
49 (0) 6021/7259
49 (0) 6021-76910

Code Blue Records
590 Fifth Ave., 16th Floor
New York, NY 10036
(212) 575-6732
(212) 575-6595

Cold Wind Records
PO Box 54199
Minneapolis, MN 55454
(612) 724-7002

Fax: (612) 338-5850

Collectables Record Corp.
PO Box 35
Narberth, PA 19072
(610) 649-7650
Fax: (610) 649-0315

Columbia/Legacy
550 Madison Ave.
New York, NY 10022-3211
(212) 833-8000
Fax: (212) 833-7731

Concord Records
PO Box 845
Concord, PA 94522
(510) 682-6770
Fax: (510) 682-3508

Cottontail West Records
PO Box 191041
Los Angeles, CA 90019
(213) 731-5548

Criminal Records
PO Box 25542
Portland, OR 97225
(503) 244-5827
Fax: (503) 289-2836

CrossCut Records
PO Box 106524
28065 Bremen, Germany
01149 (421)498-7588
Fax: 01149 (421) 498-7589

DA Music
362 Pinehurst Ln.
Marietta, GA 30068
(404) 977-4172
Fax: (404) 977-4173

Dallas Blues Society Records
PO Box 190406
Dallas, TX 75219
(214) 521-2583

Dead Reckoning
Box 159178
Nashville, TN 37215
(800) 442-DEAD

Delmark Records
4121 N. Rockwell St.
Chicago, IL 60618
(312) 539-5001
Fax: (312) 539-5004

Delta Man Music
PO Box 8874

Newport Beach, CA 92658

Deluge Records
PO Box 2877
Waterville, ME 04903
(207) 873-2663

Demon Records Ltd.
Canal House, Stars Estate,
    Transport Ave.
Brentford, Middlesex
England TW8 OQP
44 181 847 2481
Fax: 44 181 568 8223

DJM Records
535 E. Main St., Suite 191
Santa Paula, CA 93060
(888) 356-2583

Document Records
Eildouerstrasse 2343/5
A-1220 Vienna, Austria
43-1-257-1377

Drive Entertainment
10351 Santa Monica Blvd, Ste.
    404
Los Angeles, CA 90025
(310) 553-3490

Earwig Records
1818 W. Pratt Blvd.
Chicago, IL 60626
(312) 262-0278
Fax: (312) 262-0285

Ecko Records
5242 Helene Cove
Memphis TN 38117
(901) 761-7197
E-mail: lucz24@prodigy.com

Evidence Music
1100 E. Hector St., #392
Conshohocken, PA 19428
(215) 832-0844
Fax: (215) 832-0807

Excello
10390 Santa Monica Blvd.,
    Ste. 210
Los Angeles, CA 90025
(310) 556-7744
Fax: (310) 556-1299

Fat Possum Records
PO Box 1923
Oxford, MS 38655
(601) 236-3110

Fedora Records
3840 N. Forestiere St.
Fresno, CA 93722
(209) 276-8317

Fish Tail Records
PO Box 2561
Iowa City, IA 52244
(319) 338-3614

Flat Baroque Records
36 East 12th Street
New York, NY 10003
(800) 647-9125

Focus Records
3300 Bee Caves Rd., Ste. 650-
    201
Austin, TX 78746
(512) 327-7221
Fax: (512) 327-1664

Fountainbleu Entertainment
91-38 114 St.
Richmond Hill, NY 11418
(718) 847-3281
Fax: (212) 930-4685

Global Village
245 W. 29th St.
New York, NY 1001
(212) 695-6024
Fax: (212) 695-6025

Goldband Records
PO Box 1485
Lake Charles, IA 70602
(318) 439-4295
Fax: (318) 491-0994

Goldwax Records
PO Box 270655
Nashville, TN 37277-0665
(615) 321-3402
Fax: (615) 321-2422

Great Southern Records
PO Box 13977
New Orleans, LA 70185
(504) 524-7164

Gunsmoke Records
2623 Roosevelt Hwy., Ste. D-3
College Park, GA 30337
(404) 768-0488

Ham-Bone Records
Box 16161
Galveston, TX 77552
(409) 740-0322

Hard Attack Records
PO Box 367
Pacific Palisades, CA 90272
(310) 459-7177
Fax: (310) 459-2155

Have Mercy Records
PO Box 660245
Sacramento, CA 95866
(916) 486-3729

HighTone Records
220 4th St., #101
Oakland, CA 94607
(510) 763-8500

High Water Recording Co.
Dept.of Music
University of Memphis
Memphis, TN 38152
(901) 6778-3317
Fax: (901) 678-3299

Hipshake Productions
47-27 39th Pl.
Long Island City, NY 11104

Hot Fox Records
PO Box 1205
88618 Pfullendorf, Germany

House of Blues Records
203 Carondelet St., Ste 610
New Orleans, LA 70130
(504) 523-7320
Fax: (504) 523-7323

Icehouse Records
1981 Fletcher Creek Dr.
Memphis, TN 38133
(901) 388-1108
Fax: (901) 388-2366

Ichiban Records
3991 Royal Dr. NW
Kennesaw, GA 30144
(404) 419-1414
Fax: (404) 419-1230

IMG/King Records
1900 Elm Hill Pike
Nashville, TN 37210
(800) 251-4040

Indigo Recordings
31-39 Camden Rd.
London, England NW1 9LF
071-267-6899
Fax: 071-267-6746

**Inside Sounds/Memphis
Archives**
Box 171283
Memphis, TN 38187
(901) 682-2063

Integrity Music
PO Box 2285
Huntington Beach, CA 92647
(714) 846-1251

Interstate Music, Ltd.
PO Box 2285
Huntington Beach, CA 92647
(714) 846-1251

Iris Records
PO Box 422
Port Washington, NY 11050
(516) 944-7905

**I.T. Records/Blues in School
Programs**
3533 S. Calumet Ave.
Chicago, IL 60653

J & B Productions, Inc.
3109 Medgar Evers Blvd.
Jackson, MS 32913

Jass Records
140 W. 22nd St., 12th Fl
New York, NY 10011

Jewel/Paula/Ronn Records
PO Box 1125, 1700 Centenary
Shreveport, LA 71163-1125
(800) 446-2865
(318) 227-2228
Fax: (318) 227-0304

JSP Records
PO Box 1584
London N3 3NW, England
44 81 346 8663
Fax: 44 81 346 8848

Justice Records
PO Box 980369
Houston, TX 77098
(713) 520-6669
Fax: (713) 525-4444

Just In Time Records
5455 Pare, Ste. 101
Montreal, Quebec H4P 1P7,
    Canada
(514) 738-9533
Fax: (514) 737-9780

Kansas City Blues Society Records
PO Box 32131
Kansas City, MO 64171

Kicking Mule Records
PO Box 158
Alderpoint, CA 95411
(707) 926-5312
Fax: (707) 923-3009

King Biscuit Flower Hour Records
Box 6700 FDR Station
New York, NY 10150-6700

KingSnake Records
205 Lake Blvd.
Sanford, FL 32773
(407) 323-6767
Fax: (407) 321-6078

La Louisianne Records
711 Stevenson St.
Lafayette, LA 70501
(318) 234-5577
Fax: (318) 233-2595

Lanor Records
PO Box 233
Church Point, LA 70525
(318) 684-2176
Fax: (318) 684-2176

LaserLight Digital
2500 Broadway, #380
Santa Monica, CA 90404

Laurie Records
450 Livingston St.
Norwood, NJ 07648
(212) 427-9584

Liberty Records
3322 West End Ave.
Nashville, TN 37203
(615) 269-2000

Lockwood Records
7203 Lawnview Ave.
Cleveland, OH 44103
(216) 431-0420

Lollipop Tapes
PO Box 1991, Canal St. Station
New York, NY 10013
(212) 255-5298
E-mail: louisx@aol.com

Lunacy Records
417 N. Virginia

Oklahoma City, OK 73106
(405) 236-0643
Fax: (405) 236-0686
E-mail: copesetic@thornet.com

Mafioso Records
H-2085 Pilisvorosvar
Csobankai ut 24, Hungary
36 60 347 588
36 26 330 652
Fax: 36 26 330 652

Magnum Music Group
Magnum House, High St.,
  Lane End
Wycombe, Bucks HP14 35G
England

Maison de Soul Records
PO Drawer 10
Ville Platte, LA 70586
(318) 363-2184
Fax: (318) 363-5622

Malaco Records
3023 W. Northside Dr.
Jackson, MS 39213
(601) 982-4522
Fax: (601) 982-4528

Mardi Gras Records
3331 St. Charles Ave.
New Orleans, LA 70115
(504) 895-0441
Fax: (504) 891-4214

Mar-Vic Music Co.
PO Box 56042
Los Angeles, CA 90056-0042
(213) 293-0587
Fax: (213) 295-4113

M.C. Records
PO Box 1788, Huntington
  Station
New York, NY 11746
(516) 763-5767
Fax: (516) 549-7504
E-mail: b583@gramercy.ios.
  com

MCA Records
70 Universal City, CA 91608
(818) 777-4000

Mean Mountain Music
926 W. Oklahoma Ave.
Milwaukee, WI 53215

Memphis Archives
Box 171282
Memphis, TN 38187
(901) 682-2063

Messaround Records
PO Box 1392
Burlingame, CA 94010
(408) 335-5968
(415) 879-0192

Midnight Creeper
PO Box 1001
Oxford, MS 38655
(601) 238-2581
Fax: (601) 238-2565
E-mail: streemus@water
  valley.net

Minor Incarnations
PO Box 120064
Nashville, TN 37212
(615) 269-5885

Mr. R&B Records
c/o Bernholm, Blekingegatan
  25
118 56 Stockholm, Sweden
(08) 642-6358

MM & K Productions
6836 Avenida Rotella
San Jose, CA 95139
(408) 629-4546

Mobile Fidelity Sound Lab
105 Morris St.
Sebastapol, CA 95472
(800) 423-5759
(707) 829-0134
Fax: (707) 829-3746
E-mail: mofi@mofi.com

Modern Blues Recordings
PO Box 248
Pearl River, NY 10965
(914) 735-3944
Fax: (914) 620-1737

Monad Records
25 S. Broadway
Tarrytown, NY 10591
(914) 332-0930
Fax: (914) 332-4203

Mongrel Music
123 Townsend St., Ste. 445
San Francisco, CA 94107
(415) 512-7877
Fax: (415) 512-1439
E-mail: mongrel m@aol.com

Mosaic Records
35 Melrose Place
Stamford, CT 06902
(212) 353-2334
(203) 327-7111
Fax: (203) 323-3526

Mouthpiece Records
2217 Nicollet Ave. S.
Minneapolis, MN 55404
(612) 874-2431
Fax: (612) 874-2472

Munich Records
Vadaring 90
6702 EB Wageningen, The
  Netherlands
(31) (0) 8370-21444
Fax: (31) (0) 8370-22959

Muse Records
106 West 71st
New York, NY 10023
(212) 873-2020
Fax: (212) 877-0407

Music Maker Recordings
41 E. 62nd St.
New York, NY 10021
(212) 207-4016
Fax: (212) 206-4434

Nashboro
10390 Santa Monica Blvd.,
  Ste. 210
Los Angeles, CA 90025
(310) 556-7744
Fax: (310) 5561299

Nehemia Records
15 White Birch Circle
Bloomfield, CT 06002
(203) 243-1661
Fax: (203) 243-2450

Nesek International
PO Box 588
Florham Park, NJ 07932
(201) 386-5670
Fax: (201) 386-5679

New Moon Blues
PO Box 3214
Chapel Hill, NC 27515
(919) 967-1997
Fax: (919) 933-7875

Night Train International
200 W. 72nd St., Ste. 56
New York, NY 10023

(212) 721-7215
Fax: (212) 721-6150

Nighthawk Records
PO Box 15856
St. Louis, MO 63114
(314) 576-1569
Fax: (314) 576-6960

No Cover Productions
PO Box 187
Clawson, MI 48017
(810) 398-6877
E-mail: TJMJ64A@prodigy.com

Nonesuch Records
590 5th Ave.
New York, NY 10019
(212) 575-6720

November Records
1211 Avenue of the Americas,
#26
New York, NY 10036-8701
(212) 343-0799
Fax: (212) 343-0899

Oahu Records
2765 Drake Rd.
Columbus, OH 43219
(614) 476-1180

Ocean Records
PO Box 1504
Arroyo Grande, CA 93421
(805) 481-3913

OKeh Records
550 Madison Ave.
New York, NY 10022-3211
(212) 833-8000

Okra-Tone Records
232 Sunflower St.
Clarksdale, MS 38614
(800) 627-2209

Oldie Blues Productions
PO Box 12538
1100 AM Amsterdam, The
Netherlands
020-696111

Orleans Records
828 Royal St., #536
New Orleans, LA 70116
(504) 837-5042
Fax: (504) 867-9601

Overture Music
47551 Iroquois Ct.

Novi, MI 48374-3635
(810) 349-0115
Fax: (810) 349-9140

P-Vine Reocrds
Tomigaya 2-41-10, Shibuya-ku
Tokyo 151, Japan
3-3460-8611
Fax: 3-3460-8618

Palindrome Records
PO Box 1979
San Antonio, TX 78297
(210) 271-9789
Fax: (210) 225-6410

Parsifal Records
Gulden Vlieslaan 67
Brugge, Belgium 8000
32-50-339516
Fax: 32-50-333386
E-mail: info@parsifal.be

Pathway CDs
PO Box 43185
Oakland, CA 94624
(510) 536-1706

Pineapple Records
PO Box 95967
Seattle, WA 98145-2967

Pinnacle Records
1702-H Meridian Ave., Box 135
San Jose, CA 95125
(408) 356-9977

Planet Blue Records
3840 Broadway
Rockford, IL 61108
(815) 398-0569
Fax: (815) 398-6069

**Pointblank/Charisma
Records**
338 N. Foothill Rd.
Beverly Hills, CA 90201
(310) 278-1181

PolyGram/Verve Records
825 8th Ave., 26th fl.
New York, NY 10019
(212) 333-8000
Fax: (212) 333-8194

Powerhouse Records
PO Box 2455
Falls Church, VA 22042
(703) 534-9179
Fax: (703) 536-2528

Private Music
8750 Wilshire Blvd.
Beverly Hills, CA 90211
(310) 358-4517

Proof Records
PO Box 1348
Diamond City, AR 72630
(501) 422-HARP
Fax: (501) 422-7200

Qualiton Imports
24-02 40th Ave.
Long Island City, NY 11101
(718) 937-8515
Fax: (718) 729-3239
E-mail: john@qualiton.com

RaveOn Productions
226 Cleveland Dr.
Croton, NY 10520
(914) 271-3405
Fax: (914) 271-3901
E-mail: raveonrecs@aol.com

Razor & Tie Records
214 Sullivan St., #4A
New York, NY 10012
(212) 473-9173
Fax: (212) 473-9174

Red Beans Records
2240 N. Magnolia
Chicago, IL 60614

Red Hot Records
PO Box 10256
Kansas City, MO 64171
(816) 333-2633
Fax: (816) 333-3614

Red House Records
PO Box 4044
St. Paul, MN 55104
(612) 379-1089
Fax: (612) 379-0945

Red Lightnin' Ltd.
The White House
N. Lopham Diss
Norfolk 1P22 2LU, England
30-379-687-693
Fax: 30-379-687-559

Relic Records
PO Box 572
Hackensack, NJ 07602
(201) 342-6475

Remedy Records
PO Box 307
Paradise, PA 17562
(717) 442-4490
Fax: (717) 442-8073

Rhino Records
10635 Santa Monica Blvd.
Los Angeles, CA 90025
(800) 35-RHINO
(310) 474-4778
Fax: (310) 441-6575

The Right Stuff
1750 N. Vine St.
Hollywood, CA 90028-5274
(213) 692-1100

Ripsaw Records
4545 Connecticut Ave. NW,
#805
Washington, DC 20008
(202) 362-2286

Rising Son Blues
PO Box 268752
Chicago, IL 60626
(312) 508-0545

Rivera Records
PO Box 1848
Orange, CA 92668
(714) 639-0400
Fax: (714) 639-7523

Roesch Records
25-13 Old Kings Hwy N., Ste.
272
Darien, CT 06820
(203) 838-5023
Fax: (203) 838-0337

Rollin' and Tumblin' Records
PO Box 7488
Louisville, KY 40257
(502) 897-2277

Rooster Blues Records
232 Sunflower Ave.
Clarksdale, MS 38614
(601) 627-2209
Fax: (601) 627-9861
E-mail: rooster232@aol.com

Rosetta Records, Inc.
115 W. 16th St., #267
New York, NY 10011
(212) 243-3583

Rounder Records
One Camp St.
Cambridge, MA 02140
(617) 354-0700
Fax: (617) 491-1970

RSA Records
PO Box 447
Highfalls, NY 12440
(914) 687-0912

Rykodisc
Shetland Park
27 Congress St./Pickering
  Wharf
Bldg. C
Salem, MA 01970
(508) 744-7678
Fax: (508) 741-4506

Say Mo' Music
PO Box 616
Meadville, PA 16335
(814) 337-0941

Schoolkids Records
523 E. Liberty
Ann Arbor, MI 48104
(313) 994-8031
Fax: (313) 930-0071

Schubert Records
PO Box 250144, Bayenstr. 15
5000 Koln, Germany
(0221) 322729
Fax: (0221) 322916

Sequel Records
West Heath Yard
174 Mill Lane
London NW6 1TB, England
071 433 1641
Fax: 071 431 4368

Seyne Records
93 Garfield Ave.
Lynn, MA 01905
(617) 581-1931

Shanachie Entertainment
37 E. Clinton St.
Newton, NJ 07860
(201) 579-7763
Fax: (201) 579-7083

Sharkstooth Records
412 Orange St.
Selinsgrove, PA 17870

Shattered Music
8833 Sunset Blvd.
West Hollywood, CA 90069
(310) 652-9599
Fax: (310) 652-9644

Silver Shadow Records
PO Box 275
Long Lake, MN 55356

Silvertone Records
137-139 W. 25th St., 11th Fl.
New York, NY 10001
(212) 727-0016
Fax: (212) 645-3783

Slippery Noodle Inn Records
372 S. Meridian St.
Indianapolis, IN 46225
(317) 631-6974
Fax: (317) 631-6903

Smithsonian/Folkways
955 L'Enfant Plaza, Ste. 2600
Washington, D.C. 20560
(202) 287-3251
Fax: (202) 287-3699
E-mail: cfpcs.fw@ic.si.edu

Sonet Records, Ltd.
78 Stanley Gardens
London W37 5N, England
01-746-1234
Fax: 01-740-9899

Son Pat Records
PO Box 526
Lancaster, CA 93584

Sony Music
550 Madison Ave.
New York, NY 10022-3211
(212) 833-8000
Fax: (212) 833-7120

SOR
1300 Division St., 3rd fl.
Nashville, TN 37203
(800) 264-2054
(615) 255-6282

Soul-Po-Tion Records
PO Box 3388
Albany, GA 31706
(912) 438-8497

Sound of New Orleans
5584 Canal Blvd.
New Orleans, LA 70124
(504) 484-7222

Fax: (504) 483-9018

Sound of the Fifties
Prinsengracht 669
1017 JT Amsterdam, The
  Netherlands
(020) 623-9745
Fax: (020) 620-5187

Southland Records
1206 Decatur St.
New Orleans, LA 70116
(504) 525-1776
Fax: (504) 523-2629

Stash Records
140 W. 22nd St., 12th fl.
New York, NY 10011
(212) 477-6277

STYB Music Enterprise
PO Box 890
Hollywood, CA 90078-0890
(213) 759-0361

Sugar Hill Records
PO Box 55300
Durham, NC 27717-5300
(919) 489-4349
Fax: (919) 489-6080

Survival Records
PO Box 7032
Marietta, GA 30065
(770) 436-8631
Fax: (770) 432-6239

Swingmaster Records
Kruitlaan 21
NL 9711 TW Groningen, The
  Netherlands

Telarc International
23307 Commerce Park Rd.
Cleveland, OH 44122
(216) 464-2313
Fax: (216) 464-4108

Terra Nova Records
720 Monroe St., Ste. E4-15
Hoboken, NY 07030
(201) 222-2727

Testament Records
220 4th St., #101
Oakland, CA 94607
(510) 763-8500

Texas Road Recording Co.
Rt. 1, Box 311
Checotah, OK 74426

(918) 473-2411

Thunderbird Productions
345 Lake Ave., Ste. F
Santa Cruz, CA 95062
(408) 479-7170
Fax: (408) 479-7448

Tone-Cool Records
129 Parker St.
Newton, MA 02159
(617) 965-1718
Fax: (617) 244-7344

Topaz Productions
PO Box 2725
Oakland, CA 94602
(510) 482-9234

TopCat Records
PO Box 670234
Dallas, TX 75367
(214) 484-4141
Fax: (214) 620-8333
E-mail: blueman@computek.
  net

Trix Records
106 West 71st
New York, NY 10023
(212) 873-2020
Fax: (212) 877-0407

Tuff City Records
200 W. 72nd St., Ste. 56
New York, NY 10023
(212) 721-7215
Fax: (212) 721-6150

Upright Records
Rt. 1, Box 202
Beverly, OH 45715
(614) 984-4821
(813) 323-3716

Uptown Video Records
35 E. Olive
Fresno, CA 93728

**Van der Linden Recordings
Co.**
5331 S. Greenwood
Chicago, IL 60615
(312) 288-2926

Vanguard Records
1299 Ocean Ave., Ste. 800
Santa Monica, CA 90401
(310) 451-5727
Fax: (310) 394-4148

E-mail: vangardred@aol.com

Vas-Kat Records
PO Box 1414
Hattiesburg, MS 39403-1414
(601) 582-9599

Vent Records
4 South 55th Pl.
Birmingham, AL 35212
(205) 592-2222

Vee-Jay Limited Partnership
8857 W. Olympic Blvd., Ste.
200
Beverly Hills, CA 90211
(310) 657-9814
Fax: (310) 657-2331

Viceroots Records
547 W. 27th St., 6th fl.

New York, NY 10001
(212) 465-2357
Fax: (212) 279-6520

Vital Music
2591 Pomona Blvd.
(909) 613-1323
Fax: (909) 594-9652

Wa Nui Records
4257 Sierra Dr.
Honolulu, HI 96816
(808) 837-7800
Fax: (808) 732-9576

Waldoxy Records
3023 W. Northside Dr.
Jackson, MS 39213
(601) 982-4522
Fax: (601) 982-2944
E-mail: malaco@misnet.com

E-mail: wanui@aloha.net

Warner Bros.
3300 Warner Blvd.
Burbank, CA 91505-4694
(818) 846-9090
Fax: (818) 846-8474

Watermelon Records
Box 49056
Austin, TX 78765
(512) 472-6192

The Wax Museum
1505 Elizabeth Ave.
Charlotte, NC 28204
(704) 377-0700
Fax: (704) 377-0701

Wildcat Records
950 N. Kings Rd., #266

W. Hollywood, CA 90069
(213) 858-9200

Winner Records
PO Box 151095
San Rafael, CA 94915-1095
(415) 453-7712
Fax: (415) 258-0692
E-mail: wpc@netcom.com

Wolf Records
PO Box 375
A 1120 Vienna, Austria
(222) 001-43-1-512-4803
Fax: 001-043-513-5549

Yazoo Records
37 E. Clinton St.
Newton, NY 07860
(212) 334-0284
Fax: (212) 334-5207

$$\frac{4}{5}$$
1

The following albums by individual artists or groups achieved the highest rating possible—5 bones—from our discriminating MusicHound Blues writers. You can't miss with any of these recordings.

The Aces
Chicago Beat (Black & Blue, 1970)

Mose Allison
Allison Wonderland: The Mose Allison Anthology (Rhino, 1994)

The Allman Brothers Band
At Fillmore East (Capricorn, 1971)

The Animals
The Best of the Animals (MGM, 1966/Abkco, 1987)
The Most of the Animals (Raven, 1989)

Billy Boy Arnold
Back Where I Belong (Alligator, 1992)
Bo Diddley—Bo's Blues (Ace, 1993)
Crying and Pleading (Charly, 1980/1994)

James "Kokomo" Arnold
Kokomo Arnold Vol. 1 (Document, 1991)

LaVern Baker
LaVern Baker Sings Bessie Smith (Atco, 1958/1988)
Soul on Fire (Atlantic, 1991)

Barbecue Bob
Complete Recorded Works, 1927–30 (Document, 1991)

Roosevelt "Booba" Barnes
The Heartbroken Man (Rooster Blues, 1990)

Will Batts
The Sounds of Memphis 1933–39 (Story of Blues, 1987)

Beck
Odelay (Geffen, 1996)

Chuck Berry
The Chess Box (Chess/MCA, 1988)
Chuck Berry Is on Top (Chess, 1959)
The Great Twenty-Eight (Chess, 1982)

Scrapper Blackwell
Complete Recorded Works in Chronological Order, Vols. 1–2 (Document, 1993)

Bobby "Blue" Bland
I Pity the Fool/The Duke Recordings, Vol. 1 (MCA, 1992)
Turn on Your Love Light (MCA, 1994)
Two Steps from the Blues (MCA, 1961/1989)

Blind Blake
The Master of Ragtime Guitar (Indigo Records, 1996)

Zuzu Bollin
Texas Bluesman (Antone's, 1992)

Ishmon Bracey
Ishmon Bracey and Charley Taylor, 1928–29 (Document, 1991)

Big Bill Broonzy
Big Bill's Blues (Portrait)

Blues in the Mississippi Night (Rykodisc, 1990)
Good Time Tonight (Columbia/Legacy, 1990)

Charles Brown
The Complete Aladdin Recordings of Charles Brown (Mosaic, 1994)

Clarence "Gatemouth" Brown
The Original Peacock Recordings (Rounder, 1990)

James Brown
Live at the Apollo, 1962 (King, 1963/Polydor, 1990)
Star Time (Polydor, 1991)

Roy Brown
Good Rockin' Tonight (Rhino, 1994)

Roy Buchanan
Buch and the Snake Stretchers: One of Three (Genes, 1991)

Solomon Burke
Home in Your Heart (Rhino/Atlantic, 1992)

Eddie Burns
Treat Me Like I Treat You (Moonshine, 1982)

Paul Butterfield Blues Band
The Box Set (Elektra, 1997)
East-West Live (Winner, 1997)
The Paul Butterfield Blues Band (Elektra, 1965)

Paul Butterfield's Better Days
Better Days (Bearsville, 1973)

Eddie C. Campbell
That's When I Know (Blind Pig, 1994)

James Carr
Essential James Carr (Razor & Tie, 1995)

Leroy Carr
Leroy Carr 1930–35 (Magpie, 1990)

Ray Charles
Anthology (Rhino, 1988)
The Best of Ray Charles: The Atlantic Years (Rhino, 1994)
The Birth of Soul: The Complete Atlantic Rhythm & Blues Recordings, 1952–59 (Rhino, 1991)
Genius + Soul: The 50th Anniversary Collection (Rhino, 1997)
Modern Sounds in Country and Western Music (ABC, 1963)

C.J. Chenier
The Big Squeeze (Alligator, 1996)
Too Much Fun (Alligator, 1995)

Clifton Chenier
Zydeco Dynamite (Rhino, 1993)

W.C. Clark
Heart of Gold (Black Top, 1994)

William Clarke
Blowin' Like Hell (Alligator, 1990)

Otis Clay
The Best of Otis Clay—The Hi Records Years (The Right Stuff, 1996)
The 45's (Cream/Hi, 1993)
Soul Man—Live in Japan (Bullseye Blues, 1991)

Albert Collins
Complete Imperial Recordings (EMI, 1991)
Frostbite (Alligator, 1980)
Frozen Alive (Alligator, 1981)

Robert Covington
Blues in the Night (Red Beans, 1988/Evidence, 1995)

CeDell Davis
Feel Like Doin' Something Wrong (Fat Possum, 1994)

The Rev. Gary Davis
The Complete Early Recordings of the Reverend Gary Davis (Yazoo, 1994)
Pure Religion and Bad Company (Smithsonian/Folkways, 1991)

Jimmy Dawkins
Chicago Blues (Arhoolie, 1990)
Fast Fingers (Delmark, 1969)
Hot Wire 81 (Evidence, 1994)

Derek & the Dominos
Layla and Other Assorted Love Songs (Polydor, 1970)

Bo Diddley
Bo Diddley/Go Bo Diddley (Chess/MCA, 1996)
Bo Diddley: His Best (MCA/Chess, 1997)
The EP Collection (See for Miles, 1991)

Willie Dixon
The Chess Box (MCA/Chess, 1988)

Fats Domino
Antoine "Fats" Domino (Tomato, 1992)
Fats Domino: The Fat Man—25 Classics (EMI, 1996)
My Blue Heaven (EMI, 1990)
Out of New Orleans (Bear Family, 1993)
They Call Me the Fat Man (EMI, 1991)

Thomas A. Dorsey
Come on Mama Do That Dance (Yazoo)
Thomas A. Dorsey—Precious Lord (Columbia, 1973/1994)

Chris Duarte
Texas Sugar/Strat Magic (Silvertone, 1994)

Champion Jack Dupree
Blues from the Gutter (Atlantic, 1958)

Bob Dylan
Blonde on Blonde (Columbia, 1966)
Blood on the Tracks (Columbia, 1975)
Highway 61 Revisited (Columbia, 1965)

Sleepy John Estes
I Ain't Gonna Be Worried No More, 1929–41 (Yazoo, 1992)

H-Bomb Ferguson
Wiggin' Out (Earwig, 1994)

Charles Ford Band
The Charles Ford Band (Arhoolie, 1972)

Blind Boy Fuller
East Coast Piedmont Style (Columbia/Legacy, 1991)
Truckin' My Blues Away (Yazoo, 1990)

Jesse Fuller
Jazz, Folk Songs, Spirituals & Blues (Good Time Jazz, 1958/Original Blues Classics, 1993)

Anson Funderburgh & the Rockets Featuring Sam Myers
Live at the Grand Emporium (Black Top, 1995)

Al Green
Call Me (The Right Stuff, 1972)
Greatest Hits (The Right Stuff, 1996)
Let's Stay Together (The Right Stuff, 1972)

Guitar Gabriel
Guitar Gabriel, Vol. 1 (Music Maker, 1994)
My South, My Blues (Gemini, 1970/Jambalaya, 1988)

Guitar Slim
Sufferin' Mind (Specialty, 1969)

James Harman
Do Not Disturb (Black Top, 1991)

Slim Harpo
Hip Shakin': The Excello Collection (AVI/Excello)

Corey Harris
Fish Ain't Bitin' (Alligator, 1997)

Wynonie Harris
Bloodshot Eyes: The Best of Wynonie Harris (Rhino, 1994)

Ted Hawkins
Songs from Venice Beach (Evidence, 1995)

Jessie Mae Hemphill
Feelin' Good (High Water, 1990)
She-Wolf (Vogue, 1981)

Jimi Hendrix
Are You Experienced? (MCA, 1967/1993)
Axis: Bold As Love (MCA, 1967/1993)

Billie Holiday
The Complete Decca Recordings (GRP, 1991)

Homesick James
Blues on the South Side (Original Blues Classics, 1990)

John Lee Hooker
The Real Folk Blues (Chess, 1966)
The Ultimate Collection (Rhino, 1991)

Lightnin' Hopkins
Blues Train (Mainstream, 1991)
The Complete Aladdin Sessions (EMI, 1991)
The Gold Star Sessions, Vol. 1 (Arhoolie, 1990)

The Gold Star Sessions, Vol. 2 (Arhoolie, 1990)
The Herald Recordings (Collectables, 1989)
The Herald Recordings, Vol. 2 (Collectables, 1993)
Lightnin' Hopkins (Smithsonian/Folkways, 1990)
Lightnin' in New York (Candid, 1988)
Swarthmore Concert (Bluesville Prestige/Fantasy, 1993)
Texas Blues (Arhoolie, 1994)

Howlin' Wolf
Change My Way (MCA/Chess, 1990)
Howlin' Wolf: His Best (MCA/Chess, 1997)
Howlin' Wolf Rides Again (Flair/Virgin, 1991)
Moaning at Midnight (MCA/Chess, 1989)

Ivory Joe Hunter
Since I Met You Baby: The Best of Ivory Joe Hunter (Razor & Tie, 1994)

Mississippi John Hurt
Avalon Blues: The Complete 1928 OKeh Recordings (Columbia/Legacy, 1996)

J.B. Hutto
Hawk Squat (Delmark, 1968)

Elmore James
The Sky Is Crying: The History of Elmore James (Rhino, 1993)

Skip James
Complete Early Recordings (Yazoo, 1994)
She Lyin' (Genes, 1964/1993)

Blind Lemon Jefferson
Blind Lemon Jefferson (Milestone, 1992)
Blind Lemon Jefferson: Complete Works 1926–29 (Document, 1991)

Buddy Johnson
Walk 'Em (Ace, 1996)

Lonnie Johnson
He's a Jelly Roll Baker (Bluebird, 1992)
Me and My Crazy Self (Charly, 1991)
The Originator of Modern Guitar Blues (Blues Boy, 1980)
Steppin' on the Blues (Columbia/Legacy, 1991)

Robert Johnson
King of the Delta Blues Singers (Columbia, 1961)
Robert Johnson: The Complete Recordings (Columbia, 1990)

Tommy Johnson
Tommy Johnson: Complete Recorded Works in Chronological Order, 1928–29 (Document, 1994)

Tutu Jones
Blue Texas Soul (Bullseye Blues, 1996)

Janis Joplin (with Big Brother & the Holding Company)
Cheap Thrills (Columbia, 1968)

Louis Jordan
The Best of Louis Jordan (MCA, 1989)
Let the Good Times Roll (Bear Family, 1992)

Jack Kelly
The Sounds of Memphis (Story of Blues, 1987)

Albert King
Born Under a Bad Sign (Atlantic, 1967)

B.B. King
The Best of B.B. King, Vol. One (Flair/Virgin, 1991)
Live at the Regal (MCA, 1971)

Earl King
Glazed (Black Top, 1987)
Hard River to Cross (Black Top, 1993)

Freddie King
Blues Guitar Hits (Ace, 1993)
Hideaway: The Best of Freddie King (Rhino, 1993)
Just Pickin' (Modern, 1986)
King of the Blues (EMI, 1996)

Mark Knopfler (with Dire Straits)
Communique (Warner Bros., 1979)
Making Movies (Warner Bros., 1980)

Lazy Lester
Harp and Soul (Alligator/King Snake, 1988)
I'm a Lover, Not a Fighter (Excello/AVI, 1994)

Led Zeppelin
Houses of the Holy (Atlantic, 1973)
Led Zeppelin IV (Atlantic, 1971)
Led Zeppelin: The Complete Studio Recordings (Atlantic, 1993)

J.B. Lenoir
Fine Blues (Official, 1989)
I Don't Know (Chess, 1969/Vogue, 1989)
Natural Man (Chess/MCA, 1990)
Vietnam Blues (Evidence, 1995)

Furry Lewis
Furry Lewis—1927–29 (Document, 1990)
Shake 'Em on Down (Fantasy, 1972)

Smiley Lewis
I Hear You Knocking: The Best of Smiley Lewis (Collectables, 1995)
Shame Shame Shame—Complete Smiley Lewis (Bear Family, 1993)

Lightnin' Slim
Rooster Blues/Bell Ringer (Ace, 1996)

Little Walter
Confessin' the Blues (MCA/Chess, 1974/1996)
Essential Little Walter (MCA/Chess, 1993)
Hate to See You Go (MCA/Chess, 1968/1990)
Little Walter: His Best (MCA/Chess, 1997)

Johnny Littlejohn
Chicago Blues Stars (Arhoolie, 1968/1991)

Robert Junior Lockwood
Blues Live in Japan: Robert Lockwood and the Aces (Advent LP, 1976)
Contrasts (Trix, 1991)

Lonesome Sundown
I'm a Mojo Man (Excello/AVI, 1994)

Joe Hill Louis
The Be-Bop Boy (Bear Family, 1992)

Louisiana Red
The Blues Purity of Louisiana Red (Blue Labor, 1975)
Louisiana Red Sings the Blues (Atco, 1971/Blue Sting, 1994)
The Low Down Back Porch Blues (Roulette, 1962/Sequel, 1992)

Willie Love
Clownin' with the World (Alligator, 1993)

Percy Mayfield
Poet of the Blues (Specialty, 1990)

Tommy McClennan
The Bluebird Recordings 1941–42 (BMG, 1997)

The McCoy Brothers
The McCoy Brothers, 1934–44 (RST, 1992)

Jay McShann
Hootie's Jumpin' Blues (Stony Plain, 1997)

Blind Willie McTell
Atlanta Twelve String (Atlantic, 1991)

4
5 *five-bone albums*
4

Blind Willie McTell: Complete Recorded Works 1927–35, Vols. 1–3 (Document, 1990)
The Definitive Blind Willie McTell (Columbia/Legacy, 1994)

Memphis Minnie
Hoodoo Lady (1933–37) (Columbia/Roots 'n' Blues, 1991)
I Ain't No Bad Gal 1941 (CBS/Portrait Masters, 1988)
Me and My Chauffeur 1935–46 (E.P.M. Blues Collection, 1997)

Memphis Slim
Memphis Slim at the Gate of Horn (Vee-Jay, 1959/1993)

Big Maceo Merriweather
The King of Chicago Blues Piano (Arhoolie, 1992)

Amos Milburn
Blues Barrelhouse and Boogie Woogie (Capitol, 1996)
Down the Road Apiece (Alliance, 1997)

Roy Milton
Grandfather of R&B (Mr. R&B, 1994)

Mississippi Heat
Learned the Hard Way (Van der Linden, 1994)
Straight from the Heart (Van der Linden, 1993/1996)
Thunder in My Heart (Van der Linden, 1995)

Mississippi Sheiks
Stop and Listen (Yazoo, 1992)

Little Brother Montgomery
Complete Recorded Works 1930–36 (Document, 1992)

John Mooney
Late Last Night (Bullseye Blues/Rounder, 1990)
Telephone King (Blind Pig, 1983/Powerhouse, 1991)

Maria Muldaur
Maria Muldaur (Reprise, 1973/Warner Archives, 1993)

Robert Nighthawk
Drop Down Mama (MCA/Chess, 1970/1990)
Robert Lee McCoy (Robert Nighthawk): Complete Recorded Works in Chronological Order (Wolf, 1990)

Robert Nighthawk—Live on Maxwell Street (Rounder, 1980/1991)

Johnny Otis
Creepin' with the Cats (Ace, 1991)
The Original Johnny Otis Show (Savoy, 1994)

Junior Parker
Mystery Train (Rounder, 1990)

Charley Patton
King of the Delta Blues (Yazoo/Shanachie, 1991)

Elvis Presley
The Complete Sun Sessions (RCA, 1987)
Elvis' Golden Records, Vol. 1 (RCA, 1958)
Elvis' Golden Records, Vol. 3 (RCA, 1963)
Elvis—The King of Rock 'n' Roll—The Complete '50s Masters (RCA, 1992)
50,000,000 Elvis Fans Can't Be Wrong: Elvis' Golden Records, Vol. 2 (RCA, 1960)

Lloyd Price
Lawdy! (Specialty, 1991)
Vol. 2: Heavy Dreams (Specialty, 1993)

Professor Longhair
The Professor Longhair Anthology (Rhino, 1993)

Snooky Pryor
Snooky Pryor (Paula/Flyright, 1990)

Tad Robinson
One to Infinity (Delmark, 1994)

Jimmy Rogers
Chicago Bound (MCA/Chess, 1990)
Jimmy Rogers: The Complete Chess Reissue (MCA/Chess, 1997)

Rolling Stones
Big Hits/High Tide and Green Grass (Abkco, 1966)
Exile on Main Street (Virgin, 1972)
Let It Bleed (Abkco, 1969)
The Singles Collection (Abkco, 1989)

Roomful of Blues
Turn It On! Turn It Up! (Bullseye Blues/Rounder, 1995)

Bobby Rush
One Monkey Don't Stop No Show (Waldoxy, 1995)

Otis Rush
1956–58 Cobra Recordings (Paula, 1991)

Right Place, Wrong Time (Bullfrog/Hightone, 1976)

Johnny Shines
Hey Ba-Ba-Re-Bop (Rounder, 1992)
Traditional Delta Blues (Biograph, 1991)

Frankie Lee Sims
Lucy Mae Blues (Specialty, 1992)

Percy Sledge
It Tears Me Up (Rhino/Atlantic, 1992)

Bessie Smith
Bessie Smith (Time-Life, 1982)
The Complete Recordings, Vol. 2 (Columbia/Legacy, 1991)
The Complete Recordings, Vol. 3 (Columbia/Legacy, 1992)

Pine Top Smith
Boogie Woogie and Barrelhouse Piano 1928–32 (Document, 1992)

Charlie Spand
Charlie Spand: The Complete Paramounts in Chronological Order, 1929–31 (Document, 1992)

Otis Spann
Down to Earth: The Bluesway Recordings (MCA, 1995)
Live the Life (Testament, 1997)
Otis Spann (Storyville, 1992)
Otis Spann Is the Blues (Candid, 1960)
Otis Spann's Chicago Blues (Testament, 1997)

Dave Specter
Left Turn on Blue (Delmark, 1996)

Studebaker John
Too Tough (Blind Pig, 1994)

Sunnyland Slim
Rediscovered Blues (Capitol, 1996)
Sunnyland Slim/Bluesmasters Vol. 8 (Blue Horizon LP, 1969)

Tampa Red
Tampa Red, 1938–40 (BMG/Bluebird, 1997)

Hound Dog Taylor
Beware of the Dog! (Alligator, 1976)

Little Johnny Taylor
The Galaxy Years (Ace, 1992)
Greatest Hits (Fantasy, 1982)

Sonny Terry & Brownie McGhee
Brownie McGhee and Sonny Terry Sing
    (Smithsonian/Folkways,
    1958/Rounder, 1990)

Rosetta Tharpe
Sister R. Tharpe (MCA, 1975)
Sister R. Tharpe (Rosetta, 1988)
Sister Rosetta Tharpe (Frèmeaux & Associ-
    ates, 1994)
*Sister Rosetta Tharpe: Complete Recorded
    Works* (Document, 1995)

Henry "Ragtime Texas" Thomas
Henry Thomas 1927–29 (Document, 1991)
Texas Worried Blues (Yazoo, 1990)

Irma Thomas
*Sweet Soul Queen of New Orleans: The
    Irma Thomas Collection* (Razor & Tie,
    1996)

Henry Townsend
Mule (Nighthawk, 1980)

Big Joe Turner
Greatest Hits (Rhino, 1987)

Ike Turner
I Like Ike! The Best of Ike Turner (Rhino,
    1994)
*Proud Mary—The Best of Ike and Tina
    Turner* (Sue/EMI, 1991)

T-Bone Walker
*The Complete Capitol/Black and White
    Recordings* (Capitol, 1995)
The Complete Imperial Recordings (EMI
    America, 1991)
*The Complete Recordings of T-Bone
    Walker, 1940–52* (Mosaic, 1990)
I Want a Little Girl (Delmark, 1973)

Robert Ward
Fear No Evil (Black Top, 1990)

Dinah Washington
Back to the Blues (Roulette, 1997)
*The Complete Dinah Washington on Mer-
    cury, Vol. 1 (1946–49)* (Mercury, 1987)
*Dinah Washington—The Complete Vol-
    ume 1* (Official, 1988)
*First Issue: The Dinah Washington Story
    (The Original Recordings)* (Mercury,
    1993)
What a Diff'rence a Day Makes (Mobile Fi-
    delity Sound Lab, 1997)

Muddy Waters
*Complete Plantation Recordings: The His-
    toric 1941–42 Library of Congress
    Field Recordings* (MCA/Chess, 1993)
Fathers & Sons (MCA/Chess, 1989)
His Best: 1947–55 (MCA/Chess, 1997)
Muddy "Mississippi" Waters Live
    (CBS/Blue Sky, 1989)

Curley Weaver
Georgia Guitar Wizard (1928–35) (Story of
    Blues, 1987)

Junior Wells
Hoodoo Man Blues (Delmark, 1965)

Bukka White
The Complete Bukka White
    (Columbia/Legacy, 1994)
Legacy of the Blues (Sonet, 1969)

Lynn White
Take Your Time (Waylo/MMS, 1995)

Robert Wilkins
The Original Rolling Stone (Yazoo, 1989)

Robert Pete Williams
Free Again (Prestige, 1960/Fantasy, 1992)
I'm As Blue As a Man Can Be—Vol. 1
    (Arhoolie, 1994)
Louisiana Blues (Takoma, 1980)
When a Man Takes the Blues—Vol. 2
    (Arhoolie, 1994)

Sonny Boy Williamson I
*Sonny Boy Williamson: Complete
    Recorded Works, 1937–47* (Document,
    1991)

Sonny Boy Williamson II
King Biscuit Time (Arhoolie, 1990)
Sonny Boy Williamson: His Best
    (MCA/Chess, 1997)

Chuck Willis
*Let's Jump Tonight! The Best of Chuck
    Willis, 1951–56* (Columbia/Legacy,
    1994)

Jimmy Witherspoon
Blowin' in from Kansas City (Flair/Virgin,
    1991)

Mitch Woods
Solid Gold Cadillac (Blind Pig, 1991)

Big John Wrencher
*Big John Wrencher & His Maxwell Street
    Blues Boys* (Barrelhouse, 1974/Blue
    Sting, 1995)
The Chicago String Band (Testament,
    1970/1994)

O.V. Wright
The Soul of O.V. Wright (MCA, 1992)
The Wright Stuff/Live (Hi/Demon, 1990)

Johnny Young
Chicago Blues (Arhoolie,
    1966/1968/1990)
Johnny Young & His Friends (Testament,
    1975/1994)
Lake Michigan Ain't No River (Rounder,
    1973)

ZZ Top
Deguello (Warner Bros., 1979)

If you're looking for some great blues by a variety of performers, these compilation albums would be a good place to start.

Box Sets

American Folk Blues Festival 𝄞𝄞𝄞𝄞 (Evidence, 1995)

Anthology of American Folk Music 𝄞𝄞𝄞𝄞𝄞 (Smithsonian/Folkways, 1997)

The Atlantic Blues Box 𝄞𝄞𝄞𝄞𝄞 (Atlantic, 1986)

Atlantic Rhythm & Blues 𝄞𝄞𝄞𝄞𝄞 (Atlantic, 1985)

The Blues: A Smithsonian Collection of Classic Blues Singers 𝄞𝄞𝄞𝄞𝄞 (Sony, 1993)

Blues Classics 𝄞𝄞𝄞𝄞 (MCA, 1996)

Blues in the Night 𝄞𝄞𝄞𝄞 (LaserLight, 1992)

The Blues Is Alright, Vol. 1 & 2 𝄞𝄞𝄞𝄞𝄞 (Malaco, 1993)

Blues Men 𝄞𝄞𝄞𝄞 (LaserLight, 1996)

Chess Rhythm and Soul 𝄞𝄞𝄞𝄞 (MCA/Chess, 1994)

The Cobra Records Story 𝄞𝄞𝄞𝄞𝄞 (Capricorn, 1993)

The Complete Stax-Volt Singles, 1959–1968 𝄞𝄞𝄞𝄞𝄞 (Atlantic, 1991)

The Fire/Fury Records Story 𝄞𝄞𝄞𝄞 (Capricorn, 1992)

Full Spectrum Blues 𝄞𝄞𝄞𝄞 (Star Sounds, 1996)

The Jewel/Paula Records Story 𝄞𝄞𝄞𝄞 (Capricorn, 1994)

Mean Old World: The Blues from 1940 to 1994 𝄞𝄞𝄞𝄞𝄞 (Smithsonian, 1996)

The Mercury Blues and Rhythm Story 𝄞𝄞𝄞𝄞 (Mercury, 1997)

The R&B Box 𝄞𝄞𝄞𝄞 (Rhino, 1994)

The Roots 'N Blues Retrospective 𝄞𝄞𝄞𝄞 (Columbia, 1992)

Sounds of the South 𝄞𝄞𝄞𝄞𝄞 (Atlantic, 1993)

The Specialty Story 𝄞𝄞𝄞𝄞 (Specialty, 1994)

Sun Records: The Blues Years, 1950–1958 𝄞𝄞𝄞𝄞𝄞 (Charly, 1996)

The Sun Records Collection 𝄞𝄞𝄞𝄞𝄞 (Rhino, 1994)

The Swingtime Records Story 𝄞𝄞𝄞𝄞𝄞 (Capricorn, 1994)

Cajun/Zydeco

Alligator Stomp, Vol. 1–3 𝄞𝄞𝄞𝄞 (Rhino, 1992)

Cajun, Vol. 1: Abbeville Breakdown 𝄞𝄞𝄞𝄞𝄞 (Columbia, 1990)

Cajun Dance Hall Special 𝄞𝄞𝄞𝄞 (Rounder, 1992)

Cajun Dance Party Fais Do-Do 𝄞𝄞𝄞𝄞 (Columbia, 1994)

Cajun Music and Zydeco 𝄞𝄞𝄞𝄞 (Rounder, 1992)

Cajun and Zydeco Mardi Gras 𝄞𝄞𝄞𝄞 (Maison de Soul, 1992)

15 Louisiana Zydeco Classics 𝄞𝄞𝄞𝄞𝄞 (Arhoolie, 1997)

I Went to the Dance, Vol. 1 & 2 𝄞𝄞𝄞𝄞𝄞 (Arhoolie, 1990)

Stomp Down Zydeco 𝄞𝄞𝄞𝄞𝄞 (Rounder, 1992)

Zydeco Blues and Boogie 𝄞𝄞𝄞𝄞 (Ryko, 1989)

Zydeco: The Early Years 𝄞𝄞𝄞𝄞 (Arhoolie, 1989)

Chicago Blues

Atlantic Blues Chicago 𝄞𝄞𝄞𝄞𝄞 (Atlantic, 1986)

The Best of the Chicago Blues 𝄞𝄞𝄞𝄞 (Vanguard, 1987)

Chicago Blues 𝄞𝄞𝄞𝄞 (JSP, 1991)

Chicago Blues Anthology 𝄞𝄞𝄞𝄞𝄞 (Chess, 1984)

Chicago Blues Bash 𝄞𝄞𝄞𝄞 (LaserLight, 1982)

Chicago Blues from CJ Records, Vol. 1 𝄞𝄞𝄞𝄞 (Wolf, 1997)

Chicago Blues Live, Vol. 1 𝄞𝄞𝄞𝄞𝄞 (Wolf, 1997)

Chicago Blues Nights 𝄞𝄞𝄞𝄞 (Storyville, 1994)

Chicago Blues, 1951–1953 𝄞𝄞𝄞𝄞 (Paula, 1991)

Chicago Blues Session 𝄞𝄞𝄞𝄞𝄞 (Sequel, 1996)

Chicago: The Blues Today 𝄞𝄞𝄞𝄞 (Vanguard, 1996)

Chicago Boogie, 1947 𝄞𝄞𝄞𝄞 (St. George, 1983)

Chicago Boss Guitars 𝄞𝄞𝄞𝄞 (Paula, 1991)

Chicago's Blues Legends 𝄞𝄞𝄞𝄞 (Wolf)

Cool Playing Blues—Chicago Style 𝄞𝄞𝄞𝄞 (Relic, 1989)

Feelin' Down on the South Side 𝄞𝄞𝄞𝄞 (Prestige, 1995)

Genuine Houserockin' Music, Vol. 1–4 𝄞𝄞𝄞𝄞 (Alligator, 1987)

Hand Me Down Blues—Chicago Style 𝄞𝄞𝄞𝄞 (Relic, 1989)

Honkers & Bar Walkers, Vol. 1 & 2 (Delmark, 1992)

Living Chicago Blues, Vol. 1–5 (Alligator, 1991)

Modern Chicago Blues (Testament, 1994)

The New Bluebloods: The Next Generation of Chicago Blues (Alligator, 1987)

Rare Chicago Blues, 1962–1968 (Rounder, 1993)

Sweet Home Chicago (Delmark, 1994)

Windy City Blues (LaserLight, 1992)

Christmas

Alligator Records Christmas Collection (Alligator, 1992)

Blues, Mistletoe and Santa's Little Helper (Black Top, 1996)

Blue Yule (Rhino, 1991)

Bullseye Blues Christmas (Bullseye Blues, 1995)

Creole Christmas (Epic, 1990)

Even Santa Gets the Blues (Pointblank, 1995)

Greatest R&B Christmas Hits (Rhino, 1990)

Hipsters' Holiday (Rhino, 1989)

Ichiban Blues Christmas, Vol. 1 & 2 (Ichiban, 1992)

It's Christmas Time Again (Stax, 1989)

Mr. Santa Boogie (Savoy, 1985)

Santa Is a Bluesman, Vol. 1 & 2 (Rollin' and Tumblin', 1993)

Vee-Jay Christmas (Vee-Jay, 1992)

Delta Blues

Best of Country Blues: Southern Camptown Blues (Wolf, 1990)

Bloodstains on the Wall (Specialty, 1994)

Blues Masters: The Essential Blues Collection (Rhino, 1992)

Canned Heat Blues: Master of the Delta Blues (BMG, 1992)

Country Negro Jam Session (Arhoolie, 1993)

Deep Blues Soundtrack (Atlantic, 1992)

Delta Blues, 1951 (Trumpet, 1990)

From West Helena to Chicago: Mostly Unplugged (Wolf, 1994)

Giants of Country Blues Guitar (Wolf, 1991)

The Greatest in Country Blues, 1927–1930 (Blues Documents, 1992)

I Have to Paint My Face: Mississippi, 1960 (Arhoolie, 1995)

King Biscuit Blues: The Helena Blues Legacy (Blue Sun, 1996)

Legends of the Blues, Vol. 2 (Columbia, 1991)

Masters of the Delta Blues: The Friends of Charlie Patton (Yazoo, 1991)

Mississippi Delta Blues in the 1960s (Arhoolie, 1994)

Mississippi Delta Blues Jam in Memphis, Vol. 1 (Arhoolie, 1993)

Mississippi Delta Blues, Vol. 1: Blow My Blues Away (Arhoolie, 1994)

Mississippi Masters (Yazoo, 1994)

Prison Blues of the South (LaserLight, 1994)

The Roots of Rap (Yazoo, 1996)

Roots of Rhythm and Blues: A Tribute to the Robert Johnson Era (Columbia, 1992)

Sound of the Delta (Testament, 1994)

The Spirit Lives On: Deep South Country Blues and Spirituals in the 1990s (Hot Fox, 1994)

Straight from the Delta (RexMusic, 1996)

White Country Blues (Columbia, 1993)

General Blues Collections

Alone with the Blues (Drive, 1994)

A Riot in Blues (Mainstream, 1971)

A Taste of the Blues (Vee-Jay)

A Taste of Tradition (Tradition, 1996)

Beauty of the Blues (Columbia, 1991)

Big Blues Honks and Wails (Prestige, 1995)

Blue Gold (Cymekob, 1996)

The Blues, Vol. 1–6 (MCA/Chess, 1986)

Blues Around Midnight (Flair, 1991)

Blues at Newport (Vanguard, 1989)

Blues Fest: Modern Blues of the '70s (Rhino, 1995)

Blues Fest: Modern Blues of the '80s (Rhino, 1995)

Blues Fest: Modern Blues of the '90s (Rhino, 1995)

Blues Guitar Greats (Delmark, 1997)

Blues Live from Mountain Stage (Blue Plate, 1993)

Blues Master Essential Blues Collection, Vol. 1–15 (Rhino, 1992)

Blues Upside Your Head (Charly, 1986)

Blues Ways (Drive, 1995)

Blues with a Feeling: Newport Folk Festival Classics (Vanguard, 1993)

Bluesmen and Rhythm Kings (Ichiban, 1996)

Can't Keep from Cryin': Topical Blues on the Death of President Kennedy (Testament, 1994)

The Class of 15 ((MCA/Chess, 1995)

Classic Blues, Vol. 1 & 2 (Ronn, 1993)

A Collection of the Blues: Classic Blues Singers, Vol. 1 (DA Music, 1994)

Compact Jazz: Best of Blues (Polydor, 1989)

Danceland Years (Pointblank Classics, 1995)

Essential Blues (House of Blues, 1995)

Great Blues Guitarists: String Dazzlers (Columbia, 1991)

The Great Blues Men (Vanguard, 1988)

Knights of the Blues Table (Viceroy, 1996)

Legends of the Blues, Vol. 1 (Columbia, 1990)

Let It Pour (Deluge, 1996)

Livin' with the Blues (Capitol, 1995)

Messed Up in Love and Other Tales of Woe (Columbia, 1996)

Motherless Children: A Collection of Bottleneck Gospel Blues (Time & Strike, 1996)

News & the Blues: Telling It Like It Is (Columbia, 1990)

Nothing But the Blues (Drive, 1995)

The Real Blues Brothers (Dunhill, 1995)

Rediscovered Blues (Capitol, 1995)

The Roots of Jazz: The Blues Era, Vol. 1 & 2 (MU Jazz Classics)

Singin' the Blues (Drive, 1997)

Slow and Moody, Black and Bluesy (Virgin, 1994)

Steeped in the Blues Tradition (Tradition, 1996)

Strike a Deep Chord: Blues for the Homeless (Justice, 1992)

Up Jumped the Blues (Music Club, 1996)

Gospel

Best of Nashboro Gospel 🦴🦴🦴 (AVI/Excello, 1994)
Great Gospel Gems 🦴🦴🦴 (Specialty, 1991)
Great Gospel Men 🦴🦴🦴 (Shanachie, 1993)
Great Gospel Women 🦴🦴🦴 (Shanachie, 1993)
Good News: 22 Gospel Greats 🦴🦴🦴🦴 (Charly, 1987)
Great 1955 Shrine Concert 🦴🦴🦴🦴 (Specialty, 1993)
In the Spirit: The Gospel and Jubilee Recordings on Trumpet 🦴🦴🦴🦴 (Alligator, 1994)
It's Jesus, Y'All 🦴🦴🦴 (AVI/Excello, 1994)
Jubilation: Great Gospel Performances, Vol. 1 🦴🦴🦴 (Rhino, 1992)
Paula's Greatest Gospel Hits, Vol. 1 🦴🦴🦴 (Paula, 1996)
Preachin' the Gospel Holy Blues 🦴🦴🦴🦴 (Columbia, 1991)
Women of Gospel's Golden Age, Vol. 1 🦴🦴🦴🦴 (Specialty, 1994)

Harmonica

Chicago Blues Harmonica 🦴🦴🦴🦴 (Wolf, 1996)
Chicago Blues Harmonicas 🦴🦴🦴 (Paula, 1991)
Excello Harmonica Blues Variety 🦴🦴🦴 (AVI/Excello, 1994)
Good Time Blues: Harmonicas, Kazoos, Washboards & Cow-Bells 🦴🦴🦴 (Columbia, 1990)
Got Harp If You Want It 🦴🦴🦴 (Blue Rock-'It, 1990)
Harmonica Blues 🦴🦴🦴 (Yazoo, 1991)
Harmonica Blues Kings 🦴🦴🦴🦴 (Delmark, 1986)
Harmonica Blues, Vol. 1: West Coast Wailers 🦴🦴🦴 (Parisifal, 1996)
Harmonica Masters 🦴🦴🦴🦴 (Yazoo, 1996)
Harp Attack 🦴🦴🦴 (Alligator, 1991)
Low Blows: An Anthology of Chicago Harmonica Blues 🦴🦴🦴🦴 (Rooster Blues, 1994)
West Coast Wailers 🦴🦴🦴 (Double Trouble, 1997)

The Ladies

Antone's Women 🦴🦴🦴 (Antone's, 1992)
Blue Ladies 🦴🦴🦴🦴 (Memphis Archives, 1995)
Chicago's Finest Blues Ladies 🦴🦴🦴 (Wolf, 1995)
FemFest, 1994 🦴🦴🦴 (Stanhope House, 1995)
Four Women Blues 🦴🦴🦴 (RCA, 1997)
Mississippi Girls 🦴🦴🦴🦴 (Story of Blues, 1991)
Roll Over, Ms. Beethoven 🦴🦴🦴 (Prestige, 1995)
The Soul of Texas Blueswomen 🦴🦴🦴 (Collectables, 1991)
Texas Blues Women 🦴🦴🦴🦴 (Topcat, 1996)
Women of Blue Chicago 🦴🦴🦴 (Delmark, 1996)

New Orleans

Best of Louisiana Music 🦴🦴🦴 (Rounder, 1993)
Best of New Orleans R&B 🦴🦴🦴🦴 (Rhino, 1988)
Carnival Time 🦴🦴🦴🦴 (Rounder, 1988)
Chess New Orleans 🦴🦴🦴 (MCA/Chess, 1995)
Creole Kings of New Orleans 🦴🦴🦴🦴 (Specialty, 1993)
Crescent City Soul 🦴🦴🦴 (EMI, 1996)
Jazz and Heritage Festival, 1976 🦴🦴🦴 (Rhino, 1989)
Keys to the Crescent City 🦴🦴🦴 (Rounder, 1991)
Louisiana Piano Rhythms 🦴🦴🦴🦴 (Rhino/Tomato, 1993)
Louisiana Spice 🦴🦴🦴 (Rounder, 1995)
The Mardi Gras Indians Super Sunday Showdown 🦴🦴🦴🦴 (Rounder, 1992)
Mardi Gras Party 🦴🦴🦴 (Rounder, 1991)
New Orleans Party Classics 🦴🦴🦴🦴 (Rhino, 1992)
Night Train to New Orleans 🦴🦴🦴 (Night Train, 1996)
The Soul of New Orleans 🦴🦴🦴🦴 (Charly, 1996)
The Ultimate Session: Crescent City Gold 🦴🦴🦴 (Windham Hill, 1994)
We Got a Party: The Best of Ronn, Vol. 1 🦴🦴🦴🦴 (Rounder, 1988)

Piano

Best of Piano Blues 🦴🦴🦴🦴 (Wolf, 1995)
Blue Ivory 🦴🦴🦴 (Blind Pig, 1991)
Blues Piano Orgy 🦴🦴🦴 (Delmark, 1996)
Chicago Piano from Cobra & Job 🦴🦴🦴🦴 (Paula, 1991)
15 Piano and Blues & Boogie Classics 🦴🦴🦴 (Arhoolie, 1997)

57 Diff'rent Kind of Blues 🦴🦴🦴 (Piano Mania, 1996)
Great Boogie Woogie News 🦴🦴🦴 (Document, 1995)
Juke Joint Jump: A Boogie Woogie Celebration 🦴🦴🦴🦴 (Columbia, 1996)
Legends of Boogie Woogie 🦴🦴🦴🦴 (Specialty, 1992)
Piano Night at Tipitina's, 1994 🦴🦴🦴 (Overture, 1995)
Piano Night at Tipitina's, 1995 🦴🦴🦴 (Overture, 1996)

R&B

The '50s Juke Joint Blues 🦴🦴🦴 (Flair/Virgin, 1995)
The '50s R&B Vocal Groups 🦴🦴🦴 (Flair/Virgin, 1995)
Juke Box R&B 🦴🦴🦴 (Flair/Virgin, 1995)
Master King Series 🦴🦴🦴🦴 (Rhino, 1993)
R&B Confidential No. 1 🦴🦴🦴 (Flair/Virgin, 1995)
Rock Before Elvis 🦴🦴🦴🦴 (Hoy Hoy, 1993)

Record Label Collections

Abco Records Chicago 🦴🦴🦴 (Wolf, 1995)
All Night They Play the Blues 🦴🦴🦴🦴 (Specialty, 1992)
The Alligator Records 20th Anniversary Collection 🦴🦴🦴🦴 (Alligator, 1991)
The Alligator Records 20th Anniversary Tour 🦴🦴🦴🦴 (Alligator, 1993)
Alligator 25th Anniversary Collection 🦴🦴🦴🦴 (Alligator, 1996)
Antone's 10th Anniversary Anthology, Vol. 1 🦴🦴🦴 (Antone's, 1986)
Antone's 20th Anniversary Collection 🦴🦴🦴🦴 (Discovery, 1996)
The Best of Duke-Peacock Blues 🦴🦴🦴🦴 (MCA, 1992)
The Best of Excello Records 🦴🦴🦴🦴 (Excello, 1994)
The Best of Fat Possum 🦴🦴🦴🦴 (Fat Possum/Capricorn, 1997)
Black Top Blues Vocal Dynamite 🦴🦴🦴 (Black Top, 1995)
Black Top Blues-a-Rama, Vol. 1–7 🦴🦴🦴 (Black Top, 1990)
Black Top Instrumental Dynamite 🦴🦴🦴 (Black Top, 1996)
Blind Pig 20th Anniversary Collection 🦴🦴🦴🦴 (Blind Pig, 1997)
Blue Flames: A Sun Blues Collection 🦴🦴🦴 (Rhino, 1990)
Blues Before Sunrise 🦴🦴🦴 (Delmark, 1997)

Blues Cocktail Party! (Black Top, 1981)

Blues Costume Party (Black Top, 1995)

Blues Deluxe (Alligator, 1989)

Blues from the Dolphins of Hollywood (Specialty, 1991)

Blues Guitar Greats (Delmark, 1996)

Blues Hangover: Excello Blues Rarities (AVI/Excello, 1995)

Blues on a Fuse (Sequel, 1993)

The Bluesville Years Vol. 1–10 (Prestige/Bluesville, 1996)

Bringing You the Best in Blues (Antone's, 1989)

Chess Blues Classics 1947–1956 (MCA/Chess, 1997)

Chess Blues Classics 1957–1967 (MCA/Chess, 1997)

Deep Blue: 25 Years of Blues On Rounder (Rounder, 1995)

Dark Clouds Rollin; Excello Swamp Blues Classics (AVI/Excello, 1995)

Duke-Peacocks' Greatest Hits (MCA, 1992)

Earwig 16th Anniversary Sampler (Earwig, 1995)

Elko Blues (Wolf, 1995)

EveJim's Collector Edition (EveJim, 1996)

Evidence Blues Sampler One and Two (Evidence, 1993)

Excello Records, Vol. 1 & 2 (Rhino, 1990)

Excello Vocal Groups (AVI/Excello, 1995)

40th Anniversary Blues (Delmark, 1993)

The Great Tomato Blues Package (Tomato, 1989)

Hi Times: The Hi Records R&B Years (Hi/Right Stuff, 1995)

Jubilee & Josie R&B Vocal Groups (Sequel, 1996)

Jubilee Jezebels (Sequel, 1996)

Jumpin' and Jivin' (Specialty, 1997)

Jumpin' at Jubilee (Sequel, 1995)

King All Stars (Ichiban, 1991)

Legends of Jump Blues (Specialty, 1994)

Motown's Blue Evolution (Motown, 1996)

Prime Chops (Blind Pig, 1990)

Saxophony, Jubilee Honkers and Shouters (Sequel, 1995)

Shout, Brother, Shout: 1950s R&B from the Trumpet Records Label (Alligator, 1994)

Shouting the Blues (Specialty, 1992)

The Stax Blues Brothers (Stax, 1988)

Superblues: All Time Classic Blues Hits (Stax, 1991)

Testament Records Sampler (Testament/HighTone, 1995)

This Is Blues: JSP Sampler (JSP, 1992)

The Tomato Delta Blues Package (Tomato, 1993)

Too Hot For Me (JSP, 1997)

20 Years of Stony Plain (Stony Plain, 1996)

Up Jumped the Blues (JSP, 1997)

Regional

Alabama Blues Showcase (Vent, 1995)

Beale Street Get Down (Prestige, 1995)

Best of Kansas City (K-Tel, 1994)

Blues Blue, Blues White (Prestige, 1995)

Blues, Sweet Carolina Blues (Prestige, 1995)

Gulf Coast Blues (Black Top, 1990)

Hard Times: L.A. Blues Anthology (Black Magic, 1991)

In the Key of Blues (Prestige, 1995)

Iowa Blues, Vol. 3 (Hot Fudge, 1997)

Jackson Blues (Yazoo, 1991)

Kansas City Blues (Red Hot, 1994)

Memphis Blues Caravan, Vol. 1 & 2 (Memphis Archives, 1994)

Memphis Country Blues (Memphis Archives, 1994)

Memphis Masters (Yazoo, 1994)

Memphis Town (Memphis Archives, 1994)

More Bay Area Blues (Taxim, 1997)

Motor City Blues at the Ann Arbor Festival (Schoolkids, 1994)

St. Louis Town (Yazoo, 1991)

Southern Journey, Vol. 1–10 (Rounder, 1997)

Uptown Down South (AVI/Excello, 1995)

Virginia Traditions: Western Piedmont Blues (Global Village)

Sex and Booze

Booze and Blues (Columbia, 1996)

The Copulatin' Blues Compact Disc (Stash, 1976)

If It Ain't a Hit (Zu-Zazz, 1990)

Raunchy Business: Hot Nuts and Lollipops (Columbia, 1991)

Risky Blues (King, 1971)

Risque Rhythm: Nasty 50s R&B (Rhino, 1991)

Them Dirty Blues (Jass, 1989)

Slide Guitar

(Almost) Everybody Slides (Ryko, 1993)

The Best of Slide Guitar (Wolf, 1995)

Sacred Steel: Traditional Sacred African-American Steel Guitar Music in Florida (Arhoolie, 1997)

Slide Guitar Blues (Icehouse, 1995)

The Slide Guitar: Bottles, Knives & Steel (Columbia, 1990)

The Slide Guitar Bottles, Knives & Steel, Vol. 2 (Columbia, 1993)

Slidin' Some Slide (Bullseye Blues, 1993)

Texas Blues

Hot Rhythm and Blues Texas Style (Topcat, 1992)

Ruff Stuff: The Roots of Texas Blues Guitar (Catfish, 1993)

Texas Blues: Bill Quinn's Gold Star Recordings (Arhoolie, 1992)

Texas Blues Party (Wolf, 1995)

Texas Blues Party (Wolf, 1995)

Texas Bluesmen (Topcat, 1993)

Texas Guitar Blues (Capitol, 1995)

Texas Music, Vol. 1: Postwar Blues Combos (Rhino, 1995)

Tributes

Paint It Blue: Songs of the Rolling Stones (House of Blues, 1997)

Songs of Janis Joplin (House of Blues, 1997)

Til the Night Is Gone: Tribute to Doc Pomus (Forward, 1995)

Tribute to Magic Sam (Evidence, 1997)

Tribute to Elmore James (Icehouse, 1997)

A Tribute to Stevie Ray Vaughan (Epic, 1996)

Z Zelebration: A Tribute to the Late Great Z.Z. Hill (Malaco, 1995) musicHound blues

Indexes

Band Member Index

Producer Index

Roots Index

Category Index

4
6
3

The Producer Index compiles the albums in Music-Hound Blues that have a producer noted for them. (These are usually recommended discs, but we like to credit the producer for albums in the "What to Avoid" section, too, so a few of these could be downright dogs!) Under each producer's name is the name of the artist or group's entry (or entries) in which the album can be found, followed by the album title. If an album is produced by more than one individual/group, the album name will be listed separately under the names of each of the individuals/groups who has a hand in producing it.

Herb Abramson
Otis Blackwell, *All Shook Up*
Louisiana Red, *Louisiana Red Sings the Blues*
Blind Willie McTell, *Atlanta Twelve String*

Mark Abramson
Michael Bloomfield, *East-West*

Paul Butterfield Blues Band, *East-West*

Joe Adams
Ray Charles, *Anthology*
Ray Charles, *Modern Sounds in Country and Western Music*

Terry Adams
Johnnie Johnson, *Johnnie B. Bad*

George Adins
Lonnie Brooks, *Live at Pepper's 1968*

Peter Afterman
Elvis Presley, *Honeymoon in Vegas*

Chuck Ainlay
Mark Knopfler, *Golden Heart*
Mark Knopfler, *On the Night*

Chris Albertson
Lonnie Johnson, *Blues and Ballads*
Lonnie Johnson, *Blues, Ballads & Jumpin' Jazz*
Little Brother Montgomery, *Chicago's Living Legends—Piano, Vocal & Band*

Kavichandran Alexander
Ry Cooder, *A Meeting by the River*
Taj Mahal, *Mumtaz Mahal*

Leonard Allen
Robert Nighthawk, *Bricks in My Pillow*

Allman Brothers Band
The Allman Brothers Band, *Brothers and Sisters*

Jeff "Red" Alperin
Paul Oscher, *The Deep Blues of Paul Oscher*

Billy Altman
Arthur "Big Boy" Crudup, *That's All Right Mama*
Lonnie Johnson, *He's a Jelly Roll Baker*

Dave Alvin
Dave Alvin, *Blue Blvd.*
Dave Alvin, *Museum of Heart*
Dave Alvin, *Tulare Dust: A Songwriters' Tribute to Merle Haggard*
Candye Kane, *Diva la Grande*

Phil Alvin
Phil Alvin, *County Fair 2000*
Phil Alvin, *Un "Sung Stories"*

Buzz Amato
Chick Willis, *Back to the Blues*

Roy Ames
Goree Carter, *Unsung Hero*

Clifford Antone
James Cotton, *Mighty Long Time*

Pinetop Perkins, *Pinetop's Boogie Woogie*

Michael Appleton
Mark Knopfler, *Live at the BBC*

Billy Boy Arnold
Billy Boy Arnold, *Eldorado Cadillac*

Hiroshi Asada
Otis Clay, *Soul Man—Live in Japan*

Moses Asch
Leadbelly, *The Original Asch Recordings*

James Austin
Mose Allison, *Allison Wonderland: The Mose Allison Anthology*
Roy Brown, *Good Rockin' Tonight*
Clifton Chenier, *Zydeco Dynamite*
Wynonie Harris, *Bloodshot Eyes: The Best of Wynonie Harris*
John Lee Hooker, *The Ultimate Collection*
Elmore James, *The Sky Is Crying: The History of Elmore James*
Freddie King, *Hideaway: The Best of Freddie King*
Professor Longhair, *The Professor Longhair Anthology*

Black Music Review Editors
Lurrie Bell, *The Blues Caravan Live at Pit Inn*

Otis Blackwell
Otis Blackwell, *All Shook Up*

Dedrick Blanchard
Lee "Shot" Williams, *I Like Your Style*

Allan Blazek
J. Geils Band/Bluestime, *Blow Your Face Out*
J. Geils Band/Bluestime, *Hotline*

Adam Block
Charles Brown, *Driftin' Blues: The Best of Charles Brown*

Rory Block
Rory Block, *The Early Tapes 1975/1976*
Rory Block, *High Heeled Blues*

Mike Bloomfield
Otis Rush, *Mourning in the Morning*

Niko Bolas
Willie Dixon, *Willie Jones*

Larry Borenstein
Isidore "Tuts" Washington, *The Larry Borenstein Collection — Vol. 3*

Earl Bostic
Pleasant "Cousin Joe" Joseph, *Pleasant Joseph: The Complete Recordings, 1945–47*

Joe Boyd
James Booker, *Junco Partner*
Maria Muldaur, *Maria Muldaur*
Maria Muldaur, *Pottery Pie*
Maria Muldaur, *Waitress in a Donut Shop*

Doyle Bramhall
Doyle Bramhall, *Bird Nest on the Ground*

Delaney Bramlett
Eric Clapton, *Eric Clapton*

Fred Breitberg
Sugar Blue, *Blue Blazes*
Sugar Blue, *In Your Eyes*

Andy Breslau
The Holmes Brothers, *In the Spirit*
The Holmes Brothers, *Lotto Land*
The Holmes Brothers, *Promised Land*

Frank Briggs
Bukka White, *The Complete Bukka White*

Craig Brock
Paul DeLay, *Ocean of Tears*

Steve Brodie
John Ellison, *The Very Best of John Ellison & the Soul Brothers Six*

Bruce Bromberg
Dave Alvin, *Blue Blvd.*
Dave Alvin, *Museum of Heart*
Robert Cray, *Bad Influence*
Robert Cray, *Strong Persuader*
Ted Hawkins, *Happy Hour*
Ted Hawkins, *Watch Your Step*
Lonesome Sundown, *Been Gone Too Long*
Lonesome Sundown, *From La. to L.A.*
Joe Louis Walker, *Live at Slim's, Vol. One*
Joe Louis Walker, *Volume Two*
Phillip Walker, *The Bottom of the Top*
Phillip Walker, *Someday You'll Have These Blues*

Lonnie Brooks
Lonnie Brooks, *Turn on the Night*
Lonnie Brooks, *Wound Up Tight*

Michael Brooks
Lonnie Johnson, *Giants of Jazz: The Guitarists*
Bessie Smith, *Bessie Smith*

John Broven
Buddy Johnson, *Walk 'Em*

Michael Brovsky
Dave Van Ronk, *Songs for Aging Children*

Clarence Brown
Clarence "Gatemouth" Brown, *The Original Peacock Recordings*

James Brown
James Brown, *Live at the Apollo, 1962*
James Brown, *Messing with the Blues*
James Brown, *Soul Pride: The Instrumentals 1960–69*

Joe Brown
Little Brother Montgomery, *Unissued Chicago Blues of the 1950s from Cobra and JOB*

Sarah Brown
Lavelle White, *Miss Lavelle*

Terry Brown
Sammy Price, *Barrelhouse and Blues*

William Brown
Lynn White, *At Her Best*

Denny Bruce
Marcia Ball, *Soulful Dress*

Stephen Bruton
Sue Foley, *Big City Blues*

Roy Buchanan
Roy Buchanan, *When a Guitar Plays the Blues*

Norton Buffalo
Norton Buffalo, *R&B*
Norton Buffalo, *Travellin' Tracks*
Roy Rogers, *Travellin' Tracks*

Mike Bullock
Jonny Lang, *Smokin'*

Samuel Burckhardt
Robert Covington, *Chicago Jump*
Sunnyland Slim, *Chicago Jump*

Solomon Burke
Solomon Burke, *Soul Alive!*

Malcolm Burn
Chris Whitley, *Living with the Law*

Lillian Burnett
Eddie Shaw, *Have Blues Will Travel*

Pat Burnett
Phil Alvin, *Un "Sung Stories"*

T-Bone Burnett
Delbert McClinton, *Delbert & Glen*
Gillian Welch, *Revival*

Aron Burton
Aron Burton, *Past, Present & Future*
Aron Burton, *Usual Dangerous Guy*

Dominique Buscail
Sugar Blue, *Crossroads*

Henry Bush
Albert King, *I'll Play the Blues for You*
Little Milton, *What It Is*

Paul Butterfield
Paul Butterfield's Better Days, *Better Days*
Paul Butterfield's Better Days, *It All Comes Back*

Jean Buzelin
Memphis Minnie, *Me and My Chauffeur 1935–46*
Rosetta Tharpe, *Sister Rosetta Tharpe*

Joseph Byrd
Ry Cooder, *Jazz*

Ozzie Cadena
Big Maybelle, *Blues, Candy & Big Maybelle*

Chris Cain
Chris Cain, *Late Night City Blues*

Jorge Calderon
Terry Evans, *Puttin' It Down*

J.J. Cale
John Hammond Jr., *Trouble No More*

Stephen Calt
Thomas A. Dorsey, *Come on Mama Do That Dance*

Lonnie Johnson, *Stompin' at the Penny*

Taj Mahal, *World Music*

Blind Willie McTell, *The Definitive Blind Willie McTell*

Memphis Minnie, *Hoodoo Lady (1933–37)*

Bessie Smith, *The Complete Recordings, Vol. 1*

Bessie Smith, *The Complete Recordings, Vol. 2*

Bessie Smith, *The Complete Recordings, Vol. 3*

Bessie Smith, *The Complete Recordings, Vol. 4*

Bessie Smith, *The Complete Recordings, Vol. 5: The Final Chapter*

Chuck Colbert Jr.
Cash McCall, *Omega Man*

Bryan Cole
Nappy Brown, *Aw! Shucks*

Jimmy Dawkins, *B Phur Real*

Luther "Houserocker" Johnson, *Takin' a Bite Outta the Blues*

Jerry McCain, *Struttin' My Stuff*

Francine Reed, *I Want You to Love Me*

Drink Small, *Round Two*

Chick Willis, *Back to the Blues*

Gary B.B. Coleman
Buster Benton, *Money's the Name of the Game*

Buster Benton, *Why Me*

Peter Coleman
Mike Henderson, *First Blood*

Steve Coleridge
Henry Gray, *Don't Start That Stuff*

Phil Collins
Eric Clapton, *August*

Eric Clapton, *Behind the Sun*

Joanna Connor
Joanna Connor, *Believe It!*

Joanna Connor, *Big Girl Blues*

Joachim Cooder
Ry Cooder, *Music by Ry Cooder*

Ry Cooder
Ry Cooder, *Bop Till You Drop*

Ry Cooder, *Chicken Skin Music*

Ry Cooder, *Crossroads*

Ry Cooder, *Get Rhythm*

Ry Cooder, *Jazz*

Ry Cooder, *Johnny Handsome*

Ry Cooder, *The Long Riders*

Ry Cooder, *Music by Ry Cooder*

Ry Cooder, *Paris, Texas*

Ry Cooder, *Ry Cooder*

Kent Cooper
Lefty Dizz, *Walked All Night Long*

Louisiana Red, *The Blues Purity of Louisiana Red*

Sugar Blue, *Too Wet to Plow*

James Cotton
James Cotton, *High Compression*

Tommy Couch
Bobby "Blue" Bland, *Sad Street*

Z.Z. Hill, *Blues Master*

Z.Z. Hill, *Down Home Blues*

Z.Z. Hill, *In Memorium*

Little Milton, *I'm a Gambler*

Mississippi Fred McDowell, *I Do Not Play No Rock 'n' Roll*

McKinley Mitchell, *The Complete Malaco Recordings*

John Court
Michael Bloomfield, *A Long Time Coming*

Paul Butterfield Blues Band, *In My Own Dream*

Paul Butterfield Blues Band, *The Resurrection of Pigboy Crabshaw*

Peter Crawford
Robert Covington, *Blues in the Night*

Robert Cray
Robert Cray, *Shame + Sin*

Robert Cray, *Some Rainy Morning*

Robert Cray, *Sweet Potato Pie*

Steve Cropper
Cate Brothers, *Cate Brothers*

Cate Brothers, *In One Eye and out the Other*

Joe Louis Walker, *Blues of the Month Club*

Michael Cuscuna
Charles Brown, *The Complete Aladdin Recordings of Charles Brown*

Buddy Guy, *Buddy Guy & Junior Wells Play the Blues*

Bonnie Raitt, *Give It Up*

Steve Cushing
Lurrie Bell, *Mercurial Son*

Jimmie Lee Robinson, *Lonely Traveller*

Peter Dammann
Paul DeLay, *Take It from the Turnaround*

Ike Darby
Lynn White, *At Her Best*

Debbie Davies
Debbie Davies, *Loose Tonight*

Debbie Davies, *Picture This*

CeDell Davis
CeDell Davis, *The Best of CeDell Davis*

Don Davis
Robert Ward, *Hot Stuff*

Guy Davis
Guy Davis, *Call Down the Thunder*

Quint Davis
Professor Longhair, *House Party New Orleans Style*

Professor Longhair, *Mardi Gras in Baton Rouge*

Jimmy Dawkins
Jimmy Dawkins, *Feel the Blues*

Jimmy Dawkins, *Kant Sheck Dees Bluze*

Jimmy Dawkins Band
Jimmy Dawkins, *Blisterstring*

Pat Dawson
George "Mojo" Buford, *Still Blowin' Strong*

Percy Strother, *A Good Woman Is Hard to Find*

Norman Dayron
Michael Bloomfield, *Living in the Fast Lane*

Maxwell Street Jimmy Davis, *Chicago Breakdown*

Maxwell Street Jimmy Davis, *Maxwell Street Jimmy Davis*

Maxwell Street Jimmy Davis, *Rare Blues*

Johnny Jones, *Johnny Jones with Billy Boy Arnold*

Robert Nighthawk, *Masters of Modern Blues—Robert Nighthawk and Houston Stackhouse*

Robert Nighthawk, *Robert Nighthawk—Live on Maxwell Street*

Robert Pete Williams, *Louisiana Blues*

Jerry Del Giudice
Carey Bell, *Mellow Down Easy*

Eddie C. Campbell, *That's When I Know*

Eddy Clearwater, *Help Yourself*

Joanna Connor, *Believe It!*

Lester "Big Daddy" Kinsey, *Heart Attack*

Magic Slim, *Scufflin'*

John Mooney, *Comin' Your Way*

Studebaker John, *Too Tough*

Hubert Sumlin, *Heart and Soul*

Roosevelt Sykes, *The Original Honeydripper*

Jimmy Thackery, *Empty Arms Motel*

Charles Delaney
Jimmy Dawkins, *Jimmy Dawkins*

Delaware Destroyers
George Thorogood & the Destroyers, *The Baddest of George Thorogood & the Destroyers*

Paul DeLay
Paul DeLay, *Take It from the Turnaround*

Paul DeLay Band
Paul DeLay, *Ocean of Tears*

David Denny
Norton Buffalo, *The Legendary Sy Klopps Blues Band: Walter Ego*

Ed Denson
Skip James, *She Lyin'*
Bukka White, *1963 Isn't 1962*
Bukka White, *Legacy of the Blues*

Charles Derrick
Drink Small, *The Blues Doctor*

Rick Derringer
Johnny Winter, *Johnny Winter and . . . Live*
Johnny Winter, *Still Alive and Well*

Jim Dickinson
Ry Cooder, *Into the Purple Valley*
G. Love & Special Sauce, *Coast to Coast Motel*

Bo Diddley
Bo Diddley, *Bo Diddley: His Best*

Scott Dirks
Billy Boy Arnold, *Eldorado Cadillac*
Carey Bell, *Deep Down*
Jimmy Burns, *Leaving Here Walking*

Disques Black & Blue
Buster Benton, *Blues at the Top*
Eddy Clearwater, *Blues Hang Out*
Jimmy Johnson, *Bar Room Preacher*
Johnny Littlejohn, *Blues at the Top*
Johnny Littlejohn, *Sweet Little Angel*
Hubert Sumlin, *My Guitar and Me*

Carlo Ditta
Rockie Charles, *Born for You*
Guitar Slim Jr., *The Story of My Life*

Floyd Dixon
Floyd Dixon, *Hitsville Look Out: Here's Mr. Magnificent*

Floyd Dixon, *Mr. Magnificent Strikes Again*

Willie Dixon
Charles Brown, *Southern Blues 1957–63*
Willie Dixon, *The Chess Box*
Henry Gray, *Ain't Gonna Be Your Dog*
Henry Gray, *Howlin' Wolf—The Genuine Article*
Howlin' Wolf, *Ain't Gonna Be Your Dog*
Howlin' Wolf, *Howlin' Wolf: His Best*
Little Walter, *Essential Little Walter*
Johnny Littlejohn, *Chicago Blues Stars*
Koko Taylor, *Koko Taylor*
Sonny Boy Williamson II, *Sonny Boy Williamson: His Best*
Johnny Young, *Chicago Blues*
Mighty Joe Young, *Chickenheads*

Maurice Dollison
Otis Clay, *I'm Satisfied*

John Dolphin
Floyd Dixon, *Marshall Texas Is My Home*

The Dominos
Derek & the Dominos, *Layla and Other Assorted Love Songs*

Neil Dorfsman
Mark Knopfler, *On the Night*

Joel Dorn
Mose Allison, *Allison Wonderland: The Mose Allison Anthology*
The Allman Brothers Band, *Beginnings*
Billie Holiday, *The Complete Commodore Recordings*
Roomful of Blues, *First Album*
Roomful of Blues, *Two Classic Albums: Roomful of Blues with Joe Turner/with Eddie "Cleanhead" Vinson*

Double Trouble
Stevie Ray Vaughan, *In Step*
Stevie Ray Vaughan, *Live Alive*

Stevie Ray Vaughan, *Soul to Soul*
Stevie Ray Vaughan, *Texas Flood*

Alan Douglas
George "Mojo" Buford, *Luther Georgia Boy Snake Johnson: The Muddy Waters Blues Band*
Jimi Hendrix, *Voodoo Soup*
Albert King, *Red House*

Jerry Douglas
Roy Book Binder, *Bookeroo!*

Tom Dowd
The Allman Brothers Band, *At Fillmore East*
The Allman Brothers Band, *Beginnings*
The Allman Brothers Band, *Eat a Peach*
The Allman Brothers Band, *An Evening With, First Set*
The Allman Brothers Band, *Where It All Begins*
Cate Brothers, *Fire on the Tracks*
Eric Clapton, *461 Ocean Boulevard*
Eric Clapton, *Layla and Other Assorted Love Songs*
Derek & the Dominos, *Layla and Other Assorted Love Songs*
Ronnie Earl, *The Colour of Love*
Tinsley Ellis, *Fire It Up*
Buddy Guy, *Buddy Guy & Junior Wells Play the Blues*

Dan Doyle
Johnny Copeland, *Texas Twister*
Johnny Copeland, *When the Rain Starts Fallin'*

Pete Drake
Tracy Nelson, *Tracy Nelson Country*

Frank Driggs
Robert Johnson, *King of the Delta Blues Singers*
Robert Johnson, *Robert Johnson: The Complete Recordings*

Tim Duffy
Guitar Gabriel, *Deep in the South*
Guitar Gabriel, *Do You Know What It Means to Have a Friend—Toot Blues*
Guitar Gabriel, *Guitar Gabriel, Vol. 1*
Guitar Gabriel, *A Living Past*

Henri Dufresne
Sammy Price, *King of Boogie Woogie*

Dust Brothers
Beck, *Odelay*

Paul Duvive
Clarence Spady, *Charlie Spand (1940)/Big Maceo (1941–52)*

Omar Dykes
Omar Dykes, *Courts of Lulu*
Omar Dykes, *Southern Style*
Omar Dykes, *World Wide Open*

Bob Dylan
Bob Dylan, *Shot of Love*

C. Michael Dysinger
Tracy Nelson, *Move On*

Snooks Eaglin
Snooks Eaglin, *Live in Japan*

Ronnie Earl
Ronnie Earl, *Blues Guitar Virtuoso Live in Europe*
Ronnie Earl, *Language of the Soul*
Hubert Sumlin, *Hubert Sumlin's Blues Party*

Lars Edegran
Little "Sonny" Jones, *New Orleans Jems*

Esmond Edwards
Mose Allison, *Middle Class White Boy*
Chuck Berry, *The London Chuck Berry Sessions*
Eddie Kirkland, *It's the Blues Man!*
Little Brother Montgomery, *Tasty Blues*

Gary Edwards
Tommy Ridgley, *How Long*

Honeyboy Edwards
David "Honeyboy" Edwards,
I've Been Around

Kevin Eggers
Fats Domino, *Antoine "Fats"
Domino*

Big Chief Ellis
Big Chief Ellis, *Big Chief Ellis
Featuring Tarheel Slim*

Ray Ellis
Billie Holiday, *Lady in Satin*
Billie Holiday, *Last Recordings*

Ahmet Ertegun
LaVern Baker, *Blues Ballads*
LaVern Baker, *Blues Side of
Rock 'n' Roll*
LaVern Baker, *Precious Memo-
ries*
LaVern Baker, *Soul on Fire*
Ray Charles, *The Best of Ray
Charles: The Atlantic
Years*
Floyd Dixon, *Marshall Texas Is
My Home*
Buddy Guy, *Buddy Guy & Ju-
nior Wells Play the Blues*
Blind Willie McTell, *Atlanta
Twelve String*

Nesuhi Ertegun
LaVern Baker, *LaVern Baker
Sings Bessie Smith*
Ray Charles, *The Best of Ray
Charles: The Atlantic
Years*
Ray Charles, *Live*
Big Joe Turner, *Big Joe Rides
Again*
Big Joe Turner, *The Boss of the
Blues*

Rick Estrin
Little Charlie & the Nightcats,
The Big Break
Little Charlie & the Nightcats,
Straight Up

David Evans
Jessie Mae Hemphill, *Feelin'
Good*
Jessie Mae Hemphill, *She-
Wolf*
Robert Wilkins, *Remember Me*

Terry Evans
Terry Evans, *Puttin' It Down*

Hans W. Ewert
Henry Gray, *They Call Me Little
Henry*

John Fahey
Skip James, *She Lyin'*
Bukka White, *1963 Isn't 1962*
Bukka White, *Legacy of the
Blues*

Michael Falzarano
Hot Tuna, *Classic Hot Tuna
Acoustic*
Hot Tuna, *Classic Hot Tuna
Electric*

Georgie Fame
Mose Allison, *Tell Me Something*

Rachel Faro
Satan & Adam, *Harlem Blues*

Ricky Fataar
Boz Scaggs, *Some Change*

Leonard Feather
Pleasant "Cousin Joe" Joseph,
*Pleasant Joseph: The
Complete Recordings,
1945–47*

Sid Feller
Ray Charles, *Anthology*
Ray Charles, *Modern Sounds
in Country and Western
Music*

Ron Ferminack
Isidore "Tuts" Washington,
*The Best of Smiley Lewis,
I Hear You Knockin'*

Joe Ferry
Guy Davis, *Call Down the
Thunder*

R.S. Field
Sonny Landreth, *Outward
Bound*
Sonny Landreth, *South of I-10*
John Mayall, *A Sense of Place*

Suzy Fink
Buddy Scott, *Bad Avenue*

Guy Fletcher
Mark Knopfler, *Missing . . .
Presumed Having a Good
Time*
Mark Knopfler, *On the Night*

Bruce Flett
Bluebirds, *Swamp Stomp*

Buddy Flett
Bluebirds, *South from Mem-
phis*
Bluebirds, *Swamp Stomp*

Hannes Folterbauer
L.V. Banks, *Teddy Bear*
Blind Blake, *Blind Blake: The
Accompanist*
Willie Kent, *Live at B.L.U.E.S.*
Johnny Littlejohn, *Johnny Lit-
tlejohn's Blues Party*
John Primer, *Poor Man Blues:
Chicago Blues Session
Volume 6*

Jon Foose
Long John Hunter, *Border
Town Legend*

Pat Ford
Chris Cain, *Somewhere Along
the Way*
Charles Ford Band/Ford Blues
Band/Robben Ford, *Ford
and Friends*
Charles Ford Band/Ford Blues
Band/Robben Ford,
*Luther Tucker and the
Ford Blues Band*
Charlie Musselwhite, *Ace of
Harps*

Rob Fraboni
John Mooney, *Against the Wall*

Michael Robert Frank
The Aces, *Louis Myers—Tell
My Story Movin'*
Aron Burton, *Past, Present &
Future*
Lester Davenport, *When the
Blues Hit You*
Jimmy Dawkins, *Kant Sheck
Dees Bluze*
David "Honeyboy" Edwards,
Delta Bluesman
H-Bomb Ferguson, *Wiggin'
Out*
Frank Frost & Sam Carr, *Mid-
night Prowler*
Big Jack Johnson, *Daddy,
When Is Mama Comin'
Home?*
Big Jack Johnson, *The Oil Man*
Vance Kelly, *Good Candy*

Little Brother Montgomery, *At
Home*
John Primer, *Stuff You Got to
Watch*

Michael Freeman
Eddy Clearwater, *Help Your-
self*
Deborah Coleman, *I Can't
Lose*
Magic Slim, *Scufflin'*

Max Freitag
Richard Berry, *The Best of Flip
Records, Vols. 1–3*

Steve Freund
Henry Gray, *Lucky Man*
Andrew "B.B." Odom, *Goin' to
California*
Snooky Pryor, *Snooky Pryor*

Glenn Frey
Lou Ann Barton, *Old Enough*

Barry Friedman
Michael Bloomfield, *East-West*
Paul Butterfield Blues Band,
East-West

Bart Friedman
Johnny Young, *Fat Mandolin*

Frank Frost
Frank Frost & Sam Carr, *Midnight Prowler*

Aaron Fuchs
James Booker, *Gonzo: More
Than All the 45s*

Lowell Fulson
Lowell Fulson, *Hung Down
Head*

Anson Funderburgh
Pat Boyack, *Armed and Dan-
gerous*
Anson Funderburgh & the
Rockets Featuring Sam
Myers, *My Love Is Here to
Stay*
Anson Funderburgh & the
Rockets Featuring Sam
Myers, *Rack 'Em Up*
Anson Funderburgh & the
Rockets Featuring Sam
Myers, *Sins*
Anson Funderburgh & the
Rockets Featuring Sam

Tracy Nelson, *Sweet Soul Music*

Allen Jones
Albert King, *I'll Play the Blues for You*

Casey Jones
Albert Collins, *Frostbite*

Paul Jones
Paul DeLay, *Burnin'*

Tutu Jones
Paul "Wine" Jones, *I'm for Real*

Ernst Mikael Jorgensen
Elvis Presley, *Command Performances: The Essential '60s Masters II*
Elvis Presley, *Elvis—The King of Rock 'n' Roll—The Complete '50s Masters*
Elvis Presley, *From Nashville to Memphis: The Essential '60s Masters I*
Elvis Presley, *Live a Little, Love a Little/Charro!/The Trouble with Girls/Change of Habit*
Elvis Presley, *Walk a Mile in My Shoes: The Essential '70s Masters*

Seth Justman
J. Geils Band/Bluestime, *Flashback: The Best of the J. Geils Band*
J. Geils Band/Bluestime, *Freeze-Frame*
J. Geils Band/Bluestime, *Love Stinks*
J. Geils Band/Bluestime, *Showtime!*

Shel Kagen
Lightnin' Hopkins, *Swarthmore Concert*

Candye Kane
Candye Kane, *Diva la Grande*

Bruce Kaplan
Johnny Young, *Lake Michigan Ain't No River*

Mike Kappus
John Hammond Jr., *Trouble No More*

Jorma Kaukonen
Hot Tuna, *Burgers*
Hot Tuna, *First Pull Up—Then Pull Down*

Mark Kazanoff
W.C. Clark, *Heart of Gold*
W.C. Clark, *Texas Soul*
Bob Margolin, *Down in the Alley*
Bob Margolin, *My Blues & My Guitar*

Orrin Keepnews
Billie Holiday, *The Complete Commodore Recordings*
Blind Lemon Jefferson, *Blind Lemon Jefferson*
Ma Rainey, *Ma Rainey*

Ricky Keller
Nappy Brown, *Tore Up*
Tinsley Ellis, *Georgia Blue*

Vance Kelly
Vance Kelly, *Call Me*
Vance Kelly, *Joyriding on the Subway*

Bob Kempf
David Maxwell, *Maximum Blues Piano*

Don Kent
Garfield Akers, *Mississippi Masters*
Sleepy John Estes, *I Ain't Gonna Be Worried No More 1929–41*
Peg Leg Howell, *The Black Country Music of Georgia 1927–36*
Mississippi Sheiks, *Stop and Listen*

Willie Kent
Willie Kent, *Live at B.L.U.E.S.*
Johnny Littlejohn, *Johnny Littlejohn's Blues Party*

Abe Kesh
Chuck Berry, *Live at the Fillmore Auditorium*

George Kilby Jr.
Pinetop Perkins, *Portrait of a Delta Bluesman*

Chris Kimsey
Colin James, *Bad Habits*

Rolling Stones, *Flashpoint*

King Curtis
Freddie King, *Freddie King Is a Bluesmaster*
Freddie King, *My Feeling for the Blues*

Donald Kinsey
Lester "Big Daddy" Kinsey, *Edge of the City*
Kinsey Report, *Edge of the City*
Kinsey Report, *Midnight Drive*

Kinsey Family
Lester "Big Daddy" Kinsey, *Can't Let Go*
Kinsey Report, *Can't Let Go*
Kinsey Report, *Midnight Drive*

Eddie Kirkland
Eddie Kirkland, *All around the World*
Eddie Kirkland, *Front and Center*

Mark Knopfler
Mark Knopfler, *Alchemy*
Mark Knopfler, *Golden Heart*
Mark Knopfler, *Making Movies*
Mark Knopfler, *Missing . . . Presumed Having a Good Time*
Mark Knopfler, *Neck and Neck*
Mark Knopfler, *On the Night*
Mark Knopfler, *Screenplaying*

Karl Emil Knudsen
Sippie Wallace, *Women Be Wise*
Robert Pete Williams, *Blues Masters Vol. 1*

Dan Kochakian
Vann "Piano Man" Walls, *They Call Me Piano Man*

Lester Koenig
Jesse Fuller, *Jazz, Folk Songs, Spirituals & Blues*
Jesse Fuller, *San Francisco Bay Blues*

Robert Koester
Luther Allison, *Love Me Mama*
Carey Bell, *Carey Bell's Blues Harp*
Big Time Sarah, *Blues in the Year One-D-One*

Karen Carroll, *Professor Strut*
Karen Carroll, *Stock Yards Stomp*
Eddy Clearwater, *Chicago Ain't Nothin' but a Blues Band*
Jimmy Dawkins, *Fast Fingers*
Sleepy John Estes, *Broke and Hungry*
Sleepy John Estes, *Electric Sleep*
Jesse Fortune, *Fortune Tellin' Man*
Lacy Gibson, *Crying for My Baby*
J.B. Hutto, *Hawk Squat*
Pete Johnson, *Central Avenue Boogie*
Curtis Jones, *Lonesome Bedroom Blues*
Willie Kent, *Ain't It Nice*
Willie Kent, *Long Way to Ol' Miss*
Little Walter, *The Blues World of Little Walter*
Little Brother Montgomery, *Blues Piano Orgy*
Robert Nighthawk, *Bricks in My Pillow*
Barkin' Bill Smith, *Bluebird Blues*
Speckled Red, *Dirty Dozens*
Sunnyland Slim, *Blues Piano Orgy*
Roosevelt Sykes, *Gold Mine*
Roosevelt Sykes, *Hard Drivin' Blues*
Roosevelt Sykes, *Raining in My Heart*
T-Bone Walker, *I Want a Little Girl*
Junior Wells, *Hoodoo Man Blues*
Junior Wells, *On Tap*
Mighty Joe Young, *A Touch of Soul*

Al Kooper
Michael Bloomfield, *The Live Adventures of Michael Bloomfield and Al Kooper*
Michael Bloomfield, *Super Session*
Al Kooper, *Rekooperation—A Nonverbal Scenic Selection of Soul Souvenirs*

Guitar Shorty, *Get Wise to Yourself*
Guitar Shorty, *Topsy Turvy*
James Harman, *Cards on the Table*
James Harman, *Do Not Disturb*
James Harman, *Two Sides to Every Story*
Earl King, *Hard River to Cross*
Maria Muldaur, *Louisiana Love Call*
Darrell Nulisch, *Business As Usual*
Bobby Parker, *Bent out of Shape*
Bobby Parker, *Shine Me Up*
Rod Piazza, *Alphabet Blues*
Bobby Radcliff, *Black Top Bluesarama*
Bobby Radcliff, *Dresses Too Short*
Bobby Radcliff, *There's a Cold Grave in Your Way*
Bobby Radcliff, *Universal Blues*
Johnny Reno, *Born to Blow*
Tommy Ridgley, *Since the Blues Began*
Hubert Sumlin, *Hubert Sumlin's Blues Party*
Jesse Thomas, *Looking for That Woman*
Phillip Walker, *Working Girl Blues*
Robert Ward, *Fear No Evil*
Robert Ward, *Twiggs County Soul Man*
Rusty Zinn, *Sittin' and Waitin'*

Joe Scott
Bobby "Blue" Bland, *Two Steps from the Blues*

Ken Scott
Jeff Beck, *There and Back*

Nauman Scott
Jesse Thomas, *Looking for That Woman*

Son Seals
Son Seals, *Chicago Fire*
Son Seals, *Live and Burning*
Son Seals, *Live: Spontaneous Combustion*
Son Seals, *Nothing but the Truth*

Zenas Sears
Ray Charles, *The Best of Ray Charles: The Atlantic Years*
Ray Charles, *Live*

John Sebastian
Rory Block, *High Heeled Blues*

Anthony Seeger
Leadbelly, *Last Sessions*

Robert Seeman
Eddie Burns, *Detroit*
David "Honeyboy" Edwards, *White Windows*

Marshall Sehorn
Earl King, *Street Parade*

Richard Seidel
Eddie "Cleanhead" Vinson, *Blues, Boogie and Bop: The 1940s Mercury Sessions*
Dinah Washington, *First Issue: The Dinah Washington Story (The Original Recordings)*

Ivory Lee Semien
Hop Wilson, *Houston Ghetto Blues*

Roger Semon
Elvis Presley, *Command Performances: The Essential '60s Masters II*
Elvis Presley, *Elvis — The King of Rock 'n' Roll — The Complete '50s Masters*
Elvis Presley, *From Nashville to Memphis: The Essential '60s Masters I*
Elvis Presley, *Live a Little, Love a Little/Charro!/The Trouble with Girls/Change of Habit*
Elvis Presley, *Walk a Mile in My Shoes: The Essential '70s Masters*

Bob Shad
Lightnin' Hopkins, *Blues Train*
Janis Joplin/Big Brother & the Holding Company, *Big Brother & the Holding Company*

Sonny Terry & Brownie McGhee, *Hometown Blues*

Ray Shanklin
Little Johnny Taylor, *Greatest Hits*

Eddie Shaw
Eddie Shaw, *Have Blues Will Travel*

Jay Sheffield
Radio Kings, *It Ain't Easy*
Radio Kings, *Live at B.B. Kings*

Peter Shertser
Billy Boy Arnold, *Checkin' It Out*

Lonnie Shields
Lonnie Shields, *Portrait*

Johnny Shines
Johnny Shines, *Hangin' On*

Dick Shurman
Andrew Brown, *On the Case*
Roy Buchanan, *When a Guitar Plays the Blues*
Eddie C. Campbell, *King of the Jungle*
Albert Collins, *Frostbite*
Albert Collins, *Frozen Alive*
Johnny Copeland, *Showdown!*
Robert Cray, *Showdown!*
Lacy Gibson, *Switchy Titchy*
Johnny Heartsman, *The Touch*
Hip Linkchain, *Airbusters*
Fenton Robinson, *Nightflight*
Lee "Shot" Williams, *Lee "Shot" Williams Sings Big Time Blues*
Johnny Winter, *Guitar Slinger*

Ben Sidran
Mose Allison, *Tell Me Something*

Peter K. Siegel
Roy Buchanan, *Roy Buchanan*
Roy Buchanan, *Second Album*

Chris Silagyi
Dave Alvin, *Blue Blvd.*
Dave Alvin, *Museum of Heart*

Ramon Silva
Roy Buchanan, *You're Not Alone*

Eddie Silvers
Otis Clay, *That's How It Is (When You're in Love)*

Kim Simmonds
Savoy Brown, *Bring It Home*
Savoy Brown, *Looking In*
Savoy Brown, *Raw Sienna*

John Simon
Janis Joplin/Big Brother & the Holding Company, *Cheap Thrills*

Lew Simpkins
Robert Nighthawk, *Bricks in My Pillow*

Jim Simpson
Big John Wrencher, *B.J. Wrencher with Eddie Taylor & Bluehounds*

John Sinclair
Little Sonny, *Blues with a Feeling*

Patrick Sky
Mississippi John Hurt, *Today!*

Al Smith
Carey Bell, *Last Night*
Pleasant "Cousin Joe" Joseph, *Cousin Joe from New Orleans*
Jimmy Reed, *Jimmy Reed*
Jimmy Reed, *Jimmy Reed at Carnegie Hall*
Roosevelt Sykes, *Dirty Double Mother*
Johnny Young, *I Can't Keep My Foot from Jumping*
Johnny Young, *Johnny Young Plays and Sings the Blues with His Gut Bucket Mandolin*

Francis Wilford Smith
Leroy Carr, *Leroy Carr 1930–35*
Leroy Carr, *Leroy Carr Vol. 2*

Gary Smith
Sonny Rhodes, *I Don't Want My Blues Colored Bright*

Willie Smith
Legendary Blues Band, *U B Da Judge*

Lester Snell
Lynn White, *At Her Best*

Lynn White, *The New Me*

John Snyder
Johnny Adams, *Fanning the Flames*
Billy Branch, *Blues Keep Following Me Around*
Charles Brown, *Honey Dripper*
Charles Brown, *These Blues*
Clarence "Gatemouth" Brown, *Gate Swings*
Johnny Copeland, *Jungle Swing*
James Cotton, *Living the Blues*
Larry Garner, *Baton Rouge*
Larry Garner, *You Need to Live a Little*
Alvin Youngblood Hart, *Come on in This House*
Etta James, *Mystery Lady*
Lady Bianca, *Best Kept Secret*
Maria Muldaur, *Fanning the Flames*
Lucky Peterson, *I'm Ready*
Melvin Taylor, *Melvin Taylor and the Slack Band*
Carl Weathersby, *Don't Lay Your Blues on Me*
Junior Wells, *Come on in This House*

James Solberg
James Solberg, *One of These Days*
James Solberg, *See That My Grave Is Kept Clean*

Maynard Solomon
John Hammond Jr., *The Best of John Hammond*

Otis Spann
Johnny Young, *Fat Mandolin*

Pete Special
Big Twist & the Mellow Fellows, *Live from Chicago! Bigger Than Life!!*
Big Twist & the Mellow Fellows, *Playing for Keeps*

Special Sauce
G. Love & Special Sauce, *Coast to Coast Motel*
G. Love & Special Sauce, *G. Love & Special Sauce*

Dave Specter
Tad Robinson, *Blueplicity*

Tad Robinson, *Live in Europe*
Dave Specter, *Bluebird Blues*
Dave Specter, *Blueplicity*
Dave Specter, *Left Turn on Blue*
Dave Specter, *Live in Europe*

Abner Spector
Willie Dixon, *I Am the Blues*

Jon Spencer
Jon Spencer Blues Explosion, *Now I Got Worry*
Jon Spencer Blues Explosion, *Orange*

Victoria Spivey
Buster Benton, *The All Star Blues World of Maestro Willie Dixon*

Richard Spottswood
Big Chief Ellis, *Big Chief Ellis Featuring Tarheel Slim*
Mississippi John Hurt, *Avalon Blues 1963*
Mississippi John Hurt, *Worried Blues*

Pierre M. Sprey
Drink Small, *Electric Blues Doctor Live*
Sunnyland Slim, *Live at the D.C. Blues Society*

Heiner Stadler
Lefty Dizz, *Walked All Night Long*
Louisiana Red, *The Blues Purity of Louisiana Red*
Sugar Blue, *Too Wet to Plow*

Roebuck Staples
Pops Staples, *Peace to the Neighborhood*

John Stedman
Eddie C. Campbell, *Baddest Cat in the Block*
Jimmy Dawkins, *All Blues*
Phil Guy, *Breaking out on Top*
Phil Guy, *Tina Nu*
Johnny Littlejohn, *When Your Best Friends Turn Their Back on You*
Louisiana Red, *King Bee*
Jimmie Lee Robinson, *Bandera Rockabillies*
Jimmie Lee Robinson, *Chicago Jump*

Isaiah "Doc" Ross, *I Want All My Friends to Know*
Byther Smith, *Addressing the Nation with the Blues*
Phillip Walker, *Big Blues from Texas*
U.P. Wilson, *Whirlwind*

Robert Steffany
Big Maybelle, *The Last of Big Maybelle*

Karl Stephenson
Beck, *Mellow Gold*

Wolf Stephenson
Bobby "Blue" Bland, *Sad Street*
Z.Z. Hill, *Blues Master*
Z.Z. Hill, *Down Home Blues*
Z.Z. Hill, *In Memorium*
Little Milton, *I'm a Gambler*
McKinley Mitchell, *The Complete Malaco Recordings*

Jim Stewart
Eddie Floyd, *Knock on Wood*

Chris Strachwitz
Black Ace, *I'm the Boss Card in Your Hand*
Juke Boy Bonner, *Life Gave Me a Dirty Deal*
Joe Callicott, *Mississippi Delta Blues Vol. 2*
C.J. Chenier, *My Baby Don't Wear No Shoes*
Clifton Chenier, *Bogalusa Blues*
Clifton Chenier, *Bon Ton Roulet*
Clifton Chenier, *Live! At the Long Beach and San Francisco Blues Festivals*
Clifton Chenier, *Live at St. Mark's*
Clifton Chenier, *Louisiana Blues and Zydeco*
Clifton Chenier, *Out West*
K.C. Douglas, *Big Road Blues*
K.C. Douglas, *K.C. Douglas: The Country Boy*
K.C. Douglas, *K.C.'s Blues*
Snooks Eaglin, *Country Boy down in New Orleans*
Charles Ford Band/Ford Blues Band/Robben Ford, *The Charles Ford Band*

Henry Gray, *Louisiana Blues Album*
Earl Hooker, *Two Bugs and a Roach*
Lightnin' Hopkins, *The Gold Star Sessions, Vol. 1*
Lightnin' Hopkins, *The Gold Star Sessions, Vol. 2*
Lightnin' Hopkins, *Texas Blues*
Pete Johnson, *Joe Turner with Pete Johnson's Orchestra*
Furry Lewis, *Mississippi Delta Blues Jam, Vol. 1*
Johnny Littlejohn, *Chicago Blues Stars*
Mississippi Fred McDowell, *Good Morning Little School Girl*
Mississippi Fred McDowell, *Mississippi Delta Blues*
Mississippi Fred McDowell, *This Ain't No Rock 'n' Roll*
Big Maceo Merriweather, *The King of Chicago Blues Piano*
Whistlin' Alex Moore, *From North Dallas to the East Side*
Charlie Musselwhite, *Memphis Charlie*
Piano Red, *Atlanta Bounce*
Robert Shaw, *The Ma Grinder*
Mercy Dee Walton, *Troublesome Mind*
Katie Webster, *I Know That's Right*
Peetie Wheatstraw, *Kokomo Arnold/Peetie Wheatstraw*
Bukka White, *Sky Songs*
Robert Pete Williams, *Angola Prisoner's Blues*
Robert Pete Williams, *I'm As Blue As a Man Can Be— Vol. 1*
Robert Pete Williams, *When a Man Takes the Blues— Vol. 2*
Sonny Boy Williamson II, *King Biscuit Time*
Johnny Young, *Chicago Blues*

Percy Strother
Percy Strother, *A Good Woman Is Hard to Find*
Percy Strother, *The Highway Is My Home*

Keith Sykes
Bluebirds, *Swamp Stomp*

Bill Szymczyk
J. Geils Band/Bluestime, *Bloodshot*
J. Geils Band/Bluestime, *Blow Your Face Out*
J. Geils Band/Bluestime, *Hotline*
J. Geils Band/Bluestime, *Nightmares . . . and Other Tales from the Vinyl Jungle*
B.B. King, *Completely Well*

Bruce Talbot
Cecil Gant, *Mean Old World: The Blues from 1940 to 1994*

Shel Talmy
Blues Project, *Lazarus*

Hound Dog Taylor
Hound Dog Taylor, *Hound Dog Taylor and the Houserockers*

Ian Taylor
Gary Moore, *Blues Alive*
Gary Moore, *Blues for Greeny*

Jack Taylor
Big Maybelle, *The Last of Big Maybelle*

Koko Taylor
Koko Taylor, *Force of Nature*
Koko Taylor, *I Got What It Takes*
Koko Taylor, *Queen of the Blues*

P. Taylor
Big Maybelle, *The Last of Big Maybelle*

Skip Taylor
Canned Heat, *Future Blues*

John Telfer
Johnny Adams, *Lost in the Stars: The Music of Kurt Weill*

Ten Years After
Ten Years After, *Cricklewood Green*

Jimmy Thackery
John Mooney, *Sideways in Paradise*
Jimmy Thackery, *Empty Arms Motel*

Bob Thiele
Memphis Minnie, *I Ain't No Bad Gal 1941*
Otis Spann, *Down to Earth: The Bluesway Recordings*

Tabby Thomas
Tabby Thomas, *Rockin' Tabby Thomas Greatest Hits Volume 1*

Troy Thompson
Otis Clay, *The Only Way Is Up*

Russ Titelman
Eric Clapton, *From the Cradle*
Ry Cooder, *Paradise and Lunch*

Steve Tomashefsky
Jimmy Dawkins, *Blisterstring*
Jimmy Johnson, *Johnson's Whacks*
Otis Rush, *So Many Roads*

Richard Topp
Buddy Johnson, *Walk 'Em*

Eli Toscano
Little Brother Montgomery, *Unissued Chicago Blues of the 1950s from Cobra and JOB*

Allen Toussaint
Dr. John, *In the Right Place*
Earl King, *Street Parade*

Pete Townshend
John Lee Hooker, *The Iron Man*

Tre
Tre, *Delivered for Glory—Reclaiming the Blues*

Mark Trehus
Koerner, Ray & Glover, *One Foot in the Groove*

Didier Tricard
Jimmy Dawkins, *Hot Wire 81*
Lefty Dizz, *Somebody Stole My Christmas*

Buddy Guy, *Alone and Acoustic*
Buddy Guy, *Stone Crazy*
Lucky Peterson, *Ridin'*
Melvin Taylor, *Blues on the Run*

Ike Turner
Howlin' Wolf, *Howlin' Wolf Rides Again*

James Tuttle
Omar Dykes, *World Wide Open*

Rudy Van Gelder
Curtis Jones, *Trouble Blues*

Dave Van Ronk
Dave Van Ronk, *Sunday Street*

Stevie Ray Vaughan
Stevie Ray Vaughan, *In Step*
Stevie Ray Vaughan, *Live Alive*
Stevie Ray Vaughan, *Soul to Soul*
Stevie Ray Vaughan, *Texas Flood*

Billy Vera
Jay McShann, *Kansas City Blues 1944–49*
Memphis Slim, *Memphis Slim at the Gate of Horn*
Lloyd Price, *Lawdy!*
Lloyd Price, *Vol. 2: Heavy Dreams*
Mercy Dee Walton, *One Room Country Shack*

Mike Vernon
Eddie Boyd, *Five Long Years*
George "Wild Child" Butler, *Stranger*
Eric Clapton, *Bluesbreakers— John Mayall with Eric Clapton*
Jimmy Dawkins, *Montreux Blues Festival*
Jimmy Dawkins, *Transatlantic 770*
David "Honeyboy" Edwards, *Delta Bluesman*
Fleetwood Mac, *English Rose*
Fleetwood Mac, *Fleetwood Mac in Chicago 1969*
Lightnin' Slim, *Blue Lightning*

John Mayall, *Bluesbreakers— John Mayall with Eric Clapton*
Larry McCray, *Delta Hurricane*
Jay Owens, *The Blues Soul of Jay Owens*
Jay Owens, *Movin' On*
Savoy Brown, *Blue Matter*
Savoy Brown, *Getting to the Point*
Savoy Brown, *A Step Further*
Sunnyland Slim, *Sunnyland Slim/Bluesmasters Vol. 8*
Ten Years After, *Stonehenge*

Robert G. Vernon
Fats Domino, *Antoine "Fats" Domino*

Jimmy Vivino
Johnnie Johnson, *Johnnie Be Back*

Marcel Vos
Andrew Brown, *Big Brown's Chicago Blues*
Andrew Brown, *On the Case*
Eddie Burns, *Treat Me Like I Treat You*
Eddie C. Campbell, *Mind Trouble*

Steve Wagner
Karen Carroll, *Had My Fun*
Pete Johnson, *Central Avenue Boogie*
Willie Kent, *Ain't It Nice*
Tad Robinson, *Gotcha!*
Tad Robinson, *One to Infinity*
Barkin' Bill Smith, *Bluebird Blues*
Barkin' Bill Smith, *Gotcha!*

Dennis Walker
John Campbell, *One Believer*
Robert Cray, *Bad Influence*
Robert Cray, *Midnight Stroll*
Robert Cray, *Strong Persuader*
Ted Hawkins, *Happy Hour*
Ted Hawkins, *Watch Your Step*

Joe Louis Walker
Little Charlie & the Nightcats, *Night Vision*
Joe Louis Walker, *Blue Soul*
Joe Louis Walker, *Blues of the Month Club*
Joe Louis Walker, *Live at Slim's, Vol. One*

Joe Louis Walker, *Volume Two*

Phillip Walker
Phillip Walker, *Big Blues from Texas*

Robert Walker
Robert "Bilbo" Walker, *Promised Land*

Joe Walsh
Albert King, *Red House*

Matt Walters
Leadbelly, *Last Sessions*

Bob Ward
Pinetop Perkins, *Portrait of a Delta Bluesman*

John Ward
Lee "Shot" Williams, *Hot Shot*

Neil Ward
Ronnie Earl, *Grateful Heart: Blues and Ballads*

Don Wardell
Elvis Presley, *Elvis in Concert*

Lenny Waronker
Ry Cooder, *Into the Purple Valley*
Ry Cooder, *Paradise and Lunch*
Maria Muldaur, *Maria Muldaur*
Maria Muldaur, *Sweet Harmony*
Maria Muldaur, *Waitress in a Donut Shop*

Don Was
Delbert McClinton, *Never Been Rocked Enough*
Bonnie Raitt, *Luck of the Draw*
Bonnie Raitt, *Nine Lives*
Rolling Stones, *Stripped*

Jim Waters
Jon Spencer Blues Explosion, *Now I Got Worry*
Jon Spencer Blues Explosion, *Orange*

Chris Watkins
Preacher Boy, *Preacher Boy & the Natural Blues*

David Watson
Doyle Bramhall, *Bird Nest on the Ground*

Johnny "Guitar" Watson
Johnny "Guitar" Watson, *Ain't That a Bitch*
Johnny "Guitar" Watson, *Real Mother*

Katie Webster
Katie Webster, *No Foolin'!*
Katie Webster, *Two-Fisted Mama!*

Harry Weinger
James Brown, *Star Time*

Bob Weinstock
Mose Allison, *Greatest Hits*
Mose Allison, *Local Color*

Richard Weiser
Isidore "Tuts" Washington, *Shame, Shame, Shame*

Richard Weize
Louis Jordan, *Let the Good Times Roll*

Pete Welding
The Aces, *Louis Myers—I'm a Southern Man*
Connie Curtis "Pee Wee" Crayton, *Pee Wee's Blues*
Maxwell Street Jimmy Davis, *Maxwell Street Jimmy Davis*
Maxwell Street Jimmy Davis, *Modern Chicago Blues*
Snooks Eaglin, *The Complete Imperial Recordings*
Lightnin' Hopkins, *The Complete Aladdin Sessions*
J.B. Hutto, *Masters of Modern Blues*
Eddie Lee Jones, *Yonder Go That Old Black Dog*
Floyd Jones, *Masters of Modern Blues*
Mississippi Fred McDowell, *Amazing Grace*
Mississippi Fred McDowell, *My Home Is in the Delta*
Memphis Slim, *Chicago Blues Masters, Vol. 1: Muddy Waters and Memphis Slim*
Amos Milburn, *Blues Barrelhouse and Boogie Woogie*
Charlie Musselwhite, *The Blues Never Die*

Robert Nighthawk, *Masters of Modern Blues—Robert Nighthawk and Houston Stackhouse*
Isaiah "Doc" Ross, *Call the Doctor*
Johnny Shines, *Standing at the Crossroads*
Otis Spann, *Live the Life*
Houston Stackhouse, *Masters of Modern Blues*
Sunnyland Slim, *Rediscovered Blues*
Sonny Terry & Brownie McGhee, *Whoopin' the Blues: The Capitol Recordings, 1947–50*
T-Bone Walker, *The Complete Capitol/Black and White Recordings*
Big John Wrencher, *The Chicago String Band*
Johnny Young, *Johnny Young & His Friends*

Jann Wenner
Boz Scaggs, *Boz Scaggs*

Robert West
Eddie Floyd, *I Found a Love*
Robert Ward, *Hot Stuff*

Jerry Wexler
Lou Ann Barton, *Old Enough*
Ray Charles, *The Best of Ray Charles: The Atlantic Years*
Floyd Dixon, *Marshall Texas Is My Home*
Champion Jack Dupree, *Blues from the Gutter*
Mark Knopfler, *Communique*

Adam White
Billy Stewart, *One More Time*

Cliff White
Wilbert Harrison, *Da-De-Ya-Da*

Lynn White
Lynn White, *At Her Best*
Lynn White, *Cheatin'*
Lynn White, *Home Girl*

Ken Whiteley
John Hammond Jr., *Nobody but You*

Kirk Whiting
Mary Lane, *Appointment with the Blues*

P. Whittacker
Smokin' Joe Kubek Band with Bnois King, *Axe Man*

Neil Wilburn
Marcia Ball, *Circuit Queen*

Miles Wilkinson
Marcia Ball, *Blue House*

Carey Williams
Alvin Youngblood Hart, *Big Mama's Door*

Jerry Williams
Z.Z. Hill, *The Brand New Z.Z. Hill*

Lee "Shot" Williams
Lee "Shot" Williams, *Hot Shot*

Lesley Williams
Etta Baker, *One-Dime Blues*

Mayo Williams
Louis Jordan, *The Best of Louis Jordan*

Chick Willis
Chick Willis, *I Got a Big Fat Woman*

Hal Willner
Johnny Adams, *Lost in the Stars: The Music of Kurt Weill*

Alan Wilson
Son House, *Death Letter Blues*

Dale Wilson
Ted Hawkins, *Happy Hour*

Joe Wilson
Cephas & Wiggins, *Cool Down*

Kim Wilson
Jerry Portnoy, *Home Run Hitter*
Rusty Zinn, *Sittin' and Waitin'*
Rusty Zinn, *That's Life*
Rusty Zinn, *Tigerman*

Tom Wilson
Blues Project, *Projections*

Johnny Winter
Sonny Terry & Brownie McGhee, *Whoopin'*
Muddy Waters, *Muddy "Mississippi" Waters Live*
Johnny Winter, *Captured Live*
Johnny Winter, *Johnny Winter and . . . Live*

Muff Winwood
Mark Knopfler, *Dire Straits*

Charley Wirz
Doyle Bramhall, *Bird Nest on the Ground*

Steve Wisner
Eddie C. Campbell, *King of the Jungle*
Eddie C. Campbell, *Mind Trouble*

Joe Wissert
J. Geils Band/Bluestime, *Flashback: The Best of the J. Geils Band*
Boz Scaggs, *Silk Degrees*

Thom Wolke
Guy Davis, *Stomp Down Rider*

Kevin Wommack
Omar Dykes, *Courts of Lulu*
Omar Dykes, *World Wide Open*

Mitch Woods
Mitch Woods, *Keeper of the Flame*
Mitch Woods, *Mr. Boogie's back in Town*
Mitch Woods, *Solid Gold Cadillac*
Mitch Woods, *Steady Date*

John Wooler
Hadda Brooks, *Time Was When*

John Work
Muddy Waters, *Complete Plantation Recordings: The Historic 1941–42 Library of Congress Field Recordings*

Benjamin Wright
Otis Clay, *The Only Way Is Up*

Chris Wright
Ten Years After, *Watt*

Craig Wroten
Walter "Wolfman" Washington, *Sada*

Bill Wyman
Junior Wells, *Drinkin TNT 'N' Smokin' Dynamite*

Kazu Yanagida
Eddie "Cleanhead" Vinson, *Blues, Boogie and Bop: The 1940s Mercury Sessions*

Chris Youlden
Savoy Brown, *Raw Sienna*

Brian Young
Michael Hill, *Have Mercy!*

Ernie Young
Jerry McCain, *That's What They Want: The Best of Jerry McCain*

Mighty Joe Young
Koko Taylor, *I Got What It Takes*
Mighty Joe Young, *Mighty Man*

David Z
Jonny Lang, *Lie to Me*
Kenny Wayne Shepherd, *Ledbetter Heights*

Bryan Zee
Preacher Boy, *Gutters and Pews*
Preacher Boy, *Preacher Boy & the Natural Blues*

Lee Allen Zeno
Dalton Reed, *Louisiana Soul Man*

John Zwierzko
Sugar Blue, *In Your Eyes*

Which artists or groups have had the most influence on the acts included in MusicHound Blues? The Roots Index will help you find out. Under each artist or group's name—not necessarily a blues act— are listed the acts found in MusicHound Blues that were influenced by that artist or group. By the way, Muddy Waters is the influence champ: he appears in the ◀◀ section of a whopping 80 artists or groups.

Johnny Ace
Bobby "Blue" Bland

Johnny Adams
Dalton Reed
Tad Robinson

Cannonball Adderley
Noble "Thin Man" Watts

Larry Adler
George "Harmonica" Smith

Garfield Akers
Joe Callicott
Robert Wilkins

Arthur Alexander
Tad Robinson

Texas Alexander
Lowell Fulson
Lightnin' Hopkins
J.T. "Funny Paper" Smith

Luther Allison
Joanna Connor
Michael Hill
Little Jimmy King
Jonny Lang

Mose Allison Jr.
Saffire—The Uppity Blues
   Women

Duane Allman
Tab Benoit
Ronnie Earl
Sonny Landreth

Allman Brothers Band
Joanna Connor

Dave Alvin
Mike Henderson

Albert Ammons
David Maxwell

Gene Ammons
Greg Piccolo

Pink Anderson
Roy Book Binder

Alphonse "Bois Sec" Ardoin
Clifton Chenier

Amadee Ardoin
Clifton Chenier

Louis Armstrong
Billie Holiday

Ivory Joe Hunter
Louis Jordan
Sammy Price
Ikey Robinson
Jimmy Rushing
Sippie Wallace
Ethel Waters

Billy Boy Arnold
Billy Bizor

Eddy Arnold
Elvis Presley

Kokomo Arnold
Black Ace
Casey Bill Weldon

Lynn August
C.J. Chenier

Gene Autry
Roy Brown

Bachman-Turner Overdrive
Tinsley Ellis

Trevor Bacon
Bullmoose Jackson

Joan Baez
Koerner, Ray & Glover
Bonnie Raitt

Chet Baker
Johnny Reno

Marcia Ball
Michelle Willson

Hank Ballard
Eddie Floyd
Etta James

Hank Ballard & the Midnighters
James Brown

The Band
Eric Clapton

L.V. Banks
Tre

Dick Bankston
Ishmon Bracey

Barbecue Bob
Curley Weaver

Roosevelt "Booba" Barnes
James "Super Chikan"
   Johnson

Dave Bartholomew
Earl King
Tommy Ridgley

Count Basie
Ray Charles
Buddy Johnson
Johnnie Johnson
Roy Milton
Roomful of Blues
Jimmy Rushing
Vann "Piano Man" Walls

Beach Boys
J. Geils Band

Beale Street Sheiks
Memphis Minnie

Beastie Boys
Beck

The Beatles
Jimi Hendrix
Led Zeppelin
Steve Miller
Rolling Stones

Sidney Bechet
Jeannie & Jimmy Cheatham
Alberta Hunter
Sippie Wallace

Jeff Beck
Barry Goldberg
Harvey Mandel

Harry Belafonte
Richard Berry

Carey Bell
Charlie Musselwhite
Sugar Blue

T.D. Bell
W.C. Clark

Fred Below
Robert Covington

Jesse Belvin
Richard Berry

Brook Benton
Johnny Laws
Barkin' Bill Smith

Buster Benton
Johnny Laws

Sammy Berfect
Davell Crawford

Chuck Berry
Richard Berry
Eddy Clearwater
Robert Cray
Luther "Houserocker"
   Johnson
Led Zeppelin
Jerry McCain
Johnny B. Moore
Popa Chubby
Elvis Presley
Rolling Stones
Chris Smither
George Thorogood & the
   Destroyers
Robert "Bilbo" Walker
"Boogie" Bill Webb
Johnny Winter

Robert Bertrand
Professor Longhair

Dickey Betts
Ronnie Earl

Big Maybelle
Michelle Willson

Black Ace
Hop Wilson

Payton Blackwell
Scrapper Blackwell

Scrapper Blackwell
Bumble Bee Slim
Leroy Carr
Peetie Wheatstraw

Willie Blackwell
Baby Boy Warren

Eubie Blake
Speckled Red

Raymond Blakes
Bluebirds

Bobby "Blue" Bland
Johnny Adams
L.V. Banks
Doyle Bramhall
Nappy Brown
Harold Burrage
Paul Butterfield Blues Band
Paul Butterfield's Better Days
Cate Brothers
Larry Davis
Z.Z. Hill
Frankie Lee
Little Milton
Mighty Sam McClain
Delbert McClinton
Larry McCray
McKinley Mitchell
Jay Owens
Lucky Peterson
Tad Robinson
Doug Sahm
Little Johnny Taylor
Walter "Wolfman"
   Washington
Lee "Shot" Williams

The Blasters
Radio Kings

**Travis "Harmonica Slim"
Blaylock**
Harmonica Slim

Blind Blake
Roy Book Binder
Cephas & Wiggins

Blind Boy Fuller
Peg Leg Howell
John Jackson
Blind Willie McTell
Jesse Thomas
Josh White

Blind Percy
Jimmie Lee Robinson

Rory Block
Keb' Mo'
Paul Rishell

Michael Bloomfield
Elvin Bishop
Charles Ford Band
Barry Goldberg
Harvey Mandel

Blues Incorporated
Chicken Shack

Blues Project
Al Kooper

Jimmy Blythe
Thomas A. Dorsey

Dock Boggs
Bob Dylan

Scott Bohanna
Muddy Waters

Tommy Bolin
Sonny Landreth

Zuzu Bollin
U.P. Wilson

James Booker
Davell Crawford
Dr. John

Booker T. & the MGs
Barry Goldberg
Big Jack Johnson
Ron Levy
Little Sonny

Roger Boykin
Smokin' Joe Kubek Band with
   Bnois King

Ishmon Bracey
The McCoy Brothers

Billy Branch
Carl Weathersby

Hadda Brooks
Saffire—The Uppity Blues
   Women

Big Bill Broonzy
The Aces
John Brim
Bumble Bee Slim
Arthur "Big Boy" Crudup
Guy Davis
Bill "Jazz" Gillum
Steve James
J.B. Lenoir
Memphis Slim
Jimmy Rogers
Rosetta Tharpe
Washboard Sam
Bukka White

Buster Brown
Billy Bizor

Charles Brown
Mose Allison
Eddie Boyd
Nappy Brown
Ray Charles
Floyd Dixon
Big Chief Ellis
Ivory Joe Hunter
Luther "Houserocker"
   Johnson
Curtis Jones
Johnny Jones
Lovie Lee
Jimmy McCracklin
Amos Milburn
Matt "Guitar" Murphy
Doc Pomus
Sammy Price
Saffire—The Uppity Blues
   Women
Chuck Willis
Jimmy Witherspoon
Billy Wright

Clarence "Gatemouth" Brown
Albert Collins
Johnny Copeland
Larry Davis
Carol Fran & Clarence
   Hollimon
Anson Funderburgh & the
   Rockets Featuring Sam
   Myers
Grady Gaines
Guitar Slim
Long John Hunter

Harmonica Slim
The Holmes Brothers
Colin James
Eddie Kirkland
Little Milton
Mississippi Fred McDowell
Bonnie Raitt
Otis Rush
Ten Years After
George Thorogood & the
    Destroyers
Robert Ward
The Yardbirds

Joel Hopkins
Lightnin' Hopkins

Lightnin' Hopkins
Dave Alvin
Billy Bizor
Juke Boy Bonner
Lonnie Brooks
Jimmy Burns
Clarence Carter
John Hammond Jr.
Harmonica Fats & Bernie Pearl
Janis Joplin
J.B. Lenoir
Lightnin' Slim
Frankie Lee Sims
Drink Small
Chris Smither
Baby Tate
Hop Wilson
ZZ Top

Big Walter Horton
Carey Bell
Billy Branch
George "Mojo" Buford
James Harman
Shakey Jake Harris
Mississippi Heat
Charlie Musselwhite
Paul Oscher
Studebaker John
Junior Wells
Big John Wrencher

Son House
Rory Block
Michael Bloomfield
Big Bill Broonzy
Willie Brown
Bo Carter
Sam Chatmon
Willie Dixon
Sleepy John Estes

Jesse Fuller
Clifford Gibson
Bill "Jazz" Gillum
Skip James
Robert Johnson
Charley Jordan
Koerner, Ray & Glover
John Mooney
Preacher Boy
Johnnie "Geechie" Temple
James "Son" Thomas
Muddy Waters
Curley Weaver
Big Joe Williams

Howlin' Wolf
Dave Alvin
L.V. Banks
Roosevelt "Booba" Barnes
Billy Branch
Jimmy Burns
Paul Butterfield Blues Band
Paul Butterfield's Better Days
Eddie C. Campbell
John Campbell
Canned Heat
Omar Dykes
Tinsley Ellis
Anson Funderburgh & the
    Rockets Featuring Sam
    Myers
Screamin' Jay Hawkins
Mary Lane
Lovie Lee
Joe Hill Louis
Taj Mahal
John Mayall
Junior Parker
James Peterson
Lonnie Pitchford
Preacher Boy
Radio Kings
Bonnie Raitt
Bobby Rush
Doug Sahm
Curtis Salgado
Savoy Brown
Johnny Shines
Dave Specter
Jon Spencer Blues Explosion
Tre
Carl Weathersby
Smokey Wilson
The Yardbirds

Willie Hudson
Robert Pete Williams

Ivory Joe Hunter
Solomon Burke
Jimmy Liggins
Tommy Ridgley

Long John Hunter
Phillip Walker

Mississippi John Hurt
Beck
Rory Block
Roy Book Binder
Hot Tuna
Sonny Landreth
Chris Smither
Dave Van Ronk

J.B. Hutto
Lil' Ed & the Blues Imperials

The Impressions
The Holmes Brothers

The Ink Spots
Elvis Presley

Dan Jackson
Robert Pete Williams

Jim Jackson
Joe Callicott
William Harris
Jack Kelly
Memphis Jug Band
Memphis Minnie
Charley Patton
Robert Wilkins

Mahalia Jackson
Lady Bianca

Papa Charlie Jackson
Big Bill Broonzy

Wanda Jackson
Lou Ann Barton

Illinois Jacquet
Joe Liggins
Big Jay McNeely
Johnny Reno

Elmore James
Elvin Bishop
Michael Bloomfield
Bluebirds
Ry Cooder
Robert "Big Mojo" Elem
Fleetwood Mac
Dave Hole
J.B. Hutto

Luther "Georgia Boy" Johnson
Lester "Big Daddy" Kinsey
Sonny Landreth
Legendary Blues Band
Lil' Ed & the Blues Imperials
Hip Linkchain
Little Milton
Johnny Littlejohn
Jerry McCain
Mississippi Heat
Gary Moore
Johnny B. Moore
Jay Owens
John Primer
Moses Rascoe
Sonny Rhodes
Studebaker John
Tarheel Slim
Hound Dog Taylor
James "Son" Thomas
Ike Turner
Chick Willis
Hop Wilson
Smokey Wilson
Billy Wright

Etta James
Marcia Ball
Big Time Sarah
Fleetwood Mac
Shirley King
Francine Reed
Koko Taylor
Valerie Wellington
Michelle Willson

Skip James
Koerner, Ray & Glover
Jack Owens
Johnnie "Geechie" Temple

Blind Lemon Jefferson
Juke Boy Bonner
Big Bill Broonzy
The Rev. Gary Davis
Lowell Fulson
Harmonica Fats & Bernie Pearl
Ted Hawkins
Dave Hole
John Lee Hooker
Lightnin' Hopkins
Peg Leg Howell
Curtis Jones
B.B. King
Leadbelly
J.B. Lenoir
Mississippi Fred McDowell
Charley Patton

Robert Cray
Jesse Fortune
Guitar Slim
Guitar Slim Jr.
Buddy Guy
Harmonica Slim
Jimi Hendrix
Z.Z. Hill
Big Jack Johnson
Luther "Houserocker"
    Johnson
Vance Kelly
Willie Kent
Albert King
Freddie King
Shirley King
Eddie Kirkland
Mark Knopfler
Smokin' Joe Kubek Band with
    Bnois King
Bryan Lee
Little Milton
Mighty Sam McClain
Larry McCray
Gary Moore
Doc Pomus
Duke Robillard
Fenton Robinson
Otis Rush
Mem Shannon
Koko Taylor
Tre
Jimmie Vaughan
Joe Louis Walker
Phillip Walker
Robert Ward
Lynn White
Little Sonny

Earl King
Rockie Charles
Guitar Slim Jr.
Phil Guy
Bryan Lee
Savoy Brown
Walter "Wolfman"
    Washington

Freddie King
Luther Allison
Aron Burton
Chicken Shack
Eric Clapton
Joanna Connor
Robert Cray
Debbie Davies
Derek & the Dominos
Ronnie Earl

Fabulous Thunderbirds
Anson Funderburgh & the
    Rockets Featuring Sam Myers
Rory Gallagher
Tutu Jones
Smokin' Joe Kubek Band with
    Bnois King
Bryan Lee
Magic Sam
Magic Slim
Bob Margolin
Bobby Radcliff
Radio Kings
Kenny "Blue" Ray
Sonny Rhodes
Savoy Brown
Jimmie Vaughan
Joe Louis Walker
Mighty Joe Young

King Curtis
Johnny Reno

The Kinks
Led Zeppelin

Big Daddy Kinsey
Big Twist & the Mellow
    Fellows
Kinsey Report

Kinsey Report
Big Twist & the Mellow
    Fellows

Ransom Knowling
The Aces

King Kolax
J.T. Brown

Al Kooper
Barry Goldberg
Mighty Sam McClain

Alex Korner
The Animals

Stacey La Guardia
Pete Johnson

Rube Lacy
Walter Vincson

Mary Lane
Vance Kelly

Lazy Lester
Kenny Neal

Leadbelly
Beck
Snooks Eaglin
Frank Frost & Sam Carr
Jesse Fuller
John Jackson
Moses Rascoe
Baby Tate
Sonny Terry & Brownie
    McGhee
Josh White

Scott LeFaro
Hot Tuna

J.B. Lenoir
Robert "Big Mojo" Elem
Bobby Rush
Byther Smith

Furry Lewis
Steve James
Memphis Minnie

Jerry Lee Lewis
Cate Brothers
Mike Henderson

Meade Lux Lewis
David Maxwell

Noah Lewis
Sonny Boy Williamson I

Pete Lewis
Roy Buchanan

Smiley Lewis
Jimmy Dawkins
J. Geils Band
Little "Sonny" Jones

Joe Liggins
Dr. John
Jimmy Liggins

Lightnin' Slim
Juke Boy Bonner
Silas Hogan
Raful Neal

David Lindley
Sonny Landreth

Mance Lipscomb
Guy Davis
Bob Dylan
Harmonica Fats & Bernie Pearl
Steve James

Little Milton
L.V. Banks
Roosevelt "Booba" Barnes
Jimmy Johnson
Luther "Guitar Junior"
    Johnson
Casey Jones
Hip Linkchain
Lucky Peterson
John Primer

Little Richard
Harold Burrage
Davell Crawford
Grady Gaines
Jimi Hendrix
Z.Z. Hill
Piano C. Red
Elvis Presley

Little Sunny & the Skyliners
Doug Sahm

Little Walter
The Aces
Little Willie Anderson
Billy Boy Arnold
Carey Bell
Billy Bizor
Paul Butterfield Blues Band
Paul Butterfield's Better Days
Willie Cobbs
James Cotton
Lester Davenport
Frank Frost & Sam Carr
Anson Funderburgh & the
    Rockets Featuring Sam
    Myers
Harmonica Slim
Slim Harpo
Shakey Jake Harris
Lester "Big Daddy" Kinsey
Lazy Lester
Little Charlie & the Nightcats
Little Sonny
Johnny Mars
John Mayall
Mississippi Heat
Charlie Musselwhite
Raful Neal
Darrell Nulisch
Paul Oscher
Peg Leg Sam
Rod Piazza
Jerry Portnoy
Gary Primich
Snooky Pryor
Radio Kings

The Category Index repre-
sents an array of cate-
gories put together to
suggest some of the many
groupings under which
blues music and blues
acts can be classified. The
Hound welcomes your ad-
ditions to the existing categories in this index and
also invites you to send in
your own funny, sarcastic,
prolific, poignant, or exciting ideas for brand new
categories.

Acoustic Blues
Pink Anderson
Kokomo Arnold
John Henry Barbee
Scrapper Blackwell
Rory Block
Roy Book Binder
Big Bill Broonzy
Bumble Bee Slim
Bo Carter
Cephas & Wiggins
Ry Cooder
Bob Dylan
Sleepy John Estes
Jesse Fuller
John Hammond Jr.
Corey Harris
Buddy Boy Hawkins
Ted Hawkins
Jessie Mae Hemphill

John Lee Hooker
Lightnin' Hopkins
Son House
Skip James
Blind Lemon Jefferson
Robert Johnson
Tommy Johnson
Koerner, Ray & Glover
Leadbelly
Furry Lewis
Robert Junior Lockwood
Louisiana Red
Taj Mahal
John Mayall
Mississippi Fred McDowell
Mississippi John Hurt
Mississippi Sheiks
Keb' Mo'
Charley Patton
Peg Leg Sam
Lonnie Pitchford
Yank Rachell
Paul Rishell
Doctor Ross
Satan & Adam
Drink Small
Sonny Terry & Brownie
    McGhee
Henry Thomas
Dave Van Ronk
Washboard Sam
Big Joe Williams

Animals
The Animals
The Bluebirds
Norton Buffalo
Bumble Bee Slim

Chicken Shack
Charles "Cow-Cow" Daven-
    port
Pat Hare
Clarence "Frogman" Henry
Howlin' Wolf
James "Super Chikan" John-
    son
Son Seals
Hound Dog Taylor
Walter "Wolfman" Washing-
    ton

Big Ones
Big Bill Broonzy
Papa Chubby
Arthur "Big Boy" Crudup
Fats Domino
Big Chief Ellis
Big Walter "Shakey" Horton
Big Jack Johnson
Big Daddy Kinsey
Big Jay McNeely
Big Maceo Merriweather
Big Mama Thornton
Big Three Trio
Big Joe Turner
Big Joe Williams
Big John Wrencher
Big Maybelle
Big Time Sarah
Big Twist

Blind
Blind Blake
Blind Boy Fuller
Blind Roosevelt Graves
Blind Lemon Jefferson

Blind Willie Johnson
Blind Willie McTell

Blues Rock
The Animals
Blues Project
Canned Heat
Chicken Shack
Robert Cray
Cream
Dr. John
Chris Duarte
Bob Dylan
Fabulous Thunderbirds
Fleetwood Mac
Rory Gallagher
J. Geils Band
John Hammond Jr.
Jimi Hendrix
John Mayall
Steve Miller
Rolling Stones
Savoy Brown
Kenny Wayne Shepherd
Ten Years After
George Thorogood
Stevie Ray Vaughan
Johnny Winter
Yardbirds
ZZ Top

The Boys
Billy Boy Arnold
Juke Boy Bonner
Blind Boy Fuller
Buddy Boy Hawkins
Luther "Snake Boy" Johnson
Preacher Boy

Bobby Parker
James Peterson
Lucky Peterson
Rod Piazza
Bonnie Raitt
Jimmy Reed
Fenton Robinson
Jimmy Rogers
Otis Rush
Son Seals
Kenny Wayne Shepherd
Johnny Shines
Tarheel Slim
Eddie Taylor
Stevie Ray Vaughan
Joe Louis Walker
Phillip Walker
T-Bone Walker
Robert Ward
Muddy Waters
Johnny "Guitar" Watson
Junior Wells
Chick Willis
Smokey Wilson

Father & Son
L.V. Banks & Tre
Clifton & C.J. Chenier
Raful & Kenny Neal
James & Lucky Peterson
Johnny & Shuggie Otis

Food
Barbecue Bob
Chicken Shack
Hot Tuna
Candye Kane
G. Love & Special Sauce
Hambone Willie Newbern
Sugar Blue
T-Bone Walker

Guitars
Guitar Gabriel
Guitar Shorty
Guitar Slim
Guitar Slim Jr.
Eddie "Guitar" Burns
Joe "Guitar" Hughes
Luther "Guitar Junior" Johnson
Matt "Guitar" Murphy
Johnny "Guitar" Watson

Harmonicats
Billy Boy Arnold
Carey Bell
Billy Branch

Buster Brown
Mojo Buford
Paul Butterfield
Gus Cannon
William Clarke
James Cotton
Paul deLay
Frank Frost
James Harman
Harmonica Fats
Harmonica Slim
Slim Harpo
Big Walter Horton
Howlin' Wolf
Lazy Lester
Little Walter
Jerry McCain
Charlie Musselwhite
Sam Myers
Raful Neal
Rod Piazza
Jerry Portnoy
Gary Primich
Snooky Pryor
Jimmy Reed
Dr. Isaiah Ross
Will Shade
George "Harmonica" Smith
Sonny Terry
Junior Wells
Phil Wiggins
Sonny Boy Williamson I
Sonny Boy Williamson II
Kim Wilson
Big John Wrencher

Johnsons
Big Jack Johnson
Blind Willie Johnson
Buddy Johnson
James "Super Chikan" Johnson
Jimmy Johnson
Johnnie Johnson
Lonnie Johnson
Luther "Guitar Jr." Johnson
Luther "Houserocker" Johnson
Luther "Snake Boy" Johnson
Robert Johnson
Syl Johnson
Tommy Johnson

Jump Blues
Tiny Bradshaw
Jackie Brenston
Nappy Brown
Roy Brown

H-Bomb Ferguson
Bill Haley
Lionel Hampton
Wynonie Harris
Joe Houston
Bullmoose Jackson
Louis Jordan
Jimmy Liggins
Joe Liggins
Big Jay McNeely
Jay McShann
Roy Milton
Johnny Otis
Louis Prima
Roomful of Blues
Big Mama Thornton
Big Joe Turner
Eddie "Cleanhead" Vinson
Mitch Woods

Juniors
Guitar Slim Jr.
John Hammond Jr.
Luther "Guitar Junior" Johnson
Junior Kimbrough
Junior Parker
Junior Wells
Robert Junior Lockwood

Littles
Lil' Ed
Lil' Son Jackson
Little Willie Anderson
Little Charlie & the Nightcats
Little Sammy Davis
Little Sonny Jones
Little Jimmy King
Little Milton
Little Brother Montgomery
Little Sonny
Little Johnnie Taylor
Little Walter
Little Sonny Willis
"Pee Wee" Crayton
Billie "The Kid" Emerson

Louisiana Blues
Jimmy Anderson
Tab Benoit
James Booker
Chick Carbo
Rockie Charles
Boozoo Chavis
Clifton Chenier
Dr. John
Fats Domino
Snooks Eaglin

Carol Fran & Clarence Hollimon
Guitar Slim
Guitar Slim Jr.
Slim Harpo
Clarence "Frogman" Henry
Silas Hogan
Little Sonny Jones
Earl King
Sonny Landreth
Lazy Lester
Smiley Lewis
Lightnin' Slim
Lonesome Sundown
Lloyd Price
Professor Longhair
Irma Thomas
Rockin' Tabby Thomas
Walter "Wolfman" Washington
Katie Webster

Married
Jim & Jeannie Cheatum
Carol Fran & Clarence Hollimon

Mississippians
Roosevelt "Booba" Barnes
Jackie Brenston
Willie Lee Brown
Little Eddie Burns
R.L. Burnside
Gus Cannon
Sam Carr
Bo Carter
Sam Chatmon
Willie Cobbs
James Cotton
Willie Dixon
David "Honeyboy" Edwards
Frank Frost
Jessie Mae Hemphill
John Lee Hooker
Son House
Elmore James
Skip James
Big Jack Johnson
Luther "Guitar Jr." Johnson
Robert Johnson
Tommy Johnson
Eddie Jones
Paul "Wine" Jones
Junior Kimbrough
B.B. King
Robert Junior Lockwood
Louisiana Red
Tommy McClennan

Lowell Fulson
Ted Hawkins
Johnny Heartsman
Jimmy Liggins
Percy Mayfield
Jimmy McCracklin
Big Jay McNeely
Amos Milburn
Roy Milton

Johnny Otis
Rod Piazza
Joe Louis Walker
T-Bone Walker
Johnny "Guitar" Watson
Smokey Wilson
Rusty Zinn

Younger Generation
Beck

Lurrie Bell
Deborah Coleman
Davell Crawford
Sue Foley
Corey Harris
Alvin Youngblood Hart
Michael Hill Blues Mob
Jonny Lang
G. Love & Special Sauce

Omar & the Howlers
Popa Chubby
Preacher Boy
Kenny Wayne Shepherd
Jon Spencer Blues Explosion
Tre
Gillian Welch
Rusty Zinn

CATEGORY INDEX

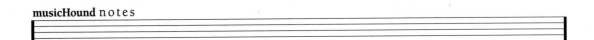

musicHound notes

FREE MUSIC from the **HOUSE of BLUES**

1. YOU CAN'T ALWAYS GET WHAT YOU WANT
LUTHER ALLISON
From *Paint It Blue: Songs of the Rolling Stones*
Time: 4:40

Blues master Allison recorded this Rolling Stones' tribute in July 1997, less than a week before being diagnosed with inoperable lung and brain cancer. He died August 12, 1997. Winner of three W.C. Handy Blues Awards in 1997, including his second consecutive Entertainer of the Year honor, Allison often closed his shows with a medley that included this 1968 classic.

2. PIECE OF MY HEART
OTIS CLAY
From *Songs of Janis Joplin: Blues Down Deep*
Time: 4:25

Based in Chicago, Clay says that he recorded this song quickly and with intensity, in the manner of Joplin. "Knowing how Janis Joplin approached a song, is similar to what we did. She gave it everything. Everything. Janis Joplin reminded me of Otis Redding. They were the type of singers who let the chips fall where they may."

3. SOMEBODY'S GONE
THE BLIND BOYS OF ALABAMA
From *Holdin' On*
Time: 3:43

The Blind Boys of Alabama began performing in 1937. Ever since they met as fellow students at the Talladega Institute for the Deaf and Blind in Alabama, they've had one goal. Says founding member Clarence Fountain, "We just wanted to sing gospel. We wanted to be popular too, but we wanted to sing gospel." This tune is from their first album on the House of Blues label.

4. THE LORD WILL MAKE A WAY SOMEHOW
CISSY HOUSTON
From *Face to Face*
Time: 4:22

Once popularized by Al Green, this song is called "dynamite!" by Houston. The album was winner of the Grammy Award for the Best Gospel Album and one of the first CDs to grace the House of Blues label. "I did not want to go into a studio with music I wasn't in love with. And, I didn't want to be associated with a record company that didn't have confidence in my music. That's why I've stayed away from recording for so long." Part of the Sweet Inspirations in the 1960s, Houston has had the pleasure of singing background on daughter Whitney's hits.

5. GAMBLERS BLUES
LUTHER ALLISON
From *Where Have You Been?*
Live in Montreux 1976–1994
Time: 6:50

The album documents Allison's two decades of recording and performance in Europe, focusing on performances at his "favorite European music festival," Montreux Jazz in Switzerland.

6. ALL MY MONEY BACK
BLUES BROTHERS & FRIENDS
From *Live from Chicago's House of Blues*
Time: 3:22

The original Blues Brothers—Elwood Blues and Cousin Zee—team up with the mighty Blues Brothers Band and special guest Lonnie Brooks at the Brothers' very own venue in Chicago. Their sound, a fusion of Chicago electrified urban music and the hot horn-driven Memphis soul sound, shines on this track.

7. BIG LEGGED MAMAS ARE BACK IN STYLE AGAIN
TAJ MAHAL
From *Taj Mahal: An Evening of Acoustic Music*
Time: 4:31

Recorded during his 1993 tour of Germany, this is an up close and personal recording by the versatile multi-instrumentalist and vocalist that *Billboard* magazine calls "one of the genre's most eloquent voices." This gem shows why Mahal's legacy has endured for more than 35 albums and why he's revered by artists as diverse as George Clinton, the Neville Brothers, and the Rolling Stones.